Landmark Documents on the U.S. Congress

Landmark Documents on the U.S. Congress

RAYMOND W. SMOCK, Editor

 CONGRESSIONAL QUARTERLY INC.
WASHINGTON, D.C.

For my father

Richard Smock

A dedicated Congress watcher.

Copyrights and acknowledgments—Cover photo: Scott J. Ferrell; Documents 4, 5: Merrill Jensen, Robert A. Becker, Gordon DenBoer, et al., *The Documentary History of the First Federal Elections 1788–1790*. Reprinted by permission of the University of Wisconsin Press. Document 7: William B. Allen, ed., *Works of Fisher Ames, as Published by Seth Ames*. Reprinted by permission of LibertyClassics. Documents 6, 8–13, 15, 17: *Documentary History of the First Federal Congress*. Reprinted by permission of Johns Hopkins University Press. Document 22: Noble E. Cunningham Jr., ed., *Circular Letters of Congressmen To their Constituents*. Reprinted by permission of the University of North Carolina Press. Document 125: Bryan B. Sterling and Frances N. Sterling, *Will Rogers' World: America's Foremost Political Humorist Comments on the Twenties and Thirties—and the Eighties and the Nineties*. Reprinted by permission of M. Evans and Company, Inc. Document 143: Joe Martin, *My First Fifty Years in Politics*. Reprinted by permission of McGraw-Hill, Inc. Document 173: Poem courtesy of P. Nemerov.

LIBRARY OF CONGRESS CATALOGING-IN-PUBLICATION DATA
Landmark documents on the U.S. Congress / edited by
    Raymond W. Smock.
        p.   cm.
    Includes bibliographical references (p.   ) and index.
    ISBN 1-56802-399-5 (cloth : alk. paper)
    1. United States. Congress—History—Sources. I. Smock, Raymond.
JK1041.L36   1998
328.73'09—dc21   98-36908

Table of Contents

Acknowledgments   x

Introduction   xi

DOCUMENTS

1. JAMES MADISON'S NOTES OF DEBATE IN THE FEDERAL CONVENTION OF 1787 (May–September 1787)   1

2. THE PREAMBLE AND ARTICLE I OF THE CONSTITUTION OF THE UNITED STATES (September 17, 1787)   25

3. *THE FEDERALIST* (1787–1788)   28

4. AN ORDINANCE CALLING FOR THE FIRST FEDERAL ELECTIONS (September 13, 1788)   45

5. JAMES MADISON DESCRIBES FACTIONS IN THE HOUSE OF REPRESENTATIVES (March 1, 1789)   46

6. THE FIRST QUORUMS OF THE HOUSE AND SENATE (April 1 and 6, 1789)   47

7. FISHER AMES DESCRIBES THE FIRST CONGRESS (April 4, 1789)   49

8. THE FIRST RULES OF THE HOUSE OF REPRESENTATIVES (April 7, 13, and 14, 1789)   49

9. THE FIRST RULES OF THE UNITED STATES SENATE (April 16, 1789)   53

10. VICE PRESIDENT JOHN ADAMS ADDRESSES THE SENATE (April 21, 1789)   54

11. SENATOR WILLIAM MACLAY'S ACCOUNT OF THE DUTIES OF THE VICE PRESIDENT (April 25, 1789)   55

12. SENATOR WILLIAM MACLAY'S DESCRIPTION OF THE INAUGURATION OF GEORGE WASHINGTON (April 30, 1789)   56

13. THE HOUSE AND SENATE AGREE ON THE PROPER TITLE FOR THE PRESIDENT OF THE UNITED STATES (May 14, 1789)   57

14. THE FIRST LAW TO PASS CONGRESS: THE OATH OF OFFICE ACT (June 1, 1789)   58

15. THE HOUSE DEBATES JAMES MADISON'S RESOLUTION ON THE BILL OF RIGHTS (June 8, 1789)   59

16. FIRST TARIFF BILL (July 4, 1789)   67

17. SENATOR WILLIAM MACLAY'S DESCRIPTION OF THE PRESIDENT'S FIRST ENCOUNTER WITH THE SENATE'S POWER OF ADVICE AND CONSENT (August 22 and 24, 1789)   69

18. AN ACT PROVIDING FOR COMPENSATION OF MEMBERS OF THE HOUSE AND SENATE (September 22, 1789)   71

19. THE JUDICIARY ACT OF 1789 (September 24, 1789)   73

20. AN ACT ESTABLISHING THE CENSUS (March 1, 1790)   74

21. ESTABLISHING A PERMANENT SEAT OF GOVERNMENT (July 16, 1790)   76

22. AN EARLY CONGRESSIONAL NEWSLETTER (January 10, 1791)   77

23. THE FIRST DOMESTIC REVENUE ACT (March 3, 1791)   78

24. THE FIRST CONGRESSIONAL INVESTIGATION: THE DEFEAT OF THE ARMY UNDER GENERAL ST. CLAIR (March 27, 1792)   79

25. AN ACT ESTABLISHING A MINT (April 2, 1792)   81

26. THE FIRST PRESIDENTIAL VETO (April 5, 1792)   83

27. AN ACCOUNT OF THE LAYING OF THE CORNERSTONE OF THE CAPITOL (September 18, 1793)   84

28. THE ESTABLISHMENT OF THE UNITED STATES NAVY (March 27, 1794)   86

29. THE JAY TREATY (November 19, 1794)   88

30. A REPORT OF THE LYON-GRISWOLD DISPUTE (February 2, 1798)   91

31. A PETITION OF ABSALOM JONES AND OTHERS (December 30, 1799)   92

32. THE HOUSE OF REPRESENTATIVES ELECTS THE PRESIDENT OF THE UNITED STATES (February 11–17, 1801)   94

33. A HOUSE REPORT REGARDING THE ESTABLISHMENT OF THE LIBRARY OF CONGRESS (December 21, 1801)   96

34. EXCERPTS FROM *JEFFERSON'S MANUAL OF PARLIAMENTARY PRACTICE* (1801)   98

DOCUMENTS

35. MEMORIAL OF SUNDRY CITIZENS IN THE CITY OF WASHINGTON IN THE DISTRICT OF COLUMBIA
    (January 26, 1803) 99

36. SENATE DEBATE ON THE LOUISIANA PURCHASE (November 2–3, 1803) 100

37. THE TWELFTH AMENDMENT TO THE CONSTITUTION (Submitted, December 9, 1803;
    Ratified, September 25, 1804) 102

38. ANN ALRICKS PETITIONS CONGRESS FOR A DIVORCE (ca. January 24, 1804) 102

39. CREATION OF THE HOUSE COMMITTEE ON PUBLIC LANDS (December 17, 1805) 103

40. THE CUMBERLAND ROAD ACT (March 29, 1806) 104

41. PETITION OF THE WARRIORS OF THE UPPER AND LOWER SANDUSKIES (October 4, 1806) 105

42. CREATION OF THE HOUSE DISTRICT OF COLUMBIA COMMITTEE (January 21 and 27, 1808) 106

43. THE ORIGINS OF THE GERRYMANDER (March 26, 1812) 107

44. DECLARATION OF WAR WITH GREAT BRITAIN AND IRELAND (June 18, 1812) 108

45. A LETTER EXPLAINING THE DESTRUCTION OF HOUSE RECORDS DURING THE BURNING OF THE CAPITOL
    (September 15, 1814) 109

46. A RESOLUTION TO PURCHASE THE LIBRARY OF THOMAS JEFFERSON (October 7, 1814) 110

47. THE TREATY OF GHENT (December 24, 1814) 111

48. AN ESTABLISHMENT OF STANDING COMMITTEES IN THE SENATE (December 5, 1816) 113

49. COMPENSATION OF MEMBERS OF CONGRESS (December 18, 1816) 114

50. A REPORT ON THE PUBLICATION OF A HISTORY OF CONGRESS (March 30, 1818) 116

51. AN ACT TO ESTABLISH THE DESIGN OF THE FLAG OF THE UNITED STATES (April 4, 1818) 117

52. *McCULLOUGH V. MARYLAND* (1819) 118

53. THE MISSOURI COMPROMISE (1819–1821) 125

54. *GIBBONS V. OGDEN* (1824) 127

55. ROBERT HAYNE'S REPLY TO DANIEL WEBSTER (January 21 and 25, 1830) 132

56. DANIEL WEBSTER'S SECOND REPLY TO ROBERT HAYNE (January 26 and 27, 1830) 138

57. ALEXIS DE TOCQUEVILLE'S DESCRIPTION OF THE HOUSE AND SENATE (January 1832) 149

58. SENATOR HENRY CLAY DEFENDS THE AMERICAN SYSTEM (February 2, 3, and 6, 1832) 150

59. THE ADOPTION OF THE GAG RULE REGARDING PETITIONS AND MEMORIALS ON SLAVERY (May 26, 1836) 158

60. THE SENATE DEBATES THE ESTABLISHMENT OF A GALLERY FOR REPORTERS (July 3, 1841) 159

61. CHARLES DICKENS'S DESCRIPTION OF CONGRESS (1841) 160

62. SENATOR HENRY CLAY'S VALEDICTORY TO THE SENATE (March 31, 1842) 163

63. SENATE AND HOUSE DEBATE ON THE DECLARATION OF WAR WITH MEXICO (May 11, 1846) 166

64. REPRESENTATIVE DAVID WILMOT DEFENDS HIS PROVISO (February 8, 1847) 169

65. DANIEL WEBSTER ON THE CONSTITUTION AND THE UNION (March 7, 1850) 171

66. SENATOR HENRY CLAY ON THE DEATH OF JOHN C. CALHOUN (April 1, 1850) 175

67. SENATOR THOMAS HART BENTON OPPOSES THE COMPROMISE OF 1850 (June 10, 1850) 177

68. THE KANSAS-NEBRASKA ACT (May 30, 1854) 181

69. HOUSE SELECT COMMITTEE REPORT ON THE BEATING OF SENATOR CHARLES SUMNER (June 2, 1856) 183

70. *SCOTT V. SANFORD* (THE DRED SCOTT DECISION) (1857) 185

71. AN ACCOUNT OF A BRAWL ON THE FLOOR OF THE HOUSE OF REPRESENTATIVES (February 6, 1858) 193

72. THE HOUSE OF REPRESENTATIVES LAUNCHES AN INVESTIGATION OF PRESIDENT JAMES BUCHANAN
    (March 5, 1860) 195

73. SENATOR JEFFERSON DAVIS'S FAREWELL ADDRESS TO THE SENATE (January 21, 1861) 197

74. JAMES G. BLAINE'S DESCRIPTION OF CONGRESS AT THE BEGINNING OF THE CIVIL WAR (March 1861) 199

75. THE FIRST FEDERAL INCOME TAX (August 5, 1861) 202

76. THE THIRTEENTH AMENDMENT TO THE CONSTITUTION (Submitted, January 31, 1865;
    Ratified, December 6, 1865) 204

77. REPRESENTATIVE THADDEUS STEVENS ON RECONSTRUCTION (December 18, 1865) 205

DOCUMENTS

78. The Civil Rights Act of 1866 (April 9, 1866)   209

79. The Fourteenth Amendment to the Constitution (Submitted, June 13, 1866; Ratified, July 9, 1868)   211

80. The Reconstruction Act of 1867 (March 2, 1867)   212

81. Representative Thaddeus Stevens on the Impeachment of Andrew Johnson (March 2, 1868)   213

82. The Articles of Impeachment of Andrew Johnson (March 4, 1868)   216

83. The Fifteenth Amendment to the Constitution (Submitted, February 26, 1869; Ratified, February 17, 1870)   221

84. *Haver v. Yaker* (1869)   222

85. The House Debates Investigation of the Credit Mobilier Scandal (December 2, 1872)   223

86. The "Salary Grab" Act of 1873 (March 3, 1873)   225

87. Susan B. Anthony Petitions Congress Regarding Her Fine for Illegal Voting (January 22, 1874)   228

88. Reorganization of the Government of the District of Columbia (June 20, 1874)   230

89. Representative James G. Blaine Defends Himself Against Charges of Corruption: The Mulligan Letters (June 5, 1875)   232

90. Establishing the Electoral Commission of 1877 (January 29, 1877)   238

91. James A. Garfield Describes Congress (July 1877)   241

92. Reform of the Rules of the House (January 6, 1880)   243

93. *Kilbourn v. Thompson* (1880)   244

94. An Argument Against Reducing Congressional Salaries (February 16, 1882)   247

95. House Report on the Reform of the Civil Service (December 12, 1882)   249

96. The Civil Service Reform Act (January 16, 1883)   251

97. Woodrow Wilson on the U.S. Senate (1885)   254

98. Woodrow Wilson Describes the Role of the Speaker of the House (1885)   256

99. James Bryce on the U.S. House of Representatives (1888)   257

100. James Bryce on the U.S. Senate (1888)   262

101. Speaker Thomas B. Reed Changes the Rules of the House (January 29, 1890)   266

102. A Newspaper Account of a Shooting at the Capitol (March 1, 1890)   270

103. Declaration of War with Spain (April 25, 1898)   273

104. Senator Albert J. Beveridge on U.S. Policy Regarding the Philippines (January 9, 1900)   274

105. Senator George Frisbie Hoar on Self-Government for the Philippines (April 17, 1900)   282

106. The Sixteenth Amendment to the Constitution (Submitted, July 12, 1909; Ratified, February 25, 1913)   284

107. The Revolt Against Speaker Joseph Cannon (March 19, 1910)   284

108. Limiting the Size of the House of Representatives (August 8, 1911)   299

109. The Seventeenth Amendment to the Constitution (Submitted, May 13, 1912; Ratified, May 31, 1913)   300

110. Senator Boies Penrose on a Senate Investigation into Campaign Financing (The Clapp Committee) (August 21, 1912)   301

111. A Newspaper Account of a Bombing at the Capitol (July 3, 1915)   304

112. The Declaration of War Against Germany (April 4, 1917)   307

113. The Eighteenth Amendment to the Constitution (Submitted, December 18, 1917; Ratified, January 29, 1919)   309

114. The Nineteenth Amendment to the Constitution (Submitted, June 4, 1919; Ratified, August 26, 1920)   310

115. The National Prohibition Act (The Volstead Act) (October 28, 1919)   310

116. Senator William E. Borah Opposes the League of Nations (November 19, 1919)   315

117. The Budget and Accounting Act of 1921 (June 10, 1921)   320

118. Senator William E. Borah Opposes the Versailles Treaty (September 26, 1921)   323

119. Speaker Nicholas Longworth on Congress (January 2, 1926)   325

120. *McGrain v. Daugherty* (January 17, 1927)   328

DOCUMENTS

121. An Act Designating the National Anthem (March 3, 1931)   330

122. The Twentieth Amendment to the Constitution (Submitted, March 2, 1932; Ratified, February 6, 1933)   331

123. The Twenty-First Amendment to the Constitution (Submitted, February 20, 1933; Ratified, December 5, 1933)   332

124. Senator Huey Long's "Every Man a King" Speech (February 23, 1934)   333

125. Will Rogers on Congress (May 12, 1935)   336

126. *National Labor Relations Board v. Jones and Laughlin Steel Corporation* (April 12, 1937)   337

127. Senator Burton K. Wheeler Opposes President Roosevelt's Court-Packing Scheme (July 9, 1937)   341

128. A Report on Un-American Activities (The Dies Committee) (1939)   352

129. Senator Harry S. Truman Calls for Investigation of the National Defense Program (February 10, 1941)   355

130. The Lend-Lease Act (March 11, 1941)   359

131. President Franklin D. Roosevelt Asks Congress to Declare War on Japan (December 8 , 1941)   361

132. Congress Declares War on Japan (December 8, 1941)   362

133. Congress Declares War on Germany and Italy (December 11, 1941)   365

134. Debate Regarding the Establishment of the House Un-American Activities Committee (January 3, 1945)   367

135. Senator Arthur Vandenberg on United States Foreign Policy (January 10, 1945)   374

136. The Atomic Energy Act (August 1, 1946)   379

137. The Legislative Reorganization Act of 1946 (August 2, 1946)   384

138. The Presidential Succession Act (July 18, 1947)   400

139. Senator Joseph R. McCarthy on Communists in Government Service (February, 9, 1950)   401

140. Senator Margaret Chase Smith's Declaration of Conscience (June 1, 1950)   404

141. General Douglas MacArthur Speaks Before a Joint Meeting of Congress (April 19, 1951)   407

142. Conclusions of the Kefauver Committee on Organized Crime (May 1, 1951)   410

143. Speaker Joseph Martin's Account of a Shooting on the Floor of the House (March 1, 1954)   413

144. An Excerpt from the Army-McCarthy Hearings (June 9, 1954)   415

145. The Creation of the Interstate Highway System (The Federal-Aid Highway Act of 1956) (June 26, 1956)   419

146. *Watkins v. United States* (June 17, 1957)   421

147. Senator Strom Thurmond's Record-Setting Filibuster (August 28–29, 1957)   426

148. The Civil Rights Act of 1957 (September 9, 1957)   430

149. Creation of the House Committee on Science and Astronautics and the Senate Committee on Aeronautical and Space Sciences (July 21 and 24, 1958)   432

150. The Twenty-Third Amendment to the Constitution (Submitted, June 17, 1960; Ratified, April 3, 1961)   433

151. A Joint Meeting of Congress to Honor Astronaut John H. Glenn Jr. (February 26, 1962)   434

152. Senator Everett Dirksen on the Civil Rights Act of 1964 (June 10, 1964)   437

153. Senator Wayne Morse Opposes the Tonkin Gulf Resolution (August 5, 1964)   440

154. *Powell v. McCormack* (June 16, 1969)   446

155. A Joint Meeting of Congress to Honor the Apollo 11 Astronauts (September 16, 1969)   448

156. Senator Frank Church on the War in Vietnam and Cambodia (May 1, 1970)   451

157. Senate Debate on the McGovern-Hatfield Amendment (September 1, 1970)   457

158. The Legislative Reorganization Act of 1970 (October 26, 1970)   463

159. The Twenty-Sixth Amendment to the Constitution (Submitted, March 23, 1971; Ratified, July 5, 1971)   468

160. *Gravel v. United States* (June 29, 1972)   469

DOCUMENTS

161. A RESOLUTION TO ESTABLISH THE SENATE WATERGATE COMMITTEE (February 7, 1973)   472

162. THE WAR POWERS RESOLUTION (November 7, 1973)   475

163. THE REORGANIZATION OF THE DISTRICT OF COLUMBIA GOVERNMENT (December 24, 1973)   478

164. THE CONGRESSIONAL BUDGET AND IMPOUNDMENT CONTROL ACT OF 1974 (July 12, 1974)   482

165. THE HOUSE JUDICIARY COMMITTEE DEBATES THE IMPEACHMENT OF PRESIDENT RICHARD M. NIXON (July 24, 1974)   487

166. THE ARTICLES OF IMPEACHMENT AGAINST PRESIDENT RICHARD M. NIXON (August 4, 1974)   495

167. THE BOLLING-MARTIN REPORT ON REFORM OF HOUSE COMMITTEES (October 8, 1974)   497

168. *BUCKLEY V. VALEO* (January 30, 1976)   506

169. THE HOUSE INVESTIGATION OF KOREAN-AMERICAN RELATIONS (KOREAGATE) (October 31, 1978)   532

170. *IMMIGRATION AND NATURALIZATION SERVICE V. CHADHA* (June 23, 1983)   539

171. SPEAKER TIP O'NEILL'S WORDS ARE TAKEN DOWN DURING DEBATE WITH REPRESENTATIVE NEWT GINGRICH (May 15, 1984)   542

172. SENATE HEARINGS ON THE SUPREME COURT NOMINATION OF ROBERT H. BORK (September 15 and 18, 1987)   548

173. A POEM TO THE CONGRESS OF THE UNITED STATES (March 2, 1989)   563

174. THE RESIGNATION SPEECH OF SPEAKER JIM WRIGHT (May 31, 1989)   564

175. SENATOR ROBERT BYRD ON THE WAR IN THE PERSIAN GULF (January 12, 1991)   572

176. CONGRESS AUTHORIZES USE OF MILITARY FORCE AGAINST IRAQ (January 14, 1991)   577

177. THE SENATE SELECT COMMITTEE ON ETHICS REPORTS ON THE INVESTIGATION OF THE KEATING 5 (November 20, 1991)   578

178. THE TWENTY-SEVENTH AMENDMENT TO THE CONSTITUTION (Submitted, September 25, 1789; Ratified, May 18, 1992)   583

179. *NIXON V. UNITED STATES* (January 13, 1993)   584

180. CONCLUSIONS OF THE SPECIAL PROSECUTOR REGARDING THE IRAN-CONTRA INVESTIGATION (August 4, 1993)   587

181. STATEMENTS OF PRESIDENTS BUSH AND REAGAN REGARDING THEIR ROLE IN IRAN-CONTRA (December 3, 1993)   597

182. SENATOR ROBERT C. BRYD OPPOSES THE LINE-ITEM VETO (October 18, 1993)   603

183. THE HOUSE REPUBLICANS' CONTRACT WITH AMERICA (September 27, 1994)   608

184. NEWT GINGRICH ADDRESSES THE HOUSE UPON HIS ELECTION AS SPEAKER (January 4, 1995)   610

185. FINAL REPORT OF THE SENATE WHITEWATER INVESTIGATION (MAJORITY VIEWS) (June 17, 1996)   614

186. FINAL REPORT OF THE SENATE WHITEWATER INVESTIGATION (MINORITY VIEWS) (June 17, 1996)   619

187. A RULING ON THE ELECTION OF SPEAKER NEWT GINGRICH (January 7, 1997)   622

188. *CLINTON V. CITY OF NEW YORK* (June 25, 1998)   624

189. A RESOLUTION AUTHORIZING AN IMPEACHMENT INVESTIGATION OF PRESIDENT WILLIAM JEFFERSON CLINTON (October 8, 1998)   627

190. THE RESIGNATION OF SPEAKER NEWT GINGRICH (November 6, 1998)   628

Bibliography   631

Index   635

Acknowledgments

Many individuals provided me with invaluable help and guidance in preparing *Landmark Documents on the U.S. Congress,* and I would like to offer my sincere appreciation and thanks to those who were especially helpful. Shana Wagger of Congressional Quarterly first approached me to ask if I would be interested in preparing a volume such as this. Her enthusiasm for the project was contagious, and I am grateful to her for her many professional courtesies and solid editorial advice during the preparation of this book. Others on Congressional Quarterly's staff who made the writing of this book a great pleasure rather than a chore include Grace Hill, David Tarr, and my outstanding editor, Kerry Kern.

I cannot thank enough the fine professionals and my dear friends in the Senate Historical Office, who never failed to be of assistance whenever I called on them during the course of preparing this volume. Richard A. Baker, the Senate historian, encouraged this project from the start and was always there when I needed his advice and guidance on Senate history. Donald A. Ritchie, the associate historian of the Senate, never failed to go the extra mile to help. He critically read the manuscript and offered many suggestions for improving the headnotes and the selection of documents. For any student of Congress, the Senate Historical Office stands as a landmark of its own in providing excellent service to Congress and the nation when it comes to the rich and colorful history of the Senate.

The selection of documents included in this volume benefited from the wisdom of a number of senior congressional scholars and experts on Congress who were willing to weigh in with their favorite documents and challenge me on some of my selections. These include Charles W. Johnson III, the House parliamentarian; Roger H. Davidson, professor of government and politics at the University of Maryland; Michael L. Gillette and Kenneth T. Kato of the National Archive's Center for Legislative Records; and Charlene Bangs Bickford and Kenneth R. Bowling of the First Federal Congress Project at George Washington University.

Much of the research for this volume was conducted from the reading room of the U.S. Senate Library, situated in the Capitol itself. I was fortunate to be able to work in this friendly and totally professional atmosphere. For a scholar of Congress, the Senate Library is the closet thing to dying and going to heaven. My deep appreciation for many favors and expert guidance goes to the entire staff, including the Senate librarian Greg Harness, Zoe Collier, Kimberly Edwards, Lauren Gluckman, Donnee Gray, Nancy Kervin, Richard Ramponi, and Karin Sedestrom.

I owe a special debt of gratitude to Suni Johnson, a fellow historian who served as research assistant for this project and performed many tasks with great skill as a fact checker, bibliographer, occasional transcriber, and organizer of thousands of pages of photocopies and notes that were generated in the course of the work on this volume.

Others who shared their special expertise were Bruce A. Ragsdale, chief historian of the Federal Judicial Center, and Joel D. Treese, editor of the *Congressional Staff Directory,* both former colleagues of mine in the Office of the Historian of the House of Representatives; William C. Allen, architectural historian in the Office of the Architect of the Capitol; and John P. Kaminski, Gaspare J. Saladino, and Richard Leffler of the Ratification of the U.S. Constitution Project at the University of Wisconsin, Madison.

The usual disclaimer applies, that none of the wonderful people who assisted in making this book possible are responsible for any faults or errors it may contain. I reserve those for myself.

To my wife Phyllis goes my abiding love and my deep appreciation of her steadfast support of my career as a historian. She has made life itself a joy.

Introduction

What is a landmark document on the United States Congress? It can be many things, but in all instances it is a document that reveals something important about the way Congress works. It can tell us about the people who served in the House and Senate or how Congress has grown and changed since the adoption of the U.S. Constitution. Congress is the place where the nation's political will is hammered out every day. Landmark documents on Congress are also important signposts in American history, in our culture, and in our way of life over the past two centuries.

I vividly recall an incident that took place outside the private office of Speaker Thomas P. "Tip" O'Neill shortly after I was appointed the first historian of the House of Representatives in September 1983. I had just come from my first meeting with the Speaker and other House leaders who had supported the creation of a history office in the House of Representatives. When the meeting was over I left the office and entered a deserted, quiet corridor that led toward the House chamber. Suddenly, a figure emerged at the other end of the hall and gestured to me, his voice echoing down the marble walls and tiled floors. "Doctor, doctor, one minute please, I want to talk to you." It was the venerable chairman of the House Rules Committee, eighty-three-year-old Claude Pepper of Florida, whose committee had conducted the national search for the House historian. He apologized for being late for the meeting.

Chairman Pepper then told me a story. He said President Franklin D. Roosevelt had once told him about a lesson he had learned as a youth from his schoolmaster, Endicott Peabody. Peabody described history as a series of peaks and valleys, but if you drew a line along the peaks there would be evidence of upward progress. Without endorsing Peabody's progressive view of history, Pepper looked me square in the eye and said, "I hope you will write about the peaks *and* the valleys."

This volume of landmark documents in the rich two-century history of Congress includes major examples of peaks and valleys in the history of this important institution—from lofty discussions of the meaning of representative government in the words of the Founders of this nation to descriptions of brawls on the floor of the House; from great speeches and debates over major issues before the nation to examples of partisan bickering and scandal. *Landmark Documents on the U.S. Congress* provides a portrait of Congress that includes the sorts of things I think Claude Pepper had in mind when he gave me my first challenge as House historian fifteen years ago.

This volume was prepared with several audiences in mind. During the almost twelve years I served as House historian, my office received numerous inquiries from members of Congress, their staffs, members of the press, school children, and the general public on a wide range of topics related to the history of the House and Congress in general. We were asked a wide variety of questions, many relating to the first or last time something happened in Congress. When did the income tax begin? When was the last time Congress had a pay raise? Has Congress ever impeached a president? Who were the greatest orators in the Senate? Frequently the questions were about the role of Congress as described in the Constitution. While we answered many questions about the Senate, we preferred to refer callers to the Senate Historical Office, our counterpart on the Senate side of the Capitol. They, in turn, would refer questions about the history of the House to my office. Working in a harmonious and collegial relationship, our two small offices managed to cover the entire institution.

This volume is designed to serve as a documentary reference to some of the major aspects of the history of both the House and Senate. The focus is on the history of Congress and its development as a branch of government. It is my basic assumption that Congress is a central institution in the lives of all who are citizens of the United States. From this assumption flows my belief that a basic understanding of Congress and how it works is the hallmark of a responsible citizen in a nation where the power to govern ultimately resides in the citizens themselves and their chosen representatives. This volume is about some of the people who have served in Congress, about the rules the House and Senate use to govern themselves, and about the committees of Congress. And, it is about some of the profound ways that Congress has shaped American history and culture.

Landmark Documents on the U.S. Congress is also designed to provide examples of fundamental documents that can be used to teach about Congress at virtually any educational level, from elementary school through college. During my tenure as House historian I was involved in a number of teacher-training seminars, where teachers told me that they could benefit from having a compendium of important documents that they could use to teach about Congress. Some schools start the process as early as the fourth grade. No American history textbook or text on U.S. government or civics has had the luxury of providing more than a handful of documents, usually limited to the Constitution, the Declaration of Independence, and perhaps a few other key documents. This volume fills the gap for those who would like to explore history for themselves through the words of those who made it.

The sense of discovery that comes from exposure to authentic documentary sources is one of the best ways I know to make history come alive. Not all the documents in this edition are lively and exciting, but all are significant in explaining some aspect of how Congress works and how it affects us. Some of the documents included here are long and complex because not all documents can be reduced to a few essential lines or paragraphs without destroying their essence. Congress is a place where words are the main product. Sometimes this means many words; other times it can be just a sentence or two. The power of a document is not determined by its length. For example, one sentence in the Thirteenth Amendment says: "Neither slavery nor involuntary servitude, except as a punishment for crime whereof the party shall have been duly convicted, shall exist within the United States, or any place subject to their jurisdiction" (see document 76). Before that one sentence could be added to the Constitution, hundreds of thousands of Americans would die on the battlefield.

There are 190 documents in this volume, ranging over time from 1787 to 1998. These include some major laws, because Congress, first and foremost, is the place where laws are made. But this volume does not focus on laws or attempt to present all the possible candidates for the status of landmark legislation from Congress. The laws included here are selected to show that when Congress passes legislation it is fulfilling its constitutional duty and in so doing it affects our daily lives. The next time you travel on an interstate highway, think for a moment how the vast interconnected system of highways came to be and how it has affected our towns, cities, industries, and how we get from place to place (see document 145). *Landmark Documents on the U.S. Congress* contains debates on the floor of the House and Senate, great speeches, declarations of war, important committee hearings and investigations, Supreme Court decisions affecting Congress and its powers, arguments over congressional salaries, the tug-of-war between the executive and legislative branches of government, descriptions of bombings and shootings in the Capitol, constitutional amendments, documents on the relationship of Congress to the District of Columbia, and petitions from ordinary citizens. The volume presents some views of Congress from foreign visitors and American observers at different periods of time, ranging from the French aristocrat Alexis de Tocqueville, who visited Washington in 1832, to the English writer Charles Dickens in 1841, to the young scholar Woodrow Wilson in 1885, and to the humorist Will Rogers in 1935.

Article I, Section 8 of the U.S. Constitution, which describes the powers of Congress, forms the main organizing principle of this volume. While it would be impossible to cover in one volume every nuance of the enumerated and implied powers of Congress mentioned in the Constitution, my goal was to select documents that were examples of how Congress functions under the Constitution. Where it said in Article I, Section 8, Clause 13 that Congress should "provide and maintain a Navy," I selected a document on the establishment of the United States Navy in 1794 (see document 28). When the Constitution stated that Congress has the power "to coin Money," I included the act that established the United States Mint in 1790 (see document 25).

The headnote to each document offers my reasons for including the document as a landmark and provides historical background and context to explain or identify persons or events referred to in the text. No attempt has been made to identify every person or event in each document. The goal has been to let the document stand on its own as close to the original as possible without further editorial intrusion. Misspellings, grammatical errors, British spellings, and abbreviations that appeared in the original document have been retained, with clarifications in brackets when needed. The full names of members of Congress only identified by last name in the documents can be found in the index. In many instances the documents included are the complete texts. In other cases, especially with many of the longer documents, excerpts are presented, with ellipses used to indicate that some text has been omitted. While footnotes in the original documents have been deleted, any material they provided that was essential to understanding the text has been clarified in the headnote.

The majority of the documents in this volume were gleaned from official government records, many widely available in libraries and to a greater extent each year on the Internet. Congress has kept some record of its debates from the earliest Congress, although the quality and accuracy of these compilations varies. Congressional debates were compiled in the *Registry of Debates,* the *Annals of Congress,* and, beginning in 1833, in the *Congressional Globe,* which was, in turn, superseded in 1873 by the *Congressional Record.* The House and Senate have each kept a journal of their official proceedings beginning with the first Congress in 1789.

Readers should note that the Library of Congress has recently launched a major digital project, "A Century of Lawmaking for a New Nation, U.S. Congressional Documents and Debates 1774–1873." This undertaking will eventually place on-line the complete text of the House and Senate journals, the *Annals of Congress,* and other compilations that will provide electronic access to the fundamental publications of Congress through the year 1873 to anyone with an Internet connection.

Finally, I hope this volume contributes to an increased interest in the study of the history of Congress. History is made every day by this fascinating and ever-changing institution. The actions taken by the representatives and senators affect our lives in many ways. As Howard Nemerov, poet laureate of the United States, said before a joint meeting of Congress on the occasion of the two hundredth anniversary of Congress in 1989:

> Here at the fulcrum of us all,
> The feather of truth against the soul
> Is weighed, and had better be found to balance
> Lest our enterprise collapse in silence.

If the poet's vision is correct, and I believe it is, Congress is indeed our political fulcrum, the place where we, as a nation, try to balance our conflicting desires. It is up to all of us to play a part in keeping that balance, "lest our enterprise collapse in silence."

Raymond W. Smock
Lanham, Maryland
November 11, 1998

Landmark Documents on the U.S. Congress

*History is the witness that testifies to
the passage of time; it illumines reality;
vitalizes memory, provides guidance in daily
life, and brings us tidings of antiquity.*—Cicero

1 James Madison's Notes of Debate in the Federal Convention of 1787

May–September 1787

James Madison's Notes of Debate in the Federal Convention of 1787 *is the best single document for understanding the intentions of the Framers of the Constitution and how they expected Congress to function. Since Madison was an eyewitness and major participant in the deliberations of the convention that met in Philadelphia between May and September 1787 to draft the U.S. Constitution, his notes represent the most complete record of the secret deliberations.*

Madison has often been called the "father of the Constitution." It is hard to overestimate his importance in shaping the draft of the Constitution that was sent to the states for ratification and in implementing the Constitution during his four terms in the House of Representatives.

Madison's Notes of Debate *was not published until 1840, more than half a century after the convention. It covered virtually all aspects of the convention's work. The excerpts that follow, however, focus on the main elements in the creation of the House and Senate. The first excerpt deals with who should elect the House of Representatives—the people or the state legislatures. Some delegates felt that popular election would overburden the public, which was easily misled by demagogues and corruption. Others maintained that the real power of government emanated from the people and they should directly elect their representatives. In the case of the Senate, the prevailing sentiment was for indirect election by state legislatures to avoid too much direct democracy. Throughout the debate the House was referred to as the first branch and the Senate as the second branch.*

The debate over the nature of the two-house legislature was crucial to the success of the delegates assembled in Philadelphia. Had they not reached a compromise between the large and small states on the composition of the House and Senate and how each would be elected, the effort to establish a new constitution could have failed. Fortunately, on July 16, 1787, the delegates agreed, breaking the major logjam in their deliberations. The Connecticut Compromise, or the "Great Compromise," as it came to be known, was a crucial moment in the history of this nation. The small states won equal representation in the Senate, while the House was apportioned by population.

In addition to their importance for understanding the creation of the House and Senate, these notes record the essential debates on the fundamental nature of representative democracy. They contain arguments of enduring value. These debates can be read with profit on such contemporary issues as the potential impact of digital technology on the nature of elections and the decision-making processes of government. Some recent critics of Congress have suggested, for example, that we may want to bypass Congress altogether and adopt some kind of national plebiscite (that is, establish direct voting on laws by the people without the intervention of an elected representative). To put the question in an extreme form: Could ordinary citizens sitting at computers linked to the Internet make bet- *ter national policy and better law than 535 elected representatives and senators in Washington? Before such a question is ever taken seriously, a careful reading of the debates of the Federal Convention of 1787 is in order.*

Madison's Notes of Debate *contain numerous abbreviations of common words, such as "wd." for "would" or "shd." for "should." His spelling of words and names of the delegates is often inconsistent, as he worked in haste to record the debates while being an active participant himself. Madison is also inconsistent in abbreviating the names of the states when votes are recorded. No attempt has been made to standardize these variations. This text follows the printing of the notes as they appeared in* Documents Illustrative of the Formation of the American States, *edited by Charles C. Tansill and published as a government document in 1927. The original text contains footnotes created by Madison and many others were later added by the editor of the 1927 printing. These footnotes have been omitted in the excerpts that follow. In a few instances an abbreviation in the text that is not clear from the context is clarified in brackets. Occasionally Madison used the abbreviation "nem. com.," when describing a vote of the delegates. This means the motion passed "without dissent."*

· · · ·

THURSDAY MAY 31

RESOL: 4. first clause "that the members of the first branch of the National Legislature ought to be elected by the people of the several States" being taken up,

MR. SHERMAN opposed the election by the people, insisting that it ought to be by the State Legislatures. The people he said, immediately should have as little to do as may be about the Government. They want information and are constantly liable to be misled.

MR. GERRY. The evils we experience flow from the excess of democracy. The people do not want virtue, but are the dupes of pretended patriots. In Massts. it had been fully confirmed by experience that they are daily misled into the most baneful measures and opinions by the false reports circulated by designing men, and which no one on the spot can refute. One principal evil arises from the want of due provision for those employed in the administration of Governmt. It would seem to be a maxim of democracy to starve the public servants. He mentioned the popular clamour in Massts. for the reduction of salaries and the attack made on that of the Govr. though secured by the spirit of the Constitution itself. He had he said been too republican heretofore: he was still however republican, but had been taught by experience the danger of the levelling spirit.

MR. MASON, argued strongly for an election of the larger branch by the people. It was to be the grand depository of the democratic principle of the Govtt. It was, so to speak, to be our

House of Commons—It ought to know & sympathise with every part of the community; and ought therefore to be taken not only from different parts of the whole republic, but also from different districts of the larger members of it, which had in several instances particularly in Virga., different interests and views arising from difference of produce, of habits &c &c. He admitted that we had been too democratic but was afraid we sd. incautiously run into the opposite extreme. We ought to attend to the rights of every class of the people. He had often wondered at the indifference of the superior classes of society to this dictate of humanity & policy; considering that however affluent their circumstances, or elevated their situations, might be, the course of a few years, not only might but certainly would, distribute their posterity throughout the lowest classes of Society. Every selfish motive therefore, every family attachment, ought to recommend such a system of policy as would provide no less carefully for the rights and happiness of the lowest than of the highest orders of Citizens.

Mr. Wilson contended strenuously for drawing the most numerous branch of the Legislature immediately from the people. He was for raising the federal pyramid to a considerable altitude, and for that reason wished to give it as broad a basis as possible. No government could long subsist without the confidence of the people. In a republican Government this confidence was peculiarly essential. He also thought it wrong to increase the weight of the State Legislatures by making them the electors of the national Legislature. All interference between the general and local Governmts. should be obviated as much as possible. On examination it would be found that the opposition of States to federal measures had preceded much more from the officers of the States, than from the people at large.

Mr. Madison considered the popular election of one branch of the National Legislature as essential to every plan of free Government. He observed that in some of the States one branch of the Legislature was composed of men already removed from the people by an intervening body of electors. That if the first branch of the general legislature should be elected by the State Legislatures, the second branch elected by the first—the Executive by the second together with the first; and other appointments again made for subordinate purposes by the Executive, the people would be lost sight of altogether; and the necessary sympathy between them and their rulers and officers, too little felt. He was an advocate for the policy of refining the popular appointments by successive filtrations, but thought it might be pushed too far. He wished the expedient to be resorted to only in the appointment of the second branch of the Legislature, and in the Executive & judiciary branches of the Government. He thought too that the great fabric to be raised would be more stable and durable, if it should rest on the solid foundation of the people themselves, than if it should stand merely on the pillars of the Legislatures.

Mr. Gerry did not like the election by the people. The maxims taken from the British constitution were often fallacious when applied to our situation which was extremely different.

Experience he said had strewn that the State legislatures drawn immediately from the people did not always possess their confidence. He had no objection however to an election by the people if it were so qualified that men of honor & character might not be unwilling to be joined in the appointments. He seemed to think the people might nominate a certain number out of which the State legislatures should be bound to choose.

Mr. Butler thought an election by the people an impracticable mode.

On the question for an election of the first branch of the national Legislature by the people.

Massts. ay. Connect. divd. N. York ay. N. Jersey no. Pena. ay. Delawe. divd. Va. ay. N.C. ay. S.C. no. Georga. ay.

. . . .

The Committee proceeded to Resolution 5. "that the second, [or senatorial] branch of the National Legislature ought to be chosen by the first branch out of persons nominated by the State Legislatures."

Mr. Spaight contended that the 2d branch ought to be chosen by the State Legislatures and moved an amendment to that effect.

Mr. Butler apprehended that the taking so many powers out of the hands of the States as was proposed, tended to destroy all that balance and security of interests among the States which it was necessary to preserve; and called on Mr. Randolph the mover of the propositions, to explain the extent of his ideas, and particularly the number of members he meant to assign to this second branch.

Mr. Rand observed that he had at the time of offering his propositions stated his ideas as far as the nature of general propositions required; that details made no part of the plan, and could not perhaps with propriety have been introduced. If he was to give an opinion as to the number of the second branch, he should say that it ought to be much smaller than that of the first; so small as to be exempt from the passionate proceedings to which numerous assemblies are liable. He observed that the general object was to provide a cure for the evils under which the U. S. laboured; that in tracing these evils to their origin every man had found it in the turbulence and follies of democracy: that some check therefore was to be sought for age this tendency of our Governments: and that a good Senate seemed most likely to answer the purpose.

Mr. King reminded the Committee that the choice of the second branch as proposed (by Mr. Spaight) viz. by the State Legislatures would be impracticable, unless it was to be very numerous, or *the idea of proportion* among the States was to be disregarded. According to this *idea*, there must be 80 or 100 members to entitle Delaware to the choice of one of them.—Mr. Spaight withdrew his motion.

Mr. Wilson opposed both a nomination by the State Legislatures, and an election by the first branch of the national Legislature, because the second branch of the latter, ought to be independent of both. He thought both branches of the National Legislature ought to be chosen by the people, but was not prepared with a specific proposition. He suggested the mode of chusing the Senate of N. York to wit of uniting several election districts, for one branch, in chusing members for the other branch, as a good model.

MR. MADISON observed that such a mode would destroy the influence of the smaller States associated with larger ones in the same district; as the latter would chose from within themselves, altho' better men might be found in the former. The election of Senators in Virga. where large & small counties were often formed into one district for the purpose, had illustrated this consequence Local partiality, would often prefer a resident within the County or State, to a candidate of superior merit residing out of it. Less merit also in a resident would be more known throughout his own State.

Mr. Sherman favored an election of one member by each of the State Legislatures.

MR. PINKNEY moved to strike out the "nomination by the State legislatures." On this question.

Massts. no. Cont. no. N. Y. no. N. J. no. Pena. no. Del divd. Va. no. N. C. no. S. C. no. Georg no.

On the whole question for electing by the first branch out of nominations by the State Legislatures, Mass. ay. Cont. no. N Y. no. N. Jersey. no. Pena. no. Del. no. Virga. ay. N. C. no. S. C. ay. Ga. no.

So the clause was disagreed to & a chasm left in this part of the plan.

The sixth Resolution stating the cases in which the national Legislature ought to legislate was next taken into discussion: On the question whether each branch shd. originate laws, there was an unanimous affirmative without debate. On the question for transferring all the Legislative powers of the existing Congs. to this Assembly, there was also a silent affirmative nem. con.

On the proposition for giving "Legislative power in all cases to which the State Legislatures were individually incompetent."

MR. PINKNEY & MR. RUTLEDGE objected to the vagueness of the term *incompetent*, and said they could not well decide how to vote until they should see an exact enumeration of the powers comprehended by this definition.

MR. BUTLER repeated his fears that we were running into an extreme in taking away the powers of the States, and called on Mr. Randolph for the extent of his meaning.

MR. RANDOLPH disclaimed any intention to give indefinite powers to the national Legislature, declaring that he was entirely opposed to such an inroad on the State jurisdictions, and that he did not think any considerations whatever could ever change his determination. His opinion was fixed on this point.

MR. MADISON said that he had brought with him into the Convention a strong bias in favor of an enumeration and definition of the powers necessary to be exercised by the national Legislature; but had also brought doubts concerning its practicability. His wishes remained unaltered; but his doubts had become stronger. What his opinion might ultimately be he could

not yet tell. But he should shrink from nothing which should be found essential to such a form of Govt. as would provide for the safety, liberty and happiness of the community. This being the end of all our deliberations, all the necessary means for attaining it must, however reluctantly, be submitted to.

On the question for giving powers, in cases to which the States are not competent, Massts. ay. Cont. divd. [Sharman no Elseworth ay] N. Y. ay. N. J. ay. Pa. ay. Del. ay. Va. ay. N. C. ay. S. Carolina ay. Georga. ay.

. . . .

WEDNESDAY JUNE 6TH. IN COMMITTEE OF THE WHOLE

MR. PINKNEY according to previous notice & rule obtained, moved "that the first branch of the national Legislature be elected by the State Legislatures, and not by the people." contending that the people were less fit Judges in such a case, and that the Legislatures would be less likely to promote the adoption of the new Government, if they were to be excluded from all share in it.

MR. RUTLEDGE 2ded the motion.

MR. GERRY. Much depends on the mode of election. In England, the people will probably lose their liberty from the smallness of the proportion having a right of suffrage. Our danger arises from the opposite extreme: hence in Massts. the worst men get into the Legislature. Several members of that Body had lately been convicted of infamous crimes. Men of indigence, ignorance & baseness, spare no pains, however dirty to carry their point agst. men who are superior to the artifices practised. He was not disposed to run into extremes. He was as much principled as ever agst. aristocracy and monarchy. It was necessary on the one hand that the people should appoint one branch of the Govt. in order to inspire them with the necessary confidence. But he wished the election on the other to be so modified as to secure more effectually a just preference of merit. His idea was that the people should nominate certain persons in certain districts, out of whom the State Legislatures shd. make the appointment.

MR. WILSON. He wished for vigor in the Govt., but he wished that vigorous authority to flow immediately from the legitimate source of all authority. The Govt. ought to possess not only 1st the *force*, but 2dly. *the mind or sense* of the people at large. The Legislature ought to be the most exact transcript of the whole Society. Representation is made necessary only because it is impossible for the people to act collectively. The opposition was to be expected he said from the *Governments*, not from the Citizens of the States. The latter had parted as was observed [by Mr. King] with all the necessary powers; and it was immaterial to them, by whom they were exercised, if well exercised. The State officers were to be the losers of power. The people he supposed would be rather more attached to the national Govt. than to the State Govts. as being more important in itself, and more flattering to their pride. There is no danger of improper elections if made by *large* districts. Bad elections proceed from the small-ness of the districts which give an opportunity to bad men to in-trigue themselves into office.

MR. SHERMAN. If it were in view to abolish the State Govts. the elections ought to be by the people. If the State Govts. are to be continued, it is necessary in order to preserve harmony be-tween the National & State Govts. that the elections to the for-mer shd. be made by the latter. The right of participating in the National Govt. would be sufficiently secured to the people by their election of the State Legislatures. The objects of the Union, he thought were few. 1. defence agst. foreign danger. 2 agst. in-ternal disputes & a resort to force. 3. Treaties with foreign na-tions. 4 regulating foreign commerce, & drawing revenue from it. These & perhaps a few lesser objects alone rendered a Con-federation of the States necessary. All other matters civil & crim-inal would be much better in the hands of the States. The people are more happy in small than large States. States may indeed be too small as Rhode Island, & thereby be too subject to faction. Some others were perhaps too large, the powers of Govt. not be-ing able to pervade them. He was for giving the General Govt. power to legislate and execute within a defined province.

COL. MASON. Under the existing Confederacy, Cong. repre-sent the *States* not the *people* of the States: their acts operate on the *States,* not on the individuals. The case will be changed in the new plan of Govt. The people will be represented; they ought therefore to choose the Representatives. The requisites in actual representation are that the Reps. should sympathize with their constituents; shd. think as they think, & feel as they feel; and that for these purposes shd. even be residents among them. Much he sd. had been alledged agst. democratic elections. He admitted that much might be said; but it was to be considered that no Govt. was free from imperfections & evils; and that im-proper elections in many instances, were inseparable from Re-publican Govts. But compare these with the advantage of this Form in favor of the rights of the people, in favor of human na-ture. He was persuaded there was a better chance for proper elections by the people, if divided into large districts, than by the State Legislatures. Paper money had been issued by the lat-ter when the former were against it. Was it to be supposed that the State Legislatures then wd. not send to the Natl. legislature patrons of such projects, if the choice depended on them.

MR. MADISON considered an election of one branch at least of the Legislature by the people immediately, as a clear principle of free Govt. and that this mode under proper regulations had the additional advantage of securing better representatives, as well as of avoiding too great an agency of the State Govern-ments in the General one.—He differed from the member from Connecticut [Mr. Sharman] in thinking the objects mentioned to be all the principal ones that required a National Govt. Those were certainly important and necessary objects; but he com-bined with them the necessity of providing more effectually for the security of private rights, and the steady dispensation of Jus-tice. Interferences with these were evils which had more perhaps

than any thing else, produced this convention. Was it to be sup-posed that republican liberty could long exist under the abuses of it practiced in some of the States. The gentleman [Mr. Shar-man] had admitted that in a very small State, faction & oppres-sion wd. prevail. It was to be inferred then that wherever these prevailed the State was too small. Had they not prevailed in the largest as well as the smallest tho' less than in the smallest; and were we not thence admonished to enlarge the sphere as far as the nature of the Govt. would admit. This was the only defence agst. the inconveniencies of democracy consistent with the democratic form of Govt. All civilized Societies would be di-vided into different Sects, Factions, & interests, as they hap-pened to consist of rich & poor, debtors & creditors, the landed, the manufacturing, the commercial interests, the inhabitants of this district or that district, the followers of this political leader or that political leader, the disciples of this religious Sect or that religious Sect. In all cases where a majority are united by a com-mon interest or passion, the rights of the minority are in dan-ger. What motives are to restrain them? A prudent regard to the maxim that honesty is the best policy is found by experience to be as little regarded by bodies of men as by individuals. Respect for character is always diminished in proportion to the number among whom the blame or praise is to be divided. Conscience, the only remaining tie, is known to be inadequate in individu-als: in large numbers, little is to be expected from it. Besides, Re-ligion itself may become a motive to persecution & oppres-sion.—These observations are verified by the Histories of every Country antient & modern. In Greece & Rome the rich & poor, the creditors & debtors, as well as the patricians & plebians alternately oppressed each other with equal unmercifulness. What a source of oppression was the relation between the par-ent cities of Rome, Athens & Carthage, & their respective provinces: the former possessing the power, & the latter being sufficiently distinguished to be separate objects of it? Why was America so justly apprehensive of Parliamentary injustice? Be-cause G. Britain had a separate interest real or supposed, & if her authority had been admitted, could have pursued that inter-est at our expence. We have seen the mere distinction of colour made in the most enlightened period of time, a ground of the most oppressive dominion ever exercised by man over man. What has been the source of those unjust laws complained of among ourselves? Has it not been the real or supposed interest of the major number? Debtors have defrauded their creditors. The landed interest has borne hard on the mercantile interest. The Holders of one species of property have thrown a dispro-portion of taxes on the holders of another species. The lesson we are to draw from the whole is that where a majority are united by a common sentiment, and have an opportunity, the rights of the minor party become insecure. In a Republican Govt. the Majority if united have always an opportunity. The only remedy is to enlarge the sphere, & thereby divide the com-munity into so great a number of interests & parties, that in the 1st place a majority will not be likely at the same moment to have a common interest separate from that of the whole or of the minority; and in the 2d place, that in case they shd. have such an interest, they may not be apt to unite in the pursuit of it. It was incumbent on us then to try this remedy, and with that view to frame a republican system on such a scale & in such a form as will controul all the evils wch. have been experienced.

MR. DICKENSON considered it as essential that one branch of the Legislature shd. be drawn immediately from the people; and as expedient that the other shd. be chosen by the Legislatures of the States. This combination of the State Govt. with the national Govt. was as politic as it was unavoidable. In the formation of the Senate we ought to carry it through such a refining process as will assimilate it as near as may be to the House of Lords in England. He repeated his warm eulogiums on the British Constitution. He was for a strong National Govt. but for leaving the States a considerable agency in the System. The objection agst. making the former dependent on the latter might be obviated by giving to the Senate an authority permanent & irrevocable for three, five or seven years. Being thus independent they will speak & decide with becoming freedom.

MR. READ. Too much attachment is betrayed to the State Governts. We must look beyond their continuance. A national Govt. must soon of necessity swallow all of them up. They will soon be reduced to the mere office of electing the National Senate. He was agst. patching up the old federal System: he hoped the idea wd. be dismissed. It would be like putting new cloth on an old garment. The confederation was founded on temporary principles. It cannot last: it cannot be amended. If we do not establish a good Govt. on new principles, we must either go to ruin, or have the work to do over again. The people at large are wrongly suspected of being averse to a Genl. Govt. The aversion lies among interested men who possess their confidence.

MR. PIERCE was for an election by the people as to the 1st branch & by the States as to the 2d branch; by which means the Citizens of the States wd. be represented both *individually & collectively.*

General PINKNEY wished to have a good National Govt. & at the same time to leave a considerable share of power in the States. An election of either branch by the people scattered as they are in many States, particularly in S. Carolina was totally impracticable. He differed from gentlemen who thought that a choice by the people wd. be a better guard agst. bad measures, than by the Legislatures. A majority of the people in S. Carolina were notoriously for paper money as a legal tender; the Legislature had refused to make it a legal tender. The reason was that the latter had some sense of character and were restrained by that consideration. The State Legislatures also he said would be more jealous, & more ready to thwart the National Govt., if excluded from a participation in it. The Idea of abolishing these Legislatures wd. never go down.

MR. WILSON, would not have spoken again, but for what had fallen from Mr. Read; namely, that the idea of preserving the State Govts. ought to be abandoned. He saw no incompatibility between the National & State Govts. provided the latter were restrained to certain local purposes; nor any probability of their being devoured by the former. In all confederated Systems antient & modern the reverse had happened; the Generality being destroyed gradually by the usurpations of the parts composing it.

On the question for electing the 1st branch by the State Legislatures as moved by Mr. Pinkney: it was negatived:

Mass. no. Ct. ay. N.Y. no. N.J. ay. Pa. no. Del. no. Md. no. Va. no. N.C. no. S.C. ay. Geo. no.

. . . . .

THURSDAY JUNE 7TH.
IN COMMITTEE OF THE WHOLE

. . . .

The Clause providing for yo appointment of the 2d branch of the national Legislature, having lain blank since the last vote on the mode of electing it, to wit, by the 1st branch, Mr. Dickenson now moved "that the members of the 2d branch ought to be chosen by the individual Legislatures."

MR. SHARMAN seconded the motion; observing that the particular States would thus become interested in supporting the national Governmt and that a due harmony between the two Governments would be maintained. He admitted that the two ought to have separate and distinct jurisdictions, but that they ought to have a mutual interest in supporting each other.

MR. PINKNEY. If the small States should be allowed one Senator only, the number will be too great, there will be 80 at least.

MR. DICKENSON had two reasons for his motion. 1. because the sense of the States would be better collected through their Governments; than immediately from the people at large; 2. because he wished the Senate to consist of the most distinguished characters, distinguished for their rank in life and their weight of property, and bearing as strong a likeness to the British House of Lords as possible; and he thought such characters more likely to be selected by the State Legislatures, than in any other mode. The greatness of the number was no objection with him. He hoped there would be 80 and twice 80. of them. If their number should be small, the popular branch could not be balanced by them. The legislature of a numerous people ought to be a numerous body.

MR. WILLIAMSON, preferred a small number of Senators, but wished that each State should have at least one. He suggested 25 as a convenient number. The different modes of representation in the different branches, will serve as a mutual check.

MR. BUTLER was anxious to know the ratio of representation before he gave any opinion.

MR. WILSON. If we are to establish a national Government, that Government ought to flow from the people at large. If one branch of it should be chosen by the Legislatures, and the other by the people, the two branches will rest on different foundations, and dissensions will naturally arise between them. He wished the Senate to be elected by the people as well as the other branch, and the people might he divided into proper districts for the purpose & moved to postpone the motion of Mr. Dickenson, in order to take up one of that import.

MR. MORRIS 2ded him.

MR. READ proposed "that the Senate should be appointed by the Executive Magistrate out of a proper number of persons to be nominated by the individual legislatures." He said he thought it his duty, to speak his mind frankly. Gentlemen he hoped would not be alarmed at the idea. Nothing short of this approach towards a proper model of Government would answer the purpose, and he thought it best to come directly to the point at once.— His proposition was not seconded nor supported.

MR. MADISON, if the motion [of Mr. Dickenson] should be agreed to, we must either depart from the doctrine of proportional representation; or admit into the Senate a very large number of members. The first is inadmissible, being evidently unjust. The second is inexpedient. The use of the Senate is to consist in its proceeding with more coolness, with more system, & with more wisdom, than the popular branch. Enlarge their number and you communicate to them the vices which they are meant to correct. He differed from Mr. D. who thought that the additional number would give additional weight to the body. On the contrary it appeared to him that their weight would be in an inverse ratio to their number. The example of the Roman Tribunes was applicable. They lost their influence and power, in proportion as their number was augmented. The reason seemed to be obvious: They were appointed to take care of the popular interests & pretensions at Rome, because the people by reason of their numbers could not act in concert; were liable to fall into factions among themselves, and to become a prey to their aristocratic adversaries. The more the representatives of the people therefore were multiplied, the more they partook of the infirmities of their constituents, the more liable they became to be divided among themselves either from their own indiscretions or the artifices of the opposite faction, and of course the less capable of fulfilling their trust. When the weight of a set of men depends merely on their personal characters; the greater the number the greater the weight. When it depends on the degree of political authority lodged in them the smaller the number the greater the weight. These considerations might perhaps be combined in the intended Senate; but the latter was the material one

MR. GERRY. 4 modes of appointing the Senate have been mentioned. 1. by the 1st branch of the National Legislature. This would create a dependence contrary to the end proposed. 2. by the National Executive. This is a stride towards monarchy that few will think of. 3. by the people. The people have two great interests, the landed interest, and the commercial including the stockholders. To draw both branches from the people will leave no security to the latter interest; the people being chiefly composed of the landed interest, and erroneously supposing, that the other interests are adverse to it. 4 by the Individual Legisla-

tures. The elections being carried thro' this refinement, will be most likely to provide some check in favor of the commercial interest agst. the landed; without which oppression will take place, and no free Govt. can last long where that is the case. He was therefore in favor of this last.

MR. DICKENSON. The preservation of the States in a certain degree of agency is indispensable. It will produce that collision between the different authorities which should be wished for in order to check each other. To attempt to abolish the States altogether, would degrade the Councils of our Country, would be impracticable, would be ruinous. He compared the proposed National System to the Solar System, in which the States were the planets, and ought to be left to move freely in their proper orbits. The Gentleman from Pa. [Mr. Wilson] wished he said to extinguish these planets. If the State Governments were excluded from all agency in the national one, and all power drawn from the people at large, the consequence would be that the national Govt. would move in the same direction as the State Govt. now do, and would run into all the same mischiefs. The reform would only unite the 13 small streams into one great current pursuing the same course without any opposition whatever. He adhered to the opinion that the Senate ought to be composed of a large number, and that their influence from family weight & other causes would be increased thereby. He did not admit that the Tribunes lost their weight in proportion as their no. was augmented and gave a historical sketch of this institution. If the reasoning of [Mr. Madison] was good it would prove that the number of the Senate ought to be reduced below ten, the highest no. of the Tribunitial corps.

MR. WILSON. The subject it must be owned is surrounded with doubts and difficulties. But we must surmount them. The British Governmt cannot be our model. We have no materials for a similar one. Our manners, our laws, the abolition of entails and of primogeniture, the whole genius of the people, are opposed to it. He did not see the danger of the States being devoured by the Nationl. Govt. On the contrary, he wished to keep them from devouring the national Govt. He was not however for extinguishing these planets as was supposed by Mr. D.—neither did he on the other hand, believe that they would warm or enlighten the Sun. Within their proper orbits they must still be suffered to act for subordinate purposes for which their existence is made essential by the great extent of our Country. He could not comprehend in what manner the landed interest we be rendered less predominant in the Senate, by an election through the medium of the Legislatures then by the people themselves. If the legislatures, as was now complained, sacrificed the commercial to the landed interest, what reason was there to expect such a choice from them as would defeat their own views. He was for an election by the people in large districts which wd. be most likely to obtain men of intelligence & uprightness; subdividing the districts only for the accomodation of voters.

MR. MADISON could as little comprehend in what manner family weight, as desired by Mr. D. would be more certainly conveyed into the Senate through elections by the State legislatures, than in some other modes. The true question was in what mode the best choice wd. be made? If an election by the people, or thro' any other channel than the State Legislatures promised as uncorrupt & impartial a preference of merit, there could surely be no necessity for an appointment by those Legislatures. Nor was it apparent that a more useful check would be derived thro' that channel than from the people thro' some other. The great evils complained of were that the State Legislatures run into schemes of paper money &c. whenever solicited by the people, & sometimes without even the sanction of the people. Their influence then, instead of checking a like propensity in the National Legislature, may be expected to promote it. Nothing can be more contradictory than to say that the Natl. Legislature with[ou]t a proper check, will follow the example of the State Legislatures, & in the same breath, that the State Legislatures are the only proper check.

MR. SHARMAN opposed elections by the people in districts, as not likely to produce such fit men as elections by the State Legislatures.

MR. GERRY insisted that the commercial & monied interest wd. be more secure in the hands of the State Legislatures, than of the people at large. The former have more sense of character, and will be restrained by that from injustice. The people are for paper money when the Legislatures are agst. it. In Massts. the County Conventions had declared a wish for a depreciating paper that wd. sink itself. Besides, in some States there are two Branches in the Legislature, one of which is somewhat aristocratic. There wd. therefore be so far a better chance of refinement in the choice. There seemed, he thought to be three powerful objections agst. elections by districts. 1. it is impracticable; the people cannot be brought to one place for the purpose; and whether brought to the same place or not, numberless frauds wd. be unavoidable. 2. small States forming part of the same district with a large one, or large part of a large one, wd. have no chance of gaining an appointment for its citizens of merit. 3 a new source of discord wd. be opened between different parts of the same district.

MR. PINKNEY thought the 2d branch ought to be permanent & independent, & that the members of it wd. be rendered more so by receiving their appointment from the State Iegislatures. This mode wd. avoid the rivalships & discontents incident to the election by districts. He was for dividing the States into three classes according to their respective sizes, & for allowing to the 1st class three members—to the 2d two, & to the 3d one.

On the question for postponing Mr. Dickinson's motion referring the appointment of the Senate to the State Legislatures, in order to consider MR. WILSON's for referring it to the people

Mass. no. Cont. no. N. Y. no. N. J. no. Pa. ay Del. no. Md. no. Va. no. N. C. no. S. C. no. Geo. no.

COL. MASON. whatever power may be necessary for the Natl. Govt. a certain portion must necessarily be left in the States. It is impossible for one power to pervade the extreme parts of the U. S. so as to carry equal justice to them. The State Legislatures also ought to have some means of defending themselves agst. encroachments of the Natl. Govt. In every other department we have studiously endeavored to provide for its self-defence. Shall we leave the States alone unprovided with the means for this purpose? And what better means can we provide than the giving them some share in, or rather to make them a constituent part of, the Natl. Establishment. There is danger on both sides no doubt; but we have only seen the evils arising on the side of the State Govts. Those on the other side remain to be displayed. The example of Congs does not apply. Congs. had no power to carry their acts into execution as the Natl. Govt. will have.

On MR. DICKINSON's motion for an appointment of the Senate by the State-Legislatures.

Mass. ay. Ct. ay. N. Y. ay. Pa. ay Del. ay. Md. ay. Va. ay N. C. ay. S. C. ay. Geo. ay.

. . . .

MONDAY. JUNE 11TH. MR. ABRAHAM BALDWIN FROM GEORGIA TOOK HIS SEAT. IN COMMITTEE OF THE WHOLE

The clause concerning the rule of suffrage in the natl. Legislature postponed on Saturday was resumed.

MR. SHARMAN proposed that the proportion of suffrage in the 1st branch should be according to the respective numbers of free inhabitants; and that in the second branch or Senate, each State should have one vote and no more. He said as the States would remain possessed of certain individual rights, each State ought to be able to protect itself: otherwise a few large States will rule the rest. The House of Lords in England he observed had certain particular rights under the Constitution, and hence they have an equal vote with the House of Commons that they may be able to defend their rights.

MR. RUTLIDGE proposed that the proportion of suffrage in the 1st branch should be according to the quotas of contribution. The justice of this rule he said could not be contested. MR. BUTLER urged the same idea: adding that money was power; and that the States ought to have weight in the Govt. in proportion to their wealth.

MR. KING & MR. WILSON, in order to bring the question to a point moved "that the right of suffrage in the first branch of the national Legislature ought not to be according the rule established in the articles of Confederation, but according to some equitable ratio of representation." The clause so far as it related to suffrage in the first branch was postponed in order to consider this motion.

MR. DICKENSON contended for the *actual* contributions of the States as the rule of their representation & suffrage in the first branch. By thus connecting the interest of the States with their duty, the latter would be sure to be performed.

MR. KING remarked that it was uncertain what mode might be used in levying a national revenue; but that it was probable, imposts would be one source of it. If the *actual* contributions were to be the rule the non-importing States, as Cont. & N. Jersey, wd. be in a bad situation indeed. It might so happen that they wd. have no representation. This situation of particular States had been always one powerful argument in favor of the 5 Per Ct. impost.

The question being abt. to be put Docr. FRANKLIN sd. he had thrown his ideas of the matter on a paper wch MR. WILSON read to the Committee in the words following—

MR. CHAIRMAN

It has given me great pleasure to observe that till this point, the proportion of representation, came before us, our debates were carried on with great coolness & temper. If any thing of a contrary kind, has on this occasion appeared, I hope it will not be repeated; for we are sent here to *consult*, not to *contend*, with each other; and declarations of a fixed opinion, and of determined resolution, never to change it, neither enlighten nor convince us. Positiveness and warmth on one side, naturally beget their like on the other; and tend to create and augment discord & division in a great concern, wherein harmony & Union are extremely necessary to give weight to our Councils, and render them effectual in promoting & securing the common good.

I must own that I was originally of opinion it would be better if every member of Congress, or our national Council, were to consider himself rather as a representative of the whole, than as an Agent for the interests of a particular State; in which case the proportion of members for each State would be of less consequence, & it would not be very material whether they voted by States or individually. But as I find this is not to be expected, I now think the number of Representatives should bear some proportion to the number of the Represented; and that the decisions shd. be by the majority of members, not by the majority of States. This is objected to from an apprehension that the greater States would then swallow up the smaller. I do not at present clearly see what advantage the greater States could propose to themselves by swallowing the smaller, and therefore do not apprehend they would attempt it. I recollect that in the beginning of this Century, when the Union was proposed of the two Kingdoms, England & Scotland, the Scotch Patriots were full of fears, that unless they had an equal number of Representatives in Parliament, they should be ruined by the superiority of the English. They finally agreed however that the different proportions of importance in the Union, of the two Nations should be attended to, whereby they were to have only forty members in the House of Commons, and only sixteen in the House of Lords; A very great inferiority of numbers! And yet to this day I do not recollect that any thing has been done in the Parliament of Great Britain to the prejudice of Scotland; and whoever looks over the lists of public officers, Civil & military of that nation will find I believe that the North Britons enjoy at least their full proportion of emolument.

But, Sir, in the present mode of voting by States, it is equally in the power of the lesser States to swallow up the greater; and this is mathematically demonstrable. Suppose for example, that 7 smaller States had each 3 members in the House, and the 6

larger to have one with another 6 members; and that upon a question, two members of each smaller State should be in the affirmative and one in the Negative; they will make

Affirmatives . . . . 14 . . . . Negatives   7
And that all the larger
States should be unani-
mously in the Negative,
they would make . . . . Negatives   <u>36</u>

   In all 43

It is then apparent that the 14 carry the question against the 43, and the minority overpowers the majority, contrary to the common practice of Assemblies in all Countries and Ages.

The greater States Sir are naturally as unwilling to have their property left in the disposition of the smaller, as the smaller are to have theirs in the disposition of the greater. An honorable gentleman has, to avoid this difficulty, hinted a proposition of equalizing the States. It appears to me an equitable one, and I should, for my own part, not be against such a measure, practicable. Formerly, indeed, when almost every province had a different Constitution, some with greater others with fewer privileges, it was of importance to the borderers when their boundaries were contested, whether by running the division lines, they were placed on one side or the other. At present when such differences are done away, it is less material. The Interest of a State is made up of the interests of its individual members. If they are not injured, the State is not injured. Small States are more easily well & happily governed than large ones. If therefore in such an equal division, it should be found necessary to diminish Pennsylvania, I should not be averse to the giving a part of it to N. Jersey, and another to Delaware. But as there would probably be considerable difficulties in adjusting such a division; and however equally made at first, it would be continually varying by the augmentation of inhabitants in some States, and their fixed proportion in others; and thence frequent occasion for new divisions, I beg leave to propose for the consideration of the Committee another mode, which appears to me, to be as equitable, more easily carried into practice, and more permanent in its nature.

Let the weakest State say what proportion of money or force it is able and willing to furnish for the general purposes of the Union.

Let all the others oblige themselves to furnish each an equal proportion.

The whole of these joint supplies to be absolutely in the disposition of Congress.

The Congress in this case to be composed of an equal number of Delegates from each State.

And their decisions to be by the Majority of individual members voting.

If these joint and equal supplies should on particular occasions not be sufficient, Let Congress make requisitions on the richer and more powerful States for farther aids, to be voluntarily afforded, leaving to each State the right of considering the necessity and utility of the aid desired, and of giving more or less as it should be found proper.

This mode is not new, it was formerly practiced with success by the British Government with respect to Ireland and the Colonies. We sometimes gave even more than they expected, or thought just to accept; and in the last war carried on while we were united, they gave us back in 5 years a million Sterling. We should probably have continued such voluntary contributions, whenever the occasions appeared to require them for the common good of the Empire. It was not till they chose to force us, and to deprive us of the merit and pleasure of voluntary contributions that we refused & resisted. Those contributions however were to be disposed of at the pleasure of a Government in which we had no representative. I am therefore persuaded, that they will not be refused to one in which the Representation shall be equal

My learned Colleague [Mr. Wilson] has already mentioned that the present method of voting by States, was submitted to originally by Congress, under a conviction of its impropriety, inequality, and injustice. This appears in the words of their Resolution. It is of Sept. 6. 1774. The words are

"Resolved that in determining questions in this Congs each Colony or province shall have one vote: The Congs. not being possessed of or at present able to procure materials for ascertaining the importance of each Colony."

On the question for agreeing to Mr. Kings and Mr. Wilsons motion it passed in the affirmative

Massts. ay. Ct. ay. N. Y. no. N. J. no. Pa. ay. Del. no. Md. divd. Va. ay. N. C. ay. S. C. ay. Geo. ay.

It was then moved by Mr. Rutlidge 2ded. by Mr. Butler to add to the words "equitable ratio of representation" at the end of the motion just agreed to, the words "according to the quotas of contribution." On motion of Mr. Wilson seconded by Mr. C. Pinckney, this was postponed; in order to add, after, after the words "equitable ratio of representation" the words following "in proportion to the whole number of white & other free Citizens & inhabitants of every age sex & condition including those bound to servitude for a term of years and three fifths of all other persons not comprehended in the foregoing description, except Indians not paying taxes, in each State," this being the rule in the Act of Congress agreed to by eleven States, for apportioning quotas of revenue on the States, and requiring a Census only every 5–7, or 10 years.

Mr. Gerry thought property not the rule of representation. Why then shd. the blacks, who were property in the South, be in the rule of representation more than the Cattle & horses of the North.

On the question,— Mass: Con: N. Y. Pen: Maryd. Virga. N.C. S.C. & Geo: were in the affirmative: N. J. & Del: in the negative.

Mr. Sharman moved that a question be taken whether each State shall have one vote in the 2d branch. Every thing he said depended on this. The smaller States would never agree to the plan on any other principle than an equality of suffrage in this branch. Mr. Elsworth seconded the motion. On the question for allowing each State one vote in the 2d branch.

Massts. no. Cont. ay. N. Y. ay. N. J. ay. Pa no. Del. ay. Md. ay. Va. no. N. C. no. S. C. no. Geo. no.

Mr. Wilson & Mr. Hamilton moved that the right of suffrage in the 2d branch ought to be according to the same rule as in the 1st branch. On this question for making the ratio of representation the same in the 2d as in the 1st branch it passed in the affirmative:

Massts. ay. Cont. no. N. Y. no. N. J. no. Pa. ay. Del. no. Md. no. Va. ay. N.C. ay. S.C. ay. Geo. ay.

. . . .

THURSDAY JUNE 21. IN CONVENTION

. . . .

The *third* resolution of the Report taken into consideration.

Genl. Pinckney moved "that the 1st branch, instead of being elected by the people, shd. be elected in such manner as the Legislature of each State should direct." He urged 1. that this liberty would give more satisfaction, as the Legislatures could then accomodate the mode to the conveniency & opinions of the people. 2. that it would avoid the undue influence of large Counties which would prevail if the elections were to be made in districts as must be the mode intended by the Report of the Committee. 3. that otherwise disputed elections must be referred to the General Legislature which would be attended with intolerable expence and trouble to the distant parts of the republic.

Mr. L. Martin seconded the Motion.

Col. Hamilton considered the motion as intended manifestly to transfer the election from the people to the State Legislatures, which would essentially vitiate the plan. It would increase that State influence which could not be too watchfully guarded agst. All too must admit the possibility, in case the Genl. Govt. shd. maintain itself, that the State Govts. might gradually dwindle into nothing. The system therefore shd. not be engrafted on what might possibly fail.

Mr. Mason urged the necessity of retaining the election by the people. Whatever inconveniency may attend the democratic principle, it must actuate one part of the Govt. It is the only security for the rights of the people.

Mr. Sherman, would like an election by the Legislatures best, but is content with plan as it stands.

Mr. Rutlidge could not admit the solidity of the distinction between a mediate & immediate election by the people. It was the same thing to act by oneself, and to act by another. An election by the Legislature would be more refined than an election immediately by the people: and would be more likely to correspond with the sense of the whole community. If this Convention had been chosen by the people in districts it is not to be supposed that such proper characters would have been preferred. The Delegates to Congs. he thought had also been fitter men than would have been appointed by the people at large.

MR. WILSON considered the election of the 1st branch by the people not only as the corner Stone, but as the foundation of the fabric: and that the difference between a mediate & immediate election was immense. The difference was particularly worthy of notice in this respect: that the Legislatures are actuated not merely by the sentiment of the people; but have an official sentiment opposed to that of the Genl. Govt. and perhaps to that of the people themselves.

MR. KING enlarged on the same distinction. He supposed the Legislatures wd. constantly choose men subservient to their own views as contrasted to the general interest; and that they might even devise modes of election that wd. be subversive of the end in view. He remarked several instances in which the views of a State might be at variance with those of the Genl. Govt.: and mentioned particularly a competition between the National & State debts, for the most certain & productive funds.

GENL. PINKNEY was for making the State Govt. a part of the General System. If they were to be abolished, or lose their agency, S. Carolina & other States would have but a small share of the benefits of Govt.

On the question for Genl. Pinkney motion to substitute election of 1st branch in such mode as the Legislatures should appoint, instead of its being elected by the people."

Massts. no. Cont. ay. N. Y. no. N. J. ay. Pa. no. Del. ay. Md. divd. Va. no. N. C. no. S. C. ay Geo. no.

GENERAL PINKNEY then moved that the 1st branch be elected *by the people* in such mode as the Legislatures should direct; but waved it on its being hinted that such a provision might be more properly tried in the detail of the plan.

On the question for ye election of the 1st branch by the *people*."

Massts. ay. Cont. ay. N.Y. ay. N.J. no. Pa. ay. Del. ay. Md. divd. Va. ay. N.C. ay. S.C. ay Geo. ay.

Election of the 1st branch "for the term of three years," considered

MR. RANDOLPH moved to strike out, "three years" and insert "two years"—he was sensible that annual elections were a source of great mischiefs in the States, yet it was the want of such checks agst. the popular intemperance as were now proposed, that rendered them so mischievous. He would have preferred annual to biennial, but for the extent of the U.S. and the inconveniency which would result from them to the representatives of the extreme parts of the Empire. The people were attached to frequency of elections. All the Constitutions of the States except that of S. Carolina, had established annual elections.

MR. DICKENSON. The idea of annual elections was borrowed from the antient usage of England, a country much less extensive than ours. He supposed biennial would be inconvenient. He preferred triennial: and in order to prevent the inconveniency of an entire change of the whole number at the same moment, suggested a rotation, by an annual election of one third.

MR. ELSEWORTH was opposed to three years, supposing that even one year was preferable to two years. The people were fond of frequent elections and might be safely indulged in one branch of the Legislature. He moved for 1 year.

MR. STRONG seconded & supported the motion.

MR. WILSON being for making the 1st branch an effectual representation of the people at large, preferred an annual election of it. This frequency was most familiar & pleasing to the people. It would be not more inconvenient to them, than triennial elections, as the people in all the States have annual meetings with which the election of the National representatives might be made to co-incide. He did not conceive that it would be necessary for the Natl. Legisl: to sit constantly; perhaps not half—perhaps not one fourth of the year.

MR. MADISON was persuaded that annual elections would be extremely inconvenient and apprehensive that biennial would be too much so: he did not mean inconvenient to the electors; but to the representatives. They would have to travel seven or eight hundred miles from the distant parts of the Union; and would probably not be allowed even a reimbursement of their expences. Besides, none of those who wished to be re-elected would remain at the seat of Governmt.; confiding that their absence would not affect them. The members of Congs. had done this with few instances of disappointment. But as the choice was here to be made by the people themselves who would be much less complaisant to individuals, and much more susceptible to impressions from the presence of a Rival candidate, it must be supposed that the members from the most distant States would travel backwards & forwards at least as often as the elections should be repeated. Much was to be said also on the time requisite for new members who would always form a large proportion, to acquire that knowledge of the affairs of the States in general without which their trust could not be usefully discharged.

MR. SHERMAN preferred annual elections, but would be content with biennial. He thought the Representatives ought to return home and mix with the people. By remaining at the seat of Govt. they would acquire the habits of the place which might differ from those of their Constituents.

COL. MASON observed that the States being differently situated such a rule ought to be formed as would put them as nearly as possible on a level. If elections were annual the middle States would have a great advantage over the extreme ones. He wished them to be biennial; and the rather as in that case they would coincide with the periodical elections of S. Carolina as well of the other States.

COL. HAMILTON urged the necessity of 3 years. There ought to be neither too much nor too little dependence, on the popular sentiments. The checks in the other branches of Govert. would be but feeble, and would need every auxiliary principle that could be interwoven. The British House of Commons were elected septennially, yet the democratic spirit of the Constitution had not ceased. Frequency of elections tended to make the people listless to them; and to facilitate the success of little cabals. This evil was complained of in all the States. In Virga. it had been lately found necessary to force the attendance & voting of the people by severe regulations.

On the question for striking out "three years"

Massts. ay. Cont. ay. N.Y. no. N.J. divd. Pa. ay. Del. no. Md. no. Va. ay. N.C. ay. S.C. ay. Geo. ay.

The motion for "two years" was then inserted nem. con. Adjd.

FRIDAY JUNE 22. IN CONVENTION

The clause in Resol. 3. "to receive fixed stipends to be paid out of the Nationl. Treasury" considered.

MR. ELSEWORTH, moved to substitute payment by the States out of their own Treasurys: observing that the manners of different States were very different in the Stile of living and in the profits accruing from the exercise of like talents. What would be deemed therefore a reasonable compensation in some States, in others would be very unpopular, and might impede the system of which it made a part.

MR. WILLIAMSON favored the idea. He reminded the House of the prospect of new States to the Westward. They would be poor—would pay little into the common Treasury—and would have a different interest from the old States. He did not think therefore that the latter ought to pay the expences of men who would be employed in thwarting their measures & interests.

MR. GHORUM, wished not to refer the matter to the State Legislatures who were always paring down salaries in such a manner as to keep out of offices men most capable of executing the functions of them. He thought also it would be wrong to fix the compensations by the constitutions, because we could not venture to make it as liberal as it ought to be without exciting an enmity agst. the whole plan. Let the Natl. Legisl: provide for their own wages from time to time; as the State Legislatures do. He had not seen this part of their power abused, nor did he apprehend an abuse of it.

MR. RANDOLPH feared we were going too far, in consulting popular prejudices. Whatever respect might be due to them, in lesser matters, or in cases where they formed the permanent character of the people, he thought it neither incumbent on nor honorable for the Convention, to sacrifice right & justice to that consideration. If the States were to pay the members of the Natl. Legislature, a dependence would be created that would vitiate the whole System. The whole nation has an interest in the attendance & services of the members. The Nationl. Treasury therefore is the proper fund for supporting them.

MR. KING, urged the danger of creating a dependence on the States by leavg. to them the payment of the members of the Natl. Legislature. He supposed it wd. be best to be explicit as to the compensation to be allowed. A reserve on that point, or a reference to the Natl. Legislature of the quantum, would excite greater opposition than any sum that would be actually necessary or proper.

MR. SHERMAN contended for referring both the quantum and the payment of it to the State Legislatures.

MR. WILSON was agst. *fixing* the compensation as circumstances would change and call for a change of the amount. He thought it of great moment that the members of the Natl. Govt. should be left as independent as possible of the State Govts. in all respects.

MR. MADISON concurred in the necessity of preserving the compensations for the Natl. Govt. independent on the State Govts. but at the same time approved of *fixing* them by the Constitution, which might be done by taking a standard which wd. not vary with circumstances. He disliked particularly the policy suggested by Mr. Williamson of leaving the members from the poor States beyond the Mountains, to the precarious & parsimonious support of their constituents. If the Western States hereafter arising should be admitted into the Union, they ought to be considered as equals & as brethren. If their representatives were to be associated in the Common Councils, it was of common concern that such provisions should be made as would invite the most capable and respectable characters into the service.

MR. HAMILTON apprehended inconveniency from *fixing* the wages. He was strenuous agst. making the National Council dependent on the Legislative rewards of the States. Those who pay are the masters of those who are paid. Payment by the States would be unequal as the distant States would have to pay for the same term of attendance and more days in travelling to & from the seat of the Govt. He expatiated emphatically on the difference between the feelings & views of the *people*—& the *Governments* of the States arising from the personal interest & official inducements which must render the latter unfriendly to the Genl. Govt.

MR. WILSON moved that the Salaries of the 1st branch *"be ascertained by the National Legislature,"* and be paid out of the Natl. Treasury.

MR. MADISON, thought the members of the Legisl. too much interested to ascertain their own compensation. It wd. be indecent to put their hands into the public purse for the sake of their own pockets.

On this question Mas. no. Cont. no. N.Y. divd. N.J. ay. Pa. ay. Del. no. Md. no. Va. no. N.C. no. S.C. no. Geo. divd.

On the question for striking out "Natl. Treasury" as moved by MR. ELSEWORTH.

MR. HAMILTON renewed his opposition to it. He pressed the distinction between State Govts. & the people. The former wd. be the rivals of the Genl. Govt. The State legislatures ought not therefore to be the paymasters of the latter.

MR. ELSEWORTH. If we are jealous of the State Govts. they will be so of us. If on going home I tell them we gave the Gen: Govtt. such powers because we cd. not trust you, will they adopt it, and witht. yr. approbation it is a nullity.

Massts. ay. Cont. ay. N.Y. divd.; N.J. no Pena. no. Del. no. Md. no. Va. no. N.C. ay. S.C. ay. Geo. divd.

On a question for substituting "adequate compensation" in place of "fixt stipends" it was agreed to nem. con. the friends of the latter being willing that the practicability of *fixing* the compensation should be considered hereafter in forming the details.

It was then moved by MR. BUTLER that a question be taken on both points jointly; to wit "adequate compensation to be paid out of the Natl. Treasury." It was objected to as out of order, the parts having been separately decided on. The Presidt. referd. the question of order to the House, and it was determined to be in order. Con. N.J. Del. Md. N.C. S.C.—ay— N.Y. Pa. Va. Geo.—no—Mass: divided. The question on the sentence was then postponed by S. Carolina in right of the State.

COL. MASON moved to insert "twenty-five years of age as a qualification for the members of the 1st branch." He thought it absurd that a man to day should not be permitted by the law to make a bargain for himself, and tomorrow should be authorized to manage the affairs of a great nation. It was the more extraordinary as every man carried with him in his own experience a scale for measuring the deficiency of young politicians; since he would if interrogated be obliged to declare that his political opinions at the age of 21. were too crude & erroneous to merit an influence on public measures. It had been said that Congs. had proved a good school for our young men. It might be so for any thing he knew but if it were, he chose that they should bear the expence of their own education.

MR. WILSON was agst. abridging the rights of election in any shape. It was the same thing whether this were done by disqualifying the objects of choice, or the persons chusing. The motion tended to damp the efforts of genius, and of laudable ambition. There was no more reason for incapacitating *youth* than *age*, where the requisite qualifications were found. Many instances might be mentioned of signal services rendered in high stations to the public before the age of 25: The present Mr. Pitt and Lord Bolingbroke were striking instances.

On the question for inserting "25 years of age."

Massts. no. Cont. ay. N.Y. divd. N.J. ay. Pa. no. Del. ay. Md. ay. N.C. ay. S.C. ay. Geo. no.

MR. GHORUM moved to strike out the last member of 3 Resol: concerning ineligibility of members of the 1st branch to off'ces during the term of their membership & for one year after. He considered it as unnecessary & injurious. It was true abuses had been displayed in G. B. but no one cd. say how far they might have contributed to preserve the due influence of the Govt. nor what might have ensued in case the contrary theory had been tried.

MR. BUTLER opposed it. This precaution agst. intrigue was necessary. He appealed to the example of G. B. where men got into Parlt. that they might get offices for themselves or their friends. This was the source of the corruption that ruined their Govt.

MR. KING, thought we were refining too much. Such a restriction on the members would discourage merit. It would also give a pretext to the Executive for bad appointments, as he might always plead this as a bar to the choice he wished to have made.

MR. WILSON was agst. fettering elections, and discouraging merit. He suggested also the fatal consequence in time of war, of

rendering perhaps the best Commanders ineligible: appealing to our situation during the late war, and indirectly leading to a recollection of the appointment of the Commander in Chief out of Congress.

COL. MASON was for shutting the door at all events agst. corruption. He enlarged on the venality and abuses in this particular in G. Britain: and alluded to the multiplicity of foreign Embassies by Congs. The disqualification he regarded as a corner stone in the fabric.

COL. HAMILTON. There are inconveniences on both sides. We must take man as we find him, and if we expect him to serve the public must interest his passions in doing so. A reliance on pure patriotism had been the source of many of our errors. He thought the remark of MR. GHORUM a just one. It was impossible to say what wd. be effect in G. B. of such a reform as had been urged. It was known that one of the ablest politicians [MR. HUME,] had pronounced all that influence on the side of the crown, which went under the name of corruption, an essential part of the weight which maintained the equilibrium of the Constitution.

On Mr. Ghorum's Motion for striking out "ineligibility,"

Masts. ay. Cont. no. N.Y. divd. N.J. ay. Pa. divd. Del. divd. Mard. no. Va. no. N.C. ay. S.C. no. Geo. ay. Adjd.

SATURDAY JUNE 23. IN CONVENTION

The 3. Resol: resumed.

On Question yesterday postponed by S. Carol: for agreeing to the whole sentence "for allowing an adequate compensation to be paid out of the *Treasury of the U. States*"

Masts. ay. Cont. no. N.Y. no. N.J. ay. Pena. ay Del. no. Md. ay. Va. ay. N.C. no. S.C. no. Geo divided. So the question was lost, & the sentence not inserted:

GENL. PINKNEY moves to strike out the ineligibility of members of the 1st branch to offices established "by a particular State." He argued from the inconveniency to which such a restriction would expose both the members of the 1st branch, and the States wishing for their services; from the smallness of the object to be attained by the restriction.

It wd. seem from the ideas of some that we are erecting a Kingdom to be divided agst. itself, he disapproved such a fetter on the Legislature.

MR. SHERMAN seconds the motion. It wd. seem that we are erecting a Kingdom at war with itself. The Legislature ought not to be fettered in such a case. on the question

Masts. no. Cont. ay. N.Y. ay. N.J. ay. Pa. no. Del. no. Md. ay. Va. ay. N.C. ay. S.C. ay. Geo. ay.

MR. MADISON renewed his motion yesterday made & waved to render the members of the 1st branch "ineligible during their term of service, & for one year after—to such offices only as should be established, or the emoluments thereof, augmented by the Legislature of the U. States during the time of their being members." He supposed that the unnecessary creation of offices, and increase of salaries, were the evils most experienced, & that if the door was shut agst. them: it might properly be left open for the appointt. of members to other offices as an encouragemt. to the Legislative service.

MR. ALEX: MARTIN seconded the motion.

MR. BUTLER. The amendt. does not go far eno' & wd. be easily evaded.

MR. RUTLEDGE, was for preserving the Legislature as pure as possible, by shutting the door against appointments of its own members to offices, which was one source of its corruption.

MR. MASON. The motion of my colleague is but a partial remedy for the evil. He appealed to him as a witness of the shameful partiality of the Legislature of Virginia to its own members. He enlarged on the abuses & corruption in the British Parliament, connected with the appointment of its members. He cd. not suppose that a sufficient number of Citizens could not be found who would be ready, without the inducement of eligibility to offices, to undertake the Legislative service. Genius & virtue it may be said, ought to be encouraged. Genius, for aught he knew, might, but that virtue should be encouraged by such a species of venality, was an idea, that at least had the merit of being new.

MR. KING remarked that we were refining too much in this business; and that the idea of preventing intrigue and solicitation of offices was chimerical. You say that no member shall himself be eligible to any office. Will this restrain him from availing himself of the same means which would gain appointments for himself, to gain them for his son, his brother, or any other object of his partiality. We were losing therefore the advantages on one side, without avoiding the evils on the other.

MR. WILSON supported the motion. The proper cure he said for corruption in the Legislature was to take from it the power of appointing to offices. One branch of corruption would indeed remain, that of creating unnecessary offices, or granting unnecessary salaries, and for that the amendment would be a proper remedy. He animadverted on the impropriety of stigmatizing with the name of venality the laudable ambition of rising into the honorable offices of the Government; an ambition most likely to be felt in the early & most incorrupt period of life, & which all wise & free Govts. had deemed it sound policy, to cherish, not to check. The members of the Legislature have perhaps the hardest & least profitable task of any who engage in the service of the state. Ought this merit to be made a disqualification?

MR. SHERMAN, observed that the motion did not go far enough. It might be evaded by the creation of a new office, the translation to it of a person from another office, and the appointment of a member of the Legislature to the latter. A new Embassy might be established to a new Court, & an ambassador taken from another, in order to *create* a vacancy for a favorite member. He admitted that inconveniencies lay on both sides. He hoped there wd. be sufficient inducements to the public service without resorting to the prospect of desireable offices, and on the whole was rather agst. the motion of MR. MADISON.

MR. GERRY thought there was great weight in the objection of MR. SHERMAN. He added as another objection agst. admitting the eligibility of members in any case that it would produce intrigues of ambitious men for displacing proper officers, in order to create vacancies for themselves. In answer to Mr. King he observed that although members, if disqualified themselves might still intrigue & cabal for their sons, brothers &c, yet as their own interest would be dearer to them, than those of their nearest connections, it might be expected they would go greater lengths to promote it.

MR. MADISON had been led to this motion as a middle ground between an eligibility in all cases, and an absolute disqualification. He admitted the probable abuses of an eligibility of the members, to offices, particularly within the gift of the Legislature He had witnessed the partiality of such bodies to their own members, as had been remarked of the Virginia assembly by his colleague [COL. MASON]. He appealed however to him, in turn to vouch another fact not less notorious in Virginia, that the backwardness of the best citizens to engage in the Legislative service gave but too great success to unfit characters. The question was not to be viewed on one side only. The advantages & disadvantages on both ought to be fairly compared. The objects to be aimed at were to fill all offices with the fittest characters, & to draw the wisest & most worthy citizens into the Legislative service. If on one hand, public bodies were partial to their own members; on the other they were as apt to be misled by taking characters on report, or the authority of patrons and dependents. All who had been concerned in the appointment of strangers on those recommendations must be sensible of this truth. Nor wd. the partialities of such Bodies be obviated by disqualifying their own members. Candidates for office would hover round the seat of Govt. or be found among the residents there, and practice all the means of courting the favor of the members. A great proportion of the appointments made by the States were evidently brought about in this way. In the general Govt. the evil must be still greater, the characters of distant states, being much less known throughout the U. States than those of the distant parts of the same State. The elections by Congress had generally turned on men living at the seat of the fedl. Govt. or in its neighbourhood.—As to the next object, the impulse to the Legislative service, was evinced by experience to be in general too feeble with those best qualified for it. This inconveniency wd. also be more felt in the Natl. Govt. than in the State Govts. as the sacrifices reqd. from the distant members, wd. be much greater, and the pecuniary provisions, probably, more disproportiate. It wd. therefore be impolitic to add fresh objections to the Legislative service by an absolute disqualification of its members. The point in question was whether this would be an objection with the most capable citizens. Arguing from experience he concluded that it would. The Legislature of Virga. would probably have been without many of its best members, if in that situation, they had been ineligible to Congs. to the Govt. & other honorable offices of the State.

MR. BUTLER thought Characters fit for office wd. never be unknown.

COL. MASON. If the members of the Legislature are disqualified, still the honors of the State will induce those who aspire to them to enter that service, as the field in which they can best display & improve their talents, & lay the train for their subsequent advancement.

MR. JENIFER remarked that in Maryland, the Senators chosen for five years, cd. hold no other office & that this circumstance gained them the greatest confidence of the people.

On the question for agreeing to the motion of Mr. Madison.

Massts. divd. Ct. ay. N.Y. no. N.J. ay. Pa. no. Del. no. Md. no. Va. no. N.C. no. S.C. no. Geo. no.

MR. SHERMAN movd. to insert the words "and incapable of holding" after the words "eligible to offices" wch. was agreed to without opposition.

The word "established" & the words "Natl. Govt." were struck out of Resolution 3d.:

MR. SPAIGHT called for a division of the question, in consequence of which it was so put, as that it turned in the first member of it, *"on the ineligibility of the members during the term for which they were elected"* —whereon the States were,

Massts. divd. Ct. ay. N.Y. ay. N.J. ay. Pa. no. Del. ay. Md. ay. Va. ay. N.C. ay. S.C. ay. Geo. no.

On the 2d member of the sentence extending ineligibility of members to one year after the term for which they were elected COL. MASON thought this essential to guard agst. evasions by resignations, and stipulations for office to be fulfilled at the expiration of the legislative term. MR. GERRY, had known such a case. MR. HAMILTON. Evasions cd. not be prevented—as by proxies—by friends holding for a year, & then opening the way &c. MR. RUTLIDGE admitted the possibility of evasions but was for controuling them as possible. Mass. no. Ct. no. N.Y. ay. N.J. no. Pa. divd. Del. ay. Mard. ay Va. no. N.C. no. S.C. ay. Geo. no.

Adjd.

MONDAY. JUNE 25. IN CONVENTION

. . . .

The mode of constituting the 2d branch being under consideration.

The word "national" was struck out and "United States" inserted.

MR. GHORUM, inclined to a compromise as to the rule of proportion. He thought there was some weight in the objections of the small States. If Va. should have 16. votes & Del[aw]re with several other States together 16. those from Virg[ini]a would be more likely to unite than the others, and would therefore have an undue influence. This remark was applicable not only to States, but to Counties or other districts of the same State. Accordingly the Constitution of Massts. had provided that the representatives of the larger districts should not be in an exact ratio to their numbers. And experience he thought had strewn the provision to be expedient.

MR. READ. The States have heretofore been in a sort of partnership. They ought to adjust their old affairs before they open a new account. He brought into view the appropriation of the common interest in the Western lands, to the use of particular States. Let justice be done on this head; let the fund be applied fairly & equally to the discharge of the general debt, and the smaller States who had been injured; would listen then perhaps to those ideas of just representation which had been held out.

MR. GHORUM. Did not see how the Convention could interpose in the case. Errors he allowed had been committed on the subject. But Congs. were now using their endeavors to rectify them. The best remedy would be such a Government as would have vigor enough to do justice throughout. This was certainly the best chance that could be afforded to the smaller States.

MR. WILSON. the question is shall the members of the 2d branch be chosen by the Legislatures of the States? When he considered the amazing extent of Country the immense population which is to fill it, the influence which the Govt. we are to form will have, not only on the present generation of our people & their multiplied posterity, but on the whole Globe, he was lost in the magnitude of the object. The project of Henry the 4th & his Statesmen was but the picture in miniature of the great portrait to be exhibited. He was opposed to an election by the State Legislatures. In explaining his reasons it was necessary to observe the twofold relation in which the people would stand. 1. as Citizens of the Genl. Govt. 2. as Citizens of their particular State. The Genl. Govt. was meant for them in the first capacity: the State Govts. in the second. Both Govts. were derived from the people—both meant for the people—both therefore ought to be regulated on the same principles. The same train of ideas which belonged to the relation of the Citizens to their State Govts. were applicable to their relation to the Genl. Govt. and in forming the latter, we ought to proceed, by abstracting as much as possible from the idea of State Govts. With respect to the province & objects of the Genl. Govt. they should be considered as having no existence. The election of the 2d branch by the Legislatures, will introduce & cherish local interests & local prejudices. The Genl. Govt. is not an assemblage of States, but of individuals for certain political purposes—it is not meant for the States, but for the individuals composing them; the *individuals* therefore not the *States*, ought to be represented in it: A proportion in this representation can he preserved in the 2d as well as in the 1st branch; and the election can be made by electors chosen by the people for that purpose. He moved an amendment to that effect which was not seconded.

MR. ELSEWORTH saw no reason for departing from the mode contained in the Report. Whoever chooses the member, he will be a Citizen of the State he is to represent & will feel the same spirit & act the same part whether he be appointed by the people or the Legislature. Every State has its particular views & prejudices, which will find their way into the general councils, through whatever channel they may flow. Wisdom was one of the characteristics which it was in contemplation to give the second branch. Would not more of it issue from the Legislatures; than from an immediate election by the people. He urged the necessity of maintaining the existence & agency of the States. Without their co-operation it would be impossible to support a Republican Govt. over so great an extent of Country. An army could scarcely render it practicable. The largest States are the worst Governed. Virg[ini]a is obliged to acknowledge her incapacity to extend her Govt. to Kentucky. Mas[sachuset]ts can not keep the peace one hundred miles from her capitol and is now forming an army for its support. How long Pen[n]a. may be free from a like situation can not be foreseen. If the principles & materials of our Govt. are not adequate to the extent of these single States; how can it be imagined that they can support a single Govt. throughout the U. States. The only chance of supporting a Genl. Govt. lies in engrafting it on that of the individual States.

DOCR. JOHNSON urged the necessity of preserving the State Govts. which would be at the mercy of the Genl. Govt. on MR. WILSON's plan.

MR. MADISON thought it wd. obviate difficulty if the present revel: were postponed. & the 8th taken up, which is to fix the right of suffrage in the 2d branch.

DOCR. [MR.] WILLIAMSON professed himself a friend to such a system as would secure the existence of the State Govts. The happiness of the people depended on it. He was at a loss to give his vote as to the Senate untill he knew the number of its members. In order to ascertain this, he moved to insert these words after "2d branch of the Natl. Legislature"—"who shall bear such proportion to the no. of the 1st branch as 1 to [blank space]." He was not seconded.

MR. MASON. It has been agreed on all hands that an efficient Govt. is necessary that to render it such it ought to have the faculty of self-defence, that to render its different branches effectual each of them ought to have the same power of self defence. He did not wonder that such an agreement should have prevailed in these points. He only wondered that there should be any disagreement about the necessity of allowing the State Govts. the same self-defence. If they are to be preserved as he conceived to be essential, they certainly ought to have this power, and the only mode left of giving it to them, was by allowing them to appoint the 2d branch of the Natl. Legislature.

MR. BUTLER observing that we were put to difficulties at every step by the uncertainty whether an equality or a ratio of representation wd. prevail finally in the 2d branch, moved to postpone the 4th Resol: & to proceed to the Resol: on that point. MR. MADISON seconded him.

On the question

Massts no. Cont no. N. Y. ay. N. J. no. Pa. no. Del. no. Md. no. Va. ay. N. C. no. S. C. ay. Geo. ay.

On a question to postpone the 4 and take up the 7. Resol: ays—Mard. Va. N.C. S.C. Geo:—Noes Mas. Ct. N.Y. N.J. Pa. Del:

On the question to agree "that the members of the 2d branch be chosen by the indivl. Legislatures" Masts ay. Cont. ay. N. Y. ay. N. J. ay. Pa. no. Del. ay. Md. ay. Va. no. N. C. ay. S. C. ay. Geo. ay.

On a question on the clause requiring the age of 30 years at least—"it was agreed to unanimously:

On a question to strike out—the words "sufficient to ensure their independency" after the word "term" it was agreed to.

That the 2d branch hold their offices for term of seven years, considered

MR. GHORUM suggests a term of "4 years," ¼ to be elected every year.

MR. RANDOLPH. supported the idea of rotation, as favorable to the wisdom & stability of the Corps, which might possibly be always sitting, and aiding the Executive. And moves after "7 years" to add, "to go out in fixt proportion" which was agreed to.

MR. WILLIAMSON. suggests "6 years," as more convenient for Rotation than 7 years.

MR. SHERMAN seconds him.

MR. REED proposed that they sd hold their offices "during good" behaviour. Mr. R. Morris seconds him.

GENL. PINKNEY proposed "4 years." A longer term wd. fix them at the seat of Govt. They wd. acquire an interest there, perhaps transfer their property & lose sight of the States they represent. Under these circumstances the distant States wd. labour under great disadvantages.

MR. SHERMAN moved to strike out "7 years" in order to take questions on the several propositions.

On the question to strike out "seven"

Masts. ay. Cont. ay. N. Y. ay. N. J. ay. Pa. no. Del no. Md. divd. Va. no. N. C. ay. S. C. ay. Geo. ay.

On the question to insert "6 years, which failed 5 Sts. being ay. 5 no. & 1 divided

Masts. no. Cont. ay. N. Y. no. N. J. no. Pa. ay. Del ay. Md. divd. Va. ay. N. C. ay. S. C. no. Geo. no.

On a motion to adjourn, the votes were 5 for 5 agst. it & 1 divided,—Con. N. J. Pa. Del. Va.—ay. Massts. N. Y. N. C. S. C. Geo: no. Maryd. divided.

On the question for "5 years" it was lost.

Masts. no. Cont. ay. N. Y. no. N. J. no. Pa. ay. Del. ay. Md. divd. Va. ay. N. C. ay. S. C. no. Geo no.

Adjd.

TUESDAY. JUNE 26. IN CONVENTION

The duration of the 2d branch under consideration.

MR. GHORUM moved to fill the blank with "six years," one third of the members to go out every second year.

MR. WILSON 2ded the motion.

GENL. PINKNEY opposed six years in favor of four years. The States he said had different interests. Those of the Southern, and of S. Carolina in particular were different from the Northern. If the Senators should be appointed for a long term, they wd. settle in the State where they exercised their functions; and would in a little time be rather the representatives of that than of the State appoint[in]g them.

MR. READ movd. that the term be nine years. This wd. admit of a very convenient rotation, one third going out triennially. He wd. still prefer "during good behaviour," but being little supported in that idea, he was willing to take the longest term that could be obtained.

MR. BROOME 2ded. the motion.

MR. MADISON. In order to judge of the form to be given to this institution, it will be proper to take a view of the ends to be served by it. These were first to protect the people agst. their rulers: secondly to protect the people agst. the transient impressions into which they themselves might be led. A people deliberating in a temperate moment, and with the experience of other nations before them, on the plan of Govt. most likely to secure their happiness, would first be aware, that those charge with the public happiness, might betray their trust. An obvious precaution agst. this danger wd. be to divide the trust between different bodies of men, who might watch & check each other. In this they wd. be governed by the same prudence which has prevailed in organizing the subordinate departments of Govt., where all business liable to abuses is made to pass thro' separate hands, the one being a check on the other. It wd. next occur to such a people, that they themselves were liable to temporary errors, thro' want of information as to their true interest, and that men chosen for a short term, & employed but a small portion of that in public affairs, might err from the same cause. This reflection wd. naturally suggest that the Govt. be so constituted, as that one of its branches might have an opp[ortunit]y of acquiring a competent knowledge of the public interests. Another reflection equally becoming a people on such an occasion, wd. be that they themselves, as well as a numerous body of Representatives, were liable to err also, from fickleness and passion. A necessary fence agst. this danger would be to select a portion of enlightened citizens, whose limited number, and firmness might seasonably interpose agst. impetuous councils. It ought finally to occur to a people deliberating on a Govt. for themselves, that as different interests necessarily result from the liberty meant to be secured, the major interest might under sudden impulses be tempted to commit injustice on the minority. In all civilized Countries the people fall into different classes hav[in]g a real or supposed difference of interests. There will be creditors & debtors, farmers, merch[an]ts & manufacturers. There will be particularly the distinction of rich & poor. It was true as had been observd [by Mr. Pinkney] we had not among us those hereditary distinctions, of rank which were a great source of the contests in the ancient Govts. as well as the modern States of Europe, nor those extremes of wealth or poverty which characterize the latter. We cannot however be regarded even at this time, as one homogeneous mass, in which every thing that affects a part will affect in the same manner the whole. In framing a system which we wish to last for ages, we shd. not lose sight of the changes which ages will produce. An increase of population will of necessity increase the proportion of those who will labour under all the hardships of life, & secretly sigh for a more equal distribution of its blessings. These may in time outnumber those who are placed above the feelings of indigence. According to the equal laws of suffrage, the power will slide into the hands of the former. No agrarian attempts have yet been made in in this Country, but symtoms, of a leveling spirit, as we have understood, have sufficiently appeared in a certain quarters to give notice of the future danger. How is this danger to be guarded agst. on republican principles? How is the danger in all cases of interested coalitions to oppress the minority to be guarded agst? Among other means by the establishment of a body in the Govt. sufficiently respectable for its wisdom & virtue, to aid on such emergences, the preponderance of justice by throwing its weight into that scale. Such being the objects of the second branch in the proposed Govt. he thought a considerable duration ought to be given to it. He did not conceive that the term of nine years could threaten any real danger; but in pursuing his particular ideas on the subject, he should require that the long term allowed to the 2d branch should not commence till such a period of life, as would render a perpetual disqualification to be re-elected little inconvenient either in a public or private view. He observed that as it was more than probable we were now digesting a plan which in its operation wd. decide for ever the fate of Republican Govt. we ought not only to provide every guard to liberty that its preservation cd require, but be equally careful to supply the defects which our own experience had particularly pointed out.

MR. SHERMAN. Govt. is instituted for those who live under it. It ought therefore to be so constituted as not to be dangerous to their liberties. The more permanency it has the worse if it be a bad Govt. Frequent elections are necessary to preserve the good behavior of rulers. They also tend to give permanency to the Government, by preserving that good behavior, because it ensures their re-election. In Connecticut elections have been very frequent, yet great stability & uniformity both as to persons & measures have been experienced from its original establishmt to the present time; a period of more than 130 years. He wished to have provision made for steadiness & wisdom in the system to be adopted; but he thought six or four years would be sufficient. He skid be content with either.

MR. READ wished it to be considered by the small States that it was their interest that we should become one people as much as possible; that State attachments shd. be extinguished as much as possible; that the Senate shd. be so constituted as to have the feelings of Citizens of the whole.

MR. HAMILTON. He did not mean to enter particularly into the subject. He concurred with Mr. Madison in thinking we were now to decide for ever the fate of Republican Government; and that if we did not give to that form due stability and wisdom, it would be disgraced & lost among ourselves, disgraced & lost to mankind for ever. He acknowledged himself not to think favorably of Republican Government; but addressed his remarks to those who did think favorably of it, in order to prevail on them to tone their Government as high as possible. He professed himself to be as zealous an advocate for liberty as any man whatever, and trusted he should be as willing a martyr to it though he differed as to the form in which it was most eligible.—He concurred also in the general observations of [Mr. Madison] on the subject, which might be supported by others if it were necessary. It was certainly true: that nothing like an equality of property existed: that an inequality would exist as long as liberty existed, and that it would unavoidably result from that very liberty itself. This inequality of property constituted the great & fundamental distinction in Society. When the Tribunitial power had levelled the boundary between the *patricians* & *plebeians,* what followed? The distinction between rich & poor was substituted. He meant not however to enlarge on the subject. He rose principally to remark that [Mr. Sherman] seemed not to recollect that one branch of the proposed Govt. was so formed, as to render it particularly the guardians of the poorer orders of Citizens; nor to have adverted to the true causes of the stability which had been exemplified in Cont. Under the British system as well as the federal, many of the great powers appertaining to Govt. particularly all those relating to foreign Nations were not in the hands of the Govt. there. Their internal affairs also were extremely simple, owing to sundry causes many of which were peculiar to that Country. Of late the Govermt. had entirely given way to the people, and had in fact suspended many of its ordinary functions in order to prevent those turbulent scenes which had appeared elsewhere. He asks Mr. S. whether the State at this time, dare impose & collect a tax on ye people ? To these causes & not to the frequency of elections, the effect, as far as it existed ought to be chiefly ascribed.

MR. GERRY. wished we could be united in our ideas concerning a permanent Govt. All aim at the same end, but there are great differences as to the means. One circumstance He thought should be carefully attended to. There were not 1/1000 part of our fellow citizens who were not agst. every approach towards Monarchy. Will they ever agree to a plan which seems to make such an approach. The Convention ought to be extremely cautious in what they hold out to the people. Whatever plan may be proposed will be espoused with warmth by many out of respect to the quarter it proceeds from as well as from an approbation of the plan itself. And if the plan should be of such a nature as to rouse a violent opposition, it is easy to foresee that discord & confusion will ensue, and it is even possible that we may become a prey to foreign powers. He did not deny the position of Mr. Madison, that the majority will generally violate justice when they have an interest in so doing; But did not think there was any such temptation in this Country. Our situation was different from that of G. Britain: and the great body of lands yet to be parcelled out & settled would very much prolong the difference. Notwithstanding the symtoms of injustice which had marked many of our public Councils, they had not proceeded so far as not to leave hopes, that there would be a sufficient sense of justice & virtue for the purpose of Govt. He admitted the evils arising from a frequency of elections: and would agree to give the Senate a duration of four or five years. A longer term would defeat itself. It never would be adopted by the people.

MR. WILSON did not mean to repeat what had fallen from others, but wd. add an observation or two which he believed had not yet been suggested. Every nation may be regarded in two relations 1. to its own citizens. 2. to foreign nations. It is therefore not only liable to anarchy & tyranny within, but has wars to avoid & treaties to obtain from abroad. The Senate will probably be the depositary of the powers concerning the latter objects. It ought therefore to be made respectable in the eyes of foreign Nations. The true reason why G. Britain has not yet listened to a commercial treaty with us has been, because she had no confidence in the stability or efficacy of our Government. 9 years with a rotation, will provide these desirable qualities; and give our Govt. an advantage in this respect over Monarchy itself. In a monarchy much must always depend on the temper of the man. In such a body, the personal character will be lost in the political. He wd. add another observation. The popular objection agst. appointing any public body for a long term was that it might by gradual encroachments prolong itself first into a body for life, and finally become a hereditary one. It would be a satisfactory answer to this objection that as $\frac{1}{3}$ would go out triennially, there would be always three divisions holding their places for unequal terms, and consequently acting under the influence of different views, and different impulses—On the question for 9 years, $\frac{1}{3}$ to go out triennially

Massts. no. Cont. no. N. Y. no. N. J. no. Pa. ay. Del. ay. Md. no. Va. ay. N. C. no. S. C. no. Geo. no.

On the question for 6 years $\frac{1}{3}$ to go out biennially

Massts. ay. Cont. ay. N. Y. no. N. J. no. Pa. ay. Del. ay. Md. ay. Va. ay. N. C. ay. S. C. no. Geo. no.

"To receive fixt stipends by which they may be compensated for their services." considered

General PINKNEY proposed "that no Salary should be allowed." As this [the Senatorial] branch was meant to represent the wealth of the Country, it ought to be composed of persons of wealth; and if no allowance was to be made the wealthy alone would undertake the service. He moved to strike out the clause.

DOCTR. FRANKLIN seconded the motion. He wished the Convention to stand fair with the people. There were in it a number of young men who would probably be of the Senate. If lucrative appointments should be recommended we might be chargeable with having carved out places for ourselves. On the question, Masts. Connecticut Pa. Md. S. Carolina ay. N.Y. N.J. Del. Virga. N.C. Geo. no.

MR. WILLIAMSON moved to change the expression into these words towit "to receive a compensation for the devotion of their time to the public Service." The motion was seconded by Mr. Elseworth. And was agreed to by all the States except S. Carol[in]a. It seemed to be meant only to get rid of the word "fixt" and leave greater room for modifying the provision on this point.

MR. ELSEWORTH moved to strike out "to be paid out of the nati[ona]l Treasury" and insert "to be paid by their respective States." If the Senate was meant to strengthen the Govt. it ought to have the confidence of the States. The States will have an interest in keeping up a representation, and will make such provision for supporting the members as will ensure their attendance.

MR. MADISON considered this a departure from a fundamental principle, and subverting the end intended by allowing the Senate a duration of 6 years. They would if this motion should be agreed to, hold their places during pleasure; during the pleasure of the State Legislatures. One great end of the institution was, that being a firm, wise and impartial body, it might not only give stability to the Genl. Govt. in its operations on individuals, but hold an even balance among different States. The motion would make the Senate like Congress, the mere Agents & Advocates of State interests & views, instead of being the impartial umpires & Guardians of justice and general Good. Congs had lately by the establishment of a board with full powers to decide on the mutual claims be- between the U. States & the individual States, fairly acknowledged themselves to be unfit for discharging this part of the business referred to them by the Confederation.

MR. DAYTON considered the payment of the Senate by the States as fatal to their independence. he was decided for paying them out of the Natl. Treasury.

On the question for payment of the Senate to be left to the States as moved by Mr. Elseworth.

Massts. no. Cont. ay. N. Y. ay. N. J. ay. Pa. no. Del. no. Md. no. Va. no. N. C. no. S. C. ay. Geo. ay.

COL. MASON. He did not rise to make any motion, but to hint an idea which seemed to be proper for consideration. One important object in constituting the Senate was to secure the rights of property. To give them weight & firmness for this purpose, a considerable duration in office was thought necessary. But a longer term than 6 years, would be of no avail in this respect, if needy persons should be appointed. He suggested therefore the propriety of annexing to the office a qualification of property. He thought this would be very practicable; as the rules of taxation would supply a scale for measuring the degree of wealth possessed by every man.

A question was then taken whether the words "to be paid out of the public treasury," should stand."

Massts. ay. Cont. no. N. Y. no. N. J. no. Pa. ay. Del. ay. Md. ay. Va. ay. N. C. no. S. C. no. Geo. no.

MR. BUTLER moved to strike out the ineligibility of Senators to *State offices.*

MR. WILLIAMSON seconded the motion.

MR. WILSON remarked the additional dependence this wd. create in the Senators on the States. The longer the time he observed allotted to the officer, the more compleat will be the dependence, if it exists at all.

GENL. PINKNEY was for making the States as much as could be conveniently done, a part of the Genl. Govt: If the Senate was to be appointed by the States, it ought in pursuance of the same idea to be paid by the States: and the States ought not to be barred from the opportunity of calling members of it into offices at home. Such a restriction would also discourage the ablest men from going into the Senate.

MR. WILLIAMSON moved a resolution so penned as to admit of the two following questions. 1. whether the members of the Senate should be ineligible to & incapable of holding offices *under the U. States*

2. Whether &c. under the *particular States.*

On the Question to postpone in order to consider Williamson's Resol[utio]n. Masts. no. Cont. ay. N. Y. no.

N. J. no. Pa. ay. Del. ay. Md. ay. Va. ay. N. C. ay. S. C. ay. Geo. ay.

MR. GERRY & MR. MADISON—move to add to Mr. Williamsons 1, Quest: "and for 1 year thereafter." On this amend[men]t

Masts. no. Cont. ay. N. Y. ay. N. J. no. P[a]. no. Del. ay. Md. ay. Va. ay. N. C. ay. S. C. ay. Geo. no.

On MR. Will-son's 1 Question as amended v[i]z. inelig: & incapable &c. &c for 1 year &c. ag[ree]d. [to] unanimously.

On the 2. question as to ineligibility &c. to State offices.

Mas. ay. Ct. no. N. Y. no. N. J. no. P[a]. ay. Del. no. Md. no. Va. ay. N. C. no. S. C. no. Geo. no.

The 5. Resol: "that each branch have the right of originating acts" was agreed to nem: con:

Adjd.

FRIDAY JULY 6TH. IN CONVENTION

. . . .

The 1st clause relating to the originating of money bills was then resumed.

MR. GOVERNR. MORRIS was opposed to a restriction of this right in either branch, considered merely in itself and as unconnected with the point of representation in the 2d branch. It will disable the 2d branch from proposing its own money plans, and giving the people an opportunity of judging by comparison of the merits of those proposed by the 1st branch.

MR. WILSON could see nothing like a concession here on the part of the smaller States. If both branches were to say yes or no, it was of little consequence which should say yes or no first, which last. If either was indiscriminately to have the right of originating, the reverse of the Report, would he thought be most proper; since it was a maxim that the least numerous body was the fittest for deliberation; the most numerous for decision. He observed that this discrimination had been transcribed from the British into several American constitutions. But he was persuaded that on examination of the American experiments it would be found to be a trifle light as air. Nor could he ever discover the advantage of it in the Parliamentary history of G. Britain. He hoped if there was any advantage in the privilege, that it would be pointed out.

MR. WILLIAMSON thought that if the privilege were not common to both branches it ought rather to be confined to the 2d as the bills in that case would be more narrowly watched, than if they originated with the branch having most of the popular confidence.

MR. MASON. The consideration which weighed with the Committee was that the 1st branch would be the immediate representatives of the people, the 2d would not. Should the latter have the power of giving away the people's money, they might soon forget the source from whence they received it. We might soon have an aristocracy. He had been much concerned at the principles which had been advanced by some gentlemen, but had the satisfaction to find they did not generally prevail. He was a friend to proportional representation in both branches; but supposed that some points must be yielded for the sake of accomodation.

MR. WILSON. If he had proposed that the 2d branch should have an independent disposal of public money, the observations of [Col. Mason] would have been a satisfactory answer. But nothing could be farther from what he had said. His question was how is the power of the 1st branch increased or that of the 2d diminished by giving the proposed privilege to the former? Where is the difference, in which branch it begins if both must concur, in the end?

MR. GERRY would not say that the concession was a sufficient one on the part of the small States. But he could not but regard it in the light of a concession. It wd. make it a constitutional principle that the 2d branch were not possessed of the Confidence of the people in money matters, which wd. lessen their weight & influence. In the next place if the 2d branch were dispossessed of the privilege, they wd. be deprived of the opportunity which their continuance in office 3 times as long as the 1st branch would give them of making three successive essays in favor of a particular point.

MR. PINKNEY thought it evident that the Concession was wholly on one side, that of the large States, the privilege of originating money bills being of no account.

MR. GOVR. MORRIS had waited to hear the good effects of the restriction. As to the alarm sounded, of an aristocracy, his creed was that there never was, nor ever will be a civilized Society without an aristocracy. His endeavor was to keep it as much as possible from doing mischief. The restriction if it has any real operation will deprive us of the services of the 2d branch in digesting & proposing money bills of which it will be more capable than the 1st branch. It will take away the responsibility of the 2d branch, the great security for good behavior. It will always leave a plea, as to an obnoxious money bill that it was disliked, but could not be constitutionally amended; nor safely rejected. It will be a dangerous source of disputes between the two Houses. We should either take the British Constitution altogether or make one for ourselves. The Executive there has dissolved two Houses as the only cure for such disputes. Will our Executive be able to apply such a remedy? Every law directly or indirectly takes money out of the pockets of the people. Again What use may be made of such a privilege in case of great emergency? Suppose an Enemy at the door, and money instantly & absolutely necessary for repelling him, may not the popular branch avail itself of this duress to extort concessions from the Senate destructive of the Constitution itself. He illustrated this danger by the example of the Long Parliament's expects. for subverting the H. of Lords; concluding on the whole that the restriction would be either useless or pernicious.

DOCR. FRANKLIN did not mean to go into a justification of the Report; but as it had been asked what would be the use of restraining the 2d branch from medling with money bills, he could not but remark that it was always of importance that the people should know who had disposed of their money, & how it had been disposed of. It was a maxim that those who feel, can

best judge. This end would, he thought, be best attained, if money affairs were to be confined to the immediate representatives of the people. This was his inducement to concur in the report. As to the danger or difficulty that might arise from a negative in the 2d where the people wd. not be proportionally represented, it might easily be got over by declaring that there should be no such Negative: or if that will not do, by declaring that there shall be no such branch at all.

MR. MARTIN said that it was understood in the Committee that the difficulties and disputes which had been apprehended, should be guarded agst. in the detailing of the plan.

MR. WILSON. The difficulties & disputes will increase with the attempts to define & obviate them. Queen Anne was obliged to dissolve her Parliamt. in order to terminate one of these obstinate disputes between the two Houses. Had it not been for the mediation of the Crown, no one can say what the result would have been. The point is still *sub judice* in England. He approved of the principles laid down by the Hon'ble President [Doctr. Franklin] his Colleague, as to the expediency of keeping the people informed of their money affairs. But thought they would know as much, and be as well satisfied, in one way as in the other.

GENL. PINKNEY was astonished that this point should have been considered as a concession. He remarked that the restriction to money bills had been rejected on the merits singly considered, by 8 States agst. 3. and that the very States which now called it a concession, were then agst. it as nugatory or improper in itself.

On the Question whether the clause relating to money bills in the Report of the Come. consisting of a member from each State, shd. stand as part of the Report—

Massts. dividd. Cont. ay. N.Y. divd. N.J. ay. Pa. no. Del. ay. Md. ay. Va. no. N.C. ay. S.C. no. Geo. divd.

A Question was then raised whether the question was carried in the affirmative: there being but 5 ays out of 11. States present. The words of the rule are (see May 28).

On the question: Mas. Cont. N.J. Pa. Del. Md. N.C. S.C. Geo ay

N.Y. Va. no

. . . .

MONDAY. JULY 16. IN CONVENTION

On the question for agreeing to the whole Report as amended & including the equality of votes in the 2d branch. it passed in the Affirmative.

Mas. divided Mr. GERRY, Mr. Strong, ay. Mr. King Mr. Ghorum no. Cont. ay. N. J. ay. Pena. no. Del. ay. Md. ay. Va. no. N. C. ay. Mr. Spaight no. S. C. no. Geo. no.

[Here enter the whole in the words entered in the Journal July 16]

The whole, thus passed is in the words following viz

"Resolved that in the original formation of the Legislature of the U. S. the first branch thereof shall consist of sixty five members, of which number N. Hampshire shall send 3. Massts. 8. Rh. I. 1. Connt. 5. N. Y. 6. N. J. 4. Pena. 8. Del. 1. Maryd. 6. Virga. 10. N. C. 5. S. C. 5. Geo. 3.—But as the present situation of the States may probably alter in the number of their inhabitants, the Legislature of the U. S. shall be authorized from time to time to apportion the number of Reps; and in case any of the States shall hereafter be divided, or enlarged by, addition of territory, or any two or more States united, or any new States created with the limits of the U. S. the Legislature of the U. S. shall possess authority to regulate the number of Reps in any of the foregoing cases, upon the principle of their number of inhabitants, according to the provisions hereafter mentioned, namely—provided always that representation ought to be proportioned according to direct taxation; and in order to ascertain the alteration in the direct taxation, which may be required from time to time by the changes in the relative circumstances of the States—

Resolved, that a Census be taken within six years from the 1st meeting of the Legislature of the U. S. and once within the term of every 10 years afterwards of all the inhabitants of the U. S. in the manner and according to the ratio recommended by Congress in their Resolution of April 18. 1783, and that the Legislature of the U. S. shall proportion the direct taxation accordingly—

"Resolved, that all bills for raising or appropriating money, and for fixing the salaries of officers of the Govt. of the U. S. shall originate in the first branch of the Legislature of the U. S. and shall not be altered or amended in the 2d branch: and that no money shall be drawn from the public Treasury, but in pursuance of appropriations to be originated in the 1st branch.

"Resolvd. that in the 2d branch of the Legislature of the U. S. each State shall have an equal vote."

The 6th Resol: in the Report from the Com[mitte]e of the whole House, which had been postponed in order to consider the 7 & 8th Resol[utio]ns: was now resumed. see the Resol[utio]n

The 1st member "That the Natl. Legislature ought to possess the Legislative Rights vested in Congs. by the Confederation." was agreed to nem. Con.

The next, "And moreover to legislate in all cases to which the separate States are incompetent; or in which the harmony of the U. S. may be interrupted by the exercise of individual legislation," being read for a question

MR. BUTLER calls for some explanation of the extent of this power: particularly of the word incompetent. The vagueness of the terms rendered it impossible for any precise judgment to be formed.

MR. GHORUM. The vagueness of the terms constitutes the propriety of them. We are now establishing general principles, to be extended hereafter into details which will be precise & explicit.

MR. RUTLIDGE, urged the objection started by Mr. Butler and moved that the clause should be committed to the end that a specification of the powers comprised in the general terms, might be reported.

On the question for a commitment, the States were equally divided.

Mas. no. Cont. ay. N. J. no. Pa. no. Del. no. Md. ay. Va. ay. N. C. no. S. C. ay. Geo. ay: So it was lost.

MR. RANDOLPH. The vote of this morning [involving an equality of suffrage in 2d branch] had embarrassed the business extremely. All the powers given in the Report from the Com[mitte]e of the whole, were founded on the supposition that a Proportional representation was to prevail in both branches of the Legislature. When he came here this morning his purpose was to have offered some propositions that might if possible have united a great majority of votes, and particularly might provide agst. the danger suspected on the part of the smaller States, by enumerating the cases in which it might lie, and allowing an equality of votes in such cases. But finding from the preceding vote that they persist in demanding an equal vote in all cases, that they have succeeded in obtaining it, and that N. York if present would probably be on the same side, he could not but think we were unprepared to discuss this subject further. It will probably be in vain to come to any final decision with a bare majority on either side. For these reasons he wished the Convention might adjourn, that the large States might consider the steps proper to be taken in the present solemn crisis of the business, and that the small States might also deliberate on the means of conciliation.

MR. PATTERSON, thought with Mr. R. that it was high time for the Convention to adjourn that the rule of secrecy ought to be rescinded, and that our Constituents should be consulted. No conciliation could be admissible on the part of the smaller States on any other ground than that of an equality of votes in the 2d branch. If Mr. Randolph would reduce to form his motion for an adjounrment sine die, he would second it with all his heart.

GENL. PINKNEY wished to know of Mr. R. whether he meant an adjournment sine die, or only an adjournment for the day. If the former was meant, it differed much from his idea. He could not think of going to S. Carolina and returning again to this place. Besides it was chimerical to suppose that the States if consulted would ever accord separately, and beforehand.

MR. RANDOLPH, had never entertained an idea of an adjournment sine die; & was sorry that his meaning had been so readily & strangely misinterpreted. He had in view merely an adjournment till tomorrow, in order that some conciliatory experiment might if possible be devised, and that in case the smaller States should continue to hold back, the larger might then take such measures, he would not say what, as might be necessary.

MR. PATTERSON seconded the adjournment till tomorrow, as an opportunity seemed to be wished by the larger States to deliberate further on conciliatory expedients.

On the question for adjourning till tomorrow, the States were equally divided.

Mas. no. Cont. no. N. J. ay. Pa. ay. Del. no. Md. ay. Va. ay. N. C. ay. S. C. no. Geo. no. So it was lost.

MR. BROOME thought it his duty to declare his opinion agst. an adjournment sine die, as had been urged by Mr. Patterson. Such a measure he thought would be fatal. Something must be done by the Convention, tho' it should be by a bare majority.

MR. GERRY observed that Mas[sachuset]ts was opposed to an adjournment, because they saw no new ground of compromise. But as it seemed to be the opinion of so many States that a trial shd– be made, the State would now concur in the adjournmt.

MR. RUTLIDGE could see no need of an adjourn[men]t because he could see no chance of a compromise. The little States were fixt. They had repeatedly & solemnly declared themselves to be so. All that the large States then had to do, was to decide whether they would yield or not. For his part he conceived that altho' we could not do what we thought best, in itself, we ought to do something. Had we not better keep the Govt. up a little longer, hoping that another Convention will supply our omissions, than abandon every thing to hazard. Our Constituents will be very little satisfied with us if we take the latter course.

MR. RANDOLPH & MR. KING renewed the motion to adjourn till tomorrow.

On the question. Mas. ay. Cont. no. N. J. ay. Pa. ay. Del. no. Md. ay. Va. ay. N. C. ay. S. C. ay. Geo. divd.

Adjourned

On the morning following before the hour of the convention a number of the members from the larger States, by common agreement met for the purpose of consulting on the proper steps to be taken in consequence of the vote in favor of an equal Representation in the 2d branch, and the apparent inflexibility of the smaller States on that point. Several members from the latter States also attended. The time was wasted in vague conversation on the subject, without any specific proposition or agreement. It appeared indeed that the opinions of the members who disliked the equality of votes differed so much as to the importance of that point, and as to the policy of risking a failure of any general act of the Convention, by inflexibly opposing it. Several of them supposing that no good Govermnt could or would be built on that foundation, and that as a division of the Convention into two opinions was unavoidable; it would be better that the side comprising the principal States, and a majority of the people of America, should propose a scheme of Govt. to the States, than that a scheme should be proposed on the other side, would have concurred in a firm opposition to the smaller States, and in a separate recommendation, if eventually necessary. Others seemed inclined to yield to the smaller States, and to concur in such an act however imperfect & exceptionable, as might be agreed on by the Convention as a body, tho' decided by a bare majority of States and by a minority of the people of the U. States. It is probable that the result of this consultation satisfied the smaller States that they had nothing to apprehend from a union of the larger, in any plan whatever agst. the equality of votes in the 2d branch.

MONDAY. AUGUST 13. IN CONVENTION

. . . .

Art. IV. Sec 5. being reconsidered.

MR. RANDOLPH moved that the clause be altered so as to read—"Bills for raising money for the *purpose of revenue* or for appropriating the same shall originate in the House of Repre-sentatives and shall not be so amended or altered by the Senate as to increase or diminish the sum to be raised, or change the mode of levying it, or the objects of its appropriation."—He would not repeat his reasons, but barely remind the members from the smaller States of the compromise by which the larger States were entitled to this privilege.

COL. MASON. This amendment removes all the objections urged agst. the section as it stood at first. By specifying *purposes of revenue,* it obviated the objection that the Section extended to all bills under which money might incidentally arise. By autho-rising amendments in the Senate it got rid of the objections that the Senate could not correct errors of any sort, & that it would introduce into the House of Reps. the practice of tacking foreign matter to money bills. These objections being removed, the arguments in favor of the proposed restraint on the Senate ought to have their full force. 1. the Senate did not represent the *people,* but the *States* in their political character. It was improper therefore that it should tax the people. The reason was the same agst. their doing it; as it had been agst. Congs. doing it. Nor was it in any respect necessary in order to cure the evils of our Republican system. He admitted that notwithstanding the superiority of the Republican form over every other, it had its evils. The chief ones, were the danger of the majority oppressing the minority, and the mischievous influence of demagogues. The Genl. Government of itself will cure these. As the States will not concur at the same time in their unjust & oppressive plans, the General Govt. will be able to check & defeat them, whether they result from the wickedness of the majority, or from the mis-guidance of demagogues. Again, the Senate is not like the H. of Reps. chosen frequently and obliged to return frequently among the people. They are to be chosen by the Sts for 6 years, will probably settle themselves at the seat of Govt. will pursue schemes for their own aggrandizement—will be able by wearyg. out the H. of Reps. and taking advantage of their impatience at the close of a long Session, to extort measures for that purpose. If they should be paid as he expected would be yet determined & wished to be so, out of the Natl. Treasury, they will particu-larly extort an increase of their wages. A bare negative was a very different thing from that of originating bills. The practice in En-gld. was in point. The House of Lords does not represent nor tax the people, because not elected by the people. If the Senate can originate, they will in the recess of the Legislative Sessions, hatch their mischievous projects, for their own purposes, and have their money bills ready cut & dried, (to use a common phrase) for the meeting of the H. of Reps. He compared the case to Poyning's law—and signified that the House of Reps. might be rendered by degrees like the Parliament of Paris, the mere depository of the decrees of the Senate. As to the compromise so much had passed on that subject that he would say nothing about it. He did not mean by what he had said to oppose the permanency of the Senate. On the contrary he had no repug-nance to an increase of it—nor to allowing it a negative, though the Senate was not by its present constitution entitled to it. But in all events he would contend that the purse strings should be in the hands of the Representatives of the people.

Mr. Wilson was himself directly opposed to the equality of votes granted to the Senate by its present Constitution. At the same time he wished not to multiply the vices of the system. He did not mean to enlarge on a subject which had been so much canvassed, but would remark as an insuperable objection agst. the proposed restriction of money bills to the H. of Reps. that it would be a source of perpetual contentions where there was no mediator to decide them. The Presidt. here could not like the Executive Magistrate in England interpose by a prorogation, or dissolution. This restriction had been found pregnant with altercation in every State where the Constitution had established it. The House of Reps. will insert other things in money bills, and by making them conditions of each other, destroy the deliberative liberty of the Senate. He stated the case of a Preamble to a money bill sent up by the House of Commons in the reign of Queen Anne, to the H. of Lords, in which the conduct of the displaced Ministry, who were to be impeached before the Lords, was condemned; the Commons thus extorting a premature judgmt. without any hearing of the Parties to be tried, and the H. of Lords being thus reduced to the poor & disgraceful expedient of opposing to the authority of a law, a protest on their Journals agst. its being drawn into precedent. If there was any thing like Poynings law in the present case, it was in the attempt to vest the exclusive right of originating in the H. of Reps. and so far he was agst. it. He should be equally so if the right were to be exclusively vested in the Senate. With regard to the purse strings, it was to be observed that the purse was to have two strings, one of which was in the hands of the H. of Reps. the other in those of the Senate. Both houses must concur in untying, and of what importance could it be which untied first, which last. He could not conceive it to be any objection to the Senate's preparing the bills, that they would have leisure for that purpose and would be in the habits of business. War, Commerce, & Revenue were the great objects of the Genl. Government. All of them are connected with money. The restriction in favor of the H. of Represts. would exclude the Senate from originating any important bills whatever—

Mr. Gerry considered this as a part of the plan that would be much scrutinized. Taxation & representation are strongly associated in the minds of the people, and they will not agree that any but their immediate representatives shall meddle with their purses. In short the acceptance of the plan will inevitably fail, if the Senate be not restrained from originating Money bills.

Mr. Governr. Morris All the arguments suppose the right to originate money & to tax, to be exclusively vested in the Senate.—The effects commented on may be produced by a Negative only in the Senate. They can tire out the other House, and extort their concurrence in favorite measures, as well by withholding their negative, as by adhering to a bill introduced by themselves.

Mr. Madison thought If the substitute offered by Mr. Randolph for the original section is to be adopted it would be proper to allow the Senate at least so to amend as to *diminish* the sum to be raised. Why should they be restrained from checking the extravagance of the other House? One of the greatest evils incident to Republican Govt. was the spirit of contention & faction. The proposed substitute, which in some respects lessened the objections agst. the section, had a contrary effect with respect to this particular. It laid a foundation for new difficulties and disputes between the two houses. The word *revenue* was ambiguous. In many acts, particularly in the regulations of trade, the object would be twofold. The raising of revenue would be one of them. How could it be determined which was the primary or predominant one; or whether it was necessary that revenue shd. be the sole object, in exclusion even of other incidental effects. When the Contest was first opened with G. B. their power to regulate trade was admitted. Their power to raise revenue rejected. An accurate investigation of the subject afterward proved that no line could be drawn between the two cases. The words *amend or alter,* form an equal source of doubt & altercation. When an obnoxious paragraph shall be sent down from the Senate to the House of Reps—it will be called an origination under the name of an amendment. The Senate may actually couch extraneous matter under that name. In these cases, the question will turn on the *degree* of connection between the matter & object of the bill and the alteration or amendment offered to it. Can there be a more fruitful source of dispute, or a kind of dispute more difficult to be settled? His apprehensions on this point were not conjectural. Disputes had actually flowed from this source in Virga. where the Senate can originate no bill. The words "so as to *increase or diminish* the sum to be raised," were liable to the same objections. In levying indirect taxes, which it seemed to be understood were to form the principal revenue of the new Govt. the sum to be raised, would be increased or diminished by a variety of collateral circumstances influencing the consumption, in general, the consumption of foreign or of domestic articles—of this or that particular species of articles, and even by the mode of collection which may be closely connected with the productiveness of a tax.—The friends of the section had argued its necessity from the permanency of the Senate. He could not see how this argumt. applied. The Senate was not more permanent now than in the form it bore in the original propositions of Mr. Randolph and at the time when no objection whatever was hinted agst. its originating money bills. Or if in consequence of a loss of the present question, a proportional vote in the Senate should be reinstated as has been urged as the indemnification the permanency of the Senate will remain the same.—If the right to originate be vested exclusively in the House of Reps. either the Senate must yield agst. its judgment to that House, in which case the Utility of the check will be lost—or the Senate will be inflexible & the H. of Reps. must adapt its money bill to the views of the Senate, in which case, the exclusive right will be of no avail.—As to the Compromise of which so much had been said, he would make a single observation. There were 5 States which had opposed the equality of votes in the Senate, viz. Masts. Penna. Virga. N. Carolina & S. Carola. As a compensation for the sacrifice extorted from them on this head, the exclusive origination of money bills in the other House had been tendered. Of the five States a majority viz. Penna. Virga. & S. Carola. have uniformly voted agst. the proposed compensation, on its own merits, as rendering the plan of Govt. still more objectionable. Massts. has been divided. N. Carolina alone has set a value on the compensation, and voted on that principle. What obligation then can the small States be under to concur agst. their judgments in reinstating the section?

Mr. Dickenson. Experience must be our only guide. Reason may mislead us. It was not Reason that discovered the singular & admirable mechanism of the English Constitution. It was not Reason that discovered or ever could have discovered the odd & in the eye of those who are governed by reason, the absurd mode of trial by Jury. Accidents probably produced these discoveries, and experience has give a sanction to them. This is then our guide. And has not experience verified the utility of restraining money bills to the immediate representatives of the people. Whence the effect may have proceeded he could not say; whether from the respect with which this privilege inspired the other branches of Govt. to the H. of Commons, or from the turn of thinking it gave to the people at large with regard to their rights, but the effect was visible & could not be doubted— Shall we oppose to this long experience, the short experience of 11 years which we had ourselves, on this subject. As to disputes, they could not be avoided any way. If both Houses should originate, each would have a different bill to which it would be attached, and for which it would contend.—He observed that all the prejudices of the people would be offended by refusing this exclusive privilege to the H. of Repress. and these prejudices shd. never be disregarded by us when no essential purpose was to be served. When this plan goes forth it will be attacked by the popular leaders. Aristocracy will be the watchword; the Shibboleth among its adversaries. Eight States have inserted in their Constitutions the exclusive right of originating money bills in favor of the popular branch of the Legislature. Most of them however allowed the other branch to amend. This he thought would be proper for us to do.

Mr. Randolph regarded this point as of such consequence, that as he valued the peace of this Country, he would press the adoption of it. We had numerous & monstrous difficulties to combat. Surely we ought not to increase them. When the people behold in the Senate, the countenance of an aristocracy; and in the president, the form at least of a little monarch, will not their alarms be sufficiently raised without taking from their immediate representatives, a right which has been so long appropriated to them.—The Executive will have more influence over the Senate, than over the H. of Reps. Allow the Senate to originate in this case, & that influence will be sure to mix itself in their deliberations & plans. The Declaration of War he conceived ought not to be in the Senate composed of 26 men only, but rather in the other House. In the other House ought to be placed the origination of the means of war. As to Commercial regulations which may involve revenue, the difficulty may be avoided by restraining the definition to bills, for the *mere* or *sole,* purpose of raising revenue. The Senate will be more likely to be corrupt

than the H. of Reps. and should therefore have less to do with money matters. His principal object however was to prevent popular objections against the plan, and to secure its adoption.

Mr. Rutledge. The friends of this motion are not consistent in their reasoning. They tell us that we ought to be guided by the long experience of G. B. & not our own experience of 11 years: and yet they themselves propose to depart from it. The *H. of Commons* not only have the exclusive right of originating, but the *Lords* are not allowed to alter or amend a money bill. Will not the people say that this restriction is but a mere tub to the whale. They cannot but see that it is of no real consequence; and will be more likely to be displeased with it as an attempt to bubble them, than to impute it to a watchfulness over their rights. For his part, he would prefer giving the exclusive right to the Senate, if it was to be given exclusively at all. The Senate being more conversant in business, and having more leisure, will digest the bills much better, and as they are to have no effect, till examined & approved by the H. of Reps. there can be no possible danger. These clauses in the Constitutions of the States had been put in through a blind adherence to the British model. If the work was to be done over now, they would be omitted. The experiment in S. Carolina, where the Senate cannot originate or amend money bills, has shewn that it answers no good purpose; and produces the very bad one of continually dividing & heating the two houses. Sometimes indeed if the matter of the amendment of the Senate is pleasing to the other House they wink at the encroachment; if it be displeasing, then the Constitution is appealed to. Every Session is distracted by altercations on this subject. The practice now becoming frequent is for the Senate not to make formal amendments; but to send down a schedule of the alterations which will procure the bill their assent.

Mr. Carrol. The most ingenious men in Maryd. are puzzled to define the case of money bills, or explain the Constitution on that point; tho' it seemed to be worded with all possible plainness & precision. It is a source of continual difficulty & squabble between the two houses.

Mr. McHenry mentioned an instance of extraordinary subterfuge, to get rid of the apparent force of the Constitution.

On Question on the first part of the motion as to the exclusive originating of Money bills in H. of Reps.

N. H. ay. Mas. ay. Ct. no. N.J. no. Pa. no. Del. no. Md. no. Virga. ay. Mr. Blair & Mr. M. no. Mr. R. Col. Mason and Genl. Washington ay N.C. ay. S.C. no. Geo. no.

Question on Originating by H. of Reps. *& amending* by Senate, as reported Art. IV. Sect. 5.

N.H. ay. Mas. ay. Ct. no. N.J. no. Pa. no. Del. no. Md. no. Va. ay. N.C. ay. S.C. no. Geo. no.

Question on the last clause of Sect: 5—Art. IV—viz "No money shall be drawn from the Public Treasury, but in pursuance of *appropriations* that shall originate in the House of Reps. It passed in the negative

N.H. no. Mas. ay. Con. no. N.J. no. Pa. no. Del. no. Md. no. Va. no. N.C. no. S.C. no. Geo. no.

Adjd.

SATURDAY SEPTEMBER 8TH. IN CONVENTION

. . . .

The clause referring to the Senate, the trial of impeachments agst. President, for Treason & bribery, was taken up.

COL. MASON. Why is the provision restrained to Treason & bribery only? Treason as defined in the Constitution will not reach many great and dangerous offenses. Hastings is not guilty of Treason. Attempts to subvert the Constitution may not be Treason as above defined. As bills of attainder which have saved the British Constitution are forbidden, it is the more necessary to extend: the power of impeachments. He movd to add after "bribery" "or maladministration." MR. GERRY seconded him.

MR. MADISON So vague a term will be equivalent to a tenure during pleasure of the Senate.

MR. GOVR. MORRIS, it will not be put in force & can do no harm. An election of every four years will prevent maladministration.

COL. MASON withdrew "maladministration" & substitutes "other high crimes & misdemeanors agst. the State"

On the question thus altered

N. H. ay. Mas. ay. Ct. ay. N. J. no. Pa. no. Del. no. Md. ay. Va. ay. N. C. ay. S. C. ay. Geo. ay.

MR. MADISON, objected to a trial of the President by the Senate, especially as he was to be impeached by the other branch of the Legislature, and for any act which might be called a misdemesnor [sic]. The President under these circumstances was made improperly dependent. He would prefer the Supreme Court for the trial of impeachments, or rather a tribunal of which that should form a part.

MR. GOVR. MORRIS thought no other tribunal than the Senate could be trusted. The supreme Court were too few in number and might be warped or corrupted. He was agst. a dependence of the Executive on the Legislature, considering the Legislative tyranny the great danger to be apprehended; but there could be no danger that the Senate would say untruly on their oaths that the President was guilty of crimes or facts, especially as in four years he can be turned out.

MR. PINKNEY disapproved of making the Senate the Court of Impeachments, as rendering the President too dependent on the Legislature. If he opposes a favorite law, the two Houses will combine agst. him, and under the influence of heat and faction throw him out of office.

MR. WILLIAMSON thought there was more danger of too much lenity than too much rigour towards the President, considering the number of cases in which the Senate was associated with the President.

MR. SHERMAN regarded the Supreme Court as improper to try the President, because the Judges would be appointed by him.

On motion by MR. MADISON to strike out the words—"by the Senate" after the word "conviction"

N. H. no. Mas. no. Ct. no. N. J. no. Pa. ay. Del. no. Md. no. Va. ay. N. C. no. S. C. no. Geo. no.

In the amendment of Col: Mason just agreed to, the word "State" after the words "misdemeanors against" was struck out, and the words "United States" inserted unanimously, in order to remove ambiguity.

On the question to agree to clause as amended,

N. H. ay. Mas. ay. Cont ay N. J. ay. Pa. no. Del ay Md. ay. Va. ay. N. C. ay. S. C. ay. Geo. ay.

On motion "The vice-President and other Civil officers of the U. S. shall be removed from office on impeachment and conviction as aforesaid" was added to the clause on the subject of impeachments.

The clause of the report made on the 5th Sepr & postponed was taken up, to wit—"All bills for raising revenue shall originate in the House of Representatives; and shall be subject to alterations and amendments by the Senate. No money shall be drawn from the Treasury but in consequence of appropriations made by law."

It was moved to strike out the words "and shall be subject to alterations and amendments by the Senate" and insert the words used in the Constitution of Massachussetts on the same subject—as "but the Senate may propose or concur with amendments as in other bills"—which was agreed too nem: con:

On the question On the first part of the clause—"All bills for raising revenue shall originate in the house of Representatives"

N. H. ay. Mas. ay. Ct. ay. N. J. ay Pa. ay. Del. no. Md. no. Va. ay. N.C.ay. S.C. ay. Geo. ay.

MR. GOVR. MORRIS moved to add to clause (3) of the report made on Sepr 4. the words "and every member shall be on oath" which being agreed to, and a question taken on the clause so amended viz—"The Senate of the U. S. shall have power to try all impeachments; but no person shall be convicted without the concurrence of two thirds of the members present; and every member shall be on oath"

N. H. ay. Mas. ay. Ct. ay. N. J. ay. Pa. no. Del. ay. Md. ay. Va. no. N. C. ay. S. C. ay. Geo. ay.

MR. GERRY repeated his motion above made on this day, in the form following "The Legislature shall have the sole right of establishing offices not herein 2 provided for," which was again negatived: Mas. Cont & Geo. only being ay.

MR. McHENRY observed that the President had not yet been any where authorised to convene the Senate, and moved to amend Art. X. sect. 2. by striking out the words "he may convene them [the Legislature] on extraordinary occasions" & insert "He may convene both or either of the Houses on extraordinary occasions." This he added would also provide for the case of the Senate being in Session at the time of convening the Legislature.

MR. WILSON said he should vote agst. the motion, because it implied that the senate might be in Session, when the Legislature was not, which he thought improper.

On the question

N. H. ay. Mas. no. Ct. ay. N. J. ay. Pa. no. Del. ay. Md. ay. Va. no. N. C. ay. S. C. no. Geo. ay.

A Committee was then appointed by Ballot to revise the stile of and arrange the articles which had been agreed to by the House. The committee consisted of Mr. Johnson, Mr. Hamilton, Mr. Govr. Morris, Mr. Madison and Mr. King.

MR. WILLIAMSON moved that previous to this work of the Committee the clause relating to the number of the House of Representatives skid be reconsidered for the purpose of increasing the number.

MR. MADISON 2ded the Motion

MR. SHERMAN opposed it. he thought the provision on that subject amply sufficient.

COL: HAMILTON expressed himself with great earnestness and anxiety in favor of the motion. He avowed himself a friend to a vigorous Government, but would declare at the same time, that he held it essential that the popular branch of it should be on a broad foundation. He was seriously of opinion that the House of Representatives was on so narrow a scale as to be really dangerous, and to warrant a jealousy in the people for their liberties. He remarked that the connection between the President & Senate would tend to perpetuate him, by corrupt influence. It was the more necessary on this account that a numerous representation in the other branch of the Legislature should be established.

On the motion of Mr. Williamson to reconsider, it was negatived

N. H. no.   Mas. no.   Ct. no.   N. J. no.   Pa. ay.   Del. ay. Md. ay.   Va. ay.   N. C. ay.   S. C. no.   Geo. no.

Adjd.

Excerpts from debates at the Federal Convention of 1787, as reported by James Madison in *Documents Illustrative of the Formation of the Union of the American States*, ed. Charles G. Tansill, House Doc. 398, 69th Congress, 1st session (Washington: Government Printing Office, 1927), 109–745, passim.

2   The Preamble and Article I of the Constitution of the United States

September 17, 1787

When it comes to defining landmark documents on the U.S. Congress, the Constitution is by far the most fundamental and important single document of all. This is especially true of Article I, which creates the bicameral legislature known as Congress and describes its powers and functions. The Constitution has been the vital touchstone to the daily workings of all three branches of the federal government for more than two centuries.

Anyone desiring to understand how Congress works can do no better than begin with Article I. Since this compilation of documents focuses on Congress, the entire Constitution is not reproduced here for purposes of saving space for other documents not as readily available in print. Subsequent amendments to the Constitution that relate directly to Congress can be found in this volume, but they are placed in their historical context in chronological order to convey how the Constitution has slowly, and rarely, been amended over time. The Preamble is included here because nowhere can one find a clearer and more eloquent description of the general purposes of government.

The delegates to the Federal Convention who met in Philadelphia from May to September 1787 began their deliberations with the idea of modifying the Articles of Confederation, which served as the first constitution of the United States. Quickly, however, the old plan was scrapped in favor of an entirely new governmental structure that would ensure a republican form of government that could encompass thirteen different states and accommodate the needs for future expansion westward.

On September 17, 1787, the delegates approved the new Constitution and sent it to the states for ratification. The deliberations and debates had been held in secret. On the day the delegates completed their handiwork, some of them gathered on the street outside Independence Hall. A woman by the name of Elizabeth Powell stopped Benjamin Franklin, the oldest delegate at age eighty-one, and asked him "Well, Doctor, what have we got, a republic or a monarchy?" Franklin replied, "A republic—if you can keep it."

We the people of the United States, in Order to form a more perfect Union, establish Justice, insure domestic Tranquility, provide for the common defence, promote the general Welfare, and secure the Blessings of Liberty to ourselves and our Posterity, do ordain and establish this Constitution for the United States of America.

ARTICLE. I.

SECTION 1. All legislative Powers herein granted shall be vested in a Congress of the United States, which shall consist of a Senate and House of Representatives.

SECTION. 2.   1 The House of Representatives shall be composed of Members chosen every second Year by the People of the several States, and the Electors in each State shall have the Qualifications requisite for Electors of the most numerous Branch of the State Legislature.

2 No Person shall be a Representative who shall not have attained to the Age of twenty five Years, and been seven Years a Citizen of the United States, and who shall not, when elected, be an Inhabitant of that State in which he shall be chosen.

3 Representatives and direct Taxes shall be apportioned among the several States which may be included within this Union, according to their respective Numbers, which shall be determined by adding to the whole Number of free Persons, including those bound to Service for a Term of Years, and excluding Indians not taxed, three fifths of all other Persons. The actual Enumeration shall be made within three Years after the first

Meeting of the Congress of the United States, and within every subsequent Term of ten Years, in such Manner as they shall by Law direct. The Number of Representatives shall not exceed one for every thirty Thousand, but each State shall have at Least one Representative; and until such enumeration shall be made, the State of New Hampshire shall be entitled to chuse three, Massachusetts eight, Rhode-Island and Providence Plantations one, Connecticut five, New-York six, New Jersey four, Pennsylvania eight, Delaware one, Maryland six, Virginia ten, North Carolina five, South Carolina five, and Georgia three.

4 When vacancies happen in the Representation from any State, the Executive Authority thereof shall issue Writs of Election to fill such Vacancies.

The House of Representatives shall chuse their Speaker and other Officers; and shall have the sole Power of Impeachment.

SECTION. 3. 1 The Senate of the United States shall be composed of two Senators from each State, chosen by the Legislature thereof, for six Years; and each Senator shall have one Vote.

2 Immediately after they shall be assembled in Consequence of the first Election, they shall be divided as equally as may be into three Classes. The Seats of the Senators of the first Class shall be vacated at the Expiration of the second Year, of the second Class at the Expiration of the fourth Year, and of the third Class at the Expiration of the sixth Year, so that one third may be chosen every second Year; and if Vacancies happen by Resignation, or otherwise, during the Recess of the Legislature of any State, the Executive thereof may make temporary Appointments until the next Meeting of the Legislature, which shall then fill such Vacancies.

3 No Person shall be a Senator who shall not have attained to the Age of thirty Years, and been nine Years a Citizen of the United States, and who shall not, when elected, be an Inhabitant of that State for which he shall be chosen.

4 The Vice President of the United States shall be President of the Senate, but shall have no Vote, unless they be equally divided.

5 The Senate shall chuse their other Officers, and also a President pro tempore, in the Absence of the Vice President, or when he shall exercise the Office of President of the United States.

6 The Senate shall have the sole Power to try all Impeachments. When sitting for that Purpose, they shall be on Oath or Affirmation. When the President of the United States is tried, the Chief Justice shall preside: And no Person shall be convicted without the Concurrence of two thirds of the Members present.

7 Judgment in Cases of Impeachment shall not extend further than to removal from Office, and disqualification to hold and enjoy any Office of honor, Trust or Profit under the United States: but the Party convicted shall nevertheless be liable and subject to Indictment, Trial, Judgment and Punishment, according to Law.

SECTION. 4. 1 The Times, Places and Manner of holding Elections for Senators and Representatives, shall be prescribed in each State by the Legislature thereof, but the Congress may at any time by Law make or alter such Regulations, except as to the Places of chusing Senators.

2 The Congress shall assemble at least once in every Year, and such Meeting shall be on the first Monday in December, unless they shall by Law appoint a different Day.

SECTION. 5. 1 Each House shall be the Judge of the Elections, Returns and Qualification of its own Members, and a Majority of each shall constitute a Quorum to do Business; but a smaller Number may adjourn from day to day, and may be authorized to compel the Attendance of absent Members, in such Manner, and under such Penalties as each House may provide.

2 Each House may determine the Rules of its Proceeding, punish its Members for disorderly Behaviour, and, with the Concurrence of two thirds, expel a Member.

3 Each House shall keep a Journal of its Proceedings, and from time to time publish the same, excepting such Parts as may in their Judgment require Secrecy; and the Yeas and Nays of the Members of either House on any question shall, at the Desire of one fifth of those Present, be entered on the Journal.

4 Neither House, during the Session of Congress, shall, without the Consent of the other, adjourn for more than three days, nor to any other Place than that in which the two Houses shall be sitting.

SECTION. 6. 1 The Senators and Representatives shall receive a Compensation for their Services, to be ascertained by Law, and paid out of the Treasury of the United States. They shall in all Cases, except Treason, Felony and Breach of the Peace, be privileged from Arrest during their Attendance at the Session of their respective Houses, and in going to and returning from the same; and for any Speech or Debate in either House, they shall not be questioned in any other Place.

2 No Senator or Representative shall, during the Time for which he was elected, be appointed to any civil Office under the Authority of the United States, which shall have been created, or the Emoluments whereof shall have been Increased during such time; and no Person holding any Office under the United States, shall be a Member of either House during his Continuance in Office.

SECTION. 7. 1 All Bills for raising Revenue shall originate in the House of Representatives; but the Senate may propose or concur with Amendments as on other Bills.

2 Every Bill which shall have passed the House of Representatives and the Senate, shall, before it become a Law, be presented to the President of the United States; If he approve he shall sign it, but if not he shall return it, with his Objections to that House in which it shall have originated, who shall enter the Objections at large on their Journal, and proceed to reconsider it. If after such Reconsideration two thirds of that House shall agree to pass the Bill, it shall be sent, together with the Objections, to the other House, by which it shall likewise be reconsidered, and if approved by two thirds of that House, it shall become a Law. But in all such Cases the Votes of both Houses shall be determined by yeas and Nays, and the Names of the Persons voting for and against the Bill shall be entered on the Journal of each House respectively. If any Bill shall not be returned by the President within ten Days (Sundays excepted) after it shall have been presented to him, the Same shall be a Law, in like Manner

as if he had signed it, unless the Congress by their Adjournment prevent its Return, in which Case it shall not be a Law.

3 Every Order, Resolution, or Vote to which the Concurrence of the Senate and House of Representatives may be necessary (except on a question of Adjournment) shall be presented to the President of the United States, and before the Same shall take Effect, shall be approved by him, or being disapproved by him, shall be repassed by two thirds of the Senate and House of Representatives, according to the Rules and Limitations prescribed in the Case of a Bill.

SECTION. 8. 1 The Congress shall have Power To lay and collect Taxes, Duties, Imposts and Excises, to pay the Debts and provide for the common Defence and general Welfare of the United States; but all Duties, Imposts and Excises shall be uniform throughout the United States;

2 To borrow Money on the credit of the United States;

3 To regulate Commerce with foreign Nations, and among the several States, and with the Indian Tribes;

4 To establish an uniform Rule of Naturalization, and uniform Laws on the subject of Bankruptcies throughout the United States

5 To coin Money, regulate the Value thereof, and of foreign Coin, and fix the Standard of Weights and Measures;

6 To provide for the Punishment of counterfeiting the Securities and current Coin of the United States;

7 To establish Post Offices and post Roads;

8 To promote the Progress of Science and useful Arts, by securing for limited Times to Authors and Inventors the exclusive Right to their respective Writings and Discoveries;

9 To constitute Tribunals inferior to the supreme Court;

10 To define and punish Piracies and Felonies committed on the high Seas, and Offences against the Law of Nations;

11 To declare War, grant Letters of Marque and Reprisal, and make Rules concerning Captures on Land and Water;

12 To raise and support Armies, but no Appropriation of Money to that Use shall be for a longer Term than two Years;

13 To provide and maintain a Navy;

14 To make Rules for the Government and Regulation of the land and naval Forces

15 To provide for calling forth the Militia to execute the Laws of the Union, suppress Insurrections and repel Invasions;

16 To provide for organizing, arming, and disciplining, the Militia, and for governing such Part of them as may be employed in the Service of the United States, reserving to the States respectively, the Appointment of the Officers, and the Authority of training the Militia according to the discipline prescribed by Congress;

17 To exercise exclusive Legislation in all Cases whatsoever, over such District (not exceeding ten Miles square) as may, by Cession of particular States, and the Acceptance of Congress, become the Seat of the Government of the United States, and to exercise like Authority over all Places purchased by the Consent of the Legislature of the State in which the Same shall be, for the Erection of Forts, Magazines, Arsenals, dock-Yards, and other needful Buildings;—And

18 To make all Laws which shall be necessary and proper for carrying into Execution the foregoing Powers, and all other Powers vested by this Constitution in the Government of the United States, or in any Department or Officer thereof.

SECTION. 9. 1 The Migration or Importation of such Persons as any of the States now existing shall think proper to admit, shall not be prohibited by the Congress prior to the Year one thousand eight hundred and eight, but a Tax or duty may be imposed on such Importation, not exceeding ten dollars for each Person.

2 The Privilege of the Writ of Habeas Corpus shall not be suspended, unless when in Cases of Rebellion or Invasion the public Safety may require it.

3 No Bill of Attainder or ex post facto Law shall be passed.

4 No Capitation, or other direct, Tax shall be laid, unless in Proportion to the Census or Enumeration herein before directed to be taken.

5 No Tax or Duty shall be laid on Articles exported from any State.

6 No Preference shall be given by any Regulation of Commerce or Revenue to the Ports of one State over those of another: nor shall Vessels bound to, or from, one State, be obliged to enter clear, or pay Duties in another.

7 No Money shall be drawn from the Treasury, but in Consequence of Appropriations made by Law; and a regular Statement and Account of the Receipts and Expenditures of all public Money shall be published from time to time.

8 No Title of Nobility shall be granted by the United States: And no Person holding any Office of Profit or Trust under them shall, without the Consent of the Congress, accept of any present, Emolument, Office, or Title, of any kind whatever, from any King, Prince, or foreign State.

SECTION. 10. 1 No State shall enter into any Treaty, Alliance, or Confederation; grant Letters of Marque and Reprisal; coin Money; emit Bills of Credit; make any Thing but gold and silver Coin a Tender in Payment of Debts; pass any Bill of Attainder ex post facto Law, or Law impairing the Obligation of Contracts or grant any Title of Nobility.

2 No State shall, without the Consent of the Congress, lay any Imposts or Duties on Imports or Exports, except what may be absolutely necessary for executing it's inspection Laws: and the net Produce of all Duties and Imposts, laid by any State on Imports or Exports, shall be for the Use of the Treasury of the United States; and all such Laws shall be subject to the Revision and Controul of the Congress.

3 No State shall, without the Consent of Congress, lay any Duty of Tonnage, keep Troops, or Ships of War in time of Peace, enter into any Agreement or Compact with another State, or with a foreign Power, or engage in War, unless actually invaded, or in such imminent Danger as will not admit of delay.

The Constitution of the United States of America, as Amended, House Doc. 102–188, 102nd Congress, 2d session (Washington: Government Printing Office, 1992), 1–6. Notes on the text and other footnotes in this printing of the Constitution have been omitted. Numbers designating clauses have been preserved for convenience of reference, although these did not appear in the engrossed copy signed by the delegates in 1787.

3   *The Federalist*

1787–1788

The Federalist was a series of eighty-eight essays written by James Madison, Alexander Hamilton, and John Jay between October 1787 and February 1788. The essays, written under the pen name of "Publius," appeared in various New York newspapers. In some instances it is not clear which of the three men wrote individual essays. While these commentaries on the nature of the U.S. Constitution and the new government it describes were written to influence the ratification of the Constitution in the State of New York, their impact was much more widely felt. The essays were recognized then as powerful and eloquent arguments on the nature of the new federal system of government and on the importance of the concept of popular sovereignty, the idea that power is derived from the people.

The Federalist remains one of the finest examples of political discourse in American history. The essays have been reprinted in numerous editions in the past two centuries, and today they can even be found thriving on the Internet at several web sites, including the Library of Congress address: http://lcweb2.loc.gov/const/fed/fedpapers.html#browse. The selections that follow focus on the nature of the House and Senate.

FEDERALIST 52
Author: Alexander Hamilton or James Madison

. . . .

I shall begin with the House of Representatives. The first view to be taken of this part of the government relates to the qualifications of the electors and the elected. Those of the former are to be the same with those of the electors of the most numerous branch of the State legislatures.

The definition of the right of suffrage is very justly regarded as a fundamental article of republican government. It was incumbent on the convention, therefore, to define and establish this right in the Constitution. To have left it open for the occasional regulation of the Congress, would have been improper for the reason just mentioned. To have submitted it to the legislative discretion of the States, would have been improper for the same reason; and for the additional reason that it would have rendered too dependent on the State governments that branch of the federal government which ought to be dependent on the people alone. To have reduced the different qualifications in the different States to one uniform rule, would probably have been as dissatisfactory to some of the States as it would have been difficult to the convention. The provision made by the convention appears, therefore, to be the best that lay within their option.

It must be satisfactory to every State, because it is conformable to the standard already established, or which may be established, by the State itself. It will be safe to the United States, because, being fixed by the State constitutions, it is not alterable by the State governments, and it cannot be feared that the peo-ple of the States will alter this part of their constitutions in such a manner as to abridge the rights secured to them by the federal Constitution. The qualifications of the elected, being less carefully and properly defined by the State constitutions, and being at the same time more susceptible of uniformity, have been very properly considered and regulated by the convention. A representative of the United States must be of the age of twenty-five years; must have been seven years a citizen of the United States; must, at the time of his election, be an inhabitant of the State he is to represent; and, during the time of his service, must be in no office under the United States. Under these reasonable limitations, the door of this part of the federal government is open to merit of every description, whether native or adoptive, whether young or old, and without regard to poverty or wealth, or to any particular profession of religious faith. The term for which the representatives are to be elected falls under a second view which may be taken of this branch. In order to decide on the propriety of this article, two questions must be considered: first, whether biennial elections will, in this case, be safe; secondly, whether they be necessary or useful. First. As it is essential to liberty that the government in general should have a common interest with the people, so it is particularly essential that the branch of it under consideration should have an immediate dependence on, and an intimate sympathy with, the people. Frequent elections are unquestionably the only policy by which this dependence and sympathy can be effectually secured.

. . . .

I conceive it to be a very substantial proof, that the liberties of the people can be in no danger from *biennial* elections . . . it has . . . been shown that the federal legislature will not only be restrained by its dependence on its people, as other legislative bodies are, but that it will be, moreover, watched and controlled by the several collateral legislatures, which other legislative bodies are not . . . no comparison can be made between the means that will be possessed by the more permanent branches of the federal government for seducing, if they should be disposed to seduce, the House of Representatives from their duty to the people, and the means of influence over the popular branch possessed by the other branches of the government above cited. With less power, therefore, to abuse, the federal representatives can be less tempted on one side, and will be doubly watched on the other. *PUBLIUS.*

FEDERALIST 53
Author: Alexander Hamilton or James Madison

To the People of the State of New York:

I shall here, perhaps, be reminded of a current observation, "that where annual elections end, tyranny begins." If it be true, as has often been remarked, that sayings which become proverbial are generally founded in reason, it is not less true, that when once established, they are often applied to cases to which the reason of them does not extend. I need not look for a proof beyond the case before us. What is the reason on which this proverbial observation is founded? No man will subject himself to the ridicule of pretending that any natural connection subsists between the sun or the seasons, and the period within which human virtue can bear the temptations of power. Happily for mankind, liberty is not, in this respect, confined to any single point of time; but lies within extremes, which afford sufficient latitude for all the variations which may be required by the various situations and circumstances of civil society.... Where no Constitution, paramount to the government, either existed or could be obtained, no constitutional security, similar to that established in the United States, was to be attempted. Some other security, therefore, was to be sought for; and what better security would the case admit, than that of selecting and appealing to some simple and familiar portion of time, as a standard for measuring the danger of innovations, for fixing the national sentiment, and for uniting the patriotic exertions? The most simple and familiar portion of time, applicable to the subject was that of a year; and hence the doctrine has been inculcated by a laudable zeal, to erect some barrier against the gradual innovations of an unlimited government, that the advance towards tyranny was to be calculated by the distance of departure from the fixed point of annual elections. But what necessity can there be of applying this expedient to a government limited, as the federal government will be, by the authority of a paramount Constitution? Or who will pretend that the liberties of the people of America will not be more secure under biennial elections, unalterably fixed by such a Constitution, than those of any other nation would be, where elections were annual, or even more frequent, but subject to alterations by the ordinary power of the government? The second question stated is, whether biennial elections be necessary or useful. The propriety of answering this question in the affirmative will appear from several very obvious considerations. No man can be a competent legislator who does not add to an upright intention and a sound judgment a certain degree of knowledge of the subjects on which he is to legislate. A part of this knowledge may be acquired by means of information which lie within the compass of men in private as well as public stations. Another part can only be attained, or at least thoroughly attained, by actual experience in the station which requires the use of it. The period of service, ought, therefore, in all such cases, to bear some proportion to the extent of practical knowledge requisite to the due performance of the service. The period of legislative service established in most of the States for the more numerous branch is, as we have seen, one year. The question then may be put into this simple form: does the period of two years bear no greater proportion to the knowledge requisite for federal legislation than one year does to the knowledge requisite for State legislation? The very statement of the question, in this form, suggests the answer that ought to be given to it. In a single State, the requisite knowledge relates to the existing laws which are uniform throughout the State, and with which all the citizens are more or less conversant; and to the general affairs of the State, which lie within a small compass, are not very diversified, and occupy much of the attention and conversation of every class of people. The great theatre of the United States presents a very different scene. The laws are so far from being uniform, that they vary in every State; whilst the public affairs of the Union are spread throughout a very extensive region, and are extremely diversified by the local affairs connected with them, and can with difficulty be correctly learnt in any other place than in the central councils to which a knowledge of them will be brought by the representatives of every part of the empire. Yet some knowledge of the affairs, and even of the laws, of all the States, ought to be possessed by the members from each of the States. How can foreign trade be properly regulated by uniform laws, without some acquaintance with the commerce, the ports, the usages, and the regulations of the different States? How can the trade between the different States be duly regulated, without some knowledge of their relative situations in these and other respects? How can taxes be judiciously imposed and effectually collected, if they be not accommodated to the different laws and local circumstances relating to these objects in the different States? How can uniform regulations for the militia be duly provided, without a similar knowledge of many internal circumstances by which the States are distinguished from each other? These are the principal objects of federal legislation, and suggest most forcibly the extensive information which the representatives ought to acquire. The other interior objects will require a proportional degree of information with regard to them. It is true that all these difficulties will, by degrees, be very much diminished. The most laborious task will be the proper inauguration of the government and the primeval formation of a federal code. Improvements on the first draughts will every year become both easier and fewer. Past transactions of the government will be a ready and accurate source of information to new members. The affairs of the Union will become more and more objects of curiosity and conversation among the citizens at large. And the increased intercourse among those of different States will contribute not a little to diffuse a mutual knowledge of their affairs, as this again will contribute to a general assimilation of their manners and laws. But with all these abatements, the business of federal legislation must continue so far to exceed, both in novelty and difficulty, the legislative business of a single State, as to justify the longer period of service assigned to those who are to transact it. A branch of knowledge which belongs to the acquirements of a federal representative, and which has not been mentioned is that of foreign affairs. In regulating our own commerce he ought to be not only acquainted with the treaties between the United States and other nations, but also with the commercial policy and laws of other nations. He ought not to be altogether ignorant of the law of nations; for that, as far as it is a proper object of municipal legislation, is submitted to the federal government.

. . . .

There are other considerations, of less importance, perhaps, but which are not unworthy of notice. The distance which many of the representatives will be obliged to travel, and the arrangements rendered necessary by that circumstance, might be much more serious objections with fit men to this service, if limited to a single year, than if extended to two years. No argument can be drawn on this subject, from the case of the delegates to the existing Congress. They are elected annually, it is true; but their re-election is considered by the legislative assemblies almost as a matter of course. The election of the representatives by the people would not be governed by the same principle. A few of the members, as happens in all such assemblies, will possess superior talents; will, by frequent reelections, become members of long standing; will be thoroughly masters of the public business, and perhaps not unwilling to avail themselves of those advantages. The greater the proportion of new members, and the less the information of the bulk of the members the more apt will they be to fall into the snares that may be laid for them. This remark is no less applicable to the relation which will subsist between the House of Representatives and the Senate. It is an inconvenience mingled with the advantages of our frequent elections even in single States, where they are large, and hold but one legislative session in a year, that spurious elections cannot be investigated and annulled in time for the decision to have its due effect. If a return can be obtained, no matter by what unlawful means, the irregular member, who takes his seat of course, is sure of holding it a sufficient time to answer his purposes. Hence, a very pernicious encouragement is given to the use of unlawful means, for obtaining irregular returns. Were elections for the federal legislature to be annual, this practice might become a very serious abuse, particularly in the more distant States. Each house is, as it necessarily must be, the judge of the elections, qualifications, and returns of its members; and whatever improvements may be suggested by experience, for simplifying and accelerating the process in disputed cases, so great a portion of a year would unavoidably elapse, before an illegitimate member could be dispossessed of his seat, that the prospect of such an event would be little check to unfair and illicit means of obtaining a seat. All these considerations taken together warrant us in affirming, that biennial elections will be as useful to the affairs of the public as we have seen that they will be safe to the liberty of the people.
PUBLIUS.

FEDERALIST 54
Author: Alexander Hamilton or James Madison

To the People of the State of New York:

The next view which I shall take of the House of Representatives relates to the appointment of its members to the several States which is to be determined by the same rule with that of direct taxes. It is not contended that the number of people in each State ought not to be the standard for regulating the proportion of those who are to represent the people of each State. The establishment of the same rule for the appointment of taxes, will probably be as little contested; though the rule itself in this case, is by no means founded on the same principle. In the former case, the rule is understood to refer to the personal rights of the people, with which it has a natural and universal connection.

In the latter, it has reference to the proportion of wealth, of which it is in no case a precise measure, and in ordinary cases a very unfit one. But notwithstanding the imperfection of the rule as applied to the relative wealth and contributions of the States, it is evidently the least objectionable among the practicable rules, and had too recently obtained the general sanction of America, not to have found a ready preference with the convention. All this is admitted, it will perhaps be said; but does it follow, from an admission of numbers for the measure of representation, or of slaves combined with free citizens as a ratio of taxation, that slaves ought to be included in the numerical rule of representation? Slaves are considered as property, not as persons. They ought therefore to be comprehended in estimates of taxation which are founded on property, and to be excluded from representation which is regulated by a census of persons. This is the objection, as I understand it, stated in its full force. I shall be equally candid in stating the reasoning which may be offered on the opposite side. "We subscribe to the doctrine," might one of our Southern brethren observe, "that representation relates more immediately to persons, and taxation more immediately to property, and we join in the application of this distinction to the case of our slaves. But we must deny the fact, that slaves are considered merely as property, and in no respect whatever as persons. The true state of the case is, that they partake of both these qualities: being considered by our laws, in some respects, as persons, and in other respects as property. In being compelled to labor, not for himself, but for a master; in being vendible by one master to another master; and in being subject at all times to be restrained in his liberty and chastised in his body, by the capricious will of another, the slave may appear to be degraded from the human rank, and classed with those irrational animals which fall under the legal denomination of property. In being protected, on the other hand, in his life and in his limbs, against the violence of all others, even the master of his labor and his liberty; and in being punishable himself for all violence committed against others, the slave is no less evidently regarded by the law as a member of the society, not as a part of the irrational creation; as a moral person, not as a mere article of property. The federal Constitution, therefore, decides with great propriety on the case of our slaves, when it views them in the mixed character of persons and of property. This is in fact their true character. It is the character bestowed on them by the laws under which they live; and it will not be denied, that these are the proper criterion; because it is only under the pretext that the laws have transformed the negroes into subjects of property, that a place is disputed them in the computation of numbers; and it is admitted, that if the laws were to restore the rights which have been taken away, the negroes could no longer be refused an equal share of representation with the other inhabitants.... Upon what principle, then, ought they to be taken into the federal estimate of representation? In rejecting them altogether, the Constitution would, in this respect, have followed the very laws which have been appealed to as the proper guide. "This objection is repelled by a single observation. It is a fundamental principle of the proposed Constitution, that as the aggregate number of representatives allotted to the several States is to be determined by a federal rule, founded on the aggregate number of inhabitants, so the right of choosing this allotted number in each State is to be exercised by such part of the inhabitants as the State itself may designate. The qualifications on which the right of suffrage depend are not, perhaps, the same in any two States. In some of the States the difference is very material. In every State, a certain proportion of inhabitants are deprived of this right by the constitution of the State, who will be included in the census by which the federal Constitution apportions the representatives.

... Let the case of the slaves be considered, as it is in truth, a peculiar one. Let the compromising expedient of the Constitution be mutually adopted, which regards them as inhabitants, but as debased by servitude below the equal level of free inhabitants, which regards the *slave* as divested of two fifths of the *man*. "After all, may not another ground be taken on which this article of the Constitution will admit of a still more ready defense? We have hitherto proceeded on the idea that representation related to persons only, and not at all to property. But is it a just idea?

Government is instituted no less for protection of the property, than of the persons, of individuals. The one as well as the other, therefore, may be considered as represented by those who are charged with the government. Upon this principle it is, that in several of the States, and particularly in the State of New York, one branch of the government is intended more especially to be the guardian of property, and is accordingly elected by that part of the society which is most interested in this object of government. In the federal Constitution, this policy does not prevail. The rights of property are committed into the same hands with the personal rights. Some attention ought, therefore, to be paid to property in the choice of those hands. "For another reason, the votes allowed in the federal legislature to the people of each State, ought to bear some proportion to the comparative wealth of the States." States have not, like individuals, an influence over each other, arising from superior advantages of fortune. If the law allows an opulent citizen but a single vote in the choice of his representative, the respect and consequence which he derives from his fortunate situation very frequently guide the votes of others to the objects of his choice; and through this imperceptible channel the rights of property are conveyed into the public representation. A State possesses no such influence over other States. It is not probable that the richest State in the Confederacy will ever influence the choice of a single representative in any other State. Nor will the representatives of the larger and richer States possess any other advantage in the federal legislature, over the representatives of other States, than what may result from their superior number alone. As far, therefore, as their superior wealth and weight may justly entitle them to any advantage, it ought to be secured to them by a superior share of representation.... As the accuracy of the census to be obtained by the Congress will necessarily depend, in a considerable degree on the disposition, if not on the co-operation, of the States, it is of great importance that the States should feel as little bias as possible, to swell or to reduce the amount of their numbers. Were their share of representation alone to be governed by this rule, they would have an interest in exaggerating their inhabitants. Were the rule to decide their share of taxation alone, a contrary temptation would prevail. By extending the rule to both objects, the States will have opposite interests, which will control and balance each other, and produce the requisite impartiality.
PUBLIUS.

FEDERALIST 55
Author: Alexander Hamilton or James Madison

To the People of the State of New York:

The number of which the House of Representatives is to consist, forms another and a very interesting point of view, under which this branch of the federal legislature may be contemplated.

Scarce any article, indeed, in the whole Constitution seems to be rendered more worthy of attention, by the weight of character and the apparent force of argument with which it has been assailed.

The charges exhibited against it are, first, that so small a number of representatives will be an unsafe depositary of the public interests; secondly, that they will not possess a proper knowledge of the local circumstances of their numerous constituents; thirdly, that they will be taken from that class of citizens which will sympathize least with the feelings of the mass of the people, and be most likely to aim at a permanent elevation of the few on the depression of the many; fourthly, that defective as the number will be in the first instance, it will be more and more disproportionate, by the increase of the people, and the obstacles which will prevent a correspondent increase of the representatives. In general it may be remarked on this subject, that no political problem is less susceptible of a precise solution than that which relates to the number most convenient for a representative legislature; nor is there any point on which the policy of the several States is more at variance, whether we compare their legislative assemblies directly with each other, or consider the proportions which they respectively bear to the number of their constituents.... Nothing can be more fallacious than to found our political calculations on arithmetical principles. Sixty or seventy men may be more properly trusted with a given degree of power than six or seven. But it does not follow that six or seven hundred would be proportionably a better depositary. And if we carry on the supposition to six or seven thousand, the whole reasoning ought to be reversed. The truth is, that in all cases a certain number at least seems to be necessary to secure the benefits of free consultation and discussion, and to guard against too easy a combination for improper purposes; as, on the other hand, the number ought at most to be kept within a certain limit, in order to avoid the confusion and intemperance of a multitude. In all very numerous assemblies, of whatever character composed, passion never fails to wrest the sceptre from reason.

Had every Athenian citizen been a Socrates, every Athenian assembly would still have been a mob.

It is necessary also to recollect here the observations which were applied to the case of biennial elections. For the same reason that the limited powers of the Congress, and the control of the State legislatures, justify less frequent elections than the public safely might otherwise require, the members of the Congress need be less numerous than if they possessed the whole power of legislation, and were under no other than the ordinary restraints of other legislative bodies. With these general ideas in our mind, let us weigh the objections which have been stated against the number of members proposed for the House of Representatives. It is said, in the first place, that so small a number cannot be safely trusted with so much power. The number of which this branch of the legislature is to consist, at the outset of the government, will be sixty five. Within three years a census is to be taken, when the number may be augmented to one for every thirty thousand inhabitants; and within every successive period of ten years the census is to be renewed, and augmentations may continue to be made under the above limitation. It will not be thought an extravagant conjecture that the first census will, at the rate of one for every thirty thousand, raise the number of representatives to at least one hundred. Estimating the negroes in the proportion of three fifths, it can scarcely be doubted that the population of the United States will by that time, if it does not already, amount to three millions. At the expiration of twenty-five years, according to the computed rate of increase, the number of representatives will amount to two hundred, and of fifty years, to four hundred. This is a number which, I presume, will put an end to all fears arising from the smallness of the body. I take for granted here what I shall, in answering the fourth objection, hereafter show, that the number of representatives will be augmented from time to time in the manner provided by the Constitution. On a contrary supposition, I should admit the objection to have very great weight indeed. The true question to be decided then is, whether the smallness of the number, as a temporary regulation, be dangerous to the public liberty? Whether sixty-five members for a few years, and a hundred or two hundred for a few more, be a safe depositary for a limited and well-guarded power of legislating for the United States? I must own that I could not give a negative answer to this question, without first obliterating every impression which I have received with regard to the present genius of the people of America, the spirit which actuates the State legislatures, and the principles which are incorporated with the political character of every class of citizens I am unable to conceive that the people of America, in their present temper, or under any circumstances which can speedily happen, will choose, and every second year repeat the choice of, sixty-five or a hundred men who would be disposed to form and pursue a scheme of tyranny or treachery. I am unable to conceive that the State legislatures, which must feel so many motives to watch, and which possess so many means of counteracting, the federal legislature, would fail either to detect or to defeat a conspiracy of the latter against the liberties of their common constituents. I am equally unable to conceive that there are at this time, or can be in any short time, in the United States, any sixty-five or a hundred men capable of recommending themselves to the choice of the people at large, who would either desire or dare, within the short space of two years, to betray the solemn trust committed to them. What change of circumstances, time, and a fuller population of our country may produce, requires a prophetic spirit to declare, which makes no part of my pretensions. But judging from the circumstances now before us, and from the probable state of them within a moderate period of time, I must pronounce that the liberties of America cannot be unsafe in the number of hands proposed by the federal Constitution. From what quarter can the danger proceed? Are we afraid of foreign gold? If foreign gold could so easily corrupt our federal rulers and enable them to ensnare and betray their constituents, how has it happened that we are at this time a free and independent nation? The Congress which conducted us through the Revolution was a less numerous body than their successors will be; they were not chosen by, nor responsible to, their fellow citizens at large; though appointed from year to year, and recallable at pleasure, they were generally continued for three years, and prior to the ratification of the federal articles, for a still longer term.

They held their consultations always under the veil of secrecy; they had the sole transaction of our affairs with foreign nations; through the whole course of the war they had the fate of their country more in their hands than it is to be hoped will ever be the case with our future representatives; and from the greatness of the prize at stake, and the eagerness of the party which lost it, it may well be supposed that the use of other means than force would not have been scrupled. Yet we know by happy experience that the public trust was not betrayed; nor has the purity of our public councils in this particular ever suffered, even from the whispers of calumny. Is the danger apprehended from the other branches of the federal government?

But where are the means to be found by the President, or the Senate, or both? Their emoluments of office, it is to be presumed, will not, and without a previous corruption of the House of Representatives cannot, more than suffice for very different purposes; their private fortunes, as they must all be American citizens, cannot possibly be sources of danger. The only means, then, which they can possess, will be in the dispensation of appointments. Is it here that suspicion rests her charge? Sometimes we are told that this fund of corruption is to be exhausted by the President in subduing the virtue of the Senate. Now, the fidelity of the other House is to be the victim. The improbability of such a mercenary and perfidious combination of the several members of government, standing on as different foundations as republican principles will well admit, and at the same time accountable to the society over which they are placed, ought alone to quiet this apprehension. But, fortunately, the Constitution has provided a still further safeguard. The members of the Congress are rendered ineligible to any civil offices that may be created, or of which the emoluments may be increased, during the term of their election.

. . . As there is a degree of depravity in mankind which requires a certain degree of circumspection and distrust, so there are other qualities in human nature which justify a certain portion of esteem and confidence. Republican government presupposes the existence of these qualities in a higher degree than any other form. Were the pictures which have been drawn by the political jealousy of some among us faithful likenesses of the human character, the inference would be, that there is not sufficient virtue among men for self-government; and that nothing less than the chains of despotism can restrain them from destroying and devouring one another.

PUBLIUS.

FEDERALIST 56

Author: Alexander Hamilton or James Madison

To the People of the State of New York:

The second charge against the House of Representatives is, that it will be too small to possess a due knowledge of the interests of its constituents. As this objection evidently proceeds from a comparison of the proposed number of representatives with the great extent of the United States, the number of their inhabitants, and the diversity of their interests, without taking into view at the same time the circumstances which will distinguish the Congress from other legislative bodies, the best answer that can be given to it will be a brief explanation of these peculiarities. It is a sound and important principle that the representative ought to be acquainted with the interests and circumstances of his constituents. But this principle can extend no further than to those circumstances and interests to which the authority and care of the representative relate. An ignorance of a variety of minute and particular objects, which do not lie within the compass of legislation, is consistent with every attribute necessary to a due performance of the legislative trust. In determining the extent of information required in the exercise of a particular authority, recourse then must be had to the objects within the purview of that authority. What are to be the objects of federal legislation? Those which are of most importance, and which seem most to require local knowledge, are commerce, taxation, and the militia. A proper regulation of commerce requires much information, as has been elsewhere remarked; but as far as this information relates to the laws and local situation of each individual State, a very few representatives would be very sufficient vehicles of it to the federal councils. Taxation will consist, in a great measure, of duties which will be involved in the regulation of commerce. . . . The representatives of each State will not only bring with them a considerable knowledge of its laws, and a local knowledge of their respective districts, but will probably in all cases have been members, and may even at the very time be members, of the State legislature, where all the local information and interests of the State are assembled, and from whence they may easily be conveyed by a very few hands into the legislature of the United States. The observations made on the subject of taxation apply with greater force to the case of the militia. For however different the rules of discipline may be in different States, they are the same throughout each particular State; and depend on circumstances which can differ but little in different parts of the same State. The attentive reader will discern that the reasoning here used, to prove the sufficiency of a moderate number of representatives, does not in any respect contradict what was urged on another occasion with regard to the extensive information which the representatives ought to possess, and the time that might be necessary for acquiring it. This information, so far as it may relate to local objects, is rendered necessary and difficult, not by a difference of laws and local circumstances within a single State, but of those among different States. Taking each State by itself, its laws are the same, and its interests but little diversified. A few men, therefore, will possess all the knowledge requisite for a proper representation of them. Were the interests and affairs of each individual State perfectly simple and uniform, a knowledge of them in one part would involve a knowledge of them in every other, and the whole State might be competently represented by a single member taken from any part of it. On a comparison of the different States together, we find a great dissimilarity in their laws, and in many other circumstances connected with the objects of federal legislation, with all of which the federal representatives ought to have some acquaintance. Whilst a few representatives, therefore, from each State, may bring with them a due knowledge of their own State, every representative will have much information to acquire concerning all the other States.

. . . .

PUBLIUS.

FEDERALIST 57

Author: Alexander Hamilton or James Madison

To the People of the State of New York:

The third charge against the House of Representatives is, that it will be taken from that class of citizens which will have least sympathy with the mass of the people, and be most likely to aim at an ambitious sacrifice of the many to the aggrandizement of the few. Of all the objections which have been framed against the federal Constitution, this is perhaps the most extraordinary.

Whilst the objection itself is levelled against a pretended oligarchy, the principle of it strikes at the very root of republican government. The aim of every political constitution is, or ought to be, first to obtain for rulers men who possess most wisdom to discern, and most virtue to pursue, the common good of the society; and in the next place, to take the most effectual precautions for keeping them virtuous whilst they continue to hold their public trust. The elective mode of obtaining rulers is the characteristic policy of republican government. The means relied on in this form of government for preventing their degeneracy are numerous and various. The most effectual one, is such a limitation of the term of appointments as will maintain a proper responsibility to the people. Let me now ask what circumstance there is in the constitution of the House of Representatives that violates the principles of republican government, or favors the elevation of the few on the ruins of the many? Let me ask whether every circumstance is not, on the contrary, strictly conformable to these principles, and scrupulously impartial to the rights and pretensions of every class and description of citizens? Who are to be the electors of the federal representatives? Not the rich, more than the poor; not the learned, more than the ignorant; not the haughty heirs of distinguished names, more than the humble sons of obscurity and unpropitious fortune. The electors are to be the great body of the people of the United States. They are to be the same who exercise the right in every State of electing the corresponding branch of the legislature of the State. Who are to be the objects of popular choice? Every citizen whose merit may recommend him to the esteem and confidence of his country. No qualification of wealth, of birth, of religious faith, or of civil profession is permitted to fetter the judgement or disappoint the inclination of the people. If we consider the situation of the men on whom the free suffrages of their fellow-citizens may confer the representative trust, we shall find it involving every security which can be devised or desired for their fidelity to their constituents. In the first place, as they will have been distinguished by the preference of their fellow-citizens, we are to presume that in general they will be somewhat distinguished also by those qualities which entitle them to it, and which promise a sincere and scrupulous regard to the nature of their engagements. In the second place, they will enter into the public service under circumstances which cannot fail to produce a temporary affection at least to their constituents. There is in every breast a sensibility to marks of honor, of favor, of esteem, and of confidence, which, apart from all considerations of interest, is some pledge for grateful and benevolent returns.

Ingratitude is a common topic of declamation against human nature; and it must be confessed that instances of it are but too frequent and flagrant, both in public and in private life. But the universal and extreme indignation which it inspires is itself a proof of the energy and prevalence of the contrary sentiment.

In the third place, those ties which bind the representative to his constituents are strengthened by motives of a more selfish nature. His pride and vanity attach him to a form of government which favors his pretensions and gives him a share in its honors and distinctions. Whatever hopes or projects might be entertained by a few aspiring characters, it must generally happen that a great proportion of the men deriving their advancement from their influence with the people, would have more to hope from a preservation of the favor, than from innovations in the government subversive of the authority of the people. All

these securities, however, would be found very insufficient without the restraint of frequent elections. Hence, in the fourth place, the House of Representatives is so constituted as to support in the members an habitual recollection of their dependence on the people. Before the sentiments impressed on their minds by the mode of their elevation can be effaced by the exercise of power, they will be compelled to anticipate the moment when their power is to cease, when their exercise of it is to be reviewed, and when they must descend to the level from which they were raised; there forever to remain unless a faithful discharge of their trust shall have established their title to a renewal of it. I will add, as a fifth circumstance in the situation of the House of Representatives, restraining them from oppressive measures, that they can make no law which will not have its full operation on themselves and their friends, as well as on the great mass of the society. This has always been deemed one of the strongest bonds by which human policy can connect the rulers and the people together. It creates between them that communion of interests and sympathy of sentiments, of which few governments have furnished examples; but without which every government degenerates into tyranny. If it be asked, what is to restrain the House of Representatives from making legal discriminations in favor of themselves and a particular class of the society? I answer: the genius of the whole system; the nature of just and constitutional laws; and above all, the vigilant and manly spirit which actuates the people of America, a spirit which nourishes freedom, and in return is nourished by it. If this spirit shall ever be so far debased as to tolerate a law not obligatory on the legislature, as well as on the people, the people will be prepared to tolerate any thing but liberty. Such will be the relation between the House of Representatives and their constituents. Duty, gratitude, interest, ambition itself, are the chords by which they will be bound to fidelity and sympathy with the great mass of the people.

It is possible that these may all be insufficient to control the caprice and wickedness of man. But are they not all that government will admit, and that human prudence can devise? Are they not the genuine and the characteristic means by which republican government provides for the liberty and happiness of the people? Are they not the identical means on which every State government in the Union relies for the attainment of these important ends?

. . . .

PUBLIUS.

FEDERALIST 58
Author: James Madison

To the People of the State of New York:

The remaining charge against the House of Representatives, which I am to examine, is grounded on a supposition that the number of members will not be augmented from time to time, as the progress of population may demand. It has been admitted, that this objection, if well supported, would have great weight. The following observations will show that, like most other objections against the Constitution, it can only proceed from a partial view of the subject, or from a jealousy which discolors and disfigures every object which is beheld. Those who urge the objection seem not to have recollected that the federal Constitution will not suffer by a comparison with the State constitutions, in the security provided for a gradual augmentation of the number of representatives. The number which is to prevail in the first instance is declared to be temporary. Its duration is limited to the short term of three years. Within every successive term of ten years a census of inhabitants is to be repeated. The unequivocal objects of these regulations are, first, to readjust, from time to time, the apportionment of representatives to the number of inhabitants, under the single exception that each State shall have one representative at least; secondly, to augment the number of representatives at the same periods, under the sole limitation that the whole number shall not exceed one for every thirty thousand inhabitants. . . . Notwithstanding the equal authority which will subsist between the two houses on all legislative subjects, except the originating of money bills, it cannot be doubted that the House, composed of the greater number of members, when supported by the more powerful States, and speaking the known and determined sense of a majority of the people, will have no small advantage in a question depending on the comparative firmness of the two houses. This advantage must be increased by the consciousness, felt by the same side of being supported in its demands by right, by reason, and by the Constitution; and the consciousness, on the opposite side, of contending against the force of all these solemn considerations. It is farther to be considered, that in the gradation between the smallest and largest States, there are several, which, though most likely in general to arrange themselves among the former are too little removed in extent and population from the latter, to second an opposition to their just and legitimate pretensions. Hence it is by no means certain that a majority of votes, even in the Senate, would be unfriendly to proper augmentations in the number of representatives. It will not be looking too far to add, that the senators from all the new States may be gained over to the just views of the House of Representatives, by an expedient too obvious to be overlooked. As these States will, for a great length of time, advance in population with peculiar rapidity, they will be interested in frequent reapportionments of the representatives to the number of inhabitants. The large States, therefore, who will prevail in the House of Representatives, will have nothing to do but to make reapportionments and augmentations mutually conditions of each other; and the senators from all the most growing States will be bound to contend for the latter, by the interest which their States will feel in the former. These considerations seem to afford ample security on this subject, and ought alone to satisfy all the doubts and fears which have been indulged with regard to it. . . . One observation, however, I must be permitted to add on this subject as claiming, in my judgment, a very serious attention. It is, that in all legislative assemblies the greater the number composing them may be, the fewer will be the men who will in fact direct their proceedings. In the first place, the more numerous an assembly may be, of whatever characters composed, the greater is known to be the ascendency of passion over reason. In the next place, the larger the number, the greater will be the proportion of members of limited information and of weak capacities. Now, it is precisely on characters of this description that the eloquence and address of the few are known to act with all their force. In the ancient republics, where the whole body of the people assembled in person, a single orator, or an artful statesman, was generally seen to rule with as complete a sway as if a sceptre had been placed in his single hand. On the same principle, the more multitudinous a representative assembly may be rendered, the more it will partake of the infirmities incident to collective meetings of the people.

Ignorance will be the dupe of cunning, and passion the slave of sophistry and declamation. The people can never err more than in supposing that by multiplying their representatives beyond a certain limit, they strengthen the barrier against the government of a few. Experience will forever admonish them that, on the contrary, *after securing a sufficient number for the purposes of safety, of local information, and of diffusive sympathy with the whole society,* they will counteract their own views by every addition to their representatives. The countenance of the government may become more democratic, but the soul that animates it will be more oligarchic. The machine will be enlarged, but the fewer, and often the more secret, will be the springs by which its motions are directed. As connected with the objection against the number of representatives, may properly be here noticed, that which has been suggested against the number made competent for legislative business. It has been said that more than a majority ought to have been required for a quorum; and in particular cases, if not in all, more than a majority of a quorum for a decision. That some advantages might have resulted from such a precaution, cannot be denied. It might have been an additional shield to some particular interests, and another obstacle generally to hasty and partial measures. But these considerations are outweighed by the inconveniences in the opposite scale. In all cases where justice or the general good might require new laws to be passed, or active measures to be pursued, the fundamental principle of free government would be reversed. It would be no longer the majority that would rule: the power would be transferred to the minority. Were the defensive privilege limited to particular cases, an interested minority might take advantage of it to screen themselves from equitable sacrifices to the general weal, or, in particular emergencies, to extort unreasonable indulgences. Lastly, it would facilitate and foster the baneful practice of secessions; a practice which has shown itself even in States where a majority only is required; a practice subversive of all the principles of order and regular government; a practice which leads more directly to public convulsions, and the ruin of popular governments, than any other which has yet been displayed among us. *PUBLIUS.*

FEDERALIST 59
Author: Alexander Hamilton

To the People of the State of New York:

The natural order of the subject leads us to consider, in this place, that provision of the Constitution which authorizes the national legislature to regulate, in the last resort, the election of its own members. It is in these words: "The *times, places,* and *manner* of holding elections for senators and representatives shall be prescribed in each State by the legislature thereof; but the Congress may, at any time, by law, make or alter *such regulations,* except as to the *places* of choosing senators." This provision has not only been declaimed against by those who condemn the Constitution in the gross, but it has been censured by those who have objected with less latitude and greater moderation; and, in one instance it has been thought exceptionable by a gentleman who has declared himself the advocate of every other part of the system. I am greatly mistaken, notwithstanding, if there be any article in the whole plan more completely defensible than this. Its propriety rests upon the evidence of this plain proposition, that *every government ought to contain in itself the means of its own preservation.* . . . Nothing can be more evident, than that an exclusive power of regulating elections for the national government, in the hands of the State legislatures, would leave the existence of the Union entirely at their mercy. They could at any moment annihilate it, by neglecting to provide for the choice of persons to administer its affairs. It is to little purpose to say, that a neglect or omission of this kind would not be likely to take place. The constitutional possibility of the thing, without an equivalent for the risk, is an unanswerable objection. Nor has any satisfactory reason been yet assigned for incurring that risk. The extravagant surmises of a distempered jealousy can never be dignified with that character. If we are in a humor to presume abuses of power, it is as fair to presume them on the part of the State governments as on the part of the general government. And as it is more consonant to the rules of a just theory, to trust the Union with the care of its own existence, than to transfer that care to any other hands, if abuses of power are to be hazarded on the one side or on the other, it is more rational to hazard them where the power would naturally be placed, than where it would unnaturally be placed. . . . It may be easily discerned also that the national government would run a much greater risk from a power in the State legislatures over the elections of its House of Representatives, than from their power of appointing the members of its Senate. The senators are to be chosen for the period of six years; there is to be a rotation, by which the seats of a third part of them are to be vacated and replenished every two years; and no State is to be entitled to more than two senators; a quorum of the body is to consist of sixteen members. The joint result of these circumstances would be, that a temporary combination of a few States to intermit the appointment of senators, could neither annul the existence nor impair the activity of the body; and it is not from a general and permanent combination of the States that we can have any thing to fear. The first might proceed from sinister designs in the leading members of a few of the State legislatures; the last would suppose a fixed and rooted disaffection in the great body of the people, which will either never exist at all, or will, in all probability, proceed from an experience of the inaptitude of the general government to the advancement of their happiness in which event no good citizen could desire its continuance. But with regard to the federal House of Representatives, there is intended to be a general election of members once in two years. If the State legislatures were to be invested with an exclusive power of regulating these elections, every period of making them would be a delicate crisis in the national situation, which might issue in a dissolution of the Union, if the leaders of a few of the most important States should have entered into a previous conspiracy to prevent an election. . . . It ought never to be forgotten, that a firm union of this country, under an efficient government, will probably be an increasing object of jealousy to more than one nation of Europe; and that enterprises to subvert it will sometimes originate in the intrigues of foreign powers, and will seldom fail to be patronized and abetted by some of them. Its preservation, therefore ought in no case that can be avoided, to be committed to the guardianship of any but those whose situation will uniformly beget an immediate interest in the faithful and vigilant performance of the trust.
PUBLIUS.

FEDERALIST 62
Author: Alexander Hamilton or James Madison

To the People of the State of New York:

Having examined the constitution of the House of Representatives, and answered such of the objections against it as seemed to merit notice, I enter next on the examination of the Senate.

The heads into which this member of the government may be considered are: I. The qualification of senators; II. The appointment of them by the State legislatures; III. The equality of representation in the Senate; IV. The number of senators, and the term for which they are to be elected; V. The powers vested in the Senate.

I. The qualifications proposed for senators, as distinguished from those of representatives, consist in a more advanced age and a longer period of citizenship. A senator must be thirty years of age at least; as a representative must be twenty-five. And the former must have been a citizen nine years; as seven years are required for the latter. The propriety of these distinctions is explained by the nature of the senatorial trust, which, requiring greater extent of information and stability of character, requires at the same time that the senator should have reached a period of life most likely to supply these advantages; and which, participating immediately in transactions with foreign nations, ought to be exercised by none who are not thoroughly weaned from the prepossessions and habits incident to foreign birth and education. The term of nine years appears to be a prudent mediocrity between a total exclusion of adopted citizens, whose merits and talents may claim a share in the public confidence, and an indiscriminate and hasty admission of them, which might create a channel for foreign influence on the national councils.

II. It is equally unnecessary to dilate on the appointment of senators by the State legislatures. Among the various modes which might have been devised for constituting this branch of the government, that which has been proposed by the convention is probably the most congenial with the public opinion. It is recommended by the double advantage of favoring a select appointment, and of giving to the State governments such an agency in the formation of the federal government as must secure the authority of the former, and may form a convenient link between the two systems.

III. The equality of representation in the Senate is another point, which, being evidently the result of compromise between the opposite pretensions of the large and the small States, does not call for much discussion. If indeed it be right, that among a people thoroughly incorporated into one nation, every district ought to have a PROPORTIONAL share in the government, and that among independent and sovereign States, bound together by a simple league, the parties, however unequal in size, ought to have an EQUAL share in the common councils, it does not appear to be without some reason that in a compound republic, partaking both of the national and federal character, the government ought to be founded on a mixture of the principles of proportional and equal representation. But it is superfluous to try, by the standard of theory, a part of the Constitution which is allowed on all hands to be the result, not of theory, but "of a spirit of amity, and that mutual deference and concession which the peculiarity of our political situation rendered indispensable." A common government, with powers equal to its objects, is called for by the voice, and still more loudly by the political situation, of America. A government founded on principles more consonant to the wishes of the larger States, is not likely to be obtained from the smaller States. The only option, then, for the former, lies between the proposed government and a government still more objectionable. Under this alternative, the advice of prudence must be to embrace the lesser evil; and, instead of indulging a fruitless anticipation of the possible mischiefs which may ensue, to contemplate rather the advantageous consequences which may qualify the sacrifice.

In this spirit it may be remarked, that the equal vote allowed to each State is at once a constitutional recognition of the portion of sovereignty remaining in the individual States, and an instrument for preserving that residuary sovereignty. So far the equality ought to be no less acceptable to the large than to the small States; since they are not less solicitous to guard, by every possible expedient, against an improper consolidation of the States into one simple republic.

Another advantage accruing from this ingredient in the constitution of the Senate is, the additional impediment it must prove against improper acts of legislation. No law or resolution can now be passed without the concurrence, first, of a majority of the people, and then, of a majority of the States. It must be acknowledged that this complicated check on legislation may in some instances be injurious as well as beneficial; and that the peculiar defense which it involves in favor of the smaller States, would be more rational, if any interests common to them, and distinct from those of the other States, would otherwise be exposed to peculiar danger. But as the larger States will always be able, by their power over the supplies, to defeat unreasonable exertions of this prerogative of the lesser States, and as the faculty and excess of law-making seem to be the diseases to which our governments are most liable, it is not impossible that this part of the Constitution may be more convenient in practice than it appears to many in contemplation.

IV. The number of senators, and the duration of their appointment, come next to be considered. In order to form an accurate judgment on both of these points, it will be proper to inquire into the purposes which are to be answered by a senate; and in order to ascertain these, it will be necessary to review the inconveniences which a republic must suffer from the want of such an institution.

First. It is a misfortune incident to republican government, though in a less degree than to other governments, that those who administer it may forget their obligations to their constituents, and prove unfaithful to their important trust. In this point of view, a senate, as a second branch of the legislative assembly, distinct from, and dividing the power with, a first, must be in all cases a salutary check on the government. It doubles the security to the people, by requiring the concurrence of two distinct bodies in schemes of usurpation or perfidy, where the ambition or corruption of one would otherwise be sufficient. This is a precaution founded on such clear principles, and now so well understood in the United States, that it would be more than superfluous to enlarge on it. I will barely remark, that as the improbability of sinister combinations will be in proportion to the dissimilarity in the genius of the two bodies, it must be politic to distinguish them from each other by every circumstance which will consist with a due harmony in all proper measures, and with the genuine principles of republican government.

Secondly. The necessity of a senate is not less indicated by the propensity of all single and numerous assemblies to yield to the impulse of sudden and violent passions, and to be seduced by factious leaders into intemperate and pernicious resolutions. Examples on this subject might be cited without number; and from proceedings within the United States, as well as from the history of other nations. But a position that will not be contradicted, need not be proved. All that need be remarked is, that a body which is to correct this infirmity ought itself to be free from it, and consequently ought to be less numerous. It ought, moreover, to possess great firmness, and consequently ought to hold its authority by a tenure of considerable duration.

Thirdly. Another defect to be supplied by a senate lies in a want of due acquaintance with the objects and principles of legislation. It is not possible that an assembly of men called for the most part from pursuits of a private nature, continued in appointment for a short time, and led by no permanent motive to devote the intervals of public occupation to a study of the laws, the affairs, and the comprehensive interests of their country, should, if left wholly to themselves, escape a variety of important errors in the exercise of their legislative trust. It may be affirmed, on the best grounds, that no small share of the present embarrassments of America is to be charged on the blunders of our governments; and that these have proceeded from the heads rather than the hearts of most of the authors of them. What indeed are all the repealing, explaining, and amending laws, which fill and disgrace our voluminous codes, but so many monuments of deficient wisdom; so many impeachments exhibited by each succeeding against each preceding session; so many admonitions to the people, of the value of those aids which may be expected from a well-constituted senate?

A good government implies two things: first, fidelity to the object of government, which is the happiness of the people; secondly, a knowledge of the means by which that object can be best attained. Some governments are deficient in both these qualities; most governments are deficient in the first. I scruple not to assert, that in American governments too little attention has been paid to the last. The federal Constitution avoids this error; and what merits particular notice, it provides for the last in a mode which increases the security for the first.

Fourthly. The mutability in the public councils arising from a rapid succession of new members, however qualified they may be, points out, in the strongest manner, the necessity of some stable institution in the government. Every new election in the States is found to change one half of the representatives. From this change of men must proceed a change of opinions; and from a change of opinions, a change of measures. But a continual change even of good measures is inconsistent with every rule of prudence and every prospect of success. The remark is verified in private life, and becomes more just, as well as more important, in national transactions.

To trace the mischievous effects of a mutable government would fill a volume. I will hint a few only, each of which will be perceived to be a source of innumerable others.

In the first place, it forfeits the respect and confidence of other nations, and all the advantages connected with national character. An individual who is observed to be inconstant to his plans, or perhaps to carry on his affairs without any plan at all, is marked at once, by all prudent people, as a speedy victim to his own unsteadiness and folly. His more friendly neighbors may pity him, but all will decline to connect their fortunes with his; and not a few will seize the opportunity of making their fortunes out of his. One nation is to another what one individual is to another; with this melancholy distinction perhaps, that the former, with fewer of the benevolent emotions than the latter, are under fewer restraints also from taking undue advantage from the indiscretions of each other. Every nation, consequently, whose affairs betray a want of wisdom and stability, may calculate on every loss which can be sustained from the more systematic policy of their wiser neighbors. But the best instruction on this subject is unhappily conveyed to America by the example of her own situation. She finds that she is held in no respect by her friends; that she is the derision of her enemies; and that she is a prey to every nation which has an interest in speculating on her fluctuating councils and embarrassed affairs.

The internal effects of a mutable policy are still more calamitous. It poisons the blessing of liberty itself. It will be of little avail to the people, that the laws are made by men of their own choice, if the laws be so voluminous that they cannot be read, or so incoherent that they cannot be understood; if they be repealed or revised before they are promulgated, or undergo such incessant changes that no man, who knows what the law is to-day, can guess what it will be to-morrow. Law is defined to be a rule of action; but how can that be a rule, which is little known, and less fixed?

Another effect of public instability is the unreasonable advantage it gives to the sagacious, the enterprising, and the moneyed few over the industrious and uniformed mass of the people. Every new regulation concerning commerce or revenue, or in any way affecting the value of the different species of property, presents a new harvest to those who watch the change, and can trace its consequences; a harvest, reared not by themselves, but by the toils and cares of the great body of their fellow-citizens. This is a state of things in which it may be said with some truth that laws are made for the *few*, not for the *many*.

In another point of view, great injury results from an unstable government. The want of confidence in the public councils damps every useful undertaking, the success and profit of which may depend on a continuance of existing arrangements. What prudent merchant will hazard his fortunes in any new branch of commerce when he knows not but that his plans may be rendered unlawful before they can be executed? What farmer or manufacturer will lay himself out for the encouragement given to any particular cultivation or establishment, when he can have no assurance that his preparatory labors and advances will not render him a victim to an inconstant government? In a word, no great improvement or laudable enterprise can go forward which requires the auspices of a steady system of national policy.

But the most deplorable effect of all is that diminution of attachment and reverence which steals into the hearts of the people, towards a political system which betrays so many marks of infirmity, and disappoints so many of their flattering hopes. No government, any more than an individual, will long be respected without being truly respectable; nor be truly respectable, without possessing a certain portion of order and stability.
PUBLIUS.

FEDERALIST 63
Author: Alexander Hamilton or James Madison

To the People of the State of New York:

A fifth desideratum, illustrating the utility of a senate, is the want of a due sense of national character. Without a select and stable member of the government, the esteem of foreign powers will not only be forfeited by an unenlightened and variable policy, proceeding from the causes already mentioned, but the national councils will not possess that sensibility to the opinion of the world, which is perhaps not less necessary in order to merit, than it is to obtain, its respect and confidence.

An attention to the judgment of other nations is important to every government for two reasons: the one is, that, independently of the merits of any particular plan or measure, it is desirable, on various accounts, that it should appear to other nations as the offspring of a wise and honorable policy; the second is, that in doubtful cases, particularly where the national councils may be warped by some strong passion or momentary interest, the presumed or known opinion of the impartial world may be the best guide that can be followed. What has not America lost by her want of character with foreign nations; and how many errors and follies would she not have avoided, if the justice and propriety of her measures had, in every instance, been previously tried by the light in which they would probably appear to the unbiased part of mankind?

Yet however requisite a sense of national character may be, it is evident that it can never be sufficiently possessed by a numerous and changeable body. It can only be found in a number so small that a sensible degree of the praise and blame of public measures may be the portion of each individual; or in an assembly so durably invested with public trust, that the pride and consequence of its members may be sensibly incorporated with the reputation and prosperity of the community. . . .

I add, as a *sixth* defect the want, in some important cases, of a due responsibility in the government to the people, arising from that frequency of elections which in other cases produces this responsibility. This remark will, perhaps, appear not only new, but paradoxical. It must nevertheless be acknowledged, when explained, to be as undeniable as it is important.

Responsibility, in order to be reasonable, must be limited to objects within the power of the responsible party, and in order to be effectual, must relate to operations of that power, of which a ready and proper judgment can be formed by the constituents. The objects of government may be divided into two general classes: the one depending on measures which have singly an immediate and sensible operation; the other depending on a succession of well-chosen and well-connected measures, which have a gradual and perhaps unobserved operation. The importance of the latter description to the collective and permanent welfare of every country, needs no explanation. And yet it is evident that an assembly elected for so short a term as to be unable to provide more than one or two links in a chain of measures, on which the general welfare may essentially depend, ought not to be answerable for the final result, any more than a steward or tenant, engaged for one year, could be justly made to answer for places or improvements which could not be accomplished in less than half a dozen years. Nor is it possible for the people to estimate the SHARE of influence which their annual assemblies may respectively have on events resulting from the mixed transactions of several years. It is sufficiently difficult to preserve a personal responsibility in the members of a *numerous* body, for such acts of the body as have an immediate, detached, and palpable operation on its constituents.

The proper remedy for this defect must be an additional body in the legislative department, which, having sufficient permanency to provide for such objects as require a continued attention, and a train of measures, may be justly and effectually answerable for the attainment of those objects.

Thus far I have considered the circumstances which point out the necessity of a well-constructed Senate only as they relate to the representatives of the people. To a people as little blinded by prejudice or corrupted by flattery as those whom I address, I shall not scruple to add, that such an institution may be sometimes necessary as a defense to the people against their own temporary errors and delusions. As the cool and deliberate sense of the community ought, in all governments, and actually will, in all free governments, ultimately prevail over the views of its rulers; so there are particular moments in public affairs when the people, stimulated by some irregular passion, or some illicit advantage, or misled by the artful misrepresentations of interested men, may call for measures which they themselves will afterwards be the most ready to lament and condemn. In these critical moments, how salutary will be the interference of some temperate and respectable body of citizens, in order to check the misguided career, and to suspend the blow meditated by the people against themselves, until reason, justice, and truth can regain their authority over the public mind? What bitter anguish would not the people of Athens have often escaped if their government had contained so provident a safeguard against the tyranny of their own passions? Popular liberty might then have escaped the indelible reproach of decreeing to the same citizens the hemlock on one day and statues on the next.

. . . The people can never wilfully betray their own interests; but they may possibly be betrayed by the representatives of the people; and the danger will be evidently greater where the whole legislative trust is lodged in the hands of one body of men, than where the concurrence of separate and dissimilar bodies is required in every public act.

The difference most relied on, between the American and other republics, consists in the principle of representation; which is the pivot on which the former move, and which is supposed to have been unknown to the latter, or at least to the ancient part of them. The use which has been made of this difference, in reasonings contained in former papers, will have shown that I am disposed neither to deny its existence nor to undervalue its importance. I feel the less restraint, therefore, in observing, that the position concerning the ignorance of the ancient governments on the subject of representation, is by no means precisely true in the latitude commonly given to it.

. . . .

In answer to all these arguments, suggested by reason, illustrated by examples, and enforced by our own experience, the jealous adversary of the Constitution will probably content himself with repeating, that a senate appointed not immediately by the people, and for the term of six years, must gradually acquire a dangerous pre-eminence in the government, and finally transform it into a tyrannical aristocracy.

To this general answer, the general reply ought to be sufficient, that liberty may be endangered by the abuses of liberty as well as by the abuses of power; that there are numerous instances of the former as well as of the latter; and that the former, rather than the latter, are apparently most to be apprehended by the United States. But a more particular reply may be given.

Before such a revolution can be effected, the Senate, it is to be observed, must in the first place corrupt itself; must next corrupt the State legislatures; must then corrupt the House of Representatives; and must finally corrupt the people at large. It is evident that the Senate must be first corrupted before it can attempt an establishment of tyranny. Without corrupting the State legislatures, it cannot prosecute the attempt, because the periodical change of members would otherwise regenerate the whole body. Without exerting the means of corruption with equal success on the House of Representatives, the opposition of that coequal branch of the government would inevitably defeat the attempt; and without corrupting the people themselves, a succession of new representatives would speedily restore all things to their pristine order. Is there any man who can seriously persuade himself that the proposed Senate can, by any possible means within the compass of human address, arrive at the object of a lawless ambition, through all these obstructions?

. . . .

As far as antiquity can instruct us on this subject, its examples support the reasoning which we have employed. In Sparta, the Ephori, the annual representatives of the people, were found an overmatch for the senate for life, continually gained on its authority and finally drew all power into their own hands. The Tribunes of Rome, who were the representatives of the people, prevailed, it is well known, in almost every contest with the senate for life, and in the end gained the most complete triumph over it. The fact is the more remarkable, as unanimity was required in every act of the Tribunes, even after their number was augmented to ten. It proves the irresistible force possessed by that branch of a free government, which has the people on its side. To these examples might be added that of Carthage, whose senate, according to the testimony of Polybius, instead of drawing all power into its vortex, had, at the commencement of the second Punic War, lost almost the whole of its original portion.

Besides the conclusive evidence resulting from this assemblage of facts, that the federal Senate will never be able to transform itself, by gradual usurpations, into an independent and aristocratic body, we are warranted in believing, that if such a revolution should ever happen from causes which the foresight of man cannot guard against, the House of Representatives, with the people on their side, will at all times be able to bring back the Constitution to its primitive form and principles. Against the force of the immediate representatives of the people, nothing will be able to maintain even the constitutional authority of the Senate, but such a display of enlightened policy, and attachment to the public good, as will divide with that branch of the legislature the affections and support of the entire body of the people themselves.

PUBLIUS.

FEDERALIST 64
Author: John Jay
To the People of the State of New York:

. . . .

The second section [of the Constitution] gives power to the President, "*by and with the advice and consent of the senate, to make treaties, provided two thirds of the senators present concur.*"

The power of making treaties is an important one, especially as it relates to war, peace, and commerce; and it should not be delegated but in such a mode, and with such precautions, as will afford the highest security that it will be exercised by men the best qualified for the purpose, and in the manner most conducive to the public good. The convention appears to have been attentive to both these points: they have directed the President to be chosen by select bodies of electors, to be deputed by the people for that express purpose; and they have committed the appointment of senators to the State legislatures. This mode has, in such cases, vastly the advantage of elections by the people in their collective capacity, where the activity of party zeal, taking the advantage of the supineness, the ignorance, and the hopes and fears of the unwary and interested, often places men in office by the votes of a small proportion of the electors.

As the select assemblies for choosing the President, as well as the State legislatures who appoint the senators, will in general be composed of the most enlightened and respectable citizens, there is reason to presume that their attention and their votes will be directed to those men only who have become the most distinguished by their abilities and virtue, and in whom the people perceive just grounds for confidence. The Constitution manifests very particular attention to this object. By excluding men under thirty-five from the first office, and those under thirty from the second, it confines the electors to men of whom the people have had time to form a judgment, and with respect to whom they will not be liable to be deceived by those brilliant appearances of genius and patriotism, which, like transient meteors, sometimes mislead as well as dazzle. If the observation be well founded, that wise kings will always be served by able ministers, it is fair to argue, that as an assembly of select electors possess, in a greater degree than kings, the means of extensive and accurate information relative to men and characters, so will their appointments bear at least equal marks of discretion and discernment. The inference which naturally results from these considerations is this, that the President and senators so chosen will always be of the number of those who best understand our national interests, whether considered in relation to the several States or to foreign nations, who are best able to promote those interests, and whose reputation for integrity inspires and merits confidence. With such men the power of making treaties may be safely lodged.

Although the absolute necessity of system, in the conduct of any business, is universally known and acknowledged, yet the high importance of it in national affairs has not yet become sufficiently impressed on the public mind. They who wish to commit the power under consideration to a popular assembly, composed of members constantly coming and going in quick succession, seem not to recollect that such a body must necessarily be inadequate to the attainment of those great objects, which require to be steadily contemplated in all their relations and circumstances, and which can only be approached and achieved by measures which not only talents, but also exact information, and often much time, are necessary to concert and to execute. It was wise, therefore, in the convention to provide, not only that the power of making treaties should be committed to able and honest men, but also that they should continue in place a sufficient time to become perfectly acquainted with our national concerns, and to form and introduce a system for the management of them. The duration prescribed is such as will give them an opportunity of greatly extending their political information, and of rendering their accumulating experience more and more beneficial to their country. Nor has the convention discovered less prudence in providing for the frequent elections of senators in such a way as to obviate the inconvenience of periodically transferring those great affairs entirely to new men; for by leaving a considerable residue of the old ones in place, uniformity and order, as well as a constant succession of official information will be preserved.

There are a few who will not admit that the affairs of trade and navigation should be regulated by a system cautiously formed and steadily pursued; and that both our treaties and our laws should correspond with and be made to promote it. It is of much consequence that this correspondence and conformity be carefully maintained; and they who assent to the truth of this position will see and confess that it is well provided for by making concurrence of the Senate necessary both to treaties and to laws.

It seldom happens in the negotiation of treaties, of whatever nature, but that perfect *secrecy* and immediate *despatch* are sometimes requisite. These are cases where the most useful intelligence may be obtained, if the persons possessing it can be relieved from apprehensions of discovery. Those apprehensions will operate on those persons whether they are actuated by mercenary or friendly motives; and there doubtless are many of both descriptions, who would rely on the secrecy of the President, but who would not confide in that of the Senate, and still less in that of a large popular Assembly. The convention have done well, therefore, in so disposing of the power of making treaties, that although the President must, in forming them, act by the advice and consent of the Senate, yet he will be able to manage the business of intelligence in such a manner as prudence may suggest.

They who have turned their attention to the affairs of men, must have perceived that there are tides in them; tides very irregular in their duration, strength, and direction, and seldom found to run twice exactly in the same manner or measure. To discern and to profit by these tides in national affairs is the business of those who preside over them; and they who have had much experience on this head inform us, that there frequently are occasions when days, nay, even when hours, are precious. The loss of a battle, the death of a prince, the removal of a minister, or other circumstances intervening to change the present posture and aspect of affairs, may turn the most favorable tide into a course opposite to our wishes. As in the field, so in the cabinet, there are moments to be seized as they pass, and they who preside in either should be left in capacity to improve them. So often and so essentially have we heretofore suffered from the want of secrecy and despatch, that the Constitution would have been inexcusably defective, if no attention had been paid to those objects. Those matters which in negotiations usually require the most secrecy and the most despatch, are those preparatory and auxiliary measures which are not otherwise important in a national view, than as they tend to facilitate the attainment of the objects of the negotiation. For these, the President will find no difficulty to provide; and should any circumstance occur which requires the advice and consent of the Senate, he may at any time convene them. Thus we see that the Constitution provides that our negotiations for treaties shall have every advantage which can be derived from talents, information, integrity, and deliberate investigations, on the one hand, and from secrecy and despatch on the other.

. . . .

As all the States are equally represented in the Senate, and by men the most able and the most willing to promote the interests of their constituents, they will all have an equal degree of influence in that body, especially while they continue to be careful in appointing proper persons, and to insist on their punctual attendance. In proportion as the United States assume a national form and a national character, so will the good of the whole be more and more an object of attention, and the government must be a weak one indeed, if it should forget that the good of the whole can only be promoted by advancing the good of each of the parts or members which compose the whole. It will not be in the power of the President and Senate to make any treaties by which they and their families and estates will not be equally bound and affected with the rest of the community; and, having no private interests distinct from that of the nation, they will be under no temptations to neglect the latter.

As to corruption, the case is not supposable. He must either have been very unfortunate in his intercourse with the world, or possess a heart very susceptible of such impressions, who can think it probable that the President and two thirds of the Senate will ever be capable of such unworthy conduct. The idea is too gross and too invidious to be entertained. But in such a case, if it should ever happen, the treaty so obtained from us would, like all other fraudulent contracts, be null and void by the law of nations.

With respect to their responsibility, it is difficult to conceive how it could be increased. Every consideration that can influence the human mind, such as honor, oaths, reputations, conscience, the love of country, and family affections and attachments, afford security for their fidelity. In short, as the Constitution has taken the utmost care that they shall be men of talents and in-

tegrity, we have reason to be persuaded that the treaties they make will be as advantageous as, all circumstances considered, could be made; and so far as the fear of punishment and disgrace can operate, that motive to good behavior is amply afforded by the article on the subject of impeachments.
PUBLIUS.

FEDERALIST 65
Author: Alexander Hamilton

To the People of the State of New York:

. . . .

A well-constituted court for the trial of impeachments is an object not more to be desired than difficult to be obtained in a government wholly elective. The subjects of its jurisdiction are those offenses which proceed from the misconduct of public men, or, in other words, from the abuse or violation of some public trust. They are of a nature which may with peculiar propriety be denominated *political,* as they relate chiefly to injuries done immediately to the society itself. The prosecution of them, for this reason, will seldom fail to agitate the passions of the whole community, and to divide it into parties more or less friendly or inimical to the accused. In many cases it will connect itself with the pre-existing factions, and will enlist all their animosities, partialities, influence, and interest on one side or on the other; and in such cases there will always be the greatest danger that the decision will be regulated more by the comparative strength of parties, than by the real demonstrations of innocence or guilt.

The delicacy and magnitude of a trust which so deeply concerns the political reputation and existence of every man engaged in the administration of public affairs, speak for themselves. The difficulty of placing it rightly, in a government resting entirely on the basis of periodical elections, will as readily be perceived, when it is considered that the most conspicuous characters in it will, from that circumstance, be too often the leaders or the tools of the most cunning or the most numerous faction, and on this account, can hardly be expected to possess the requisite neutrality towards those whose conduct may be the subject of scrutiny.

The convention, it appears, thought the Senate the most fit depositary of this important trust. Those who can best discern the intrinsic difficulty of the thing, will be least hasty in condemning that opinion, and will be most inclined to allow due weight to the arguments which may be supposed to have produced it.

What, it may be asked, is the true spirit of the institution itself? Is it not designed as a method of *national inquest* into the conduct of public men? If this be the design of it, who can so properly be the inquisitors for the nation as the representatives of the nation themselves? It is not disputed that the power of originating the inquiry, or, in other words, of preferring the impeachment, ought to be lodged in the hands of one branch of the legislative body. Will not the reasons which indicate the propriety of this arrangement strongly plead for an admission of the other branch of that body to a share of the inquiry? The model from which the idea of this institution has been borrowed, pointed out that course to the convention. In Great Britain it is the province of the House of Commons to prefer the impeachment, and of the House of Lords to decide upon it. Several of the State constitutions have followed the example. As well the latter, as the former, seem to have regarded the practice of impeachments as a bridle in the hands of the legislative body upon the executive servants of the government. Is not this the true light in which it ought to be regarded?

Where else than in the Senate could have been found a tribunal sufficiently dignified, or sufficiently independent? What other body would be likely to feel *confidence enough in its own situation,* to preserve, unawed and uninfluenced, the necessary impartiality between an *individual* accused, and the *representatives of the people, his accusers?*

Could the Supreme Court have been relied upon as answering this description? It is much to be doubted, whether the members of that tribunal would at all times be endowed with so eminent a portion of fortitude, as would be called for in the execution of so difficult a task; and it is still more to be doubted, whether they would possess the degree of credit and authority, which might, on certain occasions, be indispensable towards reconciling the people to a decision that should happen to clash with an accusation brought by their immediate representatives. A deficiency in the first, would be fatal to the accused; in the last, dangerous to the public tranquillity. The hazard in both these respects, could only be avoided, if at all, by rendering that tribunal more numerous than would consist with a reasonable attention to economy. The necessity of a numerous court for the trial of impeachments, is equally dictated by the nature of the proceeding. This can never be tied down by such strict rules, either in the delineation of the offense by the prosecutors, or in the construction of it by the judges, as in common cases serve to limit the discretion of courts in favor of personal security. There will be no jury to stand between the judges who are to pronounce the sentence of the law, and the party who is to receive or suffer it. The awful discretion which a court of impeachments must necessarily have, to doom to honor or to infamy the most confidential and the most distinguished characters of the community, forbids the commitment of the trust to a small number of persons.

These considerations seem alone sufficient to authorize a conclusion, that the Supreme Court would have been an improper substitute for the Senate, as a court of impeachments. There remains a further consideration, which will not a little strengthen this conclusion. It is this: The punishment which may be the consequence of conviction upon impeachment, is not to terminate the chastisement of the offender. After having been sentenced to a perpetual ostracism from the esteem and confidence, and honors and emoluments of his country, he will still be liable to prosecution and punishment in the ordinary course of law. Would it be proper that the persons who had disposed of his fame, and his most valuable rights as a citizen in one trial, should, in another trial, for the same offense, be also the disposers of his life and his fortune? Would there not be the greatest reason to apprehend, that error, in the first sentence, would be the parent of error in the second sentence? That the strong bias of one decision would be apt to overrule the influence of any new lights which might be brought to vary the complexion of another decision? Those who know anything of human nature, will not hesitate to answer these questions in the affirmative; and will be at no loss to perceive, that by making the same persons judges in both cases, those who might happen to be the objects of prosecution would, in a great measure, be deprived of the double security intended them by a double trial. The loss of life and estate would often be virtually included in a sentence which, in its terms, imported nothing more than dismission from a present, and disqualification for a future, office. It may be said, that the intervention of a jury, in the second instance, would obviate the danger. But juries are frequently influenced by the opinions of judges. They are sometimes induced to find special verdicts, which refer the main question to the decision of the court. Who would be willing to stake his life and his estate upon the verdict of a jury acting under the auspices of judges who had predetermined his guilt?

Would it have been an improvement of the plan, to have united the Supreme Court with the Senate, in the formation of the court of impeachments? This union would certainly have been attended with several advantages; but would they not have been overbalanced by the signal disadvantage, already stated, arising from the agency of the same judges in the double prosecution to which the offender would be liable? To a certain extent, the benefits of that union will be obtained from making the chief justice of the Supreme Court the president of the court of impeachments, as is proposed to be done in the plan of the convention; while the inconveniences of an entire incorporation of the former into the latter will be substantially avoided. This was perhaps the prudent mean. I forbear to remark upon the additional pretext for clamor against the judiciary, which so considerable an augmentation of its authority would have afforded.

Would it have been desirable to have composed the court for the trial of impeachments, of persons wholly distinct from the other departments of the government? There are weighty arguments, as well against, as in favor of, such a plan. To some minds it will not appear a trivial objection, that it could tend to increase the complexity of the political machine, and to add a new spring to the government, the utility of which would at best be questionable. But an objection which will not be thought by any unworthy of attention, is this: a court formed upon such a plan, would either be attended with a heavy expense, or might in practice be subject to a variety of casualties and inconveniences. It must either consist of permanent officers, stationary at the seat of government, and of course entitled to fixed and regular stipends, or of certain officers of the State governments to be called upon whenever an impeachment was actually depending. It will not be easy to imagine any third mode materi-

ally different, which could rationally be proposed. As the court, for reasons already given, ought to be numerous, the first scheme will be reprobated by every man who can compare the extent of the public wants with the means of supplying them. The second will be espoused with caution by those who will seriously consider the difficulty of collecting men dispersed over the whole Union; the injury to the innocent, from the procrastinated determination of the charges which might be brought against them; the advantage to the guilty, from the opportunities which delay would afford to intrigue and corruption; and in some cases the detriment to the State, from the prolonged inaction of men whose firm and faithful execution of their duty might have exposed them to the persecution of an intemperate or designing majority in the House of Representatives. Though this latter supposition may seem harsh, and might not be likely often to be verified, yet it ought not to be forgotten that the demon of faction will, at certain seasons, extend his sceptre over all numerous bodies of men.

But though one or the other of the substitutes which have been examined, or some other that might be devised, should be thought preferable to the plan in this respect, reported by the convention, it will not follow that the Constitution ought for this reason to be rejected. If mankind were to resolve to agree in no institution of government, until every part of it had been adjusted to the most exact standard of perfection, society would soon become a general scene of anarchy, and the world a desert. Where is the standard of perfection to be found? Who will undertake to unite the discordant opinions of a whole community, in the same judgment of it; and to prevail upon one conceited projector to renounce his *infallible* criterion for the *fallible* criterion of his more *conceited neighbor*? To answer the purpose of the adversaries of the Constitution, they ought to prove, not merely that particular provisions in it are not the best which might have been imagined, but that the plan upon the whole is bad and pernicious.

PUBLIUS.

FEDERALIST 66
Author: Alexander Hamilton

To the People of the State of New York:

A review of the principal objections that have appeared against the proposed court for the trial of impeachments, will not improbably eradicate the remains of any unfavorable impressions which may still exist in regard to this matter.

The *first* of these objections is, that the provision in question confounds legislative and judiciary authorities in the same body, in violation of that important and well established maxim which requires a separation between the different departments of power. The true meaning of this maxim has been discussed and ascertained in another place, and has been shown to be entirely compatible with a partial intermixture of those departments for special purposes, preserving them, in the main, distinct and unconnected. This partial intermixture is even, in some cases, not only proper but necessary to the mutual defense of the several members of the government against each other. An absolute or qualified negative in the executive upon the acts of the legislative body, is admitted, by the ablest adepts in political science, to be an indispensable barrier against the encroachments of the latter upon the former. And it may, perhaps, with no less reason be contended, that the powers relating to impeachments are, as before intimated, an essential check in the hands of that body upon the encroachments of the executive. The division of them between the two branches of the legislature, assigning to one the right of accusing, to the other the right of judging, avoids the inconvenience of making the same persons both accusers and judges; and guards against the danger of persecution, from the prevalency of a factious spirit in either of those branches. As the concurrence of two thirds of the Senate will be requisite to a condemnation, the security to innocence, from this additional circumstance, will be as complete as itself can desire.

. . . .

A *second* objection to the Senate, as a court of impeachments, is, that it contributes to an undue accumulation of power in that body, tending to give to the government a countenance too aristocratic. The Senate, it is observed, is to have concurrent authority with the Executive in the formation of treaties and in the appointment to offices: if, say the objectors, to these prerogatives is added that of deciding in all cases of impeachment, it will give a decided predominancy to senatorial influence. To an objection so little precise in itself, it is not easy to find a very precise answer. Where is the measure or criterion to which we can appeal, for determining what will give the Senate too much, too little, or barely the proper degree of influence? Will it not be more safe, as well as more simple, to dismiss such vague and uncertain calculations, to examine each power by itself, and to decide, on general principles, where it may be deposited with most advantage and least inconvenience?

If we take this course, it will lead to a more intelligible, if not to a more certain result. The disposition of the power of making treaties, which has obtained in the plan of the convention, will, then, if I mistake not, appear to be fully justified by the considerations stated in a former number, and by others which will occur under the next head of our inquiries. The expediency of the junction of the Senate with the Executive, in the power of appointing to offices, will, I trust, be placed in a light not less satisfactory, in the disquisitions under the same head. And I flatter myself the observations in my last paper must have gone no inconsiderable way towards proving that it was not easy, if practicable, to find a more fit receptacle for the power of determining impeachments, than that which has been chosen. If this be truly the case, the hypothetical dread of the too great weight of the Senate ought to be discarded from our reasonings.

But this hypothesis, such as it is, has already been refuted in the remarks applied to the duration in office prescribed for the senators. It was by them shown, as well on the credit of historical examples, as from the reason of the thing, that the most *popular* branch of every government, partaking of the republican genius, by being generally the favorite of the people, will be as generally a full match, if not an overmatch, for every other member of the Government.

But independent of this most active and operative principle, to secure the equilibrium of the national House of Representatives, the plan of the convention has provided in its favor several important counterpoises to the additional authorities to be conferred upon the Senate. The exclusive privilege of originating money bills will belong to the House of Representatives. The same house will possess the sole right of instituting impeachments: is not this a complete counterbalance to that of determining them? The same house will be the umpire in all elections of the President, which do not unite the suffrages of a majority of the whole number of electors; a case which it cannot be doubted will sometimes, if not frequently, happen. The constant possibility of the thing must be a fruitful source of influence to that body. The more it is contemplated, the more important will appear this ultimate though contingent power, of deciding the competitions of the most illustrious citizens of the Union, for the first office in it. It would not perhaps be rash to predict, that as a mean of influence it will be found to outweigh all the peculiar attributes of the Senate.

A *third* objection to the Senate as a court of impeachments, is drawn from the agency they are to have in the appointments to office. It is imagined that they would be too indulgent judges of the conduct of men, in whose official creation they had participated. The principle of this objection would condemn a practice, which is to be seen in all the State governments, if not in all the governments with which we are acquainted: I mean that of rendering those who hold offices during pleasure, dependent on the pleasure of those who appoint them. With equal plausibility might it be alleged in this case, that the favoritism of the latter would always be an asylum for the misbehavior of the former. But that practice, in contradiction to this principle, proceeds upon the presumption, that the responsibility of those who appoint, for the fitness and competency of the persons on whom they bestow their choice, and the interest they will have in the respectable and prosperous administration of affairs, will inspire a sufficient disposition to dismiss from a share in it all such who, by their conduct, shall have proved themselves unworthy of the confidence reposed in them. Though facts may not always correspond with this presumption, yet if it be, in the main, just, it must destroy the supposition that the Senate, who will merely sanction the choice of the Executive, should feel a bias, towards the objects of that choice, strong enough to blind them to the evidences of guilt so extraordinary, as to have induced the representatives of the nation to become its accusers.

If any further arguments were necessary to evince the improbability of such a bias, it might be found in the nature of the agency of the Senate in the business of appointments.

It will be the office of the President to *nominate*, and, with the advice and consent of the Senate, to *appoint*. There will, of course, be no exertion of *choice* on the part of the Senate. They may defeat one choice of the Executive, and oblige him to make another; but they cannot themselves *choose,* they can only ratify or reject the choice of the President. They might even entertain a preference to some other person, at the very moment they were assenting to the one proposed, because there might be no positive ground of opposition to him; and they could not be sure, if they withheld their assent, that the subsequent nomination would fall upon their own favorite, or upon any other person in their estimation more meritorious than the one rejected. Thus it could hardly happen, that the majority of the Senate would feel any other complacency towards the object of an appointment than such as the appearances of merit might inspire, and the proofs of the want of it destroy.

A *fourth* objection to the Senate in the capacity of a court of impeachments, is derived from its union with the Executive in the power of making treaties. This, it has been said, would constitute the senators their own judges, in every case of a corrupt or perfidious execution of that trust. After having combined with the Executive in betraying the interests of the nation in a ruinous treaty, what prospect, it is asked, would there be of their being made to suffer the punishment they would deserve, when they were themselves to decide upon the accusation brought against them for the treachery of which they have been guilty?

This objection has been circulated with more earnestness and with greater show of reason than any other which has appeared against this part of the plan; and yet I am deceived if it does not rest upon an erroneous foundation.

The security essentially intended by the Constitution against corruption and treachery in the formation of treaties, is to be sought for in the numbers and characters of those who are to make them. The *joint agency* of the Chief Magistrate of the Union, and of two thirds of the members of a body selected by the collective wisdom of the legislatures of the several States, is designed to be the pledge for the fidelity of the national councils in this particular. The convention might with propriety have meditated the punishment of the Executive, for a deviation from the instructions of the Senate, or a want of integrity in the conduct of the negotiations committed to him; they might also have had in view the punishment of a few leading individuals in the Senate, who should have prostituted their influence in that body

as the mercenary instruments of foreign corruption: but they could not, with more or with equal propriety, have contemplated the impeachment and punishment of two thirds of the Senate, consenting to an improper treaty, than of a majority of that or of the other branch of the national legislature, consenting to a pernicious or unconstitutional law, a principle which, I believe, has never been admitted into any government. How, in fact, could a majority in the House of Representatives impeach themselves? Not better, it is evident, than two thirds of the Senate might try themselves. And yet what reason is there, that a majority of the House of Representatives, sacrificing the interests of the society by an unjust and tyrannical act of legislation, should escape with impunity, more than two thirds of the Senate, sacrificing the same interests in an injurious treaty with a foreign power? The truth is, that in all such cases it is essential to the freedom and to the necessary independence of the deliberations of the body, that the members of it should be exempt from punishment for acts done in a collective capacity; and the security to the society must depend on the care which is taken to confide the trust to proper hands, to make it their interest to execute it with fidelity, and to make it as difficult as possible for them to combine in any interest opposite to that of the public good.

So far as might concern the misbehavior of the Executive in perverting the instructions or contravening the views of the Senate, we need not be apprehensive of the want of a disposition in that body to punish the abuse of their confidence or to vindicate their own authority. We may thus far count upon their pride, if not upon their virtue. And so far even as might concern the corruption of leading members, by whose arts and influence the majority may have been inveigled into measures odious to the community, if the proofs of that corruption should be satisfactory, the usual propensity of human nature will warrant us in concluding that there would be commonly no defect of inclination in the body to divert the public resentment from themselves by a ready sacrifice of the authors of their mismanagement and disgrace.

PUBLIUS.

4   An Ordinance Calling for the First Federal Elections

September 13, 1788

With New Hampshire's ratification of the Constitution on June 21, 1788, the required number of states had approved the Constitution. The Continental Congress, which after 1781 was called "the United States in Congress assembled," began to take steps for the transfer of power to the new government. This involved setting dates for the first presidential election and the first meeting of the First Federal Congress. The debate over this apparently simple res-

olution was furious, not because the dates under consideration were controversial, but because the site of this new government was a hotly contested issue. The long struggle to decide a permanent seat of government had begun. The delegates settled on a temporary home for the new government in New York City but left the final decision about where the government would reside to the First Federal Congress.

This ordinance does not mention New York City by name. It is referred to only as "the Present Seat of Congress." Elections for the House and Senate are not mentioned, but the assumption was that once the Constitution was ratified, Article I, Section 4, would require each state to establish a procedure and a date for holding the first congressional elections.

WHEREAS the Convention assembled in Philadelphia, pursuant to the Resolution of Congress of the 21st February, 1787, did, on the 17th of September in the same year, report to the United States in Congress assembled, a Constitution for the People of the United States; whereupon Congress, on the 28th of the same September, did resolve unanimously, "That the said report, with the Resolution and Letter accompanying the same, be transmitted to the several Legislatures, in order to be submitted to a Convention of Delegates chosen in each State by the people thereof, in conformity to the Resolves of the Convention made and provided in the case:" And whereas the Constitution so reported by the Convention, and by Congress transmitted to the several Legislatures, has been ratified in the manner therein declared to be sufficient for the establishment of the same, and such Ratification duly authenticated have been received by Congress, and are filed in the Office of the Secretary—therefore,

RESOLVED, That the first Wednesday in January next, be the day for appointing Electors in the several States, which before the said day shall have ratified the said Constitution; that the first Wednesday in February next, be the day for the Electors to assemble in their respective States, and vote for a President; and that the first Wednesday in March next, be the time, and the present Seat of Congress the place for commencing Proceedings under the said Constitution.

Merrill Jensen, Robert A. Becker, Gordon DenBoer, et al., *The Documentary History of the First Federal Elections 1788–1790*, 4 vols. (Madison: University of Wisconsin Press, 1976–1989), vol. 1: 132–133.

5   James Madison Describes Factions in the House of Representatives

March 1, 1789

While seeking a seat in the first House of Representatives from his home state of Virginia, James Madison told George Washington that he had an "extreme distaste" for personally campaigning for office. He preferred to go to New York City, where he could study documents in preparation for the launching of the new government. But friends and associates convinced him that he needed to be in Virginia and campaign for office.

In an era before the development of an organized party system, campaigning was far less contentious than it would become in the early 1800s. Madison and his opponent, James Monroe, often appeared together at political gatherings. Madison won the election held February 2, 1789, and a few weeks later wrote to his friend Edmund Randolph of how he had underestimated the importance of actively campaigning. In this letter, written just three days before the new government convened for the first time, Madison predicted that factions would interfere with the business of governing. The factions he described, and others that developed in the first few decades of the new government, would lead to highly organized political parties. The appearance of a party system would dramatically shape the nature of politics in the United States—a development that the Framers of the Constitution had not paid much attention to when drafting the Constitution.

In the first federal elections, the major "partisan" division in the country was between the Federalists, who supported the new Constitution, and the anti-Federalists, who opposed the new government for various reasons, including fear of encroachment on state power or the lack of a bill of rights as part of the Constitution.

MADISON TO EDMUND RANDOLPH
Alexandria, Va., March 1, 1789

. . . .

This is the first convenient opportunity I have had for dropping you a line since I last came into the State. Your sanction to my remaining in N. York during the crisis of the elections, conveyed through Col: Carrington, never came to hand till I had arrived in Orange. It coincided so fully with my inclination, and indeed with my judgment, that had it been received in due time, I do not know but I should have disregarded all the pressing exhortations which stood opposed to your opinion. I am persuaded however that my appearance in the district was more necessary to my election than you then calculated. In truth it has been evinced by the experiment, that my absence would have left a room for the calumnies of antifederal partizans which would have defeated much better pretensions than mine. In Culpeper which was the critical County, a continued attention was necessary to repel the multiplied falsehoods which circulated—Whether I ought to be satisfied or displeased with my success, I shall hereafter be more able to judge. My present anticipations are not flattering. I see on the lists of Representatives a very scanty proportion who will share in the drudgery of business. And I foresee contentions first between federal & antifederal parties, and then between Northern & Southern parties, which give additional disagreeableness to the prospect. Should the State-Elections give an antifederal colour to the Legislatures, which from causes not antifederal in the people, may well happen, difficulties will again start up in this quarter, which may have a still more serious aspect on the Congressional proceedings. . . .

Merrill Jensen, Robert A. Becker, Gordon DenBoer, et al., *The Documentary History of the First Federal Elections 1788–1790,* 4 vols. (Madison: University of Wisconsin Press, 1976–1989), vol. 2: 347–348.

6   The First Quorums of the House and Senate

April 1 and 6, 1789

To function at full capacity, a parliamentary body must have a quorum, that is, a sufficient number of members present to conduct business. Article I, Section 5 of the Constitution states that a majority of the members of each body of Congress constitutes a quorum.

When the First Federal Congress met for the first time on March 4, 1789, it was the cause of great celebration in New York City. The city was decked out with flags and bunting, church bells rang throughout the city, and cannons were fired to announce the beginning of new government under the new Constitution. But on that day only thirteen representatives and eight senators arrived to launch the new government. Since a quorum could not be achieved in either body, both adjourned without conducting any business. For nearly a month the House and Senate would meet and, finding a quorum not present, quickly adjourn. One of the first House members to arrive, Fisher Ames of Massachusetts, wrote to a friend: "We lose credit, spirit, everything. The public will forget the government before it is born."

On April 1, 1789, the House achieved its first quorum and got down to business, although it was not lost on some members that the government began on "Fool's Day." The House proceeded to elect its first Speaker, Frederick A. C. Muhlenberg of Pennsylvania, and its first Clerk, John Beckley of Virginia. Five days later the Senate achieved its first quorum, making it possible for House members to join the senators in their chamber to count the electoral ballots. For the purposes of conducting the electoral count, the Senate elected John Langdon of New Hampshire its first president pro tempore (a temporary presiding officer). With the count completed, Congress could officially notify George Washington and John Adams that they had been elected president and vice president, respectively. At last the new government was up and running.

[THE FIRST QUORUM OF THE HOUSE]
Wednesday, April 1, 1789

The House met according to adjournment.

Two other members, to wit, James Schureman, from New-Jersey, and Thomas Scott, from Pennsylvania, appeared and took their seats.

And a quorum, consisting of a majority of the whole number, being present,

RESOLVED, That this House will proceed to the choice of a Speaker by ballot.

The House accordingly proceeded to ballot for a Speaker, and upon examining the ballots, a majority of the votes of the whole House was found in favor of FREDERICK AUGUSTUS MUHLENBERG, one of the representatives for the state of Pennsylvania.

Whereupon the said Frederick Augustus Muhlenberg was conducted to the chair, from whence he made his acknowledgements to the House for so distinguished an honor.

The House then proceeded in the same manner to the appointment of a Clerk, and upon examining the ballots, a majority of the votes of the whole House was found in favor of MR. JOHN BECKLEY.

On motion,

ORDERED, That the members of this House do severally deliver in their credentials at the Clerk's table.

And then the House adjourned until to-morrow morning eleven o'clock.

[THE FIRST QUORUM OF THE SENATE]

THE SENATE assembled.

Present

From New-Hampshire	Mr. Langdon and
	Mr. Wingate
Massachusetts	Mr. Strong
Connecticut	Mr. Johnson and
	Mr. Ellsworth
New-Jersey	Mr. Paterson and
	Mr. Elmer
Pennsylvania	Mr. Maclay and
	Mr. Morris
Delaware	Mr. Bassett
Virginia	Mr. Lee
Georgia	Mr. Few

BEING A QUORUM, consisting of a majority of the whole number of Senators of the United States.

The credentials of the afore-mentioned members were read, and ordered to be filed.

The Senate proceeded by ballot to the choice of a President, for the sole purpose of opening and counting the votes for President of the United States.

JOHN LANGDON, Esquire, was elected.

ORDERED, That Mr. Ellsworth inform the House of Representatives that a quorum of the Senate is formed; that a President is elected for the sole purpose of opening the certificates and counting the votes of the Electors of the several States in the choice of a President and Vice President of the United States; and that the Senate is now ready in the Senate Chamber, to proceed, in the presence of the House, to discharge that duty: And that the Senate have appointed one of their members to sit at the Clerk's table to make a list of the votes as they shall be declared; submitting it to the wisdom of the House to appoint one or more of their members for the like purpose—Who reported, that he had delivered the message.

Mr. Boudinot, from the House of Representatives, communicated the following verbal message to the Senate:—

"MR. PRESIDENT,

"I AM directed by the House of Representatives to inform the Senate, that the House is ready forthwith to meet the Senate, to attend the opening and counting the votes of the Electors for President and Vice President of the United States."—And he withdrew.

ORDERED, That Mr. Paterson be a teller on the part of the Senate.

The Speaker and the House of Representatives attended in the Senate Chamber, for the purpose expressed in the message delivered by Mr. Ellsworth—And after some time withdrew.

The Senate then proceeded by ballot to the choice of a President of their body PRO TEMPORE.

JOHN LANGDON, Esq. was duly elected.

The President elected for the purpose of counting the votes, declared to the Senate, that the Senate and House of Representatives had met, and that he, in their presence, had opened and counted the votes of the Electors for President and Vice President of the United States—which were as follow:—

	George Washington, Esq.	John Adams, Esq.	Samuel Huntington, Esq.	John Jay, Esq.	John Hancock, Esq.	Robert H. Harrison, Esq.	George Clinton, Esq.	John Rutledge, Esq.	John Milton, Esq.	James Armstrong, Esq.	Edward Telfair, Esq.	Benjamin Lincoln, Esq.
New-Hampshire	5	5	—	—	—	—	—	—	—	—	—	—
Massachusetts	10	10	—	—	—	—	—	—	—	—	—	—
Connecticut	7	5	2	—	—	—	—	—	—	—	—	—
New-Jersey	6	1	—	5	—	—	—	—	—	—	—	—
Pennsylvania	10	8	—	—	2	—	—	—	—	—	—	—
Delaware	3	—	—	3	—	—	—	—	—	—	—	—
Maryland	6	—	—	—	—	6	—	—	—	—	—	—
Virginia	10	5	—	1	1	—	3	—	—	—	—	—
South-Carolina	7	—	—	—	1	—	—	6	—	—	—	—
Georgia	5	—	—	—	—	—	—	—	2	1	1	1²
	69	34	2	9	4	6	3	6	2	1	1	1

Whereby it appears, that
GEORGE WASHINGTON, Esq.
Was unanimously elected President,—And
JOHN ADAMS, ESQ.
Was duly elected VICE PRESIDENT,
OF THE UNITED STATES AMERICA.

Mr. Madison came from the House of Representatives with the following verbal message:—

Mr. President,

"I AM directed by the House of Representatives to inform the Senate, that the House have agreed, that the notifications of the election of the President and of the Vice President of the United States, should be made by such persons, and in such manner, as the Senate shall be pleased to direct."—And he withdrew.

Whereupon the Senate appointed Charles Thomson, Esq. to notify George Washington, Esq. of his election to the Office of President of the United States of America, and Mr. Sylvanus Bourn to notify John Adams, Esq. of his election to the Office of Vice President of the said United States.

The instructions to the Messengers are in the following words.

In SENATE, April 6, 1789

SIR,

THE Senate of the United States have appointed you to wait upon General Washington, with a certificate of his being elected to the Office of President of the United States of America. You will therefore prepare to set out as soon as possible, and apply to the Board of Treasury for such sums as you may judge necessary for the expenses of the journey.

JOHN LANGDON, President pro tem.

To Charles Thomson, Esq.

In SENATE, April 6, 1789

SIR,

THE Senate of the United States have appointed you to wait on John Adams, Esq. with a certificate of his being elected to the Office of Vice President of the United States. You are therefore to set out with the dispatches herewith sent you as soon as possible, and to apply to the Treasury Board for one hundred dollars towards defraying the expenses of your journey.

JOHN LANGDON, President pro tem.

To Mr. Sylvanus Bourn

ORDERED, That Mr. Paterson, Mr. Johnson, Mr. Lee, and Mr. Ellsworth be a committee to prepare the certificates of the election of the President and of the Vice President of the United States; and to prepare letters to George Washington, Esq. and to John Adams, Esq. to accompany the said certificates respectively.

House: *House of Representatives Journal,* reprinted from *Documentary History of the First Federal Congress, 1789–1791,* 14 vols. to date (Baltimore: Johns Hopkins University Press, 1972–), vol. 3: 7; Senate: *Senate Legislative Journal, Documentary History of the First Federal Congress,* vol. 1: 7–11.

7 Fisher Ames Describes the First Congress

April 4, 1789

Fisher Ames (1758–1808), a representative from Massachusetts, was one of the most prolific and effective members of the House of Representatives during the first four Congresses, from 1789 to 1797. A lawyer and former member of the Massachusetts House of Representatives, Ames graduated from Harvard at the age of sixteen. During his years of public service, Ames became known as an outstanding orator. His letters and speeches have provided an eye-witness account of the early Congress.

Ames was a Federalist who wanted to see the Constitution successfully launched. In his letters he often expressed frustration at the slow pace of enacting the new government. In describing members of the first House of Representatives, he said there were "few shining geniuses," but there were some and it could be easily argued that Fisher Ames was among them.

Modern critics of Congress often point to "professional" or "career" politicians as a source of what is wrong with Congress, preferring some ideal of the "citizen legislator." Fisher Ames, looking at the first Congress, took comfort that like himself many of the legislators "have been in government before, and they are not disposed to embarrass business, nor are they, for the most part, men of intrigue."

Ames last great contribution in the House came in 1796, when he gave a brilliant speech in support of Jay's Treaty. Following his remarks, the House voted 51–49 to approve appropriations for implementing that treaty.

LETTER TO GEORGE RICHARDS MINOT
April 4, 1789

Dear Sir,

I PRESUME that you have heard that the House of Representatives met on Wednesday, the 1st, a quorum of thirty attending. They have met daily, and are still occupied in the little business of making arrangements. A committee is employed to form rules and orders. Slower progress will be made in this, by reason of the Senate not having yet a quorum to act upon any bill, in case the House should prepare one. Besides, I am inclined to believe, that there is in every popular assembly a strong resemblance of character—the same refining, quiddling scepticism. The House is composed of sober, solid, old-charter folks, as we often say. At least, I am sure there are many such. They have been in government before, and they are not disposed to embarrass business, nor are they, for the most part, men of intrigue. Yet my friend, I foresee our General Court nicely. I think the debates upon questions of order will be frequent and animated. It may become necessary to consult the Aruspices, whether a man shall be called doorkeeper or sergeant-at-arms. I have given a reason why the delay arising from this source is not to be regretted, the Senate not having formed. Indeed, the little passions that occasion it will be speedily satiated or wearied, and the great business before us will soon make us sufficiently serious. This in confidence, my friend. However, though I am rather less awed and terrified at the sight of the members than I expected to be, I assure you I like them very well. There are few shining geniuses; there are so many that have experience, the virtues of the heart, and the habits of business. It will be quite a republican assembly. It looks like one. Many who expected a Roman senate, when the doors shall be opened, will be disappointed. Admiration will lose its feast. In return for this breach of poetry, I presume the *antis* will laugh at their own fears. They will see that the aristocracy may be kept down some years longer. My dear friend, by these hasty hints I have tried to give my ideas of the character of the House. You will be better satisfied with it than with newspaper stuff. The Senate will be a very respectable body. Heaven knows when they will act. Report is (and has been so these three weeks,) that several senators are just at hand. Let me hear from you frequently. I am rather more happy in your friendship for being vain of it. Your letters will gratify my vanity and comfort my heart; your neglect would make it ache.

I am, dear sir, your friend and humble servant.

Works of Fisher Ames, as Published by Seth Ames, ed. William B. Allen, 2 vols. (Indianapolis: LibertyClassics, 1983), vol. 1: 563–564.

8 The First Rules of the House of Representatives

April 7, 13, and 14, 1789

Nothing is more important to the workings of a parliamentary body than its rules and how they are used. The most effective and influential legislators are the ones who master the rules. The rules of procedure that were established in the First Congress have been modified many times over the past two hundred years, but they still have great bearing on understanding how the House operates today.

The first rules of procedure were brought to the floor of the House in two sections, less than a week apart, and passed after three separate days of consideration. These rules established the fundamental practice that would govern the House to the present day. At the beginning of each new Congress every two years, the House must adopt its entire rule package anew. The Senate, on the other hand, modifies its rules less frequently because it is a continu-

ing body that does not remake itself at the beginning of each new Congress.

Today the House rule book includes footnotes, explanations of precedents, a reprinting of Thomas Jefferson's Manual of Parliamentary Practice (see document 34), excerpts from certain acts of Congress related to the budget and other matters, and a detailed index. It contains more than 1,250 pages—all building upon or modifying the basic formula laid down in 1789.

Elias Boudinot acted as chairman of the eleven-member ad hoc rules committee that created the first House rules. Boudinot, a representative from New Jersey, played a prominent role in the American Revolutionary War and served in the Continental Congress, including two terms as president of the Continental Congress in 1782 and 1783. He served from 1789 to 1795 in the first three federal Congresses and then worked for ten years as director of the U.S. Mint.

During consideration of the second part of the House rules, several of the rules were held over and not approved until April 14, when the House added a rule on the duties of the sergeant-at-arms and added amounts to be paid for arrests and travel expenses of that office. At the suggestion of the rules committee, the House established a joint committee on rules with the Senate on May 14, 1789.

The symbol of the office of sergeant-at-arms, mentioned in the rule passed April 14, became known as the Mace, one of the oldest and most symbolically important artifacts of the House. The first Mace was destroyed when British troops burned the Capitol in 1814. A second Mace, made of painted pine wood, was used until 1841, when the current Mace of ebony rods surmounted by a silver eagle astride a world globe came into use. Each day the sergeant-at-arms carries the Mace into the House chamber as a symbol that the House is in session.

Item 7 of the rules package taken up April 13 provided for a standing committee on elections. The Committee on Elections was the first standing committee created by the House. This committee, although modified several times, survived until 1947, when its functions were absorbed by the newly created House Administration Committee.

TUESDAY, APRIL 7, 1789

MR. BOUDINOT, from the committee appointed to prepare such Rules and Orders of proceedings as may be proper to be observed in this House made the following report:—

"The committee to whom it was referred to prepare such Standing Rules and Orders of proceedings as may be proper to be observed in this House, have, according to order, prepared the same and agreed to the following report:

Resolved, That it is the opinion of this committee that the rules and orders following are proper to be established as the Standing Rules and Orders of House, to wit:

I.— Touching the duty of the Speaker.

He shall take the chair every day at the hour to which the House shall have adjourned on the preceding day, shall imme-diately call the members to order, and on the appearance of a quorum, shall cause the journal of the preceding day to be read.

He shall preserve decorum and order; may speak to points of order in preference to other members, rising from his seat for that purpose, and shall decide questions of order, subject to an appeal to the House by any two members.

He shall rise to put a question, but may state it sitting.

Questions shall be distinctly put in this form, viz: "As many as are of opinion that—(as the question may be) say Aye: And, after the affirmative voice is expressed—"As many as are of a contrary opinion, say No."

If the Speaker doubts, or a division be called for, the House shall divide; those in the affirmative going to the right, and those in the negative to the left of the chair. If the Speaker still doubt, or a count be required, the Speaker shall name two members, one from each side, to tell the numbers in the affirmative; which being reported, he shall then name two others, one from each side to tell those in the negative; which being also reported, he shall rise and state the decision to the House.

The Speaker shall appoint committees, unless it be determined by the House that the committee shall consist of more than three members, in which case the appointment shall be by ballot of the House.

In all cases of ballot by the House, the Speaker shall vote; in other cases he shall not vote, unless the House be equally divided, or unless his vote, if given to the minority will make the division equal, and in case of such equal division, the question shall be lost.

When the House adjourns, the members shall keep their seats until the Speaker go forth; and then the members shall follow.

II.—Of Decorum and Debate.

When any member is about to speak in debate, on deliver any matter to the House, he shall rise from his seat, and respectfully address himself to Mr. Speaker.

If any member, in speaking or otherwise, transgress the rules of the House, the Speaker shall, or any member may, call to order; in which case the member called to order shall immediately sit down, unless permitted to explain, and the House shall, if appealed to, decide on the case, but without debate. If there be no appeal, the decision of the Chair shall be submitted to. If the decision be in favor of the member called to order, he shall be at liberty to proceed; if otherwise, and the case require it, he shall be liable to the censure of the House.

When two or more members happen to rise at once, the Speaker shall name the member who is first to speak.

No member shall speak more than twice to the same question, without leave of the House; nor more than once, until every member choosing to speak shall have spoken.

Whilst the Speaker is putting any question, or addressing the House, none shall walk out of or across the House; nor either in such case, or when a member is speaking, shall entertain private discourse, or read any printed book or paper; nor whilst a member is speaking, shall pass between him and the chair.

No member shall vote on any question, in the event of which he is immediately and particularly interested; or in any other case where he was not present when the question was put.

Every member who shall be in the House when a question is put, shall vote on the one side or the other, unless the House, for special reasons, shall excuse him.

When a motion is made and seconded, it shall be stated by the Speaker; or being in writing, it shall be handed to the Chair, and read aloud by the Clerk before debated.

Every motion shall be reduced to writing, if the Speaker or any member desire it.

After a motion is stated by the Speaker, or read by the Clerk, it shall be deemed to be in possession of the House, but may be withdrawn at any time before a decision or amendment.

When a question is under debate, no motion shall be received, unless to amend it, to commit it for the previous question, or to adjourn.

A motion to adjourn shall always be in order, and shall be decided without debate.

The previous question shall be in this form: "Shall the main question be now put?" It shall only be admitted when demanded by five members, and until it is decided, shall preclude all amendment and further debate of the main question.

On a previous question no member shall speak more than once without leave.

Any member may call for the division of a question, where the sense will admit of it.

A motion for commitment, until it is decided, shall preclude all amendment of the main question.

Motions and reports may be committed at the pleasure of the House.

No new motion or proposition shall be admitted, under color of amendment, as a substitute for the motion or proposition under debate.

Committees consisting of more than three members shall be ballotted for by the House, if, upon such ballot, the number required shall not be elected by a majority of the votes given, the House shall proceed to a second ballot, in which a plurality of votes shall prevail; and in case a greater number than are required to compose or complete the committee shall have an equal number of votes, the House shall proceed to a further ballot or ballots.

In all other cases of ballot than for committees, a majority of the votes given shall be necessary to an election: and where there shall not be such majority on the first ballot, the ballot shall be repeated until a majority be obtained.

In all cases where others than members of the House may be eligible, there shall be a previous nomination.

If a question depending be lost by adjournment of the House, and revived on the succeeding day, no member who has spoken twice on the day preceding shall be permitted again to speak without leave.

Every order, resolution, or vote, to which the concurrence of the Senate shall be necessary, shall be read to the House, and laid on the table, on a day preceding that in which the same shall be moved, unless the House shall otherwise expressly allow.

Petitions, memorials, and other papers addressed to the House, shall be presented through the Speaker, or by a member in his place, and shall not be debated or decided on the day of their first being read, unless where the House shall direct otherwise, but shall lie on the table, to be taken up in the order they were read.

Any fifteen members (including the Speaker, if there be one,) shall be authorized to compel the attendance of absent members.

Upon calls of the House, or in taking the ayes and noes on any question, the names of the members shall be called alphabetically.

III.—Of Bills.

Every bill shall be introduced by motion for leave, or by an order of the House on the report of a committee; and, in either case, a committee to prepare the same shall be appointed. In cases of a general nature, one day's notice, at least, shall be given of the motion to bring in a bill; and every such motion may be committed.

Every bill shall receive three several readings in the House previous to its passage; and all bills shall be despatched in order as they were introduced, unless where the House shall direct otherwise; but no bill shall be twice read on the same day without special order of the House.

The first reading of a bill shall be for information, and if opposition be made to it, the question shall be, " Shall the bill be rejected?" If no opposition be made, or the question to reject be negatived, the bill shall go to its second reading without a question.

Upon the second reading of a bill, the Speaker shall state it as ready for commitment or engrossment, and, if committed, then a question shall be, whether to a Select Committee, or to a Committee of the Whole House, if to a Committee of the whole House, the House shall determine on what day. But if the bill be ordered to be engrossed, the House shall appoint a day when it shall be read the third time. After commitment, and a report thereof to the House, a bill may be re-committed, or at any time before its passage.

All bills ordered to be engrossed shall be executed in a fair round hand.

The enacting style of bills shall be, *"Be it enacted by the Senators and Representatives of the United States in Congress assembled."*

When a bill shall pass, it shall be certified by the Clerk, noting the day of its passing at the foot thereof.

No bill amended by the Senate shall be committed.

IV.—Of Committees of the whole House.

It shall be a standing order of the day throughout the session, for the House to resolve itself into a Committee of the whole House on the state of the Union.

In forming a Committee of the whole House, the Speaker shall leave his chair and a Chairman to preside in committee shall be appointed.

Upon bills committed to a committee of the whole House, the bill shall be first read throughout by the Clerk, and then again read and debated by clauses, leaving the preamble to be last considered. The body of the bill shall not be defaced or interlined; but all amendments, noting the page and line, shall be duly entered by the Clerk, on a separate paper, as the same shall be agreed to by the committee, and so reported to the House. After report, the bill shall again be subject to be debated and amended by clauses, before a question to engross it be taken.

All amendments made to an original motion in committee shall be incorporated with the motion, and so reported.

All amendments made to a report committed to a Committee of the Whole, shall be noted and reported as in the case of bills.

All questions, whether in committee or in the House shall be propounded in the order they were moved, except that, in filling up blanks, the largest sum and longest day shall be first put.

The rules of proceeding in the House shall be observed in committee, so far as they may be applicable except that limiting the times of speaking."

. . . .

MONDAY, APRIL 13, 1789

. . . .

The House proceeded to consider the report from the committee appointed to prepare such further rules and orders of proceeding as may be proper to be observed in this House, which lay on the table, and the said report was read and is as followeth:

Resolved, That it is the opinion of this committee, that the rules and orders following ought to be established as additional standing rules and orders of this House, to wit:

1. That any member may excuse himself from serving on any committee at the time of his appointment, if he is then a member of two other committees.

2. That no member absent himself from the service of the House unless he have leave, or be sick and unable to attend.

3. Upon a call of the House, for which at least one day's notice shall be requisite, the names of the members shall be called over by the clerk, and the absentees noted, after which the names of the absentees shall be again called over; the doors shall then be shut, and those for whom no excuses, or insufficient excuses are made, may by order of the House be taken into custody.

4. It shall be the office and duty of a serjeant at arms to attend the House during its sitting, to execute the commands of the House from time to time, and all such process issued by authority thereof as shall be directed to him by the Speaker, and either by himself, or special messengers appointed by him, to take and detain in his custody, members or other persons ordered by the House to be taken or committed.

5. A proper symbol of office shall be provided for the serjeant at arms, of such form and device as the Speaker shall direct, which shall be placed on the clerk's table during the sitting of the House, but when the House is in committee, shall be placed under the table; the serjeant at arms shall moreover always bear the said symbol when executing the immediate commands of the House during its sitting, returning the same to the clerk's table when the service is performed.

6. Every member or other person ordered into custody, shall pay to the serjeant at arms for every arrest, and for each day's custody and releasement; also per mile for travelling expences going and returning, unless the payment thereof shall be remitted by the House.

7. A standing committee of elections shall be appointed to consist of seven members; it shall be the duty of the said committee to examine and report upon the certificates of election, or other credentials of the members returned to serve in this House, and to take into their consideration all such matters as shall, or may come in question and be referred to them by the House, touching returns and elections, and to report their proceedings with their opinion thereupon to the House.

8. The Clerk of the House shall take an oath for the true and faithful discharge of the duties of his office, to the best of his knowledge and abilities.

Resolved, That it is the opinion of this committee, that joint rules ought to be established between the two Houses to provide for the mode of communicating messages, of holding and conducting conferences, and all other cases of proceeding requiring previous mutual agreement.

The first resolution being read a second time, and debated by paragraphs, the first, second, third, seventh, and eighth clauses were, on the question put, thereupon agreed to by this House.

The fourth, fifth, and sixth clauses were severally read a second time, and ordered to be re-committed to the same committee.

The second resolution was read a second time, and ordered to lie on the table.

On motion,

The House proceeded to ballot for a standing committee of elections.

The members elected, Mr. Clymer, Mr. Ames, Mr. Benson, Mr. Carroll, Mr. White, Mr. Huntington, and Mr. Gilman.

. . . .

TUESDAY, APRIL 14, 1789

. . . .

Mr. Boudinot reported from the committee to whom was recommitted certain clauses of the report for establishing additional rules and orders of proceeding to be observed in this House, that the committee had according to order re-considered the same, and agreed to a report thereupon, which he delivered in at the clerk's table, where the same was twice read, the blanks therein filled up, and on a question put thereupon, agreed to by the House as followeth:

Resolved, That it is the opinion of this committee, that the rules and orders following ought to be established as additional sending rules and orders of this House, to wit:

A serjeant at arms shall be appointed to hold his office during the pleasure of the House, whose duty shall be to attend the House during its sitting, to execute the commands of the House from time to time, and all such process issued by authority thereof as shall be directed to him by the Speaker.

A proper symbol of office shall be provided for the serjeant at arms, of such form and device as the Speaker shall direct, which shall be borne by the serjeant when in the execution of his office.

The fees of the serjeant at arms shall be, for every arrest the sum of two dollars; for each day's custody and releasement one dollar; and for travelling expences, going and returning, one tenth of a dollar per mile.

. . . .

House of Representatives Journal, reprinted from *Documentary History of the First Federal Congress, 1789–1791,* 14 vols. to date (Baltimore: Johns Hopkins University Press, 1972–), vol. 3: 11–15,18–21.

9   The First Rules of the United States Senate

April 16, 1789

In his four-volume text The Senate, 1789–1989, *Senator Robert C. Byrd (D-W.Va.) opens his chapter on Senate rules with the observation "that the only difference between a lynching and a fair trial is procedure." Rules define the way a parliamentary body can proceed with its business. They provide order and make it possible for persons who disagree strongly on subjects to have a way to move ahead, as long as all parties play by the same rules. Those who pay attention to rules also will be in a position to exercise more power than those who do not master them.*

The first Senate rules came from a committee of five senators, all of whom were lawyers with significant prior experience. Oliver Ellsworth of Connecticut had served in the Continental Congress, as had Richard Henry Lee of Virginia (who was also a signer of the Declaration of Independence). The other three members—Caleb Strong of Massachusetts, William Maclay of Pennsylvania, and Richard Bassett of Delaware—had been delegates to the Constitutional Convention.

The Senate rules, like those of the House, grew in part out of requirements in the Constitution. The first Senate rule begins with a reference to the "President," which is the president of the Senate. The Constitution stipulates that the "Vice President of the United States shall be President of the Senate. . . ." The first president of the Senate, Vice President John Adams, found this juxtaposition of titles and duties to be somewhat confusing (see document 11).

The Senate adopted its first nineteen rules on April 16, 1789. Two days later, a twentieth rule was added that required that any petition or memorial introduced into the Senate be explained briefly by the person introducing the measure before it would be formally read. The first twenty rules of the Senate constituted about six hundred words. The Senate's rules have been modified, expanded, and contracted over the past two centuries. In 1877, Senate rules reached their highest number at seventy-eight. As of 1998 there are forty-three, with the last added in 1992. Although the rules are few in number, the precedents—the ways that the Senate has acted under the rules—are far more numerous.

Tuesday, April 16.

. . . .

The report of the committee appointed to determine upon rules for conducting business in the Senate, was agreed to. Whereupon,

Resolved, That the following rules, from No. I to XIX, inclusive, be observed:

I. The President having taken the chair, and a quorum being present, the journal of the proceeding day shall be read, to the end that any mistake may be corrected that shall have been made in the entries.

II. No member shall speak to another, or otherwise interrupt the business of the Senate, or read any printed paper while the journals or public papers are reading, or when any member is speaking in any debate.

III. Every member, when he speaks, shall address the chair, standing in his place, and when he has finished, shall sit down.

IV. No member shall speak any more than twice in any one debate on the same day, without leave of the Senate.

V. When two members rise at the same time, the President shall name the person to speak; but in all cases the member first rising shall speak first.

VI. No motion shall be debated until the same shall be seconded.

VII. When a motion shall be made and seconded, it shall be reduced to writing, if desired by the President, or any member, delivered in at the table, and read by the President before the same shall be debated.

VIII. While a question is before the Senate, no motion shall be received unless for an amendment, for the previous question, or for postponing the main question, or to commit it, or to adjourn.

IX. The previous question being moved and seconded, the question from the chair shall be: "Shall the main question be now put?" And if the nays prevail, the main question shall not then be put.

X. If a question in debate contain several points, any member may have the same divided.

XI. When the yeas and nays shall be called for by one-fifth of the members present, each member called upon shall, unless for special reasons he be excused by the Senate, declare, openly and without debate, his assent or dissent to the question. In taking the yeas and nays, and upon the call of the House, the names of the members shall be taken alphabetically.

XII. One day's notice at least shall be given of an intended motion for leave to bring in a bill.

XIII. Every bill shall receive three readings previous to its being passed, and the President shall give notice at each, whether it be the first, second, or third; which readings shall be on three different days, unless the Senate unanimously direct otherwise.

XIV. No bill shall be committed or amended until it shall have been twice read, after which it may be referred to a committee.

XV. All committees shall be appointed by ballot, and a plurality of votes shall make a choice.

XVI. When a member shall be called to order, he shall sit down until the President shall have determined whether he is in order or not; and every question of order shall be decided by the President, without debate; but, if there be a doubt in his mind, he may call for the sense of the Senate.

XVII. If a member be called to order for words spoken, the exceptional words shall immediately be taken down in writing, that the President may be better enabled to judge the matter.

XVIII. When a blank is to be filled, and different sums shall be proposed, the question shall be taken on the highest sum first.

XIX. No member shall absent himself from the service of the Senate without leave of the Senate first obtained.

Senate Legislative Journal, reprinted from *Documentary History of the First Federal Congress, 1789–1791*, 14 vols. to date (Baltimore: Johns Hopkins University Press, 1972–), vol. 1: 18–21.

10   Vice President John Adams Addresses the Senate

April 21, 1789

When Vice President John Adams appeared for the first time in the Senate chamber to assume his duties as president of the Senate, he was greeted by the Senate president pro tempore, John Langdon of New Hampshire, who congratulated Adams on his election as vice president and conducted him to the chair of the presiding officer. Adams's address to the Senate reveals his reverence for the Senate and for President George Washington. He humbly admitted that he was used to participating in debate rather than being a presiding officer, but promised to do his best.

The matters on Adams mind as he assumed his duties were serious ones. He was aware that whatever he did he would be setting the precedent for future presidents of the Senate. Adams's confusion over his dual role as president of the Senate and vice president of the United States can be seen in an account of his actions by Senator William Maclay (see document 11).

GENTLEMEN OF THE SENATE,

INVITED to this respectable situation by the suffrages of our fellow-citizens, according to the Constitution, I have thought it my duty cheerfully and readily to accept it. Unaccustomed to refuse any public service, however dangerous to my reputation, or disproportioned to my talents, it would have been inconsistent to have adopted another maxim of conduct, at this time, when the prosperity of the country, and the liberties of the people, require perhaps, as much as ever the attention of those that possess any share of the public confidence.

I should be destitute of sensibility, if, upon my arrival in this city, and presentation to this Legislature, and especially to this Senate, I could see, without emotion, so many of those char-

acters, of whose virtuous exertions I have so often been a witness—from whose countenances and examples I have ever derived encouragement and animation—whose disinterested friendship has supported me, in many intricate conjunctures of public affairs, at home and abroad:—Those celebrated defenders of the liberties of this country, whom menaces could not intimidate, corruption seduce, nor flattery allure: Those intrepid assertors of the rights of mankind, whose philosophy and policy, have enlightened the world, in twenty years, more that it was ever before enlightened in many centuries, by ancient schools, or modern universities.

I must have been inattentive to the course of events, if I were either ignorant of the same, or insensible to the merit of those other characters in the Senate, to whom it has been my misfortune to have been, hitherto, personally unknown.

It is with satisfaction, that I congratulate the people of America on the formation of a national Constitution, and the fair prospect of a consistent administration of a government of laws. On the acquisition of an House of Representatives, chosen by themselves; of a Senate thus composed by their own State Legislatures; and on the prospect of an executive authority, in the hands of one whose portrait I will not attempt to draw— Were I blessed with powers to do justice to his character, it would be impossible to increase the confidence or affection of his country, or make the smallest addition to his glory. This can only be effected by the discharge of the present exalted trust on the same principles, with the same abilities and virtues, which have uniformly appeared in all his former conduct, public or private. May I nevertheless, be indulged to enquire, if we look over the catalogue of the first magistrates of nations, whether they have been denominated President or Consuls, Kings or Princes, where shall we find one, whose commanding talents and virtues, whose over-ruling good fortune have so completely united all hearts and voices in his favor? Who enjoyed the esteem and admiration of foreign nations and fellow-citizens with equal unanimity? Qualities so uncommon, are no common blessings to the country that possesses them. By those great qualities, and their benign effects, has Providence marked out the head of this nation, with an hand so distinctly visible, as to have been seen by all men, and mistaken by none.

It is not for me to interrupt your deliberations by any general observations on the state of the nation, or by recommending, or proposing any particular measures. It would be superfluous, to gentlemen of your great experience, to urge the necessity of order.—It is only necessary to make an apology for myself. Not wholly without experience in public assemblies, I have been more accustomed to take a share in their debates, than to preside in their deliberations. It shall be my constant endeavor to behave toward every member of this *most honorable* body with all that consideration, delicacy, and decorum which becomes the dignity of his station and character: But, if from inexperience, or inadvertency, anything should ever escape me, inconsistent with propriety, I must entreat you, by imputing it to its true cause, and not to any want of respect, to pardon and excuse it.

A trust of the greatest magnitude is committed to this Legislature—and the eyes of the world are upon you. Your country expects from your deliberations, in concurrence with the other branches of government, consideration abroad, and contentment at home—prosperity, order, justice, peace, and liberty:—And may God Almighty's providence assist you to answer their just expectations.

Adjourned to 11 o'clock to-morrow morning.

Senate Legislative Journal, reprinted from *Documentary History of the First Federal Congress, 1789–1791*, 14 vols. to date (Baltimore: Johns Hopkins University Press, 1972–), vol. 1: 21–23.

11 Senator William Maclay's Account of the Duties of the Vice President

April 25, 1789

During its first six years, the Senate met in secret sessions and made little record of its debate in that chamber in those crucial formative years. But thanks to the diary kept by Senator William Maclay (1737–1804) of Pennsylvania, we have some vivid descriptions of what happened behind closed doors. Maclay's views of what he witnessed were tempered by a crotchety personality bordering on meanness when dealing with those he did not like. Sometimes his own health or general attitude on a particular day could greatly affect the manner in which he described Senate proceedings. He could be refreshingly candid and witty one day and cantankerous and pessimistic the next. Maclay grew to dislike John Adams, the Senate president, and seemed to delight in making Adams look bad in his diary.

In this diary entry Maclay complained about the work of Samuel Otis, the Senate's secretary (even though historians have since praised Otis for his record keeping). He then launched into a description of John Adams's speech to the Senate on his duties as presiding officer. Adams seemed in a quandary over reconciling his dual roles of president of the Senate and vice president of the United States, a dilemma heightened by the preparations for the upcoming inauguration of George Washington, which would occur in the Senate chamber five days later (see document 12). Spelling, punctuation, and capitalization appear as in the original diary, although strikeouts in the original text have been omitted.

attended the House   Ceremonies endless ceremonies the whole business of the day.   I did not embark warmly this day. Otis our Secretary makes a most miserable hand of it, the grossest Mistakes made on our minutes and it cost Us an hour or Two to rectify them.   I was up as often I believe as was necessary and certainly threw so much light on Two Subjects, that the debate ended on each.   The President as usual made us two or three Speeches from the Chair.   I will endeavour to recollect one of them.   It was on the reading of a Report. Which mentioned that the President should be received in the Senate Chamber and proceed thence to the House of Representatives to be Sworn—   Gentlemen I do not know whether the framers of the Constitution had in View the Two Kings of Sparta or the Two Consuls of rome when they formed it.   one to have all the power while he held it, and the other to be nothing; nor do I know whether the Architect that formed our room, and the wide Chair in it, (to hold two I suppose) had the Constitution before him,   Gentlemen I feel great difficulty how to act,   I am possesed of two seperate powers, the one in esse, and the other in posse.   I am Vice President in this I am nothing, but I may be everything, but I am President also of the Senate.   When the President comes into the Senate, what shall I be, I cannot be then, no Gentlemen I cannot, I cannot—   I wish Gentlemen to think what I shall be;   here as if oppressed with a Sense of his distressed situation, he threw himself back in his Chair.   A Solemn Silence ensued.   God forgive me, for it was involuntary, but the profane Muscles of my face, were in Tune for laughter, in spite of my indisposition   Elsworth thumbed over the Sheet constitution, and turned it for some time;   at length he rose, and addressed the Chair with the most profound gravity. Mr. President I have looked over the Constitution (paused) and I find Sir, it is evident & Clear Sir, that wherever the Senate is to be, then Sir you must be at the head of them. but further Sir, (here he looked agast, as if some tremendous Gulph had Yaned before him) I, shall, not, pretend, to, say. Thursday next is appointed for Swearing in the President   I am

worse of my rheumatism, but perhaps it is owing to the [cha]nge of Weather. for the Wind is at North West and Cold. . . .

The Diary of William Maclay and Other Notes on Senate Debates, March 4, 1789–March 3, 1791, ed. Kenneth Bowling and Helen E. Veit, vol. IX of the *Documentary History of the First Federal Congress* (Baltimore: Johns Hopkins University Press, 1988), 5–6.

12 Senator William Maclay's Description of the Inauguration of George Washington

April 30, 1789

Congress has always figured prominently in the inauguration of the president of the United States. Senator William Maclay captured in the pages of his private diary the high drama of the first inauguration, held April 30, 1790, in New York City for George Washington. The power and enduring value of this account is its candid description of George Washington as he took the oath of office. Maclay saw the president as nervous and agitated. The senator was disappointed and somewhat embarrassed by the mediocre manner in which Washington read his speech. He even commented on Washington's rather plain clothing, which the president had carefully chosen so as not to offend American manufacturers. All he wore that day had been made in America. As in his account of the Senate speech of John Adams (see document 11), Maclay again portrays the vice president as a befuddled person unable to figure out what role he should play in the inauguration.

This diary entry offers a glimpse of the full range of the first inaugural ceremony, which included a church service while Congress was technically still in session. The president was sworn in by Robert Livingston, the chancellor of New York from 1777 to 1801. Spelling, punctuation, and capitalization appear as in the original diary, although strikeouts in the original text have been omitted.

This is the great important day. Goddess of Etiquette assist me while I describe it.   The Senate stood adjourned to half after 11 O'Clock,   about 10 dressed in my best Cloaths; went for Mr. Morris Lodgings, but met his Son' who told me, that his father would not be in Town untill Saturday.   turned into the Hall.   the Croud already great.   the Senate met.   The President rose in the most solemn Manner, never son of *Adam* seemed impressed with deeper gravity.   Yet what shall I think of him,   he often in the midst of his most important Airs, I believe when he is at a loss for expressions, (and this he often is, wrapped up I suppose in the Contemplation of his own importance) suffers an unmeaning kind of vacant laugh to escape him. This was the Case today, and really to me bore the Air of ridiculing the Farce he was acting.   "Gentlemen I wish for the direction of the Senate   the President will I suppose address the

Congress   how shall I behave,   how shall we receive   it shall it be standing or sitting,"   here followed a considerable deal of talk from him, which I could make nothing of,   Mr. Lee began with the House of Commons (as is usual with him) then the House of Lords then the King & then back again.   the result of his information was that the Lords sat and the Commons Stood. on the delivery of the Kings Speech.   Mr. Izard got up and told how often he had been in the Houses of Parliament.   he said a great deal of what he had seen there.   made however this sagacious discovery, that the Commons stood because they had no seats to sit on. being arrived at the Bar of the House of lords.   it was discovered after some time that the King sat too, and had his robes and crown on.   Mr. President got up again & said he had been very often indeed, at the Parliament on those Occasions, but there always was such a Croud, and *ladies along,* that for his part he could not say how it was.   Mr. Carrol got up to declare that he thought it of no consequence how it was in great Britain, they were no rule to us &ca.   But all at once the Secretary who had been out, wispered to the Chair that the Clerk from the Representatives was at the door with a Communication.   and Gentlemen of the Senate how shall he be received?   a Silly kind of Resolution of the Committee on that Business, had been laid on the Table some days ago,   the amount of it was that each house should communicate to the other what and how they choose.   it concluded however something in this way, that everything should be done with all the *propriety* that was *proper.* the question was shall this be adopted, that we may know how to receive the Clk.   it was objected. this will throw no light on the Subject, it will leave you where you are.   Mr. Lee brought the House of Commons before Us again.   he reprobated the Rule declared that the Clerk should not come within the Bar of the House, That the proper mode was for the Sergeant at Arms with the Mace on his shoulder should to meet the Clerk at the door and receive his Communications we are not however provided for this ceremonious way of doing business, having neither Mace nor Sergeant, nor masters in chancery, who carry down Bills— from the English Lords.

Mr. Izard got up, and labored unintelligibly to show the great distinction, between a Communication and a delivery of a thing. but he was not minded. Mr. Elsworth showed enough that if The Clerk was not permitted to deliver the Communication, the Speaker might as well send it inclosed. repeated accounts came the Speaker and representatives were at the door. confusion insued. the members left their Seats. Mr. Read rose and called the attention of the Senate to the neglect that had been shewed to Mr. Thomson late Secretary. Mr. Lee rose to answer him, but I could not hear one word he said. the Speaker was introduced followed by the Representatives. here we sat an hour and ten minutes, before the President arrived— this delay was owing to Lee, Izard and Dalton, who had staid with us untill the Speaker came in, instead of going to attend the President. the President advanced between the Senate and Representatives bowing to each. he was placed in the Chair by the President of the Senate. the Senate with their President on the right the Speaker and Representatives on his left. the President of the Senate rose and address'd a short Sentence to him. The import of it was that he should now take the Oath of Office as President. he seemed to have forgot half of what he was to say for he made a dead pause and stood for some time, to appearance, in a vacant mood. he finished with a formal bow. and the President was conducted out of the middle Window into the Gallery and the Oath administered by the Chancellor. Notice that the Business done, was communicated to the Croud by Proclamation &ca., who gave three Cheers, and repeated it on the Presidents bowing to them— as the Company returned into the Senate Chamber, the President took the Chair, and the Senate and Representatives their Seats, he rose & all arose also. and addressed them (see the address) this great Man was agitated and embarrassed more than ever he was by the levelled Cannon or pointed Musket. he trembled, and several times could scarce make out to read, tho it must be supposed he had often read it before. he put the part of the fingers of his left hand, into the side, of what I think the Taylors call the fall, of his Breeches. changing the paper into his left hand, after some time, he then did the same with some of the fingers of his right hand. When he came to the Words *all the World,* he made a flourish with his right hand, which left rather an ungainly impression. I sincerely, for my part, wished all set ceremony in the hands of the dancing Masters. and that this first of Men, had read off, his address, in the plainest Manner without ever taking his Eyes From, the paper. for I felt hurt, that he was not first in every thing. he was dressed in deep brown, with Metal buttons, with an Eagle on them, White Stockings a Bag and Sword— from the Hall there was a grand Procession to St. Pauls Church where prayers were said by the Bishop. the Procession was well conducted and without accident, as far as I have heard, the Militias were all under Arms. lined the Street near the Church, made a good figure and behaved well The Senate returned to their Chamber after Service, formed & took up the Address. Our President called it *his most gracious Speech.* I cannot approve of this. a Committee was appointd on it, Johnson, Carrol, Patterson. adjourned. in the Evening there were grand fire Works. The Spanish Ambassadors House was adorned with Transparent paintings, The French Ministers House was illuminated, and had some transparent pieces the Hall was grandly illuminated. and after all this the People went to bed.

The Diary of William Maclay and Other Notes on Senate Debates, March 4, 1789–March 3, 1791, ed. Kenneth Bowling and Helen E. Veit, vol. IX of the *Documentary History of the First Federal Congress* (Baltimore: Johns Hopkins University Press, 1988), 11–13.

13   The House and Senate Agree on the Proper Title for the President of the United States

May 14, 1789

The debate over the proper title for the president of the United States may seem a trivial matter today, but it was a topic of much concern to members of the First Congress, whose every act seemed to be precedent setting. Vice President John Adams was among those who championed a fancier title that would compete in splendor with titles of other heads of state, most of whom were monarchs. The House considered the matter and reported on May 5, 1789, that it was not proper to add additional titles for the president beyond what was in the Constitution. The House preferred to shun the trappings of monarchy.

After considerable debate, and a conference committee between House and Senate members that could not agree on the matter, the Senate finally agreed to adopt the view of the House. Ever since that time the head of the executive branch has simply been called the president of the United States.

During deliberations, some members of the First Congress and the press had fun at the expense of Vice President John Adams by proposing a few fanciful titles for him, such as "His Rotundity" or "His Superfluous Excellency."

The committee, appointed the 9th instant, to determine "under what title it will be proper for the Senate to address the President," and to confer with a committee of the House of Representatives "upon the disagreeing votes of the Senate and

House," informed the Senate that they had conferred with a committee of the House of Representatives, but could not agree upon a report.

The committee, appointed the 9th instant, "to consider and report under what title it will be proper for the Senate to address the President of the United States of America," reported:

"That, in the opinion of the committee, it will be proper thus to address the President: *His Highness, The President of the United States of America, and Protector of their Liberties.*"

Which report was postponed; and the following resolve was agreed to, to wit:

"From a decent respect for the opinion and practice of civilized nations, whether under monarchical or republican forms of Government, whose custom is to annex titles of respectability to the office of their Chief Magistrate; and that, on intercourse with foreign nations, a due respect for the majesty of the people of the United States may not be hazarded by any appearance of singularity, the Senate have been induced to be of opinion, that it would be proper to annex a respectable title to the office of President of the United States; but, the Senate, desirous of preserving harmony with the House of Representatives, where the practice lately observed in presenting an address to the President was without the addition of titles, think it proper, for the present, to act in conformity with the practice of that House: therefore,

"*Resolved,* That the present address be '*To the President of the United States,*' without addition of title."

Senate Legislative Journal, reprinted from *Documentary History of the First Federal Congress, 1789–1791,* 14 vols. to date (Baltimore: Johns Hopkins University Press, 1972–), vol. 1: 44–45,

14 The First Law to Pass Congress: The Oath of Office Act

June 1, 1789

Members of Congress, executive branch officers, and judicial branch officers are required to take an oath of office, as provided in Article VI, Clause 3, of the Constitution. The first law that Congress passed was an oath of office act that spelled out the language of the oath and set up a procedure for administering it, as required by the Constitution. Congress has amended the language of the oath a few times since 1789, but the general idea of swearing or affirming allegiance to the Constitution remains the same. The oath taken by the president of the United States is similar, but the language of the presidential oath is contained in the Constitution itself in Article II, Section 1, Clause 8, and therefore did not require separate legislation.

The current oath of office for members of Congress and other top government officials is: "I do solemnly swear that I will support and defend the Constitution of the United States against all enemies, foreign and domestic; that I will bear true faith and allegiance to the same; that I take this obligation freely, without any mental reservation or purpose of evasion, and that I will well and faithfully discharge the duties of the office on which I am about to enter. So help me God."

The addition of the phrase "So help me God," now a part of the official oath by law, began out of tradition fostered first by the House of Representatives and then by President George Washington. Neither the first Oath of Office Act in 1789 nor the language of the presidential oath in the Constitution contained any reference to God. Reference to God in the oath to be taken by members of Congress was considered and approved by a House committee, appointed April 6, 1789. The early version of the oath contained two references to God: "I do solemnly swear (or affirm, as the case may be) in the presence of Almighty God, that I will support the Constitution of the United States. So help me God" (Annals of Congress, House, 1st Congress, 1st session, April 6, 1789, 97). The first oath administered to the members of the House of Representatives on April 7, 1789, contained these references to God three weeks before George Washington added the phrase "So help me God," during his inauguration April 30, 1789.*

STATUTE I.

Chapter 1.—An Act to regulate the Time and Manner of administering certain Oaths.

SEC. 1. *Be it enacted by the Senate and [House of] Representatives of the United States of America in Congress assembled,* That the oath or affirmation required by the sixth article of the Constitution of the United States, shall be administered in the form following, to wit: "I, A. B. do solemnly swear or affirm (as the case may be) that I will support the Constitution of the United States." The said oath or affirmation shall be administered within three days after the passing of this act, by any one member of the Senate, to the President of the Senate, and by him to all the members and to the secretary; and by the Speaker of the House of Representatives, to all the members who have not taken a similar oath, by virtue of a particular resolution of the said House, and to the clerk: and in case of the absence of any member from the service of either House, at the time prescribed for taking the said oath or affirmation, the same shall be administered to such member, when he shall appear to take his seat.

SEC. 2. *And be it further enacted,* That at the first session of Congress after every general election of Representatives, the oath or affirmation aforesaid, shall be administered by any one member of the House of Representatives to the Speaker; and by him to all the members present, and to the clerk, previous to entering on any other business; and to the members who shall afterwards appear, previous to taking their seats. The President of the Senate for the time being, shall also administer the said oath or affirmation to each Senator who shall hereafter be elected, previous to his taking his seat: and in any future case of a President of the Senate, who shall not have taken the said oath or affirmation, the same shall be administered to him by any one of the members of the Senate.

SEC. 3. *And be it further enacted,* That the members of the several State legislatures, at the next sessions of the said legislatures, respect lively, and all executive and judicial officers of the several States, who have been heretofore chosen or appointed, or who shall be chosen or appointed before the first day of August next, and who shall then be in office, shall, within one month thereafter, take the same oath or affirmation, except where they shall have taken it before; which may be administered by any person authorized by the law of the State, in which such office shall be holder, to administer oaths. And the members of the several State legislatures, and all executive and judicial officers of the several States, who shall be chosen or appointed after the said first day of August, shall, before they proceed to execute the duties of their respective offices, take the foregoing oath or affirmation, which shall be administered by the person or persons, who by the law of the State shall be authorized to administer the oath of office; and the person or persons so administering the oath hereby required to be taken,

shall cause a record or certificate thereof to be made, in the same manner, as, by the law of the State, he or they shall be directed to record or certify the oath of office.

SEC. 4. *And be further enacted,* That all officers appointed, or hereafter to be appointed under the authority of the United States, shall, before they act in their respective offices, take the same oath or affirmation, which shall be administered by the person or persons who shall be authorized by law to administer to such officers their respective oaths of office; and such officers shall incur the same penalties in case of failure as shall be imposed by law in case of failure in taking their respective oaths of office.

SEC. 5. *And be it further enacted,* That the secretary of the Senate, and the clerk of the House of Representatives for the time being, shall, at the time of taking the oath or affirmation aforesaid, each take an oath or affirmation in the words following, to wit: "I, A. B. secretary of the Senate, or clerk of the House of Representatives (as the case may be) of the United States of America, do solemnly swear or affirm, that I will truly and faithfully discharge the duties of my said office, to the best of my knowledge and abilities."

APPROVED June 1, 1789.

Statutes at Large, 1 (1789–1799), 1st Congress, 1st session, June 1, 1789, 23.

---

15   The House Debates James Madison's Resolution on the Bill of Rights

June 8, 1789

When James Madison was a delegate to the Federal Convention in 1787 he did not believe a bill of rights was a necessary component of the new Constitution. While most of the delegates agreed with him, fellow Virginian George Mason and a few others felt strongly that a statement of rights that would protect citizens from the power of government was a vital element to the successful ratification of the Constitution. Mason refused to sign the copy of the Constitution adopted by the Convention on September 17, 1787, because it did not contain a bill of rights. During the ratification process, many states objected to the lack of a bill of rights. It became the rallying point for anti-Federalists, who fought against ratification of the Constitution.

Madison and many other delegates had underestimated the power of this issue. His eyes opened by political necessity, Madison changed his mind and became a supporter of the idea during his campaign for a seat in the First Congress. Once elected, Madison kept his promise and introduced a resolution that the House take up the matter of a bill of rights in the Committee of the Whole. Madison's resolution offered numerous insertions and changes in the body of the Constitution, as well as a proposal to alter the numbering of some of the original articles in the Constitution. All

the ingredients were there to establish what has come to be known as the Bill of Rights.

With the new government only nine weeks old, and the new Constitution still untested, the process of amending the Constitution began amidst much skepticism and opposition in the House. In subsequent weeks and months the House debated numerous amendments, which were eventually forged into seventeen items that were sent onto the Senate in August. A month later the Senate and House agreed to twelve amendments that they sent to the states for ratification. Ten were adopted by 1791. Of the two original amendments not ratified, one dealt with apportionment in the House and the other dealt with congressional pay increases. The pay increase amendment was finally added as the Twenty-Seventh Amendment to the Constitution in 1992, two hundred and three years after it was first proposed (see document 178).

In the debate of June 8, 1789, the day Madison resolved to take up the matter of a bill of rights, he and other supporters of a bill of rights had an uphill battle on their hands. Many members of the House opposed the bill of rights, while others felt Congress should attend to the far more pressing business of establishing the new government. This debate, the beginning of the first attempt to amend the Constitution, remains as a true landmark in the annals of Congress.

MR. MADISON

This day Mr. Speaker, is the day assigned for taking into consideration the subject of amendments to the constitution. As I considered myself bound in honor and in duty to do what I have done on this subject, I shall proceed to bring the amendments before you as soon as possible, and advocate them until they shall be finally adopted or rejected by a constitutional majority of this house. With a view of drawing your attention to this important object, I shall move that this house do now resolve itself into a committee of the whole on the state of the union; by which an opportunity will be given, to bring forward some propositions, which I have strong hopes will meet with the unanimous approbation of this house, after the fullest discussion and most serious regard. I therefore move you, that the house now go into a committee on this business.

MR. SMITH [S.C.?]

Was not inclined to interrupt the measures which the public were so anxiously expecting, by going into a Committee of the Whole at this time. He observed there were two modes of introducing this business to the house: One by appointing a select committee to take into consideration the several amendments proposed by the state conventions; this he thought the most likely way to shorten the business. The other was, that the gentleman should lay his propositions on the table, for the consideration of the members; that they should be printed, and taken up for discussion at a future day. Either of these modes would enable the house to enter upon business better prepared than could be the case by a sudden transition from other important concerns to which their minds were strongly bent. He therefore hoped that the honorable gentleman would consent to bring the subject forward in one of those ways, in preference to going into a committee of the whole. For, said he, it must appear extremely impolitic to go into the consideration of amending the government, before it is organized, before it has begun to operate. Certainly, upon reflection is must appear to be premature. I wish, therefore, gentlemen would consent to the delay: for the business which lies in an unfinished state—I mean particularly the collection bill—is necessary to be passed; else all we have hitherto done is of no effect. If we go into the discussion of this subject, it will take us three weeks or a month; and during all this time, every other business must be suspended, because we cannot proceed with either accuracy or despatch when the mind is perpetually shifted from one subject to another.

MR. JACKSON

I am of opinion we ought not to be in a hurry with respect to altering the constitution. For my part, I have no idea of speculating in this serious manner on theory; if I agree to alterations in the mode of administering this Government, I shall like to stand on the sure ground of experience and not be treading air. What experience have we had of the good or bad qualities of this constitution? Can any gentleman affirm to me one proposition that is a certain and absolute amendment? I deny that he can. Our constitution, sire, is like a vessel just launched, and lying at the wharf; she is untried, you can hardly discover any one of her properties; it is not known how she will answer her helm, or lay her course; whether she will bear with safety the precious freight to be deposited in her hold. But, in this state, will the prudent merchant attempt alterations? Will he employ workmen to tear off the planking and take asunder the frame? He certainly will not. Let us, gentlemen, fit out our vessel, set up her masts, and expand her sails, and be guided by the experiment in our alterations. If she sails upon an uneven keel, let us right her by adding weight where it is wanting. In this way, we may remedy her defects to the satisfaction of all concerned; but if we proceed now to make alterations, we may deface a beauty, or deform a well proportioned piece of workmanship. In short, Mr. Speaker, I am not for amendments at this time; but if gentlemen should think it a subject deserving of attention, they will surely not neglect the more important business which is now unfinished before them. Without we pass the collection bill we can get no revenue, and without revenue the wheels of government cannot move. I am against taking up the subject at present, and shall therefore be totally against the amendments, if the government is not organized, that I may see whether it is grievous or not.

. . . .

Let the constitution have a fair trial; let it be examined by experience, discover by that test what its errors are, and then talk of amending; but to attempt it now is doing it at a risk, which is certainly imprudent. I have the honor of coming from a State that ratified the constitution by unanimous vote of a numerous convention the people of Georgia have manifested their attachment to it by adopting a State Constitution framed upon the same plan as this. But although they are thus satisfied, I shall not be against such amendments as well gratify the inhabitants of other States, provided they are judged of by experience and not merely on theory. For this reason, I wish the consideration of the subject postponed until the first of March, 1790.

MR. GOODHUE

I believe it would be perfectly right in the gentleman who spoke last, to move postponement to the time he has mentioned; because he is opposed to the consideration of amendments altogether. But I believe it will be proper to attend to the subject earlier; because it is the wish of many of our constituents, that something should be added to the constitution, to secure a stronger manner their liberties from the inroads of power. Yet I think the present time premature; inasmuch as we have other business before us, which is incomplete, but essential to the public interest. When that is finished, I shall concur in taking up the subject of amendments.

MR. BURKE

Thought amendments to the constitution necessary, but this was not the proper time to bring them forward. He wished the government completely organized before they entered upon this ground. The law for collecting the revenue is immediately necessary; the treasury department must be established; till this and other important subjects are determined, he was against taking this up. He said it might interrupt the harmony of the house, which was necessary to be preserved in order to despatch the great objects of legislation. He hoped it would be postponed for the present, and pledged himself to bring it forward hereafter, if nobody else would.

MR. MADISON

The gentleman from Georgia (Mr. Jackson) is certainly right in his opposition to my motion for going into a committee of the whole, because he is unfriendly to the object I have in contemplation; but I cannot see that the gentlemen who wish for amendments to be proposed at the present session, stand on good ground when they object to the house going into committee on this business.

When I first hinted to the house my intention of calling their deliberations to this object, I mentioned the pressure of other important subjects, and submitted the propriety of postponing this till the more urgent business was despatched; but finding that business not despatched, when the order of the day for considering amendments arrived, I thought it a good reason for a farther delay; I moved the postponement accordingly. I am sorry the same reason still exists in some degree, but it operates with less force, when it is considered that it is not now proposed to enter into a full and minute discussion of every part of the subject, but merely to bring it before the House, that our constituents may see we pay a proper attention to a subject they have much at heart; and if it does not give that full gratification which is to be wished, they will discover that it proceeds from the urgency of business of a very important nature. But if we continue to postpone from time to time, and refuse to let the subject come into view, it may occasion suspicions, which, though not well founded, may tend to inflame or prejudice the public mind against our decisions. They may think we are not sincere in our desire to incorporate such amendments in the constitution as well secure those rights, which they consider as not sufficiently guarded. The applications for amendments come from a very respectable number of our constituents, and it is certainly proper for congress to consider the subject, in order to quiet that anxiety which prevails in the public mind. Indeed, I think it would have been of advantage to the government if it had been amendments the first business we entered upon; it would have stifled the voice of complaint, and made friends of many who doubted the merits of the constitution. Our future measures would then have been more generally agreeably supported; but the justifiable anxiety to put the government into operation prevented that; it therefore remains for us to take it up as soon as possible. I wish then to commence the consideration at the present moment; I hold it to be my duty to in some form or other without delay. I only wish to introduce the great work, and, as I said before, I do not expect it will be decided immediately; but if some step is taken in the business, it will give reason to believe that we may come to a final result. This will inspire a reasonable hope in the advocates for amendments, that full justice will be done to the important subject; and I have reason to believe their expectation will not be defeated. I hope the house will not decline my motion for going into a committee.

MR. SHERMAN

I am willing that this matter should be brought before the house at a proper time. I suppose a number of gentlemen think it their duty to bring it forward; so that there is no apprehension it will be passed over in silence: Other gentlemen may be disposed to let the subject rest until the more important objects of government are attended to; and I should conclude, from the nature of the case, that the people expect the latter from us in preference to altering the constitution; because they have ratified that instrument, in order that the government may begin to operate. If this was not their wish, they might as well have rejected the constitution, as North-Carolina has done, until the amendments took place. The state I have the honor to come from adopted this system by a very great majority, because they wished for the government; but they desired no amendments. I suppose this was the case in other states; it will therefore be imprudent to neglect much more important concerns for this. The executive part of the government wants organization; the business of the revenue is incomplete, to say nothing of the judiciary business. Now, will gentlemen give up these points to go into a discussion of amendments, when no advantage can arise from them? For my part, I question if any alteration which can be now proposed would be an amendment, in the true sense of the word; but nevertheless, I am willing to let the subject be introduced. If the gentleman only desires to go into committee for the purpose of receiving his propositions, I shall consent; but I have strong objections to being interrupted in completing the more important business; because I am well satisfied it will alarm the fears of twenty of our constituents where it will please one.

MR. WHITE

I hope the house will not spend much time on this subject, till the more pressing business is despatched; but, at the same time, I hope we shall not dismiss it altogether, because I think a majority of the people who have ratified the constitution, did it under the expectation that congress would, at some convenient time, examine its texture and point out where it was defective, in order that it might be judiciously amended. Whether, while we are without experience, amendments can be digested in such a manner as to give satisfaction to a constitutional majority of this house, I will not pretend to say; but I hope the subject may be considered with all convenient speed. I think it would tend to tranquilize the public mind; therefore I shall vote in favor of going into a committee of the whole, and, after receiving the subject, shall be content to refer it to a special committee to arrange and report. I fear, if we refuse to take up the subject, it will irritate many of our constituents, which I do not wish to do. If we cannot, after mature consideration, gratify their wishes, the cause of complaint will be lessened, if not removed. But a doubt on this head will not be a good reason why we should refuse to inquire. I do not say this as it affects my immediate constituents, because I believe a majority of the district which elected me do not require alterations; but I know there are people in other parts who will not be satisfied unless some amendments are proposed.

. . . .

MR. PAGE

My colleague tells you he is ready to submit to the committee of the whole his ideas on this subject. If no objection had been made to his motion, the whole business might have been finished before this. He has done me the honor of showing me certain propositions which he has drawn up; they are very important, and I sincerely wish the house may receive them. After they are published, I think the people will wait with patience till we are at leisure to resume them. But it must be very disagreeable to them to have it postponed from time to time, in the manner it has been for six weeks past; they will be tired out by a fruitless expectation. Putting myself into the place of those who favor amendments, I should suspect congress did not mean seriously to enter upon the subject; that it was vain to expect redress from them. I should begin to turn my attention to the alternative contained in the fifth article, and think of joining the Legislatures of those states which have applied for calling a new convention. How dangerous such as expedient would be I need not mention; but I venture to affirm, that unless you take early notice of this subject, you will not have power to deliberate. The people will clamor for a new convention; they will not trust the house any longer. Those, therefore, who dread the assembling of a convention, will do well to acquiesce in the present motion, and lay the foundation of a most important work. I do not think we need consume more than half an hour in the committee of the whole; this is not so much time but we may conveniently spare it, considering the nature of the business. I do not wish to divert the attention of congress from the organization of the government, nor do I think it need be done, if we comply with the present motion.

. . . .

MR. MADISON

I am sorry to be accessory to the loss of a single moment of time by the house. If I had been indulged in my motion, and we had gone into a committee of the whole, I think we might have rose and resumed the consideration of other business before this time; that is, so far as it depended upon what I proposed to bring forward. As that mode seems not to give satisfaction, I will withdraw the motion, and move you, sir, that a select committee be appointed to consider and report such amendments as are proper for congress to propose to the legislatures of the several states, conformably to the 5th article of the constitution. I will state my reasons why I think it proper to propose amendments, and state the amendments themselves, so far as I think they ought to be proposed. If I thought I could fulfil the duty which I owe to myself and my constituents, to let the subject pass over in silence, I most certainly should not trespass upon the indulgence of this house. But I cannot do this, and am therefore compelled to beg a patient hearing to what I have to lay before you. And I do most sincerely believe, that if congress will devote but one day to this subject, so far as to satisfy the public that we do not disregard their wishes, it will have a salutary influence on the public councils, and prepare the way for a favorable reception of our future measures. It appears to me that this house is bound by every motive of prudence, not to let the first session pass over without proposing to the state legislatures, some things to be incorporated into the constitution, that will render it as acceptable to the whole people of the United States, as it has been found acceptable to a majority of them. I wish, among other reasons why something should be done, that those who had been friendly to the adoption of this constitution may have the opportunity of proving to those who were opposed to it that they were as sincerely devoted to liberty and a republican government, as those who charged them with wishing the adoption of this constitution in order to lay the foundation of an aristocracy or despotism. It will be a desirable thing to extinguish from the bosom of every member of the community, any apprehensions that there are those among his countrymen who wish to deprive them of the liberty for which they valiantly fought and honorably bled. And if there are amendments desired of such a nature as will not injure the constitution, and they can be ingrafted so as to give satisfaction to the doubting part of our fellow-citizens, the friends of the federal government will evince that spirit of deference and concession for which they have hitherto been distinguished.

It cannot be a secret to the gentlemen in this house, that, notwithstanding the ratification of this system of government by eleven of the thirteen United States, in some cases unanimously, in others by large majorities; yet still there is a great number of our constituents who are dissatisfied with it; among whom are many respectable for their talents and patriotism, and respectable for the jealousy they have for their liberty, which, though mistaken in its object, is laudable in its motive. There is a great body of the people falling under this description, who at present feel much inclined to join their support to the cause of federalism, if they were satisfied on this one point. We ought not to disregard their inclination, but, on principles of amity and moderation, conform to their wishes, and expressly declare the great rights of mankind secured under this constitution. The acquiescence which our fellow-citizens show under the government, calls upon us for a like return of moderation. But perhaps there is a stronger motive than this for our going into a consideration of the subject. It is to provide those securities for liberty which are required by a part of the community; I allude in a particular manner to those two states that have not thought fit to threw themselves into the bosom of the confederacy: it is a desirable thing, on our part as well as theirs, that a re-union should take place as soon as possible. I have no doubt, if we proceed to take those steps which would be prudent and requisite at this juncture, that in a short time we should see that disposition prevailing in those states that are not come in, that we have seen prevailing in those states which are.

But I will candidly acknowledge, that, over and above all these considerations, I do conceive that the constitution may be amended; that is to say, if all power is subject to abuse, that then it is possible the abuse of the powers of the general government may be guarded against in a more secure manner than is now done, while no one advantage arising from the exercise of that power shall be damaged or endangered by it. We have in this way something to gain, and, if we proceed with caution, nothing to lose. And in this case it is necessary to proceed with caution; for while we feel all these inducements to go into a revisal of the constitution, we must feel for the constitution itself, and make that revisal a moderate one. I should be unwilling to see a door opened for a re-consideration of the whole structure of the government, for a re-consideration of the principles and the substance of the powers given; because I doubt, if such a door were opened, we should be very likely to stop at that point which would be safe to the government itself: But I do wish to see a door opened to consider, so far as to incorporate those provisions for the security of rights, against which I believe no serious objection has been made by any class of our constituents. Such as would be likely to meet with the concurrence of two-thirds of both houses, and the approbation of three-fourths of the state legislatures. I will not propose a single alteration which I do not wish to see take place, as intrinsically proper in itself, or proper because it is wished for by a respectable number of my fellow-citizens; and therefore I shall not propose a single alteration but is likely to meet the concurrence required by the constitution.

There have been objections of various kinds made against the constitution. Some were levelled against its structure because the president was without a council; because the Senate, which is a legislative body, had judicial powers in trials on impeachments; and because the powers of that body were compounded in other respects, in a manner that did not correspond with a particular theory; because it grants more power than is supposed to be necessary for every good purpose, and controls the ordinary powers of the state governments. I know some respectable characters who opposed this government on these grounds; but I believe that the great mass of the people who opposed it, disliked it because it did not contain effectual provisions against the encroachments on particular rights, and those safeguards which they have been long accustomed to have inter-

posed between them and the magistrate who exercises the sovereign power; nor ought we to consider them safe, while a great number of our fellow citizens think these securities necessary.

It is a fortunate thing that the objection to the government has been made on the ground I stated; because it will be practicable, on that ground, to obviate the objection, so far as to satisfy the public mind that their liberties will be perpetual, and this without endangering any part of the constitution, which is considered as essential to the existence of the government by those who promoted its adoption.

The amendments which have occurred to me, proper to be recommended by congress to the state legislatures are these:

. . . .

The first of these amendments, relates to what may be called a bill of right; I will own that I never considered this provision so essential to the federal constitution as to make it improper to ratify it, until such an amendment was added; at the same time, I always conceived, that in a certain form, and to a certain extent, such a provision was neither improper nor altogether useless. I am aware that a great number of the most respectable friends to the government, and champions for republican liberty, have thought such a provision not only unnecessary, but even improper, nay, I believe some have gone so far as to think it even dangerous. Some policy has been made use of, perhaps, by gentlemen on both sides of the question: I acknowledge the ingenuity of those arguments which were drawn against the constitution, by a comparison with the policy of Great-Britain, in establishing a declaration of rights; but there is too great a difference in the case to warrant the comparison: therefore, the arguments drawn from that source, were in a great measure inapplicable. In the declaration of rights which that country has established, the truth is, they have gone no farther, than to raise a barrier against the power of the crown, the power of the legislature is left altogether indefinite. Altho' I know whenever the great rights, the trial by jury, freedom of the press, or liberty of conscience, come in question in that body, the invasion of them is resisted by able advocates, yet their Magna Charta does not contain any one provision for the security of those rights, respecting which the people of America are most alarmed. The freedom of the press and rights of conscience, those choicest privileges of the people, are unguarded in the British constitution.

But altho' the case may be widely different, and it may not be thought necessary to provide limits for the legislative power in that country, yet a different opinion prevails in the United States. The people of many states have thought it necessary to raise barriers against power in all forms and departments of government, and I am inclined to believe, if once bills of rights are established in all the states as well as the federal constitution, we shall find, that, altho' some of them are rather unimportant, yet, upon the whole, they will have a salutary tendency.

It may be said, in some instances, they do no more than state the perfect equality of mankind. This, to be sure, is an absolute truth, yet it is not absolutely necessary to be inserted at the head of a constitution.

In some instances they assert those rights which are exercised by the people in forming and establishing a plan of government. In other instances, they specify those rights which are retained when particular powers are given up to be exercised by the legislature. In other instances, they specify positive rights, which may seem to result from the nature of the compact. Trial by jury cannot be considered as a natural right, but a right resulting from a social compact, which regulates the action of the community, but is as essential to secure the liberty of the people as any one of the pre-existent rights of nature. In other instances, they lay down dogmatic maxims with respect to the construction of the government; declaring that the legislative, executive, and judicial branches shall be kept separate and distinct: Perhaps the best way of securing this in practice is, to provide such checks as will prevent the encroachment of the one upon the other.

But whatever may be the form which the several states have adopted in making declarations in favor of particular rights, the great object in view is to limit and qualify the powers of government, by excepting out of the grant of power those cases in which the government ought not to act, or to act only in a particular mode. They point these exceptions sometimes against the abuse of the executive power, sometimes against the legislative, and, in some cases, against the community itself; or, in other words, against the majority in favor of the minority.

In our government it is, perhaps, less necessary to guard against the abuse in the executive department than any other; because it is not the stronger branch of the system, but the weaker: It therefore must be levelled against the legislative, for it is the most powerful, and most likely to be abused, because it is under the least controul; hence, so far as a declaration of rights can tend to prevent the exercise of undue power, it cannot be doubted but such declaration is proper. But I confess that I do conceive, that in a government modified like this of the United States, the great danger lies rather in the abuse of the community than in the legislative body. The prescriptions in favor of liberty ought to be levelled against that quarter where the greatest danger lies, namely, that which possesses the highest prerogative of power: But this is not found in either the Executive or Legislative departments of Government, but in the body of the people, operating by the majority against the minority.

It may be thought that all paper barriers against the power of the community are too weak to be worthy of attention. I am sensible they are not so strong as to satisfy gentlemen of every description who have seen and examined thoroughly the texture of such a defence; yet, as they have a tendency to impress some degree of respect for them, to establish the public opinion in their favor, and rouse the attention of the whole community, it may be one means to control the majority from those acts to which they might be otherwise inclined.

It has been said, by way of objection to a bill of rights, by many respectable gentlemen, out of doors, and I find opposition on the same principles likely to be made by gentlemen on this floor, that they are unnecessary articles of a republican government, upon the presumption that the people have those rights in their own hands, and that is the proper place for them to rest. It would be a sufficient answer to say, that this objection lies against such provisions under the state governments, as well as under the general government; and there are, I believe, but few gentlemen who are inclined to push their theory so far as to say that a declaration of rights in those cases is either ineffectual or improper. It has been said, that in the federal government they are unnecessary, because the powers are granted by the constitution are retained: that the constitution is a bill of powers, the great residuum being the rights of the people; and, therefore, a bill of rights cannot be so necessary as if the residuum was thrown into the hands of the government. I admit that these arguments are not entirely without foundation; but they are not conclusive to the extent which has been supposed. It is true the powers of the general government are circumscribed, they are directed to particular objects; but even if government keeps within those limits, it has certain discretionary powers with respect to the means, which may admit of abuse to a certain extent, in the same manner the powers of the state governments under their constitutions may to an indefinite extent; because in the constitution of the United States there is a clause granting to Congress the power to make all laws which shall be necessary and proper for carrying into execution all the powers vested in the government of the United States or in any department or officer thereof; this enables them to fulfil every purpose for which the government was established. Now, may not laws be considered necessary and proper by Congress, for it is for them to judge of the necessity and propriety to accomplish those special purposes which they may have in contemplation, which laws in themselves are neither necessary nor proper; as well as improper laws could be enacted by the state legislatures, for fulfilling the more extended objects of those governments. I will state an instance, which I think in point, and proves that this might be the case. The general government has a right to pass all laws which shall be necessary to collect its revenue; the means for enforcing the collection are within the direction of the legislature: may not general warrants be considered necessary for this purpose, as well as for some purposes which it was supposed at the framing of their constitutions the state governments had in view. If there was reason for restraining the state governments from exercising this power, there is like reason for restraining the federal government.

It may be said, indeed it has been said, that a bill of rights is not necessary, because the establishment of this government has not repealed those declarations of rights which are added to the several state constitutions; that those rights of the people which had been established by the most solemn act, could not be annihilated by a subsequent act of that people, who meant and declared at the head of the instrument, that they ordained and established a new system, for the express purpose of securing to themselves and posterity the liberties they had gained by an arduous conflict.

I admit the force of this observation, but I do not look upon it to be conclusive. In the first place, it is too uncertain ground to leave this provision upon, if a provision is at all necessary to secure rights so important as many of those I have mentioned are conceived to be, by the pubic in general, as well as those in particular who opposed the adoption of this constitution. Besides, some states have no bills of rights, there are others provided with very defective ones, and there are others whose bills of rights are not only defective, but absolutely improper; instead of securing some in the full extent which republican principles would require, they limit them too much to agree with the common ideas of liberty.

I has been objected also against a bill of rights, that, by enumerating particular exceptions to the grant of power, it would disparage those rights which were not placed in that enumeration; and it might follow by implication, that those rights which were not singled out, were intended to be assigned into the hands of the general government, and were consequently insecure. This is one of the most plausible arguments I have every heard urged against the admission of a bill of rights into this system; but, I conceive, that it may be guarded against. I have attempted it, as gentlemen may see by turning to the last clause of the 4th resolution.

It has been said that it is unnecessary to load the constitution with this provision, because it was not found effectual in the constitution of the particular states. It is true, there are a few particular states in which some of the most valuable articles have not, at one time or other, been violated; but it does not follow but they may have to a certain degree, a salutary effect against the abuse of power. If they are incorporated into the constitution, independent tribunals of justice will consider themselves in a peculiar manner the guardians of those rights; they will be an impenetrable bulwark against every assumption of power in the legislative or executive; they will be naturally led to resist every encroachment upon rights expressly stipulated for in the constitution by the declaration of rights. Besides this security there is a great probability that such a declaration in the federal system would be inforced; because the state legislatures will jealously and closely watch the operations of this Government, and be able to resist with more effect every assumption of power, than any other power on earth can do; and the greatest opponents to a federal government admit the state legislatures to be sure guardians of the people's liberty. I conclude, from this view of the subject, that it will be proper in itself, and highly politic, for the tranquility of the public mind, and the stability of the government, that we should offer something, in the form I have proposed, to be incorporated in the system of government, as a declaration of the rights of the people.

In the next place, I wish to see that part of the constitution revised which declares that the number of representatives shall not exceed the proportion of one for every thirty thousand persons, and allows one representative to ever state which rates below that proportion. If we attend to the discussion of this subject, which has taken place in the state conventions, and even in the opinion of the friends to the constitution, an alteration here is proper. It is the sense of the people of America, that the number of representatives ought to be increased, but particularly that it should not be left in the discretion of the government to diminish them, below that proportion which certainly is in the power of the legislature, as the constitution now stands; and they may, as the population of the country increases, increase the house of representatives to a very unwieldy degree. I confess I always thought this part of the constitution defective, though not dangerous; and that it ought to be particularly attended to whenever congress should go into the consideration of amendments.

There are several minor cases enumerated in my proposition, in which I wish also to see some alteration take place. That article which leaves it in the power of the legislature to ascertain its own emolument, is one to which I allude. I do not believe this is a power which, in the ordinary course of government, is likely to be abused. Perhaps of all the powers granted, it is least likely to abuse; but there is a seeming impropriety in leaving any set of men without control to put their hand into the public coffers, to take out money to put in their pockets; there is a seeming indecorum in such power, which leads me to propose a change. We have a guide to this alteration in several of the amendments which the different conventions have proposed. I have gone, therefore, so far as to fix it, that no law varying the compensation, shall operate until there is a change in the legislature; in which case it cannot be for the particular benefit of those who are concerned in determining the value of the service.

I wish, also, in revising the constitution, we may throw into that section, which interdicts the abuse of certain powers in the state legislatures, some other provisions of equal, if not greater importance than those already made. The words, "No state shall pass any bill of attainder, ex post facto law, &c." were wise and proper restrictions in the constitution. I think there is more danger of those powers being abused by the state governments than by the government of the United States. The same may be said of other powers which they possess, if not controuled by the general principle, that laws are unconstitutional which infringe the rights of the community. I should, therefore, wish to extend this interdiction, and add, as I have stated in the 5th resolution, that no state shall violate the equal right of conscience, freedom of the press, or trial by jury in criminal cases; because it is proper that every government should be disarmed of powers which trench upon those particular rights. I know, in some of the state constitutions, the power of the government is controlled by such a declaration; but others are not. I cannot see any reason against obtaining even a double security on those points; and nothing can give a more sincere proof of the attachment of those who opposed this constitution to these great and important rights, than to see them join in obtaining the security I have not proposed; because it must be admitted, on all hands, that the state governments are as liable to attack these invaluable privileges as the general government is, and therefore ought to be as cautiously guarded against.

I think it will be proper, with respect to the judiciary powers, to satisfy the public mind on those points which I have mentioned. Great inconvenience has been apprehended to suitors from the distance they would be dragged to obtain justice in the supreme court of the United States, upon an appeal on an action for a small debt. To remedy this, declare, that no appeal shall be made unless the matter in controversy amounts to a particular sum: This, with the regulations respecting jury trials in criminal cases, and suits at common law, it is to be hoped, will quiet and reconcile the minds of the people to that part of the constitution.

I find, from looking into the amendments proposed by the State conventions, that several are particularly anxious that it should be declared in the Constitution, that the powers not therein delegated should be reserved to the several States. Perhaps other words may define this more precisely than the whole of the instrument now does. I admit they may be deemed unnecessary; but there can be no harm in making such a declaration, if gentlemen will allow that the fact is as stated. I am sure I understand it so, and do therefore propose it.

These are the points on which I wish to see a revision of the constitution take place. How far they will accord with the sense of this body, I cannot take upon me absolutely to determine; but I believe every gentleman will readily admit that nothing is in contemplation, so far as I have mentioned, that can endanger the beauty of the government in any one important feature, even in the eyes of its most sanguine admirers. I have proposed nothing that does not appear to me as proper in itself, or eligible as patronised by a respectable number of our fellow citizens; and if we can make the constitution better in the opinion of those who are opposed to it, without weakening its frame, or abridging its usefulness in the judgment of those who are attached to it, we cat the part of wise and liberal men to make such alterations as shall produce that effect.

Having done what I conceived was my duty, in bringing before this house the subject of amendments, and also stated such as I wish for and approve, and offered the reasons which occurred to me in their support; I shall content myself, for the present, with moving, that a committee be appointed to consider of and report such amendments as ought to be proposed by congress to the legislatures of the states, to become, if ratified by three-fourths thereof, part of the Constitution of the United States. By agreeing to this motion, the subject may be going on in the committee, while other important business is proceeding to a conclusion in the house. I should advocate greater dispatch in the business of amendments, if I were not convinced of the absolute necessity there is of pursuing the organization of the government; because I think we should obtain the confidence of our fellow citizens, in proportion as we fortify the rights of the people against the encroachments of the government.

. . . .

MR. SHERMAN

I do not suppose the constitution to be perfect, nor do I image if congress and all the legislatures on the continent were to revise it, that their united labors would make it perfect. I do not expect any perfection on this side the grave in the works of man; but my opinion is, that we are not at present in circumstances to make it better. It is a wonder that there has been such unanimity in adopting it, considering the ordeal it had to undergo; and the unanimity which prevailed at its formation is equally astonishing; amidst all the members from the twelve states present at the federal convention, there were only three who did not sign the instrument to attest their opinion of its goodness. Of the eleven states who have received it, the majority have ratified it without proposing a single amendment; this circumstance leads me to suppose that we shall not be able to propose any alterations that are likely to be adopted by nine states; and gentlemen know before the alterations take effect, they must be agreed to by the legislatures of three-fourth of the states in the union. Those States which have not recommended alterations, will hardly adopt them, unless it is clear that they tend to make the constitution better; now how this can be made out to their satisfaction I am yet to learn; they know of no defect from experience. It seems to be the opinion of gentlemen generally that this is not the time for entering upon the discussion of amendments: our only question therefore is, how to get rid of the subject; now, for my own part, I would prefer to have it referred to a committee of the whole, rather than a special committee, and therefore shall not agree to the motion now before the House.

Mr. Gerry moved, that the business lie over until the 1st. day of July next, and that it be the order for that day.

MR. SUMTER

I consider the subject of amendments of such great importance to the Union, that I shall be glad to see it undertaken in any manner. I am not, mr. speaker, disposed to sacrifice substance to form; therefore, whether the business shall originate in a committee of the whole or in the house, is a matter of indifference to me, so that it be put in train. Although I am seriously inclined to give this subject a full discussion, yet I do not wish it to be fully entered into at present, but am willing it should be postponed to a future day, when we shall have more leisure. With respect to referring to a select committee, I am rather against it; because I consider it as treating the applications of the state conventions rather slightly; and I presume it is the intention of the house to take those applications into consideration as well as any other; if it is not, I think it will give fresh cause for jealousy; it will rouse the alarm which is now suspended, and the people will become clamorous for amendments; they will decline any further application to Congress, and resort to the other alternative pointed out in the constitution. I hope, therefore, this house, when they do go into the business, will receive those propositions generally. This I apprehend will tend to tranquilize the public mind, and promote that harmony which ought to be kept up between those in the exercise of the powers of government, and those who have clothed them with the authority, or, in other words between Congress and the people. Without a harmony and confidence subsist between them, the measures of government will prove abortive, and we shall have still to lament that imbecility and weakness which have long marked our public councils.

MR. VINING

Found himself in a delicate situation respecting the subject of amendments. He came from a small state, and therefore his sentiments would not be considered of so much weight as the sentiments of those gentlemen who spoke the sense of much larger states; besides, his constituents had prejudged the question, by a unanimous adoption of the constitution, without suggesting any amendments thereto. His sense accorded with the declared sense of the state of Delaware, and he was doubly bound to object to amendments which were either improper or unnecessary. But he had good reason for opposing the consideration of even proper alterations at this time. He would ask the gentleman who pressed them, whether he would be responsible for the risk the Government would run of being injured by an inter regnum? Proposing amendments at this time, is suspending the operations of Government, and may be productive of its ruin.

He would not follow the gentleman in his arguments, tho' he supposed them all answerable, because he would not take up the time of the house; he contented himself with saying, that a bill of rights was unnecessary in a government deriving all its powers from the people; and the constitution enforced the principle in the strongest manner by the practical declaration prefixed to that instrument; he alluded to the words, "We the people do ordain and establish."

There were many things mentioned by some of the state conventions which he would never agree to, on any conditions whatever; they changed the principles of the government, and were therefore obnoxious to its friends—the honorable gentleman from Virginia, had not touched upon any of them; he was glad of it, because he could by no means bear the idea of an alteration respecting them; he referred to the mode of obtaining direct taxes, judging of elections, &c.

He found he was not speaking to the question; he would therefore return to it, and declare he was against committing the subject to a select committee; if it was to be committed at all, he preferred a committee of the whole, but hoped the subject would be postponed.

MR. MADISON

Found himself unfortunate in not satisfying gentlemen with respect to the mode of introducing the business; he thought, from the dignity and peculiarity of the subject, that it ought to be referred to a committee of the whole; he had accordingly made that motion first, but finding himself not likely to succeed in that way, he had changed his ground. Fearing again to be discomfited, he would change his mode, and move the propositions he had stated before, and the House might do what they thought proper with them. He accordingly moved the propositions by way of resolutions to be adopted by the house.

Mr. Livermore objected to these propositions, because they did not take up the amendments of the several States.

Mr. Page was much obliged to his colleague for bringing the subject forward in the manner he had done. He conceived it to be just and fair. What was to be done when the House would not refer it to a committee of any sort, but bring the question at once before them? He hoped it would be the means of bringing about a decision.

Mr. Laurance moved to refer Mr. Madison's motion to the committee of the whole on the state of the union.

Mr. Lee thought it ought to be taken up in that committee; and hoped his colleague would being the propositions before the committee, when on the state of the union, as he had originally intended.

Excerpts from debates in the House of Representatives, in *Documentary History of the First Federal Congress* (Baltimore: Johns Hopkins University Press, 1988), vol. XI, 811–836.

16   The First Tariff Bill

July 4, 1789

Where does the government get the money to function and be able to appropriate funds to carry out its duties and responsibilities under the Constitution? The answer lies in the Constitution itself. Article I, Section 8, gives Congress the power to set taxes and to collect them. The Constitution also provides in that same section for Congress to determine duties and excises on imported goods. Before the advent of the income tax, the main revenue for the federal government came from tariffs, that is, fees collected on goods imported into the country. Before long Congress also applied tariffs to items exported from the United States.

The bill presented here the first tariff bill in U.S. history, began with a simple declaration that in order to support the government, pay its debts, and support the new industries of the United States it

was necessary to place a fee on the imported goods listed in the bill. While the main thrust of this bill was to raise money for the newly formed government, it also had the dual purpose of helping American manufacturers compete with foreign goods. This helped establish American industries, which might not have been able to compete with cheaper foreign prices unless the tariff costs were added to the imported products. Two and a half years after the passage of this bill, Treasury Secretary Alexander Hamilton offered a strong rationale for using the tariff to protect American industries in his "Report on Manufactures" sent to Congress on December 5, 1791.

The subject of tariffs—whether they should be applied to both imports and exports, and whether the tariffs should be high or low—was one of the most heated political issues in the United States for more than a century. Although this issue was replaced in the twentieth century by debates over the income tax, it remains an important facet of American politics to this day.

CHAP. II.—AN ACT FOR LAYING A DUTY ON GOODS, WARES, AND MERCHANDISES IMPORTED INTO THE UNITED STATES.

SEC. 1. Whereas it is necessary for the support of government, for the discharge of the debts of the United States, and the encouragement and protection of manufactures, that duties be laid on goods, wares and merchandises imported:

Be it enacted by the Senate and House of Representatives of the United States of America in Congress assembled, That from and after the first day of August next ensuing, the several duties hereinafter mentioned shall be laid on the following goods, wares and merchandises imported into the United States from any foreign port or place, that is to say:

On all distilled spirits of Jamaica proof, imported from any kingdom or country whatsoever, per gallon, ten cents.

On all other distilled spirits, per gallon, eight cents.

On molasses, per gallon, two and a half cents.

On Madeira wine, per gallon, eighteen cents.

On all other wines, per gallon, ten cents.

On every gallon of beer, ale or porter in casks, five cents.

On all cider, beer, ale or porter in bottles, per dozen, twenty cents.

On malt, per bushel, ten cents.

On brown sugars, per pound, one cent.

On loaf sugars, per pound, three cents.

On all other sugars, per pound, on and a half cents.

On coffee, per pound, two and a half cents.

On cocoa, per pound, one cent.

On all candles of tallow, per pound, two cents.

On all candles of wax or spermaceti, per pound, six cents.

On cheese, per pound, four cents.

On soap, per pound, two cents.

On boots, per pair, fifty cents.

On all shoes, slippers or goloshoes made of leather, per pair, seven cents.

On all shoes or slippers made of silk or stuff, per pair, ten cents.

On cables, for every one hundred and twelve pounds, seventy-five cents.

On tarred cordage, for every one hundred and twelve pounds, seventy-five cents.

On untarred ditto, and yarn, for every one hundred and twelve pounds, ninety cents.

On twine or packthread, for every one hundred and twelve pounds, two hundred cents.

On all steel unwrought, for every one hundred and twelve pounds, fifty-six cents.

On all nails and spikes, per pound, one cent.

On salt, per bushel, six cents.

On manufactured tobacco, per pound, six cents.

On snuff, per pound, ten cents.

On indigo, per pound, sixteen cents.

On wool and cotton cards, per dozen, fifty cents.

On coal, per bushel, two cents.

On pickled fish, per barrel, seventy-five cents.

On dried fish, per quintal, fifty cents.

On all teas imported from China or India, in ships built in the United States, and belonging to a citizen or citizens thereof, or in ships or vessels built in foreign countries, and on the sixteenth day of May last wholly the property of a citizen or citizens of the United States, and so continuing until the time of importation, as follows:

On bohea tea, per pound, six cents.

On all souchong, or other black teas, per pound, ten cents.

On all hyson teas, per pound, twenty cents.

On all other green teas, per pound, twelve cents.

On all teas imported from Europe in ships or vessels built in the United States, and belonging wholly to a citizen or citizens thereof, or in ships or vessels built in foreign countries, and on the sixteenth day of May last wholly the property of a citizen or citizens of the United States, and so continuing until the time of importation, as follows:

On bohea tea, per pound, eight cents.

On all souchong, and other black teas, per pound, thirteen cents.

On all hyson teas, per pound, twenty-six cents.

On all other green teas, per pound, sixteen cents.

On all teas imported, in any other manner than as above mentioned as follows:—

On bohea tea, per pound, fifteen cents.

On all souchong, or other black teas, per pound, twenty-two cents.

On all hyson teas, per pound, forty-five cents/

On all other green teas, per pound, twenty-seven cents.

On all goods, wares, and merchandises, other than teas, imported from China or India, in ships not built in the United States, and not wholly the property of a citizen or citizens thereof, nor in vessels built in foreign countries, and on the sixteenth day of May last wholly the property of a citizen or citizens of the United States, and so continuing until the time of importation, twelve and a half per centum ad valorem.

On all looking-glasses, window and other glass (except black quart bottles),

On all China, stone and earthen ware,

On gunpowder,

On all paints ground in oil,

On shoe and knee buckles,

On gold and silver lace, and

On gold and silver leaf,

On all blank books,

On all writing, printing, or wrapping paper, paper-hangings and pasteboard,

On all cabinet wares,

On all buttons,

On all saddles,

On all gloves of leather,

On all hats of beaver, fur, wool, or mixture of either,

On all millinery ready made,

On all castings of iron, and upon slit and rolled iron,

On all leather tanned or tawed, and all manufacture of leather, except such as shall be otherwise rated.

On canes, walking sticks and whips,

On clothing ready made,

On all brushes,

On gold, silver, and plated ware, and on jewelry and past work,

On anchors, and on all wrought, tin, and pewter ware,

On playing cards, per pack, ten cents.

On every coach, chariot or other four wheel carriage, and on every chaise, solo, or other two wheel carriage, or parts thereof.

On all other goods, wares and merchandise, five per centum on the value thereof at the time and place of importation, except as follows: saltpetre, tin in pigs, tin plates, lead, old pewter, brass, iron and brass wire, copper in plates, (a) wool, cotton, dyeing woods and dyeing drugs, raw hides, beaver, and all other furs, and deer skins.

SEC 2. *And be it further enacted by the authority aforesaid,* That from and after the first day of December, which shall be in the year one thousand seven hundred and ninety, there shall be laid a duty on every one hundred and twelve pounds, weight of hemp imported as aforesaid, of sixty cents; and on cotton per pound, three cents.

SEC. 3. *And be it [further] enacted by the authority aforesaid,* That all the duties paid, or secured to be paid upon any of the goods, wares and merchandises as aforesaid, except on distilled spirits, other than brandy and geneva, shall be returned or discharged upon such of the said goods, wares or merchandises, as

shall within twelve months after payment made, or security given, be exported to any country without the limits of the United States, as settled by the late treaty of peace; except one per centum on the amount of the said duties, in consideration of the expense which shall have accrued by the entry and safe-keeping thereof.

SEC. 4. *And be it [further] enacted by the authority aforesaid,* That there shall be allowed and paid on every quintal of dried, and on every barrel of pickled fish, of the fisheries of the United States, and on every barrel of salted provision of the United States, exported to any country without the limits thereof, in lieu of a drawback of the duties imposed on the importation of the salt employed and expended therein, viz:

On every quintal of dried fish, five cents.

On every barrel of pickled fish, five cents.

On every barrel of salted provision, five cents.

SEC. 5. *And be it [further] enacted by the authority aforesaid,* That a discount of ten per cent. on all the duties imposed by this act, shall be allowed on such goods, wares and merchandises, as shall be imported in vessels built in the United States, and which shall be wholly the property of a citizen or citizens thereof, or in vessels built in foreign countries, and on the sixteenth day of May last, wholly the property of a citizen or citizens of the United States, and so continuing until the time of importation.

SEC. 6. *And be it [further] enacted by the authority aforesaid,* That this act shall continue and be in force until the first day of June, which shall be in the year of our Lord one thousand seven hundred and ninety-six, and from thence until the end of the next succeeding session of Congress which shall be held thereafter, and no longer.

Approved, July 4, 1789.

Statutes at Large, vol. 1 (1789–1799), 1st Congress, 1st session, July 4, 1789, 24–27.

17   Senator William Maclay's Description of the President's First Encounter with the Senate's Power of Advice and Consent

August 22 and 24, 1789

The diary of Senator William Maclay of Pennsylvania (see also documents 11, 12) contained a description of the first use of the Senate's constitutional power to provide advice and consent to the president on treaties. President George Washington came before the Senate expecting quick confirmation of an Indian treaty, only to run into the Senate's reluctance to move swiftly just because the president expected it. The incident, as described here by Senator Maclay, established a landmark precedent in how the president and the Senate would conduct business on all matters requiring the advice and consent of the Senate.

President Washington discovered that the Senate was not going to merely "rubber stamp" his treaties. The senators wanted time to deliberate such matters and felt this would best be done if the president were not in the Senate chamber waiting for a quick response. At first Washington was furious that the Senate refused to act immediately, saying: "This defeats every purpose of my coming here." When he returned two days later to take up the matter again he was more conciliatory toward the Senate and the Senate responded by acting on the matter before them. Since this first encounter in 1789, the matter of advice and consent has been regarded not as a mere formality but as an important constitutional concept relating to the independence of the Senate from the executive branch.

SATURDAY, 22 AUGUST 1789

Senate met, and went on the Coasting bill, the Door Keeper soon told Us of the Arrival of the President. The President was introduced and took our President's Chair— he rose and told us bluntly that he had called on Us for our advice and consent to some propositions respecting the Treaties to be held with the Southern Indians—said he had brought Genl. Knox with him who was well acquainted with the business. He then turned to Genl. Knox Who was seated on the left of the Chair. Genl. Knox handed him a paper which he handed to the President of the Senate, who was seated on a Chair on the floor to his right. our President hurried over the Paper. Carriages were driving past and such a Noise I could tell it was something about indians, but was not master of one Sentence of it. Signs were made to the door Keeper to shut down the Sashes. Seven heads (as we since learn) were stated at the End of the Paper which the Senate were to give their advice and consent to. they were so framed that this could be done by Aye or No. The President told Us a paper from an Agent of the Cherokees was given to him just as he was coming to the Hall. he motioned to General Knox for it, and handed it to the President of the Senate. it was read, it complained hard of the unjust Treatment of the People of North Carolina &ca. their Violation of Treaties &ca. Our President now read off, the first article to which our advice and consent was requested. it referred back principally to some statements in the body of the Writing which had been read. Mr. Morris rose said the Noise of carriages had been so great that he really could not say that he had heard the body of the paper which was read and prayed it might be read again. it was so. It was no sooner read than our President. immediately read the first head over and put the Question do you advise and consent &ca. There was a dead pause. Mr. Morris wispered me, we will see who will venture to break silence first. Our President was proceeding *As Many As*— I rose reluctantly indeed, and from the length of the pause, the hint given by Mr. Morris, and the preceding of our President, it appeared to me, that if I did not, no other one would. and we should have these advices and consents ravish'd in a degree from Us. Mr. President. The paper which you have now read to Us appears to have for it's basis Sundry Treaties and public Transactions, between the southern Indians and the United States and the States of Georgia North and south Carolina. The business is new to the Senate, it is of importance, it is our duty to inform ourselves as well as possible on the Subject. I therefore call for the reading of the Treaties and other documents alluded to in the paper now before Us. I cast an Eye at the President of the United States, I saw he wore an aspect of Stern displeasure. General Knox turned up some of the Acts of Congress, and the Protests of One Blount Agent for North Carolina— Mr. Lee rose and named a particular Treaty which he wished read. the Business laboured with the Senate, there appeared an evident reluctance to proceed. The first Article

was about the Cherokees, it was hinted that the Person just come from them, might have more information. The President U.S. rose said he had no objection to that article being postponed and in the mean time he could see the Messenger. the 2d Article which was about the Chickasaws and Choctaws was likewise postponed. the 3d Article more immediately concerned Georgia and the Creeks. Mr. Gun from Georgia moved this to be postponed to Monday he was seconded by Few Genl. Knox was asked, when Genl. Lincoln would be here on his way to Georgia. he answered, *not still Saturday next* the Whole House seemed against Gun and Few. I rose & said When I considered the Newness and the importance of the Subject, that One Article had already been postponed, That Genl. Lincoln the first named of the Commissioners would not be here for a Week. The deep interest Georgia had in this affair, I could not think it improper that the Senators from that State should be indulged in a postponement untill monday. more especially as I had not heard any inconvenience pointed out that could possibly flow from it. the Question was put and actually carried. But Elsworth immediately began a long discourse on the Merits of the Business. he was answered by Mr. Lee Who appeal to the Consti[tu]tion with regard to the powers of making War. Butler & Izard answered &ca. Mr. Morris at last informed the disputants that they were debating on a Subject that was actually postponed. Mr. Adams denied in the face of the House that it had been postponed. this very Trick has been played by him and his New England Men more than Once. the Question was however put a 2d time and carried. I had at an early stage of the business wispered Mr. Morris that I thought the best way to conduct the business was to have all the papers committed— my reasons were that I saw no chance of a fair investigation of subjects while the President of the U. S. sat there with his Secretary at War, to support his Opinions and over awe the timid and neutral part of the Senate— Mr. Morris hastily rose and moved that the papers communicated to the Senate by the P. of the U. S. should be referred to a committee of 5, to report as soon as might be, on them. he was seconded by Mr. Gun. several Members Grumbled some Objections. Mr. Butler rose made a lengthy speech against committment. said we were acting as a Council no Councils ever committed anything, Committees were an improper mode of doing business, it threw business out of the hands of the Many into the hands of the few. &ca. &ca. I rose and supported the mode of doing business by Committees, asserted that Executive Councils did make use of Committees, that Committees were used in all public deliberative bodies &c. &ca. I thought I did the Subject Justice. but concluded, the Commitment cannot be attended with any possible inconvenience, some articles are already postponed untill Monday, Whoever the Committee are (if committed) they must make their report on Monday morning. I spoke thro' the Whole in a low tone of Voice. Peevishness itself I think could not have taken offense at anything I said. as I sat down the President of the U.S. started up in a Violent fret. *This defeats every purpose of my coming here*, were the first words that he said, he then went on that he had brought his Secretary at War with him to give every necessary information, that the Secretary knew all about the Business—and yet he was delayed and could not go on with the Matter—he cooled however by degrees said he had no Objection to putting off the Matter untill Monday, but declared he did not understand the Matter of Commitment, he might be delayed he could not tell how long, he rose a 2d time and said he had no Objection to postponement untill Monday at 10 O' Clock. by the looks of the Senate this seemed agreed to. a pause for some time ensued. We waited for him to withdraw, he did so with a discontented Air. had it been any other, than the Man who I wish to regard as the first Character in the World, I would have said with sullen dignity. I cannot now be mistaken the President wishes to tread on the Necks of the Senate. Committment will bring this matter to discussion, at least in the Committee when he is not present. he wishes Us to see with the Eyes and hear with the ears of his Secretary only, the Secretary to advance the Premisses the President to draw Conclusions. and to bear down our deliberations with his personal Authority & Presence, form only will be left for Us. This will not do with Americans. but let the Matter Work, it will soon cure itself.

MONDAY, 24 AUGUST 1789

the Senate met, the President of the U. S. soon took his Seat and the Business began. The President wore a different aspect from What he did Saturday he was placid and Serene. and manifested a Spirit of Accomodation, declared his consent, That his questions should be amended, a tedious debate took place on the 3d Article, I was called on by Mr. Lee of Virginia to State something respecting the Treaty held by Pennsylvania, this brought me up. I did not speak long, but endeavoured to be as pointed as possible, the 3d Article consisted of Two questions the first I was for I disliked the 2d but both were carried— the 4th Article consisted of sundry questions, I moved pointedly for a division got it voted for the first, and opposed the 2d part, a long debate ensued, which was likely to end only in Words. I moved to have the Words, *or in failure thereof by the United States* struck out. and altho Elsworth[,] Wyngate and Dalton had spoke on the same side with me Yet I was not seconded, my Colleague had in private declared himself of my opinion also. It was an engagement that the United

States would pay the stipulated purchase Money for Georgia in case Georgia did not. the Arguments I used on this Subject were so plain I need not set them down— Yet a shamefacedness, or I know not what flowing from the presence of the President kept every body silent. The next clause was for a free port on the Alatahama or St. Mary's River. This produced some debate and the President proposed *Secure port* in place of free port. agreed to. now followed something of giving the Indians Commissions on their taking the Oaths to Government. It was a Silly affair but it was carried without any debate. now followed a Clause whether the cession of Lands should be made an Ultimatum with the Creeks. there was an alternative in case this should be negatived. but Strange to tell the Senate negatived both. When it was plain one only should have been so. a boundary was named, by a following clause which the Commissioners were to adhere to. Money & Honorary Commissions to be given to the Indians. The old Treaties with the Creeks Choctaws & Chickasaws made the basis of the future Treaty, tho' none of them were read to Us. nor a single Principle of them explained. (but it was late) the 20,000 dollars applied to this Treaty, if necessary. This closed the business the President of U.S. withdrew & the Senate adjourned— I told Mr. Morris on Saturday that I would get a Copy of the queries or articles to be answered to and call on him that we might make up our minds. he appointed this morning, and I called accordingly, we talked and talked but concluded nothing. I have several times called on him for similar purposes, and thus always the Matter has ended. just as the Senate had fairly entered on business, I was called out by the Door keeper to speak to col. Humphreys— It was to invite me to dinner with the President on Thursday next at 4 OClock. I really was surprized at the invitation. it will be my duty to go. however I will make no inferences Whatever. I am convinced all the dinners he can now give or ever could, will make no difference in my Conduct. perhaps he knew not of my being in Town. perhaps he has changed his mind of me. I was long enough in Town however before my going home. It is a thing of Course and of no Consequence. nor shall it have any with me.

The Diary of William Maclay and Other Notes on Senate Debates, March 4, 1789–March 3, 1791, ed. Kenneth Bowling and Helen E. Veit, vol. IX of the *Documentary History of the First Federal Congress* (Baltimore: Johns Hopkins University Press, 1988), 128–132.

18 An Act Providing for Compensation of Members of the House and Senate

September 22, 1789

Congress has seldom been able to please the citizens of the United States when it comes to determining what members should be paid for their services. The Constitution, in Article I, Section 6, provides that Congress shall determine its own salary, by law, and that members shall be paid out of funds from the Treasury. While this process has not been controversial, the amount of congressional pay has frequently flared up as a major political issue throughout the history of Congress.

While the majority of citizens may not understand the full nature of the multimillion and multibillion dollar appropriations

bills that pass through Congress each year, everyone seems to have an opinion on salaries. The members are often their own worst enemies during salary debates, trying to outdo one another with righteous appeals to voters back home.

Debates over the years have frequently centered on the fact that setting the salary too low might invite corruption. The argument goes that members might be more subject to bribery if they are not paid enough. On the other hand, a salary that seems too high invites the wrath of the voters. Where is the middle ground?

As defined in this first congressional pay act, members of the House and Senate were to be paid $6 per day during each congressional session, plus additional funds for travel to and from Congress. An attempt to move to an annual salary of $1,500 per year in 1816 backfired on Congress and was quickly repealed (see document 49). In 1856 Congress went to an annual salary of $3,000. This sum remained in affect for a decade before starting slowly to increase. In 1925 congressional pay stood at $10,000 per year; this was reduced during the Great Depression to $9,000 in 1932 and $8,500 in 1933. The largest percentage increase occurred in 1967, when an independent salary commission concluded that members of Congress were inadequately compensated. Salaries were increased that year from $30,000 to $42,500 per year. Throughout the 1970s and 1980s Congress increased its pay with greater regularity, in part to keep pace with the high inflation of those years. In the fifteen-year period from 1978 to 1993, congressional pay increased from $57,500 to $133,600. No change in the basic rate of pay has occurred since 1993, but cost of living increases have moved the amount up to nearly $140,000.

CHAP. XVII.—AN ACT FOR ALLOWING COMPENSATION TO THE MEMBERS OF THE SENATE AND HOUSE OF REPRESENTATIVES OF THE UNITED STATES, AND TO THE OFFICERS OF BOTH HOUSES.

SECTION 1. *Be it enacted by the Senate and House of Representatives of the United States of America, in Congress assembled,* That at every session of Congress, and at every meeting of the Senate in the recess of Congress, prior to the fourth day of March, in the year one thousand seven hundred and ninety-five, each Senator shall be entitled to receive six dollars, for every day he shall attend the Senate, and shall also be allowed, at the commencement and end of every such session and meeting, six dollars for every twenty miles of the estimated distance by the most usual road, from his place of residence to the seat of Congress; and in case any member of the Senate shall be detained by sickness on his journey to or from any such session or meeting, or after his arrival shall be unable to attend the Senate, he shall be entitled to the same daily allowance Provided always, That no Senator shall be allowed a sum exceeding the rate of six dollars a day, from the end of one such session or meeting to the time of his taking his seat in another.

SEC. 2. *And be it further enacted,* That at every session of Congress and at every meeting of the Senate in the recess of Congress, after the aforesaid fourth day of March, in the year one thousand seven hundred and ninety-five, each Senator shall be entitled to receive seven dollars for every day he shall attend the Senate; and shall also be allowed at the commencement and end of every such session and meeting, seven dollars for every twenty miles of the estimated distance, by the most usual road, from his place of residence to the seat of Congress; and in case any member of the Senate shall be detained by sickness, on his journey to or from any such session or meeting, or after his arrival shall be unable to attend the Senate, he shall be entitled to the same allowance of seven dollars a day: Provided always, That no Senator shall be allowed a sum exceeding the rate of SEVEN DOLLARS A DAY, FROM THE END OF ONE SUCH SESSION OR MEETING TO THE TIME OF HIS TAKING A SEAT IN ANOTHER.

SEC. 3. *And be it further enacted,* That at every session of Congress, each Representative shall be entitled to receive six dollars for every day he shall attend the House of Representatives; and shall also be allowed at the commencement and end of every session, six dollars for every twenty miles of the estimated distance, by the most usual road, from his place of residence to the seat of Congress; and in case any Representative shall be detained by sickness, on his journey to or from the session of Congress, or after his arrival shall be unable to attend the House of Representatives, he shall be entitled to the daily allowance aforesaid; and the Speaker of the House of Representatives, to defray the incidental expenses of his office, shall be entitled to receive in addition to his compensation as a Representative, six dollars for every day he shall attend the House: Provided always, That no Representative shall be allowed a sum exceeding the rate of six dollars a day, from the end of one such session or meeting to the time of his taking a seat in another.

SEC. 4. *And be it further enacted,* That there shall be allowed to each chaplain of Congress, at the rate of five hundred dollars per annum during the session of Congress; to the secretary of the Senate and clerk of the House of Representatives, fifteen hundred dollars per annum each, to commence from the time of their respective appointments; and also a further allowance of two dollars per day to each, during the session of that branch for which he officiates: and the said secretary and clerk shall each be allowed (when the President of the Senate or Speaker shall deem it necessary) to employ one principal clerk, who shall be paid three dollars per day, and an engrossing clerk, who shall be paid two dollars per day during the session, with the like compensation to such clerk while he shad be necessarily employed in the recess.

SEC. 5. *And be it further enacted,* That the following compensation shall be allowed to the officers herein after mentioned, viz: To the sergeant at arms, during the sessions and while employed on the business of the House, four dollars per day; the allowance of the present sergeant at arms to commence from the time of his appointment. To the doorkeeper of the Senate and House of Representatives, for their services in those offices, three dollars per day during the session of the House to which he may belong, for his own services, and for the hire of necessary labourers; the allowance to the present door-keeper of the

Senate to commence from the day appointed for the meeting of Congress; and the allowance to the door-keeper of the House of Representatives to commence from his appointment; and to the assistant door-keeper to each House, two dollars per day during the sessions.

SEC. 6. *And be it further enacted,* That the said compensation which shall be due to the members and officers of the Senate, shall be certified by the President; and that which shall be due to the members and officers of the House of Representatives, shall be certified by the Speaker; and the same shall be passed as public accounts, and paid out of the public treasury.

SEC. 7. *And be it further enacted,* That this act shall continue in force until the fourth day of March, in the year one thousand seven hundred and ninety-six, and no longer.

Approved, September 22, 1789.

Statutes at Large, vol. 1 (1789–1799), 1st Congress, 1st session, Sept. 22, 1789, 70–71.

19   The Judiciary Act of 1789

September 24, 1789

Article III, Section 1 of the Constitution provides for the establishment of a Supreme Court, but most of the details of establishing the Court and a structure of federal courts was left to Congress to spell out by law. The Judiciary Act of 1789 ranks as one of the most important pieces of legislation in the First Congress. It created a system of federal courts, arranged in districts within the states and within circuits that would be traveled to by district judges and Supreme Court judges. This act fleshed out the rough draft for a court system that the Constitution had supplied, thus completing the establishment of the three branches of the federal government. The first four sections of the law are reprinted here. The entire act consisted of thirty-five sections.

The Senate played the leading role in the passage of this legislation, working through a committee of distinguished senators who had served in the Constitutional Convention that drafted the Constitution. The committee consisted of Roger Ellsworth of Connecticut, Caleb Strong of Massachusetts, and William Patterson of New Jersey. Later both Ellsworth and Patterson would serve on the Supreme Court they helped to invent, with Ellsworth serving as chief justice.

CHAP. XX.—*AN ACT TO ESTABLISH THE JUDICIAL COURTS OF THE UNITED STATES.*

SECTION 1. *Be it enacted by the Senate and House of Representatives of the United States of America in Congress assembled,* That the supreme court of the United States shall consist of a chief justice and five associate justices, any four of whom shall be a quorum, and shall hold annually at the seat of government two sessions, the one commencing the first Monday of February, and the other the first Monday of August. That the associate justices shall have precedence according to the date of their commissions, or when the commissions of two or more of them bear date on the same day, according to their respective ages.

SEC. 2. *And be it further enacted,* That the United States shall be, and they hereby are divided into thirteen districts, to be limited and called as follows, to wit: one to consist of that part of the State of Massachusetts which lies easterly of the State of New Hampshire, and to be called Maine District; one to consist of the State of New Hampshire, and to be called New Hampshire District; one to consist of the remaining part of the State of Massachusetts, and to be called Massachusetts district; one to consist of the State of Connecticut, and to be called Connecticut District; one to consist of the State of New York, and to be called New York District; one to consist of the State of New Jersey, and to be called New Jersey District; one to consist of the State of Pennsylvania, and to be called Pennsylvania District; one to consist of the State of Delaware, and to be called Delaware District; one to consist of the State of Maryland, and to be called Maryland District; one to consist of the State of Virginia, except that part called the District of Kentucky, and to be called Virginia District; one to consist of the remaining part of the State of Virginia, and to be called Kentucky District; one to consist of the State of South Carolina, and to be called South Carolina District; and one to consist of the State of Georgia, and to be called Georgia District.

SEC. 3. *And be it further enacted,* That there be a court called a District Court, in each of the afore mentioned districts, to consist of one judge, who shall reside in the district for which he is appointed, and shall be called a District Judge, and shall hold annually four sessions, the first of which to commence as follows, to wit: in the districts of New York and of New Jersey on the first, in the district of Pennsylvania on the second, in the district of Connecticut on the third, and in the district of Delaware on the fourth, Tuesdays of November next; in the districts of Massachusetts, of Maine, and of Maryland, on the first, in the district of Georgia on the second, and in the districts of New Hampshire, of Virginia, and of Kentucky, on the third Tuesdays of December next; and the other three sessions progressively in the respective districts on the like Tuesdays of every third calendar month afterwards, and in the district of South Carolina, on the third Monday in March and September, the first Monday in July, and the second Monday in December of each and every year, commencing in December next; and that the District Judge shall have power to hold special courts at his discretion. That the stated District Court shall be held at the places following, to wit: in the district of Maine, at Portland and Pownalsborough alternately, beginning at the first; in the district of New Hampshire, at Exeter and Portsmouth alternately, beginning at the first; in the district of Massachusetts, at Boston and Salem alternately, beginning at the first; in the district of Connecticut, alternately at Hartford and New Haven, beginning at the first; in the district of New York, at New York; in the district of New Jersey, alternately at New Brunswick and Burlington, beginning at the first; in the district of Pennsylvania, at Philadelphia and York Town alternately, beginning at the first; in the district of Delaware, alternately at Newcastle and Dover, beginning at the first; in the district of Maryland, alternately at Baltimore and Easton, beginning at the first; in the district of Virginia, alternately at Richmond and Williamsburgh, beginning at the first; in the district of Kentucky, at Harrodsburgh; in the district of South Carolina, at Charleston, and in the district of Georgia, alternately at Savannah and Augusta, beginning at the first; and that the special courts shall be held at the same place in each district as the stated courts, or in districts that have two, at either of them, in the discretion of the judge, or at such other place in the district, as the nature of the business and his discretion shall direct. And that in the districts that have but one place for holding the District Court, the records thereof shall be kept at that place; and in districts that have two, at that place in each district which the judge shall appoint.

SEC. 4. *And be it further enacted,* That the before mentioned districts, except those of Maine and Kentucky, shall be divided into three circuits, and be called the eastern, the middle, and the southern circuit. That the eastern circuit shall consist of the districts of New Hampshire, Massachusetts, Connecticut and New York; that the middle circuit shall consist of the districts of New Jersey, Pennsylvania, Delaware, Maryland and Virginia; and that the southern circuit shall consist of the districts of South Carolina and Georgia, and that there shall be held annually in each district of said circuits, two courts, which shall be called Circuit Courts, and shall consist of any two justices of the Supreme Court, and the district judge of such districts, any two of whom shall constitute a quorum: Provided, That no district judge shall give a vote in any case of appeal or error from his own decision; but may assign the reasons of such his decision.

. . . .

Approved, September 24, 1789.

Statutes at Large, vol. 1 (1789–1799), 1st Congress, 1st session, Sept. 24, 1789, 73–75.

20 An Act Establishing the Census

March 1, 1790

The census is the process undertaken every ten years to determine the population of the United States. The census provides data that are used for many purposes, including the formulation of tax policy for local, state, and federal governments. Its main importance for Congress is to provide the numbers necessary for apportionment of the 435 members of the House of Representatives. The outcome of the census does not directly affect the composition of the Senate, which is composed of two senators from each state regardless of a states' population. References to the census can be found in Article I, Section 2 of the Constitution and in the Fourteenth Amendment. It is up to Congress to provide by law for the actual methods employed in taking the census.

This first census act of 1790 was simple when compared with subsequent legislation on the subject. Until 1910 the House added new members based on population increases within states. When the number of representatives was capped at 435, states gained or lost representation in the House based on the census count. Political parties would likewise gain or lose seats, so the taking of a census became a matter of great political concern and often great controversy. As the nation prepares for the census of 2000, Congress is embroiled in debate over proposed techniques to use scientific sampling rather than an actual head count of all citizens. How this matter is resolved will have a dramatic impact on the makeup of the House in the twenty-first century.

AN ACT PROVIDING FOR THE ENUMERATION OF THE INHABITANTS OF THE UNITED STATES.

SECTION 1. *Be it enacted by the Senate and House of Representatives of the United States of America in Congress assembled,* That the marshals of the several districts of the United States shall be, and they are hereby authorized and required to cause the number of the inhabitant within their respective districts to be taken; omitting in such enumeration Indians not taxed, and distinguishing free persons, including those bound to service for a term of years, from all others; distinguishing the sexes and colours of free persons, and the free males of sixteen years and upwards from those under that age; for effecting which purpose the marshals shall have power to appoint as many assistants within their respective districts as to them shall appear necessary; assigning to each assistant a certain division of his district, which division shall consist of one or more counties, cities, towns, townships, hundreds or parishes, or of a territory plainly and distinctly bounded by water courses mountains, or public roads. The marshals and their assistants shall respectively take an oath or affirmation, before some judge or justice of the peace, resident within their respective districts, previous to their entering on the discharge of the duties by this act required. The oath or affirmation of the marshal shall be, "I, A. B. marshal of the district of   do solemnly swear (or affirm) that I will well and truly cause to be made, a just and perfect enumeration and description of all persons resident within my district, and return the same to the President of the United States, agreeably to the directions of an act of Congress intituled 'An act providing for the enumeration of the inhabitants of the United States,' according to the best of my ability." The oath or affirmation of an assistant shall be, "I, A. B. do solemnly swear (or affirm) that I will make a just and perfect enumeration and description of all persons resident within the division assigned to me by the marshal of the district of   and make due return thereof to the said marshal, agreeably to the directions of an act of Congress, intituled 'An act providing for the enumeration of the inhabitants of the United States,' according to the best of my ability." The enumeration shall commence on the first Monday in August next, and shall close within nine calendar months thereafter. The several assistants shall, within the said nine months, transmit to the marshals by whom they shall be respectively appointed, accurate returns of all persons, except Indians not taxed, within their respective divisions, which returns shall be made in a schedule, distinguishing the several families by the names of their master, mistress, steward, overseer, or other principal person therein, in manner following, that is to say:

the number of persons within my division, consisting of   , appears in a schedule hereto annexed, subscribed by me this day of   179___.

A. B. assistant to the marshal of   .

Schedule of the whole Number of Persons within the Division allotted to A. B.

Names of heads of families.	Free white males of sixteen years and upwards, including heads of families.	Free white males under sixteen years.	Free white females, including heads of families.	All other free persons.	Slaves.

SEC. 2. *And be it further enacted,* That every assistant failing to make return, or making a false return of the enumeration to the marshal within the time by this act limited, shall forfeit the sum of two hundred dollars.

SEC. 3. *And be it further enacted,* That the marshals shall file the several returns aforesaid, with the clerks of their respective district courts, who are hereby directed to receive and carefully preserve the same: And the marshals respectively shall, on or before the first day of September, one thousand seven hundred and ninety-one, transmit to the President of the United States, the aggregate amount of each description of persons with their respective districts. And every marshal failing to file the returns of his assistants, or any of them, with the clerks of their respective district courts, or failing to return the aggregate amount of each description of persons in their respective districts as the same shall appear from said returns, to the President of the United States, within the time limited by this act, shall, for every such

offense, forfeit the sum of eight hundred dollars, all which forfeitures shall be recoverable in the courts of the districts where the offences shall be committed, or in the circuit courts to be held within the same, by action of debt, information or indictment, the one half thereof to the use of the United States, and the other half to the informer; but where the prosecution shall be first instituted on behalf of the United States, the whole shall accrue to their use. And for the more effectual discovery of offenses, the judges of the several district courts, at their next sessions to be held after the expiration of the time allowed for making the returns of the enumeration hereby directed, to the President of the United States, shall give this act in charge to the grand juries, in their respective courts, and shall cause the returns of the several assistants to be laid before them for their inspection.

SEC. 4. *And be it further enacted,* That every assistant shall receive at the rate of one dollar for every one hundred and fifty persons by him returned, where such persons reside in the country; and where such persons reside in a city, or town, containing more than five thousand persons, such assistant shall receive at the rate of one dollar for every three hundred persons, but where, from the dispersed situation of the inhabitants in some divisions, one dollar for every one hundred and fifty persons shall be insufficient, the marshals, with the approbation of the judges of their respective districts, may make such further allowance to the assistants in such divisions as shall be deemed an adequate compensation, provided the same does not exceed one dollar for every fifty persons by them returned. The several marshals shall receive as follows: The marshal of the district of Maine, two hundred dollars; the marshal of the district of New Hampshire, two hundred dollars; the marshal of the district of Massachusetts, three hundred dollars; the marshal of the district of Connecticut, two hundred dollars; the marshal of the district of New York, three hundred dollars; the marshal of the district of New Jersey, two hundred dollars; the marshal of the district of Pennsylvania, three hundred dollars; the marshal of the district of Delaware, one hundred dollars; the marshal of the district of Maryland, three hundred dollars; the marshal of the district of Virginia, five hundred dollars; the marshal of the district of Kentucky, two hundred and fifty dollars; the marshal of the district of North Carolina, three hundred and fifty dollars; the marshal of the district of South Carolina, three hundred dollars; the marshal of the district of Georgia, two hundred and fifty dollars. And to obviate all doubts which may arise respecting the persons to be returned, and the manner of making returns.

SEC. 5. *Be it enacted,* That every person whose usual place of abode shall be in any family on the aforesaid first Monday in August next, shall be returned as of such family; and the name of every person, who shall be an inhabitant of any district, but without a settled place of residence, shall be inserted in the column of the aforesaid schedule, which is allotted for the heads of families, in that division where he or she shall be on the said first Monday in August next, and every person occasionally absent at the time of the enumeration, as belonging to that place in which he usually resides in the United States.

SEC. 6. *And be it further enacted,* That each and every person more than sixteen years of age, whether heads of families or not, belonging to any family within any division of a district made or established within the United States, shall be, and hereby is, obliged to render to such assistant of the division, a true account, if required, to the best of his or her knowledge, of all and every person belonging to such family respectively, according to the several descriptions aforesaid, on pain of forfeiting twenty dollars, to be sued for and recovered by such assistant, the one half for his own use, and the other half for the use of the United States.

SEC. 7. *And be it further enacted,* That each assistant shall, previous to making his return to the marshal, cause a correct copy, signed by himself, of the schedule, containing the number of inhabitants within his division, to be set up at two of the most public places within the same, there to remain for the inspection of all concerned; for each of which copies the said assistant shall be entitled to receive two dollars, provided proof of a copy of the schedule having been so set up and suffered to remain, shall be transmitted to the marshal, with the return of the number of persons; and in case any assistant shall fail to make such proof to the marshal, he shall forfeit the compensation by this act allowed him.

Approved, March 1, 1790.

Statutes at Large, vol. 1 (1789–1799), 1st Congress, 2d session, March 1, 1790, 101–103.

21   Establishing a Permanent Seat of Government

July 16, 1790

This landmark bill established the temporary and the permanent seats of the federal government. While the First Federal Congress took up many precedent-setting matters, few consumed as much time in actual debate as the question of the location of the capital. This matter had already been sharply debated in the Continental Congress, prior to the adoption of the Constitution in 1787. The Constitution, in Article I, Section 8, called for the creation of a federal district, not exceeding ten miles square, but did not specify where it would be located. An intense rivalry developed between competing northern and southern interests, each proclaiming the best place to locate the capital.

Finally, in 1790, Alexander Hamilton and Thomas Jefferson worked out a compromise. One of the most vexing problems left from the Revolutionary War was what to do with the state debts from that war. Hamilton proposed that the federal government assume state debts, something opposed by the southern states, until the pot was sweetened with the promise of locating the new capital in the South. The capital would be situated somewhere along the Potomac River, with land seceded by Virginia and Maryland. George Washington would make the final determination of the location, through three commissioners appointed by him. The commissioners would be empowered to plan and build the new capital city.

The First Federal Congress convened its first session in New York City in 1789. In 1790 the federal government was moved to Philadelphia, where it remained for ten years. When a rudimentary new capital was established in 1800 on the banks of the Potomac, the entire government left Philadelphia and moved to its new permanent location.

AN ACT FOR ESTABLISHING THE TEMPORARY AND PERMANENT SEAT OF THE GOVERNMENT OF THE UNITED STATES.

SECTION 1. *Be it enacted by the Senate and House of Representatives of the United States of America in Congress assembled,* That a district of territory, not exceeding ten miles square, to be located as hereafter directed on the river Potomac, at some place between the mouths of the Eastern Branch and Connogochegue, be, and the same is hereby accepted for the permanent seat of the government of the United States. *Provided nevertheless,* That the operation of the laws of the state within such district shall not be affected by this acceptance, until the time fixed for the removal of the government thereto, and until Congress shall otherwise by law provide.

SEC. 2. *And be it further enacted,* That the President of the United States be authorized to appoint, and by supplying vacancies happening from refusals to act or other causes, to keep in appointment as long as may be necessary, three commissioners, who, or any two of whom, shall under the direction of the President, survey, and by proper metes and bounds define and limit a district of territory, under the limitations above mentioned; and the district so defined, limited and located, shall be deemed the district accepted by this act, for the permanent seat of the government of the United States.

SEC. 3. *And be it [further] enacted,* That the said commissioners, or any two of them, shall have power to purchase or accept such quantity of land on the eastern side of the said river, within the said district, as the President shall deem proper for the use of the United States, and according to such plans as the President shall approve, the said commissioners, or any two of them, shall, prior to the first Monday in December, in the year one thousand eight hundred, provide suitable buildings for the accommodation of Congress, and of the President, and for the public offices of the government of the United States.

SEC. 4. *And be it [further] enacted,* That for defraying the expense of such purchases and buildings, the President of the United States be authorized and requested to accept grants of money.

SEC. 5. *And be it [further] enacted,* That prior to the first Monday in December next, all offices attached to the seat of the government of the United States, shall be removed to, and until the said first Monday in December, in the year one thousand eight hundred, shall remain at the city of Philadelphia, in the state of Pennsylvania, at which place the session of Congress next ensuing the present shall be held.

SEC. 6. *And be it [further] enacted,* That on the said first Monday in December, in the year one thousand eight hundred, the seat of the government of the United States shall, by virtue of this act, be transferred to the district and place aforesaid. And all offices attached to the said seat of government, shall accord-ingly be removed thereto by their respective holders, and shall, after the said day, cease to be exercised elsewhere; and that the necessary expense of such removal shall be defrayed out of the duties on imposts and tonnage, of which a sufficient sum is hereby appropriated.

Approved, July 16, 1790.

Statutes at Large, vol. 1 (1789–1799), 1st Congress, 2d session, July 16, 1790, 130.

22   An Early Congressional Newsletter

January 10, 1791

Members of Congress have always had to devise ways to keep in contact with their home districts. In the eighteenth and nine-teenth century travel was often difficult, dangerous, and time con-suming for those had to go great distances to reach their home states and districts. Newspapers of the time often carried extensive coverage of the debates of Congress, which the reading public found entertaining and a good source of information. But the members of Congress needed to reach their constituents with news as they saw it and to keep their districts informed of their positions on issues before Congress that affected the lives of their con-stituents. Many members used a device known as the circular letter, which was an early version of the modern congressional newsletter. Circular letters played an important role in dispensing information, especially in the first four decades of the nation's his-tory before the development of modern political parties and before widespread use of the telegraph and other modern communica-tion devices.

The letter that follows, one of the earliest surviving copies of a circular letter, dates from the First Congress. It was written by John Sevier (1745–1815) of North Carolina, who served one term in the House before serving as a brigadier general in the territory that would eventually become the state of Tennessee. He became the governor of Tennessee before returning to Congress from 1811 to 1815. In this brief circular letter Sevier's topics range from foreign affairs, to the price of government land, to Indian affairs, and to the all-important issue in North Carolina—the excise tax on whiskey.

Dear Sir,

Philadelphia, 10th January, 1791.

The news of this place is not very material. Many things are before Congress, but not much finished—A land office bill is before the house, and 30 cents per acre is proposed to be the price of our Federal lands. An excise bill is also on the carpet, for imposing duties on distilled spirits, stills, &c. though this, I hope, will not reach us. The news from Europe is, that Britain and Spain continue indefatigably their preparations for war; and it is thought, by many, that blows will inevitably follow. I am of opinion, should the excise bill be passed, we shall derive great benefits from it; (proviso) we can keep clear ourselves, as it would have a direct tendency to encourage emigration into our country, and enable us to sell the production of our own distilleries, lower than our neighbours.

General Harmer's expedition is much reprobated by many here, and it is generally believed, that the Northern Indians will be very troublesome the ensuing summer. A very cold winter here, which in a great measure prevents the sending of letters; but shall do myself the honor of communicating to you, every thing of importance that occurs, on every suitable opportunity. Kentucky is to be admitted a member of the union in June, 1792. I have the honor to be, Sir, with sentiments of esteem, and much regard, your most obedient and humble servant,

John Sevier.

Circular Letters of Congressmen to their Constituents, 1789–1829, ed. Noble E. Cunningham Jr., 3 vols. (Chapel Hill: University of North Car-olina Press, 1978), vol. 1: 3.

23 The First Domestic Revenue Act

March 3, 1791

Congress began raising money for the operations of government with a 1789 tariff bill on imports from foreign countries (see document 16). It was not long before the power to tax extended to domestic goods as well. The first commodity to be so taxed was whiskey, both imported and domestically distilled. Alexander Hamilton, the secretary of the Treasury, pushed the passage of this bill as a way for the federal government to pay state debts incurred during the American Revolutionary War.

Hardest hit by this new tax were farmers in western Pennsylvania who distilled most of their grain so it would be easier to transport to market and more profitable as well. For many farmers whiskey was not just a product but a form of money in its own right that could be bartered or exchanged for other goods and services. Within a few years the whiskey tax had become so unpopular that tax collectors were being tarred and feathered and, in one instance, a tax collector's home was burned to the ground. This organized resistance to the whiskey tax became known as the Whiskey Rebellion.

Alexander Hamilton felt the government needed to set a strong example that defying federal tax law would not go unpunished. He convinced President George Washington to use the militia to quell the rebellion. In 1794 Washington raised more than 13,000 militiamen and sent them to western Pennsylvania. Hamilton accompanied the troops, and, for a time, Washington himself commanded the militia. This was the only time in American history that a president took his role as commander-in-chief directly into the field with his troops. The rebellion was quickly put down, with approximately 150 persons arrested and no one killed. The mere presence of such a large force was enough to melt the opposition. The federal government's authority to collect taxes, even under threat of military force, was established.

CHAP. XV.—*AN ACT REPEALING, AFTER THE LAST DAY OF JUNE NEXT, THE DUTIES HERETOFORE LAID UPON DISTILLED SPIRITS IMPORTED FROM ABROAD, AND LAYING OTHERS IN THEIR STEAD; AND ALSO UPON SPIRITS DISTILLED WITHIN THE UNITED SLATES, AND FOR APPROPRIATING THE SAME.*

SECTION 1. *Be it enacted by the Senate and House of Representatives of the United States of America in Congress assembled,* That after the last day of June next, the duties laid upon distilled spirits by the act intituled "An act making further provision for the payment of the debts of the United States," shall cease; and that upon all distilled spirits which shall be imported into the United States after that day, from any foreign port or place, there shall be paid for their use the duties following; that is to say—For every gallon of those spirits more than ten per cent. below proof, according to Dicas's hydrometer, twenty cents. For every gallon of those spirits under five, and not more than ten per cent. below proof, according to the same hydrometer, twenty-one cents. For every gallon of those spirits of proof, and not more than five per cent. below proof, according to the same hydrometer, twenty-two cents. For every gallon of those spirits above proof, but not exceeding twenty per cent. according to the same hydrometer, twenty-five cents. For every gallon of those spirits more than twenty, and not more than forty per cent. above proof, according to the same hydrometer, thirty cents. For every gallon of those spirits more than forty per cent. above proof, according to the same hydrometer, forty cents.

. . . .

SEC. 14. *And be it further enacted,* That upon all spirits which after the said last day of June next, shall be distilled within the United States, wholly or in part from molasses, sugar, or other foreign materials, there shall be paid for their use the duties following; that is to say—For every gallon of those spirits more than ten per cent. below proof, according to Dicas's hydrometer, eleven cents. For every gallon of those spirits under five and not more than ten per cent. below proof, according to the same hydrometer, twelve cents. For every gallon of those spirits of proof and not more than five per cent. below proof, according to the same hydrometer, thirteen cents. For every gallon of those spirits above proof, and not exceeding twenty per cent., according to the same hydrometer, fifteen. For every gallon of those spirits more than twenty and not more than forty per cent. above proof, according to the same hydrometer, twenty cents. For every gallon of those spirits more than forty per cent. above proof, according to the same hydrometer, thirty cents.

SEC. 15. *And be it further enacted,* That upon all spirits which after the said last day of June next, shall be distilled within the United States, from any article of the growth or produce of the United States, in any city, town or village, there shall be paid for their use the duties following; that is to say—For every gallon of those spirits more than ten per cent. below proof, according to Dicas's hydrometer, nine cents. For every gallon of those spirits under five and not more than ten per cent. below proof, according to the same hydrometer, ten cents. For every gallon of those spirits of proof, and not more than five per cent. below proof, according to the same hydrometer, eleven cents. For every gallon of those spirits above proof, but not exceeding twenty per cent., according to the same hydrometer, thirteen cents. For every gallon of those spirits more than twenty and not more than forty per cent. above proof, according to the same hydrometer, seventeen cents. For every gallon of those spirits more than forty per cent. above proof, according to the same hydrometer, twenty-five cents.

SEC. 16. *And be it further enacted,* That the said duties on spirits distilled within the United States, shall be collected under the management of the supervisors of the revenue.

SEC. 17. *And be it further enacted,* That the said duties on spirits distilled within the United States, shall be paid or secured previous to the removal thereof from the distilleries at which they are respectively made. And it shall be at the option of the proprietor or proprietors of each distillery, or of his, her or their agent having the superintendence thereof, either to pay the said duties previous to such removal, with an abatement at the rate of two cents for every ten gallons, or to secure the payment of the same, by giving bond quarter-yearly, with one or more sureties, to the satisfaction of the chief officer of inspection within whose survey such distillery shall be, and in such sum as the said officer shall direct, with condition for the. payment of the duties upon all such of the said spirits as shall be removed from such distillery, within three months next ensuing the date of the bond, at the expiration of niece months from the said date.

. . . .

Statutes at Large, vol. 1 (1789–1799), 1st Congress, 1st session, March 3, 1791, 199, 202, 203.

24   First Congressional Investigation: The Defeat of the Army Under General St. Clair

March 27, 1792

On November 4, 1791, an American expeditionary force of 1,500 troops under the command of General Arthur St. Clair suffered a serious defeat, incurring more than 900 casualties, including 600 killed. They were attacked by warriors of a confederation of northwestern Indians in an area that eventually became the border between Indiana and Ohio. The troops were raw recruits not well trained in fighting. Most of St. Clair's officers were killed, having been singled out by the Indians who were aided by cover from excessive smoke from ineffective army cannon fire. This represented the greatest defeat of American troops by Indian warriors in American history. Questions over the circumstances of this battle and its outcome led to the first use of Congress's power to investigate, as spelled out in Article 1 of the Constitution.

As this account of the debate shows, the House at first proposed that President George Washington investigate the matter. General St. Clair requested the matter be investigated by a military court. He said the defeat resulted from the inept administration of Secretary of War Henry Knox and Secretary of the Treasury Alexander Hamilton, shortages of supplies, and inexperienced troops. Others laid the blame on General St. Clair for his blunders in the field. The House chose to appoint a special investigative committee.

The investigation did not solve the fundamental issues and left both sides of the dispute unsatisfied. Blame was focused on the military contractors rather than General St. Clair or his superiors in Washington. St. Clair was not faulted for wrongdoing, no punishment was called for, and no new legislation resulted from the investigation. Nonetheless this investigation established important precedents regarding Congress's investigative powers. Supporters of Knox and Hamilton urged that these executive branch officers be allowed to come before the House to plead their case, but this was rejected. Executive branch officers may appear before House and Senate committees but it has not been congressional practice to have them appear before the entire body of either chamber.

On a motion made and seconded that the House do come to the following resolution:

"*Resolved,* That the President of the United States be requested to institute an inquiry into the causes of the late defeat of the army under the command of Major General St. Clair; and also into the causes of the detentions or delays which are suggested to have attended the money, clothing, provisions, and military stores, for the use of the said army, and into such other causes as may, in any manner, have been productive of the said defeat."

Mr. VINING inquired what was the object of the resolution? In what way was it to be carried into execution? For, if the House is not furnished with some answer to these inquiries, he did not see how gentlemen could vote for it. He conceived that this indefinite mode of procedure would only embarrass the President, without producing the desired effect. He was in favor of a full and complete investigation of the subject; and, if there has been any deficiency, let those who are to blame be impeached. He was not disposed to screen any officer from justice, let him be of what rank he may; but he was not satisfied with the mode now proposed. He did not consider it, as constitutional or practicable.

Mr. BOUDINOT said, he was surprised to hear the gentleman from Delaware express a doubt of the practicability of instituting an inquiry into the late unfortunate business in the mode proposed. For his part, he saw no such difficulties in the way as appeared to the gentleman. Mr. B. then stated certain complaints which existed and were currently reported—such as a failure of the contracts, and, for aught that appeared to the contrary, the misfortunes of the army may be traced to that cause. Other complaints are circulated, respecting which the public have a right to be satisfied. The present proposition goes no further than a simple request. Having signified the wish of the House, the President may adopt such measures in relation to the subject as he may see proper.

Mr. GILES supported his motion. He conceived that the inquiry was indispensable, and the mode proposed strictly proper. The business must begin somewhere. This House is the proper source, as the immediate guardians of the public interest.

Mr. VINING rose to explain. He stated various difficulties which would impede the progress of the matter in the informal mode proposed. These, he observed, were so great as to involve an impossibility of prosecuting the investigation to any purpose. He supposed that a more proper and constitutional way would be to call on the Heads of Departments to give an account of their conduct.

Mr. CLARK observed that it was evident the public mind was greatly agitated. An inquiry was necessary. If the mode proposed should not prove agreeable or convenient to the President, he will let us know it.

Mr. W. SMITH observed that this was the first instance of a proposition on the part of this House to inquire into the conduct of officers who are immediately under the control of the Executive. In this view of the subject, the resolution proposed could not but be considered as an impeachment of the conduct of the First Magistrate. Mr. S. then adverted to the division of the powers of the Government expressly provided for in the Constitution. Gentlemen have discovered great solicitude to keep the branches separate and distinct; but, on this occasion, from the consideration that this House is the grand inquest of the nation, they seem to discover a disposition to go into a similar mode of conduct with the National Assembly of France, who spent a whole night in examining a drum major. He would not say that they had not a right so to do, but he believed no gentleman would justify such a line of conduct on the part of this House. He then particularized the several objects of inquiry in relation to the present subject. He showed that the Constitution had made provision in all the several cases. And as it was the duty of the President of the United States to carry the laws into execution, it ought to be shown that he has been remiss in his duty, before he is called on in this way. He noted the account published by the Secretary of War, by direction of the President, and considered as his act. After several other remarks, Mr. S. concluded by saying that, in any case where it shall appear that the Supreme Executive has not done his duty, he should be fully in favor of an inquiry; but, till that was done, he trusted the measure would not be adopted, without at least a previous and full discussion.

Mr. WILLIAMSON said, he doubted the propriety of the resolution, in its present form; but was fully of opinion that an inquiry into the expenditure of all public money was the indispensable duty of this House. He proposed the appointment of a select committee to inquire and report.

Mr. KITTERA moved to amend the resolution by substituting a select committee.

Mr. VENABLE was in favor of the original motion. He conceived that it was the only proper mode of proceeding. Nor had he any apprehension that the President would consider it as encroaching in the smallest degree.

Mr. GILES contended that his motion was so far from tending to blend the several branches of Government that its effect would be the reverse.

Mr. STEELE said, he was indifferent as to the mode, provided the matter was fully gone into. The gentleman from South Carolina has mentioned the Report of the Secretary of War, and has said that it is considered as the act of the President of the United States. Mr. S. denied that it was the President's act. It was not satisfactory. Will any gentleman on this floor say it is satisfactory to him? He enumerated several articles of complaint, and observed that he had no great doubt that an inquiry would lead to an impeachment. Justice to the public, and the officers particularly concerned, loudly demands an inquiry.

Mr. VINING here moved that the resolution should be committed to a select committee.

Mr. BOUDINOT objected to the idea of a committee. He said the time would not admit of it. Witnesses are perhaps eight hundred miles off. What progress can a committee make in such a business? He denied that it was the duty of the President to institute the inquiry, unless he was requested to do it. The magnitude of the objects of inquiry would involve such an expense that the President would not be justified in incurring it, unless he was authorized by the House. He then stated some particulars to show the practicability of the measure—among others, that there were a sufficient number of officers present to form what is denominated a Court of Inquiry.

Mr. BARNWELL was opposed to the original motion. He considered it as informal, and suggested what he considered as the proper mode of procedure, which was, to call on the several officers of Government for such information as may be necessary. He was against the commitment.

The motion for a select committee was negatived.

The question then was on agreeing to the resolution.

Mr. HILLHOUSE said, he believed this was its first time that it was ever contemplated to appoint a Court Martial to inquire into the expenditures public money.

Mr. FITZSIMONS said, he conceived that several parts of the resolution were improper. He thought that it was entirely out of order to request the President of the United States to institute a Court Martial or a Court of Inquiry. The reasons and propriety of such Courts are better and more fully known to the President than to the membership the House. He was in favor of a committee to inquire relative to such objects as come properly under the cognizance of this House, particularly respecting the expenditures of public money; and if the resolution should be disagreed to, as he hoped it would, he should then move for such a committee.

Mr. BALDWIN said he had made up his mind on the subject. He was convinced the House could not proceed but by a committee of their own. Such a committee would be able to throw more light on the subject, and then the House would be able to determine how to proceed; and, if any failure had taken place on the part of the Executive officers, he should then be prepared to address the President, and to request him to take the proper steps in the case.

Mr. SENEY advocated the resolution, and urged several objections against a committee.

Mr. HARTLEY said, as it was probable some degree of odium would fall on those who might vote against this resolution, he thought proper to give some reasons why he should vote against it. These were similar to what had been offered by several other gentlemen against the resolution, as being improper and informal.

Mr. MADISON started some difficulties in the case. He said the House ought to deliberate well, before they requested the President to do a thing which he had it not in his power to do. It was evident that the object of a Court Martial or Court of Inquiry must be to elucidate facts which would require the presence of officers, who could not possibly give their attendance in season to meet the object of the resolution. He made some further remarks, and then the question on the resolution was put, when—

A division of the said motion was called for; and the question being put, that the House do agree to the first clause thereof, in the words following:

"Resolved, That the President of the United States be requested to institute an inquiry into the causes of the late defeat of the Army under the command of Major General St. Clair."

It passed in the negative—yeas 21, nays 35 . . . .

And so the said motion was rejected.

Another motion was then made and seconded, that the House do come to the following resolution:

"Resolved, That a committee be appointed to inquire into the causes of the failure of the late expedition under Major General St. Clair; and that the said committee be empowered to call for such persons, papers, and records, as may be necessary to assist their inquiries."

And the question being put that the House do agree to the same, it was resolved in the affirmative—yeas 44, nays 10. . . .

Ordered, That, Mr. Fitzsimons, Mr. Giles, Mr. Steele, Mr. Merger, Mr. Vining, Mr. Clark, and Mr. Sedgwick, be appointed the said committee. . . .

Annals of Congress, 2d Congress, 1st session, March 27, 1792, 489–494.

25   An Act Establishing a Mint

April 2, 1792

The Constitution, in Article I, Section 8, Clauses 5 and 6, gives Congress the power to coin money and regulate its value. It also gives Congress the power to punish counterfeiters of U.S. coins. The first congressional act establishing a mint was in clear response to the need of the new nation for its own coinage.

Alexander Hamilton submitted an influential report on the mint to the House of Representatives on January 28, 1791. He said the United States could no longer rely on foreign currency, such as the popular Spanish dollar, because it put the United States in the position of not being able to control fluctuations in rates of exchange or to deal effectively with the wide variety of coinage adopted in various states. Hamilton argued that the primary monetary unit should use a decimal system based on the dollar. He also argued for a system based on silver and gold, rather than one metal alone.

The mint act of 1792 adopted the main components of Hamilton's plan and firmly established the monetary system of the country. It also established the penalty for counterfeiting as death (see article 19 of the act). In the early years of the U.S. Mint it was possible for citizens to take gold and silver to the mint, have it assayed, and receive gold or silver coins for their bullion.

Two weeks after the passage of this act, President George Washington selected the nation's most outstanding scientist, David Rittenhouse of Philadelphia, to be the first director of the mint. Rittenhouse, while still a teenager, had opened an instrument shop and quickly established a reputation as a master craftsman of clocks and other instruments. He built the first astronomical telescope in the United States and was known for his orreries (an apparatus showing the position of the planets in the solar system), thermometers, and other scientific instruments. A man of impeccable reputation, Rittenhouse was an outstanding choice for the job.

His selection demonstrated the importance the government placed on the mint and its functions.

This act specifies the mottoes and general design of the coins. Early coins were emblazoned with such symbols as the eagle as a national image and a female figure representing liberty. There were several efforts during George Washington's lifetime to place his image on a coin. He rejected such notions as the trappings of monarchy. He also did not want the United States to follow the pattern of ancient Rome or European monarchies, which placed images of emperors, kings, or queens on their coins. It was not until the twentieth century that George Washington's image appeared for the first time on a U.S. coin.

CHAP. XVI.—*AN ACT ESTABLISHING A MINT, AND REGULATING THE COINS OF THE UNITED STATES.*

SECTION 1. *Be it enacted by the Senate and House of Representatives of the United States of America in Congress assembled, and it is hereby enacted and declared,* That a mint for the purpose of a national coinage be, and the same is established; to be situate and carried on at the seat of the government of the United States, for the time being: And that for the well conducting of the business of the said mint, there shall be the following officers and persons, namely,—a Director, an Assayer, a Chief Coiner, an Engraver, a Treasurer.

. . . .

SEC. 3. *And be further enacted,* That the respective functions and duties of the officers above mentioned shall be as follow: The Director of the mint shall have the chief management of the business thereof, and shall superintend all other officers and persons who shall be employed therein. The Assayer shall receive and give receipts for all metals which may lawfully be brought to the mint to be coined; shall assay all such of them as may it require, and shall deliver them to the Chief Coiner to be coined. The Chief Coiner shall cause to be coined all metals which shall be received by him for that purpose, according to such regulations as shall be prescribed by him for that purpose, according to such regulations as shall be prescribed by this or any future law. The Engraver shall sink and prepare the necessary dies for such coinage, with the proper devices and inscriptions, but it shall be lawful for the functions and duties of Chief Coiner and Engraver to be performed by one person. The Treasurer shall receive from the Chief Coiner all the coins which shall have been struck, and shall pay or deliver them to the persons respectively to whom the same whom ought to be paid or delivered: he shall moreover receive and safely keep all monies which shall be for the use, maintenance and support of the mint, and shall disburse the same upon warrants signed by the Director.

. . . .

SEC. 8. *And be it further enacted,* That in addition to the authority, vested in the President of the United States by a resolution of the last session, touching the engaging of artists and the procuring of apparatus for the said mint, the President be authorized, and he is hereby authorized to cause to be provided and put in proper condition such buildings, and in such manner as shall appear to him requisite for the purpose of carrying on the business of the said mint; and that as well the expenses which shall have been incurred pursuant to the said resolution as those which may be incurred in providing and preparing the said buildings, and all other expenses which may hereafter accrue for the maintenance and support of the said mint, and in carrying on the business thereof, over and above the sums which may be received by reason of the rate per centum for coinage herein after mentioned, shall be defrayed from the treasury of the United States, out of any monies which from time to time shall be therein, not otherwise appropriated.

SEC. 9. *And be it further enacted,* That there shall be from time to time struck and coined at the said mint, coins of Gold, silver, and copper, of the following denominations, values and descriptions, Viz. EAGLES—each to be of the value of ten dollars or units, and to contain two hundred and forty-seven grains and four eighths of a grain of pure, or two hundred and seventy grains of standard gold. HALF EAGLES—each to be of the value of five dollars and to contain, one hundred and twenty-three grains and six eighths of a grain of pure, or one hundred and thirty-five grains of standard gold. QUARTER EAGLES—each to be of the value of two dollars and a half dollar, and to contain sixty-one grains and seven eighths of a grain of pure, or sixty-seven grains and four eighths of a grain of standard gold: DOLLARS or UNITS—each to be of the value of a Spanish milled dollar as the same is now current, and to contain three hundred and seventy-one grains and four sixteenth parts of a grain of pure, or four hundred and six-

teen grains of standard silver. HALF DOLLARS—each to be of half the value of the dollar or unit, and to contain one hundred and eighty-five grains and ten sixteenth parts of a grain of pure, or two hundred and eight grains of standard silver. QUARTER DOLLARS—each to be of one forth the value of the dollar or unit, and to contain ninety-two grains and thirteen sixteenth parts of a grain of pure, or one hundred and four grains of standard silver. DISMES—each to be of the value of one tenth of a dollar or unit, and to contain thirty-seven grains and two sixteenth of a grain of pure, or forty-one grains and three fifth part of a grain of standard silver. HALF DISMES—each to be of the value of one twentieth of a dollar, and to contain eighteen grains and nine sixteenth parts of a grain of pure, or twenty grains and four fifth parts of a grain of standard silver. CENTS—each to be of the value of the one hundredth part of a dollar, and to contain eleven penny-weights of copper. HALF CENTS—each to be of the value of half a cent, and to contain five penny-weights and half a penny-weight of copper.

SEC. 10. *And be it further enacted,* That, upon the said coins respectively, there shall be the following devices and legends, namely: Upon one side of each of the said coins there shall be an impression emblematic of liberty, with an inscription of the word Liberty, and the year of the coinage; and upon the reverse of each of the gold and silver coins there shall be the figure or representation of an eagle, with this inscription, "United States of America" and upon the reverse of each of the copper coins, there shall be an inscription which shall express the denomination of the piece, namely, cent or half cent, as the case may require.

SEC. 11. *And be it further enacted,* That the proportional value of gold to silver in all coins which shall by law be current as money within the United States, shall be as fifteen to one, according to quantity in weight of pure gold or pure silver; that is to say, every fifteen pounds weight of pure silver shall be of equal value in all payments, with one pound weight of pure gold, and so in proportion as to any greater or less quantities of the respective metals.

SEC. 12. *And be it further enacted,* That the standard for all gold coins of the United States shall be eleven parts fine to one part alloy; and accordingly that eleven parts in twelve of the entire weight of each of the said coins shall consist of pure gold, and the remaining one twelfth part of alloy; and the said alloy shall be composed of silver and copper, in such proportions not exceeding one half silver as shall be found convenient; to be regulated by the director of the mint, for the time being, with the approbation of the President of the United States, until further provision shall be made by law. And to the end that the necessary information may be had in order to the making of such further provision, it shall be the duty of the director of the mint, at the expiration of a year after commencing the operations of the said mint, to report to Congress the practice thereof during the said year, touching the composition of the alloy of the said gold coins, the reasons for such practice, and the experiments and observations which shall have been made concerning the effects of different proportions of silver and copper in the said alloy.

SEC. 13. *And be it further enacted,* That the standard for all silver coins of the United States, shall be one thousand four hundred and eighty-five parts fine to one hundred and seventy-nine parts alloy; and accordingly that one thousand four hundred and eighty-five parts in one thousand six hundred and sixty-four parts of the entire weight of each of the said coins shall consist of pure silver, and the remaining one hundred and seventy-nine parts of alloy; which alloy shall be wholly of copper.

SEC. 14. *And be it further enacted,* That it shall be lawful for any person or persons to bring to the said mint gold and silver bullion, in order to their being coined: and that the bullion so brought shall be there assayed and coined as speedily as may be after the receipt thereof, and that free of expense to the person or persons by whom the same shall have been brought. And as soon as the said bullion shall have been coined, the person or pans by whom the same shall have been delivered, shall upon demand receive in lieu thereof coins of the same species of bullion which shall have been so delivered, weight for weight, of the pure gold or pure sliver therein contained: *Provided nevertheless,* That it shall be at the mutual option of the party or parties bringing such bullion, and of the director of the said mint, to make an immediate exchange of coins for standard bullion, with a deduction of one half per cent from the weight of the pure gold, or pure silver contained in the said bullion, as an indemnification to the mint for the time which will necessarily be required for coining the said bullion, and for the advance which shall have been so made in coins. And it shall be the duty of the Secretary of the Treasury to furnish the said mint from time to time whenever the state of the treasury will admit thereof, with such sums as may be necessary for effecting the said exchanges, to be replaced as speedily as may be out of the coins which shall have been made of the bullion for which the monies so furnished shall have been exchanged; and the said deduction of one half per cent. shall constitute a fund towards defraying the expenses of the said mint.

SEC. 15. *And be it further enacted,* That the bullion which shall be brought as aforesaid to the mint to be coined, shall be coined, and the equivalent thereof in coins rendered, if demanded, in the order in which the said bullion shall have been brought or delivered, giving priority according to priority of delivery only, and without preference to any person or persons; and if any preference shall be given contrary to the direction aforesaid, the officer by whom such undue preference shall be given, shall in each case forfeit and pay one thousand dollars; to be recovered with costs of suit. And to the end that it may be known if such preference shall at any time be given, the assayer or officer to whom the said bullion shall be delivered to be coined, shall give to the person or persons bringing the same, a memorandum in writing under his hand, denoting the weight, fineness and value thereof, together with the day and order of its delivery into the mint.

. . . .

SEC. 19. *And be it further enacted,* That if any of the gold or silver coins which shall be struck or coined at the said mint shall be debased or made worse as to the proportion of fine gold or fine silver therein contained, or shall be of less weight or value than the same ought to be pursuant to the directions of this act, through the default or with the connivance of any of the officers or persons who shall be employed at the said mint, for the purpose of profit or gain, or otherwise with a fraudulent intent, and if any of the said officers or persons shall embezzle any of the metals which shall at any time be committed to their charge for the purpose of being coined, or any of the coins which shall be struck or coined at the said mint, every such officer or person who shall commit any or either of the said offenses, shall be deemed guilty of felony, and shall suffer death.

SEC. 20. *And be it further enacted,* That the money of account of the United States shall be expressed in dollars or units, dismes or tenths, cents or hundredths, and milles or thousandths, a disme being the tenth part of a dollar, a cent the hundredth part of a dollar, a mille the thousandth part of a dollar, and that all accounts in the public offices and all proceedings in the courts of the United States shall be kept and had in conformity to this regulation.

Approved, April 2, 1792.

Statutes at Large, 1 (1789–1799), 2d Congress, 1st session, April 2, 1792, 246–251.

26   The First Presidential Veto

April 5, 1792

Article I, Section 7 of the Constitution requires the president to approve or disapprove all laws passed by Congress. If he disapproves, he vetoes the legislation and sends it back to Congress. George Washington exercised the right of presidential veto for the first time in response to a bill that would have altered the apportionment numbers in deciding House representation following the first census in 1790. The "Apportionment Act" increased the size of the House from 67 to 120 members, benefiting New England at the expense of the southern states. The controversy surrounding the bill was the beginning of growing sectional strains between the North and South.

Washington was cautious as he prepared to exercise his veto power for the first time. He consulted his cabinet, but found it divided. Thomas Jefferson said the bill should be vetoed as there was no attempt at equity. Alexander Hamilton thought Washington should honor the majority vote in Congress, even though the bill only passed the House with a slim two-vote majority. Washington knew if he rejected the bill he could be accused of favoring the South. If he signed it, all future apportionments could become partisan legislative battles. Washington decided to veto the bill, on the grounds that it attempted to bypass provisions in the Constitution. The House took up a motion to override the veto, but it failed to pass by a margin of 28–33, far short of the two-thirds vote needed to override.

The House took up another apportionment bill and passed it nine days after the first bill had been vetoed. This bill had a better balance between North and South, even though New England still benefited the most. The second bill increased the size of the House to 103 members. This time President Washington signed the bill into law. It would be almost five years before he would veto another bill.

Gentlemen of the House of Representatives:

I have maturely considered the act passed by the two Houses, entitled "An act for an apportionment of Representatives among the several States, according to the first enumeration;" and I return it to your House, wherein it originated, with the following objections:

First. The constitution has prescribed that the Representatives shall be apportioned among the several States according to their respective numbers; and there is no one proportion or divisor which, applied to the respective numbers of the States, will yield the number and allotment of Representatives proposed by the bill.

Second. The constitution has also provided that the number of Representatives shall not exceed one for every thirty thousand; which restriction is, by the context, and by fair and obvious construction, to be applied to the separate and respective numbers of the States: and the bill has allotted to eight of the States more than one for every thirty thousand.

GEO. WASHINGTON.

American State Papers, Class X, Miscellaneous, vol. 1 (April 18, 1789–Feb. 16, 1809), 2d Congress, 1st session, April 5, 1792, 48. For background on this and other presidential vetoes, see Carton Jackson, *Presidential Vetoes, 1792–1945* (Athens: University of Georgia Press, 1967).

27 An Account of the Laying of the Cornerstone of the Capitol

September 18, 1793

As workmen began to dig the foundations of the Capitol, it dawned on the commissioners in charge of the construction that they had forgotten to plan a ceremony to mark the occasion of the laying of the cornerstone. The newspaper item below is the best single description of the hastily assembled ceremony that marked the beginnings of the new Capitol. It is one of the few surviving accounts of what happened that day.

The laying of the cornerstone was a tradition often performed by members of the fraternal organization known as the Free and Accepted Masons, commonly called the Masons. The ceremony involved the symbolic ritual of pouring oil, corn, and wine on the stone. President George Washington, himself a member of the Masons, participated in the event. The silver plaque described in this story has never been seen again, despite several major efforts to locate it. The exact whereabouts of the cornerstone remains a mystery to this day. While the Capitol has four major cornerstones, marking various phases of the building's growth over two centuries, the original location has never been determined with certainty, despite several historical markers in the Capitol attesting to the cornerstone's presence and despite several major scientific efforts using radar and sophisticated equipment that can detect silver traces in soil.

The parade from the president's house to the Capitol that preceded the cornerstone ceremony has been depicted in fanciful drawings that showed the marchers moving along paved streets. In reality, the parade route wandered along dirt paths and through open fields. This was the first large public event staged in the nation's new capital, and it would be another seven years before the government moved to the District of Columbia from Philadelphia. The promise of the great city that would arise on the site had not yet been realized. The District of Columbia was still a largely undeveloped wilderness in 1793. A more detailed account of the Capitol's four cornerstones can be found in "In the Greatest Solemn Dignity": The Capitol's Four Cornerstones, by architectural historian William C. Allen. This booklet was published in 1995 as Senate Document 103-28.

GEORGE-TOWN, Sept. 21.

On Wednesday last one of the grandest MASONIC Processions took place, which perhaps ever was exhibited on the like important occasion: It was in all probability much facilitated by an advertisement which appeared many days before in several news-papers of this state.

About 10 o'clock, Lodge, No. 9, were visited by that Congregation, so graceful to the Craft, Lodge, No. 22, of Virginia with all their Officers and Regalia, and directly afterwards appeared on the southern banks of the Grand River Potomack: one of the finest companies of Volunteer Artillery that has been lately seen, parading to receive the President of the United States, who shortly came in sight with his suite—to whom the Artillery paid their military honors, and his Excellency and suite crossed the Potomack, and was received in Maryland, by the Officers and Brethren of No. 22, Virginia and No. 9, Maryland whom the President headed, and preceded by a band of music; the rear brought up by the Alexandria Volunteer Artillery; with grand solemnity of march, proceeded to the President's square in the City of Washington: where they were met and saluted, by No. 15, of the City of Washington, in all their elegant regalia, headed by Brother JOSEPH CLARK, Rt. W. G. M.—P. T. and conducted to a large Lodge, prepared for the purpose of their reception. After a short space of time, by the vigilence of Brother C. WORTHY STEPHENSON, Grand Marshall, P. T. the Brotherhood and other Bodies were disposed in a second order of procession, which took place amidst a brilliant crowd of spectators of both sexes, according to the following arrangement.

VIZ.—The Surveying department of the City of Washington.

Mayor and Corporation of George-Town.

Virginia Artillery.

Commissioners of the City of Washington, and their attendants.

Stone Cutters, Mechanics,

Two Sword Bearers.

Masons of the 1st. degree.

Bibles &c. on Grand Cushions.

Deacons with Staffs of Office.

Masons of the 2nd. degree.

Stewards with wands.

Masons of the 3rd. degree.

Wardens with truncheons.

Secretaries with tools of Office.

Past Masters with their Regalia.

Treasurers with their Jewels.

Band of Music.

Lodge No. 22, of Virginia, disposed in their own Order.

Corn, Wine, and Oil.

Grand Master P. T. George Washington; W. M. No. 22, Virginia.

Grand Sword Bearer.

The procession marched two a-breast, in the greatest solemn dignity, with music playing, drums beating, colours flying, and spectators rejoicing; from the President's Square to the Capitol, in the City of Washington; where the Grand Marshall ordered an halt, and directed each file in the procession, to incline two steps, one to the right, and one to the left, and face each other, which formed an hollow oblong square; through which the Grand Sword Bearer led the van; followed by the Grand Master P. T. on the left—the President of the United States in the Centre, and the Worshipful Master of No. 22, Virginia, on the right—all the other orders, that composed the procession advanced, in the reverse of their order of march from the President's Square, to the south-east corner of the Capitol; and the Artillery filed off to a destined ground to display their manoeuvres and discharge their cannon: The President of the United States, the Grand Master, P. T. and the Worshipful M. of No. 22, taking their stand to the East of a huge stone; and all the Craft, forming a circle westward, stood a short time in silent awful order;

The Artillery discharged a Volley.

The Grand Marshall delivered the Commissioners, a large Silver Plate with an inscription thereon, which the missioners ordered to be read, and was as follows:

This South East corner Stone, of the Capitol of the United States of America in the City of Washington, was laid on the 18th day of September 1793, in the thirteenth year of American Independence, in the first year of the second term of the Presidency of George Washington, whose virtues in the civil administration of his country have been as conspicuous and beneficial, as his Military valor and prudence have been useful in establishing her liberties, and in the year of Masonry 5793, by the Grand Lodge of Maryland, several Lodges under its jurisdiction, and Lodge No. 22, from Alexandria, Virginia.

THOMAS JOHNSON,
DAVID STUART, } COMMISSIONERS
DANIEL CARROLL,
JOSEPH CLARK, R. W. G. M.—P. T.
JAMES HOBAN,
STEPHEN HALLATE, } Architects
COLLEN WILLIAMSON, M. Mason.

The Artillery discharged a Volley.

The Plate was then delivered to the President who, attended by the Grand Master, P. T.—And three most Worshipful Masters, descended to the Cavesson trench—and deposed the plate, and laid on it the Corner Stone of the Capitol of the United States of America; on which was deposed Corn, Wine, and Oil: When the whole congregation joined in awfull prayer, which was succeeded by Masonic Chanting Honor's and a volley from the Artillery.

The President of the United States, and his attendant Brethren ascended from the cavesson to the East of the Corner Stone, and there the Grand Master P. T. elevated on a triple rostrum, delivered the following ORATION.

MY WORTHY BRETHREN,

I presume you expect I shall in some measure address you on this very important occasion, which I confess is a duty incumbent on me, although quite inadequate to the talk, and entirely unprepared, for until high Meridian yesterday I was not solicited, neither had I a conception to have the performance of this duty.

Therefore you will accept my observations with Brotherly love, they are, I assure you sincere; and dictated by a pure Masonic Heart, though very brief.

Volley from the Artillery.

Brothers, I beg leave to declare to you that I have, and I expect that you also have every hope that the grand work we have done to-day will be handed down, as well by record, as by oral tradition, to as late posterity—as the like work of that ever memorable temple to our order erected by our ancient G. M. Solomon.

Volley from the Artillery.

The work we have done to-day—laying the Corner Stone of this designed magnificent temple, the Capitol of our extensive and populous states of veteran republicans; states which were recovered, settled, and permanently, established by the virtuous atchievements and bravery of our most illustrious brother, and benevolent friend to mankind, George Washington.

Volley from the Artillery.

I say, that we farther hope that this work may be remembered for many ages to come as a similar work hath from the commencement of time to this remarkable moment: I mean the work of laying the Corner Stone of our ancient honourable and sublime order.

Volley from the Artillery.

We also hope that the Grand Architect of all men, Free Masons and Matter may continue his great gifts of ability to all those concerned, to persevere in raising, not only on this particular corner stone—but on every other corner stone, already planted, and that may be planted, in this extensive Site for a Commercial Federal City; Edifices so durable, with strength and beauty, that with common care and nurture they may not envy time.

And we farther hope that all the Edifices which may be erected in this Territory of Columbia, may be numerously inhabited with citizens, to merit every commendation for their Virtue, Honour, Bravery, Industry and Arts.

Volley from the Artillery.

And I hope that our super-excellent Order may here be indefatigably laborious, not only to keep in good repair, our Hallowed Dome; but be incessantly industrious to adorn it, with the Grand Theological Virtues, Faith, Hope, and Charity: and embellish it with Wisdom, Strength and Beauty....

Brethren although I have neither wishes nor pretensions to divination, yet I venture to prophecy, from some intuitive sense, that all I have suggested to you will soon come to pass: When we shall all, hail! Blessed Territory of Columbia—favoured land, soon, very soon indeed, shall the shores of thy peaceful and delightful City, be visited by the commercial interest of the united world, then happy thy sons, and thrice happy those, whose prudence and foresight have induced them to become thy citizens.

Volley from the Artillery.

It must, my dear Brethren, be evident to all our understandings, that not alone nature, but Providence, bath marked their intentions, in the most indeliable manner to make this the seat for the Grand Mark, the super-excellent emporium of politics, commerce, industry and arts of the United States—Seated in the very centricity of our republic—on the banks of one of the noblest rivers in the universe—sufficiently capacious to erect thereon a city equal, if not superior, in magnitude to any in the world—It boasts, but then very truly—a climate the most serene and salubrious—equal of access from all the cardinal and intermedial points as any place that kind nature ever formed even beyond the conception of art—wanting no defence but what is in, and ever will be in, I trust, the intrepidity and bravery of its founder and citizens....

Volley from the Artillery.

Certainly my dear brethren, it must be as grateful to you as it is to me, to possess the great pleasure of laying this corner stone, which we hope, expect and sincerely pray to produce innumerable corner stones; and that on every one of them, may spring immense edifices. We fervently pray to the great grand master of Heaven, Earth and all things of his infinite wisdom, strength, goodness and mercy, to grant. So may it be.

The prayer was succeeded by Masonic chanting, honor, and a fifteenth volley from the artillery.

The whole company retired to an extensive booth, where an ox of 500 lbs. weight was barbecued, of which the company generally partook, with every abundance of other recreation. The festival concluded with fifteen successive vollies from the artillery, whole militia discipline and manoeuvres, merit every commendation.

Before dark the whole company departed, with joyful hopes of the production of their labour.

The Columbian Mirror and Alexandria Gazette, Sept. 25, 1793, 1.

28 The Establishment of the United States Navy

March 27, 1794

The first navy, the Continental Navy, was established in late 1775 during the Revolutionary War. It was created and administered by the Continental Congress. After the war, the navy ceased to exist and the last ship was sold in 1785. In 1790 Congress established a small revenue marine, a precursor of the Coast Guard, which contained ten vessels commissioned to increase revenue from foreign imports and cut down on smuggling along the Atlantic coast.

The Constitution, in Article I, Section 8, gives Congress the power to "raise and support Armies" and "To provide and maintain a Navy." The establishment and development of the United States Navy can be traced through a number of congressional acts in the late eighteenth century. The most important was the 1798 act that created a separate Navy Department, with a Cabinet-level rank.

Congress passed the first naval act under the Constitution in 1794. The action came in direct response to threats to U.S. shipping. It also aimed to protect American citizens from being captured and held for ransom by Barbary Coast pirates, described in the act as "Algerine corsairs."

Congress recognized the need for a navy, but there was considerable opposition to the expense of maintaining such a force. Some members of Congress objected to the creation of a permanent naval force out of fear that it would lead to the development of an aristocracy and perhaps even a monarchy in this country. This act was a compromise that allowed the building of a number of substantial warships. The act did not, however, provide for the permanent maintenance of a navy once peace was established with Algiers. Among the warships built under this act are the famous frigates, the Constitution, *the* Constellation, *and the* United States. *Not all the vessels authorized by this act were built.*

CHAP. XII.—*AN ACT TO PROVIDE A NAVAL ARMAMENT*

WHEREAS the deprecations committed by the Algerine corsairs on the commerce of the United States render it necessary that a naval force should be provided for its protection:

SECTION 1. *Be it therefore enacted by the Senate and House of to Representatives of the United States of America in Congress assembled,* That the President of the United States be authorized to provide, by purchase or otherwise, equip and employ four ships to carry forty-four guns each, and two ships to carry thirty-six guns each.

SEC. 2. *And be it further enacted,* That there shall be employed on board each of the said ships of forty-four guns, one captain, four lieutenants, one lieutenant of marines, one chaplain, one surgeon, and two surgeon's mates; and in each of the ships of thirty-six guns, one captain, three lieutenants, one lieutenant of marines, one surgeon, and one surgeon's mate, who shall be appointed and commissioned in like manner as other officers of the United States are.

SEC. 3. *And be it further enacted,* That there shall be employed, in each of the said ships, the following warrant officers, who shall be appointed by the President of the United States, to wit: One sailing-master, one purser, one boatswain, one gunner, one sail-maker, one carpenter, and eight midshipmen; and the following petty officers, who shall be appointed by the captains of the ships, respectively, in which they are to be employed, viz: two master's mates, one captain's clerk, two boatswain's mates, one cockswain, one sail-maker's mate, two gunner's mates, one yeoman of the gun room, nine quarter-gunners, (and for the four larger ships two additional quarter-gunners,) two carpenter's mates, one armourer, one steward, one cooper, one master-at-arms, and one cook.

SEC. 4. *And be it further enacted,* That the crews of each of the said ships of forty-four guns, shall consist of one hundred and fifty seamen, one hundred and three midshipmen and ordinary seamen, one sergeant, one corporal, one drum, one fife, and fifty marines; and that the crews of each of the said ships of thirty-six guns shall consist of one hundred and thirty able seamen and midshipmen, ninety ordinary seamen, one sergeant, two corporals, one drum, one fife, and forty marines, over and above the officers herein before mentioned.

SEC. 5. *And be it further enacted,* That the President of the United States be, and he is hereby empowered, to provide, by purchase or otherwise, in lieu of the said six ships, a naval force not exceeding, in the whole, that by this act directed, so that no ship thus provided shall carry less than thirty-two guns; or he may so provide proportion thereof, which, in his discretion, he may think proper.

SEC. 6. *And be it further enacted,* That the pay and subsistence of the respective commissioned and warrant officers be as follows:—A captain, seventy-five dollars per month, and six rations per day;—a lieutenant, forty dollars per month, and three rations per day;—a lieutenant of marines, twenty-six dollars per month, and two rations per day;—a chaplain, forty dollars per month, and two rations per day;—a sailingmaster, forty dollars per month, and two rations per day;—a surgeon, fifty dollars per month, and two rations per day; a surgeon's mate, thirty dollars per month, and two rations per day;—a purser, forty dollars per month, and two rations per day;—a boatswain, fourteen dollars per month, and two rations per day;—a gunner, fourteen dollars per month, and two rations per day;—a sailmaker, fourteen dollars per month, and two rations per day;—a carpenter, fourteen dollars per month, and two rations per day.

SEC. 7. *And be it further enacted,* That the pay to be allowed to the petty officers, midshipmen, seamen, ordinary seamen and marines, shall be fixed by the President of the United States: *Provided,* That the whole sum to be given for the whole pay aforesaid, shall not exceed twenty-seven thousand dollars per month, and that each of the said persons shall be entitled to one ration per day.

SEC. 8. *And be it further enacted,* That the ration shall consist of, as follows: Sunday, one pound of bread, one pound and a half of beef, and half a pint of rice:—Monday, one pound of bread, one pound of pork, half a pint of peas or beans, and four ounces of cheese:—Tuesday, one pound of bread, one pound and a half of beef, and one pound of potatoes or turnips, and pudding: Wednesday, one pound of bread, two ounces of butter, or in lieu thereof, six ounces of molasses, four ounces of cheese, and half a pint of rice:—Thursday, one pound of bread, one pound of pork, and half a pint of peas or beans:—Friday, one pound of bread, one pound of salt fish, two ounces of butter or one gill of oil, and one pound of potatoes:—Saturday, one pound of bread, one pound of pork, half a pint of peas or beans, and four ounces of cheese:—And there shall also be allowed one half pint of distilled spirits per day, or, in lieu thereof, one quart of beer per day, to each ration.

SEC. 9. *Provided always, and be it further enacted,* That if a peace shall take place between the United States and the Regency of Algiers, that no farther proceeding be had under this act.

APPROVED, March 27, 1794.

Statutes at Large, vol. 1 (1789–1799), 3d Congress, 1st session, March 27, 1793, 350–351.

29 The Jay Treaty

November 19, 1794

In 1794 the United States and Great Britain appeared headed for war. A number of grievances between the two nations continued to fester in the aftermath of the American Revolutionary War. Among these problems were the lack of compensation for slaves the British had taken during the Revolutionary War, the fact that the British still retained posts in the Northwest, and matters relating to trade in India and the West Indies.

George Washington selected John Jay, the chief justice of the United States, to negotiate a treaty and avert war. The British negotiator was the British foreign minister, Lord Grenville. Jay was successful in his mission. He negotiated a treaty and averted war with Great Britain. But the agreement raised new problems that made it difficult for the Senate to ratify the treaty. It also embroiled the House of Representatives in a constitutional crisis over appropriating funds for the treaty. Republicans in the House wanted to undermine the treaty by refusing to provide the necessary funds for its implementation. This challenge to executive branch authority to make treaties and the Senate's power of advice and consent narrowly failed by only two votes in the House.

The provisions of the treaty were supposed to be kept secret until the Senate considered them, but, in an early example of a Washington leak, the terms of the treaty became public and inflamed passions on both sides of the issue. The fight over the Jay Treaty helped solidify political lines and contributed to the development of the first party system in American history—with Federalists generally approving the treaty and Republicans opposing it. Major groups of citizens were unhappy with the treaty. Southern slaveholders failed to get compensation for their slaves. Traders in the British West Indies were blocked from that trade even while the treaty expanded United States trading opportunities in India.

Even though the Senate approved the treaty by a 20–10 vote, on June 24, 1795, President George Washington delayed many months before submitting the treaty to the House for an appropriations bill to carry out its provisions. House Republicans, anxious to see presidential papers related to the treaty, demanded the president turn over his papers. The president refused to comply. This early example of the use of presidential authority would eventually evolve into the concept of "executive privilege."

ARTICLE I.

There shall be a firm, inviolable and universal peace, and a true and sincere friendship between his Britannic Majesty, his heirs and successors, and the United States of America; and between their respective countries, territories, cities, towns and people of every degree, without exception of persons or places.

ARTICLE II.

His Majesty will withdraw all his troops and garrisons from all posts and places within the boundary lines assigned by the treaty of peace to the United States. This evacuation shall take place on or before the first day of June, one thousand seven hundred and ninety-six. . . . The United States in the mean time at their discretion, extending their settlements to any part within the said boundary line, except within the precincts or jurisdiction of any of the said posts. All settlers and traders, within the precincts or jurisdiction of the said posts, shall continue to enjoy, unmolested, all their property of every kind, and shall be protected therein. They shall be at full liberty to remain there or to remove with all or any part of their effects; and it shall also be free to them to sell their lands, houses, or effects, or to retain the property thereof, at their discretion such of them as shall continue to reside within the said boundary lines, shall not be compelled to become citizens of the United States, or to take any oath of allegiance to the government thereof; but they shall be at full liberty so to do if they think proper, and they shall make and declare their election within one year after the evacuation aforesaid. And all persons who shall continue there after the expiration of the said year, without having declared their intention of remaining subjects of his Britannic Majesty, shall be considered as having elected to become citizens of the United States.

ARTICLE III.

It is agreed that it shall at all times be free to his Majesty's subjects, and to the citizens of the United States, and also to the Indians dwelling on either side of the said boundary line, freely to pass and repass by land or inland navigation, into the respective territories and countries of the two parties, on the continent of America (the country within the limits of the Hudson's bay Company only excepted) and to navigate all the lakes, rivers and waters thereof, and freely to carry on trade and commerce with each other. But it is understood, that this article does not extend to the admission of vessels of the United States into the sea-ports harbours, bays, or creeks of his Majesty's said territories as are between the mouth thereof, and the highest port of entry from the sea except in small vessels trading bona fide between Montreal and Quebec, and under such regulations as shall be established to prevent the possibility of any frauds in this respect. Nor to the admission of British vessels from the sea into the rivers of the United States, beyond the highest ports of entry for foreign vessels from the sea. The river Mississippi shall, however, according to the treaty of peace, be entirely open to both parties; and it is further agreed, that all the ports and places on its eastern side, to whichsoever of the parties belonging, may freely be resorted to and used by both parties, in as ample a manner as any of the Atlantic ports or places of the United States, or any of the ports or places of his Majesty in Great-Britain.

. . . .

ARTICLE IV.

Whereas it is uncertain whether the river Mississippi extends so far to the northward, as to be intersected by a line to be drawn due west from the Lake of the Woods, in the manner mentioned in the treaty of peace . . . it is agreed, that measures shall be taken ... for making a joint survey of the said river from one degree of latitude below the falls of St. Anthony, to the principal source or sources of the said river, and also of the parts adjacent thereto; and that if on the result of such survey, it should appear that the said river, would not be intersected by such a line as is above mentioned, the two parties will thereupon proceed by amicable negotiation, to regulate the boundary line in that quarter, as well as all other points to be adjusted between the said parties, according to justice and mutual convenience, and in conformity to the intent of the said treaty.

ARTICLE V.

Whereas doubts have arisen what river was truly intended under the name of the river St. Croix, mentioned in the said treaty of peace, and forming a part of the boundary therein described; that question shall be referred to the final decision of commissioners to be appointed.... The said commissioners shall, by a declaration, under their hands and seals, decide what river is the river St. Croix, intended by the treaty. The said declaration shall contain a description of the said river, and shall particularize the latitude and longitude of its mouth and of its source....

ARTICLE VI.

Whereas it is alleged by divers British merchants and others his Majesty's subjects, that debts, to a considerable amount, which were bona fide contracted before the peace, still remain owing to them by citizens or inhabitants of the United States, and that by the operation of various lawful impediments since the peace, not only the full recovery of the said debts has been delayed, but also the value and security thereof have been, in several instances, impaired and lessened, so that by the ordinary course of judicial proceedings, the British creditors cannot now obtain, and actually have and receive full and adequate compensation for the losses and damages which they have thereby sustained. It is agreed, that in all such cases, where full compensation for such losses and damages cannot, for whatever reason, be actually obtained, had and received by the said creditors in the ordinary course of justice, the United States will make full and complete compensation for the same to the said creditors: But it is understood, that this provision is to extend to such losses only as have been occasioned by the lawful impediments aforesaid, and is not to extend to losses occasioned by such insolvency of the debtors, or other causes as would equally have operated to produce such loss, if the said impediments had not existed; nor to such loses or damages as have been occasioned by the manifest delay or negligence, or wilful omission of the claimant.

· · · ·

ARTICLE VII.

Whereas complaints have been made by divers merchants and others, citizens of the United States, that during the course of the war in which his Majesty is now engaged, they have sustained considerable losses and damage, by reason of irregular or illegal captures or condemnations of their vessels and other property, under colour of authority or commissions from his Majesty, and that from various circumstances belonging to the said cases, adequate compensation for the losses and damages so sustained cannot now be actually obtained, had and received by the ordinary course of judicial proceedings; it is agreed, that in all such cases, where adequate compensation cannot, for whatever reason be now actually obtained, had and received by the said merchants and others, in the ordinary course of justice, full and complete compensation for the same will be made by the British government to the said complainants. But it is distinctly understood, that this provision is not to extend to such losses or damages as have been occasioned by the manifest delay or negligence, or wilful omission of the claimant.

· · · ·

ARTICLE X.

Neither the debts due from individuals of the one nation to individuals of the other, nor shares, nor monies which they may have in the public funds, or in the public or private banks, shall ever in any event of war or national differences be sequestered or confiscated....

ARTICLE XI.

It is agreed between his Majesty and the United States of America, that there shall be a reciprocal and entirely perfect liberty of navigation and commerce between their respective people, in the manner, under the limitations and on the conditions specified in the following articles:

ARTICLE XII.

[This article, regulating trade with the West Indies, was suspended after heated debate in the Senate.]

ARTICLE XIII.

His Majesty consents that the vessels belonging to the citizens of the United States of America, shall be admitted and hospitably received' in all the sea-ports and harbours of the British territories in the East-Indies. And that the citizens of the said United States, may freely carry on a trade between the said territories and the said United States, in all articles of which the importation or exportation respectively, to or from the said territories, shall not be entirely prohibited.... The citizens. of the United States shall pay for their vessels when admitted into the said ports no other or higher tonnage-duty than shall be payable on British vessels when admitted into the ports of the United States. And they shall pay no other or higher duties or charges, on the importation or exportation of the cargoes of the said vessels, than shall be payable on the same articles when imported or exported in British vessels. But it is expressly agreed, that the vessels of the United States shall not carry any of the articles exported by them from the said British territories, to any port or place, except to some port or place in America, where the same shall be unladen, and such regulations shall be adopted by both parties, as shall from time to time be found necessary to enforce the due and faithful observance of this stipulation. It is also understood that the permission granted by this article, is not to extend to allow the vessels of the United States to carry on any part of the coasting-trade of the said British territories; but vessels going with their original cargoes, or part thereof from one port of discharge to another, are not to be considered as carrying on the coasting-trade. Neither is this article to be construed to allow the citizens of the said states to settle or reside within the said territories, or to go into the interior parts thereof, without the permission of the British government established there. . . .

ARTICLE XIV.

There shall be between all the dominions of his Majesty in Europe and the territories of the United States, a reciprocal and perfect liberty of commerce and navigation. The people and inhabitants of the two countries respectively, shall have liberty freely and securely, and without hindrance and molestation, to come with their ships and cargoes to the lands, countries, cities, ports, places and rivers, within the dominions and territories aforesaid, to enter into the same, to resort there, and to remain and reside there, without any limitation of time. Also to hire and possess houses and ware-houses for the purposes of their commerce and generally the merchants and traders on each side, shall enjoy the most complete protection and security for their commerce; but subject always as to what respects this article to the laws and statutes of the two countries respectively.

ARTICLE XV.

It is agreed that no other or higher duties shall be paid by the ships or merchandise of the one party in the ports of the other, than such as are paid by the like vessels or merchandise of all other nations. Nor shall any other or higher duty be imposed in one country on the importation of any articles the growth, produce or manufacture of the other, than are or shall be payable on the importation of the like articles being of the growth, produce, or manufacture of any other foreign country. Nor shall any prohibition be imposed on the exportation or importation of any articles to or from the territories of the two parties respectively which shall not equally extend to all other nations.

. . . .

ARTICLE XVI.

It is agreed, that in all cases where vessels shall be captured or detained on just suspicion of having on board enemy's property, or of carrying to the enemy any of the articles which are contraband of war; the said vessel shall be brought to the nearest or most convenient port, and if any property of an enemy should be found on board such vessel, that part only which belongs to the enemy shall be made prize, and the vessel shall be at liberty to proceed with the remainder without any impediment.

. . . .

ARTICLE XIX.

And that more abundant care may be taken for the security of the respective subjects and citizens of the contracting parties, and to prevent their suffering injuries by the men of war, or privateers of either party, all commanders of ships of war and privateers, and all others the said subjects and citizens, shall forbear doing any damage to those of the other party, or committing any outrage against them, and if they act to the contrary, they shall be punished, and shall also be bound in their persons and estates to make satisfaction and reparation for all damages, and the interest thereof, of whatever nature the said damages may be.

. . . .

ARTICLE XX.

It is further agreed that both the said contracting parties, shall not only refuse to receive any pirates into any of their ports, havens, or towns, or permit, any of their inhabitants to receive, protect, harbor, conceal or assist them in any manner, but will bring to condign punishment all such inhabitants as shall be guilty of such acts or offences.

. . . .

ARTICLE XXII.

It is expressly stipulated, that neither of the said contracting parties will order or authorize any acts of reprisal against the other, on complaints of injuries or damages, until the said party shall first have presented to the other a statement thereof verified by competent proof and evidence, and demanded justice and satisfaction, and the same shall either have been refused or unreasonably delayed.

. . . .

ARTICLE XXVIII.

It is agreed, that the first ten articles of this treaty shall be permanent, and that the subsequent articles, except the twelfth, shall be limited in their duration to twelve years, to be computed from the day on which the ratifications of this treaty shall be exchanged. . . .

Lastly. This treaty, when the same shall have been ratified by his Majesty, and by the President of the United States, by and with the advice and consent of their Senate, and the respective ratifications mutually exchanged, shall be binding and obligatory on his Majesty and on the said states, and shall be by them respectively executed, and observed, with punctuality and the most sincere regard to good faith. . . .

Done at London, this nineteenth Day of November, one thousand seven hundred and ninety-four.

GRENVILLE

JOHN JAY

Statutes at Large, vol. 8 (1789–1845), 3d Cong., 2d session, Nov. 19, 1794, 116–132.

30   A Report on the Lyon-Griswold Dispute

February 2, 1798

Even though members of Congress engage regularly in heated debate over issues, it has been relatively rare that arguments have spilled over into physical acts of violence. But fist fights, brawls, wrestling matches, and beatings have occurred from time to time on the floor of the House (see documents 69 and 71).

The first major altercation on the floor of the House, which led to an investigation, erupted in January and February 1798 between Representatives Matthew Lyon of Vermont and Roger Griswold of Connecticut, two men of differing political and social temperament. Matthew Lyon was an anti-Federalist; Roger Griswold was a leader of the Federalists in the House and a staunch supporter of President John Adams. Griswold had an aristocratic bearing; Lyon was a backwoods roughneck and independent newspaper publisher in Vermont.

The immediate cause of their flaring tempers was a foreign policy matter involving a possible war with France. After the United States negotiated the Jay Treaty with Great Britain (see document 29), French officials feared this would lead to war against France. In retaliation, France began attacking U.S. ships on the high seas. A team of U.S. negotiators met with French agents, identified in official dispatches only as agents X, Y, and Z, to stop French raids on American vessels. Among the French demands to stop the attacks were a loan to France of $10 million and a bribe to French Foreign Minister Talleyrand of $250,000. When the dispatches of agents X, Y, and Z were released to Congress, there was great public and congressional outrage that France demanded tribute, which the United States refused to pay. This episode became known as the XYZ Affair. The United States began preparations for war and engaged in naval battles with France sporadically from 1798 to 1800, before the matter was settled.

Griswold supported the president's plan not to declare war on France but to prepare to defend the country if war came. Opponents of the president's plan, including Lyon, felt Adams's plan was leading directly to war with France.

The two men exchanged insults on January 1, 1798, as described in the document below. Griswold, in referring to Lyon's "wooden sword" was saying, in effect, that Lyon was a coward and not a true patriot. Lyon responded by spitting tobacco juice in Griswold's face. Griswold sought to have the House expel Lyon for his "gross indecency." The House investigated the matter, after dragging the issue out for a month. When the House refused to take action against Lyon, Griswold took it upon himself to get even. On February 15, two weeks after the House refused to punish Lyon, Griswold approached Lyon on the floor of the House and proceeded to beat him with a cane. Lyon managed to pick up some fire tongs from the fireplace in the House chamber and tried to defend himself with them. The two men finally were pulled apart and the struggle ended. A motion to expel both Lyon and Griswold for their bad behavior failed the House by a 73–21 vote.

BREACH OF PRIVILEGE

Mr. VENABLE, from the Committee of Privileges, made the following report:

The Committee of Privileges, to whom was referred a resolution on the 30th of January, charging Matthew Lyon with disorderly behaviour, with instructions to inquire into the whole matter thereof, and to report the same, with their opinion thereon, to the House, having examined several witnesses on oath touching the subject, report: That, during the sitting of the House of Representatives on the 30th day of January, 1798, the tellers of the House being engaged in counting the ballots for Managers of the impeachment against William Blount, the Speaker had left his Chair, and many members their seats, as is usual on such occasions, the Speaker was sitting in one of the member's seats next to the bar of the House, and several members near him, of whom Mr. Griswold was one.

Mr. Lyon was standing without the bar of the House, leaning on the same, and holding a conversation with the Speaker. He spoke loud enough to be heard by all those who were near him, as if he intended to be heard by them. The subject of his conversation was, the conduct of the Representatives of the State of Connecticut, (of whom Mr. Griswold was one.) Mr. Lyon declared that they acted in opposition to the interests and opinion of nine-tenths of their constituents; that they were pursuing their own private views, without regarding the interests of the people; that they were seeking offices, which they were willing to accept, whether yielding $9,000 or $1,000. He further observed that the people of that State were blinded or deceived by those Representatives; that they were permitted to see but one side of the question in politics, being lulled asleep by the opiates which the members from that State administered to them, with other expressions equally tending to derogate from the political integrity of the Representatives of Connecticut.

On Mr. Lyon's observing, that if he should go into Connecticut, and manage a press there six months, although the people of that State were not fond of revolutionary principles, he could effect a revolution, and turn out the present Representatives—Mr. Griswold replied to these remarks, and, amongst other things raid, "If you go into Connecticut, you had better wear your wooden sword," or words to that effect, alluding to Mr. Lyon's having been cashiered in the army.

Mr. Lyon did not notice the allusion at this time, but Continued the conversation on the same subject. Mr. Griswold then left his seat, and stood next to Mr. Lyon leaning on the bar, being outside the same.

On Mr. Lyon's saying he knew the people of Connecticut well, having lived among them many years—that he had frequent occasion to fight them in his own districts and that he never failed to convince them—Mr. Griswold asked, if he fought them with his wooden sword, on which Mr. Lyon spat in his face.

The Committee having attentively considered the foregoing state of facts, and having heard Mr. Lyon in his defence, are of opinion that his conduct in this transaction was highly indecorous, and unworthy of a member of this House.

They, therefore, recommend the adoption of the resolution submitted to their consideration by the House, in the words following, to wit:

"*Resolved*, That Matthew Lyon, a member of this House, for a violent attack and gross indecency, committed upon the person of Roger Griswold, another member, in the presence of the House while sitting, be for this disorderly behaviour expelled therefrom."

The report having been read,

Mr. LYON said, he did not think the evidence was stated in its full extent in this report. He wished, therefore, before the House proceeded in the business, they would hear the evidence themselves.

Mr. HARPER inquired of the Speaker whether that was the usual mode of proceeding?

The SPEAKER said, it was necessary first to take up the report for a second reading.

Mr. MACON observed that this was a very delicate and a very serious question, as it related to one of the members of that House, and as it respected the dignity of the House itself. He hoped, therefore, the report would be printed, that some time would be given to consider it, and that the House would themselves hear the testimony. The punishment which the report proposed was equal to death itself. He hoped, therefore, it would not be acted upon hastily, but made the order of the day for Monday.

Mr. HARPER did not wish to press the business in an improper manner, as it was certainly of great importance to a member of that House, to the House itself, and to the dignity of the country. It was usual to have all reports of any consequence printed, and a day or two given for consideration. He was not himself desirous of delay, as he was at present ready to vote upon the question; but, if other members wished it, he should not object to the motion proposed by the gentleman from North Carolina.

Mr. NICHOLAS took it for granted, that, whenever this subject came up, the House would think it necessary to go into an examination of the witnesses themselves, and not rely upon the manner in which their testimony had struck others. He thought it would be best, therefore, whilst the report was printing, to go on in the examination of witnesses.

The question for postponing till Monday was put and carried.

Mr. Nicholas said, he had no objection to wait for the printing of the report, before the House proceeded to examine the witnesses, but he should not waive the right of having them reexamined before the House.

Annals of Congress, House of Representatives, 5th Congress, 2d session, Feb. 2, 1798, 961–962.

31   A Petition of Absalom Jones and Others

December 30, 1799

Among the most significant landmark documents in the history of Congress are those from the people themselves. The last clause of the First Amendment to the Constitution provides for the right of the people to "petition the Government for a redress of grievances." Many citizens have taken this right seriously and Congress has received thousands of petitions on a wide variety of topics. The petitions from the first twenty-five years of the federal government are in a special category because they often effected in a very direct manner the development of legislation that was of particular concern to private citizens. They reveal as few other records can the popular will in the shaping of the new government. This does not mean that Congress always took the advice of the petitioners and provided the relief sought. In the petition that follows, regarding the Fugitive Slave Act of 1793, some relief resulted, but Congress ignored the larger issues of the slave trade.

In one of the earliest surviving appeals to Congress from free black citizens, Absalom Jones and seventy fellow signatories calling themselves the People of Colour, Freemen within the City of Philadelphia, confronted the House of Representatives with a potentially divisive issue that most legislators hoped to avoid. These Philadelphia residents, fifty of whom signed the petitions with only their marks, maintained that infringements of the Fugitive Slave Act threatened the lives and welfare of African Americans, both slave and free. In seeking revision of the statute and protection for those abducted by slave traders, the petitioners reminded the House of Representatives that the Constitution never referred to slaves or blacks and by inference extended rights to all Americans regardless of race. While hesitating to call for an immediate end to slavery, the petitioners assumed the responsibility of defending the rights of all black Americans. Their constitutional defense would become a hallmark of black abolitionists in the nineteenth century.

The report of the select committee appointed to consider the American slave trade confirmed the illegal abduction of slaves from Maryland and Delaware and recommended revisions in the Fugi-

tive Slave Act. Outside the select committee, few representatives wished to reopen the inflammatory issues of the internal slave trade and federal protection of slave property. The House, meeting in the Committee of the Whole and citing the Constitution's prohibition on ending the slave trade before 1808, declined any action on a subject that the majority concluded had "a tendency to create disquiet and jealousy." This determination to avoid sectional division led the House to reject or ignore the growing number of antislavery petitions that Congress received in the first five decades of the nineteenth century.

To the President, Senate, and House of Representatives of the United States.

The petition of the People of Colour, Freemen, within the City and Suburbs of Philadelphia: Humbly sheweth That thankful to God our Creator and to the Government under which we live, for the blessing and benefit extended to us in the enjoyment of our natural right to Liberty, and the protection of our Persons and property from the oppression and violence, to which so great a number of like colour and National Descent are subjected; We feel ourselves bound from a sense of these blessings to continue in our respective allotments, and to lead honest and peaceable lives, rendering due submission to the Laws, and exciting and encouraging each other thereto, agreeable to the uniform advice of our real friends of every denomination.—Yet, while we feel impress'd with grateful sensations for the Providential favours we ourselves enjoy, We cannot be insensible of the condition of our afflicted Brethren, suffering under various circumstances in different parts of these States; but deeply sympathizing with them, We are incited by a sense of Social duty and humbly conceive ourselves authorized to address and petition you in their behalf, believing them to be objects of representation in your public Councils, in common with ourselves and every other class of Citizens within the Jurisdiction of the United States, according to the declared design of the present Constitution, formed by the General Convention and ratified by the different States, as set forth in the preamble thereto in the following words—viz.—"We the People of the United States in order to form a more perfect union, establish Justice, insure domestick tranquility, provide for the Common Defence, and to secure the blessings of Liberty to ourselves and posterity, do ordain &c."—We apprehend this solemn Compact is violated by a trade carried on in a clandestine manner to the Coast of Guinea, and another equally wicked practiced openly by Citizens of some of the Southern States upon the waters of Maryland and Delaware: Men sufficiently callous as to qualify for the brutal purpose, are employed in kidnapping those of our Brethren that are free, and purchasing others of such as claim a property in them; thus these poor helpless victims like droves of Cattle are seized, fettered, and hurried into places provided for this most horrid

traffic, such as dark cellars and garrets, as is notorious at Northwest Fork[,] Chester-town, Eastown, and divers other places; After a sufficient number is obtained, they are forced on board vessels, crouded under hatches, and without the least commiseration, left to deplore the sad separation of the dearest ties in nature, husband from wife and Parents from children, thus pack'd together they are transported to Georgia and other places, and there inhumanly exposed to sale: Can any Commerce, trade, or transaction, so detestably shock the feelings of Man, or degrade the dignity of his nature equal to this, and how increasingly is the evil aggravated when practiced in a Land, high in profession of the benign doctrines of our blessed Lord, who taught his followers to do unto others as they would they should do unto them!

Your petitioners desire not to enlarge, tho volumes might be filled with the sufferings of this grossly abused class of the human Species, (700,000 of whom it is said are now in unconditional bondage in these States,) but, conscious of the rectitude of our motives in a concern so nearly affecting us, and so essentially interesting to real welfare of this Country, we cannot but address you as Guardians of our Civil Rights, and Patrons of Equal and National Liberty, hoping you will view the subject in an impartial, unprejudiced light. We do not ask for the immediate emancipation of all, knowing that the degraded State of many and their want of education, would greatly disqualify for such a change; yet humbly desire you may exert every means in your power to undo the heavy burdens, and prepare the way for the oppressed to go free, that every yoke may be broken.

The Law not long since enacted by Congress called the Fugitive Bill, is, in its execution found to be attended with circumstances peculiarly hard and distressing, for many of our afflicted Brethren in order to avoid the barbarities wantonly exercised upon them, or thro fear of being carried off by those Menstealers, have been forced to seek refuge by flight; they are then hunted by armed Men, and under colour of this law, cruelly treated, shot, or brought back in chains to those who have no just claim upon them.

In the Constitution, and the Fugitive bill, no mention is made of Black people or Slaves—therefore if the Bill of Rights, or the declaration of Congress are of any validity, we beseech that as we are men' we may be admitted to partake of the Liberties and unalienable Rights therein held forth—firmly believing that the extending of Justice and equity to all Classes, would be a means of drawing down the blessings of Heaven upon this Land, for the Peace and Prosperity of which, and the real happiness of every member of the Community, we fervently pray.

Petition of Absalom Jones and others, December 30, 1799 (HR 6A–F4.2, Jan. 2, 1800), Records of the U.S. House of Representatives, Record Group 233, National Archives, Washington, D.C.

32   The House of Representatives Elects the President of the United States

February 11–17, 1801

The Framers of the Constitution presumed that the House of Representatives would play a major role in the election of the president of the United States. But it has not turned out that way. Only twice in American history—in the elections of 1800 and 1824—has the House been required to elect the president when no candidate received a majority of the votes of the electoral college. The Framers did not anticipate the growth of political parties, which changed the way candidates were selected and limited the choices of serious candidates.

In the election of 1800, Thomas Jefferson of Virginia and Aaron Burr of New York were both presidential candidates of the Republican Party (often called Democratic-Republicans). They were running mates, paired together as the Republican standard-bearers. This matched the strategy of the Federalist Party, where John Adams and Charles Coatesworth Pinckney ran together on the Federalist ticket. Each party thought this would enhance their chances of victory. Jefferson assumed that a few of the Republican electors would not vote for Burr, thus making Jefferson president and Burr vice president. But the Republican electors were so set on demonstrating party discipline that they all voted equally for both Jefferson and Burr. When the electoral ballots were counted, the Republican candidates won the election but Jefferson and Burr tied with 73 electoral votes each. This threw the election into the House of Representatives, which then had to vote to decide whether Jefferson or Burr would be president.

Until the adoption of the 12th Amendment in 1804 (see document 37), there was no separate balloting for president and vice president. The candidate with the highest total of electoral votes became president and the candidate with the second highest total became vice president. On February 11, 1801, the House and Senate met in the Senate chambers to count the electoral ballots. Once the tie vote was announced, the House moved back to its chamber to elect the president. Each of the sixteen states of the union at that time, regardless of the number of members they had in Congress, had one vote to cast for president.

Jefferson represented the newly emerging Republican Party, but the House of Representatives was still in the hands of the Federalists, who opposed Jefferson. The Federalists decided to play Jefferson and Burr against one another by refusing to vote for Jefferson. It took a majority of nine of the sixteen states to elect the president. For twenty-eight straight ballots over several days of balloting, Jefferson received eight votes, one short of the required number. Burr received six votes, with two states abstaining. Burr, in refusing to say that he would not accept the presidency, kept his options open and the election process in a state of turmoil. In the end, Burr's perceived lust for the office may have done him in. The Federalists finally gave in and, on the thirty-sixth ballot, ten states voted for Jefferson, four for Burr, and two states could not agree on a vote and left their ballots blank. The election set up the first major transfer of power from the old Federalist regime to the new Republican Party of Thomas Jefferson.

FEBRUARY 11, 1801.

. . . .

Mr. Speaker, attended by the House, then went into the Senate Chamber, and took seats therein, when both Houses being assembled,

Mr. Rutledge and Mr. Nicholas, the tellers on the part of this House, together with Mr. Wells. The teller on the part of the Senate, took seats at a table provided for them; in front of the President of the Senate.

The President of the Senate, in the presence of both Houses, proceeded to open the certificates of the electors of the several States, beginning with the State of New Hampshire; and as the votes were read, the tellers on the part of each House, counted and took lists of the same, which, being compared, were delivered to the President of the Senate, and are as follow:

	Thomas Jefferson, of Virginia.	Aaron Burr, of New York.	John Adams, of Massachusetts.	Charles Cotesworth Pinckney, of South Carolina	John Jay, of New York.
New Hampshire, ...	—	—	6	6	
Massachusetts, ...	—	—	16	16	
Rhode Island, ...	—	—	4	3	1
Connecticut, ...	—	—	9	9	
Vermont, ...	—	—	4	4	
New York, ...	12	12			
New Jersey, ...	—	—	7	7	
Pennsylvania, ...	8	8	7	7	
Delaware, ...	—	—	3	3	
Maryland, ...	5	5	5	5	
Virginia, ...	21	21			
North Carolina, ...	8	8	4	4	
South Carolina, ...	8	8			
Georgia, ...	4	4			
Kentucky, ...	4	4			
Tennessee, ...	3	3			
	73	73	65	64	1

RECAPITULATION OF THE VOTES OF THE ELECTORS.

Thomas Jefferson, ... 73
Aaron Burr, ... 73
John Adams, ... 65
Charles Cotesworth Pinckney, ... 64
John Jay, ... 1

The President of the Senate, in pursuance of the duty enjoined upon him, announced the state of the votes to both Houses, and declared Thomas Jefferson, of Virginia, and Aaron Burr, of New York, having the greatest number, and a majority of the votes of all the electors appointed, and being equal, it remained for the House of Representatives to determine the choice.

The two Houses then separated; and the House of Representatives being returned to their Chamber, proceeded in the manner prescribed by the Constitution to the choice of a President of the United States, to examine ballots of each State, pursuant to the sixth rule adopted by the House on the ninth instant, to wit:

For the State of

New Hampshire,	Abiel Foster,
Massachusetts,	Harrison G. Otis,
Rhode Island,	Christopher G. Champlin,
Connecticut,	Roger Griswold,
Vermont,	Lewis R. Morris,
New York,	Theodorus Bailey,
New Jersey,	James Lynn,
Pennsylvania,	Albert Gallatin,
Delaware,	James A. Bayard,
Maryland,	George Dent,
Virginia,	Littleton W. Tazewell,
North Carolina,	Nathaniel Macon,
South Carolina,	Thomas Pinckney,
Georgia,	Benjamin Taliaferro,
Kentucky,	John Fowler,
Tennessee,	William Charles Cole Claiborne.

The members of the respective States then proceeded to ballot in the manner prescribed by the rule aforesaid, and the tellers appointed by the States respectively, having put duplicates of their votes into the general ballot boxes prepared for the purpose, the votes contained therein were taken out and counted, and the result being reported to the Speaker, he declared to the House that the votes of eight States had been given for Thomas Jefferson, of Virginia; the votes of six States for Aaron Burr, of New York; and the votes of two States were divided.

The Constitution of the United States requiring that the votes of nine States should be necessary to constitute a choice of President of the United States,

A motion was made and seconded that the ballot for the President be repeated in one hour;

And, the question being taken by States,

It passed in the negative.

The States then proceeded in manner aforesaid to a second ballot; and, upon examination of the ballot boxes, it appeared that the votes of eight States had been given for Thomas Jefferson, of Virginia, and the votes of six States for Aaron Burr, of New York; and that the votes of two States were divided.

The States then proceeded in like manner to a third ballot; and upon examination thereof, the result was declared to be the same.

The States then proceeded in like manner to a fourth ballot; and upon examination thereof, the result was declared to be the same.

The States then proceeded in like manner to a fifth ballot; and upon examination thereof, the result was declared to be the same.

The States then proceeded in like manner to a sixth ballot; and upon examination thereof, the result was declared to be the same.

The States then proceeded in like manner to a seventh ballot; and upon examination thereof, the result was declared to be the same.

A motion was then made and seconded that the States proceed again to ballot in one hour;

And the question being taken thereupon,

It was resolved in the affirmative,

The votes of the States being,

Ayes, ... 12,

Noes, ... 4.

The time agreed upon by the last mentioned vote being expired, the States proceeded, in manner aforesaid, to the eighth ballot; and, upon examination thereof, the result was declared to be the same, to wit:

The votes of eight States for Thomas Jefferson, of Virginia;

The vote of six States for Aaron Burr, of New York;

And the votes of two States were divided.

The States then proceed to a ninth, tenth, eleventh, twelfth, thirteenth, fourteenth, and fifteenth ballots; and upon examination of the ballots respectively, the result was declared to be the same.

A motion was then made and seconded that the States proceed to ballot at ten o'clock;

And, the question being taken thereupon,

It passed in the negative,

The votes of the States being,

Ayes, ... 7,

Noes, ... 9.

. . . .

FEBRUARY 12, 1801—1 O'CLOCK, A.M.

The time agreed upon by the last mentioned vote being expired, the States proceeded in manner aforesaid to the twentieth ballot; and upon examination thereof, the result was declared to be the same.

Ordered, That the ballot be repeated at two o'clock.

The agreed upon by the last mentioned vote being expired, the States proceeded in manner aforesaid tot he twenty-second ballot; and, upon examination thereof, the result was declared to be the same.

Ordered, That the ballot be repeated at half after two o'clock.

The time agreed upon by the last mentioned vote being expired, the States proceeded in manner aforesaid tot he twenty-second ballot; and, upon examination thereof, the result was declared to be the same.

. . . .

FEBRUARY 13, 1801.

The time agreed upon by the last mentioned vote being expired, the States proceeded in manner aforesaid to the twenty-ninth ballot; and, upon examination thereof, the result was declared to be the same.

Ordered, That the ballot be repeated to-morrow at twelve o'clock, and not before.

FEBRUARY 14, 1801.

The time agreed upon by the last mentioned vote being expired, the States proceeded in manner aforesaid to the thirtieth ballot; and, upon examination thereof, the result was declared to be the same.

. . . .

FEBRUARY 16, 1801.

The time agreed upon by the last mentioned vote being expired, the States proceeded in manner aforesaid to the thirty-fourth ballot; and, upon examination thereof, the result was declared to be the same.

Ordered, That the ballot be repeated to-morrow at twelve o'clock, and not before.

FEBRUARY 17, 1801.

The time being agreed upon by the last mentioned vote being expired, the States proceeded in manner aforesaid to the

thirty-fifth ballot; and, upon examination thereof, the result was declared to be the same.

Ordered, That the ballot be repeated at one o'clock.

The time agreed upon by the last mentioned vote being expired, the States proceeded in manner aforesaid to the thirty-sixth ballot; and, upon examination thereof, and the result being reported by the tellers to the Speaker, the Speaker declared to the House that the votes of ten States had been given for Thomas Jefferson of Virginia; the votes of four States for Aaron Burr, of New York; and the votes of two States had been given in blank; and that, consequently, Thomas Jefferson of Virginia, had been, agreeably to the Constitution, elected President of the United States, for the term of four years, commencing on the fourth day of March next.

Ordered, that Mr. Pinckney, Mr. Tazewell, and Mr. Bayard, be appointed a committee to wait on the President of the United States, and notify him that Thomas Jefferson is elected President of the United States, for the term commencing on the fourth of March next.

Ordered, That a message be sent to the Senate to inform them that Thomas Jefferson has been duly elected President of the United States, for the term of four years, commencing on the fourth day of March next; and that the Clerk of the House do go with the said message.

. . . .

House Journal, 3 (1797–1801), 6th Congress, 2d session, Feb. 11–17, 1801, 798–803.

33   A House Report Regarding the Establishment of the Library of Congress

December 21, 1801

As the federal government prepared to move to Washington, D.C., in 1800, Congress passed legislation that contained an appropriation of $5,000 for the purchase of books for the use of Congress. This marked the birth of the Library of Congress, one of the great libraries of the world. When Congress began to actually purchase books and maps, the real work of creating a library began. This 1801 report discusses the business of establishing a library and providing a mechanism to make it operational, including fines for members who did not return books on time.

The Library of Congress had a number of major setbacks along the way to greatness. In 1814 British troops burned the Capitol and the library was completely destroyed. It was revived when Thomas Jefferson offered to sell his extensive personal library to Congress to replace what had been lost (see document 46).

Mr. RANDOLPH, from the joint committee appointed to take into consideration the statement made by the Secretary of the Senate, respecting books and maps purchased pursuant to a late act of Congress, and to make report respecting the future arrangement of the same, made the following report:

That, in their opinion, the following resolutions contain the proper regulations upon the subject committed to them; they therefore present them for consideration.

1st. *Resolved, by the Senate and House of Representatives of the United States of America,* in Congress assembled, That the books and maps purchased by directions of the act of Congress passed the 24th day of April, 1800, be placed in the Capitol, in the room which was occupied by the House of Representatives during the last session of the sixth Congress; and that the books shall be numbered, labelled, and set up in portable cases with handles to them, for the purpose of easy removal, with wire-netting doors, and locks. And that the books or libraries which have heretofore been kept separately, by each House, shall be removed and set up with those lately purchased, and be numbered and labelled with them; making one library of the whole.

2d. *And it is further resolved,* That the Secretary of the Senate, and the clerk of the House of Representatives for the time being, be, and they are hereby, authorized to take charge of the room, books, and maps aforesaid; and they are hereby authorized and directed to make suitable arrangements in said room for the library and maps; to procure proper furniture for the room; to procure the cases; number and label the books, and set them up in their cases; to procure for their own use, and the use of both Houses of Congress, printed catalogues of all the books, with the labelled number of each, and of the maps; to place on each book some proper mark or marks, to designate it as belonging to the Congressional library; to procure printed blank receipts for members to sign them they take books from the room; and to arrange and hang up the maps: all to be done under the inspection and direction of the President of the Senate and Speaker of the House of Representatives for the time being.

3d. *And it is further resolved,* That the Secretary of the Senate, and Clerk of the House of Representatives, shall be responsible for the safe-keeping of the room, furniture, books, and maps aforesaid; and shall not permit any map to be taken out of said room by any person, nor any book, except by members of the Senate and House of Representatives for the time being; and no member shall be permitted to take any book out of said room until he shall sign a receipt for the same, the form of which follows, viz:

Received this _____ day of _____ of the keepers of the Congressional library (here the book and its number are to be described,) which I promise to return within _____ days from this date; or forfeit the sum of _____ dollars, to be paid to said keepers, or either of them, or to their successors, or either of them. Witness my hand.

4th. *And it is further resolved,* That no member shall have at. any one time more than three books out of said library; and a folio volume shall be returned within _____ days; a quarto within _____ days; and an octavo within _____ days after the date of the receipt, respectively; and in case of such return, the receipt shall be cancelled; but in case of forfeiture, the keepers shall immediately collect the penalty.

5th. *And it is further resolved,* That the keepers of said library shall, one of them, attend, or shall cause some proper person for whose conduct they shall be responsible, to attend in said room from the hour of eleven in the morning until three in the after-noon, of each day, Sundays excepted, during each session of Congress, for the purpose of delivering and receiving said books. And the keepers of said library, shall receive for their services, including the safe-keeping of the room, furniture, books, and maps, delivering and receiving the books, and collecting forfeitures, _____ dollars annually; to be paid out of the fund annually appropriated for the contingent expenses of both Houses of Congress.

6th. *And it is further resolved,* That the keepers of said library shall, at the commencement or every session of Congress, exhibit a statement to each House, of the condition of said room, furniture, books, and maps, with information of the sum of forfeitures, if any, which they have collected; and of the necessary expenses for fuel, &c. in said room, during the period next preceding each statement, which then remains unsettled, that their accounts may be liquidated and approved by Congress; and the balance shall be paid out of the fund appropriated for the contingent expenses of both Houses of Congress.

7th. *And be it is further resolved,* That the keepers of said library shall cause a printed copy of the third, fourth, and fifth of the foregoing resolutions to be pasted up in some conspicuous place in said room, which shall be there at all times for the information of the members.

And the committee further report, for the consideration of Congress, the following resolutions:

Resolved, That the Secretary of the Senate be, and he is hereby, directed to make sale of the trunks in which the books lately purchased were imported; that he exhibit to both Houses of Congress an account of the proceeds, including a statement of the actual expenditures incurred under the act of the 24th of April, 1800, as well by the purchase of books and maps, and incidental expenses, as for the expenses of fitting up the room, procuring furniture, cases, &c., as mentioned in the second of the foregoing resolutions; and the residue of the five thousand dollars, appropriated by said act shall be laid out by the Secretary of the Senate, and Clerk of the House of Representatives, for books and maps, or books alone, under the direction of a joint committee to be appointed for that purpose, to consist of _____ members from the Senate, and _____ members from the House of Representatives.

Resolved, That Congress, by law, annually appropriate the sum of _____ dollars to be laid out for books and maps, or books alone, by the Secretary of the Senate, and Clerk of the House of Representatives; under the direction of a joint committee to be appointed by them for that purpose.

American State Papers, vol. 1, Class X, Miscellaneous, Dec. 21, 1801, 253.

34 Excerpts from *Jefferson's Manual of Parliamentary Practice*

1801

When Thomas Jefferson became vice president of the United States in 1797, he also assumed the role of president of the Senate. As the Senate's presiding officer, he felt a keen obligation to be well prepared to deal with the parliamentary practices of that body. He was also aware that his predecessor, John Adams, was often criticized for his inconsistent practices while presiding over the Senate. Jefferson approached his assignment with scholarly zeal and in the course of his four-year tenure as vice president compiled an influential volume of parliamentary rules, procedures, precedents, and practices. Much of the material was drawn from numerous volumes on procedure in the British parliament and from state legislatures in the United States. He combined these sources with his understanding of the U.S. Constitution, a decade of experience of observing the House and Senate, and his lengthy notes on parliamentary procedure—some of which he had prepared twenty-five years earlier during his service in the Virginia House of Burgesses.

The end product, which became known as Jefferson's Manual of Parliamentary Practice, *was published for the first time in 1801. It became a standard reference on parliamentary procedure in the Senate, for which it was originally intended. In 1837 the House of Representatives adopted a rule that declared* Jefferson's Manual *should "govern the House in all cases to which they are applicable and in which they are not inconsistent with the standing rules and orders of the House and joint rules of the Senate and House of Representatives." That 1837 ruling is still in force.*

The Jefferson's Manual *has been in print in one form or another for almost two centuries, a testimony to its continuing utility and status as a classic of parliamentary practice. However, it has been superseded in many respects and does not constitute the official parliamentary rules of either House or Senate today. It remains an important touchstone for anyone interested in understanding parliamentary procedure (and human nature, for that matter). In the excerpts that follow, Jefferson explains the power of having rules and adhering to them and offers some practical advice for members of Congress who may find their speeches falling on deaf ears.*

(1) SEC. I. THE IMPORTANCE OF ADHERING TO RULES.

[1.1] Mr. Onslow, the ablest among the Speakers of the House of Commons, used to say it was a maxim he had often heard when he was a young man, from old and experienced members, that nothing tended more to throw power into the hands of administration and those who acted with the majority of the House of Commons, than a neglect of, or departure from, the rules of proceeding: that these forms, as instituted by our ancestors, operated as a check and controul on the actions of the majority, and that they were in many instances, a shelter and protection to the minority, against the attempts of power. So far the maxim is certainly true, and is founded in good sense, that as it is always in the power of the majority, by their numbers, to stop any improper measures proposed on the part of their opponents, the only weapons, by which the minority can defend themselves against similar attempts from those in power, are the forms and rules of proceeding, which have been adopted as they were found necessary from time to time, and are become the law of the house; by a strict adherence to which, the weaker party can only be protected from those irregularities and abuses, which these forms were intended to check, and which the wantonness of power is but too often apt to suggest to large and successful majorities. . . .

[1.2] And whether these forms be in all cases the most rational or not, is really not of so great importance. It is much more material that there should be a rule to go by, than what that rule is; that there may be an uniformity of proceeding in business, not subject to the caprice of the Speaker, or captiousness of the members. It is very material that order, decency, and regularity be preserved in a dignified public body. . . .

[17.12] No one is to disturb another in his speech by hissing, coughing, spitting, speaking or whispering to another. . . . nor to stand up or interrupt him. . . . nor to pass between the Speaker and the speaking member, nor to go across the house. . . . or to walk up and down it, or to take books or papers from the table, or write there. . . .

[17.13] Nevertheless, if a member finds that it is not the inclination of the House to hear him, and that by conversation or any other noise they endeavour to drown his voice, it is his most prudent way to submit to the pleasure of the House, and sit down; for it scarcely ever happens that they are guilty of this piece of ill manners without sufficient reason, or inattentive to a member who says any thing worth their hearing. . . .

Thomas Jefferson, *A Manual of Parliamentary Practice for the Use of the Senate of the United States* (1801). Reprinted as *Senate Doc. 103–8,* 102d Congress, 2d session (Washington: Government Printing Office, 1993), 1, 28. Jefferson's citations to sources have been omitted. *Jefferson's Manual* is also printed as part of the *Rules of the House of Representatives,* published as a House document shortly after the beginning of each new Congress.

35   Memorial of Sundry Citizens of the City of Washington in the District of Columbia

January 26, 1803

The relocation of the federal government to the District of Columbia in 1800 presented Congress with many problems. Members arrived to find the city still rough and unfinished. One of their first responsibilities was to devise a system of administration for the federal district. The Constitution gave Congress the authority "to exercise exclusive Legislation in all cases whatsoever" over a district established as the seat of government. Once the District of Columbia was established, residents who formerly lived under the laws of Maryland or Virginia sought to return to their old jurisdictions, while citizens of the new Washington City petitioned for the same political privileges enjoyed by every state: self-government and voting rights.

The petition reproduced here was signed by Robert Brent, Washington's first mayor, who had been appointed under the act of incorporation of 1802, which established the first city government with a mayor appointed by the president. Brent and his fellow citizens had concluded that Congress, despite the best of intentions, could not adequately govern a local municipality at the same time that it attended to affairs of state. The Washington inhabitants requested permission to hold a convention to draft a local system of government, much as territories did when they applied for statehood. In 1804 Congress amended the act of incorporation to make the city council elective but failed to give the federal district representation in the national legislature or a vote in presidential elections. Not until the passage of the 23rd Amendment in 1961 (see document 150) were citizens of the District of Columbia able to vote in presidential elections. Other issues of home rule and full congressional representation for citizens of the District of Columbia remain contentious to the present day.

To the Senate and House of Representatives of the United States of America, in Congress assembled. The Memorial of the citizens of Washington convened on the 26th day of January 1803:

That your Memorialists, in common with the other inhabitants of the Territory of Columbia, are seriously impressed with the unfavorable circumstances in which they are placed, and still more seriously impressed with the apprehension of greater evils likely to ensue. Their short experience has forcibly confirmed the wisdom of all the political institutions of America by which the Citizens of an independent republic, except in the solitary case of Columbia, are invested with the powers of self government; powers commensurate to the protection of their rights, and the promotion of their happiness. Notwithstanding, however, the deprivation of this inestimable right, they have hitherto submitted without a murmur to provisions established by the collected wisdom of the nation, in the hope that their interests under the guardianship of the general government, would be solicitously consulted and faithfully promoted. But an experience of more than two years has proved that hope illusive. Of the unfeigned desire of the legislature of the United States to discharge every duty assigned them by the Constitution, they entertain no doubts; but it is their belief that a Legislative body, instituted for the accomplishment of great national objects, and unaquainted with the minute and local circumstances attending the Territory of Columbia, cannot be considered as possessed of that peculiar knowledge which is required in Legislating for them. Nor are your Memorialists insensible to the impropriety of claiming, to the neglect of National concerns, and at a great expence, so large a portion of time as such legislation would demand.

Under these convictions, and with impressions derived from the known friendship of Congress, your Memorialists request that they may be authorized in common with their fellow Citizens to elect delegates to a Convention to establish a system of government for themselves, if such shall appear their sense, expressed through the organ of their representatives so assembled; or, if such shall not appear to be the sense of the Territory they be empowered to recommend to the adoption of Congress such other measures as shall in their opinion best promote the general welfare of their constituents.

As Citizens of the United States, as members of a great and independent empire, founded on equal rights and diffusing equal happiness and protection, we appeal to the magnanimity, the patriotism, and the justice of Congress. We ask that which they can give without derogating from their dignity or impairing their power: and, that, without which our industry and resources, active and extensive as they are must be without avail.

Other objects of an interesting though subordinate nature, in our opinion claim the early attention of Congress. To them as exhibited in the annexed statement we respectfully invite their attention, trusting that their pressing importance will obtain the contemplated legislative redress during the present session. In behalf & at the request of the Citizens present

Robert Brent, Chairman

Memorial of sundry citizens of the City of Washington in the District of Columbia, Jan. 26, 1803 (HR 7A–F4.2, Jan. 28, 1803), Records of the U.S. House of Representatives, Record Group 233, National Archives, Washington, D.C.

36 Senate Debate on the Louisiana Purchase

November 2–3, 1803

In one of the greatest land deals in history, the United States bought 885,000 square miles of land from France for the sum of $15 million. This one transaction—a vast territory extending from the Mississippi River to the Rocky Mountains—doubled the size of the United States. At first President Thomas Jefferson wanted a constitutional amendment to allow him to purchase foreign territory, but pressure to complete the deal before Napoleon of France had a change of heart led Jefferson to submit the Louisiana Purchase Treaty to the Senate, which quickly confirmed the deal on October 26, 1803, by a vote of 27–7.

Once the treaty had been approved, difficult problems remained over how to implement it and what to do with this vast uncharted wilderness. No one knew the exact boundaries of the vast wilderness or what they would find there. Some members of Congress worried that the purchase could offend Spain and lead to war if Spain claimed any of the territory as her own. Almost before the ink was dry on the Senate's ratification of the Louisiana Purchase, and before the money for the purchase had been approved, the Senate began debating the meaning of what they had just done. While the Louisiana Purchase Treaty is truly a major landmark document of American history, the debate selected here is important for what it reveals about the magnitude of this purchase and what it would mean to future generations of Americans.

The expression "the devil is in the details" is often applied to the legislative process. This expression is borne out in the debate that follows. Some senators expressed deep concern that in purchasing the land from France, the United States might have created a situation that would lead to war with Spain. Others feared that frontiersmen would try to quickly settle the territory before the United States had firm control of the land and that these citizens would eventually wander so far from the seat of government that they might not hold allegiance to the United States.

LOUISIANA TREATY

The Senate resumed the second reading of the bill, entitled "An act authorizing the creation of a stock to the amount of eleven millions two hundred and fifty thousand dollars, for the purpose of carrying into effect the convention of the 30th of April, 1803, between the United States of America and the French Republic, and making provision for the payment of the same;" and having amended the bill—

On the question, Shall the bill pass?

Mr. WHITE moved that the further consideration of the bill be postponed until the second Monday in December next, stating as the ground of the motion he had the honor to make, that the question was then involved in much difficulty and doubt. He could not accede to the immediate passage of the bill—that by the day he had named the Senate would be able to act more understandingly on the subject, as it would then probably be ascertained whether we are likely to obtain the quiet possession of New Orleans and Louisiana under the treaty or not, and there would still remain a great sufficiency of time to make the necessary provisions on our part for carrying the treaty into execution, if it should be deemed necessary.

. . . .

But Mr. President, it is now a well known fact, that Spain considers herself injured by this treaty, and if it should be in her power to prevent it, will not agree to the cession of New Orleans and Louisiana to the United States. She considers herself absolved from her contract with France, in consequence of the latter having neglected to comply with certain stipulations in the Treaty of St. Ildefonso, to be performed on her part, and of having violated her engagement never to transfer this country into other hands. Gentlemen may say this money is to be paid upon the responsibility of the President of the United States, and not until after the delivery of possession to us of the territory; but why cast from ourselves all the responsibility upon this subject and impose the whole weight upon the President, which may hereafter prove dangerous and embarrassing to him? Why make the President the sole and absolute judge of what shall be a faithful delivery of possession under the treaty? What he may think a delivery of possession sufficient to justify payment of this money, we might not; and I have no hesitation in saying that if, in acquiring this territory under the treaty, we have to fire a single musket, to charge a bayonet, or to lose a drop of blood, it will not be such a cession on the part of France as should justify to the people of this country the payment of any, and much less so enormous a sum of money. What would the case be, sir? It would be buying of France authority to make war upon Spain; it would be giving the First Consul fifteen million dollars to stand aloof until we can settle our differences with His Catholic Majesty. . . . I wish not to be understood as predicting that the French will not cede to us the actual and quiet possession of the territory. I hope to God they may, for possession of it we must have—I mean of New Orleans, and of such other positions on the Mississippi as may be necessary to secure to us forever the complete and uninterrupted navigation of that river. This I have ever been in favor of; I think it essential to the peace of the United States, and to the prosperity of our Western country. But as to Louisiana, this new, immense, unbounded world, if it should ever be incorporated into this Union, which I have no idea can be done but by altering the Constitution, I believe it will be the greatest curse that cold at present befall us; it may be productive of innumerable evils, and especially of one that I fear even to look upon. Gentlemen on all sides, with very few exceptions, agree that the settlement of this country will be highly injurious and dangerous to the United States; but as to what has been suggested of removing the Creeks and other nations of Indians from the eastern to the western banks of the Mississippi, and of making the fertile regions of Louisiana a howling wilderness, never to be trodden by the foot of civilized man, it is impracticable. . . . To every man acquainted with the adventurous, roving, and enterprising temper of our people, and with the manner in which our Western country has been settled, such an idea must be chimerical. The inducements will be so strong that it will be impossible to restrain our citizens from crossing the river. Louisiana must and will become settled, if we hold it, and with the very population that would otherwise occupy part of our present territory. Thus our citizens will be removed to the immense distance of two or three thousand miles from the capital of the Union, where they will scarcely ever feel the rays of the General Government; their affections will become alienated; they will gradually begin to view us as strangers; they will form other commercial connexions, and our interests will become distinct.

. . . .

THURSDAY, November 3.

. . .

[Mr. JACKSON] Sir, it has been observed by a gentleman in debate yesterday, (Mr. White,) that Louisiana would become a grievance to us, and that we might as well attempt to prevent fish from swimming in water, as to prevent our citizens from going across the Mississippi. The honorable gentleman is not so well acquainted with the frontier citizens as I am. I see an honorable gentleman in my view, who knows whether or not what I am going to assert be the fact—he was part of the time high in office, (Mr. Pickering.) The citizens of the State I represent, scattered along an Indian frontier of from three to four thousand miles, have been restrained, except in one solitary instance, by two or three companies of infantry and a handful of dragoons, from crossing over artificial lines and water-courses, sometimes dry, into the Indian country, after their own cattle, which no human prudence could prevent from crossing to a finer and more luxuriant range, and this too at a time when the feelings of Georgians were alive to the injuries they had received by the New York Treaty with the Creek Indians, which took Tallassee county from them, after even three Commissioners appointed by the United States had reported to the President that it was *bona fide* the property of Georgia, and sold under as fair a contract as could be formed by a civilized with an uncivilized society. If the Georgians, under these circumstances, were restrained from going on their ground, cannot means be devised to prevent citizens crossing into Louisiana? The frontier people are not the people they are represented; they will listen to reason, and respect the laws of their country; it cannot be their wish, it is not their interest to go to Louisiana, or see it settled for years to come; the settlement of it at present would part father and son, brother and brother, and friend and friend, and lessen the value of their lands beyond all calculation. If Spain acts an amicable part, I have no doubt myself but the Southern tribes of Indians can be persuaded to go there; it will be advantageous for themselves; they are now hemmed in on every side; their chance of game decreasing daily; ploughs and looms, whatever may be said, have no charms for them; they want a wider field for the chase, and Louisiana presents it. Spain may, in such case, discard her fears for her Mexican dominions, for half a century at least; and we should fill up the space the Indians removed from, with settlers from Europe, and thus preserve the density of population within the original States. For sir, I will agree with the honorable gentleman, (Mr. White,) that it will be as impossible to prevent fish in the water from swimming, as to prevent the distressed of every country from flying to this asylum of the oppressed of the human race. They will come from the ambitious and distracted States of Europe to our mild and happy Government, if they commit themselves to the mercy of the ocean, or on a few planks nailed together, In a century, sir, we shall be well populated, and prepared to extend our settlements, and that world of itself will present itself to our approaches, and instead of the description given of it by the honorable gentleman, of making it a howling wilderness, where no civilized foot shall ever tread, if we could return at the proper period we should find it the seat of science and civilization.

Mr. President, in whatever shape I view this bill, I conceive it all-important that it should pass without a moment's delay. We have a bargain now in our power, which, once missed, we never shall have again. Let us close our part of the contract by the passage of this bill, let us leave no opportunity for any Power to charge us with a want of hood faith; and having executed our stipulations in good faith we can appeal to God for the justice of our cause; and I trust that, confiding in that justice, there is virtue, patriotism, and courage sufficient in the American nation, not only to take possession of Louisiana, but to keep that possession against the encroachments or attacks of any Power on Earth.

. . . .

Annals of Congress, Senate, 8th Congress, 1st session, Nov. 2 and 3, 1803, 31–74.

37 The Twelfth Amendment to the Constitution

Submitted to the States, December 9, 1803; Ratified, September 25, 1804

Following in the wake of the constitutional crises created when the presidential election of 1800 was decided by the House of Representatives (see document 32), Congress initiated a reform of the way presidential elections would be decided. The result was the Twelfth Amendment, which revised Article II, Section 1, Clause 3, of the Constitution. The growth of organized political parties created problems for the presidential election process that the Framers of the Constitution had not anticipated. As early as 1796 conflicts emerged when John Adams, a Federalist, ended up with Thomas Jefferson, a Republican, as his vice president since there was no separate balloting for president and vice president.

The Twelfth Amendment called for separate balloting for the president and vice president. If no candidate for president received a majority of the electoral votes, the House of Representatives would elect the president from the top three contenders (not the top five, as was the earlier case). If no candidate for vice president received a majority of the electoral votes, the Senate would elect the vice president from the top two contenders. There was some opposition to this amendment on the grounds that it violated the intention of the Framers of the Constitution, who had assumed that most elections of the president would be decided by the House because there would be numerous candidates and no one candidate would receive the necessary majority of electoral votes needed for victory.

Congress submitted the amendment to the states for ratification on December 9, 1803. Ratification by the required number of states occurred on June 15, 1804. The election of the president under the provisions of the 12th Amendment has occurred only once, in the election of 1824.

[ARTICLE XII.]

The Electors shall meet in their respective states, and vote by ballot for President and Vice-President, one of whom, at least, shall not be an inhabitant of the same state with themselves; they shall name in their ballots the person voted for as President and in distinct ballots the person voted for as Vice-President and they shall make distinct lists of all persons voted for as President, and of all persons voted for as Vice-President, and of the number of votes for each, which lists they shall sign and certify, and transmit sealed to the seat of the government of the United States, directed to the President of the Senate,—The President of the Senate shall, in the presence of the Senate and House of Representatives, open all the certificates and the votes shall then be counted;—The person having the greatest number of votes for President, shall be the President, if such number be a majority of the whole number of Electors appointed; and if no person have such majority, then from the persons having the highest numbers not exceeding three on the list of those voted for as President, the House of Representatives shall choose immediately, by ballot, the President. But in choosing the President, the votes shall be taken by states, the representation from each state having one vote; a quorum for this purpose shall consist of a member or members from two-thirds of the states, and a majority of all the states shall be necessary to a choice. And if the House of Representatives shall not choose a President whenever the right of choice shall devolve upon them, before the fourth day of March next following, then the Vice-President shall act as President, as in the case of the death or other constitutional disability of the President.—The person having the greatest number of votes as Vice-President, shall be the Vice-President, if such number be a majority of the whole number of Electors appointed, and if no person have a majority, then from the two highest numbers on the list, the Senate shall choose the Vice-President; a quorum for the purpose shall consist of two-thirds of the whole number of Senators, and a majority of the whole number shall be necessary to a choice. But no person constitutionally ineligible to the office of President shall be eligible to that of Vice-President of the United States.

The Constitution of the United States of America as Amended, House Doc. 102–188, 102d Congress, 2d session (Washington: Government Printing Office, 1992), 15.

38 Ann Alricks Petitions Congress for a Divorce

ca. January 24, 1804

The Constitution gave Congress authority over individual claims as well as broad issues of national policy. There were many cases where veterans and others with private claims against the government petitioned Congress to correct their grievances pursuant to the Fifth Amendment, which stipulates that private property cannot be taken without compensation. In assuming this role Congress took on a judicial function that would later be the prerogative of federal courts. In the case of petitions from the District of Columbia, Congress had special obligations and exclusive jurisdiction under Article I, Section 8, Clause 17.

In this unusual petition, Congress was asked to help with a divorce. Ann Alricks recognized that her plea was not among the "great national concerns," but she appealed to Congress as the only body with authority to end her hopeless marriage. In direct response to this and other divorce pleas, the House passed legislation granting the circuit court of the District of Columbia the power to grant divorces.

To the Honorable the Congress of the United States now setting.

The petition and memorial of Ann Alricks of the town and county of Alexandria in the District of Columbia respectfully sheweth; That in February 1794 she intermarried with a Mr. West Alricks at that time a merchant in very good business and of respectable connections. That when your Petitioner was married she was only fifteen years of age. That she lived with her husband until September 1797 a period of almost four years when they parted by mutual consent, having lived very unhappily together, and have never since lived together. She forbears from all crimination but four years experience have evinced the melancholy truth, that Mr. Alricks and herself can never make each other happy, or ever live together. Your Petitioner is left with two infant female children, without any means of support for them, or for herself, but what she receives from the bounty of a very aged widowed mother, whose property is dependent upon her life, and from the kindness of a sister, whose power to aid her may not continue long.

That after your Petitioner and her husband had separated, he remained in this neighbourhood several years, and always declared his intention to petition the Legislature of Virginia for a divorce, in which your petitioner would most cheerfully have joined him, and she has now in her possession letters, from him

to her mother, requesting her aid and concurrence in such a measure, but your Petitioner further shows, that some eighteen months or two years ago, he left this part of the Country, and went she knows not whither, and that he has not been since heard of.

That your Petitioner being yet possessed of youth and health, and not destitute of respectable friends and connections, indulges the hope, that a prudent and discreet conduct, might enable her to better much her situation, was she freed from these matrimonial obligations contracted with Mr. Alricks, almost in her infancy, which have long since become equally embarrassing and intollerable to them both.

As your Petitioner is a resident of the District of Columbia, she is advised that it belongs exclusively to this honorable body, to grant her the relief she prays for, and though assembled principally for great national concerns, she respectfully expresses a hope, that the trappings of an individual will not be deemed by you an object unworthy of your attention.

She therefore respectfully solicits your Honor to take her case into consideration to release her from those matrimonial engagements which she has entered into with Mr. West Alricks, and to declare their marriage null and void.

And your Petitioner as in duty bound shall pray &c.

Ann Alricks

Petition of Ann Alricks, of the town and county of Alexandria, in the District of Columbia (HR 8A–F5.5, Jan. 24, 1804), Records of the U.S. House of Representatives, Record Group 233, National Archives, Washington, D.C. The petition had no date but the docketing by a House clerk shows the petition was referred to a committee on Jan. 24, 1804.

39   Creation of the House Committee on Public Lands

December 17, 1805

In order to understand the workings of the House and Senate it is vital to learn how Congress organizes itself into committees. In the earliest Congresses, most committees were appointed to handle specific bills. They were not permanent committees, which are referred to in congressional parlance as "standing committees." As the nation grew and the work of Congress became more complex, both the House and Senate devised a system of standing committees to conduct the business of lawmaking. The House, the larger body, began the process earlier, but by 1816 the Senate also developed a committee system roughly parallel to that of the House. The first standing committee in the House, the Committee on Elections, was established in 1789 (see document 8).

The creation of specific standing committees often reflected the larger contours of American history. For example, the Committee on Public Lands was created two years after the Louisiana Purchase (see document 36), which doubled the size of the United States and raised many questions about the management of the

new territories and the sale of public land. The House Committee on Public Lands grew in importance over the years, assuming jurisdiction over issues related to mineral and water rights, forests, game, national parks, conservation, and other topics. The committee existed with this name from 1805 to 1951, when its name was changed to the Committee on Interior and Insular Affairs.

The creation of the Committee on Public Lands did not come easy. The first attempt to establish the committee on January 3, 1805, failed to pass the House. Reproduced here is a brief account of the debate twelve months later over the creation of the committee. One House member, George M. Bedinger, a Jeffersonian Republican from Kentucky, objected to the new committee because it would lead to a concentration of power within the committee at the expense of those members who were not a part of the committee. This is an early example of Congress's recognition that it would have to specialize to some degree in order to conduct the increasingly complex business before it. In doing so some members gave up some leg-

islative power. The argument that carried the day was that a committee with experienced members would make more uniform and enlightened decisions, which would benefit the country.

RULES OF THE HOUSE.

The House again went into Committee of the Whole on the standing rules of the House.

After making a slight amendment in one of the rules, the Committee rose and reported their agreement to the rules, with certain amendments.

The House immediately took up the report.

On the amendment offered by Mr. FINDLEY, relative to the appointment of a standing committee respecting the lands of the United States, a debate of some length ensued, in which the amendment was supported by Messrs. GREGG, NICHOLSON, and SMILIE; and opposed by Mr. BEDINGER.

Mr. BEDINGER suggested his fears, lest a standing committee, vested with the entire business connected with the public lands, should gain such an ascendancy over the sentiments and decisions of the House, by the confidence reposed in them, as to impair the salutary vigilance with which it became every member to attend to so interesting a subject.

On the other hand it was contended that the business of the House would, on this point, be greatly facilitated by the institution of a standing committee' whose decisions would be uniform, who would from a long experience become more enlightened than a select committee, and who would be enabled to despatch the business confided to them with greater celerity.

The amendment was agreed to—. . . .

Annals of Congress, 9th Congress, 1st session, Dec. 17, 1805, 286.

40   The Cumberland Road Act

March 29, 1806

The development of a system of roads was one of the highest priorities of the federal government in its early years. Post roads, which were routes used to carry the mail, helped bind the country together and maintain a means of internal communication. The development of the Cumberland Road, often called the National Road, marked the beginning of the national highway system in the United States. The Cumberland Road was a far cry from the modern highways of today. Originally an Indian trail, this road from Cumberland, Maryland, into the Ohio Territory was used by traders and settlers moving west as early as the 1750s.

By the early 1800s the Cumberland Road was in a state of complete disrepair. Congress passed a bill in 1802 allowing money from the sale of land in Ohio to be used to improve the Cumberland Road. The Cumberland Road Act of 1806 marked the beginning of those improvements. By the 1820s, a plan was devised to convert the road into a turnpike, with tolls paying for the costs of maintenance. President James Monroe vetoed the Cumberland Road Bill in 1822 because he feared Congress would go on a spree of internal improvements without concern for the costs.

In this first major piece of internal improvements legislation in 1806, Congress took its first step toward a national highway system. A century and a half later, Congress would face similar problems on a far more massive scale with the creation of the interstate highways system (see document 145).

CHAP. XIX.—AN ACT TO REGULATE THE LAYING OUT AND MAKING A ROAD FROM CUMBERLAND, IN THE STATE OF MARYLAND, TO THE STATE OF OHIO.

Be it enacted by the Senate and House of Representatives of the United States of America in Congress assembled, That the President of the United States be, and he is hereby authorized to appoint, by and with the advice and consent of the Senate, three discreet and disinterested citizens of the United States, to lay out a road from Cumberland, or a point on the northern bank of the river Potomac in the state of Maryland, between Cumberland and the place where the main road leading from Gwinn's to Winchester, in Virginia, crossed the river, to the state of Ohio: whose duty it shall be, as soon as may be, after their appointment, to repair to Cumberland aforesaid, and view the ground, from the points on the river Potomac herein before designated, to the river Ohio; and to lay out in such direction as they shall judge, under all circumstances, the most proper, a road from thence to the river Ohio, to strike the same at the most convenient place, between a point on its eastern bank, opposite to the northern boundary of Steubenville, in said state of Ohio, and the mouth of Grave creek, which empties into the said river, a little below Wheeling, in Virginia.

SEC. 2. *And be it further enacted,* That the aforesaid road shall be laid out four rods in width, and designated on each side by a plain and distinguishable mark on a tree, or by the erection of a stake or monument, sufficiently conspicuous, in every quarter of a mile of the distance, at least, where the road pursues a straight course so far or farther, and on each side, at every point where an angle occurs in its course.

. . . .

SEC. 4. *And be it further exacted,* That all parts of the road which the President shall direct to be made, in case the trees are standing, shall be cleared the whole width of four rods; and the road shall be raised in the middle of the carriage way with stone, earth, or gravel and sand, or a combination of all of them, leaving or making, as the case may be, a ditch or water-course on each side, and contiguous to said carriage way: and in no instance shall there be an elevation in said road, when finished, greater than an angle of five degrees with the horizon. But the manner of making said road , in every other particular, is left to the direction of the President.

SEC. 5. *And be it further enacted,* That said commissioners shall each receive four dollars per day, while employed as aforesaid, in full for their compensation, including all expenses. And they are hereby authorized chainmen, and one marker, for whose faithfulness and accuracy, they, the said commissioners, shall be responsible, to attend them in laying out said road, who shall receive in full satisfaction for their wages, including all expenses, the surveyor three dollars per day, and each chainman and the marker, one dollar per day, while they shall be employed in said business; of which fact, a certificate signed by said commissioners all be deemed sufficient evidence.

SEC. 6. *And be it further enacted,* That the sum of thirty thousand appropriated, to defray the expense of laying out and making said road. And the President is hereby authorized to draw, from time to time, on the treasury, for such parts, or at any one time, for the whole of said sum, as he shall judge the service requires. Which sum of thirty thousand dollars, shall be paid, first, out of the fund of two per cent, reserved for laying out and making roads to the state of Ohio, by virtue of the seventh section of an act passed on the thirtieth day of April, one thousand eight hundred and two, intituled "An act to enable the people of the eastern division of the territory northwest of the river Ohio, to form a constitution and state government, and for the admission of such state into the Union, on an equal footing with the original states and for other purposes." Three per cent of the appropriation contained in said seventh section, being directed by a subsequent law, to the laying out, opening, and making roads within the said state of Ohio. And secondly, out of any money in the treasury not otherwise appropriated, chargeable upon, and reimbursable at the treasury by said fund of two per cent, as the same shall accrue.

. . . .

Approved, March 29, 1806.

Statutes at Large, 2 (1799–1813), 9th Congress, 1st session, March 29, 1806, 357–359.

41　Petition of the Warriors of the Upper and Lower Sanduskies

October 4, 1806

Like many appeals to Congress from Native Americans, the petition of the warriors of the Upper and Lower Sanduskies, who lived in territory that is now in the state of Ohio, is more significant as an expression of the predicament of the indigenous population than as an influence on legislation. The people of the Sanduskies turned to Congress following an unanswered appeal to the president and the War Department, which had jurisdiction over Indian affairs before 1849. The leaders of the Sanduskies sought assurances for the title to their ancestral lands and assured Congress of their hopes for a settled life in close proximity to white settlers. The petition also expressed the fear that white settlement would inevitably displace the Native American population.

While it is unclear who drafted this petition, its language is striking and eloquently conveys the position of the Sanduskies. It was common among Native Americans and other petitioners, especially those who could not read or write in English, to enlist a scribe or agent to prepare the petition for signatures. The original petition contained the actual signatures of the chiefs, shown as pictographs of birds, turtles, deer, and other graphic representations, along with phonetic spellings of their names.

Representative Joseph B. Varnum, a Federalist from Massachusetts, submitted the Sanduskie's petition, which was referred to the Committee on Public Lands. Neither the committee nor the House took any further action.

The Petition of the Warriors of the Upper & Lower Sanduskies; To the Honbl. the Congress of the United States of America.

Fathers Listen. Last August a year our Chiefs had a Petition drawn and sent to our Great Father the President of the U.S. to relinquish the one half of the Reserve at the foot of the Rappids at Lower Sandusky, and to give the other half to the Missionary who should be sent to live with us.

Fathers Listen. The Warriors have now taken it upon themselves to renew the Petition sent by the Chiefs. The Warriors and the Women now cry to the Fathers of the United States; We beg of Congress to do us the great favour we now ask for. We the Warriors and Women now speak with one voice to the Seventeen States. Fathers, we now beg of you that you will relinquish to us, the whole of the Reserve in this place.

Our reason for asking this great favour of our Fathers are these. It is the place where we were born, where our ancestors were born; and where they, and many of our Relations lie buried. It is our most ardent wish, to live the remainder of our days in this place; and to have our Graves here with our ancestors and Relations. Another Reason of our asking our Fathers to give us this little piece of land, is this, We are desirous to have the Gospel preached to us, and to have our Children learn to read; and we want to cultivate our land with the plough; and raise Cattle, and have a Mill to grind our Corn. In order to injoy these previledges, we must build houses and some fields: But we are affraid to build houses or to make homes & fields—for our Fathers may order this land to be sold to their white Children, and then we might immediately leave all we have done and be made poor at once; and have no houses to live in, nor fields to raise corn in, until we can clear land, and make them; which will be very heard for us as we have numbers of very Old people, and families of Children. We are in great trouble about receiving the Gospel, and having our Children instructed; lest we should soon be turned away from this place.

Fathers Listen. What we ask of our Fathers is but a small mattr with them; They have lately bought a great piece of our best hunting ground and will we expect aftr they have settled that with their white Children, ask us for more of our land. We hope our Fathers will listen to our cry, and the cry of our Women and grant us our request. It will make us happy, and not injure our Fathers nor their white Children.

Fathers Listen. Another reason why we ask our Fathers for this favour, is this. Last year our Chiefs sent a request to our Fathers the Ministers in Pensylvania to send them a Good Minister to teach us Religion, and a School Teacher for our Children. In answer to their request; In the spring they sent us a Minister,

with three labouring men, with a team, and farming tools. They ploughed all our ground for planting of Corn; and have helped us about our houses, and farms, and are ready to help us all they can. Our Father the Minister gives us good Counsel, and helps us with medison when we are sick. They are building a School-house for our Children, and will soon have it done. We wish them to live with us; they treat us kindly, & do us no injury, and we shall be more happy for their living with us. But if our Fathers take this land from us it will break us up, & make us very miserable. It is our wish (the Warriors) that our Fathers the Members of Congress should see the Petition, our Chiefs sent last year to our Great Father the President. We are informed by our Father present, that it lies in the War Office, where Congress can see it, if they wish for it. And we do cry to our Fathers in Congress, not to listen to any Petition which may be sent in opposition to this, the Prayer of their Red Children. The petition which was sent last year, in opposition, to the one sent by our Chiefs; the Wiandot People of our Towns do not know from whom it was sent.

Petition of the Warriors of the Upper and Lower Sanduskies, Oct. 4, 1806 (HR 9A-F5.1, Dec. 22, 1806), Records of the U.S. House of Representatives, Record Group 233, National Archives, Washington, D.C.

42   Creation of the House District of Columbia Committee

January 21 and 27, 1808

A special home for the federal government was created when land originally allotted to Maryland and Virginia was annexed to form a federal district. This created many problems for those persons who lived in the new District of Columbia and found themselves without representation in Congress (see documents 35 and 38). Since Congress had control of the district under the provisions of Article I, Section 8 of the Constitution, it had to devise ways to oversee and govern it.

As these burdens grew the House created a committee to focus on the problems of running the District of Columbia. Representative Philip Barton Key, a Federalist from Maryland, introduced the resolution to create the District of Columbia Committee and became the committee's first chairman.

THURSDAY, JANUARY 21.

Mr. KEY offered the following resolution:

Resolved, That a standing committee be appointed to be called a Committee of the District of Columbia, to consist of — members. It shall be the duty of this committee to take into consideration all petitions and memorials relating to the affairs of the District of Columbia, and to report from time to time, by bill or otherwise.

Mr. K. said, he would take the liberty of suggesting the reasons of this motion. The District of Columbia was governed by the laws of Maryland on the east, and by the laws of Virginia on the west of the Potomac, which existed at time of cession to the United States. The various modifications made in the state laws since that period, had no operation in the territory which they ceded. It was desired that the laws be rendered uniform and equal in their operation throughout the territory. The object of the resolution was to simplify the business related tot he District. It would be recollected that Congress alone could legislate on this subject; the great measures of national concern had prior claim on the attention of the House; for this reason he had moved the appointment of a general committee.

The resolution was ordered to lie on the table for one day.

. . . .

WEDNESDAY, JANUARY 27.

. . . .

The House took up for consideration the resolution lately offered by Mr. Key for the erection of a standing committee of the House to inquire and report on all concerns relative to the District of Columbia.

Mr. FINDLEY observed that he had long been in favor of appointing a committee of this kind. The citizens of the District of Columbia were not and could not be represented on this floor. He wished to see the business consolidated, so that they might be justly heard.

Mr. KEY said his object in this motion had merely been to render more simple to the House the legislating for the Dis-

trict. It would save many committees from being raised, and promote consistency and uniformity in the laws relating to the District.

The resolution was then agreed to without a division, and Messrs. Key, Van Dyke, Love, Holland, Brown, Livermore, and Taylor appointed to the committee. . . .

Annals of Congress (1807–1808, part 2), 10th Congress, 1st session, Jan. 21 and 27, 1808, 1486–1487, 1512.

43   The Origins of the Gerrymander

March 26, 1812

The term gerrymander *has become a standard word found in dictionaries and in wide use since its origins in a political cartoon published in the* Boston Gazette *in 1812. To gerrymander a congressional district means to draw its boundaries in such a manner that one particular political party, race, or ethnic group has a distinct advantage over another in elections.*

The word was first used to poke fun at Elbridge Gerry, the governor of Massachusetts. The electoral districts of Essex County, Massachusetts, had been drawn in such a way that a cartoonist, Elkanah Tisdale, portrayed the districts as a dragon-like monster, which he called the "gerrymander"—a combination of the governor's name and the second part of the word salamander. *The Federalist Party quickly adopted the word to criticize what they saw as unfair political divisions designed to undermine their party's political strength.*

Since congressional redistricting for seats in the House of Representatives is accomplished largely through state laws, the dominant political party in a state often has the most influence in determining electoral districts. Gerrymandering can take various forms. District boundaries can be drawn specifically to increase the concentration of voters from one party or, alternatively, to dilute party strength by dividing the district so no one party has a distinct advantage.

A new species of *Monster,* which appeared in *Essex South District* in January last.

"O generation of Vipers! *who hath warned you of the wrath to come?"*

The horrid Monster, of which this drawing is a correct representation, appeared in the County of Essex, during the last session of the Legislature. Various and manifold have been the speculations and conjectures among learned naturalists respecting the *genus* and origin of this astonishing production. Some believe it to be the real *Basilisk,* a creature which had been supposed to exist only in the poet's imagination. Others pronounce it the *Serpens Monocepliaus* of Pliny, or single-headed *Hydra,* a terrible animal of pagan extraction. Many are of the opinion that is the *Griffin* or *Hippogriff* of romance, which flourished in the dark ages, and has come hither to assist the knight of the rueful countenance in restoring that gloomy period of ignorance, fiction and imposition. Some think it the great Red Dragon, or Bunyun's *Apollyon* or the *Monsirum Herrendum* of Virgil, and all believe it a creature of infernal origin, both from its aspect, and from the circumstances of its birth.

But the learned Doctor Watergruel who is famous for peeping under the skins of nature, has decided that it belongs to the *Salamander* tribe, and gives many plausible reasons for this opinion. He says that though the Devil himself must undoubtedly have been concerned, either directly or indirectly in the procreation of this monster, yet many possible causes must have concurred to give it existence, amongst which must be reckoned the present combustible and venomous state of affairs. There have been, (says the Doctor) many fiery ebullitions of party spirit, many explosions of democratic wrath and fulminations of gubernatorial vengeance within the year past, which would naturally produce an uncommon degree of inflammation and acrimony in the body politic. But as the Salamander cannot be generated except in the most potent degree of heat, he thinks these malignant causes, could not alone have produced such diabolical effects. He therefore ascribes the real birth and material existence of this monster, in all its horrors, to the alarm which his Excellency the Governor and his friends experienced last season, while they were under the influence of the Dog-star & the Comet—and while his Excellency was pregnant with his last speech, his libelous message, and a numerous litter of new judges and other animals, of which he has since been happily delivered. This fright and purturbation was occasioned by an incendiary letter threatening him with fire-brands, arrows and death; (if his proclamation to be credited) which was sent to him by some mischievous wight, probably some rouge of his own party, to try the strength of his Excellency's mind. Now his Excellency, being somewhat like a tender-horn, and his party very liable to take fire, they must of course have been thrown into a most fearful panic, extremely dangerous to persons in their situation, and calculated to produce the most disastrous effects upon their unborn progeny.

From these premises the sagacious Doctor most solemnly avers that there can be no doubt that this monster is a genuine Salamander, though by no means perfect in all its members; a circumstance however which goes far to prove its legitimacy. But as this creature has been engendered and brought forth under the slimiest auspices, he proposes that a name should be given to it, expressive of its genus, and at the same time conveying an elegant and very appropriate compliment to his Excellency the Governor, who is known to be the zealous patron and promoter of whatever is new, astonishing and erratic, especially of domestic growth and manufacture. For these reasons and for other valuable considerations, the Doctor has decreed that this monster shall be denominated a Gerry-mander, a name that must exceedingly gratify the parental bosom of our Chief Magistrate, and prove so highly flattering to his ambition, that the Doctor may confidently expect in return for his ingenuity and fidelity, some benefits a little more substantial than the common reward of virtue.

That asstute naturalist Lubricostus however in the 26th section of his invaluable notes on the Salamander, clearly shows that this word is a corruption of the Latin, Salimania; expressing the characteristic dislike and almost hydrophobic antipathy of that animal for sea salt: "Oweinge (to use the words of the author) to the properties and virtues of the sayde minerale, as is well knowen to moste folke, in dampeinge the heate of that elemente of fyre, wherein the sayde beaste doth abide, so that if a piece of salt, or any marine thinge be placed neare it, it dothe fret it sorely, and enrage it to such madnesse that it dothe incontinently throw from its mouthe a venomous spittle, which dothe tarnishe and destroy all that is of worth or value that it fallethe upon: A further and most manyfest proofe of which deadlie hatred appearethe in that, whereas, on and neare the rationed salt mountayne, so called, amydst alle the marvells and wonders with which it dothe abounde, not any of this Lizarde species hath been discoverable thereyne." We therefore propose, with the utmost deference to the ingenious Doctor's opinion, that the term *Gerry-mania* be substituted for Gerrymander, as highly descriptive both of the singular ferocity if the monster in question, and the influence which the moon at certain periods, more especially on the approach of April, is supposed to exert over it.

A friend of ours has further suggested that there is a peculiar felicity at the present time in adopting the term Gerry-mania, as according to his definition, Gerry is derived form the French Guerre, or the Italian Guerra (war) and that it therefore possesses the double advantage of expressing the characteristic ferocity of this monster, and that magnanimous rage for war which seems to have taken such possession of our worthy Chief Magistrate and his friends. But we mention this merely as an ingenious speculation, being well convinced ourselves, notwithstanding appearances, of the truly pacific sentiments of that great man, whose *mild* and *charitable* denunciations of his political opponents have had such a wonderful effect in convincing their reason, allaying the spirit of the party, and in reconciling all conflicting opinions.

The Boston Gazette, March 26, 1812, 2.

44 Declaration of War with Great Britain and Ireland

June 18, 1812

Article I, Section 8 of the Constitution gives Congress the power to declare war. The first time that power was officially and formally used was in this declaration of war with Great Britain and Ireland, initiating the War of 1812. The number of times Congress has formally declared war is relatively rare when compared with the number of times U.S. troops have engaged in various kinds of warfare. There have been only four formal declarations of war: the War of 1812, the Spanish-American War, World War I, and World War II. But there have been more than 200 instances when American troops have been involved in some type of warfare. Some of these nondeclared wars have been major endeavors costing thousands of lives, including the Korean War and the Vietnam War.

The War of 1812 lasted from 1812 to 1815. It was promoted by President James Madison and the so-called War Hawks in Congress, led by Henry Clay. Clay was serving his first term in the House of Representatives, where he was elected Speaker. While later declarations of war would come at dramatic moments with widespread support in Congress, there was serious opposition to the War of 1812. The House vote to declare war was 79–49. In the Senate the vote was 19–13. When optimism over a quick and decisive victory faded with the harsh realities of Britain's earnestness to push the war, Congress became less interested in pursuing the war and more divided regarding war policy. In August 1814, when British troops burned the White House and the Capitol, American fortunes were at a low ebb. Luckily, the peace treaty, known as the Treaty of Ghent, and a major battle held after the peace treaty was agreed to gave Americans the right to brag that the war had been successfully concluded (see document 47).

AN ACT DECLARING WAR BETWEEN THE UNITED KINGDOM OF GREAT BRITAIN AND IRELAND AND THE DEPENDENCIES THEREOF, AND THE UNITED STATES OF AMERICA AND THEIR TERRITORIES.

Be it enacted, &c., That war be and the same is hereby declared to exist between the United Kingdom of Great Britain and Ireland and the dependencies thereof, and the United States of America and their Territories; and that the President of the United States is hereby authorized to use the whole land and naval force of the United States to carry the same into effect, and to issue to private armed vessels of the United States commissions of marque and general reprisal, in such form as he shall think proper, and under the seal of the United States, against the vessels, goods, and effects, of the Government of the said United Kingdom of Great Britain and Ireland, and the subjects thereof.

Approved. June 18, 1812.

Annals of Congress (1811–1812), 12th Congress, 1st session, June 18, 1812, 2322–2323.

45   A Letter Explaining the Destruction of House Records During the Burning of the Capitol

September 15, 1814

On August 24, 1814, during the War of 1812, British troops invaded the city of Washington and burned the Capitol, the White House, and several other public buildings. The damage to the Capitol was severe. Capitol architect Benjamin Henry Latrobe described the building in early 1815 as "a most magnificent ruin." The interiors of the House and Senate wings were gutted, although the walls remained standing thanks to a heavy rainstorm that doused the flames and prevented complete destruction. Inside the building, however, flames consumed the congressional library and many of the records of the House of Representatives. On the Senate side, the Senate secretary and his clerks managed to find wagons and haul to safety most of the important Senate records.

The House clerk, Patrick Magruder, was away from the Capitol at the time of the fire attending to his poor health at various spas in Virginia and Pennsylvania. Nonetheless, he was held responsible for the loss of House records. It is difficult to assess exactly how much valuable material was lost during the fire, but many irreplaceable journals, committee records, petitions from citizens, financial records, and private correspondence were consumed in the flames. The House clerk was forced to resign over his mishandling of the situation, becoming one more casualty of the War of 1812. In the document that follows, two of the House clerk's staff, writing to the clerk, describe what happened on the day of the fire. They, too, were away from their duties at the Capitol for a time, because they were in the militia that was called up to defend the city and only a furlough from their commander allowed them to return to the Capitol to attend to its records. The clerk submitted this letter of explanation to the House and called for an investigation of the matter. This document is the most direct explanation of what happened that day at the Capitol and it speaks of lost documents that can never be recovered.

To Patrick Magruder, Esq.,
    Clerk to the House of Representatives.

City of Washington, *September 15, 1814.*
Sir:

In order to correct any erroneous statements or representations which may go, or have gone out to the public, in relation to the destruction of your office, we deem it our duty to make the following statement of facts:

At the time you left the city, (which was in the latter part of July,) for the springs in Virginia and Pennsylvania, for the recovery of your health, all was quiet, and we believe no fears were entertained for the safety of the seat of Government. Indeed, nothing was heard of the enemy, except his marauding parties in the Chesapeake, and what was seen in the newspapers, of troops being ordered from Europe to America.

About the middle of August it was stated that the enemy was is the bay, in great force, and, an the 19th of that month, the whole body of the militia of the District of Columbia was called out, under which call every clerk of the office was taken into the fold, except Mr. Frost, and marched to meet the enemy.

On the 21st, the first of the undersigned clerks was furloughed, by Brigadier General Smith, at the request of Colonel George Magruder, for the purpose of returning to the duty, to take care of, and save such part of the books and papers of the clerk's office, as he might be able to effect, in case the enemy should get possession of the place; he arrived here the night of that day.

His orders from Colonel George Magruder were, not to begin packing up until it was ascertained that the clerks at the War Office were engaged in that business; and it was not until

12 o'clock, on Monday, the 22d, that we were informed that they had begun to move the effects of that office, although we were subsequently told that it had commenced the day before.

We immediately went to packing up, and Mr. Burch went out in search of wagons and other carriages, for the transportation of the books and papers; every wagon, and almost every cart, belonging to the city, had been previously impressed into the service of the United States, for the transportation of the baggage of the army; the few he was able to find were loaded with the private effects of individuals, who were moving without the city; those he attempted to hire out, but, not succeeding, he claimed a right to impress them; but, having no legal authority, or military force to aid him, he, of course, did not succeed. He then sent off three messengers into the country, one of whom obtained from Mr. John Wilson, whose residence is six miles from the city, the use of a cart and four oxen; it did not arrive at the office, until after dark on Monday night, when it was immediately laden with the most valuable records and papers, which were taken, on the same night, nine miles, to a secret place in the country. We continued to remove as many of the most valuable books and papers, having removed the manuscript records, as we were able to do with one cart, until the morning of the day of the battle of Bladensburg, after which we were unable to take away any thing further.

Every thing belonging to the office, together with the library of Congress, we venture to say, might have been removed in time, if carriages could have been procured; but it was altogether impossible to procure them, either or hire, or by force.

The most material papers which have been lost are, the last volumes of the manuscript records of the Committee of Ways and Means, Claims and Pensions, and Revolutionary Claims; the clerks were engaged in bringing up these records previous to the alarm, and it was not certain that the enemy would get to the city, and being desirous to have them completed, they were not packed away with the rest, but were kept out, that they might be finished by the meeting of Congress; but with the intention of taking them to a private residence, if such a removal should be found necessary. After the defeat of our troops at Bladensburg, removed them to a house commonly called General Washington's, which house being unexpectedly consumed by fire, these records were thus unfortunately lost.

The secret journal of Congress was also consumed; it was kept in a private drawer in the office, and in the hurry of removal was forgotten. Its contents, however, have been, in most cases, published by order of the House.

The manuscript papers, which have not been saved, were mostly of a private nature, consisting chiefly of petitions, and unimportant papers, presented previous to the year 1799.

We regret very much the loss of your private accounts and vouchers, amongst which, we are sorry to add, were the receipts and accounts of the expenditure of the contingent moneys of the House of Representatives; they were in the private drawer of Mr. George Magruder, which being locked, and the key not in our possession, we delayed to break it open until the last extremity, after which it escaped our recollection.

It is well known to one of us, (Mr. Burch,) that the receipts were from the first of January last, and embraced nearly the whole amount of the appropriation for the contingent expenses of the House.

A number of the printed books were also consumed, but they were all duplicates of those that have been preserved.

We have thus given you a full account of our proceedings during the troublesome scene, and we flatter ourselves you will not see in them any thing to disapprove, as we were guided solely by a zealous endeavor to discharge our duty to you, and to the public.

S. BURCH,
J. T. FROST.

American State Papers, vol. 2, Class X, Miscellaneous, 13th Congress, 3d session, Sept. 15, 1814, 245–246.

46 A Resolution to Purchase the Library of Thomas Jefferson

October 7, 1814

Less than two months after British troops invaded and burned the United States Capitol, destroying the library that had been assembled for the use of members of Congress, Thomas Jefferson offered to sell his complete library, one of the finest private libraries in the nation, to rebuild the congressional library. Jefferson wrote to his agent, Samuel H. Smith, on September 21, 1814, "I learn from the newspapers that the vandalism of our enemy has triumphed at Washington over science as well as the arts, by the destruction of the public library, with the noble edifice in which it was deposited."

He offered his library for sale, sent along a catalog of his books, and noted that his library had been fifty years in the making.

The resolution below was the first step leading to the congressional purchase of Jefferson's library. Some anti-Jeffersonians in the House objected to the purchase of the library largely on the grounds that it contained many books by controversial writers, such as Voltaire. The price agreed upon was $23,950—a very reasonable figure for this collection of 6,487 volumes. The vote to purchase the library passed the House by an 81–71 margin. On Janu-

ary 21, 1815, President James Madison appointed George Watterson to become the first full-time librarian. Nine days later Madison signed the bill authorizing the purchase into law. Jefferson's books then made their way to the Capitol by horse cart from Monticello. These events mark the rebirth of the Library of Congress, which has risen from the ashes of war to become one of the great libraries of the world. Although Jefferson's library formed an incredibly important core for the new congressional library, over the years those books have been lost.

Today the Library of Congress is no longer housed in the Capitol. It sits on more than 64 acres of land adjacent to the Capitol complex and includes three main buildings, named for presidents Jefferson, Madison, and Adams. The library contains hundreds of miles of bookshelves, more than 12 million books, 39 million manuscripts, and more than 16 million films, videos, photographs, and other visuals.

In the Senate of the United States, *October 7, 1814.*

Mr. GOLDSBOROUGH, from the joint committee on the library of Congress, reported:

That they have received, through Mr. Samuel H. Smith, an offer Mr. Jefferson, late President of the United States, of the whole of his library for Congress, in such a mode, and upon such terms, as they consider highly advantageous to the nation, and worthy the distinguished gentleman who tenders it. But the means placed at the disposal of the committee being very limited and totally inadequate to the purchase of such a library as that now offered, the committee must have recourse to Congress, either to extend their powers, or to adopt such other plan as they may think most proper.

Should it be the sense of Congress to confide this matter to the committee, they respectfully submit the following resolution:

Resolved, by the Senate and House of Representatives of the United States of America in Congress Assembled, That the joint Library Committee of the two Houses of Congress be, and they are hereby, authorized and empowered to contract, on their part, for the purchase of the library of Mr. Jefferson, late President of the United States, for the use of both Houses of Congress.

American State Papers, vol. 2, Class 10, Miscellaneous, 13th Congress, 3d session, Oct. 7, 1814, 246. A letter of transmittal from Samuel H. Smith, dated Oct. 3, 1814, and Thomas Jefferson's letter to Smith of Sept. 14, 1814, offering to sell his library also appear in the *American State Papers* along with the above resolution.

47   The Treaty of Ghent

December 24, 1814

Sometimes a bad war can lead to a successful peace. Such was the case with the War of 1812. Almost as soon as the United States declared war on Great Britain in June 1812, President James Madison made peace overtures to his British adversaries. In 1813 he tried to convince Great Britain to allow the Russian government to act as intermediaries to end the war. The United States was not faring well in the war and needed a way to end it. When the British sought direct negotiations, Madison quickly accepted the offer. The treaty was negotiated in the city of Ghent, in present-day Belgium. The American negotiators were John Quincy Adams, the son of former president John Adams who would later serve as president himself; Henry Clay, who resigned as House Speaker to negotiate the peace treaty; Jonathan Russell, Madison's chargé d'affaires in England; James A. Bayard, who resigned his Senate seat from Delaware to participate; and Albert Gallatin, the U.S. Secretary of the Treasury, who turned out to be the shrewdest and most effective of the negotiators.

At first the British negotiators made a series of demands that included withdrawing U.S. warships from the Great Lakes, ending fishing privileges of American fishermen in Canadian waters, creating a large Indian reservation in the Northwest territory, and giving up some U.S. land. None of these provisions was acceptable to the United States. Eventually the treaty ceased hostilities without concessions on the part of the United States and both sides agreed to return to the status quo ante bellum, that is, the return to conditions as they existed before the war began. While the Treaty of Ghent declared the war to be a draw from a legal and diplomatic position, it was nonetheless hailed as a victory in the United States. President Madison submitted the treaty to the Senate in February 1815 and the Senate quickly and unanimously approved it.

At the same time that negotiators in Ghent were putting their signatures on the document that technically ended the war on Christmas Eve 1814, General Andrew Jackson was engaged in battle with British forces near New Orleans. Days later, on January 8, 1815, as the treaty made its slow journey from Europe to the United States, Jackson's troops engaged the British in a decisive battle that claimed 2,000 British lives to only 13 on the American side.

TREATY OF PEACE AND AMITY BETWEEN HIS BRITANNIC MAJESTY AND THE UNITED STATES OF AMERICA.

His Britannic Majesty and the United States of America, desirous of terminating the war which has unhappily subsisted between the two countries, and of restoring, upon principles of perfect reciprocity, peace, friendship, and good understanding between them, have for that purpose appointed their respective plenipotentiaries; that is to say, His Britannic Majesty, on his part, has appointed the right honorable James Lord Gambier, late admiral of the white, now admiral of the red squadron of His Majesty's fleet, Henry Goulburn, Esquire, a member of the Imperial Parliament, and Under Secretary of State, and William Adams, Esquire, doctor of civil laws: and the President of the United States, by and with the advice and consent of the Senate thereof, has appointed John Quincy Adams, James A. Bayard, Henry Clay, Jonathan Russell, and Albert Gallatin, citizens of the United States, who, after a reciprocal communication of their respective full powers, have agreed upon the following articles:

ARTICLE 1. There shall be a firm and universal peace between His Britannic Majesty and the United States, and between their respective countries, territories, cities, towns, and people of every degree, without exception of places or persons. All hostilities, both by sea and land, shall cease as soon as this treaty shall have been ratified by both parties, as hereinafter mentioned. All territory, places, and possessions whatsoever taken by either party from the other during the war, or which may be taken after the signing of this treaty, excepting only the islands hereinafter mentioned, shall be restored without delay, and without causing any destruction or carrying away any of the artillery or other public property originally captured in the said forts or places, and which shall remain therein upon the exchange of the ratifications of this treaty, or any slaves or other private property. And all archives, records, deeds, and papers, either of a public nature or belonging to private persons, which in the course of the war may have fallen into the hands of the officers of either party, shall be, as far as may be practicable, forthwith restored and delivered to the proper authorities and persons to whom they respectively belong. Such of the islands in the bay of Passamaquoddy as are claimed by both parties shall remain in the possession of the party in whose occupation they may be at the time of the exchange of the ratifications of this treaty. No disposition made by this treaty, as to such possession of the islands and territories claimed by both parties, shall in any manner whatever be construed to affect the right of either.

ART. 2. Immediately after the ratifications of this treaty by both parties, as hereinafter mentioned, orders shall be sent to the armies, squadrons, officers, subjects, and citizens of the two Powers to cease from all hostilities; and to prevent all causes of complaint which might arise on account of the prizes which may be taken at sea after the said ratifications of this treaty, it is reciprocally agreed that all vessels and effects which may be taken after the space of twelve days from the said ratifications, upon all parts of the coast of North America, from the latitude of twenty-three degrees north to the latitude of fifty degrees north, and as far eastward in the Atlantic ocean as the thirty-sixth degree of west longitude from the meridian of Greenwich, shall be restored on each side; that the time shall be thirty-six days in all other parts of the Atlantic ocean north of the equinoctial line or equator, and the same time for the British and Irish channels, for the Gulf of Mexico, and all parts of the West Indies; forty days for the North seas, for the Baltic, and for all parts of the Mediterranean; sixty days for the Atlantic ocean south of the equator as far as the latitude of the Cape of Good Hope; ninety days for every part of the world south of the equator; and one hundred and twenty days for all other parts of the world, without exception.

ART. 3. All prisoners of war taken on either side, as well as by land as by sea, shall be restored as soon as practicable after the ratifications of this treaty, as hereinafter mentioned, on their paying the debts which they may have contracted during their captivity. The two contracting parties respectively engage to discharge, in specie, the advances which may have been made by the other for the sustenance and maintenance of such prisoners.

ART. 4. Whereas it was stipulated by the second article in the treaty of peace of one thousand seven hundred and eighty-three between his Britannic Majesty and the United States of America, that the boundary of the United States should comprehend all islands within twenty leagues of any party of the shores of the United States, and lying between lines to be drawn due east from the points where the aforesaid boundaries between Nova Scotia on the one part, and East Florida on the other, shall respectively touch the bay of Fundy and the Atlantic ocean, excepting such islands as now are, or heretofore have been, within the limits of Nova Scotia; and whereas several islands in the bay of Passamaquoddy, which is part of the bay of Fundy, and the island of Grand Maman, in the said bay of Fundy, are claimed by the United States as being comprehended within their aforesaid boundaries, which said islands are claimed as belonging to His Britannic Majesty, as having been at the time of, and previous to, the aforesaid treaty of one thousand seven hundred and eighty-three; and if the said commissioners shall agree in their decision, both parties shall consider such decision as final and conclusive. . . .

ART. 9. The United States of America engage to put an end, immediately after the ratification of the present treaty, to hostilities with all the tribes or nations of Indians with whom they may be at war at the time of such ratification, and forthwith to restore to such tribes or nations, respectively, all the possessions, rights, and privileges which they may have enjoyed, or been entitled to, in one thousand eight hundred and eleven, previous to such hostilities: provided always, that such tribes or nations shall agree to desist from all hostilities against the United States of America, their citizens and subjects, upon the ratification of the present treaty being notified to such tribes or nations, and shall so desist accordingly. And His Britannic Majesty engages, on his part, to put an end, immediately after the ratification of the present treaty, to hostilities with all the tribes or nations of Indians with whom he may be at war at the time of such ratification, and forthwith to restore to such tribes or nations, respectively, all the possessions rights, and privileges, which they may have enjoyed, or been entitled to, in one thousand eight hundred and eleven, previous to such hostilities: provided always, that such tribes or nations shall agree to desist from all hostilities against His Britannic Majesty and his subjects, upon the ratification of the present treaty being notified to such tribes or nations, and shall so desist accordingly.

ART. 10. Whereas the traffic in slaves is irreconcilable with the principles of humanity and justice; and whereas both His Majesty and the United States are desirous of continuing their efforts to promoted its entire abolition, it is hereby agreed that both the contracting parties shall use their best endeavors to accomplish so desirable an object.

ART. 11. This treaty, when the same shall have been ratified on both sides, without alteration by either of the contracting parties, and the ratifications mutually exchanged, shall be binding on both parties, and the ratifications shall be exchanged at Washington in the space of four months from this day, or sooner if practicable.

In faith whereof, the respective plenipotentiaries, have signed this treaty, and have hereunto affixed our seals.

Done, in triplicate, at Ghent, the twenty-fourth day of December, one thousand eight hundred and fourteen.

GAMBIER.
HENRY GOULBURN
WILLIAM ADAMS
JOHN QUINCY ADAMS
J. A. BAYARD
HENRY CLAY
JONATHAN RUSSELL
ALBERT GALLATIN

American State Papers, Class 1, Foreign Relations, vol. 3 (10th–13th Congress), Dec. 24, 1814, 745–748.

48   The Establishment of Standing Committees in the Senate

December 5, 1816

The Senate, being a much smaller body than the House, did not feel the need until after the War of 1812 to create permanent standing committees to divide its workload. The evolving committee systems of the House and Senate can be seen as indicators of the growing complexity of the nation and the rising need for a division of labor and the development of increasing expertise in specific areas of legislation.

By 1816 the House had nine standing committees, including a Ways and Means Committee that was a temporary (or "ad hoc") committee from 1789 to 1795 and then a standing committee beginning in 1795. The Senate had only four standing committees in 1816, all of which dealt with internal housekeeping matters rather than with broad areas of legislation. These were the Joint Committee on Enrolled Bills (1789), the Joint Committee on the Library (1806), the Joint Committee on Engrossed Bills (1806), and the Committee to Audit and Control the Contingent Expenses of the Senate (1807).

In 1816 the Senate made a major revision of its committee structure that dramatically changed how it conducted its business. The resolution reproduced here from the collection of the National Archives was printed for distribution in the Senate in 1816, during the discussion of the committee system. It contained some handwritten markings, the most interesting of which is that the Senate resolution originally called for its committee on financial matters to be the Ways and Means Committee, the term used in the House. But the words "Ways and Means" were crossed out and the word "finance" was substituted—a distinction that survives to the present day.

Senator James Barbour of Virginia introduced this resolution on December 5, 1816. The Senate adopted it five days later, and in a matter of days senators were elected to the new committees. On December 18, 1816, the Senate added another committee to its rooster, the Committee on the District of Columbia.

IN SENATE OF THE UNITED STATES
December 5, 1816.

Mr. Barbour submitted the following motion for consideration, which was twice read by unanimous consent.

Resolved, That it shall be one of the rules of the Senate that the following standing committees be appointed at each session.

A Committee on Foreign Relations.
A Committee on ~~Ways and Means.~~ finance
A Committee on Commerce and Manufactures.
A Committee on Military Affairs.
A Committee on the Militia.
A Committee on Naval Affairs.
A Committee on Public Lands.
A Committee of Claims.
A Committee on the Judiciary.
A Committee on the Post-Office, and Post-Roads.
A Committee on Pensions.

"Motion for the appointment of standing committees," Dec. 15, 1816, SEN 14A–B6, RG 46, 14th Congress, 1st session, National Archives, Washington, D.C.

49   Compensation of Members of Congress

December 18, 1816

Deciding what is proper compensation for a member of Congress has been one of the most contentious issues Congress has faced since the beginning of the federal government (see document 18). One of the proposed amendments to the Constitution in 1789 addressed this issue by providing for an election of the House to occur before a pay raise went into effect, thus giving the voters an opportunity to voice their approval or disapproval of any increase. While this amendment was not ratified in 1789, it was revived and ratified 203 years later, in 1992, and became the Twenty-Seventh Amendment to the Constitution (see document 178).

In this 1816 document, a congressional committee expressed its difficulty in understanding why the pay issue seemed to have blown up in their faces. A bill passed March 16, 1816, changed for the first time the way members were paid and provided an increase retroactive to December 1815. From 1789 to 1815 members of the House and Senate had received $6 per day for their service. House and Senate salaries have been equal except on a few brief occasions, such as from 1795 to 1796, when Senators earned $7 per day.

The 1816 bill changed from a daily rate of pay to an annual salary of $1,500. This caused such public outcry that a number of members who voted for the increase were defeated at the polls in the next election. Legend has it that Daniel Webster was one of those defeated over the salary issue of 1816, but this is not true. He simply did not run for reelection.

Congress was forced to retreat. In 1817 it abandoned the annual salary and returned to a daily (per diem) salary of $8. It would be another thirty-eight years before Congress got up enough nerve to give itself another pay raise. In 1855 the public finally accepted the notion of an annual salary, which stood at $3,000 per year until the end of the Civil War in 1865.

The author of this report, Representative Richard M. Johnson of Kentucky, a Democratic-Republican, later served in the Senate and became vice president of the United States in the Van Buren administration.

The committee to whom was referred the consideration of the expediency of repealing or modifying the law passed at the last session relative to the compensation of members of Congress ask leave to report.

The power vested in Congress by the constitution of providing for the pay of its own members is doubtless a delicate trust, and it might have been apprehended, as well from the nature of the subject, as from former experience, and the most judicious exercise of that trust would not be exempt from some degree of public animadversion. The committee, however, cannot perceive, either in the increase of compensation provided by the late act, or in the mode of making that compensation, cause of excitement or alarm adequate to the effects which are understood to have been produced. The addition which this law has made to the public expenditure is not considerable, and, if it

had been created by other measures of Government, would not probably, of itself, have been thought worthy of great attention. And the change in the mode of compensation, even if it be not attended with real and manifest advantages, does not still appear to be wrong so clearly and in such dangerous measures as to furnish grounds for any high degree of public inquietude. The committee, therefore, cannot but be of opinion that the law in question has not been considered without some mixture of misapprehension of its principles and objects, and that a more accurate knowledge of its provisions, and more mature reflection on its design and tendency, if they should not end in a conviction of its usefulness, would yet result in a different and far more moderate estimate of its probable evils. It would not become the committee to claim any infallibility for the body of which they are members, nor to take it for granted that every law which it may pass must necessarily be a wise and wholesome act of legislation. Human errors and imperfections find their way into all bodies; and there is, doubtless, existing in the judgment of the community a power under whose revision this and other acts of Government must and ought to pass. If, however, on a review of this subject, the House should still be of opinion that the law in question, or some equivalent provision, has become essentially necessary for the useful exercise of the powers of Government, and for the safety, security, and honor of the people themselves, its members may still hope that in not hastily departing from it they will be justified by the enlightened sense and generous sentiments of the nation. The abandonment of a measure, which, according to their most conscientious conviction, is intimately connected with the general good, would be no mode of obtaining favor with the American people.

If, in passing the law in question, the House of Representatives discharged any portion of its duty, it acted upon general and public principles, with an entire disregard to the convenience of its own members any further than their convenience was supposed to be connected with the public serve. It treated the question, not as one between themselves and the public, but as exclusively of public and national concern. It regarded it as a subject of general policy by which the nation, and the nation only, was to be affected; as much as any other act of legislation whatever. Any imputation so gross as to impeach its conduct in this essential particular, a feeling of self-respect must compel the House to pass over in silence, and its members must rely on their known character as members of the Government, and as citizens of the community to disprove it. The House would not presume to judge whether its services, in the various and important matters upon which it has acted, have deserved any consideration or respect from the public; but for those services, such as they are, it has not sought nor would accept any reward which could be measured out to it in a mere pecuniary compensation. And while the members of the House would certainly not think of claiming any merit for passing the law in question, any more than for the discharge of what they thought their duty in any other case, the committee do not see that they have any cause for taking humiliation upon themselves on account of having passed an act which they believed would be essentially useful to the country, but which they must have foreseen would be exposed itself, and might expose its authors, to misapprehension and misrepresentation of all sorts. Holding offices in the immediate gift of the people, of short duration, and at a time when the people were soon to exercise, in most districts, their accustomed privilege of a new election, if these offices had been objects of their regard, and if they had permitted personal considerations to influence their conduct, it is obvious that all such considerations pointed to a course different from that which they pursued. They must have known that no measure could be more easily misconstrued and perverted to the purposes of obloquy and reproach. The committee cannot yet believe that a faithful discharge of duty, in the face of these probably consequences, is to be reckoned among dangerous political errors.

. . . .The statute book of the Government exhibits a constant and progressive increase of compensation in all the departments of Government, with the exception of the Legislature and the Supreme Judiciary. On the recommendation of the Executive, or its branches, the Legislature has repeatedly augmented the provisions for that Department, patiently raising the pay of clerks and of writers far above that of its own members, without agitating either itself or the country with any question about its own compensation. From the heads of Departments to the lowest clerkships in the public offices, a general augmentation has obtained throughout. A long enumeration of instances is not necessary; one may suffice. When members of Congress were first paid six dollars a day, the salary of the Attorney General was $1,500 a year. This salary has since been increased to $3,000; and the Executive has, at the present session, found it necessary to recommend a still further increase, as essential to the public service. If the duties of that officer have increased, so have the duties of members of Congress, in at least an equal proportion; and which of the two stations requires the greatest sacrifice of private pursuits may be easily discerned.

. . . .

Of all the powers with which the people have invested the Government, that of legislation is, undoubtedly, the chief. In addition to its own important ordinary duties, the Legislature is the only power which can create other powers. Departments with all their duties, and offices with all their emoluments, can emanate from the Legislature alone. Over the most numerous branch of the Legislature, therefore, the people have retained the power of frequent election; and with this branch alone they have trusted the original exercise of the right of taxation. The members of the House of Representatives are the special delegates and agent s of the people in this high trust. They, and they alone, proceed immediately from the suffrage of the people; they, and they alone, can touch the mainspring of the public

prosperity. They are elected to be the guardians of the public rights and liberties. Can the people then have any greater or clearer interest than that the seats of these their representatives should be honorable and independent stations, in order that they may have the power of filling them with able and independent men? Is it according to the principles of our Government that the legislative office should sink in character and importance below any office, even the highest, in the gift of the Executive? Or can any thing be more unpropitious to the success of a free representative Government than that the representatives of the people should estimate any thing higher than their own seats, or should find inducements to look to any other favor than the favor of their constituents?

It would be a most unnatural state of things in a republic if the people should place greater reliance anywhere else than in their own immediate representatives; or if, on the other hand, representatives should revolve round any other centre than the interests of their constituents. Through their representatives the direct influence and control of the people can alone be felt. In them the rays of their power are collected; and there can be no better criterion by which to judge of the real influence of the people in the Government, than by the degree of respectability and importance attached to the representative character. Evil, indeed, to the republic will that time be, should it ever arrive, when representatives in Congress, instead of being agents of the people to exercise an influence in Government, shall become instruments of Government to influence the people.

It is probably the necessary tendency of government that patronage and influence should accumulate wherever the executive power is deposited, and this accumulation may be expected to increase with the progress of the Government and the increasing wealth of the nation. To guard, as far as possible, against the effect of this on the Legislature, the constitution has prohibited members of Congress from holding, while members, any office under executive appointment. But it has not restrained them from resigning their seats to accept such appointments, nor from accepting them after their term of service has expired; nor has it prohibited the grant of such offices to their relations, connexions, or dependants. There are hundreds of offices in the gift of the Executive, which, as far as pecuniary emolument is concerned, are preferable to seats in Congress. Indeed, there are none, except of the very lowest class, which in that respect are not preferable.

Is it for the interest of the people that their representatives should be placed in this condition? Is it expedient that better service should be commanded for any other department than for the hall of legislation? Or admitting that offices of high trust and responsibility in the State—such as will be commonly regarded less from motives of pecuniary emolument than from the love of honorable distinction and devotion to the public service—should possess more attractions than the legislative office; is it still fit or expedient that subordinate places in Government, such as have no recommendation but the salaries and perquisites belonging to them, should have the same influence? And yet not only is it well known that persons at every election decline being candidates for the Legislature, but the Government has not been without instances in which members of either House have relinquished their seats in the Congress of the United States to accept offices of a very low grade. Can the public interest require the establishment of a habit of filling such places by candidates taken from the legislative body? Or what is the value to the people of the right of representation if they have nothing to give which their representatives will not relinquish for even the smaller appointments of the executive power? It cannot but tend more, one would think, to the permanent safety of the republic that no such hopes or motives should exist; that there should be no inducements of this nature either to an unfaithful and compliant discharge of official duty, or to a more indirect but not less pernicious exercise of the influence of a public character and a public station.

The geographical extent of the United States furnishes a case out of all analogy with any thing which has heretofore existed either in any State Government or the Government of any other country. There are members of Congress who reside more than a thousand miles from the seat of Government. A great proportion live at more than half that distance. If these members are accompanied by their families to a session of Congress, even the present compensation, with the strictest economy, does not defray their expenses. To live within the means provided for them, they must come as exiles from their own homes; they must abandon not only all private pursuits, but the enjoyment of all domestic relations, and live like strangers and temporary lodgers in the metropolis of their own country. How far it is wise in Government to demand of those who enter its service this sacrifice of all social feelings, those who have the deepest knowledge of our nature are most competent to judge. It is a sacrifice which will not ordinarily and for any length of time be made by such as have the dearest and strongest ties to their country, and the greatest possible stake in its prosperity.

One further observation is obvious. If an adequate provision be not made for members of Congress, the office will fall exclusively into the hands of one or the other of two descriptions of persons: either of the most affluent of the country only, who can bear the charges of it without any compensation, or of those who would accept it, not for the compensation legally belonging to it, but from the hope of turning it to account by other means. A reasonable allowance, neither extravagant on the one hand nor parsimonious on the other, would seem to be the best security against these various evils. Influenced by these considerations, Congress was at the last session of opinion that the compensation to members had become inadequate. The committee are still of the same opinion. In many cases it was not equal to the expense incurred by individuals in their attendance on the Legislature; and in all cases it must be presumed that the labor and intelligence bestowed on the discharge of his official duties by an able and faithful member of Congress could not but yield a much more profitable result if employed in private pursuits.

If the view which the committee have taken of this subject be not altogether an erroneous one; if great changes in relation to the value of money and the price of living have taken place in the country; if it has been found necessary to provide for this change by an increase of the compensation of other officers throughout the General and State Governments; and, more than all, if it be desirable to maintain the constitutional importance of the legislative office; to open to the people a wide field for the selection of representatives; to put at their command the experience have best fitted them to promote their interests and maintain their rights, then the object of the law in question was not only a useful but a highly important and commendable object.

In regard to the mode of accomplishing that object, it has not been, and is not, easy to reconcile opinions. On the whole, the committee are of opinion that, under all the circumstances, it is advisable to provide that the increase of pay should be made in the form of an addition to the former daily allowance. They therefore recommend that, in lieu of all other compensations, there be paid to members of Congress and delegates of Territories _____ dollars per day for their actual attendance, and _____ dollars for every twenty miles' travel to and from the seat of Government; and they report a bill for that purpose.

American State Papers, vol. 2, Class X, Miscellaneous, 14th Congress, 2d session, Dec. 18, 1816, 403.

50   A Report on the Publication of a History of Congress

March 30, 1818

The Constitution requires the House and Senate to keep a journal of their proceedings. This has been done since the first Congress in 1789. The journals are extremely important, but they are summaries of what occurs in the chambers of each body and not an attempt to capture the full content of debate. Since the first Congress newspaper reporters and recorders of debate hired by Congress have recorded a rich legacy of what was actually said on the floor of the House or Senate. But Congress was not always interested in keeping all the records

they should have or in making those records available to the public. Historians of Congress owe a great debt to two enterprising men in the early part of the nineteenth century who made great efforts to recover and publish the early debates of Congress. These men were Joseph Gales Jr. and William W. Seaton, both stenographic reporters who covered Congress, Gales in the Senate and Seaton in the House.

In 1810 the two men took over an important Washington newspaper, The National Intelligencer, *which published extensive coverage of House and Senate debates. Because of their contacts with House and Senate members, they gained contracts to be the official printers for the House and Senate. In 1818 they proposed a monumental multivolume publication that would bring together the fragmentary and often unpublished debates of the early Congresses. This was a private printing venture on a large scale and Gales and Seaton sought government support for the project. The "history of Congress" referred to in this report was eventually published in 42 volumes between 1834 and 1856 as the* Annals of Congress. *Gales and Seaton were also responsible for the publication of the* American State Papers *series and the* Register of Debates, *a forerunner of the modern* Congressional Record. *Both men later served terms as mayors of Washington, D.C.*

In the debate over the report on Gales and Seaton's plan to publish the Annals of Congress, *one member—Josiah Butler of New Hampshire—argued against the publication on the grounds that he could not see any "great public advantage" from it and that it would be too expensive. He said the only persons that would be interested in it would be those members of Congress who would be pleased "to read their own speeches, and see their names floating down the current of time in this great political ark, the History of Congress." Thanks to Gales and Seaton, even Representative Butler's objections to their work have been saved and are still floating down the currents of time. The* Annals of Congress *have proven to be one of the most valuable resources we have on the early years of Congress. The* Annals *are currently coming on-line on the Internet at the Library of Congress Web site.*

Mr. ROBERTSON, of Louisiana, from the committee to whom was referred the memorial of Gales and Seaton, reported:

That the memorialists are engaged in publishing a History of the Congress of the United States from the commencement of the Government to the present day, and a continuation of the same history, to keep pace with the present and future transactions of that body. The memorialists solicit the aid of the Government in this their laborious and expensive undertaking. The committee are fully impressed with the importance of this work. Nothing can be more useful than a correct legislative history of the United States. It is a source of much regret that one has not heretofore existed; and, now that it is proposed to be published,

there can be no hesitation in giving it encouragement. The views and opinions of the great actors on the theatre of Government are not less necessary to be known than their acts themselves. The utility of judicial reports is very generally admitted; and, if the reasons of the judge ought to accompany his exposition of the law, how much more proper is it that this should be the case in respect to the views of the legislator, the author of the law itself. To a right understanding of statutes, nothing is more essential than a knowledge of the causes and motives which produced their enactment; and this can in no way be so satisfactorily obtained as by a resort to contemporaneous debate.

That the aid of Congress is necessary to this work arises out of the great labor and expense attending it, whilst, at the same time, no adequate remuneration can be expected from its sale. The agriculturist, the merchant, the mechanic, and the physician, who purchase other books, will feel comparatively but little interest in this, however useful it may be to the politician, the historian, and the lawyer. The work will not afford amusement to the general reader, but without it the archives of the nation are defective.

Congress has not been backward in giving aid to publications of a similar character. Of the new edition of the Laws of the United States a subscription was directed of one thousand copies before the work was commenced. Three or four hundred have been since purchased of that work, and it is now proposed to purchase eight hundred copies more. A subscription was, in like manner, authorized to Wait's edition of the public documents; and it is further proposed to purchase an equal number of copies of an additional volume of that work about to be published. The policy is not less just than liberal which provides for the widest attainable diffusion of whatever concerns the development of the springs and principles of our Government.

With such views it is that, at the present session, the publication of the journals of the convention and of the secret journal of the old Congress has been authorized; and, with such views, the committee ask leave to report a bill authorizing a subscription to the History of Congress.

American State Papers (11th–17th Congress), vol. 2, Class 10, Miscellaneous, 15th Congress, 1st session, March 30, 1818, 510.

51 An Act to Establish the Design of the Flag of the United States

April 4, 1818

This simple piece of legislation defined the nature and design of the nation's most important symbol, the flag of the United States. As the nation grew beyond the original thirteen colonies, the design of the U.S. flag underwent changes in the number of stars and stripes, although the general design of red and white stripes and white stars on a blue field remained the same as it was during the Revolutionary War, when the Continental Congress established

the first flag on June 14, 1777. As early as 1795, after Kentucky and Vermont were added to the Union and the number of stripes was increased to fifteen, some members of Congress argued that there ought to be a permanent design established. In 1818 Congress established the pattern for design changes that has remained in operation to the present day. Subsequent flag laws have followed the 1818 law. Since 1912 the president has specified the actual design by executive order. *Beginning in the 1920s, a code regarding flag etiquette, promoted by patriotic groups following World War I, was in wide use and eventually made law in 1942. Flag Day, June 14, became a national holiday in 1916.*

The Constitution does not specifically authorize Congress to establish a flag, but it was clearly understood that this matter fell under the implied powers of Congress. The first law regarding flag desecration was passed in 1905 to limit the commercial use of flags on trademarks. In recent years the issue of burning the American flag as a protest against U.S. actions or policies has led some members of Congress to call for a constitutional amendment that would prohibit flag burning. The Supreme Court, in the case of Texas v. Johnson *(1989), upheld the right of citizens to engage in flag burning as an exercise of their First Amendment rights of free speech. While the number of flags that have been burned in protest is minuscule, this issue has generated much emotion in Congress and among citizens.*

CHAP. XXXIV.—*AN ACT TO ESTABLISH THE FLAG OF THE UNITED STATES.*

Be it enacted by the Senate and House of Representatives of the United States of America, in Congress assembled, That from and after the fourth day of July next, the flag of the United States be thirteen horizontal stripes, alternate red and white: that the union be twenty stars, white in a blue field.

SEC. 2. *And be it further enacted,* That on the admission of every new state into the Union, one star be added to the union of the flag; and that such addition shall take effect on the fourth day of July then next succeeding such admission.

APPROVED, April 4, 1818.

Statutes at Large, 3 (1818–1823), 15th Congress, 1st session, April 4, 1818, 415.

52   *McCullough v. Maryland*

1819

The decision of the Supreme Court in the case of McCullough v. Maryland *proved to be one of the most significant cases in American history in helping to establish a strong national government. This decision gave Congress broad powers over the actions of state governments. Chief Justice John Marshall, who rendered the decision, served as chief justice from 1801 to 1835. During his long and forceful tenure on the Supreme Court he made numerous decisions that strengthened the Federalist view that the Constitution was framed for the purpose of creating a strong national government.*

This case was brought by James W. McCullough, a cashier at the Baltimore branch of the Second Bank of the United States. McCullough sued the state of Maryland for imposing an annual tax on the federally chartered Second Bank. Banks chartered by the state of Maryland did not have to pay the tax. The Supreme Court decided that the Maryland law taxing the Second Bank of the United States was unconstitutional. Congress, Marshall concluded, had the power to incorporate banks and the Constitution should be interpreted in such a manner as to give Congress broad authority to make laws necessary to carry out its constitutional responsibilities. In so ruling, Marshall countered the "strict construction" view held by most state governments that the only powers Congress had were those explicitly spelled out in the Constitution.

Even though President Andrew Jackson vetoed the bill to recharter the Second Bank of the United States in 1832, the decision in this case set a long-lasting precedent that overshadowed Jackson's veto. McCullough v. Maryland *has been cited frequently in subsequent decisions of the Supreme Court well into the twentieth century, including challenges to New Deal legislation in the 1930s.*

MARSHALL, Chief Justice, delivered the opinion of the Court.

In the case now to be determined, the defendant, a sovereign State, denies the obligation of a law enacted by the legislature of the Union, and the plaintiff, on his part, contests the validity of an act which has been passed by the legislature of that State. The Constitution of our country, in its most interesting and vital parts, is to be considered, the conflicting powers of the Government of the Union and of its members, as marked in that Constitution, are to be discussed, and an opinion given which may essentially influence the great operations of the Government. No tribunal can approach such a question without a deep sense of its importance, and of the awful responsibility involved in its decision. But it must be decided peacefully, or remain a source of hostile legislation, perhaps, of hostility of a still more serious nature; and if it is to be so decided, by this tribunal alone can the decision be made. On the Supreme Court of the United States has the Constitution of our country devolved this important duty.

The first question made in the cause is—has Congress power to incorporate a bank?

It has been truly said that this can scarcely be considered as an open question entirely unprejudiced by the former proceedings of the Nation respecting it. The principle now contested was introduced at a very early period of our history, has been recognised by many successive legislatures, and has been acted upon by the Judicial Department, in cases of peculiar delicacy, as a law of undoubted obligation.

. . . .

The power now contested was exercised by the first Congress elected under the present Constitution. The bill for incorporating the Bank of the United States did not steal upon an unsuspecting legislature and pass unobserved. Its principle was completely understood, and was opposed with equal zeal and ability. After being resisted first in the fair and open field of debate, and afterwards in the executive cabinet, with as much persevering talent as any measure has ever experienced, and being supported by arguments which convinced minds as pure and as intelligent as this country can boast, it became a law. The original act was permitted to expire, but a short experience of the embarrassments to which the refusal to revive it exposed the Government convinced those who were most prejudiced against the measure of its necessity, and induced the passage of the present law. It would require no ordinary share of intrepidity to assert that a measure adopted under these circumstances was a bold and plain usurpation to which the Constitution gave no countenance. These observations belong to the cause; but they are not made under the impression that, were the question entirely new, the law would be found irreconcilable with the Constitution.

In discussing this question, the counsel for the State of Maryland have deemed it of some importance, in the construction of the Constitution, to consider that instrument not as emanating from the people, but as the act of sovereign and independent States. The powers of the General Government, it has been said, are delegated by the States, who alone are truly sovereign, and must be exercised in subordination to the States, who alone possess supreme dominion. It would be difficult to sustain this proposition. The convention which framed the Constitution was indeed elected by the State legislatures. But the instrument, when it came from their hands, was a mere proposal, without obligation or pretensions to it. It was reported to the then existing Congress of the United States with a request that it might be submitted to a convention of delegates, chosen in each State by the people thereof, under the recommendation of its legislature, for their assent and ratification.

This mode of proceeding was adopted, and by the convention, by Congress, and by the State legislatures, the instrument was submitted to the people. They acted upon it in the only manner in which they can act safely, effectively and wisely, on such a subject—by assembling in convention. It is true, they assembled in their several States—and where else should they have assembled? No political dreamer was ever wild enough to think of breaking down the lines which separate the States, and of compounding the American people into one common mass. Of consequence, when they act, they act in their States. But the measures they adopt do not, on that account, cease to be the measures of the people themselves, or become the measures of the State governments.

From these conventions the Constitution derives its whole authority. The government proceeds directly from the people; is "ordained and established" in the name of the people, and is declared to be ordained, in order to form a more perfect union, establish justice, insure domestic tranquillity, and secure the blessings of liberty to themselves and to their posterity.

The assent of the States in their sovereign capacity is implied in calling a convention, and thus submitting that instrument to the people. But the people were at perfect liberty to accept or reject it, and their act was final. It required not the affirmance, and could not be negatived, by the State Governments. The Constitution, when thus adopted, was of complete obligation, and bound the State sovereignties.

It has been said that the people had already surrendered all their powers to the State sovereignties, and had nothing more to give. But surely the question whether they may resume and modify the powers granted to Government does not remain to be settled in this country. Much more might the legitimacy of the General Government be doubted had it been created by the States. The powers delegated to the State sovereignties were to be exercised by themselves, not by a distinct and independent sovereignty created by themselves. To the formation of a league such as was the Confederation, the State sovereignties were certainly competent. But when, "in order to form a more perfect union," it was deemed necessary to change this alliance into an effective Government, possessing great and sovereign powers and acting directly on the people, the necessity of referring it to the people, and of deriving its powers directly from them, was felt and acknowledged by all. The Government of the Union then (whatever may be the influence of this fact on the case) is, emphatically and truly, a Government of the people. In form and in substance, it emanates from them. Its powers are granted by them, and are to be exercised directly on them, and for their benefit.

This Government is acknowledged by all to be one of enumerated powers. The principle that it can exercise only the powers granted to it would seem too apparent to have required to be enforced by all those arguments which its enlightened friends, while it was depending before the people, found it necessary to urge; that principle is now universally admitted. But the question respecting the extent of the powers actually granted is perpetually arising, and will probably continue to arise so long as our system shall exist. In discussing these questions, the conflicting powers of the General and State Governments must be brought into view, and the supremacy of their respective laws, when they are in opposition, must be settled.

If any one proposition could command the universal assent of mankind, we might expect it would be this—that the Government of the Union, though limited in its powers, is supreme within its sphere of action. This would seem to result necessarily from its nature. It is the Government of all; its powers are delegated by all; it represents all, and acts for all. Though any one State may be willing to control its operations, no State is willing to allow others to control them. The nation, on those subjects on which it can act, must necessarily bind its component parts. But this question is not left to mere reason; the people have, in express terms, decided it by saying, "this Constitution, and the laws of the United States, which shall be made in pursuance thereof," "shall be the supreme law of the land," and by requiring that the members of the State legislatures and the officers of the executive and judicial departments of the States shall take the oath of fidelity to it. The Government of the United States, then, though limited in its powers, is supreme, and its laws, when made in pursuance of the Constitution, form the supreme law of the land, "anything in the Constitution or laws of any State to the contrary notwithstanding."

Among the enumerated powers, we do not find that of establishing a bank or creating a corporation. But there is no phrase in the instrument which, like the Articles of Confederation, excludes incidental or implied powers and which requires that everything granted shall be expressly and minutely described. Even the 10th Amendment, which was framed for the purpose of quieting the excessive jealousies which had been excited, omits the word "expressly," and declares only that the powers "not delegated to the United States, nor prohibited to the States, are reserved to the States or to the people," thus leaving the question whether the particular power which may become the subject of contest has been delegated to the one Government, or prohibited to the other, to depend on a fair construction of the whole instrument. The men who drew and adopted this amendment had experienced the embarrassments resulting from the insertion of this word in the Articles of Confederation, and probably omitted it to avoid those embarrassments. A Constitution, to contain an accurate detail of all the subdivisions of which its great powers will admit, and of all the means by which they may be carried into execution, would partake of the prolixity of a legal code, and could scarcely be embraced by the human mind. It would probably never be understood by the public. Its nature, therefore, requires that only its great outlines should be marked, its important objects designated, and the minor ingredients which compose those objects be deduced from the nature of the objects themselves. That this idea was entertained by the framers of the American Constitution is not only to be inferred from the nature of the instrument, but from the language. Why else were some of the limitations found in the 9th section of the 1st article introduced? It is also in some degree warranted by their having omitted to use any restrictive term which might prevent its receiving a fair and just interpretation. In considering this question, then, we must never forget that it is a Constitution we are expounding.

Although, among the enumerated powers of Government, we do not find the word "bank" or "incorporation," we find the great powers, to lay and collect taxes; to borrow money; to regulate commerce; to declare and conduct a war; and to raise and support armies and navies. The sword and the purse, all the external relations, and no inconsiderable portion of the industry of the nation are intrusted to its Government. It can never be pretended that these vast powers draw after them others of inferior importance merely because they are inferior. Such an idea can never be advanced. But it may with great reason be contended that a Government intrusted with such ample powers, on the due execution of which the happiness and prosperity of the Nation so vitally depends, must also be intrusted with ample

means for their execution. The power being given, it is the interest of the Nation to facilitate its execution. It can never be their interest, and cannot be presumed to have been their intention, to clog and embarrass its execution by withholding the most appropriate means. Throughout this vast republic, from the St. Croix to the Gulf of Mexico, from the Atlantic to the Pacific, revenue is to be collected and expended, armies are to be marched and supported. The exigencies of the Nation may require that the treasure raised in the north should be transported to the south that raised in the east, conveyed to the west, or that this order should be reversed. Is that construction of the Constitution to be preferred which would render these operations difficult, hazardous and expensive? Can we adopt that construction (unless the words imperiously require it) which would impute to the framers of that instrument, when granting these powers for the public good, the intention of impeding their exercise, by withholding a choice of means? If, indeed, such be the mandate of the Constitution, we have only to obey; but that instrument does not profess to enumerate the means by which the powers it confers may be executed; nor does it prohibit the creation of a corporation, if the existence of such a being be essential, to the beneficial exercise of those powers. It is, then, the subject of fair inquiry how far such means may be employed.

It is not denied that the powers given to the Government imply the ordinary means of execution. That, for example, of raising revenue and applying it to national purposes is admitted to imply the power of conveying money from place to place as the exigencies of the Nation may require, and of employing the usual means of conveyance. But it is denied that the Government has its choice of means, or that it may employ the most convenient means if, to employ them, it be necessary to erect a corporation. On what foundation does this argument rest? On this alone: the power of creating a corporation is one appertaining to sovereignty, and is not expressly conferred on Congress. This is true. But all legislative powers appertain to sovereignty. The original power of giving the law on any subject whatever is a sovereign power, and if the Government of the Union is restrained from creating a corporation as a means for performing its functions, on the single reason that the creation of a corporation is an act of sovereignty, if the sufficiency of this reason be acknowledged, there would be some difficulty in sustaining the authority of Congress to pass other laws for the accomplishment of the same objects. The Government which has a right to do an act and has imposed on it the duty of performing that act must, according to the dictates of reason, be allowed to select the means, and those who contend that it may not select any appropriate means that one particular mode of effecting the object is excepted take upon themselves the burden of establishing that exception.

The creation of a corporation, it is said, appertains to sovereignty. This is admitted. But to what portion of sovereignty does it appertain? Does it belong to one more than to another? In America, the powers of sovereignty are divided between the Government of the Union and those of the States. They are each sovereign with respect to the objects committed to it, and neither sovereign with respect to the objects committed to the other. We cannot comprehend that train of reasoning, which would maintain that the extent of power granted by the people is to be ascertained not by the nature and terms of the grant, but by its date. Some State Constitutions were formed before, some since, that of the United States. We cannot believe that their relation to each other is in any degree dependent upon this circumstance. Their respective powers must, we think, be precisely the same as if they had been formed at the same time. Had they been formed at the same time, and had the people conferred on the General Government the power contained in the Constitution, and on the States the whole residuum of power, would it have been asserted that the Government of the Union was not sovereign, with respect to those objects which were intrusted to it, in relation to which its laws were declared to be supreme? If this could not have been asserted, we cannot well comprehend the process of reasoning which maintains that a power appertaining to sovereignty cannot be connected with that vast portion of it which is granted to the General Government, so far as it is calculated to subserve the legitimate objects of that Government. The power of creating a corporation, though appertaining to sovereignty, is not, like the power of making war or levying taxes or of regulating commerce, a great substantive and independent power which cannot be implied as incidental to other powers or used as a means of executing them. It is never the end for which other powers are exercised, but a means by which other objects are accomplished. No contributions are made to charity for the sake of an incorporation, but a corporation is created to administer the charity; no seminary of learning is instituted in order to be incorporated, but the corporate character is conferred to subserve the purposes of education. No city was ever built with the sole object of being incorporated, but is incorporated as affording the best means of being well governed. The power of creating a corporation is never used for its own sake, but for the purpose of effecting something else. No sufficient reason is therefore perceived why it may not pass as incidental to those powers which are expressly given if it be a direct mode of executing them.

But the Constitution of the United States has not left the right of Congress to employ the necessary means for the execution of the powers conferred on the Government to general reasoning. To its enumeration of powers is added that of making all laws which shall be necessary and proper for carrying into execution the foregoing powers, and all other powers vested by this Constitution in the Government of the United States or in any department thereof.

The counsel for the State of Maryland have urged various arguments to prove that this clause, though in terms a grant of power, is not so in effect, but is really restrictive of the general right which might otherwise be implied of selecting means for executing the enumerated powers.

. . . .

But the argument on which most reliance is placed is drawn from that peculiar language of this clause. Congress is not empowered by it to make all laws which may have relation to the powers conferred on the Government, but such only as may be "necessary and proper" for carrying them into execution. The word "necessary" is considered as controlling the whole sentence, and as limiting the right to pass laws for the execution of the granted powers to such as are indispensable, and without which the power would be nugatory. That it excludes the choice of means, and leaves to Congress in each case that only which is most direct and simple.

Is it true that this is the sense in which the word "necessary" is always used? Does it always import an absolute physical necessity so strong that one thing to which another may be termed necessary cannot exist without that other? We think it does not. If reference be had to its use in the common affairs of the world or in approved authors, we find that it frequently imports no more than that one thing is convenient, or useful, or essential to another. To employ the means necessary to an end is generally understood as employing any means calculated to produce the end, and not as being confined to those single means without which the end would be entirely unattainable. Such is the character of human language that no word conveys to the mind in all situations one single definite idea, and nothing is more common than to use words in a figurative sense. Almost all compositions contain words which, taken in a their rigorous sense, would convey a meaning different from that which is obviously intended. It is essential to just construction that many words which import something excessive should be understood in a more mitigated sense—in that sense which common usage justifies. The word "necessary" is of this description. It has not a fixed character peculiar to itself. It admits of all degrees of comparison, and is often connected with other words which increase or diminish the impression the mind receives of the urgency it imports. A thing may be necessary, very necessary, absolutely or indispensably necessary. To no mind would the same idea be conveyed by these several phrases. The comment on the word is well illustrated by the passage cited at the bar from the 10th section of the 1st article of the Constitution. It is, we think, impossible to compare the sentence which prohibits a State from laying "imposts, or duties on imports or exports, except what may be absolutely necessary for executing its inspection laws," with that which authorizes Congress "to make all laws which shall be necessary and proper for carrying into execution" the powers of the General Government without feeling a conviction that the convention understood itself to change materially the meaning of the word "necessary," by prefixing the word "absolutely." This word, then, like others, is used in various senses, and, in its construction, the subject, the context, the intention of the person using them are all to be taken into view.

Let this be done in the case under consideration. The subject is the execution of those great powers on which the welfare of a Nation essentially depends. It must have been the intention of those who gave these powers to insure, so far as human prudence could insure, their beneficial execution. This could not be done by confiding the choice of means to such narrow limits as not to leave it in the power of Congress to adopt any which might be appropriate, and which were conducive to the end. This provision is made in a Constitution intended to endure for ages to come, and consequently to be adapted to the various crises of human affairs. To have prescribed the means by which Government should, in all future time, execute its powers would have been to change entirely the character of the instrument and give it the properties of a legal code. It would have been an unwise attempt to provide by immutable rules for exigencies which, if foreseen at all, must have been seen dimly, and which can be best provided for as they occur. To have declared that the best means shall not be used, but those alone without which the power given would be nugatory, would have been to deprive the legislature of the capacity to avail itself of experience, to exercise its reason, and to accommodate its legislation to circumstances.

. . . .

But the argument which most conclusively demonstrates the error of the construction contended for by the counsel for the State of Maryland is founded on the intention of the convention as manifested in the whole clause. To waste time and argument in proving that, without it, Congress might carry its powers into execution would be not much less idle than to hold a lighted taper to the sun. As little can it be required to prove that, in the absence of this clause, Congress would have some choice of means. That it might employ those which, in its judgment, would most advantageously effect the object to be accomplished. That any means adapted to the end, any means which tended directly to the execution of the Constitutional powers of the Government, were in themselves Constitutional. This clause, as construed by the State of Maryland, would abridge, and almost annihilate, this useful and necessary right of the legislature to select its means. That this could not be intended is, we should think, had it not been already controverted, too apparent for controversy.

The result of the most careful and attentive consideration bestowed upon this clause is that, if it does not enlarge, it cannot be construed to restrain, the powers of Congress, or to impair the right of the legislature to exercise its best judgment in the selection of measures to carry into execution the Constitutional powers of the Government. If no other motive for its insertion can be suggested, a sufficient one is found in the desire to remove all doubts respecting the right to legislate on that vast mass of incidental powers which must be involved in the Constitution if that instrument be not a splendid bauble.

We admit, as all must admit, that the powers of the Government are limited, and that its limits are not to be transcended. But we think the sound construction of the Constitution must allow to the national legislature that discretion with respect to the means by which the powers it confers are to be carried into execution which will enable that body to perform the high duties assigned to it in the manner most beneficial to the people. Let the end be legitimate, let it be within the scope of the Constitution, and all means which are appropriate, which are plainly adapted to that end, which are not prohibited, but consist with the letter and spirit of the Constitution, are Constitutional.

. . . .

If a corporation may be employed, indiscriminately with other means, to carry into execution the powers of the Government, no particular reason can be assigned for excluding the use of a bank, if required for its fiscal operations. To use one must be within the discretion of Congress if it be an appropriate mode of executing the powers of Government. That it is a convenient, a useful, and essential instrument in the prosecution of its fiscal operations is not now a subject of controversy.

. . . .

But were its necessity less apparent, none can deny its being an appropriate measure; and if it is, the decree of its necessity, as has been very justly observed, is to be discussed in another place. Should Congress, in the execution of its powers, adopt measures which are prohibited by the Constitution, or should Congress, under the pretext of executing its powers, pass laws for the accomplishment of objects not intrusted to the Government, it would become the painful duty of this tribunal, should a case requiring such a decision come before it, to say that such an act was not the law of the land. But where the law is not prohibited, and is really calculated to effect any of the objects intrusted to the Government, to undertake here to inquire into the decree of its necessity would be to pass the line which circumscribes the judicial department and to tread on legislative ground. This Court disclaims all pretensions to such a power.

After this declaration, it can scarcely be necessary to say that the existence of State banks can have no possible influence on the question. No trace is to be found in the Constitution of an intention to create a dependence of the Government of the Union on those of the States, for the execution of the great powers assigned to it. Its means are adequate to its ends, and on those means alone was it expected to rely for the accomplishment of its ends. To impose on it the necessity of resorting to means which it cannot control, which another Government may furnish or withhold, would render its course precarious, the result of its measures uncertain, and create a dependence on other Governments which might disappoint its most important designs, and is incompatible with the language of the Constitution. But were it otherwise, the choice of means implies a right to choose a national bank in preference to State banks, and Congress alone can make the election.

After the most deliberate consideration, it is the unanimous and decided opinion of this Court that the act to incorporate the Bank of the United States is a law made in pursuance of the Constitution, and is a part of the supreme law of the land.

. . . .

It being the opinion of the Court that the act incorporating the bank is constitutional, and that the power of establishing a branch in the State of Maryland might be properly exercised by the bank itself, we proceed to inquire:

2. Whether the State of Maryland may, without violating the Constitution, tax that branch?

That the power of taxation is one of vital importance; that it is retained by the States; that it is not abridged by the grant of a similar power to the Government of the Union; that it is to be concurrently exercised by the two Governments—are truths which have never been denied. But such is the paramount character of the Constitution that its capacity to withdraw any subject from the action of even this power is admitted. The States are expressly forbidden to lay any duties on imports or exports except what may be absolutely necessary for executing their inspection laws. If the obligation of this prohibition must be conceded—if it may restrain a State from the exercise of its taxing power on imports and exports—the same paramount character would seem to restrain, as it certainly may restrain, a State from such other exercise of this power as is in its nature incompatible with, and repugnant to, the constitutional laws of the Union. A law absolutely repugnant to another as entirely repeals that other as if express terms of repeal were used.

On this ground, the counsel for the bank place its claim to be exempted from the power of a State to tax its operations. There is no express provision for the case, but the claim has been sustained on a principle which so entirely pervades the Constitution, is so intermixed with the materials which compose it, so interwoven with its web, so blended with its texture, as to be incapable of being separated from it without rending it into shreds.

This great principle is that the Constitution and the laws made in pursuance thereof are supreme; that they control the Constitution and laws of the respective States, and cannot be controlled by them. From this, which may be almost termed an axiom, other propositions are deduced as corollaries, on the truth or error of which, and on their application to this case, the cause has been supposed to depend. These are, 1st. That a power to create implies a power to preserve; 2d. That a power to destroy, if wielded by a different hand, is hostile to, and incompatible with these powers to create and to preserve; 3d. That, where this repugnancy exists, that authority which is supreme must control, not yield to that over which it is supreme.

. . . .

The power of Congress to create and, of course, to continue the bank was the subject of the preceding part of this opinion, and is no longer to be considered as questionable.

That the power of taxing it by the States may be exercised so as to destroy it is too obvious to be denied. But taxation is said to be an absolute power which acknowledges no other limits than those expressly prescribed in the Constitution, and, like sovereign power of every other description, is intrusted to the discretion of those who use it. But the very terms of this argument admit that the sovereignty of the State, in the article of taxation itself, is subordinate to, and may be controlled by, the Constitution of the United States. How far it has been con-

trolled by that instrument must be a question of construction. In making this construction, no principle, not declared, can be admissible which would defeat the legitimate operations of a supreme Government. It is of the very essence of supremacy to remove all obstacles to its action within its own sphere, and so to modify every power vested in subordinate governments as to exempt its own operations from their own influence. This effect need not be stated in terms. It is so involved in the declaration of supremacy, so necessarily implied in it, that the expression of it could not make it more certain. We must, therefore, keep it in view while construing the Constitution.

The argument on the part of the State of Maryland is not that the States may directly resist a law of Congress, but that they may exercise their acknowledged powers upon it, and that the Constitution leaves them this right, in the confidence that they will not abuse it.

. . . .

The sovereignty of a State extends to everything which exists by its own authority or is introduced by its permission, but does it extend to those means which are employed by Congress to carry into execution powers conferred on that body by the people of the United States? We think it demonstrable that it does not. Those powers are not given by the people of a single State. They are given by the people of the United States, to a Government whose laws, made in pursuance of the Constitution, are declared to be supreme. Consequently, the people of a single State cannot confer a sovereignty which will extend over them.

. . . .

That the power to tax involves the power to destroy; that the power to destroy may defeat and render useless the power to create; that there is a plain repugnance in conferring on one Government a power to control the constitutional measures of another, which other, with respect to those very measures, is declared to be supreme over that which exerts the control, are propositions not to be denied. But all inconsistencies are to be reconciled by the magic of the word *confidence.* Taxation, it is said, does not necessarily and unavoidably destroy. To carry it to the excess of destruction would be an abuse, to presume which would banish that confidence which is essential to all Government. But is this a case of confidence? Would the people of any one State trust those of another with a power to control the most insignificant operations of their State Government? We know they would not. Why, then, should we suppose that the people of any one State should be willing to trust those of another with a power to control the operations of a Government to which they have confided their most important and most valuable interests? In the Legislature of the Union alone are all represented. The Legislature of the Union alone, therefore, can be trusted by the people with the power of controlling measures which concern all, in the confidence that it will not be abused. This, then, is not a case of confidence, and we must consider it is as it really is.

If we apply the principle for which the State of Maryland contends, to the Constitution generally, we shall find it capable of changing totally the character of that instrument. We shall find it capable of arresting all the measures of the Government, and of prostrating it at the foot of the States. The American people have declared their Constitution and the laws made in pursuance thereof to be supreme, but this principle would transfer the supremacy, in fact, to the States. If the States may tax one instrument, employed by the Government in the execution of its powers, they may tax any and every other instrument. They may tax the mail; they may tax the mint; they may tax patent rights; they may tax the papers of the custom house; they may tax judicial process; they may tax all the means employed by the Government to an excess which would defeat all the ends of Government. This was not intended by the American people. They did not design to make their Government dependent on the States.

. . . If the controlling power of the States be established, if their supremacy as to taxation be acknowledged, what is to restrain their exercising control in any shape they may please to give it? Their sovereignty is not confined to taxation; that is not the only mode in which it might be displayed. The question is, in truth, a question of supremacy, and if the right of the States to tax the means employed by the General Government be conceded, the declaration that the Constitution and the laws made in pursuance thereof shall be the supreme law of the land is empty and unmeaning declamation.

In the course of the argument, the Federalist has been quoted, and the opinions expressed by the authors of that work have been justly supposed to be entitled to great respect in expounding the Constitution. No tribute can be paid to them which exceeds their merit; but in applying their opinions to the cases which may arise in the progress of our Government, a right to judge of their correctness must be retained; and to understand the argument, we must examine the proposition it maintains and the objections against which it is directed. The subject of those numbers from which passages have been cited is the unlimited power of taxation which is vested in the General Government. The objection to this unlimited power, which the argument seeks to remove, is stated with fulness and clearness. It is, that an indefinite power of taxation in the latter (the Government of the Union) might, and probably would, in time, deprive the former (the Government of the States) of the means of providing for their own necessities, and would subject them entirely to the mercy of the National Legislature. As the laws of the Union are to become the supreme law of the land; as it is to have power to pass all laws that may be necessary for carrying into execution the authorities with which it is proposed to vest it; the National Government might, at any time, abolish the taxes imposed for State objects upon the pretence of an interference with its own. It might allege a necessity for doing this, in order to give efficacy to the national revenues; and thus, all the resources of taxation might, by degrees, become the subjects of federal monopoly, to the entire exclusion and destruction of the State Governments.

. . . .

It has also been insisted that, as the power of taxation in the General and State Governments is acknowledged to be concurrent, every argument which would sustain the right of the General Government to tax banks chartered by the States, will equally sustain the right of the States to tax banks chartered by the General Government. But the two cases are not on the same reason. The people of all the States have created the General Government, and have conferred upon it the general power of taxation. The people of all the States, and the States themselves, are represented in Congress, and, by their representatives, exercise this power. When they tax the chartered institutions of the States, they tax their constituents, and these taxes must be uniform. But when a State taxes the operations of the Government of the United States, it acts upon institutions created not by their own constituents, but by people over whom they claim no control. It acts upon the measures of a Government created by others as well as themselves, for the benefit of others in common with themselves. The difference is that which always exists, and always must exist, between the action of the whole on a part, and the action of a part on the whole—between the laws of a Government declared to be supreme, and those of a Government which, when in opposition to those laws, is not supreme.

. . . .

The Court has bestowed on this subject its most deliberate consideration. The result is a conviction that the States have no power, by taxation or otherwise, to retard, impede, burden, or in any manner control the operations of the constitutional laws enacted by Congress to carry into execution the powers vested in the General Government. This is, we think, the unavoidable consequence of that supremacy which the Constitution has declared. We are unanimously of opinion that the law passed by the Legislature of Maryland, imposing a tax on the Bank of the United States is unconstitutional and void. . . .

. . . It is, therefore, adjudged and ordered that the said judgment of the said Court of Appeals of the State of Maryland in this case be, and the same hereby is, reversed and annulled. And this Court, proceeding to render such judgment as the said Court of Appeals should have rendered, it is further adjudged and ordered that the judgment of the said Baltimore County Court be reversed and annulled, and that judgment be entered in the said Baltimore County Court for the said James W. McCulloch.

17 U.S. 316 (1819). Text courtesy of *Selected Historic Decisions of the U.S. Supreme Court* (CD-ROM, 1997 edition), a publication of the Legal Information Institute, Cornell Law School.

53 The Missouri Compromise

1819–1821

The Missouri Compromise was Congress's first major attempt to deal with the issue of the expansion of slavery in the United States. It marks a significant juncture in the struggle between the North and South over the limits to which slavery could be extended into new states. The Missouri Compromise was not one piece of legislation or one document but a series of actions in 1819, 1820, and 1821 that constitute an agreement that a majority of pro- and antislavery advocates in Congress and the state of Missouri finally approved.

Following the Louisiana Purchase in 1803, southern parts of the Louisiana Territory quickly became areas for the expansion of slavery. By the time Missouri, a part of the Louisiana Territory, sought admission to statehood in 1819, many in the North felt the expansion of slavery could no longer be ignored. Underlying the issue was a struggle over political control of Congress. The South wanted to maintain a balance of slave and free states in the Senate. The southern states feared the growing power of the North and the emergence of free western states, which, if left unchecked, could further isolate and reduce the political power of the South.

In February 1819, as legislation granting Missouri statehood was introduced in the House, Representative James Tallmadge Jr. (R-N.Y.) offered an amendment that prohibited further importation of slaves into Missouri and called for the gradual emancipation of all slaves in Missouri. This dramatically heightened the stakes in the growing debate over slavery in the United States and led to a crisis that threatened to divide the United States into slave states and free states. Under the Tallmadge amendment, Missouri would be admitted as a slave state, but eventually it would become a free state. The House approved the Tallmadge amendment, with the vote splitting along sectional lines—the South opposing it, the North accepting it. It was defeated in the Senate, which temporarily halted Missouri's bid for statehood in 1819.

When Congress took up the matter again, the Senate was even stronger in opposition to slavery in Missouri. The Taylor amendment, introduced by Senator Waller Taylor (R-Ind.) on January 26, 1820, banned slavery except for those already held in slavery. Shortly thereafter in the Senate, Senator Jesse B. Thomas (R-Ind.) introduced the Thomas amendment (February 13, 1820), which banned slavery in Missouri altogether. Both the Taylor and Thomas amendments contained provisions for returning runaway slaves to their owners under provisions of the Fugitive Slave Act. Congress was at odds with officials in Missouri who drafted a state constitution that allowed slavery in the state. The Missouri Constitution of July 19, 1820, prohibited the state from abolishing slavery without the consent of the owners or without compensating slave owners. It also prohibited the state from banning the importation of slaves.

The compromise that finally emerged admitted Maine as a free state and allowed Missouri to enter the Union as a slave state, thus maintaining the balance of slave and free states. The Missouri En-abling Act of March 6, 1820, permitted slavery in Missouri. It offered something for those opposed to the extension of slavery by declaring that the southern boundary of Missouri at latitude 36°30' would be extended across the country as a line dividing free territory from slave territory, No slavery would be allowed north of that line, except in the state of Missouri. This ensured that most of the territory of the Louisiana Purchase would eventually be composed of free states.

The matter was not completely settled until February 1821. The Missouri Constitution of July 19, 1820, which Congress had earlier approved, contained a clause that prohibited free blacks from moving into the state. Some northern politicians objected to this clause on the grounds that it violated the U.S. Constitution's guarantee that citizens of any state are guaranteed equal privileges in all states. Representative Henry Clay (R-Ky.) convinced Missouri never to enforce this constitutional provision. This provision was incorporated in the Resolution for the Admission of Missouri, which became law on March 2, 1821. Missouri later struck this offensive clause from its constitution.

This Missouri Compromise helped hold the Union together for another thirty years. But events in the 1850s, including the Kansas-Nebraska Act in 1854 (see document 68) and the Dred Scott Decision in 1857 (see document 70), completely unraveled the Missouri Compromise, paving the way to civil war.

THE TALLMADGE AMENDMENT
February 13, 1819

And provided also, *That the further introduction of slavery or involuntary servitude be prohibited, except for the punishment of crimes, whereof the party shall be duly convicted; and that all children of slaves, born within the said state; after the admission thereof into the Union, shall be free, but may be held to service until the age of twenty-five years.*

THE TAYLOR AMENDMENT
January 26, 1820

The reading of the bill proceeded as far as the fourth section; when

Mr. Taylor, of New York, proposed to amend the bill by incorporating in that section the following provision:

Section 4, line 25, insert the following after the word "States," "And shall ordain and establish, that there shall be neither slavery nor involuntary servitude in the said State, otherwise than in the punishment of crimes, whereof the party shall have been duly convicted: *Provided, always,* That any person escaping into the same, from whom labor or service is lawfully claimed in any other State, such fugitive may be lawfully reclaimed, and conveyed to the person claiming his or her labor or service as aforesaid: *And provided, also,* That the said provision shall not be construed to alter the condition or civil rights of any person now held to service or labor in the said Territory."

THE THOMAS AMENDMENT
February 17, 1820

"*And be it further enacted,* That in all that territory ceded by France to the United States, under the name of Louisiana, which lies north of thirty-six degrees and thirty minutes north latitude, excepting only such part thereof as is included within the limits of the State contemplated by this act, slavery and involuntary servitude, otherwise in the punishment of crimes whereof the party shall have been duly convicted, shall be and is hereby forever prohibited: *Provided always,* That any person escaping into the same, from whom labor or service is lawfully claimed in any State or Territory of the United States, such fugitive may be lawfully reclaimed, and conveyed to the person claiming his or her labor or service, as aforesaid."

MISSOURI ENABLING ACT
March 6, 1820

. . . An act to authorize the people of the Missouri territory to form a constitution and state government, and for the admission of such state into the Union on an equal footing with the original states, and to prohibit slavery in certain territories.

Be it enacted by the Senate and House of Representatives of the United States of America in Congress assembled, That the inhabitants of that portion of the Missouri territory included within in the boundaries hereinafter designated, be, and they are hereby, authorized to form for themselves a constitution and state government, and to assume such name as they shall deem proper; and the said state, when formed, shall be admitted into the Union, upon an equal footing with the original states, in all respects whatever.

SEC. 2. *And be it further enacted,* That the said state shall consist of all the territory within the following boundaries, to wit: Beginning in the middle of the Mississippi river, on the parallel of thirty-six degrees of north latitude; thence west, along that parallel of latitude, to the St. Francois river; thence up, and following the course of that river, in the middle of the main channel thereof, to the parallel of latitude of thirty-six degrees and thirty minutes; thence west, along the same, to a point where the said parallel is intersected by a meridian line passing through the middle of the mouth of the Missouri river, thence, from the point aforesaid north, along the said meridian line, to the intersection of the parallel of latitude which passes through the rapids of the river Des Moines, making the said line to correspond with the Indian boundary line; thence east, from the point of intersection last aforesaid, along the said parallel of latitude, to the middle of the channel of the main fork of the said river Des Moines; thence down and along the main channel of the said river Des Moines, to the mouth of the same, where it empties into the Mississippi river; thence down, and following

the course of the Mississippi river, in the middle of the main channel thereof, to the place of beginning. . . .

SEC. 3. *And be it further enacted,* That all free white male citizens of the United States, who shall have arrived at the age of twenty-one years, and have resided in said territory three months previous to the day of election, and all other persons qualified to vote for representatives to the general assembly of said territory, shall be qualified to be elected, and they are hereby qualified and authorized to vote, and choose representatives to form a convention. . . .

SEC. 8. *And it be further enacted,* That in all that territory ceded by France to the United States, under the name of Louisiana, which lies north of thirty-six degrees and thirty minutes north latitude, not included within the limits of the state, contemplated by this act, slavery and involuntary servitude, otherwise than in the punishment of crimes, whereas the parties shall have been duly convicted, shall be, and is hereby, forever prohibited: *Provided always,* That any persons escaping into the same, from whom labor or service is lawfully claimed, in any state or territory of the United States, such fugitive may be lawfully reclaimed and conveyed to the person claiming his or her labor or service as aforesaid.

RESOLUTION FOR THE ADMISSION OF MISSOURI
March 2, 1821

Resolved by the Senate and House of Representatives of the United States of America, in Congress assembled, That Missouri shall be admitted into this union on an equal footing with the original states, in all respects whatever, upon the fundamental condition, that the fourth clause of the twenty-sixth section of the third article of the constitution submitted on the part of the said state to Congress, shall never be construed to authorize the passage of any law, and that no law shall be passes in conformity thereto, by which any citizen, of either of the states of this Union, shall be excluded from the enjoyment of any of the privileges and immunities to which such citizen is entitled under the constitution of the United States: *Provided,* That the legislature of the said state, by a solemn public act, shall declare the assent of the said state to the said fundamental condition, and shall transmit to the President of the United States, on or before the fourth Monday in November next, an authentic copy of the said act; upon the receipt whereof, the President, by proclamation, shall announce the fact; whereupon, and without any further proceeding on the part of Congress, the admission of the said state into this Union shall be considered complete.

Journal of the House of Representatives, 15th Congress, 2d session, Feb. 16, 1819, 272; *Annals of Congress,* 16th Congress, 1st session, Jan. 26, 1820, 947; *Annals of Congress,* 16th Congress, 1st session, Feb. 17, 1820, 427–428; *Statutes at Large,* 3, 16th Congress, 1st session, March 6, 1820, 545–548; *Statutes at Large,* 3, 16th Congress, 1st session, March 2, 1821, 645.

54 *Gibbons v. Ogden*

1824

The Supreme Court's decision in Gibbons v. Ogden *has had a profound impact on the ability of Congress to regulate commerce. The Constitution, in Article I, Section 8, Clause 3, gave Congress the power to "regulate Commerce with foreign Nations, and among the several States. . . ." This clause has been the subject of a great deal of interpretation and litigation for almost two centuries. This Court decision gave Congress broad power to regulate commerce. It struck another blow at the strict constructionists who wanted Congress to be limited to the powers specifically described in the Constitution.*

Gibbons v. Ogden *was cited in the creation of the Interstate Commerce Commission in 1887 and in the Sherman Antitrust Act of 1890, which sought to curb monopolies. It was used as precedent for federal regulation of wages and child labor in the 1930s and 1940s. Because of the federal government's authority under the "commerce clause" (Article I, Section 8, Clause 3 of the Constitution), Congress was able to attack racial discrimination in public places such as restaurants and in public transportation in the 1960s.*

This case began in a dispute over trade carried by steamboats. The state of New York licensed steamboats that used its ports. New York favored certain steamboat companies in the state and this created a state monopoly for those lucky enough to get a license. Thomas Gibbons, a steamboat operator in New York waters, had a federally granted license. He was sued by Aaron Gibbons, a New York licensee, to keep Gibbons out of New York waters because he violated state law by not having the proper license.

Justice John Marshall, in another of his strong decisions in favor of the power of the federal government over state governments, argued that federal laws were superior to state laws regarding the regulation of commerce. Marshall extended the definition of commerce to include not just trade but transportation and navigation as well. The results of the decision have been far reaching in terms of building a national infrastructure of roads and waterways that went beyond the ability of any one state to control or operate. It helped to create a strong feeling of nationalism that molded the country into one nation rather than a collection of separate states. While the dispute began in the age of the steamboat, its affects are felt today in many aspects of federal regulation of commerce, including air travel.

Mr. Chief Justice MARSHALL delivered the opinion of the Court, and, after stating the case, proceeded as follows:

The appellant contends that this decree is erroneous because the laws which purport to give the exclusive privilege it sustains are repugnant to the Constitution and laws of the United States.

They are said to be repugnant:

1st. To that clause in the Constitution which authorizes Congress to regulate commerce.

2d. To that which authorizes Congress to promote the progress of science and useful arts.

The State of New York maintains the Constitutionality of these laws, and their Legislature, their Council of Revision, and their Judges, have repeatedly concurred in this opinion. It is supported by great names—by names which have all the titles to consideration that virtue, intelligence, and office can bestow. No tribunal can approach the decision of this question without feeling a just and real respect for that opinion which is sustained by such authority, but it is the province of this Court, while it respects, not to bow to it implicitly, and the Judges must exercise, in the examination of the subject, that understanding which Providence has bestowed upon them, with that independence which the people of the United States expect from this department of the government.

As preliminary to the very able discussions of the Constitution which we have heard from the bar, and as having some influence on its construction, reference has been made to the political situation of these States anterior to its formation. It has been said that they were sovereign, were completely independent, and were connected with each other only by a league. This is true. But, when these allied sovereigns converted their league into a government, when they converted their Congress of Ambassadors, deputed to deliberate on their common concerns and to recommend measures of general utility, into a Legislature, empowered to enact laws on the most interesting subjects, the whole character in which the States appear underwent a change, the extent of which must be determined by a fair consideration of the instrument by which that change was effected.

This instrument contains an enumeration of powers expressly granted by the people to their government. It has been said that these powers ought to be construed strictly. But why ought they to be so construed? Is there one sentence in the Constitution which gives countenance to this rule? In the last of the enumerated powers, that which grants expressly the means for carrying all others into execution, Congress is authorized "to make all laws which shall be necessary and proper" for the purpose. But this limitation on the means which may be used is not extended to the powers which are conferred, nor is there one sentence in the Constitution which has been pointed out by the gentlemen of the bar or which we have been able to discern that prescribes this rule. We do not, therefore, think ourselves justified in adopting it. What do gentlemen mean by a "strict construction?" If they contend only against that enlarged construction, which would extend words beyond their natural and obvious import, we might question the application of the term, but should not controvert the principle. If they contend for that narrow construction which, in support or some theory not to be found in the Constitution, would deny to the government those powers which the words of the grant, as usually understood, import, and which are consistent with the general views and objects of the instrument; for that narrow construction which would cripple the government and render it unequal to the object for which it is declared to be instituted, and to which the powers given, as fairly understood, render it competent; then we cannot perceive the propriety of this strict construction, nor adopt it as the rule by which the Constitution is to be expounded. As men whose intentions require no concealment generally employ the words which most directly and aptly express the ideas they intend to convey, the enlightened patriots who framed our Constitution, and the people who adopted it, must be understood to have employed words in their natural sense, and to have intended what they have said. If, from the imperfection of human language, there should be serious doubts respecting the extent of any given power, it is a well settled rule that the objects for which it was given, especially when those objects are expressed in the instrument itself, should have great influence in the construction. We know of no reason for excluding this rule from the present case. The grant does not convey power which might be beneficial to the grantor if retained by himself, or which can enure solely to the benefit of the grantee, but is an investment of power for the general advantage, in the hands of agents selected for that purpose, which power can never be exercised by the people themselves, but must be placed in the hands of agents or lie dormant. We know of no rule for construing the extent of such powers other than is given by the language of the instrument which confers them, taken in connexion with the purposes for which they were conferred.

The words are, "Congress shall have power to regulate commerce with foreign nations, and among the several States, and with the Indian tribes."

The subject to be regulated is commerce, and our Constitution being, as was aptly said at the bar, one of enumeration, and not of definition, to ascertain the extent of the power, it becomes necessary to settle the meaning of the word. The counsel for the appellee would limit it to traffic, to buying and selling, or the interchange of commodities, and do not admit that it comprehends navigation. This would restrict a general term, applicable to many objects, to one of its significations. Commerce, undoubtedly, is traffic, but it is something more: it is intercourse. It describes the commercial intercourse between nations, and parts of nations, in all its branches, and is regulated by prescribing rules for carrying on that intercourse. The mind can scarcely conceive a system for regulating commerce between nations which shall exclude all laws concerning navigation, which shall be silent on the admission of the vessels of the one nation into the ports of the other, and be confined to prescribing rules for the conduct of individuals in the actual employment of buying and selling or of barter.

If commerce does not include navigation, the government of the Union has no direct power over that subject, and can make no law prescribing what shall constitute American vessels or requiring that they shall be navigated by American seamen. Yet this power has been exercised from the commencement of the government, has been exercised with the consent of all, and has been understood by all to be a commercial regulation. All

America understands, and has uniformly understood, the word "commerce" to comprehend navigation. It was so understood, and must have been so understood, when the Constitution was framed. The power over commerce, including navigation, was one of the primary objects for which the people of America adopted their government, and must have been contemplated in forming it. The convention must have used the word in that sense, because all have understood it in that sense, and the attempt to restrict it comes too late.

If the opinion that "commerce," as the word is used in the Constitution, comprehends navigation also, requires any additional confirmation, that additional confirmation is, we think, furnished by the words of the instrument itself.

. . . .

The 9th section of the 1st article declares that "no preference shall be given, by any regulation of commerce or revenue, to the ports of one State over those of another." This clause cannot be understood as applicable to those laws only which are passed for the purposes of revenue, because it is expressly applied to commercial regulations, and the most obvious preference which can be given to one port over another in regulating commerce relates to navigation. But the subsequent part of the sentence is still more explicit. It is, "nor shall vessels bound to or from one State be obliged to enter, clear, or pay duties, in another." These words have a direct reference to navigation.

. . . .

The word used in the Constitution, then, comprehends, and has been always understood to comprehend, navigation within its meaning, and a power to regulate navigation is as expressly granted as if that term had been added to the word "commerce."

To what commerce does this power extend? The Constitution informs us, to commerce "with foreign nations, and among the several States, and with the Indian tribes."

It has, we believe, been universally admitted that these words comprehend every species of commercial intercourse between the United States and foreign nations. No sort of trade can be carried on between this country and any other to which this power does not extend. It has been truly said that "commerce," as the word is used in the Constitution, is a unit every part of which is indicated by the term.

If this be the admitted meaning of the word in its application to foreign nations, it must carry the same meaning throughout the sentence, and remain a unit, unless there be some plain intelligible cause which alters it.

The subject to which the power is next applied is to commerce "among the several States." The word "among" means intermingled with. A thing which is among others is intermingled with them. Commerce among the States cannot stop at the external boundary line of each State, but may be introduced into the interior.

It is not intended to say that these words comprehend that commerce which is completely internal, which is carried on between man and man in a State, or between different parts of the same State, and which does not extend to or affect other States. Such a power would be inconvenient, and is certainly unnecessary.

Comprehensive as the word "among" is, it may very properly be restricted to that commerce which concerns more States than one. The phrase is not one which would probably have been selected to indicate the completely interior traffic of a State, because it is not an apt phrase for that purpose, and the enumeration of the particular classes of commerce to which the power was to be extended would not have been made had the intention been to extend the power to every description. The enumeration presupposes something not enumerated, and that something, if we regard the language or the subject of the sentence, must be the exclusively internal commerce of a State. The genius and character of the whole government seem to be that its action is to be applied to all the external concerns of the nation, and to those internal concerns which affect the States generally, but not to those which are completely within a particular State, which do not affect other States, and with which it is not necessary to interfere for the purpose of executing some of the general powers of the government. The completely internal commerce of a State, then, may be considered as reserved for the State itself.

But, in regulating commerce with foreign nations, the power of Congress does not stop at the jurisdictional lines of the several States. It would be a very useless power if it could not pass those lines. The commerce of the United States with foreign nations is that of the whole United States. Every district has a right to participate in it. The deep streams which penetrate our country in every direction pass through the interior of almost every State in the Union, and furnish the means of exercising this right. If Congress has the power to regulate it, that power must be exercised whenever the subject exists. If it exists within the States, if a foreign voyage may commence or terminate at a port within a State, then the power of Congress may be exercised within a State.

This principle is, if possible, still more clear, when applied to commerce "among the several States." They either join each other, in which case they are separated by a mathematical line, or they are remote from each other, in which case other States lie between them. What is commerce "among" them, and how is it to be conducted? Can a trading expedition between two adjoining States, commence and terminate outside of each? And if the trading intercourse be between two States remote from each other, must it not commence in one, terminate in the other, and probably pass through a third? Commerce among the States must, of necessity, be commerce with the States. In the regulation of trade with the Indian tribes, the action of the law, especially when the Constitution was made, was chiefly within a State. The power of Congress, then, whatever it may be, must be exercised within the territorial jurisdiction of the several States. The sense of the nation on this subject is unequivocally manifested by the provisions made in the laws for transporting goods by land between Baltimore and Providence, between New York and Philadelphia, and between Philadelphia and Baltimore.

We are now arrived at the inquiry—What is this power?

It is the power to regulate, that is, to prescribe the rule by which commerce is to be governed. This power, like all others vested in Congress, is complete in itself, may be exercised to its utmost extent, and acknowledges no limitations other than are prescribed in the Constitution. These are expressed in plain terms, and do not affect the questions which arise in this case, or which have been discussed at the bar. If, as has always been understood, the sovereignty of Congress, though limited to specified objects, is plenary as to those objects, the power over commerce with foreign nations, and among the several States, is vested in Congress as absolutely as it would be in a single government, having in its Constitution the same restrictions on the exercise of the power as are found in the Constitution of the United States. The wisdom and the discretion of Congress, their identity with the people, and the influence which their constituents possess at elections are, in this, as in many other instances, as that, for example, of declaring war, the sole restraints on which they have relied, to secure them from its abuse. They are the restraints on which the people must often they solely, in all representative governments.

The power of Congress, then, comprehends navigation, within the limits of every State in the Union, so far as that navigation may be in any manner connected with "commerce with foreign nations, or among the several States, or with the Indian tribes." It may, of consequence, pass the jurisdictional line of New York and act upon the very waters to which the prohibition now under consideration applies.

But it has been urged with great earnestness that, although the power of Congress to regulate commerce with foreign nations and among the several States be coextensive with the subject itself, and have no other limits than are prescribed in the Constitution, yet the States may severally exercise the same power, within their respective jurisdictions. In support of this argument, it is said that they possessed it as an inseparable attribute of sovereignty, before the formation of the Constitution, and still retain it except so far as they have surrendered it by that instrument; that this principle results from the nature of the government, and is secured by the tenth amendment; that an affirmative grant of power is not exclusive unless in its own nature it be such that the continued exercise of it by the former possessor is inconsistent with the grant, and that this is not of that description.

. . . .

In discussing the question whether this power is still in the States, in the case under consideration, we may dismiss from it the inquiry whether it is surrendered by the mere grant to Congress, or is retained until Congress shall exercise the power. We may dismiss that inquiry because it has been exercised, and the regulations which Congress deemed it proper to make are now in full operation. The sole question is can a State regulate commerce with foreign nations and among the States while Congress is regulating it?

. . . .

Although Congress cannot enable a State to legislate, Congress may adopt the provisions of a State on any subject. When the government of the Union was brought into existence, it found a system for the regulation of its pilots in full force in every State. The act which has been mentioned adopts this system, and gives it the same validity as if its provisions had been specially made by Congress. But the act, it may be said, is prospective also, and the adoption of laws to be made in future presupposes the right in the maker to legislate on the subject.

The act unquestionably manifests an intention to leave this subject entirely to the States until Congress should think proper to interpose, but the very enactment of such a law indicates an opinion that it was necessary, that the existing system would not be applicable to the new state of things unless expressly applied to it by Congress. But this section is confined to pilots within the "bays, inlets, rivers, harbours, and ports of the United States," which are, of course, in whole or in part, also within the limits of some particular state. The acknowledged power of a State to regulate its police, its domestic trade, and to govern its own citizens may enable it to legislate on this subject to a considerable extent, and the adoption of its system by Congress, and the application of it to the whole subject of commerce, does not seem to the Court to imply a right in the States so to apply it of their own authority. But the adoption of the State system being temporary, being only "until further legislative provision shall be made by Congress," shows conclusively an opinion that Congress could control the whole subject, and might adopt the system of the States or provide one of its own.

A State, it is said, or even a private citizen, may construct light houses. But gentlemen must be aware that if this proves a power in a State to regulate commerce, it proves that the same power is in the citizen. States or individuals who own lands may, if not forbidden by law, erect on those lands what buildings they please, but this power is entirely distinct from that of regulating commerce, and may, we presume, be restrained if exercised so as to produce a public mischief.

. . . .

Since, however, in exercising the power of regulating their own purely internal affairs, whether of trading or police, the States may sometimes enact laws the validity of which depends on their interfering with, and being contrary to, an act of Congress passed in pursuance of the Constitution, the Court will enter upon the inquiry whether the laws of New York, as expounded by the highest tribunal of that State, have, in their application to this case, come into collision with an act of Congress and deprived a citizen of a right to which that act entitles him. Should this collision exist, it will be immaterial whether those laws were passed in virtue of a concurrent power "to regulate commerce with foreign nations and among the several States" or in virtue of a power to regulate their domestic trade and police. In one case and the other, the acts of New York must yield to the law of Congress, and the decision sustaining the privilege they confer against a right given by a law of the Union must be erroneous.

This opinion has been frequently expressed in this Court, and is founded as well on the nature of the government as on the words of the Constitution. In argument, however, it has been contended that, if a law passed by a State, in the exercise of its acknowledged sovereignty, comes into conflict with a law passed by Congress in pursuance of the Constitution, they affect the subject and each other like equal opposing powers.

But the framers of our Constitution foresaw this state of things, and provided for it by declaring the supremacy not only of itself, but of the laws made in pursuance of it. The nullity of any act inconsistent with the Constitution is produced by the declaration that the Constitution is the supreme law. The appropriate application of that part of the clause which confers the same supremacy on laws and treaties is to such acts of the State Legislatures as do not transcend their powers, but, though enacted in the execution of acknowledged State powers, interfere with, or are contrary to, the laws of Congress made in pursuance of the Constitution or some treaty made under the authority of the United States. In every such case, the act of Congress or the treaty is supreme, and the law of the State, though enacted in the exercise of powers not controverted, must yield to it.

In pursuing this inquiry at the bar, it has been said that the Constitution does not confer the right of intercourse between State and State. That right derives its source from those laws whose authority is acknowledged by civilized man throughout the world. This is true. The Constitution found it an existing right, and gave to Congress the power to regulate it. In the exercise of this power, Congress has passed "an act for enrolling or licensing ships or vessels to be employed in the coasting trade and fisheries, and for regulating the same." The counsel for the respondent contend that this act does not give the right to sail from port to port, but confines itself to regulating a preexisting right so far only as to confer certain privileges on enrolled and licensed vessels in its exercise.

It will at once occur that, when a Legislature attaches certain privileges and exemptions to the exercise of a right over which its control is absolute, the law must imply a power to exercise the right. The privileges are gone if the right itself be annihilated. It would be contrary to all reason, and to the course of human affairs, to say that a State is unable to strip a vessel of the particular privileges attendant on the exercise of a right, and yet may annul the right itself; that the State of New York cannot prevent an enrolled and licensed vessel, proceeding from Elizabethtown, in New Jersey, to New York, from enjoying, in her course, and on her entrance into port, all the privileges conferred by the act of Congress, but can shut her up in her own port, and prohibit altogether her entering the waters and ports of another State. To the Court, it seems very clear that the whole act on the subject of the coasting trade, according to those principles which govern the construction of statutes, implies unequivocally an authority to licensed vessels to carry on the coasting trade.

. . . .

If, as our whole course of legislation on this subject shows, the power of Congress has been universally understood in America to comprehend navigation, it is a very persuasive, if not a conclusive, argument to prove that the construction is correct, and if it be correct, no clear distinction is perceived between the power to regulate vessels employed in transporting men for hire and property for hire. The subject is transferred to Congress, and no exception to the grant can be admitted which is not proved by the words or the nature of the thing. A coasting vessel employed in the transportation of passengers is as much a portion of the American marine as one employed in the transportation of a cargo, and no reason is perceived why such vessel should be withdrawn from the regulating power of that government which has been thought best fitted for the purpose generally. The provisions of the law respecting native seamen and respecting ownership are as applicable to vessels carrying men as to vessels carrying manufactures, and no reason is perceived why the power over the subject should not be placed in the same hands. The argument urged at the bar rests on the foundation that the power of Congress does not extend to navigation as a branch of commerce, and can only be applied to that subject incidentally and occasionally. But if that foundation be removed, we must show some plain, intelligible distinction, supported by the Constitution or by reason, for discriminating between the power of Congress over vessels employed in navigating the same seas. We can perceive no such distinction.

If we refer to the Constitution, the inference to be drawn from it is rather against the distinction. The section which restrains Congress from prohibiting the migration or importation of such persons as any of the States may think proper to admit until the year 1808 has always been considered as an exception from the power to regulate commerce, and certainly seems to class migration with importation. Migration applies as appropriately to voluntary as importation does to involuntary arrivals, and, so far as an exception from a power proves its existence, this section proves that the power to regulate commerce applies equally to the regulation of vessels employed in transporting men, who pass from place to place voluntarily, and to those who pass involuntarily.

If the power reside in Congress, as a portion of the general grant to regulate commerce, then acts applying that power to vessels generally must be construed as comprehending all vessels. If none appear to be excluded by the language of the act, none can be excluded by construction. Vessels have always been employed to a greater or less extent in the transportation of passengers, and have never been supposed to be, on that account, withdrawn from the control or protection of Congress. Packets which ply along the coast, as well as those which make voyages between Europe and America, consider the transportation of passengers as an important part of their business. Yet it has never been suspected that the general laws of navigation did not apply to them.

. . . .

The questions, then, whether the conveyance of passengers be a part of the coasting trade and whether a vessel can be protected in that occupation by a coasting license are not, and cannot be, raised in this case. The real and sole question seems to be whether a steam machine in actual use deprives a vessel of the privileges conferred by a license.

In considering this question, the first idea which presents itself is that the laws of Congress for the regulation of commerce do not look to the principle by which vessels are moved. That subject is left entirely to individual discretion, and, in that vast and complex system of legislative enactment concerning it, which embraces everything that the Legislature thought it necessary to notice, there is not, we believe, one word respecting the peculiar principle by which vessels are propelled through the water, except what may be found in a single act granting a particular privilege to steamboats. With this exception, every act, either prescribing duties or granting privileges, applies to every vessel, whether navigated by the instrumentality of wind or fire, of sails or machinery. The whole weight of proof, then, is thrown upon him who would introduce a distinction to which the words of the law give no countenance.

If a real difference could be admitted to exist between vessels carrying passengers and others, it has already been observed that there is no fact in this case which can bring up that question. And, if the occupation of steamboats be a matter of such general notoriety that the Court may be presumed to know it, although not specially informed by the record, then we deny that the transportation of passengers is their exclusive occupation. It is a matter of general history that, in our western waters, their principal employment is the transportation of merchandise, and all know that, in the waters of the Atlantic, they are frequently so employed.

. . . .

Powerful and ingenious minds, taking as postulates that the powers expressly granted to the government of the Union are to be contracted by construction into the narrowest possible compass and that the original powers of the States are retained if any possible construction will retain them may, by a course of well digested but refined and metaphysical reasoning founded on these premises, explain away the Constitution of our country and leave it a magnificent structure indeed to look at, but totally unfit for use. They may so entangle and perplex the understanding as to obscure principles which were before thought quite plain, and induce doubts where, if the mind were to pursue its own course, none would be perceived. In such a case, it is peculiarly necessary to recur to safe and fundamental principles to sustain those principles, and when sustained, to make them the tests of the arguments to be examined. . . .

This Court is therefore of opinion that the decree of the Court of New York for the Trial of Impeachments and the Correction of Errors affirming the decree of the Chancellor of that State, which perpetually enjoins the said Thomas Gibbons, the appellant, from navigating the waters of the State of New York with the steamboats the *Stoudinger* and the *Bellona* by steam or fire, is erroneous, and ought to be reversed, and the same is hereby reversed and annulled, and this Court doth further DIRECT, ORDER, and DECREE that the bill of the said Aaron Ogden be dismissed, and the same is hereby dismissed accordingly.

22 U.S. 1 (1824). Text courtesy of *Selected Historic Decisions of the U.S. Supreme Court* (CD-ROM, 1997 edition), a publication of the Legal Information Institute, Cornell Law School.

55   Robert Hayne's Reply to Daniel Webster

January 21 and 25, 1830

Beginning January 18, 1830, and concluding nine days later, the Webster-Hayne debate stands as one of the greatest exchanges in the history of the United States Senate. Contemporaries recognized the high drama of the moment, and subsequent generations of American school teachers in the nineteenth century would train children to commit parts of this debate to memory, so great was its impact on the public conscience in an era that found both entertainment and educational value in outstanding orations and political debate.

The issue that sparked the debate was a discussion of public land policy. Several weeks earlier Samuel A. Foot, an anti-Jackson senator from Connecticut, introduced a resolution in the Senate to limit the sale of western public land to land already on the market. The debate quickly turned into a clash between the sections of the country when westerner Thomas Hart Benton (D-Mo.) accused New England of trying to cut off western expansion to protect cheap sources of labor in the Northeast. Benton, always a defender of western interests, offered an alliance with the South to fend off the political power of his New England rivals and thwart that region's efforts to enact a tariff that would protect New England industries at the expense of westerner and southern interests.

Into the breech stepped Robert Y. Hayne (D-S.C.). At age thirty-eight, he was among the youngest senators, but nonetheless a person of considerable skill as an orator. Hayne had served in the Senate since 1823 and before that he was speaker of the South Carolina House. Hayne was a champion of state's rights, a defender of slavery, and a protégé of John C. Calhoun and his doctrine of nullification. Calhoun was vice president of the United States at the time and presided over this debate in his capacity as president of the Senate. Hayne called for a ban on the sale of western lands because such sales enriched the federal government at the expense of the states and the western territories. Hayne argued that the states—not the federal government—should control the sale of their land.

Daniel Webster (Whig-Mass.) entered the debate on January 20. Webster began his remarks with the public land issue and the tariff question, the original bone of contention, but then took the debate to broader themes of the evils of slavery and the importance of the Union. Webster took pride in the fact that a man from Massachusetts, Nathan Dane, had drafted the Northwest Ordinance of 1787, which banned slavery in that territory. Webster, while not calling for the end of slavery, made it clear that New England's history was filled with examples of wisdom and enlightenment in opposing the evils of the slavery.

Angered by Webster's attempt to isolate the South on the issue of slavery and to form alliances with the West at the expense of the South, Hayne proceeded to answer Webster in a long, powerful oration that was delivered in two parts on January 21 and January 25, 1830. Rising to the occasion the next day, Webster began his second reply to Hayne, which also took part of two days to deliver (see document 56). Taken together, the two speeches offer a sharp contrast of views between the North and South, with Hayne defending states rights and slavery while Webster defended the Constitution, the Union, and spoke of the evils of slavery. This debate set the stage for many others that would follow in the years ahead as growing sectional differences and the debate over slavery came to dominate the politics of the nation. Two years after this debate Hayne would resign the Senate to become governor of South Carolina, which opened the door for the return of John C. Calhoun to the Senate.

In the excerpts that follow, most of the speech is in Hayne's own words as printed in the Register of Debates. But it was not unusual in the early nineteenth century for the recorders of debates to mix the actual words spoken with third-person summaries, in which case the reporter used "[said Mr. H.]"

. . . .

In 1825, the gentleman [Daniel Webster] told the world, that the public lands "ought not to be treated as a treasure." He now tells us, that "they must be treated as so much treasure." What the deliberate opinion of the gentleman on this subject may be, belongs not to me to determine; but, I do not think he can, with the shadow of justice or propriety, impugn my sentiments, while his own recorded opinions are identical with my own. When the gentleman refers to the conditions of the grants under which the United States have acquired these lands, and insists that, as they are declared to be "for the common benefit of all the States," they can only be treated as so much treasure, I think he has applied a rule of construction too narrow for the case. If, in the deeds of cession, it has been declared that the grants were intended for "the common benefit of all the States," it is clear, from other provisions, that they were not intended merely as so much property: for, it is expressly declared that the object of the grants is the erection of new states; and the United States, in accepting the trust, bind themselves to facilitate the foundation of the states, to be admitted into the Union with all the rights and privileges of the original states. This, sir, was the great end to which all parties looked, and it is by the fulfilment of this high trust, that "the common benefit of all the States" is to be best promoted. Sir, let me tell the gentleman, that, in the part of the country in which I live, we do not measure political benefits by the money standard. We consider as more valuable than gold— liberty, principle, and justice. But, sir, if we are bound to act on the narrow principles contended for by the gentleman, I am wholly at a loss to conceive how he can reconcile his principles with his own practice. The lands are, it seems, to be treated "as so much treasure," and must be applied to the "common benefit of all the States." Now, if this be so, whence does he derive the right to appropriate them for partial and local objects? How can the gentleman consent to vote away immense bodies of these funds—for canals in Indiana and Illinois, to the Louisville and Portland Canal, to Kenyon College in Ohio, to schools for the deaf and dumb, and other objects of a similar description? If grants of this character can fairly be considered as made "for the common benefit of all the States," it can only be because all the States are interested in the welfare of each—a principle which, carried to the full extent, destroys all distinction between local and national objects, and is certainly broad enough to embrace the principle for which I have ventured to contend. Sir, the true difference between us, I take to be this: the gentleman wishes to treat the public lands as a great treasure, just as so much money in the treasury, to be applied to all objects, constitutional and unconstitutional, to which the public money is now constantly applied. I consider it as a sacred trust, which we ought to fulfil, on the principles for which I have contended.

The senator from Massachusetts has thought proper to present in strong contrast the friendly feelings of the East towards the West, with sentiments of an opposite character displayed by the South in relation to appropriations for internal improvement. Now, sir, let it be recollected that the South have made no professions; I have certainly made none in their behalf, of regard for the West. It has been reserved to the gentleman from Massachusetts, while he vaunts his own personal devotion to western interests, to claim for the entire section of country to which he belongs, an ardent friendship for the West, as manifested by their support of the system of internal improvement, while he casts in our teeth the reproach that the South has manifested hostility to western interests in opposing appropriations for such objects. That gentleman, at the same time, acknowledged that the South entertains constitutional scruples on this subject. Are we then, sir, to understand, that the gentleman considers it a just subject of reproach, that we respect our oaths, by which we are bound "to preserve, protect, and defend, the constitution of the United States?" Would the gentleman have us manifest our love to the West by trampling under foot our constitutional scruples? Does he not perceive, if the South is to be reproached with unkindness to the West, in voting against appropriations, which the gentleman admits, they could not vote for without doing violence to their constitutional opinions, that he exposes himself to the question, whether, if he was in our situation, he could vote for these appropriations, regardless of his scruples? No, sir, I will not do the gentleman so great injustice. He has fallen into this error from not having duly weighed the force and effect of the reproach which he was endeavoring to cast upon the South. In relation to the other point, the friendship manifested by New England towards the West in their support of the system of internal improvement, the gentleman will pardon me for saying that I think he is equally unfortunate in having introduced that topic. As that gentleman has forced it upon us, however, I cannot suffer it to pass unnoticed. When the gentleman tells us that the appropriations for internal improvement in the West would, in almost every instance, have failed, but for New England votes, he has forgotten to tell us the when, the how, and the wherefore, this new-born zeal for the West sprung up in the bosom of New England. If we look back only a few years, we will find, in both houses of Congress, an uniform and steady opposition, on the part of the members from the eastern states, generally, to all appropriations of this character. At the time I became a member of this house, and for some time afterwards, a decided majority of the New England senators were opposed to the very measures which the senator from Massachusetts tells us they now cordially support. Sir, the journals are before me, and an examination of them will satisfy every gentleman of that fact.

It must be well known to everyone whose experience dates back as far as 1825, that, up to a certain period, New England was generally opposed to appropriations for internal improvements in the West. The gentleman from Massachusetts may be himself an exception, but if he went for the system before 1825, it is certain that his colleagues did not go with him. In the session of 1824 and 1825, however, (a memorable era in the history of this country) a wonderful change took place in New England, in relation to the western interests. Sir, an extraordinary union of sympathies and of interests was then effected, which brought the East and the West into close alliance. The book from which I have before read contains the first public annunciation of that happy reconciliation of conflicting interests, personal and political, which brought the East and West together, and locked in a fraternal embrace the two great orators of the East and West. Sir, it was on the 18th of January, 1825, while the result of the presidential election, in the House of Representatives, was still doubtful, while the whole country was looking with intense anxiety to that legislative hall where the mighty drama was so soon to be acted, that we saw the leaders of two great parties in the House and in the nation "taking sweet counsel together," and in a celebrated debate on the Cumberland Road fighting side by side for western interests. It was on that memorable occasion that the senator from Massachusetts held out the white flag to the West, and uttered those liberal sentiments, which he, yesterday, so indignantly repudiated. Then it was that that happy union between the members of the celebrated coalition was consummated, whose immediate issue was a president from one quarter of the Union, with the succession (as it was supposed) secured to another. The "American System," before, a rude, disjointed, and misshapen mass, now assumed form and consistency; then it was, that it became "the settled policy of the Government" that this system should be so administered as to create a reciprocity of interests, and a reciprocal distribution of government favors—East and West, (the tariff and internal improvements)—while the South—yes, sir, the impracticable South, was to be "out of your protection." The gentleman may boast as much as he pleases of the friendship of New England for the West, as displayed in their support of internal improvement; but, when he next introduces that topic, I trust that he will tell us when that friendship commenced, how it was brought about, and why it was established. Before I leave this topic, I must be permitted to say, that the true character of the policy now pursued by the gentleman from Massachusetts and his friends, in relation to appropriations of land and money, for the benefit of the West, is, in my estimation, very similar to that pursued by Jacob of old towards his brother Esau; "it robs them of their birthright for a mess of pottage."

The gentleman from Massachusetts, in alluding to a remark of mine, that, before any disposition could be made of the public lands, the national debt (for which they stand pledged) must be first paid, took occasion to intimate "that the extraordinary fervor which seems to exist in a certain quarter (meaning the South, sir) for the payment of the debt, arises from a disposition to weaken the ties which bind the people to the Union." While the gentleman deals us this blow, he professes an ardent desire to see the debt speedily extinguished. He must excuse me, however, for feeling some distrust on that subject until I find this disposition manifested by something stronger than professions. I shall look for acts, decided and unequivocal acts: for the performance of which an opportunity will very soon (if I am not greatly mistaken) be afforded. Sir, if I were at liberty to judge of the course which that gentleman would pursue, from the principles which he has laid down in relation to this matter, I should be bound to conclude that he will be found acting with those with whom it is a darling object to prevent the payment of the public debt. He tells us he is desirous of paying the debt, "because we are under an obligation to discharge it." Now, sir, suppose it should happen that the public creditors, with whom we have contracted the obligation, should release us from it, so far as to declare their willingness to wait for payment for fifty years to come, provided only the interest shall be punctually discharged. The gentleman from Massachusetts will then be released from the obligation which now makes him desirous of paying the debt; and, let me tell the gentleman, the holders of the stock will not only release us from this obligation, but they will implore, nay, they will even pay us not to pay them. But,

adds the gentleman, "so far as the debt may have an effect in binding the debtors to the country, and thereby serving as a link to hold the States together, he would be glad that it should exist forever." Surely then, sir, on the gentleman's own principles, he must be opposed to the payment of the debt.

Sir, let me tell that gentleman that the South repudiates the idea that a pecuniary dependence on the federal government is one of the legitimate means of holding the states together. A moneyed interest in the government is essentially a base interest; and just so far as it operates to bind the feelings of those who are subjected to it to the government; just so far as it operates in creating sympathies and interests that would not otherwise exist; is it opposed to all the principles of free government, and at war with virtue and patriotism. Sir, the link which binds the public creditors, as such, to their country, binds them equally to all governments, whether arbitrary or free. In a free government, this principle of abject dependence, if extended through all the ramifications of society, must be fatal to liberty. Already have we made alarming strides in that direction. The entire class of manufacturers, the holders of stocks, with their hundreds of millions of capital, are held to the government by the strong link of pecuniary interests; millions of people, entire sections of country, interested, or believing themselves to be so, in the public lands, and the public treasure, are bound to the government by the expectation of pecuniary favors. If this system is carried much further, no man can fail to see that every generous motive of attachment to the country will be destroyed, and in its place will spring up those low, grovelling, base, and selfish feelings which bind men to the footstool of a despot by bonds as strong and as enduring as those which attach them to free institutions. Sir, I would lay the foundation of this government in the affections of the people; I would teach them to cling to it by dispensing equal justice, and, above all, by securing the "blessings of liberty to themselves and to their posterity."

The honorable gentleman from Massachusetts has gone out of his way to pass a high eulogium on the state of Ohio. In the most impassioned tones of eloquence, he described her majestic march to greatness. He told us that, having already left all the other states far behind, she was now passing by Virginia, and Pennsylvania, and about to take her station by the side of New York. To all this, sir, I was disposed most cordially to respond. When, however, the gentleman proceeded to contrast the state of Ohio with Kentucky, to the disadvantage of the latter, I listened to him with regret; and when he proceeded further to attribute the great, and, as he supposed, acknowledged superiority of the former in population, wealth, and general prosperity, to the policy of Nathan Dane, of Massachusetts, which had secured to the people of Ohio (by the Ordinance of '87) a population of freemen, I will confess that my feelings suffered a revulsion, which I am now unable to describe in any language sufficiently respectful towards the gentleman from Massachusetts. In contrasting the state of Ohio with Kentucky, for the purpose of pointing out the superiority of the former, and of attributing that superiority to the existence of slavery, in the one state, and its absence in the other, I thought I could discern the very spirit of the Missouri question intruded into this debate, for objects best known to the gentleman himself. Did that gentleman, sir, when he formed the determination to cross the southern border, in order to invade the state of South Carolina, deem it prudent, or necessary, to enlist under his banners the prejudices of the world, which, like Swiss troops may be engaged in any cause, and are prepared to serve under any leader? Did he desire to avail himself of those remorseless allies, the passions of mankind, of which it may be more truly said, than of the savage tribes of the wilderness, "that their known rule of warfare is an indiscriminate slaughter of all ages, sexes, and conditions?" Or was it supposed, sir, that, in a premeditated and unprovoked attack upon the South, it was advisable to begin by gentle admonition of our supposed weakness, in order to prevent us from making that firm and manly resistance due to our own character, and our dearest interest? Was the significant hint of the weakness of slaveholding states, when contrasted with the superior strength of free states—like the glare of the weapon half drawn from its scabbard—intended to enforce the lessons of prudence and of patriotism, which the gentleman has resolved, out of his abundant generosity, gratuitously to bestow upon us? [said Mr. H.] The impression which has gone abroad, of the weakness of the South, as connected with the slave question, exposes us to such constant attacks, has done us so much injury, and is calculated to produce such infinite mischiefs, that I embrace the occasion presented by the remarks of the gentleman from Massachusetts, to declare that we are ready to meet the question promptly and fearlessly. It is one from which we are not disposed to shrink, in whatever form or under whatever circumstances it may be pressed upon us. We are ready to make up the issue with the gentleman, as to the influence of slavery on individual and national character—on the prosperity and greatness, either of the United States, or of particular states. Sir, when arraigned before the bar of public opinion, on this charge of slavery, we can stand up with conscious rectitude, plead not guilty, and put ourselves upon God and our country. Sir, we will not consent to look at slavery in the abstract. We will not stop to inquire whether the black man, as some philosophers have contended, is of an inferior race, nor whether his color and condition are the effects of a curse inflicted for the offences of his ancestors. We deal in no abstractions. We will not look back to inquire whether our fathers were guiltless in introducing slaves into this country. If an inquiry should ever be instituted in these matters, however, it will be found that the profits of the slave trade were not confined to the South. Southern ships and southern sailors were not the instruments of bringing slaves to the shores of America, nor did our merchants reap the profits of that "accursed traffic." But, sir, we will pass over all this. If slavery, as it now exists in this country, be an evil, we of the present day found it ready made to our hands. Finding our lot cast among a people, whom God had manifestly committed to our care, we did not sit down to speculate on abstract questions of theoretical liberty. We met it as a practical question of obligation and duty. We resolved to make the best of the situation in which Providence had placed us, and to fulfil the high trust which had devolved upon us as the owners of slaves, in the only way in which such a trust could be fulfilled, without spreading misery and ruin throughout the land. We found that we had to deal with a people whose physical, moral, and intellectual habits and character, totally disqualified them from the enjoyment of the blessings of freedom. We could not send them back to the shores from whence their fathers had been taken; their numbers forbade the thought, even if we did not know that their condition here is infinitely preferable to what it possibly could be among the barren sands and savage tribes of Africa; and it was wholly irreconcilable with all our notions of humanity to tear asunder the tender ties which they had formed among us, to gratify the feelings of a false philanthropy. What a commentary on the wisdom, justice, and humanity, of the southern slave owner is presented by the example of certain benevolent associations and charitable individuals elsewhere. Shedding weak tears over sufferings which had existence only in their own sickly imaginations, these "friends of humanity" set themselves systematically to work to seduce the slaves of the South from their masters. By means of missionaries and political tracts, the scheme was in a great measure successful. Thousands of these deluded victims of fanaticism were seduced into the enjoyment of freedom in our northern cities. And what has been the consequence? Go to these cities now, and ask the question. Visit the dark and narrow lanes, and obscure recesses, which have been assigned by common consent as the abodes of those outcasts of the world—the free people of color. Sir, there does not exist, on the face of the whole earth, a population so poor, so wretched, so vile, so loathsome, so utterly destitute of all the comforts, conveniences, and decencies of life, as the unfortunate blacks of Philadelphia, and New York, and Boston. Liberty has been to them the greatest of calamities, the heaviest of curses. Sir, I have had some opportunities of making comparisons between the condition of the free negroes of the North and the slaves of the South, and the comparison has left not only an indelible impression of the superior advantages of the latter, but has gone far to reconcile me to slavery itself. Never have I felt so forcibly that touching description, "the foxes have holes, and the birds of the air have nests, but the son of man hath not where to lay his head," as when I have seen this unhappy race, naked and houseless, almost starving in the streets, and abandoned by all the world. Sir, I have seen in the neighborhood of one of the most moral, religious, and refined cities of the North, a family of free blacks, driven to the caves of the rock, and there obtaining a precarious subsistence from charity and plunder.

When the gentleman from Massachusetts adopts and reiterates the old charge of weakness as resulting from slavery, I must be permitted to call for the proof of those blighting effects which he ascribes to its influence. I suspect that when the subject is closely examined, it will be found that there is not much force even in the plausible objection of the want of physical power in slaveholding states. The power of a country is compounded of its population and its wealth; and, in modern times, where, from the very form and structure of society, by far the greater portion of the people must, even during the continuance of the most desolating wars, be employed in the cultivation of the soil, and other peaceful pursuits, it may be well doubted whether slaveholding states, by reason of the superior value of their productions, are not able to maintain a number of troops in the field, fully equal to what could be supported by states with a larger white population, but not possessed of equal resources.

It is a popular error to suppose, that, in any possible state of things, the people of a country could ever be called out *en masse,* or that a half, or a third, or even a fifth part of the physical force of any country could ever be brought into the field. The difficulty is not to procure men, but to provide the means of maintaining them; and in this view of the subject, it may be asked whether the southern states are not a source of strength and power, and not of weakness, to the country? whether they have not contributed, and are not now contributing, largely, to the wealth and prosperity of every state in this Union? From a statement which I hold in my hand, it appears that, in ten years (from 1818 to 1827 inclusive) the whole amount of the domestic exports of the United States was $521,811,045. Of which, three articles, the product of slave labor, namely, cotton, rice, and tobacco, amounted to $339,203,032; equal to about two-thirds of the whole. It is not true, as has been supposed, that the advantages of this labor is confined almost exclusively to the southern states. Sir, I am thoroughly convinced that, at this time, the states North of the Potomac actually derive greater profits from the labor of our slaves, than we do ourselves. It appears, from our public documents, that, in seven years, (from 1821 to 1827 inclusive) the six southern states exported to the amount of $190,337,281; and imported to the value of $55,646,301. Now, the difference between these two sums, near $140 million, passed through the hands of the northern merchants, and enabled them to carry on their commercial operations with all the world. Such part of these goods as found its way back to our hands, came charged with the duties, as well as the profits of the merchant, the ship owner, and a host of others, who found employment in carrying on these immense exchanges; and, for such part as was consumed at the North, we received in exchange northern manufactures, charged with an increased price, to cover all the taxes which the northern consumer had been compelled to pay on the imported article. It will be seen, therefore, at a glance, how much slave labor has contributed to the wealth and prosperity of the United States; and how largely our northern brethren have participated in the profits of that labor.

. . . .

There is a spirit, which, like the father of evil, is constantly "walking to and fro about the earth, seeking whom it may devour." It is the spirit of false philanthropy. The persons whom it possesses do not indeed throw themselves into the flames, but they are employed in lighting up the torches of discord throughout the community. Their first principle of action is to leave their own affairs, and neglect their own duties, to regulate the affairs and the duties of others. Theirs is the task to feed the hungry and clothe the naked, of other lands, whilst they thrust the naked, famished, and shivering beggar from their own doors; to instruct the heathen, while their own children want the bread of life. When this spirit infuses itself into the bosom of a statesman, (if one so possessed can be called a statesman) it converts him at once into a visionary enthusiast. Then it is that he indulges in golden dreams of national greatness and prosperity. He discovers that "liberty is power;" and not content with vast schemes of improvement at home, which it would bankrupt the treasury of the world to execute, he flies to foreign lands, to fulfil obligations to "the human race," by inculcating the principles of "political and religious liberty," and promoting the "general welfare" of the whole human race. It is a spirit which has long been busy with the slaves of the South, and is even now displaying itself in vain efforts to drive the government from its wise policy in relation to the Indians. It is this spirit which has filled the land with thousands of wild and visionary projects, which can have no effect but to waste the energies and dissipate the resources of the country. It is the spirit, of which the aspiring politician dexterously avails himself, when, by inscribing on his banner the magical words "liberty and philanthropy," he draws to his support that entire class of persons who are ready to bow down at the very names of their idols.

But, sir, whatever difference of opinion may exist as to the effect of slavery on national wealth and prosperity, if we may trust to experience, there can be no doubt that it has never yet produced any injurious effect on individual or national character. Look through the whole history of the country, from the commencement of the Revolution down to the present hour; where are there to be found brighter examples of intellectual and moral greatness, than have been exhibited by the sons of the South? From the Father of his Country, down to the distinguished chieftain who has been elevated, by a grateful people, to the highest office in their gift, the interval is filled up by a long line of orators, of statesmen, and of heroes, justly entitled to rank among the ornaments of their country, and the benefactors of mankind. Look at "the Old Dominion," great and magnanimous Virginia, "whose jewels are her sons." Is there any state in this Union which has contributed so much to the honor and welfare of the country? Sir, I will yield the whole question; I will acknowledge the fatal effects of slavery upon character, if any one can say that, for noble disinterestedness, ardent love of country, exalted virtue, and a pure and holy devotion to liberty, the people of the southern states have ever been surpassed by any in the world.

. . . .

Sir, the party to which I am proud of having belonged from the very commencement of my political life to the present day, were the Democrats of '98. Anarchists, Antifederalists, revolutionists, I think they were sometimes called. They assumed the name of Democratic Republicans in 1812, and have retained their name and their principles up to the present hour. True to their political faith, they have always, as a party, been in favor of limitations of power; they have insisted that all powers not delegated to the federal government are reserved, and have been constantly struggling, as they are now struggling, to preserve the rights of the states, and prevent them from being drawn into the vortex, and swallowed up by one great consolidated government. Sir, anyone acquainted with the history of parties in this country will recognize in the points now in dispute between the senator from Massachusetts and myself, the very grounds which have, from the beginning, divided the two great parties in this country, and which (call these parties by what names you will, and amalgamate them as you may) will divide them forever. The true distinction between those parties is laid down in a celebrated manifesto issued by the convention of the Federalists of Massachusetts, assembled in Boston, in February, 1824, on the occasion of organizing a party opposition to the reelection of Governor Eustis. The gentleman will recognize this as "the canonical book of political scripture," and it instructs us, that "when the American colonies redeemed themselves from British bondage, and became so many independent nations, they proposed to form a national union." (Not a federal union, sir, but a national union.) "Those who were in favor of a union of the States in this form became known by the name of federalists; those who wanted no union of the States, or disliked the proposed form of union, became known by the name of antifederalists. By means which need not be enumerated, the antifederalists became, after the expiration of twelve years, our national rulers; and, for a period of sixteen years, until the close of Mr. Madison's administration in 1817, continued to exercise the exclusive direction of our public affairs." Here, sir, is the true history of the origin, rise, and progress, of the party of national republicans, who date back to the very origin of the government, and who, then, as now, chose to consider the Constitution as having created not a federal but a national union; who regarded "consolidation" as no evil, and who doubtless consider it "a consummation devoutly to be wished," to build up a great "central Government," "one and indivisible." Sir, there have existed, in every age and every country, two distinct orders of men—the lovers of freedom, and the devoted advocates of power. The same great leading principles, modified only by peculiarities of manners, habits, and institutions, divided parties in the ancient republics, animated the Whigs and Tories of Great Britain, distinguished in our own times the liberals and ultras of France, and may be traced even in the bloody struggles of unhappy Spain. Sir, when the gallant Riego, who devoted himself, and all that he possessed, to the liberties of his country, was dragged to the scaffold, followed by the tears and lamentations of every lover of freedom throughout the world, he perished amidst the deafening cries of "Long live the absolute King!" The people whom I represent are the descendants of those who brought with them to this country, as the most precious of their possessions, "an ardent love of liberty;" and while that shall be preserved, they will always be found manfully struggling against the consolidation of the government, as the worst of evils.

. . . .

The honorable gentleman from Massachusetts [Mr. Webster] while he exonerates me personally from the charge, intimates that there is a party in the country who are looking to disunion. Sir, if the gentleman had stopped there, the accusation would "have passed by me as the idle wind which I regard not." But, when he goes on to give to his accusation a local habitation and a name, by quoting the expression of a distinguished citizen of South Carolina, [Dr. Cooper] "that it was time for the South to calculate the value of the Union," and, in the language of the bitterest sarcasm, adds, "surely then the Union cannot last longer than July, 1831," it is impossible to mistake either the allusion or the object of the gentleman. Now I call upon every one who hears me to bear witness that this controversy is not of my seeking. The Senate will do me the justice to remember, that, at the time this unprovoked and uncalled for attack was made upon the South, not one word has been uttered by me in disparagement of New England, nor had I made the most distant allusion, either to the senator from Massachusetts, or the state he represents. But, sir, that gentleman has thought proper, for purposes best known to himself, to strike the South through me, the most unworthy of her servants. He has crossed the border, he has invaded the state of South Carolina, is making war upon her citizens, and endeavoring to overthrow her principles and her institutions. Sir, when the gentleman provokes me to such a conflict, I meet him at the threshold. I will struggle while I have life, for our altars and our firesides, and if God gives me strength, I will drive back the invader discomfited. Nor shall I stop there. If the gentleman provokes the war, he shall have war. Sir, I will not stop at the border; I will carry the war into the enemy's territory, and not consent to lay down my arms, until I shall have obtained "indemnity for the past, and security for the future." It is with unfeigned reluctance that I enter upon the performance of this part of my duty. I shrink almost instinctively from a course, however necessary, which may have a tendency to excite sectional feelings, and sectional jealousies. But, sir, the task has been forced upon me, and I proceed right onward to the performance of my duty; be the consequences what they may, the responsibility is with those who have imposed upon me this necessity. The senator from Massachusetts has thought proper to cast the first stone, and if he shall find, according to a homely adage, "that he lives in a glass house," on his head be the consequences.

. . . .

Register of Debates in Congress, Senate, 21st Congress, 1st session, January 21 and 25, 1830, 43–58.

56   Daniel Webster's Second Reply to Robert Hayne

January 26 and 27, 1830

The cause of the Union and the name of Daniel Webster be-
came one and inseparable with the stirring concluding lines of this
speech, "Liberty and Union, now and for ever, one and insepara-
ble!" This is regarded as one of the best single speeches ever deliv-
ered on the floor of the U.S. Senate. This speech, and Webster's
equally famous "7th of March" speech twenty years later (see doc-
ument 65) ensured Webster's place in Senate history as its greatest
orator. To friend and foe alike he was called "the godlike Daniel,"
for his intense gaze, his great voice, his unsurpassed skill as a ora-
tor, and his awesome stern presence.

The context for these remarks can be found in the headnote to
the previous document, Robert Hayne's Reply to Daniel Webster
(see document 55). The forty-eight-year-old Webster, although
only in his third year in the Senate, had a well-deserved reputation
as a master orator long before he delivered this speech. He gained
national fame with his skills as a lawyer, arguing landmark
Supreme Court cases in 1819, Dartmouth College v. Woodward
and McCullough v. Maryland *(see document 52). His earlier con-*
gressional career in the House of Representatives, serving first from
New Hampshire and then from Massachusetts, was filled with
memorable debates.

While Webster replied to the specific arguments of Hayne,
speaking from twelve pages of notes, his arguments were polished
long before this particular debate in many conversations on these
subjects and in earlier debates, some going back to his arguments
in McCullough v. Maryland. *Because of the nature of the report-*
ing of debates in the 1830s, no precise and complete text exists of
what either Webster or Hayne said during this debate. It was not
uncommon for senators and the reporters of Senate debates to later
edit, and sometimes embellish, the remarks that were actually ut-
tered on the floor. In this well-documented speech, the original
shorthand notes of the reporter survive along with the printed ver-
sion of the speech. The two versions differ considerably. It is clear
that Webster edited his own remarks for publication to enhance
their impact on readers who were not on hand to hear the power of
his oratory. The version of Webster's speech excerpted here is from
Robert C. Byrd's The Senate, 1789–1989, *which used an 1880 edi-*
tion of Webster's speeches for the text. For the best and most de-
tailed scholarly treatment of the speech itself and the various ver-
sions, see Charles M. Wiltse and Harold D. Moser (eds.), The
Papers of Daniel Webster: Speeches and Formal Writings, 1800-
1833, *vol. 1 (Hanover, N.H.: University Press of New England,*
1974–1989), 285–393. For an excellent account of the Webster-
Hayne debate, see Robert V. Remini, Daniel Webster, the Man
and His Time *(New York: W.W. Norton, 1997), 312–331.*

Mr. President,—When the mariner has been tossed for
many days in thick weather, and on an unknown sea, he naturally avails himself of the first pause in the storm, the earliest
glance of the sun, to take his latitude, and ascertain how far the
elements have driven him from his true course. Let us imitate
this prudence, and, before we float farther on the waves of this
debate, refer to the point from which we departed, that we may
at least be able to conjecture where we now are. I ask for the
reading of the resolution before the Senate.

The Secretary read the resolution, as follows:—

"*Resolved*, That the Committee on Public Lands be instructed
to inquire and report the quantity of public lands remaining un-
sold within each State and Territory, and whether it be expedient
to limit for a certain period the sales of the public lands to such
lands only as have heretofore been offered for sale, and are now
subject to entry at the minimum price. And, also, whether the
office of Surveyor-General, and some of the land offices, may
not be abolished without detriment to the public interest; or
whether it be expedient to adopt measures to hasten the sales
and extend more rapidly the surveys of the public lands."

We have thus heard, Sir, what the resolution is which is actually before us for consideration; and it will readily occur to every
one, that it is almost the only subject about which something
has not been said in the speech, running through two days, by
which the Senate has been entertained by the gentleman from
South Carolina. Every topic in the wide range of our public affairs, whether past or present,—every thing, general or local,
whether belonging to national politics or party politics,—seems
to have attracted more or less of the honorable member's attention, save only the resolution before the Senate. He has spoken
of every thing but the public lands; they have escaped his notice.
To that subject, in all his excursions, he has not paid even the
cold respect of a passing glance.

When this debate, Sir, was to be resumed on Thursday morning, it so happened that it would have been convenient for me to
be elsewhere. The honorable member, however, did not incline
to put off the discussion to another day. He had a shot, he said,
to return, and he wished to discharge it. That shot, Sir, which he
thus kindly informed us was coming, that we might stand out of
the way, or prepare ourselves to fall by it and die with decency,
has now been received. Under all advantages, and with expectation awakened by the tone which preceded it, it has been discharged, and has spent its force. It may become me to say no
more of its effect, than that, if nobody is found, after all, either
killed or wounded, it is not the first time, in the history of human affairs, that the vigor and success of the war have not quite
come up to the lofty and sounding phrase of the manifesto.

The gentleman, Sir, in declining to postpone the debate, told
the Senate, with the emphasis of his hand upon his heart, that
there was something rankling *here*, which he wished to relieve.
[Mr. Hayne rose, and disclaimed having used the word
rankling.] It would not, Mr. President, be safe for the honorable
member to appeal to those around him, upon the question
whether he did in fact make use of that word. But he may have

been unconscious of it. At any rate, it is enough that he disclaims it. But still, with or without the use of that particular word, he had yet something *here,* he said, of which he wished to rid himself by an immediate reply. In this respect, Sir, I have a great advantage over the honorable gentleman. There is nothing *here,* Sir, which gives me the slightest uneasiness; neither fear, nor anger, nor that which is sometimes more troublesome than either, the consciousness of having been in the wrong. There is nothing, either originating *here,* or now received *here* by the gentleman's shot. Nothing originating here, for I had not the slightest feeling of unkindness towards the honorable member. Some passages, it is true, had occurred since our acquaintance in this body, which I could have wished might have been otherwise; but I had used philosophy and forgotten them. I paid the honorable member the attention of listening with respect to his first speech; and when he sat down, though surprised, and I must even say astonished, at some of his opinions, nothing was farther from my intention than to commence any personal warfare. Through the whole of the few remarks I made in answer, I avoided, studiously and carefully, every thing which I thought possible to be construed into disrespect. And, Sir, while there is thus nothing originating *here* which I have wished at any time, or now wish, to discharge, I must repeat, also, that nothing has been received *here* which *rankles,* or in any way gives me annoyance. I will not accuse the honorable member of violating the rules of civilized war; I will not say, that he poisoned his arrows. But whether his shafts were, or were not, dipped in that which would have caused rankling if they had reached their destination, there was not, as it happened, quite strength enough in the bow to bring them to their mark. If he wishes now to gather up those shafts, he must look for them elsewhere; they will not be found fixed and quivering in the object at which they were aimed.

The honorable member complained that I had slept on his speech. I must have slept on it, or not slept at all. The moment the honorable member sat down, his friend from Missouri [Thomas Hart Benton] rose, and, with much honeyed commendation of the speech, suggested that the impressions which it had produced were too charming and delightful to be disturbed by other sentiments or other sounds, and proposed that the Senate should adjourn. Would it have been quite amiable in me, Sir, to interrupt this excellent good feeling? Must I not have been absolutely malicious, if I could have thrust myself forward, to destroy sensations thus pleasing? Was it not much better and kinder, both to sleep upon them myself, and to allow others also the pleasure of sleeping upon them? But if it be meant, by sleeping upon his speech, that I took time to prepare a reply to it, it is quite a mistake. Owing to other engagements, I could not employ even the interval between the adjournment of the Senate and its meeting the next morning, in attention to the subject of this debate. Nevertheless, Sir, the mere matter of fact is undoubtedly true. I did sleep on the gentleman's speech, and slept soundly. And I slept equally well on his speech of yesterday, to which I am now replying. It is quite possible that in this respect, also, I possess some advantage over the honorable member, at-

tributable, doubtless, to a cooler temperament on my part; for, in truth, I slept upon his speeches remarkably well.

But the gentleman inquires why *he* was made the object of such a reply. Why was *he* singled out? If an attack has been made on the East, he, he assures us, did not begin it; it was made by the gentleman from Missouri. Sir, I answered the gentleman's speech because I happened to hear it; and because, also, I chose to give an answer to that speech, which, if unanswered, I thought most likely to product [sic] injurious impressions. I did not stop to inquire who was the original drawer of the bill. I found a responsible indorser before me, and it was my purpose to hold him liable, and to bring him to his just responsibility, without delay. But, Sir, this interrogatory of the honorable member was only introductory to another. He proceeded to ask me whether I had turned upon him, in this debate, from the consciousness that I should find an overmatch, if I ventured on a contest with his friend from Missouri. If, Sir, the honorable member, *modestiae gratia,* had chosen thus to defer to his friend, and to pay him a compliment, without intentional disparagement to others, it would have been quite according to the friendly courtesies of debate, and not at all ungrateful to my own feelings. I am not one of those, Sir, who esteem any tribute of regard, whether light and occasional, or more serious and deliberate, which may be bestowed on others, as so much unjustly withholden from themselves. But the tone and manner of the gentleman's question forbid me thus to interpret it. I am not at liberty to consider it as nothing more than a civility to his friend. It had an air of taunt and disparagement, something of the loftiness of asserted superiority, which does not allow me to pass it over without notice. It was put as a question for me to answer, and so put as if it were difficult for me to answer, whether I deemed the member from Missouri an overmatch for myself, in debate here. It seems to me, Sir, that this is extraordinary language, and an extraordinary tone, for the discussions of this body.

Matches and overmatches! Those terms are more applicable elsewhere than here, and fitter for other assemblies than this. Sir, the gentleman seems to forget where and what we are. This is a Senate, a Senate of equals, of men of individual honor and personal character, and of absolute independence. We know no masters, we acknowledge no dictators. This is a hall for mutual consultation and discussion; not an arena for the exhibition of champions. I offer myself, Sir, as a match for no man; I throw the challenge of debate at no man's feet. But then, Sir, since the honorable member has put the question in a manner that calls for an answer, I will give him an answer; and I tell him, that, holding myself to be the humblest of the members here, I yet know nothing in the arm of his friend from Missouri, either alone or when aided by the arm of *his* friend from South Carolina, that need deter even me from espousing whatever opinions I may choose to espouse, from debating whenever I may choose to debate, or from speaking whatever I may see fit to say, on the floor of the Senate. Sir, when uttered as matter of commendation or compliment, I should dissent from nothing which the honorable member might say of his friend. Still less do I put forth any pretensions of my own. But when put to me as matter of taunt, I throw it back, and say to the gentleman, that he could possibly say nothing less likely than such a comparison to wound my pride of personal character. The anger of its tone rescued the remark from intentional irony, which otherwise, probably, would have been its general acceptation. But, Sir, if it be imagined that by this mutual quotation and commendation; if it be supposed that, by casting the characters of the drama, assigning to each his part, to one the attack, to another the cry of onset; or if it be thought that, by a loud and empty vaunt of anticipated victory, any laurels are to be won here; if it be imagined, especially, that any, or all these things will shake any purpose of mine, I can tell the honorable member, once for all, that he is greatly mistaken, and that he is dealing with one of whose temper and character he has yet much to learn. Sir, I shall not allow myself, on this occasion, I hope on no occasion, to be betrayed into any loss of temper; but if provoked, as I trust I never shall be, into crimination and recrimination, the honorable member may perhaps find that, in that contest, there will be blows to take as well as blows to give; that others can state comparisons as significant, at least, as his own, and that his impunity may possibly demand of him whatever powers of taunt and sarcasm he may possess. I commend him to a prudent husbandry of his resources.

. . . .

In the course of my observations the other day, Mr. President, I paid a passing tribute of respect to a very worthy man, Mr. [Nathan] Dane of Massachusetts. It so happened that he drew the Ordinance of 1787, for the government of the Northwestern Territory. A man of so much ability, and so little pretence; of so great a capacity to do good, and so unmixed a disposition to do it for its own sake; a gentleman who had acted an important part, forty years ago, in a measure the influence of which is still deeply felt in the very matter which was the subject of debate, might, I thought, receive from me a commendatory recognition. But the honorable member was inclined to be facetious on the subject. He was rather disposed to make it matter of ridicule, that I had introduced into the debate the name of one Nathan Dane, of whom he assures us he had never before heard. Sir, if the honorable member had never before heard of Mr. Dane, I am sorry for it. It shows him less acquainted with the public men of the country than I had supposed. Let me tell him, however, that a sneer from him at the mention of the name of Mr. Dane is in bad taste. It may well be a high mark of ambition, Sir, either with the honorable gentleman or myself, to accomplish as much to make our names known to advantage, and remembered with gratitude, as Mr. Dane has accomplished. But the truth is, Sir, I suspect, that Mr. Dane lives a little too far north. He is of Massachusetts, and too near the north star to be reached by the honorable gentleman's telescope. If his sphere had happened to range south of Mason and Dixon's line, he might, probably, have come within the scope of his vision.

I spoke, Sir, of the Ordinance of 1787, which prohibits slavery, in all future times, northwest of the Ohio, as a measure of great wisdom and foresight, and one which had been attended with highly beneficial and permanent consequences. I suppose that, on this point, no two gentlemen in the Senate could entertain different opinions. But the simple expression of this sentiment has led the gentleman, not only into a labored defence of slavery, in the abstract, and on principle, but also into a warm accusation against me, as having attacked the system of domestic slavery now existing in the Southern States. For all this, there was not the slightest foundation, in any thing said or intimated by me. I did not utter a single word which any ingenuity could torture into an attack on the slavery of the South. I said, only, that it was highly wise and useful, in legislating for the Northwestern country while it was yet a wilderness, to prohibit the introduction of slaves; and I added, that I presumed there was no reflecting and intelligent person, in the neighboring State of Kentucky, who would doubt that, if the same prohibition had been extended, at the same early period, over that commonwealth, her strength and population would, at this day, have been far greater than they are. If these opinions be thought doubtful, they are nevertheless, I trust, neither extraordinary nor disrespectful. They attack nobody and menace nobody. And yet, Sir, the gentleman's optics have discovered, even in the mere expression of this sentiment, what he calls the very spirit of the Missouri question! He represents me as making an onset on the whole South, and manifesting a spirit which would interfere with, and disturb, their domestic condition!

Sir, this injustice no otherwise surprises me, than as it is committed here, and committed without the slightest pretence of ground for it. I say it only surprises me as being done here; for I know full well, that it is, and has been, the settled policy of some persons in the South, for years, to represent the people of the North as disposed to interfere with them in their own exclusive and peculiar concerns. This is a delicate and sensitive point in Southern feeling; and of late years it has always been touched, and generally with effect, whenever the object has been to unite the whole South against Northern men or Northern measures. This feeling, always carefully kept alive, and maintained at too intense a heat to admit discrimination or reflection, is a lever of great power in our political machine. It moves vast bodies, and gives to them one and the same direction. But it is without adequate cause, and the suspicion which exists is wholly groundless. There is not, and never has been, a disposition in the North to interfere with these interests of the South. Such interference has never been supposed to be within the power of government; nor has it been in any way attempted. The slavery of the South has always been regarded as a matter of domestic policy, left with the States themselves, and with which the federal government had nothing to do. Certainly, Sir, I am, and ever have been, of that opinion. The gentleman, indeed, argues that slavery, in the abstract, is no evil. Most assuredly I need not say I differ with him, altogether and most widely, on that point. I regard domestic slavery as one of the greatest evils, both moral and political. But whether it be a malady, and whether it be curable, and if so, by what means; or, on the other hand, whether it be the *vulnus immedicabile* of the social system, I leave it to those whose right and duty it is to inquire and to decide. And this I believe, Sir, is, and uniformly has been, the sentiment of the North.

. . . .

I hope I am above violating my principles, even under the smart of injury and false imputations. Unjust suspicions and undeserved reproach, whatever pain I may experience from them, will not induce me, I trust, to overstep the limits of constitutional duty, or to encroach on the rights of others. The domestic slavery of the Southern States I leave where I find it,—in the hands of their own governments. It is their affair, not mine. Nor do I complain of the peculiar effect which the magnitude of that population has had in the distribution of power under this federal government. We know, Sir, that the representation of the States in the other house is not equal. We know that great advantage in that respect is enjoyed by the slave-holding States; and we know, too, that the intended equivalent for that advantage, that is to say, the imposition of direct taxes in the same ratio, has become merely nominal, the habit of the government being almost invariably to collect its revenue from other sources and in other modes. Nevertheless, I do not complain; nor would I countenance any movement to alter this arrangement of representation. It is the original bargain, the compact; let it stand; let the advantage of it be fully enjoyed. The Union itself is too full of benefit to be hazarded in propositions for changing its original basis. I go for the Constitution as it is, and for the Union as it is. But I am resolved not to submit in silence to accusations, either against myself individually or against the North, wholly unfounded and unjust; accusations which impute to us a disposition to evade the constitutional compact, and to extend the power of the government over the internal laws and domestic condition of the States. All such accusations, wherever and whenever made, all insinuations of the existence of any such purposes, I know and feel to be groundless and injurious. And we must confide in Southern gentlemen themselves; we must trust to those whose integrity of heart and magnanimity of feeling will lead them to a desire to maintain and disseminate truth, and who possess the means of its diffusion with the Southern public; we must leave it to them to disabuse that public of its prejudices. But in the mean time, for my own part, I shall continue to act justly, whether those towards whom justice is exercised receive it with candor or with contumely.

. . . .

In my remarks on Wednesday, I contended that we could not give away gratuitously all the public lands; that we held them in trust; that the government had solemnly pledged itself to dispose of them as a common fund for the common benefit, and to sell and settle them as its discretion should dictate. Now, Sir, what contradiction does the gentleman find to this senti-ment in the speech of 1825? He quotes me as having then said, that we ought not to hug these lands as a very great treasure. Very well, Sir, supposing me to be accurately reported in that expression, what is the contradiction? I have not now said, that we should hug these lands as a favorite source of pecuniary income. No such thing. It is not my view. What I have said, and what I do say, is, that they are a common fund, to be disposed of for the common benefit, to be sold at low prices for the accommodation of settlers, keeping the object of settling the lands as much in view as that of raising money from them. This I say now, and this I have always said. Is this hugging them as a favorite treasure? Is there no difference between hugging and hoarding this fund, on the one hand, as a great treasure, and, on the other, of disposing of it at low prices, placing the proceeds in the general treasury of the Union? My opinion is, that as much is to be made of the land as fairly and reasonably may be, selling it all the while at such rates as to give the fullest effect to settlement. This is not giving it all away to the States, as the gentleman would propose; nor is it hugging the fund closely and tenaciously, as a favorite treasure; but it is, in my judgment, a just and wise policy, perfectly according with all the various duties which rest in government. So much for my contradiction. And what is it? Where is the ground of the gentleman's triumph? What inconsistency in word or doctrine has he been able to detect? Sir, if this be a sample of that discomfiture with which the honorable gentleman threatened me, commend me to the word *discomfiture* for the rest of my life.

But, after all, this is not the point of the debate; and I must now bring the gentleman back to what is the point.

The real question between me and him is, Has the doctrine been advanced at the South or the East, that the population of the West should be retarded, or at least need not be hastened, on account of its effect to drain off the people from the Atlantic States? Is this doctrine, as has been alleged, of Eastern origin? That is the question. Has the gentleman found any thing by which he can make good his accusation? I submit to the Senate, that he has entirely failed; and, as far as this debate has shown, the only person who has advanced such sentiments is a gentleman from South Carolina, and a friend of the honorable member himself. The honorable gentleman has given no answer to this; there is none which can be given. The simple fact, while it requires no comment to enforce it, defies all argument to refute it. I could refer to the speeches of another Southern gentleman, in years before, of the same general character, and to the same effect, as that which has been quoted; but I will not consume the time of the Senate by the reading of them.

So then, Sir, New England is guiltless of the policy of retarding Western population, and of all envy and jealousy of the growth of the new States. Whatever there be of that policy in the country, no part of it is hers. If it has a local habitation, the honorable member has probably seen by this time where to look for it; and if it now has received a name, he has himself christened it.

We approach, at length, Sir, to a more important part of the honorable gentleman's observations. Since it does not accord with my views of justice and policy to give away the public lands altogether, as a mere matter of gratuity, I am asked by the honorable gentleman on what ground it is that I consent to vote them away in particular instances. How, he inquires, do I reconcile with these professed sentiments, my support of measures appropriating portions of the lands to particular roads, particular canals, particular rivers, and particular institutions of education in the West? This leads, Sir, to the real and wide difference in political opinion between the honorable gentleman and myself. On my part, I look upon all these objects as connected with the common good, fairly embraced in its object and its terms; he, on the contrary, deems them all, if good at all, only local good. This is our difference. The interrogatory which he proceeded to put, at once explains this difference. "What interest," asks he, "has South Carolina in a canal in Ohio?" Sir, this very question is full of significance. It develops the gentleman's whole political system; and its answer expounds mine. Here we differ. I look upon a road over the Alleghanies, a canal round the falls of the Ohio, or a canal or railway from the Atlantic to the Western waters, as being an object large and extensive enough to be fairly said to be for the common benefit. The gentleman thinks otherwise, and this is the key to his construction of the powers of the government. He may well ask what interest has South Carolina in a canal in Ohio. On his system, it is true, she has no interest. On that system, Ohio and Carolina are different governments, and different countries; connected here, it is true, by some slight and ill-defined bond of union, but in all main respects separate and diverse. On that system, Carolina has no more interest in a canal in Ohio than in Mexico. The gentleman, therefore, only follows out his own principles; he does no more than arrive at the natural conclusions of his own doctrines; he only announces the true results of that creed which he has adopted himself, and would persuade others to adopt, when he thus declares that South Carolina has no interest in a public work in Ohio.

Sir, we narrow-minded people of New England do not reason thus. Our *notion* of things is entirely different. We look upon the States, not as separated, but as united. We love to dwell on that union, and on the mutual happiness which it has so much promoted, and the common renown which it has so greatly contributed to acquire. In our contemplation, Carolina and Ohio are parts of the same country; States, united under the same general government, having interests, common, associated, intermingled. In whatever is within the proper sphere of the constitutional power of this government, we look upon the States as one. We do not impose geographical limits to our patriotic feeling or regard; we do not follow rivers and mountains, and lines of latitude, to find boundaries, beyond which public improvements do not benefit us. We who come here, as agents and representatives of these narrow-minded and selfish men of New England, consider ourselves as bound to regard with an equal eye the good of the whole, in whatever is within our powers of legislation. Sir, if a railroad or canal, beginning in South Carolina and ending in South Carolina, appeared to me to be of national importance and national magnitude, believing, as I

do that the power of government extends to the encouragement of works of that description, if I were to stand up here and ask, What interest has Massachusetts in a railroad in South Carolina? I should not be willing to face my constituents. These same narrow-minded men would tell me, that they had sent me to act for the whole country, and that one who possessed too little comprehension, either of intellect or feeling, one who was not large enough, both in mind and in heart, to embrace the whole, was not fit to be intrusted with the interest of any part.

Sir, I do not desire to enlarge the powers of the government by unjustifiable construction, nor to exercise any not within a fair interpretation. But when it is believed that a power does exist, then it is, in my judgment, to be exercised for the general benefit of the whole. So far as respects the exercise of such a power, the States are one. It was the very object of the Constitution to create unity of interests to the extent of the powers of the general government. In war and peace we are one; in commerce, one; because the authority of the general government reaches to war and peace, and to the regulation of commerce. I have never seen any more difficulty in erecting lighthouses on the lakes, than on the ocean; in improving the harbors of inland seas, than if they were within the ebb and flow of the tide; or in removing obstructions in the vast streams of the West, more than in any work to facilitate commerce on the Atlantic coast. If there be any power for one, there is power also for the other; and they are all and equally for the common good of the country.

. . . .

I go to other remarks of the honorable member; and I have to complain of an entire misapprehension of what I said on the subject of the national debt, though I can hardly perceive how any one could misunderstand me. What I said was, not that I wished to put off the payment of the debt, but, on the contrary, that I had always voted for every measure for its reduction, as uniformly as the gentleman himself. He seems to claim the exclusive merit of a disposition to reduce the public charge. I do not allow it to him. As a debt, I was, I am for paying it, because it is a charge on our finances, and on the industry of the country. But I observed, that I thought I perceived a morbid fervor on that subject, an excessive anxiety to pay off the debt, not so much because it is a debt simply, as because, while it lasts, it furnishes one objection to disunion. It is, while it continues, a tie of common interest. I did not impute such motives to the honorable member himself, but that there is such a feeling in existence I have not a particle of doubt. The most I said was, that if one effect of the debt was to strengthen our Union, that effect itself was not regretted by me, however much others might regret it. The gentleman has not seen how to reply to this, otherwise than by supposing me to have advanced the doctrine that a national debt is a national blessing. Others, I must hope, will find much less difficulty in understanding me. I distinctly and pointedly cautioned the honorable member not to understand me as expressing an opinion favorable to the continuance of the debt. I repeated this caution, and repeated it more than once; but it was thrown away.

On yet another point, I was still more unaccountably misunderstood. The gentleman had harangued against "consolidation." I told him, in reply, that there was one kind of consolidation to which I was attached, and that was the consolidation of our Union; that this was precisely that consolidation to which I feared others were not attached, and that such consolidation was the very end of the Constitution, the leading object, as they had informed us themselves, which its framers had kept in view. I turned to their communication, and read their very words, "the consolidation of the Union," and expressed my devotion to this sort of consolidation. I said, in terms, that I wished not in the slightest degree to augment the powers of this government; that my object was to preserve, not to enlarge; and that by consolidating the Union I understood no more than the strengthening of the Union, and perpetuating it. Having been thus explicit, having thus read from the printed book the precise words which I adopted, as expressing my own sentiments, it passes comprehension how any man could understand me as contending for an extension of the powers of the government, or for consolidation in that odious sense in which it means an accumulation, in the federal government, of the powers properly belonging to the States.

I repeat, Sir, that, in adopting the sentiment of the framers of the Constitution, I read their language audibly, and word for word; and I pointed out the distinction, just as fully as I have now done, between the consolidation of the Union and that other obnoxious consolidation which I disclaimed. And yet the honorable member misunderstood me. The gentleman had said that he wished for no fixed revenue,—not a shilling. If by a word he could convert the Capitol into gold, he would not do it. Why all this fear of revenue? Why, Sir, because, as the gentleman told us, it tends to consolidation. Now this can mean neither more nor less than that a common revenue is a common interest, and that all common interests tend to preserve the union of the States. I confess I like that tendency; if the gentleman dislikes it, he is right in deprecating a shilling of fixed revenue. So much, Sir, for consolidation.

. . . .

Professing to be provoked by what he chose to consider a charge made by me against South Carolina, the honorable member, Mr. President, has taken up a new crusade against New England. Leaving altogether the subject of the public lands, in which his success, perhaps, had been neither distinguished nor satisfactory, and letting go, also, of the topic of the tariff, he sallied forth in a general assault on the opinions, politics, and parties of New England, as they have been exhibited in the last thirty years. This is natural. The "narrow policy" of the public lands had proved a legal settlement in South Carolina, and was not to be removed. The "accursed policy" of the tariff, also, had established the fact of its birth and parentage in the same State. No wonder, therefore, the gentleman wished to carry the war, as he expressed it, into the enemy's country. Prudently willing to quit these subjects, he was, doubtless, desirous of fastening on others, which could not be transferred south of Mason and Dixon's line. The politics of New England became his theme; and it was in this part of his speech, I think, that he menaced me with such sore discomfiture. Discomfiture! Why, Sir, when he attacks any thing which I maintain, and overthrows it, when he turns the right or left of any position which I take up, when he drives me from any ground I choose to occupy, he may then talk of discomfiture, but not till that distant day. What has he done? Has he maintained his own charges? Has he proved what he alleged? Has he sustained himself in his attack on the government, and on the history of the North, in the matter of the public lands? Has he disproved a fact, refuted a proposition, weakened an argument, maintained by me? Has he come within beat of drum of any position of mine? O, no; but he has "carried the war into the enemy's country"! Carried the war into the enemy's country! Yes, Sir, and what sort of a war has he made of it? Why, Sir, he has stretched a drag-net over the whole surface of perished pamphlets, indiscreet sermons, frothy paragraphs, and fuming popular addresses; over whatever the pulpit in its moments of alarm, the press in its heats, and parties in their extravagance, have severally thrown off in times of general excitement and violence. He has thus swept together a mass of such things as, but that they are now old and cold, the public health would have required him rather to leave in their state of dispersion. For a good long hour or two, we had the unbroken pleasure of listening to the honorable member, while he recited with his usual grace and spirit, and with evident high gusto, speeches, pamphlets, addresses, and all the *et caeteras* of the political press, such as warm heads produce in warm times; and such as it would be "discomfiture" indeed for any one, whose taste did not delight in that sort of reading, to be obliged to peruse. This is his war. This it is to carry war into the enemy's country. It is in an invasion of this sort, that he flatters himself with the expectation of gaining laurels fit to adorn a Senator's brow!

. . . .

Mr. President, in carrying his warfare, such as it is, into New England, the honorable gentleman all along professes to be acting on the defensive. He chooses to consider me as having assailed South Carolina, and insists that he comes forth only as her champion, and in her defence. Sir, I do not admit that I made any attack whatever on South Carolina. Nothing like it. The honorable member, in his first speech, expressed opinions, in regard to revenue and some other topics, which I heard both with pain and with surprise. I told the gentleman I was aware that such sentiments were entertained *out* of the government, but had not expected to find them advanced in it; that I knew there were persons in the South who speak of our Union with indifference or doubt, taking pains to magnify its evils, and to say nothing of its benefits; that the honorable member himself, I was sure, could never be one of these; and I regretted the expression of such opinions as he had avowed, because I thought their obvious tendency was to encourage feelings of disrespect to the Union, and to impair its strength. This, Sir, is the sum and substance of all I said on the subject. And this constitutes the attack which called on the chivalry of the gentleman, in his own opinion, to harry us with such a foray among the party pamphlets and party proceedings of Massachusetts! If he means that I spoke with dissatisfaction or disrespect of the ebullitions of individuals in South Carolina, it is true. But if he means that I assailed the character of the State, her honor, or patriotism, that I reflected on her history or her conduct, he has not the slightest ground for any such assumption.

... I thank God, that, if I am gifted with little of the spirit which is able to raise mortals to the skies, I have yet none, as I trust, of that other spirit, which would drag angels down. When I shall be found, Sir, in my place here in the Senate, or elsewhere, to sneer at public merit, because it happens to spring up beyond the little limits of my own State or neighborhood; when I refuse, for any such cause, or for any cause, the homage due to American talent, to elevated patriotism, to sincere devotion to liberty and the country; or, if I see an uncommon endowment of Heaven, if I see extraordinary capacity and virtue, in any of the South, and if, moved by local prejudice or gangrened by State jealousy, I get up here to abate the tithe of a hair from his just character and just fame, may my tongue cleave to the roof of my mouth!

Sir, let me recur to pleasing recollections; let me indulge in refreshing remembrance of the past; let me remind you that, in early times, no States cherished greater harmony, both of principle and feeling, than Massachusetts and South Carolina. Would to God that harmony might again return! Shoulder to shoulder they went through the Revolution, hand in hand they stood round the administration of Washington, and felt his own great arm lean on them for support. Unkind feeling, if it exist, alienation, and distrust are the growth, unnatural to such soils, of false principles since sown. They are weeds, the seeds of which that same great arm never scattered.

Mr. President, I shall enter on no encomium upon Massachusetts; she needs none. There she is. Behold her, and judge for yourselves. There is her history; the world knows it by heart. The past, at least, is secure. There is Boston, and Concord, and Lexington, and Bunker Hill; and there they will remain for ever. The bones of her sons, falling in the great struggle for Independence, now lie mingled with the soil of every State from New England to Georgia; and there they will lie for ever. And Sir, where American Liberty raised its first voice, and where its youth was nurtured and sustained, there it still lives, in the strength of its manhood and full of its original spirit. If discord and disunion shall wound it, if party strife and blind ambition shall hawk at and tear it, if folly and madness, if uneasiness under salutary and necessary restraint, shall succeed in separating it from that Union, by which alone its existence is made sure, it will stand, in the end, by the side of that cradle in which its infancy was rocked; it will stretch forth its arm with whatever of vigor it may still retain over the friends who gather round it; and it will fall at last, if fall it must, amidst the proudest monuments of its own glory, and on the very spot of its origin.

There yet remains to be performed, Mr. President, by far the most grave and important duty, which I feel to be devolved on me by this occasion. It is to state, and to defend, what I conceive to be the true principles of the Constitution under which we are here assembled. I might well have desired that so weighty a task should have fallen into other and abler hands. I could have wished that it should have been executed by those whose character and experience give weight and influence to their opinions, such as cannot possibly belong to mine. But, Sir, I have met the occasion, not sought it; and I shall proceed to state my own sentiments, without challenging for them any particular regard, with studied plainness, and as much precision as possible.

I understand the honorable gentleman from South Carolina to maintain, that it is a right of the State legislatures to interfere, whenever, in their judgment, this government transcends its constitutional limits, and to arrest the operation of its laws.

I understand him to maintain this right, as a right existing *under* the Constitution, not as a right to overthrow it on the ground of extreme necessity, such as would justify violent revolution.

I understand him to maintain an authority, on the part of the States, thus to interfere, for the purpose of correcting the exercise of power by the general government, of checking it, and of compelling it to conform to their opinion of the extent of its powers.

I understand him to maintain, that the ultimate power of judging of the constitutional extent of its own authority is not lodged exclusively in the general government, or any branch of it; but that, on the contrary, the States may lawfully decide for themselves, and each State for itself, whether, in a given case, the act of the general government transcends its power.

I understand him to insist, that, if the exigency of the case, in the opinion of any State government, require it, such State government may, by its own sovereign authority, annul an act of the general government which it deems plainly and palpably unconstitutional.

This is the sum of what I understand from him to be the South Carolina doctrine, and the doctrine which he maintains. I propose to consider it, and compare it with the Constitution. Allow me to say, as a preliminary remark, that I call this the South Carolina doctrine only because the gentleman himself has so denominated it. I do not feel at liberty to say that South Carolina, as a State, has ever advanced these sentiments. I hope she has not, and never may. That a great majority of her people are opposed to the tariff laws, is doubtless true. That a majority, somewhat less than that just mentioned, conscientiously believe these laws unconstitutional, may probably also be true. But that any majority holds to the right of direct State interference at State discretion, the right of nullifying acts of Congress by acts of State legislation, is more than I know, and what I shall be slow to believe.

. . . .

We, Sir, who oppose the Carolina doctrine, do not deny that the people may, if they choose, throw off any government when it becomes oppressive and intolerable, and erect a better in its stead. We all know that civil institutions are established for the public benefit, and that when they cease to answer the ends of their existence they may be changed. But I do not understand the doctrine now contended for to be that, which, for the sake of distinction, we may call the right of revolution. I understand the gentleman to maintain, that, without revolution, without civil commotion, without rebellion, a remedy for supposed abuse and transgression of the powers of the general government lies in a direct appeal to the interference of the State governments.

[Mr. Hayne here rose and said: He did not contend for the mere right of revolution, but for the right of constitutional resistance. What he maintained was, that in case of a plain, palpable violation of the Constitution by the general government, a State may interpose; and that this interposition is constitutional.

Mr. Webster resumed:—]

So, Sir, I understood the gentleman, and am happy to find that I did not misunderstand him. What he contends for is, that it is constitutional to interrupt the administration of the Constitution itself, in the hands of those who are chosen and sworn to administer it, by the direct interference, in form of law, of the States, in virtue of their sovereign capacity. The inherent right in the people to reform their government I do not deny; and they have another right, and that is, to resist unconstitutional laws, without overturning the government. It is no doctrine of mine that unconstitutional laws bind the people. The great question is, Whose prerogative is it to decide on the constitutionality or unconstitutionality of the laws? On that, the main debate hinges. The proposition, that, in case of a supposed violation of the Constitution by Congress, the States have a constitutional right to interfere and annul the law of Congress, is the proposition of the gentleman. I do not admit it. If the gentleman had intended no more than to assert the right of revolution for justifiable cause, he would have said only what all agree to. But I cannot conceive that there can be a middle course, between submission to the laws, when regularly pronounced constitutional, on the one hand, and open resistance, which is revolution or rebellion, on the other. I say, the right of a State to annul a law of Congress cannot be maintained, but on the ground of the inalienable right of man to resist oppression; that is to say, upon the ground of revolution. I admit that there is an ultimate violent remedy, above the Constitution and in defiance of the Constitution, which may be resorted to when a revolution is to be justified. But I do not admit, that, under the Constitution and in conformity with it, there is any mode in which a State government, as a member of the Union, can interfere and stop the progress of the general government, by force of her own laws, under any circumstances whatever. This leads us to inquire into the origin of this government and the source of its power. Whose agent is it? Is it the creature of the State legislatures, or the creature of the people? If the government of the United States be the agent of the State governments, then they may control it, provided they can agree in the manner of controlling it; if it be the agent of the people, then the people alone can control it, restrain it, modify, or reform it. It is observable enough, that the doctrine for which the honorable gentleman contends leads him to the necessity of maintaining, not only

that this general government is the creature of the States, but that it is the creature of each of the States severally, so that each may assert the power for itself of determining whether it acts within the limits of its authority. It is the servant of four-and-twenty masters, of different wills and different purposes, and yet bound to obey all. This absurdity (for it seems no less) arises from a misconception as to the origin of this government and its true character. It is, Sir, the people's Constitution, the people's government, made for the people, made by the people, and answerable to the people. The people of the United States have declared that the Constitution shall be the supreme law. We must either admit the proposition, or dispute their authority. The States are, unquestionably, sovereign, so far as their sovereignty is not affected by this supreme law. But the State legislatures, as political bodies, however sovereign, are yet not sovereign over the people. So far as the people have given power to the general government, so far the grant is unquestionably good, and the government holds of the people, and not of the State governments. We are all agents of the same supreme power, the people. The general government and the State governments derive their authority from the same source. Neither can, in relation to the other, be called primary, though one is definite and restricted, and the other general and residuary. The national government possesses those powers which it can be shown the people have conferred on it, and no more. All the rest belongs to the State governments, or to the people themselves. So far as the people have restrained State sovereignty, by the expression of their will, in the Constitution of the United States, so far, it must be admitted, State sovereignty is effectually controlled. I do not contend that it is, or ought to be, controlled farther. The sentiment to which I have referred propounds that State sovereignty is only to be controlled by its own "feeling of justice"; that is to say, it is not to be controlled at all, for one who is to follow his own feelings is under no legal control. Now, however men may think this ought to be, the fact is, that the people of the United States have chosen to impose control on State sovereignties. There are those, doubtless, who wish they had been left without restraint; but the Constitution has ordered the matter differently. To make war, for instance, is an exercise of sovereignty; but the Constitution declares that no State shall make war. To coin money is another exercise of sovereign power, but no State is at liberty to coin money. Again, the Constitution says that no sovereign State shall be so sovereign as to make a treaty. These prohibitions, it must be confessed, are a control on the State sovereignty of South Carolina, as well as of the other States, which does not arise "from her own feelings of honorable justice." The opinion referred to, therefore, is in defiance of the plainest provisions of the Constitution.

. . . .

I must now beg to ask, Sir, Whence is this supposed right of the States derived? Where do they find the power to interfere with the laws of the Union? Sir, the opinion which the honorable gentleman maintains is a notion founded in a total misapprehension, in my judgment, of the origin of this government, and of the foundation on which it stands. I hold it to be a popular government, erected by the people; those who administer it, responsible to the people; and itself capable of being amended and modified, just as the people may choose it should be. It is as popular, just as truly emanating from the people, as the State governments. It is created for one purpose; the State governments for another. It has its own powers; they have theirs. There is no more authority with them to arrest the operation of a law of Congress, than with Congress to arrest the operation of their laws. We are here to administer a Constitution emanating immediately from the people, and trusted by them to our administration. It is not the creature of the State governments. It is of no moment to the argument, that certain acts of the State legislatures are necessary to fill our seats in this body. That is not one of their original State powers, a part of the sovereignty of the State. It is a duty which the people, by the Constitution itself, have imposed on the State legislatures; and which they might have left to be performed elsewhere, if they had seen fit. So they have left the choice of President with electors; but all this does not affect the proposition that this whole government, President, Senate, and House of Representatives, is a popular government. It leaves it still all its popular character. The governor of a State (in some of the States) is chosen, not directly by the people, but by those who are chosen by the people, for the purpose of performing, among other duties, that of electing a governor. Is the government of the State, on that account, not a popular government? This government, Sir, is the independent offspring of the popular will. It is not the creature of State legislatures; nay, more, if the whole truth must be told, the people brought it into existence, established it, and have hitherto supported it, for the very purpose, amongst others, of imposing certain salutary restraints on State sovereignties. The States cannot now make war; they cannot contract alliances; they cannot make, each for itself, separate regulations of commerce; they cannot lay imposts; they cannot coin money. If this Constitution, Sir, be the creature of State legislatures, it must be admitted that it has obtained a strange control over the volitions of its creators.

The people, then, Sir, erected this government. They gave it a Constitution, and in that Constitution they have enumerated the powers which they bestow on it. They have made it a limited government. They have defined its authority. They have restrained it to the exercise of such powers as are granted; and all others, they declare, are reserved to the States or the people. But, Sir, they have not stopped here. If they had, they would have accomplished but half their work. No definition can be so clear, as to avoid possibility of doubt; no limitation so precise, as to exclude all uncertainty. Who, then, shall construe this grant of the people? Who shall interpret their will, where it may be supposed they have left it doubtful? With whom do they repose this ultimate right of deciding on the powers of the government? Sir, they have settled all this in the fullest manner. They have left it with the government itself, in its appropriate branches. Sir, the very chief end, the main design, for which the whole Constitu-

tion was framed and adopted, was to establish a government that should not be obliged to act through State agency, or depend on State opinion and State discretion. The people had had quite enough of that kind of government under the Confederation. Under that system, the legal action, the application of law to individuals, belonged exclusively to the States. Congress could only recommend; their acts were not of binding force, till the States had adopted and sanctioned them. Are we in that condition still? Are we yet at the mercy of State discretion and State construction? Sir, if we are, then vain will be our attempt to maintain the Constitution under which we sit.

But, Sir, the people have wisely provided, in the Constitution itself, a proper, suitable mode and tribunal for settling questions of constitutional law. There are in the Constitution grants of powers to Congress, and restrictions on these powers. There are, also, prohibitions on the States. Some authority must, therefore, necessarily exist, having the ultimate jurisdiction to fix and ascertain the interpretation of these grants, restrictions, and prohibitions. The Constitution has itself pointed out, ordained, and established that authority. How has it accomplished this great and essential end? By declaring, Sir, that *"the Constitution, and the laws of the United States made in pursuance thereof, shall be the supreme law of the land, any thing in the constitution or laws of any State to the contrary notwithstanding."*

This, Sir, was the first great step. By this the supremacy of the Constitution and laws of the United States is declared. The people so will it. No State law is to be valid which comes in conflict with the Constitution, or any law of the United States passed in pursuance of it. But who shall decide this question of interference? To whom lies the last appeal? This, Sir, the Constitution itself decides also, by declaring, *"that the judicial power shall extend to all cases arising under the Constitution and laws of the United States."* These two provisions cover the whole ground. They are, in truth, the keystone of the arch! With these it is a government; without them it is a confederation. In pursuance of these clear and express provisions, Congress established, at its very first session, in the judicial act, a mode for carrying them into full effect, and for bringing all questions of constitutional power to the final decision of the Supreme Court. It then, Sir, became a government. It then had the means of self-protection; and but for this, it would, in all probability, have been now among things which are past. Having constituted the government, and declared its powers, the people have further said, that, since somebody must decide on the extent of these powers, the government shall itself decide; subject, always, like other popular governments, to its responsibility to the people. And now, Sir, I repeat, how is it that a State legislature acquires any power to interfere? Who, or what, gives them the right to say to the people, "We, who are your agents and servants for one purpose, will undertake to decide, that your other agents and servants, appointed by you for another purpose, have transcended the authority you gave them!" The reply would be, I think, not impertinent,—"Who made you a judge over another's servants? To their own masters they stand or fall."

Sir, I deny this power of State legislatures altogether. It cannot stand the test of examination. Gentlemen may say, that, in an extreme case, a State government might protect the people from intolerable oppression. Sir, in such a case, the people might protect themselves, without the aid of the State governments. Such a case warrants revolution. It must make, when it comes, a law for itself. A nullifying act of a State legislature cannot alter the case, nor make resistance any more lawful. In maintaining these sentiments, Sir, I am but asserting the rights of the people. I state what they have declared, and insist on their right to declare it. They have chosen to repose this power in the general government, and I think it my duty to support it, like other constitutional powers.

For myself, Sir, I do not admit the competency of South Carolina, or any other State, to prescribe my constitutional duty; or to settle, between me and the people, the validity of laws of Congress, for which I have voted. I decline her umpirage. I have not sworn to support the Constitution according to her construction of its clauses. I have not stipulated, by my oath of office or otherwise, to come under any responsibility, except to the people, and those whom they have appointed to pass upon the question, whether laws, supported by my votes, conform to the Constitution of the country. And, Sir, if we look to the general nature of the case, could any thing have been more preposterous, than to make a government for the whole Union, and yet leave its powers subject, not to one interpretation, but to thirteen or twenty-four interpretations? Instead of one tribunal, established by all, responsible to all, with power to decide for all, shall constitutional questions be left to four-and-twenty popular bodies, each at liberty to decide for itself, and none bound to respect the decisions of others; and each at liberty, too, to give a new construction on every new election of its own members? Would any thing, with such a principle in it, or rather with such a destitution of all principle, be fit to be called a government? No, Sir. It should not be denominated a Constitution. It should be called, rather, a collection of topics for everlasting controversy; heads of debate for a disputatious people. It would not be a government. It would not be adequate to any practical good, or fit for any country to live under.

To avoid all possibility of being misunderstood, allow me to repeat again, in the fullest manner, that I claim no powers for the government by forced or unfair construction. I admit that it is a government of strictly limited powers; of enumerated, specified, and particularized powers; and that whatsoever is not granted, is withheld. But notwithstanding all this, and however the grant of powers may be expressed, its limit and extent may yet, in some cases, admit of doubt; and the general government would be good for nothing, it would be incapable of long existing, if some mode had not been provided in which those doubts, as they should arise, might be peaceably, but authoritatively, solved.

And now, Mr. President, let me run the honorable gentleman's doctrine a little into its practical application. Let us look at his probable *modus operandi*. If a thing can be done, an ingenious man can tell *how* it is to be done, and I wish to be informed *how* this State interference is to be put in practice, without violence, bloodshed, and rebellion. We will take the existing case of the tariff law. South Carolina is said to have made up her opinion upon it. If we do not repeal it (as we probably shall not), she will then apply to the case the remedy of her doctrine. She will, we must suppose, pass a law of her legislature, declaring the several acts of Congress, usually called the tariff laws, null and void, so far as they respect South Carolina, or the citizens thereof. So far, all is a paper transaction, and easy enough. But the collector at Charleston is collecting the duties imposed by these tariff laws. He, therefore, must be stopped. The collector will seize the goods if the tariff duties are not paid. The State authorities will undertake their rescue, the marshal, with his posse, will come to the collector's aid, and here the contest begins. The militia of the State will be called out to sustain the nullifying act. They will march, Sir, under a very gallant leader; for I believe the honorable member himself commands the militia of that part of the State. He will raise the NULLIFYING ACT on his standard, and spread it out as his banner! It will have a preamble, setting forth, that the tariff laws are palpable, deliberate, and dangerous violations of the Constitution! He will proceed, with this banner flying, to the custom-house in Charleston,

"All the while, Sonorous metal blowing martial sounds."

Arrived at the custom-house, he will tell the collector that he must collect no more duties under any of the tariff laws. This he will be somewhat puzzled to say, by the way, with a grave countenance, considering what hand South Carolina herself had in that of 1816. But, Sir, the collector would not, probably, desist, at his bidding. He would show him the law of Congress, the treasury instruction, and his own oath of office. He would say, he should perform his duty, come what come might.

Here would ensue a pause; for they say that a certain stillness precedes the tempest. The trumpeter would hold his breath awhile, and before all this military array should fall on the custom-house, collector, clerks, and all, it is very probable some of those composing it would request of their gallant commander in chief to be informed a little upon the point of law; for they have, doubtless, a just respect for his opinions as a lawyer, as well as for his bravery as a soldier. They know he has read Blackstone and the Constitution, as well as Turenne and Vauban. They would ask him, therefore, something concerning their rights in this matter. They would inquire, whether it was not somewhat dangerous to resist a law of the United States. What would be the nature of their offence, they would wish to learn, if they, by military force and array, resisted the execution in Carolina of a law of the United States, and it should turn out, after all, that the law *was constitutional*? He would answer, of course, Treason. No lawyer could give any other answer. John Fries, he would tell them, had learned that, some years ago. How, then, they would ask, do you propose to defend us? We are not afraid of bullets, but treason has a way of taking people off that we do not much relish. How do you propose to defend us? "Look at my floating banner," he would reply; "see there the *nullifying law!*" Is it your opinion, gallant commander, they would then say, that, if we should be indicted for treason, that same floating banner of yours would make a good plea in bar? "South Carolina is a sovereign State," he would reply. That is true; but would the judge admit our plea? "These tariff laws," he would repeat, "are unconstitutional, palpably, deliberately, dangerously." That may all be so; but if the tribunal should not happen to be of that opinion, shall we swing for it? We are ready to die for our country, but it is rather an awkward business, this dying without touching the ground! After all, that is a sort of hemp tax worse than any part of the tariff.

Mr. President, the honorable gentleman would be in a dilemma, like that of another great general. He would have a knot before him which he could not untie. He must cut it with his sword. He must say to his followers, "Defend yourselves with your bayonets"; and this is war,—civil war.

Direct collision, therefore, between force and force, is the unavoidable result of that remedy for the revision of unconstitutional laws which the gentleman contends for. It must happen in the very first case to which it is applied. Is not this the plain result? To resist by force the execution of a law, generally, is treason. Can the courts of the United States take notice of the indulgence of a State to commit treason? The common saying, that a State cannot commit treason herself, is nothing to the purpose. Can she authorize others to do it? If John Fries had produced an act of Pennsylvania, annulling the law of Congress, would it have helped his case? Talk about it as we will, these doctrines go the length of revolution. They are incompatible with any peaceable administration of the government. They lead directly to disunion and civil commotion; and therefore it is, that at their commencement, when they are first found to be maintained by respectable men, and in a tangible form, I enter my public protest against them all.

. . . .

But, Sir, although there are fears, there are hopes also. The people have preserved this, their own chosen Constitution, for forty years, and have seen their happiness, prosperity, and renown grow with its growth, and strengthen with its strength. They are now, generally strongly attached to it. Overthrown by direct assault, it cannot be; evaded, undermined, NULLIFIED, it will not be, if we, and those who shall succeed us here, as agents and representatives of the people, shall conscientiously and vigilantly discharge the two great branches of our public trust, faithfully to preserve, and wisely to administer it.

Mr. President, I have thus stated the reasons of my dissent to the doctrines which have been advanced and maintained. I am conscious of having detained you and the Senate much too long. I was drawn into the debate with no previous deliberation, such as is suited to the discussion of so grave and important a subject. But it is a subject of which my heart is full, and I have not been willing to suppress the utterance of its spontaneous sentiments. I cannot, even now, persuade myself to relinquish it, without expressing once more my deep conviction, that since it respects nothing less than the Union of the States, it is of most vital and essential importance to the public happiness. I profess, Sir, in my career hitherto, to have kept steadily in view the prosperity and honor of the whole country, and the preservation of our Federal Union. It is to that Union we owe our safety at home, and our consideration and dignity abroad. It is to that Union that we are chiefly indebted for whatever makes us most proud of our country. That Union we reached only by the discipline of our virtues in the severe school of adversity. It had its origin in the necessities of disordered finance, prostrate commerce, and ruined credit. Under its benign influences, these great interests immediately awoke, as from the dead, and sprang forth with newness of life. Every year of its duration has teemed with fresh proofs of its utility and its blessings; and although our territory has stretched out wider and wider, and our population spread farther and farther, they have not outrun its protection or its benefits. It has been to us all a copious fountain of national, social, and personal happiness.

I have not allowed myself, Sir, to look beyond the Union, to see what might lie hidden in the dark recess behind. I have not coolly weighed the chances of preserving liberty when the bonds that unite us together shall be broken asunder. I have not accustomed myself to hang over the precipice of disunion, to see whether, with my short sight, I can fathom the depth of the abyss below; nor could I regard him as a safe counsellor in the affairs of this government, whose thoughts should be mainly bent on considering, not how the Union may be best preserved, but how tolerable might be the condition of the people when it should be broken up and destroyed. While the Union lasts, we have high, exciting, gratifying prospects spread out before us, for us and our children. Beyond that I seek not to penetrate the veil. God grant that in my day, at least, that curtain may not rise! God grant that on my vision never may be opened what lies behind! When my eyes shall be turned to behold for the last time the sun in heaven, may I not see him shining on the broken and dishonored fragments of a once glorious Union; on States dissevered, discordant, belligerent; on a land rent with civil feuds, or drenched, it may be, in fraternal blood! Let their last feeble and lingering glance rather behold the gorgeous ensign of the republic, now known and honored throughout the earth, still full high advanced, its arms and trophies streaming in their original lustre, not a stripe erased or polluted, nor a single star obscured, bearing for its motto, no such miserable interrogatory as "What is all this worth?" nor those other words of delusion and folly, "Liberty first and Union afterwards"; but everywhere, spread all over in characters of living light, blazing on all its ample folds, as they float over the sea and over the land, and in every wind under the whole heavens, that other sentiment, dear to every true American heart,—Liberty *and* Union, now and for ever, one and inseparable!

Excerpted from Robert C. Byrd, *The Senate, 1789–1989,* 4 vols. (Washington, D.C.: Government Printing Office), vol. 3: 37–77. Senator Byrd used the version in Edwin P. Whipple (ed.), *The Great Speeches and Orations of Daniel Webster* (Boston, 1880), 227–269.

57 Alexis de Tocqueville's Description of the House and Senate

January 1832

Alexis de Tocqueville, a brilliant French aristocrat, age twenty-six when he arrived in America, toured the United States for nine months in 1831 and 1832. He returned to France and wrote Democracy in America *(1835), which remains to this day a classic study of American politics and the American character. It is a broad look at America as it was in the 1830s, encompassing the economy, people, politics, structure of government, religion, and, most of all, an exploration of the contours of American democracy. Tocqueville's work was controversial in his time and continues to be so, but it had great influence in the United States and abroad. It remains a fascinating and often quoted source on many aspects of American life.*

Tocqueville and his companion August de Beaumont visited most major cities and most of the twenty-four states of the Union during their tour. Near the end of their journey they arrived in Washington, D.C., in mid-January 1832 and stayed until February 3 of that year. While in Washington they spent a great deal of time visiting the chambers of the House and Senate and listening to debate. Their evenings were filled with entertainment, dances, dinners, and meetings with prominent citizens, including former president of the United States John Quincy Adams, then a member of the House.

They could not have arrived at a more interesting time for the nation. Andrew Jackson and the new forces of democracy his presidency unleashed were in full sway in the nation's capital. Henry Clay's American System (see document 58) was being assailed by Jackson, who sought a smaller federal government with most power remaining in the states and regions of the country. The Union was threatened by South Carolina "nullifyers," led by Vice President John C. Calhoun, who would soon resign the vice presidency to take a seat in the Senate. The political turmoil that Tocqueville observed made him fear that democracy would not survive its more rough and tumble aspects.

One of Tocqueville's shortcomings as an observer was his aristocratic bias, which made him suspect of the direct aspects of democracy, as exemplified by the way House members were elected. The Senate struck him as more civilized and restrained because senators were not elected directly by the people but by those elected to state legislatures. Tocqueville thought the only salvation for the House was to have it elected indirectly like the Senate or the nation would flounder on the "shoals of democracy." He underestimated the resilience of the American political process. His prediction that direct election was dangerous seems to have been written for consumption abroad. In the United States the trend went in the opposite direction. Beginning in 1913, senators, like House members, were elected directly by the people.

Senator Thomas Hart Benton (D-Mo.), who was in the Senate in 1832 when Tocqueville visited it, later wrote in his memoir Thirty Years View *that he thought Tocqueville made a terrible mistake in assuming the House was inferior to the Senate. Benton pointed out that for most of American history up to the 1830s the* real power of government resided in the House and that many of the senators Tocqueville seemed so impressed with had earlier service in the House.

There are certain laws of a democratic nature which contribute, nevertheless, to correct in some measure these dangerous tendencies of democracy. On entering the House of Representatives at Washington, one is struck by the vulgar demeanor of that great assembly. Often there is not a distinguished man in the whole number. Its members are almost all obscure individuals, whose names bring no associations to mind. They are mostly village lawyers, men in trade, or even persons belonging to the lower classes of society. In a country in which education is very general, it is said that the representatives of the people do not always know how to write correctly.

At a few yards' distance is the door of the Senate, which contains within a small space a large proportion of the celebrated men of America. Scarcely an individual is to be seen in it who has not had an active and illustrious career: the Senate is composed of eloquent advocates, distinguished generals, wise magistrates, and statesmen of note, whose arguments would do honor to the most remarkable parliamentary debates of Europe.

How comes this strange contrast, and why are the ablest citizens found in one assembly rather than in the other? Why is the former body remarkable for its vulgar elements, while the latter seems to enjoy a monopoly of intelligence and talent? Both of these assemblies emanate from the people; both are chosen by universal suffrage; and no voice has hitherto been heard to assert in America that the Senate is hostile to the interests of the people. From what cause, then, does so startling a difference arise? The only reason which appears to me adequately to account for it is that the House of Representatives is elected by the people directly, while the Senate is elected by elected bodies. The whole body of the citizens name the legislature of each state, and the Federal Constitution converts these legislatures into so many electoral bodies, which return the members of the Senate. The Senators are elected by an indirect application of the popular vote; for the legislatures which appoint them are not aristocratic or privileged bodies, that elect in their own right, but they are chosen by the totality of the citizens; they are generally elected every year, and enough new members may be chosen every year to determine the senatorial appointments. But this transmission of the popular authority through an assembly of chosen men operates an important change in it by refining its discretion and improving its choice. Men who are chosen in this manner accurately represent the majority of the nation which governs them; but they represent only the elevated thoughts that are current in the community and the generous propensities that prompt its nobler actions rather than the petty passions that disturb or the vices that disgrace it.

The time must come when the American republics will be obliged more frequently to introduce the plan of election by an elected body into their system of representation or run the risk of perishing miserably among the shoals of democracy.

I do not hesitate to avow that I look upon this peculiar system of election as the only means of bringing the exercise of political power to the level of all classes of the people. Those who hope to convert this institution into the exclusive weapon of a party, and those who fear to use it, seem to me to be equally in error.

Alexis de Tocqueville, *Democracy in America*, 2 vols. (New York: Alfred Knopf, 1963), vol. 1: 204–205. Originally published in 1835 and 1840.

58   Senator Henry Clay Defends the American System

February 2, 3, and 6, 1832

Henry Clay of Kentucky dominated the national politics of the United States in the first half of the nineteenth century. His service extended from his early days in the U.S. Senate beginning in 1806, even though he was technically too young to serve in the Senate; to his election to the Speakership of the House on the first day of his service in that body beginning in 1811; as a negotiator of the Treaty of Ghent, which ended the War of 1812; as Secretary of State in the administration of John Quincy Adams (1825–1829); and as a three-time unsuccessful presidential candidate, in 1824, 1832, and 1844. This brief recitation of his career does not convey the enormous energy and the popularity of the man. Clay was a man of large passions and sharp contrasts. He could be a rough-and-tumble westerner who gambled, drank whiskey, and engaged in duels, or he could be a skilled politician and a national statesman. He was loathed by his enemies and loved by his admirers as few men have been in American history.

Clay's "American System" was an ambitious series of programs designed to foster economic growth in the United States. Clay was an ardent nationalist who believed the government should play an active and aggressive role in promoting the interests of the nation. This view clashed with those who preferred a laissez-faire, free trade system, where government stayed out of the management of the economy, leaving it to state and regional commercial interests. The American System was based on three pillars: a protective tariff that aided the development of American industry; federal development of roads, canals, and other internal improvements designed to tie the various regions of the nation together and promote commerce; and a national bank to provide further support to commercial interests across the various regions of America.

Beginning in 1816 and for the next twelve years Congress supported the three pillars of Clay's program. With the inauguration of Andrew Jackson in 1829, however, the American System came unraveled as Jackson ushered in an era of limited government and a willingness to let regional autonomy rule in economic matters. Jackson despised the national bank and vetoed the bill that would have reauthorized its charter. The clash between the forces of Jackson and Clay led to the emergence of a new Whig party, with Clay as its leading spokesman. Clay's return to the Senate in 1831 gave him a national platform from which to attack Jackson and plan for his own presidential ambitions. For the next two decades he would be a powerful force in the Senate.

While Clay had served briefly in the Senate many years earlier and had a masterful career as Speaker of the House, this speech was his first upon returning to the Senate after many years of absence. The speech itself took a good part of three days to deliver, with the galleries packed to hear the voice of one of the great orators in American history. Despite the statistics, some of dubious value, and the often endless details that filled his speeches, Clay was a marvelously entertaining speaker. It was high drama and high theater when Clay took to the floor of the Senate. In this case, the speech was doubly dramatic because it attacked Jackson's policies and defended his own American System. Clay was also staking out a claim to run against Jackson for president in 1832.

In one sentiment, Mr. President, expressed by the honorable gentleman from South Carolina, [Mr. HAYNE] though, perhaps, not in the sense intended by him, I entirely concur. I agree with him, that the decision on the system of policy embraced in this debate involves the future destiny of this growing country. One way, I verily believe, it would lead to deep and general distress, general bankruptcy, and national ruin, without benefit to any part of the Union. The other, the existing prosperity will be preserved and augmented, and the nation will continue rapidly to advance in wealth, power, and greatness, without prejudice to any section of the confederacy.

Thus viewing the question, I stand here as the humble but zealous advocate, not of the interests of one state, or seven states only, but of the whole Union. And never before have I felt more intensely the overpowering weight of that share of responsibility which belongs to me in these deliberations. Never before have I had more occasion than I now have, to lament my want of those intellectual powers, the possession of which might enable me to unfold to this Senate, and to illustrate to this people, great truths intimately connected with the lasting welfare of my country. I should, indeed, sink, overwhelmed and subdued, beneath the appalling magnitude of the task which lies before me, if I did not feel myself sustained and fortified by a thorough consciousness of the justness of the cause which I have espoused, and by a persuasion, I hope not presumptuous, that it has the approbation of that Providence who has so often smiled upon these United States.

Eight years ago, it was my painful duty to present to the other house of Congress an unexaggerated picture of the general distress pervading the whole land. We must all yet remember some of its frightful features. We all know that the people were then oppressed and borne down by an enormous load of debt; that the value of property was at the lowest point of depression; that ruinous sales and sacrifices were everywhere made of real estate; that stop laws and relief laws and paper money were adopted to save the people from impending destruction; that a deficit in the public revenue existed, which compelled government to seize upon, and divert from its legitimate object, the appropriation to the sinking fund, to redeem the national debt; and that our commerce and navigation were threatened with a complete paralysis. In short, sir, if I were to select any term of seven years since the adoption of the present constitution, which exhibited a scene of the most widespread dismay and desolation, it would be exactly that term of seven years which immediately preceded the establishment of the tariff of 1824.

I have now to perform the more pleasing task of exhibiting an imperfect sketch of the existing state of the unparalleled prosperity of the country. On a general survey, we behold cultivation extended, the arts flourishing, the face of the country improved, our people fully and profitably employed, and the public countenance exhibiting tranquility, contentment, and happiness. And, if we descend into particulars, we have the agreeable contemplation of a people out of debt; land rising slowly in value, but in a secure and salutary degree; a ready, though not extravagant market for all the surplus productions of our industry; innumerable flocks and herds browsing and gamboling on ten thousand hills and plains, covered with rich and verdant grasses; our cities expanded, and whole villages springing up, as it were, by enchantment; our exports and imports increased and increasing; our tonnage, foreign and coastwise, swelling and fully occupied; the rivers of our interior animated by the perpetual thunder and lightning of countless steamboats; the currency sound and abundant; the public debt of two wars nearly redeemed; and, to crown all, the public treasury overflowing, embarrassing Congress, not to find subjects of taxation, but to select the objects which shall be liberated from the impost. If the term of seven years were to be selected of the greatest prosperity which this people have enjoyed since the establishment of their present constitution, it would be exactly that period of seven years which immediately followed the passage of the tariff of 1824.

This transformation of the condition of the country from gloom and distress to brightness and prosperity, has been mainly the work of American legislation, fostering American industry, instead of allowing it to be controlled by foreign legislation, cherishing foreign industry. The foes of the American System, in 1824, with great boldness and confidence, predicted, 1st. The

ruin of the public revenue, and the creation of a necessity to resort to direct taxation. The gentleman from South Carolina, [Mr. HAYNE,] I believe, thought that the tariff of 1824 would operate a reduction of revenue to the large amount of eight millions of dollars. 2d. The destruction of our navigation. 3d. The desolation of commercial cities. And 4th. The augmentation of the price of objects of consumption, and further decline in that of the articles of our exports. Every prediction which they made has failed—utterly failed. Instead of the ruin of the public revenue, with which they then sought to deter us from the adoption of the American System, we are now threatened with its subversion, by the vast amount of the public revenue produced by that system. Every branch of our navigation has increased.

. . . .

It is now proposed to abolish the system to which we owe so much of the public prosperity, and it is urged that the arrival of the period of the redemption of the public debt has been confidently looked to as presenting a suitable occasion to rid the country of the evils with which the system is alleged to be fraught. Not an inattentive observer of passing events, I have been aware that, among those who were most eagerly pressing the payment of the public debt, and, upon that ground, were opposing appropriation to other great interests, there were some who cared less about the debt than the accomplishment of other objects. But the people of the United States have not coupled the payment of *their* public debt with the destruction of the protection of *their* industry, against foreign laws and foreign industry. They have been accustomed to regard the extinction of the public debt as relief from a burden, and not as the infliction of a curse. If it is to be attended or followed by the subversion of the American system, and an exposure of our establishments and our productions to the unguarded consequences of the selfish policy of foreign powers, the payment of the public debt will be the bitterest of curses. Its fruit will be like the fruit

> Of that forbidden tree, whose mortal taste
> Brought death into the world, and all our wo,
> With loss of Eden.

If the system of protection be founded on principles erroneous in theory, pernicious in practice—above all, if it be unconstitutional, as is alleged, it ought to be forthwith abolished, and not a vestige of it suffered to remain. But, before we sanction this sweeping denunciation, let us look a little at this system, its magnitude, its ramifications, its duration, and the high authorities which have sustained it. We shall see that its foes will have accomplished comparatively nothing, after having achieved their present aim of breaking down our iron founderies, our woollen, cotton, and hemp manufactories, and our sugar plantations. The destruction of these would undoubtedly lead to the sacrifice of immense capital, the ruin of many thousands of our fellow citizens, and incalculable loss to the whole community. But their prostration would not disfigure, nor produce greater effect upon the *whole* system of protection, in all its branches, than the destruction of the beautiful domes upon the Capitol would occasion to the magnificent edifice, which they surmount. Why, sir, there is scarcely an interest, scarcely a vocation in society, which is not embraced by the beneficence of this system.

It comprehends our coasting tonnage and trade, from which all foreign tonnage is absolutely excluded.

It includes all our foreign tonnage, with the inconsiderable exception made by treaties of reciprocity with a few foreign powers.

It embraces our fisheries, and all our hardy and enterprising fishermen.

It extends to almost every mechanic art: to tanners, cordwainers, tailors, cabinetmakers, hatters, tinners, brass-workers, clock-makers, coach-makers, tallow-chandlers, trace-makers, rope-makers, cork-cutters, tobacconists, whip-makers, paper-makers, umbrella-makers, glass-blowers, stocking-weavers, button-makers, saddle and harness-makers, cutlers, brush-makers, bookbinders, dairymen, milk-farmers, blacksmiths, type-founders, musical instrument-makers, basket-makers, milliners, potters, chocolate-makers, floor-cloth makers, bonnet-makers, hair-cloth makers, copper-smiths, pencil-makers, bellows-makers, pocket book-makers, card-makers, glue-makers, mustard-makers, lumber-sawyers, saw-makers, scale-beam-makers, scythe-makers, wood-saw-makers, and many others. The mechanics enumerated enjoy a measure of protection adapted to their several conditions, varying from 20 to 50 percent. The extent and importance of some of these artisans may be estimated by a few particulars. The tanners, curriers, boot and shoe-makers, and other workers in hides, skins, and leather, produce an ultimate value per annum of $40 millions; the manufacturers of hats and caps produce an annual value of $15 millions; the cabinetmakers, $12 millions; the manufacturers of bonnets and hats for the female sex, lace, artificial flowers, combs, etc., $7 millions; and the manufacturers of glass, $5 millions.

It extends to all lower Louisiana, the delta of which might as well be submerged again in the Gulf of Mexico, from which it has been a gradual conquest, as now to be deprived of the protecting duty upon its great staple.

It affects the cotton planter himself, and the tobacco planter, both of whom enjoy protection.

The total amount of the capital vested in sheep, the land to sustain them, wool, woollen manufactures, and woollen fabrics, and the subsistence of the various persons directly or indirectly employed in the growth and manufacture of the article of wool, is estimated at $167 million, and the number of persons at 150,000.

The value of iron, considered as a raw material, and of its manufactures, is estimated at $26 million per annum. Cotton goods, exclusive of the capital vested in the manufacture, and of the cost of the raw material, are believed to amount, annually, to about $20 million.

These estimates have been carefully made by practical men, of undoubted character, who have brought together and embodied their information. Anxious to avoid the charge of exaggeration, they have sometimes placed their estimates below what was believed to be the actual amount of these interests. With regard to the quantity of bar and other iron annually produced, it is derived from the known works themselves; and I know some in western states which they have omitted in their calculations.

Such are some of the items of this vast system of protection, which it is now proposed to abandon. We might well pause and contemplate, if human imagination could conceive the extent of mischief and ruin from its total overthrow, before we proceed to the work of destruction. Its duration is worthy, also, of serious consideration. Not to go behind the Constitution, its date is coeval with that instrument. It began on the ever memorable 4th day of July—the 4th day of July, 1789. The second act which stands recorded in the statute book, bearing the illustrious signature of George Washington, laid the cornerstone of the whole system. That there might be no mistake about the matter, it was then solemnly proclaimed to the American people and to the world, that it was *necessary* for "the encouragement and *protection* of manufactures," that duties should be laid. It is in vain to urge the small amount of the measure of protection then extended. The great principle was then established by the fathers of the Constitution, with the Father of his Country at their head. And it cannot now be questioned, that, if the government had not then been new and the subject untried, a greater measure of protection would have been applied, if it had been supposed necessary. Shortly after, the master minds of Jefferson and Hamilton were brought to act on this interesting subject. Taking views of it appertaining to the departments of foreign affairs and of the treasury, which they respectively filled, they presented, severally, reports which yet remain monuments of their profound wisdom, and came to the same conclusion of protection to American industry. Mr. Jefferson argued that foreign restrictions, foreign prohibitions, and foreign high duties, ought to be met, at home, by American restrictions, American prohibitions, and American high duties. Mr. Hamilton, surveying the entire ground, and looking at the inherent nature of the subject, treated it with an ability which, if ever equalled, has not been surpassed, and earnestly recommended protection.

. . . .

Thus, sir, has this great system of protection been gradually built, stone upon stone, and step by step, from the 4th July, 1789, down to the present period. In every stage of its progress it has received the deliberate sanction of Congress. A vast majority of the people of the United States has approved, and continues to approve it. Every chief magistrate of the United States, from Washington to the present, in some form or other, has given to it the authority of his name; and, however the opinions of the existing president are interpreted south of Mason and Dixon's line, on the north they are, at least, understood to favor the establishment of a *judicious* tariff.

The question, therefore, which we are now called upon to determine, is not whether we shall establish a new and doubtful system of policy, just proposed, and for the first time presented to our consideration; but whether we shall break down and destroy a long established system, patiently and carefully built up, and sanctioned, during a series of years, again and again, by the nation and its highest and most revered authorities. And are we not bound deliberately to consider whether we can proceed to this work of destruction without a violation of the public faith? The people of the United States have justly supposed that the policy of protecting *their* industry, against *foreign* legislation and *foreign* industry, was fully settled, not by a single act, but by repeated and deliberate acts of government, performed at distant and frequent intervals. In full confidence that the policy was firmly and unchangeably fixed, thousands upon thousands have invested their capital, purchased a vast amount of real and other estate, made permanent establishments, and accommodated their industry. Can we expose to utter and irretrievable ruin this countless multitude, without justly incurring the reproach of violating the national faith?

. . . .

When gentlemen have succeeded in their design of an immediate or gradual destruction of the American System, what is their substitute? Free trade! Free trade! The call for free trade, is as unavailing as the cry of a spoiled child, in its nurse's arms, for the moon or the stars that glitter in the firmament of heaven. It never has existed; it never will exist. Trade implies at least two parties. To be free, it should be fair, equal, and reciprocal. But if we throw our ports wide open to the admission of foreign productions, free of all duty, what ports, of any other foreign nation, shall we find open to the free admission of our surplus produce? We may break down all barriers to free trade on our part, but the work will not be complete until foreign powers shall have removed theirs. There would be freedom on one side, and restrictions, prohibitions, and exclusions, on the other. The bolts, and the bars, and the chains, of all other nations will remain undisturbed. It is, indeed, possible that our industry and commerce would accommodate themselves to this unequal and unjust state of things: for such is the flexibility of our nature, that it bends itself to all circumstances. The wretched prisoner, incarcerated in a jail, after a long time, becomes reconciled to his solitude, and regularly notches down the passing days of his confinement.

Gentlemen deceive themselves. It is not free trade that they are recommending to our acceptance. It is, in effect, the British colonial system that we are invited to adopt; and, if their policy prevail, it will lead substantially to the recolonization of these states, under the commercial dominion of Great Britain.

. . . .

I will now, Mr. President, proceed to a more particular consideration of the arguments urged against the protective system, and an inquiry into its practical operation, especially on the cotton-growing country. And, as I wish to state and meet the argument fairly, I invite correction of my statement of it, if nec-essary. It is alleged that the system operates prejudicially to the cotton planter, by diminishing the foreign demands for his staple; that we cannot sell to Great Britain, unless we buy from her; that the import duty is equivalent to an export duty, and falls upon the cotton grower; that South Carolina pays a disproportionate quota of the public revenue; that an abandonment of the protective policy would lead to an augmentation of our exports of an amount not less than one hundred and fifty millions of dollars; and, finally, that the South cannot partake of the advantages of manufacturing, if there be any.

. . . .

The argument comprehends two errors, one of fact and the other of principle. It assumes that we do not in fact purchase of Great Britain. What is the true state of the case? There are certain, but very few articles which it is thought sound policy requires that we should manufacture at home, and on these the tariff operates. But, with respect to all the rest, and much the larger number of articles of taste, fashion, or utility, they are subject to no other than revenue duties, and are freely introduced. I have before me, from the treasury, a statement of our imports from England, Scotland, and Ireland, including ten years preceding the last, and three quarters of the last year, from which it will appear that, although there are some fluctuations in the amount of the different years, the largest amount imported in any one year has been since the tariff of 1824, and that the last year's importation, when the returns of the fourth quarter shall be received, will probably be the greatest in the whole term of eleven years.

Now, if it be admitted that there is a less amount of the protected articles imported from Great Britain, she may be, and probably is, compensated for the deficiency by the increased consumption in America of the articles of her industry not falling within the scope of the policy of our protection. The establishment of manufactures among us excites the creation of wealth, and this gives new powers of consumption, which are gratified by the purchase of foreign objects. A poor nation can never be a great consuming nation. Its poverty will limit its consumption to bare subsistence.

The erroneous principle which the argument includes, is, that it devolves on us the duty of taking care that Great Britain shall be enabled to purchase from us, without exacting from Great Britain the corresponding duty. If it be true, on one side, that nations are bound to shape their policy in reference to the ability of foreign powers, it must be true on both sides of the Atlantic. And this reciprocal obligation ought to be emphatically regarded towards the nation supplying the raw material, by the manufacturing nation, because the industry of the latter gives four or five values to what had been produced by the industry of the former.

But, does Great Britain practise towards us upon the principles which we are now required to observe in regard to her? The exports to the United Kingdom, as appears from the same treasury statement just adverted to, during eleven years, from 1821 to 1831, and exclusive of the fourth quarter of the last year, fall short of the amount of imports by upwards of $46 million, and the total amount, when the returns of that quarter are received, will exceed $50 million! It is surprising how we have been able to sustain, for so long a time, a trade so very unequal. We must have been absolutely ruined by it, if the unfavorable balance had not been neutralized by more profitable commerce with other parts of the world. Of all nations Great Britain has the least cause to complain of the trade between the two countries. Our imports from that single power are nearly one-third of the entire amount of our importations from all foreign countries together. Great Britain constantly acts on the maxim of buying only what she wants and cannot produce, and selling to foreign nations the utmost amount she can. In conformity with this maxim, she excludes articles of prime necessity produced by us—equally if not more necessary than any of her industry which we tax, although the admission of those articles would increase our ability to purchase from her, according to the argument of gentlemen.

. . . .

If the establishment of American manufactures, therefore, had the sole effect of creating a new, and an American, demand for cotton, *exactly* to the same extent in which it lessened the British demand, there would be no just cause of complaint against the tariff. The gain in one place would precisely equal the loss in the other. But the true state of the matter is much more favorable to the cotton grower. It is calculated that the cotton manufactories of the United States absorb at least 200 thousand bales of cotton annually. I believe it to be more. The two ports of Boston and Providence alone received, during the last year, near 110 thousand bales. The amount is annually increasing. The raw material of that 200 thousand bales is worth $6 millions, and there is an additional value conferred by the manufacturer, of $18 millions; it being generally calculated that, in such cotton fabrics as we are in the habit of making, the manufacture constitutes three-fourths of the value of the article. If, therefore, these $24 millions worth of cotton fabrics were not made in the United States, but were manufactured in Great Britain, in order to obtain them, we should have to add to the already enormous disproportion between the amount of our imports and exports, in the trade with Great Britain, the further sum of $24 millions, or, deducting the price of the raw material, $18 millions! And will gentlemen tell me how it would be possible for this country to sustain such a ruinous trade?

. . . .

An abandonment of the American System, it is urged, would lead to an addition to our exports of $150 millions. The amount of $150 millions of cotton, in the raw state, would produce $450 millions in the manufactured state, supposing no greater measure of value to be communicated, in the manufactured form, than that which our industry imparts. Now, sir, where would markets be found for this vast addition to the supply? Not in the United States, certainly, nor in any other quarter of the globe, England having already everywhere pressed her cotton manufactures to the utmost point of repletion. We must look out for new worlds, seek for new and unknown races of mortals, to consume this immense increase of cotton fabrics.

. . . .

But it is contended, in the last place, that the South cannot, from physical and other causes, engage in the manufacturing arts. I deny the premises, and I deny the conclusion. I deny the fact of inability, and, if it existed, I deny the conclusion that we must, therefore, break down our manufactures, and nourish those of foreign countries. The South possesses, in an extraordinary degree, two of the most important elements of manufacturing industry—water power and labor. The former gives to our whole country a most decided advantage over Great Britain. But a single experiment, stated by the gentleman from South Carolina, in which a faithless slave put the torch to a manufacturing establishment, has discouraged similar enterprises. We have, in Kentucky, the same description of population, and we employ them, and almost exclusively employ them, in many of our hemp manufactories. A neighbor of mine, one of our most opulent and respectable citizens, has had one, two, if not three, manufactories burnt by incendiaries; but he persevered, and his perseverance has been rewarded with wealth. We found that it was less expensive to keep night watches, than to pay premiums for insurance, and we employed them.

Let it be supposed, however, that the South cannot manufacture; must those parts of the Union which *can* be therefore prevented? Must we support those of foreign countries? I am sure that injustice would be done to the generous and patriotic nature of South Carolina, if it were believed that she envied or repined at the success of other portions of the Union in branches of industry to which she might happen not to be adapted. Throughout her whole career she has been liberal, national, high-minded.

The friends of the American System have been reminded, by the honorable gentleman from Maryland, [Mr. SMITH,] that they are the majority, and he has admonished them to exercise their power in moderation. The *majority* ought never to trample upon the feelings, or violate the just rights of the minority. They ought never to triumph over the fallen, nor to make any but a temperate and equitable use of their power. But these counsels come with an ill grace from the gentleman from Maryland. He, too, is a member of a *majority*—a political majority. And how has the administration of that majority exercised their power in this country? Recall to your recollection the 4th of March, 1829, when the lank, lean, famished forms, from fen and forest, and the four quarters of the Union, gathered together in the halls of patronage, or stealing, by evening's twilight, into the apartments of the president's mansion, cried out, with ghastly faces, and in sepulchral tones, Give us bread! Give us treasury pap! Give us our reward! England's bard was mistaken, ghosts will sometimes come, called or uncalled. Go to the families who were driven from the employments on which they were dependent for subsistence, in consequence of their exercise of the dearest right of freemen. Go to mothers, whilst hugging to their bosoms their starving children. Go to fathers, who, after being disqualified, by long public service, for any other business, were stripped of their humble places, and then sought, by the minions of authority, to be stripped of all that was left them—their good names—and ask, what mercy was shown to them! As for myself, born in the midst of the revolution, the first air that I ever breathed on my native soil of Virginia having been that of liberty and independence, I never expected justice nor desired mercy at their hands; and scorn the wrath, and defy the oppression of power!

I regret, Mr. President, that one topic has, I think unnecessarily, been introduced into this debate. I allude to the charge brought against the manufacturing system, as favoring the growth of aristocracy. If it were true, would gentlemen prefer supporting foreign accumulations of wealth, by that description of industry, rather than their own country? But is it correct? The joint stock companies of the North, as I understand them, are nothing more than associations, sometimes of hundreds, by means of which the small earnings of many are brought into a common stock; and the associates, obtaining corporate privileges, are enabled to prosecute, under one superintending head, their business to better advantage. Nothing can be more essentially democratic, or better devised to counterpoise the influence of individual wealth. In Kentucky, almost every manufactory known to me is in the hands of enterprising self-made men, who have acquired whatever wealth they possess by patient and diligent labor. Comparisons are odious, and, but in defence, would not be made by me. But is there more tendency to aristocracy in a manufactory, supporting hundreds of freemen, or in a cotton plantation, with its not less numerous slaves, sustaining, perhaps, only two white families—that of the master and the overseer?

I pass, with pleasure, from this disagreeable topic to two general propositions which cover the entire ground of debate. The first is, that, under the operation of the American System, the objects which it protects and fosters are brought to the consumer at cheaper prices than they commanded prior to its introduction, or than they would command if it did not exist. If that be true, ought not the country to be contented and satisfied with the system, unless the second proposition, which I mean presently also to consider, is unfounded? And that is, that the tendency of the system is to sustain, and that it has upheld the prices of all our agricultural and other produce, including cotton.

And is the fact not indisputable, that all essential objects of consumption, affected by the tariff, are cheaper and better, since the act of 1824, than they were for several years prior to that law? I appeal, for its truth, to common observation and to all practical men. I appeal to the farmer of the country, whether he does not purchase, on better terms, his iron, salt, brown sugar, cotton goods, and woollens, for his laboring people. And I ask the cotton planter if he has not been better and more cheaply supplied with his cotton bagging. In regard to this latter article, the gentleman from South Carolina was mistaken in supposing that I complained that, under the existing duty, the Kentucky manufacturer could not compete with the Scotch. The Kentuckian furnishes a more substantial and a cheaper article, and at a more uniform and regular price. But it was the frauds, the violations of law, of which I did complain; not smuggling, in the common sense of that practice, which has something bold, daring, and enterprising in it, but mean, barefaced cheating by fraudulent invoices and false denomination.

I plant myself upon this FACT of cheapness and superiority, as upon impregnable ground. Gentlemen may tax their ingenuity, and produce a thousand speculative solutions of the fact but the fact itself will remain undisturbed.

. . . .

This brings me to consider what I apprehend to have been the most efficient of all the causes in the reduction of the prices of manufactured articles; and that is, *competition*. By competition, the total amount of the supply is increased, and by increase of the supply a competition in the sale ensues, and this enables the consumer to buy at lower rates. Of all human powers operating on the affairs of mankind, none is greater than that of competition. It is action and reaction. It operates between individuals in the same nation, and between different nations. It resembles the meeting of the mountain torrent, grooving, by its precipitous motion, its own channel, and ocean's tide. Unopposed, it sweeps everything before it; but, counterpoised, the waters become calm, safe, and regular. It is like the segments of a circle or an arch; taken separately, each is nothing; but, in their combination, they produce efficiency, symmetry, and perfection. By the American System this vast power has been excited in America, and brought into being to act in cooperation or collision with European industry. Europe acts within itself, and with America; and America acts within itself, and with Europe. The consequence is the reduction of prices in both hemispheres. Nor is it fair to argue, from the reduction of prices in Europe, to her own presumed skill and labor, exclusively. We affect her prices, and she affects ours. This must always be the case, at least in reference to any articles as to which there is not a total nonintercourse; and if our industry, by diminishing the demand for her supplies, should produce a diminution in the price of those supplies, it would be very unfair to ascribe that reduction to her ingenuity, instead of placing it to the credit of our own skill and excited industry.

Practical men understand very well this state of the case, whether they do or do not comprehend the causes which produce it. I have in my possession a letter from a respectable merchant, well known to me, in which he says, after complaining of the operation of the tariff of 1828 on the articles to which it applies, some of which he had imported, and that his purchases having been made in England before the passage of that tariff was known, it produced such an effect upon the English market, that the articles could not be resold without loss; he adds: "for *really* it appears that, when additional duties are laid upon an article, it then becomes *lower* instead of *higher*." This could not probably happen where the supply of the foreign article did not exceed the home demand, unless upon the supposition of the increased duty having *excited* or *stimulated* the measure of the home production.

The great law of *price* is determined by supply and demand. Whatever affects either, affects the price. If the supply is increased, the demand remaining the same, the price declines; if the demand is increased, the supply remaining the same, the price advances; if both supply and demand are undiminished, the price is stationary, and the price is influenced exactly in proportion to the degree of disturbance to the demand or supply. It is therefore a great error to suppose that an existing or new duty *necessarily* becomes a component element, to its exact amount, of price. If the proportions of demand and supply are varied by the duty, either in augmenting the supply, or diminishing the demand, or vice versa, price is affected, to the extent of that variation. But the duty never becomes an integral part of the price, except in the instances where the demand and the supply remain, after the duty is imposed, precisely what they were before, or the demand is increased, and the supply remains stationary.

Competition, therefore, wherever existing, whether at home or abroad, is the parent cause of cheapness. If a high duty excites production at home, and the quantity of the domestic article exceeds the amount which had been previously imported, the price will fall.

. . . .

Gentlemen have allowed to the manufacturing portions of the community no peace; they have been constantly threatened with the overthrow of the American System. From the year 1820, if not from 1816, down to this time, they have been held in a condition of constant alarm and insecurity. Nothing is more prejudicial to the great interests of a nation than unsettled and varying policy. Although every appeal to the national legislature has been responded to, in conformity with the wishes and sentiments of the great majority of the people, measures of protection have only been carried by such small majorities, as to excite hopes on the one hand, and fears on the other. Let the country breathe; let its vast resources be developed; let its energies be fully put forth; let it have tranquility; and, my word for it, the degree of perfection in the arts which it will exhibit will be greater than that which has been presented, astonishing as our progress has been. Although some branches of our manufactures might, and, in foreign markets, now do, fearlessly contend with similar foreign fabrics, there are many others, yet in their infancy, struggling with the difficulties which encompass them. We should look at the *whole* system, and recollect that time, when we contemplate the great movements of a nation, is very different from the short period which is allotted for the duration of individual life. The honorable gentleman from South Carolina well and eloquently said, in 1824, "No great interest of any country ever yet grew up in a day; no new branch of indus-

try can become firmly and profitably established, but in a long course of years; every thing, indeed, great or good, is matured by slow degrees; that which attains a speedy maturity is of small value, and is destined to a brief existence. It is the order of Providence that powers gradually developed shall alone attain permanency and perfection. Thus must it be with our national institutions, and national character itself."

I feel, most sensibly, Mr. President, how much I have trespassed upon the Senate. My apology is, a deep and deliberate conviction that the great cause under debate involves the prosperity and the destiny of the Union. But the best requital I can make for the friendly indulgence which has been extended to me by the Senate, and for which I shall ever retain sentiments of lasting gratitude, is, to proceed, with as little delay as practicable, to the conclusion of a discourse which has not been more tedious to the Senate than exhausting to me. I have now to consider the remaining of the two propositions which I have already announced. That is,

2dly. That, under the operation of the American system, the products of our agriculture command a higher price than they would do without it, by the creation of a home market; and, by the augmentation of wealth produced by manufacturing industry, which enlarges our powers of consumption, both of domestic and foreign articles. The importance of the home market is among the established maxims which are universally recognised by all writers and all men. However some may differ as to the relative advantages of the foreign and the home market, none deny to the latter great value and high consideration. It is nearer to us, beyond the control of foreign legislation, and undisturbed by those vicissitudes to which all international intercourse is more or less exposed. The most stupid are sensible of the benefit of a residence in the vicinity of a large manufactory, or a market town, of a good road, or of a navigable stream, which connects their farms with some great capital. If the pursuits of all men were perfectly the same, although they would be in possession of the greatest abundance of the particular produce of their industry, they might, at the same time, be in extreme want of other necessary articles of human subsistence. The uniformity of the general occupation would preclude all exchanges—all commerce. It is only in the diversity of the vocations of the members of a community that the means can be found for those salutary exchanges which conduce to the general prosperity; and the greater that diversity, the more extensive and the more animating is the circle of exchange. Even if foreign markets were freely and widely open to the reception of our agricultural produce, from its bulky nature, and the distance of the interior, and the dangers of the ocean, large portions of it could never profitably reach the foreign market. But let us quit this field of theory, clear as it is, and look at the practical operation of the system of protection, beginning with the most valuable staple of our agriculture. . . .

Let us suppose that the home demand for cotton, which has been created by the American System, were to cease, and that the 200,000 bales, that the home market now absorbs, were thrown into the glutted markets of foreign countries, would not the effect inevitably be to produce a further and great reduction in the price of the article? If there be any truth in the facts and principles which I have before stated, and endeavored to illustrate, it cannot be doubted that the existence of American manufactures has tended to increase the demand, and extend the consumption of the raw material; and that, but for this increased demand, the price of the article would have fallen, possibly one-half, lower than it now is. The error of the opposite argument is, in assuming one thing, which, being denied, the whole fails; that is, it assumes that the *whole* labor of the United States would be profitably employed, without manufactures. Now, the truth is, that the system *excites* and *creates* labor, and this labor creates wealth, and this new wealth communicates additional ability to consume, which acts on all the objects contributing to human comfort and enjoyment. The amount of cotton imported into the two ports of Boston and Providence alone, (during the last year, and it was imported exclusively for the home manufacture,) was 109,517 bales. . . .

I could extend and dwell on the long list of articles—the hemp, iron, lead, coal, and other items, for which a demand is created in the home market, by the operation of the American System; but I should exhaust the patience of the Senate. *Where, where,* should we find a market for all these articles, if it did not exist at home? What would be the condition of the largest portion of our people and of the territory, if this home market were annihilated? How could they be supplied with objects of prime necessity? What would not be the certain and inevitable decline in the price of all these articles, but for the home market? And allow me, Mr. President, to say, that, of all the agricultural parts of the United States which are benefited by the operation of this system, none are equally so with those which border the Chesapeake Bay, the lower parts of North Carolina, Virginia, and the two shores of Maryland. Their facilities of transportation and proximity to the North give them decided advantages.

But if all this reasoning were totally fallacious—if the price of manufactured articles were really higher under the American System, than without it, I should still argue that high or low prices were themselves relative—relative to the ability to pay them. It is in vain to tempt, to tantalize us with the lower prices of European fabrics than our own, if we have nothing wherewith to purchase them. If, by the home exchanges, we can be supplied with necessary, even if they are dearer and worse, articles of American production than the foreign, it is better than not to be supplied at all. And how would the large portion of our country which I have described, be supplied, but for the home exchanges? A poor people destitute of wealth or of exchangeable commodities, has nothing to purchase foreign fabrics. To them they are equally beyond their reach, whether their cost be a dollar or a guinea. It is in this view of the matter that Great Britain, by her vast wealth—her *exerted* and *protected* industry—is enabled to bear a burden of taxation which, when compared to that of other nations, appears enormous; but which, when her immense riches are compared to theirs, is light

and trivial. The gentleman from South Carolina has drawn a lively and flattering picture of our coasts, bays, rivers, and harbors; and he argues that these proclaimed the design of Providence that we should be a commercial people. I agree with him. We differ only as to the means. He would cherish the foreign, and neglect the internal trade. I would foster both. What is navigation without ships, or ships without cargoes? By penetrating the bosoms of our mountains, and extracting from them their precious treasures; by cultivating the earth, and *securing* a home market for its rich and abundant products; by employing the water power with which we are blessed; by stimulating and protecting our native industry, in all its forms; we shall but nourish and promote the prosperity of commerce, foreign and domestic.

I have hitherto considered the question in reference only to a state of peace; but a season of war ought not to be entirely overlooked. We have enjoyed near twenty years of peace; but who can tell when the storm of war shall again break forth? Have we forgotten, so soon, the privations to which not merely our brave soldiers and our gallant tars were subjected, but the whole community, during the last war, for the want of absolute necessaries? To what an enormous price they rose? And how inadequate the supply was, at any price? The statesman, who justly elevates his views, will look behind as well as forward, and at the existing state of things; and he will graduate the policy which he recommends, to all the probable exigencies which may arise in the republic. Taking this comprehensive range, it would be easy to show that the higher prices of peace, if prices were higher in peace, were more than compensated by the lower prices of war, during which supplies of all essential articles are indispensable to its vigorous, effectual, and glorious prosecution. I conclude this part of the argument with the hope that my humble exertions have not been altogether unsuccessful in showing—

1. That the policy which we have been considering ought to continue to be regarded as the genuine American System.

2. That the free trade system, which is proposed as its substitute, ought really to be considered as the British colonial system.

3. That the American System is beneficial to all parts of the Union, and absolutely necessary to much the larger portion.

4. That the price of the great staple of cotton, and of all our chief productions of agriculture, has been sustained and upheld, and a decline averted by the protective system.

5. That, if the foreign demand for cotton has been at all diminished by the operation of that system, the diminution has been more than compensated in the additional demand created at home.

6. That the constant tendency of the system, by creating competition among ourselves, and between American and European industry, reciprocally acting upon each other, is to reduce prices of manufactured objects.

7. That, in point of fact, objects within the scope of the policy of protection have greatly fallen in price.

8. That if, in a season of peace, these benefits are experienced in a season of war, when the foreign supply might be cut off, they would be much more extensively felt.

9. And, finally, that the substitution of the British colonial system for the American System, without benefiting any section of the Union, by subjecting us to a foreign legislation, regulated by foreign interests, would lead to the prostration of our manufactures, general impoverishment, and ultimate ruin.

. . . .

And now, sir, I would address a few words to the friends of the American System in the Senate. The revenue *must, ought* to be reduced. The country will not, after, by the payment of the public debt, $10 or $12 millions become unnecessary, bear such an annual surplus. Its distribution would form a subject of perpetual contention. Some of the opponents of the system understand the stratagem by which to attack it, and are shaping their course accordingly. It is to crush the system by the accumulation of revenue, and by the effort to persuade the people that they are unnecessarily *taxed,* whilst those would really *tax* them who would break up the *native* sources of supply, and render them dependent upon the *foreign.* But the revenue *ought* to be reduced, so as to accommodate it to the fact of the payment of the public debt. And the alternative is, or may be, to *preserve* the protecting system, and repeal the duties on the *unprotected* articles, or to preserve the duties on *unprotected* articles, and endanger, if not *destroy,* the system. Let us then adopt the measure before us, which will benefit all classes: the farmer, the professional man, the merchant, the manufacturer, the mechanic, and the cotton planter more than all. A few months ago, there was no diversity of opinion as to the expediency of this measure. All, then, seemed to unite in the selection of these objects, for a repeal of duties which were not produced within the country.

Such a repeal did not touch our domestic industry, violated no principle, offended no prejudice.

Can we not all, whatever may be our favorite theories, cordially unite on this *neutral* ground? When that is occupied, let us look beyond it, and see if anything can be done, in the field of protection, to modify, to improve it, or to satisfy those who are opposed to the system. Our southern brethren believe that it is injurious to them, and ask its repeal. We believe that its abandonment will be prejudicial to them, and *ruinous* to every other section of the Union. However strong their convictions may be, they are not stronger than ours. Between the points of the preservation of the system and its absolute repeal, there is no principle of union. If it can be *shown* to operate immoderately on any quarter; if the measure of protection to any article can be demonstrated to be undue and inordinate, it would be the duty of Congress to interpose and apply a remedy. And none will cooperate more heartily than I shall, in the performance of that duty. It is quite probable that beneficial modifications of the system may be made, without impairing its efficacy. But, to make it fulfil the purposes of its institution, the measure of protection ought to be adequate. If it be not, all interests will be injuriously affected. The manufacturer, crippled in his exertions, will produce less perfect and dearer fabrics, and the consumer will feel the consequence. This is the spirit, and these are the principles only, on which it seems to me that a settlement of this great question can be made satisfactorily to all parts of our Union.

Register of Debates in Congress, Senate, 22d Congress, 1st session, February 2, 3, and 6, 1832, 257–295.

59   The Adoption of the Gag Rule Regarding Petitions and Memorials on Slavery

May 26, 1836

Few decisions of Congress have been as fraught with peril as this brief item, which imposed a ban on the introduction of petitions in the House related to slavery. The "gag rule," as it was called because it gagged, or cut off, debate, was an extreme measure for a parliamentary body designed to be the place where conflicting voices are heard and where debate helps shape solutions to political problems. The gag rule was a powerful example of the hardening of views between the North and the South over slavery. Slavery became an issue that could not be resolved by debate alone. The issue was eventually addressed in a bloody civil war.

The immediate cause of the gag rule was the frustration of the majority of House members to a growing, orchestrated, petition drive on the part of northern abolitionists to eliminate slavery and the slave trade in the District of Columbia. The House reacted by refusing to take up any petition or other statement related to slavery. Despite repeated attempts to abolish it, the gag rule stayed in force until December 3, 1844, when a resolution introduced by John Quincy Adams finally passed. Adams, the only president of

the United States ever to serve in the House of Representatives after his term as president, dedicated himself to the elimination of the gag rule. His speeches in opposition to the hated rule led friend and foe alike to dub him "Old Man Eloquent."

And whereas it is extremely important and desirable that the agitation of this subject should be finally arrested, for the purpose of restoring tranquility to the public mind, your committee respectfully recommend the adoption of the following additional resolution, viz:

Resolved, That all petitions, memorials, resolutions, propositions, or papers, relating in any way, or to any extent whatever, to the subject of slavery, or the abolition of slavery, shall, without being either printed or referred, be laid upon the table, and that no further action whatever shall be had thereon.

Congressional Globe, House, 24th Congress, 1st session, May 26, 1836, 505.

60   The Senate Debates the Establishment of a Gallery for Reporters

July 3, 1841

There is a long and colorful history of public access to the workings of Congress and of the role of reporters covering Congress. The best account of the early history of reporters covering Congress is Donald A. Ritchie's Press Gallery: Congress and the Washington Correspondents *(1991). The House and Senate approached public access differently in the early years of the nation. The House had a small public gallery from the first Congress in 1789; the Senate met in secret until 1795, allowing no member of the public and no reporters to record their proceedings. Many senators of the early congresses held the public gallery in the House in disdain, saying it only caused members of the House to play to the galleries, where their speeches were often met with applause or with booing and hissing. (These same arguments were used almost two centuries later by those opposed to television cameras in the House and Senate.)*

Early press coverage of congressional debates was uneven and often casually done either from seats in the gallery or from positions on the floors of the House or Senate chamber, where reporters could hear better. The Senate took up the matter of a gallery for reporters in 1839, after receiving complaints and requests from reporters from distant places, who claimed they were not given accommodations equal to those of reporters from Washington, D.C., and nearby towns. But after a close vote of 17–20, the press gallery proposal was dropped. In the 1839 debate Senator John Niles (D-Conn.) said he was surprised that the Senate would want to "sanction, and in some manner indorse, the vile slanders that issued daily from these letter-writers, by assigning them seats within the Chamber." He went on to describe reporters as "miserable slanderers—hirelings, hanging on to the skirts of literature, earning a miserable subsistence from their vile and dirty misrepresentations of the proceedings here, and many of them writing for both sides."

On July 3, 1841, the Senate again debated the question of establishing a press gallery and agreed to a resolution to form a select committee to look into the matter and report back to the Senate. On July 8, 1841, five days after the debate that follows, the Senate approved a change in Senate Rule 47, thus establishing a separate gallery for reporters and removing reporters from the floor of the Senate, a practice that continues to the present day.

Today, only the official recorders of debate, employees of the Senate or the House, are allowed to record Senate and House proceedings from the floors of the respective chambers. In the modern age of televised coverage of both bodies, reporters are seldom seen in the press galleries unless there is a special event, such as a State of the Union address in the House, or the likelihood of a dramatic event, such as a filibuster in the Senate.

Mr. BAYARD said he wished to offer a resolution in relation to the Reporters. Some modification of the 47th rule was evidently called for. It was desirable that a fair distribution of the liberty granted to reporters should be made. One of the prominent city papers had given over all pretension to reporting the proceedings, and confined itself to a very brief outline of the business.

He moved that the 47th rule be referred to a select committee of five, to be appointed by the Chair.

Mr. WALKER observed that last session he had offered a somewhat similar resolution in relation to the Reporters admitted on the floor of the Senate. It was his wish to see the proceedings of this chamber fairly and impartially reported for the information of the people; but he believed that never would be done until Congress employed Reporters of its own for the purpose. It was seen every day that the various letter writers who professed to give to the country statements of the business of Congress, misrepresented every thing so as to mislead the public mind. The people never could rely upon having correct reports of the proceedings in Congress till Reporters shall be employed by Congress itself for this purpose.

The resolution was adopted.

Mr. CLAY said that, as a matter in connection with the subject now under the action of the Senate, he would remark that one of the city papers which he seldom reads, had been put into his hands since he came into the Senate chamber this morning. He was surprised to find in that paper—not, indeed, under the head of the ordinary reports of proceedings—but in a sort of running analysis of what occurred yesterday, a misrepresentation, calculated to would the feelings of an honorable Senator, and to present himself (Mr. CLAY) in the erroneous attitude of endeavoring to fasten on that Senator a denial of an assertion or contradiction, which would reflect upon his character for veracity. Nothing could be farther from his (Mr. CLAY's) heart and thoughts than the slightest intention to place that honorable Senator in any such position. The good natured editor of the paper to which he (Mr. CLAY) alluded, in his zeal to sow dissension between that honorable Senator and him, (Mr. CLAY,) not only professed to give the words which passed, but also to give his (Mr. CLAY's) very looks, motions, and actions; not only had done this, but had attributed to him that he had left his own seat and taken that of the Senator from Illinois, within one seat of the Senator from Massachusetts, in anticipation of an incident that subsequently occurred. Now the fact was, that he had gone to the passage opposite to the door, which was one of the few places in the chamber where a mouthful of fresh air might be occasionally enjoyed, and the worthy Senator from Illinois (Mr. YOUNG) had offered him his seat, and insisted on his taking it, he presumed from the fact that he, (Mr. C.) was much the older man. [Mr. YOUNG assented] It was under these circumstances he had taken his seat, and not with any view of making a rude attempt to force the honorable Senator from Massachusetts to retract any expression of opinion. He would recall the Senate to the manner in which the incident had occurred. The Senator from Virginia was going on to charge him (Mr. CLAY) with having called the Senator from Massachusetts to order. He (Mr. CLAY) rose to correct the Senator from Virginia, and to state that he did not know that his inquiry would or would not lead to the fact of whether that Senator had been out of order. While thus explaining the object for which he (Mr. CLAY) had interrupted the Senator from Virginia, the editor presents him in the attitude of trying to make the Senator from Massachusetts admit that what he had stated was not true. His (Mr. Clay's) inquiry was stated in such a manner as to make it appear that he wanted to know whether the Senator from Massachusetts had not contradicted himself instead of what he (Mr. CLAY) really wanted to know, which was, wether the result of his conviction proceeded from his own conclusions or from any authority that could defeat the measure. It would be recollected that he was directly opposed to the introduction of the Executive opinions, and therefore could have had no intention of extorting them. It has been concurred in that the introduction of such opinions was improper. All he had been desirous of knowing from the Senator was the amount of information, and from what quarter he obtained it, which had led him to the conviction that there would be no Bank this session without the adoption of the amendment proposed by the Senator from Virginia. This was his sole purpose. Nothing on earth was farther from his purpose than to urge his inquiry with a view of placing his friend, the Senator from Massachusetts, in a questionable position. In conclusion, he hoped he would be allowed to express, in common with other Senators whose sentiments had become known to him since he entered the chamber, the satisfaction he experienced on learning that the difference of opinion which yesterday threatened to interrupt the harmonious relations between his friends, the Senators from Virginia, had been mutually explained, so as not to leave a trace of unpleasant misunderstanding between them. He trusted that in the further progress of this bill, a resolution which he had imposed on himself would be concurred in by those opposed to the measure, as well as by those in favor of it, to avoid all interruptions to that harmony which best comported with the dignity of this grave and deliberative body.

Mr. ARCHER, in some brief remarks, adverted to the discussion between himself and colleague yesterday, disavowing all unkind feelings on his part.

Mr. RIVES responded in the same amicable spirit.

Mr. LINN observed that he had a few remarks to make on the subject now before the Senate. He would not have felt disposed to say a word on this occasion had not the Senator from Kentucky, in his marks, appealed to both sides of the chamber, and deprecated the strong language called up by allusions to exciting topics. For the last ten or twelve years that the party which supported the late Administration had been in possession of power, the Opposition to that Administration had been allowed, without limitation, the widest range of language—even when its violent and indecent abuse of General Jackson and his friends seemed to pass the bounds of all forbearance. It was well know that the friends of that Administration were particularly scrupulous to observe towards the then Opposition not only the marked forbearance but all the kind feelings or consideration which properly belongs to a party in possession of power. Allowances were made for the excited feelings of a minority: and it was felt that forbearance was a duty. Now the tables are turned. The supporters of the late Administration are here now in the minority. And what is the reciprocity evinced by the majority? Was it not fresh in the recollection of the Senate how that great and good man, now trembling on the verge of the grave, so much loved and revered by the American people, was treated yesterday in the remarks which emanated from the friends of the present Administration? Now, he (Mr. LINN) felt no disposition to depart without provocation from the courtesy which was most becoming and most in accordance with the dignity of the chamber to which he had the honor to belong. No man respected more than he did the obligations of courtesy; but he felt it due to himself and to the principles of the party to which he belonged, to declare unequivocally that he would always maintain his right to use the strongest, the most decided, and the most unsparing language in regard to the party in power, so far as it was connected with their official acts. He again adverted to the abuse of General Jackson, and particularly on yesterday, and concluded with a strong asseveration that he would, on all occasions, in this chamber and out of it, wherever and whenever he head his venerated name assailed, defend it with all the energies that God had given him.

Congressional Globe (weekly), 27th Congress, 1st session, July 10, 1841, 145.

61 Charles Dickens's Description of Congress

1841

The great English writer Charles Dickens (1812–1870) visited the United States in 1841 and wrote a fascinating account of his travels, American Notes, *first published in 1842. In one chapter he described Washington, Congress, and the White House with the keen eye of someone familiar with Parliament. Earlier in Dickens's career he had been a reporter of debates in the House of Commons.*

But unlike the Frenchman Alexis de Tocqueville, who visited Congress nine years earlier (see document 57), Dickens was less concerned with the nature of democracy and more concerned with the personal habits he saw among members of Congress, especially their vile habit of chewing tobacco and spitting pretty much where they pleased. He described the nation's capital as "the head-

quarters of tobacco-tinctured saliva." He confessed that the frequent sight of men chewing and spitting sickened him.

Dickens's colorful account is the type of observation that is often lost in the official records of Congress. Written in an era when classical references were far more common in literature and speech than is true today, his reference to Washington, D.C., as a Barmecide Feast may need some explanation. It is taken from a story in The Arabian Nights' Entertainments, *where Barmecide, a Persian nobleman, prepared an imaginary feast for a guest, using real dishes but without food on them. As Dickens looked out on the panorama of Washington, designed by the Frenchman Pierre L'Enfant, he saw an unfinished illusion of empire, not the real thing. The design of the city, with its spacious avenues that ran to nowhere, was not unlike dishes without food, an apt description of Washington in the 1840s.*

. . . .

It is sometimes called the City of Magnificent Distances, but it might with greater propriety be termed the City of Magnificent Intentions; for it is only on taking a bird's-eye view of it from the top of the Capitol that one can at all comprehend the vast designs of its projector, an aspiring Frenchman. Spacious avenues that begin in nothing, and lead nowhere; streets, mile-long, that only want houses, roads, and inhabitants; public buildings that need but a public to be complete; and ornaments of great thoroughfares, which only lack great thoroughfares to ornament—are its leading features. One might fancy the season over, and most of the houses gone out of town for ever with their masters. To the admirers of cities it is a Barmecide Feast; a pleasant field for the imagination to rove in; a monument raised to a deceased project, with not even a legible inscription to record its departed greatness.

Such as it is, it is likely to remain. It was originally chosen for the seat of Government as a means of averting the conflicting jealousies and interests of the different States; and very probably, too, as being remote from mobs: a consideration not to be slighted, even in America. It has no trade or commerce of its own: having little or no population beyond the President and his establishment: the members of the legislature, who reside there during the session; the Government clerks and officers employed in the various departments; the keepers of the hotels and boarding-houses; and the tradesmen who supply their tables. It is very unhealthy. Few people would live in Washington, I take it, who were not obliged to reside there; and the tides of emigration and speculation, those rapid and regardless currents, are little likely to flow at any time towards such dull and sluggish water.

The principal features of the Capitol are, of course, the two Houses of Assembly. But there is, besides, in the centre of the building, a fine rotunda, ninety-six feet in diameter, and ninety-six high, whose circular wall is divided into compartments, ornamented by historical pictures. Four of these have for their subjects prominent events in the revolutionary struggle. They were painted by Colonel Trumbull, himself a member of Washington's staff at the time of their occurrence; from which circumstance they derive a peculiar interest of their own. In this same hall Mr. Greenough's large statue of Washington has been lately placed. It has great merits, of course, but it struck me as being rather strained and violent for its subject. I could wish, however, to have seen it in a better light than it can ever be viewed in where it stands.

There is a very pleasant and commodious library in the Capitol; and from a balcony in front, the bird's-eye view, of which I have just spoken, may be had, together with a beautiful prospect of the adjacent country. In one of the ornamented portions of the building there is a figure of Justice; whereunto, the Guide Book says, "the artist at first contemplated giving more of nudity, but he was warned that the public sentiment in this country would not admit of it, and in his caution he has gone, perhaps, to the opposite extreme." Poor Justice! she has been made to wear much stranger garments in America than those she pines in in the Capitol. Let us hope that she has changed her dressmaker since they were fashioned, and that the public sentiment of the country did not cut out the clothes she hides her lovely figure in just now.

The House of Representatives is a beautiful and spacious hall of semicircular shape, supported by handsome pillars. One part of the gallery is appropriated to the ladies, and there they sit in front rows, and come in, and go out, as at a play or concert. The chair is canopied, and raised considerably above the floor of the House; and every member has an easy-chair and a writing-desk to himself: which is denounced by some people out of doors as a most unfortunate and injudicious arrangement, tending to long' sittings and prosaic speeches. It is an elegant chamber to look at, but a singularly bad one for all purposes of hearing. The Senate, which is smaller, is free from this objection, and is exceedingly well adapted to the uses for which it is designed. The sittings, I need hardly add, take place in the day; and the parliamentary forms are modelled on those of the old country.

I was sometimes asked, in my progress through other places, whether I had not been very much impressed by the heads of the lawmakers at Washington; meaning not their chiefs and leaders, but literally their individual and personal heads, whereon their hair grew, and whereby the phrenological character of each legislator was expressed; and I almost as often struck my questioner dumb with indignant consternation by answering, "No, that I didn't remember being at all overcome." As I must, at whatever hazard, repeat the avowal here, I will follow it up by relating my impressions on this subject in as few words as possible.

In the first place—it may be from some imperfect development of my organ of veneration—I do not remember having ever fainted away, or having even been moved to tears of joyful pride, at sight of any legislative body. I have borne the grouse of Commons like a man, and have yielded to no weakness, but slumber, in the House of Lords. I have seen elections for borough and county, and have never been impelled (no matter which party won) to damage my hat by throwing it up into the air in triumph, or to crack my voice by shouting forth any reference to our Glorious Constitution, to the noble purity of our independent voters, or the unimpeachable integrity of our independent members. Having withstood such strong attacks upon my fortitude, it is possible that I may be of a cold and insensible temperament, amounting to iciness, in such matters; and therefore my impressions of the live pillars of the Capitol at Washington must be received with such grains of allowance as this free confession may seem to demand.

Did I see in this public body an assemblage of men, bound together in the sacred names of Liberty and Freedom, and so asserting the chaste dignity of those twin goddesses, in all their discussions, as to exalt at once the Eternal Principles to which their names are given, and their own character, and the character of their countrymen, in the admiring eyes of the whole world?

It was but a week since an aged, gray-haired man, a lasting honour to the land that gave him birth, who has done good service to his country, as his forefathers did, and who will be remembered scores upon scores of years after the worms bred in its corruption are but so many grains of dust—it was but a week since this old man had stood for days upon his trial before this very body, charged with having dared to assert the infamy of that traffic which has for its accursed merchandise men and women, and their unborn children. Yes. And publicly exhibited in the same city all the while; gilded, framed, and glazed; hung up for general admiration; shown to strangers, not with shame, but pride; its face not turned towards the wall, itself not taken down and burned; is the Unanimous Declaration of the Thirteen United States of America, which solemnly declares that All Men are created Equal; and are endowed by their Creator with the Inalienable Rights of Life, Liberty, and the Pursuit of Happiness!

It was not a month since this same body had sat calmly by, and heard a man, one of themselves, with oaths which beggars in their drink reject, threaten to cut another's throat from ear to ear. There he sat among them; not crushed by the general feeling of the assembly, but as good a man as any.

There was but a week to come, and another of that body, for doing his duty to those who sent him there; for claiming in a Republic the Liberty and Freedom of expressing their sentiments, and making known their prayer; would be tried, found guilty, and have strong censure passed upon him by the rest. His was a grave offence indeed; for, years before, he had risen up and said, "A gang of male and female slaves for sale, warranted to breed like cattle, linked to each other by iron fetters, are passing now along the open street beneath the windows of your Temple of Equality! Look!" But there are many kinds of hunters engaged in the Pursuit of Happiness, and they go variously armed. It is the Inalienable Right of some among them to take the field after *their* Happiness, equipped with cat and cart-whip, stocks, and iron collar, and to shout their view halloa (always in praise of Liberty) to the music of clanking chains and bloody stripes.

Where sat the many legislators of coarse threats; of words and blows such as coalheavers deal upon each other, when they forget their breeding? On every side. Every session had its anecdotes of that kind, and the actors were all there.

Did I recognise in this assembly a body of men who, applying themselves in a new world to correct some of the falsehoods and vices of the old, purified the avenues to Public Life, paved the dirty ways to Place and Power, debated and made laws for the Common Good, and had no party but their Country?

I saw in them the wheels that move the meanest perversion of virtuous Political Machinery that the worst tools ever wrought. Despicable trickery at elections; under-handed tamperings with public officers; cowardly attacks upon opponents, with scurrilous newspapers for shields, and hired pens for daggers; shameful trucklings to mercenary knaves, whose claim to be considered is, that every day and week they sow new crops of ruin with their venal types, which are the dragon's teeth of yore, in everything but sharpness; aidings and abettings of every bad inclination in the popular mind, and artful suppressions of all its good influences: such things as these, and, in a word, Dishonest Faction in its most depraved and most unblushing form, stared out from every corner of the crowded hall.

Did I see among them the intelligence and refinement: the true, honest, patriotic heart of America? Here and there were drops of its blood and life, but they scarcely coloured the stream of desperate adventurers which sets that way for profit and for pay. It is the game of these men, and of their profligate organs, to make the strife of politics so fierce and brutal, and so destructive of all self-respect in worthy men, that sensitive and delicate-minded persons shall be kept aloof and they, and such as they, be left to battle out their selfish views unchecked. And thus this lowest of all scrambling fights goes on, and they who in other countries would, from their intelligence and station, most aspire to make the laws, do here recoil the farthest from that degradation.

That there are, among the representatives of the people in both Houses, and among all parties, some men of high character and great abilities, I need not say. The foremost among those politicians who are known in Europe have been already described, and I see no reason to depart from the rule I have laid down for my guidance, of abstaining from all mention of individuals. It will be sufficient to add that, to the most favourable accounts that have been written Them, I more than fully and most heartily subscribe; and that personal intercourse and free communication have bred within me, not the result predicted in the very doubtful proverb, but increased admiration and respect. They are striking men to look at, hard to deceive, prompt to act, lions in energy, Crichtons in varied accomplishments, Indians in fire of eye and gesture, Americans in strong and generous impulse; and they as well represent the honour and wisdom of their country at home, as the distinguished gentleman who is now its minister at the British Court sustains its highest character abroad.

I visited both Houses nearly every day during my stay in Washington. On my initiatory visit to the House of Representatives, they divided against a decision of the chair; but the chair won. The second time I went, the member who was speaking, being interrupted by a laugh, mimicked it, as one child would in quarrelling with another, and added "that he would make honourable gentlemen opposite sing out a little more on the other side of their mouths presently." But interruptions are rare; the speaker being usually heard in silence. There are more quarrels than with us, and more threatenings than gentlemen are accustomed to exchange in any civilised society of which we have record: but farmyard imitations have not as yet been imported from the Parliament of the United Kingdom. The feature in oratory which appears to be the most practiced, and most relished, is the constant repetition of the same idea, or shadow of an idea, in fresh words; and the inquiry out of doors is not, "What did he say?" but, "How long did he speak?" These, however, are but enlargements of a principle which prevails elsewhere.

The Senate is a dignified and decorous body, and its proceedings are conducted with much gravity and order. Both Houses are handsomely carpeted; but the state to which these carpets are reduced by the universal disregard of the spittoon with which every honourable member is accommodated, and the extraordinary improvements on the pattern which are squirted and dabbled upon it in every direction, do not admit of being described. I will merely observe, that I strongly recommend all strangers not to look at the floor; and if they happen to drop anything, though it be their purse, not to pick it up with an ungloved hand on any account.

It is somewhat remarkable too, at first, to say the least, to see so many honourable members with swelled faces; and it is scarcely less remarkable to discover that this appearance is caused by the quantity of tobacco they contrive to stow within the hollow of the cheek. It is strange enough, too, to see an honourable gentleman leaning back in his tilted chair, with his legs on the desk before him, shaping a convenient "plug" with his penknife, and when it is quite ready for use, shooting the old one from his mouth as from a pop-gun, and clapping the new one in its place.

I was surprised to observe that even steady old chewers of great experience are not always good marksmen, which has rather inclined me to doubt that general proficiency with the rifle, of which we have heard so much in England. Several gentlemen called upon me who, in the course of conversation, frequently missed the spittoon at five paces; and one (but he was certainly short-sighted) mistook the closed sash for the open window at three.

Charles Dickens, *American Notes,* 2 vols. (New York: St. Martin's, 1985), vol. 1: 106–111. Originally published in 1842.

62   Senator Henry Clay's Valedictory to the Senate

March 31, 1842

In one of the most dramatic moments in Senate history, speaking before the full Senate and a packed gallery, the great Henry Clay (Whig-Ky.) resigned his seat in the Senate. He was tired, in poor health, and frustrated by his inability to get along with President John Tyler, a fellow Whig who detested him. Eyewitnesses reported that there was hardly a dry eye in the chamber, including Clay's, when the speech ended.

Clay resigned to prepare his final campaign for the presidency, having run in 1824 and 1832. He was no more successful in 1844, but he returned once more to the Senate in 1849, where he served until his death on June 29, 1852, ending almost a half century as one of the most dominant and influential politicians of the first half of the nineteenth century. Clay's funeral was held in the Senate chamber and his body was the first to lay in state in the Rotunda of the Capitol.

And now [continued Mr. CLAY], allow me to announce, formally and officially, my retirement from the Senate of the United States, and to present the last motion which I shall ever make within this body; but, before making that motion, I trust I shall be pardoned for availing myself of this occasion to make a few observations. At the time of my entry into this body, which took place in December, 1806, I regarded it, and still regard it, as a body which may be compared, without disadvantage, to any of a similar character which has existed in ancient or modern times; whether we look at it in reference to its dignity, its powers, or the mode of its constitution; and I will also add, whether it be regarded in reference to the amount of ability which I shall leave behind me when I retire from this chamber. In instituting a comparison between the Senate of the United States and similar political institutions, of other countries, of France and England for example, [he was sure] the comparison might be made without disadvantage to the American Senate. In respect to the constitution of these bodies: in England, with only the exception of the peers from Ireland and Scotland, and in France with no exception, the component parts, the members of these bodies, hold their places by virtue of no delegated authority, but derive their powers from the crown, either by ancient creation of nobility transmitted by force of hereditary descent, or by new patents as occasion required an increase of their numbers. But here, Mr. President, we have the proud title of being the representatives of sovereign states or commonwealths. If we look at the powers of these bodies in France and England, and the powers of this Senate, we shall find that the latter are far greater than the former. In both those countries they have the legislative power, in both the judicial with some modifications, and in both perhaps a more extensive judicial power than is possessed by this Senate; but then the vast and undefined and undefinable power, the treatymaking power, or at least a participation in the conclusions of treaties with foreign powers, is possessed by this Senate, and is possessed by neither of the others. Another power, too, and one of infinite magnitude, that of distributing the patronage of a great nation, which is shared by this Senate with the executive magistrate. In both these respects we stand upon ground different from that occupied by the houses of peers of England and of France. And I repeat that with respect to the dignity which ordinarily prevails in this body, and with respect to the ability of its members during the long period of my acquaintance with it, without arrogance or presumption, we may say, in proportion to its numbers, the comparison would not be disadvantageous to us compared with any Senate either of ancient or modern times. Sir, I have long—full of attraction as public service in the Senate of the United States is—a service which might fill the aspirations of the most ambitious heart—I have nevertheless long desired to seek that repose which is only to be found in the bosom of one's family—in private life—in one's home. It was my purpose to have terminated my senatorial career in November, 1840, after the conclusion of the political struggle which characterized that year. But I learned very soon, what my own reflections indeed prompted me to suppose would take place, that there would be an extra session; and being desirous, prior to my retirement, to cooperate with my friends in the Senate in restoring, by the adoption of measures best calculated to accomplish that purpose, that degree of prosperity to the country, which had been, for a time, destroyed, I determined upon attending the extra session, which was called, as was well known, by the lamented Harrison. His death, and the succession which took place in consequence of it, produced a new aspect in the affairs of the country. Had he lived, I do not entertain a particle of doubt that those measures which, it was hoped, might be accomplished at that session, would have been consummated by a candid cooperation between the executive branch of the government and Congress; and, sir, allow me to say, (and it is only with respect to the extra session) that I believe if there be any one free from party feelings, and free from bias and from prejudice, who will look at its transactions in a spirit of candor and of justice, but must come to the conclusion to which, I think, the country generally will come, that if there be anything to complain of in connection with that session, it is not as to what was done and concluded, but as to that which was left unfinished and unaccomplished. After the termination of that session, had Harrison lived, and had the measures which it appeared to me it was desirable to have accomplished, been carried, it was my intention to have retired; but I reconsidered that determination, with the vain hope that, at the regular session of Congress, what had been unaccomplished at the extra session, might then be effected, either upon the terms proposed or in some manner which would be equivalent. But events were announced after the extra session—events resulting, I believe, in the failure to accomplish certain objects at the extra session—events which seemed to throw upon our friends everywhere present defeat—this hope, and the occurrence of these events, induced me to attend the regular session, and whether in adversity or in prosperity, to share in the fortunes of my friends. But I came here with the purpose, which I am now about to effectuate, of retiring as soon as I thought I could retire with propriety and decency, from the public councils.

From the year 1806, the period of my entering upon this noble theatre of my public service, with but short intervals, down to the present time, I have been engaged in the service of my country. Of the nature and value of those services which I may have rendered during my long career of public life, it does not become me to speak. History, if she deigns to notice me, and posterity—if a recollection of any humble service which I may have rendered shall be transmitted to posterity—will be the best, truest, and most impartial judges; and to them I defer for a decision upon their value.

But, upon one subject, I may be allowed to speak. As to my public acts and public conduct, they are subjects for the judgment of my fellow citizens; but my private motives of action—that which prompted me to take the part which I may have done, upon great measures during their progress in the national councils, can be known only to the Great Searcher of the human heart and myself; and I trust I shall be pardoned for repeating again a declaration which I made thirty years ago; that whatever error I may have committed—and doubtless I have committed many during my public service—I may appeal to the Divine Searcher of hearts for the truth of the declaration which I now make, with pride and confidence, that I have been actuated by no personal motives—that I have sought no personal aggrandizement—no promotion from the advocacy of those various measures on which I have been called to act—that I have had an eye, a single eye, a heart, a single heart, ever devoted to what appeared to be the best interests of the country. Yet, sir, during this long period, I have not escaped the fate of other public men, in this and other countries. I have been often, Mr. President, the object of bitter and unmeasured detraction and calumny. I have borne it, I will not say always with composure, but I have borne it without creating any disturbance. I have borne it, waiting in unshaken and undoubting confidence, that the triumphs of truth and justice would ultimately prevail; and that time would settle all things as they ought to be settled. I have borne them under the conviction, of which no injustice, no wrong, no injury could deprive me, that I did not deserve them, and that He to whom we are all to be finally and ultimately responsible, would acquit me, whatever injustice I might experience at the hands of my fellow men.

But I have not been unsustained during this long course of public service. Every where on this widespread continent have I enjoyed the benefit of possessing warm-hearted, and enthusiastic, and devoted friends—friends who knew me, and appreciated justly the motives by which I have been actuated. To them, if I had language to make suitable acknowledgments, I would now take leave to present them, as being all the offering that I can make for their long continued, persevering and devoted friendship. But, sir, if I have a difficulty in giving utterance to an expression of the feelings of gratitude which fill my heart towards my friends, dispersed throughout this continent, what shall I say—what can I say—at all commensurate with my feelings of gratitude towards that state whose humble servitor I am? I migrated to the state of Kentucky nearly forty-five years ago. I went there as an orphan, who had not yet attained his majority—who had never recognised a father's smile—poor, penniless, without the favor of the great—with an imperfect and inadequate education, limited to the means applicable to such a boy; but scarcely had I set foot upon that generous soil, before I was caressed with parental fondness—patronized with bountiful munificence—and I may add to this, that her choicest honors, often unsolicited, have been freely showered upon me; and when I stood, as it were, in the darkest moments of human existence—abandoned by the world, calumniated by a large portion of my own countrymen, she threw around me her impenetrable shield, and bore me aloft, and repelled the attacks of malignity and calumny, by which I was assailed. Sir, it is to me an unspeakable pleasure that I am shortly to return to her friendly limits; and that I shall finally deposit (and it will not be long before that day arrives) my last remains under her generous soil, with the remains of her gallant and patriotic sons who have preceded me.

Mr. President, a recent epithet, (I do not know whether for the purpose of honor or of degradation,) has been applied to me; and I have been held up to the country as a dictator! Dictator! The idea of dictatorship is drawn from Roman institutions; and there, when it was created, the person who was invested with this tremendous authority, concentrated in his own person the whole power of the state. He exercised unlimited control over the property and lives of the citizens of the commonwealth. He had the power of raising armies, and of raising revenue by taxing the people. If I have been a dictator, what have been the powers with which I have been clothed? Have I possessed an army, a navy, revenue? Have I had the distribution of the patronage of the government? Have I, in short, possessed any power whatever? Sir, if I have been a dictator, I think those who apply the epithet to me must at least admit two things: In the first place, that my dictatorship has been distinguished by no cruel executions, stained by no deeds of blood, soiled by no act of dishonor. And they must no less acknowledge, in the second place, (though I do not know when its commencement bears date, but I suppose, however, that it is intended to be averred, from the commencement of the extra session,) that if I have been invested with, or have usurped the dictatorship, I have at least voluntarily surrendered the power within a shorter period than was assigned by the Roman laws for its continuance.

Mr. President, if to have sought, at the extra session and at this, by cooperation with my friends, to carry out those great measures which the majority of 1840 desired to see adopted and executed—if to have desired to see the currency and exchanges of this country once more regulated—if to have desired to replenish the empty coffers of the treasury, by an imposition of suitable duties—if to have desired to extend relief to the unfortunate bankrupts of the country, ruined, in a great measure, by the operation of the previous policy of the government—if to have desired, by cooperation with my friends, to limit and restrain and regulate the executive action, because it had become dangerous towards the other departments of the government in my opinion, and in the opinion of the majority of 1840—if to have desired to preserve the honor and credit of the country untarnished by adequate and suitable provisions for revenue, sufficient for fulfilling all the public engagements—if the faithful purpose of executing all these measures—if an ardent desire to carry out and redeem every pledge which was fairly made by my friends when struggling for the acquisition of power—if I say these efforts and this cooperation constitute my dictatorship, then I suppose I must bear the odium or the honor of the epithet whichever it may be considered.

Mr. President, that my nature is warm, my temper ardent, my disposition in the public service enthusiastic, I am ready to own. But those who suppose they may have seen any proof of dictation in my conduct, have only mistaken that ardor for what I at least supposed to be patriotic exertions for fulfilling the wishes and expectations by which I hold this seat; they have only mistaken the one for the other.

Mr. President, during my long and arduous services in the public councils, and especially during the last eleven years, in the Senate, the same ardor of temperament has characterized my actions, and has no doubt led me, in the heat of debate, in endeavoring to maintain my opinions in reference to the best course to be pursued in the conduct of public affairs, to use language offensive and susceptible of ungracious interpretation towards my brother senators.

If there be any who entertain a feeling of dissatisfaction resulting from any circumstance of this kind, I beg to assure them that I now make the amplest apology. And, on the other hand, I assure the Senate, one and all, without exception and without reserve, that I leave the Senate chamber without carrying with me to my retirement a single feeling of dissatisfaction towards the Senate itself or any one of its members. I go from it under the hope that we shall mutually consign to perpetual oblivion whatever of personal animosities or jealousies may have arisen between us during the repeated collisions of mind with mind.

And now, allow me to submit the motion which is the object that induced me to arise upon this occasion. It is to present the credentials of my friend and successor, who is present to take my place. If, Mr. President, any void could be created by my withdrawal from the Senate of the United States, it will be filled to overflowing by my worthy successor, whose urbanity, gallant bearing, steady adherence to principle, rare and uncommon powers of debate, are well known already in advance to the whole Senate. I move that the credentials be received, and at the proper moment that the oath required be administered. And now, in retiring as I am about to do from the Senate, I beg leave to deposit with it my fervent wishes, that all the great and patriotic objects for which it was instituted, may be accomplished—that the destiny designed for it by the framers of the Constitution may be fulfilled—that the deliberations now and hereafter, in which it may engage for the good of our common country, may eventuate in the restoration of its prosperity, and in the preservation and maintenance of her honor abroad, and her best interests at home. I retire from you, Mr. President, I know, at a period of infinite distress and embarrassment. I wish I could have taken leave of the public councils under more favorable auspices: but without meaning to say at this time, upon whom reproaches should fall on account of that unfortunate condition, I think I may appeal to the Senate and to the country for the truth of what I say, when I declare that at least no blame on account of these embarrassments and distresses can justly rest at my door. May the blessings of Heaven rest upon the heads of the whole Senate, and every member of it; and may every member of it advance still more in fame, and when they shall retire to the bosoms of their respective constituencies, may they all meet there that most joyous and grateful of all human rewards, the exclamation of their countrymen, "well done thou good and faithful servants." Mr. President, and Messieurs Senators, I bid you, one and all, a long, a last, a friendly farewell.

Congressional Globe, Senate, 27th Congress, 2d session, March 31, 1842, 376–377.

63   Senate and House Debate on the Declaration of War with Mexico

May 11, 1846

President James K. Polk was an expansionist president who sought to gain territory from Mexico and did not mind going to war to get it. Congress, likewise, had expansionist ambitions, even though some members complained that the reasons for going to war with Mexico were trumped up to make Mexico look like the aggressor. The origins of the war with Mexico can be traced to the struggle to annex Texas in 1836. By the 1840s the idea of "Manifest Destiny" had claimed the imagination of many Americans. This grandiose concept held that God had ordained the United States to expand its empire from sea to sea. Polk, an early champion of the annexation of Texas, used the idea of Manifest Destiny as his campaign theme in the presidential election of 1844. Texas became a state shortly after Polk was inaugurated in 1845.

Polk sent a letter to Congress outlining the situation with Mexico. It was read before Congress on May 11, 1846. The previous month Mexican troops had attacked U.S. soldiers under the command of General Zachary Taylor, after much provocation by the Americans. Once shots had been fired, Polk lost no time declaring that American blood had been shed on American soil—even though it was unclear exactly where the blood had been shed. Polk's assertion that a state of war existed between the United States and Mexico touched off a brief congressional debate focusing on the language of the statement and on the maintenance of constitutional balance regarding the right of Congress to declare war. Polk's message did not ask explicitly for a declaration of war. He asked for congressional support in funding the military and a call to enlist more volunteers in Texas. The tone of his message implied that a state of war existed. After listening to the president's message, the House took less than half an hour to approve Polk's request and pass a resolution that was the equivalent of a declaration of war, by an overwhelming majority of 173–14. The Senate likewise wasted no time approving the resolution the same day by a vote of 40–2.

Among those participating in the debate who were critical of Polk but who ended up voting for war anyway were John C. Calhoun (D-S.C.) in the Senate and Garrett Davis (Whig-Ky.) in the House. Calhoun said Polk's message that war existed was deceptive since only the legislative branch of government had the constitutional power to declare war. Davis pointed an accusing finger at Polk for instigating a confrontation and then placing the blame on Mexico.

The war with Mexico ended in 1848, after many military triumphs by the United States. As the war progressed, Congress became less reluctant to support Polk's conduct of the war. The war resulted in huge territorial gains for the United States, including California, New Mexico, Arizona, and parts of Colorado and Wyoming. It left Mexico shorn of half its territory. Despite some token payments for the land acquired, Mexico was devastated financially and politically. In the United States the acquisition of the new territory raised anew the specter of the expansion of slavery into the new territories. House member David Wilmot (D-Pa.) devised a proviso to keep slavery out of any land acquired in the war with Mexico (see document 64).

[SENATE DEBATE]

. . . .

Mr. CALHOUN then rose, and said: The question now submitted to us is one of the gravest character and the importance of the consequences which may result from it we cannot now determine. I do hope that this body will give to it that high, full, and dispassionate consideration which is worthy the character of the body and the high constitutional functions which it is called on to exercise. I trust that we will weigh everything calmly and deliberately, and do all that the Constitution, interests, and honor of the country may require. I hope that in the present state of the question nothing further will be done than is usual—that is, to print the document for the use of the Senate, and after we have had the subject under consideration, it will be time enough to determine the number of copies to be printed. I say this because no man can make up his opinion from the mere reading of the message, and the printing of an extra number may seem to be a committal of this body in favor of all which is contained in the message. It is eminently proper that, in this case, the deliberate sense of the body should be expressed. It is always understood that printing a large number of documents is an endorsement. At all events, I think it would be undignified in the Senate to print on this occasion more than the usual number.

Mr. SPEIGHT said, I rise to respond to every sentence—every word—which has been uttered by the honorable Senator from South Carolina. My motive in moving to print an extra number of copies of the message and accompanying documents was the suggestion of Senators around me. I had supposed that the country would be anxious to read those documents, and I cannot see why the printing of it should be necessarily considered as an endorsement of that message. But I take occasion to state here in my place that I endorse every word of that message. I approve of it. The President has recommended what I am prepared to carry out. It is useless to conceal the fact that he has recommended no declaration of war. He only asks Congress to place at his disposal a sufficient military force to repel any invasion of the territory of the United States.

I apprehend that there is not a single Senator who will not cordially respond to that portion of the message; and I am confident I only do justice to the Senator form South Caroline, [Mr. Calhoun,] when I say that none will more cordially respond to it than himself. If I apprehended that my motion was at all inconsistent with the dignity of the Senate, I need not say that I would at once withdraw it. Far be it from me to entertain any desire to precipitate the action of the body in this important affair. But the document will appear in the newspapers, and there will be a general anxiety in the country to read it; and I cannot see the impropriety of printing such a number of extra copies as will ensure the most extended circulation of the message. It is an important document, and we seem to have approached an important crisis, and I agreed with the Senator that we should meet it firmly, calmly, and with deliberation, For my part, I am prepared so to meet the crisis.

. . . .

Mr. ALLEN. . . . these are facts about which there can be no dispute; and if ever there was a case in which it becomes important to give an extended circulation to a great public fact, this is that case. What is it? The honorable Senator has told us that the President recommends no declaration of war; but he did not tell us what the President has told us, which is the far more important fact, that war actually exists, and he asks the Congress of the United States to acknowledge that fact by such a public act as shall nationalize the troops, and put the United States in that relation to the nations of the world which she has a right to assume, as growing out of a state of war. Sir, it has been said that time for deliberation is necessary; but the time of deliberation should be measured by the crises presented by the state of facts

upon which that deliberation is to be had; and what is the crises here! The crises is existing war. The deliberation can tend to no point, if it have a useful object, except the great point of the defence of the country against invasion. And as for the suggestion thrown out that the arm of the Government should be limited to its own soil—that we should be required to fight over one square of the board, while Mexico fights over the whole board—seems to me to involve a most suicidal policy. How can this war be brought to a successful issue? How can any permanent peace be expected to result from all this conflict with Mexico, unless she is given distinctly to understand that when she makes war upon the United States she incurs all the penalties which the condition of war inflicts upon nations? But I am sensible that this is digressive. I desire that these documents may be printed in large numbers, for the reasons that I have given; and for the sake of testing the sense of the Senate, I ask the yeas and nays.

. . . .

Mr. MOREHEAD said: I regret that I cannot concur with my friend from Delaware in his suggestion as to the proper direction which this document should take. I think that in the first instance the reference should be made to the Committee on Foreign Relations; and I do so because I concur with the Senator from South Carolina, [Mr. Calhoun,] that before war does exist, according to the Constitution of the United States, there must be some action on the part of Congress. Thus far, if war does now exist—if the people of the United States now find themselves in a state of war with Mexico, it is a war which has not been brought about or declared by the legislative department of the United States, to which constitutionally the power of declaring war belongs. It does, therefore, seem to me that before we can occupy a proper position in the estimation of the nations of the world—(whose opinion on subjects of this sort, I think, we dare not disregard, at all events it is our duty to pay respect to it)—before we assume a hostile position, which in all probability it will be our duty to assume—this subject ought to be referred to that committee which in all cases of this sort has charge of these subjects; that this ought to be done before the Congress of the United States shall recognise the existence of war, and perform that part assigned to them by the Constitution. It is with this view, and with regret, that I cannot concur with the Senator from Delaware, and I hope that the subject will take the usual direction.

Mr. J. M. CLAYTON. It is perfectly clear in my mind that this Message should go to the Committee on Military Affairs, and not to that on Foreign Relations. The President has announced to the Senate of the United States that there is war—that war does exist between this country and Mexico, and he calls upon us for millions of money to aid him in carrying on that war; he pronounces it necessary, and demands of us the needful supplies. He also asks for tens of thousands of volunteers. Now I am quite willing—although I so not take upon myself any portion of the responsibility of this war—that devolves upon the President and upon him alone, with those who have brought it about—but I say I am quite ready to fight it out. I will not undertake to decide, in the first instance, whether it was right or not; but I go for the soldiers and the millions at once, to support the honor of the country and army. The Committee on Foreign Relations can decide at their leisure any grave questions touching the constitutionality of this war. We shall have all that undoubtedly in debate here from day to day; but the first duty of the Senate, in my judgement, is to vote the supplies. Well, what has the Committee of Foreign Relations to do with that? What does it know about the manner of furnishing these supplies? That is the appropriate duty of the Committee of Military Affairs. I would say to my friend from South Carolina—if he will allow me to call him my friend—that I entertain opinions perhaps closely allied to his own on this general subject. I do not mean to express any opinion as to the sending of troops o the Rio Grande, by voting for the supplies. The President has announced the existence of war. What is the first duty of Congress? I hold that its first duty is to vote the supplies; to lose no time in defending the country. . . .

Mr. ARCHER proceeded. It has been stated, on the highest authority that the President of the United States cannot declare war. The intervention of Congress is absolutely indispensable to constitute war. What is the import of the message received this morning? A certain state of facts has reached the President, which has rendered it necessary for him, in the discharge of his duty, to inform Congress of the necessity of inquiring what action of Congress may be necessary, and whether there shall or shall not be war on the part of the United States, Does the existence of hostilities on one of the frontiers of the United States necessarily put us in a state of war with any foreign Power? Clearly not. Suppose we have misunderstood the state of things on the Rio Grande, and that the Mexican authorities have acted justifiably under the circumstances: the danger of admitting the doctrine that a state of war can exist except by the constitutional action of the Government of the United States will then be evident. There can be no question about that. There can be no war till the ascertained facts be submitted to the Congress of the United States, to be pronounced upon by them, and till they authorize war. That is the question. . . .

Mr. BENTON said: I apprehend that there are two very distinct questions presented to the consideration of the Senate in the message of the President. He announces the fact of the invasion of the territory of the United States, that's one thing.

He then proposes to Congress to carry on war against Mexico on a scale commensurate with the exigency of the occasion, in order to bring it to an immediate close. These are two distinct subjects; and on these two subjects a different form of action is, I think, required. It is not merely the constitutional authority, but the duty of the President to repel invasion at once, and by all the means which the law has put into his hands. He has a regular army and navy for that purpose. The act of Congress of 1795 authorized him to call out the militia from the neighboring States for that purpose; but their services is limited to a period of three months; and as often as emergencies of this kind have occurred, it has been deemed proper, both for the purpose of getting troops more promptly into action, and also, such as could be retained in the service for a longer period—it has, I say, been usual for Congress on all such occasions, when in session, and when not in session, it has been usual for the President to call for volunteers. . . .

[HOUSE DEBATE]

. . . .

Mr. GARRETT DAVIS. . . . Sir, if the bill contained any recitation upon that point in truth and justice, it should be that this war was begun by the President. The river Nueces is the true western boundary of Texas. The country between that stream and the Del Norte is part of Mexico; and that Power had people and establishments on it. Months ago the President, of his own will, orders General Taylor and his army to take post at Corpus Christi, on the west bank of the Nueces, where they remained until a considerable time after the beginning of this session of Congress. In March last, under the positive orders of the President, he moves through the disputed country upon Del Norte. The Mexican authorities meet him at several points with the declaration that he has invaded their country, and with protests against the aggression. They warn him that unless he retires east of the Nueces, he will be deemed to be making war upon Mexico, and they will resort to force. He refers to the positive orders of the Executive, and in the execution of them he presses on to Matamoras; strongly fortifies a position overlooking the city, and mounts a battery of cannon within three hundred yards of it, bearing upon its public square, and from whence he could, in a few hours, batter it down. He then blockades the port of Matamoras, orders off English and American vessels, and directs the capture of a Spanish schooner. The Mexican commander treats all these as acts of war; and, on the 25th of April, General Taylor is informed, by a messenger from the Mexican camp, that hostilities exist, that the Mexicans will prosecute them according to the usages of civilized nations. That night a detachment of the Mexican army crosses the Rio Grande, General Taylor sends out a scouting party to reconnoitre, which attacks the Mexicans, and is defeated and captured by the Mexicans, and thus war is raging in bloody earnestness. It is our own President who began the war. He has been carrying it on for months in a series of acts. Congress, which is vested exclusively by the Constitution with the war-making power, he has not deigned to consult, much less to ask it for authority. Now, forsooth, when it has unexpectedly broke forth in bloody reverses, a position must be taken by the friends of the President in Congress to protect him by charging Mexico with being the author of the war; and he, in cold blood, teaches others to sacrifice a brave and veteran officer, whenever it may become necessary to cover his mistakes and incompetency.

I have yet another objection to this bill. All that is proposed to be voted by this bill is to be trusted to him. He is to conduct this war. He is our Commander-in-Chief, our *Generalissimo* of army and navy. He knows, or ought to know, how much money and how many men the present exigency requires; and yet he has not named any sum or any number of troops, as has been invariably the usage in such cases by all former Presidents. He leaves us to act upon our information and judgement in the premises. Are we to understand that he abandons the responsibilities and duties as President and Commander-in-Chief in the conduct of this war? Does he intend to be understood by Congress as saying to them, (what must be now apparent to the whole nation,) "I am unequal to the high position which I now occupy. I know not how to advise you as to the amount of money and the number of men you must raise to rescue the military renown of the country from the passing cloud which now covers it. In this important matter you must assume my duties and my responsibilities, and adopt the necessary measures to vindicate the suffering honor of the nation?" If this be the position of the President, he has exhibited more good sense in assuming it than in all the acts of his Administration besides; if it be not, he exhibits his usual reprehensible secretiveness.

But, Mr. Speaker, the essence of this measure is the supplies. They will all be required before the nation gets out of this difficulty. I will vote for the supplies of the bill with a hearty alacrity, at the same time protesting against its falsehoods. Since the play has begun, I am for fighting Mexico on our soil, on hers, everywhere, until we drive her across the Rio Grande, and retrieve our ancient renown. I am then for withdrawing our army to the east side of the Nueces, and then settling by treaty all our points of dispute with that weak and distracted country upon the most liberal terms.

. . . .

Mr. BAYLY rose and said:

Mr. Speaker: I ask to be excused from voting. I cannot vote in silence, without placing myself in a false position. I consider this bill virtually a declaration of war, made without Executive recommendation; for I do not understand the message, from hearing it read, as recommending a declaration of war, and made, too, when we do not know that the invasion of our territory and the aggressive acts are sanctioned by the Mexican Government. They may yet be disavowed, and reparation made. I am unwilling, therefore, at this time, and under the circumstances, to vote for a declaration of war. I do not think such a declaration necessary to meet the emergency. On the other hand, I am anxious to vote such supplies of men and money as will afford succor to our army, and repel the invasion. I must, as I am now situated, decline to do this, or vote for the bill before the House, I shall vote for the bill, if not excused, as I can never withhold supplies, under the circumstances, as the greater evil. Mr. B. then withdrew his request to be excused.

The question, "Shall this bill pass?" was then taken, and decided as follows:

. . . .

So the bill was passed in the following form, viz [Declaration of War with Mexico]:

Whereas, by the act of the Republic of Mexico, a state of war exists between that Government and the United States:

Be it enacted by the Senate and House of Representatives of the United States of American in Congress assembled, That, for the purpose of enabling the Government of the United States to prosecute said war to a speedy and successful termination, the President be, and he is hereby, authorized to employ the militia, naval, and military forces of the United States, and to call for and accept the services of any number of volunteers, not exceeding fifty thousand, who may offer their services, either as cavalry, artillery, or riflemen, to serve twelve months after they shall have arrived at the place of rendezvous, or to the end of the war, unless sooner discharged; and that the sum of ten millions of dollars out of any moneys in the Treasury, or to come into the Treasury, not otherwise apportioned, for the purpose of carrying the provisions of this act into effect.

SEC. 2. *And be it further enacted,* That the militia, when called into the service of the United States by virtue of this act, or any other act, may, if in the opinion of the President of the United States the public interest requires it, be compelled to serve for a term not exceeding six months, after their arrival at the place of rendezvous, in any one year, unless sooner discharged.

SEC. 3. *And it be further enacted,* That the said volunteers shall furnish their own clothes, and if cavalry, their own horses; and when mustered into service shall be armed and equipped at the expense of the United States.

SEC. 4. *And be it further enacted,* That said volunteers shall, when called into actual service, and while remaining therein, be subject to the rules and articles of war, and shall be in all respects, except as to clothing and pay, placed on the same footing with similar corps of the United States Army; and in lieu of clothing every non-commissioned officer and private, in any company, who may this offer himself, shall be entitled, when called into actual service, to receive in money a sum equal to the cost of clothing of a non-commissioned officer or private (as the case may be) in the regular troops of the United States. . . .

Congressional Globe, 29th Congress, 1st session, May 11, 1846, 782–795.

64 Representative David Wilmot Defends His Proviso

February 8, 1847

The Wilmot Proviso was an amendment to an appropriations bill in 1846 that never passed through Congress and never became law. Yet it was an important landmark in the growing debate over slavery, which would eventually lead to the Civil War. David Wilmot (D-Pa.), a thirty-two-year-old House member serving his *first term, feared that an appropriation bill requested by President James K. Polk, ostensibly to promote peace with Mexico, would be used to acquire more territory from Mexico and foster the expansion of slavery. His amendment stated that in any land acquired from Mexico "neither slavery nor involuntary servitude shall exist in any part of the territory, except for crime, where of the party shall first be duly convicted." Wilmot argued that he was not trying to abolish slavery but to prevent its extension into free territory.*

The proviso passed the House with support from northerners opposed to slavery. It ran into stiff opposition from southerners in the Senate and failed to pass that body. Wilmot tried several times to attach his proviso to other House bills, but all failed. One of the supporters of the proviso was a first-term member in the House, Abraham Lincoln, who claimed he voted for the principle of the proviso forty-two times during his one term in the House of Representatives from 1847 to 1849. In the presidential election of 1848 the Wilmot Proviso was rejected by both Whigs and Democrats, leading to the creation of a third party, the Free Soil Party, a precursor to the Republican Party. Wilmot became a leader in the creation of the Republican Party and later served briefly in the U.S. Senate. He became active in trying to stem the tide of civil war and in 1863 was appointed by President Lincoln as a judge of the U.S. Claims Court, where he served until his death in 1868.

Sir, it will be recollected by all present, that, at the last session of Congress, an amendment was moved by me to a bill of the same character as this, in the form of a proviso, by which slavery should be excluded from any territory that might subsequently be acquired by the United States from the republic of Mexico.

Sir, on that occasion, that proviso was sustained by a very decided majority of this House. Nay, sir, more it was sustained, if I mistake not, by a majority of the Republican party on this floor. I am prepared I think, to show that the entire South were then willing to acquiesce in what appeared to be, and, in so far as the action of this House was concerned, what was the legislative will and declaration of the Union on this subject. It passed this House. Sir, there were no threats of disunion sounded in our ears. It passed here and went to the Senate, and it was the judgment of the public, and of men well informed, that, had it not been defeated there for want of time, it would have passer that body and become the established law of the land. . . .

. . . There was then no cry that the Union was to be severed in con sequence. The South, like brave men defeated, bowed to the voice and judgment of the nation. No, sir, no cry of disunion then. Why now? The hesitation and the wavering of northern men on this question has encouraged the South to assume a bolder attitude. This cry of disunion proceeds from no resolve of the South. It comes, sir, from the cowardice of the North. . . .

But, sir, the issue now presented is not whether slavery shall exist unmolested where it now is, but whether it shall be carried to new and distant regions, now free, where the footprint of a slave cannot be found. This, sir, is the issue. Upon it I take my stand, and from it I cannot be frightened or driven by idle charges of abolitionism. I ask not that slavery be abolished. I demand that this Government preserve the integrity of free territory against the aggressions of slavery—against its wrongful usurpations. Sir, I was in favor of the annexation of Texas. . . . The Democracy of the North, almost to a man, went for annexation sir, here was an empire larger than France given up to slavery. Shall further concessions be made by the North? Shall we give up free territory, the inheritance of free labor?

Must we yield this also? Never, sir, never, until we ourselves are fit to be slaves. The North may be betrayed by her Representatives, but upon this great question she will be true to herself—true to posterity. Defeat! Sir, there can be no defeat. Defeat to-day will but arouse the teeming millions of the North, and lead to a more decisive and triumphant victory to-morrow.

But, sir, we are told, that the joint blood and treasure of the whole country being expended in this acquisition, therefore it should be divided, and slavery Now, sir, we are told that California is ours; that New Mexico is ours—won by the valor of our arms. They are free. Shall they remain free? Shall these fair provinces be the inheritance and homes of the white labor of freemen or the black labor of slaves? This, sir, is the issue this the question. The North has the right, and her representatives here have the power. . . . But the South contend, that in their emigration to this free territory, they have the right to take and hold slaves, the same as other property. Unless the amendment I have offered be adopted, or other early legislation is had upon this subject, they will do so. Indeed, they unitedly, as one man, have declared their right and purpose so to do, and the work has already begun. Slavery follows in the rear of our armies. Shall the war power of our Government be exerted to produce such a result? Shall this Government depart from its neutrality on this question, and lend its power and influence to plant slavery in these territories? There is no question of abolition here, sir. Shall the South be permitted, by aggression, by invasion of the right, by subduing free territory, and planting slavery upon it, to wrest these provinces from northern freemen, and turn them to the accomplishment of their own sectional purposes and schemes? This is the question. Men of the North answer. Shall it be so? Shall we of the North submit to it? If we do, we are coward slaves, and deserve to have the manacles fastened upon our own limbs.

Appendix to the Congressional Globe, 29th Congress, 2d session, Feb. 8, 1847, 3–15.

65 Senator Daniel Webster on the Constitution and the Union

March 7, 1850

Nearing the end of a long and distinguished career as a nationally known lawyer, a member of both the House and Senate, and secretary of state (1841–1843), Daniel Webster would resign from the Senate in July 1850 to again assume the role of secretary of state in the administration of his friend Millard Fillmore. In this speech, one of Webster's greatest (see also document 56), he entered into one last round of debate with the two other giants of the Senate, Henry Clay and John C. Calhoun. These three were often called the "Great Triumvirate" for their dominance of the Senate during its golden age of oratory. A month earlier Henry Clay had delivered a two-day long defense of the Compromise of 1850, which led to a response from John C. Calhoun. Calhoun was too ill to deliver his remarks himself and had to sit silently while another senator, James Mason, read his speech. Calhoun urged the Senate not to forsake the South and its institutions (including slavery) to the interests of the industrial North.

In his reply to Calhoun, Webster sought to appeal to southern moderates and took the position that slavery was not a moral issue with him. He was willing to tolerate it where it traditionally existed in the South, but he was opposed to its spread to new territories and states. His attempt to attract southerners to his argument backfired in the North, where abolitionists, who wanted no compromise on slavery, claimed that Webster had betrayed their cause. Supporters of Calhoun also found no comfort in the speech. But the speech did appeal to moderates in both the North and South and received much acclaim mixed in with the criticism from both sides of the issue.

Webster carefully edited the speech and saw to it that it was reprinted and distributed widely throughout the country as a pamphlet. It was a central part of the public debate on the Compromise of 1850 and the question of the preservation of the Union. In his farewell to the Senate four months later, Webster again urged the Senate to find a way to compromise to hold the Union together.

With Calhoun's death just three weeks after the "7th of March" speech (see document 66) and the death of Henry Clay and Webster in 1852, the Great Triumvirate was gone. While the Senate would produce many great leaders and skilled debaters in the future, few would ever match the drama or the power of these three men. The best accounts of the careers of Clay, Calhoun, and Webster can be found in Robert V. Remini's biographies—Henry Clay: Statesman for the Union (New York: W. W. Norton, 1991) and Daniel Webster: The Man and His Time (New York: W. W. Norton, 1997)—and Merrill D. Peterson's book, The Great Triumvirate: Webster, Clay, and Calhoun (New York: Oxford University Press, 1987).

Mr. President, I wish to speak today, not as a Massachusetts man, nor as a northern man, but as an American, and a member of the Senate of the United States. It is fortunate that there is a Senate of the United States; a body not yet moved from its propriety, not lost to a just sense of its own dignity, and its own high responsibilities, and a body to which the country looks with confidence, for wise, moderate, patriotic, and healing counsels. It is not to be denied that we live in the midst of strong agitations, and are surrounded by very considerable dangers to our institutions of government. The imprisoned winds are let loose. The East, the West, the North, and the stormy South, all combine to throw the whole sea into commotion, to toss its billows to the skies, and to disclose its profoundest depths. I do not affect to regard myself, Mr. President, as holding, or as fit to hold, the helm in this combat with the political elements; but I have a duty to perform, and I mean to perform it with fidelity—not without a sense of surrounding dangers, but not without hope. I have a part to act, not for my own security or safety, for I am looking out for no fragment upon which to float away from the wreck, if wreck there must be, but for the good of the whole, and the preservation of the whole; and there is that which will keep me to my duty during this struggle, whether the sun and the stars shall appear, or shall not appear, for many days. I speak today for the preservation of the Union. "Hear me for my cause." I speak today, out of a solicitous and anxious heart, for the restoration to the country of that quiet and that harmony which make the blessings of this Union so rich and so dear to us all. These are the topics that I propose to myself to discuss; these are the motives, and the sole motives, that influence me in the wish to communicate my opinions to the Senate and the country; and if I can do anything, however little, for the promotion of these ends, I shall have accomplished all that I desire.

Mr. President, it may not be amiss to recur very briefly to the events which, equally sudden and extraordinary, have brought the political condition of the country to what it now is. In May, 1846, the United States declared war against Mexico. Her armies, then on the frontiers, entered the provinces of that republic, met and defeated all her troops, penetrated her mountain passes, and occupied her capital. The marine force of the United States took possession of her forts and her towns on the Atlantic and on the Pacific. In less than two years a treaty was negotiated, by which Mexico ceded to the United States a vast territory, extending seven or eight hundred miles along the shores of the Pacific, and reaching back over the mountains, and across the desert, until it joined the frontier of the state of Texas. It so happened, that, in the distracted and feeble state of the Mexican government, before the declaration of war by the United States against Mexico had become known in California, the people of California, under the lead of American officers, overthrew the existing provincial government of California, the Mexican authorities, and run up an independent flag. When the news arrived at San Francisco, that war had been declared by the United States against Mexico, this independent flag was pulled down, and the stars and stripes of this Union hoisted in its stead. So, sir, before the war was over, the powers of the United States, military and naval, had possession of San Francisco and upper California, and a great rush of emigrants, from various parts of the world, took place into California, in 1846 and 1847. But now, behold another wonder.

In January of 1848, the Mormons, it is said, or some of them, made a discovery of an extraordinarily rich mine of gold; or, rather, of a very great quantity of gold, hardly fit to be called a mine, for it was spread near the surface—on the lower part of the south or American branch of the Sacramento. They seem to have attempted to conceal their discovery for some time; but soon another discovery, perhaps of greater importance, was made, of gold in another part of the American branch of the Sacramento, and near Sutter's Fort, as it is called. The fame of these discoveries spread far and wide. They excited more and more the spirit of emigration toward California, which had already been excited; and persons crowded in hundreds, and flocked toward the Bay of San Francisco. This, as I have said, took place in the winter and spring of 1848. The digging commenced in the spring of that year; and from that time to this, the work of searching for gold has been prosecuted with a success not heretofore known in the history of this globe. We all know, sir, how incredulous the American public was at the accounts which reached us at first of these discoveries; but we all know now that these accounts received, and continue to receive, daily confirmation; and down to the present moment, I suppose the assurances are as strong, after the experience of these several months, of mines of gold apparently inexhaustible in the regions near San Francisco, in California, as they were at any period of the earlier dates of the accounts. It so happened, sir, that although in the time of peace it became a very important subject for legislative consideration and legislative decision, to provide a proper territorial government for California, yet, differences of opinion in the councils of the government prevented the establishment of any such territorial government for California, at the last session of Congress. Under this state of things, the inhabitants of San Francisco and California—then amounting to a great number of people—in the summer of last year, thought it to be their duty, to establish a local government. Under the proclamation of General Riley, the people chose delegates to a convention. That convention met at Monterey. They formed a constitution for the state of California, and it was adopted by the people of California in their primary assemblages. Desirous of immediate connection with the United States, its senators were appointed and representatives chosen, who have come hither, bringing with them the authentic constitution of the state of California; and they now present themselves, asking in behalf of their state, that the state may be admitted into this Union as one of the United States. This constitution, sir, contains an express prohibition against slavery, or involuntary servitude, in the state of California. It is said, and I suppose truly, that of the members who composed that convention, some sixteen were natives, and had been residents of, the slaveholding states, and about twenty-two were from the nonslaveholding states, and the remaining

ten members were either native Californians, or old settlers in that country. This prohibition against slavery, it is said was inserted with entire unanimity.

. . . .

And it is this circumstance, sir, the prohibition of slavery by that convention, which has contributed to raise—I do not say it has wholly raised—the dispute as to the propriety of the admission of California into the Union under this constitution. It is not to be denied, Mr. President—nobody thinks of denying—that, whatever reasons were assigned at the commencement of the late war with Mexico, it was prosecuted for the purpose of the acquisition of territory, and under the alleged argument that the cession of territory was the only form in which proper compensation could be made to the United States, by Mexico, for the various claims and demands which the people of this country had against that government. At any rate, it will be found that President Polk's message at the commencement of the session of December, 1847, avowed, that the war was to be prosecuted until some acquisition of territory was made. And, as the acquisition was to be south of the line of the United States, in warm climates and countries, it was naturally, I suppose, expected by the South, that whatever acquisitions were made in that region would be added to the slaveholding portion of the United States. Events have turned out as was not expected, and that expectation has not been realized; and therefore some degree of disappointment and surprise has resulted, of course. In other words, it is obvious that the question which has so long harassed the country, and at times very seriously alarmed the minds of wise and good men, has come upon us for a fresh discussion—the question of slavery in these United States.

. . . .

Now, sir, upon the general nature, and character, and influence of slavery there exists a wide difference between the northern portion of this country and the southern. It is said, on the one side, that if not the subject of any injunction or direct prohibition in the New Testament, slavery is a wrong; that it is founded merely in the right of the strongest; and that it is an oppression, like unjust wars—like all those conflicts by which a mighty nation subjects a weaker nation to their will; and that slavery, in its nature, whatever may be said of it in the modifications which have taken place, is not in fact according to the meek spirit of the Gospel. It is not kindly affectioned; it does not "seek another's, and not its own." It does not "let the oppressed go free." These are sentiments that are cherished, and recently with greatly augmented force, among the people of the northern states. It has taken hold of the religious sentiment of that part of the country, as it has more or less taken hold of the religious feelings of a considerable portion of mankind. The South, upon the other side, having been accustomed to this relation between the two races all their lives, from their birth; having been taught, in general, to treat the subjects of this bondage with care and kindness—and I believe, in general, feeling for them great care and kindness—have yet not taken this view of the subject which I have mentioned. There are thousands of religious men, with consciences as tender as any of their brethren at the North, who do not see the unlawfulness of slavery; and there are more thousands, perhaps, that, whatsoever they may think of it in its origin, and as a matter depending upon natural right, yet take things as they are, and, finding slavery to be an established relation of the society in which they live, can see no way in which—let their opinions on the abstract question be what they may—it is in the power of the present generation to relieve themselves from this relation. And, in this respect, candor obliges me to say, that I believe they are just as conscientious, many of them—and of the religious people, all of them—as they are in the North, in holding different opinions.

. . . .

There are men, who, in times of that sort, and disputes of that sort, are of opinion, that human duties may be ascertained with the exactness of mathematics. They deal with morals as with mathematics, and they think what is right, may be distinguished from what is wrong, with the precision of an algebraic equation. They have, therefore, none too much charity toward others who differ with them. They are apt, too, to think that nothing is good but what is perfect, and that there are no compromises or modifications to be made in submission to difference of opinion, or in deference to other men's judgment. If their perspicacious vision enables them to detect a spot on the face of the sun, they think that a good reason why the sun should be struck down from heaven. They prefer the chance of running into utter darkness, to living in heavenly light, if that heavenly light be not absolutely without any imperfection. There are impatient men—too impatient always to give heed to the admonition of St. Paul, "that we are not to do evil that good may come"—too impatient to wait for the slow progress of moral causes in the improvement of mankind. They do not remember, that the doctrines and the miracles of Jesus Christ have, in eighteen hundred years, converted only a small portion of the human race; and among the nations that are converted to Christianity, they forget how many vices and crimes, public and private, still prevail, and that many of them—public crimes especially, which are offences against the Christian religion—pass without exciting particular regret or indignation. Thus wars are waged, and unjust wars. I do not deny that there may be just wars. There certainly are; but it was the remark of an eminent person, not many years ago, on the other side of the Atlantic, that it was one of the greatest reproaches to human nature, that wars were sometimes necessary. The defense of nations sometimes causes a war against the injustice of other nations.

Now, sir, in this state of sentiment, upon the general nature of slavery, lies the cause of a great portion of those unhappy divisions, exasperations, and reproaches which find vent and support in different parts of the Union. Slavery does exist in the United States. It did exist in the states before the adoption of this Constitution, and at that time.

. . . .

On other occasions, in debates here, I have expressed my determination to vote for no acquisition, or cession, or annexation, north or south, east or west. My opinion has been, that we have territory enough, and that we should follow the Spartan maxim, "Improve, adorn what you have, seek no farther." I think that it was in some observations that I made here on the three-million loan bill, that I avowed this sentiment. In short, sir, the sentiment has been avowed quite as often, in as many places, and before as many assemblages, as any humble sentiments of mine ought to be avowed.

But now that, under certain conditions, Texas is in, with all her territories, as a slave state, with a solemn pledge that if she is divided into many states, those states may come in as slave states south of 36° 30', how are we to deal with this subject? I know no way of honorable legislation, when the proper time comes for the enactment, but to carry into effect all that we have stipulated to do. I do not entirely agree with my honorable friend from Tennessee [Mr. Bell], that, as soon as the time comes when she is entitled to another representative, we should create a new state. The rule in regard to it I take to be this: that, when we have created new states out of territories, we have generally gone upon the idea, that when there is population enough to form a state—sixty thousand, or some such thing—we would create a state; but it is quite a different thing when a state is divided, and two or more states made out of it. It does not follow, in such a case, that the same rule of apportionment should be applied. That, however, is a matter for the consideration and discretion of Congress, when the proper time arrives. I may not then be here—I may have no vote to give on the occasion; but I wish it to be distinctly understood, today, that according to my view of the matter, this government is solemnly pledged, by law and contract, to create new states out of Texas, with her consent, when her population shall justify such a proceeding, and so far as such states are formed out of Texan territory lying south of 36°30', to let them come in as slave states. The time of admission, and requisite population, must depend, of course, on the discretion of Congress. But when new states shall be formed out of Texas, they have a fixed right to come into the Union as slave states. That is the meaning of the resolution which our friends, the northern Democracy, have left us to fulfill; and I, for one, mean to fulfill it, because I will not violate the faith of the government.

Now, as to California and New Mexico, I hold slavery to be excluded from those territories by a law even superior to that which admits and sanctions it in Texas—I mean the law of nature—of physical geography—the law of the formation of the earth. That law settles forever, with a strength beyond all terms of human enactment, that slavery cannot exist in California or New Mexico. Understand me, sir—I mean slavery as we regard it; slaves in gross, of the colored race, transferable by sale and delivery, like other property. I shall not discuss the point, but leave it to the learned gentlemen who have undertaken to discuss it;

but I suppose there is no slave of that description in California now. I understand that *peonism,* a sort of penal servitude, exists there; or, rather, a voluntary sale of a man and his offspring for debt, as it is arranged and exists in some parts of California and New Mexico. But what I mean to say is, that African slavery, as we see it among us, is as utterly impossible to find itself, or to be found in Mexico, as any other natural impossibility.

. . . .

Now, Mr. President, I have established, so far as I proposed to go into any line of observation to establish, the proposition with which I set out, and upon which I propose to stand or fall; and that is, that the whole territory of the states in the United States, or in the newly acquired territory of the United States, has a fixed and settled character, now fixed and settled by law, which cannot be repealed in the case of Texas without a violation of public faith, and cannot be repealed by any human power in regard to California or New Mexico; that, under one or other of these laws, every foot of territory in the states, or in the territories, has now received a fixed and decided character.

Sir, if we were now making a government for New Mexico, and anybody should propose a Wilmot Proviso, I should treat it exactly as Mr. Polk treated that provision for excluding slavery from Oregon. Mr. Polk was known to be in opinion decidedly averse to the Wilmot Proviso; but he felt the necessity of establishing a government for the territory of Oregon, and, though the proviso was there, but he knew it would be entirely nugatory; and, since it must be entirely nugatory, since it took away no right, no describable, no estimable, no weighable, or tangible, right of the South, he said he would sign the bill for the sake of enacting a law to form a government in that territory, and let that entirely useless, and, in that connection, entirely senseless, proviso remain. For myself, I will say that we hear much of the annexation of Canada; and if there be any man, any of the northern Democracy, or any one of the Free Soil party, who supposes it necessary to insert a Wilmot Proviso in a territorial government of New Mexico, that man will of course be of opinion that it is necessary to protect the everlasting snows of Canada from the foot of slavery, by the same overpowering wing of an act of Congress. Sir, wherever there is a particular good to be done, wherever there is a foot of land to be staid back from becoming slave territory—I am ready to assert the principle of the exclusion of slavery. I am pledged to it from the year 1837; I have been pledged to it again and again; and I will perform those pledges; but I will not do a thing unnecessary, that wounds the feelings of others, or that does disgrace to my own understanding.

. . . .

Mr. President, I should much prefer to have heard, from every member on this floor, declarations of opinion that this Union could never be dissolved, than the declaration of opinion that in any case, under the pressure of any circumstances, such a dissolution was possible. I hear with pain and anguish, and dis-

tress, the word secession, especially when it falls from the lips of those who are eminently patriotic, and known to the country, and known all over the world, for their political services. Secession! Peaceable secession! Sir, your eyes and mine are never destined to see that miracle. The dismemberment of this vast country without convulsion! The breaking up of the fountains of the great deep without ruffling the surface! Who is so foolish—I beg everybody's pardon—as to expect to see any such thing? Sir, he who sees these states, now revolving in harmony around a common centre, and expects to see them quit their places and fly off without convulsion, may look the next hour to see the heavenly bodies rush from their spheres, and jostle against each other in the realms of space, without producing the crush of the universe. There can be no such thing as a peaceable secession. Peaceable secession is an utter impossibility. Is the great Constitution under which we live here—covering this whole country—is it to be thawed and melted away by secession, as the snows on the mountain melt under the influence of a vernal sun—disappear almost unobserved, and die off? No, sir! no, sir! I will not state what might produce the disruption of the states; but, sir, I see as plainly as I see the sun in heaven—I see that disruption must produce such a war as I will not describe, in its twofold character.

Peaceable secession! peaceable secession! The concurrent agreement of all the members of this great republic to separate! A voluntary separation, with alimony on one side and on the other. Why, what would be the result? Where is the line to be drawn? What states are to secede? What is to remain American? What am I to be—an American no longer? Where is the flag of the Republic to remain? Where is the eagle still to tower? or is he to cower, and shrink, and fall to the ground? Why, sir, our ancestors—our fathers and our grandfathers, those of them that are yet living among us with prolonged lives—would rebuke and reproach us; and our children, and our grandchildren, would cry out, Shame upon us! if we, of this generation, should dishonor these ensigns of the power of the government, and the harmony of the Union, which is every day felt among us with so much joy and gratitude. What is to become of the army? What is to become of the navy? What is to become of the public lands? How is each of the thirty states to defend itself? I know, although the idea has not been stated distinctly, there is to be, a southern confederacy. I do not mean, when I allude to this statement, that anyone seriously contemplates such a state of things. I do not mean to say that it is true, but I have heard it suggested elsewhere, that that idea has originated in a design to separate. I am sorry, sir, that it has ever been thought of, talked of, or dreamed of, in the wildest flights of human imagination. But the idea must be of a separation, including the slave states upon one side, and the free states on the other. Sir, there is not—I may express myself too strongly, perhaps—but some things, some moral things are almost as impossible as other natural or physical things; and I hold the idea of a separation of these states—those that are free to form one government, and those that are slaveholding to form another—as a moral impossibility. We could not separate the states by any such line, if we were to draw it. We could not sit down here today, and draw a line of separation, that would satisfy any five men in the country. There are natural causes that would keep and tie us together, and there are social and domestic relations which we could not break, if we would, and which we should not, if we could. Sir, nobody can look over the face of this country at the present moment—nobody can see where its population is the most dense and growing—without being ready to admit, and compelled to admit, that, ere long, the strength of America will be in the valley of the Mississippi.

Well, now, sir, I beg to inquire what the wildest enthusiast has to say, on the possibility of cutting off that river, and leaving free states at its source and its branches, and slave states down near its mouth? Pray, sir, pray, sir, let me say to the people of this country, that these things are worthy of their pondering and of their consideration. Here, sir, are five millions of freemen in the free states north of the river Ohio: can anybody suppose that this population can be severed by a line that divides them from the territory of a foreign and an alien government, down somewhere, the Lord knows where, upon the lower banks of the Mississippi? What will become of Missouri? Will she join the *arrondissement* of the slave states? Shall the man from the Yellowstone and the Platte be connected in the new republic with the man who lives on the southern extremity of the cape of Florida? Sir, I am ashamed to pursue this line of remark. I dislike it—I have an utter disgust for it. I would rather hear of natural blasts and mildews, war, pestilence, and famine, than to hear gentlemen talk of secession. To break up! To break up this great government! to dismember this great country! to astonish Europe with an act of folly, such as Europe for two centuries has never beheld in any government! No, sir! no, sir! There will be no secession. Gentlemen are not serious when they talk of secession.

. . . .

And now, Mr. President, instead of speaking of the possibility or utility of secession, instead of dwelling in these caverns of darkness, instead of groping with those ideas so full of all that is horrid and horrible, let us come out into the light of day; let us enjoy the fresh air of liberty and Union; let us cherish those hopes which belong to us; let us devote ourselves to those great objects that are fit for our consideration and our action; let us raise our conceptions to the magnitude and the importance of the duties that devolve upon us; let our comprehension be as broad as the country for which we act, our aspirations as high as its certain destiny; let us not be pigmies in a case that calls for men. Never did there devolve, on any generation of men, higher trusts than now devolve upon us for the preservation of this Constitution, and the harmony and peace of all who are destined to live under it. Let us make our generation one of the strongest, and the brightest link, in that golden chain which is destined, I fully believe, to grapple the people of all the states to this Constitution for ages to come. It is a great popular constitutional government, guarded by legislation, by law, and by judicature, and defended by the whole affections of the people. No monarchical throne presses these states together; no iron chain of despotic power encircles them; they live and stand upon a government popular in its form, representative in its character, founded upon principles of equality, and calculated, we hope, as to last forever. In all its history, it has been beneficent; it has trodden down no man's liberty; it has crushed no state. Its daily respiration is liberty and patriotism; its yet youthful veins are full of enterprise, courage, and honorable love of glory and renown. Large before, the country has now, by recent events, become vastly larger. This Republic now extends, with a vast breadth, across the whole continent. The two great seas of the world wash the one and the other shore. We realize on a mighty scale, the beautiful description of the ornamental edging of the buckler of Achilles—

Now, the broad shield complete the artist crowned,
With his last hand, and poured the ocean round;
In living silver seemed the waves to roll,
And beat the buckler's verge, and bound the whole.

Congressional Globe, 31st Congress, 1st session, appendix, March 7, 1850, 269–276. This is Webster's revised version of the speech. For the full text, see also Robert C. Byrd, *The Senate, 1789–1989*, 4 vols. (Washington, D.C.: Government Printing Office), vol. 3: 267–289.

66   Senator Henry Clay on the Death of John C. Calhoun

April 1, 1850

The custom of memorializing members upon their death has long been part of congressional oratory. In this speech Henry Clay remembers his friend and colleague John C. Calhoun. These two giants of the Senate had spent almost four decades together serving the federal government, beginning their political careers in the House of Representatives. Along with Daniel Webster, these three men were reputed to be the most eloquent speakers and the greatest political theorists of their age and were referred to as the "Great

Triumvirate." Calhoun's death marked the beginning of the end of an era, with Clay and Webster both dying two years later.

Clay and Calhoun had worked side by side as "War Hawks," in support of the War of 1812, and together drafted the compromise tariff that resolved the nullification crisis during Andrew Jackson's presidency. At the time of Calhoun's death the Senate was in the middle of yet another constitutional crisis, one that pitted Clay and Calhoun against each other. Calhoun's death cleared the way for Clay's last great effort, the Compromise of 1850, to which Calhoun had been the most vocal opponent, even though he was too ill to deliver his own speeches. Whether acting in accord or finding themselves on opposite ends of a political battle, it is clear the two men had great respect for one another. Biographer Robert Remini in Henry Clay: Statesman for the Union *(New York: W. W. Norton, 1991) provides a quotation of Calhoun's opinion of Clay, which may be apocryphal, but nonetheless true in sentiment: "I don't like Clay. He is a bad man, an imposter, a creator of wicked schemes. I wouldn't speak to him, but by God! I love him."*

Mr. CLAY. Mr. President, prompted by my own feelings of profound regret, and requested at the same time by some highly esteemed friends, I wish, in rising to second the resolutions which have been offered, and which have just been read, to add a few words to what has so well and so justly said by the surviving colleague of the illustrious deceased.

My personal acquaintance with him, Mr. President, commenced upwards of thirty-eight years ago. We entered at the same time, together, the House of Representatives at the other end of the building. The Congress of which we thus became members was that amongst whose deliberations and acts was the declaration of war against the most powerful nation, as it respects us, in the world. During the preliminary discussions that arose in the preparation for that great event, as well as during those that took place when the resolution was finally adopted, no member displayed a more lively and patriotic sensibility to the wrongs which led to that momentous event than the deceased whose death we now all so much deplore. Ever active, ardent, able, no one was in advance of him in advocating the cause of his country, and denouncing the foreign injustice which compelled us to appeal to arms. Of all Congresses with which I have had any acquaintance since my entry into the service of the Federal Government, in none, in my humble opinion, has been assembled such a galaxy of eminent and able men as were in the House of Representatives of that Congress which declared the war, and in that immediately following the peace; and amongst that splendid assemblage none shone more bright and brilliant than the star which is now set.

It was my happiness, sir, during a large part of the life of the departed, to concur with him on all great questions of national policy. And, at a later period, when it was my fortune to differ from him as to measures of domestic policy, I had the happiness to agree with him generally as to those which concerned our foreign relations, and especially as to the preservation of the peace of the country. During the long session at which the war was declared, we were messmates, as were other distinguished members of Congress from his own patriotic State. I was afforded, by the intercourse which resulted from that fact, as well as the subsequent intimacy and intercourse which arose between us, an opportunity to form an estimate, not merely of his public, but of his private life; and no man with whom I have ever been acquainted, exceeded him in habits of temperance and regularity, and in all the freedom, frankness, and affability of social intercourse, and in all the tenderness and respect and

affection which he manifested towards that lady who now mourns more than any other, the sad event that has just occurred. Such, Mr. President, was the high estimate I formed of his transcendent talents, that, if at the end of his service in the executive department under Mr. Monroe's administration, he had been called to the highest office in the Government, I should have felt perfectly assured that under his auspices, the honor, the prosperity, and the glory of our country would have been safely placed.

Sir, he is gone! No more shall we witness form yonder seat the flashes of that keen and penetrating eye of his, darting through this chamber. No more shall we behold that torrent of clear, concise, compact logic, poured out from his lips, which, if it did not always carry conviction to our judgement, commanded our great admiration. Those eyes and those lips are closed forever!

And when, Mr. President, will that great vacancy which has been created by the event we are now alluding, when will it be filled by an equal amount of ability, patriotism, and devotion, to what he conceived to be the best interests of his country?

Sir, this is not the appropriate occasion, nor would I be the appropriate person to attempt a delineation of his character, or the powers of his enlightened mind. I will only say, in a few words, that he possessed an elevated genius of the highest order; that in felicity of generalization of the subjects of which his mind treated, I have seen him surpassed by no one; and the charm and captivating influence of his colloquial powers have been felt by all who have conversed with him. I was his senior, Mr. President, in years—in nothing else. According to the course of nature, I ought to have proceeded him. It has been decreed otherwise; but I know that I shall linger here only a short time and shall soon follow him.

And how brief, how short is the period of human existence allotted even to the youngest amongst us! Sir, ought we not to profit by the contemplation of this melancholy occasion? Ought we not to draw from it the conclusion how unwise it is to indulge in the acerbity of unbridled debate? How unwise to yield ourselves to the sway of the animosities of party feeling? how wrong it is to indulge in those unhappy and hot strifes which too often exasperate our feelings and mislead our judgements in the discharge of the high and responsible duties we are called to perform? How unbecoming, if not presumptuous, it is in us, who are the tenants of an hour in this earthly abode, to wrestle and struggle together with a violence which would not be justifiable if it were our perpetual home!

In conclusion, sir, while I beg leave to express my cordial sympathies and sentiments of the deepest condolence to all who stand in near relation to him, I trust we shall all be instructed by the eminent virtues and merits of his exalted character, and be taught, by his bright example, to fulfill our great public duties by the lights of our own judgement and the dictates of our own consciences, as he did, according to his honest and best conceptions of those duties, faithfully, and to the last.

Congressional Globe, 31st Congress, 1st session, April 1, 1850, 624–625.

67   Senator Thomas Hart Benton Opposes the Compromise of 1850

June 10, 1850

Senator Thomas Hart Benton (D-Mo.) went against the grain when he opposed the Compromise of 1850 and assailed Henry Clay for an omnibus bill that Benton considered unnecessary and harmful to the nation. Benton's own state of Missouri had been the product of earlier compromises on the issue of slavery in 1819 and 1820. In 1850, nearing the end of a thirty-year career in the Senate, the large and magisterial Benton knew that he was standing not just against Henry Clay, but against his own constituents in Missouri who were in favor of the compromise. When John Kennedy wrote Profiles in Courage, *he praised Benton for his willingness to sacrifice his own political career for what he saw as the good of the country.*

Benton's career symbolized the torment the issue of slavery caused the nation. Benton himself was a slaveholder who brought slaves with him to Washington, D.C., as servants. Yet he opposed the extension of slavery into the new territories acquired by an expanding nation. He blamed both the abolitionists and the slaveholders for the rising discord in the nation.

Less than two months before this speech Benton was ridiculed on the floor of the Senate by Mississippi senator Henry Foote, who accused Benton of being old and cowardly and taunted him on his impending defeat in the upcoming election. The verbal fireworks between the two men escalated to the point that on April 17, 1850, the sixty-eight-year-old Benton approached Foote as if to assault him. Benton was restrained and turned away only to have Foote draw a pistol on him. Benton threw open his coat to show that he was not carrying a weapon and shouted: "I have no pistol! Let him fire! Let the assassin fire!" Foote did not fire but the Senate and the nation was shocked at such behavior in the Senate chamber. A Senate committee considered censuring both Foote and Benton but took no action. The war of words between the two men continued for the rest of the session, symbolic of the rapidly escalating political tensions on the issue of slavery.

Benton was defeated for reelection to the Senate in 1850 but was elected to the House of Representatives two years later, where he served a term before being defeated for reelection to the House and losing a bid to become governor of Missouri. He retired from politics and wrote a two-volume memoir of his thirty years in government. Benton died in 1858.

I make the motion which supersedes all other motions, and which, itself, can only be superseded by a motion still more stringent—the motion to lie on the table. I move the indefinite postponement of this bill, and in the form required by our rules, which is to a day certain beyond the session; and, to make sure of that, I propose a day beyond the life of the present Congress. It is the proper motion to test the sense of the Senate on the fate of a measure, and to save time which might be lost in useless amendments. I have waited a month for the larger amendments to be voted upon, and now deem it my duty to proceed with my motion, with a view to proceed with the bills singly, if this bill, of many in one, shall be put out of the way; but will withdraw it at any time to admit of votes on vital points. It is a bill of thirty-nine sections—forty, save one—an ominous number; and which, with the two little bills which attend it, is called a compromise, and is pressed upon us as a remedy for the national calamities. Now, all this labor of the committee, and all this remedy, proceed upon the assumption that the people of the United States are in a miserable, distracted condition; that it is their mission to relieve this national distress, and that these bills are the sovereign remedy for that purpose. Now, in my opinion, all this is a mistake, both as to the condition of the country, the mission of the committee, and the efficacy of their remedy. I do not believe in this misery, and distraction, and distress, and strife, of the people. On the contrary, I believe them to be very quiet at home, attending to their crops, such of them as do not mean to feed out of the public crib; and that they would be perfectly happy if the politicians would only permit them to think so. I know of no distress in the country, no misery, no strife, no distraction, none of those five gaping wounds of which the senator from Kentucky made enumeration on the five fingers of his left hand, and for the healing of which, all together, and all at once, and not one at a time, like the little Doctor Taylor, he has provided this capacious plaster in the shape of five old bills tacked together.... I know nothing of all these "gaping wounds," nor of any distress in the country since we got rid of the bank of the United States, and since we got possession of the gold currency. Since that time I have heard of no pecuniary or business distress, no rotten currency, no expansions and contractions, no deranged exchanges, no decline of public stocks, no laborers begging employment, no produce rotting upon the hands of the farmer, no property sacrificed at forced sales, no loss of confidence, no three per centum a month interest, no call for a bankrupt act. Never were the people—the business-doing and the working people—as well off as they are today. As for political distress, *"it is all in my eye."* It is all among the politicians. Never were the political blessings of the country greater than at present: civil and religious liberty eminently enjoyed; life, liberty, and property protected; the North and the South returning to the old belief, that they were made for each other; and peace and plenty reigning throughout the land. This is the condition of the country—happy in the extreme; and I listen with amazement to the recitals which I have heard on this floor of strife and contention, gaping wounds and streaming blood, distress and misery. I feel mystified. The senator from Kentucky [Mr. Clay], chairman of the committee, and reporter of the bill, and its pathetic advocate, formerly delivered us many such recitals, about the times that the tariff was to be increased, the national bank charter to be renewed, the deposits to be restored, or a bankrupt act to be passed. He has been absent for some years; and, on returning among us, seems to begin where he left off. He treats us to the old dish of distress! Sir, it is a mistake. There is none of it; and if there was, the remedy would be in the hands of the people—in the hearts of the people—who love their country, and mean to take care of it—and not in the contrivances of politicians, who mistake their own for their country's distresses. It is all a mistake. It looks to me like a joke. But when I recollect the imposing number of the committee, and how "distinguished" they all were, and how they voted themselves free from instructions, and allowed the Senate to talk, but not to vote, while they were out, and how long they were deliberating: when I recollect all these things, I am constrained to believe the committee are in earnest. And as for the senator himself, the chairman of the committee, the perfect gravity with which he brought forward his remedy—these bills and the report—the pathos with which he enforced them, and the hearty congratulations which he addressed to the Senate, to the United States, and all mankind on the appointment of his committee, preclude the idea of an intentional joke on his part. In view of all this, I find myself compelled to consider this proceeding as serious, and bound to treat it parliamentarily; which I now proceed to do.

. . . .

I proceed to the destruction of this monster. The California bill is made the scapegoat of all the sins of slavery in the United States—that California which is innocent of all these sins. It is made the scapegoat; and as this is the first instance of an American attempt to imitate that ancient Jewish mode of expiating national sins, I will read how it was done in Jerusalem, to show how exactly our committee have imitated that ancient expiatory custom. I read from an approved volume of Jewish antiquities:

The goat being tied in the northeast corner of the court of the temple, and his head bound with scarlet cloth to signify sin; the high-priest went to him, and laid his hands on his head, and confessed over it all the iniquities of the children of Israel, and all their transgressions in all their sins, putting them all on the head of the goat. After which, he was given to the person appointed to lead him away, who, in the early ages of the custom, led him into the desert, and turned him loose to die; but as the goat sometimes escaped from the desert, the expiation, in such cases, was not considered complete; and to make sure of his death, the after-custom was to lead him to a high rock, about twelve miles from Jerusalem, and push him off of it backwards, to prevent his jumping, the scarlet cloth being first torn from his head, in token that the sins of the people were taken away.

This was the expiation of the scapegoat in ancient Jerusalem: an innocent and helpless animal, loaded with sins which were not his own and made to die for offences which he had never committed. So of California. She is innocent of all the evils of slavery in the United States, yet they are all to be packed upon her back, and herself sacrificed under the heavy load. First, Utah and New Mexico are piled upon her, each pregnant with all the transgressions of the Wilmot Proviso—a double load in itself—and enough, without further weight, to bear down California. Utah and New Mexico are first piled on; and the reason given for it by the committee is thus stated in their authentic report:

The committee recommend to the Senate the establishment of those territorial governments; and, in order more effectually to secure that desirable object, they also recommend that the bill for their establishment be incorporated in the bill for the admission of California, and that, united together, they both be passed.

This is the reason given in the report; and the first thing that strikes me, on reading it, is its entire incompatibility with the reasons previously given for the same act. In his speech in favor of raising the committee, the senator from Kentucky [Mr. Clay] was in favor of putting the territories upon California for her own good—for the good of California herself—as the speedy way to get her into the Union, and the safe way to do it, by preventing an opposition to her admission which might otherwise defeat it altogether. This was his reason then, and he thus delivered it to the Senate.

He would say now to those who desired the speedy admission of California, the shortest and most expeditious way of attaining the desired object was to include her admission in a bill giving governments to the territories. He made this statement because he was impelled to do so from what had come to his knowledge. If her admission as a separate measure be urged, an opposition is created which may result in the defeat of any bill for her admission.

These are the reasons which the senator then gave for urging the conjunction of the state and the territories—quickest and safest for California: her admission the supreme object, and the conjunction of the territories only a means of helping her along and saving her. And unfounded as I deemed these reasons at the time, and now know them to be, they still had the merit of giving preference where it was due—to the superior object—to California herself, a state, without being a state of the Union, and suffering all the ills of that anomalous condition. California was then the superior object; the territories were incidental figures and subordinate considerations, to be made subservient to her salvation. Now all this is reversed. The territories take the superior place. They become the object: the state the incident. They take the first—she the second place! And to make sure of their welfare—make more certain of giving governments to them—*inuendo*, such governments as the committee prescribe—the conjunction is now proposed and enforced. This is a change of position, with a corresponding change of reasons. Doubtless the senator from Kentucky has a right to change his own position, and to change his reasons at the same time; but he has no right to ask other Senators to change with him, or to require them to believe in two sets of reasons, each contradictory to the other. It is my fortune to believe in neither. I did not believe in the first set when they were delivered; and time has shown that I was right. Time has disposed of the argument of speed. That reason has expired under the lapse of time. Instead of more speedy, we all now know that California has been delayed three months, waiting for this conjunction: instead of defeat if she remained single, we all know now that she might have been passed singly before the committee was raised, if the Senator from Kentucky had remained on his original ground, on my side; and everyone knows that the only danger to California now comes from the companionship into which she has been forced. I do not believe in either set of reasons. I do not admit the territorial governments to be objects of superior interest to the admission of California. I admit them to be objects of interest, demanding our attention, and that at this session; but not at the expense of California, nor in precedence of her, nor in conjunction with her, nor as a condition for her admission. She has been delayed long, and is now endangered by this attempt to couple with her the territories, with which she has no connection, and to involve her in the Wilmot Proviso question, from which she is free. The senator from Kentucky has done me the favor to blame me for this delay. He may blame me again when he beholds the catastrophe of his attempted conjunctions; but all mankind will see that the delay is the result of his own abandonment of the position which he originally took with me. The other reason which the senator gave in his speech for the conjunction is not repeated in the report—the one which addressed itself to our nervous system, and menaced total defeat to California if urged in a bill by herself. He has not renewed that argument to our fears, so portentously exhibited three months ago; and it may be supposed that the danger has passed by, and that Congress is now free. But California is not bettered by it, but worsted. Then it was only necessary to her salvation that she should be joined to the territories; so said the speech. Now she is joined to Texas also; and must be damned if not strong enough to save Texas, and Utah, and New Mexico, and herself into the bargain! . . .

Mr. President: all the evils of incongruous conjunctions are exemplified in this conjunction of the territorial government bills with the California state admission bill. They are subjects not only foreign to each other, but involving different questions, and resting upon principles of different natures. One involves the slavery and antislavery questions: the other is free from them. One involves constitutional questions: the other does not. One is a question of right, resting upon the Constitution of the United States and the treaty with Mexico: the other is a question of expediency, resting in the discretion of Congress. One is the case of a state, asking for an equality of rights with the other states: the other is a question of territories, asking protection from states. One is a sovereignty—the other a property. So that, at all points, and under every aspect, the subjects differ; and it is well known that there are senators here who can unite in a vote for the admission of California, who cannot unite in any vote for the territorial governments; and that, because these governments involve the slavery questions, from all which the California bill is free. That is the rock on which men and parties split here. Some deny the power of Congress *in toto* over the subject of slavery in territories: such as they can support no bill which touches that question, one way or the other. Others admit the power, but deny the expediency of its exercise. Others again claim both the power and the exercise. Others again are under legislative instructions—some to vote one way, some the other. Finally, there are some opposed to giving any govern-

ments at all to these territories, and in favor of leaving them to grow up of themselves into future states. Now, what are the senators, so circumstanced, to do with these bills conjoined? Vote for all—and call it a compromise! as if oaths, duty, constitutional obligation, and legislative instructions, were subjects of compromise. No! rejection of the whole is the only course; and to begin anew, each bill by itself, the only remedy.

. . . .

As for California—far from feeling her sensibility affected by her being associated with other kindred measures—she ought to rejoice and be highly gratified that, in entering into the Union, she may have contributed to the tranquility and happiness of the great family of States, of which it is to be hoped she may one day be a distinguished member.

. . . .

Mr. President, the moralist informs us, that there are some subjects too light for reason—too grave for ridicule; and in such cases, the mere moralist may laugh or cry, as he deems best. But not so with the legislator—his business is not laughing or crying. Whimpering, or simpering, is not his mission. Work is his vocation, and gravity his vein; and in that vein I proceed to consider this interjection of Texas, with all her multifarious questions, into the bowels of the California bill.

. . . .

In the first place, this Texas bill is a compact, depending for its validity on the consent of Texas, and is put into the California bill as part of a compromise and general settlement of all the slavery questions; and, of course, the whole must stand together, or fall together. This gives Texas a veto upon the admission of California. This is unconstitutional, as well as unjust; for, by the Constitution, new states are to be admitted by Congress, and not by another state; and, therefore, Texas should not have a veto upon the admission of California.

. . . .

I avoid all argument about right—the eventual right of Texas to any part of what was New Mexico before the existence of Texas. I avoid that question. Amicable settlement of contested claim, and not adjudication of title, is now my object. I need no argument from any quarter to satisfy me that the Texas questions ought to be settled. I happened to know that before Texas was annexed, and brought in bills and made speeches for that purpose, at that time. I brought in such bills six years ago, and again at the present session; and whenever presented single, either by myself or any other person, I shall be ready to give it a generous consideration; but, as part of the California bill, I wash my hands of it.

I am against disturbing actual possession, either that of New Mexico or of Texas; and, therefore, am in favor of leaving to each all its population, and an ample amount of compact and homogeneous territory. With this view, all my bills and plans for a divisional line between New Mexico and Texas—whether of 1844 or 1850—left to each all its settlements, all its actual possessions, all its uncontested claim; and divided the remainder by a line adapted to the geography and natural divisions of the country, as well as suitable to the political and social condition of the people themselves. This gave a longitudinal line between them; and the longitude of 100 degrees in my bill of 1844, and 102 degrees in my bill of 1850—and both upon the same principle of leaving possessions intact, Texas having extended her settlements in the meantime. The proposed line of the committee violates all these conditions. It cuts deep and arbitrarily into the actual possessions of New Mexico, such as she held them before Texas had existence; and so conforms to no principle of public policy, private right, territorial affinity, or local propriety.

. . . .

And here I find the largest objection to the extension of slavery—to planting it in new regions where it does not now exist—bestowing it on those who have it not. The incurability of the evil is the greatest objection to the extension of slavery. It is wrong for the legislator to inflict an evil which can be cured: how much more to inflict one that is incurable, and against the will of the people who are to endure it forever! I quarrel with no one for supposing slavery a blessing: I deem it an evil and would neither adopt it nor impose it on others. Yet I am a slaveholder, and among the few members of Congress who hold slaves in this District. The French proverb tells us that nothing is new but what has been forgotten. So of this objection to a large emancipation. Every one sees now that it is a question of races, involving consequences which go to the destruction of one or the other: it was seen fifty years ago, and the wisdom of Virginia balked at it then. It seems to be above human wisdom. But there is a wisdom above human! and to that we must look. In the meantime, not extend the evil.

In refusing to extend slavery into these seventy thousand square miles, I act in conformity not only to my own long-established principles, but also in conformity to the long-established practice of Congress. . . .

Thus, five times in four years, the respective houses of Congress refused to admit even a temporary extension, or rather re-extension of slavery into Indiana Territory, which had been before the Ordinance of '87 a slave territory, holding many slaves at Vincennes. These five refusals to suspend the Ordinance of '87, were so many confirmations of it. All the rest of the action of Congress on the subject, was to the same effect or stronger. The Missouri Compromise line was a curtailment of slave territory; the Texas annexation resolutions were the same; the Ordinance of '87 itself, so often confirmed by Congress, was a curtailment of slave territory—in fact its actual abolition; for it is certain that slavery existed in fact in the French settlements of the Illinois at that time; and that the ordinance terminated it. I act then in conformity to the long, uniformly established policy of Congress, as well as in conformity to my own principles, in

refusing to vote the extension of slavery, which the committee's line would involve.

And here, it does seem to me that we, of the present day, mistake the point of the true objection to the extension of slavery. We look at it as it concerns the rights, or interests, of the inhabitants of the states! and not as it may concern the people to whom it is to be given! and to whom it is to be an irrevocable gift—to them, and posterity! Mr. Randolph's report, in the case of Indiana, took the true ground. It looked to the interest of the people to whom the slavery was to go, and refused them an evil, although they begged for it. . . .

This is the end of the committee's labor—five old bills gathered up from our table, tacked together, and christened a compromise! Now compromise is a pretty phrase at all times, and is a good thing in itself, when there happens to be any parties to make it, any authority to enforce it, any penalties for breaking it, or anything to be compromised. The compromises of the Constitution are of that kind; and they stand. Compromises made in court, and entered of record, are of that kind; and they stand. Compromises made by individuals on claims to property are likewise of that character; and they stand. I respect all such compromises. But where there happens to be nothing to be compromised, no parties to make a compromise, no power to enforce it, no penalty for its breach, no obligation on anyone—not even its makers—to observe it, and when no two human beings can agree about its meaning, then a compromise becomes ridiculous and pestiferous. I have no respect for it, and eschew it. It cannot stand, and will fall; and in its fall will raise up more ills than it was intended to cure. And of this character I deem this farrago of incongruous matter to be, which has been gathered up and stuck together, and offered to us "all or none," like "fifty-four forty." It has none of the requisites of a compromise, and the name cannot make it so.

In the first place, there are no parties to make a compromise. We are not in convention, but in Congress; and I do not admit a geographical division of parties in this chamber, although the Committee of Thirteen was formed upon that principle—six from the South, half a dozen from the North, and one from the borders of both—sitting on a ridge pole, to keep the balance even. I recognize no such parties. I know no North, and I know no South; and I repulse and repudiate, as a thing to be forever condemned, this first attempt to establish geographical parties in this chamber, by creating a committee formed upon that principle. In the next place, there is no sanction for any such compromise—no authority to enforce it—none to punish its violation. In the third place, there is nothing to be compromised. A compromise is a concession, a mutual concession of contested claims between two parties. I know of nothing to be conceded on the part of the slaveholding states in regard to their slave property. Their rights are independent of the federal government, and admitted in the Constitution—a right to hold their slaves *as property,* a right to pursue and recover them *as property,* a right to it as a *political element* in the weight of these states, by making five count three in the national representation. These are our rights by an instrument which we are bound to respect, and I will concede none of them, nor purchase any of them. I never purchase as a concession what I hold as a right, nor accept an inferior title when I already hold the highest. Even if this congeries of bills was a compromise, in fact, I should be opposed to it, for the reasons stated. But the fact itself is to me apocryphal. What is it but the case of five old bills introduced by different members as common legislative measures—caught up by the senator from Kentucky, and his committee, bundled together, and then called a compromise! Now, this mystifies me. The same bills were ordinary legislation in the hands of their authors; they become a sacred compromise in the hands of their new possessors. They seemed to be of no account as laws; they become a national panacea as a compromise. The difference seems to be in the change of name. The poet tells us that a rose will smell as sweet by any other name. That may be true of roses, but not of compromises. In the case of the compromise, the whole smell is in the name; and here is the proof. The senator from Illinois [Mr. DOUGLAS] brought in three of these bills: they emitted no smell. The senator from Virginia brought in another of them—no smell in that. The senator from Missouri, who now speaks to the Senate, brought in the fifth—*ditto*, no smell about it. The olfactory nerve of the nation never scented their existence. But no sooner are they jumbled together, and called a compromise, than the nation is filled with their perfume. People smell it all over the land, and, like the inhalers of certain drugs, become frantic for the thing.

. . . .

No, sir! no more slavery compromises. Stick to those we have in the Constitution, and they will be stuck to! Look at the four votes—those four on the propositions which I submitted. No abolition of slavery in the states: none in the fort, arsenals, navy yards and dockyards: none in the District of Columbia: no interference with the slave trade between the states. These are the votes given on this floor, and which are above all Congress compromises, because they abide the compromises of the Constitution.

. . . .

Mr. President, it is time to be done with this comedy of errors. California is suffering for want of admission. New Mexico is suffering for want of protection. The public business is suffering for want of attention. The character of Congress is suffering for want of progress in business. It is time to put an end to so many evils; and I have made the motion intended to terminate them, by moving the indefinite postponement of this unmanageable mass of incongruous bills, each an impediment to the other, that they may be taken up one by one, in their proper order, to receive the decision which their respective merits require.

Congressional Globe, Senate, 31st Congress, 1st session, June 10, 1850, 676–684. For the full text, see also Robert C. Byrd, *The Senate, 1789–1989,* 4 vols. (Washington, D.C.: Government Printing Office), vol. 3: 323–345.

68   The Kansas-Nebraska Act

May 30, 1854

The Kansas-Nebraska Act completely undermined the Missouri Compromise (see document 53) and set the stage for the coming of the Civil War. The act, originally introduced by Senator Stephen Douglas (D-Ill.), declared that citizens of the new territories of Kansas and Nebraska, even though they were above latitude 36°30'—the line separating slave territory from free territory— had the right to determine if the new territories should allow slavery or be free. This concept of allowing citizens to determine the status of slavery in the new territories and states was known as "popular sovereignty." It became the rallying cry of those seeking to extend slavery north of latitude 36°30'.

Those in favor of the act claimed it would ease tensions over slavery, but just the opposite resulted. The debate over the act led to deep divisions within the existing political parties and led to the emergence of a new party in the North, the Republicans. Before long, localized civil war broke out in Kansas, where pro- and anti-slavery forces fought over the issue. The fighting in "Bleeding

Kansas" was a dress rehearsal for the larger civil war that would engulf the nation in 1861.

CHAP. LIX.—*AN ACT TO ORGANIZE THE TERRITORIES OF NEBRASKA AND KANSAS.*

Be it enacted by the Senate and House of Representatives of the United States of America in Congress assembled, That all that part of the territory of the United States included within the following limits, except such portions thereof as are hereinafter expressly exempted from the operations of this act, to wit: beginning at a point in the Missouri River where the fortieth parallel of north latitude crosses the same; thence west on said parallel to the east boundary of the Territory of Utah, on the summit of the Rocky Mountains; thence on said summit northward to the forty-ninth parallel of north latitude; thence east on said parallel to the western boundary of the territory of Minnesota; thence southward on said boundary to the Missouri River; thence down the main channel of said river to the place of beginning, be, and the same is hereby, created into a temporary government by the name of the Territory of Nebraska; and when admitted as a State or States, the said Territory, or any portion of the same, shall be received into the Union with or without slavery, as their constitution may prescribe at the time of their admission: Provided, That nothing in this act contained shall be construed to inhibit the government of the United States from dividing said Territory into two or more Territories, in such manner and at such times as Congress shall deem convenient and proper, or from attaching any portion of said Territory to any other State or Territory of the United States: *Provided further,* That nothing in this act contained shall be construed to impair the rights of person or property now pertaining to the Indians in said Territory, so long as such rights shall remain unextinguished by treaty between the United States and such Indians, or to include any territory which, by treaty with any Indian tribe, is not, without the consent of said tribe, to be included within the territorial limits or jurisdiction of any State or Territory; but all such territory shall be excepted out of the boundaries, and constitute no part of the Territory of Nebraska, until said tribe shall signify their assent to the President of the United States to be included within the said Territory of Nebraska, or to affect the authority of the government of the United States to make any regulations respecting such Indians, their lands, property, or other rights, by treaty, law, or otherwise, which it would have been competent to the government to make if this act had never passed.

. . . .

SEC. 10. *And be it further enacted,* That the provisions of an act entitled "An act respecting fugitives from justice, and persons escaping from the service of their masters," approved February twelve, seventeen hundred and ninety-three, and the provisions of the act entitled "An act to amend, and supplementary to, the aforesaid act," approved September eighteen, eighteen hundred and fifty, be, and the same are hereby, declared to extend to and be in full force within the limits of said Territory of Nebraska.

. . . .

SEC. 14. *And be it further enacted,* That a delegate to the House of Representatives of the United States, to serve for the term of two years, who shall be a citizen of the United States, may be elected by the voters qualified to elect members of the Legislative Assembly, who shall be entitled to the same rights and privileges as are exercised and enjoyed by the delegates from the several other Territories of the United States to the said House of Representatives, but the delegate first elected shall hold his seat only during the term of the Congress to which he shall be elected. The first election shall be held at such time and places, and be conducted in such manner, as the Governor shall appoint and direct; and at all subsequent elections the times, places, and manner of holding the elections, shall be prescribed by law. The person having the greatest number of votes shall be declared by the Governor to be duly elected; and a certificate thereof shall be given accordingly. That the Constitution, and all Laws of the United States which are not locally inapplicable, shall have the same force and effect within the said Territory of Nebraska as elsewhere within the United States, except the eighth section of the act preparatory to the admission of Missouri into the Union, approved March sixth, eighteen hundred and twenty, which, being inconsistent with the principle of non-intervention by Congress with slavery in the States and Territories, as recognized by the legislation of eighteen, hundred and fifty, commonly called the Compromise Measures, is hereby declared inoperative and void; it being the true intent and meaning of this act not to legislate slavery into any Territory or State, nor to exclude it therefrom, but to leave the people thereof perfectly free to form and regulate their domestic institutions in their own way, subject only to the Constitution of the United States: Provided, That nothing herein contained shall be construed to revive or put in force any law or regulation which may have existed prior to the act of sixth March, eighteen hundred and twenty, either protecting, establishing, prohibiting, or abolishing slavery.

. . . .

SEC. 19. *And be it further enacted,* That all that part of the Territory of the United States included within the following limits, except such portions thereof as are hereinafter expressly exempted from the operations of this act, to wit, beginning at a point on the western boundary of the State of Missouri, where the thirty-seventh parallel of north latitude crosses the same; thence west on said parallel to the eastern boundary of New Mexico; thence north on said boundary to latitude thirty-eight; thence following said boundary westward to the east boundary of the Territory of Utah, on the summit of the Rocky Mountains; thence northward on said summit to the fortieth parallel of latitude; thence east on said parallel to the western boundary of the State of Missouri; thence south with the western boundary of said State to the place of beginning, be, and the same is hereby, created into a temporary government by the name of the Territory of Kansas; and when admitted as a State or States, the said Territory, or any portion of the same, shall be received into the Union with or without slavery, as their Constitution may prescribe at the time of their admission: Provided, That nothing in this act contained shall be construed to inhibit the government of the United States from dividing said Territory into two or more Territories, in such manner and at such times as Congress shall deem convenient and proper, or from attaching any portion of said Territory to any other State or Territory of the United States: Provided further, That nothing in this act contained shall be construed to impair the rights of person or property now pertaining to the Indians in said Territory, so long as such rights shall remain unextinguished by treaty between the United States and such Indians, or to include any territory which, by treaty with any Indian tribe, is not, without the consent of said tribe, to be included within the territorial limits or jurisdiction of any State or Territory; but all such territory shall be excepted out of the boundaries, and constitute no part of the Territory of Kansas, until said tribe shall signify their assent to the President of the United States to be included within the said Territory of Kansas, or to affect the authority of the government of the United States to make any regulation respecting such Indians, their lands, property, or other rights, by treaty, law, or otherwise, which it would have been competent to the government to make if this act had never passed. . . .

Statutes at Large, 10 (1851–1855) 33rd Cong., 1st Sess., May 30, 1854, 277–290.

69 House Select Committee Report on the Beating of Senator Charles Sumner

June 2, 1856

On May 22, 1856, Senator Charles Sumner of Massachusetts was seated at his desk in the Senate chamber when he was approached by Representative Preston Brooks of South Carolina, who then proceeded to beat Senator Sumner with a cane. This incident of violence in Congress was one of the most severe examples of the growing tensions during the 1850s over the issue of slavery. It was a harbinger of the collapse of civil debate and a growing willingness to resort to violence, physical and verbal, which would eventually lead to the Civil War, when debate over sectional differences no longer seemed possible.

The events that led to the beating had to do with the tensions and civil war in Kansas, where pro- and antislavery forces were fighting to decide the fate of Kansas as a slave or free state. On May 19, 1856, Sumner delivered a powerful and emotional speech called "The Crime Against Kansas" in which he made uncharacteristically strong personal attacks on several Democratic senators, among them Senator Andrew Butler of South Carolina, whom he ridiculed for his false sense of southern chivalry and whom he accused of choosing as his mistress "the harlot, Slavery."

One of Butler's distant relatives, Preston Brooks, took it upon himself to defend the honor of his kinsman and fellow South Carolinian. Three days after Sumner's speech, Brooks, accompanied by another South Carolina representative, Laurence Keitt, marched into the Senate chamber, which was not in session at the time, and beat Sumner so badly that the cane broke in several places. Sumner's desk, although bolted to the floor, was wrenched from its moorings as he tried to escape the beating. He was left bleeding and in critical condition. His injuries, both psychological and physical, kept him out of the Senate for three years, although he was overwhelmingly reelected to a new term beginning in 1857.

Sumner's beating turned this rather ordinary senator into a national celebrity in the North. His speech on Kansas was widely reprinted, where its attacks on slaveholders and slavery found a sympathetic audience. When Sumner returned to the Senate it was as a leader of the Radical Republicans, a bold and outspoken champion of abolition, and a staunch advocate of racial equality.

Preston Brooks became a hero of sorts himself. The House investigation found him guilty of a serious breech of House rules and the investigating committee voted to expel him from the House.

However, the full House could not muster the necessary two-thirds vote to expel him. On July 15, 1856, Brooks resigned from the House and then ran for reelection to fill his own vacant seat. Two weeks after his resignation he was triumphantly returned to the House, where he served until January 27, 1857, when he died in office at the age of thirty-seven. His accomplice, Laurence Keitt, also resigned his seat and was quickly reelected. A third accomplice, Henry Edmundson of Virginia, who was not on the floor at the time of the beating, was not punished.

The select committee appointed under the resolution of the House, passed on the 23d day of May, 1856, to investigate the subject of the assault alleged to have been made in the Senate chamber, by the Hon. Preston S. Brooks, and other members of the House, upon the Hon. Charles Sumner, a senator from the State of Massachusetts, and to whom the House referred the proceedings of the Senate, announcing that they—a co-ordinate branch of Congress—"make complaint to the House of Representatives of the assault committed by one of its members—the Hon. Preston S. Brooks—upon the Hon. Charles Sumner, a senator from the State of Massachusetts," having taken such testimony as was accessible to them, beg leave to make the following report, with the accompanying testimony:

The committee, upon a full investigation of the subject, concur in the following conclusions, which the Senate seem unanimously to have declared:

1. "That the Hon. Preston S. Brooks, a member of the House of Representatives from the State of South Carolina, did, on the 22d day of the present month, after the adjournment of the Senate, and while Mr. Sumner was seated at his desk in the Senate chamber, assault him with considerable violence, striking him numerous blows on or about the head with a walking stick, which cut his head, and disabled him for the time being from attending to his duties in the Senate."

2. "That this assault was a breach of the privileges of the Senate."

3. That "the Senate, for a breach of its privileges, cannot arrest a member of the House of Representatives, and, *a fortiori*, cannot try and punish him; that such authority devolves upon

the House of which he is a member," and, therefore, "that it is not within the jurisdiction of the Senate, and can only be punished by the House of Representatives, of which Mr. Brooks is a member."

The committee therefore report back the complaint of the Senate, with the journal of their proceedings and the testimony taken in the premises, pursuant to the resolution of the House.

The testimony discloses the following facts:

On Monday and Tuesday, the 19th and 20th days of May, 1856, Mr. Sumner delivered a speech in the Senate, in reply to a senator from South Carolina, (Mr. Butler,) and other senators, an authenticated copy of which is appended to the accompanying testimony, and forms a part of this report.

It appears that, as early as Tuesday, before the speech was concluded, Mr. Brooks took exception to the remarks of the senator; and that on Wednesday morning, after the delivery of the speech, he declared to Mr. Edmundson, of the House, by whom he was casually met, in the Capitol grounds, a short time before the meeting of the two Houses, that he had determined to punish Mr. Sumner, unless he made an ample apology for the language he had uttered in his speech, and expressed a desire that Mr. Edmundson should be present as a witness to the transaction; that they thereupon took a seat near the walk leading from Pennsylvania avenue to the Capitol, and there remained some fifteen minutes, awaiting the approach of Mr. Sumner; and he not making his appearance, they then proceeded to the Capitol.

On Thursday morning he was again casually met by Mr. Edmundson at the western entrance of the Capitol grounds, on Pennsylvania avenue, a point which commands a view of all the approaches to the Capitol from that portion of the city in which Mr. Sumner resides. Here Mr. Brooks informed Mr. Edmundson that he was on the lookout for Mr. Sumner, and again declared his purpose to resent the language of Mr. Sumner's speech; and after remaining for a short period, Mr. Sumner not approaching, the two again proceeded to the Capitol.

After the reading of the journal of the House on Thursday, the death of the honorable Mr. Miller, of Missouri, was announced, addresses delivered, the customary resolutions adopted, and thereupon the House adjourned.

When the message was received by the Senate from the House, announcing the death of Mr. Miller, a tribute of respect was paid to the deceased by Senator Geyer, in an address, and that body thereupon also adjourned. Most of the Senators left the Senate chamber, a few only remaining. Mr. Sumner continued in his seat engaged in writing. Mr. Brooks approached, and, addressing a few words to him, immediately commenced the attack by inflicting blows upon his bare head, whilst he was in a sitting posture, with a large and heavy cane. Stunned and blinded by the first blow, and confined by his chair and desk, Mr. Sumner made several ineffectual efforts to rise, and finally succeeded by wrenching his desk from its fastenings. The blows were re-pealed by Mr. Brooks with great rapidity and extreme violence, while Mr. Sumner, almost unconscious, made further efforts of self-defence, until he fell to the floor under the attack, bleeding and powerless.

The wounds were severe and calculated to endanger the life of the Senator who remained for several days in a critical condition. It appears that the blows were inflicted with a cane, the material of which was about the specific gravity of hickory or whalebone, one inch in diameter at the larger end, and tapering to the diameter of about five-eighths of an inch at the smaller end. It is not too much to say that the weapon used was of a deadly character, and that the blows were indiscriminately dealt, at the hazard of the life of the assailed.

The committee have extended to the parties implicated the fullest facilities for taking exculpatory testimony. There is no proof to show, nor has it been in any way intimated, that Mr. Brooks at any time, in any manner, directly or indirectly, notified Mr. Sumner of his intention to make the assault. There is no evidence that Mr. Sumner ever carried weapons, either for the purpose of attack or defence; on the contrary, it appears that he did not anticipate personal violence until at the instant he received the first blow, and that he was not armed or otherwise prepared in any respect for self-defence.

There is no evidence beyond the character of the attack tending to show an intention on the part of Mr. Brooks to kill the Senator, his expressions being that he did not intend to kill, but to punish him; but the committee cannot but regard the assault as a most flagrant violation, not only of the privileges of the Senate and of the House, as co-ordinate branches of the legislative department of the government, and the personal rights and privileges of the Senator, but of the rights of his constituents and of our character as a nation. It was premeditated during a period of at least two days, without any other provocation than words lawfully spoken in debate in the Senate chamber, not ruled out of order by the President of the Senate, nor objected to by any Senator as violative of the rules established for the government and order of that body.

The act cannot, therefore, be regarded by the committee otherwise than as an aggravated assault upon the inestimable right of freedom of speech guarantied by the Constitution. It asserts for physical force a prerogative over governments, constitutions, and laws; and, if carried to its ultimate consequences, must result in anarchy and bring in its train all the evils of a "reign of terror."

The committee therefore, in conformity to the spirit of the resolution of the House, and their sense of public duty, are constrained to recommend to the House the passage of such a resolution as will vindicate its own character and rebuke the member who has, so unhappily for himself and the country, perpetrated this great wrong.

The committee do not discuss the powers of the House to punish its disorderly members, nor do they undertake to argue the general question as to what constitutes a breach of privilege. The passage of the resolution raising the committee is regarded as a declaration on the part of the House of its power to call its members to account for such acts as violate the privileges of the

Senate. This assault having been committed by a member upon a Senator "whilst remaining in his seat in the Senate chamber in the performance of the duties pertaining to his official station," and for words there spoken in debate, the committee have no doubt of the right or power of the House to adopt the resolutions which they recommend.

No testimony has been taken, nor are the committee aware of any, which shows that any other member of the House was either actively engaged in the assault or designed to commit any violence upon Mr. Sumner, nor that any other member knew the "precise time when" or "the place where" Mr. Brooks would assail him. It does appear, however, that the Hon. Henry A. Edmundson, of Virginia, and the Hon. Lawrence M. Keitt, of South Carolina, members of the House, had been previously informed of the purpose of Mr. Brooks to commit the assault upon Mr. Sumner, and that they anticipated that the assault would take place in or near the Senate chamber about the time the occurrence did take place. Mr. Keitt was in the Senate chamber and Mr. Edmundson in a room adjoining it at the time the attack was made; and it is proved that Mr. Keitt rushed up with a cane in a threatening manner when the bystanders attempted to protect Mr. Sumner from the blows of Mr. Brooks, and that Mr. Edmundson entered the chamber soon after Mr. Sumner fell.

The committee do not feel themselves justified in expressing the opinion upon the testimony that either of these members was a principal or accessory in the assault, but regard their conduct in the transaction—and particularly in not taking steps to prevent the perpetration of the wrong, or to inform the Senator of his danger—as reprehensible. The committee, therefore, recommend the adoption of the following resolutions:

Whereas, the Senate of the United States have transmitted to this House a message, complaining that Preston S. Brooks, a Representative from the State of South Carolina, committed upon the person of Charles Sumner, a Senator from the State of Massachusetts, while seated at his desk in the Senate chamber, after the adjournment of that body on the 22d of May last, a violent assault, which disabled him from attending to his duties in the Senate, and declaring that the said assault was a breach of the privileges of that body: And whereas, from respect to the privileges of the House, the Senate have further declared that, inasmuch as the said Preston S. Brooks is a member of this House, they cannot arrest, and, *a fortiori*, cannot try or punish him for a breach of their privileges, that they cannot proceed further in the case than to make their complaint to this House, and that the power to arrest, try, and punish, devolves solely on this body And whereas, upon full investigation, it appears to this House that the said Preston S. Brooks has been guilty of the assault complained of by the Senate, with most aggravated circumstances of violence; that the same was a breach of the privileges not only of the Senate, but of the Senator assailed, and of this House, as a co-ordinate branch of the legislative department of government, in direct violation of the Constitution of the United States, which declares that Senators and Representatives "for any speech or debate in either House shall not be questioned in any other place:" And whereas, this House is of opinion that it has the power and ought to punish the said Preston S. Brooks for the said assault, not only as a breach of the privileges of the Senator assailed, and of the Senate and House, as declared by the Constitution, but as an act of disorderly behavior: And whereas, it further appears, from such investigation, that Henry A. Edmundson, a Representative from the State of Virginia, and Lawrence M. Keitt, a Representative from the State of South Carolina, some time previous to the said assault, were informed that it was the purpose of the said Preston S. Brooks to commit violence upon the person of said Charles Sumner, for words used by him in debate, as a Senator in the Senate, and took no measures to discourage or prevent the same; but, on the contrary, anticipating the commission of such violence, were present on one or more occasions to witness the same, as friends of the assailant: therefore

Resolved, That Preston S. Brooks be, and he is forthwith, expelled from this House as a Representative from the State of South Carolina.

Resolved, That this House hereby declare its disapprobation of the said act of Henry A. Edmundson and Lawrence M. Keitt in regard to the said assault.

Lewis D. Campbell
F. E. Spinner
A. C. M. Pennington

House of Representatives, *House Report No. 182,* 34th Congress, 1st session, June 12, 1856, 1–5.

70   *Scott v. Sanford* (The Dred Scott Decision)

1857

*Few decisions in the history of the Supreme Court have been as momentous as the Dred Scott decision in terms of its impact on American history and in terms of its affect on the actions of Congress. For decades Congress had failed to work out a satisfactory solution to the expansion of slavery into new territories. Patchwork compromises in 1820 and 1850 bought time for further debate but did not get Congress closer to a resolution on the issue. The lengthy debate over the Wilmot Proviso in 1846 and 1847 also revealed Congress's failure to work out a solution (see document 64). After 1850, and especially after the Kansas-Nebraska Act of 1854 and the ensuing civil war in Kansas, the nation and Congress were un-*able to overcome the growing division of opinion and the heightening passions on the subject of slavery.

Finally, the issue came before the Supreme Court in a case that developed from incidents in 1846 when Dred Scott and his wife Harriet, held as slaves in Missouri, brought a suit to obtain their freedom based on the fact that his master, John F. A. Sanford, had taken him to free territory in the state of Illinois and then to parts of U.S. territory where slavery was prohibited by the Missouri Compromise of 1820. Lower courts upheld Sanford's right to transport his slaves as he saw fit, and the case eventually came before the Supreme Court.

Roger B. Taney served as chief justice of the United States from 1836 to 1864, succeeding the great John Marshall. Taney became one of the most controversial chief justices in history, largely because of his unpopular and politically devastating decision in the Dred Scott case. Taney argued that slaves were not citizens and did not have the rights of citizens. Furthermore, he maintained that Congress did not have the authority to ban slavery from the territories, as it had done in the Missouri Compromise. The Dred Scott decision declared the Missouri Compromise unconstitutional. The impact of this decision outraged members of the newly formed Republican Party and badly divided the Democratic Party. Taney's decision also ran against the earlier Marshall court decisions that favored broad powers for Congress to act in such matters. At the same time Taney declared Congress's authority to limit slavery's expansion unconstitutional, he recognized the power of Congress to determine citizenship.

For the remaining seven years of his life, Taney was criticized and condemned for this decision. Congress remained hopelessly divided on the issue of slavery and was unable to mount a challenge to the Dred Scott decision before the Civil War began less than four years later. It took a bloody war and the extraordinary events of Reconstruction and three amendments to the Constitution (the Thirteenth, Fourteenth, and Fifteenth Amendments) to reverse the Dred Scott decision.

Mr. CHIEF JUSTICE TANEY delivered the opinion of the court.

This case has been twice argued. After the argument at the last term, differences of opinion were found to exist among the members of the court, and as the questions in controversy are of the highest importance, and the court was at that time much pressed by the ordinary business of the term, it was deemed advisable to continue the case and direct a re-argument on some of the points in order that we might have an opportunity of giving to the whole subject a more deliberate consideration. It has accordingly been again argued by counsel, and considered by the court; and I now proceed to deliver its opinion.

There are two leading questions presented by the record:

1. Had the Circuit Court of the United States jurisdiction to hear and determine the case between these parties? And

2. If it had jurisdiction, is the judgment it has given erroneous or not?

The plaintiff in error, who was also the plaintiff in the court below, was, with his wife and children, held as slaves by the defendant in the State of Missouri, and he brought this action in the Circuit Court of the United States for that district to assert the title of himself and his family to freedom.

The declaration is in the form usually adopted in that State to try questions of this description, and contains the averment necessary to give the court jurisdiction; that he and the defendant are citizens of different States; that is, that he is a citizen of Missouri, and the defendant a citizen of New York.

The defendant pleaded in abatement to the jurisdiction of the court, that the plaintiff was not a citizen of the State of Missouri, as alleged in his declaration, being a negro of African descent, whose ancestors were of pure African blood and who were brought into this country and sold as slaves.

To this plea the plaintiff demurred, and the defendant joined in demurrer. The court overruled the plea, and gave judgment that the defendant should answer over. And he thereupon put in sundry pleas in bar, upon which issues were joined, and at the trial the verdict and judgment were in his favor. Whereupon the plaintiff brought this writ of error.

Before we speak of the pleas in bar, it will be proper to dispose of the questions which have arisen on the plea in abatement.

That plea denies the right of the plaintiff to sue in a court of the United States, for the reasons therein stated.

If the question raised by it is legally before us, and the court should be of opinion that the facts stated in it disqualify the plaintiff from becoming a citizen, in the sense in which that word is used in the Constitution of the United States, then the judgment of the Circuit Court is erroneous, and must be reversed.

. . . .

This difference arises, as we have said, from the peculiar character of the Government of the United States. For although it is sovereign and supreme in its appropriate sphere of action, yet it does not possess all the powers which usually belong to the sovereignty of a nation. Certain specified powers, enumerated in the Constitution, have been conferred upon it, and neither the legislative, executive, nor judicial departments of the Government can lawfully exercise any authority beyond the limits marked out by the Constitution. And in regulating the judicial department, the cases in which the courts of the United States shall have jurisdiction are particularly and specifically enumerated and defined, and they are not authorized to take cognizance of any case which does not come within the description therein specified. Hence, when a plaintiff sues in a court of the United States, it is necessary that he should show, in his pleading, that the suit he brings is within the jurisdiction of the court, and that he is entitled to sue there. And if he omits to do this, and should, by any oversight of the Circuit Court, obtain a judgment in his favor, the judgment would be reversed in the appellate court for want of jurisdiction in the court below. The jurisdiction would not be presumed, as in the case of a common law English or State court, unless the contrary appeared. But the record, when it comes before the appellate court, must show affirmatively that the inferior court had authority under the Constitution to hear and determine the case. And if the plaintiff claims a right to sue in a Circuit Court of the United States under that provision of the Constitution which gives jurisdiction in controversies between citizens of different States, he must distinctly aver in his pleading that they are citizens of different States, and he cannot maintain his suit without showing that fact in the pleadings.

. . . .

If, however, the fact of citizenship is averred in the declaration, and the defendant does not deny it and put it in issue by plea in abatement, he cannot offer evidence at the trial to disprove it, and consequently cannot avail himself of the objection in the appellate court unless the defect should be apparent in some other part of the record. For if there is no plea in abatement, and the want of jurisdiction does not appear in any other part of the transcript brought up by the writ of error, the undisputed averment of citizenship in the declaration must be taken in this court to be true. In this case, the citizenship is averred, but it is denied by the defendant in the manner required by the rules of pleading, and the fact upon which the denial is based is admitted by the demurrer. And, if the plea and demurrer, and judgment of the court below upon it, are before us upon this record, the question to be decided is whether the facts stated in the plea are sufficient to show that the plaintiff is not entitled to sue as a citizen in a court of the United States.

. . . .

This is certainly a very serious question, and one that now for the first time has been brought for decision before this court. But it is brought here by those who have a right to bring it, and it is our duty to meet it and decide it.

The question is simply this: can a negro whose ancestors were imported into this country and sold as slaves become a member of the political community formed and brought into existence by the Constitution of the United States, and as such become entitled to all the rights, and privileges, and immunities, guaranteed by that instrument to the citizen, one of which rights is the privilege of suing in a court of the United States in the cases specified in the Constitution?

It will be observed that the plea applies to that class of persons only whose ancestors were negroes of the African race, and imported into this country and sold and held as slaves. The only matter in issue before the court, therefore, is, whether the descendants of such slaves, when they shall be emancipated, or who are born of parents who had become free before their birth, are citizens of a State in the sense in which the word "citizen" is used in the Constitution of the United States. And this being the only matter in dispute on the pleadings, the court must be understood as speaking in this opinion of that class only, that is, of those persons who are the descendants of Africans who were imported into this country and sold as slaves.

. . . .

We proceed to examine the case as presented by the pleadings.

The words "people of the United States" and "citizens" are synonymous terms, and mean the same thing. They both describe the political body who, according to our republican institutions, form the sovereignty and who hold the power and conduct the Government through their representatives. They are what we familiarly call the "sovereign people," and every citizen is one of this people, and a constituent member of this sovereignty. The question before us is whether the class of persons described in the plea in abatement compose a portion of this people, and are constituent members of this sovereignty? We think they are not, and that they are not included, and were not intended to be included, under the word "citizens" in the Constitution, and can therefore claim none of the rights and privileges which that instrument provides for and secures to citizens of the United States. On the contrary, they were at that time considered as a subordinate and inferior class of beings who had been subjugated by the dominant race, and, whether emancipated or not, yet remained subject to their authority, and had no rights or privileges but such as those who held the power and the Government might choose to grant them.

. . . .

In discussing this question, we must not confound the rights of citizenship which a State may confer within its own limits and the rights of citizenship as a member of the Union. It does not by any means follow, because he has all the rights and privileges of a citizen of a State, that he must be a citizen of the United States. He may have all of the rights and privileges of the citizen of a State and yet not be entitled to the rights and privileges of a citizen in any other State. For, previous to the adoption of the Constitution of the United States, every State had the undoubted right to confer on whomsoever it pleased the character of citizen, and to endow him with all its rights. But this character, of course, was confined to the boundaries of the State, and gave him no rights or privileges in other States beyond those secured to him by the laws of nations and the comity of States. Nor have the several States surrendered the power of conferring these rights and privileges by adopting the Constitution of the United States. Each State may still confer them upon an alien, or anyone it thinks proper, or upon any class or description of persons, yet he would not be a citizen in the sense in which that word is used in the Constitution of the United States, nor entitled to sue as such in one of its courts, nor to the privileges and immunities of a citizen in the other States. The rights which he would acquire would be restricted to the State which gave them. The Constitution has conferred on Congress the right to establish an uniform rule of naturalization, and this right is evidently exclusive, and has always been held by this court to be so. Consequently, no State, since the adoption of the Constitution, can, by naturalizing an alien, invest him with the rights and privileges secured to a citizen of a State under the Federal Government, although, so far as the State alone was concerned, he would undoubtedly be entitled to the rights of a citizen and clothed with all the rights and immunities which the Constitution and laws of the State attached to that character.

It is very clear, therefore, that no State can, by any act or law of its own, passed since the adoption of the Constitution, introduce a new member into the political community created by the Constitution of the United States. It cannot make him a member of this community by making him a member of its own. And, for the same reason, it cannot introduce any person or description of persons who were not intended to be embraced in this new political family which the Constitution brought into existence, but were intended to be excluded from it.

The question then arises, whether the provisions of the Constitution, in relation to the personal rights and privileges to which the citizen of a State should be entitled, embraced the negro African race, at that time in this country or who might afterwards be imported, who had then or should afterwards be made free in any State, and to put it in the power of a single State to make him a citizen of the United States and endue him with the full rights of citizenship in every other State without their consent? Does the Constitution of the United States act upon him whenever he shall be made free under the laws of a State, and raised there to the rank of a citizen, and immediately clothe him with all the privileges of a citizen in every other State, and in its own courts?

The court think the affirmative of these propositions cannot be maintained. And if it cannot, the plaintiff in error could not be a citizen of the State of Missouri within the meaning of the Constitution of the United States, and, consequently, was not entitled to sue in its courts.

It is true, every person, and every class and description of persons who were, at the time of the adoption of the Constitution, recognised as citizens in the several States became also citizens of this new political body, but none other; it was formed by them, and for them and their posterity, but for no one else. And the personal rights and privileges guarantied to citizens of this new sovereignty were intended to embrace those only who were then members of the several State communities, or who should afterwards by birthright or otherwise become members according to the provisions of the Constitution and the principles on which it was founded. It was the union of those who were at that time members of distinct and separate political communities into one political family, whose power, for certain specified purposes, was to extend over the whole territory of the United States. And it gave to each citizen rights and privileges outside of his State which he did not before possess, and placed him in every other State upon a perfect equality with its own citizens as to rights of person and rights of property; it made him a citizen of the United States.

It becomes necessary, therefore, to determine who were citizens of the several States when the Constitution was adopted. And in order to do this, we must recur to the Governments and institutions of the thirteen colonies when they separated from Great Britain and formed new sovereignties, and took their places in the family of independent nations. We must inquire who, at that time, were recognised as the people or citizens of a State whose rights and liberties had been outraged by the English Government, and who declared their independence and assumed the powers of Government to defend their rights by force of arms.

In the opinion of the court, the legislation and histories of the times, and the language used in the Declaration of Independence, show that neither the class of persons who had been imported as slaves nor their descendants, whether they had become free or not, were then acknowledged as a part of the people, nor intended to be included in the general words used in that memorable instrument.

It is difficult at this day to realize the state of public opinion in relation to that unfortunate race which prevailed in the civilized and enlightened portions of the world at the time of the Declaration of Independence and when the Constitution of the United States was framed and adopted. But the public history of every European nation displays it in a manner too plain to be mistaken.

They had for more than a century before been regarded as beings of an inferior order, and altogether unfit to associate with the white race either in social or political relations, and so far inferior that they had no rights which the white man was bound to respect, and that the negro might justly and lawfully be reduced to slavery for his benefit. He was bought and sold, and treated as an ordinary article of merchandise and traffic whenever a profit could be made by it. This opinion was at that time fixed and universal in the civilized portion of the white race. It was regarded as an axiom in morals as well as in politics which no one thought of disputing or supposed to be open to dispute, and men in every grade and position in society daily and habitually acted upon it in their private pursuits, as well as in matters of public concern, without doubting for a moment the correctness of this opinion.

. . . .

The opinion thus entertained and acted upon in England was naturally impressed upon the colonies they founded on this side of the Atlantic. And, accordingly, a negro of the African race was regarded by them as an article of property, and held, and bought and sold as such, in every one of the thirteen colonies which united in the Declaration of Independence and afterwards formed the Constitution of the United States. The slaves were more or less numerous in the different colonies as slave labor was found more or less profitable. But no one seems to have doubted the correctness of the prevailing opinion of the time.

The legislation of the different colonies furnishes positive and indisputable proof of this fact.

. . . .

The language of the Declaration of Independence is equally conclusive:

. . . .

We hold these truths to be self-evident: that all men are created equal; that they are endowed by their Creator with certain unalienable rights; that among them is life, liberty, and the pursuit of happiness; that to secure these rights, Governments are instituted, deriving their just powers from the consent of the governed.

The general words above quoted would seem to embrace the whole human family, and if they were used in a similar instrument at this day would be so understood. But it is too clear for dispute that the enslaved African race were not intended to be included, and formed no part of the people who framed and adopted this declaration, for if the language, as understood in that day, would embrace them, the conduct of the distinguished men who framed the Declaration of Independence would have been utterly and flagrantly inconsistent with the principles they asserted, and instead of the sympathy of mankind to which they so confidently appealed, they would have deserved and received universal rebuke and reprobation.

Yet the men who framed this declaration were great men— high in literary acquirements, high in their sense of honor, and incapable of asserting principles inconsistent with those on which they were acting. They perfectly understood the meaning of the language they used, and how it would be understood by others, and they knew that it would not in any part of the civilized world be supposed to embrace the negro race, which, by common consent, had been excluded from civilized Governments and the family of nations, and doomed to slavery. They spoke and acted according to the then established doctrines and principles, and in the ordinary language of the day, and no one misunderstood them. The unhappy black race were separated from the white by indelible marks, and laws long before established, and were never thought of or spoken of except as property, and when the claims of the owner or the profit of the trader were supposed to need protection.

This state of public opinion had undergone no change when the Constitution was adopted, as is equally evident from its provisions and language.

. . . .

But there are two clauses in the Constitution which point directly and specifically to the negro race as a separate class of persons, and show clearly that they were not regarded as a portion of the people or citizens of the Government then formed.

One of these clauses reserves to each of the thirteen States the right to import slaves until the year 1808 if it thinks proper. And the importation which it thus sanctions was unquestionably of persons of the race of which we are speaking, as the traffic in slaves in the United States had always been confined to them. And by the other provision the States pledge themselves to each other to maintain the right of property of the master by delivering up to him any slave who may have escaped from his service, and be found within their respective territories. By the first above-mentioned clause, therefore, the right to purchase and hold this property is directly sanctioned and authorized for twenty years by the people who framed the Constitution. And by the second, they pledge themselves to maintain and uphold the right of the master in the manner specified, as long as the Government they then formed should endure. And these two provisions show conclusively that neither the description of persons therein referred to nor their descendants were embraced in any of the other provisions of the Constitution, for certainly these two clauses were not intended to confer on them or their posterity the blessings of liberty, or any of the personal rights so carefully provided for the citizen.

. . . .

Indeed, when we look to the condition of this race in the several States at the time, it is impossible to believe that these rights and privileges were intended to be extended to them.

. . . .

The legislation of the States therefore shows in a manner not to be mistaken the inferior and subject condition of that race at the time the Constitution was adopted and long afterwards, throughout the thirteen States by which that instrument was framed, and it is hardly consistent with the respect due to these States to suppose that they regarded at that time as fellow citizens and members of the sovereignty, a class of beings whom they had thus stigmatized, whom, as we are bound out of respect to the State sovereignties to assume they had deemed it just and necessary thus to stigmatize, and upon whom they had impressed such deep and enduring marks of inferiority and degradation, or, that, when they met in convention to form the Constitution, they looked upon them as a portion of their constituents or designed to include them in the provisions so carefully inserted for the security and protection of the liberties and rights of their citizens. It cannot be supposed that they intended to secure to them rights and privileges and rank, in the new political body throughout the Union which every one of them denied within the limits of its own dominion. More especially, it cannot be believed that the large slaveholding States regarded them as included in the word citizens, or would have consented to a Constitution which might compel them to receive them in that character from another State. For if they were so received, and entitled to the privileges and immunities of citizens, it would exempt them from the operation of the special laws and from the police regulations which they considered to be necessary for their own safety. It would give to persons of the negro race, who were recognised as citizens in any one State of the Union, the right to enter every other State whenever they pleased, singly or in companies, without pass or passport, and without obstruction, to sojourn there as long as they pleased, to go where they pleased at every hour of the day or night without molestation, unless they committed some violation of law for which a white man would be punished; and it would give them the full liberty of speech in public and in private upon all subjects upon which its own citizens might speak; to hold public meetings upon political affairs, and to keep and carry arms wherever they went. And all of this would be done in the face of the subject race of the same color, both free and slaves, and inevitably producing discontent and insubordination among them, and endangering the peace and safety of the State.

. . . .

It is impossible, it would seem, to believe that the great men of the slaveholding States, who took so large a share in framing the Constitution of the United States and exercised so much influence in procuring its adoption, could have been so forgetful or regardless of their own safety and the safety of those who trusted and confided in them.

. . . .

The right of naturalization was therefore, with one accord, surrendered by the States, and confided to the Federal Government. And this power granted to Congress to establish an uniform rule of naturalization is, by the well understood meaning of the word, confined to persons born in a foreign country, under a foreign Government. It is not a power to raise to the rank of a citizen anyone born in the United States who, from birth or parentage, by the laws of the country, belongs to an inferior and subordinate class.

. . . .

Congress might, as we before said, have authorized the naturalization of Indians because they were aliens and foreigners. But, in their then untutored and savage state, no one would have thought of admitting them as citizens in a civilized community. And, moreover, the atrocities they had but recently committed, when they were the allies of Great Britain in the Revolutionary war, were yet fresh in the recollection of the people of the United States, and they were even then guarding themselves against the threatened renewal of Indian hostilities. No one supposed then that any Indian would ask for, or was capable of enjoying, the privileges of an American citizen, and the word white was not used with any particular reference to them.

Neither was it used with any reference to the African race imported into or born in this country; because Congress had no power to naturalize them, and therefore there was no necessity for using particular words to exclude them.

. . . .

The conduct of the Executive Department of the Government has been in perfect harmony upon this subject with this course of legislation. The question was brought officially before the late William Wirt, when he was the Attorney General of the United States, in 1821, and he decided that the words "citizens of the United States" were used in the acts of Congress in the same sense as in the Constitution, and that free persons of color were not citizens within the meaning of the Constitution and laws; and this opinion has been confirmed by that of the late Attorney General, Caleb Cushing, in a recent case, and acted upon by the Secretary of State, who refused to grant passports to them as "citizens of the United States."

But it is said that a person may be a citizen, and entitled to that character, although he does not possess all the rights which may belong to other citizens—as, for example, the right to vote, or to hold particular offices—and that yet, when he goes into another State, he is entitled to be recognised there as a citizen, although the State may measure his rights by the rights which it allows to persons of a like character or class resident in the State, and refuse to him the full rights of citizenship.

This argument overlooks the language of the provision in the Constitution of which we are speaking.

Undoubtedly a person may be a citizen, that is, a member of the community who form the sovereignty, although he exercises no share of the political power and is incapacitated from holding particular offices. Women and minors, who form a part of the political family, cannot vote, and when a property qualification is required to vote or hold a particular office, those who have not the necessary qualification cannot vote or hold the office, yet they are citizens.

So, too, a person may be entitled to vote by the law of the State, who is not a citizen even of the State itself. And in some of the States of the Union, foreigners not naturalized are allowed to vote. And the State may give the right to free negroes and mulattoes, but that does not make them citizens of the State, and still less of the United States. And the provision in the Constitution giving privileges and immunities in other States does not apply to them.

Neither does it apply to a person who, being the citizen of a State, migrates to another State. For then he becomes subject to the laws of the State in which he lives, and he is no longer a citizen of the State from which he removed. And the State in which he resides may then, unquestionably, determine his status or condition, and place him among the class of persons who are not recognised as citizens, but belong to an inferior and subject race, and may deny him the privileges and immunities enjoyed by its citizens.

But so far as mere rights of person are concerned, the provision in question is confined to citizens of a State who are temporarily in another State without taking up their residence there. It gives them no political rights in the State as to voting or holding office, or in any other respect. For a citizen of one State has no right to participate in the government of another. But if he ranks as a citizen in the State to which he belongs, within the meaning of the Constitution of the United States, then, whenever he goes into another State, the Constitution clothes him, as to the rights of person, will all the privileges and immunities which belong to citizens of the State. And if persons of the African race are citizens of a State, and of the United States, they would be entitled to all of these privileges and immunities in every State, and the State could not restrict them, for they would hold these privileges and immunities under the paramount authority of the Federal Government, and its courts would be bound to maintain and enforce them, the Constitution and laws of the State to the contrary notwithstanding. And if the States could limit or restrict them, or place the party in an inferior grade, this clause of the Constitution would be unmeaning, and could have no operation, and would give no rights to the citizen when in another State.

. . . .

And, upon a full and careful consideration of the subject, the court is of opinion, that, upon the facts stated in the plea in abatement, Dred Scott was not a citizen of Missouri within the meaning of the Constitution of the United States, and not entitled as such to sue in its courts, and consequently that the Circuit Court had no jurisdiction of the case, and that the judgment on the plea in abatement is erroneous.

. . . .

We proceed, therefore, to inquire whether the facts relied on by the plaintiff entitled him to his freedom.

. . . .

In considering this part of the controversy, two questions arise: 1. Was he, together with his family, free in Missouri by reason of the stay in the territory of the United States hereinbefore mentioned? And 2. If they were not, is Scott himself free by reason of his removal to Rock Island, in the State of Illinois, as stated in the above admissions?

We proceed to examine the first question.

The act of Congress upon which the plaintiff relies declares that slavery and involuntary servitude, except as a punishment for crime, shall be forever prohibited in all that part of the territory ceded by France, under the name of Louisiana, which lies north of thirty-six degrees thirty minutes north latitude, and not included within the limits of Missouri. And the difficulty which meets us at the threshold of this part of the inquiry is whether Congress was authorized to pass this law under any of the powers granted to it by the Constitution; for if the authority is not given by that instrument, it is the duty of this court to declare it void and inoperative, and incapable of conferring freedom upon anyone who is held as a slave under the have of anyone of the States.

The counsel for the plaintiff has laid much stress upon that article in the Constitution which confers on Congress the power "to dispose of and make all needful rules and regulations respecting the territory or other property belonging to the United States," but, in the judgment of the court, that provision has no bearing on the present controversy, and the power there given, whatever it may be, is confined, and was intended to be confined, to the territory which at that time belonged to, or was claimed by, the United States, and was within their boundaries as settled by the treaty with Great Britain, and can have no influence upon a territory afterwards acquired from a foreign Government. It was a special provision for a known and particular territory, and to meet a present emergency, and nothing more.

. . . .

The Constitution has always been remarkable for the felicity of its arrangement of different subjects and the perspicuity and appropriateness of the language it uses. But if this clause is construed to extend to territory acquired by the present Government from a foreign nation, outside of the limits of any charter from the British Government to a colony, it would be difficult to say why it was deemed necessary to give the Government the power to sell any vacant lands belonging to the sovereignty which might be found within it, and, if this was necessary, why

the grant of this power should precede the power to legislate over it and establish a Government there, and still more difficult to say why it was deemed necessary so specially and particularly to grant the power to make needful rules and regulations in relation to any personal or movable property it might acquire there. For the words other property necessarily, by every known rule of interpretation, must mean property of a different description from territory or land. And the difficulty would perhaps be insurmountable in endeavoring to account for the last member of the sentence, which provides that "nothing in this Constitution shall be so construed as to prejudice any claims of the United States or any particular State," or to say how any particular State could have claims in or to a territory ceded by a foreign Government, or to account for associating this provision with the preceding provisions of the clause, with which it would appear to have no connection.

. . . .

It is thus clear from the whole opinion on this point that the court did not mean to decide whether the power was derived from the clause in the Constitution or was the necessary consequence of the right to acquire. They do decide that the power in Congress is unquestionable, and in this we entirely concur, and nothing will be found in this opinion to the contrary. The power stands firmly on the latter alternative put by the court—that is, as "the inevitable consequence of the right to acquire territory."

. . . .

This brings us to examine by what provision of the Constitution the present Federal Government, under its delegated and restricted powers, is authorized to acquire territory outside of the original limits of the United States, and what powers it may exercise therein over the person or property of a citizen of the United States while it remains a Territory and until it shall be admitted as one of the States of the Union.

There is certainly no power given by the Constitution to the Federal Government to establish or maintain colonies bordering on the United States or at a distance to be ruled and governed at its own pleasure, nor to enlarge its territorial limits in any way except by the admission of new States. That power is plainly given, and if a new State is admitted, it needs no further legislation by Congress, because the Constitution itself defines the relative rights and powers and duties of the State, and the citizens of the State, and the Federal Government. But no power is given to acquire a Territory to be held and governed permanently in that character.

And indeed the power exercised by Congress to acquire territory and establish a Government there, according to its own unlimited discretion, was viewed with great jealousy by the leading statesmen of the day. And in the *Federalist No. 38,* written by Mr. Madison, he speaks of the acquisition of the Northwestern Territory by the confederated States, by the cession from Virginia, and the establishment of a Government there, as an exercise of power not warranted by the Articles of Confederation, and dangerous to the liberties of the people. And he urges the adoption of the Constitution as a security and safeguard against such an exercise of power.

We do not mean, however, to question the power of Congress in this respect. The power to expand the territory of the United States by the admission of new States is plainly given, and, in the construction of this power by all the departments of the Government, it has been held to authorize the acquisition of territory not fit for admission at the time, but to be admitted as soon as its population and situation would entitle it to admission. It is acquired to become a State, and not to be held as a colony and governed by Congress with absolute authority, and, as the propriety of admitting a new State is committed to the sound discretion of Congress, the power to acquire territory for that purpose, to be held by the United States until it is in a suitable condition to become a State upon an equal footing with the other States, must rest upon the same discretion. It is a question for the political department of the Government, and not the judicial, and whatever the political department of the Government shall recognise as within the limits of the United States, the judicial department is also bound to recognise and to administer in it the laws of the United States so far as they apply, and to maintain in the Territory the authority and rights of the Government and also the personal rights and rights of property of individual citizens as secured by the Constitution. All we mean to say on this point is that, as there is no express regulation in the Constitution defining the power which the General Government may exercise over the person or property of a citizen in a Territory thus acquired, the court must necessarily look to the provisions and principles of the Constitution and its distribution of powers for the rules and principles by which its decision must be governed.

. . . .

But the power of Congress over the person or property of a citizen can never be a mere discretionary power under our Constitution and form of Government. The powers of the Government and the rights and privileges of the citizen are regulated and plainly defined by the Constitution itself. And when the Territory becomes a part of the United States, the Federal Government enters into possession in the character impressed upon it by those who created it. It enters upon it with its powers over the citizen strictly defined, and limited by the Constitution, from which it derives its own existence and by virtue of which alone it continues to exist and act as a Government and sovereignty. It has no power of any kind beyond it, and it cannot, when it enters a Territory of the United States, put off its character and assume discretionary or despotic powers which the Constitution has denied to it. It cannot create for itself a new character separated from the citizens of the United States and the duties it owes them under the provisions of the Constitution. The Territory being a part of the United States, the Government and the citizen both enter it under the authority of the Constitution, with their respective rights defined and marked out, and the Federal Government can exercise no power over his person or property beyond what that instrument confers, nor lawfully deny any right which it has reserved.

. . . .

Upon these considerations, it is the opinion of the court that the act of Congress which prohibited a citizen from holding and owning property of this kind in the territory of the United States north of the line therein mentioned is not warranted by the Constitution, and is therefore void, and that neither Dred Scott himself nor any of his family were made free by being carried into this territory, even if they had been carried there by the owner with the intention of becoming a permanent resident.

. . . .

So in this case. As Scott was a slave when taken into the State of Illinois by his owner, and was there held as such, and brought back in that character, his status as free or slave depended on the laws of Missouri, and not of Illinois.

. . . .

Upon the whole, therefore, it is the judgment of this court that it appears by the record before us that the plaintiff in error is not a citizen of Missouri in the sense in which that word is used in the Constitution, and that the Circuit Court of the United States, for that reason, had no jurisdiction in the case, and could give no judgment in it. Its judgment for the defendant must, consequently, be reversed, and a mandate issued directing the suit to be dismissed for want of jurisdiction.

60 U.S. 393 (1856). Text courtesy of *Selected Historic Decisions of the U.S. Supreme Court* (CD-ROM, 1997 edition), a publication of the Legal Information Institute, Cornell Law School.

71   An Account of a Brawl on the Floor of the House of Representatives

February 6, 1858

While this account of a major brawl on the floor of the House of Representatives was written with humor and sarcasm regarding the behavior of the members and the reporters who watched the melee unfold, it was also a vivid reminder of the increasing tensions in Congress as the sectional feud between North and South over slavery continued to grow in the years immediately preceding the Civil War. This shoving and wrestling match was, perhaps, the largest such disturbance of its kind in the history of Congress.

The main participants were Galusha Grow, a Free Soil Democrat from Pennsylvania, who would, during the Civil War, serve a term as Speaker of the House as a Republican; Speaker of the House James Orr, a Democrat from South Carolina; John Hickman of Pennsylvania, described as a "Douglas Democrat," who would soon join the Republican Party; and the troublemaker Laurence Keitt, Democrat of South Carolina, who had a reputation for starting fights. Keitt was present two years earlier when Senator Charles Sumner was badly beaten on the floor of the Senate (see document 69). Also involved were John Quitman, a Democrat from Mississippi and former governor of that state; two Republican members from Wisconsin, Cadwallader Washburn and John Potter; and a States Rights Democrat from Mississippi, William Barksdale. No stranger to violent behavior, Potter was known by his nickname "Bowie Knife" Potter. Once, when challenged to a duel, Potter selected Bowie knives as the weapon of choice.

Once the brawl started, it was the North versus the South. The fight, involving more than fifty members, ended in laughter, when Potter grabbed at the scalp of Barksdale, only to pull off Barksdale's wig. When Potter yelled, "I've scalped him," the heated tempers were quickly cooled by the comedy of the situation. Frank Leslie's Illustrated Newspaper, from which this account is taken, featured a large engraving of the fight on its front page, complete with the moment of truth when Potter grabbed Barksdale's wig.

The sergeant-at-arms of the House is said to have "waved his spread eagle over their heads," a reference to the Mace of the House—a beautiful silver eagle, with wings spread, sitting astride a globe and mounted atop thirteen ebony rods. On rare occasions, such as this one, when the House is completely out of order, it is the House custom for the sergeant-at-arms to lift the Mace from its pedestal and present it before the offending members. Usually this action is sufficient reminder that order must be restored.

THE CONGRESSIONAL ROW.

On Friday night, in the year of our Lord eighteen hundred and fifty-eight, and the morning of Saturday, which was February sixth, before cock crowing, and yet after midnight, just about the time, according to poetical authority, that graveyards yawn, the United States House of Representatives was the scene of a spirited discussion on the "State of the Union." The members of that "deliberative body," who are generally as averse to any useful employment as New York policemen are to temperance practices, and who for the ostensible object of business generally assemble in the middle of the day, for the want of something better to do on the occasion referred to, concluded, in place of the futile experiment of exercising their brains, that they would test their physical endurance and see who could keep out of bed the longest. The contest was very interesting "to outsiders," and presented a scene, which, for all that is lamentable in human nature and our national fame, was, even for a Washington city row, pre-eminently disgusting.

The members exhibited towards the close of the [f]earful struggle some curious pictures; some were doubled up and others were doubled down. The "Western delegates" usually hung over the backs of their chairs, displaying open mouths and giving utterance to dreadful sounds; they had learned this attitude and expression in the wayside groggeries. The "Eastern men," in their slumbers, assumed reverential attitudes, and seemed to be lost in some devotional exercise. The "chivalry" seemed to be restive and fighting mosquitoes, and they were, therefore, the widest awake of any of their fellow-sufferers. Speaker Orr maintained his dignified good-nature, and though lost to "outward things," his right arm mechanically brought down his gavel upon his desk, unintentionally but truthfully indicating that the body before him was continually "out of order." The clerks, whose business it was to call the "yeas and nays," first gabbled at their work like so many geese, then became less articulate, and finally, at their "herculean task," broke down altogether. The newspaper reporters in the side galleries, under the delusion that they were in a vast oyster saloon in a state of drunken demoralization, went to cracking smutty jokes and pelting each other with spit balls, the solid contents of which were the President's Kansas message, degluted with Virginian weed and lager bier.

A few innocent members of the House, who had just arrived at congressional honors, were honestly impressed with the idea that their work for the public was indeed no sinecure, and that this making the delaying or passing of an act depend upon the muscles of the eyelids, was no trifling demand upon their integrity. These "honest men" (perhaps four out of the whole representation) having been accustomed to regular habits, suffered great inconvenience, and many felt that it was even taxing their patriotism, in spite of the eight dollars a day and little outside jobs, to keep them up after ten o'clock; while the "old stagers," who have made politics what "sneak thieves" do thimblerigging—a perfect business—having been through many campaigns, and thus become case-hardened to all "irregularities," felt no more inconvenience in sleeping in their chairs in the Representative Hall, than they would, if they had reposed in their accustomed places at the corner grocery, on a wooden bench, or a pine table-top.

For many hours had the house been in session. It is incredible what a number of "private drinks" had been indulged in to sustain the failing strength of its members, it would create a run on the hog market if it were known how much bacon, encased in bread slices, was consumed on that memorable occasion, nor would it be within the power of any mathematician to enumerate the plugs of tobacco that were masticated, or the vile cigars that were etherialized in smoke, or, when half consumed, as "old soldiers" trampled on to the floor. The whole thing was a kind of mental and physical fermentation; it had gone on silently, engendering diseased life, and like a slippery cheese was to grow "lively," by the very exuberance of a newly-hatched existence. The time and the hour came. Mr. Grow, of Pennsylvania, passed over physically, to "the Democratic side of the House," for the purpose of conferring, probably about "pairing off to liquor," with Mr. Hickman, "a Douglas Democrat" when, having finished his conference, he was passing down the side aisle, on his way back to kits seat. At the moment Gen. Quitman, asked unanimous consent "to submit a motion out of order" (as if a motion at that time and under those circumstances could have been anything else than *out of order*). Mr. Grow, raising himself from his somnolent state, according to usual custom, said, "I object, Mr. Speaker; let us go on in regular order." Whereupon Mr. Keitt, of South Carolina, who was near Mr. Grow, rather roughly suggested that the gentleman should go over to his own side, if he wanted to object; whereat Mr. Grow, inflamed with the general principle of constitutional liberty, for which our ancestors principally fought and died (always excepting those who sold things to both sides and thus founded some of the oldest and wealthiest families in the country), resented this intrusion from the gentleman of the Palmetto State, and boldly and fearlessly asserted that he was in a "free hall—that a man could be where he pleased in it," forgetting that he could not be in two places at the same time, nor occupy the same space already filled by another honorable gentleman—nor could he be nowhere in the hall, for nature abhors a vacuum; and with such a general but incorrect expression of the great principle of American liberty, he continued to walk slowly down the hall.

Mr. Keitt who was probably in a somnambulic state, as subsequent events seem to suggest, rushed into the "area of freedom," and turning round faced up the aisle just as Mr. Grow reached the bottom of it and with an authoritative air, asked Mr. Grow what he meant by his answer? Mr. Grow, under the circumstances with remarkable presence of mind, remembered what he had last said, and reseated the broad declaration that he was in a free hall. This proposition, so pertinaciously insisted upon by the gentleman from Pennsylvania, aroused Mr. Keitt's ire—for he, Mr. Keitt, knew full well that it wasn't a "free hall," that nobody had a legal right on the floor except members of Congress and certain hangers-on at their button-holes, including at times the leading cabinet officers; and so outraged had he become, that he clenched at something in his indignation. Words now grew "fast and, furious;" Grow persisted in the ridiculous idea that he could go where he pleased in the hall, implying that he could get into an inkstand or the Speaker's tobacco-box; Mr Keitt, equally enthusiastic, contradicted this oft asserted proposition, and in the excitement "fell on the floor."

Now the melée became general; the members, who had previously been stewing and sweating in their sleep, and all probably dreaming that they were in some personal danger, like a fellows suddenly precipitated in the water, commenced "striking out." In the twinkling of an eye—very slow twinkling, it must be remembered—some forty or fifty Republicans came dashing across the hall, headed by Potter of Wisconsin, who leaped into the midst of the arena with an agility commendable to behold and then commenced a series of muscular demonstrations that would have been very alarming had they followed the bite of a mad dog; the effect of all this was a general distribution of side licks, back handers, and stomach winders, that acted wonderfully as specifies in waking up the gentlemen most interested. That the whole thing might have the air of an Indian pow-wow, Potter seized Barksdale, of Mississippi, by the hair of the head, and awful to relate, *tore the scalp entirely off*—whereupon, Washburn, of Wisconsin, having his reminiscences of fights with the red man revived within him, pitched into the ring, causing an immense rolling over on the floor of numerous specimens of the collected wisdom of the nation.

Meantime the speaker battered the front of his new desk into mince meat, and wore off the sharp edges of his hammer, crying out at the top of his voice "Order! order!" which was as practical as if a katydid should by its piping try to drown thunder. The Sergeant-at-Arms, believing in the bird of Jove, seized an emblem of that valorous "critter" and rushed into the body of the hall, but as the Sergeant-at-Arms didn't bargain to prevent the members of Congress fighting and rowdying as much as they pleased, he merely waved his spread eagle over their heads, and so judiciously managed, that he left the impression that he was on both sides of the quarrel, and would no more hurt the feelings of a representative by enforcing the rules formed for the good of the House, than he would refuse the forty-ninth stiff cocktail, necessary to carry him through the fatigues of the day.

In infinitely less time than our facts can be detailed—in the short conventional space of three minutes—this curry began and ended. As the excitement wore off the members presented the appearance of hot mutton fat suddenly brought in contact with the north wind. Every man looked more or less as if he had been caught in a dirty scrape, and only found relief in the fact that his compatriots were as guilty as himself, and therefore wouldn't peach. The next day Mr. Keitt, who has, it seems, true magnanimity enough to acknowledge a fault, rose in his place and took the responsibility of setting the first brick in motion that so agitated the rest of the pile, whereupon the whole country comes out in laudation of Mr. Keitt, and pronounces him a real brick and he acquires great glory; while those gentlemen who always behave themselves (four or five) are never heard of, and are consequently considered very poor and very inefficient members of Congress. So much for the last Congressional row, a thing which it is useless to treat seriously, and yet in its moral effect is doing constant damage to our fame at home, and will damage our standing as a nation "with the rest of mankind."

Frank Leslie's Illustrated Newspaper, February 20, 1858, 177–178.

72   The House of Representatives Launches an Investigation of President James Buchanan

March 5, 1860

Congressional investigations of sitting presidents of the United States are always dramatic and fraught with partisan politics. One of the most mean-spirited investigations of a president occurred in 1860, when President James Buchanan, a Democrat, ran afoul of northern Republicans in the House. The Covode Committee, named after its Republican chairman "Honest John" Covode of Pennsylvania, conducted an investigation so broad in scope and vague in charges that almost anything corrupt anywhere in government was laid at Buchanan's feet. The committee called more than a hundred witnesses. President Buchanan complained that the investigation was motivated by bitter partisanship and was an unconstitutional infringement on the executive branch.

John Covode was a little known member of Congress in his third term when he introduced the resolution calling for the Speaker to appoint a committee "for the purpose of investigating whether the President of the United States, or any other officer of the Government, has, by money, patronage, or other improper means, sought to influence the action of Congress. . . ." The resolution called for an investigation of any laws the president may have broken or refused to enforce. Specifically, it called for an examination of abuses in the navy yards of Philadelphia and the post offices of Chicago. Covode used a letter the president had written two years earlier, in which he said money was used to coerce elections in Pennsylvania, to launch an open-ended campaign finance investigation in Pennsylvania and other states.

The Select Committee to Investigate Alleged Corruption in Government issued its report in June 1860. Much corruption was discovered in private government printing contracts. Some voting fraud was found in the 1856 Pennsylvania elections. A few Democratic "bag men" were exposed, one of whom said he gave $100,000 to Democratic campaigns over four years but could not remember the details of who got the money and how because he did not keep books.

None of the corruption could be directly connected to the president. The press reported every detail of the case. Buchanan actually garnered some public sympathy because of the flawed, vague resolution that launched the investigation. One of the two Democratic members of the investigating committee, Miles Taylor of Louisiana, branded the Covode Committee "a secret Star Chamber."

Despite the committee's findings, there was never any attempt to impeach the president. The Republicans were content to damage the president before the fall presidential election that year. The Senate had a Democratic majority, which further weakened the chances of successfully impeaching the president. Perhaps the best thing to come from the 1860 investigation was Republican-led reform of the government's corrupt private-sector printing contracts. This led to the establishment of the Government Printing Office in 1860. Covode became a popular speaker and fund-raiser for the Republican Party. He would emerge again into the national lime-light eight years later when he was the first to call for the impeachment of another president, Andrew Johnson.

Buchanan left the presidency as one of the most vilified presidents in American history. At his successor's inauguration, Buchanan expressed his feelings about leaving office to Abraham Lincoln: "My dear, sir, if you are as happy on entering the White House as I on leaving, you are a very happy man indeed."

The House debate that followed the introduction of the Covode resolution, reproduced here, showed that tempers flared and parliamentary order broke down. Members even tried to give speeches while a roll call vote was underway. The resolution was approved largely on a party-line vote, although some Democrats voted for it, saying they were confident the president had nothing to hide.

Mr. COVODE. I ask the unanimous consent of the House for leave to introduce the resolutions I send to the Clerk's desk to be read.

The Clerk read as follows:

Resolved, That a committee of five members be appointed by the Speaker, for the purpose of investigating whether the President of the United States, or any other officer of the Government, has, by money, patronage, or other improper means, sought to influence the action of Congress, or any committee thereof, for or against the passage of any law appertaining to the rights of any state or Territory; also, to inquire into and investigate whether any officer or officers of the Government have, by combination or otherwise, prevented or defeated, or attempted to prevent or defeat, the execution of any law or laws now upon the statute-book, and whether the President has failed or refused to compel the execution of any law thereof; and that said committee shall investigate and inquire into the abuses at the Chicago or other post offices, and at the Philadelphia and other navy-yards, and into any abuses in connection with the public buildings other public works of the United States.

And resolved further, That, as the President, in his letter to the Pittsburg[h] centenary celebration of the 25th November, 1858, speaks of the employment of money to coerce elections, said committee shall inquire into and ascertain the amount so used in Pennsylvania, and any other State or States, in what districts it was expended, and by whom, and by whose authority it was done, and from what source the money was derived, and to report the names of the parties implicated; and that, for the purpose aforesaid, said committee shall have the power to send for persons and papers, and to report at any time.

Before the Clerk concluded the reading of the resolutions, "Messrs. FLORENCE and WHITELEY objected.

Mr. COVODE. Then I move to suspend the rules, that the resolutions may be introduced.

Mr. FLORENCE. I want a statement of the grounds upon which those resolutions are introduced here. If there is any evidence, let it be specified; and if there are any specified charges, I am as ready to vote for an investigation as any member here.

The SPEAKER *pro tempore,* (Mr. Colfax in the chair.) The resolutions will be read through.

Mr. FLORENCE. Enough has been read to let us know what the resolutions are.

The SPEAKER *pro tempore*. The resolutions must be read through.

Mr. HINDMAN. We have not heard the first portion of the resolutions distinctly enough to understand it, and I hope they will be read again.

The SPEAKER *pro tempore*. The Clerk will read the entire resolutions when gentlemen take their seats and order is restored.

Mr. UNDERWOOD. I rise to a point of order. It is, that it is not in order in this House for any member to propose an investigation upon vague, loose, and indefinite charges; but it is his duty to state the grounds distinctly upon which he predicates his inquiry. If the gentleman who offered these resolutions will state to the House, upon his responsibility as a member of the House, that he knows, or has been informed and believes, that offers have been made to bribe, as insinuated in that resolution, nobody will object. But I do object to charges against any officer of the Government by insinuation.

Mr. BINGHAM. I object to this debate. It is all out of order.

Mr. UNDERWOOD. When gentlemen will not make their charges upon their responsibility as Representatives upon this floor, I must object.

Mr. FLORENCE. I submit a point of order.

The Speaker *pro tempore*. The gentleman from Georgia has submitted a point of order; and until that is disposed of, no other question is in order. The Chair overrules the point of order.

Mr. FLORENCE. For the reason mentioned by the gentleman from Georgia—that there is a vague and indefinite something in those resolution—I object to them. There is no use of reading them. If my colleague wants the rules suspended, he can have them, if he can get votes enough; but l will not sit in my place quietly, when such innuendoes as those are leveled against honest men. [Laughter.]

Mr. COVODE. If it will relieve my colleague, I will leave the navy-yards out.

Mr. FLORENCE. I have nothing to do with the navy-yards. I court investigation everywhere, and condemn corruption in the navy-yards as soon as I would anywhere else; and my colleague knows it. I am against corruption everywhere. Give me a reason for this investigation, and I will vote for it.

Mr. MORRIS, of Pennsylvania. I do not mean to debate the resolutions; but wish simply to say, if these charge are vague and unfounded, they can be prove to be so by the investigation.

The Clerk then read the resolutions again, as above inserted.

Mr. COVODE. I call for the yeas and nays upon the suspension of the rules.

Mr. BURNETT. I wish to vote correctly upon this question; and for that purpose, desire to say to the gentleman from Pennsylvania—

Mr. GROW. I rise to a point of order. Upon a motion to suspend the rules debate is not in order.

The SPEAKER *pro tempore*. The Chair sustains the point of order.

Mr. BURNETT. If the gentleman will make the charges specific, I will vote for the investigation; but I cannot vote for an investigation upon such vague charges as those contained in those resolutions.

Mr. COVODE. This is no time to make the charges specific.

The yeas and nays were ordered.

The question was put, and it was decided in the affirmative—yeas 117, nays 45 . . . .

So the rules were suspended, (two thirds voting in favor thereof.)

During the call,

Mr. ASHMORE, when his name was called, said: I desire to vote for an investigation if the charges are properly made—

Mr. GROW. I call the gentleman to order.

Mr. ASHMORE. The gentleman from Pennsylvania has no right to call me to order. The gentleman has taken it upon himself, frequently, since I have been here, to interfere with me, [cries of "Order !" "Order!"] and I would be obliged to him if he would keep his tongue silent where I am concerned. [Loud cries of "Order!"] I desire to vote for the resolutions if gentlemen will assert upon their responsibility that—

Mr. BINGHAM. I call the gentleman to order, and I call upon the Chair to enforce the rules.

Mr. ASHMORE, (amidst loud and continued cries of "Order!") I will not vote for an investigation merely upon insinuations and imputations like these upon the character of public officers, made by those who will not take the responsibility of doing, and who have not the manliness to do what gentlemen ought to do. I say I will vote for the resolutions whenever the charges are properly specified. Now, I vote "no."

Mr. HINDMAN. I am paired off, upon all questions which have a political bearing, with the gentleman from Pennsylvania, [Mr. Killinger;] I therefore decline to vote upon this proposition.

Mr. LANDRUM stated that he was paired off with Mr. Carter.

Mr. CRAIGE, of North Carolina, said: While I am ordinarily willing to vote for an investigation of any charges made against any officer of the Government, ["Order !" "Order !"] or any department of it, I am determined not to vote for a resolution which condemns in advance, [renewed cries of "Order!"] as this resolution does, the highest officer in the Government—the President of the United States.

Mr. GROW. I call the gentleman to order. No debate is in order while the roll is being called, and I call upon the Speaker to enforce the rule.

The SPEAKER *pro tempore*. The point of order is well taken; and the Chair hopes gentlemen will preserve order.

Mr. WINSLOW. I hope the House will indulge me in saying—

Mr. GROW: I object to debate.

Mr. WINSLOW (amidst loud and continued cries of "Order!") said: I feel some hesitation about my vote. These resolutions are very vague and indefinite, large in their terms, and framed like a French indictment, covering a deal of ground and abounding in a multitude of general charges. I have perfect confidence in the integrity of the President and his Cabinet. Let any specific charge be brought against him, or them, and I will cheerfully yield the fullest investigation and accord the promptest action. I will do nothing to hinder, but everything to facilitate it. I cannot, however, vote for a committee on these sweeping charges. I vote "no."

Mr. BOCOCK. Is debate in order?

The SPEAKER *pro tempore*. It is not.

Mr. BOCOCK. I shall give some reasons for my vote hereafter, not now. I vote "no."

Mr. HARRIS, of Virginia. Not having the slightest confidence in the accuracy of the charges preferred, I vote "ay."

Mr. SOMES stated that he should have voted "ay," had he been within the bar when his name was called.

Mr. COBB. If my party is guilty of corruption, let it be ferreted out. I vote "ay."

Mr. MILES. Is my vote recorded? for I wish to be upon the record as voting against clap-trap and humbug.

Mr. FLORENCE. Is my vote recorded? I am as much opposed ["Order!" "Order!"] to corruption ["Order!" "Order!"] as any gentleman upon this floor.

The SPEAKER *pro tempore*. Debate is not in order; and the Chair hopes gentlemen will preserve decorum.

Mr. FLORENCE. I will preserve decorum, of course.

Mr. PEYTON. I wish to change my vote. I voted under a misapprehension, supposing that definite charges had been made against the Administration, but learning that the charges are general, I change my vote, and vote "no."

Mr. JOHN COCHRANE. Because no charge are preferred upon which an investigation can be founded—

Mr. GROW and others called the gentleman to order.

Mr. JOHN COCHRANE. I suppose my friends will say I am in order, when I vote "no."

Mr. GROW. No debate is in order.

Mr. JOHN COCHRANE. I am proposing vote "no." The gentlemen furnish me with the reason for it. Will the Clerk call my name?

The CLERK. Mr. Cochrane.

Mr. JOHN COCHRANE. No. [Laughter.]

Mr. SMITH, of Virginia, I simply want to say, ["Order!" "Order!"] the resolution is unworthy of the men who drew it. ["Order!" "Order!"] Yes, sir, unworthy of the men who drew it. I vote "no."

Mr. MONTGOMERY. I desire to vote. I was not within the bar when my name was called.

Mr. FLORENCE. I must object, though I would like to have the gentleman's vote upon our side, for I suppose he would vote against this thing.

The result of the vote was then announced, as above recorded.

Mr. COVODE. I call for the previous question upon the adoption of the resolutions.

Mr. NOELL. I desire to offer an amendment, and ask that it may be read for information.

Mr. COVODE. I cannot yield for that purpose.

Mr. NOELL. I ask to have the amendment read for information.

Mr. BINGHAM. I object.

The previous question was seconded, and the main question ordered to be put; and under the operation thereof, the resolutions were adopted.

Mr. COVODE moved to reconsider the vote by which the resolutions were adopted, and also moved to lay the motion to reconsider on the table.

The latter motion was agreed to.

Congressional Globe, 36th Congress, 1st session, March 5, 1860, 997–998.

73   Senator Jefferson Davis's Farewell Address to the Senate

January 21, 1861

In the aftermath of the election of Abraham Lincoln, the South believed compromise over slavery was at an end. One by one, starting with South Carolina in December 1860, southern states left the Union in a process known as secession. On January 21, 1861, three more states—Mississippi, Florida, and Alabama—left the Union. The senators from Florida and Alabama made final remarks that day, but it was the senator from Mississippi, Jefferson Davis (1808–1889), the last to speak, who captured the high drama of the moment. Davis was the most distinguished of those who spoke that day. He was a West Point graduate who served earlier in the House of Representatives, as a commander in the Mexican War, as secretary of war in the Pierce Administration, and twice in the U.S. Senate, from 1847 to 1851 and 1857 to 1861. He did not try to of-fer an elaborate defense of secession. He based his remarks on his belief that states were sovereign entities and that Mississippi had the right to "declare her separation from the United States." When he completed his remarks, he and his colleagues from Alabama and Florida solemnly walked out of the Senate chamber while some in the galleries applauded and others wept.

Within a month of leaving the Senate, Jefferson Davis became the first and only president of the Confederate States of America. As other southern states seceded from the Union, the politeness and confusion that greeted Davis's departure were replaced with a sterner approach, as southern senators were formally expelled from the body for treason against the United States. As the Confederacy crumbled in the spring of 1865, Davis escaped from his capital in

Richmond, Virginia, and was captured by Union troops on May 10, 1865. He spent two years in a federal prison, charged with treason and complicity in Lincoln's assassination, although he was never tried. When he was paroled, he returned to Mississippi, where he spent much of his time writing an account of the Confederate government. His work was published in 1881. It was not until 1978 that Congress posthumously restored Davis's status as a citizen of the United States.

I rise, Mr. President, for the purpose of announcing to the Senate that I have satisfactory evidence that the state of Mississippi, by a solemn ordinance of her people in convention assembled, has declared her separation from the United States. Under these circumstances, of course my functions are terminated here. It has seemed to me proper, however, that I should appear in the Senate to announce that fact to my associates, and I will say but very little more. The occasion does not invite me to go into argument; and my physical condition would not permit me to do so if it were otherwise; and yet it seems to become me to say something on the part of the state I here represent, on an occasion so solemn as this.

It is known to senators who have served with me here, that I have for many years advocated, as an essential attribute of state sovereignty, the right of a State to secede from the Union. Therefore, if I had not believed there was justifiable cause; if I had thought that Mississippi was acting without sufficient provocation, or without an existing necessity, I should still, under my theory of the government, because of my allegiance to the state of which I am a citizen, have been bound by her action. I, however, may be permitted to say that I do think she has justifiable cause, and I approve of her act. I conferred with her people before that act was taken, counseled them then that if the state of things which they apprehended should exist when the convention met, they should take the action which they have now adopted.

I hope none who hear me will confound this expression of mine with the advocacy of the right of a state to remain in the Union, and to disregard its constitutional obligations by the nullification of the law. Such is not my theory. Nullification and secession, so often confounded, are indeed antagonistic principles. Nullification is a remedy which it is sought to apply within the Union, and against the agent of the states. It is only to be justified when the agent has violated his constitutional obligation, and a state, assuming to judge for itself, denies the right of the agent thus to act, and appeals to the other states of the Union for a decision; but when the states themselves, and when the people of the states, have so acted as to convince us that they will not regard our constitutional rights, then, and then for the first time, arises the doctrine of secession in its practical application.

A great man who now reposes with his fathers, and who has been often arraigned for a want of fealty to the Union, advocated the doctrine of nullification, because it preserved the Union. It was because of his deep-seated attachment to the Union, his determination to find some remedy for existing ills short of a severance of the ties which bound South Carolina to the other states, that Mr. Calhoun advocated the doctrine of nullification, which he proclaimed to be peaceful, to be within the limits of state power, not to disturb the Union, but only to be a means of bringing the agent before the tribunal of the states for their judgment.

Secession belongs to a different class of remedies. It is to be justified upon the basis that the states are sovereign. There was a time when none denied it. I hope the time may come again, when a better comprehension of the theory of our government, and the inalienable rights of the people of the states, will prevent anyone from denying that each state is a sovereign, and thus may reclaim the grants which it has made to any agent whomsoever.

I therefore say I concur in the action of the people of Mississippi, believing it to be necessary and proper, and should have been bound by their action if my belief had been otherwise; and this brings me to the important point which I wish on this last occasion to present to the Senate. It is by this confounding of nullification and secession that the name of a great man, whose ashes now mingle with his mother earth, has been invoked to justify coercion against a seceded state. The phrase "to execute the laws," was an expression which General Jackson applied to the case of a state refusing to obey the laws while yet a member of the Union. That is not the case which is now presented. The laws are to be executed over the United States, and upon the people of the United States. They have no relation to any foreign country. It is a perversion of terms, at least it is a great misapprehension of the case, which cites that expression for application to a state which has withdrawn from the Union. You may make war on a foreign state. If it be the purpose of gentlemen, they may make war against a state which has withdrawn from the Union; but there are no laws of the United States to be executed within the limits of a seceded state. A state finding herself in the condition in which Mississippi has judged she is, in which her safety requires that she should provide for the maintenance of her rights out of the Union, surrenders all the benefits (and they are known to be many), deprives herself of the advantages (they are known to be great), severs all the ties of affection (and they are close and enduring), which have bound her to the Union; and thus divesting herself of every benefit, taking upon herself every burden, she claims to be exempt from any power to execute the laws of the United States within her limits.

I well remember an occasion when Massachusetts was arraigned before the bar of the Senate, and when then the doctrine of coercion was rife and to be applied against her because of the rescue of a fugitive slave in Boston. My opinion then was the same that it is now. Not in a spirit of egotism, but to show that I am not influenced in my opinion because the case is my own, I refer to that time and that occasion as containing the opinion which I then entertained, and on which my present conduct is based. I then said, if Massachusetts, following her through a stated line of conduct, chooses to take the last step which separates her from the Union, it is her right to go, and I will neither vote one dollar nor one man to coerce her back; but will say to her, God speed, in memory of the kind associations which once existed between her and the other states.

It has been a conviction of pressing necessity, it has been a belief that we are to be deprived in the Union of the rights which our fathers bequeathed to us, which has brought Mississippi into her present decision. She has heard proclaimed the theory that all men are created free and equal, and this made the basis of an attack upon her social institutions; and the sacred Declaration of Independence has been invoked to maintain the position of the equality of the races. That Declaration of Independence is to be construed by the circumstances and purposes for which it was made. The communities were declaring their independence; the people of those communities were asserting that no man was born—to use the language of Mr. Jefferson—booted and spurred to ride over the rest of mankind; that men were created equal—meaning the men of the political community; that there was no divine right to rule; that no man inherited the right to govern; that there were no classes by which power and place descended to families, but that all stations were equally within the grasp of each member of the body-politic. These were the great principles they announced; these were the purposes for which they made their declaration; these were the ends to which their enunciation was directed. They have no reference to the slave; else, how happened it that among the items of arraignment made against George III was that he endeavored to do just what the North has been endeavoring of late to do—to stir up insurrection among our slaves? Had the Declaration announced that the negroes were free and equal, how was the prince to be arraigned for stirring up insurrection among them? And how was this to be enumerated among the high crimes which caused the colonies to sever their connection with the mother country? When our Constitution was formed, the same idea was rendered more palpable, for there we find provision made for that very class of persons as property; they were not put upon the footing of equality with white men—not even upon that of paupers and convicts; but, so far as representation was concerned, were discriminated against as a lower caste, only to be represented in the numerical proportion of three-fifths.

Then, senators, we recur to the compact which binds us together; we recur to the principles upon which our government was founded; and when you deny them, and when you deny to us the right to withdraw from a government which thus perverted threatens to be destructive of our rights, we but tread in the path of our fathers when we proclaim our independence, and take the hazard. This is done not in hostility to others, not to injure any section of the country, not even for our own pecuniary benefit; but from the high and solemn motive of defending and protecting the rights we inherited, and which it is our sacred duty to transmit unshorn to our children.

I find in myself, perhaps, a type of the general feeling of my constituents towards yours. I am sure I feel no hostility to you, senators from the North. I am sure there is not one of you, whatever sharp discussion there may have been between us, to whom I cannot now say, in the presence of my God, I wish you well; and such, I am sure, is the feeling of the people whom I represent towards those whom you represent. I therefore feel that I but express their desire when I say I hope, and they hope, for peaceful relations with you, though we must part. They may be mutually beneficial to us in the future, as they have been in the past, if you so will it. The reverse may bring disaster on every portion of the country; and if you will have it thus, we will invoke the God of our fathers, who delivered them from the power of the lion, to protect us from the ravages of the bear; and thus, putting our trust in God, and in our own firm hearts and strong arms, we will vindicate the right as best we may.

In the course of my service here, associated at different times with a great variety of senators, I see now around me some with whom I have served long; there have been points of collision; but whatever of offense there has been to me, I leave here; I carry with me no hostile remembrance. Whatever offense I have given which has not been redressed, or for which satisfaction has not been demanded, I have, senators, in this hour of our parting, to offer you my apology for any pain which, in heat of discussion, I have inflicted. I go hence unencumbered of the remembrance of any injury received, and having discharged the duty of making the only reparation in my power for any injury offered.

Mr. President, and senators, having made the announcement which the occasion seemed to me to require, it only remains for me to bid you a final adieu.

Congressional Globe, Senate, 36th Congress, 2d session, Jan. 21, 1861, 487.

74 James G. Blaine's Description of Congress at the Beginning of the Civil War

March 1861

James G. Blaine (1830–1893), a Republican from Maine, was one of the most popular and gifted American politicians of the second half of the nineteenth century. A former teacher of the blind and a newspaper editor in Maine, Blaine entered politics at the state level in 1859. When the Civil War broke out he was serving as speaker of the Maine House of Representatives. Blaine served in the U.S. House of Representatives from 1863 to 1876, holding important positions as chairman of the Rules Committee and as Speaker from 1869 to 1875. He served as a senator from Maine from 1876 to 1881 and was an unsuccessful presidential candidate in 1876,

1880, and 1884. Blaine also served as secretary of state in the cabinets of three presidents, James A. Garfield, Chester A. Arthur, and Benjamin Harrison. In the 1880s he wrote a two-volume memoir, Twenty Years of Congress: From Lincoln to Garfield, *which ranks as one of the best political memoirs of the nineteenth century. It is still cited frequently by historians and political scientists.*

In this entry from Twenty Years of Congress, *Blaine characterized the 37th Congress, which convened as the Civil War began. Drawing on his skills as a former newspaper man and his years of experience in Congress, where he met and knew the principal characters he described, Blaine painted a vivid portrait of Congress as it entered those perilous times. Although this account was written more than twenty years after the events it described, it is clear that Blaine had an excellent grasp of historical detail and great respect for the talent he saw in both the House and the Senate. Blaine reminded us that Congress is not an abstract entity that is easily described. It is composed of individuals with varying backgrounds and experience, different personalities, and clashing ideas. To know any Congress one has to know the people and not just the statistics of the body.*

The Thirty-seventh Congress assembled according to the President's proclamation, on the fourth day of July, 1861. There had been no ebb in the tide of patriotic enthusiasm which overspread the loyal States after the fall of Sumter. Mr. Lincoln's sagacity in fixing the session so late had apparently been well approved. The temper of the senators and representatives as they came together could not have been better for the great work before them. Startling events, following each other thick and fast had kept the country in a state of absorbing excitement, and Congress saw around it on every side the indications of a sanguinary struggle to come. Even after the firing on Sumter, anxious and thoughtful men had not given up all hope of an adjustment. The very shock of arms in the harbor of Charleston, it was believed, by many, might upon sober second thought induce Southern men to pause and consider and negotiate before taking the fatal plunge. Such expectations were vain. The South felt that their victory was pre-ordained. Jefferson Davis answered Mr. Lincoln's call for seventy-five thousand men by a proclamation ordering the enlistment of one hundred thousand. The Confederacy was growing in strength daily. State after State was joining it, and energy and confidence prevailed throughout all its borders. The situation grew every day more embarrassing and more critical. Without waiting for the action of Congress, Mr. Lincoln had called for forty-two thousand additional volunteers, and added eleven new regiments, numbering some twenty-two thousand men, to the regular army. A blockade of the Southern ports had been ordered on the 19th of April, and eighteen thousand men had been added to the navy.

No battle of magnitude or decisive character had been fought when Congress assembled; but there had been activity on the skirmish line of the gathering and advancing forces and, at many points, bloody collision. In Baltimore, on the historic 19th of April, the mob had endeavored to stop the march of Massachusetts troops hurrying to the protection of the National Capital. In Missouri General Nathaniel Lyon had put to flight the disloyal governor, and established the supremacy of National authority. In Western Virginia General McClellan had met with success in some minor engagements, and on the upper Potomac the forces under General Robert Patterson had gained some advantages. A reverse of no very serious character had been experienced at Big Bethel, near Hampton Roads, by the troops under General Benjamin F. Butler. General Robert C. Schenck, in command of a small force, had met with a repulse a few miles from Washington, near Vienna in the State of Virginia. These incidents were not in themselves of special importance, but they indicated an aggressive energy on the part of the Confederates, and foreshadowed the desperate character which the contest was destined to assume. Congress found itself legislating in a fortified city, with patrols of soldiers on the streets and with a military administration which had practically superseded the civil police in the duty of maintaining order and protecting life. The situation was startling and serious, and for the first time people began to realize that we were to have a war with bloody fighting and much suffering, with limitless destruction of property, with costly sacrifice of life.

The spirit in both branches of Congress was a fair reflection of that which prevailed in the North. Andrew Johnson of Tennessee was the only senator who appeared from the eleven seceding States. John C. Breckinridge was present from Kentucky, somewhat mortified by the decisive rebuke which he had received in the vote of his State. The first important act of the Senate was the seating of James H. Lane and Samuel C. Pomeroy as senators from the new State of Kansas which had been admitted at the last session of Congress as a free State, in a bill which, with historic justice, Mr. Buchanan was called upon to approve, after he had announced to Congress, during the first year of his administration, that Kansas, was as much a slave State as South Carolina. The first question of moment growing out of the Rebellion was the presentation of credentials by Messrs. Willey and Carlile, who claimed seats as senators from Virginia, the right to which was certified by the seal of the State with the signature of Francis H. Pierpont as governor. The credentials indicated that Mr. Willey was to take the seat vacated by Mr. Mason, and Mr. Carlile that vacated by Mr. Hunter. The loyal men of Virginia, especially from the western counties, finding that the regularly organized government of the State had joined the Rebellion, extemporized, a government composed of the Union men of the Legislature which had been in session the preceding winter in Richmond. This body had met in Wheeling and elected two men as senators who had stood firmly for the union in the convention which had forced Virginia into secession. Their admission to the Senate was resisted by Mr. James A. Bayard, then senator from Delaware, and by the few other Democratic senators who still held seats. But after discussion, Mr. Willey and Mr. Carlile were sworn in, and thus the first step was taken which led soon after to the partition of the Old Dominion and the creation of the new State of West Virginia. The free

States had a unanimous representation of Republican Senators, with the exception of John R. Thompson from New Jersey, Jesse D. Bright from Indiana, James W. Nesmith from Oregon, and the two senators from California, Milton S. Latham and James A. McDougall the latter of whom was sworn in as the successor of William M. Gwin.

The Senate, though deprived by secession of many able men from the South, presented an imposing array of talent, statesmanship, and character. . . .

The prominence of New England in the Senate was exceptional. So many positions of influence were assigned to her that it created no small degree of jealousy and ill-feeling in other sections. The places according to the somewhat rigid rules of precedence in that body, but this fact did not induce senators, from the Middle and Western States to acquiesce with grace. The chairmanship of the Committee on Foreign Relations was given to Mr. Sumner; Mr. Fessenden was placed at the head of the Finance Committee, which then included Appropriations; Mr. Wilson was made chairman of Military Affairs; Mr. John P. Hale, chairman of Naval Affairs; Mr. Collamer, chairman of Post-office and Post-road; Mr. Foster of Connecticut, chairman of Pensions; Mr. Clark of New Hampshire, chairman of Claims; Mr. Simmons of Rhode Island, chairman of Patents; Mr. Foot of Vermont, chairman of Public Buildings and Grounds; Mr. Anthony, chairman of Printing; Mr. Dixon of Connecticut, chairman of Contingent Expenses. Mr. Lot M. Morrill who had just entered the public service from Maine, was the only New England senator left without a chairmanship. There were in all twenty-two committees in the Senate. Eleven were given to New England. But even this ratio does not exhibit the case in its fun strength. The Committees on Foreign Relations, Finance, Military Affairs, and Naval Affairs; shaped almost the entire legislation in time of war, and thus New England occupied a most commanding position. The retirement of Mr. Seward, Mr. Chase, and Mr. Cameron from the Senate to enter the Cabinet undoubtedly increased the number of important positions assigned to New England. Twenty-two States were represented in the Senate, and it was impossible to make sixteen of them, including the four leading States of the Union, recognize the justice of placing the control of National legislation in the hands of six States in the far North-East. It was not a fortunate arrangement for New England, since it provoked prejudices which proved injurious in many ways, and lasted for many years.

The House of Representatives was promptly organized by the election of Galusha A. Grow of Pennsylvania as Speaker. Mr. Grow came from the Wilmot district, on the northern border of the State, where the anti-slavery sentiment had taken earliest and deepest root. As Connecticut had in the Colonial period claimed a large part of the area of North Pennsylvania, her emigration tended in that direction, and this fact had given a distinct and more radical type to the population. Mr. Grow was himself a native of Connecticut. He was chosen Speaker because

of his activity in the anti-slavery struggles of the House, and because of his aptitude for the duties of the chair. Francis P. Blair, Jr., of Missouri was a rival candidate, and was supported by strong influences. It was not considered expedient to hold a party caucus, and the Democratic minority declined to present a candidate. On the roll call, Mr. Grow received 71 votes, Mr. Blair 40, while 48 votes, principally of Democratic representatives were cast for different gentlemen who were in no sense candidates. Accepting Mr. Grow's plurality as the best form of nomination t6 the office, a huge number of the friends of Mr. Blair changed then votes before the result was authoritatively declared, and Mr. Grow was announced as receiving 99 votes, a majority of all the members. Two members appeared from Virginia. The other Confederate States were without representation. Emerson Etheridge of Tennessee was chosen Clerk, in compliment to his fidelity and courage as a Union man.

The House was filled with able men, many of whom had parliamentary experience. The natural leader, who assumed his place by common consent, was Thaddeus Stevens, a man of strong peculiarities of character, able, trained, and fearless. Born in Vermont and educated at Dartmouth, he had passed all his adult years in Pennsylvania, and was thoroughly identified with the State which he had served with distinction both in her own Legislature and in Congress. He had the reputation of being somewhat unscrupulous as to Political methods, somewhat careless in personal conduct, somewhat lax in personal morals; but to the one great object of his life, the destruction of slavery and the elevation of the slave, he was supremely devoted. From the pursuit of that objective nothing could deflect him. Upon no phase of it would he listen to compromise. Any man who was truly anti-slavery was his friend. Whoever espoused the cause and proved faithless in never so small a degree, became his enemy, inevitably and irreconcilably. Towards his own race he seemed often to be misanthropic. He was learned in the law, and for a third of a century had held high rank at the bar of a State distinguished for great lawyers. He was disposed to be taciturn. A brilliant talker, he did not relish idle and aimless conversation. He was much given to reading, study, and reflection, and to the retirement which enabled him, to gratify his tastes. As was said of Mr. Emerson, Mr. Stevens loved solitude and understood its uses.

Upon all political questions, Mr. Stevens was an authority. He spoke with ease and readiness, using a style some what resembling of the crisp, clear sententiousness of Dean Swift. Seldom, even in the most careless moment, did a sentence escape his lips, that would not bear the test of grammatical and rhetorical criticism. He possessed the keenest wit, and was unmerciful in its use towards those whom he did not like. He illustrated in concrete form the difference between wit and humor. He did not indulge in the latter. He did not enjoy a laugh. When his sharp sallies would set the entire House in uproar, he was as impassive, his visage as solemn, as if he were pronouncing a funeral oration. His memory of facts, dates, and figures was exact, and in argument he knew the book and chapter and page for reference. He was fond of young men, invited their society, encouraged and generously aided them. He was easily moved by the distress of others. He was kind, charitable, lavish of his money in the relief of poverty. He had characteristics which seemed contradictory, but which combined to make one of the memorable figures in the Parliamentary history of the United States, a man who had the courage to meet any opponent, and who was never overmatched in intellectual conflict.

. . . .

The organization of the House was so promptly effected that the President's message was received on the same day. Throughout the country there was an eagerness to hear Mr. Lincoln's views on the painful situation. The people had read with deep sympathy the tender plea to the South contained in his Inaugural address. The next occasion on which they had heard from him officially was his proclamation for troops after the fall of Sumter. Public opinion in the North would undoubt-

edly be much influenced by what the President should now say. Mr. Lincoln was keenly alive to the importance of his message, and he weighed every word he wrote. He maintained, as he always did, calmness of tone, moderation in expression. He appealed to reason, not to prejudice. He spoke as one who knew that he would be judged by the public opinion of the world. It was his fortune to put his name to many state papers of extraordinary weight, but never to one of graver import than his first message to Congress.

The President informed Congress that he would not call their attention "to any ordinary subject of legislation." In fact there were but two things for Congress to do in the national exigency—provide for the enlistment of an army and for the raising of money necessary to the conduct of a great war. . . .

James G. Blaine, *Twenty Years of Congress: From Lincoln to Garfield with a Review of the Events Which Led to the Political Revolution of 1860*, 2 vols. (Norwich, Conn.: Henry Bill Publishing, 1884), vol. 1: 313–332.

75   The First Federal Income Tax

August 5, 1861

The Constitution gives Congress the "Power To lay and collect Taxes, Duties, Imposts, and Excises" for the purpose of paying the debts of the United States, to provide for defense of the nation, and for the "general welfare" of the country and its people. Throughout the history of the United States, no subject has been a more central, and a more contentious, part of political debate than that of taxes, regardless of the form of the tax. As Benjamin Franklin wrote in 1789: "Our Constitution is in actual operation; everything appears to promise that it will last; but in this world nothing is certain but death and taxes."

Dating from colonial times, the most common form of personal tax imposed upon citizens was the property tax, a tax that has persisted throughout American history. Other taxes, such as excise taxes on whiskey and tobacco, have been in use for hundreds of years. The main revenue of government throughout the nineteenth century was custom duties on imported goods, known as tariffs. The idea of a tax on income dates from colonial times, but its first real use came during the Civil War when duties on imported goods fell sharply at the same time that the costs of conducting the war were rising by leaps and bounds.

This first income tax law was part of the general revenue act that passed Congress in July 1861 and became law on August 5 that year. Provisions for the income tax were not mentioned until Section 49 of the law. Strangely enough, no revenue resulted from this first income tax law. Section 49 was quickly repealed in 1862 and replaced with another income tax law, which was modified again in 1864. Even though there was much opposition in Congress to an income tax, the rapidly mounting debts of the Civil

War convinced the majority of members that it was necessary. The income tax generated a great deal of revenue for the government. It lasted until 1872, when it was repealed. A tax on income would not appear again until ratification of the Sixteenth Amendment to the Constitution was completed in 1913 (see document 106).

. . . .

SEC. 49. *And be it further enacted,* That, from and after the first day of January next, there shall be levied, collected, and paid, upon the annual income of every person residing in the United States, whether such income is derived from any kind of property, or from any profession, trade, employment, or vocation carried on in the United States or elsewhere, or from any other source whatever, if such annual income exceeds the sum of eight hundred dollars, a tax of three per centum on the amount of such excess of such income above eight hundred dollars *Provided,* That upon such portion of said income as shall be derived from interest upon treasury notes or other securities of the United States, there shall be levied, collected, and paid a tax of one and one half per centum. Upon the income, rents, or dividends accruing, upon any property, securities, or stocks owned in the United States by any citizen of the United States residing abroad, there shall be levied, collected, and paid ft tax of five per centum, excepting that portion of said income derived from interest on treasury notes and other securities of the Government of the United States, which shall pay one and one half per centum. The tax herein provided shall be assessed upon the annual income of the persons hereinafter named for the year next preceding the time for assessing said tax, to wit, the year next preceding, the first of January, eighteen hundred and sixty-two; and the said taxes, when so assessed and made public, shall become a lien on the property or other sources of said income for the amount of the same, with the interest and other expenses of collection until paid: *Provided,* That in estimating said income, all national, state, or local taxes assessed upon the property, from which the income is derived, shall be first deducted.

SEC. 50. *And be it further enacted,* That it shall be the duty of the President of the United States, and he is hereby authorized, by and with the advice and consent of the Senate, to appoint one principal assessor and one principal collector in each of the States and Territories of the United States, and in the District of Columbia, to assess and collect the internal duties or income tax imposed by this act with authority in each of said officers to appoint so many assistants as the public service may require, to be approved by the Secretary of the Treasury. The said taxes to be assessed and collected under such regulations as the Secretary of the Treasury may prescribe. The said collectors, herein authorized to be appointed, shall give bonds, to the satisfaction of the Secretary of the Treasury, in such sums as he may prescribe, for the faithful performance of their respective duties. And the Secretary of the Treasury shall prescribe such reasonable compensation for the assessment and collection of said internal duties or income tax as may appear to him just and proper; not, however, to exceed in any case the sum of two thousand five hundred dollars per annum for the principal officers herein referred to, and twelve hundred dollars per annum for an assistant. The assistant collectors herein provided shall give bonds to the satisfaction of the principal collector for the faithful performance of their duties. The Secretary of the Treasury is further authorized to select and appoint one or more depositaries in each State for the deposit and safe-keeping of the moneys arising from the taxes herein imposed when collected, and the receipt of the proper officer of such depository to the collector for the moneys deposited by him shall be the proper voucher for such collector in the settlement of his account at the Treasury Department. And he is further authorized and empowered to make such officer or depositary the disbursing agent of the Treasury for the payment of all interest due to the citizens of such State upon the treasury notes or other government securities issued by authority of law. And he shall also prescribe the forms of returns to be made to the department by all assessors and collectors appointed under the authority of this act He shall also prescribe the forms of oath or obligation to be taken by the several officers authorized or directed to be appointed and commissioned by the President under this act, before a competent magistrate duly authorized to administer oaths, and the form of the return to be made thereon to the Treasury Department

SEC. 51. *And be it further enacted,* That the tax herein imposed by the forty-ninth section of this act shall be due and payable on or before the thirtieth day of June, in the year eighteen hundred and sixty-two, and all sums due and unpaid at that day shall draw interest thereafter at the rate of six per cen-

tum per annum; and if any person or persons shall neglect or refuse to pay after due notice said tax assessed against him, her, or them, for the space of more than thirty days after the same is due and payable, it shall be lawful for any Collector or assistant collector charged with the duty of collecting such tax, and they are hereby authorized, to levy the same on the visible property of any such person, or so much thereof as may be sufficient to pay such tax, with the interest due thereon, and the expenses incident to such levy and sale, first giving thirty days' public notice of the time and place of the sale thereof; and in case of the failure of an person or persons authorized to act as agent or agents for the collection of the rents or other income of any person residing abroad shall neglect or refuse to pay the tax assessed thereon (having had due notice) for more than thirty days after the thirtieth of June, eighteen hundred and sixty-two, the collector or his assistant, for the district where such property is located, or rents or income is payable, shall be and hereby is authorized to levy upon the property itself, and to sell the same, or so much thereof as may be necessary to pay the tax assessed, together with the interest and expenses incident to such levy and sale, first giving thirty days' public notice of the time and place of sale. And in all cases of the sale of property herein authorized, the conveyance by the officer authorized to make the sale, duly executed, shall give a valid title to the purchaser, whether the property sold be real or personal. And the several collectors and assistants appointed under the authority of this act may, if they find no property to satisfy the taxes assessed upon any person by authority of the forty-ninth section of this act, and which such person neglects to pay as hereinbefore provided, shall have power, and it shall be their duty, to examine under oath the person assessed under this act, or any other person, and may sell at public auction, after ten days' notice, any stock, bonds, or choses in action, belonging to said person, or so much thereof as will pay such tax and the expenses of such sale; and in case he refuses to testify, the said several collectors and assistants shall have power to arrest such person and commit him to prison, to be held in custody until the same shall be paid, with interest thereon, at the rate of six per centum per annum, from the time when the same was payable as aforesaid, and all fees and charges of such commitment and custody. And the place of custody shall in all cases be the same provided by law for the custody of persons committed for any cause by the authority of the United States, and the warrant of the collector, stating the cause of commitment, shall be sufficient authority to the proper officer for receiving and keeping such person in custody until the amount of said tax and interest, and all fees and the expense of such custody, shall have been fully paid and discharged; which fees and expenses shall be the same as are chargeable under the laws of the United States in other cases of commitment and custody. And it shall be the duty of such collector to pay the expenses of such custody, and the same, with his fees shall be allowed on settlement of his accounts. And the person so committed shall have the same right to be discharged from such custody as may be allowed by the laws of the State or Territory, or the District of Columbia, where he is so held in custody, to persons committed under the laws of such State or Territory, or District of Columbia, for the non-payment of taxes, and in the manner provided by such laws; he may be discharged at any time by order of the Secretary of the Treasury.

SEC. 52. *And be it further enacted,* That should any of the people of any of the States and Territories of the United States, or the District of Columbia be in actual rebellion against the authority of the Government of the United States at the time this act goes into operation, so that the laws of the United States cannot be executed therein, it shall be the duty of the President, and he is hereby authorized, to proceed to execute the provisions of this act within the limits of such State or Territory, or District of Columbia, so soon as the authority of the United States therein is re-established, and to collect the sums which would have been due from the persons residing or holding property or stocks therein, with the interest due, at the rate of six per centum per annum thereon until paid in the manner and under the regulations prescribed in the foregoing *in the foregoing* sections of this act.

. . . .

Statutes at Large, 12 (1859–1863), 37th Congress, 1st session, Aug. 5, 1861, 309–311.

76   The Thirteenth Amendment to the Constitution

Submitted to the States, January 31, 1865; Ratified, December 6, 1865

The first of three constitutional amendments written with the purpose of ending slavery and guaranteeing the rights of the ex-slaves (see also documents 79 and 83), the Thirteenth Amendment finally laid to rest the issue of slavery, at least from the technical standpoint of the Constitution and American law. This amendment freed the slaves in the border states and those states occupied by federal troops—areas that were not covered under Lincoln's Emancipation Proclamation. Its language, drawn from similar wording in the Northwest Ordinance of 1787, abolished all slavery in the United States. The amendment included a clause that gave Congress the power to enforce the abolition of slavery by drafting "appropriate legislation." This provision had the potential to alter federal-state relations by giving Congress power to intervene in state matters. But Congress expected each state to assume the responsibility for guaranteeing that slavery was abolished within its borders.

The amendment passed the Senate on March 3, 1864, but did not pass the House until the lame-duck session of January 1865. In the meantime, Abraham Lincoln used adoption of the Thirteenth Amendment as part of his platform for reelection in 1864. But Lincoln did not live to see the Thirteenth Amendment ratified. He died of an assassin's bullet on April 15, 1865. The Thirteenth Amendment was not ratified until December 6 that year.

While the northern states (with the exception of Delaware) quickly ratified the amendment, President Andrew Johnson's plan of reconstruction required the states of the Confederacy to ratify the amendment before they could be readmitted to the Union. With federal troops occupying the South, most southern states reluctantly complied. Several states did not get around to ratifying the Thirteenth Amendment until the twentieth century. Delaware rejected the Thirteenth Amendment in 1865 but finally ratified it in 1901. Kentucky did not ratify the amendment until 1976. Mississippi rejected the amendment in 1865 and has never voted to ratify it.

Even with the majority of states approving the Thirteenth Amendment, the struggle for freedom was not over. Once Reconstruction ended in 1877 and federal troops withdrew from the South, southern state legislatures began redrafting their state constitutions and laws to disenfranchise black citizens. Slavery may have been abolished, but its legacy lived on in the second-class status accorded the newly freed slaves. The enforcement portion of the Thirteenth Amendment would gain importance again in the twentieth century, when the federal government used it to bolster enforcement of racial discrimination cases during the Civil Rights movement of the 1950s and 1960s.

ARTICLE XIII.

SECTION 1. Neither slavery nor involuntary servitude, except as a punishment for crime whereof the party shall have been duly convicted, shall exist within the united states, or any place subject to their jurisdiction.

SECTION 2. Congress shall have the power to enforce this article by appropriate legislation.

The Constitution of the United States of America as Amended, House Doc. 102–188, 102d Congress, 2d session (Washington: Government Printing Office, 1992), 16.

77   Representative Thaddeus Stevens on Reconstruction

December 18, 1865

In 1865 Thaddeus Stevens (R-Pa.) was the most powerful man in the House of Representatives and one of the most powerful men in the entire federal government. As House floor leader, chairman of the House Ways and Means Committee, and then chairman of the newly created House Appropriations Committee in 1865, Stevens had a great deal to say about how the nation would handle the problems of reconstructing the Union after the Civil War. At age seventy-three, and in failing health, he expended all his energy on pushing the congressional plan of Reconstruction as the fiery leader of the Radical Republicans. Stevens hated slavery and had long been an outspoken critic of southern slaveholders. With the war over and federal troops occupying the South, Stevens was not about to let the slave-holding states back into the Union until all traces of slavery were abolished. He was angry with President Andrew Johnson's accommodation to the interests of slave-holders and the president's willingness to let ex-Confederates assume positions of government authority in the South.

As Congress convened in December 1865, Stevens lost little time attacking the president's reconstruction plans by outlining his own plan. This speech is a landmark in the annals of Congress for its clear statement of the congressional plan for Reconstruction and for its visionary analysis of the United States as a nation where all men—regardless of color—should have the same protection under law.

Steven's speech documented his hatred of former chief justice of the United States Roger B. Taney, who, in 1857, had sided with slave-holders in the famous Dred Scott case (see document 70). The speech ends with Steven's presumption that Taney, who died the previous year, was burning in hell for his defense of slavery and his assumption that the United States was a "white man's government."

Stevens supported and led the effort to impeach Andrew Johnson but was too ill to play an active role in the actual proceedings. He died in August 1868, three months after Johnson's acquittal. Steven's left instructions that he be buried in a cemetery that was not segregated by race, and his tombstone in Lancaster, Pennsylvania, reads:

I repose in this quiet and secluded spot,
Not from any natural preference for solitude
But, finding other Cemeteries limited as to Race
    by Charter Rules,
I have chosen this that I might illustrate
    in my death
The Principles which I advocated
    Through a long life:
EQUALITY OF MAN BEFORE HIS CREATOR.

A candid examination of the power and proper principles of reconstruction can be offensive to no one, and may possibly be profitable by exciting inquiry. One of the suggestions of the message which we are now considering has special reference to this. Perhaps it is the principle most interesting to the people at this time. The President assumes, what no one doubts, that the late rebel States have lost their constitutional relations to the Union, and are incapable of representation in Congress, except by permission of the Government. It matters but little, with this admission, whether you call them States out of the Union, and now conquered territories, or assert that because the Constitution forbids them to do what they did do, that they are therefore only dead as to all national and political action, and will remain so until the Government shall breathe into them the breath of life anew and permit them to occupy their former position. In other words, that they are not out of the Union, but are only dead carcasses lying within the Union. In either case, it is very plain that it requires the action of Congress to enable them to form a State government and send representatives to Congress. Nobody, I believe, pretends that with their old constitutions and frames of government they can be permitted to claim their old rights under the Constitution. They have torn their constitutional States into atoms, and built on their foundations fabrics of a totally different character. Dead men cannot raise themselves. Dead States cannot restore their own existence "as it was." Whose especial duty is it to do it? In whom does the Constitution place the power? Not in the judicial branch of Government, for it only adjudicates and does not prescribe laws. Not in the Executive, for he only executes and cannot make laws. Not in the Commander-in-Chief of the armies, for he can only hold them under military rule until the sovereign legislative power of the conqueror shall give them law.

There is fortunately no difficulty in solving the question. There are two provisions in the Constitution, under one of which the case must fall. The fourth article says:

New States may be admitted by the Congress into this Union.

In my judgment this is the controlling provision in this case. Unless the law of nations is a dead letter, the late war between two acknowledged belligerents severed their original compacts, and broke all the ties that bound them together. The future condition of the conquered power depends on the will of the conqueror. They must come in as new States or remain as conquered provinces. Congress—the Senate and House of Representatives, with the concurrence of the President—is the only power that can act in the matter. But suppose, as some dreaming theorists imagine, that these States have never been out of the Union, but have only destroyed their State governments so as to be incapable of political action; then the fourth section of the fourth article applies, which says:

The United States shall guaranty to every State in this Union a republican form of government.

Who is the United States? Not the judiciary; not the President; but the sovereign power of the people, exercised through their representatives in Congress, with the concurrence of the Executive. It means the political Government—the concurrent action of both branches of Congress and the Executive. The separate action of each amounts to nothing, either in admitting new States or guarantying republican governments to lapsed or outlawed States. Whence springs the preposterous idea that either the President, or the Senate, or the House of Representatives, acting separately, can determine the right of States to send members or Senators to the Congress of the Union?

To prove that they are and for four years have been out of the Union for all legal purposes, and being now conquered, subject to the absolute disposal of Congress, I will suggest a few ideas and adduce a few authorities. If the so-called "confederate States of America" were an independent belligerent, and were so acknowledged by the United States and by Europe, or had assumed and maintained an attitude which entitled them to be considered and treated as a belligerent, then, during such time, they were precisely in the condition of a foreign nation with whom we were at war; nor need their independence as a nation be acknowledged by us to produce that effect. In the able opinion delivered by that accomplished and loyal jurist, Mr. Justice Grier, in the prize cases, all the law on these points is collected and clearly stated. (2 Black, page 66.) Speaking of civil wars, and following Vattel, he says:

When the party in rebellion occupy and hold in a hostile manner a certain portion of territory; have declared their independence; have cast off their allegiance; have organized armies; have commenced hostilities against their former sovereign, the world acknowledges them as belligerents, and the contest a war.

And

The parties belligerent in a public war are independent nations. But it is not necessary, to constitute war, that both parties should be acknowledged as independent nations or foreign States. A war may exist where one of the belligerents claims sovereign rights as against the other.

The idea that the States could not and did not make war because the Constitution forbids it, and that this must be treated as a war of individuals, is a very injurious and groundless fallacy. Individuals cannot make war. They may commit murder, but that is no war. Communities, societies, States, make war. Phillimore says, (volume three, page 68:)

War between private individuals who are members of a society cannot exist. The use of force in such a case is trespass and not war.

But why appeal to reason to prove that the seceded States made war as States, when the conclusive opinion of the Supreme Court is at hand? In the prize cases already cited, the Supreme Court say:

Hence, in organizing this rebellion, they have acted as States claiming to be sovereign over all persons and property within their respective limits, and asserting a right to absolve their citizens from their allegiance to the Federal Government. Several of these States have combined to form a new confederacy, claiming to be acknowledged by the world as a sovereign State. Their right to do so is now being decided by wager of battle. The ports and territory of each of these States are held in hostility to the General Government. It is no loose, unorganized insurrection, having no defined boundary or possession. It has a boundary marked by lines of bayonets, and which can be crossed only by force. South of this line is enemies' territory, because it is claimed and held in possession by an organized hostile and belligerent power.

Again, the court say, what I have been astonished that any one should

The proclamation of blockade is itself official and conclusive evidence to the court that a state of war existed.

Now, what was the legal result of such war?

The conventions, the treaties, made with a nation are broken or annulled by a war arising between the contracting parties.—Vattel, 372; Halleck, 371, section 23.

If gentlemen suppose that this doctrine applies only to national and not to civil wars, I beg leave to refer them to Vattel, page 423. He says:

A civil war breaks the bands of society and government, or at least suspends their force and effect; it produces in the nation two independent parties, who consider each other as enemies, and acknowledge no common judge. These two parties must therefore be considered as thenceforward constituting, at least for a time, two separate bodies; two distinct societies. They stand, therefore, in precisely the same predicament as two nations who engage in a contest, and being unable to come to an agreement, have recourse to arms.

At page 427:

And when a nation becomes divided into two parties absolutely independent, and no longer acknowledge a common superior, the State is dissolved, and the war between the two parties stands on the same ground, in every respect, as a public war between two different nations.

But must the belligerent be acknowledged as an independent nation, as some contend? That is answered in the case referred to in 2 Black, as follows:

It is not the less a civil war, with belligerent parties in hostile array, because it may be called an "insurrection" by one side, and the insurgents be considered as rebels or traitors. It is not necessary that the independence of the revolted province or State be acknowledged in order to constitute it a party belligerent in a war, according to the law of nations.

This doctrine, so clearly established by publicists, and so distinctly stated by Mr. Justice Crier, has been frequently reiterated since by the Supreme Court of the United States. In Mr. Alexander's case (2 Wallace, 419) the present able Chief Justice, delivering the opinion of the court, says:

We must be governed by the principle of public law so often announced from this bench as applicable to civil and international wars, that all the people of each State or district in insurrection against the United States must be regarded as enemies until by the action of the Legislature and Executive, or otherwise, that relation is thoroughly and permanently changed.

After such clear and repeated decisions it is something worse than ridiculous to hear men of respectable standing attempting to nullify the law of nations, and declare the Supreme Court of the United States in error, because, as the Constitution forbids it, the States could not go out of the Union in fact. A respectable gentleman was lately reciting this argument, when he suddenly stopped and said, "Did you hear of that atrocious murder committed in our town? A rebel deliberately murdered a Government official." The person addressed said, "I think you are mistaken." "How so? I saw it myself." "You are wrong, no murder was or could be committed, for the law forbids it."

The theory that the rebel States, for four years a separate power and without representation in Congress, were all the time here in the Union, is a good deal less ingenious and respectable than the metaphysics of Berkeley, which proved that neither the world nor any human being was in existence. If this theory were simply ridiculous it could be forgiven; but its effect is deeply injurious to the stability of the nation. I cannot doubt that the late confederate States are out of the Union to all intents and purposes for which the conqueror may choose so to consider them.

But on the ground of estoppel, the United States have the clear right to elect to adjudge them out of the Union. They are estopped both by matter of record and matter in Dais. One of the first resolutions passed by seceded South Carolina in January, 1861, is as follows:

Resolved, unanimously, That the separation of South Carolina from the Federal Union is final, and she has no further interest in the Constitution of the United States; and that the only appropriate negotiations between her and the Federal Government are as to their mutual relations as foreign States.

Similar resolutions appear upon all their State and confederate government records. The speeches of their members of congress, their generals and executive officers, and the answers of their government to our shameful sueings for peace, went upon the defiant ground that no terms would be offered or received except upon the prior acknowledgment of the entire and permanent independence of the confederate States. After this, to deny that we have a right to treat them as a conquered belligerent, severed from the Union in fact, is not argument but mockery. Whether it be our interest to do so is the only question hereafter and more deliberately to be considered.

But suppose these powerful but now subdued belligerents, instead of being out of the Union, are merely destroyed, and are now lying about, a dead corpse, or with animation so suspended as to be incapable of action, and wholly unable to heal themselves by any, unaided movements of their own. Then they may fall under the provision of the Constitution which says "the United States shall guaranty to every State in the Union a republican form of government." Under that power can the judiciary, or the President, or the Commander-in-Chief of the Army, or the Senate or House of Representatives, acting separately, restore them to life and readmit them into the Union? I insist that if each acted separately, though the action of each was identical with all the others, it would amount to nothing. Nothing but the joint action of the two Houses of Congress and the concurrence of the President could do it. If the Senate admitted their Senators, and the House their members, it would have no effect on the future action of Congress. The Fortieth Congress might reject both. Such is the ragged record of Congress for the last four years.

In *Luther vs. Borden* (7 Howard, 1–42) the Supreme Court say:

Under this article of the Constitution [the one above cited] it rests with Congress to decide what government is the established one in a State. For as the United States guaranty to each State a republican government, Congress must necessarily decide what government is established in the State before it can determine whether it is republican or not.

Congress alone can do it. But Congress does not mean the Senate, or the House of Representatives, and President, all acting severally. Their joint action constitutes Congress. Hence a law of Congress must be passed before any new State can be admitted; or any dead ones revived. Until then no member can be lawfully admitted into either House. Hence it appears with how little knowledge of constitutional law each branch is urged to admit members separately from these destroyed States. The provision that "each House shall be the judge of the elections, returns, and qualifications of its own members," has not the most distant bearing on this question. Congress must create States and declare when they are entitled to be represented. Then each House must judge whether the members presenting themselves from a recognized State possess the requisite qualifications of age, residence, and citizenship; and whether the election and returns are according to law. The Houses, separately, can judge of nothing else. It seems amazing that any man of legal education could give it any larger meaning.

It is obvious from all this that the first duty of Congress is to pass a law declaring the condition of these outside or defunct States, and providing proper civil governments for them. Since the conquest they have been governed by martial law. Military rule is necessarily despotic, and ought not to exist longer than is absolutely necessary. As there are no symptoms that the people of these provinces will be prepared to participate in constitutional government for some years, I know of no arrangement so proper for them as territorial governments. There they can learn the principles of freedom and eat the fruit of foul rebellion. Under such governments, while electing members to the Territorial Legislatures, they will necessarily mingle with those to whom Congress shall extend the right of suffrage. In Territories Congress fixes the qualifications of electors; and I know of no better place nor better occasion for the conquered rebels and the conqueror to practice justice to all men, and accustom themselves to make and to obey equal laws.

As these fallen rebels cannot at their option reenter the heaven which they have disturbed, the garden of Eden which they have deserted, and flaming swords are set at the gates to secure their exclusion, it becomes important to the welfare of the nation to inquire when the doors-shall be reopened for their admission.

According to my judgment they ought never to be recognized as capable of acting in the Union, or of being counted as valid States, until the Constitution shall have been so amended as to make it what its framers intended; and so as to secure perpetual ascendancy to the party of the Union; and so as to render our republican Government firm and stable forever. The first of those amendments is to change the basis of representation among the States from Federal numbers to actual voters. Now all the colored freemen in the slave States, and three fifths of the slaves, are represented, though none of them have votes. The States have nineteen representatives of colored slaves. If the slaves are now free then they can add, for the other two fifths, thirteen more, making the slave representation thirty-two. I suppose the free blacks in those States will give at least five more, making the representation of non-voting people of color about thirty-seven. The whole number of representatives now from the slave States is seventy. Add the other two fifths and it will be eighty-three.

If the amendment prevails, and those States withhold the right of suffrage from persons of color, it will deduct about thirty-seven, leaving them but forty-six. With the basis unchanged, the eighty-three southern members, with the Democrats that will in the best times be elected from the North, will always give them a majority in Congress and in the Electoral College. They will at the very first election take possession of the White House and the halls of Congress. I need not depict the ruin that would follow. Assumption of the rebel debt or repudiation of the Federal debt would be sure to follow. The oppression of the freedmen; the reamendment of their State constitutions, and the reestablishment of slavery would be the inevitable result. That they would scorn and disregard their present constitutions, forced upon them in the midst of martial law, would be both natural and just. No one who has any regard for freedom of elections can look upon those governments, forced upon them in duress, with any favor. If they should grant the right of suffrage to persons of color, I think there would always be Union white men enough in the South, aided by the blacks, to divide the representation, and thus continue the Republican ascendancy. If they should refuse to thus alter their election laws it would reduce the representatives of the late slave States to about forty-five and render them powerless for evil.

It is plain that this amendment must be consummated before the defunct States are admitted to be capable of State action, or it never can be.

The proposed amendment to allow Congress to lay a duty on exports is precisely in the same situation. Its importance cannot well be overstated. It is very obvious that for many years the South will not pay much under our internal revenue laws. The only article on which we can raise any considerable amount is cotton. It will be grown largely at once. With ten cents a pound export duty it would be furnished cheaper to foreign markets than they could obtain it from any other part of the world. The late war has shown that. Two million bales exported, at five hundred pounds to the bale, would yield $100,000,000. This seems to be the chief revenue we shall ever derive from the South. Besides, it would be a protection to that amount to our domestic manufactures. Other proposed amendments—to make all laws uniform; to prohibit the assumption of the rebel debt—are of vital importance, and the only thing that can prevent the combined forces of copperheads and secessionists from legislating against the interests of the Union whenever they may obtain an accidental majority.

But this is not all that we ought to do before these inveterate rebels are invited to participate in our legislation. We have turned, or are about to turn, loose four million slaves without a hut to shelter them or a cent in their pockets. The infernal laws of slavery have prevented them from acquiring an education, understanding the commonest laws of contract, or of managing the ordinary business of life. This Congress is bound to provide for them until they can take care of themselves. If we do not furnish them with homesteads, and hedge them around with protective laws; if we leave them to the legislation of their late masters, we had better have left them in bondage. Their condition would be worse than that of our prisoners at Andersonville. If we fail in this great duty now, when we have the power, we shall deserve and receive the execration of history and of all future ages.

Two things are of vital importance.

1. So to establish a principle that none of the rebel States shall be counted in any of the amendments of the Constitution until they are duly admitted into the family of States by the law-making power of their conqueror. For more than six months the amendment of the Constitution abolishing slavery has been ratified by the Legislatures of three fourths of the States that acted on its passage by Congress, and which had Legislatures, or which were States capable of acting, or required to act on the question.

I take no account of the aggregation of white-washed rebels, who without any legal authority have assembled in the capitals of the late rebel States and simulated legislative bodies. Nor do I regard with any respect the cunning byplay into which they deluded the Secretary of State by frequent telegraphic announcements that "South Carolina had adopted the Amendment;" "Alabama has adopted the amendment, being the twenty-seventh State," &c. This was intended to delude the people, and accustom Congress to hear repeated the names of these extinct States as if they were alive, when, in truth, they have now no more existence than the revolted cities of Latium, two thirds of whose people were colonized and their property confiscated, and their right of citizenship withdrawn by conquering and avenging Rome.

2. It is equally important to the stability of this Republic that it should now be solemnly decided what power can revive, recreate, and reinstate these provinces into the family of States, and invest them with the rights of American citizens. It is time that Congress should assert its sovereignty, and assume something of the dignity of a Roman senate. It is fortunate that the President invites Congress to take this manly attitude. After stating with great frankness in his able message his theory, which, however, is found to be impracticable, and which I believe very few now consider tenable, he refers the whole matter to the judgment of Congress. If Congress should fail firmly and wisely to discharge that high duty it is not the fault of the President.

This Congress owes it to its own character to set the seal of reprobation upon a doctrine which is becoming too fashionable, and unless rebuked will be the recognized principle of our Government. Governor Perry and other provisional governors and orators proclaim that "this is the white man's Government." The whole copperhead party, pandering to the lowest prejudices of the ignorant, repeat the cuckoo cry, "This is the white man's Government." Demagogues of all parties, even some high in authority, gravely shout, "This is the white man's Government." What is implied by this? That one race of men are to have the exclusive right forever to rule this nation, and to exercise all acts of sovereignty, while all other races and nations and colors are to be their subjects, and have no voice in making the laws and choosing the rulers by whom they are to be governed. Wherein does this differ from slavery except in degree? Does not this contradict all the distinctive principles of the Declaration of Independence? When the great and good men promulgated that instrument, and pledged their lives and sacred honors to defend it, it was supposed to form an epoch in civil government. Before that time it was held that the right to rule was vested in families, dynasties, or races, not because of superior intelligence or virtue, but because of a divine right to enjoy exclusive privileges.

Our fathers repudiated the whole doctrine of the legal superiority of families or races, and proclaimed the equality of men before the law. Upon that they created a revolution and built the Republic. They were prevented by slavery from perfecting the superstructure whose foundation they had thus broadly laid. For the sake of the Union they consented to wait, but never relinquished the idea of its final completion. The time to which they looked forward with anxiety has come. It is our duty to complete their work. If this Republic is not now made to stand on their great principles, it has no honest foundation, and the Father of all men will still shake it to its center. If we have not yet been sufficiently scourged for our national sin to teach us to do justice to all God's creatures, without distinction of race or color, we must expect the still more heavy vengeance of an offended Father, still increasing his inflictions as he increased the severity of the plagues of Egypt until the tyrant consented to do justice. And when that tyrant repented of his reluctant consent, and attempted to reenslave the people, as our southern tyrants are attempting to do now, he filled the Red sea with broken chariots and drowned horses, and strewed the shores with dead carcasses.

Mr. Chairman, I trust the Republican party will not be alarmed at what I am saying. I do not profess to speak their sentiments, nor must they be held responsible for them. I speak for myself, and take the responsibility, and will settle with my intelligent constituents.

This is not a "white man's Government," in the exclusive sense in which it is used. To say so is political blasphemy, for it violates the fundamental I principles of our gospel of liberty. This is man's Government; the Government of all men alike; not that all men will have equal power and sway within it. Accidental circumstances, natural and acquired endowment and ability, will vary their fortunes. But equal rights to all the privileges of the Government is innate in every immortal being, no matter what the shape or color of the tabernacle which it inhabits.

If equal privileges were granted to all, I should not expect any but white men to be elected to office for long ages to come. The prejudice engendered by slavery would not soon permit merit to be preferred to color. But it would still be beneficial to the weaker races. In a country where political divisions will always exist, their power, joined with just white men, would greatly modify, if it did not entirely prevent, the injustice of majorities. Without the right of suffrage in the late slave States, (I do not speak of the free States,) I believe the slaves had far better been left in bondage. I see it stated that very distinguished advocates of the right of suffrage lately declared in this city that they do not expect to obtain it by congressional legislation, but only by administrative action, because, as one gallant gentleman said, the States had not been out of the Union. Then they will never get it. The President is far sounder than they. He sees that administrative action has nothing to do with it. If it ever is to come, it must be constitutional amendments or congressional action in the Territories, and in enabling acts.

How shameful that men of influence should mislead and miseducate the public mind! They proclaim, "This is the white man's Government," and the whole coil of copperheads echo the same sentiment, and upstart, jealous Republicans join the cry. Is it any wonder ignorant foreigners and illiterate natives should learn this doctrine, and be led to despise and maltreat a whole race of their fellow-men?

Sir, this doctrine of a white man's Government is as atrocious as the infamous sentiment that damned the late Chief Justice to everlasting fame; and, I fear, to everlasting fire.

Congressional Globe, 39th Congress, 1st session, Dec. 18, 1865, 72–75.

78   The Civil Rights Act of 1866

April 9, 1866

Immediately after the Civil War, Congress had to deal with the many serious problems of reconstructing the Union, addressing the economic crisis of a nation torn apart by war, and grappling with the problems of several million newly freed slaves. From the standpoint of African Americans, the future of the race was at stake. Would the United States live up to the noble language of the Declaration of Independence, that "all men are created equal"? The immediate response of the former Confederate states was to pass in 1865 and 1866 a series of "black codes" that were designed to control the black population through a series of oppressive laws that denied African Americans the equal protection of the law.

While the passage of the Thirteenth, Fourteenth, and Fifteenth Amendments to the Constitution signaled the beginning of a new era with the abolition of slavery and the promise of civil rights for the newly freed slaves, constitutional change alone was not enough ensure equal protection under the law. Each of these amendments contained a clause giving Congress the power to pass laws that would enforce the language of the amendments. The first such law designed to guarantee newly freed slaves the right of citizenship and "full and equal benefit of all laws" was the Civil Rights Act of 1866, which was followed by other civil rights laws in 1870, 1871, and 1875.

The Civil Rights Act of 1866 did not dramatically change the lives of the newly freed slaves. It proved difficult to enforce because of the persistence of racism in American society and in American politics. The act is important as a symbol of the intent of Congress to play a leading role in defining and protecting the rights of all citizens, regardless of color. It marks the beginning of a long social, political, and legal struggle to ban racial discrimination from the United States, a struggle that would eventually encompass the Civil Rights Movement of the 1950s and 1960s and one that continues to the present day.

CHAP. XXXI.—AN ACT TO PROTECT ALL PERSONS IN THE UNITED STATES IN THEIR CIVIL RIGHTS, AND FURNISH THE MEANS OF THEIR VINDICATION.

Be it enacted by the Senate and House of Representatives of the United States of America in Congress assembled, That all persons born in the United States and not subject to any foreign power, excluding Indians not taxed, are hereby declared to be citizens of the United States; and such citizen; of every race and color, without regard to any previous condition of slavery or involuntary servitude, except as a punishment for crime whereof the party shall have been duly convicted, shall have the same right, in every State and Territory in the United States, to make and enforce contracts, to sue, be parties, and give evidence, to inherit, purchase, lease, sell, hold, and convey real and personal property, and to full and equal benefit of all laws and proceedings for the security of person and property, as is enjoyed by white citizens, and shall be subject to like punishment, pains, and penalties, and to none other, any law, statute, ordinance, regulation, or custom, to the contrary notwithstanding.

Sec. 2. *And be it further enacted,* That any person who, under color of any law, statute, ordinance, regulation, or custom, shall subject, or cause to be subjected, any inhabitant of any State or Territory to the deprivation of any right secured or protected by this act, or to different punishment, pains, or penalties on account of such person having at any time been held in a condition of slavery or involuntary servitude, except as a punishment for crime whereof the party shall have been duly convicted, or by reason of his color or race, than is prescribed for the punishment of white persons, shall be deemed guilty of a misdemeanor, and, on conviction, shall be punished by fine not exceeding one thousand dollars, or imprisonment not exceeding one year, or both, in the discretion of the court.

Sec. 3. *And be it further enacted,* That the district courts of the United States, within their respective districts shall have, exclusively of the courts of the several States, cognizance of all crimes and offences committed against the provisions of this act, and also, concurrently with the circuit courts of the United States, of all causes, civil and criminal, affecting persons who are denied or cannot enforce in the courts or judicial tribunals of the State or locality where they may be any of the rights secured to them by the first section of this act; and if any suit or prosecution, civil or criminal, has been or shall be commenced in any State court, against any such person, for any cause whatsoever, or against any officer, civil or military, or other person, for any arrest or imprisonment, trespasses, or wrongs done or committed by virtue or under color of authority derived from this act or the act establishing a Bureau for the relief of Freedmen and Refugees, and all acts amendatory thereof, or for refusing to do any act upon the ground that it would be inconsistent with this act, such defendant shall have the right to remove such cause for trial to the proper district or circuit court in the manner prescribed by tile "Act relating, to habeas corpus and regulating judicial proceedings in certain cases," approved March three, eighteen hundred and sixty-three, and all acts amendatory thereof. The jurisdiction in civil and criminal matters hereby conferred on the district and circuit courts of the United States shall be exercised and enforced in conformity with the laws of the United States, so far as such laws are suitable to carry the same into effect; but in all cases where such laws are not adapted to the object, or are deficient in the provisions necessary to furnish suitable remedies and punish offences against law, the common law, as modified and changed by the constitution and statutes of the State wherein the court having jurisdiction of the cause, civil or criminal, is held, so far as the same is not inconsistent with the Constitution and laws of the United States, shall be extended to and govern said courts in the trial and disposition of such cause, and, if of a criminal nature, in the infliction of punishment on the party found guilty.

Sec. 4. *And be it further enacted,* That the district attorneys, marshals, and deputy marshals of the United States, the commissioners appointed by the circuit and territorial courts of the United States, with powers of arresting, imprisoning, or bailing offenders against the laws of the United States, the officers and agents of the Freedmen's Bureau, and every other officer who may be specially empowered by the President of the United States, shall be, and they are hereby, specially authorized and required, at the expense of the United States, to institute proceedings against all and every person who shall violate the provisions of this act and cause him or them to be arrested and imprisoned, or bailed, as the case may be, for trial before such court of the United States or territorial court as by this act has cognizance of the offence. And with a view to affording, reasonable protection to all persons in their constitutional right of equality before the law, without distinction of race or color, or previous condition of slavery or involuntary servitude, except as a punishment for crime, whereof the party shall have been duly convicted, and to the prompt discharge of the duties of this act, it shall be the duty of the circuit courts of the United States and the superior courts of the Territories of the United States, from time to time, to increase the number of commissioners, so as to afford a speedy and convenient means for the arrest and examination of persons charged with a violation of this act; and such commissioners are hereby authorized and required to exercise and discharge all the powers and duties conferred on them by this act and the same duties with regard to offences created by this act, as they are authorized by law to exercise with regard to other offences against the laws of the United States.

. . . .

SEC. 8. *And be it further enacted,* That whenever the President of the United States have reason to believe that offences have been or are likely to be committed against the provisions of this act within any judicial district, it shall be lawful for him, in his discretion, to direct the; judge, marshal, and district attorney of such district to attend at such place with the district, and for such time as he may designate, for the purpose of the more speedy arrest and trial of persons charged with a violation of this act; and it shall be the duty of every judge or other officer, when an such requisition shall be received by him, to attend at the place and for the time, therein designated.

SEC. 9. *And be it further enacted,* That it shall be lawful for the President of the United States, or such person as he may empower for that purpose, to employ such part of the land or naval forces of the United States, or of the militia, as shall be necessary to prevent the violation and enforce the due execution of this act.

SEC. 10. *And be further enacted,* That upon all questions of law arising in any cause under the provisions of this act a final appeal may be taken to the Supreme Court of the United States.

Statutes at Large, 14 (1865–1867), 39th Congress, 1st session, April 9, 1866, 27–29.

79 The Fourteenth Amendment to the Constitution

Submitted to the States, June 13, 1866; Ratified, July 9, 1868

In 1866 Congress was in the hands of the Republican Party, representing the northern states, while the president of the United States, Andrew Johnson, was a former Democrat sympathetic to the South. The story of the clash of interests between President Johnson and the Radical Republicans in Congress was one of the most exciting chapters of American political history. By 1868 the Republicans in the House had lost all patience with the president and impeached him. The Senate came within one vote of removing the president from office (see documents 81 and 82).

In this tumultuous setting, Congress drafted the Fourteenth Amendment to the Constitution. It is not surprising that this amendment has continued to be controversial. It was born out of political controversy. It had its origins in the extreme disagreement between Congress and President Johnson over the requirements that should be placed on the rebellious southern states before they could reenter the Union. President Johnson preferred a more lenient approach that allowed the southern states to keep their power and decide for themselves how best to deal with the newly freed slaves. Republicans in Congress wanted stronger measures that punished the South for slavery and required a federal solution to the question of citizenship for African Americans. The Fourteenth Amendment overturned the hated Dred Scott decision (see document 70) by proclaiming that every person born or naturalized in the United States was a citizen.

The five sections of the amendment gained importance in later legislation. The "due process" clause in Section 1 has become binding on all states, guarding citizens rights against arbitrary action by individual states. Section 1 also established that all citizens are entitled to "equal protection under the laws." Section 2 punished states that denied blacks the right to vote by reducing their representation in Congress. Section 3 banned former federal officeholders, including members of Congress, from holding federal office again unless Congress approved it with a two-thirds majority of both Houses. Section 4 guaranteed the payment of war debts to the loyal states and denied payment to the states that had seceded. Section 5 gave Congress the power to enforce the amendment.

The Reconstruction Act of 1867 required that before a state could be readmitted to the Union it must approve the Fourteenth Amendment (see document 80).

ARTICLE XIV.

SECTION 1. All persons born or naturalized in the United States and subject to the jurisdiction hereof, are citizens of the United States and the State wherein they reside. No State shall make or enforce any law which shall abridge the privileges or immunities of citizens of the United States; nor shall any State deprive any person of life, liberty, or property, without due process of law; nor deny to any person within its jurisdiction the equal protection of the laws.

SECTION 2. Representatives shall be apportioned among the several States according to their respective numbers, counting the whole number of persons in each State, excluding Indians not taxed. But when the right to vote at any election for the choice of electors for President and Vice President of the United States, Representatives of Congress, the Executive and Judicial officers of a State, or the members of the Legislature thereof, is denied to any male inhabitants of such State, being twenty-one years of age, and citizens of the United States, or in any way abridged, except for participation in rebellion, or other crime, the basis of representation therein shall be reduced in the proportion which the number of male citizens twenty-one years of age in each State.

SECTION 3. No person shall be a Senator or Representative in Congress, or elector of President or Vice President, or hold any office, civil or military, under the United States, or under any State, who, having previously taken an oath, as a member of any State legislature, or as an executive or judicial officer of any State, to support the Constitution of the United States, shall have engaged in insurrection or rebellion against the same, or given aid or comfort to the enemies thereof. But Congress may by a vote of two-thirds of each House, remove such disability.

SECTION 4. The validity of the public debt of the United States, authorized by law, including debts incurred for payment of pensions and bounties for services in suppressing insurrection or rebellion, shall not be questioned. But neither the United States or any State shall assume or pay any debt or obligation incurred in aid of insurrection or rebellion against the United States, or claim for the loss or emancipation of any slave; but all such debts, obligations and claims shall be held illegal and void.

SECTION 5. The Congress shall have power to enforce, by appropriate legislation, the provisions of this article.

The Constitution of the United States of America as Amended, House Doc. 102–188, 102d Congress, 2d session (Washington: Government Printing Office, 1992), 16–17.

80   The Reconstruction Act of 1867

March 2, 1867

The battle of wills between a Congress controlled by the Radical Republicans and the executive branch under President Andrew Johnson heated up over the question of which branch would play the dominant role in charting the course of reconstructing the Union. In the first Reconstruction Act of March 2, 1867, Congress outlined its plan for military rule of the former Confederacy and the procedures required for the rebel states to rejoin the Union. The states had to approve the Fourteenth Amendment, which was pending ratification when this bill passed Congress. The same day that Congress passed this bill, President Johnson vetoed it, saying he had reasons for disagreeing with the bill that were "so grave that I hope my statement of them may have some influence on the minds of the patriotic and enlightened men with whom the decision must rest."

President Johnson objected to the bill because it created military rule in the southern states that virtually replaced the state governments with military commanders who had the power of monarchs. The president considered the bill extreme because the former Confederate states were no longer at war and should be treated as peaceful states, not hostile entities. He also objected to provisions of the bill that required the former Confederate states to ratify the Fourteenth Amendment, saying: "The negroes have not asked for the privilege of voting; the vast majority of them have no idea what it means." These statements only further inflamed the Radical Republicans in their attempt to guarantee the right of all citizens to equal treatment under the law. Congress managed to override the president's veto and the bill became law.

Three weeks later, on March 23, Congress passed a second Reconstruction Act, only to have President Johnson veto that legislation on the same day Congress passed it. Again, Congress overrode the veto of the president. A third Reconstruction Act, which cleared up some of the language in the two earlier bills, passed Congress on

July 19, 1867. With the passage of these bills, Congress was in full control of the course of Reconstruction.

CHAP. CLIII.—AN ACT TO PROVIDE FOR MORE EFFICIENT GOVERNMENT OF THE REBEL STATES.

Whereas no legal State governments or adequate protection for life or property now exists in the rebel States of Virginia, North Carolina, South Carolina, Georgia, Mississippi, Alabama, Louisiana, Florida, Texas, and Arkansas; and whereas it is necessary that peace and good order should be enforced in said States until loyal and republican State governments can be legally established: Therefore,

Be it enacted by the Senate and House of Representatives of the United States of America in Congress assembled, That said rebel States shall be divided into military districts and made subject to the military authority of the United States as hereinafter prescribed, and for that purpose Virginia shall constitute the first district; North Carolina and South Carolina the second district; Georgia, Alabama, and Florida the third district; Mississippi and Arkansas the fourth district; and Louisiana and Texas the fifth district.

SEC. 2. And be it further enacted, That it shall be the duty of the President to assign to the command of each said districts an officer of the Army, not below the rank of brigadier general, and detail a sufficient military force to enable such an officer to perform his duties and enforce his authority within the district to which he is assigned.

SEC. 3. And be it further enacted, That it shall be the duty of each officer assigned as aforesaid to protect all persons in their rights of person and property, to suppress insurrection, disorder, and violence, and to punish, or cause to be punished, all disturbers of the public peace and criminals; and to this end he may allow local civil tribunals to take jurisdiction of and to try offenders, or, when in his judgement it may be necessary for the trial of offenders, he shall have power to organize military commissions or tribunals for that purpose, and all interference under color of State authority under this act shall be null and void.

SEC. 4. *And be it further enacted,* That all persons put under military arrest by virtue of this act shall be tried without unnecessary delay, and no cruel or unusual punishment shall be inflicted, and no sentence of any military commission or tribunal hereby authorized, affecting the life or liberty of any person, shall be executed until it is approved by the officer in command of the district, and the laws and regulation for the government of the Army shall not be affected by this act, except so far as they conflict with its provisions: *Provided,* That no sentence of death under the provisions of this act shall be carried into effect without the approval of the President.

SEC. 5. *And be it further enacted,* That when the people of any one of said rebel States shall have formed a constitution of government in conformity with the Constitution of the United States in all respects, framed by a convention of delegates elected by the male citizens of said State, twenty-one years old and upward, of whatever race, color, or previous condition, who have resident in said State for one year previous to the day of such election, except such as may be disfranchised for participation in the rebellion or for felony at common law, and when such constitution shall provide that the elective franchise shall be enjoyed by all persons as have the qualifications herein stated for electors of delegates, and when such constitution shall be ratified by a majority of the persons voting on the question of ratification who, are qualified as electors for delegates, and when such constitution has been submitted to Congress for examination and approval, and Congress shall have approved the same, and when

the State, by vote of its Legislature, elected under said constitution, shall have adopted the amendment to the Constitution of the United States, proposed by the Thirty-Ninth Congress, and known as article fourteen, and when said article shall have become a part of the Constitution of the United States, said State shall become entitled to representation in Congress, and Senators and Representatives shall be admitted therefrom on their taking the oath prescribed by law, and then and thereafter the preceding sections of this act shall be inoperative in said State: *Provided,* That no person excluded from the privilege of holding office by said proposed amendment to the Constitution of the United States shall be eligible to election as a member of the convention to frame the constitution for any of the said rebel States, nor shall any such person vote for members of such convention.

SEC. 6. *And be it further enacted,* That, until the people of said rebel States shall be by law be admitted to representation in the Congress of the United States, any civil governments which may exist therein shall be deemed provisional only, and in all respects subject to the Paramount authority of the United States at any time to abolish, modify, control or supersede the same; and in all elections to any office under such provisional governments all persons shall be entitled to vote, and none others, who are entitled to vote, under the fifth provision of this act; and no person shall be eligible to any office under any such provisional governments who would be disqualified from holding office under the provisions of the third article of said constitutional amendment.

SCHUYLER COLFAX,
Speaker of the House of Representatives.
LA FAYETTE S. FOSTER,
President of the Senate pro tempore.

Congressional Globe, 39th Congress, 2d session, March 2, 1867, appendix, 197–198.

81   Representative Thaddeus Stevens on the Impeachment of Andrew Johnson

March 2, 1868

Thaddeus Stevens (1792–1868), a representative from Pennsylvania, epitomized the Radical Republican's no-compromise stance against slavery and southern slaveholders. He was a visionary on the subject of equal rights for all citizens regardless of color, ahead of most members of the Republican Party, including Abraham Lincoln. Stevens was among the first to call for emancipation of the slaves and the confiscation of the property of slaveholders, which would be redistributed to the slaves themselves.

In the wake of Lincoln's assassination in 1865, Stevens turned his righteous wrath on President Andrew Johnson, a southern sympathizer. Stevens could not abide Johnson's willingness to make concessions to the South and leave the slaveholding class in power.

Stevens was willing to take on the president in a colossal power struggle between the executive branch and Congress to determine which branch would control the direction of Reconstruction. His hatred for slavery and for President Johnson was clear in this speech, in which he called for the impeachment of the president and offered an amendment to the articles of impeachment that Stevens felt would ensure the success of the impeachment process.

While Stevens had called for the impeachment of the president before 1868, it was not until President Johnson ran afoul of the Tenure of Office Act in February 1868 that moderate Republicans were willing to go along with the Radicals and vote for impeachment. President Johnson believed the Tenure of Office Act, a law less than a year old at the time, was an unconstitutional infringement on executive authority. When the president consciously violated its provisions, Stevens pushed the point, making Johnson look like a criminal. Many years later the Supreme Court declared the act unconstitutional. Thaddeus Stevens used impeachment as a tool to further the political ends of his party. To Stevens, this was not a time for subtle debates on the constitutionality of a law but a time to oust a president from office and eliminate a major roadblock to congressional plans for Reconstruction.

MR. STEVENS, of Pennsylvania. Never was a great malefactor so gently treated as Andrew Johnson. The people have been unwilling to blot the records of their country by mingling his crimes with their shame—shame for endurance for so long a time of his great crimes and misdemeanors. The committee have omitted entirely his wicked abuse of the patronage of the Government, his corruption of the voters of the nation by seducing them with the offers of office, and intimidating them by threats of expulsion, all for the purpose of making them abandon their honest principles and adopt the bastard policy which had had just conceived, a crime more heinous than that which brought many ancient agitators to the block. To this he was prompted by the same motive which made the angels fall. Soon after the death of Mr. Lincoln and the surrender of the so-called confederate army and possessions, the whole government of the territory, persons and property of the territory claimed by and conquered from the so-called confederate States of America devolved upon the Congress of the United States, according to the most familiar and well-adjudicated principles of national and municipal law, leaving nothing for the President to do but execute the laws of Congress and govern them by military authority until Congress should otherwise direct. Yet Andrew Johnson, assuming to establish an empire for his own control and depriving Congress of its just prerogative did erect North Carolina and the other conquered territories into States and nations, giving them governments of his own creation and appointing over them rulers unknown to the laws of the United States and who could not by any such laws hold any office therein. He fixed the qualifications of electors, directed who should hold office, and especially directed them to send representatives to both branches of Congress, ordering Congress to admit them when they should arrive. When Congress refused and asserted its sovereign prerogative to govern those territories, except during their military occupation, by their own inherent power, he treated their pretensions as idle and refused to obey them. When Congress subsequently passed acts dated, March 2, 1867, and their supplements, to reconstruct those governments under republican forms by the votes of the people, he pronounced them unconstitutional, and after they had become laws he advised the people not to obey them, thus seeking to defeat instead of to execute the laws of Congress. All this was done after Congress had declared these outlying States as possessing no governments which Congress could recognize, and that Congress alone had the power and control over them. This

monstrous usurpation, worse than sedition and little short of treason, he adhered to, by declaring in his last annual message and at other times that there was no Congress, and that all their acts were unconstitutional. These, being much more fundamental offenses, and, in my judgment, much more worthy of punishment, because more fatal to the nation, the committee have omitted in their articles of impeachment, because they were determined to deal gently with the President. Encouraged by this impunity, the President proceeded to new acts of lawless violence and disregard of the express enactments of Congress. It is those acts, trivial by comparison, but grave in their positive character, for which the committee has chosen to call him to answer, knowing that there is enough among them, if half were omitted, to answer the great object and purpose of impeachment. That proceeding can reach only to the removal from office, and anything beyond what will effect that purpose, being unnecessary, may be looked upon as wanton cruelty. Hence the tender mercies of this committee have rested only on the most trifling crimes and misdemeanors which they and could select from the official life of Andrew Johnson.

I will begin with the articles in their inverse order and devote a few minutes to each. The tenth article charges the President with attempting to induce the commander of this military district, Major General Emory, to disregard the law, by which he considered that he was bound to act, requiring orders to be issued through the General of the Army. The President declared it to be unconstitutional and contrary to the General's commission. About the fact there can be no doubt. There could be but one purpose, and that was to use the Army, if possible, for his operations against Congress. By the ninth article it is charged that the President violated the act regulating the tenure of certain civil officers by appointing Lorenzo Thomas Secretary of War *ad interim* on the 21st day of February, 1868, and declaring that he had that day removed Edwin M. Stanton from the office of Secretary for the Department of War, the Senate being then in session, and not having consented to said removal. He ordered the said Lorenzo Thomas to seize the property of the War Department and act in place of Edwin M. Stanton, and delivered to said Thomas a letter of authority in writing authorizing him to do said acts. About the fact there can be no doubt, as the certified records aver it. What defense the President will make for this violation, direct and palpable, of the civil-tenure bill, we must wait and see.

The eighth article charges that the President conspired with Lorenzo Thomas to seize, take, and possess the property of the United States in the War Department, in violation of the act of March 2, 1867, before referred to. This fact is also proved by the records.

The seventh article charges that the President entered into a conspiracy with Lorenzo Thomas to prevent Edwin M. Stanton, Secretary for the Department of War, from holding the office of Secretary of War, to which he had been appointed under the laws of the United States. All this is proved by a letter of authority produced by General Thomas when he repeatedly demanded possession of the office from the incumbent, and needs no further proof till there be a satisfactory answer.

Article six charges that the President conspired with Thomas to seize the property of the United States in the War Department, contrary to both the act of July, 1861, and the act of March 2, before referred to. This is all proved by the same letter of authority issued by the President to said Thomas, and repeatedly produced by the latter to the Secretary of War in his attempt to gain possession of said property. As I am now only showing the evidence that will be given, it would be wrong to anticipate the defense by argument, until we see the authority upon which it rests.

Article five charges that the President conspired with Lorenzo Thomas to hinder the execution of the tenure-of-office bill, passed March 2, 1867, and to prevent Edwin M. Stanton, Secretary of War, from holding said office. The same evidence is conclusive upon this point.

The fourth article charges that the President, in conspiracy with Lorenzo Thomas and with other persons unknown, did attempt, by intimidation and threats, to prevent Edwin M. Stanton, then and there Secretary of the Department of War, from holding said office, contrary to the provisions of the act of July 31, 1866.

The third article charges that the President, on the 21st day of February, 1868, while the Senate was in session, did appoint Lorenzo Thomas Secretary of War *ad interim* without the advice and consent of the Senate, no vacancy having happened during the recess of the Senate nor then existing. The commission produced by Major General Thomas and the copy given in evidence place that fact beyond dispute.

By the second section of the second article of the Constitution the President is empowered to make appointments to office by and with the advice and consent of the Senate, but not while the Senate is in session without such consent. The appointment, therefore, of General Thomas was a palpable violation of the Constitution.

The first article charges that the President, in violation of the Constitution and laws of the United States, issued an order removing Edwin M. Stanton from the office of Secretary of War, commissioned by and with the advice and consent of the Senate, having suspended Mr. Stanton from his office during the recess of the Senate and within twenty days after the meeting of the next session of the Senate, on the 12th day of December, having reported to the Senate such suspension, with the evidence and reasons for his action, and the Senate on the 13th of January, having considered the evidence, refused to concur in the suspension, whereby the said Edwin M. Stanton, by virtue of the tenure-of-office bill, did forthwith resume the functions of his office, of which the said President had due notice, as appears from the records; whereupon the President assumed to remove the Secretary from office and to appoint Brevet Major General Lorenzo Thomas Secretary ad interim, and ordered the delivery of possession, which order was unlawfully issued, in violation of the act to regulate the tenure of certain civil offices,

and contrary to the provisions of said act, and contrary to the provisions of the Constitution of the United States, without the advice and consent of the Senate then being in session.

I had thought that the article which I hold in my hand was one of the articles reported; I had understood it was to be put in as one of the articles, but when I came to read them, after they were printed, I found that there were two articles that are nearly alike, tautological, I think; but this was not in, and I suspect it was omitted by mistake. I will therefore read it and call it one and a half as, in my judgment, it is the gist and vital portion of this whole prosecution:

On the 12th day of August, 1867, during the recess of Congress, Andrew Johnson, President of the United States did suspend from office Edwin M. Stanton, Secretary of the Department of War, he having been duly appointed and then in possession and in discharge of the duties of said office and did as he was bound to do by the act entitled "An act regulating the tenure of certain civil offices," report to the Senate at its next meeting such suspension, with his reasons for his action in the case. By the second section of said act it is provided that "if the Senate shall refuse to concur in such suspension, such officer so suspended shall forthwith resume the functions of his office, and the powers of the Person so performing its duties in his stead shall cease." While the Senate was considering the sufficiency of the reasons reported, and at other times, Andrew Johnson, President as aforesaid, formed a deliberate design and determination to prevent the execution of that portion of the law and to prevent the said Edwin M. Stanton from forthwith resuming the functions of his office, notwithstanding the Senate should decide in his favor, thereby committing a high misdemeanor in office. And when he was defeated in accomplishing his design by the integrity and fidelity of the Secretary ad interim, he sought to arrive at the same end by giving a letter of authority to one Lorenzo Thomas Adjutant General of the Army, to act as Secretary of War ad interim, and to take all the records, books, papers, and other public Property of said Department into his custody, the Senate being then in session; and he severely censured the former Secretary ad interim for not yielding to his efforts to make him betray his trust.

I wish this to be particularly noticed, for I intend to offer it as an amendment. I wish gentlemen to examine and see that this charge is nowhere contained in any of the articles reported, and unless it be inserted there can be no trial upon it; and if there be shrewd lawyers, as I know there will be, and cavilling judges, and, without this article, they do not acquit him, they are greener than I was in any case I ever undertook before the court of quarter sessions. If it be inserted his own letters show both the removal and the attempt to defeat the reinstatement of the Secretary of War, although the Senate should decide in his favor. How, then, can he or his counsel hope to escape, even if there were no other charge—it is worth all of them put together—from conviction, unless it be upon what I know they will rely on, the unconstitutionality of the tenure-of-civil-office act. Let us for a moment look and see what chance he has to escape there. I may say that the Senate have four times voted upon the constitutionality of that very bill. On the 19th day of February, 1867, the Senate passed that bill by a vote of yeas 29, nays 9. I am sorry to say that it was a party vote but every Republican voted in its favor. Let me see the recreant who will now dare to tread back upon his steps and vote upon the other side.

Gentlemen remember that we had a committee of conference upon the bill, and the votes were—yeas 22, nays 10; every Republican present voting after a long discussion, in favor of the constitutionality of the measure. Then came the veto of the President and his reasons therefor, when the bill was again submitted to the Senate and passed by yeas 35, nays 11; every Republican present voting in favor of the bill. I will not go further, although I could trace one or two other incidental votes of precisely the same character.

Now, if my article is adopted, let him hope who dares to hope that so high a body as the Senate will betray its trust, will forget its own acts, will tread back upon its own action, will disgrace itself in the face of the nation. Point me to one who dare do it, and I will show you one who will dare the infamy of posterity.

What chance, then, would Andrew Johnson have had we not left out the article I desire to move as an amendment, in order to give him a loophole of escape. Gentlemen can see how fair we are. If my article be inserted what chance has Andrew Johnson to escape, even if all the rest of the articles should fail? Unfortunate man! thus surrounded, hampered, tangled in the meshes of his own wickedness—unfortunate, unhappy man, behold your doom.

Congressional Globe, 40th Congress, 2d session, March 2, 1868, 1612–1613.

82   The Articles of Impeachment of Andrew Johnson

March 4, 1868

President Andrew Johnson is the only American president to date to be impeached in the House and be subjected to a trial in the Senate. Johnson, however, won acquittal of the charges against him by a one-vote margin. He was able to stay in office and complete his term, although the process left him politically weakened and embittered. He did not bother to attend the inauguration of his successor, Ulysses S. Grant, the following year.

Johnson's impeachment is best understood in the context of the extraordinary political turmoil in the nation as the United States tried to heal the wounds of the Civil War and bring the Confederate states back into the Union through the process known as Reconstruction. Johnson, the wartime governor of Tennessee, took office following the assassination of Abraham Lincoln. He faced a hostile and powerful Congress filled with Radical Republicans who did not like Johnson's mild handling of the defeated southern states. The Radical Republicans had their own plans for Reconstruction and President Johnson stood in their way. In a series of bills designed to curtail presidential power, Congress required the president to convey all instructions to military commanders through the commanding general, Ulysses S. Grant, who was sympathetic to the Radical Republican approach to Reconstruction. Grant was also the leading candidate for the presidential nomination on the Republican ticket in 1868. Congress further curtailed the president's ability to put his own people in key government positions when it passed the Tenure of Office Act, requiring the president to seek the advice and consent of the Senate before removing any Republican officeholders and replacing them with his own people. Johnson vetoed both of these measures as unconstitutional intrusions by Congress into the affairs of the executive branch. Congress, however, overruled Johnson's vetoes.

Johnson's Reconstruction plans were thwarted by his own secretary of war, Edwin M. Stanton, who preferred congressional plans for Reconstruction. When Johnson decided to confront Congress by replacing Stanton without the approval of the Senate, he handled the situation ineptly. He sent Adjutant General Lorenzo P. Thomas to take over Stanton's office, which the latter refused to vacate with the help of Ulysses S. Grant, who had locked the secretary's office and given the key to Stanton. The whole fiasco worked to the advantage of the Radical Republicans, who felt they had grounds for impeaching the president under the Tenure of Office Act. The bulk of the eleven-count indictment referred to violations of this one controversial law.

Johnson's trial in the Senate began March 30, 1868. His lawyers argued that impeachment should rest on legal matters, not differences over politics. They argued that the Tenure of Office Act was unconstitutional. Those in favor of convicting Johnson argued that impeachment by its very nature was political. On May 16, 1868, the Senate voted on the eleventh article of impeachment, which combined all the charges in the preceding ten. In that dramatic vote 35 senators declared Johnson guilty and 19 voted for acquittal. Since this was one vote short of the required two-thirds majority, Johnson was acquitted. Ten days later the Senate voted on two other articles of impeachment, but the vote was the same and the Senate gave up the effort.

Was Johnson guilty? The verdict of most students of the subject is no. Johnson was the victim of an overreaching Congress that wanted to remove a roadblock to its plans for Reconstruction. Those who voted for Johnson's acquittal did so for mixed reasons. Some thought the Tenure of Office Act unconstitutional. Others worried about the man who would succeed Johnson as president, Senate president pro tempore, Benjamin Wade of Ohio, one of the most radical of the Radical Republicans. In 1885 Congress repealed the Tenure of Office Act, but it was not until 1926 that Andrew Johnson received belated vindication, when the Supreme Court finally declared the act to be unconstitutional.

ARTICLE 1

That said Andrew Johnson, President of the United States, on the twenty-first day of February, in the year of our Lord one thousand eight hundred and sixty-eight, at Washington, in the District of Columbia, unmindful of the high duties of his office, of his oath of office, and of the requirement of the Constitution that he should take care that the laws be faithfully executed, did unlawfully, and in violation of the Constitution and laws of the United States issue an order in writing for the removal of Edwin M. Stanton from the office of Secretary for the Department of War, said Edwin M. Stanton having been theretofore duly appointed and commissioned, by and with the advice and consent of the Senate of the United States, as such Secretary, and said Andrew Johnson, President of the United States, on the twelfth day of August, in the year of our Lord one thousand eight hundred and sixty-seven, and during the recess of said Senate, having suspended by his order Edwin M. Stanton from said office, and within twenty days after the first day of the next meeting of said Senate, that is to say, on the twelfth day of December in the year last aforesaid having reported to said Senate such suspension with the evidence and reasons for his action in the case and the name of the person designated to perform the duties of such office temporarily until the next meeting of the Senate, and said Senate thereafterwards, on the thirteenth day of January, in the year of our Lord one thousand eight hundred and sixty-eight, having duly considered the evidence and reasons reported by said Andrew Johnson for said suspension, and having refused to concur in said suspension, whereby and by force of the provisions of an act entitled "An act regulating the tenure of certain civil offices," passed March second, eighteen hundred and sixty-seven, said Edwin M. Stanton did forthwith resume the functions of his office, whereof the said Andrew Johnson had then and there due notice, and said Edwin M. Stanton, by reason of the premises, on said twenty-first day of February, being lawfully entitled to hold said office of Secretary for the Department of War, which said order for the removal of said Edwin M. Stanton is in substance as follows, that is to say:

Executive Mansion
Washington, D. C., February 21, 1868

Sir:

By virtue of the power and authority vested in me as President by the Constitution and laws of the United States you are hereby removed from office as Secretary for the Department of War, and your functions as such will terminate upon the receipt of this communication.

You will transfer to Brevet Major General Lorenzo Thomas, Adjutant General of the army, who has this day been authorized and empowered to act as Secretary of War *ad interim*, all records, books, papers, and other public property now in your custody and charge.

Respectfully yours,
Andrew Johnson

To the Hon. Edwin M. Stanton, Washington, D. C.

Which order was unlawfully issued with intent then and there to violate the act entitled "An act regulating the tenure of certain civil offices," passed March second, eighteen hundred and sixty-seven, and with the further intent, contrary to the provisions of said act, in violation thereof, and contrary to the provisions of the Constitution of the United States, and without the advice and consent of the Senate of the United States, the said Senate then and there being in session, to remove said Edwin M. Stanton from the office of Secretary for the Department of War, the said Edwin M. Stanton being then and there Secretary for the Department of War, and being then and there in the due and lawful execution and discharge of the duties of said office whereby said Andrew Johnson, President of the United States, did then and there commit and was guilty of a high misdemeanor in office.

ARTICLE II

That on the said twenty-first day of February, in the year of our Lord one thousand eight hundred and sixty-eight, at Washington, in the District of Columbia, said Andrew Johnson, President of the United States, unmindful of the high duties of his office, of his oath of office, and in violation of the Constitution of the United States, and contrary to the provisions of an act entitled "An act regulating the tenure of certain civil offices," passed March second, eighteen hundred and sixty-seven, without the advice and consent of the Senate of the United States, said Senate then and there being in session, and without authority of law, did, with intent to violate the Constitution of the United States, and the act aforesaid, issue and deliver to one Lorenzo Thomas a letter of authority in substance as follows, that is to say:

Executive Mansion
Washington, D. C., February 21, 1868

Sir:

The Hon. Edwin M. Stanton having been this day removed from office as Secretary for the Department of War, you are hereby authorized and empowered to act as Secretary of War ad interim, and will immediately enter upon the discharge of the duties pertaining to that office.

Mr. Stanton has been instructed to transfer to you all the records, books, papers and other public property now in his custody and charge.

Respectfully yours,
Andrew Johnson

To Brevet Major General Lorenzo Thomas,
Adjutant General U.S. Army, Washington, D. C.

Then and there being no vacancy in said office of Secretary for the Department of War, whereby said Andrew Johnson, President of the United States, did then and there commit and was guilty of a high misdemeanor in office.

ARTICLE III

That said Andrew Johnson, President of the United States, on the twenty-first day of February, in the year of our Lord one thousand eight hundred and sixty-eight, at Washington, in the District of Columbia, did commit and was guilty of a high misdemeanor in office in this, that, without authority of law, while the Senate of the United States was then and there in session, he did appoint one Lorenzo Thomas to be Secretary for the Department of War *ad interim,* without the advice and consent of the Senate, and with intent to violate the Constitution of the United States, no vacancy having happened in said office of Secretary for the Department of War during the recess of the Senate, and no vacancy existing in said office at the time, and which said appointment, so made by said Andrew Johnson, of said Lorenzo Thomas, is in substance as follows, that is to say:

Executive Mansion
Washington, D. C., February 21,1868

Sir:

The Hon. Edwin M. Stanton having been this day removed from office as Secretary for the Department of War, you are hereby authorized and empowered to act as Secretary of War ad interim, and will immediately enter upon the discharge of the duties pertaining to that office.

Mr. Stanton has been instructed to transfer to you all the records, books, papers, and other public property now in his custody and charge.

Respectfully yours,
Andrew Johnson

To Brevet Major General Lorenzo Thomas,
Adjutant General U.S. Army, Washington, D. C.

ARTICLE IV

That said Andrew Johnson, President of the United States, unmindful of the high duties of his office and of his oath of office, in violation of the Constitution and laws of the United States, on the twenty-first day of February, in the year of our Lord one thousand eight hundred and sixty-eight, at Washington, in the District of Columbia, did unlawfully conspire with one Lorenzo Thomas, and with other persons to the House of Representatives unknown, with intent, by intimidation and threats, unlawfully to hinder and prevent Edwin M. Stanton, then and there the Secretary for the Department of War, duly appointed under the laws of the United States, from holding said office of Secretary for the Department of War, contrary to and in violation of the Constitution of the United States, and of the provisions of an act entitled "An act to define and punish certain conspiracies" approved July thirty-first, eighteen hundred and sixty-one, whereby said Andrew Johnson, President of the United States, did then and there commit and was guilty of a high crime in office.

ARTICLE V

That said Andrew Johnson, President of the United States, unmindful of the high duties of his office and of his oath of office, on the twenty-first day of February, in the year of our Lord one thousand eight hundred and sixty-eight, and on divers other days and times in said year, before the second day of March in the year of our Lord one thousand eight hundred and sixty-eight, at Washington, in the District of Columbia, did unlawfully conspire with one Lorenzo Thomas, and with other persons to the House of Representatives unknown, to prevent and hinder the execution of an act entitled "An act regulating

the tenure of certain civil offices," passed March second, eighteen hundred and sixty-seven, and in pursuance of said conspiracy, did unlawfully attempt to prevent Edwin M. Stanton, then and there being Secretary for the Department of War duly appointed and commissioned under the laws of the United States, from holding said office, whereby the said Andrew Johnson, President of the United States, did then and there commit and was guilty of a high misdemeanor in office.

ARTICLE VI

That said Andrew Johnson, President of the United States, unmindful of the high duties of his office and of his oath of office, on the twenty-first day of February, in the year of our Lord one thousand eight hundred and sixty-eight, at Washington, in the District of Columbia, did unlawfully conspire with one Lorenzo Thomas by force to seize, take, and possess the property of the United States in the Department of War, and then and there in the custody and charge of Edwin M. Stanton, Secretary for said department, contrary to the provisions of an act entitled "An act to define and punish certain conspiracies," approved July thirty-one, eighteen hundred and sixty-one, and with intent to violate and disregard an act entitled "An act regulating the tenure of certain civil offices," passed March second, eighteen hundred and sixty-seven, whereby said Andrew Johnson, President of the United States, did then and there commit a high crime in office.

ARTICLE VII

That said Andrew Johnson, President of the United States, unmindful of the high duties of his office and of his oath of office, on the twenty-first day of February, in the year of our Lord one thousand eight hundred and sixty-eight, at Washington, in the District of Columbia, did unlawfully conspire with one Lorenzo Thomas with intent unlawfully to seize, take, and possess the property of the United States in the Department of War, in the custody and charge of Edwin M. Stanton, Secretary for said department, with intent to violate and disregard the act entitled "An act regulating the tenure of certain civil offices," passed March second, eighteen hundred and sixty-seven, whereby said Andrew Johnson, President of the United States, did then and there commit a high misdemeanor in office.

ARTICLE VIII

That said Andrew Johnson, President of the United States, unmindful of the high duties of his office and of his oath of office, with intent unlawfully to control the disbursements of the moneys appropriated for the military service and for the Department of War, on the twenty-first day of February, in the year of our Lord one thousand eight hundred and sixty-eight, at Washington, in the District of Columbia, did unlawfully and contrary to the provisions of an act entitled "An act regulating the tenure of certain civil offices," passed March second, eighteen hundred and sixty-seven, and in violation of the Constitution of the United States, and without the advice and consent of the Senate of the United States, and while the Senate was then and there in session, there being no vacancy in the office of Secretary for the Department of War, and with intent to violate and disregard the act aforesaid, then and there issue and deliver to one Lorenzo Thomas a letter of authority in writing, in substance as follows, that is to say:

Executive Mansion
Washington, D. C., February 21, 1868

Sir:

The Hon. Edwin M. Stanton having been this day removed from office as Secretary for the Department of War, you are hereby authorized and empowered to act as Secretary of War ad interim, and will immediately enter upon the discharge of the duties pertaining to that office.

Mr. Stanton has been instructed to transfer to you all the records, books, papers, and other public property now in his custody and charge.

Respectfully, yours,
Andrew Johnson

To Brevet Major General Lorenzo Thomas,
Adjutant General United States Army, Washington, D. C.

Whereby said Andrew Johnson, President of the United States, did then and there commit and was guilty of a high misdemeanor in office.

ARTICLE IX

That said Andrew Johnson, President of the United States, on the twenty-second day of February, in the year of our Lord one thousand eight hundred and sixty-eight, at Washington, in the District of Columbia, in disregard of the Constitution, and the laws of the United States duly enacted, as commander-in-chief of the army of the United States, did bring before himself then and there William H. Emory, a major general by brevet in the army of the United States, actually in command of the department of Washington and the military forces thereof, and did then and there, as such commander-in-chief, declare to and instruct said Emory that part of a law of the United States, passed March second, eighteen hundred and sixty-seven, entitled "An act making appropriations for the support of the army for the year ending June thirtieth, eighteen hundred and sixty-eight, and for other purposes," especially the second section thereof, which provides, among other things, that "all orders and instructions relating to military operations, issued by the President or Secretary of War, shall be issued through the General of the army, and, in case of his inability, through the next in rank," was unconstitutional, and in contravention of the commission of said Emory, and which said provision of law had been therefore duly and legally promulgated by General Orders for the government and direction of the army of the United States, as the said Andrew Johnson then and there well knew, with intent thereby to induce said Emory, in his official capacity as commander of the department of Washington, to violate the provisions of said act, and to take and receive, act upon, and obey such orders as he, the said Andrew Johnson, might make

and give, and which should not be issued through the General of the army of the United States, according to the provisions of said act, and with the further intent thereby to enable him, the said Andrew Johnson, to prevent the execution of the act entitled "An act regulating the tenure of certain civil offices," passed March second, eighteen hundred and sixty-seven, and to unlawfully prevent Edwin M. Stanton, then being Secretary for the Department of War from holding said office and discharging the duties thereof, whereby said Andrew Johnson, President of the United States, did then and there commit and was guilty of a high misdemeanor in office.

And the House of Representatives, by protestation, saving to themselves the liberty of exhibiting at any time hereafter any further articles or other accusation or impeachment against the said Andrew Johnson, President of the United States, and also of replying to his answers which he shall make unto the articles herein preferred against him, and of offering proof to the same, and every part thereof, and to all and every other article, accusation, or impeachment which shall be exhibited by them, as the case shall require, DO DEMAND that the said Andrew Johnson may be put to answer the high crimes and misdemeanors in office herein charged against him, and that such proceedings, examinations, trials, and judgments may be thereupon had and given as may be agreeable to law and justice.

ARTICLE X

That said Andrew Johnson, President of the United States, unmindful of the high duties of his office, and the dignity and proprieties thereof, and of the harmony and courtesies which ought to exist and be maintained between the executive and legislative branches of the government of the United States, designing and intending to set aside the rightful authority and powers of Congress, did attempt to bring into disgrace, ridicule, hatred, contempt, and reproach the Congress of the United States, and the several branches thereof, to impair and destroy the regard and respect of all the good people of the United States for the Congress and legislative powers thereof, (which all officers of the government ought inviolably to preserve and maintain,) and to excite the odium and resentment of all the good people of the United States against Congress and the laws by it duly and constitutionally enacted; and in pursuance of his said design and intent, openly and publicly, and before divers assemblages of the citizens of the United States, convened in divers parts thereof to meet and receive said Andrew Johnson as the Chief Magistrate of the United States, did, on the eighteenth day of August, in the year of our Lord one thousand eight hundred and sixty-six, and on divers other days and times, as well before as afterward, make and deliver, with a loud voice, certain intemperate, inflammatory, and scandalous harangues, and did therein utter loud threats and bitter menaces, as well against Congress as the laws of the United States duly enacted thereby, amid the cries, jeers, and laughter of the multitudes then assembled and in hearing, which are set forth in the several specifications hereinafter written, in substance and effect, that is to say:

Specification first.

In this, that at Washington, in the District of Columbia, in the Executive Mansion, to a committee of citizens who called upon the President of the United States, speaking of and concerning the Congress of the United States, said Andrew Johnson, President of the United States, heretofore, to wit, on the eighteenth day of August, in the year of our Lord one thousand eight hundred and sixty-six, did, in a loud voice, declare, in substance and effect, among other things, that is to say:

So far as the executive department of the government is concerned, the effort has been made to restore the Union, to heal the breach, to pour oil into the wounds which were consequent upon the struggle, and (to speak in common phrase) to prepare, as the learned and wise physician would, a plaster healing in character and co-extensive with the wound. We thought, and we think, that we had partially succeeded; but, as the work progresses, as reconstruction seemed to be taking place, and the country was becoming reunited, we found a disturbing and marring element opposing us. In alluding to that element I shall go no further than your convention, and the distinguished gentleman who has delivered to me the report of its proceedings. I shall make no reference to it that I do not believe the time and occasion justify.

We have witnessed in one department of the government every endeavor to prevent the restoration of peace, harmony and union. We have seen hanging upon the verge of the government, as it were, a body called, or which assumes to be, the Congress of the United States, while, in fact, it is a Congress of only a part of the States. We have seen this Congress pretend to be for the Union, when its every step and act tended to perpetuate disunion and make a disruption of the States inevitable. . . . We have seen Congress gradually encroach, step by step, upon constitutional rights, and violate, day after day and month after month, fundamental principles of the government. We have seen a Congress that seemed to forget that there was a limit to the sphere and scope of legislation. We have seen in Congress in a minority assume to exercise power which, allowed to be consummated, would result in despotism or monarchy itself.

Specification second.

In this, that at Cleveland, in the State of Ohio, heretofore, to wit, on the third day of September, in the year of our Lord one thousand eight hundred and sixty-six, before a public assemblage of citizens and others, said Andrew Johnson, President of the United States, speaking of and concerning the Congress of the United States, did, in a loud voice, declare, in substance and effect, among other things, that is to say:

I will tell you what I did do. I called upon your Congress that is trying to break up the government. . . . In conclusion, besides that, Congress had taken much pains to poison their constituents against him. But what had Congress done? Have they done anything to restore the union of these States? No; on the contrary, they had done everything to prevent it; and because he stood now where he did when the rebellion commenced, he had been denounced as a traitor. Who had run greater risks or made greater sacrifices than himself? But Congress, factious and domineering, had undertaken to poison the minds of the American people.

Specification third.

In this, that at St. Louis, in the State of Missouri, heretofore, to wit, on the eighth day of September, in the year of our Lord one thousand eight hundred and sixty-six, before a public assemblage of citizens and others, said Andrew Johnson, President of the United States, speaking of and concerning the Congress of the United States, did, in a loud voice, declare in substance and effect, among other things, that is to say:

Go on. Perhaps if you had a word or two on the subject of New Orleans you might understand more about it than you do. And if you will go back—if you will go back and ascertain the cause of the riot at New Orleans, perhaps you will not be so prompt in calling out "New Orleans." If you will take up the riot at New Orleans, and trace it back to its source or its immediate cause, you will find out who is responsible for the blood that was shed there. If you will take up the riot at New Orleans and trace it back to the radical Congress, you will find that the riot at New Orleans was substantially planned. If you will take up the proceedings in their caucusses you will understand that they there knew that a convention was to be called which was extinct by its power having expired; that it was said that the intention was that a new government was to be organized, and on the organization of that government the intention was to enfranchise one portion of the population, called the colored population, who had just been emancipated, and at the same time disfranchise white men. When you design to talk about New Orleans you ought to understand what you are talking about. When you read the speeches that were made, and take up the facts on the Friday and Saturday before that convention sat, you will there find that speeches were made incendiary in their character, exciting in that portion of the population, the black population, to arm themselves and prepare for the shedding of blood. You will also find that that convention did assemble in violation of law, and the intention of that convention was to supersede the reorganized authorities in the State government of Louisiana, which had been recognized by the government of the United States; and every man engaged in that rebellion in that convention, with the intention of superseding and upturning the civil government which had been recognized by the government of the United States, I say that he was a traitor to the Constitution of the United States, and hence you find that another rebellion was commenced, *having its origin in the radical Congress.* . . .

So much for the New Orleans riot. And there was the cause and the origin of the blood that was shed, and every drop of blood that was shed is upon their skirts, and they are responsible for it. I could test this thing a little closer, but will not do it here to-night. But when you talk about the causes and consequences that resulted from proceedings of that kind, perhaps, as I have been introduced here, and you have provoked questions of this kind, though it does not provoke me, I will tell you a few wholesome things that have been done by this radical Congress in connection with New Orleans and the extension of the elective franchise.

I know that I have been traduced and abused. I know it has come in advance of me here as elsewhere, that I have attempted to exercise an arbitrary power in resisting laws that were intended to be forced upon the government; that I had exercised that power; that I had abandoned the party that elected me, and that I was a traitor, because I exercised the veto power in attempting, and did arrest for a time, a bill that was called a "Freedman's Bureau" bill yes, that I was a traitor. And I have been traduced, I have been slandered, I have been maligned, I have been called Judas Iscariot, and all that. Now, my countrymen, here to-night, it is very easy to indulge in epithets; it is easy to call a man Judas and cry out traitor; but when he is called upon to give arguments and facts he is very often found wanting. Judas Iscariot—Judas. There was a Judas, and he was one of the twelve apostles. Oh! yes, the twelve apostles had a Christ. The twelve apostles had a Christ, and he never could have had a Judas unless he had had twelve apostles. If I have played the Judas, who has been my Christ that I have played the Judas with? Was it Thad Stevens? Was it Wendell Phillips? Was it Charles Sumner? These are the men that stop and compare themselves with the Saviour; and everybody that differs with them in opinion, and to try to stay and arrest their diabolical and nefarious policy, is to be denounced as a Judas. . . .

Well, let me say to you, if you will stand by me in this action, if you will stand by me in trying to give the people a fair chance—soldiers and citizens—to participate in these offices, God being willing, I will kick them out. I will kick them out just as fast as I can.

Let me say to you, in concluding, that what I have said I intended to say. I was not provoked into this, and I care not for their menaces, the taunts, and the jeers. I care not for threats. I do not intend to be bullied by my enemies nor overawed by my friends. But, God willing, with your help, I will veto their measures when any of them come to me.

Which said utterances, declarations, threats, and harangues, highly censurable in any, are peculiarly indecent and unbecoming in the Chief Magistrate of the United States, by means whereof said Andrew Johnson has brought the high office of the President of the United States into contempt, ridicule, and disgrace, to the great scandal of all good citizens, whereby said Andrew Johnson, President of the United States, did commit, and was then and there guilty of a high misdemeanor in office.

ARTICLE XI

That said Andrew Johnson, President of the United States, unmindful of the high duties of his office, and of his oath of office, and in disregard of the Constitution and laws of the United States, did, heretofore, to wit, on the eighteenth day of August, A.D. eighteen hundred and sixty-six, at the city of Washington, and the District of Columbia, by public speech, declare and affirm, in substance, that the thirty-ninth Congress of the United States was not a Congress of the United States authorized by the Constitution to exercise legislative power under the same, but, on the contrary, was a Congress of only part of the States, thereby denying, and intending to deny, that the legislation of said Congress was valid or obligatory upon him, the said Andrew Johnson, except in so far as he saw fit to approve the same and also thereby denying, and intending to deny, the power of the said thirty-ninth Congress to propose amendments to the Constitution of the United States; and, in pursuance of said declaration, the said Andrew Johnson, President of the United States, afterwards, to wit, on the twenty-first day of February, A.D. eighteen hundred and sixty-eight, at the city of Washington, in the District of Columbia, did, unlawfully, and in disregard of the requirements of the Constitution, that he should take care that the laws be faithfully executed, attempt to prevent the execution of an act entitled "An act regulating the tenure of certain civil offices," passed March second, eighteen hundred and sixty-seven, by unlawfully devising and contriving, and attempting to devise and contrive means by which he should prevent Edwin M. Stanton from forthwith resuming the functions of the office of Secretary for the Department of War, notwithstanding the refusal of the Senate to concur in the suspension theretofore made by said Andrew Johnson of said Edwin M. Stanton from said office of Secretary for the Department of War; and, also, by further unlawfully devising and contriving, and attempting to devise and contrive means, then and there, to prevent the execution of an act entitled "An act making appropriations for the support of the army for the fiscal year ending June thirtieth, eighteen hundred and sixty-eight, and for other purposes," approved March second, eighteen hundred and sixty-seven; and, also, to prevent the execution of an act entitled "An act to provide for the more efficient government of the rebel States, passed March second, eighteen hundred and sixty-seven, whereby the said Andrew Johnson, President of the United States, did, then, to wit, on the twenty-first day of February, A.D., eighteen hundred and sixty-eight, at the city of Washington, commit, and was guilty of, a high misdemeanor in office.

Andrew Johnson, *Trial of Andrew Johnson, President of the United States, on Impeachment by the House of Representatives for High Crimes and Misdemeanors*, 3 vols. (Washington, D.C.: Government Printing Office, 1868), vol. 1: 6–10.

83   The Fifteenth Amendment to the Constitution

Submitted to the States, February 26, 1869; Ratified, February 17, 1870

This amendment is the third of the trio of constitutional amendments passed near the end of the Civil War and during Reconstruction to guarantee former slaves the rights of citizenship. The Thirteenth Amendment freed the slaves in the border states and those states occupied by federal troops (see document 76). The Fourteenth Amendment provided voting rights for African Americans in the former Confederate states, which, at the time of ratification, were still under military rule (see document 79). Suffrage for blacks did not come automatically in the border states or in some of the northern states.

The Fifteenth Amendment extended the right of suffrage to African Americans in all states. Supported by moderate Republicans and most of the Radical Republicans in Congress, the amendment marked the symbolic high water mark of congressional efforts to enfranchise blacks. Unfortunately, it was not enforced uniformly in the nation, especially in most of the southern states, where various devices, such as literacy tests, property qualifications, poll taxes, and outright intimidation kept black voters from the polls.

ARTICLE XV.

SECTION 1. The right of citizens of the United States to vote shall not be denied or abridged by the United States or by any State on account of race, color, or previous condition of servitude.

SECTION 2. The Congress shall have the right to enforce this article by appropriate legislation.

The Constitution of the United States of America as Amended, House Doc. 102–188, 102d Congress, 2d session (Washington: Government Printing Office, 1992), 18.

84   *Haver v. Yaker*

1869

Only a few Senate and Supreme Court specialists are familiar with Haver v. Yaker, *a relatively obscure Supreme Court decision from 1869. It is seldom mentioned in textbooks or encyclopedias, but it is a landmark document nonetheless because of the important precedents it established regarding the Senate's constitutional power to make treaties.*

The case was routine in nature and had none of the drama of some of the better known decisions of the Supreme Court. In 1853 a Swiss-born U.S. citizen, Peter Yaker, a resident of Kentucky, died leaving some real estate. His wife, Janet Yaker, an American citizen and resident of Kentucky, was the apparent heir. A group of Peter Yaker's relatives in Switzerland, including three with the last name of Haver, sued Yaker's widow, claiming that an 1850 treaty between the United States and the Swiss Confederation made it possible for Swiss citizens to inherit land in the United States. The treaty had been signed in 1850, but it was not ratified by the Senate until 1855—two years after Peter Yaker's death. Yaker's Swiss relatives did not learn of his death until 1859, when they filed this suit in Kentucky.

Under international law a treaty becomes legally binding when it is signed by the representatives of the nations conducting the treaty. But, as this case affirmed, in U.S. law a treaty is not binding until it meets the constitutional requirement of approval by the U.S. Senate. The case also made clear that the Senate had the right to amend a treaty before approving it.

David Davis (1815–1886), an associate justice of the U.S. Supreme Court from 1862 to 1877, wrote the majority opinion in the case, which favored Yaker's widow and affirmed the earlier judgment of the Kentucky courts. Davis later resigned from the Supreme Court when he was elected to the U.S. Senate as an Independent from Illinois, where he served from 1877 to 1883.

Mr. Justice DAVIS delivered the opinion of the court.

It is undoubtedly true, as a principle of international law, that, as respects the rights of either government under it, a treaty is considered as concluded and binding from the date of its signature. In this regard the exchange of ratifications has a retroactive effect, confirming the treaty from its date. But a different rule prevails where the treaty operates on individual rights. The principle of relation does not apply to rights of this character, which were vested before the treaty was ratified. In so far as it affects them, it is not considered as concluded until there is an exchange of ratifications. . . . The reason of the rule is apparent. In this country, a treaty is something more than a contract, for the Federal Constitution declares it to be the law of the land. If so, before it can become a law, the Senate, in whom rests the authority to ratify it, must agree to it. But the Senate are not required to adopt or reject it as a whole, but may modify or amend it, as was done with the treaty under consideration. As the individual citizen, on whose rights of property it operates, has no means of knowing anything of it while before the Senate, it would be wrong in principle to hold him bound by it, as the law of the land, until it was ratified and proclaimed. And to construe the law, so as to make the ratification of the treaty relate back to its signing, thereby divesting a title already vested, would be manifestly unjust, and cannot be sanctioned.

These views dispose of this case, and we are not required to determine whether this treaty, if it had become a law at an earlier date, would have secured the plaintiffs in error the interest which they claim in the real estate left by Yaker at his death.

JUDGMENT AFFIRMED.

76 U.S. 32 (1869).

85   The House Debates Investigation of the Credit Mobilier Scandal

December 2, 1872

The Credit Mobilier scandal rocked Congress in late 1872 and in 1873 with allegations of corruption at the highest levels of government. In the document below, the House of Representatives debated the implications of the scandal. A disgruntled stockholder in the Union Pacific Railroad, Henry S. McComb, accused Representative Oakes Ames (R-Mass.) of bribing members of Congress with shares of lucrative stock in the Union Pacific in order to influence their votes on legislation. The New York Sun *published the story during the presidential election of 1872, implying that McComb had correspondence from Ames proving the complicity of high-ranking officials.*

Credit Mobilier of America was an investment holding company originally chartered in France to hold funds related to railroad construction. The firm's French directors had been forced to make restitution to stockholders after they were found guilty of malfeasance in business practices in 1868. The Union Pacific Railroad acquired Credit Mobilier and used it to raise money for the transcontinental railroad, which had been stalled for decades by the high costs of the endeavor, the lack of private funding, and technical construction problems. The Construction Acts of 1862 and 1864 had offered matching government funds to private investment, along with land grants as inducements to investors, but these bills failed to draw substantial amounts of private money. The Credit Mobilier Company lured investors by promising them limited liability in case of losses. For a while the company succeeded in enriching its own holdings and providing much needed funding for the Union Pacific Railroad.

The allegations came to light when McComb became unhappy with his investments and the infighting between the boards of the Union Pacific and Credit Mobilier. Representative Ames, a holder of Union Pacific Railroad stock and a director of Credit Mobilier, did not view soliciting investment by congressional colleagues as bribery, only good business, as the venture promised high returns. He claimed since there was no pending railroad legislation at the time, there was no attempt to influence votes.

Speaker James G. Blaine (R-Maine), one of those implicated in the scandal, left the Speaker's chair to take part in the floor debate. Ten days later the House and Senate agreed to form a five-member joint investigative committee chaired by Senator Luke B. Poland (R-Vt.) that began hearings on December 12, 1872. A separate Senate committee also looked into the matter. Among those implicated in the affair, in addition to the Speaker, were Vice President of the United States Schuyler Colfax, prominent representative and later president of the United States James A. Garfield, and several other government officials and members of the House and Senate.

Once McComb's charges of bribery became public, those implicated scrambled to cover their tracks or rationalize their involvement. The reactions were mixed. Benjamin Boyer, who had been a representative from Pennsylvania from 1865 to 1869, regretted only that he had not increased his investment in Credit Mobilier. Men

such as Senator James Patterson (R-N.H.) and Speaker Blaine denied any involvement. Vice President Colfax, while unsure of the propriety or constitutional requirements of his appearing before an investigative committee of Congress, did so anyway, denying any wrongdoing in the affair. But his testimony left many questions unanswered and it ruined his political career. James A. Garfield was accused of accepting ten shares of Credit Mobilier stock and a loan of $300. In an initial statement before the Poland Committee, he denied accepting the stock and admitted to taking a loan, which he paid back. He refused to testify further. His silence ultimately saved his public career. He was reelected to Congress and went on to be elected president of the United States in 1880. Speaker Blaine was cleared of wrongdoing, although his political enemies would charge him in another scandal in 1876 (see document 89).

The Poland Committee recommended the expulsion of two House members: Oakes Ames for bribery and James Brooks (D-N.Y.) for buying the stock but placing it in his son-in-law's name. The full House did not vote to expel Ames and Brooks, who received the lesser punishment of being censured by the House. By strange coincidence, both men died within a few months of their censure. A Senate select committee recommended the expulsion of Senator Patterson for giving false testimony, but a caucus of Republican senators argued there was insufficient time left in the term to deliberate on the matter. Patterson escaped expulsion when his term in the Senate expired.

The scandal served to increase public scrutiny of government. It was the first of several major scandals that would haunt Congress and the administration of President Ulysses S. Grant in the 1870s.

ALLEGED BRIBERY OF MEMBERS.

Mr. BLAINE, (Mr. Cox occupying the chair.) Mr. Speaker, I rise to question of the highest privilege, to one that concerns the integrity of members of this House and the honor of the House itself. It is quite generally known to the members of this House that during the recent presidential campaign there was a widespread accusation of bribery of members; that members of this House were bribed to perform certain legislative acts for the benefit of the Union Pacific Railroad Company by presents of stock in a corporation known as the "Credit Mobilier." Without obtruding myself as one of eminent station, I may say that the charge struck in high places. It included the Vice President of the United States, the Vice President-elect of the United States; it included Senators of the United States, two of them ex-Senators from Tennessee and Delaware, and a present Senator from New Hampshire; it included the Secretary of the Treasury of the United States; it included honorable and prominent members of this House—my friend, the chairman of the Ways and Means, [Mr. Dawes,] my friend, the chairman of the Appropriations Committee, [Mr. Garfield,] my friend, the chairman of the Appropriations Committee, [Mr. Kelley,] the chairman of the Civil Service Committee; the gentleman from Ohio, [Mr. Bingham,] the chairman of the Judiciary committee; the gentleman from Pennsylvania, [Mr. Scofield,] the chairman of the Naval Committee; on the other side of the House, the prominent and distinguished member of the Ways and Means Committee from New York, [Mr. Brooks,] and a member from Pennsylvania (Mr. Boyer) not now in this House; and besides these, a gentleman from Massachusetts (Mr. Eliot) no longer among the living, but sleeping in what was considered an honored grave. These accusations are that the several persons received bribes from the hands of a Representative from Massachusetts, [Mr. Ames.] A charge of bribery of members is the gravest that can be made in a legislative body. It seems to me, sir, that this charge demands prompt, thorough, and impartial investigation, and I have taken the floor for the purpose of moving that investigation. Unwilling, of course, to appoint any committee of investigation to examine into a charge in which I was myself included, I have called you, sir, to the chair, an honored member of the House, honored here and honored in the country; and when on Saturday last I called upon you and advised you of this service, I placed upon you no other restriction in the appointment of a committee than that it should not contain a majority of my political friends.

I therefore send to the Clerk's desk, for adoption by the House, a preamble and accompanying resolution. If there be no gentleman desiring to discuss them, I will call the previous question.

The Clerk read as follows:

Whereas accusations have been made in the public press, founded on the alleged letter of Oakes Ames, a Representative from Massachusetts, and upon the alleged affidavit of Henry C. McComb, a citizen of Wilmington, in the State of Delaware, to the effect that members of this House were bribed by Oakes Ames to perform certain legislative acts for the benefit of the Union Pacific Railway Company by presents of stock in the Credit Mobilier of America, or by presents of a valuable character derived therefrom: Therefore,

Resolved, That a special committee of five members be appointed by the Speaker pro tempore, whose duty it shall be to investigate and ascertain whether any member of this House was bribed by Oakes Ames in any matter touching his legislative duty.

Resolved further, That the committee have the right to employ a stenographer, and that they be empowered to send for persons and papers.

The question was upon the adoption of the preamble and resolutions.

Mr. BUTLER, of Massachusetts. This resolution, by inadvertence I assume, relates only to bribery by a member of this House.

The SPEAKER pro tempore, (Mr. COX.) Does the gentleman from Maine [Mr. BLAINE] withdraw the call for the previous question?

Mr. BLAINE. Certainly.

Mr. BUTLER, of Massachusetts. I would suggest to the mover of the resolution to modify it, or I will move to amend it, so that it will read, "bribed by OAKES AMES or any other person."

Mr. BLAINE. I will modify the resolution to that effect.

Mr. BUTLER, of Massachusetts. It should be made as broad as possible.

Mr. BLAINE. Certainly. In intimating a desire to call the previous question I had no intention to cut off any amendment or remark. I said that if no other member desired to speak upon it, I would call the previous question. I will modify the resolution so that it will read, "Bribed by OAKES AMES, or any other person or corporation."

Mr. KELLEY. I would suggest to the gentleman from Maine [Mr. BLAINE] that he has not given Mr. McCombs's name correctly.

Mr. BLAINE. I do not know the gentleman. I have seen the name in print as "Henry C. McComb."

Mr. KELLEY. It is "Henry S. McCombs."

Mr. BLAINE. I will make that correction. If the gentleman who occupies the chair desires any further time in which to make up this committee, I will call the yeas and nays.

The SPEAKER pro tempore. The Chair would suggest to the gentleman from Maine [Mr. BLAINE] that the resolution has not yet been adopted, and therefore the Chair has no right, as yet, to appoint the committee. [Laughter.]

Mr. BLAINE. "The gentleman from Maine" stands corrected. [Laughter.]

The SPEAKER pro tempore. I hope this resolution will not be adopted. This question has been tried by a higher tribunal than this House The charges were made broadcast all over the country before the campaign through which we have just passed took place. Upon them the American people have spoken. We had much better go on with the business of the country than to continue such investigations as we have had.

MR. RANDALL. I hope that this resolution will be adopted. I had hoped that it would be adopted unanimity. I trust that, in the language of the Speaker, this investigation will be full, thorough, and searching. Less than that will not meet the expectation or the requirements of the people of the country. There has been a dark cloud of scandal raised over this House. It is due to such members as have not in any manner whatever been involved in any such proceedings that their characters should be lifted above suspicion; and, further, that the heavy thunderbolt of public opinion should fall upon those few, if any, who are implicated in voting for bills in which they were directly or indirectly interested.

Mr. DAWES. I agree with the gentleman from Pennsylvania, [Mr. RANDALL.] I hope this resolution will be adopted without a dissenting voice. Without expressing any opinion in reference to the result of such an investigation, it is due to the House, as well as to the members implicated, that there should be no shrinking at this time from a thorough, exhaustive, fair, and impartial investigation. In times that have passed I have borne my full share in urging upon the House the propriety of taking cognizance of charges of this kind when presented by responsible authority. I do not intend now to shrink from any such investigation; and I trust that those who stand with me to-day will feel, as I have no doubt they do, the propriety of calling upon the

House, without opposition and without dissent, to pursue this investigation as they would a judicial trial, in such a manner that the result will command, as I have no doubt it will receive, the approval of the American people.

Mr. HOLMAN. It seems to me very proper that this resolution should be adopted and this committee raised. It seems to me that the House, without dissent, with that unanimity which will arrest the attention of the country, should adopt this resolution. I think the House owes this to itself, to the individual members composing this body, and to the country. I trust this resolution will be adopted without a dissenting voice.

The preamble and resolutions, as modified, were agreed to.

Mr. BLAINE moved to reconsider the vote by which the preamble and resolutions were adopted; and also moved that the motion to reconsider be laid on the table.

The latter motion was agreed to.

The SPEAKER pro tempore. The present occupant of the chair having been advised beforehand that he would be called upon to act on this matter, has had time enough to select a committee, which he submits as the result of his best judgment, having in view the securing of a fair and impartial investigation.

The Clerk read, as follows, the names of the members constituting the committee:

LUKE P. POLAND of Vermont, NATHANIEL P. BANKS of Massachusetts, JAMES B. BECK of Kentucky, WILLIAM E. NIBLACK of Indiana, and GEORGE W. MCCRARY of Iowa.

. . . .

Congressional Globe, 42nd Congress, 3d session, Dec. 2, 1872, 11–12.

86   The "Salary Grab" Act of 1873

March 3, 1873

As the 42d Congress came to an end in March 1873, one of the last bills passed was an appropriations bill that specified the pay of government officials in all three branches. The members of Congress quickly regretted this bill. It demonstrated that once again the pay of members of Congress remained a controversial subject with many citizens. The timing of the bill could not have been worse. The Credit Mobilier scandal (see document 85) was still fresh in the minds of the public. This appropriations bill, raising congressional salaries from $5,000 to $7,500 per year retroactively to the beginning of the 42d Congress, meant that all members would have not only a pay raise in the future but a bonus of $5,000 ($2,500 per year for the 42d Congress just ended). The press quickly labeled the bill the "salary grab" act or the "back-pay steal."

To avoid being tainted by the bill, some members of Congress returned the increased pay to the U.S. Treasury—a ploy still occasionally used today by members who want to protest salary increases. Others donated the extra money to charities or to educational institutions. When the next Congress convened in December 1873, public outcry demanded that the new salary be rolled back. Congress quickly passed new legislation that returned congressional salaries to $5,000 per year, the same rate that had been in effect since 1865. The lasting effect of this monumental blunder was that it would be thirty-four years before Congress would again pass a bill increasing their pay. It was not until 1907 that congressional salaries were increased to $7,500 again, the same rate proposed in the 1873 bill. In 1882 a bill to reduce congressional pay even lower was defeated (see document 94).

CHAP. CCXXVI.—*AN ACT MAKING APPROPRIATIONS FOR THE LEGISLATIVE, EXECUTIVE AND JUDICIAL EXPENSES OF THE GOVERNMENT FOR THE YEAR ENDING JUNE THIRTIETH, EIGHTEEN HUNDRED AND SEVENTY-FOUR, AND FOR OTHER PURPOSES.*

Be it enacted by the Senate and House of Representatives of the United States of America, in Congress assembled, That the following sums be, an the same are hereby, appropriated, out of any money in the treasury not otherwise appropriated, for the service of the fiscal year ending June thirtieth, eighteen hundred and seventy-four, for the objects herein expressed, namely:

Legislative

Senate.—For compensation and mileage of senators, four hundred and five thousand dollars.

For compensation of the officers, clerks, messengers, and others receiving an annual salary in the service of the Senate, namely: secretary of the Senate, four thousand three hundred and twenty dollars; officer charged with disbursements of the Senate, five hundred and seventy-six dollars; chief clerk, three thousand dollars, and the additional sum of one thousand dollars while the said office is held by the present incumbent and no longer; principal clerk, three thousand six hundred dollars. That on and after the fourth day of March eighteen hundred and seventy-three, the President of the United States, shall receive in full, for his services during the term for which he shall have been elected, the sum of fifty thousand dollars per annum, to be paid monthly; the Vice-President of the United States shall receive in fall for his services, during the term for which he shall have been elected, the sum of ten thousand dollars per annum, to be paid monthly; and the chief justice of the Supreme Court of the United States, shall receive the sum of ten thousand five hundred dollars per annum, and the justices of the Supreme Court of the United States shall receive the sum of ten thousand dollars, per annum each, to be paid monthly: the Secretary of State, the Secretary of the Treasury, the Secretary of War, the Secretary of the Navy, the Secretary of the Interior, the Attorney-General, and the Postmaster-General, shall receive ten thousand dollars per annum each, for their service, to be paid monthly; and each assistant secretary of the Treasury, State and Interior Departments, shall receive as annual compensation, to be paid monthly, six thousand dollars: and the Speaker of the House of Representatives shall after the present Congress receive in full for all his services, compensation at the rate of ten thousand dollars per annum, and senators, representatives, and delegates in Congress, including senators, representatives and delegates in the forty-second Congress holding such office at the passage of this act and whose claim to a seat has not been adversely decided, shall receive seven thousand five hundred dollars, per annum each, and this shall be in lieu of all pay and allowance, except actual individual travelling expenses from their homes to the seat of government and return, by the most direct route of usual travel, once for each session, of the house to which such senator, member or delegate belongs to be certified to under his hand to the disbursing officer, and filed as a voucher. *Provided,* That in settling the pay and allowances of senators, members, and delegates in the forty-second Congress, all mileage shall be deducted and no allowance made for expenses of travel. And there is hereby appropriate a sum sufficient to make the annual salaries of such of the clerks in the office of the clerk of the House of Representatives as receive two thousand five hundred dollars and upwards and less then three thousand dollars, including the petition clerk and printing clerk, three thousand dollars each: and of such as receive two thousand dollars and upwards, and less than two thousand five hundred dollars, the sum of two thousand five hundred dollars each; and of such as receive eighteen hundred dollars and upwards, and less than two thousand dollars the sum of two thousand dollars each: and of the secretary of the Senate and the clerk of the House five thousand dollars each; and of the chief clerk and journal clerk of the House, while such positions are held by the present incumbents, and no longer, three thousand six hundred dollars each; and of the doorkeeper of the House, and the assistant-doorkeeper of the Senate, while the position is held by the present incumbent and no longer, three thousand dollars each; and of the postmaster to the Senate, two thousand five hundred and ninety-two dollars; assistant-postmaster, two thousand dollars; and of two mail-carriers one thousand seven hundred dollars; and of the superintendent and first assistant of the Senate document-room two thousand five hundred dollars each; and second assistant in said document-room eighteen

hundred dollars; and of the additional compensation to the reporters of the House and Senate for the Congressional Globe fifteen hundred dollars each; and of additional pay to the chief engineer of the House three hundred and sixty dollars (so as to equalize his pay with that of the chief engineer of the Senate). And it is hereby provided that the increase of compensation to the officers, clerks, and others in the employ of the Senate and House of Representatives, provided for by this act shall begin with the present Congress; and the pay of all the present employees of the Senate and the House of Representatives, including the employees in the library of Congress and those under the commissioner of public buildings and grounds, now employed in the capitol building, and also the House reporters, whose pay has not been specifically increased by this act, holding their places by appointment under the respective officers thereof or by the authority of the committee of contingent expenses of the Senate, and the committee of accounts of the House, be in fifteen per cent of their present compensation on the amount actually received and payable to them respectively from the beginning of the present Congress, or from the date of their appointment, during the present Congress, and who shall be actually employed at the passage of this act, and the amounts of money necessary to carry the foregoing provisions into effect are hereby appropriate out of any moneys in the treasury not otherwise appropriated. Principal executive clerk, minute and journal clerk, and financial clerk, in the office of the secretary of the Senate, at three thousand dollars each; librarian and seven clerks in the office of the secretary of the Senate, at two thousand five hundred dollars; keeper of the stationery, two thousand four hundred dollars; assistant keeper of the stationery, one thousand eight hundred dollars; one messenger, at one thousand two hundred and ninety-six dollars, one page, at seven hundred and twenty dollars; sergeant-at-arms and doorkeeper, four thousand three hundred and twenty dollars: *Provided,* That hereafter he shall receive, directly or indirect, no fees or other compensation or emoluments whatever for performing the duties of the office, or in connection therewith, otherwise than as aforesaid; assistant doorkeeper, two thousand five hundred and ninety-two dollars; acting assistant doorkeeper two thousand five hundred and ninety-two dollars; postmaster to the Senate, two thousand one hundred dollars; assistant postmaster and mail-carrier, one thousand seven hundred and twenty-eight dollars; two mail-carrier, at one thousand two hundred dollars each; superintendent of the document-room, two thousand one hundred and sixty dollars; two assistants in document-room, at one thousand four hundred and forty dollars each; superintendent of the folding-room, two thousand one hundred and sixty dollars; three messengers, acting as assistant doorkeepers, at one thousand eight-hundred dollars each; nineteen messengers, to be appointed and removed by the sergeant-at-arms, with the approval of the committee to audit and control the contingent the Senate at one thousand four hundred and forty dollars each; one messenger, as authorized by Senate resolution of June tenth, eighteen hundred and seventy-two, at one thousand four hundred and forty dollars; secretary to the President of the Senate, two thousand one hundred and two dollars and forty cents; clerk to the committee on finance, two thousand two hundred and twenty dollars; clerk to committee on claims, two thousand two hundred and twenty dollars; clerk of printing records, two thousand two hundred and twenty dollars; clerk to committee on appropriations, two thousand two hundred and twenty dollars; one laborer in charge of private passage, eight hundred and sixty-four dollars; one laborer in stationery-room, eight hundred and sixty-four dollars; one special policeman, one thousand two hundred and ninety-six dollars; chaplain to the Senate, nine hundred dollars; chief engineer, two thousand one hundred and sixty dollars; three assistant engineers, at one thousand eight hundred dollars each; two firemen, at one thousand and ninety-five dollars each; three laborers, at seven hundred and thirty dollars each.

For temporary clerks in the office of the secretary of the Senate, ten thousand dollars.

For contingent expenses of the Senate, namely:

For stationery and newspapers for seventy-four senators, at the rate of one hundred and twenty-five dollars each per annum, nine thousand two hundred and fifty dollars.

For stationery for committees and officers, five thousand dollars.

For clerks to committees, thirty thousand dollars.

For fourteen pages for the Senate chamber, two riding-pages, one page for the Vice-President's room, and one page for the office of the secretary of the Senate, making eighteen pages in all, at the rate of three dollars be appointed and removed the committee to audit Senate, eleven thousand.

For horses and carryalls, nine thousand dollars.

For fuel and oil for the heating-apparatus, nine thousand dollars; for furniture and repairs of furniture, ten thousand dollars; for labor, fifteen thousand dollars; for folding documents and materials therefor, eight thousand dollars; for packing-boxes, seven hundred and forty dollars; for miscellaneous items, exclusive of labor, including one hundred dollars for contingent expenses of capitol police, forty thousand dollars.

For the usual additional compensation to the reporters of the Senate for the Congressional Globe, for reporting the proceedings of the Senate for the session of the forty-third Congress, beginning on the first Monday in December, eighteen hundred seventy-three, eight hundred dollars each, four thousand dollars.

Capitol Police.—For one captain, two thousand and eighty-eight dollars; three lieutenants, at one thousand eight hundred dollars each; twenty-seven privates, at one thousand five hundred and eighty-four dollars each, forty-two thousand seven hundred and sixty-eight dollars, and eight watchmen, at one thousand dollars each, eight thousand dollars;

That the appointment of the capitol police shall hereafter be made by the sergeant-at-arms of the two houses and the architect of the capitol extension; and the captain of the capitol police force may suspend any member of said force, subject to the action of the officers above refers to; making in all fifty-eight thousand two hundred and fifty-six dollars, one-half to be paid into the contingent fund of the House of Representatives, and the other half to be paid into the contingent fund of the Senate.

House of Representatives.—For compensation and mileage of members of the House of Representatives and delegates from Territories; one million six hundred and fifty thousand dollars; the same to be available from and after the first day of March, eighteen hundred and seventy-three And hereafter representatives and delegates elect to Congress whose are delegates in due form of law have been duly filed with the clerk of House of Representatives in accordance with the provisions of the act of Congress approved March third, eighteen hundred and sixty-three, may receive their compensation monthly from the beginning of their term until the beginning of the first session of each Congress upon a certificate in the form now in use, to be signed by the clerk of the House, which certificate shall have the like force and effect as is given to the certificate of the speaker under existing laws: *Provided,* That in case, the clerk of the House of Representatives shall be notified that the election of such holder of a certificate of election will be contested, his name shall not be placed upon the roll of members-elect so as to entitle him to be paid, until he shall have been sworn in as a member, or until such contest shall be determined.

For compensation of the officers, clerks, messengers, and others receiving an annual salary in the service of the House of Representatives, namely: clerk of the House of Representatives, four thousand three hundred and twenty dollars; and that there be allowed to the officer disbursing the contingent fund and other expenses of the House of Representatives an annual sum of five hundred and seventy-six dollars; chief clerk and journal clerk, three thousand dollars each; six assistant clerks, at two thousand five hundred and ninety-two dollars each; one assistant clerk, at two thousand five hundred and twenty, dollars; ten assistant clerks, including librarian and assistant librarian, at two thousand one hundred and sixty dollars each; four assistant clerks at one thousand eight hundred dollars each; one chief messenger in the office of the clerk of the House, at five dollars and seventy-six cents per day; three messengers, at one thousand four hundred and forty dollars; one messenger in the House library, one thousand four hundred and forty dollars; one engineer, one thousand eight hundred dollars; three assistant engineers, at one thousand four hundred and forty dollars each; and the electrical apparatus for the lighting of the hall of the House, the dome, and rotunda, and old hall of Representatives shall be placed in charge of the said engineer, and operated by the person or persons under his charge, to be designated by him, subject to the control and supervision of the architect of the capitol and the commissioner of public buildings and grounds, and the offices of electrician and assistant electrician are hereby abolished six firemen, at one thousand and ninety-five dollars each per annum; for clerk to committee of ways and means, two thousand five hundred and ninety-two dollars; messenger to committee of ways and means, one thousand three hundred and fourteen dollars; clerk to committee of appropriations, two thousand five hundred and ninety-two dollars; messenger to committee on appropriations, one thousand three hundred and fourteen dollars; clerk to the committee of claims, two thousand one hundred and sixty dollars, clerk to the committee on the public lands, two thousand one hundred and sixty dollars; clerk at the speaker's table, at five dollars and seventy-six cents per day; private secretary to the speaker, two thousand one hundred and two dollars and forty cents; sergeant-at-arms, four thousand three hundred and twenty dollars: *Provided,* That hereafter he shall receive, directly or indirectly, no fees or other compensation or emolument whatever for performing the duties of the office, or in connection therewith, otherwise than as aforesaid; clerk five hundred dollars; paying teller for the sergeant-at-arms, one thousand eight hundred dollars; messenger to the sergeant-at-arms, one thousand four hundred and forty dollars; door-keeper, two thousand five hundred and ninety-two dollars; first assistant doorkeeper, two thousand five hundred and ninety-two dollars; postmaster, two thousand five hundred and ninety-two dollars; first assistant postmaster, two thousand and eighty-eight dollars; four messen-

gers, at one thousand seven hundred and twenty-eight dollars each; ten mail carriers, three at one thousand seven hundred and twenty-eight dollars each, and seven at one thousand and eighty dollars each; chaplain of the House, nine hundred dollars; two stenographers, four thousand three hundred and eighty dollars each; superintendent of the folding-room, two thousand one hundred and sixty dollars; superintendent and assistant superintendent of the document-room, at two thousand one hundred and sixty dollars each; document file-clerk, one thousand eight hundred dollars; eleven messengers, five at one thousand eight hundred dollars, and six at one thousand four hundred and forty dollars each, twelve messengers during the session, at the rate of one thousand four hundred and forty dollars each per annum, ten thousand and eighty dollars; fifteen laborers, seven hundred and twenty dollars each; seven laborers during the session, at the rate of seven hundred and dollars per annum; and one laborer at eight hundred and twenty dollars. . . .

Statutes at Large, 17 (1871–1873), 42nd Congress, 3d session, March 3, 1873, 485–490.

87   Susan B. Anthony Petitions Congress Regarding Her Fine for Illegal Voting

January 22, 1874

The long struggle on the part of women for the right to vote was not realized in full until ratification of the Nineteenth Amendment in 1920, although a few states had granted women the right to vote before that time (see document 114). In this petition to Congress, suffragist Susan B. Anthony explains how she was hauled into court for the act of voting in the presidential and congressional elections of 1872, found guilty, and fined $100 because women were not allowed to vote in New York State.

National women's suffrage organizations adopted a strategy in the 1870s that presumed women already had the right to vote. Susan B. Anthony and others argued that the Fourteenth Amendment (see document 79) declared that all persons born or naturalized in the United States were citizens and, the suffragists concluded, citizens should have the right to vote. Anthony was testing this concept when she voted in 1872. U.S. Supreme Court Justice Ward Hunt heard Anthony's case in New York in 1873 and, based on New York law, ordered the jury to find her guilty of voting—an act she had readily admitted to. Anthony hoped to go to jail to raise attention to the cause of women's suffrage, but the judge refused to send her to jail even though she refused to pay her fine.

The House and Senate each considered her petition in committees but took no further action on it, even though one senator, Aaron Sargent (R-Calif.), introduced a bill to pay the fine. Two years later the Supreme Court declared in Minor v. Happersett *that the Fourteenth Amendment did not apply to women's suffrage. Anthony and other suffragists then switched strategy and*

began a drive to amend the Constitution. It took another forty-five years before the amendment was ratified. Even though Susan B. Anthony lived to be eighty-six, she died fourteen years before the adoption of the Nineteenth Amendment. In 1997 a large marble statue of pioneer suffragists Susan B. Anthony, Elizabeth Cady Stanton, and Lucretia Mott that was part of the art collection of the U.S. Capitol was moved to the highest place of honor, the Rotunda of the Capitol, in recognition of their lifelong dedication to the cause of women's rights.

PETITION OF SUSAN B. ANTHONY,

Praying

For the remission of a fine imposed upon her by the United States court for the northern district of New York, for illegal voting.

JANUARY 22, 1874.—Referred to the Committee on the Judiciary and ordered to be printed.

To the Congress of the United States:

The petition of Susan B. Anthony, of the city of Rochester, in the county of Monroe, and State of New York, respectfully represents: That, prior to the late presidential election, your petitioner applied to the board of registry in the Eighth ward of the city of Rochester, in which city she had resided for more than twenty-five years, to have her name placed upon the register of voters; and the board of registry, after consideration of the subject, decided that your petitioner was entitled to have her name placed upon the register, and placed it there accordingly.

On the day of the election your petitioner, in common with hundreds of other American citizens, her neighbors, whose names had also been registered as voters, offered to the inspectors of election her ballots for electors of President and Vice-President, and for members of Congress, which were received and deposited in the ballot-box by the inspectors. For this act of your petitioner an indictment was found against her by the grand jury, at the sitting of the district court of the United States for the northern district of New York, at Albany, charging your petitioner, under the nineteenth section of the act of Congress of May 31, 1870, entitled "An act to enforce the rights of citizens of the United States to vote in the several States of this Union, and for other purposes," with having "*knowingly* voted without having a lawful right to vote."

To that indictment your petitioner pleaded not guilty, and the trial of the issue thus joined took place at the circuit court in Canandaigua, in the county of Ontario, before the honorable Ward Hunt, one of the justices of the Supreme Court of the United States, on the 18th day of June last.

Upon that trial the facts of voting by your petitioner, and that she was a woman, were not denied; nor was it claimed on the part of the Government that your petitioner lacked any of the qualifications of a voter, unless disqualified by reason of her sex.

It was shown on behalf of your petitioner, on the trial, that before voting she called upon a respectable lawyer and asked his opinion whether she had a right to vote, and he advised her that she had such right, and the lawyer was examined as a witness in her behalf, and testified that he gave her such advice, and that he gave it in good faith, believing that she had such a right.

It also appeared that when she offered to vote, the question whether, as a woman, she had a right to vote, was raised by the inspectors, and considered by them in her presence, and they decided that she had a right to vote, and received her vote accordingly.

It was shown on the part of the Government that, on the examination of your petitioner before the commissioner on whose warrant she was arrested, your petitioner stated that she should have voted if allowed to vote, without reference to the advice of the attorney whose opinion she asked; that she was not induced to vote by that opinion; that she had before determined to offer her vote, and had no doubt about her right to vote.

At the close of the testimony, your petitioner's counsel proceeded to address the jury, and stated that he desired to present for consideration three propositions, two of law, and one of fact:

First. That your petitioner had a lawful right to vote.

Second. That whether she had a right to vote or not, if she honestly believed that she had that right, and voted in good faith in that belief, she was guilty of no crime.

Third. That when your petitioner gave her vote she gave it in good faith, believing that it was her right to do so.

That the two first propositions presented questions for the court to decide, and the last a question for the jury.

When your petitioner's counsel had proceeded thus far, the judge suggested that the counsel had better discuss in the first place the questions of law, which the counsel proceeded to do; and, having discussed the two legal questions at length, asked then to say a few words to the jury on the question of fact. The judge then said to the counsel that he thought that had better be left until the views of the court upon the legal questions should be made known.

The district attorney thereupon addressed the court at length upon the legal questions, and at the close of his argument the judge delivered an opinion adverse to the positions of your petitioner's counsel upon both of the legal questions presented, holding that your petitioner was not entitled to vote; and that if she voted in good faith in the belief in fact that she had a right to vote, it would constitute no defense; the ground of the decision on the last point being that your petitioner was bound to know that by the law she was not a legal voter, and that even if she voted in good faith in the contrary belief, it constituted no defense to the crime with which she was charged.

The decision of the judge upon those questions was read from a written document, and at the close of the reading the judge said that the decision of those questions disposed of the case and left no question of fact for the jury, and that he should therefore direct the jury to find a verdict of guilty. The judge then said to the jury that the decision of the court had disposed of all there was in the case, and that he directed then to find a verdict of guilty; and he instructed the clerk to enter such a verdict.

At this time, before any entry had been made by the clerk, your petitioner's counsel asked the judge to submit the case to the jury, and to give the jury the following several instructions:

First. That if the defendant, at the time of voting, believed that she had a right to vote, and voted in good faith in that belief, she was not guilty of the offense charged.

Second. That in determining the question of whether she did or did not believe that she had a right to vote, the jury might take into consideration as bearing upon that question, the advice which she received from the counsel to whom she applied.

Third. That they might also take into consideration as bearing upon the same question the fact that the inspectors considered the question and came to the conclusion that she had right to vote.

Fourth. That the jury had a right to find a general verdict of guilty or not guilty, as they should believe that she had or had not been guilty of the offense described in the statute.

The judge declined to submit the case to the jury upon any question whatever, and directed them to render a verdict of guilty against your petitioner.

Your petitioner's counsel excepted to the decision of the judge upon the legal questions, and to his direction to the jury to find a verdict of guilty, insisting that it was a direction which no court had a right to give in any criminal case.

The judge then instructed the clerk to take the verdict, and the clerk said, "Gentlemen of the jury, hearken to your verdict as the court hath recorded it. You say you find the defendant guilty of the offense charged; so say you all."

No response whatever was made by the jury, either by word or sign. They had not consulted together in their seats or otherwise. Neither of them had spoken a word, nor had they been asked whether they had or had not agreed upon a verdict.

Your petitioner's counsel then asked that the clerk be requested to poll the jury. The judge said, "That cannot be allowed. Gentlemen of the jury you are discharged;" and the jurors left the box. No juror spoke a word during the trial, from the time when they were empanneled to the time of their discharge.

After denying a motion for a new trial, the judge proceeded upon the conviction thus obtained to pass sentence upon your petitioner, imposing upon her a fine for $100 and the costs of the prosecution.

Your petitioner respectfully submits that, in these proceedings, she has been denied the rights guaranteed by the Constitution to all persons accused of crime, the right of trial by jury, and the right to have the assistance of counsel for their defense. It is a mockery to call her trial a trial by jury; and unless the assistance of counsel may be limited to the argument of legal questions, without the privilege of saying a word to the jury upon the question of the guilt or innocence in fact of the party charged, or the privilege of ascertaining from the jury whether they do or do not agree to the verdict pronounced by the court in their name, she has been denied the assistance of counsel for her defense.

Your petitioner also respectfully insists that the decision of the judge that good faith on the part of your petitioner in offering her vote did not constitute a defense, was not only a violation of the deepest and most sacred principle of the criminal law, that no one can be guilty of crime unless a criminal intent exists; but was also a palpable violation of the statute under which the conviction was had; not on the ground that good faith could, in this, or in any case, justify a criminal act, but on the ground that *bad faith* in voting was an indispensable ingredient in the offense with which your petitioner was charged. Any other interpretation strikes the word "knowingly" out of the statute, the word which alone describes the essence of the offense.

The statute means, as your petitioner is advised, and humbly submits, a *knowledge in fact,* not a knowledge falsely imputed by law to a party not possessing it in fact, as the judge in this case has held Crimes cannot, either in law or in morals, be established by judicial falsehood. If there be any crime in the case, your petitioner humbly insists it is to be found in such an adjudication.

To the decision of the judge upon the question of the right of your petitioner to vote she makes no complaint. It was a question properly belonging to the court to decide, was fully and fairly submitted to the judge, and of his decision, whether right or wrong, your petitioner is well aware she cannot here complain.

But in regard to her conviction of crime, which she insists, for the reasons above given, was in violation of the principles of the common law, of common morality, of the statute under which she was charged, and of the Constitution—a crime of which she was as innocent as the judge by whom she was convicted—she respectfully asks, inasmuch as the law has provided no means of reviewing the decisions of the judge, or of correcting his errors, that the fine imposed upon your petitioner be remitted, as an expression of the sense of this high tribunal that her conviction was unjust.

Dated January 12, 1874.

SUSAN B. ANTHONY

Petition of Susan B. Anthony for Remission of Fine for Voting, Jan. 12, 1874, SEN43A-H11.3, Records of the United States Senate, 43d Congress, 1st session, National Archives and Records Administration, Washington, D.C. For a very useful documentary resource of petitions to Congress written by women, including a facsimile reproduction of this petition of Susan B. Anthony, see *Our Mothers Before Us: Women and Democracy, 1789–1920,* prepared by the National Archives and Records Administration, Washington, D.C. (1998).

88   Reorganization of the Government of the District of Columbia

June 20, 1874

The Constitution in Article I, Section 8 grants Congress the power to "exercise exclusive Legislation in all Cases whatsoever" over the District of Columbia. Since the early days of the Republic (see document 35), this constitutional provision has been the subject of much controversy. Congress has experimented with various forms of limited local government since the federal government moved to the District of Columbia in 1800.

From 1802 to 1871 the district had a mayor-council form of government, with the mayor appointed by the president of the United States and the council elected by the citizens of the district.

During and after the Civil War the population of the District of Columbia changed dramatically with the influx of black citizens, attracted in part by the fact that slavery was abolished there in 1862. As early as 1867, three years before the ratification of the Fifteenth Amendment (see document 83), black residents could vote in the district. As black residents gained political power, Congress and the white residents of the district sought to limit black participation in local government through changes in the district government and through the power of Congress to control district appropriations. By the 1870s the district was in deep financial trouble and Congress refused to appropriate the funds necessary to rectify the situation.

The congressional solution to the problem of the district's financial woes was to establish a new form of government. Congress erected briefly a form of territorial government, where the District of Columbia was organized like a territory of the United States, with a governor appointed by the president, a nonvoting representative in Congress, a territorial assembly, and a twenty-two-member house of delegates. Congress pumped money into this ambitious new system and many major internal improvements resulted, such as paved streets, water mains, and a sewer system. The high cost of these improvements and the cost of the government itself left the district deep in debt within three years.

This 1874 bill excerpted here completely reorganized the district government again, abolishing the territorial-style government and creating a commission government, with a three-member board appointed by the president of the United States. In 1875 a joint congressional committee recommended continuance of the commission government with some slight alterations that allowed residents of the District of Columbia to elect a few members of the school board. The commission form of government, with some modifications, lasted for ninety-three years, until 1967.

A growing "home rule" movement, where citizens of the district would enjoy the same rights as citizens of a state, achieved some success during the Civil Rights era of the 1960s. In 1967 Congress changed the district to a commission-council system that eventually provided limited home rule. But the real power to run the district, and the power of the purse, still resided in Congress, in the House and Senate committees that had oversight over the district's affairs. Often the chairman of these committees have had little interest in promoting the welfare of the district and have proven to be obstructionists to the idea of home rule. Home rule got a boost in 1973 (see document 164), when a black representative, Charles Diggs (D-Mich.) became chairman of the House District of Columbia Committee. Diggs introduced legislation that gave citizens of the district the right to elect a mayor and a city council that had more direct control over the daily operations of district government. Despite all the changes, Congress has never given up its control of district government through its own committees.

CHAP. 337—AN ACT FOR THE GOVERNMENT OF THE DISTRICT OF COLUMBIA, AND FOR OTHER PURPOSES.

Be it enacted by the Senate and House of Representatives of the United States of America in Congress assembled, That all provisions of law providing for an executive, for a secretary for the District, for a legislative assembly, for a board of public works, and for a Delegate in Congress in the District of Columbia are hereby repealed: *Provided,* That this repeal shall not affect the term of office of the present Delegate in Congress.

SEC. 2. That the President of the United States, by and with the advice and consent of the Senate, is hereby authorized to appoint a commission, consisting of three persons, who shall, until otherwise provided by law, exercise all the power and au-thority now lawfully vested in the governor or board of public works of said District, except as hereinafter limited; and shall be subject to all the restrictions and limitations now imposed by law on said governor or board; and shall have power to apply the taxes or other revenues of said District to the payment of the current expenses thereof, to the support of the public schools, the fire department, and the police, and to the payment of the debts of said District secured by a pledge of the securities of said District or board of public works as collateral, and also to the payment of debts due to laborers and employees of the District and board of public works; and for that purpose shall take possession and supervision of all the offices, books, papers, records, moneys, credits, securities, assets, and accounts belonging or appertaining to the business or interests of the government of the District of Columbia and the board of public works, and exercise the power and authority aforesaid; but said commission, in the exercise of such power or authority, shall make no contract, nor incur any obligation other than such contracts and obligations as may be necessary to the faithful administration of the valid laws enacted for the government of said District, to the execution of existing legal obligations and contracts, and to the protection or preservation of improvements existing, or commenced and not completed, at the time of the passage of this act. All taxes heretofore lawfully assessed and due or to become due shall be collected pursuant to law, except as herein provided; but said commissioners shall have no power to anticipate taxes by a sale or hypothecation of any such taxes, or evidence thereof: *Provided,* That nothing in this clause contained shall affect any provisions of law authorizing or requiring a deposit of certificates of assessment with the sinking-fund commissioners of said District; and said commissioners are hereby authorized to abolish any office, to consolidate two or more offices, reduce the number of employees, remove from office, and make appointments to any office authorized by law; and the compensation of all officers and employees, except teachers in the public schools, and officers and employees in the fire department, shall be reduced twenty per centum per annum. Said commissioners shall each, before entering upon the discharge of his duties, take an oath to support the Constitution of the United States and to faithfully discharge the duties imposed upon him by law; and shall each give bond in the penal sum of fifty thousand dollars, to be approved by the Secretary of the Treasury, for the faithful discharge of the duties of his office; and shall each receive for his services a compensation at the rate of five thousand dollars per annum: *Provided,* That nothing in this act shall be construed to abate or in any wise interfere with any suit pending in favor of or against the District of Columbia; *And provided further,* That in suits hereafter commenced against the District of Columbia, process may be served on any one of said commissioners, until otherwise provided by law.

SEC. 3. That the President of the United States shall detail an officer of the Engineer Corps of the Army of the United

States, who shall, subject to the general supervision and direction of the said board of commissioners, have the control and charge of the work of repair and improvement of all streets, avenues, alleys, sewers, roads, and bridges of the District of Columbia; and he is hereby vested with all the power and authority of, and shall perform the duties heretofore devolved upon, the chief engineer of the board of public works. He shall take possession of, and preserve and keep, all the instruments pertaining to said office, and all the maps, charts, surveys, books, records, and papers relating to said District or to any of the avenues, streets alleys, public spaces, squares, lots and buildings thereon, sewers, or any of them, as are now in or belonging to the office of said engineer of the board of public works, and shall, in books provided for that purpose, keep and preserve the records now required to be kept, and such as may be required by regulation of said board. He may, with the advice and consent of said board of commissioners, appoint not more than two assistant engineers from civil life, who shall each receive a salary of one thousand eight hundred dollars per annum, and shall be subject to his direction and control. He shall receive no additional compensation for such services. And he shall not be deemed by reason of anything in this act contained to hold a civil office under the laws of the United States. And no salary or compensation shall be paid to the surveyor of the District, or any of his subordinates, except such fees for special services as are allowed by law. And the offices of assistant surveyor and additional assistant surveyor of the District of Columbia are hereby abolished.

. . . .

SEC. 5. That a joint select committee shall be appointed, consisting of two Senators, to be appointed by the presiding officer of the Senate, and two members of the House, to be appointed by the Speaker of the House of Representatives, whose duty it shall be to prepare a suitable frame of government for the District of Columbia and appropriate draughts of statutes to be enacted by Congress for carrying the sale into effect, and report the same to the two Houses, respectively, on the first day of the next session thereof; and they shall also prepare and submit to Congress a statement of the proper proportion of the expenses of said government, or any branch thereof, including interest on the funded debt, which should be borne by said District and the United States, respectively, together with the reasons upon which their conclusions may be based; and in the discharge of the duty hereby imposed, said committee is authorized to employ such assistance as it may deem advisable, at an expense not to exceed the sum of five thousand dollars; and said sum, or so much thereof as may be necessary, be, and the same is hereby, appropriated for that purpose. . . .

Statutes at Large, 18 (1873–1875), 43d Congress, 1st session, June 20, 1874, 116–118.

89 Representative James G. Blaine Defends Himself Against Charges of Corruption: The Mulligan Letters

June 5, 1875

The political career of Representative James G. Blaine (R-Maine) was mired in controversy, even though he had been cleared of wrongdoing in the Credit Mobilier scandal (see document 85). The Mulligan Letters, so called because they were first exposed by a Boston bookkeeper, James Mulligan, contained business correspondence between Blaine and associates regarding stock transactions related to the Little Rock and Fort Smith Railroad in Arkansas. The letters implicated Blaine in abuse of the office of Speaker. He used his influence as Speaker to gain a land grant for the railroad. In turn, he received money and railroad stock. While few people knew the actual contents of the Mulligan Letters, Blaine's critics pointed to them as proof of corruption. Blaine added to the mystery surrounding the letters by refusing to hand them over to congressional investigators.

In a surprising and dramatic turnabout, Blaine tried to salvage his reputation by defending himself on the floor of the House and reading the Mulligan Letters into the record. He knew if he did not do something dramatic, his pursuit of the presidency of the United States would be at an end. After serving as Speaker of the Republican-controlled House from 1869 to 1875, Blaine and his Republican colleagues suddenly found themselves stripped of power and in the minority for the first time since the Civil War. Democrats regained control of the House in dramatic fashion in 1875 in one of the largest turnovers of House seats in American history. Despite this setback, Blaine was a leading contender for the Republican presidential nomination in 1876. In January 1876 Blaine spoke out against the Democrat's plan to grant amnesty for Jefferson Davis, the former president of the Confederacy. This endeared him to Republicans but angered the new Democratic majority in the House, who were not above seeking revenge against Blaine.

In taking charge of his own defense on the floor of the House, Blaine appealed directly to the public to defuse the impact of the Mulligan Letters. The galleries were packed with Blaine supporters and during the course of his remarks people in the galleries frequently cheered and applauded Blaine despite the Speaker pro tempore's efforts to maintain order. Democrats on the floor during

Blaine's defense did not make it easy for him. His chief antagonist on the floor that day was James Proctor Knott (D.-Ky.), the chairman of the House Judiciary Committee. Despite Blaine's best efforts, the Mulligan Letters continued to plague him for the rest of his political career. He failed to get his party's presidential nomination in 1876 and again in 1880. When he did become the Republican presidential candidate in 1884, his opponents kept the issue of the Mulligan Letters alive. Blaine narrowly lost the 1884 presidential election to Grover Cleveland.

PERSONAL EXPLANATION

. . . .

Mr. BLAINE. Mr. Speaker, on the 2d day of May this resolution was passed by the House:

Whereas it is publicly alleged, and is not denied by the officers of the Union Pacific Railroad Company, that that corporation did, in the year 1871 or 1872, become the owner of certain bonds of the Little Rock and Fort Smith Railroad Company, for which bonds the said Union Pacific Railroad Company paid a consideration largely in excess of their actual or market value, and that the board of directors of said Union Pacific Railroad Company, though urged, have neglected to investigate said transaction: Therefore,

Be it resolved, That the Committee on the Judiciary be instructed to inquire if any such transaction took place, and, if so, what were the circumstances and inducements thereto, from what person or persons said bonds were obtained and upon what consideration, and whether the transaction was from corrupt design or in furtherance of any corrupt object; and that the committee have power to send for persons and papers.

That resolution on its face, and in its fair intent, was obviously designed to find out whether any improper thing had been done by the Union Pacific Railroad Company; and of course, incidentally thereto, to find out with whom the transaction was made. The gentleman who offered that resolution offered it when I was not in the House, and my colleague, [Mr. Frye,] after it was objected to, went to the gentleman and stated that he would have no objection to it, as he knew I would not have if I were present in the House. The gentleman from Massachusetts, [Mr. Tarbox,] to whom I refer, took especial pains to say to my colleague that the resolution was not in any sense aimed at me. The gentleman will pardon me if I say that I had a slight incredulity upon that assurance given by him to my colleague.

No sooner was the subcommittee designated than it became entirely obvious that the resolution was solely and only aimed at me. I think there had not been three questions asked until it was obvious that the investigation was to be a personal one upon me, and that the Union Pacific Railroad or any other incident of the transaction was secondary, insignificant, and unimportant. I do not complain of that; I do not say that I had any reason to complain of it. If the investigation was to be made in that personal sense, I was ready to meet it.

The gentleman on whose statement the accusation rested, Mr. Harrison, was first called. He stated what he knew from rumor. Then there were called Mr. Rollins, Mr. Morton, and Mr. Millard from Omaha, a Government director of the Union Pacific road, and finally Thomas A. Scott. The testimony was completely and conclusively in disproof of the charge that there was any possibility that I could have had anything to do with the transaction.

I expected (and so I state to the gentleman from Virginia, the honorable chairman of the subcommittee) that I should have an early report; but the case was prolonged and prolonged and prolonged; and when last week the witnesses had seemed to be exhausted, I was somewhat surprised to be told that the committee would now turn to investigate a transaction of the Northern Pacific Railroad Company on a newspaper report that there had been some effort on my part with a friend in Boston to procure for him a share in that road, which effort had proved abortive, the money having been returned. I asked the honorable gentleman from Virginia on what authority he made that investigation—not that I cared about it; I begged him to be assured I did not; and the three witnesses that he called could not have been more favorable to me within any possibility. But I wanted to know on what authority I was to be arraigned before the country upon an investigation of that kind; and a resolution offered in this House on the 31st of January by the gentleman from California [Mr. Lutrell] was read as the authority for investigating that little transaction in Boston. I ask the House to bear with me while I read a somewhat lengthy resolution:

Whereas the several railroad companies hereinafter named, to wit, the Northern Pacific, the Kansas Pacific, the Union Pacific, the Central Branch of the Union Pacific, the Western Pacific, the Southern Pacific, the Sioux City and Pacific, the Northern Pacific, the Texas and Pacific, and all Pacific roads or branches to which bonds or other subsidies have been granted by the Government, have received from the United States, under the act of Congress of July 1, 1862, the act March 3, 1874, and the several acts amendatory thereof, money subsidies amounting to over $64,000,000, land subsidies amounting to over 220,000,000 acres of the public domain, bond subsidies amounting to $——, and interest amounting to $——, to aid in the construction of their several roads; and whereas it is but just and proper that the Government and people should understand the status of such roads and the disposition made by such companies in the construction of their roads of the subsidies granted by the Government: Therefore,

Be it resolved, That the Judiciary Committee be, and are hereby, instructed and authorized to inquire into and report to this House, first, whether the several railroad companies hereinbefore named, or any of them, have, in the construction of their railroads and telegraph lines, fully complied with the requirements of law granting money, bonds, and land subsidies to aid such companies in the construction of their railroads and telegraph lines; second, whether the several railroad companies or any of them have formed within themselves corporate or construction companies for the purpose of subletting to such corporate or construction companies contracts for building and equipping said roads or any portion thereof, and, if so, whether money, land, and bond subsidies granted by the Government have been properly applied by said companies or any of them in the construction of their road or roads; third, whether the several railroad companies or any of them have forfeited their land subsidies by failing to construct and equip their road or roads or any portion of them as required by law; and fourth, that, for the purpose of making a thorough investigation of the several Pacific railroads or any of them, the Judiciary Committee shall have full power to send for persons and papers, and, after thorough investigation shall have been made, shall report to this House such measure or bill as will secure to the Government full indemnity for all losses occasioned by fraudulent transactions or negligence on the part of said railroad companies or any of them, or on the part of any corporate or construction company, in the expenditures of moneys, bonds, or interest, or in the disposition of land donated by the Government for the construction of the roads or any of them or any portion thereof, and for the non-payment of interest lawfully due the Government, or any other claim or claims the United States may have against such railroad company or companies.

Now, that resolution embraces a very wide scope. It undoubtedly embraces a great many things which it is highly proper for the Government to look into; but I think the gentleman from California who offered that resolution will be greatly surprised to find that the first movement made under it to investigate what the Northern Pacific Railroad Company has done was to bring the whole force of that resolution to find out the circumstances of a little transaction in Boston which never became a transaction at all. I asked the gentleman from Virginia how he deduced his power. Well, he said it would take three months to go through the whole matter, but in about three months it would reach this point, and that he might as well begin on me right there. Well, he began; and three witnesses testified precisely what the circumstances were. I had no sooner got through with that, than I was advised that in another part of the Capitol, without the slightest notice in the world being given to me, with no monition, no warning to me, I was being arraigned before a committee known as the Real Estate Pool Committee, which was originally organized to examine into the affairs of the estate of Jay Cooke & Co., and whose powers were enlarge on the 3d day of April by the following resolution:

Whereas on the 24th day of January, A.D. 1876, the House adopted the following resolution:

"*Resolved*, That a special committee of five members of this House, to be selected by the Speaker, be appointed to inquire into the nature and history of said real-estate pool and the character of said settlement, with the amount paid or to be paid in settlement, with power to send for persons and papers and report to this House:" Therefore,

Be it resolved, That said committee be further authorized and directed to likewise investigate any and all matters touching the official misconduct of any officer of the Government of the United States which may come to the knowledge of said committee: *Provided*, That this resolution shall not affect any such matter now being investigated by any other committee under authority of either House of Congress; and for this purpose said committee shall have the same powers to send for persons and papers as conferred by said original resolution.

They began an investigation which I am credibly informed, and I think the chairman of that committee will not deny, was specifically aimed at me. I had no notice of it, not the remotest; no opportunity to be confronted with witnesses. I had no idea that any such thing was going on, not the slightest. So that on three distinct charges I was being investigated at the same time and having no opportunity to meet any of them; and I understand, though I was not present, that the gentleman from Virginia has this morning introduced a fourth, to find out something about the Kansas Pacific Railroad, a transaction fifteen years old if it ever existed, and has summoned numerous witnesses.

Mr. HUNTON. What was the statement the gentleman just made? I did not fully understand it.

Mr. BLAINE. That an investigation has been set on foot by the gentleman, aimed at me, in regard to the Kansas Pacific Railroad, and that witnesses have been summoned on that question, the transaction out of which it grew being fifteen years old.

Now, I say—and I say it boldly—that, under these general powers to investigate Pacific railroads and their transactions, the whole enginery of this committee is aimed personally at me; and I want that to be understood by the country. I have no objection to it; but I want you by name to organize a committee to investigate JAMES G. BLAINE. I want to meet the question squarely. That is the whole purpose and object. I will not further make personal references; for I do not wish to stir up any blood on this question; but ever since a certain debate here in January it has been known that there are gentlemen in this Hall whose feelings were peculiarly exasperated toward me. And I beg the gentleman from Kentucky, the chairman of the Judiciary Committee, to remember that when this matter affecting me went to his committee, while there were seven democratic members of that committee, he took as the majority of the subcommittee the two who were from the South and had been in the rebel army.

Mr. KNOTT. Will the gentleman allow me one word?

Mr. BLAINE. After a moment; I have not a great deal of time.

Mr. KNOTT. As the gentleman has made an insinuation, I prefer to answer it now.

Mr. BLAINE. Very well.

Mr. KNOTT. These railroad investigations were referred to that committee before I ever heard the gentleman's name insinuated in connection with them; and I will say furthermore that I had no act or part in instituting any investigation implicating the gentleman at all.

Mr. BLAINE. Then when the investigation began, the gentleman from Virginia who conducted it insisted under that resolution, which was obviously on its face limited to the seventy-five thousand dollar transaction—the transaction with the Union Pacific Railroad—he insisted on going into all the affairs of the Fort Smith Railroad as incidental thereto, and pursued that to such an extent that to such an extent that finally I had myself through my colleague, Mr. FRYE, to take an appeal to the whole committee, and the committee decided that the gentleman had no right to go there. But when he came back and resumed the examination he began again exactly in the same way, and was stopped there and then by my colleague who sits in front, not as my attorney, but as my friend.

When the famous witness Mulligan came here loaded with information in regard to the Fort Smith road, the gentleman from Virginia drew out what he knew had no reference whatever to the question of investigation. He then and there insisted on all of my private memoranda being allowed to be exhibited by that man in reference to business that had no more connection, no more relation, no more to do with that investigation than with the North Pole.

And the gentleman tried his best, also, though I believe that has been abandoned, to capture and use and control my private correspondence. This man had selected out of correspondence running over a great many letters which he thought would be peculiarly damaging to me. He came here loaded with them. He came here for a sensation. He came here primed. He came here on that particular errand. I was advised of it, and I obtained those letters under circumstances which have been notoriously scattered throughout the United States, and are known to everybody. I have them. I claim I have the entire right to those letters, not only by natural right, but upon all the precedents and principles of law, as the man who held those letters in possession held them wrongfully. The committee that attempted to take those letters from that man for use against me proceeded wrongfully. They proceeded in all boldness to a most defiant violation of the ordinary private and personal rights which belong to every American citizen, and I was willing to stand and meet the Judiciary Committee on this floor. I wanted them to introduce it. I wanted the gentleman from Kentucky and the gentleman from Virginia to introduce that question upon this floor, but they did not do it.

Mr. KNOTT, (in his seat.) I know you did.

Mr. BLAINE. Very well.

Mr. KNOTT. I know you wanted to be made a martyr of. [Laughter.]

Mr. BLAINE. And you did not want to, and there is the difference. [Laughter and applause.] I go a little further: you did not dare to.

Mr. KNOTT. We will talk about that hereafter.

Mr. BLAINE. I wanted to meet that question. I wanted to invoke all the power you had in this House on that question.

Mr. HAMILTON, of New Jersey. I rise to a question of order. Is this language parliamentary?

Mr. BLAINE. Yes; entirely so. [Laughter.]

Mr. HAMILTON, of New Jersey. I do not ask the gentleman. I ask the Speaker. I call the gentleman to order.

The SPEAKER pro tempore. The gentleman will state his point of order.

Mr. HAMILTON, of New Jersey. I want to know whether it is in order for one gentleman on this floor to say to another he dare not do so and so?

The SPEAKER pro tempore. The gentleman from New Jersey calls the gentleman from Maine to order, and under the rules the gentleman from Maine will be seated, and if there be objectionable words, they will be taken down.

Mr. KASSON. I wish to say the point of order is simply to the use of the second person, and I hope gentlemen on both sides will use the third person.

Mr. BLAINE. I did not.

Mr. KASSON. You said "you."

The SPEAKER pro tempore. The Chair will say to gentlemen who have the privilege of the House, that this display of cheering is entirely out of order.

Mr. BLAINE. It never ought to be done, and never has been done so much as during this Congress.

The SPEAKER pro tempore. The Chair will enforce the order, and the doorkeepers will assist the Chair, and, if necessary, the Sergeant-at-Arms under the rules will assist the doorkeepers. The gentleman from Maine will now proceed in order.

Mr. BLAINE. I repeat, the Judiciary Committee I understand have abandoned that issue against me. I stood up and declined not only on the conclusion of my own mind, but by eminent legal advice. I was standing behind the rights which belong to every American citizen, and if they wanted to treat the question in my person anywhere in the legislative halls or judicial halls, I was ready. Then there went forth everywhere the idea and impression that because I would not permit that man or any man whom I could prevent from holding as a menace over my head my private correspondence there must be something in it most deadly and destructive to my reputation. I would like any gentleman on this floor—and all gentlemen on this floor are presumed to be men of affairs, whose business has been varied, whose intercourse has been large—I would like any gentleman to stand up here and tell me that he is willing and ready to have his private correspondence scanned over and made public for the last eight or ten years. I would like any gentleman to say that. Does it imply guilt? Does it imply wrong-doing? Does it imply any sense of weakness that a man will protect his private correspondence? No, sir; it is the first instinct to do it, and it is the last outrage upon any man to violate it.

Now, Mr. Speaker, I say that I have defied the Power of the House to compel me to produce those letters. I speak with all respect to this House. I know its powers, and I trust I respect them. But I say this House has no more power to order what shall be done or not done with my private correspondence than it has with what I shall do in the nurture and education of my children; not a particle. The right is as sacred in the one case as it is in the other. But, sir, having vindicated that right, standing by it, ready to make any sacrifice in the defense of it, here and now if any gentleman wants to take issue with me on behalf of this House I am ready for any extremity of contest or conflict in behalf of so sacred a right. And while I am so, I am not afraid to show the letters. Thank God Almighty I am not ashamed to show them. There they are, [holding up a package of letters.] There is the very original package. And with some sense of humiliation, with a mortification that I do not pretend to conceal, with a sense of outrage which I think any man in my position would feel, I invite the confidence of 44,000,000 of my countrymen while I read those letters from this desk. [Applause.]

The SPEAKER pro tempore. The doorkeepers will enforce the rule.

Mr. BLAINE. I beg gentlemen who are my friends to make no manifestation.

The SPEAKER pro tempore. The Chair has directed the doorkeepers to enforce the rule, and to remove from the Hall persons who are not entitled to its privileges who are making these manifestations.

Mr. KELLEY. I desire to say, Mr. Speaker, that so far as my observation extends the applause was within the bar of the House.

The SPEAKER *pro tempore.* The doorkeepers are authorized to remove from the Hall any persons who violate its privileges.

Mr. BLAINE. Now as regards many of these letters I have not the slightest feeling in reading them. Some of them will require a little explanation. Some of them may possibly, as I have said, involve a feeling of humiliation. But I would a great deal rather take that than take the evil surmises and still more evil inferences which might be drawn if I did not act with this frankness.

The first letter I shall read, marked "private and personal," is as follows:

[Private and personal.]
Augusta, Maine, August 31, 1872.

MY DEAR MR. FISHER: I have been absent so much of late that I did not receive your last letter until it was several days old. When I last wrote you I was expecting to be in Boston on a political conference about this time, but I found it impossible to be there, and it is now impossible for me to leave here until after our election, which occurs Monday week, the 9th. I will try to meet you at the Parker House on the 10th or 11th, availing myself of the first possible moment for that purpose.

I cannot, however, allow a remark in your letter to pass without comment. You say that you have been trying to get a settlement with me for fifteen months, you have been trying to induce me to comply with certain demands which you made upon me, without taking into account any claims I have of a counter kind. This does not fill my idea of a *settlement,* for a *settlement* must include both sides.

No person could be more anxious for a settlement than I am, and if upon our next interview we cannot reach one, why then we try other means.

But my judgment is that I shall make you so liberal an offer of settlement that you cannot possibly refuse it.

As one of the elements which I wish to take into account is the note of $10,000 given you in 1863 for Spencer stock, I desire that you will furnish me with the items of interest on that note. My impression is that when that note was consolidated into the large note, which you will still hold, that you did not charge me full interest, possibly omitting one or two years.

I will be obliged if you will give me information on this point, for I intend to submit to you a full and explicit basis of settlement, and in making it up it is necessary that I should have this information. Please send it as promptly as you may be able to give it to me.

In haste, very truly yours,

J. G. Blaine.
Warren Fisher, Jr. , Esq.

There is an allusion there to Spencer stock. I took this letter up first because I wish to make an explanation as to that. In the month of November, 1861, I was summoned to Boston by a telegram to meet Mr. Fisher and another gentleman on some urgent business. I immediately responded. On getting there I found that they were the proprietors of a newly-invented rifle. The other gentleman was Mr. Ward Cheney, of Connecticut, recently deceased, well known for his eminence in the silk manufacture, and a gentleman of great wealth and high character. One of the ingenious mechanics in his employ named Spencer had invented a repeating rifle. It had been tested in various private ways, but it had not received the official sanction of the Government. They had employed various persons to come to Washington during the summer of 1861, the first of the war; but these various agents reported, and these gentlemen so re-

ported to me, that what they called a gun-ring in Washington were so close and were so powerful that they could not get an opportunity to bring that new arm to the attention of the Secretary of War, present venerable Senator from Pennsylvania, and they asked me if I thought I could do it. That was two years and more before I entered Congress.

I told them that I thought I could. And going back home and making preparations I immediately came to Washington, and in a very short time I had an interview with Secretary CAMERON at the War Department. He looked at the gun, was satisfied there was something in it, and gave an order to have it tested by the Ordinance Bureau. It was thoroughly tested, and in the course of two weeks the experiment was so satisfactory that they gave a preliminary order for 20,000 rifles. It was of course, as every gentleman who is familiar with the war knows, a most eminent success. It was one of the wonderful arms of the war: the Spencer rifle.

The company immediately proceeded to erect an armory in Boston, but, with all that ingenuity and capital could do, they did not produce, as every gentleman on this floor who was familiar with the operations of the war knows, half as many arms as the service wanted. They paid me not an extravagant but a moderate fee for that service, which I was then as much at liberty to take as any lawyer or agent on this floor would be in his private relations at home. I was not in Congress, was nominated to Congress, was not here for two years afterward.

The winter afterward, or next spring, Mr. Fisher and Mr. Cheney, both together, offered me $10,000 stock in the concern, and I took it.

A MEMBER. And paid for it?

Mr. BLAINE. Yes, of course; and paid for it, and owned, and had the dividends on it. I made no concealment of it. But I never was at the War Department about in any shape or form in my life. Now, if the gentleman from Missouri [Mr. Glover] wants to investigate that case I will save him all the trouble. I will just cut that short. If he wants the list of stockholders, why they are all private citizens, and very respectable ones, and the corporation is dissolved, dead, merged in the Winchester Rifle Company. I will give him all the trail there is to the whole story, and he can strike it and follow it out. The whole story, that I had so much per gun as a royalty of any sort, is simply absurd. I was an ordinary stockholder, just as a man is in a bank. A gentleman asks me if I paid for this stock. I tell him yes, I did, emphatically. The truth is the Department was only too anxious to urge in every direction to have these guns manufactured.

I take these letters up quite miscellaneously. The next is dated Augusta, Maine, August 9, 1872:

[Personal.]
Augusta, Maine, August 9, 1872.
MY DEAR MR. FISHER: On my return home yesterday I found your favor of 6th from Stonington, asking for my notes, $6,000, on account. It seems to me that a partial settlement of our matter would only lead to future trouble, or at all events to a mere postponement of our present difficulties.

I deem it highly desirable that we should have a conclusive and comprehensive settlement, and I have been eager for that these many months.

The account which you stated June 20, 1872, does not correspond precisely with the reckoning I have made of my indebtedness on the note you hold. You credit me, April 26, 1869, with $12,500 dividend from Spencer Company; but there were two subsequent dividends, one of $3,750, the other of $5,800, of which no mention is made in your statement, though I received in June, 1870, your check for $2,700 or $2,800, which was a part of these dividends, I believe. I think my "cash memorandum" of June 25, 1869, for $2,500, with which you charge me, represented at the time a part of the dividends; but being debited with that, I am entitled to a credit of the dividend.

In other words, as I reckon it, there are dividends amounting to $9,550 due me, with interest since June, 1870, of which I have received only $2,700 or $2,800, entitling me thus to a credit of some $7,500.

Besides the cash memorandum January 9, 1864, $600, which with interest amounts to $904.10, was obviously included in the consolidated note which was given to represent all my indebtedness to you and which you repeatedly assured me would be met and liquidated in good time by Spencer dividends.

You will thus see that we differ materially as to the figures. Of course each of us is aiming at precisely the facts of the case, and if I am wrong, please correct me. I am sure that you do not desire me to pay a dollar that is not due, and I am equally sure that I am more than ready to pay every cent that I owe you.

The Little Rock matter is a perpetual and never-ending embarrassment to me. I am pressed daily almost to make final settlement with those who still hold the securities—a settlement I am not able to make until I receive the bonds due on your article of agreement with me. That is to me by far the most urgent and pressing of all the demands connected with our matters, and the one of which I think in all equity should be first settled, or certainly settled as soon as any.

If the $6,000 cash is so important to you, I would be glad to assist in raising the same for you on your notes, using Little Rock bonds as collateral at same rate they are used in Boston, four for one. I think I could get the money here on four or six months on these terms. If I had the money myself, I would be glad to advance it to you, but I am as dry as a contribution box, borrowing indeed to defray my campaign expenses.

Very sincerely yours,

J. G. Blaine.

Warren Fisher, Jr., Esq., *Boston*.

That is a very important communication to the American people.

The next letter I hold is dated Augusta, Maine, July 3, 1872. The witness Mulligan said that there was nothing in this about the Northern Pacific Railroad.

. . . .

I do not wish to detain the House, but I have one or two more observations to make. The specific charge that went to the committee of which the honorable gentleman from Virginia is chairman, so far as it affects me, was whether I was a party in interest to the sixty-four-thousand-dollar transaction; and I submit that up to this time there has not been one particle of proof before the committee sustaining that charge. Gentlemen have said what they had heard somebody else say, and generally when that somebody else brought on the stand it appeared that he did not say it at all. Colonel Thomas A. Scott swore very positively and distinctly under the most rigid cross examination all about it. Let me call attention to that letter of mine which Mulligan says refers to that. I ask your attention, gentlemen, as closely as if you were a jury while I show the absurdity of that statement. It is in evidence that with the exception of a small fraction the bonds which were sold to parties in Maine were first-mortgage bonds. It is in evidence over and over again that the bonds which went to the Union Pacific road were land-grant bonds. Therefore it is a moral impossibility the bonds taken up to Maine should have gone to the Union Pacific Railroad. They were of different series, different kinds, different colors, everything different, as different as if not issued within a thousand miles of each other. So on its face it is shown it could not be so.

There has not been, I say, one positive piece of testimony in any direction. They sent to Arkansas to get some hearsay about bonds. They sent to Boston to get some hearsay. Mulligan was contradicted by Fisher, and Atkins and Scott swore directly against him. Morton, of Morton, Bliss & Co., never heard my name in the matter. Carnegee, who negotiated the note, never heard my name in that connection. Rollins said it was one of the intangible rumors he spoke of as floating in the air. Gentlemen who have lived any time in Washington need not be told that intangible rumors get considerable circulation here; and if a man is to be held accountable before the bar of public opinion for intangible rumors, who in the House will stand?

Now, gentlemen, those letters I have read were picked out of correspondence extending over fifteen years. The man did his worst, the very worst he could, out of the most intimate business correspondence of my life. I ask gentlemen if any of you, and I ask it with some feeling, can stand a severer scrutiny of or more rigid investigation into your private correspondence? That was the worst he could do.

There is one piece of testimony wanting. There is but one thing to close the complete circle of evidence. There is but one witness whom I could not have, to whom the Judiciary Committee, taking into account the great and intimate connection he had with the transaction, was asked to send a cable dispatch, and I ask the gentleman from Kentucky if that dispatch was sent to him?

Mr. FRYE. Who?

Mr. BLAINE. To Josiah Caldwell.

Mr. KNOTT. I will reply to the gentleman that Judge Hunton and myself have both endeavored to get Mr. Caldwell's address and have not yet got it.

Mr. BLAINE. Has the gentleman from Kentucky received a dispatch from Caldwell?

Mr. KNOTT. I will explain that directly.

Mr. BLAINE. I want a categorical answer.

Mr. KNOTT. I have received a dispatch purporting to be from Mr. Caldwell.

Mr. BLAINE. You did?

Mr. KNOTT. How did you know I got it?

Mr. BLAINE. When did you get it? I want the gentleman from Kentucky to answer when he got it.

Mr. KNOTT. Answer my question first.

Mr. BLAINE. I never heard of it until yesterday.

Mr. KNOTT. How did you hear it?

Mr. BLAINE. I heard you got a dispatch last Thursday morning at eight o'clock from Josiah Caldwell completely and absolutely exonerating me from this charge, and you have suppressed it. [Protracted applause upon the floor and in the galleries.] I want the gentleman from to answer. [After a pause.] Does the gentleman from Kentucky decline to answer?

The SPEAKER *pro tempore*. The gentleman will suspend until order is restored. The doorkeepers will remove from the Hall those not entitled to the floor; and the galleries will be cleared if this applause is repeated. So long as the present occupant is in the chair that rule will be enforced.

Mr. BLAINE. Mr. Speaker, I ask to offer the following resolution as a matter of privilege in this connection.

The SPEAKER *pro tempore*. The gentleman from Maine will suspend until order is restored. The Chair is not responsible for this disorder, and the doorkeepers have failed to keep out men not authorized to come into the Hall. There are in this Hall those not members double the number of members. The doorkeepers will enforce the rules of the House. Those who are not entitled to the floor will leave it. Members of the House will be seated. [After a pause.] The gentleman from Maine will proceed.

Mr. BLAINE. I want the gentleman from Kentucky to answer me, or rather to answer the House, that question.

Mr. KNOTT. I will answer that when I get ready. Go on with your speech.

Mr. BLAINE. I desire to offer the following resolution.

The Clerk read as follows:

Resolved, That the Committee on the Judiciary be instructed to report forthwith to the House whether in acting under the resolution of the House of May 2, relative to the purchase by the Pacific Railroad Company of seventy-five land-grant bonds of the Little Rock and Fort Smith Railroad, it has sent any telegram to one Josiah Caldwell, in Europe, and received a reply thereto. And, if so, to report said telegram and reply, with the date when said reply was received, and the reasons why the same has been suppressed.

Mr. BLAINE. After that add, "or whether the have heard from Josiah Caldwell in any way." Just add those words, "and what." Give it to me and I will modify it.

The SPEAKER *pro tempore*. The Clerk will read the modification of the resolution.

The Clerk read as follows:

And whether they have heard from the said Josiah Caldwell, in any other way, and to what effect.

Mr. BLAINE. The gentleman form Kentucky in responding probably, I think, from what he said, intended to convey the idea I had some illegitimate knowledge of how that dispatch was obtained. I have had no communication with Josiah Caldwell. I have had no means of knowing from the telegram office whether the telegram was received. But I tell the gentleman from Kentucky that murder will out.

Mr. GLOVER. That is true.

Mr. BLAINE. And secrets will leak. And I tell the gentleman now, and I am prepared to state to this House, that at eight o'clock on last Thursday morning, or thereabouts, the gentleman from Kentucky received and receipted for a message addressed to him from Josiah Caldwell, in London, entirely corroborating and substantiating the statements of Thomas A. Scott, which he had just read in the New York papers, and entirely exculpating me from the charges which I am bound to believe from the suppression of that report the gentleman is anxious to fasten upon me.

I call the previous question on that resolution.

[Protracted applause from the floor and the galleries.]

. . . .

Congressional Record, House, 44th Congress, 1st session, June 5, 1876, 3602–3617.

90   Establishing the Electoral Commission of 1877

January 29, 1877

The centennial year of 1876 found the Democrats holding the majority in the House of Representatives while Republicans remained in power in the Senate. The changing complexion of Congress mirrored that of a public wearying of Reconstruction legislation and the corruption and scandals in Congress and in the Grant administration.

The presidential election of 1876 turned out to be one of the strangest and most challenging in American history. Congress had to create a special electoral commission in 1877 to determine who won the presidency. The election matched Republican Rutherford B. Hayes against Democrat Samuel J. Tilden. The initial ballot count showed that Tilden carried the popular vote and held the edge in the electoral college, 184 to 165, with 20 electoral votes in dispute. Tilden needed only one more electoral vote to be declared the president of the United States; Hayes needed all 20.

Election irregularities in several states made it difficult to determine just who had won. Oregon had one contested electoral vote and the remaining 19 were in three southern states—South Carolina, Louisiana, and Florida—where there were two sets of election returns, one from each party, each claiming to be the legitimate ballots. The Democrats accused the Republican-controlled states of manipulating the votes for Hayes, while the Republicans claimed that the Democrats had intimidated black voters on Tilden's behalf.

Congress established a bipartisan commission made up of five members each from the House and Senate and five Supreme Court Justices to examine the contested ballots and declare a new president and vice president. When an independent justice, not affiliated with either the Republican or Democratic parties, resigned, Justice Joseph Bradley replaced him as a commissioner and exhibited strong Republican sympathies to accept the ballots sent from the Republican governors. In response the Democrats threatened a filibuster to hold up the decision until after the date scheduled for the inauguration.

With the process deadlocked, House and Senate leaders met at a Washington hotel to work out a deal. They gave the presidency to Hayes. The Democrats exchanged the presidency for the withdrawal of federal troops from the South. Thus the election ended Reconstruction and assured the old southern ruling class a return to control. This deal between southern Democrats and northern Republicans became known as the Compromise of 1877. It averted a serious constitutional crisis and placed Rutherford B. Hayes in the White House, even though he had lost the popular vote and had insufficient electoral votes to win the election outright.

Ten years later, in 1887, Congress passed the Electoral Count Act, which established a procedure that put the burden of determining the electoral count on the states themselves. Congress would never again be faced with two sets of ballots from some states. The method of counting electoral ballots today still follows the procedure established in the Electoral Count Act.

CHAP. 37.—AN ACT TO PROVIDE FOR AND REGULATE THE COUNTING OF VOTES FOR PRESIDENT AND VICE-PRESIDENT, AND THE DECISION OF QUESTIONS ARISING THEREON, FOR THE TERM COMMENCING MARCH FOURTH, ANNO DOMINI EIGHTEEN HUNDRED AND SEVENTY-SEVEN

Be it enacted by the Senate and House of Representatives of the United States of America in Congress assembled, That the Senate and House of Representatives shall meet in the hall of the House of Representatives, at the hour of one O'clock post meridian, on the first Thursday in February, anno Domini eighteen hundred and seventy-seven; and the President of the Senate shall be their presiding officer. Two tellers shall be previously appointed on the part of the Senate, and two on the part of the House of Representatives, to whom shall be handed, as they are opened by the President of the Senate, all the certificates, and papers purporting to be certificates, of the electoral vote which certificates and papers shall be opened, presented, and acted upon in the alphabetical order of the States, beginning with the letter A; and said tellers having then read the same in the presence and herring of the two houses, shall make a list of the votes as they shall appear from the said certificates; and the votes having been ascertained and counted as in this act provided, the result of the same shall be delivered to the President of the Senate, who shall thereupon announce the state of the vote, and the names of the persons, if any, elected, which announcement shall be deemed a sufficient declaration of the persons elected President and Vice-President of the United States, and, together with a list of the votes, be entered on the journals of the two houses. Upon such reading of any such certificate or paper when there shall be only one return from a State, the President of the Senate shall call for objections, if any. Every objection shall be made in writing, and shall state clearly and concisely , and without argument, the ground thereof, and shall be signed by at least one Senator and one member of the House of Representatives before the same shall be received. When all objections; so made to any vote or paper from a State shall have been received and read, the Senate shall thereupon withdraw, and such objections shall be submitted to the Senate for its decision; and the Speaker of the House of Representatives shall, in like manner, submit such objections to the House of Representatives for its decision ; and no electoral vote or votes from any State from which but one return has been received shall be rejected except by the affirmative vote of the two Houses. When the two Houses have voted, they shall immediately again meet, and the presiding officer shall then announce the decision of the question submitted.

SEC 2. That if more than one return, or paper purporting to be a return from a State, shall have been received by the President of the Senate, purporting to be the certificates of electoral votes given at the last preceding election for President and Vice-President in such State, (unless they shall be duplicates of the same return,) all such returns and papers shall be opened by him in the presence of the two houses when met as aforesaid, and read by the tellers, and all such returns and papers shall thereupon be submitted to the judgment and decision as to which is the true and lawful electoral vote of such State, of a commission constituted as follows, namely: During the session of each House on the Tuesday next preceding the first Thursday in February, eighteen hundred and seventy-seven, each House shall, by viva voce vote, appoint five of its members, who with the five associate justices of the Supreme Court of the United States, to be ascertained as hereinafter provided, shall constitute a commission for the decision of all question upon or in respect of such double returns named in this section. On the Tuesday next preceding the first Thursday in February, anno Domini eighteen hundred and seventy-seven, or as soon thereafter as may be, the associate justices of the Supreme Court of the United States now assigned to the first, third, eighth, and ninth circuits shall elect, in such manner as a majority of them shall deem fit, another of the associate justices of said court, which five persons shall be members of said commission; and the person longest in commission of said five justices shall be he president of said commission. The members of said commission shall respectively take and subscribe the following oath: "I, _____ _____ do solemnly swear (or affirm, as the case may be) that I will impartially examine and consider all questions submitted to the commission of which I am a member, and a true judgment give thereon, agreeably to the Constitution and the laws: so help me God;" which oath shall be filed with the Secretary of the Senate. When the commission shall have been thus organized, it shall not be in the power of either house to dissolve the same, or to withdraw any of its members; but if any such Senator or member shall die or become physically unable to perform the duties required by this act, the fact of such death or physical inability shall be by said commission, before it shall proceed further, communicated to the Senate or House of Representatives, as the case may be, which body shall immediately, and without debate proceed by viva voce vote to fill the place so vacated, and the person so appointed shall take and subscribe the oath hereinbefore prescribed, and become a member of said commission; and, in like manner, if any of said justices of the Supreme Court shall die or become physically incapable of performing the duties required by this act, the other of said justices, members of the said commission, shall immediately appoint another justice of said court a member of said commission, and, in such appointments, regard shall be had to the impartiality and freedom from bias sought by the original appointments to said commission, who shall thereupon immediately take and subscribe the oath hereinbefore prescribed, and become a member of said commission to fill the vacancy so occasioned. All the certificates and papers purporting to be certificate of the electoral votes of each State shall be opened, in the alphabetical order of the States, as provided in section one of this act; and which there shall be more than one such certificate or paper, as the certificate and papers from such State shall so be opened, (excepting duplicates of the same return,) they shall be read by the tellers, and thereupon the President of the Senate shall call for objections, if any. Every objection shall be made in writing, and shall state clearly and concisely, and without argument, the ground thereof, and shall be signed by at least one Senator and one member of the House of Representatives before the same shall be received. When all such objections so made to any certificate, vote, or paper from a State shall have been received and read, all such certificates, votes, and papers so objected to, and all papers accompanying the same, together with such objections, shall be forthwith submitted to said commission, which shall proceed to consider the same, with the same powers, if any, now possessed for that purpose or together, and, by a majority of votes from such State are the votes provided for by the Constitution of the United States, and how many and what persons were duly appointed electors in such State, and may therein take into view such petitions, depositions, and other papers, if any, as shall, by the Constitution and now existing law, be competent and pertinent in such consideration ; which decision shall be made in writing, stating briefly the ground thereof. and signed by the members of said commission agreeing therein; whereupon the two houses shall again meet; and such decision shall be read and entered in the journal of each House, and the counting of the votes shall proceed in conformity therewith,

unless. upon objection made thereto in writing by at least five Senators and five members of the House of Representatives, the two Houses shall separately concur in ordering otherwise, in which case such concurrent order shall govern. No votes or papers from any other State shall be acted upon until the objections previously made to the votes or papers from any State shall have been finally disposed of.

SEC 3. That while the two Houses shall be in meeting, as provided in this act, no debate shall be allowed and no question shall be put by the presiding officer, except to either House on a motion to withdraw; and he shall have power to preserve order.

SEC 4. That when the two Houses separate to decide upon an objection that may have been made to the counting of any electoral vote or votes from any State, or upon objection to a report of said commission or other question arising under this ac; each Senator and Representative may speak to such objection or question ten minutes, and not oftener than once; but after such debate shall have lasted two hours, it shall be the duty of each House to put the main question without further debate.

SEC 5. That at such joint meeting of the two Houses, seats shall be provided as follows: For the President of the Senate, the Speaker's chair; for the Speaker, immediately upon his left; the Senators in the body of the hall upon the right of the presiding officer; for the Representatives, in the body of the ball not provided for the Senators; for the tellers, Secretary of the Senate, and Clerk of the House of Representatives, at the Clerk's desk; for the other officers of the two Houses, in front of the Clerk's desk and upon each side of the Speaker's platform. Such joint meeting shall not be dissolved until the count of electoral votes shall be completed and the result declared; and no recess shall be taken unless a question shall have arisen in regard to counting any such votes, or otherwise under this act; in which case it shall be competent for either House, acting separately, in the manner hereinbefore provided, to direct a recess of such House not beyond the next day, Sunday excepted, at the hour of ten o'clock in the forenoon. And while any question is being considered by said commission, either House may proceed with its legislative or other business.

SEC 6. That nothing in this act shall be held to impair or affect any right now existing under the Constitution and laws to question, by proceeding in the judicial courts of the United States, the right or title of the person who shall be declared elected, or who shall claim to be President or Vice-President of the United States, if any such right exists.

SEC 7. That said commission shall make its own rules, keep a record of its proceedings, and shall have power to employ such persons as may be necessary for the transaction of its business and the execution of its powers.

Approved, January 29, 1877.

Statutes at Large, 19 (1875–1877), 44th Congress, 2d session, Jan. 29, 1877, 227–229.

91 Representative James A. Garfield Describes Congress

July 1877

James A. Garfield served as a representative from Ohio from 1863 to 1880, when he resigned to accept the Republican nomination for the presidency. His tenure in the House and his experience rising through the ranks of the committee system made him a leader in the House and a keen and thoughtful observer of Congress during the Reconstruction era.

In this excerpt from an article he published in the Atlantic Monthly, *which was later included in* The Collected Works of James Abram Garfield, *Garfield provided a glimpse of Congress shaped by an increasing workload and the ever increasing complexity of the nation, which grew rapidly in the last decades of the nineteenth century. Garfield accurately described the fact that the federal government was being felt more directly in the lives of more citizens than ever before. In response to several scandals that beset the Grant administration and Congress, Garfield warned his readers that they had to take responsibility for the election of worthy members of Congress. "If that body be ignorant, reckless, and corrupt," Garfield wrote, "it is because the people tolerate ignorance, recklessness, and corruption. If it be intelligent, brave, and pure, it is because the people demand those high qualities to represent them in the national legislature." His words on this subject remain as vital today as they were in 1877.*

. . . .

As a result of the great growth of the country and of the new legislation arising from the late war, Congress is greatly overloaded with work. It is safe to say that the business which now annually claims the attention of Congress is tenfold more complex and burdensome than it was forty years ago. For example: the twelve annual appropriation bills, with their numerous details, now consume two thirds of each short session of the House. Forty years ago, when the appropriations were made more in block, one week was sufficient for the work.

The vast extent of our country, the increasing number of States and Territories, the legislation necessary to regulate our mineral lands, to manage our complex systems of internal revenue, banking, currency, and expenditure, have so increased the work of Congress that no one man can even read the bills and the official reports relating to current legislation, much less qualify himself for intelligent action upon them. As a necessary consequence, the real work of legislation is done by the committees; and their work must be accepted or rejected without full knowledge of its merits. This fact alone renders leadership in Congress, in the old sense of the word, impossible. For many years we have had the leadership of committees and chairmen of committees; but no one man can any more be the leader of all the legislation of the Senate or of the House, than one lawyer or one physician can now be foremost in all the departments of law or medicine. The evils of loose legislation resulting from this situation must increase rather than diminish, until a remedy is provided.

John Stuart Mill held that a numerous popular assembly is radically unfit to *make good laws,* but is the best possible means *of getting good laws made.* He suggested, as a permanent part of the constitution of a free country, a legislative commission, composed of a few trained men, to draft such laws as the legislature, by general resolutions, shall direct, which draft shall be adopted by the legislature, without change, or returned to the commission to be amended. Whatever may be thought of Mr. Mill's suggestion, it is clear that some plan must be adopted to relieve Congress from the infinite details of legislation, and to preserve harmony and coherence in our laws.

Another change observable in Congress, as well as in the legislatures of other countries, is the decline of oratory. The press is rendering the orator obsolete. Statistics now furnish the materials upon which the legislator depends; and a column of figures will often demolish a dozen pages of eloquent rhetoric.

Just now, too, the day of sentimental politics is passing away, and the work of Congress is more nearly allied to the business interests of the country and to "the dismal science," as political economy is called by the "practical men" of our time. the legislation of Congress comes much nearer to the daily life of the people than ever before. Twenty years ago, the presence of the national government was not felt by one citizen in a hundred. Except in paying his postage and receiving his mail, the citizen of the interior rarely came in contact with the national authority. Now, he meets it in a thousand ways. Formerly the legislation of Congress referred chiefly to our foreign relations, to indirect taxes, to the government of the army, the navy, and the Territories. Now, a vote in Congress may, any day, seriously derange the business affairs of every citizen.

And this leads me to say that now, more than ever before, the people are responsible for the character of their Congress. If that body be ignorant, reckless, and corrupt, it is because the people tolerate ignorance, recklessness, and corruption. If it be intelligent, brave, and pure, it is because the people demand those high qualities to represent them in the national legislature. Congress lives in the blaze of "that fierce light which beats against the throne." The telegraph and the press will to-morrow morning announce at a million breakfast-tables what has been said and done in Congress to-day. Now, as always, Congress represents the prevailing opinions and political aspirations of the people. The wildest delusions of paper money, the crudest theories of taxation, the passions and prejudices that find expression in the Senate and House, were first believed and discussed at the firesides of the people, on the corners of the streets, and in the caucuses and conventions of political parties.

The most alarming feature of our situation is the fact that so many citizens of high character and solid judgment pay but little attention to the sources of political power, to the selection of those who shall make their laws. The clergy, the faculties of colleges, and many of the leading business men of the community, never attend the township caucus, the city primary, or the county convention; but they allow the less intelligent and the more selfish and corrupt members of the community to "make the states" and "run the machine" of politics. They wait until the "machine" has done its work, and then, in surprise and horror at the ignorance and corruption in public office, sigh for the return of that mythical period called the "better and purer days of the republic." It is precisely this neglect of the first steps in our political processes that has made possible the worst evils of our system. Corrupt and incompetent presidents, judges, and legislators can be removed; but when the fountains of political power are corrupted, when voters themselves become venal and elections fraudulent, there is no remedy except by awakening the public conscience. and bringing to bear upon the subject the power of public opinion and the penalties of the law. The practice of buying and selling votes at our popular elections has already gained a foothold, though it has not gone so far as in England. It is mentioned in the recent biography of Lord Macaulay, as a boast, that his four elections to the House of Commons cost him but five hundred pounds. A hundred years ago, bribery of electors was far more prevalent and shameless in England than it now is.

There have always been, and always will be, bad men in all human pursuits. There was a Judas in the college of the Apostles, an Arnold in the army of the Revolution, a Burr in our early politics; and they have had successors in all departments of modern life. But it is demonstrable, as a matter of history, that on the whole the standard of public and private morals is higher in the United States at the present time than ever before; that men in public and private stations are held to a more rigid accountability, and that the average moral tone of Congress is higher to-day than at any previous period of our history. It is certainly true that our late war disturbed the established order of society, awakened a reckless spirit of adventure and speculation, and greatly multiplied the opportunities, and increased the temptations to evil. The disorganization of the Southern States, and the temporary disfranchisement of its leading citizens, threw a portion of their representation in Congress, for a short time, into the hands of political adventurers, many of whom used their brief hold on power for personal ends, and thus brought disgrace upon the national legislature. And it is also true that the enlarged sphere of legislation so mingled public duties and private interests that it was not easy to draw the line between them. From that cause also the reputation, and in some cases the character, of public men suffered eclipse. But the earnestness and vigor with which wrong-doing is everywhere punished is a strong guaranty of the purity of those who may hold posts of authority and honor. Indeed, there is now danger

in the opposite direction; namely, that criticism may degenerate into mere slander, and put an end to its power for good by being used as a means to assassinate the reputation and destroy the usefulness of honorable men. It is as much the duty of all good men to protect and defend the reputation of worthy public servants as to detect and punish public rascals.

In a word, our national safety demands that the fountains of political power shall be made pure by intelligence, and kept pure by vigilance; that the best citizens shall take heed to the selection and election of the worthiest and most intelligent among them to hold seats in the national legislature; and that, when the choice has been made, the continuance of the representative shall depend upon his faithfulness, its ability, and his willingness to work.

In Congress, as everywhere else, careful study—thorough, earnest work—is the only sure passport to usefulness and distinction. From its first meeting in 1774 to its last in 1788, three hundred and fifty-four men sat in the Continental Congress. Of these, one hundred and eighteen—one third of the whole number—were college graduates. That third embraced much the larger number of those whose names have come down to us as the great founders of the republic. Since the adoption of the Constitution of 1787, six thousand two hundred and eighteen men have held seats in Congress; and among them all, through culture and earnest, arduous work have been the leading characteristics of those whose service has been most useful, and whose fame has been most enduring. Galloway wrote of Samuel Adams, "He eats little, drinks little, sleeps little, and thinks much, and is most decisive and indefatigable in the pursuit of his objects." This description can still be fittingly applied to all men who deserve and achieve success anywhere, but especially in public life. As a recent writer has said, in discussing the effect of Prussian culture, so we may say of culture in Congress: "The lesson is, that, whether you want him for war or peace, there is no way in which you can get so much out of a man as by training him, not in pieces, but the whole of him; and that the trained men, other things being equal, are pretty sure, in the long run, to be masters of the world."

Congress must always be the exponent of the political character and culture of the people; and if the next centennial does not find us a great nation, with a great and worthy Congress, it will be because those who represent the enterprise, the culture, and the morality of the nation do not aid in controlling the political forces which are employed to select the men who shall occupy the great places of trust and power.

Burke A. Hinsdale, ed., *The Works of James Abram Garfield*, 2 vols. (Boston: James B. Osgood and Co., 1883), vol. 2: 484–489. This excerpt was originally published as an article, "A Century of Progress," in *Atlantic Monthly* (July 1877).

92   Reform of the Rules of the House

January 6, 1880

The House of Representatives must "reinvent" itself every two years at the beginning of a new Congress by approving the rules by which it will conduct its parliamentary business and administer its committees and offices. The opening of a new Congress is usually the time when new rules are introduced and passed, but the House can revise its rules whenever it sees fit. During the 46th Congress in 1880, the House made a sweeping revision of its rules. Members had complained for years that the cumbersome, antiquated rules often impeded the flow of legislative business and kept them uninformed about when and how legislation would reach the floor. The press also criticized the House for its outdated rules and its inability to handle the increased workload of legislation. There was a general mood of reform in House and throughout the federal government following the scandal-ridden Grant administration. The specific reasons for the changes were spelled out in this report of the Committee on Rules.

By 1880 the rules of the House had grown to 166 rules, 63 of which were more than eighty years old. More significantly, the size and complexity of the House had grown as the nation had grown and it was time to find better ways to conduct the business of the House. The twenty-five categories in which the rules were arranged after the revision is a revealing outline of the administrative and parliamentary structure of the House. While House rules have undergone other major revisions since 1880, present day rules still follow, with some variations, the general outline adopted in 1880. The House Committee on Rules did its job well, reducing 166 rules to 44. In the process, the Committee on Rules itself was strengthened and made a standing committee of the House. The Rules Committee became a powerful arm of the Speaker. Some speakers, such as Thomas B. Reed (see document 101), would use the House rules and the Rules Committee vigorously, running the House with strong centralized authority.

The modern House rule book (as of the 105th Congress) is a thick compendium of useful information that includes the U.S. Constitution, Jefferson's Manual (see document 34), House Rules, the Congressional Budget Act, and other important information. As of 1998, there were 51 House rules and the entire rule book and manual is 1,336 pages in length.

The Committee on Rules, in pursuance of the resolution of the 25th of June ultimo, authorizing them to sit during the then coming recess "for the purpose of revising, codifying, and simplifying the rules of the House," ask leave to submit the following report:

The urgent necessity of a through revision of the rules of the House cannot be better illustrated and shown then by the simple statement of the fact that of the present one hundred and sixty-six rules sixty-three of that number, or portions thereof, were adopted prior to the year 1800, and that in the only revision and rearrangement of the rules ever made since that time at all ap-

proaching thoroughness, not less than thirty rules which were practically obsolete, in whole or in part, were allowed to remain among the standing rules of the House of Representatives.

In view of this fact, the committee decided that a complete revision and codification of the rules was not only a parliamentary but a practical business necessity, demanded both by the gradual change in parliamentary law and practice which has taken place since the Jefferson Manual was the standard recognized American Authority, and by reason of the increased representation in the House, and the very large increase of business transacted, which can be best illustrated by the statement of the fact that in the Sixth Congress, which convened December 2, 1799, and expired March 3, 1801, with sixteen (16) States in the Union, having one hundred and forty-one (141) Representatives in the House, (one for every 33,000 inhabitants,) there were 298 bills introduced and reported and 347 petitions presented, while in the Forty-fifth Congress which convened October 15, 1877, and expired March 3, 1879, with thirty-eight (38) States in the Union, having two hundred and ninety-three Representatives in the House, (one for every 133,000 inhabitants,) there were 6,579 bills introduced and reported and 10,467 petitions presented.

The committee determined at the very threshold of their labors—it being, indeed, the first conclusion reached by them—that their reported revision should be the unanimous action and agreement of the committee, leaving intact only such rules as the committee could not agree unanimously to adopt or to amend, reserving, however, to each member of the committee the right individually, to offer such amendments as he might, on further consideration of the subject, deem proper or desirable; and the accompanying proposed code of he standing rules for conducting business in the House of Representatives is, therefore, the unanimous report of the Committee on Rules. In submitting the same, it is proper to remark that the rights and privileges of the political minority of the House have in no respect been restricted or abridged therein, and that political or partisan considerations never entered into or disturbed its deliberations, or once divided the committee in respect to a single item or paragraph. The objective point with the committee was to secure accuracy in business, economy of time, order uniformity and impartiality, and to prepare, if possible, a simple, concise, and non-partisan code of rules, which should neither surrender the right of the majority to control and dispose of the business for which it is held responsible, or, on the other hand, to invade and restrict the powers of the minority to check temporarily, if not permanently, the action of a majority believed to be improper or unconstitutional, and to attain, of possible, the great underlying principle of all the rules and forms by which the business of a legislative assembly is governed, whether constitutional, legal, or parliamentary in the origin, namely, "to subserve the will of the assembly rather than to restrain it, to facilitate and not to obstruct the expression of its deliberate sense."

As a second conclusion the committee decided to arrange the proposed rules in such order as would make their connection and subject correspond, as nearly as practicable, consolidating in one rule the various provisions relating to the same subject, now embrace in several rules scattered about without regard to uniformity of system; and the order in which they have been arranged is as follows, namely:

1. Duties of the Speaker;
2. Election of officers;
3. Duties of the Clerk;
4. Duties of the Sergeant-at Arms;
5. Duties of Doorkeeper;
6. Duties of Postmaster;
7. Duties of Chaplain;
8. Of the members;
9. Questions of privilege;
10. Of committees;
11. Powers and duties of committees;
12. Delegate;
13. Calendars;
14. Decorum and debate;
15. Calls of the roll and House;
16. On motion—their precedence;
17. Previous question;
18. Reconsiderations;
19. Of amendments;
20. Of amendments of the Senate;
21. On bills;
22. Of petitions and memorials;
23. Of Committees of the Whole House;
24. Order of business;
25. Miscellaneous rules.

Congressional Record, House, 46th Congress, 2d session, Jan. 6, 1880, 198–199.

93   *Kilbourn v. Thompson*

1880

The Supreme Court in Kilbourn v. Thompson *declared that a member of Congress could not be sued for matters related to congressional duties and responsibilities. At the same time the decision placed limits on the investigative powers of Congress when they extended into the jurisdiction of the judicial branch of government. The decision struck a blow for individual rights by affirming that individuals brought before congressional investigative committees still had the right to sue in order to protect themselves. This case limited, but did not completely curtail, Congress's authority to arrest persons for contempt of Congress. From 1850 to 1880, the year of the* Kilbourn *decision, Congress had used, or threatened to use, the charge of contempt of Congress in forty-nine investigations. In the sixty years after the* Kilbourn *decision, Congress used the charge in only six cases. The power of Congress to compel witnesses to testify was not firmly reestablished until 1927, in the case of* McGrain v. Daugherty *(see document 120). It was not until the 1940s, however, during investigations of communist infiltration of government that Congress flexed its authority to compel witnesses to testify with some regularity.*

This case resulted from an 1876 congressional investigation of the firm of Jay Cooke and Company, a large banking house in Philadelphia that had raised more than a billion dollars through the sale of government bonds to help finance the Civil War. During the economic depression known as the Panic of 1873, Cooke's firm filed for bankruptcy. In the course of its investigation of the bankruptcy, the House committee, seeking to compel a witness to testify, asked the House to arrest for contempt of Congress one of the associates of Jay Cooke and Company, Hallet Kilbourn. The House voted to arrest Kilbourn for his refusal to testify and ordered the House sergeant-at-arms, John G. Thompson, to make the arrest. Kilbourn was locked up in the city jail in the District of Columbia, where he was held for forty-five days until obtaining a writ of habeas corpus in a federal court. He sued the sergeant-at-arms, the House Speaker, and the members of the House investigating committee for false arrest.

Associate Justice Samuel Freeman Miller (1816–1890) wrote the majority opinion of the Court. After a lengthy exploration of precedents, including an examination of the practice of the British Parliament, the Court concluded that members of Congress could not be sued. They were protected by the Constitution's speech and debate clause (Article I, Section 6, Clause 1). On the other hand, the House sergeant-at-arms could be sued for carrying out the arrest and was guilty of false arrest. Justice Miller said that Congress had no business investigating private financial matters, which should be the role of the courts, not Congress.

MR. JUSTICE MILLER, after stating the case, delivered the opinion of the court.

The argument before us has assumed a very wide range, and includes the discussion of almost every suggestion that can well be conceived on the subject. The two extremes of the controversy are the proposition on the part of the plaintiff that the House of Representatives has no power whatever to punish for a contempt of its authority, and, on the part of defendants, that such power undoubtedly exists, and when that body has formally exercised it, it must be presumed that it was right fully exercised.

This latter proposition assumes the form of expression sometimes used with reference to courts of justice of general jurisdiction that, having the power to punish for contempts, the judgment of the House that a person is guilty of such contempt is conclusive everywhere.

Conceding for the sake of the argument that there are cases in which one of the two bodies that constitute the Congress of the United States may punish for contempt of its authority or disregard of its orders, it will scarcely be contended by the most ardent advocate of their power in that respect that it is unlimited.

The powers of Congress itself, when acting through the concurrence of both branches, are dependent solely on the Constitution. Such as are not conferred by that instrument, either expressly or by fair implication from what is granted, are "reserved to the States respectively, or to the people." Of course, neither branch of Congress, when acting separately, can lawfully exercise more power than is conferred by the Constitution on the whole body, except in the few instances where authority is conferred on either House separately, as in the case of impeachments. No general power of inflicting punishment by the Congress of the United States is found in that instrument. It contains in the provision that no "person all be deprived of life, liberty, or property, without due process of law" the strongest implication against punishment by order of the legislative body. It has been repeatedly decided by this court, and by others of the highest authority, that this means a trial in which the rights of the party shall be decided by a tribunal appointed by law, which tribunal is to be governed by rules of law previously established. An act of Congress which proposed to adjudge a man guilty of a crime and inflict the punishment would be conceded by all thinking men to be unauthorized by anything in the Constitution. That instrument, however, is not wholly silent as to the authority of the separate branches of Congress to inflict punishment. It authorizes each House to punish its own members. By the second clause of the fifth section of the first article, "Each House may determine the rules of its proceedings, punish its members for disorderly behavior, and, with the concurrence of two-thirds, expel a member," and, by the clause immediately preceding, it "may be authorized to compel the attendance of absent members in such manner and under such penalties as each House may provide." These provisions are equally instructive in what they authorize and in what they do not authorize. There is no express power in that instrument conferred on either House of Congress to punish for contempts.

. . . .

We are of opinion that the right of the House of Representatives to punish the citizen for a contempt of its authority or a breach of its privileges can derive no support from the precedents and practices of the two Houses of the English Parliament, nor from the adjudged cases in which the English courts have upheld these practices. Nor, taking what has fallen from the English judges, and especially the later cases on which we have just commented, is much aid given to the doctrine that this power exists as one necessary to enable either House of Congress to exercise successfully their function of legislation.

This latter proposition is one which we do not propose to decide in the present case, because we are able to decide it without passing upon the existence or nonexistence of such power in aid of the legislative function.

As we have already said, the Constitution expressly empowers each House to punish its own members for disorderly behavior. We see no reason to doubt that this punishment may, in a proper case, be imprisonment, and that it may be for refusal to obey some rule on that subject made by the House for the preservation of order.

So also, the penalty which each House is authorized to inflict in order to compel the attendance of absent members may be imprisonment, and this may be for a violation of some order or standing rule on that subject.

Each House is, by the Constitution, made the judge of the election and qualification of its members. In deciding on these, it has an undoubted right to examine witnesses and inspect papers, subject to the usual rights of witnesses in such cases, and it may be that a witness would be subject to like punishment at the hands of the body engaged in trying a contested election, for refusing to testify, that he would if the case were pending before a court of judicature.

The House of Representatives has the sole right to impeach officers of the government, and the Senate to try them. Where the question of such impeachment is before either body acting in its appropriate sphere on that subject, we see no reason to doubt the right to compel the attendance of witnesses, and their answer to proper questions, in the same manner and by the use of the same means that courts of justice can in like cases.

Whether the power of punishment in either House by fine or imprisonment goes beyond this or not, we are sure that no person can be punished for contumacy as a witness before either House unless his testimony is required in a matter into which that House has jurisdiction to inquire, and we feel equally sure that neither of these bodies possesses the general power of making inquiry into the private affairs of the citizen.

It is believed to be one of the chief merits of the American system of written constitutional law that all the powers intrusted to government, whether State or national, are divided into the three grand departments, the executive, the legislative, and the judicial. That the functions appropriate to each of these branches of government shall be vested in a separate body of public servants, and that the perfection of the system requires that the lines which separate and divide these departments shall be broadly and clearly defined. It is also essential to the successful working of this system that the persons intrusted with power in any one of these branches shall not be permitted to encroach upon the powers confided to the others, but that each shall, by the law of its creation, be limited to the exercise of the powers appropriate to its own department, and no other. To these general propositions there are in the Constitution of the United States some important exceptions. One of these is that the President is so far made a part of the legislative power that his assent is required to the enactment of all statutes and resolutions of Congress.

This, however, is so only to a limited extent, for a bill may become a law notwithstanding the refusal of the President to approve it, by a vote of thirds of each House of Congress.

So, also, the Senate is made a partaker in the functions of appointing officers and making treaties, which are supposed to be properly executive, by requiring its consent to the appointment of such officers and the ratification of treaties. The Senate also exercises the judicial power of trying impeachments, and the House of preferring articles of impeachment.

In the main, however, that instrument, the model on which are constructed the fundamental laws of the States, has blocked out with singular precision, and in bold lines, in its three primary articles, the allotment of power to the executive, the legislative, and the judicial departments of the government. It also remains true, as a general rule, that the powers confided by the Constitution to one of these departments cannot be exercised by another.

It may be said that these are truisms which need no repetition here to give them force. But while the experience of almost a century has in general shown a wise and commendable forbearance in each of these branches from encroachments upon the others, it is not to be denied that such attempt have been made, and it is believed not always without success. The increase in the number of States, in their population and wealth, and in the amount of power, if not in its nature to be exercised by the Federal government, presents powerful and growing temptations to those to whom that exercise is intrusted to overstep the just boundaries of their own department and enter upon the domain of one of the others, or to assume powers not intrusted to either of them.

The House of Representatives having the exclusive right to originate all bills for raising revenue, whether by taxation or otherwise; having with the Senate the right to declare war, and fix the compensation of all officers and servants of the government, and vote the supplies which must pay that compensation, and being also the most numerous body of all those engaged in the exercise of the primary powers of the government—is for these reasons least of all liable to encroachments upon its appropriate domain.

By reason, also, of its popular origin and the frequency with which the short term of office of its members requires the renewal of their authority at the hands of the people—the great source of all power in this country—encroachments by that body on the domain of coordinate branches of the government would be received with less distrust than a similar exercise of unwarranted power by any other department of the government. It is all the more necessary, therefore, that the exercise of power by this body, when acting separately from and independently of all other depositaries of power, should be watched with vigilance, and when called in question before any other tribunal having the right to pass upon it, that it should receive the most careful scrutiny.

In looking to the preamble and resolution under which the committee acted, before which Kilbourn refused to testify, we are of opinion that the House of Representatives not only exceeded the limit of its own authority, but assumed a power which could only be properly exercised by another branch of the government, because it was, in its nature, clearly judicial.

The Constitution declares that the judicial power of the United States shall be vested in one Supreme Court and in such inferior courts as the Congress may from time to time ordain and establish. If what we have said of the division of the powers of the government among the three departments be sound, this is equivalent to a declaration that no judicial power is vested in the Congress or either branch of it, save in the cases specifically enumerated to which we have referred. If the investigation which the committee was directed to make was judicial in its character, and could only be properly and successfully made by a court of justice, and if it related to a matter wherein relief or redress could be had only by a judicial proceeding, we do not, after what has been said, deem it necessary to discuss the proposition that the power attempted to be exercised was one confided by the Constitution to the judicial, and not to the legislative, department of the government. We think it equally clear that the power asserted is judicial, and not legislative.

. . . .

We are of opinion, for these reasons, that the resolution of the House of Representatives authorizing the investigation was in excess of the power conferred on that body by the Constitution; that the committee, therefore, had no lawful authority to require Kilbourn to testify as a witness beyond what he voluntarily chose to tell; that the orders and resolutions of the House, and the warrant of the speaker, under which Kilbourn was imprisoned are, in like manner, void for want of jurisdiction in that body, and that his imprisonment was without any lawful authority.

. . . .

But, however that may be, the defence of the sergeant-at-arms rested on the broad ground that the House, having found the plaintiff guilty of a contempt, and the speaker, under the order of the House, having issued a warrant for his arrest, that alone was sufficient authority for the defendant to take him into custody, and this court held the plea good.

It may be said that, since the order of the House, and the warrant of the speaker, and the plea of the sergeant-at-arms do not disclose the ground on which the plaintiff was held guilty of a contempt, but state the finding of the House in general terms as a judgment of guilty, and as the court placed its decision on the ground that such a judgment was conclusive in the action against the officer who executed the warrant, it is no precedent for a case where the plea establishes, as we have shown it does in this case by its recital of the facts, that the House has exceeded its authority.

. . . .

But we do not concede that the Houses of Congress possess this general power of punishing for contempt. The cases in which they can do this are very limited, as we have already attempted to show. If they are proceeding in a matter beyond their legitimate cognizance, we are of opinion that this can be shown, and we cannot give our assent to the principle that, by the mere act of asserting a person to be guilty of a contempt, they thereby establish their right to fine and imprison him, beyond the power of any court or any other tribunal whatever to inquire into the grounds on which the order was made. . . .

"The house of representatives is not the final judge of its own power and privilege in cases in which the rights and liberties of the subject are concerned, but the legality of its action may be examined and determined by this court. That house is not the legislature, but only a part of it, and is therefore subject in its action to the laws, in common with all other bodies, officers, and tribunals within the Commonwealth. Especially is it competent and proper for this court to consider whether its proceedings are in conformity with the Constitution and laws because, living under a written constitution, no branch or department of the government is supreme, and it is the province and duty of the judicial department to determine, in cases regularly brought before them, whether the powers of any branch of the government, and even those of the legislature in the enactment of laws, have been exercised in conformity to the Constitution, and, if they have not, to treat their acts as null and void. The house of

representatives has the power under the Constitution to imprison for contempt, but the power is limited to cases expressly provided for by the Constitution or to cases where the power is necessarily implied from those constitutional functions and duties, to the proper performance of which it is essential."

In this statement of the law, and in the principles there laid down, we fully concur.

. . . .

It is not necessary to decide here that there may not be things done, in the one House or the other, of an extraordinary character, for which the members who take part in the act may be held legally responsible. If we could suppose the members of these bodies so far to forget their high functions and the noble instrument under which they act as to imitate the Long Parliament in the execution of the Chief Magistrate of the nation, or to follow the example of the French Assembly in assuming the function of a court for capital punishment, we are not prepared to say that such an utter perversion of their powers to a criminal purpose would be screened from punishment by the constitutional provision for freedom of debate. In this, as in other matters which have been pressed on our attention, we prefer to decide only what is necessary to the case in hand, and we think the plea set up by those of the defendants who were members of the House is a good defence, and the judgment of the court overruling the demurrer to it and giving judgment for those defendants will be affirmed. As to Thompson, the judgment will be reversed and the case remanded for further proceedings.

So ordered.

103 U.S. 168 (1880).

---

94   An Argument Against Reducing Congressional Salaries

February 16, 1882

Members of Congress can often be their own worst enemies. This is especially true in regard to the issue of congressional pay (see documents 18, 49, and 86). Throughout the history of Congress, some members have expressed the view that their salary is too low. Even the first Speaker of the House, Frederick A. C. Muhlenberg, complained that his salary was insufficient to pay the high costs of living in New York and Philadelphia, where the First Congress met. Over the years other members of Congress have spoken out against raises. This stand often played well in the member's own district but did not sit well with colleagues in the House or Senate. The public has generally sided with those who think members of Congress are overpaid.

Following the disaster of the "salary grab" of 1873, Congress did not increase its salary for thirty-four years. In this document from 1882, the House Committee on Reform of the Civil Service had to

address the broad issue of reducing the salaries of executive department heads, the president of the United States, and members of Congress. A House bill proposed that the president's salary be reduced from $50,000 to $30,000 per year and that congressional salaries be reduced 20 percent, from $5,000 to $4,000 per year. This bill was defeated. But the debate, as reflected in this committee report, revealed once again the emotional power of this issue. In this report Roswell G. Horr (R-Mich.) could hardly contain his outrage at the very suggestion of reducing congressional pay. Rising to his full height of indignity, Horr suggested that those who felt they were receiving too much pay should return the excess amount to the U.S. Treasury. The report explained the many duties of a member of the House of Representatives that justified the compensation they received. Many of these same arguments can be heard today whenever the issue of congressional pay comes before Congress.

. . . .

Another feature of this bill is to reduce the pay of the Senators of the United States and the members of the House from $5,000 to $4,000 per annum.

What a strange infatuation. What really could the author of such a measure have been dreaming about? No one, surely, would originate such a bill just for buncombe. The clap-trap of the demagogue can by no means find any lodging-place in this House of Representatives! It must have been the accident of inadvertency. When you take into account the labor at present required of a member of Congress, can you conceive how any man in his normal condition, in full possession of all his faculties, could for a moment suppose that the salaries of these officials as now fixed by law are excessive? The work of a member of this House which is expected of him by his constituents and demanded of him by the people, if properly performed, is by no means light. We doubt if there is a single member of this House who will claim for a single moment that the work which he is compelled to do is not largely in excess of what really ought to be required of any man. Let us, just for one moment, glance at the ordinary work of an average Congressman, as it will generally run from week to week.

First, he is expected to be, and his public duties require that he should be, in his seat, during each session, at least five hours of each working day.

In addition to this, the majority of the committees, at least all the more important committees, demand that he shall be in attendance upon their sessions say two hours each day for four days in each week; and most members are on two committees, the other one of which will take at least two hours of each week, making two hours of each day for five days in each week that has to be given to the regular meetings of the committees. In addition to this, each member on all the large committees is on from three to five subcommittees. To these subcommittees are referred the various bills which are brought before Congress. Each member of a subcommittee is expected carefully to examine and be able to report intelligently as to the merits of each bill referred to his several subcommittees. In addition to this, each member is chairman of some one subcommittee: The bills referred to the subcommittee of which he is chairman he is expected not only to examine, but he is required to make out a written report as to the merits of each one of them, which report he is expected to be able to defend before the whole committee, and also if need be, upon the floor of the House.

Many questions thus referred to members require a vast amount of reading and examination in order to enable a member to give anything like an intelligent opinion in regard to them. In addition to all this there are all the time questions of public interest arising in this House, coming from all the various committees—questions affecting the entire country, on each of which every member is expected to be prepared at least to vote intelligently, and on some of them members are required to make such preparation as well enable them intelligently to oppose or defend them upon the floor of the House. All these things require time and labor for even moderate preparation.

But still more. I think it is safe to say that each member of this House receives fifty letters each week; many receive more, very many more, and few, we presume, receive less. All these require attention. The most of them are expected to be answered, but the mere answering of them is a small part of the work which they add to our regular duties. Growing out of these letters will be found during each week a large number of errands, a vast amount of what is called department work. One-quarter of them, perhaps, will be from soldiers asking aid in their pension cases, and each soldier is clear in his own mind that the member can help his case out if he will only make it a special case and give it special attention; and each one of them will request that you shall call personally at the Pension Department and urge his particular case forward. And no one can blame these soldiers for such requests. The delay in their cases has been so great that they feel as if some such action must be taken to give them relief.

Another man writes you to look up some matter in reference to a land patent. Another says his homestead claim should be looked after and he wants you to learn and let him know why he does not receive his full title. Another has invented some machine and the department have declared this discovery to be already supplemented by some former inventor, and have refused his patent. He would like you to go through the Patent Office and look over the patent laws and see if great injustice has not been done in his case. Another has a son or brother in the Regular Army whom he would like to have discharged. Another would like to have you go to the Post-Office Department and see if extra clerk hire cannot be allowed his office. Another wants a new post-route established, and now and then some strange, singular man will seek an appointment as postmaster of some town. Another would like to have you call at the Navy Department and see if his boy cannot get into the school at Annapolis or on some training ship. Another would like to have you call on the Attorney-General of the United States. He says that some railroad company has been trespassing upon his homestead, that the legal title to the homestead is still in the United States, that consequently he is unable to sue the company in his own name, hence he wished you to call on the Attorney-General and see if that official will not bring suit in name of the government for his benefit; if he will, then he would like to have the action commenced without delay. By the time a member has given these little requests their proper attention, or it may be during the time he is looking after them, he will receive an attack from a different direction. A large number of letters will have come to hand informing him of some friend who is seeking a situation in some of the departments, or perhaps in some foreign country. The friend is worthy, is every way fitted for the position, and all concerned are satisfied that all that is now needed to insure success is your powerful influence. In conformity with these requests you are liable to be called upon, perhaps several times in one week, by these applicants in personam, and they will require you to go at once and exert your enormous powers.

I doubt if there is a member of this House who has not from time to time been thus informed of his great personal popularity and immense individual strength, until he has in the outcome been actually amazed at the small results following such gigantic efforts. When these parties call upon you, they usually demand that you shall go at once and give their case attention. And they take special pains to inform you that they are perfectly satisfied if you only work for them in dead earnest, if you will make their case a specialty, they know you will be able to secure the desired appointment. It matters not what subject is before The House; it makes no difference how much your time may be needed for the examination of public measures; it matters not what real work you should attend to, the moment one of these personal applications is made you are expected to drop everything and make a desperate dive for one of the departments that you may show your influence and demonstrate your power.

We have thus enumerated a portion only of the work demanded of almost every Congressman in each week of his life here in Washington. We think no one will claim that the picture is overdrawn. Now then, for all this work, a Congressman receives the sum of $5,000 per annum, and the bill now under consideration would reduce that amount to $4,000. Your committee are of the opinion that the salary as now fixed by law is none too high for the work demanded. Besides this, they fear that the reduction of these salaries would result only in injury to the public service. Every member of Congress is expected to live at least decently while attending to his duties. With the price of living at the present day, we submit that no man who is fitted for the place can afford to devote his time to this public work for less than members now receive. Most Congressmen are compelled to keep up two establishments, one at their homes where they live, the other here during the session of Congress, so that the amount now received is not and cannot be in excess of the actual wants of such members.

Should this bill become a law your committee fear that its effect would be to prevent many honest, able men, of moderate means, from accepting the situation; we fear that Congress would soon be made up almost entirely of the following four classes of individuals: First, men of large means, to whom the salary is a matter of small moment, men who do not rely at all upon their pay as Congressmen for their livelihood; second, men of such small caliber, intellectually, that they can command little anywhere at any other kind of work; the third, a class of men who, without regard to the amount of salary, would accept the position simply for the purpose of making money out of it in an indirect way; or, in the fourth place, men who have no families, the old bachelors of the country.

Your committee submit that it would not be safe to adopt any rule which should confine the law-making power of the government to any or even all of these classes. Certainly the wealthy alone should not possess all the political power of this land. The people should not be debarred from selecting able and good men for these positions, simply because those men could not afford to accept the situations. Many of our ablest legislators in the past have been men of very moderate means. But how about the second class? We think that no one will for a moment claim that it is desirable to increase the number of men in this House who cannot, for the want of ability, earn the amount now allowed to each member; and we know no one will claim that the Congress of the United States should be put into the hands of the third class, into the hands of men who care nothing about the amount of salary, but who accept the position simply for what can be realized out of it in an indirect and dishonest way.

As to the fourth class, we submit it that while there are many single men, men who are treading life's pathway solitary and alone, who are every way splendid men and worthy of the highest confidence, still we are firm in our belief that no premium should be offered to this mistaken manner of life; and we fear that the perpetuity of our cherished institutions would be endangered by the establishment of any law which should ever ten to increase the delusions of this class of our mistaken fellow-citizens, or to given them any additional power in the councils of the nation.

Your committee would therefore report against reducing the salaries of the members of this House. And we see no reason why the argument should not apply, perhaps with some limitations, to the members of the Senate.

At the same time, your committee would desire to recognize the sacredness of any conscientious scruples any member here may have who fears that he is not earning the full amount of his salary.

For the relief of all such members we would suggest that there is now no law on our statute books which prevents such a member from covering back into the Treasury any portion of his salary, and thereby reducing the amount so that it will conform to the demands of his conscientious scruples in this regard. We do not see why this privilege may not be used as a perfect safety-valve for all such overpressed and troubled souls!

House Report No. 466, "Salaries of the Heads of Departments," 47th Congress, 1st session, Feb. 16, 1882.

95   House Report on the Reform of the Civil Service

December 12, 1882

A process for hiring federal government employees known as the spoils, or patronage, system began with the rise of popular political parties in the 1830s and reached its peak in the 1870s during the Grant administration. The political party in control rewarded those who had supported it by placing them in public office. Such persons were not hired on their merit, but through the patronage of the party in power. Civil servants were expected to contribute both time and money to protecting the political interests of their patrons. Political favors eventually went not just to top government officials but often included the hiring of tradesmen and janitors.

In 1865 Representative Thomas A. Jenckes (R-R.I.) introduced a bill that would reform civil service jobs so that government employees would be chosen on merit rather than partisan political affiliation. Jenckes's bill required that job seekers would take a competitive examination and enter at the lowest position. Many in Congress were loathe to accept Jenckes's bill, afraid that the new guidelines would undercut their ability to maintain political power.

The idea of civil service reform gained strength with each new scandal in the post-Civil War years, sparked in part by reformers, intellectuals, and abolitionists looking for new causes in the wake of the abolition of slavery. The goal was to install in government service only "the best people"—those who had merit and not just political connections. By the early 1880s the movement boasted a large, effective Civil Service Reform Organization, which had grown in influence during the Hayes administration. The size of the federal civil service also became a cause of concern. In 1871 there were approximately 50,000 federal employees. The number increased to 100,000 by 1881. The reform movement got an unsuspected boost when President James A. Garfield was assassinated in 1881 by a disgruntled government job seeker.

This excerpt from the House Committee on Reform in the Civil Service outlined the main problems of the patronage system and offered a moderate introduction of reforms that took a middle path between those who wanted massive changes and a complete overhaul of the way government employees were hired and those who were opposed to civil service reform. The Civil Service Reform Act, known as the Pendleton Act, after its chief sponsor, Senator George Hunt Pendleton (D-Ohio), passed Congress just months after this House report (see document 96).

The Committee on Reform in the Civil Service, to whom was referred the bill H.R. 6919, and sundry other bills on the same subject, report herewith a substitute for the former, covering the subject presented by the various bills referred, and submit it to the consideration of the House.

The evils of the system of patronage in appointments to the civil service are admitted on all sides. The methods by which they are to be remedied are in dispute, and are as numerous as the shades of opinion on the subject in the country at large. They cover the whole range from life tenure of appointees to removals at the will of the appointing power, from appointments at will with patronage to appointments irrespective of location, of only the most learned who shall apply and whose qualifications shall be determined by an independent board to be created for the purpose of ascertaining those having the highest attainments.

The committee believe that no bill based on either extreme method can pass the House. They report a bill that pursues a middle course, after the application of which to the departments affected by it, it can be better known how much further it will be both safe and expedient to go. If adopted it is believed it will wholly and absolutely cure most of the evils of political patronage by members of Congress, and also the pressure of political assessments on the civil service by party organizations. It this were all, it would be much to accomplish.

The bill, however, goes much further. It provides for examinations to show veritable fitness for the appointment in question by local boards away from the personal pressure of executive authority. It preserves the right of recognition of appointments in all parts of the United States subject only to undoubted qualification in the candidate presenting himself. Once appointed, promotion is to be made by competitive examination. It prohibits during tenure of office, except for specified causes. Your committee is agreed there should be a fixed tenure, but divided as to the length of the term.

The principle features of the bill are as follows:

Original appointments to be on probation, and after an independent examination showing absolute fitness for place.

Promotions by competitive examination. All final appointments for fixed term.

No removals except for specified causes, verified by a board, the majority of whom are selected from outside the department in question, or for discontinuance of the office.

Right to a continuance for another term after the first on condition of faithful service. Officers appointed by the President and confirmed by the Senate are not to be removed during their term as fixed by law except on written report showing unfitness, signed by the chief executive of the department and approved by the President.

Giving the same term to collectors of internal revenue as now fixed for other like officers.

No solicitations or recommendations to offices in question by members of Congress or United State Judges, unless on written request for information from appointing authority.

No requests in writing or in print from any member of Congress or political committee to be addressed to them for political contributions, and no requests from any person for a particular sum, or percentage.

Violation of these prohibitions to be a punishable misdemeanor. An examination under the direction of the State Department, and a term of six years for United States consuls and for secretaries of legations, during which no removals except for unfitness, to be specifically reported by the Secretary of State and approved by the President.

There is no provision in the bill touching appointment and removal of postmasters receiving a compensation less than $1,000 per annum. In attempting to provide an extension of the same provisions to include them the committee is confronted by difficulties apparently insurmountable. These postmasters, a very numerous body, generally furnish their own rooms and pay their own rent. In most cases a change of location by order of the department involves a change of postmaster, whose office is in his own house or store. He cannot follow the office. In the rapid development west of the Alleghanies, offices must be moved conveniently to railroad stations and other new centers where business concentrates. Star routes are discontinued and changed; post-offices must change with them. We can formulate no rule to meet the variety of cases. A rule applicable to a region where centers of population do not change, and lines of communication are complete, would be totally inapplicable to a region where all is new and changing; a small difference in distance of location saves or involves the expense of the carrier to the department.

The only rule, perhaps, which can be universally applied is the simple declaration that no postmaster shall be removed for political reasons, a rule so liable to abuse that the committee hesitates to adopt it.

There are also other classes of officers not so numerous as those provided for, like special agents of the different departments, where knowledge of men, and of the particular business to be supervised by them, is the most essential qualification. They are the eyes and ears of the department in the country at large. The chief executive of the department or bureau, it seems to us, must have the liberty of the selection to be made, as they so essentially concern the integrity and success of his administration. Nor do the committee deem it necessary to assume that when Congress shall have declared a far-reaching principle of general reform in the civil service, the chief executive of a department will necessarily be the enemy of its application in his jurisdiction. We rather assume that, finding in the law the spirit of reform everywhere, the very fact that some discretion is left to him in its application will bind alike his discretion and his honor to follow in all his action the path of reform; not only his

honor, and the public welfare, but also his own comfort in administration will compel him to that line of duty, and to the retention of a faithful officer in the service.

Conscious as we are of the difficulties surrounding the question, and of the fact that this measure will not meet extreme views on either side, we still report it as the most acceptable basis of agreement, and one requiring least sacrifice of opposing methods of legislative action.

Rash and excessive innovations, required perhaps by a perfect theory, but not founded on experience with public affairs, are far more likely to derange the public service than improve it.

Your committee report the bill, not as a perfect system which will require neither extension nor amendment in the future; not as embodying all that various members of the committee would desire now; but a bill which, if adopted, will crystallize a large improvement in political action, check arbitrary official dispositions, relieve members of Congress of onerous, and most frequently ineffective, labors, which prevent due attention to legislative duty, and will elevate the tone of political life in the United States. This it will do without diminishing the efficiency of the service, while it increases its independence and honor.

House of Representatives, Committee on Reform of the Civil Service, *Report No. 1826*, 47th Congress, 2d session, Dec. 12, 1882, 1–3.

96   The Civil Service Reform Act

January 16, 1883

The Civil Service Reform Act, often referred to as the Pendleton Act (named after its chief sponsor, Democratic senator George Hunt Pendleton of Ohio), is a sweeping, far-reaching law that transformed the civil service from a corrupt system of patronage to one of increasing professionalism. It has had a major impact in removing politics from the workplace of the bulk of federal employees. Its passage was the result of reform agitation begun shortly after the Civil War (see document 95). The act expanded the merit system and marked the beginning of a regular professional civil service free of direct and blatant political influence.

This act still forms the basis of the civil service system of the federal government, although it has undergone several major revisions since its passage in 1883.

CHAP. 27—AN ACT TO REGULATE AND IMPROVE THE CIVIL SERVICE OF THE UNITED STATES.

Be it enacted by the Senate and House of Representatives of the United States of America in Congress assembled, That the President is authorized to appoint, by and with the advice and consent of the Senate, three persons, not more than two

of whom shall be adherents of the same party, as Civil Service Commissioners, and said three commissioners shall constitute the United States Civil Service Commission. Said commissioners shall hold no other official place under the United States.

The President may remove any commissioner; and any vacancy in the position of commissioner shall be so filled by the President, by and with the advice and consent of the Senate, as to conform to said conditions for the first selection of commissioners.

The commissioners shall each receive a salary of three thousand five hundred dollars a year. And each of said commissioners shall be paid his necessary traveling expenses incurred in the discharge of his duty as a commissioner.

SEC. 2. That it shall be the duty of said commissioners:

FIRST. To aid the President, as he may request, in preparing suitable rules for carrying this act into effect, and when said rules shall have been promulgated it shall be the duty of all officers of the United States in the departments and offices to which any such rules may relate to aid, in all proper ways, in carrying said rules, and any modifications thereof, into effect.

SECOND. And, among other things, said rules shall provide and declare, as nearly as the conditions of good administration will warrant, as follows:

First, for open, competitive examinations for testing the fitness of the applicants for the public service now classified hereunder. Such examinations shall be practical in their character, and so far as may be shall relate to those matters which will fairly test the relative capacity and fitness of the persons examined to discharge the duties of the service into which they seek to be appointed.

Second, that all the offices, places, and employments so arranged or to be arranged in classes shall be filled by selections according to grade from among those graded highest as the results of such competitive examinations.

Third, appointments to the public service aforesaid in the departments at Washington shall be apportioned among the several States and Territories and the District of Columbia upon the basis of population as ascertained at the last preceding census. Every application for an examination shall contain, among other things, a statement, under oath, setting forth his or her actual bona fide residence at the time of making the application, as well as how long he or she has been a resident of such place.

Fourth, that there shall be a period of probation before any absolute appointment or employment aforesaid.

Fifth, that no person in the public service is for that reason under any obligations to contribute to any political fund, or to render any political service, and that he will not be removed or otherwise prejudiced for refusing to do so.

Sixth, that no person in said service has any right to use his official authority or influence to coerce the political action of any person or body.

Seventh, there shall be non-competitive examinations in all proper cases before the commission, when competent persons do not compete, after notice has been given of the existence of the vacancy, under such rules as may be prescribed by the commissioners as to the manner of giving notice.

Eighth, that notice shall be given in writing by the appointing power to said commission of the persons selected for appointment or employment from among those who have been examined, of the place of residence of such persons, of the rejection of any such persons after probation, of transfers, resignations, and removals, and of the date thereof, and a record of the same shall be kept by said commission. And any necessary exceptions from said eight fundamental provisions of the rules shall be set forth in connection with such rules, and the reasons therefor shall be stated in the annual reports of the commission.

THIRD. Said commission shall, subject to the rules that may be made by the President, make regulations for, and have control of, such examinations, and, through its members or the examiners, it shall supervise and preserve the records of the same; and said commission shall keep minutes of its own proceedings.

FOURTH. Said commission may make investigations concerning the facts, and may report upon all matters touching the enforcement and effects of said rules and regulations, and concerning the action of any examiner or board of examiners hereinafter provided for, and its own subordinates, and those in the public service, in respect to the execution of this act.

FIFTH. Said commission shall make an annual report to the President for transmission to Congress, showing its own action, the rules and regulations and the exceptions thereto in force, the practical effects thereof, and any suggestions it may approve for the more effectual accomplishment of the purposes of this act.

SEC. 3. That said commission is authorized to employ a chief examiner, a part of whose duty it shall be, under its direction, to act with the examining boards, so far as practicable, whether at Washington or elsewhere, and to secure accuracy, uniformity, and justice in all their proceedings, which shall be at all times open to him. The chief examiner shall be entitled to receive a salary at the rate of three thousand dollars a year, and he shall be paid his necessary traveling expenses incurred in the discharge of his duty. The commission shall have a secretary, to be appointed by the President, who shall receive a salary of one thousand six hundred dollars per annum. It may, when necessary, employ a stenographer, and a messenger, who shall be paid, when employed, the former at the rate of one thousand six hundred dollars a year, and the latter at the rate of six hundred dollars a year. The commission shall, at Washington, and in one or more places in each State and Territory where examinations are to take place, designate and select a suitable number of persons, not less than three, in the official service of the United States, residing in said State or Territory, after consulting the head of the department or office in which such persons serve, to be members of boards of examiners, and may at any time substitute any other person in said service living in such State or Territory in the place of any one so selected. Such boards of examiners shall be so located as to make it reasonably convenient and inexpensive for applicants to attend before them; and where there are persons to be examined in any State or Territory, examinations shall be held therein at least twice in each year. It shall be the duty of the collector, postmaster, and other officers of the United States, at any place outside the District of Columbia where examinations are directed by the President or by said board to be held, to allow the reasonable use of the public buildings for holding such examinations, and in all proper ways to facilitate the same.

SEC. 4. That it shall be the duty of the Secretary of the Interior to cause suitable and convenient rooms and accommodations to be assigned or provided, and to be furnished, heated, and lighted, at the city of Washington, for carrying on the work of said commission and said examinations, and to cause the necessary stationery and other articles to be supplied, and the necessary printing to be done for said commission.

SEC. 5. That any said commissioner, examiner, copyist, or messenger, or any person in the public service who shall willfully and corruptly, by himself or in co-operation with one or more other persons, defeat, deceive, or obstruct any person in respect of his or her right of examination according to any such rules or regulations, or who shall willfully, corruptly, and falsely mark, grade, estimate, or report upon the examination or proper standing of any person examined hereunder, or aid in so doing, or who shall willfully and corruptly make any false representations concerning the same or concerning the person examined, or who shall willfully and corruptly furnish to any person any special or secret information for the purpose of either improving or injuring the prospects or chances of any person so examined, or to be examined, being appointed, employed, or promoted, shall for each such offense be deemed guilty of a misdemeanor, and upon conviction thereof, shall be punished by a fine of not less than one hundred dollars, nor more than one thousand dollars, or by imprisonment not less than ten days, nor more than one year, or by both such fine and imprisonment.

Sec. 6. That within sixty days after the passage of this act it shall be the duty of the Secretary of the Treasury, in as near conformity as may be to the classification of certain clerks now existing under the one hundred and sixty-third section of the Revised Statutes, to arrange in classes and several clerks and persons employed by the collector, naval officer, surveyor, and appraisers, or either of them, or being in the public service, at their respective offices in each customs district where the whole number of said clerks and persons shall be all together as many as fifty. And thereafter, from time to time, on the direction of the President, said Secretary shall make the like classification or arrangement of clerks and persons so employed, in connection with any said office or offices, in any other customs district. And, upon like request, and for the purposes of this act, said Secretary shall arrange in one or more of said classes, or of existing classes, any other clerks, agents, or persons employed under his department in any said district not now classified; and every such arrangement and classification upon being made shall be reported to the President.

Second. Within said sixty days it shall be the duty of the Postmaster-tion, [sic, Postmaster General] to separately arrange in classes the several clerks and persons employed, in the public service, at each post-office, or under any postmaster of the United States, where the whole number of said clerks and persons shall together amount to as many as fifty. And thereafter, from time to time, on the direction of the President, it shall be the duty of the Postmaster-General to arrange in like classes the clerks and persons so employed in the postal service in connection with any other post-office; and every such arrangement and classification upon being made shall be reported to the President.

Third. That from time to time said Secretary, the Postmaster-General, and each of the heads of departments mentioned in the one hundred and fifty-eighth section of the Revised Statutes, and each head of an office, shall, on the direction of the President, and for facilitating the execution of this act, respectively revise any then existing classification or arrangement of those in their respective departments and offices, and shall, for the purposes of the examination herein provided for, include one or more of such classes, so far as practicable, subordinate places, clerks, and officers in the public service pertaining to their respective departments not before classified for examination.

Sec. 7. That after the expiration of six months from the passage this act no officer or clerk shall be appointed, and no person shall be employed to enter or be promoted in either of the said classes now existing, or that may be arranged hereunder pursuant to said rules, until he has passed an examination, or is shown to be specially exempted from such examination in conformity herewith. But nothing herein contained shall be construed to take from those honorably discharged from the military or naval service any preference conferred by the seventeen hundred and fifty-fourth section of the Revised Statutes, nor to take from the President any authority not inconsistent with this act conferred by the seventeen hundred and fifty-third section of said statues; nor shall any officer not in the executive branch of the government, or any person merely employed as a laborer or workman, be required to be classified hereunder; nor, unless by direction of the Senate, shall any person who has been nominated for confirmation by the Senate be required to be classified or to pass an examination.

Sec. 8. That no person habitually using intoxicating beverages to excess shall be appointed to, or retained in, any office, appointment, or employment to which the provisions of this act are applicable.

Sec. 9. That whenever there are already two or more members of a family in the public service in the grades covered by this act, no other member of such family shall be eligible to appointment to any of said grades.

Sec. 10. That no recommendation of any person who shall apply for office or place under the provisions of this act which may be given by any Senator or member of the House of Representatives, except as to the character or residence of the applicant, shall be received or considered by any person concerned in making any examination or appointment under this act.

Sec. 11. That no Senator, or Representative, or Territorial Delegate of the Congress, or Senator, Representative, or Delegate elect, or any officer or employee of either of said houses, and no executive, judicial, military, or naval officer of the United States, and no clerk or employee of any department, branch or bureau of the executive, judicial, or military or naval service of the United States, shall, directly or indirectly, solicit or receive, or be in any manner concerned in soliciting or receiving, any assessment, subscription, or contribution for any political purpose whatever, from any officer, clerk, or employee of the United States, or any department, branch, or bureau thereof, or from any person receiving any salary or compensation from moneys derived from the Treasury of the United States.

Sec. 12. That no person shall, in any room or building occupied in the discharge of official duties by any officer or employee of the United States mentioned in this act, or in any navy-yard, fort, or arsenal, solicit in any manner whatever, or receive any contribution of money or any other thing of value for any political purpose whatever.

Sec. 13. No officer or employee of the United States mentioned in this act shall discharge, or promote, or degrade, or in manner change the official rank or compensation of any other officer or employee, or promise or threaten so to do, for giving or withholding or neglecting to make any contribution of money or other valuable thing for any political purpose.

SEC. 14. That no officer, clerk, or other person in the service of the United States shall, directly or indirectly, give or hand over to any other officer, clerk, or person in the service of the United States, or to any Senator or Member of the House of Representatives, or Territorial Delegate, any money or other valuable thing on account of or to be applied to the promotion of any political object whatever.

SEC. 15. That any person who shall be guilty of violating any provision of the four foregoing sections shall be deemed guilty of a misdemeanor, and shall, on conviction thereof, be punished by a fine not exceeding five thousand dollars, or by imprisonment for a term not exceeding three years, or by such fine and imprisonment both, in the discretion of the court.

Approved, January sixteenth, 1883.

Statutes at Large, 22 (1881–1883), 47th Congress, 2d session, Jan. 16, 1883, 403–407.

97 Woodrow Wilson on the U.S. Senate

1885

When the future president of the United States, Woodrow Wilson, was a graduate student at Johns Hopkins University, he wrote a study of how Congress operates entitled Congressional Government. *Published in January 1885, the book became an instant success and helped convince the young Wilson that he wanted to do more than study and teach about government. He wanted to become a politician.*

Congressional Government *has remained in print for more than a century and is still considered an important text on the workings of Congress. It has become one of the most frequently quoted books on Congress. Wilson saw Congress as the most important branch of government. He considered the constitutional checks and balances between the branches of government to be superficial. To Wilson the national government was more important than the states and Congress was more important that the executive and judicial branches. Wilson was influenced strongly by his study of the British Parliament through the works of British authorities. He believed the best system for the United States was a parliamentary system not unlike that of Great Britain. While he thought Congress superior to the other branches, this did not mean that he approved of the operations of the House and Senate. He believed that both bodies needed serious reform—a popular idea in the 1880s, when the federal government was undergoing changes in the wake of the Reconstruction era scandals (see documents 92, 95, 96).*

Wilson criticized the House and Senate for their inefficiency and their elaborate committee systems that worked mostly behind closed doors. He saw the House Speaker as an irresponsible autocrat with too much power. He described the Senate as devoid of the great leaders it had once produced, but praised the Senate for being an undemocratic check on the excesses of democracy.

*In the prefaces to later editions, especially the 15th edition in 1900, Wilson softened some of his harsher criticisms of Congress and admitted that Congress continued to change. Later he discovered from direct experience as president of the United States that the executive branch was more important than he earlier imagined it to be. Nonetheless, Wilson's views of Congress still maintain a pe-*culiar vitality, perhaps because we are always willing to be critical of Congress and because we always think it needs to be improved.*

In this excerpt on the U.S. Senate, Wilson strikes a chord not unlike that of James Garfield (see document 91) in concluding that the caliber of the members of the Senate is only as good as the caliber of those in the House and in other elective offices. As Wilson put it, the Senate "contains the most perfect product of our politics, whatever that product may be." Ultimately, the voters make that decision.

The Senate of the United States has been both extravagantly praised and unreasonably disparaged, according to the predisposition and temper of its various critics. In the eyes of some it has a stateliness of character, an eminency of prerogative, and, for the most part, a wisdom of practice such as no other deliberative body possesses; whilst in the estimation of others it is now, whatever it may have been formerly, but a somewhat select company of leisurely "bosses," in whose companionship the few men of character and high purpose who gain admission to its membership find little that is encouraging and nothing that is congenial. Now of course neither of these extreme opinions so much as resembles the uncolored truth, nor can that truth be obtained by a judicious mixture of their milder ingredients. The truth is, in this case as in so many others, something quite commonplace and practical. The Senate is just what the mode of its election and the conditions of public life in this country make it. Its members are chosen from the ranks of active politicians, in accordance with a law of natural selection to which the state legislatures are commonly obedient; and it is probable that it contains, consequently, the best men that our system calls into politics. If these best men are not good, it is because our system of government fails to attract better men by its prizes, not because the county affords or could afford no finer material.

It has been usual to suppose that the Senate was just what the Constitution intended it to be; that because its place in the federal system was exalted the aims and character of its members would naturally be found to be exalted as well; that because its term was long its foresight would be long also; or that because its election was not directly of the people demagogy would find no life possible in its halls. But the Senate is in fact, of course, nothing more than a part, though a considerable part, of the public service, and if the general conditions of that service be such as to starve statesmen and foster demagogues, the Senate itself will be full of the latter kind, simply because there are no others available. There cannot be a separate breed of public men reared specially for the Senate. It must be recruited from the lower branches of the representative system, of which it is only the topmost part. No stream can be purer than its sources. The Senate can have in it no better men than the best men of the House of Representatives; and if the House of Representatives attract to itself only inferior talent, the Senate must put up with the same sort. I think it safe to say, therefore, that, though it may not be as good as could be wished, the Senate is as good as it can be under the circumstances. It contains the most perfect product of our politics, whatever that product may be.

These, then, are the conditions of public life which make the House of Representatives what it is, a disintegrate mass of jarring elements, and the Senate what it is, a small, select, and leisurely House of Representatives. Or perhaps it would be nearer the whole truth to say that these are the circumstances and this the frame of government of which the two Houses form a part. Were the Senate not supplied principally by promotions from the House, it had, that is, a membership made up of men specially trained for its peculiar duties, it would probably be much more effective than it is in fulfilling the great function of instructive and business-like debate of public questions; for its duties are enough unlike those of the House to be called peculiar. Men who have acquired all their habits in the matter of dealing with legislative measures in the House of Representatives, where committee work is everything and public discussion nothing but "talking to the country," find themselves still mere declaimers when they get into the Senate, where no previous question utters its interrupting voice from the tongues of tyrannical committee-men, and where, consequently, talk is free to all. Only superior talents, such as very few men possess, could enable a Representative of long training to change his spots upon entering the Senate. Most men will not fit more than one sphere in life; and after they have been stretched or compressed to the measure of that one they will rattle about loosely or stick too tight in any other into which they may be thrust. Still, more or less adjustment takes place in every case. If a new Senator knock about too loosely amidst the free spaces of the rules of that august body, he will assuredly have some of his biggest comers knocked off and his angularities thus made smoother; if he stick fast amongst the dignified courtesies and punctilious observances of the upper chamber, he will, if he stick long enough, finally wear down to such a size, by jostling, as to attain some motion more or less satisfactory.

But it must be said, on the other hand, that even if the Senate were made up of something better than selections from the House, it would probably be able to do little more than it does in the way of giving efficiency to our system of legislation. For it has those same radical defects of organization which weaken the House. Its functions also, like those of the House, are segregated in the prerogatives of numerous Standing Committees. In this regard Congress is all of a piece. There is in the Senate no more opportunity than exists in the House for gaining such recognized party leadership as would be likely to enlarge a man by giving him a sense of power, and to steady and sober him by filling him with a grave sense of responsibility. So far as its organization controls it, the Senate, notwithstanding the one or two special excellences which make it more temperate and often more rational than the House, has no virtue which marks it as of a different nature. Its proceedings bear most of the characteristic features of committee rule. Its conclusions are suggested now by one set of its members, now by another set, and again by a third; an arrangement which is of course quite effective in its case, as in that of the House, in depriving it of that leadership which is valuable in more ways than in imparting distinct purpose to legislative action, because it concentrates party responsibility" attracts the best talents, and fixes public interest.

Some Senators are, indeed, seen to be of larger mental stature and built of stauncher moral stuff than their fellow members, and it is not uncommon for individual members to become conspicuous figures in every great event in the Senate's deliberations. The public now and again picks out here and there a Senator who seems to act and to speak with true instinct of statesmanship and who unmistakably merits the confidence of colleagues and of people. But such a man, however eminent, is never more than *a* Senator. No one is *the* Senator. No one may speak for his party as well as for himself; no, one exercises the special trust of acknowledged leadership. The Senate is merely a body of individual critics, representing most of the not very diversified types of a society substantially homogeneous; and the weight of every criticism uttered in its chamber depends upon the weight of the critic who utters it, deriving little if any addition to its specific gravity from connection with the designs of a purposeful party organization. I cannot insist too much upon this defect of congressional government, because it is evidently radical. Leadership with authority over a great ruling party is a prize to attract great competitors, and is in a free government the only prize that will attract great competitors.

Woodrow Wilson, *Congressional Government*, 15th ed. (Gloucester, Mass.: Peter Smith, 1973), 135–147. Original edition 1885.

98 Woodrow Wilson Describes the Role of the Speaker of the House

1885

In this excerpt from Woodrow Wilson's classic study of Congress, Congressional Government, *published in 1885 (see document 97 for background on the book), Wilson described the Speaker of the House with accuracy from the perspective of the 1880s, when House rules gave Speakers the power to appoint the standing committees. Wilson's observations about the Speaker's power would remain useful for another twenty-five years, when the power to appoint the members of committees was stripped from the Speaker's control in the revolt against Speaker Joseph G. Cannon (see document 107).*

One final observation about Congressional Government *can, perhaps, serve as an encouragement and also a warning to future congressional scholars. The book was published just weeks after Wilson's twenty-eighth birthday. He wrote it in less than a year. Most of the writing occurred in Baltimore, about forty miles from the Capitol. He wrote the book after extensive reading, but he had never been to Congress, never observed firsthand a session of Congress, and never attended a congressional committee meeting before he finished his book.*

It is highly interesting to note the extraordinary power accruing to Mr. Speaker through this pregnant prerogative of appointing the Standing Committees of the House. That power is, as it were, the central and characteristic inconvenience and anomaly of our constitutional system, and on that account excites both the curiosity and the wonder of the student of institutions. The most esteemed writers upon our Constitution have failed to observe, not only that the Standing Committees are the most essential machinery of our governmental system, but also that the Speaker of the House of Representatives is the most powerful functionary of that system. So sovereign is he within the wide sphere of his influence that one could wish for accurate knowledge as to the actual extent of his power. But Mr. Speaker's powers cannot be known accurately, because they vary with the character of Mr. Speaker. All Speakers have, of late years especially, been potent factors in legislation, but some have, by reason of greater energy or less conscience, made more use of their opportunities than have others.

The Speaker's privilege of appointing the Standing Committees is nearly as old as Congress itself. At first the House tried the plan of balloting for its more important Committees, ordering, in April, 1789, that the Speaker should appoint only those Committees which should consist of not more than three members; but less than a year's experience of this method of organizing seems to have furnished satisfactory proof of its impracticability, and in January, 1790, the present rule was adopted: that "All committees shall be appointed by the Speaker, unless otherwise specially directed by the House." The rules of one House of Representatives are not, however, necessarily the rules of the next. No rule lives save by biennial readoption. Each newly-elected House meets without rules for its governance, and amongst the first acts of its first session is usually the adoption of the resolution that the rules of its predecessor shall be its own rules, subject, of course, to such revisions as it may, from time to time, see fit to make. Mr. Speaker's power of appointment, accordingly, always awaits the passage of this resolution; but it never waits in vain, for no House, however foolish in other respects, has yet been foolish enough to make fresh trial of electing its Committees. That mode may do well enough for the cool and leisurely Senate, but it is not for the hasty and turbulent House.

It must always, of course, have seemed eminently desirable to all thoughtful and experienced men that Mr. Speaker should be no more than the judicial guide and moderator of the proceedings of the House, keeping apart from the heated controversies of party warfare, and exercising none but an impartial influence upon the course of legislation; and probably when he was first invested with the power of appointment it was thought possible that he could exercise that great prerogative without allowing his personal views upon questions of public policy to control or even affect his choice. But it must very soon have appeared that it was too much to expect of a man who had it within his power to direct affairs that he should subdue all purpose to do so, and should make all appointments with an eye to regarding every preference but his own; and when that did become evident, the rule was undoubtedly retained only because none better could be devised. Besides, in the early years of the Constitution the Committees were very far from having the power they now possess. Business did not then hurry too fast for discussion, and the House was in the habit of scrutinizing the reports of the Committees much more critically than it now pretends to do. It deliberated in its open sessions as well as in its private committee-rooms, and the functionary who appointed its committees was simply the nominator of its advisers, not, as is the Speaker of to-day, the nominor of its rulers.

It is plain, therefore, that the office of Speaker of the House of Representatives is in its present estate a constitutional phenomenon of the first importance, deserving a very thorough and critical examination. If I have succeeded, in what I have already said, in making clear the extraordinary power of the Committees in directing legislation, it may now go without the saying that he who appoints those Committees is an autocrat of the first magnitude. There could be no clearer proof of the great political weight of the Speaker's high commission in this regard than the keen strife which every two years takes place over the election to the speakership, and the intense interest excited throughout the country as to the choice to be made. Of late years, the newspapers have had almost as much to say about the rival candidates for that office as about the candidates for the presidency itself, having come to look upon the selection made as a sure index of the policy to be expected in legislation.

The Speaker is of course chosen by the party which commands the majority in the House, and it has sometimes been the effort of scheming, self-seeking men of that majority to secure the elevation of some friend or tool of their own to that office, from which he can render them service of the most substantial and acceptable sort. But, although these intrigues have occasionally resulted in the election of a man of insignificant parts and doubtful character, the choice has usually fallen upon some representative party man of well-known antecedents and clearly-avowed opinions; for the House cannot, and will not willingly, put up with the intolerable inconvenience of a weak Speaker, and the majority are urged by self-respect and by all the weightiest considerations of expediency, as well as by a regard for the interests of the public business, to place one of their accredited leaders in the chair. If there be differences of opinion within the party, a choice between leaders becomes a choice between policies and assumes the greatest significance. The Speaker is expected to constitute the Committees in accordance with his own political views, and this or that candidate is preferred by his party, not at all because of any supposed superiority of knowledge of the precedents and laws of parliamentary usage, but because of his more popular opinions concerning the leading questions of the day.

Mr. Speaker, too, generally uses his powers as freely and imperatively as he is expected to use them. He unhesitatingly acts as the legislative chief of his party, organizing the Committees in the interest of this or that policy, not covertly and on the sly, as one who does something of which he is ashamed, but openly and confidently, as one who does his duty. Nor does his official connection with the Committees cease upon their appointment. It is his care to facilitate their control of the business of the House, by recognizing during the consideration of a report only those members with whom the reporting committee-man has agreed to share his time, and by keeping all who address the House within the strictest letter of the rules as to the length of their speeches, as well as by enforcing all those other restrictions which forbid independent action on the part of individual members. He must see to it that the Committees have their own way. In so doing he is not exercising arbitrary powers which circumstances and the habits of the assembly enable him safely to arrogate; he is simply enforcing the plain letter and satisfying the evident spirit of the rules.

Woodrow Wilson, *Congressional Government*, 15th ed. (Gloucester, Mass.: Peter Smith, 1973), 83–86. Original edition 1885.

99   James Bryce on the U.S. House of Representatives

1888

Following a tour of this country in 1888, British scholar and diplomat James Bryce (1838–1922) wrote The American Commonwealth, *a magnificent study of the United States government. First published in 1893, it stands today as a classic study of government. Bryce set out to describe American government for his British readers, much as Alexis de Tocqueville had written earlier for a French audience (see document 57).*

Bryce brought to the task a keen, firsthand understanding of Parliament and a solid analytical eye in making comparisons between the American and British systems of government. Like an earlier English visitor, Charles Dickens (see document 61), Bryce described the air of confusion and clamor that greeted a visitor to the House chamber. Bryce found the House in the 1880s to be rambunctious and undisciplined in appearance, especially when compared to the relative stateliness and dignity of the Senate. Yet his analysis went deeper than mere appearances. He was fascinated by what he saw as a classless society and how the lack of class distinctions affected Congress. In one powerful and oft-quoted passage, Bryce said of the House: "This huge gray hall, filled with perpetual clamour, this multitude of keen and eager faces, this ceaseless coming and going of many feet, this irreverent public, watching from the galleries and forcing its way on to the floor, all speak to the beholder's mind of the mighty democracy, destined in another cen- *tury to form on half of civilized mankind, whose affairs are here debated. If the men are not great, the interests and the issues are vast and fateful. Here, as so often in America, one thinks rather of the future than of the present. Of what tremendous struggles may not this hall become the theatre in ages yet far distant, when the parliaments of Europe have shrunk to insignificance?"*

Bryce's accounts of the House and Senate (see also document 100) contrast nicely with Bryce's young American contemporary, Woodrow Wilson (see documents 97 and 98). Strangely enough, Wilson was more favorably inclined to see the American government transformed into a parliamentary system than was Bryce. Following the publication of American Commonwealth, *Bryce became widely respected in the United States. He served from 1907 to 1913 as the British ambassador to the United States.*

THE HOUSE AT WORK

AN Englishman expects to find his House of Commons reproduced in the House of Representatives. He has the more reason for this notion because he knows that the latter was modelled on the former, has borrowed many of its rules and technical expressions, and regards the procedure of the English chamber as a storehouse of precedents for its own guidance. The notion is delusive. Resemblances of course there are. But an English parliamentarian who observes the American House at work is more impressed by the points of contrast than by those of similarity. The life and spirit of the two bodies are wholly different.

The room in which the House meets is in the south wing of the Capitol, the Senate and the Supreme Court being lodged in the north wing. It is more than thrice as large as the English House of Commons, with a floor about equal in area to that of Westminster Hall, 139 feet long by 93 feet wide and 36 feet high. Light is admitted through the ceiling. There are on all sides deep galleries running backwards over the lobbies, and capable of holding two thousand five hundred persons. The proportions are so good that it is not till you observe how small a man looks at the farther end, and how faint ordinary voices sound, that you realize its vast size. The seats are arranged in curved concentric rows looking towards the Speaker, whose handsome marble chair is placed on a raised marble platform projecting slightly forward into the room, the clerks and the mace below in front of him, in front of the clerks the official stenographers, to the right the seat of the sergeant-at-arms. Each member has a revolving arm-chair, with a roomy desk in front of it, where he writes and keeps his papers. Behind these chairs runs a railing, and behind the railing is an open space into which some classes of strangers may be brought, where sofas stand against the wall, and where smoking is practised, even by strangers, though the rules forbid it.

When you enter, your first impression is of noise and turmoil, a noise like that of short sharp waves in a Highland loch, fretting under a squall against a rocky shore. The raising and dropping of desk lids, the scratching of pens, the clapping of hands to call the pages, keen little boys who race along the gangways, the pattering of many feet, the hum of talking on the floor and in the galleries, make up a din over which the Speaker with the sharp taps of his hammer, or the orators straining shrill throats, find it hard to make themselves audible. Nor is it only the noise that gives the impression of disorder. Often three or four members are on their feet at once, each shouting to catch the Speaker's attention. Others, tired of sitting still, rise to stretch themselves, while the Western visitor, long, lank, and imperturbable, leans his arms on the railing, chewing his cigar, and surveys the scene with little reverence. Less favourable conditions for oratory cannot be imagined, and one is not surprised to be told that debate was more animated and practical in the much smaller room which the House formerly occupied.

Not only is the present room so big that only a powerful and well-trained voice can fill it, but the desks and chairs make a speaker feel as if he were addressing furniture rather than men, while of the members few seem to listen to the speeches. It is true that they sit in the House instead of running frequently out into the lobbies, but they are more occupied in talking or writing, or reading newspapers, than in attending to the debate. To attend is not easy, for only a shrill voice can overcome the murmurous roar; and one sometimes finds the newspapers in describing an unusually effective speech, observe that "Mr. So-and-So's speech drew listeners about him from all parts of the

House." They could not hear him where they sat, so they left their places to crowd in the gangways near him. "Speaking in the House," says an American writer, "is like trying to address the people in the Broadway omnibuses from the kerbstone in front of the Astor House. . . . Men of fine intellect and of good ordinary elocution have exclaimed in despair that in the House of Representatives the mere physical effort to be heard uses up all the powers, so that intellectual action becomes impossible. The natural refuge is in written speeches or in habitual silence, which one dreads more and more to break."

It is hard to talk calm good sense at the top of your voice, hard to unfold a complicated measure. A speaker's vocal organs react upon his manner, and his manner on the substance of his speech. It is also hard to thunder at an unscrupulous majority or a factious minority when they do not sit opposite to you, but beside you, and perhaps too much occupied with their papers to turn round and listen to you. The Americans think this an advantage, because it prevents scenes of disorder. They may be right; but what order gains oratory loses. It is admitted that the desk encourage inattention by enabling men to write their letters; but though nearly everybody agrees that they would be better away, nobody supposes that a proposition to remove them would succeed. So too the huge galleries add to the area the voice has to fill; but the public like them, and might resent a removal to a smaller room. The smoking shocks an Englishman, but not more than the English practice of wearing hats in both Houses of Parliament shocks an American. Interruption, cries of "Divide," interjected remarks, are not more frequent—when I have been present they seemed to be much less frequent—than in the House of Commons. Approval is expressed more charily, as is usually the case in America. Instead of "Hear, hear," there is a clapping of hands and hitting of desks. Applause is sometimes given from the galleries; and occasionally at the end of a session both the members below and the strangers in the galleries above have known to join in singing some popular ditty.

There is little good speaking. I do not mean merely that fine oratory, oratory which presents valuable thoughts in eloquent words is rare, for it is rare in all assemblies. But in the House of Representatives a set speech upon any subject of importance tends to become not an exposition or an argument but a piece of elaborate and high-flown declamation. Its author is often wise enough to send direct to the reporters what he has written out, having read aloud a small part of it in the House. When it has been printed *in extenso* in the *Congressional Record* (leave to get this done being readily obtained), he has copies struck off and distributes them among his constituents. Thus everybody is pleased and time is saved.

That there is not much good business debating, by which I mean a succession of comparatively short speeches addressed to a practical question, and hammering it out by the collision of mind with mind, arises not from any want of ability among the members, but from the unfavourable conditions under which the House acts. Most of the practical work is done in the standing committees, while much of the House's time is consumed in pointless discussions, where member after member delivers himself upon large questions, not likely to be brought to a definite issue. Many of the speeches thus called forth have a value as repertories of facts, but the debate as a whole is unprofitable and languid. On the other hand the five-minute debates which take place, when the House imposes that limit of time, in Committee of the Whole on the consideration of a bill reported from a standing committee, are often lively, pointed, and effective. The topics which excite most interest and are best discussed are those of taxation and the appropriation of money, more particularly to public works, the improvement of rivers and harbours, erection of Federal buildings, and so forth. This kind of business is indeed to most of its members the chief interest of Congress, the business which evokes the finest skill of a tactician and offers the severest temptations to frail conscience. As a theatre or school either of political eloquence or political wisdom, the House has been inferior not only to the Senate but to most European assemblies. Nor does it enjoy much consideration at home. Its debates are very shortly reported in the Washington papers as well as in those of Philadelphia and New York. They are not widely read except in very exciting times, and do little to instruct or influence public opinion.

This is of course only one part of a legislature's functions. An assembly may despatch its business successfully and yet shine with few lights of genius. But the legislation on public matters which the House turns out is scanty in quantity and generally mediocre in quality. What is more, the House tends to avoid all really grave and pressing questions, skirmishing round them, but seldom meeting them in the face or reaching a decision which marks an advance. If one makes this observation to an American, he replies that at this moment there are few such questions lying within the competence of Congress, and that in his country representatives must not attempt to move faster than their constituents. This latter remark is eminently true; it expresses a feeling which has gone so far that Congress conceives its duty to be to follow and not to seek to lead public opinion. The harm actually suffered so far is not grave. But the European observer cannot escape the impression that Congress might fail to grapple with a serious public danger, and is at present hardly equal to the duty of guiding and instructing the political intelligence of the nation.

In all assemblies one must expect abundance of unreality and pretence, many speeches obviously addressed to the gallery, many bills meant to be circulated but not to be seriously proceeded with. However, the House seems to indulge itself more freely in this direction than any other chamber of equal rank. Its galleries are large, holding 2500 persons. But it talks and votes, I will not say to the galleries, for the galleries cannot hear it, but as if every section of American opinion was present in the room. It adopts unanimously resolutions which perhaps no single member in his heart approves of, but which no one cares to object to, because it seems not worth while to do so. This habit sometimes exposes it to a snub, such as that administered by

Bismarck in the matter of the resolution of condolence with the German Parliament on the death of Lasker [Eduard Lasker (1829–1884)], a resolution harmless indeed but so superfluous as to be almost obtrusive. A practice unknown to Europeans is of course misunderstood by them, and sometimes provokes resentment. Bills are frequently brought into the House proposing to effect impossible objects by absurd means, which astonish a visitor, and may even cause disquiet in other countries, while few people in American notice them, and no one thinks it worth while to expose their emptiness. American statesmen keep their pockets full of the loose cash of empty compliments and pompous phrases, and become so accustomed to scatter it among the crowd that they are surprised when a complimentary resolution or electioneering bill, intended to humour some section of opinion at home, is taken seriously aboard. The House is particularly apt to err in this way, because having no responsibility in foreign policy, and little sense of its own dignity, it applies to international affairs the habits of election meetings.

Watching the House at work, and talking to the members in the lobbies, and Englishman naturally asks himself how the intellectual quality of the body compares with that of the House of Commons. His American friends have prepared him to expect a marked inferiority. They are fond of running down congressmen. The cultivated New Englanders and New Yorkers do this out of intellectual fastidiousness, and in order to support the role which they unconsciously fall into when talking to Europeans. The rougher Western men do it because they would not have congressmen either seem or be better in any way than themselves, since that would be opposed to republican equality. A stranger who has taken literally all he hears is therefore surprised to find so much character, shrewdness, and keen though limited intelligence among the representatives. Their average business capacity is not below that of members of the House of Commons. True it is that great lights, such as usually adorn the British chamber, are absent: true also that there are fewer men who have received a high education which has developed their tastes and enlarged their horizons. The want of such men seriously depresses the average. It is raised, however, by the almost total absence of two classes hitherto well represented in the British Parliament, the rich, dull parvenu, who has bought himself into public life, and the perhaps equally unlettered young sporting or fashionable man who, neither knowing nor caring anything about politics, has come in for a county or (before 1885) a small borough, on the strength of his family estates. Few congressmen sink to so low an intellectual level as these two sets of persons, for congressmen have almost certainly made their way by energy and smartness, picking up a knowledge of men and things "all the time." In respect of width of view, of capacity for penetrating thought on political problems, representatives are scarcely above the class from which they came, that of second-rate lawyers or farmers, less often merchants or petty manufacturers. They do not pretend to be statesmen in the European sense of the word, for their careers, which have made them smart and active, have given them little opportunity for acquiring such capacities. As regards manners they are not polished, because they have not lived among polished people; yet neither are they rude, for to get on in American politics one must be civil and pleasant. The standard of parliamentary language, and of courtesy generally, has tended to rise during the last few decades; and scenes of violence and confusion such as occasionally convulse the French chamber, and were common in Washington before the War of Secession, are now rare.

On the whole, the most striking difference between the House of Representatives and European popular assemblies is its greater homogeneity. The type is marked; the individuals vary little from the type. In Europe all sorts of persons are sucked into the vortex of the legislature, nobles and landowners, lawyers, physicians, business men, artisans, journalists, men of learning, men of science. In American five representatives out of six are politicians pure and simple, members of class as well defined as any one of the above-mentioned European peoples; and this characteristic is palpable in its legislatures.

Uneasy lies the head of an ambitious congressman, for the chances are at least even that he will lose his seat at the next election. It was observed in 1788 that half of the members of each successive State legislature were new members and this average has been usually maintained in the Federal legislature, rather less than half keeping their seats from one Congress to the next. In England the proportion of members re-elected from Parliament to Parliament is much higher. Any one can see how much influence this constant change in the composition of the American House must have upon its legislative efficiency.

I have kept to the last the feature of the House which Europeans find the strangest.

It has parties, but they are headless. There is neither Government nor Opposition; neither leaders nor whips. No person holding any Federal office or receiving any Federal salary, can be a member of it. That the majority may be and often is opposed to the President and his cabinet, does not strike Americans as odd, because they proceed on the theory that the legislative ought to be distinct from the executive authority. Since no minister sits, there is no official representative of the party which for the time being holds the reins of the executive government. Neither is there any opinions expressed in debate are followed, so there are none whose duty it is to bring up members to vote, to secure a quorum, to see that people know which way the bulk of the party is going.

So far as the majority has a chief, that chief is the Speaker, who has been chosen by them as their ablest and most influential man; but as the Speaker seldom joins in debate (though he may do so by leaving the chair, having put some one else in it), the chairman of the most important committee, that of Ways and Means, enjoys a sort of eminence, and comes nearer than any one else to the position of leader of the House. But his authority does not always enable him to secure co-operation for debate among the best speakers of his party, putting up now one now another, after the fashion of an English prime minister, and thereby guiding the general course of the discussion.

The minority do not formally choose a leader, nor is there usually any one among them whose career marks him out as practically the first man, but the person whom they have put forward as their party candidate for the Speakership, giving him what is called "the complimentary nomination," has a sort of vague claim to be so regarded. This honour amounts to very little. In the forty-eighth Congress the Speaker of the last preceding Congress received such a complimentary nomination from the Republicans against Mr. Carlisle, whom the Democratic majority elected. But the Republicans immediately afterwards refused to treat their nominee as leader, and lift him on some motion which he made, in a ridiculously small minority. Of course when an exciting question comes up, some man of marked capacity and special knowledge will often become virtually leader, in either party, for the purposes of the debates upon it. But he will not necessarily command the votes of his own side.

How then does the House work?

If it were a Chamber, like those of France or Germany, divided into four or five sections of opinion, none of which commands a steady majority, it would not work at all. But parties are few in the United States, and their cohesion tight. There are usually two only, so nearly equal in strength that the majority cannot afford to dissolve into groups like those of France. Hence upon all large national issues whereon the general sentiment of the party has been declared, both the majority cannot afford to dissolve into groups like those of France. Hence upon all large national issues, whereon the general sentiment of the party has been declared, both the majority and the minority know how to vote, and vote solid.

If the House were, like the English House of Commons, to some extent an executive as well as a legislative body—one by whose co-operation and support the daily business of government had to be carried on—it could not work without leaders and whips. This it is not. It neither creates, nor controls, nor destroys, the Administration, which depends on the President, himself the offspring of a direct popular mandate.

"Still," it may be replied, "the House has important functions to discharge. Legislation comes from it. Supply depends on it. It settles the tariff, and votes money for the civil and military services, besides passing measures to cure the defects which experience must disclose in the working every government, every system of jurisprudence. How can it satisfy these calls upon it without leaders and organization?"

To a European eye, it does not seem to satisfy them. It votes the necessary supplies, but not wisely, giving sometimes too much, sometimes too little money, and taking no adequate securities for the due application of the sums voted. For many years past it has fumbled over both the tariff problem and the currency problem. It produces few useful laws and leaves on one side many grave practical questions. An Englishman is disposed to ascribe these failures to the fact that as there are no leaders, there is no one responsible for the neglect of business, the miscarriage of bills, the unwise appropriation of public funds. "In England," he says, "the ministry of the day bears the blame of whatever goes wrong in the House of Commons. Having a majority, it ought to be able to do what it desires. If it pleads that its measures have been obstructed, and that it cannot under the faulty procedure of the House of Commons accomplish what it seeks, it is met, and rushed, by the retort that in such case it ought to have the procedure changed. What else is its majority good for but to secure the efficiency of Parliament? In America there is no person against whom similar charges can be brought. Although conspicuous folly or perversity on the part of the majority tends to discredit them collectively with the public, and may damage them at the next presidential or congressional election, still responsibility, to be effective, ought to be fixed on a few conspicuous leaders. Is not the want of such men, men to whom the country can look, and whom the ordinary members will follow, the cause of some of the faults which are charged its ignoble surrenders to some petty clique, its deficient sense of dignity, its shrinking from troublesome questions, its proclivity to jobs?"

Two American statesmen to whom such a criticism was submitted, replied as follows: "It is not for want of leaders that Congress has forborne to settle the questions mentioned, but because the division of opinion in the country regarding them has been faithfully reflected in Congress. The majority has not been strong enough to get its way; and this has happened, not only because abundant opportunities for resistance arise from the methods of doing business, but still more because no distinct impulse or mandate towards any particular settlement of these questions has been received from the country. It is not for Congress to go faster than the people. When the country knows and speaks its mind, Congress will not fail to act." The significance of this reply lies in its pointing to a fundamental difference between the conception of the respective positions and duties of a representative body and of the nation at large entertained by Americans, and the conception which has hitherto prevailed in Europe. Europeans have thought of a legislature as belonging to the governing class. In America there is no such class. Europeans think that the legislature ought to consist of the best men in the country, Americans that it should be a fair average sample of the country. Europeans think that it ought to lead the nation, Americans that it ought to follow the nation.

Without some sort of organization, an assembly of three hundred and fifty men would be a mob, so necessity has provided in the system of committees a substitute for the European party organization. This system will be explained in the next chapter; for the present it is enough to observe that when a matter which has been (as all bills are) referred to a committee, come up in the House to be dealt with there, the chairman of the particular committee is treated as a leader *pro hac vice,* and member who knew nothing of the matter are apt to be guided by his speech or his advice given privately. If his advice is not available, or is suspected because he belongs to the opposite party, they seek direction from the member in charge of the bill, if he belongs to their own party, or from some other member of the committee, or from some friend whom they trust. When a debate arises unexpectedly on a question of importance, members are often puzzled how to vote. The division being taken, they get some on to move a call of yeas and nays, and while this slow process goes on, they scurry about asking advice as to their action, and give their votes on the second calling over if not ready on the first. If the issue is one of serious consequence to the party, a recess is demanded by the majority, say for two hours. The House then adjourns, each party "goes into caucus" (the Speaker possibly announcing the fact), and debates the matter with closed doors. Then the House resumes, and each party votes solid according to the determination arrived at in caucus. In spite of these expedients, surprises and scratch votes are not uncommon.

I have spoken of the din of the House of Representatives, of its air of restlessness and confusion, contrasting with the staid gravity of the Senate, of the absence of dignity both in its proceedings and in the bearing and aspect of individual members. All these things notwithstanding, there is something impressive about it, something not unworthy of the continent for which it legislates.

This huge gray hall, filled with perpetual clamour, this multitude of keen and eager faces, this ceaseless coming and going of many feet, this irreverent public, watching from the galleries and forcing its way on to the floor, all speak to the beholder's mind of the mighty democracy, destined in another century to form on half of civilized mankind, whose affairs are here debated. If the men are not great, the interests and the issues are vast and fateful. Here, as so often in America, one thinks rather of the future than of the present. Of what tremendous struggles may not this hall become the theatre in ages yet far distant, when the parliaments of Europe have shrunk to insignificance?

James Bryce, *The American Commonwealth,* 2 vols. (New York: Macmillan, 1901), vol. 1: 142–153. Original edition 1893.

100   James Bryce on the U.S. Senate

1888

When British scholar James Bryce turned his attention to the Senate (see document 99 for background on Bryce and his book American Commonwealth), *he, like other observers of Congress, found activity in the Senate to have a greater appearance of refinement when compared with the often rambunctious behavior of House members. But he went beyond this conventional analysis, based largely on appearances. He observed that those who were ashamed of the behavior in the House and saw the Senate "as a sort of Olympian dwelling-place of statesmen and sages" needed to be aware that it "is nothing of the kind. It is a company of shrewd and vigorous men who have fought their way to the front by the ordinary methods of American politics, and on many of whom the battle has left its stains. There are abundant opportunities for intrigue in the Senate, because its most important business is done in the secrecy of the committee rooms or of executive session; and many senators are intriguers."*

Writing at a time when the Senate was still elected not directly by the people but by state legislatures, Bryce found that the body's virtues rested on the fact that it represented the choice of the people (albeit indirectly) and was responsible to the people. He also thought its small size was important in forming the character of the Senate. "A small body," Bryce wrote, "educates its members better than a large one, because each member has more to do, sooner masters the business not only of his committee but of the whole body, feels a livelier sense of the significance of his own action in bringing about collective action." Bryce's description of the Senate, written more than a century ago, still provides plenty of thoughtful analysis of use to modern observers.

THE SENATE: ITS WORKING AND INFLUENCE

The Americans consider the Senate one of the successes of their Constitution, a worthy monument of the wisdom and foresight of its founders. Foreign observers have repeated this praise, and have perhaps, in their less perfect knowledge, sounded it even more loudly.

The aims with which the Senate was created, the purposes it was to fulfill, are set forth, under the form of answers to objections, in five letters (1xi.-1xv.), all by Alexander Hamilton, in the *Federalist*. These aims were the five following:

To conciliate the spirit of independence in the several States, by giving each, however small, equal representation with every other, however large, in one branch of the national government.

To create a council qualified, by its moderate size and the experience of its members, to advise and check the President in the exercise of his powers of appointing to office and concluding treaties.

To restrain the impetuosity and fickleness of the popular House, and so guard against the effects of gusts of passion or sudden changes of opinion in the people.

To provide a body of men whose greater experience, longer term of membership, and comparative independence of popular election, would make them an element of stability in the government of the nation, enabling it to maintain its character in the eyes of foreign States, and to preserve a continuity of policy at home and abroad.

To establish a Court proper for the trial of impeachments, a remedy deemed necessary to prevent abuse of power by the executive.

All of these five objects have been more or less perfectly attained; and the Senate has acquired a position in the government which Hamilton scarcely ventured to hope for. In 1788 he wrote: "Against the force of the immediate representatives of the people nothing will be able to maintain even the constitutional authority of the Senate, but such a display of enlightened policy, and attachment to the public good, as will divide the House of Representatives the affections and support of the entire body of the people themselves."

It may be doubted whether the Senate has excelled the House in attachment to the public good; but it has certainly shown greater capacity for managing the public business, and has won the respect, if not the affections, of the people, by its sustained intellectual power.

The *Federalist* did not think it necessary to state, nor have Americans generally realized, that this masterpiece of the Constitution-makers was in fact a happy accident. No one in the Convention of 1787 set out with the idea of such a Senate as ultimately emerged from their deliberations. It grew up under the hands of the Convention, as the result of the necessity for reconciling the conflicting Demands of the large and small States. The concession of equal representation in the Senate induced the small States to accept the principal of representation according to population in the House of Representatives; and a series of compromises between the advocates of popular power, as embodied in the House, and those of monarchical power, as embodied in the President, led to the allotment of attributes and functions which have made the Senate what it is. When the work which they had almost unconsciously perfected was finished, the leaders of the Convention perceived its excellence, and defended it by arguments in which we feel the note of sincere conviction. Yet the conception they formed of it differed from the reality which has been evolved. Although they had created it as a branch of the legislature, they thought of it as being first and foremost a body with executive functions. And this, at first, it was. The traditions of the executive councils, which advised the governors of the colonies while still subject to the British Crown, clung about the Senate and affected the minds of the senators. It was small body, originally of twenty-six, even in 1810 of thirty-four members only, a body not ill fitted for executive work. Its members regarding themselves as a sort of congress of ambassadors from their respective States, were accustomed to refer for advice and instructions each to his State legislature. So late as 1828, a Senator after arguing strongly against a measure declared that he would nevertheless vote for it, because he believed is State to be in its favor. For the first five years of its existence, the Senate sat with closed doors, occupying itself chiefly with the confidential business of appointments and treaties, and conferring in private with the ministers of the President. Not till 1816 did it create, in imitation of the House, those Standing Committees which the experience of the House had shown to be, in bodies where the executive ministers not sit, the necessary organs for dealing with legislative body, not less active and powerful than the other branch of Congress, is the result of a long process of evolution, a process possible (as will be more fully explained hereafter) even under the rigid Constitution of the United States, because the language of the sections which define the competence of the Senate is wide and general. But in gaining legislative authority, it has not lost its executive functions, although those which relate to treaties are largely exercised on the advice of the standing Committee on Foreign Relations. And as respects these executive functions it stands alone in the world. No European state, no British colony, entrusts to an elective assembly that direct participation in executive business which the Senate enjoys.

What is meant by saying that the Senate has proved a success?

It has succeeded by effecting that chief object of the Fathers of the Constitution, the creation of a center of gravity in the government, an authority able to correct and check on the one hand the "democratic recklessness" of the House, on the other the "monarchical ambition" of the President. Placed between the two, it is necessarily the rival and often the opponent of both. The House can accomplish nothing without its concurrence. The President can be checkmated by its resistance. These are, so to speak, negative or prohibitive successes. It has achieved less in the way of positive work, whether of initiating good legislation or of improving the measures which the House sends it. But the whole scheme of the American Constitution tends to put stability above activity, to sacrifice the productive energies of the bodies it creates to their power of resisting changes in the general fabric of the government. The Senate has succeeded in making itself eminent and respected. It has drawn the best talent of the nation, so far as that talent flows to politics, into its body, has established an intellectual supremacy, has furnished a vantage ground from which men of ability may speak with authority to their fellow-citizens.

To what causes are these successes to be ascribed? Hamilton assumed that the Senate would be weaker than the House of Representatives, because it would not so directly spring from, speak for, be looked at by, the people. This was a natural view, especially as the analogy between the position of the Senate towards the House of Representatives in America, and that of the House of Lords towards the House of Commons in Great Britain, an analogy constantly present to the men of 1787, seemed to suggest that the larger and more popular chamber must dwarf and overpower the smaller one. But the Senate has proven no less strong, and more intellectually influential, than its sister House of Congress. The analogy was unsound, because the British House of Lords is hereditary and Senate representative. In these days no hereditary assembly, be its members ever so able, ever so wealthy, ever so socially powerful, can speak with the authority which belongs to those who speak for the people. Mirabeau's famous words in the Salle des Menus at Versailles, "We are here by the will of the people, and nothing but bayonets shall send us hence," express the whole current of modern feeling. Now the Senate, albeit not chosen by direct popular election, does represent the people; and what it may lose through not standing in immediate contact with the masses, it gains in representing such ancient and powerful commonwealths as the States. A senator from New York or Pennsylvania speaks for, and is responsible to, millions of men. No wonder he has an authority beyond that of the long-descended nobles of Prussia, or the peers of Britain whose possessions stretch over whole counties.

This is the first reason for the strength of the Senate, as compared with the upper chambers of other countries. It is built on a wide and solid foundation of choice by the people and consequent responsibility to them. A second cause is to be found in its small size. A small body educates its members better than a large one, because each member has more to do, sooner masters the business not only of his committee but of the whole body, feels a livelier sense of the significance of his own action in bringing about collective action. There is less disposition to abuse the freedom of debate. Party spirit may be as intense as in great assemblies, yet it is mitigated by the wish to keep on friendly terms with those whom, however much you dislike them, you have constantly to meet, and by the feeling of a common interest in sustaining the authority of the body. A senator soon gets to know each of his colleagues—they were originally only twenty-five—and what each of them thinks of him; he becomes sensitive to their opinion; he is less inclined to pose before them, however he may pose before the public. Thus the Senate formed, in its childhood, better habits in discussing and transacting its business than would be formed by a large assembly; and these habits its mature age retains. Its comparative permanence has also worked for good. Six years, which seem a short term in Europe, are in America a long term when compared with the two years for which the House of Representatives and the Assemblies of nearly all the States are elected, long also when compared with the swiftness of change in American politics. A senator has the opportunity of thoroughly learning his work, and of proving that he has learnt it. He becomes slightly more independent of his constituency, which in America, where politicians catch at every passing breeze of opinion, is a clear gain. He is relieved a little, though only a little, of the duty of going on the stump in his State, and maintaining his influence among local politicians there.

The smallness and the permanence of the Senate have however another important on its character. They contribute to one main cause of its success, the superior intellectual quality of its members. Every European who has described it, has dwelt upon the capacity of those who compose it, and most have followed. Tocqueville in attributing this capacity to the method of double election. The choice of senators by the State legislature is supposed (but I think erroneously) to have proved a better means than direct choice by the people of discovering and selecting the fittest men. I have already remarked that the legislatures now do little more than register and formally complete a choice already made by the party managers, and perhaps ratified in the party convention, and am inclined to believe that direct popular election would work better. But apart from this recent development, and reviewing the whole hundred years' history of the Senate, the true explanation of its capacity is to be found in the superior attraction which it has for the ablest in most ambitious men. A senator has more power than a member of the House, more dignity, a longer term of service, a more independent position. Hence every Federal politician aims at senatorship, and looks on the place of Representative as a stepping-stone to what may fairly be called an Upper House, because it is the House to which Representatives seek to mount. It is no more surprising that the average capacity of the Senate should surpass that of the House, than that the average cabinet minister of Europe should be abler than the average member of the legislature.

What is more, the Senate so trains its members as to improve their political efficiency. Several years of service in a small body, with important and delicate executive work, are worth twice as many years of jostling in the crowd of representatives at the other end of the Capitol. If the Senate does not find the man who enters it already superior to the average of Federal politicians, it makes him superior. But natural selection, as has been said, usually seats upon its benches the best ability of the country that has flowed into political life, and would do so no less wore the election in form a direct one by the people at the polls.

Most of the leading men of the last sixty years have sat in the Senate, and in it were delivered most of the famous speeches which illumine, though too rarely, the wearisome debates over State rights and slavery from 1825 till 1860. One of these debates, that in the beginning of 1830, which called forth Daniel Webster's majestic defense of the Constitution, was long called par excellence "the great debate in the Senate."

Of the 76 senators who sat in the forty-eighth Congress (1883–85) 31 had sat in the other House of Congress, and 49 had served in State legislatures. In the fifty-second Congress (1891–93) out of 88 senators, 34 had sat in the House of Representatives, and 50 in State legislatures. Many had been judges or State governors; many had sat in State conventions. Nearly all had held some public function. A man must have had considerable experience of affairs, and of human nature in its less engaging aspects, before he enters this august conclave. but experience is not all gain. Practice makes perfect in evil-doing no less then in well-doing. The habits of local politics and of work in the House of Representatives by which the senators have been trained, while they develop shrewdness and quickness in all characters, tell injuriously on characters of the meaner sorts, leaving men's views narrow, and giving them a taste as well as a talent for intrigue.

The chamber in which the Senate meets is rectangular, but the part occupied by the seats is semicircular in form, the Vice-President of the United States, who acts as presiding officer, having his chair on a marble dais, slightly raised, in the center of the chord, with the senators all turned towards him as they sit in curving rows, each in a arm-dash chair, with a desk in front of it. The floor is about as large as the whole superficial area of the British House of Commons, but as there are great galleries on all four sides, running back over the lobbies, the upper part of the chamber and its total air-space much exceeds that of the English house. One of these galleries is appropriated to the President of the United States; the others to ladies, diplomatic representatives, the press, and the public. Behind the senatorial chairs and desks there is an open space in to which strangers can be brought by the Senators, who sit an talk on the sofas there placed. Members of foreign legislatures are allowed access to this outer "floor of the Senate." There is, especially when the galleries are empty, a slight echo in the room, which obliges most speakers to strain their voices. Two or three pictures on the walls somewhat relieve the cold tone of the chamber, with its marble platform and sides unpierced by windows, for the light enters through glass compartments in the ceiling.

A senator always addresses the Chair "Mr. President," and refers to other senators by their States, "the senator from Ohio," "the senator from Tennessee." When two senators rise at the same moment, the Chair calls on one, indicating him by his State, "the senator from Minnesota has the floor." Senators of the Democratic party apparently always have sat on the right of the chair, Republican senators on the left; but, as already explained, the parties do not face one another. The impression which the place makes on a visitor is one of business-like gravity, a gravity which though plain is dignified. It has the air not so much of a popular assembly as of a diplomatic congress. The English House of Lords, with it fretted roof and windows rich with the figures of departed kings, it majestic throne, its Lord Chancellor in his wig on the woolsack, its benches of lawn-sleeved bishops, its bar where the Commons throng at a great debate, is not only more gorgeous and picturesque in externals, but appeals far more powerfully to the historical imagination, for it seems to carry the middle ages down into the modern world. The Senate is modern, severe, and practical. So, too, few debates in the Senate rise to the level of the best debates in the English chamber. But the Senate seldom wears that air of listless vacuity in superannuated indolence which the House of Lords presents on all but a few nights of every session. The faces are keen and forcible, as of men who have learned to know the world, and have much to do in it; in the place seems consecrated to great affairs.

As might be expected from the small number of the audience, as well as from its character, discussions in the Senate are apt to be sensible and practical. Speeches are shorter and less fervid than those made in the House of Representatives. The least useful debates are those on show-days, when a series of set discourses are delivered on some prominent question. Each senator brings down and fires off in the air, a carefully-prepared oration, which may have little bearing on what has gone before. In fact the speeches are made not to convince the assembly,— no one dreams of that,—but to keep a man's opinions before the public and sustain his fame. The question at issue is sure to have been already settled, either in a committee or in a "caucus" of the party which commands the majority, so that these long and sonorous harangues are mere rhetorical thunder addressed to the nation outside.

The Senate now contains many men of great wealth. Some, an increasing number, are senators because they are rich; a few are rich because they are senators; while in the remaining cases the same talents which have won success in law or commerce have brought their possessor to the top in politics also. The great majority are or have been lawyers; some regularly practice before the Supreme Court. Complaints are occasionally leveled against the aristocratic tendencies which wealth is supposed to have bred, in sarcastic references are made to new avenues of Washington. While admitting that there is more sympathy for the capitalist class among these rich men than there would be in a Senate of poor men, I must add that the Senate is far from being a class body like the upper houses of England or Prussia or Spain or Denmark. It is substantially representative, by its composition as well as by legal delegation, of all parts of American society; it is far too dependent, and far too sensible that it is dependent, upon public opinion, to dream of legislating in the interest of the rich. The senators, however, indulge some social pretensions. They are the nearest approach to an official aristocracy that has yet been seen in America. They and their wives are allowed precedence at private entertainments, as well as public occasions, over members of the House, and of course over private citizens. Jefferson might turn in his grave if he knew of such an attempt to introduce European distinctions of rank into his democracy; yet as the office is temporary and the rank vanishes with the office, these pretensions are harmless; it is only the universal social quality of the country that makes noteworthy. Apart from such petty advantages, the position of a senator, who can count on re-election, is the most desirable in the political world of America. It gives as much power and influence as a man need desire. It secures for him the ear of the public. It is more permanent than the presidency or a cabinet office, requires less labour, involves less vexation, though still great vexation, by importunate office-seekers.

European writers on America have been too much inclined to idealized the Senate. Admiring its structure and function, they have assumed that the actors must be worthy of their parts. They have been encouraged in this tendency by the language of many Americans. As the Romans were never tired if repeating that the ambassador of Pyres had called the Roman senate an assembly of kings, so Americans of refinement, who are ashamed of the turbulent House of Representatives, have been wont to talk of the Senate as a sort of Olympian dwelling-place of statesmen and sages. It is nothing of the kind. It is a company of shrewd and vigorous men who have fought their way to the front by the ordinary methods of American politics, and on many of whom the battle has left its stains. There are abundant opportunities for intrigue in the Senate, because its most important business is done in the secrecy of the committee rooms or of executive session; and many senators are intriguers. There are opportunities for missing senatorial powers. Scandals have sometimes arisen from the practice of employing as counsel before the Supreme Court, senators whose influence has contributed the appointment or confirmation of the judges. There are opportunities for corruption and blackmailing, of which unscrupulous men are well known to take advantage. Such men are fortunately few; but considering how demoralized are the legislatures of a few States, their presence must be looked for; and the rest of the Senate, however it may blush for them, obliged to work with them and treat them as equals. The contagion of political vice is nowhere so swiftly potent as in legislative bodies, because you cannot taboo a man who has got a vote. You may loathe him personally, but he is the people's choice. He has a right to share in the government of the country; you are grateful to him when he saves you on a critical division; you discover that "he is not such a bad fellow when one knows him"; People remark that he gives good dinners, or has an agreeable wife; and so it goes on till falsehood and knavery are covered under the cloak of party loyalty.

As respects ability, the Senate cannot be profitably compared with the English House of Lords, because that assembly consists of some fifteen eminent and as many ordinary men attending regularly, with a multitude of undistinguished persons who rarely appear, and take no share in the deliberations. Setting the Senate beside the House of Commons, the average natural capacity of its ninety members is not above that of the ninety best men in the English House. There is more variety of talent in the latter, and a greater breadth of culture. On the other hand, the Senate excels in legal knowledge as well as in practical shrewdness. The House of Commons contains more men who could give a good address on a literary or historical subject; the Senate, together with some eminent lawyers, has more who could either deliver a rousing popular harangue or manage the business of a great trading company, these being the forms of capacity commonest among congressional politicians. An acute American observer [Bryce refers here to Woodrow Wilson's *Congressional Government;* see documents 97 and 98] says (writing in 1885):

"The Senate is just what the mode of its election and the conditions of public life in this country make it. Its members are chosen from the ranks of active politicians, in accordance with a law of natural selection to which the State legislatures are commonly obedient; and it is probable that it contains, consequently the best men that our system calls into politics. If these best men are not good, it is because our system of government fails to attract better men by its prizes, not because the country affords or could afford no finer material. The Senate is in fact, of course, nothing more than a part, though a considerable part, of the public service; and if the general conditions of that service be such as to starve statesmen and foster demagogues, the Senate itself will be full of the latter kind, simply because there are no others available."

This judgment is severe, but not unjust. Whether the senators of today are inferior in ability and integrity to those of fifty, thirty, twenty years ago, is not easy to determine. But it must be admitted, however regretfully, that they are less independent, less respected by the people, less influential with the people, than were their predecessors; and their wealth, which has made them fear the reproach of wanting popular sympathies, may count for something in this decline.

The place which the Senate holds in the constitutional system of America cannot be fully appreciated till the remaining parts of that system have been described. This much, however, be claimed for it, that it has been and is still, though perhaps less formerly, a steadying and moderating power. One cannot say in the language of European politics that it has represented aristocratic principles, or even conservative principles. Each of the great historic parties has in turn commanded a majority in it, and the difference between their strength has during the last decade been slight. On none of the great issues that have divided the nation has the Senate been, for any long period, decidedly opposed to the other House of Congress. It showed no more capacity than the House for grappling with the problems of slavery extension. It was scarcely less ready than the House to strain the Constitution by supporting Lincoln in the exercise of the so-called war powers, or subsequently by cutting down presidential authority in the struggle between Congress and Andrew Johnson, though it refused to convict him when impeached by the House. All the fluctuations of public opinion tell upon it, nor does it venture, any more than the House, to confront a popular impulse, because it is, equally with the House, subject to the control of the great parties, which seek to use while they obey the dominant sentiment of the hour.

But the fluctuations of opinion tell on it less energetically than on the House of Representatives. They reach it more slowly and gradually, owing to the system which renews it by one-third every second year, so that it sometimes happens that before the tide has risen to the top of the flood in the Senate it has already begun to ebb in the country. The Senate has been a stouter bulwark against agitation, not merely because a majority of the senators have always four years of membership before them, within which period public feeling may change, but also because the senators have been individually stronger men than the representatives. They are less democratic, not in opinion, but in temper, because they are more self-confident, because they have more to lose, because experience has taught them how fleeting a thing popular sentiment is, and how useful a thing continuity in policy is. The Senate has therefore usually kept its head better than the House of Representatives. It has expressed more adequately the judgment, as contrasted with the emotion, of the nation. In this sense it does constitute a "check and balance" in the Federal government. Of the three great functions which the Fathers of the Constitution meant it to perform, the first, that of securing the rights of the smaller States, is no longer important; while the second, that of advising or controlling the Executive in appointments as well as in treaties, has given rise to evils almost commensurate with its benefits. But the third duty is still discharged, for "the propensity of a single and numerous assembly to yield to the impulse of sudden and violent passions" is frequently, though not invariably, restrained.

James Bryce, *The American Commonwealth,* 2 vols. (New York: Macmillan, 1901), vol. 1: 111–123. Original edition 1893.

101   Speaker Thomas B. Reed Changes the Rules of the House

January 29, 1890

Thomas Brackett Reed (1839–1902), a Republican from Maine, was Speaker of the House from 1889 to 1891 and from 1895 to 1899. He was one of the most powerful and colorful speakers in the history of the House of Representatives. Reed's greatest legacy was his revision of House rules, which consolidated power in the hands of the Speaker. His rules package, known as "Reed's Rules," strengthened the ability of the majority party to carry out its own legislative agenda. Criticism of Reed's Rules came mostly from the Democrats, the minority party at the time. They called Reed a dictator and a "czar" for running roughshod over their rights as members of the House. Supporters of Reed hailed him for bringing efficiency to the House and eliminating long-standing practices that impeded the ability of the majority party to work its will. Reed once said that the only function the minority members in the House served was to draw their paychecks and help make a quorum.

One of the most dramatic changes in the rules under Reed's leadership was the elimination of the so-called disappearing quorum. In order for the House to conduct business, it must have a quorum of members present. One long-standing method of obstructing the proceedings of the House was for members to fail to answer their names during a roll call to determine a quorum. Even if members were present in the chamber when their names were called, they would not be counted unless they verbally answered. Reed put an end to this practice by ruling that if members were present in the chamber they could be counted for the purposes of a quorum even if they did not answer the roll call.

Reed first applied the rule against the disappearing quorum on January 29, 1890, during debate on a report from the Committee on Elections regarding a contested election that had awarded the contested seat to the Republican. The Democrats, as part of their objection to the procedure, chose to obstruct the proceedings by failing to answer to the quorum call. When the quorum count was taken, 163 members answered, two short of a quorum, even though there were more than 163 members on the floor at the time.

This excerpt from the Congressional Record *begins with the discussion of the quorum call underway, just minutes before Speaker Reed would say: "The Chair directs the Clerk to record the following names of members present and refusing to vote." Once this happened, members of the Democratic Party objected strenuously to this departure from the rules of the House. Some members tried to leave the chamber, while others hid under their desks. The shouting and confusion on the floor made it difficult for the House to proceed. The most telling moment in the debate that clearly demonstrated the common sense of Reed's ruling, even though it was branded as a revolutionary rules change, was when Democrat James B. McCreary of Kentucky said to Speaker Reed: "I deny your right, Mr. Speaker, to count me as present, and I desire to read from the parliamentary law on that subject." To which Reed replied: "The Chair is making a statement of the fact that the gentleman from Kentucky is present. Does he deny it?" Through all the objections and the pandemonium on the floor, Reed held firm. The House continued to boil over this issue for two more weeks. On February 14, 1890, the House formally approved Reed's ruling regarding the disappearing quorum.*

Among the chief participants in this debate on the Republican side, in addition to Speaker Reed, were Charles H. Cowles of North Carolina, John Dalzel of Pennsylvania, and John Lockwood Wilson of Washington. The Democrats, objecting to the ruling of the Speaker, included Charles F. Crisp of Georgia, Clifton Rodes Breckinridge of Arkansas, William C. Breckinridge of Kentucky, Richard P. Bland of Missouri, James B. McCreary of Kentucky, George W. Cooper of Indiana, and Benjamin A. Enloe of Tennessee.

In the next Congress, when Democrats again regained the majority, the new Speaker, Charles Crisp, who had protested against the abolition of the disappearing quorum, suddenly found it to his advantage to leave this "revolutionary" rule in place.

. . . .

Mr. COWLES. I desire to withdraw my vote. I believe I am recorded as voting in the negative.

Mr. BAYNE. I object, Mr. Speaker.

Mr. TAYLOR, of Illinois, addressed the Chair.

The SPEAKER. The gentleman from Illinois.

Mr. COWLES. Does the Speaker rule on my request?

The SPEAKER. The gentleman's vote can not be withdrawn now. The gentleman from Illinois.

Mr. COWLES. I appeal from the decision of the Chair.

Mr. TAYLOR, of Illinois. I ask whether I am recorded as voting?

Mr. COWLES. Mr. Speaker—

The SPEAKER. The gentleman from Illinois is not recorded. The Clerk will call his name.

The name of Mr. Taylor, of Illinois, being called, he voted "ay."

Mr. ROGERS. I desire to withdraw my vote.

Mr. DALZELL, Mr. BAYNE, and others objected.

Mr. ROGERS. Does the Chair rule—

The SPEAKER. The Chair does not rule at all.

Mr. ROGERS. Then I direct the Clerk to take my name off.

Mr. DALZELL. The Clerk has no right to do it.

Mr. Wilson, of Washington, addressed the Chair.

The SPEAKER. The gentleman from Washington.

Mr. WILSON, of Washington. I desire to have my vote recorded.

The SPEAKER having directed the name of Mr. Wilson, of Washington, to be called, he voted "ay."

The SPEAKER. The Clerk will recapitulate the vote.

Mr. SWEENY. I raise a point of order upon the request of the gentleman on the other side, on the ground that it requires the consent of the House, or its affirmative action, to do what is termed correcting the record.

The SPEAKER. The gentleman will suspend for a moment. The Clerk will recapitulate the vote.

During the recapitulation of the vote by the Clerk the name of Mr. Cowles was called.

Mr. COWLES. Mr. Speaker, I desire to withdraw my vote.

Mr. FARQUHAR. I object.

Mr. COVERT (when his name was called). I desire to change my vote.

The SPEAKER. The gentleman from New York desires to change his vote.

Mr. COVERT. Let my name be called.

Mr. Covert's name was called.

Mr. COVERT. I will vote later. [Laugher and applause on the Democratic side of the House.]

Mr. ROGERS. I see the Clerk still recapitulates my name. I ask to withdraw my vote.

The SPEAKER. The gentleman from Arkansas withdraws his vote.

Mr. COWLES. I desire to change my vote.

The SPEAKER. On this question the yeas are 161, the nays 2.

Mr. CRISP. No quorum.

The SPEAKER. The Chair directs the Clerk to record the following names of members present and refusing to vote: [Applause on the Republican side.]

Mr. CRISP. I appeal—[applause on the Democratic side]—I appeal from the decision of the Chair.

The SPEAKER. Mr. Blanchard, Mr. Bland, Mr. Blount, Mr. Breckinridge, of Arkansas, Mr. Breckinridge of Kentucky.

Mr. BRECKINRIDGE, of Kentucky. I deny the power of the Speaker and denounce it as revolutionary. [Applause on the Democratic side of the House, which was renewed several times.]

Mr. BLAND. Mr. Speaker—[Applause on the Democratic side.]

The SPEAKER. The House will be in order.

Mr. BLAND. Mr. Speaker, I am responsible to my constituents for the way in which I vote, and not to the Speaker of this House. [Applause.]

The SPEAKER. Mr. Brookshire, Mr. Bullock, Mr. Bynum, Mr. Carlisle, Mr. Chipman, Mr. Clements, Mr. Clunie, Mr. Compton.

Mr. COMPTON. I protest against the conduct of the Chair in calling my name.

The SPEAKER (proceeding). Mr. Covert, Mr. Crisp, Mr. Culberson of Texas [hisses on the Democratic side], Mr. Cummings, Mr. Edmunds, Mr. Enloe, Mr. Fithian, Mr. Goodnight, Mr. Hare, Mr. Hatch, Mr. Hayes.

Mr. HAYES. I appeal from any decision, so far as I am concerned.

The SPEAKER (continuing). Mr. Holman, Mr. Lawler, Mr. Lee, Mr. McAdoo, Mr. McCreary.

Mr. MCCREARY. I deny your right, Mr. Speaker, to count me as present, and I desire to read from the parliamentary law on that subject.

The SPEAKER. The Chair is making a statement of the fact that the gentleman from Kentucky is present. Does he deny it? [Laughter and applause on the Republican side.]

Mr. MCCREARY. The ruling of the Chair the other day contained the following statement [cries of "Order!"]:

This House, then, is governed by the general parliamentary law such as has been established in the same manner that the common law of England was established, by repeated decisions and the general acquiescence of the people in a system which governs all ordinary assemblies.

May's Parliamentary Practice states as follows:

A call is of little avail in taking the sense of the House, as there is no compulsory process by which members can be obliged to vote.

[Cries of "Order!" and applause.]

The SPEAKER. The gentlemen will be in order. [Laughter.] The Chair is proceeding in an orderly manner. [Renewed laughter and applause on the Republican side.] Mr. Montgomery, Mr. Moore, of Texas, Mr. Morgan.

Mr. MORGAN. I beg leave to protest against this as unconstitutional and revolutionary.

The SPEAKER (continuing). Mr. Outhwaite.

Mr. OUTHWAITE. [Cries of "Regular Order!"] I wish to state to the Chair that I was not present in the House when my name was called, and the Chair is therefore stating what is not true. [Applause and cries of "Order!"] It is not for the Chair to say whether I shall vote or not or whether I shall answer to my name when it is called. [Laughter and applause.]

The SPEAKER (continuing). Mr. Owens of Ohio, Mr. O'Ferrall.

Mr. O'FERRALL. I protest against the assumption of power by the Speaker.

Mr. COOPER, of Indiana. I ask by what right or by what rule of parliamentary law the Speaker of this House declares men present and voting who have not voted?

The SPEAKER. The Chair does not declare men voting who have not voted.

Mr. CRISP. I appeal from the decision—

Mr. BRECKINRIDGE, of Kentucky. It is disorderly; the House has ordered a vote, and the Speaker has no more right to state that fact from the Speaker's chair than he would have from the floor of the House. It is a disorderly proceeding on the part of the Speaker. [Applause on the Democratic side.]

The SPEAKER. Mr. Stewart of Texas, Mr. Tillman—

Mr. COOPER, of Indiana. Will the Chair answer the parliamentary inquiry?

The SPEAKER. Mr. Turner of Georgia—

Mr. COOPER, of Indiana. I demand an answer to the parliamentary inquiry. By what rule of parliamentary law or by what right does the Chair undertake to direct that men shall be recorded as present and voting?

The SPEAKER. The Chair will answer the gentleman, if he will be in order, in due time.

Mr. CRISP. I appeal form the decision of the Chair.

The SPEAKER. The Chair will now make a statement to the House, and the matter can proceed in orderly fashion if gentlemen will only be in order.

Mr. ENLOE. But the Speaker has undertaken to state who were present and not voting. Now, the Speaker has furnished only a partial list. There were other gentlemen present. The Speaker says he states the facts. Let him state all the facts.

The SPEAKER. The Chair, will, in due time, allow any member an appeal to the House.

Mr. COOPER, of Indiana. I demand an answer to the parliamentary inquiry.

The SPEAKER. The gentleman must not be disorderly.

MR. WHEELER, OF Alabama. Must the representatives of the people remain silent in their seats and see the Speaker of this House inaugurate revolution?

MR. CRISP. I understood the Speaker had concluded his statement.

The SPEAKER. The Chair had not concluded the statement when the gentleman from Georgia rose.

Mr. CRISP. If the Speaker has not completed his statement now, I trust that I will be recognized for the purpose of taking an appeal.

The SPEAKER. The Chair will state the question.

The question of quorum was raised, and the Chair treats this subject in orderly fashion, and will submit his opinion to the House, which, if not acquiesced in by the House, can be overruled on an appeal taken from the decision.

Mr. CRISP. By brute force.

Mr. COOPER, of Indiana. Mr. I insist upon my appeal.

The SPEAKER. The gentleman must not mistake his situation. He is not to compel the Chair to do certain things. The Chair must proceed in regular order, and the gentleman as a member of this body will undoubtedly permit the Chair to proceed.

Mr. ENLOE. If the gentleman is not in order, will the Chair state what rule is being violated?

Mr. COOPER, of Indiana. Do I understand that the Chair is about to answer my parliamentary inquiry?

The SPEAKER. There is no occasion for disorder.

Mr. COOPER, of Indiana. I understood the Chair—

The SPEAKER. The occupant of the Chair does not know what the gentleman understood, but if the House will be in order the Chair will proceed in an orderly way.

Mr. BLOUNT. Mr. Speaker, may I make an inquiry?

The SPEAKER. Will the gentleman from Georgia permit the Chair to proceed?

Mr. BLOUNT. But the inquiry I wished to make was in view of the Statement of the Chair.

I understood the Chair to say that the Chair was stating a fact. I had understood that the Chair had directed the names to be put on the roll by the Clerk.

The SPEAKER. Put on the record by the Clerk. They will be recorded as present.

Mr. FLOWER. I desire to be recorded as present and not voting.

Mr. COWLES. Mr. Speaker—

The SPEAKER. The Chair will proceed in order if gentlemen will take their seats.

Mr. COWLES. Will the Speaker permit me—

The SPEAKER. The yea-and-nay vote has been reported by the Clerk as follows—

Mr. COWLES. Mr. Speaker—

The SPEAKER. Will the gentleman have the kindness to take his seat? If he will do so, the Chair will be greatly obliged.

The Clerk announces the members voting in the affirmative as 161 and 2 who voted in the negative. The Chair thereupon, having seen the members present, having heard their names called in their presence, directed the call to be repeated, and, gentlemen not answering when thus called, the Chair directed a record of their names to be made showing the fact of their presence as bearing upon the question which has been raised, namely, whether there is a quorum of this House present to do business or not, according the Constitution of the United States; and accordingly that question is now before the House, and the Chair purposes to give a statement accompanied by a ruling, from which an appeal can be taken if any gentleman is dissatisfied therewith.

Mr. CRISP. In advance I enter an appeal. [Laughter and applause on the Democratic side.]

The SPEAKER. There has been for some considerable time a question of this nature raised in very many parliamentary assemblies. There has been a great deal of doubt, especially in this body, on the subject, and the present occupant of the chair well recollects a proposition or suggestion made ten years ago by a member from Virginia, Mr. John Randolph Tucker, an able constitutional lawyer as well as an able member of this House. That matter was somewhat discussed and a proposition was made with regard to putting it into the rules. The general opinion which seemed to prevail at that time was that it was inexpedient so to do, and some men had grave doubts whether it was proper to make such an amendment to the rules as would count the members present and not voting as a part of the quorum as well as those present and voting. The evils which resulted from the other course were not then as apparent, and no such careful study had been given to the subject as has been given to it since.

That took place in the year 1880. Since then there had been various arguments and various decisions by various eminent gentlemen upon the subject, and these decisions have very much cleared up the question, which renders it much more apparent what the rule is. One of the first places in which the question was raised was in the senate of the State of New York. The present governor of New York was the presiding officer and upon him devolved a duty similar to that which has devolved upon me today. He met that duty in precisely the same manner. The question there raised was the necessity, under their constitution, of three-fifths constituting a quorum for the passage of certain bills, and he held that that constitutional provision as to a quorum was entirely satisfied by the presence of the members, even if they did not vote, and accordingly he directed the recording officer of the senate to put down the names as a part of the record of the transaction; that is, to put down the names of the members of the senate who were present and refused to vote, in precisely the manner in which the occupant of this chair has directed the same thing to be done. That decision would be regarded as in no sense partisan, at least the Chair cites it.

There has also been a decision in the State of Tennessee, where the provision of the law require a quorum to consist of two-thirds. The house has ninety-nine members, of which two-thirds is sixty-six. In the Legislature of 1885 the house had ninety-nine members, of which two-thirds was sixty-six. A registration bill was pending which was objected to by the Republican members of the house. Upon the third reading the Republicans refused to vote, whereupon the speaker, a member of the other party, directed the clerk to count as present those not voting and declared the bill as passed upon this reading.

These two decisions, made, the first, in 1883, and, the other, in the year 1885, seem to the present occupant of the chair to cover the ground; but there is an entirely familiar process which every old member will recognize, which, in the opinion of the Chair, is incontestable evidence of the recognition at all times of the right to regard members present as constituting a part of a quorum. It has been almost an every-day occurrence at certain stages of the session for votes to be announced by the Chair containing obviously and mathematically no quorum; yet if the point was not made the bill has always been declared to be passed. Now, that can only be upon a very distinct basis, and that is, that everybody present silently agreed to the fact that there was a quorum present, while the figures demonstrated no quorum voting.

Mr. SPRINGER. We did not silently do it.

The SPEAKER. There is no ground by which under any possibility such a bill could be passed constitutionally, unless the presence of a quorum is inferred. It is inferred from the fact that no one raised the question, and the presence was deemed enough.

Now, all methods of determining a vote are of equal value. The count by the Speaker or Chairman and the count by tellers or a count by the yeas and nays are all of them of equal validity. The House has a right, upon the call of one-fifth of the members, to have a yea-and-nay vote, and then upon that the question is decided; but the decision in each of the other cases is of precisely the same validity.

Again, it has always been the practice in parliamentary bodies of this character, and especially in the Parliament of Great Britain, for the Speaker to determine the question whether there is or is not a quorum present by count. It is a question that is a determination of the actual presence of a quorum, and the determination of that is intrusted to the presiding officer in almost all instances. So that when a question is raised whether there is a quorum or not, without special arrangement for determining it, it would be determined on a count by the presiding officer. Again, there is a provision in the Constitution which declares that the House may establish rules for compelling the attendance of members. If members can be present and refuse to exercise their function, to wit, not be counted as a quorum, that provision would seem to be entirely nugatory. Inasmuch as the Constitution only provides for their attendance, that attendance is enough. If more was needed the Constitution would have provided for more.

. . . .

Congressional Record, House, 51st Congress, 1st session, Jan. 29, 1890, 949–950.

102   A Newspaper Account of a Shooting at the Capitol

March 1, 1890

On February 28, 1890, Charles E. Kincaid, a journalist for the Louisville Times, shot a former representative, William Preston Taulbee (D-Ky.), following an argument over a newspaper article Kincaid had written that implicated Taulbee in a scandal. The shooting took place in the House side of the Capitol Building. Two days later, Taulbee died from his wounds. Kincaid made no attempt to flee and readily admitted he had done the shooting. The incident served as a reminder that violence was no stranger to the halls of Congress, although such extreme violence was noteworthy because it was so rare.

The Taulbee-Kincaid incident remained the most serious shooting in the Capitol until July 24, 1998, when a mentally deranged lone gunman shot his way into the Capitol, killing two Capitol policemen and wounding a tourist. The assailant was seriously wounded in the exchange of gunfire and was immediately arrested. The slain officers, Detective John M. Gibson and Officer Jacob J. Chestnut, were honored as heroes for giving their lives in the line of duty. They were the first Capitol policemen to die while on duty in the Capitol since the force was established in 1828. The bodies of the slain officers laid in honor in the Rotunda of the Capitol on July 28, 1998, in the place reserved for the highest tribute to departed presidents, members of Congress, military leaders, top government officials, and unknown soldiers from various wars.

Today, in an era when potential threats from terrorists and others prone to violence must be taken seriously, visitors to the Capitol are subjected to security checks using metal-detecting devices like those used at airports. In the nineteenth century and well into the twentieth century it was not uncommon for ordinary citizens to carry concealed weapons in the halls of Congress and for some members of Congress to carry pistols while attending sessions of Congress. The Capitol police still confiscate about a dozen hand guns each year from visitors to the Capitol.

The earliest shooting incident at the Capitol occurred in 1835, when an insane man attempted to assassinate Andrew Jackson while he was attending a funeral service in the Rotunda of the Capitol. Both pistols misfired and Jackson was unhurt. In 1932 a gunman waved a weapon in the House gallery but Representative Melvin Maas (R-Minn.) talked him into dropping the gun without a shot being fired. In 1947 an irate former Capitol policeman fired two shots at Senator John W. Bricker (R-Ohio) near the Senate subway, but both shots missed. One of the most serious shootings in the Capitol occurred March 1, 1954, when a group of Puerto Rican extremists, situated in the House gallery, fired on members of Congress below in the House chamber (see document 143).

In the hundred years and more since the shooting of William Taulbee, the incident has remained a frequently told story regarding the history of the Capitol. Although there is no firm evidence to support it, Capitol guides, House staff members, and even members of Congress readily point to dark stains on the interior marble staircase leading from the first floor to the second-floor entrance to the House chamber, claiming they are blood stains from Taulbee's wounds.

This account, published less than two days after the shooting, does not contain the whole story of the incident. Taulbee had not yet succumbed to his wounds. But it stands as a good journalistic account of the drama as it unfolded.

NEARLY A FATAL SHOT
A Plea of Self-Defense Made

The Publication of a Washington Dispatch in the Louisville "Times" Reflecting on the Politician's Relations With a Woman the Cause of the Encounter

"I am not armed."

"Then you had better be."

And two hours after ex-Congressman Taulbee, of Kentucky, who had given the advice contained in the last quotation to Charles Kincaid, correspondent of the Louisville *Times*, was carried to Providence Hospital with a pistol ball in his face, fired there by the correspondent while the ex-Congressman was standing at the southeastern entrance of the Capitol.

The shooting is the climax of trouble which is of more than two years' standing, and which originated in the publication in the Louisville *Times* of a notorious scandal affecting the moral character and standing of ex-Congressman Taulbee, and which is remembered in Washington as the Patent Office Scandal.

Yesterday just before noon Mr. Kincaid, who sent in his card to see a Kentucky member of Congress, was waiting at the east door leading into the floor of the House. There is always a large crowd of people about the corridor. Mr. Taulbee, who had business a business engagement with Congressman McCreary, of Kentucky, and several others, came out of the House while Mr. Kincaid was standing in the outer doorway, and, walking up to him said a few words in an undertone, indistinguishable to the Doorkeeper only two or three feet away.

It is said that the lie was passed. The Doorkeeper, who was in the act of closing the doors, as is customary on a call of the House, then noticed Mr. Taulbee, who is large framed and muscular, clutch Mr. Kincaid by the lapel of the coat, and with a strong grasp held him while he said: "Kincaid, come out into the corridor with me." The reports which flow about the Capitol stated that the ex-Congressman had pulled the correspondent's nose or ear, but the Doorkeeper, who was standing there, denies this. Kincaid is a small, slightly built man, suffering from illness and some nervous ailment. His reply to Taulbee's invitation to come into the corridor was:

"I am in no condition for a physical contest with you—I am unarmed."

"Then you had better be."

Taulbee kept talking while Kincaid called upon Sam Walton, an acquaintance, to bear witness to what had occurred. Walton evidently did not desire to become involved in the trouble between the two men, for he said that he could be a witness to nothing; he only knew that some words had been exchanged. All this time the Doorkeeper was vainly endeavoring to get the men out of the way so that the doors might be closed, but was prevented by Taulbee, who declared that he had a right to enter. Taulbee and Kincaid then went their ways, the former into the House, and the latter, it is supposed, after a pistol, for, as he stated, he had none at the time.

The quarrel was not generally known even to the intimate friends of the two men, when about 1:30 o'clock, members and their friends dining in the restaurant were startled by the sharp report of a pistol fired very near the private room attached to the restaurant.

They rushed out breathlessly, while other persons came tumbling down the stairway, and soon there was an excited crowd surrounding a man holding his head, from which the blood was gushing in a steady stream, while another man was exclaiming that he had done the shooting. The bullet was fired at a range not the length of a man's arm.

Taulbee, after spending some time in the House, had come out and was descending the eastern marble stairway leading from the main to the lower floor of the building. He passed Kincaid on his way, and the latter came after him. This stairway is lighted only by one small window. And is dark and gloomy. At the time the affair occurred there were many people passing up

and down. Taulbee had nearly reached the bottom when he and Kincaid came together, but just in what manner there are conflicting stories, some claiming that Taulbee grabbed Kincaid by the ear and gave it a wrenching, while others say that Kincaid made the assault and fired as Taulbee turned his head.

The bullet entered on the right side of the right eye. The wounded man almost sank to the floor, but rallied instantly, and staggered down the few remaining steps to the landing, where he was quickly surrounded by a throng, some of whom recognized him. Congressman Yoder, a physician as well as a politician, and Dr. Clarence Adams, a young practitioner of this city, were near at hand. Under their guidance the wounded man was removed to the room of the Committee on Public Buildings and Grounds, where he was made comfortable on a lounge until he could be removed to Providence Hospital.

Kincaid made no effort to escape, but walked into the crowd surrounding the wounded man, excitedly exclaiming: "I did it; I am the man who did the shooting." Officer Bryan, of the Capitol police force, caught hold of him after he heard these words uttered, and Kincaid was taken to the New Jersey avenue station and surrendered to the local police authorities.

At the Station House.

Mr. Kincaid Declares that He was Forced into the Encounter.

When Kincaid was first carried into the station, Lieutenant Kelly gave him the freedom of his private room and office, where he was permitted to see and talk to friends. The prisoner was completely unnerved, and complained that the was suffering with severe pains in the chest and stomach, he having not fully recovered from a long and protracted illness, which left him almost a physical wreck. Mr. Kincaid said to Lieutenant Kelly that he was thankful for the kindly manner in which he was being treated.

"I will treat you just as well as the law will permit me," was the lieutenant's reply. "And that is all that any one can ask," responded Mr. Kincaid. "I do not think I could live long if locked up in a cell."

"Oh, well, I'll give you a room upstairs and two of my men to keep you company, but you must keep a stiff upper lip."

Before being taken to the room above stairs, ex-Governor McCreery, Representatives Caruth, Goodnight, Ellis, Stone, Montgomery, and others called to see him, offering assistance and counsel.

Last night when a Post reporter was admitted to the correspondent's room, he found him sitting in an easy chair, with both hands pressed to his chest.

"Under advice of my counsel, Mr. Charles Maurice Smith, I do not care to discuss the unfortunate transaction," said Mr. Kincaid, in reply to the reporter's question if he wished to make a statement. "I will say, however, that I was forced to do what I did."

After a long pause the reporter asked:

"Did Mr. Taulbee pull you ear, Mr. Kincaid?"

"He did, and also attempted to drag me around. I have been hounded down by him ever since the publication of the Pension Office scandal. I was in no way to blame for that, for the matter was printed here before I heard of it. My paper paid me to send the news, and the story being of special local interest I put it on the wires."

"The next day a friend, who is still in the newspaper business here told me to be on my guard, as Taulbee had threatened me and had said that I ought to die, or should die. Taulbee had a leaded cane and I made it a point to avoid him, as I did not wish a personal difficulty. He had not previously carried a cane, and the threats he had made in the presence of my friend caused me to be very careful. I told him that if he wished to make a statement regarding the Patent Office story that the columns of my paper were at his disposal. He did not avail himself of the offer."

"That is all you care to say?"

"I could say much more, but will not, I am being nicely treated, and scores of friends have been to see me."

As the reporter left the room Dr. G. B. Harrison called and rendered medical attention to the prisoner.

An attempt will be made to have Kincaid released on bail today, but the Government is not ready, and the matter will go over until Monday. It is said that $100,000 can be raised for the correspondent if necessary. It is likely that Representatives McCreary and Caruth will be associated with Mr. Smith in the prisoner's defense.

At Providence Hospital.

It is Not Believed that Mr. Taulbee's Wound is Fatal.

"I do not think the wound will result fatally," said Dr. Koones to a Post reporter who called at Providence Hospital last night to inquire as to the condition of Mr. Taulbee.

"The ball entered about an eighth of an inch to the right of the eye, and when Doctor Bayne probed he found that it had taken a downward course, passing near the superior maxillary bone. The ball was not located, and I suppose Doctor Bayne will make another effort to find it to-morrow. The patient is resting nicely, and we have not found it necessary to administer opiates."

"Has he spoken of the difficulty?"

"I believe not; only to say that Mr. Kincaid acted in a cowardly manner. Of course we wish him to remain as quiet as possible and will not allow him to talk more than is necessary. I think he will recover."

Messrs. Carlisle, Stone, and other former colleagues of the ex-Congressman saw him soon after the shooting, but no one was admitted to his room at the hospital, though a large number called.

Mr. Taulbee subsequently admitted he assaulted Mr. Kincaid, but said that he had no idea of attacking him when Kincaid approached him with a pistol. He did not know that Kincaid was near until he was close to him. Then he saw the pistol pulled and the flash. Mr. Taulbee had remained conscious ever since the shooting. Prosecuting Attorney Armes went to the hospital, fearing a fatal termination, in order to obtain an ante mortem statement, but the attending physician assured him that there was no danger, and Mr. Armes left without seeing the patient.

Mr. Taulbee's temperature, pulse, and respiration are almost, if not quite normal. He has little fever, is perfectly rational, and talks freely with those about him when allowed to do so. While the exact location of the ball is yet undetermined, it is the opinion of the attending surgeons that it is lodged in the superior maxillary bone not more than an inch or an inch and a half from the place where it entered. There are but slight hemorrhages from the nose and mouth, which together with the fact that, so far as is now known, the brain and the optic nerves are untouched, leads the attending surgeons to regard the case at present as entirely hopeful.

Kincaid and Taulbee.

Sketches of the One Who Shot and the One Who Was Wounded.

Mr. Kincaid is a good-looking, slight-built man of thirty-four years, and his family connections are first class, standing at the head in Kentucky. He graduated from Center College, Danville, and was judge of one of the courts of Louisville. His newspaper career began at an early age, being only twenty when he began publication of a Democratic journal in Lawrenceburg, Ky. His State honored him with the position of railroad commissioner, which position he filled with signal ability. He served as secretary of the State Central Democratic Committee for several years, and was given other positions of honor and trust. Governor Knott made him his private secretary, which position he resigned to go as commissioner of the State to Italy to bring back the body of the sculptor, Joel T. Hart, which was buried in Florence. Before accepting the position in the Louisville *Times* as Washington correspondent he was Senator Williams' private secretary. He was sent as a consular agent to St. Helens, England, in 1887, and remained there for several months. Last summer failing health caused him to take a foreign trip, and on his ocean voyage he came near dying. He has never fully recovered. He wields a fluent pen, and has contributed some excellent articles to his own and other papers.

Ex-Congressman Taulbee, the wounded man, came from one of the mountain districts of Kentucky. He is thirty-nine years old, of tall figure, with a frame sinewy and strong, but lean. He soon became known in the House as a ready talker, and was more frequently on his feet than any other member. He had an immensely powerful voice, and in the tumults which sometimes occurred in the House it could always be heard above the din. The following is a biography furnished by himself to the Congressional Directory:

"William Preston Taulbee, of Saylersville, was born in Morgan county, Kentucky, October 22, 1851, and was educated in private country schools; studied for the ministry from 1875 to 1878, and for the law from 1878 to 1881. He was elected clerk to the Magoflin county court in 1878 and re-elected in 1882. He was a member of the Forty-ninth and Fiftieth Congresses."

. . . .

Washington Post, March 1, 1890, 1.

103   Declaration of War with Spain

April 25, 1898

Despite its constitutional power to declare war, Congress has rarely exercised that power outright. The declaration of war against Spain was one of the few times Congress responded instantly to the wishes of the president. This declaration was brief and to the point. On the day of its passage it did not generate great debate in Congress, as might be expected. By the time President William McKinley sent a war message to Congress on April 25, 1898, both houses of Congress had already debated the matter. The House passed the war declaration earlier in the day and notified the Senate. In the document that follows, the Senate quickly went into a closed-door session and also voted for a declaration of war.

This seemingly quick response was proceeded by several years of dramatic, emotion-filled events. Much of the debate had been spread over three years as the American government tried to figure out a position regarding the bloody war going on in Cuba between Cuban citizens and the government of Spain, which controlled the island. American newspapers filled their pages with stories of the war. Emotions ran high in Congress, where populists sided with the insurgent Cubans against the cruelty of Spanish rule. In the presidential campaign of 1896, Republicans expressed sympathy for the Cubans and the populist Democrats called outright for Cuban independence. By 1898 more than 50,000 Cuban soldiers had been killed, along with more than 200,000 Cubans, many of whom had been placed in concentration camps, where they died from disease. When the U.S. warship the Maine, *on a peaceful visit to Havana, blew up and sank under mysterious circumstances on February 15, 1898, those clamoring for U.S. intervention used the* Maine's *destruction and the loss of 265 lives aboard ship as a rallying cry for a declaration of war.*

Two weeks before this declaration of war, on April 11, 1898, President McKinley sent a message to Congress urging U.S. intervention as the only way to stop the war, but he stopped short of asking for a declaration of war. Debate in the House and Senate during the first weeks of April 1898 was heated. On April 20 Congress passed a joint resolution recognizing the independence of the Cuban people. The resolution demanded that Spain "at once relinquish its authority and government in the Island of Cuba and withdraw its land and naval forces from Cuba and Cuban waters." Furthermore, to satisfy Senator Henry M. Teller (R-Colo.), the resolution stated that the United States "hereby disclaims any disposition or intention to exercise sovereignty, jurisdiction, or control over said Island except for the pacification thereof. . . ."

As a result of the Spanish-American War the United States acquired Puerto Rico, the Philippines, Hawaii, and Guam. It marked the beginning of the rise of the United States as a world power. From the standpoint of Congress, the war had the inadvertent effect of increasing the power of the executive branch in setting the national agenda, a role that Congress had played throughout most of American history before this time. This war marked the beginning of the shift of political power from Capitol Hill to the White House.

MESSAGE FROM THE HOUSE

A message form the House of Representatives, by Mr. W. J. BROWNING, its Chief Clerk, announced that the House had passed a bill (H. R. 10086) declaring that a war exists between the United States of America and the Kingdom of Spain; in which it requested the concurrence of the Senate.

WAR BETWEEN THE UNITED STATES AND SPAIN

The VICE-PRESIDENT. The Chair lays before the Senate a bill from the House of Representatives.

The bill (H. R. 10086) declaring war exists between the United States of American and the Kingdom of Spain was read the first time by its title and the second time at length, as follows:

Be it enacted by the Senate and the House of Representatives of the United States of America in Congress assembled, First. That war be, and the same is hereby declared to exist, and that war has existed since the 21st day of April, A.D. 1898, including said day, between the United States of America and the Kingdom of Spain.

Second. That the President of the United States be, and he hereby is, directed and empowered to use the entire land and naval forces of the United States, and to call into the actual service of the United States the militia of the several States, to such extent as may be necessary to carry this act into effect.

Mr. DAVIS. I move that the doors of the Senate be closed.

Mr. PLATT OF CONNECTICUT. I second the motion.

The VICE-PRESIDENT. The motion if seconded, and the Senate will proceed in session with closed doors.

The Senate, with closed doors, proceeded, as in Committee of the Whole, to consider the bill; and it was reported to the Senate without amendment, ordered to a third reading, and was read the third time.

The VICE-PRESIDENT. The question is, Shall the bill pass?

The bill was unanimously passed.

Congressional Record, Senate, 55th Congress, 2nd session, April 25, 1898, 4244.

104   Senator Albert J. Beveridge on U.S. Policy Regarding the Philippines

January 9, 1900

It is rare when a freshman senator takes the floor for a maiden speech to packed galleries of rapt listeners, but thirty-seven-year-old Albert J. Beveridge (R-Ind.), while new to the Senate, was not new to the art of oratory, having put himself through college by winning oratorical contests. His reputation as a stump speaker for the Republican Party had proceeded him. Almost a year elapsed from the time of his election to the Senate until his swearing in on December 4, 1899. During this time Beveridge toured the Philippines extensively in preparation for his role as a leading proponent of American imperialism.

The Philippines were ceded to the United States in 1899 in provisions of the Treaty of Paris, which ended the Spanish-American War. At the time Beveridge delivered this speech U.S. troops were engaged in warfare in the Philippines to put down an insurrection (lasting until 1902) against United States rule. Beveridge's speech was filled with the braggadocio of racial superiority and the belief that the United States was God's chosen instrument to bring order to the world. The more extreme aspects of this speech bothered many within his own party and made him the subject of ridicule by critics. Beveridge, somewhat chastened by the criticism he received, took a less extreme approach in subsequent speeches. Nonetheless, this speech remains one the single best statements of American jingoism ever uttered. When Beveridge finished the address the packed galleries burst into applause.

Responding in large part to Beveridge and other colleagues who espoused U.S. acquisition of the Philippines, Senator George Frisbie Hoar (R-Mass.) addressed the Senate several months later to present an opposite point of view (see document 105). Taken together, these two speeches contain the essence of many congressional debates since then, some continuing to this day, over the role of the United States as a world power and our relationship with Pacific nations.

Mr. President, I address the Senate at this time because senators and members of the House on both sides have asked that I give to Congress and the country my observations in the Philippines and the Far East, and the conclusions which those observations compel; and because of hurtful resolutions introduced and utterances made in the Senate, every word of which will cost and is costing the lives of American soldiers.

Mr. President, the times call for candor. The Philippines are ours forever, "territory belonging to the United States," as the Constitution calls them. And just beyond the Philippines are China's illimitable markets. We will not retreat from either. We will not repudiate our duty in the archipelago. We will not abandon our opportunity in the Orient. We will not renounce our part in the mission of our race, trustee, under God, of the civilization of the world. And we will move forward to our work, not howling out regrets like slaves whipped to their burdens, but with gratitude for a task worthy of our strength, and thanksgiving to Almighty God that He has marked us as His chosen people, henceforth to lead in the regeneration of the world.

This island empire is the last land left in all the oceans. If it should prove a mistake to abandon it, the blunder once made would be irretrievable. If it proves a mistake to hold it, the error can be corrected when we will. Every other progressive nation stands ready to relieve us.

But to hold it will be no mistake. Our largest trade henceforth must be with Asia. The Pacific is our ocean. More and more Europe will manufacture the most it needs, secure from its colonies the most it consumes. Where shall we turn for consumers of our surplus? Geography answers the question. China is our natural customer. She is nearer to us than to England, Germany, or Russia, the commercial powers of the present and the future. They have moved nearer to China by securing permanent bases on her borders. The Philippines give us a base at the door of all the East.

Lines of navigation from our ports to the Orient and Australia; from the isthmian canal to Asia; from all oriental ports to Australia, converge at and separate from the Philippines. They are a self-supporting, dividend-paying fleet, permanently anchored at a spot selected by the strategy of Providence, commanding the Pacific. And the Pacific is the ocean of the commerce of the future. Most future wars will be conflicts for commerce. The power that rules the Pacific, therefore, is the power that rules the world. And, with the Philippines, that power is and will forever be the American Republic.

China's trade is the mightiest commercial fact in our future. Her foreign commerce was $285,738,300 in 1897, of which we, her neighbor, had less than 9 percent, of which only a little more than half was merchandise sold to China by us. We ought to have 50 percent, and we will. And China's foreign commerce is only beginning. Her resources, her possibilities, her wants, all are undeveloped. She has only 340 miles of railway. I have seen trains loaded with natives and all the activities of modern life already appearing along the line. But she needs, and in fifty years will have, 20,000 miles of railway.

Who can estimate her commerce, then? That statesman commits a crime against American trade—against the American grower of cotton and wheat and tobacco, the American manufacturer of machinery and clothing—who fails to put America where she may command that trade. Germany's Chinese trade is increasing like magic. She has established ship lines and secured a tangible foothold on China's very soil. Russia's Chinese trade is growing beyond belief. She is spending the revenues of the empire to finish her railroad into Pekin itself, and she is in physical possession of the imperial province of Manchuria. Japan's Chinese trade is multiplying in volume and value. She is bending her energy to her merchant marine, and is located along China's very coast; but Manila is nearer China than Yokohama is. The Philippines command the commercial situation of the entire East. Can America best trade with China from San Francisco or New York? From San Francisco, of course. But if San Francisco were closer to China than New York is to Pittsburgh, what then? And Manila is nearer Hongkong than Habana is to Washington. And yet American statesmen plan to surrender this commercial throne of the Orient where Providence and our soldiers' lives have placed us. When history comes to write the story of that suggested treason to American supremacy and therefore to the spread of American civilization, let her in mercy write that those who so proposed were merely blind and nothing more.

But if they did not command China, India, the Orient, the whole Pacific for purposes of offense, defense, and trade, the Philippines are so valuable in themselves that we should hold them. I have cruised more than 2,000 miles through the archipelago, every moment a surprise at its loveliness and wealth. I have ridden hundreds of miles on the islands, every foot of the way a revelation of vegetable and mineral riches.

No land in America surpasses in fertility the plains and valleys of Luzon. Rice and coffee, sugar and cocoanuts, hemp and tobacco, and many products of the temperate as well as the tropic zone grow in various sections of the archipelago. I have seen hundreds of bushels of Indian corn lying in a road fringed with banana trees. The forests of Negros, Mindanao, Mindora, Paluan, and parts of Luzon are invaluable and intact. The wood of the Philippines can supply the furniture of the world for a century to come. At Cebu the best-informed man in the island told me that forty miles of Cebu's mountain chain are practically mountains of coal. Pablo Majia, one of the most reliable men on the islands, confirmed the statement. Some declare that the coal is only lignite; but ship captains who have used it told me that it is better steamer fuel than the best coal of Japan.

I have a nugget of pure gold picked up in its present form on the banks of a Philippine creek. I have gold dust washed out by crude processes of careless natives from the sands of a Philippine stream. Both indicate great deposits at the source from which they come. In one of the islands great deposits of copper exist untouched. The mineral wealth of this empire of the ocean will one day surprise the world. I base this statement partly on personal observation, but chiefly on the testimony of foreign merchants in the Philippines, who have practically investigated the subject, and upon the unanimous opinion of natives and priests. And the mineral wealth is but a small fraction of the agricultural wealth of these islands.

And the wood, hemp, copra, and other products of the Philippines supply what we need and cannot ourselves produce. And the markets they will themselves afford will be immense. Spain's export and import trade, with the islands undeveloped, was $11,534,731 annually. Our trade with the islands developed will be $125,000,000 annually, for who believes that we can not do ten times as well as Spain? Consider their imperial dimensions. Luzon is larger and richer than New York, Pennsylvania, Illinois, or Ohio. Mindanao is larger and richer than all New England, exclusive of Maine. Manila, as a port of call and exchange, will, in the time of men now living, far surpass Liverpool. Behold the exhaustless markets they command. It is as if a half dozen of our states were set down between Oceania and the Orient, and those states themselves undeveloped and unspoiled of their primitive wealth and resources.

Nothing is so natural as trade with one's neighbors. The Philippines make us the nearest neighbors of all the East. Nothing is more natural than to trade with those you know. This is the philosophy of all advertising. The Philippines bring us permanently face to face with the most sought-for customers of the world. National prestige, national propinquity, these and commercial activity are the elements of commercial success. The Philippines give the first; the character of the American people supply the last. It is a providential conjunction of all the elements of trade, of duty, and of power. If we are willing to go to war rather than let England have a few feet of frozen Alaska, which affords no market and commands none, what should we not do rather than let England, Germany, Russia, or Japan have all the Philippines? And no man on the spot can fail to see that this would be their fate if we retired.

The climate is the best tropic climate in the world. This is the belief of those who have lived in many tropic countries, with scores of whom I have talked on this point. My own experience with tropical conditions has not been exhaustive; yet, speaking from that experience, I testify that the climate of Iloilo, Sulu, Cebu, and even of Manila, greatly surpasses that of Hongkong. And yet on the bare and burning rock of Hongkong our constructing race has built one of the noblest cities of all the world and made the harbor it commands the focus of the commerce of the East. And the glory of that achievement illumines with a rarer splendor than that of Waterloo the flag that floats above it, for from Hongkong's heights civilization is irradiating all the Orient. If this be imperialism, its final end will be the empire of the Son of Man.

. . . .

It will be hard for Americans who have not studied them to understand the people. They are a barbarous race, modified by three centuries of contact with a decadent race. The Filipino is the South Sea Malay, put through a process of three hundred years of superstition in religion, dishonesty in dealing, disorder in habits of industry, and cruelty, caprice, and corruption in government. It is barely possible that a thousand men in all the archipelago are capable of self-government in the Anglo-Saxon sense.

My own belief is that there are not a hundred men among them who comprehend what Anglo-Saxon self-government even means, and there are over five million people to be governed. I know many clever and highly educated men among them, but there are only three commanding intellects and characters—Arellano, Mabini, and Aguinaldo. Arellano, the chief justice of our supreme court, is a profound lawyer and a brave and incorruptible man. Mabini, who, before his capture, was the literary and diplomatic associate of Aguinaldo, is the highest type of subtlety and the most constructive mind that race has yet produced. Aguinaldo is a clever, popular leader, able, brave, resourceful, cunning, ambitious, unscrupulous, and masterful. He is full of decision, initiative, and authority, and had the confidence of the masses. He is a natural dictator. His ideas of government are absolute orders, implicit obedience, or immediate death. He understands the character of his countrymen. He is a Malay Sylla; not a Filipino Washington.

. . . .

Here, then, senators, is the situation. Two years ago there was no land in all the world which we could occupy for any purpose. Our commerce was daily turning toward the Orient, and geography and trade developments made necessary our commercial empire over the Pacific. And in that ocean we had no commercial, naval, or military base. Today we have one of the three great ocean possessions of the globe, located at the most commanding commercial, naval, and military points in the eastern seas, within hail of India, shoulder to shoulder with China, richer in its own resources than any equal body of land on the entire globe, and peopled by a race which civilization demands shall be improved. Shall we abandon it? That man little knows the common people of the Republic, little understands the instincts of our race, who thinks we will not hold it fast and hold it forever, administering just government by simplest methods. We may trick up devices to shift our burden and lessen our opportunity; they will avail us nothing but delay. We may tangle conditions by applying academic arrangements of self-government to a crude situation; their failure will drive us to our duty in the end.

The military situation, past, present, and prospective, is no reason for abandonment. Our campaign has been as perfect as possible with the force at hand. We have been delayed, first, by a failure to comprehend the immensity of our acquisition; and, second, by insufficient force; and, third, by our efforts for peace. In February, after the treaty of peace, General Otis had only 3,722 officers and men whom he had a legal right to order into battle. The terms of enlistment of the rest of his troops had expired, and they fought voluntarily and not on legal military compulsion. It was one of the noblest examples of patriotic devotion to duty in the history of the world.

Those who complain do so in ignorance of the real situation. We attempted a great task with insufficient means; we became impatient that it was not finished before it could fairly be commenced; and I pray we may not add that other element of disaster, pausing in the work before it is thoroughly and forever done. That is the gravest mistake we could possibly make, and that is the only danger before us. Our Indian wars would have been shortened, the lives of soldiers and settlers saved, and the Indians themselves benefited had we made continuous and decisive war; and any other kind of war is criminal because ineffective. We acted toward the Indians as though we feared them, loved them, hated them—a mingling of foolish sentiment, inaccurate thought, and paralytic purpose. Let us now be instructed by our own experience.

This, too, has been Spain's course in the Philippines. I have studied Spain's painful military history in these islands. Never sufficient troops; never vigorous action, pushed to conclusive results and a permanent peace; always treating with the rebels while they fought them; always cruel and corrupt when a spurious peace was arranged. This has been Spain's way for three hundred years, until insurrection has become a Filipino habit. Never since Magellan landed did Spain put enough troops in the islands for complete and final action in war; never did she intelligently, justly, firmly, administer government in peace.

. . . .

Mr. President, that must not be our plan. This war is like all other wars. It needs to be finished before it is stopped. I am prepared to vote either to make our work thorough or even now to abandon it. A lasting peace can be secured only by overwhelming forces in ceaseless action until universal and absolutely final defeat is inflicted on the enemy. To halt before every armed force, every guerrilla band, opposing us is dispersed or exterminated will prolong hostilities and leave alive the seeds of perpetual insurrection.

Even then we should not treat. To treat at all is to admit that we are wrong. And any quiet so secured will be delusive and fleeting. And a false peace will betray us; a sham truce will curse us. It is not to serve the purposes of the hour, it is not to salve a present situation, that peace should be established. It is for the tranquility of the archipelago forever. It is for an orderly government for the Filipinos for all the future. It is to give this problem to posterity solved and settled; not vexed and involved. It is to establish the supremacy of the American Republic over the Pacific and throughout the East till the end of time.

It has been charged that our conduct of the war has been cruel. Senators, it has been the reverse. I have been in our hospitals and seen the Filipino wounded as carefully, tenderly cared for as our own. Within our lines they may plow and sow and reap and go about the affairs of peace with absolute liberty. And yet all this kindness was misunderstood, or rather not understood. Senators must remember that we are not dealing with Americans or Europeans. We are dealing with Orientals. We are dealing with Orientals who are Malays. We are dealing with Malays instructed in Spanish methods. They mistake kindness for weakness, forbearance for fear. It could not be otherwise unless you could erase hundreds of years of savagery, other hundreds of years of orientalism, and still other hundreds of years of Spanish character and custom.

Our mistake has not been cruelty; it has been kindness. It has been the application to Spanish Malays of methods appropriate to New England. Every device of mercy, every method of conciliation, has been employed by the peace-loving President of the American Republic, to the amazement of nations experienced in oriental revolt. Before the outbreak our general in command appointed a commission to make some arrangements with the natives mutually agreeable. I know the members of the commission well—General Hughes, Colonel Crowder, and General

Smith—moderate, kindly, tactful men of the world; an ideal body for such negotiation. It was treated with contempt.

We smiled at intolerable insult and insolence until the lips of every native in Manila were curling in ridicule for the cowardly Americans. We refrained from all violence until their armed bravos crossed the lines in violation of agreement. Then our sentry shot the offender, and he should have been court-martialed had he failed to shoot. That shot was the most fortunate of the war. For there is every reason to believe that Aguinaldo had planned the attack upon us for some nights later. Our sentry's shot brought this attack prematurely on. He arranged for an uprising in Manila to massacre all Americans, the plans for which, in a responsible officer's handwriting, are in our possession. This shot and its results made that awful scheme impossible. We did not strike till they attacked us in force, without provocation. This left us no alternative but war or evacuation.

The patience of our peace-loving president was not even then exhausted. A civil commission was sent to Manila, composed of the president of one of our great universities, a distinguished diplomat and an eminent college professor who had special knowledge of the country and people and also General Otis and Admiral Dewey. These men exhausted the expedients of peace, and always were met with the Malay's ready evasion, the Spaniard's habitual delay. I am personal witness that no effort was neglected by our commission to assure the Filipino people of our good intentions and beneficent purposes. The commission entertained the mestizos of Manila in a way that would have honored the Senate of the United States; the brown faces of the common people sneered. The commission treated natives, accustomed to blows, with kindest consideration; the agents of Aguinaldo told tales of our pusillanimity to the ignorant rural masses. This remarkable man sent so-called commissions, ostensibly to treat, but really to play with ours. His commissions were composed of generals in uniform. The populace gaped in open admiration when they appeared in Manila. Our representatives of peace talked to them, argued with them, entertained them; the people were impressed with their importance. President Schurman even rode with them through the city. The masses were confirmed in their reverence for their brothers who were thus honored and distinguished. Then the bespangled representatives of the Malay dictator return to their lord, and the sole effect of these pacific efforts was to make 250,000 natives in Manila think that the only way to win the respect of the American Republic is to fight it.

No, senators, the friendly methods of peace have been thoroughly tried only to make peace more difficult. The Oriental does not understand our attempt to conciliate. Every effort of our commission which did its work at Manila so earnestly, so honestly, so thoroughly and which, with Americans or Europeans, would have so brilliantly succeeded, only delayed the peace it attempted to hasten. There is not now and never was any possible course but ceaseless operations in the field and loyal support of the war at home.

The news that 60,000 American soldiers have crossed the Pacific; that, if necessary, the American Congress will make it 100,000 or 200,000 men; that, at any cost, we will establish peace and govern the islands, will do more to end the war than the soldiers themselves. But the report that we even discuss the withdrawal of a single soldier at the present time and that we even debate the possibility of not administering government throughout the archipelago ourselves will be misunderstood and misrepresented and will blow into a flame once more the fires our soldiers' blood has almost quenched.

Mr. President, reluctantly and only from a sense of duty am I forced to say that American opposition to the war has been the chief factor in prolonging it. Had Aguinaldo not understood that in America, even in the American Congress, even here in the Senate, he and his cause were supported; had he not known that it was proclaimed on the stump and in the press of a faction in the United States that every shot his misguided followers fired into the breasts of American soldiers was like the volleys fired by Washington's men against the soldiers of King George his insurrection would have dissolved before it entirely crystallized.

The utterances of American opponents of the war are read to the ignorant soldiers of Aguinaldo and repeated in exaggerated form among the common people. Attempts have been made by wretches claiming American citizenship to ship arms and ammunition from Asiatic ports to the Filipinos, and these acts of infamy were coupled by the Malays with American assaults on our government at home. The Filipinos do not understand free speech, and therefore our tolerance of American assaults on the American president and the American government means to them that our president is in the minority or he would not permit what appears to them such treasonable criticism. It is believed and stated in Luzon, Panay, and Cebu that the Filipinos have only to fight, harass, retreat, break up into small parties, if necessary, as they are doing now, but by any means hold out until the next presidential election, and our forces will be withdrawn.

All this has aided the enemy more than climate, arms, and battle. Senators, I have heard these reports myself; I have talked with the people; I have seen our mangled boys in the hospital and field; I have stood on the firing line and beheld our dead soldiers, their faces turned to the pitiless southern sky, and in sorrow rather than anger I say to those whose voices in America have cheered those misguided natives on to shoot our soldiers down, that the blood of those dead and wounded boys of ours is on their hands, and the flood of all the years can never wash that stain away. In sorrow rather than anger I say these words, for I earnestly believe that our brothers knew not what they did.

But, senators, it would be better to abandon this combined garden and Gibraltar of the Pacific, and count our blood and treasure already spent a profitable loss, than to apply any academic arrangement of self-government to these children. They are not capable of self-government. How could they be? They are not of a self-governing race. They are Orientals, Malays, instructed by Spaniards in the latter's worst estate.

They know nothing of practical government except as they have witnessed the weak, corrupt, cruel, and capricious rule of Spain. What magic will anyone employ to dissolve in their minds and characters those impressions of governors and governed which three centuries of misrule has created? What alchemy will change the oriental quality of their blood and set the self-governing currents of the American pouring through their Malay veins? How shall they, in the twinkling of an eye, be exalted to the heights of self-governing peoples which required a thousand years for us to reach, Anglo-Saxon though we are?

Let me beware how they employ the term "self-government." It is a sacred term. It is the watchword at the door of the inner temple of liberty, for liberty does not always mean self-government. Self-government is a method of liberty—the highest, simplest, best—and it is acquired only after centuries of study and struggle and experiment and instruction and all the elements of the progress of man. Self-government is no base and common thing, to be bestowed on the merely audacious. It is the degree which crowns the graduate of liberty, not the name of liberty's infant class, who have not yet mastered the alphabet of freedom. Savage blood, oriental blood, Malay blood, Spanish example— are these the elements of self-government?

We must act on the situation as it exists, not as we would wish it. I have talked with hundreds of these people, getting their views as to the practical workings of self-government. The great majority simply do not understand any participation in any government whatever. The most enlightened among them declare that self-government will succeed because the employers of labor will compel their employees to vote as their employer wills and that this will insure intelligent voting. I was assured that we could depend upon good men always being in office because the officials who constitute the government will nominate their successors, choose those among the people who will do the voting, and determine how and where elections will be held.

The most ardent advocate of self-government that I met was anxious that I should know that such a government would be tranquil because, as he said, if anyone criticised it, the government would shoot the offender. A few of them have a sort of verbal understanding of the democratic theory, but the above are the examples of the ideas of the practical workings of self-government entertained by the aristocracy, the rich planters and traders, and heavy employers of labor, the men who would run the government.

Example for decades will be necessary to instruct them in American ideas and methods of administration. Example, example; always example—this alone will teach them. As a race, their general ability is not excellent. Educators, both men and women, to whom I have talked in Cebu and Luzon, were unanimous in the opinion that in all solid and useful education they are, as a people, dull and stupid. In showy things, like carving and painting or embroidery or music, they have apparent aptitude, but even this is superficial and never thorough. They have facility of speech, too.

The three best educators on the island at different times made to me the same comparison that the common people in their stupidity are like their caribou bulls. They are not even good agriculturists. Their waste of cane is inexcusable. Their destruction of hemp fiber is childish. They are incurably indolent. They have no continuity or thoroughness of industry. They will quit work without notice and amuse themselves until the money they have earned is spent. They are like children playing at men's work.

No one need fear their competition with our labor. No reward could beguile, no force compel, these children of indolence to leave their trifling lives for the fierce and fervid industry of high-wrought America. The very reverse is the fact. One great problem is the necessary labor to develop these islands—to build the roads, open the mines, clear the wilderness, drain the swamps, dredge the harbors. The natives will not supply it. A lingering prejudice against the Chinese may prevent us from letting them supply it. Ultimately, when the real truth of the climate and human conditions is known, it is barely possible that our labor will go there. Even now young men with the right moral fiber and a little capital can make fortunes there as planters.

But the natives will not come here. Let all men dismiss that fear. The Dutch have Java, and its population, under Holland's rule, has increased from 2 million to more than 20 million people; yet the Java laborer has never competed with the laborer of Holland. And this is true of England and Germany, of every colonizing, administering power. The native has produced luxuries for the laborer of the governing country and afforded a market for what the laborer of the governing country in turn produced.

In Paluan the natives are primitive. In Sulu and Mindanao the Moros are vigorous and warlike, but have not the most elementary notions of civilization. For example, they do not understand the utility of roads. Nothing exists but paths through the jungle. I have ridden for hours in Sulu over the most primitive paths, barely discernible in the rank grass. They have not grasped the idea of private and permanent property in land, and yet there is no lovelier spot, no richer land, no better military and naval base than the Sulu group. In Paluan, Sulu, and Mindanao the strictest military government is necessary indefinitely. The inhabitants can never be made to work, can never be civilized. Their destiny cannot be foretold. But whether they will withstand civilization or disappear before it, our duty is plain.

In all other islands our government must be simple and strong. It must be a uniform government. Different forms for different islands will produce perpetual disturbance, because the people of each island would think that the people of the other islands are more favored than they. In Panay I heard murmurings that we were giving Negros an American constitution. This is a human quality, found even in America, and we must never forget that in dealing with the Filipinos we deal with children. And so our government must be simple and strong. Simple and strong! The meaning of those two words must be written in every line of Philippine legislation, realized in every act of Philippine administration. . . .

Even the elemental plan I have outlined will fail in the hands of any but ideal administrators. Spain did not utterly fail in devising—many of her plans were excellent; she failed in administering. Her officials as a class were corrupt, indolent, cruel, immoral. They were selected to please a faction in Spain, to placate members of the Cortes, to bribe those whom the government feared. They were seldom selected for their fitness. They were the spawn of government favor and government fear, and therefore of government iniquity.

The men we send to administer civilized government in the Philippines must be themselves the highest examples of our civilization. I use the word examples, for examples they must be in that word's most absolute sense. They must be men of the world and of affairs, students of their fellow men, not theorists nor dreamers. They must be brave men, physically as well as morally. They must be as incorruptible as honor, as stainless as purity, men whom no force can frighten, no influence coerce, no money buy. Such men come high, even here in America. But they must be had. Better pure military occupation for years than government by any other quality of administration. Better abandon this priceless possession, admit ourselves incompetent to do our part in the world-redeeming work of our imperial race; better now haul down the flag of arduous deeds for civilization and run up the flag of reaction and decay than to apply academic notions of self-government to these children or attempt their government by any but the most perfect administrators our country can produce. I assert that such administrators can be found.

. . . .

Mr. President, self-government and internal development have been the dominant notes of our first century; administration and the development of other lands will be the dominant notes of our second century. And administration is as high and holy a function as self-government, just as the care of a trust estate is as sacred an obligation as the management of our own concerns. Cain was the first to violate the divine law of human society which makes of us our brother's keeper. And administration of good government is the first lesson in self-government, that exalted estate toward which all civilization tends.

Administration of good government is not denial of liberty. For what is liberty? It is not savagery. It is not the exercise of individual will. It is not dictatorship. It involves government, but not necessarily self-government. It means law. First of all, it is a common rule of action, applying equally to all within its limits. Liberty means protection of property and life without price, free speech without intimidation, justice without purchase or delay, government without favor or favorites. What will best give all this to the people of the Philippines—American administration, developing them gradually toward self-government, or self-government by a people before they know what self-government means?

The Declaration of Independence does not forbid us to do our part in the regeneration of the world. If it did, the Declaration would be wrong, just as the Articles of Confederation, drafted by the very same men who signed the Declaration, was found to be wrong. The Declaration has no application to the present situation. It was written by self-governing men for self-governing men.

It was written by men who, for a century and a half, had been experimenting in self-government on this continent, and whose ancestors for hundreds of years before had been gradually developing toward that high and holy estate. The Declaration applies only to people capable of self-government. How dare any man prostitute this expression of the very elect of self-governing peoples to a race of Malay children of barbarism, schooled in Spanish methods and ideas? And you, who say the Declaration applies to all men, how dare you deny its application to the American Indian? And if you deny it to the Indian at home, how dare you grant it to the Malay abroad?

The Declaration does not contemplate that all government must have the consent of the governed. It announces that man's "inalienable rights are life, liberty, and pursuit of happiness; that to secure these rights governments are established among men deriving their just powers from the consent of the governed; that when any form of government becomes destructive of those rights, it is the right of the people to alter or abolish it." "Life, liberty, and the pursuit of happiness" are the important things; "consent of the governed" is one of the means to those ends.

If "any form of government becomes destructive of those ends, it is the right of the people to alter or abolish it," says the Declaration. "Any forms" includes all forms. Thus the Declaration itself recognizes other forms of government than those resting on the consent of the governed. The word "consent" itself recognizes other forms for "consent" means the understanding of the thing to which the "consent" is given; and there are people in the world who do not understand any form of government. And the sense in which "consent" is used in the Declaration is broader than mere understanding; for "consent" in the Declaration means participation in the government "consented" to. And yet these people who are not capable of "consenting" to any form of government must be governed.

And so the Declaration contemplates all forms of government which secure the fundamental rights of life, liberty, and the pursuit of happiness. Self-government, when that will best secure these ends, as in the case of people capable of self-government; other appropriate forms when people are not capable of self-government. And so the authors of the Declaration themselves governed the Indian without his consent; the inhabitants of Louisiana without their consent; and ever since the sons of the makers of the Declaration have been governing not by theory, but by practice, after the fashion of our governing race, now by one form, now by another, but always for the purpose of securing the great eternal ends of life, liberty, and the pursuit of happiness, not in the savage, but in the civilized meaning of those terms—life according to orderly methods of civilized society; liberty regulated by law; pursuit of happiness limited by the pursuit of happiness by every other man.

If this is not the meaning of the Declaration, our government itself denies the Declaration every time it receives the representative of any but a republican form of government, such as that of the Sultan, the Czar, or other absolute autocrats, whose governments, according to the opposition's interpretation of the Declaration, are spurious governments, because the people governed have not "consented" to them.

Senators in opposition are stopped from denying our constitutional power to govern the Philippines as circumstances may demand, for such power is admitted in the case of Florida, Louisiana, Alaska. How, then, is it denied in the Philippines? Is there a geographical interpretation to the Constitution? Do degrees of longitude fix constitutional limitations? Does a thousand miles of ocean diminish constitutional power more than a thousand miles of land?

The ocean does not separate us from the field of our duty and endeavor—it joins us, an established highway needing no repair, and landing us at any point desired. The seas do not separate the Philippine Islands from us or from each other. The seas are highways through the archipelago, which would cost hundreds of millions of dollars to construct if they were land instead of water. Land may separate men from their desire, the ocean never. Russia has been centuries in crossing Siberian wastes; the Puritans crossed the Atlantic in brief and flying weeks.

If the Boers must have traveled by land, they would never have reached the Transvaal; but they sailed on liberty's ocean; they walked on civilization's untaxed highway, the welcoming sea. Our ships habitually sailed round the cape and anchored in California's harbors before a single trail had lined the desert with the whitening bones of those who made it. No! No! The ocean unites us; steam unites us; electricity unites us; all the elements of nature unite us to the region where duty and interest call us. There is in the ocean no constitutional argument against the march of the flag, for the oceans, too, are ours. With more extended coast lines than any nation of history; with a commerce vaster than any other people ever dreamed of, and that commerce as yet only in its beginnings; with naval traditions equaling those of England or of Greece, and the work of our Navy only just begun; with the air of the oceans in our nostrils and the blood of a sailor ancestry in our veins; with the shores of all the continents calling us, the great Republic before I die will be the acknowledged lord of the world's high seas. And over them the Republic will hold dominion, by virtue of the strength God has given it, for the peace of the world and the betterment of man.

No; the oceans are not limitations of the power which the Constitution expressly gives Congress to govern all territory the nation may acquire. The Constitution declares that "Congress shall have power to dispose of and make any needful rules and regulations respecting the territory belonging to the United States." Not the Northwest Territory only; not Louisiana or Florida only; not territory on this continent only, but any territory anywhere belonging to the nation. The founders of the nation were not provincial. Theirs was the geography of the world.

They were soldiers as well as landsmen, and they knew that where our ships should go our flag might follow. They had the logic of progress, and they knew that the Republic they were planting must, in obedience to the laws of our expanding race, necessarily develop into the greater Republic which the world beholds today, and into the still mightier Republic which the world will finally acknowledge as the arbiter, under God, of the destinies of mankind. And so our fathers wrote into the Constitution these words of growth, of expansion, of empire, if you will, unlimited by geography or climate or by anything but the vitality and possibilities of the American people: "Congress shall have power to dispose of and make all needful rules and regulations respecting the territory belonging to the United States."

The power to govern all territory the nation may acquire would have been in Congress if the language affirming that power had not been written in the Constitution. For not all powers of the national government are expressed. Its principal powers are implied. The written Constitution is but the index of the living Constitution. Had this not been true, the Constitution would have failed. For the people in any event would have developed and progressed. And if the Constitution had not had the capacity for growth corresponding with the growth of the nation, the Constitution would and should have been abandoned as the Articles of Confederation were abandoned. For the Constitution is not immortal in itself, is not useful even in itself. The Constitution is immortal and even useful only as it serves the orderly development of the nation. The nation alone is immortal. The nation alone is sacred. The army is its servant. The navy is its servant. The president is its servant. This Senate is its servant. Our laws are its methods. Our Constitution is its instrument.

This is the golden rule of constitutional interpretation: The Constitution was made for the people, not the people for the Constitution.

. . . .

The nation's power to make rules and regulations for the government of its possessions is not confined to any given set of rules or regulations. It is not confined to any particular formula of laws or kind of government or type of administration. Where do senators find constitutional warrant for any special kind of government in "territory belonging to the United States." The language affirming our power to govern such territory is as broad as the requirements of all possible situations. And there is nothing in the Constitution to limit that comprehensive language. The very reverse is true. For power to administer government anywhere and in any manner the situation demands would have been in Congress if the Constitution had been silent; not merely because it is a power not reserved to the states or people; not merely because it is a power inherent in and an attribute of nationality; not even because it might be inferred from other specific provisions of the Constitution; but because it is the power most necessary for the ruling tendency of our race—the tendency to explore, expand, and grow, to sail new seas and seek new lands, subdue the wilderness, revitalize decaying peoples, and plant civilized and civilizing governments over all the globe.

For the makers of the Constitution were of the race that produced Hawkins, and Drake, and Raleigh, and Smith, and Winthrop and Penn. They were of the great exploring, pioneering, colonizing, and governing race who went forth with trade or gain or religious liberty as the immediate occasion for their voyages, but really because they could not help it; because the blood within them commanded them; because their racial tendency is as resistless as the currents of the sea or the process of the suns or any other elemental movement of nature, of which that racial tendency itself is the most majestic. And when they wrote the Constitution they did not mean to negative the most elemental characteristic of their race, of which their own presence in America was an expression and an example. You can not interpret a constitution without understanding the race that wrote it. And if our fathers had intended a reversal of the very nature and being of their race, they would have so declared in the most emphatic words our language holds. But they did not, and in the absence of such words the power would remain which is essential to the strongest tendency of our practical race, to govern wherever we are and to govern by the methods best adapted to the situation. But our fathers were not content with silence, and they wrote in the Constitution the words which affirm this essential and imperial power.

Mr. President, this question is deeper than any question of party politics; deeper than any question of the isolated policy of our country even; deeper even than any question of constitutional power. It is elemental. It is racial. God has not been preparing the English-speaking and Teutonic peoples for a thousand years for nothing but vain and idle self-contemplation and self-admiration. No! He has made us the master organizers of the world to establish system where chaos reigns. He has given us the spirit of progress to overwhelm the forces of reaction throughout the earth. He has made us adepts in government that we may administer government among savage and senile peoples. Were it not for such a force as this the world would relapse into barbarism and night. And of all our race He has marked the American people as His chosen nation to finally lead in the regeneration of the world. This is the divine mission of America, and it holds for us all the profit, all the glory, all the happiness possible to man. We are trustees of the world's progress, guardians of its righteous peace. The judgment of the Master is upon us: "Ye have been faithful over a few things; I will make you ruler over many things."

What shall history say of us? Shall it say that we renounced that holy trust, left the savage to his base condition, the wilderness to the reign of waste, deserted duty, abandoned glory, forget our sordid profit even because we feared our strength and read the charter of our powers with the doubter's eye and the quibbler's mind? Shall it say that, called by events to captain and command the proudest, ablest, purest race of history in history's noblest work, we declined that great commission? Our fathers would not have had it so. No! They founded no paralytic government, incapable of the simplest acts of administration.

They planted no sluggard people, passive while the world's work calls them. They established no reactionary nation. They unfurled no retreating flag.

That flag has never paused in its onward march. Who dares halt it now—now, when history's largest events are carrying it forward; now, when we are at last one people, strong enough for any task, great enough for any glory destiny can bestow? How comes it that our first century closes with the process of consolidating the American people into a unit just accomplished, and quick upon the stroke of that great hour presses upon us our world opportunity, world duty, and world glory, which none but a people welded into an indivisible nation can achieve or perform?

Blind indeed is he who sees not the hand of God in events so vast, so harmonious, so benign. Reactionary indeed is the mind that perceives not that this vital people is the strongest of the saving forces of the world: that our place, therefore, is at the head of the constructing and redeeming nations of the earth; and that to stand aside while events march on is a surrender of our interests, a betrayal of our duty as blind as it is base. Craven indeed is the heart that fears to perform a work so golden and so noble; that dares not win a glory so immortal.

Do you tell me that it will cost us money? When did Americans ever measure duty by financial standards? Do you tell me of the tremendous toil required to overcome the vast difficulties of our task? What mighty work for the world, for humanity, even for ourselves, has ever been done with ease? Even our bread must we eat by the sweat of our faces. Why are we charged with power such as no people ever knew, if we are not to use it in a work such as no people ever wrought? Who will dispute the divine meaning of the fable of the talents?

Do you remind me of the precious blood that must be shed, the lives that must be given, the broken hearts of loved ones for their slain? And this is indeed a heavier price than all combined. And yet as a nation every historic duty we have done, every achievement we have accomplished, has been by the sacrifice of our noblest sons. Every holy memory that glorifies the flag is of those heroes who have died that its onward march might not be stayed. It is the nation's dearest lives yielded for the flag that makes it dear to us; it is the nation's most precious blood poured out for it that makes it precious to us. That flag is woven of heroism and grief, of the bravery of men and women's tears, of righteousness and battle, of sacrifice and anguish, of triumph and of glory. It is these which make our flag a holy thing. Who would tear from that sacred banner the glorious legends of a single battle where it has waved on land or sea? What son of a soldier of the flag whose father fell beneath it on any field would surrender that proud record for the heraldry of a king? In the cause of civilization, in the service of the Republic anywhere on earth, Americans consider wounds the noblest decorations man can win, and count the giving of their lives a glad and precious duty.

Pray God that spirit never fails. Pray God the time may never come when Mammon and the love of ease shall so debase our blood that we will fear to shed it for the flag and its imperial destiny. Pray God the time may never come when American heroism is but a legend like the story of the Cid, American faith in our mission and our might a dream dissolved, and the glory of our mighty race departed.

And that time will never come. We will renew our youth at the fountain of new and glorious deeds. We will exalt our reverence for the flag by carrying it to a noble future as well as by remembering its ineffable past. Its immortality will not pass, because everywhere and always we will acknowledge and discharge the solemn responsibilities our sacred flag, in its deepest meaning, puts upon us. And so, Senators, with reverent hearts, where dwells the fear of God, the American people move forward to the future of their hope and the doing of His work.

Mr. President and Senators, adopt the resolution offered, that peace may quickly come and that we may begin our saving, regenerating, and uplifting work. Adopt it, and this bloodshed will cease when these deluded children of our islands learn that this is the final word of the representatives of the American people in Congress assembled. Reject it, and the world, history, and the American people will know where to forever fix the awful responsibility for the consequences that will surely follow such failure to do our manifest duty. How dare we delay when our soldiers' blood is flowing? [Applause in the galleries.]

Congressional Record, Senate, 56th Congress, 1st session, Jan. 9, 1900, 704–712.

105   Senator George Frisbie Hoar on Self-Government for the Philippines

April 17, 1900

Senator George Frisbie Hoar (R-Mass.) had a long and distinguished career in the House of Representatives and the Senate. At the time of this speech, Hoar, a twenty-three-year veteran of the Senate, was nearing the end of his career. He was seventy-six when he delivered this address in opposition to U.S. acquisition of the Philippines. Hoar was out of step with his party on U.S. imperialism and was one of only two Republican senators to vote against the Treaty of Paris, which ended the Spanish-American War. Hoar's speech stands in marked contrast to the jingoism of Senator Albert J. Beveridge's Senate speech (see document 104) and remains a timeless argument against one nation imposing rule upon another nation without the consent of the governed.

. . . .

We are told if we oppose the policy of our imperialistic and expanding friends we are bound to suggest some policy of our own as a substitute for theirs. We are asked what we would do in this difficult emergency. It is a question not difficult to answer. I for one am ready to answer it.

1. I would declare now that we will not take these islands to govern them against their will.

2. I would reject a cession of sovereignty which implies that sovereignty may be bought and sold and delivered without the consent of the people. Spain had no rightful sovereignty over the Philippine Islands. She could not rightfully sell it to us. We could not rightfully buy it from her.

3. I would require all foreign governments to keep out of these islands.

4. I would offer to the people of the Philippines our help in maintaining order until they have a reasonable opportunity to establish a government of their own.

5. I would aid them by advice, if they desire it, to set up a free and independent government.

6. I would invite all the great powers of Europe to unite in an agreement that that independence shall not be interfered with by us, by themselves, or by any one of them with the consent of the others. As to this I am not so sure. I should like quite as well to tell them it is not to be done whether they consent or not.

7. I would declare that the United States will enforce the same doctrine as applicable to the Philippines that we declared as to Mexico and Haiti and the South American Republics. It is true that the Monroe Doctrine, a doctrine based largely on our regard for our own interests, is not applicable either in terms or in principle to a distant Asiatic territory. But undoubtedly, having driven out Spain, we are bound, and have the right, to secure to the people we have liberated an opportunity, undisturbed and in peace, to establish a new government for themselves.

8. I would then, in a not distant future, leave them to work out their own salvation, as every nation on earth, from the beginning of time, has wrought out its own salvation. . . . To attempt to confer the gift of freedom from without, or to impose freedom from without on any people, is to disregard all the lessons of history. It is to attempt

"A gift of that which is not to be given
By all the blended powers of earth and heaven."

9. I would strike out of your legislation the oath of allegiance to us and substitute an oath of allegiance to their own country. . . .

Mr. President, there lies at the bottom of what is called imperialism a doctrine which, if adopted, is to revolutionize the world in favor of despotism. It directly conflicts with and contradicts the doctrine on which our own revolution was founded, and with which, so far, our example has revolutionized the world. It is the doctrine that when, in the judgment of any one nation or any combination of nations, the institutions which a people set up and maintain for themselves are disapproved they have a right to overthrow that government and to enter upon and possess it themselves. . . .

Our imperialistic friends seem to have forgotten the use of the vocabulary of liberty. They talk about giving good government. "We shall give them such a government as we think they are fitted for." "We shall give them a better government than they had before." Why, Mr. President, that one phrase conveys to a free man and a free people the most stinging of insults. In that little phrase, as in a seed, is contained the germ of all despotism and of all tyranny. Government is not a gift. Free government is not to be given by all the blended powers of earth and heaven. It is a birthright. It belongs, as our fathers said and as their children said, as Jefferson said and as President McKinley said, to human nature itself. There can be no good government but self government. . . .

I have failed to discover in the speech, public or private, of the advocates of this war, or in the press which supports it and them, a single expression anywhere of a desire to do justice to the people of the Philippine Islands, or of a desire to make known to the people of the United States the truth of the case. . . .

The catchwords, the cries, the pithy and pregnant phrases of which all their speech is full, all mean dominion. They mean perpetual dominion. When a man tells you that the American flag must not be hauled down where it has once floated, or demands of a shouting audience, "Who will haul it down?" if he mean anything, he means that that people shall be under our dominion forever. The man who says, "We will not treat with them till they submit; we will not deal with men in arms against the flag," says, in substance, the same thing. One thing there has been, at least, given to them as Americans not to say. There is not one of these gentlemen who will rise in his place and affirm that if he were a Filipino he would not do exactly as the Filipinos are doing; that he would not despise them if they were to do otherwise. So much, at least, they owe of respect to the dead and buried history—the dead and buried history, so far as they can slay and bury it—of their country.

Why, the tariff schemes which are proposed are schemes in our interest and not in theirs. If you propose to bring tobacco from Porto Rico or from the Philippine Islands on the ground that it is for the interest of the people whom you are undertaking to govern, for their best interests to raise it and sell it to you, every imperialist in Connecticut will be up in arms. The nerve in the pocket is still sensitive, though the nerve in the heart may be numb. You will not let their sugar come here to compete with the cane sugar of Louisiana or the beet sugar of California or the Northwest, and in determining that question you mean to think not of their interest but of yours. The good government you are to give them is a government under which their great productive and industrial interests, when peace comes, are to be totally and absolutely disregarded by their government. You are not only proposing to do that, but you expect to put another strain on the Constitution to accomplish it.

Why, Mr. President, the atmosphere of both legislative chambers, even now, is filled with measures proposing to govern and tax these people for our interest, and not for theirs. Your men who are not alarmed at the danger to constitutional liberty are up in arms when there is danger to tobacco. . . .

Is there any man so bold as to utter in seriousness the assertion that where the American flag has once been raised it shall never be hauled down? I have heard it said that to haul down or to propose to haul down this national emblem where it has once floated is poltroonery. Will any man say it was poltroonery when Paul Jones landed on the northeast coast of England that he took his flag away with him when he departed? Was Scott a poltroon, or was Polk a poltroon? Was Taylor a poltroon? Was the United States a nation of poltroons when they retired from the City of Mexico or from Vera Cruz without leaving the flag behind them? . . .

Mr. President, this talk that the American flag is never to be removed where it has once floated is the silliest and wildest rhetorical flourish ever uttered in the ears of an excited populace. No baby ever said anything to another baby more foolish.

Now, what are the facts as to the Philippine Islands and the American flag? We have occupied a single city, part of one of four hundred islands, and with a population of 120,000 or thereabouts out of 10,000,000. The Spanish forces were invested and hemmed in by the people of those islands, who had risen to assert their own freedom when we got there. Now, what kind of Americanism, what kind of patriotism, what kind of love of liberty is it to say that we are to turn our guns on that patriot people and wrest from them the freedom that was almost within their grasp and hold these islands for our own purposes in subjection and by right of conquest because the American flag ought not to be hauled down where it has once floated, or, for the baser and viler motive still, that we can make a few dollars a year out of their trade?

Congressional Record, Senate, 56th Congress, 1st session, April 17, 1900, 4303–4305.

106 The Sixteenth Amendment to the Constitution

Submitted to the States, July 12, 1909; Ratified, February 25, 1913

One sentence is all it took to amend the Constitution and give Congress the power to collect tax based on income "from whatever source derived." This is one amendment to the Constitution that touched the lives of every American.

The first use of the income tax came during the Civil War (see document 75). The burden of the Civil War income tax fell heaviest on the New England states and California, and these states led the fight to repeal the law in 1872. The income tax was resurrected again in 1894, under the leadership of populist Democrats, including William Jennings Bryan of Nebraska. An amendment to a tariff bill that year provided for another income tax, but it was quickly challenged in the Supreme Court. By a narrow 5–4 decision the Supreme Court in Pollack v. Farmers' Loan and Trust Co. *declared the income tax to be unconstitutional because it was a direct excise tax, which the Constitution required to be proportioned equally in all states.*

With the submission of the Sixteenth Amendment to the states, Congress addressed the Supreme Court's objection in the Pollack *case by saying the income tax could be collected "without apportionment among the several States, and without regard to any census or enumeration." Once the amendment had been ratified in 1913, Congress quickly passed a relatively simple income tax law only eight pages in length. The rates were modest, most Americans were exempt, and only 2 percent of Americans paid any income tax as a result of the first law, passed in October 1913. Matters*

changed quickly once the United States entered World War I. The income tax became a major source of revenue for the nation. Congress lowered exemptions and increased rates. As a result, more Americans had to pay the tax. Even so, as late as 1939 only 15 percent of Americans were filing returns. Things changed quickly with the coming of World War II. In 1942 employers began withholding taxes from paychecks. Before the war was over more than 90 percent of Americans were filing income tax returns.

Just as disagreements over high versus low tariffs dominated and shaped political discourse and the development of political parties in the nineteenth century, raising or lowering income taxes became a defining issue for twentieth century political parties, especially in the second half of the twentieth century. Politics has always been about what to do and how to pay for it. One major reason why the public is often critical of Congress is because Congress has the power to tax.

ARTICLE XVI.

The Congress shall have the power to lay and collect taxes on incomes, from whatever source derived, without apportionment among the several States, and without regard to any census or enumeration.

The Constitution of the United States of America as Amended, House Doc. 102–188, 102d Congress, 2d session (Washington: Government Printing Office, 1992), 18.

107 The Revolt Against Speaker Joseph Cannon

March 19, 1910

Beginning on St. Patrick's Day, March 17, 1910, and culminating two days later on March 19, a revolution occurred in the House of Representatives that marked a major shift in the powers of the Speaker of the House. This revolution did not involve bloodshed or violence. It was conducted through a highly dramatic parliamentary maneuver that resulted in a major change in the rules of the House. The event has become one of the most noted chapters in the history of the House of Representatives.

The Speaker of the House from 1903 to 1910 was Joseph Gurney Cannon (R-Ill.), who had served thirty-five years in the House at the time of the revolt against him. Over the years Cannon rose in power in the House to become one of the chief lieutenants of Speaker Thomas Reed (R-Maine), when major changes in House rules transformed the House (see document 101). Cannon was one of the men who ushered in and defended Reed's Rules.

When Cannon became Speaker in 1903, he, like Reed, was labeled a "czar" and a "tyrant" for his willingness to exercise his power to

appoint committees and run the House Rules Committee by serving on the committee and appointing its chairman. Cannon, known by friend and foe alike as "Uncle Joe," was a shrewd, amiable man who characterized himself as a hayseed from Danville, Illinois. He frequently said that America was a "hell of a success" and it did not need new legislation to improve it. A conservative, Cannon sought to block "progressive" legislation coming from Democrats and a growing number of progressives within his own party. Scott Rager, a Cannon scholar, has called him "the brakeman of the House" for his attempts to hold back the flood of Progressive Era legislation coming in the early years of the twentieth century. See Scott Rager, "Uncle Joe Cannon: The Brakeman of the House of Representatives, 1903–1911," in Roger H. Davidson, Susan Webb Hammond, and Raymond W. Smock (eds.), Masters of the House: Congressional Leadership Over the Centuries *(Boulder, Colo.: Westview Press, 1998).*

With the Democrats in the minority in the House, they alone could not challenge Cannon's authority. It took a young progres-

sive Republican from Nebraska, George E. Norris, to lead the attempt to overturn Cannon's iron-fisted control of the House and its committees.

On March 17, with some members already absent from the chamber because of St. Patrick's Day festivities, Norris introduced a resolution that would change the rules of the House by removing the Speaker's power to appoint the chairman of the Rules Committee and removing the Speaker from a place on the Rules Committee. Furthermore, Norris called for the Rules Committee to be elected by the members themselves rather than being appointed by the Speaker. This would, in effect, strip the Speaker of a considerable amount of power.

John Dalzell of Pennsylvania, Cannon's hand-picked Rules Committee chairman, immediately objected to Norris's resolution on a point of order saying the resolution violated House rules. Cannon delayed making a ruling on the point of order, stalling for time until more Republicans loyal to him could return to the House chamber. Republicans kept the House in session all night and until 2:00 P.M. the next afternoon. After some additional delaying tactics the House finally met on the morning of March 19, when Cannon hoped he would have sufficient votes to rule against Norris's resolution and have his ruling sustained by the House. In the meantime, behind-the-scenes negotiations were underway to find a compromise. But Cannon instructed his loyalists not to compromise. If he lost control of the Rules Committee through compromise he would lose just as much as he would if the vote went against him. He preferred to fight it out on the floor of the House.

Cannon, not surprisingly, ruled against the Norris resolution. What came as a surprise was the House vote on sustaining the Speaker's ruling. Cannon lost by a vote of 182–163. Then, when the vote came on the Norris resolution; it passed by a vote of 191–156. Insurgent Republicans and Democrats had managed to team up to defeat the Speaker and end his centralized control of the House.

Even in the midst of defeat Uncle Joe Cannon rose to the occasion with a remarkable speech. Although it seemed spontaneous, Cannon had worked it out in advance in case he lost on the Norris resolution. He took a calculated risk and offered to step down as Speaker. While some in the chamber would have been happy to see Cannon go, the insurgents had already beaten Cannon; it would serve no further purpose to drive him from office. A resolution to declare the office of Speaker vacant and to call for an immediate election of a new Speaker failed by a vote of 155–192.

Cannon kept the Speakership for another year, but he was seriously weakened. His tight control of the House had caused a serious split in his own party that continued to grow. In 1911 he turned over the Speaker's gavel to Champ Clark and the new Democratic majority in the House. The old brakeman of the House could no longer hold back the powerful forces in both political parties that ushered in the Progressive Era. In the election of 1912 Cannon lost his seat in the House in a close election. But he would return two years later and serve again as a representative from Illinois until his retirement from politics in 1923.

. . . .

The SPEAKER. The Chair is prepared to rule on the matter pending before the House, and will ask the Clerk to read the resolution presented by the gentleman from Nebraska [Mr. Norris].

The Clerk read as follows:

House resolution 502.
Resolved, That the rules of the House be amended as follows:
"The Committee on Rules shall consist of 15 members, 9 of whom shall be members of the majority party and 6 of whom shall be members of the minority party, to be selected as follows:
"The States of the Union shall be divided by a committee of three, elected by the House for that purpose, into nine groups, each group containing, as near as may be, an equal number of Members belonging to the majority party. The States of the Union shall likewise be divided into six groups, each group containing, as near may be, an equal number of Members belonging to the minority party.
"At 10 o'clock a.m. of the day following the adoption of the report of said committee each of said groups shall meet and select one of its number a member of the Committee on Rules. The place of meeting for each of said groups shall be designated by the said committee of three in its report. Each of said groups shall report to the House the name of the Member selected for membership on the Committee on Rules.
"The Committee on Rule shall select its own chairman.
"The Speaker shall not be eligible to membership on said committee.
"All rules or parts thereof inconsistent with the foregoing resolution are hereby repealed."

The SPEAKER. To that resolution the gentleman from Pennsylvania [Mr. Dalzell] made the point of order that its consideration should not be entered upon contrary to the rules of the House, as provided under a demand for the regular order.

The Chair has been somewhat criticized because in this matter he has been slow to rule. But the question which was brought so unexpectedly upon the attention of the House, in a revolutionary manner, as it seems to the Chair, to of such transcendent importance to the future procedure of the House that the fullest, even the most protracted, discussion seemed justifiable. In no other manner could the most complete information be brought to the consideration of the question, and in no other way could the largest participation of the membership of the House be assured.

The question of constitutional privilege in this House has not been reviewed, and the principles governing for the last thirty years have not, prior to this week, been questioned in this House for many years. Those principles are relatively simple. It has been held always that the ordinary legislative duties and functions of the House, exercised by authority of the constitution, must proceed according to the order prescribed by the rules. The fact that the Constitution says that the House "shall have power to" lay taxes, regulate commerce, make naturalization laws, coin money, establish post-offices, create courts, support armies and a navy, and so forth, has not given these subjects when embodied In bills any right to disturb the order of business provided by the rules. The very object of the rules is to provide an orderly way for considering those and other subjects entrusted to the House judgment. To give all those subjects constitutional privilege would be to establish constitutional chaos in the House.

There are, however, certain functions which the Constitution enjoins on Congress to do, and also fixes the time for doing these things. Thus, the clause directing the disposition of a bill vetoed by the President says that the House "shall proceed" to consider it. This has always been understood as meaning that the House should at once proceed to some act of consideration. And therefore it has been held that no rule should prevent the House from proceeding to this constitutional duty. In like manner the Constitution specifies that the Congress shall provide for a census of population and an apportionment of Representatives, and specifies the time when it shall do it— every tenth year. Therefore, on the tenth year, bills to make the required provision have been admitted without regard to the requirements of the House rules. Whether that construction proceeded too far when the Constitution gave a year within which to perform the duty, to a matter as to which there might be doubt

But for thirty years the practice was unvarying; and when confronted with the question this week, the Chair followed the practice of the House, as he would obey every other rule, without questioning the wisdom that originally created it.

To-day, however, the Chair is asked to permit a proposition for a new rule to come in, although the rules prescribing the order of business require us to proceed to other matters, and it is claimed that the Chair would be justified in doing this because the Constitution says that "each House may determine the rules of its proceeding." Whether the word "may" means "shall" or not, the Chair will not stop to examine, The Constitution fixes no time when rules shall be adopted; and as the House may, and has in one notable instance, proceeded without rules, it does not seem to the Chair that there is here given any constitutional mandate which would justify the overriding of the rules. Fortunately in this crisis the Chair is not compelled to rely crisis his own judgment, swayed as he might be by the passions and purposes of this hour. He can look back to another hour, when in a day of calm the navigators who steered the business of this House took their latitude and longitude unembarrassed by the exigencies of tempest.

The pathway of the Chair has been blazed, not by any flushed majority in a moment of factional success, not for any ends of one political party as opposed to the wishes of another political party, not under auspices which prejudice the Chair because of memories of political affiliation of his own, but on a question of order raised by a great Democratic floor leader of this House, and decided by a great Democratic Speaker.

On December 13, 1878, this identical question arose in this House. Mr. Roger Q. Mills, of Texas, proposed as a question of constitutional privilege, exactly as is proposed to-day, to offer from the floor for immediate consideration a proposition looking to the amendment of the rules. And when objection was made, as it is made to-day, Mr. Mills argued:

It is the constitutional privilege of a House of Representatives to adopt rules at any time; it is a continuing power of which the House can not divest itself.

The Members of the House did not agree with Mr. Mills, and Mr. James A. Garfield objected that it was proposed—

to carry the power of the House in this respect further than the Constitution justifies. If the position of the gentleman were correct, a Member could at any time interrupt our proceedings by bringing in a proposition for the amendment of the rules.

The great Democratic Speaker—and the Chair measures his words in memory of the fame of a man who was the peer of his associates, the civil war leaders who yet lingered on this floor— the great Speaker, Samuel J. Randall, heard the arguments for and against the claim of Mr. Mills, and decided that the proposition to amend the rules was not a case of constitutional privilege. There was criticism, grave criticism, of the rules in those days, as there is to-day, but no man in that House thought of appealing from a decision so consonant with reason.

Planting himself upon the law made for the House by Mr. Speaker Randall, appealing from the passion of this day to the just reasons of that day, the Chair sustains the point of order and holds that the resolution is not in order. [Loud and long-continued applause on the Republican side.]

Mr. NORRIS. Mr. Speaker, I appeal from the decision; and on that I move the previous question.

The SPEAKER. The gentleman from Nebraska appeals from the decision of the Chair.

Mr. DALZELL. I move to lay the appeal on the table.

Mr. GAINES. Mr. Speaker—

The SPEAKER. One moment.

Mr. GAINES. I move that the House do now adjourn.

The SPEAKER. The Chair will say to the gentleman,

Mr. NORRIS. I concede, Mr. Speaker, that the motion of the gentleman from Pennsylvania has precedence over mine.

The SPEAKER. Correct; and pending that the gentleman from West Virginia moves that the House do adjourn, which has precedence over both motions. The question was taken.

Mr. FOELKER. Yeas and nays, Mr. Speaker.

The SPEAKER. On a viva voce vote the noes seem to have it; the noes have it, and the House refuses to adjourn. The gentleman from Pennsylvania moves to lay the appeal from the decision of the Chair, made by the gentleman from Nebraska, on the table.

Mr. DALZELL and Mr. CLARK of Missouri. Yeas and nays!

The yeas and nays were ordered.

The question was taken; and there were, yeas 164, nays 182, answered "present" 6, not voting 37. . . .

So the motion to lay the appeal on the table was rejected. . . .

The result of the vote was then announced as above recorded. [Loud applause on the Democratic side.]

Mr. NORRIS: Mr. Speaker—

The SPEAKER. The gentleman from Nebraska.

Mr. NORRIS. Mr. Speaker, inasmuch as we have been debating this point of order for two days, I do not suppose anybody desires any further debate, and therefore I move the previous question on the appeal.

Mr. BURKE of Pennsylvania. Mr. Speaker, will the gentleman withhold his demand a moment?

Mr. NORRIS. I yield to the gentleman from Pennsylvania.

Mr. BURKE of Pennsylvania. I understood the gentleman from Nebraska to state that he assumed that no further discussion was desired by any of the Members of the House. I have no doubt that that is an honest assumption, but I wish to state to the gentleman that there is a desire upon the part of Members who have not discussed the point of order or the merits of the resolution, and I hope the gentleman will withhold his motion. [Cries of "No!" "No!"]

Mr. NORRIS. Mr. Speaker, I would suggest to the gentleman from Pennsylvania that this motion for the previous question on the appeal does not affect the merits, or the discussion of the merit, of the resolution itself. Why, this point of order was before the House all night, when the gentleman was in bed, and he might have been here to debate it then.

The SPEAKER. The gentleman from Nebraska moves the previous question on the appeal. The question pending before the House is, Shall the decision of the Chair stand as the judgment of the House? Upon that question the gentleman from Nebraska moves the previous question.

Mr. DALZELL. On that I demand the yeas and nays.

Mr. TAWNEY. On this we ask for the yeas and nays.

The yeas and nays were ordered.

The question was taken; and there were—yeas 183, nays 160, answered "present" 7, not voting 39. . . .

So the previous question was ordered. . . .

The SPEAKER. On this vote the ayes are 183 and the noes are 160. The previous question is ordered. The question is, Shall the decision of the Chair stand as the judgment of the House?

Mr. DALZELL. And on that we demand the yeas and nays.

The yeas and nays were ordered.

Mr. JAMES. Mr. Speaker, I ask that the question be stated again. There was so much confusion on this side of the Chamber that some Members did not hear it.

The SPEAKER pro tempore (Mr. OLMSTED). The question is, Shall the decision of the Chair stand as the judgment of the House?

The question was taken; and there were—yeas 161, nays 182, answered "present" 7, not voting 37. . . .

The SPEAKER pro tempore. The yeas are 162 and the nays are 182. The decision of the Chair does not stand as the judgment of the House. The Clerk will read the resolution now pending before the House.

The Clerk read as follows:

House resolution 502.

Resolved, That the Rules of the House be amended as follows:

"The Committee on Rules shall consist of 15 members, 9 of whom shall be members of the majority party and 6 of whom shall be members of the minority party, to be selected as follows:

"The States of the Union shall be divided, by a committee of three, containing, as near as may be, an equal number of Members belonging to the majority party. The States of the Union shall likewise be divided into six groups, each group containing, as near as may be, an equal number of members belonging to the minority party.

"At 10 o'clock ante meridian of the day following the adoption of the report of said committee each of said groups shall meet and select one of its members a member of the committee on Rules. The place of meeting for each of said groups shall be designated by the said committee of three in its report. Each of said groups shall report to the House the name of the Member selected for membership on the committee on Rules.

"The Committee on Rules shall select its own chairman.

"All rules or parts thereof inconsistent with the foregoing resolution are hereby repealed."

Mr. NORRIS. Mr. Speaker, I would like to see if we can not have an agreement as to time for debate. I would like to ask the gentleman from Pennsylvania if we an come to any agreement.

Mr. DALZELL. What time would the gentleman from Nebraska suggest?

Mr. NORRIS. I would suggest that we have an hour and a half on each side. Would that meet with the approval of the House?

Mr. DALZELL. That will be satisfactory to us.

Mr. NORRIS. Then, Mr. Speaker, I will ask unanimous or substitutes thereto, be limited to one hour and a half on each from Pennsylvania and on the other side by myself.

Mr. MANN. Reserving the right to object, Mr. Speaker, I would like to ask the gentleman what about amendments?

Mr. NORRIS: I was going to suggest a similar proposition on the amendments.

Mr. MANN. I understand, but are amendments to be disposed of at the time they are offered, or are they to be disposed of after the conclusion of the debate?

Mr. NORRIS. I did not hear the last part of the gentleman's remark.

The SPEAKER. The gentleman from Illinois desires to know when the amendments are to be offered.

Mr. MANN. Under the gentleman's proposition, any amendment might take up the entire time of debate, and would have to be disposed of—

Mr. NORRIS: I will say that I expect to offer at the beginning of the discussion a substitute for the resolution pending, and I would like to have unanimous consent that the gentleman from Pennsylvania be allowed to offer a substitute if he wishes to, or an amendment in the nature of a substitute, and that the previous question be considered as ordered on all amendments and substitutes to the resolution to final passage at the close of the debate.

Mr. RODENBERG. Mr. Speaker, I object to the request of the gentleman from Nebraska.

Mr. DALZELL. May I ask what the gentleman's objection is—to the time?

Mr. RODENBERG. Yes.

Mr. NORRIS. Did I understand that there was objection made the unanimous consent?

The SPEAKER. Yes.

Mr. NORRIS. Mr. Speaker, if the objection is of such a nature that any additional proposition should be contained in the request, I would like to hear from the gentleman. I am willing to concede any reasonable proposition as to this debate.

Mr. RODENBERG. I think the time is entirely too short on an important matter such as this.

Mr. NORRIS. How much time does the gentleman. I am willing to concede any reasonable proposition as to this debate.

Mr. RODENBERG. I think the time is entirely too short on an important matter such as this.

Mr. NORRIS. How much time does the gentleman think we ought to have?

Mr. RODENBERG. I think we ought to have at least five hours a side.

Mr. NORRIS. I would not want to agree to as long a debate as that. We have been debating this now for some time.

Mr. RODENBERG. I would compromise on two and a half hours a side.

Mr. MANN. We better have a week's time, I think.

Mr. NORRIS. Would the gentleman be willing to agree to two hours on a side?

Mr. MANN. Mr. speaker, I suggest to the gentleman that at the end of four hours or two hours or any other time he will have the right to move the previous question.

Mr. NORRIS. Well, I will have to have the floor in order to move the previous question.

Mr. MANN. The gentleman could reserve part of his time and doubtless get the floor. He is in charge of the measure, and I suppose the Speaker will recognize him at any time.

The SPEAKER. The Chair calls the attention of the gentleman from Nebraska to the fact that the previous question carries with it its own right to recognition. Under the rule there can not be a period of more than one hour during which time that right can not be exercised.

Mr. TAWNEY. Mr. Speaker, I desire to ask the gentleman from Nebraska whether this hour and a half on a side will deprive members of the opportunity of discussing amendments that may be offered to his proposition when the amendment is offered.

Mr. NORRIS. Well, I think it would not, unless the gentleman desiring to discuss any amendment had spoken prior to the time of the offering of the amendment, and then it would.

Mr. MANN. If the previous question were offered at the end of three hours, nobody would have a chance to discuss of offer an amendment.

Mr. TAWNEY. That is the reason I propounded this inquiry.

Mr. NORRIS. I suppose we can agree, then, that all amendments or substitutes must be offered within one hour of the time of the beginning of the debate, and that all voting will take place at the close of the discussion.

Mr. TAWNEY. That could only be done by unanimous consent.

Mr. NORRIS. That could only be done by unanimous consent.

Mr. KEIFER. Offer the amendments at the close of the general debate?

Mr. MANN. With no chance to discuss them? I shall object to that.

Mr. DALZELL. Mr. Speaker, I think we had better proceed under the rules. [Cries of "Regular order!"]

The SPEAKER. The regular order is demanded. The gentleman from Nebraska has the floor.

Mr. NORRIS. Mr. Speaker, while personally I prefer the resolution which I offered the other day and which is now before the House over the substitute which I intend to offer is better than the original resolution. Therefore, in accordance with their wishes, I expect to support the substitute which I now send to the Clerk's desk for the resolution that is now pending.

The SPEAKER. Does the gentleman now offer the substitute or does he desire to have it read for information?

Mr. NORRIS. I offer the substitute.

The SPEAKER. The gentleman from Nebraska offers the following amendment by way of substitute, which the Clerk will report.

The Clerk read as follows:

House resolution 502.

Resolved, That the rules of the House of Representatives be amended as follows:

"1. In Rule X, paragraph 1, strike out the words 'on Rules, to consist of five members.'

"2. Add new paragraph to Rule X, as follows:

" 'Paragraph 5. There shall be a committee on Rules, elected by the House, consisting of 10 Members, 6 of whom shall be Members of the majority party and 4 of whom shall be Members of the minority party. The Speaker shall not be a member of the committee and the committee shall elect its own chairman from its own members.'

"*Resolved further,* That within ten days after the adoption of this resolution there shall be an election of this committee, and immediately upon its election the present Committee on Rules shall be dissolved."

Mr. MARTIN of South Dakota. Mr. Speaker—

The SPEAKER. Does the gentleman yield?

Mr. NORRIS. I yield for a question.

Mr. MARTIN of South Dakota. Mr. Speaker—

Mr. MANN. Mr. Speaker—

The SPEAKER. To whom does the gentleman from Nebraska yield?

Mr. MANN. Mr. Speaker, I make the point of order the gentleman from Nebraska has not the floor.

Mr. NORRIS. Mr. Speaker, I said I would yield to the gentleman from South Dakota.

Mr. MANN. Mr. Speaker, I submit the gentleman from Nebraska—

The SPEAKER. For what purpose does the gentleman rise?

Mr. MANN. To submit that the gentleman from Nebraska is not entitled to the floor. The gentleman from Nebraska was recognized for one hour. During that time he offered an amendment. When he offered the amendment he lost the floor and is not entitled to recognition now for another hour, to which, if he were recognized, he would have in preference to recognition from the other side. If the gentleman from Nebraska can offer an amendment and obtain the floor now for an hour, he can retain the floor for the balance of the afternoon by offering amendment after amendment.

The SPEAKER. The point of order Is well taken by the gentleman from Illinois; although the gentleman from Nebraska, being the original proposer of the resolution, had not proceeded to debate, but in the moment offers a substitute by way of amendment, and it would be the duty of the Chair in that case to recognize the gentleman if he applies for recognition upon the substitute, not on the original proposition. You may say this amounts to a new recognition, but it would not be, as the gentleman had not proceeded to debate.

Mr. MANN. I understood the gentleman bad proceeded to debate.

The SPEAKER. Not on the merits of the proposition.

Mr. MARTIN of South Dakota. Mr. Speaker, I desire to offer an amendment as a substitute to the amendment of the gentleman.

Mr. NORRIS. I can not yield to the gentleman for the purpose without losing the floor, as the gentleman understands, and while I want to get an agreement in regard to time of debate and the offering of amendments, that being denied, I can not yield to the gentleman, I am sorry to say, under the parliamentary situation.

Mr. MARTIN of South Dakota. Mr. Speaker, I would then ask unanimous consent to have the amendment read as considered as pending.

Mr. NORRIS. I would say to the gentleman that In accordance with his request I expect to yield him some time, even out of the hour I have, and he can offer his amendment in that time.

Mr. GAINES. The gentleman from Nebraska could permit the gentleman from South Dakota to have his amendment read, and the gentleman from South Dakota ought to agree to that. [Cries of "Regular order!"]

The SPEAKER. The gentleman declines to yield.

Mr. NORRIS. Now, Mr. Speaker, I yield to the gentleman from Missouri [Mr. CLARK] five minutes.

Mr. DOUGLAS. Mr. Speaker, a parliamentary inquiry. I want to call the attention of the Chair—

The SPEAKER. The gentleman will state it.

Mr. DOUGLAS. Will the Chair permit the Clerk to read the number of the rule to which this substitute is an amendment?

The SPEAKER. It is probably Rule X. Without objection, not to be taken out of the time of the gentleman from Nebraska, the substitute will be again reported.

There was no objection.

The amendment was again reported.

The SPEAKER. The Chair suggests to the gentleman from Nebraska, if he will give his attention, as the Chair caught it, it seems the substitute is to paragraph 4, There is a paragraph 4. Does the gentleman desire to add an additional paragraph by making it paragraph 5?

Mr. NORRIS. It is paragraph 5, I think.

The SPEAKER. It was read as paragraph 4. The gentleman can modify, without objection, his substitute.

Mr. NORRIS. It ought to be five.

Mr. CLARK of Missouri. Mr. Speaker, no man in this presence realizes more thoroughly than I do the seriousness as well as the importance of this occasion. I want to make one personal remark; whether it will be popular or not I do not know, and to tell you the truth I do not care. This is not a personal light, so far as I am concerned, or ever has been, against the Hon. Joseph G. Cannon, from the State of Illinois, personally. [Loud applause on both sides of the Chamber.] I can lay my hand on my heart and truthfully assert that the personal relations between that distinguished personage and myself have always been pleasant.

So far as I am concerned and as far as the men who have co-operated with me are concerned, so far as I know, this is a fight against a system. We think it is a bad system, as far as this Committee on Rules has been concerned. It does not make any difference to me that it is sanctified by time. There never has been any progress in this world except to overthrow precedents and take new positions. [Applause.] There never will be. Reformers and progressives are necessarily and inevitably iconoclasts.

I want to say another thing, so far as I am concerned. There is no other proposition pending in my mind on my own initiative or by agreement with anybody except the one that is pending here to-day. I have believed ever since I was in the House long enough to understand the work of the Committee on Rules that the fact that the Speaker of the House was chairman of that committee, and practically the Committee on Rules, gives the Speaker of this House more power than any one man ought to have over the destinies of this Republic. [Applause on the Democratic side.]

Macaulay says that Sir Robert Walpole was avaricious of power. I am not certain but that the illustrious historian might without exaggeration have extended that remark so as to Include the entire human race within its scope. It is for that very reason that restrictions, constitutional and otherwise, are placed upon public men—even upon hereditary kings, emperors, and potentates. And every such new restriction smashes precedents. We had made up our mind months ago to try to work the particular revolution that we are working here to-day, because, not to mince words, it is a revolution. I have no fear of revolutions, for men of our blood revolutionize in the right direction. The enlargement of the Committee on Rules even in itself has some beneficent features attached to it, simply that and nothing more, because it takes into consideration, as the gentleman from Wisconsin [Mr. Cooper] stated the other night, the larger portion of the country. But I am not giving any adhesion to any proposition concerning this rules business that does not remove the Speaker now, and, so far as we can control it, for all time to come, from the Committee on Rules. [Applause on the Democratic side.] That is my position, and in that I speak for the Democrats of the House and the insurgent Republicans. [Applause on the Democratic side.] We are fighting to rehabilitate the House of Representatives and to restore it to its ancient place of honor and prestige in our system of government.

I do not believe that men in this world are heard for much speaking or that much attention is paid to it after it is done, and it seems to me that I have stated our whole contention.

You can not restore to the membership of this House the quantum of power that each Member is entitled to without taking from the Speaker of the House some quantum of the power he now enjoys, because he practically enjoys it all. On this proposition I could wish that there could be a unanimous vote of this House, but that is a hope too fantastic for entertainment. We want to try this experiment. If it does not work well, Mr. Speaker, the House at any time can change it, because it has now been definitely settled that this House can do what it pleases when it wants to do it. [Applause on the Democratic side.]

Mr. NORRIS. Mr. Speaker, I yield five minutes to the gentleman from Minnesota [Mr. Nye].

Mr. NYE. Mr. Speaker, I am obliged to the gentleman from Nebraska for his courtesy, because my conscience and my judgment impel me to vote against his resolution. [Applause on the Republican side.] There are decisive moments in the history of human affairs, and destiny seems sometime to hang upon the results of a moment. I have no fear of the individual conscience, but so far as passion rather than patriotism actuates us in such moments, so far as we and the country will reap disastrous consequences from it.

What I have to say is addressed to Republicans. I have not always been in perfect accord with the leadership of this House. I am inclined to be individually independent in various matters; but I am willing to take responsibility, and if this is a vote against a system, as we are told it is, I am willing to say that we, as Republicans, are responsible for the system and should share the consequences of it. [Applause on the Republican side.]

But I fear; Mr. Speaker, this is not a fight against a system. I fear that passion and personal feeling have stirred the men who are moving in this matter to-day, and I feel that the country as well as the great party to which we belong may regret it and regret it bitterly. Parties are a necessity, and the great power and effectiveness of the Republican party has, been largely its cohesiveness. Its followers have stood shoulder to shoulder and fought the battle against a political foe. And as for me, I am willing to take the consequences. It looks too much like mutiny against captain and crew in the face of storm and night. [Loud applause on the Republican side.] I will stay with the ship—and go down If necessary. I will not hold my sent at the cost of conscience and heap personal indignity upon the chosen leader of the Republican party. [Loud applause on the Republican side.] I have not been close to our Speaker, have no intimate acquaintance with him, but for forty years not only his party but the Nation has honored him, and to-day you seek to butcher him, "to make a Roman holiday." [Loud applause on the Republican side.] I will not stand for it. Let the storm come, man the old Republican ship again, and let her face the storm, and as Holmes said in his Ironsides:

> Nail to the mast her holy flag,
> Set every threadbare sail,
> And give her to the god of storms,
> The lightning and the gale!

[Loud and long-continued applause on the Republican side.]

Mr. NORRIS. I yield two minutes to the gentleman from New York.

Mr. FOELKER. Mr. Speaker, it has been threatened that we are to be read out of the Republican party. I came to this country from Germany when quite a boy because there was no opportunity for such as I in the land of my birth. When I got to learn something of the institutions of this land, I saw at once that they had been protected, preserved, and perpetuated by the Republican party; that with the retirement of the Buchanan administration chaos and war were precipitated, which almost permanently disrupted the Union, costing hundreds of thousands of lives, millions of treasure, and left many sorrowing hearts for those who would never return. The Republican party took over the country in these conditions, and we find it led by Lincoln until the cause of the trouble was removed in the abolition of slavery, upon the consummation of which he yielded up his life a martyr to the cause which he had so espoused. Then came Grant, Hayes, Garfield, Harrison, McKinley, Roosevelt, and last, through not least, President Taft, all of whom believed in the destiny of the Republic, first as Republicans and always as Americans. As soon as I could vote I joined this party, and have always voted its ticket. An attempt may be made to read me out of it because I have not been subservient to the will of some of its leaders, but I am willing to trust my future with the people whom I came here to serve and whom I am serving to the best of my ability.

Mr. Speaker, I am going to vote to override the ruling of the Chair and ask that this matter be passed upon by the House as a body, and by the whole House.

Mr. NORRIS. I yield five minutes to the gentleman from South Dakota.

Mr. MARTIN of South Dakota. Mr. Speaker, the resolution which I shall offer as an amendment to the substitute, if I may have an opportunity to present it, is itself well known to many of the membership of this House, and will be offered at time of these proceedings when amendments can be presented.

Mr. DOUGLAS. Read it.

Mr. MARTIN of South Dakota. I have only five minutes. I will read it:

Resolved, That the Committee on Rules shall consist of 10 members, 6 of whom shall be members of the majority party and 4 of whom shall be members of the minority party, all of whom shall be elected by the House by majority vote.

The Committee on Rules shall select its own chairman.

After March 3, 1911, the same person shall not at the same time hold the office of Speaker and membership on the Committee on Rules.

All rules or parts thereof inconsistent with this resolution are hereby repealed.

The amendment, if adopted by this House, would enlarge the committee to 10, as in the Norris resolution, 6 Republicans and 4 Democrats, all to be elected by the House, and would leave for the House, at the time of the election of members of this committee, to decide whether the Speaker should be a member during the balance of this session and this Congress it announces the principle that the Speaker shall not after a certain time occupy the position of Speaker and a position upon the Committee on Rules.

I think my position upon this subject was quite clearly stated in the debate yesterday. I stated upon the point of order that while fundamentally it was doubtful as to whether the resolution of the gentleman from Indiana [Mr. Crumpacker] a day or two previous was in order upon the ground of high constitutional prerogative, that certainly if that was in order the Norris resolution was in order, and for one I should hold the House to the precedent that it had established by its deliberate vote. I should further that if it came to a vote upon the floor of the House, I should, consistently with that position, vote to overturn the decision of the Chair. That would give an opportunity to the House to consider this resolution at this time. In my judgment this is a question of high privilege. It does not rest alone upon precedents for being in order at this time. Every deliberative body reserves necessarily from the inception of its organizational control over its own committees, which tire really its servants.

This committee chances to be the House Committee on Rules. The rules of this House provide that all amendments pertaining to the rules shall be referred to the Committee on Rules; but here we have an amendment which proposes to remodel and reconstruct that committee itself, and it would be absurd and without parliamentary precedent to say that by adopting certain rules at the beginning of this Congress the House thereby gave this Committee on Rules a prerogative so far-reaching that it would pass through the entire length of this Congress of two years and make it impossible for this House to detract from that committee any portion of the power given to it.

In other words, we would be in the position of being helpless to remodel this committee, except by referring a rule to that committee for its consent. The principle of Master and servant applies to the deliberations of this body as well as to the commercial transactions of life. This House in its sovereign right undoubtedly has inherently within itself the power upon its own motion, at any particular time, to reconsider the question of the apportionment of the powers of committees and the personnel of those committees.

I think I have made it plain that there is no personal feeling upon my part in this entire proceeding, except a personal feeling of the kindest character toward the Speaker of this House and toward the membership of this Committee on Rules. By the silent evolution of power of the Speaker, without any special rule upon the subject, has become a member of the Committee on Rules and the chairman of that body. It is often said in popular language that this is a House governed by a majority. That is in part true, but it is true only in part. The Committee on Rules can pass no law without the support of the majority of the House. With the large number of bill, on our calendars most important measures may never be heard, unless the Rules Committee shall so decide. In other words, accurately speaking, the power dominant in this House resides in a majority of the House, with the consent and initiative of the Committee on Rules.

As the Speaker appoints the Committee on Rules and has the deciding vote on the committee, it is evident that the power to prefer or reject legislation of the utmost importance really rests with the Speaker himself. This is a day of popular government. The people are demanding that a portion of the power that has been by custom centered in the Speaker shall be restored to the Representatives themselves. It is a reasonable demand, and will go far toward restoring to this body the prestige and dignity it possessed in the early years of the Republic.

Mr. NORRIS. I yield five minutes to the gentleman from Wisconsin [Mr. Lenroot].

Mr. LENROOT. Mr. Speaker, I wish to address myself to the proposed amendment suggested by the gentleman from South Dakota [Mr. Martin]. His amendment, like the pending proposition, enlarges the Committee on Rules to 10 members. His proposal, like the pending proportion, recognizes and endorses the principle that the Speaker should not be a member of the Committee on Rules. However, while recognizing that principle, his proposition clearly declares that while that principle is correct, nevertheless the present Speaker of this House ought to be a member of the Committee on Rules. We believe that in the future no Speaker should be a member of the committee, and that the present Speaker ought not to be a member of that committee. [Applause.] And I wish the Republican side clearly to have in mind, if a vote shall be taken upon that proposition, exactly what the effect of it is.

Now, Mr. Speaker, much has been said about disruption In the Republican party and the peril which it is in it the present time. I say that, in my sincere judgment, the adoption of the pending proposition will do much to insure a Republican majority in the next Congress. We should remember that the Republican party is not conflict within the walls of this Capitol. We should remember that the success of the Republican party does not depend upon its so-called leaders, but upon the men upon our farms, in our shops throughout this land, in the rank and file of the Republican party, and that rank, and file desire that this body be made a representative body. They believe that this will tend to make this what it should be, a government by the people. [Applause.]

. . . .

Mr. NORRIS. I yield five minutes to the gentleman from Alabama [Mr. Clayton].

Mr. CLAYTON. The gentleman from Nebraska offered the fairest sort of a proposition at the very opening of this discussion. According to my recollection, his first proposition was for two hours of debate on the pending question, one hour to be consumed on this side and one hour on the other side.

He afterwards enlarged that proposition so as to include an hour and a half on each side for discussion. He afterwards further said, according to my recollection, that he willing to ask the house to accord two hours to each side for this discussion.

Now, these propositions were each severally and separately rejected, and it does not come with good grace from the gentleman from Pennsylvania at this time to say that he must have thirty minutes in his own right or, as has been suggested, that he have an hour in his own right.

The Speaker, those of us on this side of this Chamber who are fighting this unbridled power of the Speaker have seen the rules of this House so used, and I measure my words when I say so abused, I believe in the very nature of party exigency—so demanded by party exigency—that the whole country has forced the minority of this House and a minority of the majority of this House to strike hands with each other in order that this power of the Speaker may be curbed. That is what we are here for today. That is what we were here for the other day and night during a continuous session of more than twenty-nine hours. The Speaker is right when he said in some of his observations that this is revolutionary, for we are now conducting a parliamentary revolution.

For twelve years, Mr. Speaker, I have been a Member of this body. I have seen great measures pertaining to the revenues of the country, touching the welfare of the entire people of this country, the consumers of the country, great questions presented here, involving representative government and the liberties and the personal rights of the people; I have seen important measures relating to these great questions brought into this Chamber time after time, and a little committee, dominated by the Speaker of this House, has throttled, by special rules dictated by him, the will of this House, and thus has throttled the will of the American people, and put through, under special rules reported by his little kitchen cabinet, his committee on rules, known as the "Rules Committee," far-reaching propositions without debate, according to the minority Representatives of the people the poor privilege sometimes of twenty minutes' discussion, and very frequently no opportunity of amendment.

Mr. Douglas. Will the gentleman yield for a question?

Mr. Clayton. I have only five minutes, and the gentleman must not expect me to yield to him, for it would take a long time for me, doubtless, to answer any question that my distinguished friend might propound.

Mr. Speaker, this is a crisis in the legislative history of the country. Those of us who favor the proposition advanced by the gentleman from Nebraska [Mr. Norris] recognize that it may be denominated revolutionary. So far as the parliamentary propositions are concerned, I am willing to concede that it is revolutionary, but it is necessary to overcome this arbitrary power of the Speaker. The American people demand it. We are hereby ready to secure it, and we have the votes to enforce the resolution offered by the gentleman from Nebraska. We are responsible to our constituencies and to the American people. I do not care how our conduct may be characterized, but we stand here ready to vote up the proposition offered by the gentleman from Nebraska, and I am confident that the American people will approve our votes. [Applause on the Democratic side.]

Mr. Norris. Mr. Speaker, I yield three minutes—

Mr. Douglas. Will the gentleman yield to me for a question?

Mr. Norris. I yield three minutes to the gentleman from Ohio [Mr. Douglas]. [Laughter.]

Mr. Douglas. Mr. Speaker, I thank the gentleman for his courtesy, since he knows that I am opposed to his resolution. I want first to say a word, if I may be permitted, with reference to *my* own attitude on this question. I do not see how any Member of this House, especially if he be a lawyer and has had any experience as such, could have voted to overrule the decision of the Speaker upon this question of order without intellectual stultification. I could not do it myself, favorable as I am to an enlargement of the Committee on Rules. If I believed with the gentleman from Missouri [Mr. Clark], the leader of the minority of this House, that this proposition in no way contained an attack upon the present occupant of the Chair, I would not oppose it, and therefore it seems to me that those of us in this House who have been opposed to some of the rules and with the management of the majority of this house can vote, without any reflection upon the present occupant of the chair, for the proposition suggested by the gentleman from South Dakota. That is nothing more nor less, as I understand it, than a proposition to enlarge the Committee on Rules of this House from 5 to 10, and that after the present Congress the Speaker of the House may hot be a member of it. That is a reform which I favor.

Mr. Dalzell. I suggest to the gentleman that he is mistaken as to that.

Mr. Douglas. I so understood it.

Mr. Dalzell. The Martin resolution deposes the Speaker of the House from the chairmanship of the Committee on Rules.

Mr. Douglas. When?

Mr. Dalzell. Now.

Mr. Douglas. Not the present Speaker of the House?

Mr. McCall. I would suggest, as I understood the resolution of the gentleman, that it deposes the Speaker and simply leaves him eligible to election until the 3d of March next.

Mr. Douglas. I would like to understand what the proposition is, and I will ask the gentleman from South Dakota to read it.

Mr. Martin of South Dakota. I will read it:

Resolved, That the Committee on Rules shall consist of 10 members, 6 of whom shall be members of the majority party, and 4 of whom shall be members of the minority party, all of whom shall be elected by the House by a majority vote.

The Committee on Rules shall select its own Chairman after March 3, 1911. The same person shall not at the same time hold the office of Speaker and membership of the Committee on Rules.

Mr. Douglas. That is the amendment, as I understand the proposition.

Mr. Dalzell. It provides the committee shall select its chairman.

Mr. McCall. It provides the House shall select the 10 members, and it deposes the Speaker and simply leaves him eligible to be selected until the 3rd of March, 1911.

Mr. Douglas. That is the idea, and for that proposition I shall vote.

That is not my understanding of the proposition. As I understand, it simply increases the number of the Committee on Rules from 5 to 10, and provides that after March 3, 1911, the Speaker of the House, whoever he may be shall not be eligible to membership on that committee. If my understanding of it be correct, and I am given the opportunity, I shall vote for it.

Mr. NORRIS. Mr. Speaker, I should like to have the attention of the gentleman from Pennsylvania again with a view to securing, in agreement as to time. I would like to ask if this proposition would be agreeable to him that unanimous consent be given that the gentleman from Pennsylvania shall have one hour, for debate only, without interfering with my right to the floor at the conclusion of that hour?

Mr. MANN. Mr. Speaker, a parliamentary inquiry or question.

The SPEAKER. The gentleman will state it.

Mr. MANN. What does the gentleman mean by the hour; that the gentleman from Pennsylvania during that hour, or some person to whom he might yield, would have no right to offer an amendment or to move the previous questions.

Mr. NORRIS. I mean that; yes.

Mr. MANN. Oh, well, then I will object,

Mr. NORRIS. Mr. Speaker, I yield five minutes to the gentleman from Alabama [Mr. Underwood].

Mr. UNDERWOOD. Mr. Speaker, if this resolution is adopted by the House, we have reached the end of an era in the parliamentary history of this body. More than a decade ago, when Mr. Reed was elected Speaker of this House, the House, on account of the large number of Members here, found it Impossible under the rules then existing to do business. Speaker Reed adopted a system of rules that would allow the majority of this House to do business at any time, but in doing so lie lodged the power of the House in the Speaker, and there it has remained since that time. Now, we have no fight to make it on the personality of JOSEPH G. CANNON, of Illinois. We are fighting a system, and that system is the system that enables the Speaker, by the power vested in him, to thwart and overthrow the will of the majority membership of this House. We recognize to-day that there has to be leadership; that some man must be the leader of the minority, but we say the place for that leadership is not in the Chair. [Applause on the Democratic side.]

If this resolution goes through—ultimately, if not to-day—the Speaker of the House of Representatives will cease to be its leader and the chairman of the Committee on Rules elected by this House will become the leader of the majority party in the House. It does not deprive this House of one scintilla of the power to control its business. It does not deprive it of the right of leadership, but it divorces from the Speaker the leadership of the House. There is no great parliamentary body in the world of which the speaker is the leader. It is not so in the British Parliament; it is not so in the Senate of the United States. And yet those two great bodies are able to transact their business as efficiently as the House of Representatives has ever done. I say that, no matter how high or of what pure character a man may be who occupies the Speaker's chair of this House, that leader can not divorce the leadership and the partisanship of the leader from the Speaker when he is presiding over the deliberations of this House. This great parliamentary body is entitled to a presiding officer who wields the scales of justice between man and man, between the two contending political parties, and that is what we are standing for to-day. [Applause on the Democratic side.]

Mr. NORRIS. Mr. Speaker, I would like to inquire how much time I have remaining?

The SPEAKER. The gentleman has twenty-seven minutes remaining.

Mr. NORRIS. I yield three minutes of that time to the gentleman from Kansas [Mr. Murdock].

Mr. MURDOCK. Mr. Speaker, everyone ought to know, and I think that everyone here does know, that this substitute of Mr. Norris's to his original resolution, if it passes, changes the system of this House. Calendar Wednesday did not change the system. The Fitzgerald proposition for a recommittal of a bill did not change the system. The proposition to put the Speaker off the Committee on Rules does change the system, and changes it vitally. The committee on Rules of this House is its most powerful committee it is small, and it should be small because it must come quickly into action. The function of that committee is to bring to this House a concrete proposition a major measure for immediate action. It is not possible in the House of Representatives to recommit a matter to the Committee on Rules. The House must act upon its reports.

The Committee on Rules has the last word for action In this large body. Now, we propose to take off that committee the man who sits in the Chair and presides over the fortunes of a measure after the Committee on Rules has reported it to the House-the Speaker. We propose that the man who helps frame the concrete measure this House has to pass upon, usually without the right to amend, shall not, having helped to frame the concrete measure, walk into the body and take the Chair to preside over the fortunes of his own measure while it is under discussion for adoption or rejection. That is the change, and it is a change. It is in response to a popular impeachment of this House, and that impeachment and challenge is this: That during a long term of years of power which was originally lodged in the membership of this body has been taken over or has filtered through to the Chair. This, and not calendar Wednesday; this, and not the motion to recommit; this proposition, not particularly to enlarge the Committee on Rules, but this proposition wherein it proposes to take the Speaker off the Committee on Rules, not next March 3, but now, is a change of system. It is turning back the tide of power which has been ruling from the House to the Speaker, turning that tide so that it will run back from the Speaker to the House. [Applause.]

Mr. NORRIS. Mr. Speaker, I yield five minutes to the gentleman from New York [Mr. Fitzgerald].

Mr. FITZGERALD. Mr. Speaker, time alone will demonstrate the wisdom of the proposed change in the rules. The situation in the House during the past forty-eight house demonstrates that a substantial majority of this House, is in favor of an important and a radical change in one of its important rules. I am one of those, Mr. Speaker, who have confidence in what the majority of this House will do under any circumstances, and I am perfectly content to have the majority of this House determine every single rule of its procedure. [Applause on the Democratic side.]

There are those who differ radically as to the wisdom and the effect of this rule. There are those who differ radically the causes of this movement at this time. I would not be so hypercritical on this occasion as to assert that the views that I have long entertained as to the wisdom of electing all of the committees of the House have changed in anywise, but I have no doubt that, considering conditions not only here but in the country, it is desirable at this time to give this opportunity to test the wisdom of electing the Committee on Rules in the House. [Applause on the Democratic side.]

Mr. Speaker, even if I did not have confidence in the wisdom of this experiment, I would support this resolution for another reason. To me it is not the present system in the procedure of the House to which is due this situation to-day, but it is due largely to the fact that the majority party in control of the Government is discredited before the people of the country. [Applause on the Democratic side.] And, try its you may, you can not, despite the assertions of some gentlemen on the other side of the House, so change your procedure or so change your stripes that you will bring back to yourselves before the next election confidence on the part of the people.

This is the time to demonstrate, when our opponents are demoralized and disorganized, that it is possible for the democracy to stand united upon an important question. [Applause on the Democratic side.] I am ready, Mr. Speaker, in the demonstration of that possibility and of capacity on the part of Democratic party to subordinate any individual views I may have, and to stand here harmoniously and united with my party associates at this time. [Applause on the Democratic side.] Believing that it is not possible by any subterfuge to which resort may be had to restore the confidence of the country in the present administration before the coming election, I rejoice that this demonstration has occurred to show that our party can safely be intrusted with power. [Applause on the Democratic side.]

Mr. NORRIS. Mr. Speaker, I yield three minutes to the gentleman from California [Mr. Hayes].

Mr. HAYES. Mr. Speaker, before proceeding to discuss the merits of the proposition which is now before the House, I beg the indulgence of the House to make a brief personal reference. I am moved to the action which I take upon this floor by no personal consideration whatever. Since I may been a Member of this House I have received at all times from the speaker of the House and from the members of the Committee on Rules every courtesy and every right to which I am entitled. More than that, I am not sure but I have received more than my just deserts and merits entitle me to receive. As a Member of this House I am moved to the action which I take in the matter only by what I conceive to be the highest considerations of conscience and duty.

Mr. Speaker, I have not time to refer to historical matters, but sometimes it clears the atmosphere to refer briefly to elementary propositions. The Speaker of this House, as we know him how, as he has been known for many years past, is not a product of the Constitution. He is the product of an evolution that has gone on depositing more and more power in the hands of the Speaker until in the Fifty-ninth Congress, if my memory serves me, no matter of any kind was brought before this House, except it was a matter of privilege, without the consent of the Speaker of the House. In the Sixtieth Congress it was nearly the same. The amendment to the rules which was adopted last March, when this session of Congress opened, has made that power somewhat less. While there to now less power lodged in the Speaker to control the legislative procedure of the House, there is still, in my judgment, too much power lodged in the Speaker of this House; more than should be lodged in the hands of any man connected with the government of the Republic. The Speaker of the House of Representatives is entitled to the support of every man on this floor in the lawful and constitutional discharge of his duties, no matter by what party he may be put in the chair. But it does not follow from that premise that the Speaker of the House is therefore entitled to he the political and legislative dictator of this House in whole or in part. I believe that the House of Representatives and its membership should have the largest possible independence, free from coercion, free from fear of political punishment or death. Every Member of the House should feel perfect liberty under proper rules, at the proper time and in a proper way, to say and do those things that his conscience and his highest conception of duty prompt him to say and do; to think, to act and discharge his duties as a representative of the American people in the manner that the Constitution of the United States intended that he should. Believing this, as I do firmly, and being convinced that it will go a long way toward releasing the House from the domination of one man, I shall support the resolution of the gentleman from Nebraska. [Loud applause.]

Mr. NORRIS. I yield three minutes to the gentleman from Minnesota.

Mr. TAWNEY. Mr. Speaker, the time that I requested of the gentleman from Nebraska will be occupied by the gentleman from Pennsylvania.

Mr. NORRIS. I yield three minutes to the gentleman from Pennsylvania in addition to the three minutes that I yield to the gentleman from Minnesota.

Mr. OLMSTED. What I desire to ask is whether the gentleman will yield to me to offer an amendment.

Mr. NORRIS. I will not. . . .

Mr. NORRIS. I yield two minutes to the gentleman from Massachusetts [Mr. McCall].

Mr. McCALL. Mr. Speaker, I desire to say a few words upon the proposition before the House; but it is manifestly impossible to discuss it within the two minutes yielded to me.

This proceeding, in my opinion, is aimed at the Speaker of the House of Representatives. The proposition of the gentleman from South Dakota deposes the Speaker from his present position as a member of the Committee on Rules. Now, if it were an entirely new proposition, at the beginning of a Congress, I should consider Its adoption; but I do not propose to vote for it, and I do not consider that it is open to be passed by a House controlled by Republicans. I do not propose to vote to deliver the Speaker, bound hand and foot, over to the minority party, although I know that if you do that, he will go with heal unbowed and erect, in the simple majesty of American manhood. [Applause.] This movement does not originate in the House of Representatives. I am not undiscriminating. I do not condemn a whole class, but you are about to do the behest of a gang of literary highwaymen who are entirely willing to assassinate a reputation in order to sell a magazine. [Applause.] I believe that the Speaker of the House, by his conduct in the last three days, if the country has been permitted to know it, has shattered many of the criticisms that have been made against him; and, as I see him there, his spirit reminds me of that of the, old Ulysses starting off on his last voyage:

> Push off, and sitting well in order smite
> The sounding furrows, for my purpose holds
> To sail beyond the sunset, and the baths
> Of all the western stars, until I die.

[Applause.]

Mr. NORRIS. I yield one minute to the gentleman from North Dakota [Mr. Gronna].

Mr. GRONNA. Mr. Speaker, I yield to no man on the floor of this House in loyalty to my party and in respect for the distinguished gentleman now in the chair, and I believe that I have shown that in my former actions. But, Mr. Speaker, there is a principle involved in this. I do believe that the time has come when the rules should be changed. While I have not occupied as much time on this floor as others discussing this question, I acknowledge—looking the Speaker in the face—that I have been as enthusiastic and energetic as any Member now called an insurgent to bring this change about. Why do I favor this change? I do not believe it is any discredit to the Speaker that we declare he shall not be eligible as a member of the Committee on Rules. I have no quarrel with the Speaker personally. He has always been friendly and courteous to me. I have no fault to find with him personally, neither am I disappointed because of any requests that I have made of him, but I do believe and shall continue to believe that it is time that the American people were represented on this floor by the Members of this House and not by the Committee on Rules. [Applause.]

. . . .

Mr. NORRIS. Mr. Speaker, how much time have I remaining?

The SPEAKER. The gentleman has five and one-half minutes.

Mr. NORRIS. After I have taken three minutes I would like to have the Chair call my attention to the fact. Mr. Speaker, I have no time left me to review this situation as I wanted to do. I want to order to just two things that have been brought into this discussion. First, I want to absolutely deny that this movement to change the rules of the House is intended as any personal slap or any personal thrust at the Speaker or any other man. Those of use who favor this rule represent a principle here far beyond the personality of any man or any set of men.

I want to say that there is no feeling against the Speaker in this matter unless it is brought into it by the Speaker or his friends. I want to deny the charge that this is anti-Republican. From every hamlet, from every fireside, and from every farm of Republican constituents to-day there are going up prayers and hopes that this resolution to change the rules of the House will be successful here to-day. [Laughter and applause.]

Mr. Speaker, I move the previous question on the substitute and resolution to the final passage.

The SPEAKER. The gentleman from Nebraska moves the previous question on the resolution and the substitute to its final passage. The question is on ordering the previous question.

Mr. Tawney. And on that I demand the yeas and nays.

The yeas and nays were ordered.

The question was taken; and there were—yeas 180, nays 159, answered "present" 7, not voting 42. . . .

So the previous question was ordered.

. . . .

The SPEAKER pro tempore. The question now is upon the amendment in the nature of a substitute, offered by the gentleman from Nebraska [Mr. Norris].

Mr. MANN. On that we demand the yeas and nays.

The yeas and nays were ordered.

Mr. PRINCE. Mr. Speaker—

The SPEAKER pro tempore. For what purpose does the gentleman rise?

Mr. PRINCE. For the purpose of asking to have the substitute again reported so that we will know what we are voting on.

The SPEAKER pro tempore. Without objection, the substitute will again be reported.

There was no objection, and the Clerk again reported the substitute.

The SPEAKER pro tempore. The Clerk will call the roll.

The question was taken; and there were—yeas 193, nays 153, answered "present" 5, not voting 38. . . .

So the substitute amendment was agreed to.

. . . .

The SPEAKER. The question is on agreeing to the resolution as amended.

Mr. TAWNEY. On that Mr. Speaker, I demand the yeas and nays.

The yeas and nays were ordered.

The question was taken; and there were—yeas 191, nays 156, answered "present" 5, not voting 37. . . .

So the resolution as amended was agreed to.

. . . .

The result of the vote was announced as above recorded.

Mr. NORRIS. Mr. Speaker, I move to reconsider the vote by which the resolution was adopted and to lay that motion on the table.

The SPEAKER. The gentleman from Nebraska moves to reconsider the vote by which the resolution was agreed to and to lay that motion upon the table. Without objection it is so ordered.

There was no objection.

Mr. NORRIS. Mr. Speaker, I move that the House do now adjourn.

The SPEAKER. One moment. The Speaker asks the indulgence of the House for not exceeding three minutes to make a statement.

Mr. NORRIS. Mr. Speaker, I am willing to withhold the motion.

The SPEAKER. Gentlemen of the House of Representatives: Actions, not words, determine the conduct and the sincerity of men in the affairs of life. This is a government by the people acting through the representatives of a majority of the people. Results can not be had except by a majority, and in the House of Representatives a majority, being responsible, should have full power and should exercise that power; otherwise the majority is inefficient and does not perform its function. The office of the minority is to put the majority on its good behavior, advocating, in good faith, the policies which it professes, ever ready to take advantage of the mistakes of the majority party, and appeal to the country for its vindication.

From time to time heretofore the majority has become the minority, as in the present case, and from time to time hereafter the majority will become the minority. The country believes the Republican party has a majority of 44 in the House of Representatives at this time; yet such is not the case.

The present Speaker of the House has, to the best of his ability and judgment, cooperated with the Republican party, and so far in the history of this Congress the Republican party in the House has been enabled by a very small majority, when the test came, to legislate in conformity with the policies and the platform of the Republican party. Such action of course begot criticism—which the Speaker does not deprecate—on the part of the minority party.

The Speaker can not be unmindful of the fact, as evidenced by three previous elections to the Speakership, that in the past be has enjoyed the confidence of the Republican party of the country and of the Republican Members of the House; but the assault upon the Speaker of the House by the minority, supplemented by the efforts of the so-called insurgents, shows that the Democratic minority, aided by a number of so-called Insurgents, constituting 15 per cent of the majority party in the House, is now in the majority, and that the Speaker of the House is not in harmony with the actual majority of the House, as evidenced by the vote just taken.

There are two courses open for the Speaker to pursue one is to resign and permit the new combination of Democrats and insurgents to choose a Speaker in harmony with its aims and purposes. The other is for that combination to declare a vacancy in the office of Speaker and proceed to the election of a new Speaker. After consideration, at this stage of the session of the House, with much of important legislation pending involving the pledges of the Republican platform and their crystallization into law, believing that his resignation might consume weeks of time in the reorganization of the House, the Speaker, being in harmony with Republican policies and desirous of carrying them out, declines by his own motion to precipitate a contest upon the House in the election of a new Speaker, a contest that might greatly endanger the final passage of all legislation necessary to redeem Republican pledges and fulfill Republican promises. This is one reason why the Speaker does not resign at once; and another reason is this: in the judgment of the present Speaker, a resignation is in and of itself a confession of weakness or mistake or an apology for past actions. The Speaker is not conscious of having done any political wrong. [Loud applause on the Republican side.] The same rules are in force in this House that have been in force for two decades. The Speaker has construed the rules as he found them and as they have been construed by previous Speakers from Thomas B. Reed's incumbency down to the present time.

Heretofore the Speakers have been members of the Committee on Rules, covering a period of sixty years, and the present Speaker has neither sought new power nor has he unjustly used that already conferred upon him.

There has been much talk on the part of the minority and the insurgents of the "czarism" of the Speaker, culminating in the action taken to-day. The real truth is that there is no coherent Republican majority in the House of Representatives [Loud applause on the Republican side.] Therefore, the real majority ought to have the courage of its convictions [applause on the Republican side], and logically meet the situation that confronts it.

The Speaker does now believe, and always has believed, that this is a government through parties, and that parties can act only through majorities. The Speaker has always believed in and bowed to the will of the majority in convention, in caucus, and in the legislative hall, and to-day profoundly believes that to act otherwise is to disorganize parties, is to prevent coherent action in any legislative body, is to make impossible the reflection of the wishes of the people in statutes and in laws.

The Speaker has always said that, under the Constitution, it is a question of the highest privilege for an actual majority of the House at any time to choose new Speaker, and again notifies the House that the Speaker will at this moment, or at any other time while he remains Speaker, entertain, in conformity with the highest constitutional privilege, a motion by any Member to vacate the office of the Speakership and choose a new Speaker [loud applause on the Republican side]; and, under existing coalitions, would welcome such action upon the part of the actual majority of the House, so that power and responsibility may rest with the Democratic and insurgent Members who, by the last vote, evidently constitute a majority of this House. The Chair is now ready to entertain such motion. [Loud and long-continued applause on the Republican side; great confusion in the Hall.]

Mr. BURLESON. Mr. Speaker, I offer the following resolution.

Mr. SHERLEY. Mr. Speaker, I move that the House do now adjourn.

Mr. TAWNEY. The gentleman from Texas has been recognized.

Mr. SHERLEY. The motion is not debatable.

The SPEAKER. The gentleman from Texas.

Mr. SHERLEY. I make the point of order that the gentleman from Nebraska offered a motion to adjourn.

Mr. BURLESON. I demand the reading of my resolution.

Mr. SHERLEY (continuing). And out of courtesy to the Speaker, withheld it pending the Speaker's remarks to the House. That motion is now properly before the House.

Mr. LOUDENSLAGER. We have no rules now.

Mr. SABATH. A motion to adjourn is always in order. [Great confusion in the Hall.]

Mr. BURLESON. I ask for the reading of the resolution, and demand the previous question on its adoption.

Several Members: It has not been read.

The SPEAKER. No business can be transacted until the House is in order. For what purpose does the gentleman rise?

Mr. BURLESON. I ask for the reading of the resolution, and upon that resolution I demand the previous question.

Mr. SHERLEY. Mr. Speaker, I make the point of order that the motion—

The SPEAKER. The Chair is not advised, and is trying to find out what the motion of the gentleman from Texas is.

Mr. SHERLEY. I make the point of order that there is now pending before the House a motion to adjourn, which is not debatable. [Cries of "No! No!" and great confusion in the Hall.]

Mr. BURLESON. I demand the reading of the resolution.

The SPEAKER. The House will be in order. Gentlemen will be seated. No rights shall be lost and no unparliamentary action bad in the premises. There are matters that take precedence of a motion to adjourn. [Loud applause on the Republican side.] Speaker Carlisle and many other Speakers have so ruled. Until the Chair knows what it is that the gentleman from Texas proposes the Chair does not know whether the motion to adjourn is of superior quality.

Mr. BURLESON. I demand the reading of the resolution.

Mr. SHERLEY. I make the point of order that there is a motion to adjourn pending.

The SPEAKER. The Clerk will read.

The Clerk read as follows:

Resolved, That the office of Speaker of the House of representatives is hereby declared to be vacant, and the House of Representatives shall at once proceed to the election of a Speaker.

Mr. BURLESON. On that I move the previous question.

Mr. DWIGHT. I move the previous question.

Mr. SHERLEY. Now, Mr. Speaker, I insist that the gentleman from Nebraska had made a motion to adjourn, which he temporarily withheld; and the motion offered by the gentleman from Texas does not take precedence. The only motion before the House is the motion to adjourn.

Mr. MADDEN. I make the point of order that there is no motion pending for adjournment.

The SPEAKER. The House will be in order. The Sergeant-at-Arms will request gentlemen to take their seats. All gentlemen will be seated. [Great confusion in the Hall.]

The Sergeant-at-Arms will request gentlemen in the aisles to be seated. The House will be in order.

Does the gentleman from Nebraska make a motion to adjourn?

Mr. BURLESON. Mr. Speaker, I believe I have the floor.

Mr. NORRIS. I had made a motion to adjourn and withheld it at the request of the Speaker, so that he could make a statement. That is the situation.

The SPEAKER. The Speaker would be pleased if the gentleman would withdraw it. The Speaker now having heard what the resolution of the gentleman from Texas is, the motion to adjourn is in order; but the Speaker would be gratified if it might be withdrawn.

Mr. JAMES. A point of order.

Mr. RODENBERG. Show your nerve. [Great confusion in the House.]

Mr. JAMES. I make the point of order that the resolution is of the highest privilege, and therefore takes privilege of a motion to adjourn.

Mr. BURLESON. Mr. Speaker—

The SPEAKER. The House will please be in order. The Chair desires to say this is a question of high constitutional privilege, but if in the consideration of that question the House should desire to adjourn, the Chair is of the opinion that the House can adjourn. A conference report was admitted to interrupt a roll call; but after having interrupted the roll call, and being presented, it did not prevent the House from adjourning. That was done in Speaker Carlisle's time; and it was held that that does not deprive the House of the power to adjourn. It can be presented and pending, and all questions under the rules of consideration raised and any parliamentary motion made, but the motion to adjourn would have to be entertained by the Speaker; otherwise the House might remain in session for a week. While the Chair would be glad for the resolution to be acted upon at once, yet the Chair can not help entertaining the motion to adjourn.

Mr. HARDWICK. A parliamentary inquiry, Mr. Speaker.

Mr. MADDEN. A point of order. The point of order is, Mr. Speaker, that the gentleman from Nebraska can not make a motion to adjourn and withhold it at the same time and still have it pending.

Mr. NORRIS. I withheld it at the request of the Speaker, and nobody objected.

Mr. HARDWICK. A parliamentary inquiry. The gentleman withheld it, at the request of the Speaker, while the Speaker made a statement. Now, the motion to adjourn is always in order unless some gentleman has the floor. [Great confusion in the Hall and cries of "Vote it down!"]

The SPEAKER. Does the gentleman from Nebraska make the motion? The Chair wants to know whether he understands the gentleman made the motion to adjourn and withdrew it.

Several Members. He withdrew it.

Mr. NORRIS. I did not. I withheld it, at the request of the Speaker.

The SPEAKER. Does the gentleman renew the motion?

Mr. NORRIS. It does not need renewal. I have not withdrawn it.

Mr. JONES. If he does, I renew it.

Mr. NORRIS. It has been withheld, and I only did that as a courtesy to the Chair, that he might make a statement.

The SPEAKER. It occurs to the Chair that the gentleman from Nebraska is correct. So, as many as are in favor of the motion to adjourn will say "aye;" those opposed will say "no."

The question was taken. [Great confusion in the Hall.]

The SPEAKER. The noes have it; the House refuses to adjourn. The gentleman from Texas.

Mr. BURLESON. Mr. Speaker, the resolution I have offered is simple in its terms and easily understood.

Mr. NORRIS. Mr. Speaker, I never heard the announcement on the vote, on account of the confusion.

The SPEAKER. The gentleman from Nebraska says that the confusion was so great he did not hear the Speaker when he announced that the House refused to adjourn. The Chair recognizes the confusion was great. What is the request of the gentleman?

Mr. NORRIS. I demand the yeas and nays.

Mr. TAWNEY. I make the point of order that the demand comes too late.

Mr. NORRIS. Are you afraid of going on record? Are you afraid to see where the combination is?

The SPEAKER. The Chair thinks, on account of the confusion, that the demand should be allowed. As many as are in favor of ordering the yeas and nays will rise and stand until counted. The Chair will count all gentlemen standing. [After counting.] Fourteen gentlemen have arisen; not a sufficient number; the yeas and nays are refused, and the House declines to adjourn.

Mr. BURLESON. Mr. Speaker, the resolution I have offered is simple in its terms and easily understood. It needs no discussion in order to elucidate its purpose. I demand the previous question on the resolution.

The SPEAKER. The gentleman from Texas demands the previous question on the resolution. The question is on ordering the previous question.

Mr. DWIGHT. On that I demand the yeas and nays.

The SPEAKER. The gentleman from New York demands the yeas and nays. [Several Members on the Republican side, "No!" "No!"]

Mr. DWIGHT. I withdraw the demand.

The SPEAKER. The demand is withdrawn. As many as are in favor of ordering the previous question will rise and stand until they are counted. The Chair will count all gentlemen standing. [After counting.] Two hundred and seventy gentlemen have arisen; the ayes will be seated and the noes will rise. [After a pause.] No vote in the negative. The previous question is ordered. The question is on agreeing to the resolution.

Mr. TAWNEY. On that I demand the yeas and nays.

Mr. UNDERWOOD. I demand the yeas and nays. The question was taken, and the yeas and nays were ordered.

The SPEAKER. The resolution will be again reported.

Mr. TAWNEY. Mr. Speaker, I ask that the resolution be read again before the roll call begins.

The SPEAKER. Without objection, the resolution will be again reported.

The Clerk began to read the resolution.

Mr. TAWNEY. I demand before the reading of the resolution the House shall be brought to order, so that we may understand what it is.

The SPEAKER. The House will be in order. [After a pause.] The Clerk will report the resolution.

The Clerk read as follows:

Resolved, That the office of Speaker of the House of Representatives is hereby declared to be vacant, and the House of Representatives shall at once proceed to the election of a Speaker.

Mr. CLARK of Florida. Mr. Speaker—

The SPEAKER. Hold on a minute.

Mr. CLARK of Florida. A parliamentary inquiry.

The SPEAKER. The gentleman from New York [Mr. PAYNE] will take the Chair. [Great applause on the Republican side.]

Mr. CLARK of Florida. A parliamentary inquiry.

Mr. PAYNE took the chair amidst loud applause on the Republican side.

Mr. CLARK of Florida. A parliamentary inquiry.

The SPEAKER pro tempore. Before any business is transacted the House will be in order. All gentlemen will be seated. Gentlemen standing in front will be seated; gentlemen standing in the aisles will be seated.

Mr. CLARK of Florida. A parliamentary inquiry.

The SPEAKER pro tempore. For what purpose does the gentleman rise?

Mr. CLARK of Florida. A parliamentary inquiry.

The SPEAKER pro tempore. The gentleman will state it.

Mr. CLARK of Florida. Will it be in order to move an amendment to the resolution?

The SPEAKER pro tempore. It will not. The House has ordered the previous question.

Mr. CLARK of Florida. That Champ Clark, of Missouri, be elected Speaker. [Loud applause on the Democratic side.]

Mr. TAWNEY. That motion will be in order when the House has voted in favor of the resolution just now offered.

The SPEAKER pro tempore. The yeas and nays have been ordered on the resolution. The Clerk will call the roll. As many as are in favor of the adoption of the resolution will, as their names are called, answer "yea," those opposed will answer "nay;" and again the Chair cautions the House to keep in order during the roll call.

The question was taken; and there were—yeas 155, nays 192, answered "present" 8, not voting 33. . . .

The SPEAKER pro tempore. On this question the "ayes" are 155, the "noes" 192, "present" ' 8, and the resolution is not agreed to. [Loud applause on the Republican side.]

The Speaker resumed the chair.

Congressional Record, House, 61st Congress, 2d session, March 19, 1910, 3425–3426, 3427, 3428–3435, 3436–3438, 3439.

108   Limiting the Size of the House of Representatives

August 8, 1911

Following the thirteenth census, taken in 1910, the House reapportioned the number of House seats for each state. This reapportionment, or redistribution, of House seats was required by the Constitution (Article I, Section 2). This process requires the states to redistrict, or redraw the boundaries of each congressional district in order to spread the population as equally as possible among the districts.

Until 1910 the size of the House had grown after each of the first twelve censuses. The first House in 1789 had 65 members. It was apportioned according to the Constitution, since the first census was not taken until 1790. Following the first census the size of the House increased to 106. Following the tenth Census in 1880 the House expanded to 332. The House grew rapidly, along with the population of the United States. The solution to an ever-increasing number of seats in the House was to freeze the overall size of the body and increase the number of persons represented by each member.

The 1911 law that provided for this apportionment also set a size limit on the House of Representatives that has remained in place, with a few minor variations, to date. This law set the size of the House at 433 members, effective March 3, 1913. The law anticipated that Arizona and New Mexico would soon enter the Union and allowed them one representative each, bringing the total size of the House to 435 seats. The size of the House has remained at 435 seats except for a temporary increase to 437 seats when Alaska and Hawaii entered the Union in 1959.

At some time in the future the House may decide to revisit the question of the size of the House. With the population continuing to increase, each member now represents, on average, more than 600,000 persons. In some instances, members represent considerably more. Is 435 the correct number of seats for the twenty-first century? While many persons erroneously believe that it would take a constitutional amendment to change the size of the House, as this law demonstrates, the size of the House can be changed by simply amending the law—something the House can do any time there is a compelling reason to do so.

CHAP. 5—AN ACT FOR THE APPORTIONMENT OF REPRESENTATIVES IN CONGRESS AMONG THE SEVERAL STATES UNDER THE THIRTEENTH CENSUS.

Be it enacted by the Senate and House of Representatives of the United States of America in Congress assembled, That after the third day of March, nineteen hundred and thirteen, the House of Representatives shall be composed of four hundred and thirty-three Members, to be apportioned among the several States as follows:

Alabama, ten.

Arkansas, seven.

California, eleven.

Colorado, four.

Connecticut, five.

Delaware, one.

Florida, four.

Georgia, twelve.

Idaho, two.

Illinois, twenty-seven.

Indiana, thirteen.

Iowa, eleven.

Kansas, eight.

Kentucky, eleven.

Louisiana, eight.

Maine, four.

Maryland, six.

Massachusetts, sixteen.

Michigan, thirteen.

Minnesota, ten.

Mississippi, eight.

Missouri, sixteen.

Montana, two.

Nebraska, six.

Nevada, one.

New Hampshire, two.

New Jersey, twelve.

New York, forty-three.

North Carolina, ten.

North Dakota, three.

Ohio, twenty-two.

Oklahoma, eight.

Oregon, three.

Pennsylvania, thirty-six.

Rhode Island, three.

South Carolina, seven.

South Dakota, three.

Tennessee, ten.

Texas, eighteen.

Utah, two.

Vermont, two.

Virginia, ten.

Washington, five.

West Virginia, six.

Wisconsin, eleven.

Wyoming, one.

SEC. 2. That if the Territories of Arizona and New Mexico shall become States in the Union before the apportionment of Representatives under the next decennial census they shall have one Representative each, and if one of such Territories shall so become a State, such State shall have one Representative, which Representative or Representatives shall be in addition to the number four hundred and thirty-three, its provided in section one of this Act, and all laws and parts of laws in conflict with this section are to that extent hereby repealed.

SEC. 3. That in each State entitled under this apportionment to more than one Representative, the Representatives to the Sixty-third and each subsequent Congress shall be elected by districts composed of a contiguous and compact territory, and containing as nearly as practicable an equal number of inhabitants. The said districts shall be equal to the number of Representatives to which such State may be entitled in Congress, no district electing more than one Representative.

SEC. 4. That in case of an increase in the number of Representatives in any State under this apportionment such additional Representative or Representatives shall be elected by the State at and the other Representatives by the districts now prescribed by

law until such State shall be redistricted in the manner provided by the laws thereof and in accordance with the rules enumerated in section three of this Act; and if there be no change in the number of Representatives from a State, the Representatives thereof shall be elected from the districts now prescribed by law until such State shall be redistricted as herein prescribed.

SEC. 5. That candidates for Representative or Representatives to be elected at large in any State shall be nominated in the same manner as candidates for governor, unless otherwise provided by the laws of such State.

Approved, August 8, 1911.

Statutes at Large, 37 (1911–1913), 62d Congress, 1st session, Aug. 8, 1911, 13–14.

109 The Seventeenth Amendment to the Constitution

Submitted to the States for Ratification, May 13, 1912; Ratified, May 31, 1913

The Seventeenth Amendment changed the manner in which senators were elected by providing for direct election by the people. Until the ratification of this amendment, senators were elected by the legislatures of each state. This indirect method of election for the Senate was part of the original compromise in the Constitutional Convention of 1787 (see document 1, entries in Madison's Notes for May 31 and July 16, 1787). In Federalist 62 (see document 3), Madison or Hamilton wrote: "Among the various modes which might have been devised for constituting this branch of the government, that which has been proposed by the convention is probably the most congenial with the public opinion. It is recommended by the double advantage of favoring a select appointment, and of giving to the State governments such an agency in the formation of the federal government as must secure the authority of the former, and may form a convenient link between the two systems."

Over the years the process of having senators elected by state legislatures came under attack as being undemocratic and giving too much power to state governments to control the Senate. Tensions grew as the rural-dominated state legislatures had to cope with the growing needs of a rapidly urbanizing nation. Beginning in the 1870s and extending into the twentieth century, nineteen separate efforts to change the method of electing senators managed to pass in the House of Representatives only to be defeated in the Senate.

Early in the twentieth century, spurred by the rise of Progressive Era politics, the Democratic Party, the Populists, and the Socialists all called for direct election of senators as part of their political platforms. Public opinion began to turn in favor of direct election as a result of several scandals involving bribery of state officials and a series of sensational articles by journalist David Graham Philips

published in several issues of Cosmopolitan *magazine in 1906. Called "The Treason of the Senate," these articles accused a number of senators of being tools of special interests. Political cartoons in the first decade of the twentieth century portrayed the Senate as a millionaires' club filled with representatives not of the people but of big corporations. Insurgent progressive Republicans in the Senate finally joined the ranks of those desiring change and the Seventeenth Amendment passed both houses of Congress on May 13, 1912, and was ratified by the states a year later.*

ARTICLE XVII.

The Senate of the United States shall be composed of two Senators from each State, elected by the people thereof, for six years, and each Senator shall have one vote. The electors in each State shall have the qualifications requisite for electors of the most numerous branch of the State legislatures.

When vacancies happen in the representation of any State in the Senate, the executive authority of such State shall issue writs of election to fill such vacancies: Provided, That the legislature of any State may empower the executive thereof to make temporary appointments until the people fill the vacancies by election as the legislature may direct.

This amendment shall not be so construed as to affect the election or term of any Senator chosen before it becomes valid as part of the Constitution.

The Constitution of the United States of America as Amended, House Doc. 102–188, 102d Congress, 2d session (Washington: Government Printing Office, 1992), 19.

110   Senator Boies Penrose on a Senate Investigation into Campaign Financing (The Clapp Committee)

August 21, 1912

In May 1912 the U.S. Senate began an investigation of corporate contributions to the presidential campaigns of 1904 and 1908, which saw the elections of Republican presidents Theodore Roosevelt in 1904 and William Howard Taft in 1908. As is often the case in congressional investigations of previous elections, the driving force behind this investigation was not an objective search for truth but a desire to gain political advantage. In this instance, moderate and conservative Republicans were out to derail the ambitions of Theodore Roosevelt, a progressive Republican, to once again regain the presidency. Roosevelt's candidacy challenged the machinery of the regular Republican Party, which was committed to the reelection of Taft. Senator Moses E. Clapp (R-Minn.), a Roosevelt supporter, agreed to become chairman of the special subcommittee of the Senate Committee on Privileges and Elections that conducted the investigation.

As the Clapp Committee investigation continued, the press had a field day with charges and countercharges about the excesses of campaign financing and influence peddling by American corporations and wealthy Americans, such as J. P. Morgan. A series of sensational newspaper and magazine stories, first printed in Hearst's Magazine, exposed letters from the files of John D. Archbold, who was then vice president of Standard Oil Company. These records showed how Standard Oil had contributed to political campaigns in return for favors related to legislation in which Standard Oil had an interest. Among those implicated in taking large contributions was Senator Boies Penrose (R-Pa.), who in 1904 was the Republican Party chairman in Pennsylvania and a member of the Republican National Committee. Hearst's Magazine alleged Penrose received $25,000 from the Standard Oil Company as a campaign contribution in Pennsylvania, with the full knowledge of Theodore Roosevelt.

The charge led to a remarkable speech on the floor of the Senate in which Penrose defended himself, criticized the press for its bias, but admitted to receiving a larger contribution of $125,000 from Standard Oil, which he claimed Roosevelt knew about. The Penrose speech led to several days of Senate debate about political contributions, with the goal of undermining Roosevelt's presidential aspirations. Roosevelt responded by characterizing Penrose and Archbold, who had since become president of Standard Oil, as liars who were out to frame him. In an effort to undo the damage of these revelations and others that claimed that three-quarters of all Republican campaign funds came from corporations in 1904, Roosevelt himself made a dramatic appearance before the Clapp Committee, where he emphatically denied that the Republican Party made any promises to corporations in return for their political contributions.

The Clapp Committee never issued a report or recommended any changes in campaign laws to address the campaign abuses made during the investigation. Less than a month before the presidential election of 1912, Roosevelt was shot and wounded as he delivered a campaign speech. The Democratic candidate for president, Woodrow Wilson, as well as the Clapp Committee temporarily suspended criticism of Roosevelt after the shooting. While the Clapp Committee met again following the election of 1912, it eventually issued only two volumes of testimony and no report or recommendations for legislation. Since the Democrats captured the White House, the House, and the Senate in the 1912 elections, there was little reason to pursue the investigation of Roosevelt's earlier campaign. Despite chairman Clapp's support of Roosevelt, the committee he headed seriously damaged Roosevelt's presidential aspirations in 1912. The investigation was one of the factors that caused the Republican Party to come close to self-destruction in 1912.

Mr. PENROSE. Mr. President, I rise to a question of personal privilege. Certain letters from John D. Archbold, addressed to me, have recently been published, and an effort has been made to establish a connection between the work of the Industrial Commission, of which I was a member, and an alleged letter purporting to inclose $25,000 from John D. Archbold. These stories have been circulated in Hearst's Magazine, a sensational periodical; in the Munsey daily papers, which are Roosevelt organs; and more particularly in the North American, in Philadelphia, and the Leader, in Pittsburgh, yellow journals, the chief organs of the Flinn-Van Valkenburg-Roosevelt combine in Pennsylvania.

These letters have been in the possession of the periodical referred to about five years, since the theft of the Archbold correspondence occurred, but apparently there has been no occasion for their publication until prompted by present political exigencies. Their publication now, with the malignant insinuations accompanying them, is in the nature of political blackmail, the purpose of which is to punish, coerce, or intimidate me because of my political course.

The statement that there is any connection between the Industrial Commission and a certain check from John D. Archbold is false, malicious, and without justification.

I was one of the senatorial members of the Industrial Commission, but the work of the commission, as is well known, was performed largely by the noncongressional members of the commission. As the sessions of the commission were continuous over a considerable period, it turned out to be impossible for me at least to attend very many of the prolonged sessions. I do not believe that I was able to attend more than one or two meetings during the whole life of the commission. I certainly never participated in their deliberations or conclusions, neither did I in any way try to influence the same. The commission was engaged in a general line of investigation into industrial conditions, and in no case did anyone refuse to appear before the commission or object to appearing. The only question raised as to the appearance of witnesses where all witnesses were entirely willing to appear might have been the question of arranging the dates of appearance in individual cases to suit individual convenience or engagement, a question not unusual in protracted hearings of this character. Upon the death of Senator Kyle, the president of the commission, my name was mentioned by a large number of persons to succeed him as president, I being the ranking senatorial member and representing a great industrial State. Realizing, however, that I had not been able to attend the sessions of the commission regularly or keep up with the work, I declined to be considered for the place and the commission, as is well known, elected Mr. Clarke. The hearings of the commission were open, and there was no secrecy about their proceedings. There was no occasion to furnish anyone with any particular information, as it was open and accessible to the general public.

I now come more particularly to the letter alleged to have been written to me by John D. Archbold, inclosing a certificate of deposit in my favor for $25,000, written under date of October 13, 1904. I have reason to believe that this letter is a forgery, and I challenge its production; but it is true, and at the time it was well known, that during the presidential campaign of 1904 I did receive such a contribution from Mr. Archbold for the campaign in Pennsylvania. The contribution was part of a much larger one, which I will now explain.

I was at the time the chairman of the Republican State committee of Pennsylvania and a member of the Republican national committee, representing that State. I was at the Republican headquarters in Philadelphia in full and sole charge of the State campaign, and as a member of the national committee, I was every week in New York in close touch with many of the phases of the national campaign.

Mr. John D. Archbold had several interviews with Cornelius N. Bliss, treasurer of the Republican national committee, and with me, relative to financial assistance in the presidential campaign of 1904. Finally, after some discussion, we came to an understanding by which Mr. Archbold made a contribution of $125,000, of which $100,000 was to go to Mr. Bliss as treasurer of the Republican national committee for the national presidential campaign outside of Pennsylvania and $25,000 was to be contributed to me as State chairman for the campaign in Pennsylvania. Mr. Archbold received the receipt of Mr. Cornelius Bliss as treasurer of the Republican national committee and for the Republican national committee for the amount of $100,000. The contribution of $25,000 so received by me as chairman of the Republican State committee of Pennsylvania was expended in the presidential campaign in that State.

While the result of the election of 1904 was a splendid victory for the Republican candidate it must not be forgotten that there were times during the campaign when apprehension existed among the Republican managers and when it was felt that it was necessary to wage the contest with all possible vigor. The vigorous and effective efforts then made largely contributed to the final result. Not long after the contribution of $100,000 to Mr. Bliss for the Republican national committee, Mr. Bliss, on behalf of the committee, called again to see Mr. Archbold and asked for a further contribution of $150,000. He represented to Mr. Archbold and a large number of his associates, known as the group which was chiefly interested in the Standard Oil Co., that Mr. Roosevelt had been advised of the original contribution, and also that the chairman of the Republican national committee, Mr. Cortelyou, had been similarly advised, and that the original contribution, $100,000, was greatly appreciated by them both, but that the need of further financial assistance was badly felt at headquarters and that such further assistance would be still more keenly appreciated by both of the gentlemen referred to. The demand was urgent, insistent, I may say imperative, and purported to come directly from Mr. Roosevelt and Mr. Cortelyou. I knew personally at the time, as I was more or less in touch with the situation, that Mr. Archbold wanted to make this further contribution and felt that it was presented to him in such an imperative manner, a way that made him desire to make it, but he was overruled by his associates, who felt that sufficient had been done, and a further contribution was not made.

It should be explained that the Pennsylvania Republican State committee seldom receives any financial assistance from the Republican national committee, such as is extended to other States.

On the contrary, treasurers are appointed by the chairman of the Republican national committee in Philadelphia and in Pittsburgh, and large sums are collected in a presidential year, and this money so collected in Pennsylvania is sent direct to the Republican national committee in New York for use in other States outside of Pennsylvania. Thus the resources of the Pennsylvania State committee are frequently impoverished in presidential years. In the campaign of 1904 no contribution was made to the Pennsylvania Republican State committee by the Republican national committee, and hence the special arrangement for the Pennsylvania Republican State committee in this instance, and the transaction was part of the general plan of financial aid extended for the presidential campaign. The fact that the contribution of $25,000 for Pennsylvania made a contribution of $125,000 from Mr. Archbold and his associates to the presidential campaign was one reason given for the refusal of Mr. Archbold and his associates to comply with the additional requisition of Mr. Bliss for another $150,000.

The State ticket of Pennsylvania was not in danger in the fall of 1904, and the campaign was waged entirely to poll as large a vote as possible for electors for the presidential and vice presidential candidates and to elect to Congresses large a number of Republicans from the State as possible. The result was majority of over 500,000 in Pennsylvania for Mr. Roosevelt for President, and a delegation which was all Republican with the exception of one congressional district. Immediately after the election I received a letter from Mr. Roosevelt, expressing his warm and heartfelt thanks for the result in Pennsylvania.

Senator Quay had recently died; the burdens of the Republican organization in Pennsylvania had apparently devolved upon me. I was a good deal younger then than I am now and quite enthusiastic. The State chairmanship had been forced upon me the year previous as the result of political conditions in Pennsylvania. I did not think it likely that I should ever be compelled to take the office again and I knew I certainly would not seek it, and I was anxious on my own account in the new field opened before me to make as good a record as possible. I was therefore highly gratified by the result in the State, which broke all previous records for majorities not only in Pennsylvania but in any other State in the Union.

The malicious efforts made to misrepresent a transaction which at the time was entirely legal and proper is only part of the systematic efforts of the Flinn-Van Valkenburg combination in Pennsylvania to break me down and deceive the people through the unscrupulous methods of yellow journalism.

Mr. William Flinn, of this unsavory combination, which until recently Mr. Roosevelt would have been quick to denounce and repudiate, has made a fortune out of crooked municipal contracts and the corrupt control of municipal councils and State legislatures. Mr. E. A. Van Valkenburg, editor of the North American in Philadelphia, was arrested and indicted for bribery in my first senatorial contest in 1896 and only escaped conviction through the leniency of Senator Quay and upon the payment of about $10,000 for costs for lawyers, detectives, and for other expenses of prosecution, which amount was paid by his attorney the day before the trial was set to take place in Pottsville, the county seat of Schuylkill County.

Upon the death of Senator Quay in 1904 Mr. Flinn became a candidate to succeed him in the United States Senate. In Philadelphia during a discussion of the successorship to Senator Quay Mr. Flinn offered to Israel W. Durham, a Republican leader in Philadelphia, and to me, $1,000,000, or even $2,000,000, to favor his ambition, and the offer was known to others at the time. The offer was declined, and we refused to support his candidacy.

The governor of Pennsylvania, Hon. Samuel W. Pennypacker, desiring to uphold the honor and dignity of the State, appointed the Hon. Philander C. Knox to succeed Mr. Quay. Mr. Knox was subsequently elected by the legislature for the full term. His appointment and election and resignation from the Cabinet occurred with the full knowledge and acquiescence of Mr. Roosevelt. Mr. Flinn still desires to go to the United States Senate. His friends openly avow his ambition, and his activity for Mr. Roosevelt and the reforms to which he has recently become a convert from his unrepentant days are prompted by this desire.

The effrontery, hypocrisy, and mendacity of the Van Valkenburg-Flinn combination are disclosed by the following correspondence between John D. Archbold and William Flinn. I call attention to the following telegram sent to J. D. Archbold by William Flinn, the Roosevelt leader in Pennsylvania:

PITTSBURGH, PA., *June 7, 1904*

I tried to talk to you over the phone last night, but could not hear you. I am making an effort to go the United States Senate as M. S. Quay's successor. As it now stands the appointment will go to Allegheny County, and I expect to get it. The Republican organization of Allegheny County are desirous of my appointment and are working in. Also the Republican organization of the surrounding counties. The decision of the question is up to Senator Boles Penrose, State chairman, and Israel W. Durham. The efforts of a few of my influential friends put forth at once with Penrose and Durham will settle the question. If you will use your influence with them in my behalf I will greatly appreciate it. The decision will probably be reached Wednesday. Can you help me?

WILLIAM FLINN.

Under the same date the following reply was sent in cipher to William Flinn from John D. Archbold:

NEW YORK, *June 7, 1904*

Telegram received. Sorry that the posy did not shout friskiness. I expect to jail pop sharply parsed fanning, and until flagon prefix it is lamented for me to have flood hatred reship.

[Laughter.]

Which being translated reads as follows:

Telegram received. Sorry that the phone did not work better. I expect to have talk with Senator Penrose, and until after that it is impossible for me to have any definite view.

JOHN D. ARCHBOLD.

[Laughter.]

This is addressed to William Flinn, a noted reformer in Pennsylvania.

Thus it is discovered that while the Flinn yellow journals in Pennsylvania are expressing their abhorrence of what they denounce as a malodorous transaction on my part, within a few months of the date of the alleged letter from John D. Archbold to me, Mr. William Flinn was asking the aid of the same John D. Archbold to secure his appointment and election to the United States Senate and conducting an active correspondence with him under a cipher code.

Mr. STONE. Mr. President, while the Senator from Pennsylvania is at the confessional and in a confessing mood, it occurred to me that he might be able and willing to add something more to the gayety of the occasion. He has laid before the Senate and the country some very interesting facts as to one transaction.

The Senator was a member of the Republican national committee in the year 1904 and is familiar with its work and seemingly familiar with the financial affairs of the committee. There was a man in this country at that time very celebrated for his achievements in the industrial world, a great constructor of railroads, one of the master men in the financial centers of the country. I refer to Mr. E. H. Harriman. He came down to Washington about the time of which the Senator has been speaking to call on President Roosevelt, then the Republican candidate for President. There will be no need for me to take time in detailing the circumstances and the correspondence which followed. Mr. Harriman finally declared that he had raised $250,000, or about that, at the special instance and request of the President. The President denounced him as a liar and conferred upon him the thirty-second degree in his Ananias Club. Can the Senator from Pennsylvania tell the Senate and the country what he knows about that transaction, if he knows anything?

Mr. PENROSE. Mr. President, many years have passed since these transactions occurred. There are papers on file and a number of letters accessible, interesting documents, which I have no doubt as this discussion develops during the campaign, should any gentlemen desire to press these matters, will see the light of day, and I think it would be very beneficial to the American public to have many of these transactions exposed.

Mr. STONE. Where are those letters?

Mr. PENROSE. They are hidden in the archives of campaign committees and in cellars and vaults of business houses and offices of lawyers in different places throughout the country. I was only brought to a recollection of these interesting letters about Mr. Flinn in an unexpected way. I had knowledge at the time of their being written, and it was only by accident that I remembered them. I think the time has come, as the Senator brings the point up, when these charges should be met and that the American people should be no longer gulled by an answer which implies the other man is a liar and that a reference to a speech formerly made is a sufficient answer to the charge.

I would just like to add, and I am glad the Senator has called that to my attention, there was a garbled interview. I have carefully refrained from saying anything about this particular matter in addressing the Senate today, but I should like to have the Secretary read this answer of Mr. Roosevelt to an alleged interview which appeared as coming from me, containing in a general way the substance of what I have said to the Senate.

The PRESIDENT pro tempore. Without objection, the Secretary will read as requested.

The Secretary read as follows:

Col. Roosevelt's statement follows:

"As regards Senator Penrose's statement I have only to say that I have not, and never have had, the slightest knowledge whether he or anyone else during the campaign of 1904 raised any money to be used in carrying the State of New York.

In 1904 in Pennsylvania, if my memory is correct, Senator Quay was in charge. My relations with him were always cordial and pleasant. He vigorously supported all the policies I advocated, and, as far as I know, he never asked and I never did anything of any kind, sort, or description for him that could not be blazoned in every newspaper throughout the country."

Mr. PENROSE. Now, Mr. President, there is a deliberate statement that I only had the interest in Mr. Roosevelt's election that might have been shared by a member of this body on the Republican side, when Senator Quay had been dead for several months, when I was in correspondence with Mr. Roosevelt on more than one occasion, when I was a member of the national committee, and in constant touch with Mr. Cortelyou. Yet he deliberately states to the American people that I had nothing whatever to do with his campaign.

Mr. President, is this ingratitude, is it mendacity, is it duplicity, or is it political aphasia?

Mr. BACON. I beg the Senator's pardon if I make an inquiry of him, which of course he will use his own judgment in replying to or not. I only venture to do so because the Senator himself made a statement, if I understood it correctly, that in the State of Pennsylvania a citizen of that State offered $2,000,000 to be elected to the Senate. Did I understand the Senator correctly?

Mr. PENROSE. That statement is correct. For various reasons peculiar to the situation at that time it was generally conceded that Mr. Durham and I would have a large voice in the selection of my own colleague. Mr. Flinn, however, in his insatiable desire to go to the Senate, may have slightly exaggerated that power. That had not been used by me in any offensive way. It was stated to me by people active in the party at that time.

Mr. BACON. I ask another question with hesitation, prefacing it—

Mr. PENROSE. I am glad to have any questions addressed to me.

Mr. BACON. I give the Senator the assurance that I do not ask it with any desire to seek an answer unless it is entirely convenient to the Senator to do so. To whom was that $2,000,000 to be paid?

Mr. PENROSE. I suppose it was to be paid to Mr. Durham or to me. I did I get far enough to decide those details.

Congressional Record, Senate, 62d Congress, 2d session, Aug. 21, 1912, 11466–11468.

111   A Newspaper Account of a Bombing at the Capitol

July 3, 1915

The Capitol has experienced a number of fires, explosions, and bombings in its long and colorful history. The most devastating incident was the burning of the building at the hands of British troops during the War of 1812. On Christmas eve 1851 an accidental fire destroyed more than half the books in the Library of Congress, which were then housed in the Capitol. In 1898 a huge gas explosion and fire seriously damaged the Supreme Court chambers in the Capitol. More recently, on March 1, 1971, a bomb in a private restroom in the old Senate wing did extensive damage to a half dozen rooms. This incident may have been related to a protest against the Vietnam War, but no perpetrators were ever caught. On November 7, 1983, a bomb exploded in the Senate wing around 11:00 P.M., doing extensive damage to the main corridor off the entrance to the Senate chamber and damaging portraits hanging on the walls. Fortunately, there were no injuries. Eventually seven persons—five women and two men—were apprehended, convicted, and sentenced to long prison terms for various terrorist acts, including the Capitol bombing, which was supposedly carried out in protest of American troops in Lebanon and Granada.

The bombing described in this newspaper account from the Washington Post *occurred on the night of July 2, 1915. It was the first recorded act of terrorism in the Capitol. In this incident a disgruntled former Harvard University German instructor, Erich Muenter, planted a bomb in the Capitol to protest the fact that the United States was selling munitions to Great Britain during World War I, even though the United States had not yet declared war on Germany. After bombing the Capitol, Muenter traveled to New York, where he tried to assassinate the wealthy financier, J. P. Morgan Jr. Muenter was arrested and committed suicide in his jail cell several days later.*

BLAST SHAKES CAPITOL AND WRECKS RECEPTION ROOM ON SENATE SIDE
Windows Blown Out and Plate Glass Mirrors Shattered.

Watchmen Almost Lifted From His Chair, and Great Building Shaken as if by an Earthquake— Besides the Few Men on Guard, Only Telephone Operators on Duty Were Within the Walls—Explosion at 11:40 P.M.— No Loiterers Seen—No One Hurt.

An explosion in the Capitol last night at 11:40 o'clock shook the giant pile as if an earthquake had passed under it, practically wrecking everything in the reception room on the Senate side, where it occurred, except two heavy chandeliers. Heavy plate glass mirrors extending from the ceiling to the floor were smashed to flinders, windows were blown out, and the wainscoting and other woodwork about the room, including three telephone booths, were reduced to kindling wood. The tiling of the floor near the point where the bomb went off was torn up in great patches, while large holes were dug deep into the brick and stone walls of the sides of the room.

Fortunately none of the employees of the Capitol were on duty in that portion of the building at the time of the explosion, and no one was injured.

No Remnants of Bomb Found.

At a late hour Supt. Woods and his assistants were making an investigation.

No strangers were seen prowling around the building by any of the watch officers, and so far there has been no remnant of a bomb or other apparatus discovered.

Supt. Woods, after a hasty examination of the foundation at that end of the big building, said there had been no structural damage sustained.

The view was expressed in some quarters that a bomb may have been thrown in from the outside by some one as a protest against the foreign policy of the government in connection with the present war.

At 2:30 this morning Supt. Woods of the Capitol definitely stated that the blast that wrecked the reception room in the Senate side just before midnight was due to an explosion. It was not caused by spontaneous combustion. If it was a bomb, he declared, it must have been placed in the room by some crank who wished to cause a sensation. If it was a bomb, it was not of sufficient size to cause any damage to the construction of the building, "We are working on the case along all lines, and will continue our investigations today," Mr. Woods said.

The doors of the Capitol were closed immediately after the explosion and no one was permitted to enter while the investigation was under way.

Supt. Woods, Sergeant-at Arms-Higgins, of the Senate, and the head of the Capitol police who directed the inquiry, refused to give any theory of the cause of the explosion until the investigation was completed.

Watchman Receives a Shock.

At the time of the explosion the Capitol had been closed since dark, and no one was in the building except the few watchmen on duty and telephone operators. The watchman in the hall directly below the reception room said he was almost blown from his chair by the force of the blast. He declared that no one could have been near the room for hours.

Persons who reached the Capitol soon after the explosion occurred said they noticed the odor of burned powder which persisted 15 or 20 minutes.

The explosion was heard for several blocks.

Officer Jones' Story.

F. G. Jones, member of the night watch on duty at the time of the explosion, was seated in his chair in the basement at the east entrance of the Senate wing. Officer Jones said that the men on duty were at their posts and a dead silence marked the moment of the explosion. Describing the sensation following the terrific explosion, Officer Jones said that he was thrown with considerable violence from a big armchair into the middle of the corridor.

"My first thought was," continued the officer, "that a bomb had been exploded under the center of the big building and that the dome had crushed through the space under it. I regained my feet bewildered, hardly knowing which way to turn. The men on duty came running from every direction. As soon as we could recover from the effects of the shock we started an investigation.

Filled With Blinding Smoke.

"We quickly saw that the explosion had been on the upper or main floor of the Senate wing. There was smoke coming from the direction of the Senate chamber through the reception room. When we reached the reception room, where the explosion took place, it was filled with a black blinding smoke with the smell of a powder clearly indicating to our senses that the explosion was due to that cause.

"After the smoke had cleared away we entered the room and found the wreck of things in there, as you have seen, A short time after we entered the room, Supt. Woods, who had been in his office making some experiments, came hurrying to the scene of the wreck with several members of his staff. Chief of Police Loughton was among the first men to get to the wrecked room after the smoke had cleared, There were no members of the police force in the part of the building where the room was wrecked."

Exact Location of Wrecked Room.

The room in which the explosion took place is to the rear of the main entrance from the west to the United States Senate and back of the battery of elevators on each side of the corridor, the anteroom to the entrance to the visitors' side of the Senate being directly south of the room which is used as a reception and waiting room by visitors going to the Capitol to see members of the Senate. This room is probably 25 feet wide and 75 feet long, and runs directly north and south. It is handsomely furnished and richly decorated with frescoes in allegoric work in panels and scrolls and other similar garnishments. From the center of each end of the room hang two massive chandeliers in pyramid shape, festooned in clusters of candelabra and bronze trimmings and engraved work. These chandeliers escaped injury for the reason that they do not hang rigid, by swing, and when the great force of the explosion took place the flexibility of the hangings caused the chandeliers to sway, preventing them from being crushed.

Bomb Placed in Window.

In the west window, where the bomb had evidently been placed, there was a telephone board that was out of commission. The force of the explosion was terrific at that point, clearly indication that there was where the bomb had been placed. Adjoining the telephone exchange switchboard were three private telephone booths. All of this was wrecked and wrecked as if a madman of herculean powers with a mighty ax or sledge hammer had smashed the wood and metal work in his fury. The walls and wainscoting nearby suffered a like fate at that point and broken glass, crushed mirrors and splintered wood was piled ankle deep in a mixture of debris that told eloquently of the force of the explosion.

A Suspicious Lot of Waste.

Back at the point of the explosion were a number of telephone and electric light cables in heavy armored jackets. These were packed with a lot of greasy waste, which could not have be explained by the officers of the building, but it was suggested that it had been placed there as a means to keep the cold air out of the room in the winter time. This waste took fire from the explosion and was thrown into the middle of the room, and was burning when Officer Jones and his assistants reached the room. It is not thought that the waste had been placed there by the man who planted the bomb.

Other Evidences of Damage.

The massive double mahogany doors of the United Senate District committee room, which opens into the reception room, were crushed in as if they had been built for a dollhouse. Similar carved doors leading into the office of the sergeants-at-arms of the Senate were similarly wrecked, and the debris thrown into both of these rooms. The windows in both the committee room and the sergeant-at-arms room were broken.

Beyond the short corridor, where are located the battery of elevators and the main entrance and exit to the Senate wing at the head of the long flight of steps on the eat front, the big double doors were sprung and the large transom glass was thrown out on the Capitol front in small pieces. The frescoing in the room was damaged to some extent, but it can be restored without a heavy outlay.

Supt. Woods' Statement.

Superintendent Woods, who was working in his office in the subbasement of the center portion of the building under the dome, said that he heard the explosion as if it had been directly under him. He said that his first impression was that there had been an explosion of trains in the New Jersey yard of the Pennsylvania Railroad, nearby, and that one or both of the colliding engines had exploded, so severe was the shock that shook the building as if it was under it.

"Immediately following the explosion I got in touch with Capt. Laughton in charge of the Capitol police, and he and other members of my office and executive staff who were in the building went to investigate the cause of the explosion. We soon located the point in the Senate reception room.

No Injury Downstairs.

"As soon as I looked over the situation I began a personal investigation to determine if there had been any structural injury to the building, going into the basement and subbasements below the point of the explosion. After an hour I returned to the wrecked room satisfied that the only damage was in the reception room, where the explosion took place, and some damage in the adjoining rooms and in the corridors. This damage is superficial and can, I believe, be repaired at a small cost inside of a thousand dollars.

"The explosion was due, in my opinion," said Supt. Woods, after making a careful investigation, "to a bomb placed in the reception room under the old telephone switchboard by a crank, to create a sensation. Just what the motive was or what he hoped to accomplish by the explosion of the bomb in that room at such an hour of the night is only conjecturable."

Capt. Laughton Also Convinced.

Capt. Laughton, chief of the Capitol police, said that he fully agreed with Superintendent Woods that the explosion was the result of a bomb put there by a crank. He had thought at first that it might have been due to spontaneous combustion or possibly some condition of the electric light and telephone cables at the point of the explosion. However, he said late investigation showed conclusively that the explosion was that of a bomb placed there hours before the explosion by somebody who had brought the bomb into the building unnoticed and place it there while no one was around and made good his escape unobserved.

"Six months ago," said Capt. Laughtan, "a man writing from St. Louis, Mo. addressed a letter to Vice President Marshall during the session of Congress, while certain legislation favorable to organized labor was under final consideration, threatening that if that legislation was not passed as presented by the friends of organized labor, some day during the session of the Senate a bomb would be exploded that would register the disapproval of the laboring men in a way that would bring the statesmen and capitalists to their senses.

"This man said that the labor people had men in the Capitol building who could carry out the threat and make good the proposition.

Work of Crank, He Thinks.

"This letter was turned over to me by Vice President Marshall, and I made a careful investigation into it, with the assistance of the postoffice inspectors, and we finally arrived at the conclusion that it was the work of a crank, who had no connection with organized labor, but whose mind had been inflamed by newspaper discussion of the various bills under consideration looking to the betterment of labor people." . . .

Washington Post, July 3, 1915, 1–2.

112 The Declaration of War Against Germany

April 4, 1917

On April 2, 1917, President Woodrow Wilson called Congress into special session to issue a call for a declaration of war against Germany. In one of his most memorable speeches, the president outlined the justification for abandoning the earlier U.S. policy of neutrality against the warring nations of Europe. Germany's resumption of unrestricted submarine warfare on the high seas, which had already cost American lives, was too much to ignore. Even though Wilson had been reelected in 1916 on the slogan "he kept us out of war," changing circumstances compelled the president to abandon the policy of neutrality and ask Congress for a declaration of war.

The Senate took up the war resolution on April 4, 1917. Although there was considerable discussion on the floor of the Senate that day, most of the debate over war had actually occurred over a long period of time as Congress debated the official policy of neutrality and the possibility of war during the two proceeding years of European conflict. Most of the debate on April 4 followed along the lines of the excerpt cited here from Senator Gilbert Monell Hitchcock (D-Neb.), who, as chairman of the Senate Committee on Foreign Relations, introduced the war resolution. Many senators spoke of their abhorrence of war even as they argued for war. A small handful of senators spoke against going to war. One Republican senator from North Dakota, Asle Jorgenson Gronna, said the Senate was about to "decide one of the most momentous problems in the history of our country." He argued that the American people did not want war and that the issue was so large that only the American people themselves could decide it. He was one of only six senators to vote against war. The Senate vote on the resolution was 82–6, with 8 not voting.

On the same day the Senate passed the declaration of war resolution, the House was in turmoil over a minor matter of seating in the House galleries. In the days following Wilson's speech a larger than usual number of citizens filled the galleries in anticipation of a declaration of war. When the day came, the Senate chose to clear its galleries during the debate on the resolution, forcing even more persons who wanted to witness history to flock to the House galleries. Persons who had obtained tickets from members of Congress could not find room in the galleries, leading to complaints, embarrassment, and general confusion. The House did not take up the matter of the war declaration until the next day. Instead of voting on its own resolution, the House accepted the Senate version and passed it overwhelmingly, but not before a number of members spoke against going to war. The vote in the House was 373–50, with 9 not voting.

On December 4, 1917, Wilson spoke again before a joint meeting of Congress, this time to call for a declaration of war against Germany's allies, Austria-Hungary. "One very embarrassing obstacle that stands in our way is that we are at war with Germany but not with her allies. I therefore very earnestly recommend that the Congress immediately declare the United States in a state of war with Austria-Hungary." Congress responded with another declaration of war on December 7, 1917.

WAR WITH GERMANY

. . . .

Mr. HITCHCOCK. I ask unanimous consent that the Senate now proceed to the consideration of Senate joint resolution No. 1.

The VICE PRESIDENT. Is there objection? The Chair hears none, and lays before the Senate the joint resolution.

The Senate, as in Committee of the Whole, proceeded to consider the joint resolution (S. J. Res. 1) declaring that a state of war exists between the Imperial German Government and the Government and the people of the United States and making provision to prosecute the same, which had been reported from the Committee on Foreign Relations with an amendment.

The VICE PRESIDENT. The amendment of the committee will be stated.

The SECRETARY. The amendment is, on page 1, line 7, after the words "directed to," to strike out the words "take immediate steps not only to put the country in a thorough state of defense, but also to exert all of its power and employ all of its resources to carry on war against the Imperial German Government and to bring the conflict to a successful termination," and insert "employ the entire naval and military forces of the United States and the resources of the Government to carry on war against the Imperial German Government; and to bring the conflict to a successful termination all of the resources of the country are hereby pledged by the Congress of the United States," so as to make the joint resolution read:

Resolved by the Senate and House of Representatives of the United States of America in Congress assembled, That the state of war between the United States and the Imperial German Government which has been thrust upon the United States is hereby formally declared; and that the President be, and he is hereby, authorized and directed to employ the entire naval and military forces of the United States and the resources of the Government to carry on war against the Imperial German Government; and to bring the conflict to a successful determination all of the resources of the country are hereby pledged by the Congress of the United States.

The amendment was agreed to.

Mr. HITCHCOCK. Mr. President, What I shall say in support of the joint resolution will be short. The time for action has arrived. The time for discussion has passed. The President of the United States has already stated more clearly, more conclusively, and more effectively than I can the reasons which make this great step now to be taken necessary.

The joint resolution provides for war against the Imperial German Government. It is framed on the lines of other war declarations of Congress, in that it directs the President to employ the military and naval forces of the country to carry the war to a successful termination. It also conforms to the precedents of other declarations when Congress has entered upon the solemn business of war by declaring that a state of war already exists. It places the responsibility of this war squarely upon the shoulders of the Imperial German Government, which is charged with having committed repeated acts of war against the United States. Over and above all this, however, the measure is unquestionably also a declaration of war.

Mr. President, in presenting the joint resolution I am impressed with the solemnity of the occasion. Some may be filled with joy at the prospect of war. To me it is depressing and dreadful. The enormous cost which the people must pay, the great increased cost of living which they must meet, the enormous burden of taxes which they must bear, and the still greater heritage of debt which they must incur stagger my mind. The awful sacrifice of life that must follow sickens my heart. I am sure other Senators have the same feeling. I am sure the great body of the American people have it also.

Our country has nothing material to gain by victory. We want no more territory; we demand no indemnity. We have no historic grudges to settle and no racial antipathies to gratify.

In these respects, Mr. President, we differ from other countries already involved in this awful struggle. Pan-Slavism struggles with pan-Germanism. Italy fights to get back the Trentino. France is resolved to recover her lost provinces. Great Britain has almost within her grasp German commerce and German colonies. Russia fights to win Constantinople. Germany not only wants her place in the sun but sue wants to dominate central Europe, while Austria, Bulgaria, and Roumania all seek to extend their borders.

We alone of all the nations, Mr. President, will spend our treasure and sacrifice our lives without possibility of material gain. We are going to war, Mr. President, to vindicate our honor and to maintain our independence as a great nation. We are going to war, as the President has stated, in defense of humanity. Such quarrel as we have with the Imperial Government of Germany was not of our seeking. It was forced upon us. We did much to avoid it.

For nearly three years of this struggle our country has steadily held to its purpose to avoid war if possible. This has been true not only of the President but of Congress; and it has been true of the American people. One desperate act of the Imperial German Government after another has added to the provocation. I do not mean to say, Mr. President, that Germany has desired war with us; I do not believe it; but the German Government has been desperate and has taken desperate chances.

The invasion of Belgium shocked the sense of justice of the whole civilized world and subjected American neutrality to its first great strain. The sinking of the *Lusitania,* with hundreds of innocent passengers, men, women, and children, many of them Americans, sent a thrill of horror through America, and would have produced war had it not been for the moderation of President Wilson and his success finally in securing from the German Government an agreement to modify its methods and conform them to the rules of international law and to the dictates of humanity.

It is customary, Mr. President, to say that this agreement was violated by Germany, but it is more just and more correct to say that Germany had reserved the right to revoke it under certain conditions and exercised that right by revoking it on February first of this year. This also was an act of desperation. It was not intended to provoke war with us, but it was followed by acts of war upon us. They were not made for the deliberate purpose of injuring us, but rather to starve the English people. The effect on us, however, was the same. We were ordered off the high seas. We then dissolved diplomatic relations with Germany. We might then have gone to war. We could not submit; no great nation could remain great and independent if it did so. No great nation could maintain its place in history if it permitted another to order it off the seas, if it permitted another to bottle up its commerce, if it permitted another to dictate to it as to the exercise of its unquestioned right and to impose the penalty of murder of its citizens in case of refusal.

. . . .

The American people, Mr. President, have clung to the hope through all these months that the dread alternative might be avoided. Like the Savior of man in the garden of Gethsemane, they have prayed that the bitter cup of sacrifice might pass from them. They have prayed that it might not be necessary to make the sacrifice for the protection of humanity and the vindication of national honor. All has been in vain. All patience, all moderation, and all long-suffering have apparently been in vain—not entirely in vain, though, Mr. President, because we have avoided the horrors of war for two years or more, but the time has now come when further delay is impossible.

Mr. President, I have opposed war; I have been bitterly opposed to it. What influence I have had in my State and in this body has been exerted against it. As long as there was any hope to avoid it I used my legitimate influence for that purpose. I sup-ported armed neutrality here with the fervor that I did because I thought it offered an escape from war with honor and I even hoped to avoid war up to the eleventh hour. Yes, Mr. President, when I knew that the people of the United States were calling for war, when I knew that a majority of the Congress of the United States was overwhelmingly for war, and upon the proper occasion would vote for war—even when I knew that, Mr. President, I sought out the President of the United States and begged him if possible to cling yet longer to armed neutrality as an expedient to avoid war; but it was vain. The President was in possession of such information as made it impossible for him to listen longer to the arguments of those who sought to avoid war. He has spoken to the Congress. The country is ready, and the Congress is ready. While the vote has not yet been recorded, the decision has, as we all know, been reached. It is war.

. . . .

Congressional Record, Senate, 65th Congress, 1st session, April 4, 1917, 200–201.

113   The Eighteenth Amendment to the Constitution

Submitted to the States, December 18, 1917; Ratified, January 29, 1919

The Eighteenth Amendment was the culmination of a century-long temperance movement in the United States that saw alcohol consumption as the root of many of the nation's social, economic, political, and moral problems. Adoption in 1913 of the Sixteenth Amendment, which provided for a federal income tax (see document 106), helped pave the way for a national Prohibition act by replacing revenue that had previously been generated by a tax on liquor sales. Various Prohibition groups, such as the Anti-Saloon League, worked hard and successfully to elect members of Congress sympathetic to a liquor ban.

Hoping that delay would eventually thwart ratification of the amendment, anti-Prohibition senators who felt compelled to vote for the measure managed to add a clause stating that ratification must occur within seven years from the time of submission of the amendment to the states. This clause has become a standard addition to most subsequent constitutional amendments. In this instance the seven-year deadline, much to the surprise of anti-Prohibitionists, did nothing to stop the required three-quarters of the states from approving the amendment just thirteen months after Congress submitted it to the states. Opponents of the resolution also succeeded in adding a one-year delay of enforcement to allow the liquor industry time to adjust to the massive economic blow. In 1917 the liquor industry was the seventh largest business in the United States.

Enforced by the Volstead Act (see document 115), Prohibition proved controversial, particularly in urban areas and among recent immigrants. Banning liquor production and sales led to the growth of an elaborate underworld trade in alcohol. But contrary to popular beliefs spurred by novels, films, and television, and sus-tained by several generations of anecdotes about "speakeasies" and "bathtub gin," most Americans, whether they agreed with the law or not, generally complied with its provisions. Alcohol consumption dropped dramatically during the fourteen years of Prohibition. Enforcement of the law led to the creation of a large federal law enforcement bureaucracy. Public disfavor with law enforcement policies, perhaps more than the regulation of liquor itself, led to a demand for repeal of the Eighteenth Amendment in 1933. This is the only constitutional amendment that has ever been repealed (see document 123).

ARTICLE XVIII.

SECTION 1. After one year from the ratification of this article the manufacture, sale, or transportation of intoxicating liquors within, the importation thereof into, or the exportation thereof from the United States and all territory subject to the jurisdiction thereof for beverage purposes is hereby prohibited.

SEC. 2. The Congress and the several States shall have concurrent power to enforce this article by appropriate legislation.

SEC. 3. This article shall be inoperative unless it shall have been ratified as an amendment to the Constitution by the legislatures of the several States, as provided in the Constitution within seven years from the date of the submission hereof to the States by the Congress.

The Constitution of the United States of America as Amended, House Doc. 102–188, 102d Congress, 2d session (Washington: Government Printing Office, 1992), 19–20.

114   The Nineteenth Amendment to the Constitution

Submitted to the States, June 4, 1919; Ratified, August 26, 1920

The Nineteenth Amendment guaranteed women the right to vote. The Constitution never prohibited women from voting. It was silent on the subject. Women's ability to exercise the right to vote had been left up to the individual states. Elizabeth Cady Stanton and other suffragists began the call for nationwide enfranchisement for women in 1848, at a convention in Seneca Falls, New York. This meeting helped launch a movement that would eventually enlist numerous groups and individuals in the long, hard-fought cause of women's suffrage.

Several states allowed women to vote before the passage of the Nineteenth Amendment. The first woman to serve as a member of the House of Representatives, Republican Jeannette Rankin of Montana, began her service in the House in 1917 because Montana provided for woman's suffrage. By 1919 a majority of states *had passed laws that would allow women to vote in the next presidential election. A combination of women's increased political leverage and their support of the war effort during World War I fueled the adoption of this amendment.*

ARTICLE XIX.

The right of citizens of the United States to vote shall not be denied or abridged by the United States or by any State on account of sex.

Congress shall have power to enforce this article by appropriate legislation.

The Constitution of the United States of America as Amended, House Doc. 102–188, 102d Congress, 2d session (Washington: Government Printing Office, 1992), 20.

115   The National Prohibition Act (The Volstead Act)

October 28, 1919

In the congressional elections of 1914 and 1916, the temperance movement was finally successful in helping to elect enough members of the House and Senate who would push for a constitutional amendment to ban the manufacture and sale of alcoholic beverages. With the ratification of the Nineteenth Amendment (see document 114), Congress had to devise a method of making Prohibition work. Many citizens and members of Congress took a middle path on Prohibition. They were willing to ban hard liquor, but did not see the harm in wines and beer. Temperance advocates, on the other hand, were opposed to all forms of alcoholic beverages. A key provision of the National Prohibition Act, called the Volstead Act after its chief sponsor, Representative Andrew J. Volstead (R-Minn.), was setting the definition of an alcoholic beverage as any product containing 0.5 percent alcohol or more. This included wine and beer. This was the goal of the Anti-Saloon League, whose general counsel Wayne B. Wheeler actually drafted the main provisions of the bill. President Woodrow Wilson, a moderate on Prohibition, vetoed the bill because it banned wine and beer, but both houses of Congress overrode the veto by wide margins.

During the first decade of Prohibition more than a half million arrests were made by local, state, and federal officials to enforce compliance with the Volstead Act. Eventually many Americans began to fear police intrusion into their personal lives more than they feared the consumption of alcohol. This was especially the case after 1929, as stiffer penalties and a more elaborate federal enforcement took hold. The Volstead Act was the law of the land until the ratification of the Twenty-First Amendment (see document 123) on December 5, 1933, which repealed the Eighteenth Amendment.

. . . .

TITLE II. PROHIBITION OF INTOXICATING BEVERAGES.

SEC. 1. When used in Title II and Title III of this Act (1) The word "liquor" or the phrase "intoxicating liquor" shall be construed to include alcohol, brandy, whisky, rum, gin, beer, ale, porter, and wine, and in addition thereto any spirituous, vinous, malt, or fermented liquor, liquids, and compounds, whether medicated, proprietary, patented, or not, and by whatever name called, containing one-half of 1 per centum or more of alcohol by volume which are fit for use for beverage purposes: *Provided,* That the foregoing definition shall not extend to dealcoholized wine nor to any beverage or liquid produced by the process by which beer, ale, porter or wine is produced, if it contains less than one-half of 1 per centum of alcohol by volume, and is made as prescribed in section 37 of this title, and is otherwise denominated than as beer, ale, or porter, and is contained and sold in, or from, such sealed or labeled bottles, casks, or containers an the commissioner may by regulation prescribe.

. . . .

SEC. 2. The Commissioner of Internal Revenue, his assistants, agents, and inspectors shall investigate and report violations of this Act to the United States attorney for the district in which committed, who is hereby charged with the duty of prosecuting the offenders, subject to the direction of the Attorney General, as in the case of other offenses against the laws of the

United States; and such Commissioner of Internal Revenue, his assistants, agents, and inspectors may swear out warrants before United States commissioners or other officers or courts authorized to issue the same for the apprehension of such offenders, and may, subject to the control of the said United States attorney, conduct the prosecution at the of having the offenders held for the action of the grand jury. Section 1014 of the Revised Statutes of the applicable in the enforcement of this Act. Officers mentioned in said section 1014 are authorized to issue warrants under the limitations provided in Title XXI of the Act approved June 15, 1917 (Fortieth Statutes at Large, page 217, et seq.).

SEC. 3. No person shall on or after the date when the eighteenth amendment to the Constitution of the United States goes into effect, manufacture, sell, barter, transport, import, export, deliver, furnish or possess any intoxicating liquor except as authorized in this Act, and all the provisions of this Act shall be liberally construed to the end that the use of intoxicating liquor as a beverage may be prevented.

Liquor for nonbeverage purposes and wine or sacramental purposes, may be manufactured, purchased, sold, bartered, transported, and possessed, but only as herein provided, and the commissioner may, upon application, issue permits therefor: *Provided,* That nothing in this Act shall prohibit receipts covering distilled spirits warehouses, and no special tax liability shall attach to the business of purchasing and selling such warehouse receipts.

SEC. 4. The articles enumerated in this section shall not, after having been manufactured and prepared for the market, be subject to the provisions of this Act if they correspond with the following descriptions and limitations, namely:

(a) Denatured alcohol or denatured rum produced and used as provided by laws and regulations now or here-after in force.

(b) Medicinal preparations manufactured in accordance with formulas prescribed by the United States Pharmacopoeia, National Formulary or the American Institute of Homeopathy that are unfit for use for beverage purposes.

(c) Patented, patent, and proprietary medicines that are unfit for use for beverage purposes.

(d) Toilet and medicinal, and antiseptic preparations and solutions that are unfit for use for beverage purposes.

(e) Flavoring extracts and sirups that are unfit for use as a beverage, or for intoxicating beverage purposes.

(f) Vinegar and preserved sweet cider.

A person who manufactures any of the articles mentioned in this liquor for that purpose, but he shall secure permits to manufacture such articles and to purchase such liquor, give the bonds, keep the records, and make the reports specified the commissioner. No such manufacturer shall sell, use, or dispose of any liquor otherwise than as an ingredient of the articles authorized to be manufactured therefrom. No more alcohol shall be used in the manufacture of any extract, sirup, or the articles named in paragraphs b, c, and d of this section which may be used for beverage purposes than the quantity necessary extrac-

tion or solution of the elements contained therein and for the preservation of the article.

Any person who shall knowingly sell any of the articles mentioned in paragraphs a, b, c, and d of this section for beverage purposes, or who shall sell any of the same under circumstances from which the seller might reasonable deduce the intention of the purchaser to use them for such purposes, or shall sell any beverage containing one-half of 1 per centum or more of alcohol by volume in which any extract, sirup, or other article is used as an ingredient, shall be subject to the penalties provided in section 29 of this Title. If the commissioner shall find, after notice and hearing as provided for in section 5 of this Title, that any person has sold any flavoring extract, sirup, or beverage in violation Of this paragraph, he shall notify such person, and any known principal for whom the sale was made, to desist from selling such article; and it shall thereupon be unlawful for a period of one year thereafter for any person so notified to sell any such extract, sirup, or beverage without making an application for giving a bond, and obtaining a permit so to do, which permit may be issued upon such conditions as the commissioner may deem necessary to prevent such illegal sales, and in addition the commissioner shall require a record and report of sales.

. . . .

SEC. 6. No one shall manufacture, sell, purchase, transport, or prescribe any liquor without first obtaining. a permit from the commissioner so to do so to do, except that a person may, without a permit, purchase and use liquor for medicinal purposes when prescribed by a physician as herein provided, and except that any person who in the opinion of the commissioner is conducting a bona fide hospital or sanatorium engaged in the treatment of persons suffering from alcoholism, may, under such rules, regulations, and conditions as the commissioner shall prescribe, purchase and use, in accordance with the methods in use in such institution, liquor, to be administered to the patients of such institution under the direction of a duly qualified physician employed by such institution.

. . . .

SEC. 7. No one but a physician holding a permit to prescribe liquor shall issue any prescription for liquor. And no physician shall prescribe liquor unless after careful physical examination of the person for whose use such prescription is sought, or if such examination is found impracticable, then upon the best information obtainable, he in good faith believes that the use of such liquor as a medicine by such person is necessary and will afford relief to him from some known ailment. Not more than a pint of spirituous liquor to be taken internally should be prescribed for use by the same person within any period of ten days and no prescription shall be filled more than once. Any pharmacist filling a prescription shall at the time indorse upon it over his own signature the word "canceled," together with the date when the liquor was delivered, and then make the same a part of the record that he is required to keep as herein provided.

Every physician who issues a prescription for liquor shall keep a record, alphabetically arranged in a book prescribed by the commissioner, which shall show the date of issue, amount prescribed, to whom issued, the purpose or ailment for which it is to be used and directions for use, stating the amount and frequency of the dose.

. . . .

SEC. 10. No person shall manufacture, purchase for sale, sell, or transport any liquor without making at the time a permanent record thereof showing in detail the amount and kind of liquor manufactured, purchased, sold, or transported, together with the names and addresses of the persons to whom sold, in case of sale, and the consignor and consignee in case of transportation, and the time and place transportation. The commissioner may prescribe the form of such record, which shall at all times be open to inspection as in this Act provided.

SEC. 11. All manufacturers and wholesale or retail druggists shall keep as a part of the records required of them a copy of all permits to purchase on which a sale of any liquor is made, and no manufacturer or wholesale druggist shall sell or otherwise dispose of any liquor except at wholesale and only to persons having permits to purchase in such quantities.

SEC. 12. All persons manufacturing liquor for sale under the provisions of this title shall securely and permanently attach to every container thereof, as the same is manufactured, kind and quantity of liquor contained therein, and the date of its manufacture, together with the number of the permit authorizing the manufacture liquor in wholesale quantities label thereof; and all persons possessing such liquor in wholesale quantities shall securely keep and maintain such label thereon; and all persons selling at wholesale shall attach to every package of liquor, when sold, a label setting forth the kind and quantity of liquor contained therein, by whom manufactured, the date of the sale, and the person to whom sold; which label shall likewise be kept and maintained thereon until the liquor is used for the purpose for which such sale was authorized.

SEC. 13. It shall be the duty of every carrier to make a record at the place of shipment of the receipt of any liquor transported, and he shall deliver liquor only to persons who present to the carrier a verified copy of a permit to purchase which shall be made a part of the carrier's permanent record at the office from which delivery is made.

The agent of the common carrier is hereby authorized to administer the oath to the consignee in verification of the copy of the permit presented, who, if not personally known to the agent, shall be identified before the delivery of the liquor to him. The name an address of the person identifying the consignee shall be included in the record.

SEC. 14. It shall be unlawful for a person to use or induce any carrier, or any agent or employees thereof, to carry or ship any package or receptacle containing liquor without notifying the carrier of the true nature and character of the shipment. No carrier shall transport nor shall any person receive liquor from a carrier unless there appears on the outside of the package containing such liquor the following information:

Name and address of the consignor or seller, name and address of the consignee, kind and quantity of liquor contained therein, and number of the permit to purchase or ship the same, together with the name and address of the person using the permit.

SEC. 15. It shall be unlawful for any consignee to accept or receive any package containing any liquor upon which appears a statement known to him to be false, or for any carrier or other person to consign, ship, transport, or deliver any such package, knowing such statement to be false.

SEC. 16. It shall be unlawful to give to any carrier or any officer, agent, or person acting or assuming to act for such carrier an order requiring the delivery to any person of any liquor or package containing liquor consigned to, or purporting to claimed to be consigned to a person, when the purpose of the order is to enable any person not an actual bona fide consignee to obtain such liquor.

SEC. 17. It shall be unlawful to advertise anywhere, or by any means or method, liquor, or the manufacture, sale, keeping for sale or furnishing of the same, or where, how, from whom, or at what prices the same may be obtained. No one shall permit any sign or billboard containing such advertisement to remain upon one's premises. But nothing herein shall prohibit manufacturers and wholesale druggists holding permits to sell liquor from furnishing price lists, with description of liquor for sale, to persons permitted to purchase liquor, or from advertising alcohol in business publications or trade journals circulating generally among manufacturers of lawful alcoholic perfumes, toilet preparations, flavoring extracts, medicinal preparations, and like articles. . . .

SEC. 18. It shall be unlawful to advertise, manufacture, sell, or possess for sale any utensil, contrivance, machine, preparation, compound, tablet, substance, formula direction, or recipe advertised, designed, or intended for use in the unlawful manufacture of intoxicating liquor.

SEC. 19. No person shall solicit or receive, nor knowingly permit his employee to solicit or receive, from any person any order for liquor or give any information of how liquor may be obtained in violation of this Act.

SEC. 20. Any person who shall be injured in person, property, or otherwise by any intoxicated person, or by reason of the intoxication of any person, whether resulting in his death or not, shall have a right of action against any person who shall, by unlawfully selling to or unlawfully assisting in procuring liquor for such intoxicated person, have caused or contributed to such intoxication, and in any such action such person shall have a right to recover actual and exemplary damages. In case of the death of either party, the action or right of action given by this section shall survive to or against his or her executor or administrator, and the amount so recovered by either wife or child shall be his or her sole and separate property. Such action may be brought in any court of competent jurisdiction. In any case where parents shall be entitled to such damages, either the father or mother may sue alone therefor, but recovery by one of such parties shall be a bar to suit brought by the other.

SEC. 21. Any room, house, building, boat, vehicle, structure, or place where intoxicating liquor is manufactured, sold, kept, or bartered in violation of this title, and all intoxicating liquor and property kept and used in maintaining the same, is hereby declared to be a common nuisance, and any person who maintains such a common nuisance shall be guilty of a misdemeanor and upon conviction thereof shall be fined not more than $1,000 or be imprisoned for not more than one year, or both. If a person has knowledge or reason to believe that his room, house, building, boat, vehicle, structure, or place is occupied or used for the manufacture or sale of liquor contrary to the provisions of this title, and suffers the same to be so occupied or used, such room, house, building, boat, vehicle, structure, or place shall be subject to a lien for and may be sold to pay all fines and costs assessed against the person guilty of such nuisance for such violation, and any such lien may be enforced by action in any court having jurisdiction.

. . . .

SEC. 23. That any person who shall, with intent to effect a sale of liquor, by himself, his employee, servant, or agent, for himself or any person, company or corporation, keep or carry around on his person, or in a vehicle, or other conveyance whatever, or leave in a place for another to secure, any liquor, or who shall travel to solicit, or solicit, or take, or accept orders for the sale, shipment, or delivery of liquor in violation of this title is guilty of a nuisance and may be restrained by injunction, temporary and permanent, from doing or continuing to do any of said acts or things.

In such proceedings it shall not be necessary to show any intention on the part of the accused to continue such violations if the action is brought within sixty days following any such violation of the law.

For removing and selling property inforcing this Act the officer shall be entitled to charge and receive the same fee as the sheriff of the county would receive for levying upon and selling property under execution, and for closing the premises and keeping them closed a reasonable sum shall be allowed by the court.

Any violation of this title upon any leased premises by the lessee or occupant thereof shall, at the option of the lessor, work a forfeiture of the lease.

SEC. 24. In the case of the violation of any injunction, temporary or permanent, granted pursuant to the provisions of this title, the court, or in vacation a judge thereof, may summarily try and punish the defendant. The proceedings for punishment for contempt shall be commenced by filing with the clerk of the court from which such injunction issued information under oath setting out the alleged facts constituting the violation, whereupon the court or judge shall forthwith cause a warrant to issue under which the defendant shall be arrested. The trial may be had upon affidavits, or either party may demand the produc-

tion and oral examination of the witnesses. Any person found guilty of contempt under the provisions of this section shall be punished by a fine of not less twelve months, or by both fine and imprisonment.

SEC. 25. It shall be unlawful to have or possess any liquor or property designed for the manufacture of liquor intended for use in violating this title or which has been so used, and no property rights shall exist in any such liquor or property. A search warrant may issue as provided in Title XI of public law numbered 24 of the Sixty-fifth Congress, approved June 15, 1917, and such liquor, the containers thereof, and such property so seized shall be subject to such disposition as the court may make thereof. If it is found that such liquor or property was so unlawfully held or possessed, or had been so unlawfully used, the liquor, and all property designed for the unlawful manufacture of liquor, shall be destroyed, unless the court shall otherwise order. No search warrant shall issue to search any private dwelling occupied as such unless it is being used for the unlawful sale of intoxicating liquor, or unless it is in pat used for some business purpose such as a store, shop, saloon, restaurant, hotel, or boarding house. The term "private dwelling" shall be construed to include the room or rooms used and occupied not transiently but solely as a residence in an apartment house, hotel, or boarding house. The property seized on any such warrant shall not be taken from the officer seizing the same on any writ of replevin or other like process.

SEC. 26. When the commissioner, his assistants, inspectors, or any officer of the law shall discover any person in the act of transporting in violation of the law shall discover any person in the act of transporting in violation of the law, intoxicating liquors in any wagon, buggy, automobile, water or air craft, or other vehicle, it shall be his duty to seize any and all intoxicating liquors found therein being transported contrary to law. Whenever intoxicating liquors transported or possessed illegally shall be seized by an officer he shall take possession of the vehicle and team or automobile, boat, air or water craft, or any other conveyance, and shall arrest any person in charge thereof. Such officer shall at once proceed against the person arrested under the provisions of this title in any court having competent jurisdiction; but the said vehicle or conveyance shall be returned to the owner upon execution by him of a good and valid bond, with sufficient sureties, in a sum double the value of the property, which said bond shall be approved by said officer and shall be conditioned to return said property to the custody of said officer on the day of trial to abide the judgment of the court. The court upon conviction of the person so arrested shall order the liquor destroyed, and unless good cause to the contrary is shown by the owner, shall order a sale by public auction of the property seized, and the officer making the sale, after deducting the expenses of keeping the property, the fee for the seizure, and the cost of the sale, shall pay all liens, according to their priorities, which are established, by intervention or otherwise at said hearing or in other proceeding brought for said purpose, as being bona fide and as having been created without the lienor having any notice that the carrying vehicle was being used or was to be used for illegal transportation of liquor, and shall pay the balance of the proceeds into the Treasury of the United States as miscellaneous receipts. All liens against property sold under the provisions of this section shall be transferred from the property to the proceeds of the sale of the property. If, however, no one shall be found claiming the team, vehicle, water or air craft, or automobile, the taking of same, with a description thereof, to be advertised in some newspaper published in the city or county where taken or if there be no newspaper published in each city or county, in a newspaper having circulation in the county, once a week for two weeks and by handbills posted in three public places near the place of seizure, and if no claimant shall appear within ten days after the last publication of the advertisement, the property shall be sold and the proceeds after deducting the expenses and costs shall be paid into the Treasury of the United States is miscellaneous receipts.

. . . .

SEC. 29. Any person who manufactures or sells liquor in violation of this title shall for a first offense be fined not more than $1,000, or imprisoned not exceeding six months, and for a second or subsequent offense shall be fined not less than $200 nor more than $2,000 and be imprisoned not less than one month nor more than five years.

Any person violating the provisions of any permit, or who makes any false record, report, or affidavit required by this title, or violates any of the provisions of this title, for which offense a special penalty is not prescribed, shall be fined for a first offense not more than $500; for a second offense not less than $100 nor more than $1,000, or be imprisoned not more than ninety days; for any subsequent offense he shall be fined not less than $500 and be imprisoned not less than three months nor more than two years. It shall be the duty of the prosecuting officer to ascertain whether the defendant has been previously convicted and to plead the prior conviction in the affidavit, information, or indictment. The penalties provided in this Act against the manufacture of liquor without a permit shall not apply to nonintoxicating cider and fruit juices but such cider and fruit juices shall to persons having permits to manufacture vinegar.

SEC. 30. No person shall be excused, on the ground that it may tend to incriminate him or subject him to a penalty or forfeiture, from attending and testifying, or producing books, papers, documents, and other evidence in obedience a subpoena of any court in any suit or proceeding based upon or growing out of any alleged violation of this Act; but no natural person shall be prosecuted or subjected to any penalty or forfeiture for or on account of any transaction, matter, oath, he may so testify or produce evidence, but no person shall be exempt from prosecution and punishment for perjury committed in so testifying.

. . . .

SEC. 33. After February 1, 1920, the possession of liquors by any person not legally permitted under this title to possess liquor shall be prima facie evidence that such liquor is kept for the purpose of being sold, bartered, exchanged, given away, furnished, or otherwise disposed of in violation of the provisions of this title. Every person legally permitted under this title to have liquor shall report to the commissioner within ten days after the date when the eighteenth amendment of the Constitution of the United States goes into effect, the kind and amount of intoxicating liquors in his possession. But it shall not be unlawful to possess liquors in one's private dwelling while the same is occupied and used by him as his dwelling only and such liquor need not be reported, provided such liquors are for use only for the consumption of the owner thereof and his family residing in such dwelling and of his bona fide guests when entertained by him therein; and the burden of proof shall be upon the possessor that such liquor was lawfully acquired, possessed, and used.

. . . .

SEC. 38. The Commissioner of Internal Revenue and the Attorney General of the United States are hereby respectively authorized to appoint and employ such assistants, experts, clerks, and other employees in the District of Columbia or elsewhere, and to purchase such supplies and equipment as they may deem necessary for the enforcement of the provisions of this Act, but such assistants, experts, clerks, and other employees, except such executive officers as may be appointed by the Commissioner or the Attorney General to have immediate direction of the enforcement of the provisions of this Act, and persons authorized to issue permits, and agents and inspectors in the field service, shall be appointed under the rules and regulations prescribed by the Civil Service Act: *Provided,* That the Commissioner and Attorney General in making such appointments shall give preference to those who have served in the military or naval service in the recent war, if otherwise qualified, and there is hereby authorized to be appropriated, out of any money in the Treasury not otherwise appropriated, such sum as may be required for the enforcement of this Act including personal services in the District of Columbia, and for the fiscal year ending June 30, 1920, there is hereby appropriated out of any money in the Treasury not otherwise appropriated, the sum of $2,000,000 for the use of the Commissioner of Internal Revenue and $100,000, for the use of the Department of Justice for the enforcement of the provisions of his Act, including personal services in the District of Columbia and necessary printing and binding.

SEC. 39. In all cases wherein the property of any citizen is proceeded against or wherein a judgment affecting it might be rendered, and the citizen is not the one who in person violated the provisions of the law, summons must be issued in due form and served personally, if said person is to be found within the jurisdiction of the court.

. . . .

Statutes at Large, 41 (1919–1921), 66th Congress, 1st session, Oct. 28, 1919, 307–319.

116   Senator William E. Borah Opposes the League of Nations

November 19, 1919

The conventional wisdom about Congress is that floor debate in the House or Senate seldom changes votes. This was the view of Woodrow Wilson, whose 1885 study of Congress is still often quoted today (see document 97). Wilson and many observers since him have concluded that floor debate is merely a formal way of announcing what has occurred in committee and is designed primarily for the consumption of the nation, to educate the American people (and perhaps friends and foes in foreign lands) and allow constituents back home to judge how their representatives and senators display their views. While there is some truth in this view, it cannot explain fully the drama and the timing of some of the great floor speeches in the history of Congress. The full impact of a great speech cannot be measured only by its ability to influence votes.

When Senator William E. Borah (R-Idaho) rose to speak against the creation of a League of Nations on the last day of the first session of the 66th Congress, few who heard the speech failed to realize that it was a masterpiece of oratory and superb timing, perhaps unmatched since the days of Daniel Webster, Henry Clay, and John Calhoun. Borah was known as the "Great Opposer" for his many independent stands during his long career in the Senate (see document 118). Henry Cabot Lodge deserved the lion's share of credit for defeating the bill to create the League, in his dual roles as Senate majority leader and chairman of the Senate Foreign Relations Committee, where he loaded the bill with provisions objectionable to the League's supporters. But it was Borah who carried the day with his passionate opposition to the League in speeches all through the Midwest and from the floor of the Senate. Borah's opposition to foreign alliances, harkening back to the often-quoted words of George Washington's farewell address, where the first president warned the nation against permanent alliances with foreign nations, made Borah one of the leading isolationists of his day. The arguments in the speech can be heard to this day in the words of those who oppose such alliances as the United Nations or the North Atlantic Treaty Organization.

Mr. President, I am not misled by the debate across the aisle into the view that this treaty will not be ratified. I entertain little doubt that sooner or later—and entirely too soon—the treaty will be ratified with the league of nations in it, and I am of the opinion with the reservations in it as they are now written. There may possibly be some change in verbiage in order that there may be a common sharing of parentage, but our friends across the aisle will likely accept the league of nations with the reservations in substance as now written. I think, therefore, this moment is just as appropriate as any other for me to express my final views with reference to the treaty and the league of nations. It is perhaps the last opportunity I shall have to state, as briefly as I may, my reasons for opposing the treaty and the league.

Mr. President, after Mr. Lincoln had been elected President before he assumed the duties of the office and at a time when all indications were to the effect that we would soon be in the midst of civil strife, a friend from the city of Washington wrote him for instructions. Mr. Lincoln wrote back in a single line, "Entertain no compromise; have none of it." That states the position I occupy at this time and which I have, in an humble way, occupied from the first contention in regard to this proposal.

My objections to the league have not been met by the reservations. I desire to state wherein my objections have not been met. Let us see what our attitude will be toward Europe and what our position will be with reference to the other nations of the world after we shall have entered the league with the present reservations written therein. With all due respect to those who think that they have accomplished a different thing and challenging no man's intellectual integrity or patriotism, I do not believe the reservations have met the fundamental propositions which are involved in this contest.

When the league shall have been formed, we shall be a member of what is known as the council of the league. Our accredited representative will sit in judgment with the accredited representatives of the other members of the league to pass upon the concerns not only of our country but of all Europe and all Asia and the entire world. Our accredited representatives will be members of the assembly. They will sit there to represent the judgment of these 110,000,000 people—more than—just as we are accredited here to represent our constituencies. We cannot send our representatives to sit in council with the representatives of the other great nations of the world with mental reservations as to what we shall do in case their judgment shall not be satisfactory to us. If we go to the council or to the assembly with any other purpose than that of complying in good faith and in absolute integrity with all upon which the council or the assembly may pass, we shall soon return to our country with our self-respect forfeited and the public opinion of the world condemnatory.

Why need you gentlemen across the aisle worry about a reservation here or there when we are sitting in the council and in the assembly and bound by every obligation in morals, which the President said was supreme above that of law, to comply with the judgment which our representative and the other representatives finally form? Shall we go there, Mr. President, to sit in judgment, and in case that judgment works for peace join with our allies, but in case it works for war withdraw our cooperation? How long would we stand as we now stand, a great Republic commanding the respect and holding the leadership of the world, if we should adopt any such course?

So, sir, we not only sit in the council and in the assembly with our accredited representatives, but bear in mind that article 11 is untouched by any reservation which has been offered here; and with article 11 untouched and its integrity complete, article 10 is perfectly superfluous. If any war or threat of war shall be a matter of consideration for the league, and the league shall take such action as it deems wise to deal with it, what is the necessity of article 10? Will not external aggression be regarded as a war or threat of war? If the political independence of some nation in Europe is assailed will it be regarded as a war or threat of war? Is there anything in article 10 that is not completely covered by article 11?

It remains complete, and with our representatives sitting in the council and the assembly, and with article 11 complete, and with the assembly and the council having jurisdiction of all matters touching the peace of the world, what more do you need to bind the United States if you assume that the United States is a Nation of honor?

We have said, Mr. President, that we would not send our troops abroad without the consent of Congress. Pass by now for a moment the legal proposition. If we create Executive functions, the executive will perform those functions without the authority of Congress. Pass that question by and go to the other question. Our members of the council are there. Our members of the assembly are there. Article 11 is complete, and it authorizes the league, a member of which is our representative, to deal with matters of peace and war, and the league through its council and its assembly deals with the matter, and our accredited representative joins with the others in deciding upon a certain course, which involves a question of sending troops. What will the Congress of the United States do? What right will it have left, except the bare technical right to refuse, which as a moral proposition it will not dare to exercise? Have we not been told day by day for the last nine months that the Senate of the United States, a coordinate part of the treatymaking power, should accept this league as it was written because the wise men sitting at Versailles had so written it, and has not every possible influence and every source of power in public opinion been organized and directed against the Senate to compel it to do that thing? How much stronger will be the moral compulsion upon the Congress of the United States when we ourselves have indorsed the proposition of sending our accredited representatives there to vote for us?

Ah, but you say that there must be unanimous consent, and that there is vast protection in unanimous consent.

I do not wish to speak disparagingly; but has not every division and dismemberment of every nation which has suffered dismemberment taken place by unanimous consent for the last three hundred years? Did not Prussia and Austria and Russia by unanimous consent divide Poland? Did not the United States and Great Britain and Japan and Italy and France divide China and give Shantung to Japan? Was that not a unanimous decision? Close the doors upon the diplomats of Europe, let them sit in secret, give them the material to trade on, and there always will be unanimous consent.

How did Japan get unanimous consent? I want to say here, in my parting words upon this proposition, that I have no doubt the outrage upon China was quite as distasteful to the President of the United States as it is to me. But Japan said: "I will not sign your treaty unless you turn over to me Shantung,

to be turned back at my discretion," and you know how Japan's discretion operates with reference to such things. And so, when we are in the league, and our accredited representatives are sitting at Geneva, and a question of great moment arises, Japan, or Russia, or Germany, or Great Britain will say, "Unless this matter is adjusted in this way I will depart from your league." It is the same thing, operating in the same way, only under a different date and under a little different circumstances.

Mr. President, if you have enough territory, if you have enough material, if you have enough subject peoples to trade upon and divide, there will be no difficulty about unanimous consent.

Do our Democratic friends ever expect any man to sit as a member of the council or as a member of the assembly equal in intellectual power and in standing before the world with that of our representative at Versailles? Do you expect a man to sit in the council who will have made more pledges, and I shall assume made them in sincerity, for self-determination and for the rights of small peoples, than had been made by our accredited representative? And yet, what became of it? The unanimous consent was obtained nevertheless.

But take another view of it. We are sending to the council one man. That one man represents 110,000,000 people.

Here, sitting in the Senate, we have two from every State in the Union, and over in the other House we have Representatives in accordance with population, and the responsibility is spread out in accordance with our obligations to our constituency. But now we are transferring to one man the stupendous power of representing the sentiment and convictions of 110,000,000 people in tremendous questions which may involve the peace or may involve the war of the world.

However you view the question of unanimous consent, it does not protect us.

What is the result of all this? We are in the midst of all of the affairs of Europe. We have entangled ourselves with all European concerns. We have joined in alliance with all the European nations which have thus far joined the league, and all nations which may be admitted to the league. We are sitting there dabbling in their affairs and intermeddling in their concerns. In other words, Mr. President—and this comes to the question which is fundamental with me—we have forfeited and surrendered, once and for all, the great policy of "no entangling alliances" upon which the strength of this Republic has been founded for 150 years.

My friends of reservations, tell me where is the reservation in these articles which protects us against entangling alliances with Europe?

Those who are differing over reservations, tell me what one of them protects the doctrine laid down by the Father of his Country. That fundamental proposition is surrendered, and we are a part of the European turmoils and conflicts from the time we enter this league.

Let us not underestimate that. There has never been an hour since the Venezuelan difficulty that there has not been operating in this country, fed by domestic and foreign sources, a powerful propaganda for the destruction of the doctrine of no entangling alliances.

[*British Prime Minister David*] Lloyd George is reported to have said just a few days before the conference met at Versailles that Great Britain could give up much, and would be willing to sacrifice much, to have America withdraw from that policy. That was one of the great objects of the entire conference at Versailles, so far as the foreign representatives were concerned. [*Premier of France Georges*] Clemenceau and Lloyd George and others like them were willing to make any reasonable sacrifice which would draw America away from her isolation and into the internal affairs and concerns of Europe. This league of nations, with or without reservations, whatever else it does or does not do, does surrender and sacrifice that policy; and once having surrendered and become a part of the European concerns, where, my friends, are you going to stop?

You have put in here a reservation upon the Monroe doctrine. I think that, in so far as language could protect the Monroe doctrine, it has been protected. But as a practical proposition, as a working proposition, tell me candidly, as men familiar with the history of your country and of other countries, do you think that you can intermeddle in European affairs and keep Europe from intermeddling in your affairs?

When Mr. Monroe wrote to Jefferson, he asked him his view upon the Monroe Doctrine, and Mr. Jefferson said, in substance, our first and primary obligation should be never to interfere in European affairs; and, secondly, never to permit Europe to interfere in our affairs.

He understood, as every wise and practical man understands, that if we intermeddle in her affairs, if we help to adjust her conditions, inevitably and remorselessly Europe then will be carried into our affairs, in spite of anything you can write upon paper.

We cannot protect the Monroe doctrine unless we protect the basic principle upon which it rests, and that is the Washington policy. I do not care how earnestly you may endeavor to do so, as a practical working proposition your league will come to the United States. Will you permit me to digress long enough to read a paragraph from a great French editor upon this particular phase of the matter, Mr. Stephen Lausanne, editor of *Le Matin*, of Paris?

When the executive council of the league of nations fixes "the reasonable limits of the armament of Peru"; when it shall demand information concerning the naval program of Brazil; when it shall tell Argentina what shall be the measure of the 'contribution to the armed forces to protect the signatures of the social covenant'; when it shall demand the immediate registration of the treaty between the United States and Canada at the seat of the league, it will control, whether it wills or no, the destinies of America. And when the American States shall be obliged to take a hand in every war or menace of war in Europe (art. 11), they will necessarily fall afoul of the fundamental principle laid down by Monroe, which was that Americans should never take part in a European war.

If the league takes in the world, then Europe must mix in the affairs of America; if only Europe is included, then America will violate of necessity her own doctrine by intermixing in the affairs of Europe.

If the league includes the affairs of the world, does it not include the affairs of all the world? Is there any limitation of the jurisdiction of the council or of the assembly upon the question of peace or war? Does it not have now, under the reservations, the same as it had before, the power to deal with all matters of peace or war throughout the entire world? How shall you keep from meddling in the affairs of Europe or keep Europe from meddling in the affairs of America?

Mr. President, there is another and even a more commanding reason why I shall record my vote against this treaty. It imperils what I conceive to be the underlying, the very first principles of this Republic. It is in conflict with the right of our people to govern themselves free from all restraint, legal or moral, of foreign powers. It challenges every tenet of my political faith. If this faith were one of my own contriving, if I stood here to assert principles of government of my own evolving, I might well be charged with intolerable presumption, for we all recognize the ability of those who urge a different course. But I offer in justification of my course nothing of my own save the deep and abiding reverence I have for those whose policies I humbly but most ardently support. I claim no merit save fidelity to American principles and devotion to American ideals as they were wrought out from time to time by those who built the Republic and as they have been extended and maintained throughout these years. In opposing the treaty I do nothing more than decline to renounce and tear out of my life the sacred traditions which throughout 50 years have been translated into my whole intellectual and moral being. I will not, I cannot, give up my belief that America must, not alone for the happiness of her own people, but for the moral guidance and greater contentment of the world, be permitted to live her own life. Next to the tie which binds a man to his God is the tie which binds a man to his country, and all schemes, all plans, however ambitious and fascinating they seem in their proposal, but which would embarrass or entangle and impede or shackle her sovereign will, which would compromise her freedom of action, I unhesitatingly put behind me.

Sir, since the debate opened months ago those of us who have stood against this proposition have been taunted many times with being little Americans. Leave us the word American, keep that in your presumptuous impeachment, and no taunt can disturb us, no gibe discompose our purposes. Call us little Americans if you will, but leave us the consolation and the pride which the term American, however modified, still imparts. Take away that term and though you should coin in telling phrase your highest eulogy we would hurl it back as common slander. We have been ridiculed because, forsooth, of our limited vision. Possibly that charge may be true. Who is there here that can read the future? Time, and time alone, unerring and remorseless, will give us each our proper place in the affections of our countrymen and in the esteem and commendation of those who are to come after us. We neither fear nor court her favor. But if our vision has been circumscribed it has at all times within its compass been clear and steady. We have sought nothing save the tranquility of our own people and the honor and independence of our own Republic. No foreign flattery, no possible world glory and power have disturbed our poise or come between us and our devotion to the traditions which have made us a people or the policies which have made us a Nation, unselfish and commanding. If we have erred we have erred out of too much love for those things which from childhood you and we together have been taught to revere—yes, to defend even at the cost of limb and life. If we have erred it is because we have placed too high an estimate upon the wisdom of Washington and Jefferson, too exalted an opinion upon the patriotism of the sainted Lincoln. And blame us not therefore if we have, in our limited vision, seemed sometimes bitter and at all times uncompromising, for the things for which we have spoken, feebly spoken, the things which we have endeavored to defend, have been the things for which your fathers and our fathers were willing to die.

Senators, even in an hour so big with expectancy we should not close our eyes to the fact that democracy is something more, vastly more, than a mere form of government by which society is restrained into free and orderly life. It is a moral entity, a spiritual force, as well. And these are things which live only and alone in the atmosphere of liberty. The foundation upon which democracy rests is faith in the moral instincts of the people. Its ballot boxes, the franchise, its laws, and constitutions are but the outward manifestations of the deeper and more essential thing—a continuing trust in the moral purposes of the average man and woman. When this is lost or forfeited your outward forms, however democratic in terms, are a mockery. Force may find expression through institutions democratic in structure equal with the simple and more direct processes of a single supreme ruler. These distinguishing virtues of a real republic you can not commingle with the discordant and destructive forces of the Old World and still preserve them. You can not yoke a government whose fundamental maxim is that of liberty to a government whose first law is that of force and hope to preserve the former. These things are in eternal war, and one must ultimately destroy the other. You may still keep for a time the outward form, you may still delude yourself, as others have done in the past, with appearances and symbols, but when you shall have committed this Republic to a scheme of world control based upon force, upon the combined military force of the four great nations of the world, you will have soon destroyed the atmosphere of freedom, of confidence in the self-governing capacity of the masses, in which alone a democracy may thrive. We may become one of the four dictators of the world, but we shall no longer be master of our own spirit. And what shall it profit us as a Nation if we shall go forth to the dominion of the earth and share with others the glory of world control and lose that fine sense of confidence in the people, the soul of democracy?

Look upon the scene as it is now presented. Behold the task we are to assume, and then contemplate the method by which we are to deal with this task. Is the method such as to address itself to a Government "conceived in liberty and dedicated to the proposition that all men are created equal"? When this league,

this combination, is formed four great powers representing the dominant people will rule one-half of the inhabitants of the globe as subject peoples—rule by force, and we shall be a party to the rule of force. There is no other way by which you can keep people in subjection. You must either give them independence, recognize their rights as nations to live their own life and to set up their own form of government, or you must deny them these things by force. That is the scheme, the method proposed by the league. It proposes no other. We will in time become inured to its inhuman precepts and its soulless methods, strange as this doctrine now seems to a free people. If we stay with our contract, we will come in time to declare with our associates that force—force, the creed of the Prussian military oligarchy—is after all the true foundation upon which must rest all stable governments. Korea, despoiled and bleeding at every pore; India, sweltering in ignorance and burdened with inhuman taxes after more than a hundred years of dominant rule; Egypt, trapped and robbed of her birthright; Ireland, with seven hundred years of sacrifice for independence—this is the task, this is the atmosphere, and this is the creed in and under which we are to keep alive our belief in the moral purposes and self-governing capacity of the people, a belief without which the Republic must disintegrate and die. The maxim of liberty will soon give way to the rule of blood and iron. We have been pleading here for our Constitution. Conform this league, it has been said, to the technical terms of our charter, and all will be well. But I declare to you that we must go further and conform to those sentiments and passions for justice and freedom which are essential to the existence of democracy. You must respect not territorial boundaries, not territorial integrity, but you must respect and preserve the sentiments and passions for justice and for freedom which God in His infinite wisdom has planted so deep in the human heart that no form of tyranny however brutal, no persecution however prolonged, can wholly uproot and kill. Respect nationality, respect justice, respect freedom, and you may have some hope of peace, but not so if you make your standard the standard of tyrants and despots, the protection of real estate regardless of how it is obtained.

Sir, we are told that this treaty means peace. Even so, I would not pay the price. Would you purchase peace at the cost of any part of our independence? We could have had peace in 1776— the price was high, but we could have had it. James Otis, Sam Adams, [John] Hancock, and [Joseph] Warren were surrounded by those who urged peace and British rule. All through that long and trying struggle, particularly when the clouds of adversity lowered upon the cause, there was a cry of peace—let us have peace. We could have had peace in 1860; Lincoln was counseled by men of great influence and accredited wisdom to let our brothers—and, thank heaven, they are brothers—depart in peace. But the tender, loving Lincoln, bending under the fearful weight of impending civil war, an apostle of peace, refused to pay the price, and a reunited country will praise his name forevermore—bless it because he refused peace at the price of national honor and national integrity. Peace upon any other basis than national independence, peace purchased at the cost of any part of our national integrity, is fit only for slaves, and even when purchased at such a price it is a delusion, for it cannot last.

But your treaty does not mean peace—far, very far, from it. If we are to judge the future by the past it means war. Is there any guaranty of peace other than the guaranty which comes of the control of the war-making power by the people? Yet what great rule of democracy does the treaty leave unassailed? The people in whose keeping alone you can safely lodge the power of peace or war nowhere, at no time and in no place, have any voice in this scheme for world peace. Autocracy which has bathed the world in blood for centuries reigns supreme. Democracy is everywhere excluded. This, you say, means peace.

Can you hope for peace when love of country is disregarded in your scheme, when the spirit of nationality is rejected, even scoffed at? Yet what law of that moving and mysterious force does your treaty not deny? With a ruthlessness unparalleled your treaty in a dozen instances runs counter to the divine law of nationality. Peoples who speak the same language, kneel at the same ancestral tombs, moved by the same traditions, animated by a common hope, are torn asunder, broken in pieces, divided, and parceled out to antagonistic nations. And this you call justice. This, you cry, means peace. Peoples who have dreamed of independence, struggled and been patient, sacrificed and been hopeful, peoples who were told that through this peace conference they should realize the aspirations of centuries, have again had their hopes dashed to earth. One of the most striking and commanding figures in this war, soldier and statesman, turned away from the peace table at Versailles declaring to the world, "The promise of the new life, the victory of the great humane ideals for which the peoples have shed their blood and their treasure without stint, the fulfillment of their aspirations toward a new international order and a fairer and better world, are not written into the treaty." No; your treaty means injustice. It means slavery. It means war. And to all this you ask this Republic to become a party. You ask it to abandon the creed under which it has grown to power and accept the creed of autocracy, the creed of repression and force.

Mr. President, I turn from this scheme based upon force to another scheme, planned 143 years ago in old Independence Hall, in the city of Philadelphia, based upon liberty. I like it better. I have become so accustomed to believe in it that it is difficult for me to reject it out of hand. I have difficulty in subscribing to the new creed of oppression, the creed of dominant and subject peoples. I feel a reluctance to give up the belief that all men are created equal—the eternal principle in government that all governments derive their just powers from the consent of the governed. I can not get my consent to exchange the doctrine of George Washington for the doctrine of Frederick the Great translated into mendacious phrases of peace. I go back to that serene and masterful soul who pointed the way to power and glory for the new and then weak Republic, and whose teachings and admonitions even in our majesty and dominance we dare not disregard.

I know well the answer to my contention. It has been piped about of late from a thousand sources—venal sources, disloyal sources, sinister sources—that Washington's wisdom was of his day only and that his teachings are out of fashion—things long since sent to the scrap heap of history—that while he was great in character and noble in soul he was untrained in the arts of statecraft and unlearned in the science of government. The puny demagogue, the barren editor, the sterile professor now vie with each other in apologizing for the temporary and commonplace expedients which the Father of his Country felt constrained to adopt in building a republic!

What is the test of statesmanship? Is it the formation of theories, the utterance of abstract and incontrovertible truths, or is it the capacity and the power to give to a people that concrete thing called liberty, that vital and indispensable thing in human happiness called free institutions, and to establish over all and above all the blessed and eternal reign of order and law? If this be the test, where shall we find another whose name is entitled to be written beside the name of Washington? His judgment and poise in the hour of turmoil and peril, his courage and vision in times of adversity, his firm grasp of fundamental principles, his almost inspired power to penetrate the future and read there the result, the effect of policies, have never been excelled, if equalled, by any of the world's commonwealth builders. Peter the Great, William the Silent, and Cromwell the Protector, these and these alone perhaps are to be associated with his name as the builders of States and the founders of governments. But in exaltation of moral purpose, in the unselfish character of his work, in the durability of his policies, in the permanency of the institutions which he more than anyone else called into effect, his service to mankind stands out separate and apart in a class by itself. The works of these other great builders, where are they now? But the work of Washington is still the most potent influence for the advancement of civilization and the freedom of the race.

Reflect for a moment over his achievements. He led the Revolutionary Army to victory. He was the very first to suggest a union instead of a confederacy. He presided over and counseled with great wisdom the convention which framed the Constitution. He guided the Government through its first perilous years. He gave dignity and stability and honor to that which was looked upon by the world as a passing experiment, and finally, my friends, as his own peculiar and particular contribution to the happiness of his countrymen and to the cause of the Republic, he gave us his great foreign policy under which we have lived and prospered and strengthened for nearly a century and a half. This policy is the most sublime confirmation of his genius as a statesman. It was then, and it now is, an indispensable part of our whole scheme of government. It is to-day a vital, indispensable element in our entire plan, purpose, and mission as a nation. To abandon it is nothing less than a betrayal of the American people. I say betrayal deliberately, in view of the suffering and the sacrifice which will follow in the wake of such a course.

But under the stress and strain of these extraordinary days, when strong men are being swept down by the onrushing forces of disorder and change, when the most sacred things of life, the most cherished hopes of a Christian world seem to yield to the mad forces of discontent—just such days as Washington passed through when the mobs of Paris, wild with new liberty and drunk with power, challenged the established institutions of all the world, but his steadfast soul was unshaken—under these conditions come again we are about to abandon this policy so essential to our happiness and tranquillity as a people and our stability as a government. No leader with his commanding influence and his unquailing courage stands forth to stem the current. But what no leader can or will do, experience, bitter experience, and the people of this country in whose keeping, after all, thank God, is the Republic, will ultimately do. If we abandon his leadership and teachings, we will go back. We will return to this policy. Americanism shall not, cannot, die. We may go back in

sackcloth and ashes, but we will return to the faith of the fathers. America will live her own life. The independence of this Republic will have its defenders. Thousands have suffered and died for it, and their sons and daughters are not of the breed who will be betrayed into the hands of foreigners. The noble face of the Father of his Country, so familiar to every boy and girl, looking out from the walls of the Capitol in stern reproach, will call those who come here for public service to a reckoning. The people of our beloved country will finally speak, and we will return to the policy which we now abandon. America disenthralled and free in spite of all these things will continue her mission in the cause of peace, of freedom, and of civilization.

Congressional Record, Senate, 66th Congress, 1st session, Nov. 19, 1919, 8781–8784.

117   The Budget and Accounting Act of 1921

June 10, 1921

Today it is taken for granted that the federal government has a single annual budget, submitted to Congress by the president of the United States. But this was not the case until the passage of the Budget and Accounting Act of 1921. Individual government agencies of the executive branch, not the president, prepared their own budgets, which were submitted through the secretary of the Treasury. To compound the decentralized nature of the budget process, the secretary of the Treasury submitted the agency budgets to a number of different committees of the House and Senate, each with its own jurisdiction over certain areas of government spending.

Efforts to reform the budget process got underway in a serious manner during the presidency of William H. Taft, who launched a general study of government efficiency, known as the Taft Commission. The commission concluded that greater efficiency would come from a centralized federal budget and a single budget committee in Congress. This Republican-led reform was never adopted because Democrats gained control of the White House and Congress in the 1912 elections.

The inefficient manner of handling the budget became all the more troublesome during World War I. Budgetary reform became a campaign issue in 1918 for both parties as candidates for House and Senate seats vowed to straighten out the budget mess.

In 1919 the House created a Budget Study Committee under the chairmanship of James W. Good (R-Iowa) that prepared a bill in 1920 similar to the Budget and Accounting Act of 1921. President Woodrow Wilson vetoed the 1920 bill over disagreements related to the office of comptroller general. When Republicans regained the White House and Congress in 1921, the 1920 bill was renamed and quickly passed Congress. It was signed into law by President Warren G. Harding.

This act remains today the fundamental law governing the budget process. Only a few changes have been made to it over the years. Its main provisions call for the president to submit a single annual budget to the Congress. The act created the General Accounting Office, which was independent of the executive branch under the direction of the comptroller general. It established in the executive branch the Bureau of the Budget (later renamed the Office of Management and Budget). This act represented a major reform of the federal budget process, but it did not solve all problems related to the budget or the political nature of the budget process. In 1974, because of increasing problems between Congress and the executive branch over the control of the budget, Congress passed the Congressional Budget and Impoundment Control Act of 1974 (see document 165), which gave Congress new tools to independently analyze the president's annual budget.

CHAP. 18.—AN ACT TO PROVIDE A NATIONAL BUDGET SYSTEM AND AN INDEPENDENT AUDIT OF GOVERNMENT ACCOUNTS, AND FOR OTHER PURPOSES.

. . . .

Title II.—The Budget.

SEC. 2. The President shall transmit to Congress on the first day of each regular session, the Budget, which shall set forth in summary and in detail:

(a) Estimates of the expenditures and appropriations necessary in his judgment for the support of the Government for the ensuing fiscal year; except that the estimates for such year for the Legislative Branch of the Government and the Supreme Court of the United States shall be transmitted to the President on or before October 15th of each year, and shall be included by him in the Budget without revision;

(b) His estimates of the receipts of the Government during the ensuing fiscal year, under (1) laws existing at the time the Budget is transmitted and also (2) under the revenue proposals, if any, contained in the Budget;

(c) The expenditures and receipts of the Government during the last completed fiscal year;

(d) Estimates of the expenditures and receipts of the Government during the fiscal year in progress;

(e) The amount of annual, permanent, or other appropriations, including balances of appropriations for prior fiscal years, available for expenditure during the fiscal year in progress, as of November 1 of such year;

(f) Balanced statements of (1) the condition of the Treasury at the end of the last completed fiscal year, (2) the estimated condition of the Treasury at the end of the fiscal year in progress, and (3) the estimated condition of the Treasury at the end of the ensuing fiscal year if the financial proposals contained in the Budget are adopted;

(g) All essential facts regarding the bonded and other indebtedness of the Government; and

(h) Such other financial statements and data as in his opinion are necessary or desirable in order to make known in all practicable detail the financial condition of the Government.

SEC. 202. (a) If the estimated receipts for the ensuing fiscal year contained in the Budget, on the basis of laws existing at the time the Budget is transmitted, plus the estimated amounts in the Treasury at the close of the fiscal year in progress, available for expenditure in the ensuing fiscal year, are less than the estimated expenditures for the ensuing fiscal year contained in the Budget, the President in the Budget shall make recommendations to Congress for new taxes, loans, or other appropriate action to meet the estimated deficiency.

(b) If the aggregate of such estimated receipts and such estimated amounts in the Treasury is greater than such estimated expenditures for the ensuing fiscal year, he shall make such recommendations as his opinion the public interests require.

SEC. 203. (a) The President from time to time may transmit to Congress supplemental or deficiency estimates for such appropriations or expenditures as in his judgment (1) are necessary on account of laws enacted after the transmission of the Budget, or (2) are otherwise in the public interest. He shall accompany such estimates with a statement of the reasons therefor, including the reasons for their omission from the Budget.

(b) Whenever such supplemental or deficiency estimates reach an aggregate which, if they had been contained in the Budget, would have required the President to make a recommendation under subdivision (a) of section 202, he shall thereupon make such recommendation.

SEC. 204. (a) Except as otherwise provided in this Act, the contents, order, and arrangement of the estimates of appropriations and the statements of expenditures and estimated expenditures contained in the Budget or transmitted under section 203, and the notes and other data submitted therewith, shall conform to the requirements of existing law.

(b) Estimates for lump-sum appropriations contained in the Budget or transmitted under section 203 shall be accompanied by statements showing, in such detail and form as may be necessary to inform Congress, the manner of expenditure of such appropriations and of the corresponding appropriations for the fiscal year in progress and the last completed fiscal year. Such statements shall be in lieu of statements of like character now required by law.

. . . .

SEC. 206. No estimated or request for an appropriation and no request for an increase in an item of any such estimate or request and no recommendation as to how the revenue needs of the Government should be met, shall be submitted to Congress or any committee thereof by any officer or employee of any department or establishment, unless at the request of either House of Congress.

SEC. 207. There is hereby created in the Treasury Department a Bureau to be know as the Bureau of the Budget. There shall be in the Bureau a Director and an Assistant Director, who shall be appointed by the President and receive salaries of $10,000 and $7,500 a year, respectively.

. . . .

SEC. 209. The Bureau, when directed by the President, shall make a detailed study of the departments and establishments for the purpose of enabling the President to determine what changes (with a view of securing greater economy and efficiency in the conduct of the public service) should be made in (1) the existing organization, activities, and methods of business of such departments or establishments, (2) the appropriations therefor, (3) the assignment of particular activities to particular services, or (4) the regrouping of services. The results of such study shall be embodied in a report or reports or any part thereof with his recommendations on the matters covered thereby.

SEC. 210. The Bureau shall prepare for the President a codification of all laws or parts of laws relating to the preparation and transmission to Congress of statements of receipts and expenditures of the Government and of estimates of appropriations. The President shall transmit the same to Congress on or before the first Monday in December, 1921, with a recommendation as to the changes which, in his opinion, should be made in such laws or parts of laws.

. . . .

SEC. 212. The Bureau shall, at the request of any committee of either House of Congress having jurisdiction over revenue or appropriations, furnish the committee such aid and information as it may request.

SEC. 213. Under such regulations as the President may prescribe, (1) every department and establishment shall furnish to the Bureau such information as the Bureau may from time to time require, and (2) the Director and the Assistant Director, or any employee of the Bureau when duly authorized, shall, for the purpose of securing such information, have access to, and the right to examine any books, documents, papers, or records of any such department or establishment.

SEC. 214. (a) The head of each department and establishment shall designate an official thereof as budget officer therefor, who, in each year under his direction and on or before a date fixed by him, shall prepare the departmental estimates.

(b) Such budget officer shall also prepare, under the direction of the head of the department or establishment, such supplemental and deficiency estimates as may be required for its work.

SEC. 215. The head of each department and establishment shall revise the departmental estimates and submit them to the Bureau on or before September 15 of each year. In case of his failure so to do, the President shall cause to be prepared such estimates and data as are necessary to enable him to include in the Budget estimates and statements in respect to the work of such department or establishment.

SEC. 216. The departmental estimates and any supplemental or deficiency estimates submitted to the Bureau by the head of any department or establishment shall be prepared and submitted in such form, manner, and detail as the President may prescribe.

. . . .

Title III.—General Accounting Office.

SEC. 301. There is created an establishment of the Government to be known as the General Accounting Office, which shall be independent of the executive departments and under the control and direction of the Comptroller General of the United States. The offices of Comptroller of the Treasury and Assistant Comptroller of the Treasury are abolished, to take effect July 1, 1921. All other officers and employees of the office of the Comptroller of the Treasury shall be come officers and employees in the General Accounting Office at their grades and salaries on July 1, 1921, and all books, records, documents, papers, furniture, office equipment and other property of the office of the Comptroller of the Treasury shall become the property of the General Accounting Office. The Comptroller General is authorized to adopt a seal for the General Accounting Office.

SEC. 302. There shall be in the General Accounting Office a Comptroller General of the United States, who shall be appointed by the President with the advice and consent of the Senate, and shall receive salaries of $10,000 and $7,500 a year, respectively. The Assistant Comptroller General shall perform such duties as may be assigned to him by the Comptroller General, and during the absence or incapacity of the Comptroller General, or during a vacancy in that office, shall act as Comptroller General.

SEC. 303. Except as hereinafter provided in this section, the Comptroller General and the Assistant Comptroller General shall hold office for fifteen years. The Comptroller General shall not be eligible for reappointment. The Comptroller General or the Assistant Comptroller General may be removed at any time by joint resolution of Congress after notice and hearing, when, in the judgment of Congress, the Comptroller General or Assistant Comptroller General has become permanently incapacitated or has been inefficient, or guilty of neglect of duty, or of malfeasance in office, or of any felony or conduct involving moral turpitude, and for no other cause an in no other manner except by impeachment. Any Comptroller General or Assistant Comptroller General removed in the manner herein provided shall be ineligible for reappointment to that office. When a Comptroller General or Assistant Comptroller General attains the age of seventy years, he shall be retired from his office.

SEC. 304. All powers and duties now conferred or imposed by law upon the Comptroller of the Treasury or the six auditors of the Treasury Department, and the duties of the Division of Bookkeeping and Warrants of the Office of the Secretary of the Treasury relating to keeping the personal ledger accounts of disbursing and collecting offers, shall, so far as not inconsistent with this Act, be vested in and imposed upon the General Accounting Office and be exercised without direction from any other officer. The balances certified by the Comptroller General shall be final and conclusive upon the executive Branch of the Government. The revision by the Comptroller General of settlements made by the six auditors shall be discontinued, except as to settlements made before July 1, 1921.

. . . .

SEC. 312. (a) The Comptroller General shall investigate, at the seat of government or elsewhere, all matters relating to the receipt, disbursement, and application of public funds, and shall make to the President when requested by him, and to Congress at the beginning of each regular session, a report in writing of the work of the General Accounting Office, containing recommendations concerning the legislation he may deem necessary to facilitate the prompt and accurate rendition and settlement of accounts and concerning such other matters relating to the receipt, disbursement, and application of public funds as he may think advisable. In such regular report, or in special reports at any time when Congress is in session, he shall make recommendations looking to greater economy or efficiency in public expenditures.

(b) He shall make such investigations and reports as shall be ordered by either House of Congress or by any committee of either House having jurisdiction over revenue, appropriations, or expenditures. The Comptroller General shall also, at the request of an such committee, direct assistants from his office to furnish the committee such aid and information as it may request.

(c) The Comptroller General shall specially report to Congress every expenditure or contract made by any department or establishment in any year in violation of law.

(d) He shall submit to Congress reports upon the adequacy and effectiveness of the administrative examination of accounts and claims in the respective departments and establishments and upon the adequacy and effectiveness of departmental inspection of the offices and accounts of fiscal officers.

(e) He shall furnish such information relating to expenditures and accounting to the Bureau of the Budget as it may request from time to time.

Sec. 313. All departments and establishments shall furnish to the Comptroller General such information regarding the powers, duties, activities, organization, financial transactions, and methods of business of their respective offices as he may from time to time require of them; and the Comptroller General, or any of his assistants or employees, when duly authorized by him, shall, for the purpose of securing such information, have access to and the to examine any books, documents, papers, or records of any such department or establishment. . . .

Approved, June 10, 1921.

Statutes at Large, 41 (1921–1923), 67th Congress, 1st session, June 10, 1921, 20–27.

118   Senator William E. Borah Opposes the Versailles Treaty

September 26, 1921

In the aftermath of World War I, the United States was thrust into a role of world leadership as never before. While some, including President Woodrow Wilson, welcomed this new power and the new role in the affairs of nations, others, such as Senator William E. Borah (1865–1940), a Republican from Idaho, were dead set against it. Borah, a fervent isolationist, fought against Wilson's plan for a League of Nations (see document 116) and against the terms of the Versailles Treaty, which President Wilson and other world leaders had negotiated in France to bring a conclusion to the war. Borah was part of a small band of senators, mostly progressive Republicans from western states, known as the "Irreconcilables" because they would not compromise on the question of increased entangling alliances with foreign powers. Borah also opposed the Versailles Treaty because he considered its terms too harsh on Germany. The treaty required Germany to assume the full burden of causing the war and to pay more than $50 billion in reparations.

To counteract Senate opposition to his plans, President Wilson took his case in support of the League of Nations and the Versailles Treaty to the American people. He undertook a strenuous speaking tour that so weakened him that he suffered a stroke in October 1919 that left him partially paralyzed and from which he never fully recovered. Senate opposition to the treaty continued despite President Wilson's efforts to rally Democratic support from his sick bed in the White House. The Senate rejected the Versailles Treaty on Nov. 19, 1919, even though Germany had reluctantly signed it and there were forty other nations that endorsed it. In March 1920 the Senate again failed to ratify an amended version of the Versailles Treaty. It was not until 1921, with Warren Harding in the White House, that the United States finally declared the war with Germany at an end, but this relatively simple resolution was a far cry from the provisions of the Versailles Treaty.

Since the Versailles Treaty was a reality despite its rejection by the Senate, the Senate found it necessary to revisit some of the treaty's provisions from time to time. In the speech that follows, Senator Borah reiterated his earlier objection to the treaty and the League of Nations and found fault with the Reparation Commission established as part of the treaty. The isolationist ideas ex-pressed in the speech are at the heart of many arguments that continue to resonate among those today who are opposed to such world bodies as the United Nations or the North Atlantic Treaty Organization. In the current era of global economies, multinational treaties, and increasing global interdependence, Borah's views still contain the essence of the argument that the United States cannot be all things to all nations.

Mr. President, there is a law stronger than constitutional law, stronger than legislative law, and that is the moral law, and it finally wins. While I agree with the Senator as an actual fact that we could repudiate it, because we have the power to do it, I venture to say that if we sit upon that commission the Senate of the United States will execute the decrees which it inaugurates. We can not stand before the world and refuse to do it. Our eyes are open. We know what we are joining. We are joining a despotism; we are joining a secret body; we are joining an unlimited power; and we say to the world that we are joining it and we propose to help execute it. What will be the position of the United States if it refused to do so?

I have already referred to the proposition that the commission shall have the power to interpret the treaty; that it has the taxing power; that it determines the amount Germany shall pay; that it has entire charge of the bonding, revenue, and financial system; in short, that it has autocratic and complete power over the wealth, the health, and the life of an entire people; in fact, three peoples. It is the most absolute and despotic form of government since the time of the Roman praetors. It is clear also that this power over Germany must to a great degree control the affairs of the entire Continent of Europe.

Germany is the most powerful economic unit in Europe. The Central Powers were altogether the most powerful economic factor in Europe; and when we undertake to administer the affairs of Germany, Austria, and Hungary, we must ramify and extend our interests into every conceivable enterprise, interest, and business, and all the politics of the entire Continent of Europe. We must deal with all the nations of Europe. We must be a part of the financial system of Europe. We must deal with the exchange system of Europe. We must deal with the transportation system of Europe. We are a European power.

. . . .

But, Mr. President, my aversion to the Versailles treaty, to the principles upon which it is built, the old imperialistic policies which have brought the world into sad ruin, makes it impossible for me to ever vote for any treaty which gives even moral recognition to that instrument. That alone would prevent me from voting for this treaty.

I am not forgetful, I trust, of the times and circumstances under which the Versailles treaty was written. They were extraordinary; they were without precedent. All the suffering and passions of a terrible war, led by the intolerant spirit of triumph, were present and dominant. It was a dictated treaty, dictated by those who yet felt the agony of conflict and whose fearful hours of sacrifice, now changed to hours of victory, thought only in terms of punishment. It was too much to expect anything else. We gain nothing, therefore; indeed, we lose much by going back to criticize or assail the individuals who had to do with its making; it was a treaty born of a fiendlike struggle and also of the limitations of human nature. So let its making pass.

But three years have come and gone since the war, and we have now had time to reflect and to contemplate the future. We have escaped, I trust, to some extent the grip of the war passion and are freer to think of the things which are to come rather than upon the things which are past. We have had time not only to read this treaty and think it over, but we have had an opportunity to see its effect upon peace and civilization. We know what it is now, and if we recognize it and strengthen it or help to maintain it, we shall not be able to plead at the bar of history the extenuating circumstances which its makers may justly plead. We see now not alone the punishment it would visit upon the Central Powers, but we see the cruel and destructive punishment it has visited and is to visit upon millions, many of whom fought by our side in the war. We know it has reduced to subjection and delivered over to exploitation subject and friendly peoples; that it has given in exchange for promises of independence and freedom dependence and spoliation. But that is not the worst. "If it were done when it is done," we could turn our backs upon the past and hope to find exculpation in doing better things in the future. But we know this treaty has in it the seeds of many wars. It hangs like a storm cloud upon the horizon. It is the incarnation of force. It recognizes neither mercy nor repentance, and discriminates not at all between the guilty and the innocent, friend or foe. Its one-time defenders now are frank to admit it. It will bring sorrow to the world again. Its basic principle is cruel, unconscionable, and remorseless imperialism. Its terms will awaken again the reckoning power of retribution—the same power which brought to a full accounting those who cast lots over Poland and who tore Alsace-Lorraine from her coveted allegiance. We know that Europe can not recover so long as this treaty exists; that economic breakdown in Europe, if

not the world, awaits its execution; and that millions of men, women, and children, those now living and those yet unborn, are to be shackled, enslaved, and hungered if it remains the law of Europe. All this we know, and knowing it we not only invite the lashings of retribution, but we surrender every tenet of the American faith when we touch the cruel and maledict thing.

When the treaty was written it had incorporated in it the so-called League of Nations. I believe it correct to say the treaty proper was only accepted by Mr. Wilson because the league was attached. I have never believed, I have never supposed, he could have been induced to accept this treaty, so at variance with every principle he had advocated and all things for which he had stood, had he not believed the league in time would ameliorate its terms and humanize its conditions. In that, of course, I think he was greatly in error.

In my opinion the league, had it been effective at all, would have been but the instrument to more effectually execute the sinister mandates of the predominant instrument. Under the treaty the league would have quickly grown into an autocracy based upon force, the organized military force of the great powers of the world. But now, so far as we are concerned, the league has been stricken from the document. The sole badge of respectability, the sole hope of amelioration, so far as American advocates were concerned, now vanish. With the league stricken out, who is there left in America, reared under the principles of a free government, to defend the terms and conditions of this treaty? There it is, harsh, hideous, naked, dismembering friendly peoples, making possible and justifying the exploitation of vast populations, a check to progress and at war with every principle which the founders interwove into the fabric of this Republic and challenging every precept upon which the peace of the world may be built. For such a treaty I loathe to see my country even pay the respect of recognition, much less to take anything under its terms.

Mr. President, some nation or people must lead in a different course from the course announced by this treaty and its policies, or the human family is to sink back into hopeless barbarism. Reflect upon the situation. We see about us on every hand in the whole world around conditions difficult to describe—a world convulsed by the agonies which the follies and crimes of leaders have laid upon the people. Hate seems almost a law of life and devastation a fixed habit of the race. Science has become the prostitute of war, while the arts of statecraft are busy with schemes for pillaging helpless and subject peoples. Trade is suspended, industry is paralyzed, famine, ravenous and insatiable, gathers millions into its skeleton clutches, while unemployment spreads and discontent deepens. The malign shadows of barbarism are creeping up and over the outskirts of civilization. And this condition is due more to the policies which the political dictators of Europe have imposed than any other one thing. Repression, reprisal, blockades, disregard of solemn pledges, the scheming and grabbing for the natural resources of helpless peoples, the arming of Poland, the fitting out of expeditions into Russia, the fomenting of war between Greece and

Turkey, and, finally, the maintenance of an insurmountable obstacle to rehabilitation in the Versailles treaty—how could Europe, how can Europe, ever recover? Is there no nation to call a halt? Is there no country to announce the gospel of tolerance and to denounce the brutal creed of force and to offer to a dying world something besides intrigue and armaments?

In this stupendous and bewildered crisis America must do her part. No true American wants to see her shirk any part of her responsibility. There are no advocates of selfishness, none so fatuous as to urge that we may be happy and prosperous while the rest of the world is plunging on in misery and want. Call it providence, call it fate, but we know that in the nexus of things there must be something of a common sharing, all but universal and inexorable in the burdens which these great catastrophies place upon the human family. It is not only written in the great book but it is written in the economic laws of nature—"Bear ye one another's burdens." We do not differ as to the duty of America, we differ only as to the manner in which she shall discharge that duty.

. . . .

Mr. President, one of the revolting monstrosities born of this war, the illegitimate offspring of secret diplomacy and violence, is the absurd, iniquitous belief that you can only have peace through martial means—that force, force, is the only power left on earth with which to govern men. I denounce the hideous, diabolical idea, and I insist that this Government ought to be counted against all plans, all treaties, all programs, all policies, based upon this demoniacal belief. Let us have an American policy. Or, if the word "American" be considered by some as provincial or distasteful—a term of incivility—then let us have a humane policy, a Christian policy, a policy based upon justice, resting upon reason, guided by conscience, and made dominant by the mobilized moral forces of the world.

. . . .

Congressional Record, Senate, 67th Congress, 1st session, Sept. 26, 1921, 5800–5801.

119   Speaker Nicholas Longworth on Congress

January 2, 1926

Nicholas Longworth (R-Ohio) had twenty years of experience in the House of Representatives before becoming Speaker in December 1925. A dapper man who dressed impeccably, wore spats, and carried a gold-tipped cane, Longworth was a popular member of Washington society, having married the daughter of Theodore Roosevelt.

In one of his first interviews after becoming Speaker of the House, Longworth revealed his humor and insight into what it meant to be a member of Congress. The interview appeared in a new publication called Liberty, *a mass market magazine featuring serialized fiction, discussions of the issues of the day, movie reviews, and profiles of prominent personalities. Longworth's lighthearted analysis of what it meant to be a member of Congress has stood the test of time. He said he looked into history and found that members of Congress had always "been attacked, denounced, despised, hunted, harried, blamed, looked down upon, excoriated, and flayed." His answer to this dilemma was to recognize that a member of Congress had "no chance" to be popular, at least not for long.*

His observations about the advantages the president of the United States has over a member of Congress got to the heart of a fundamental problem in the nature of representative democracy. Presidents are elected nationally; members of Congress are elected locally. Representatives and senators often represent minorities of opinion. Within their districts or states a given opinion may be held by a majority of the voters. But when that opinion reaches the halls of Congress, or is taken up in a presidential campaign, individual members of Congress face the challenge of balancing the

views of their constituents with those of the entire nation. Often the desires of the "folks back home" can differ substantially from the desires of people in other parts of the nation. Is a representative to act only on the wishes of his or her constituents or should that representative act on behalf of the entire nation?

Longworth served as Speaker from 1925 to 1929. His personal charm, cheerful disposition, and debonair style led some observers to consider him more of a socialite and a rich playboy than a serious leader of the House. But Longworth did much to restore the office of Speaker to its place of prominence following the loss of prestige and power the office suffered when Speaker Joseph Cannon was stripped of power fifteen years earlier (see document 107). One scholar of Longworth's career, Donald C. Bacon, has called him the "genial czar" for his iron-handed rule of the House, which he carried out with humor and a consistently friendly manner.

. . . .

I have to ask to be allowed at least to feel sorry for us Congressman, . . . At bottom—the fact is—I insist sometimes on feeling proud of us. However, I also feel sorry for us—very. We are always "unpopular."

I have been a member of the House of Representatives ten terms. That is twenty years. During the whole of that time we have been attacked, denounced, despised, hunted, harried, blamed, looked down upon, excoriated, and flayed.

I refuse to take it personally. I have looked into history. I find that we did not start being unpopular when I became a Congressman. We were unpopular before that time. We were unpopular even when Lincoln was a Congressman. We were unpopular even when John Quincy Adams was a Congressman. We were unpopular even when Henry Clay was a Congressman. We have always been unpopular.

From the beginning of the republic it has been the duty of every free-born voter to look down upon us and the duty of every free-born humorist to make jokes at us.

Always there is something—and, in fact, almost always there is almost everything—wrong with us. We simply cannot be right.

Let me illustrate. Suppose we pass a lot of laws. Do we get praised? Certainly not. We then get denounced by everybody for being a "Meddlesome Congress" and for being a "Busybody Congress." Is it not so?

But suppose we take warning from the experience? Suppose that in our succeeding session we pass only a few laws. Are we any better off? Certainly not. Then everybody, instead of denouncing us for being a "Meddlesome Congress" and a "Busybody Congress," denounces us for being an "Incompetent Congress" and a "Do-Nothing Congress."

We have no escape—absolutely none.

Suppose, for instance that we follow the President. Suppose we obey him. Suppose we heed his vetoes. What do we get called? We get called a "flock of sheep." We get called "echoes of the master's voice," a "machine."

Suppose, then we turn around and get very brave, and defy the President and override his vetoes. What, then do we get called? We get called "factionists." We get called "disloyalists." We get called "disrupters of the party." We get called "demagogues."

We have no chance—just absolutely no chance. The only way for a Congressman to be happy is to realize that he has no chance.

We have no chance—we most particularly and especially have no chance—against a President. That is, we have no chance—absolutely none—against him for "popularity." It is unavoidable. It is inevitable. It cannot be otherwise.

Suppose you took the five hundred and thirty-one admittedly ablest men in the United States. Suppose you put ninety-six of them into the ninety-six chairs in the Senate. Suppose you put the four hundred and thirty-five others into the four hundred and thirty-five chairs in the House of Representatives. Suppose they were all of them geniuses. They still, as a group, would have no chance at all for the popularity against a President.

Just think it over for a minute, and see if it is not true.

In the first place, the President is elected by the whole country. He can appeal to the whole country. He can pour out all the neglect and contempt he pleases upon the minorities. He can go along with the majority sentiment—safely and triumphantly. He can be at one with the dominate feelings of the nation. Therefore, it is absolutely readily open to him to be nationally "popular."

But now compare his circumstances with those of the many Representatives and of many Senators!

Those minorities of ours—where are they? These people who have peculiar views about *this or that*—who are extremists *in favor of* something or extremists *against* something—where are they?

They are not spread out evenly through all our States and through all our Congressional districts. They are not a minority everywhere. They are concentrated. They live in geographical "blocs." A minority which amounts to nothing nationally may amount to everything in many Congressional districts and even in many States. A national small majority may often be a local big majority.

Suppose, then, you are a Senator or a Representative from a State or district where a national minority has a local majority. You stick up for that minority which for you is a majority. The President denounces your majority which for him (nationally) is a minority. Which of you is going to be nationally popular?

There is only one answer to that question.

You may retain your popularity in your home region, but all the rest of the country will rally to the President, to any President, who assails you. He will be nationally a hero, and you will be nationally a dog.

This cannot be changed. Senators and Representatives speak for the localities. A President can speak for the nation. The nation is always "right." Localities which differ with the nation are always "wrong." Therefore, a lot of Senators and Representatives must always be "wrong" and different.

That is the first great reason for our misery in Congress, compared with almost any President. The second reason is related to the first, and yet different.

Every locality in this country, besides possibly being peculiar in certain particulars, is always exactly like every other locality in one particular. It always wants everything it can get out of every rivers and harbors bill, every public buildings bill, and every other such bill, including tariff bills.

A locality containing a lemon grove always wants a high tariff on lemons. A locality containing a jackknife factory always wants a high tariff on jackknives. The two localities agree in principle. But do they, therefore, agree in detail? Certainly not. The lemon locality will call the high tariff on jackknives an "iniquity." The jackknife locality will call the high tariff on lemons an "abomination."

Now, where does all this bad language happen? It happens, it is bound to happen, in Congress. It need not happen, it does not happen, in the White House.

A President, if he is selfish on behalf of the whole country, which he represents, is "patriotic." A Senator or a member of the House of Representatives, if he is selfish on behalf of a locality which he represents, is simply merely "selfish."

See, for instance, what happens at the end of the struggle over any tariff bill. Each locality has put into the bill its own local "iniquity," its own local "abomination." These iniquities, these abominations, however, when combined, constitute a "national policy." They often, indeed, successfully constitute "national prosperity."

Congress inserts the iniquities and abominations. It gets blames and cursed. The President signs the "national prosperity." He gets praised and blessed.

He puts his name to the result, and is popular. We have to log-roll the rough-stuff makings of the result, and we are un— very un—popular.

Can you beat it?

I do not worry about it.

To mention a third unfair advantage which a President has over us poor national pillars of unpopularity in Congress, he does not have to debate. He can just mediate. We cannot escape debating. We have to stand up and expose our minds. We have to debate *scores* of topics, *hundreds* of topics—it sometimes seems to me, *thousands* of topics.

When Congress is making up its mind, it is making up five hundred and thirty-one minds. When a President is making up his mind, he is making up one mind. He can make it up privately and silently. We have to make our minds up publicly and audibly.

If a President uses any poor arguments to himself, nobody knows it. If any one of us uses a poor argument, everybody knows it.

A President has all the advantage of secret diplomacy, where every diplomat can come out and say he was wise. We have all the disadvantage of open covenants openly arrived at, where every negotiator is watched by the bleachers of the whole world and gets sprinkled with pop bottles for every error he makes.

In these circumstances I ask again: "What chance have we?"

Please understand me. I am not asking the populace in the amphitheater to spare our lives. I know that in this matter of national popularity we poor Congressman must die. I am only asking that, as you turn your thumbs down and consign us to the sword, you at least—and merely—murmur: "Poor fellow! He has no chance."

I have a special, personal reason for this request, as Speaker of the House of Representatives. I look back now with despairing interest on the experiences of various previous Speakers of the House.

I remember "Uncle Joe" Cannon. Some of my earlier years in the House of Representatives were spent under the speakership of "Uncle Joe."

President Roosevelt once praised us, and praised us highly, under the speakership of "Uncle Joe," for the large quantity and for the progressive quality of the laws which we passed.

But how did we do it?

"Uncle Joe" did it. He did it by running the House himself— with the help of a few (just a few) lieutenants.

The country called "uncle Joe" a "despot." It called him a "tyrant." It called him and his lieutenants "The Old Guard." It called his system "bossism."

It overthrew it. It wanted "liberty." It wanted "independence." It demanded "men." It demanded men who would "defy" the "boss."

We got many of them. They ran in gangs or cliques or "blocs," but they would not run in parties. The climax came in the long session of the last Congress, when there was no majority for any party.

The public should have been satisfied. But was it? Certainly not.

We were wrong again.

The public was just as dissatisfied with "blocs" as it had been at one time with parties.

It began to demand "leadership."

Our present little task in the House of Representatives is to provide "leadership" without providing "bossism."

We are obediently trying.

In order to provide "leadership" we shall have to have "party loyalty," and we are going to have it. Will the public be pleased? Shall we be popular or unpopular? History provides the answer to that question. We shall be unpopular.

In the long session of the last Congress the public told us that we did not have enough party. In this Congress will not the public tell us that we have too much party?

Probably. We have no chance.

Yet, seriously, we are not without some pride in ourselves. We are unpopular. Yet here the country is, after all that we have done to it, the strongest and most prosperous country in the world, resting on the laws which Congress in the course of its one hundred and thirty-seven years of continuous unpopularity has passed. A few people appreciate us. Among them is a gentleman whim sometimes we have charged with antagonizing. He appreciates us. He has spoken of us in words I almost hesitate to quote. They might seem to set him down as a person lacking in the intelligence which enables almost any private citizen to have contempt for us.

However, our appetite for a crumb of praise is so seldom gratified that I venture to remind my readers that, after all, Calvin Coolidge, in his inaugural address last March, did say:

"In spite of all the criticism which so often falls to the lot of Congress, there is no more effective legislative body in the world."

Liberty, 2 (Jan. 2, 1926), 32–33.

120 *McGrain v. Daugherty*

January 17, 1927

McGrain v. Daugherty *is one of the most significant Supreme Court decisions ever rendered on the subject of Congress's constitutional power to conduct investigations and compel the testimony of witnesses. The case grew out of the Teapot Dome scandal of the 1920s, which led to a long, drawn-out Senate investigation of corruption related to the leasing of U.S. oil reserves in a tract of land known as Teapot Dome in Wyoming.*

Irregularities in the leasing of the land surfaced in 1922, but it was not until 1924 that progress in unraveling the complex case began to take shape. The scandal reached some high officials of the Harding and Coolidge administrations and forced the resignation of Attorney General Harry M. Daugherty. In 1924 a Senate investigation of Daugherty's failure to prosecute those behind the Teapot Dome scandal led to a subpoena of the attorney general's brother, Mally S. Daugherty, the president of Midland National Bank in Ohio. As a private citizen, Mally Daugherty refused to appear before the committee after receiving two separate subpoenas. The Senate passed a resolution ordering the deputy sergeant-at-arms of the Senate, John J. McGrain, to arrest Daugherty and keep him in custody for his refusal to testify. Daugherty was arrested in Cincinnati, Ohio, but the federal district court released him saying the Senate had exceeded its constitutional powers. McGrain appealed the decision to the Supreme Court.

In the decision written by Justice Willis Van Devanter, the Supreme Court upheld the right of either the House or Senate to conduct investigations and compel any witnesses to testify, whether federal official or private citizen. Daugherty's attorneys argued that his rights under the Fourth Amendment had been violated because the warrant for his arrest was not properly sworn. The Supreme Court did not agree, arguing that the senators were acting within their rights as senators, doing the business of the Senate when the warrant for arrest was issued. Also at issue in the case was the question of whether a witness could be compelled to testify if the purpose of the investigation had nothing to do with legislation. The Supreme Court stated clearly that "the power of inquiry—with process to enforce it—is an essential and appropriate auxiliary to the legislative function." Congressional investigations need not be about legislation. They could be conducted solely for the purpose of gathering information, for whatever reason the House or Senate deemed appropriate. In this case the high court upheld an individual's right to refuse to answer questions about private matters that were not pertinent to the subject of the investigation.

The Teapot Dome scandal also resulted in another important Supreme Court decision in 1929 in the case of Sinclair v. United States. *Harry F. Sinclair, the president of Mammoth Oil Company, was one of the key culprits in the shady deals that led to his leasing of the Teapot Dome oil reserves. He refused to cooperate with the Senate investigation in 1924 on grounds that the Senate had no jurisdiction in the case. This led to Sinclair's indictment by a District of Columbia grand jury. When the case reached the*

Supreme Court five years later, the Court's decision further amplified the right of the Senate to conduct investigations even while some of the matter in the investigation was before the courts. The Court said the Senate had the right to investigate the oil leases and "to make any other inquiry concerning the public domain." Congress was the proprietor of public lands and had the right to investigate how public land laws and regulations affected their use. While McGrain v. Daugherty *was the more important of the two cases in regard to the congressional power to investigate, together these two Court decisions expanded considerably the ability of Congress to launch investigations that may or may not relate strictly to the development of legislation.* McGrain v. Daugherty *has been cited as authority in several major investigations involving the Justice Department, including the Watergate hearings (1973) and the Iran-contra hearings (1987).*

Mr. Justice Van Devanter delivered the opinion of the Court.

. . . .

We have given the case earnest and prolonged consideration because the principle questions involved are of unusual importance and delicacy. They are (a) whether the Senate—or the House of Representatives, both being on the same plane in this regard—has power, through its own process, to compel a private individual to appear before it or one of its committees and give testimony needed to enable it efficiently to exercise a legislative function belonging to it under the Constitution; and (b) whether it sufficiently appears that the process was being employed in this instance to obtain testimony for that purpose.

Other questions are presented, which in regular course should be taken up first.

The witness challenges the authority of the deputy to execute the warrant on two grounds—that there was no provision of law for a deputy, and that, even if there were such a provision, a deputy could not execute the warrant because it was addressed simply to the sergeant at arms. We are of the opinion that neither ground is tenable.

The Senate adopted in 1889 and has retained ever since a standing order declaring that the sergeant at arms may appoint deputies "to serve process or perform other duties" in his stead, that they shall be "officers of the Senate," and that acts done and returns made by them "shall have like effect and be of the same validity as if performed or made by the sergeant at arms in person." In actual practice the Senate has given full effect to the order, and Congress has sanctioned the practice under it by recognizing the deputies—sometimes called assistants—as officers of the Senate, by fixing their compensation, and by making appropriations to pay them. Thus there was ample provision of law for a deputy.

The fact that the warrant was addressed simply to the sergeant at arms is not of special significance. His authority was not to be tested by the warrant alone. Other criteria were to be considered. The standing order and the resolution under which the warrant was issued plainly contemplated that he was to be free to execute the warrant in person or to direct a deputy to execute it. They expressed the intention of the Senate, and the words of the warrant were to be taken, as they well could be, in a sense which would give effect to that intention. Thus understood, the warrant, admissibly could be executed by a deputy, if the sergeant at arms so directed, which he did.

. . . .

The witness points to the provision in the Fourth Amendment to the Constitution declaring "no warrants shall issue, but upon probably cause, supported by oath or affirmation," and contends that the warrant was void because the report of the committee on which it was based was unsworn. We think the contention overlooks the relation of the committee to the Senate and to the matters reported, and puts aside the accepted interpretation of the constitutional provision.

The committee was a part of the Senate, and its members were acting under their oath of office as senators. The matters reported pertained to their own knowledge. They had issued the subpoenas, had received and examined the officer's returns thereon (copies of which accompanied the report), and knew the witness had not obeyed either subpoena, or offered any excuse for his failure to do so.

The constitutional provision was not intended to establish a new principle, but to affirm and preserve a cherished rule of the common law, designed to prevent the issue of groundless warrants. In legislative practice, committee reports are regarded as made under the sanction of the oath of office of its members, and where the matters reported are within the committee's knowledge and constitute probably cause for an attachment, such reports are acted on and given effect, without requiring that they be supported by further oath or affirmation. This is not a new practice, but one which has come down from an early period. It was well recognized before the constitutional provision was adopted, has been followed ever since, and appears never to have been challenged until now. Thus it amounts to a practical interpretation, long continued, of both the original common-law rule and the affirming constitutional provision, and should be given effect accordingly.

The principle underlying the legislative practice has also been recognized and applied in judicial proceedings. This is illustrated by the settled rulings that courts, in dealing with contempts committed in their presence, may order commitments without other proof than their own knowledge of the occurrence, and that they may issue attachments, based in their own knowledge of the default, where intended witnesses or jurors fail to appear in obedience to the process shown by the officer's return to have been duly served. A further illustration is found in the rulings that grand jurors, acting under the sanction of their oath as such, may find and return indictments based solely on their own knowledge of the particular offenses, and that warrants may be issued on such indictments without further oath or affirmation, and still another is found in the practice which recognized that, where grand jurors, under their oath as such, report to the court that a witness brought before them has refused to testify, the court may act an that report, although otherwise unsworn, and order the witness brought before it by attachment.

We think the legislative practice, fortified as it is by the judicial practice, shows that the report of the committee—which was based on the committee's own knowledge and made under the sanction of the oath of office of its members—was sufficiently supported by oath to satisfy the constitutional requirement.

The witness also points to the provision in the warrant, and in the resolution under which it was issued, requiring that he be "brought before the bar of the Senate, then and there" to give testimony "pertinent to the subject under inquiry," and contends that an essential prerequisite to such an attachment was wanting, because he neither had been subpoenaed to appear and testify before the Senate nor had refused to do so. The argument in support of the contention proceeds on the assumption that the warrant of attachment "is to be treated precisely the same as if no subpoena had been issued by the committee, and the same as if the witness had not refused to testify before the committee." In our opinion the contention and the assumption are both untenable. The committee was acting for the Senate and under its authorization, and therefore the subpoenas which the committee issued and the witness refused to obey are to be treated as if issued by the Senate, The warrant was issued as an auxiliary process to compel him to give the testimony sought by the subpoenas; and its nature in this respect is not affected by the direction that his testimony be given at the bar of the Senate, instead of before the committee. If the Senate deemed it proper, in view of his contumacy, to give that direction, it was at liberty to do so.

. . . .

The first of the principal questions—the one which the witness particularly presses on our attention—is, as before shown, whether the Senate—or the House of Representatives, both being on the same plane in this regard—has power, through its own process, to compel a private individual to appear before it or one of its committees and give testimony needed to enable it efficiently to exercise a legislative function belonging to it under the Constitution.

The Constitution provides for a Congress, consisting of a Senate and House of Representatives, and invests it with "all legislative powers" granted to the United States, and with power "to make laws which shall be necessary and proper" for carrying into execution these powers and "all other powers" vested by the Constitution in the United States or in any department or officer thereof. Article 1, secs. 1, 8. Other provisions show that, while bills can become laws only after being considered and passed by both houses of Congress, each house id to be distinct from the other to have its own officers and rules, and to exercise its legislative function independently. Article 1, secs. 2, 3, 5, 7. But there is no provision expressly investing either house with power to make investigations and exact testimony, to the end that it may exercise its legislative function advisedly and effectively. So the question arises whether this power is so far incidental to the legislative function as to be implied.

In actual legislative practice, power to secure needed information by such means has long been treated as an attribute of the power to legislate. It was so regarded in the British Parliament and in the colonial Legislatures before the American Revolution, and a like view has prevailed and been carried into effect in both houses of Congress and in most of the state Legislatures.

This power was both asserted and exerted by the House of Representatives in 1792, when it appointed a select committee to inquire into the St. Clair expedition and authorized the committee to send for necessary persons, papers and records. Mr. Madison, who had taken an important part in framing the Constitution only five years before, and four of his associates in that work, were members of the House of Representatives at the time, and all voted for the inquiry. . . .

While these cases are not decisive of the question we are considering, they definitely settle two propositions which we recognize as entirely sound and having a bearing on its solution: One, that the two houses of Congress, their separate relations, possess, not only such powers as are expressly granted to them by the Constitution, but such auxiliary powers as are necessary and appropriate to make the express powers effective; and the other, that neither house is invested with "general" power to inquire into private affairs and compel disclosures, but only with such limited power of inquiry as is shown to exist when the rule of constitutional interpretation just stated is rightly applied. . . .

We are of the opinion that the power of inquiry—with process to enforce it—is an essential and appropriate auxiliary to the legislative function. It was so regarded and employed in American Legislatures before the Constitution was framed and ratified. Both houses of Congress took this view of it early in their history—the House of Representatives with the approving votes of Mr. Madison and other members whose service in the convention which framed the Constitution gives special significance to their action—and both houses have employed the

power accordingly up to the present time. The acts of 1798 and 1857, judged by their comprehensive terms, were intended to recognize the existence of this power in both houses and to enable them to employ it "more effectually" than before. So, when their practice in the matter is appraised according to the circumstances in which it was begun and to those in which it has been continued, it falls nothing short of a practical construction, long continued, of the constitutional provisions respecting their powers, and therefore should be taken as fixing the meaning of those provisions, if otherwise doubtful.

We are further of opinion that the provisions are not of doubtful meaning, but, as was held by this court in the cases we have reviewed, are intended to be effectively exercised, and therefore to carry with them such auxiliary powers as are necessary and appropriate to that end. While the power to exact information in aid of the legislative function was not involved in those cases, the rule of interpretation applied there is applicable here. A legislative body cannot legislate wisely or effectively in the absence of information respecting the conditions which the legislation is intended to affect or change; and where the legislative body does not itself possess the requisite information—which not infrequently is true—recourse must be had to others who possess it. Experience has taught that mere requests for such information which is volunteered is not always accurate or complete; so some means of compulsion are essential to obtain what is needed. All this was true before and when the Constitution was framed and adopted. I that period the power of inquiry, with enforcing process, was regarded and employed as a necessary and appropriate attribute of the power to legislate—indeed, was treated as inhering in it. Thus there is ample warrant for thinking, as we do, that the constitutional provisions which commit the legislative function to the two houses are intended to include this attribute to the end that the function may be effectively exercised.

. . . .

What has been said requires that the final order in the district court discharging the witness from custody be reversed.

Final order reversed.

273 U.S. 135 (1927).

121   An Act Designating the National Anthem

March 3, 1931

Congress declared the "Star Spangled Banner" to be the national anthem in one of the shortest laws ever written. The words to the "Star Spangled Banner" originated in a poem written by Francis Scott Key in 1814, when he witnessed the bombardment of Fort McHenry, near Baltimore, Maryland, during the War of 1812. The large flag flying over Fort McHenry was thirty feet by forty-two feet in size and managed to survive a night of shelling, inspiring Key's poem. Before long, the poem became popular as a song, sung to the tune of an eighteenth century British drinking song "To Anacreon in Heaven."

Following World War I many veterans and patriotic organizations began a movement to make the "Star Spangled Banner" the official anthem of the United States. These organizations included the Veterans of Foreign Wars, the National Flag Code Committee, the Daughters of the American Revolution, the United Daughters of the Confederacy, the Boy Scouts of America, the American Legion, and many other organizations. These organizations and others managed to gather 5 million signatures on petitions urging Congress to formalize what most Americans, and the army and navy, already considered to be the national anthem. The bill passed the House four times before it managed to pass the Senate on March 3, 1931, the last day of the 71st Congress.

The original flag that inspired Francis Scott Key's poem was donated to the Smithsonian Institution in 1912, where it became a popular tourist attraction. Over the years the ravages of time and exposure to light have taken a serious toll on the condition of the fifteen-star, fifteen-stripe Fort McHenry flag. As part of the cele-

bration of the millennium, the White House and the Smithsonian Institution designated the Fort McHenry flag a major historical treasure worthy of preservation. An elaborate effort, estimated to cost $18 million, is underway to save the flag that inspired the national anthem.

CHAP. 436.—AN ACT TO MAKE THE STAR-SPANGLED BANNER THE NATIONAL ANTHEM OF THE UNITED STATES OF AMERICA.

Be it enacted by the Senate and the House of Representatives of the United States of America in Congress assembled, That the composition consisting of the words and music known as the Star-Spangled Banner is designated the national anthem of the United States of America.

Approved, March 3, 1931.

Statutes at Large, 45 (1929–1931), 71st Congress, 3d session, March 3, 1931, 1508.

122   The Twentieth Amendment to the Constitution

Submitted to the States, March 2, 1932; Ratified, February 6, 1933

Constitutional amendments usually come from the judiciary committees of the House or Senate, but the Twentieth Amendment originated in 1923 in the House Committee on Agriculture and Forestry, under the chairmanship of George Norris (R-Neb.). Despite Norris's efforts to see this amendment adopted, opposition in his own party in the House of Representatives and in the Republican-controlled White House kept it from passing both houses of Congress until 1932.

The Twentieth Amendment is often called the "Lame Duck Amendment" because it eliminated the long time period between the election of members of Congress and the time they actually took their seats. Since defeated members remained in office until the next Congress convened, they were known as "lame ducks" because their effectiveness as members was weakened. Sometimes lame ducks used the extra time they had in Congress to cut deals that would ensure they would have a job when their term of office was up. Until the passage of the Twentieth Amendment, members defeated for re-election stayed in office for thirteen months after the November elections because the new Congress did not usually convene until the following December. The amendment designated January 3 following the November elections as the start of new terms.

The amendment also shortened the time between the election of the president of the United States and the date of the inauguration. It set January 20 as the date of the presidential inauguration. Before the passage of this amendment, the president, elected in November, would not be sworn in until the following March 4. This five-month delay did not cause major problems in earlier elections, but it became crucial during the Great Depression, when the nation faced a

dire economic emergency. The newly elected president, Franklin D. Roosevelt, had to wait from November 1932 until March 1933 before he could take decisive measures to address the national crisis.

Once submitted to the states, the amendment was ratified in less than a year. On January 3, 1935, the members of the 74th Congress were the first to be sworn in under the provisions of this amendment. Franklin Roosevelt was the last person to be inaugurated under the old system and on January 20, 1936, became the first to be inaugurated under the provisions of the Twentieth Amendment.

ARTICLE [XX].

SECTION 1. The terms of the President and Vice President shall end at noon on the 20th day of January, and the terms of Senators and Representatives at noon on the 3d day of January, of the years in which such terms would have ended if this article had not been ratified; and the terms of their successors shall then begin.

SEC. 2. The Congress shall assemble at least once in every year, and such meeting shall begin at noon on the 3d day of January, unless they shall by law appoint a different day.

SEC. 3. If, at the time fixed for the beginning of the term of the President, the President elect shall have died, the Vice President elect shall become President. If a President shall not have been chosen before the time fixed for the beginning of his term, or if the President elect shall have failed to qualify, then the Vice President elect shall act as President until a President shall have qualified; and the Congress may by law provide for the case wherein neither a President elect nor a Vice President elect shall have qualified, declaring who shall then act as President, or the manner in which one who is to act shall be selected, and such person shall act accordingly until a President or Vice President shall have qualified.

SEC. 4. The Congress may by law provide for the case of the death of any of the persons from whom the House of Representatives may choose a President whenever the right of choice shall have devolved upon them, and for the case of the death of any of the persons from whom the Senate may choose a Vice President whenever the right of choice shall have devolved upon them.

SEC. 5. Sections 1 and 2 shall take effect on the 15th day of October following the ratification of this article.

SEC. 6. This article shall be inoperative unless it shall have been ratified as an amendment to the Constitution by the legislatures of three-fourths of the several States within seven years from the date of its submission.

The Constitution of the United States of America as Amended, House Doc. 102–188, 102d Congress, 2d session (Washington: Government Printing Office, 1992), 21.

123   The Twenty-First Amendment to the Constitution

Submitted to the States, February 20, 1933; Ratified, December 5, 1933

The Twenty-First Amendment, which repealed Prohibition, is the only amendment ever ratified to undo an earlier amendment, the Eighteenth (see document 113). It is also the only amendment to be ratified in special conventions held in each state rather than by state legislatures, under provisions of Article V of the Constitution. Congress left the details of how the conventions would be run to each state. But the intention of calling for ratifying conventions was to get a better gauge of public sentiment than might be the case in the state legislatures, which often were dominated by rural interests and did not represent larger cities. The substantial immigrant populations of the larger cities opposed Prohibition.

The great experiment to end the manufacture and sale of alcoholic beverages in the United States proved to be impossible to enforce after almost fourteen years of effort. Even though alcoholic consumption declined considerably during Prohibition, the methods employed to apprehend violators of the Volstead Act (see document 115) included searching automobiles without a warrant and wiretapping. This vigorous enforcement often raised serious questions of individual rights of privacy and the constitutional guarantee "against unreasonable searches and seizures" found in Article IV of the Constitution.

In the presidential and congressional elections of 1932 the voters had a clear choice on the issue. The Democratic Party favored repeal, while the Republican Party wanted to stay the course with *Prohibition and strict enforcement of the Volstead Act. While it is not fair to say that Prohibition was the single most important issue in the 1932 election, given the many issues related to the Great Depression, it was a major factor. The election was a sweeping success for the Democratic Party that year, which gained control of the White House and both houses of Congress. In the House, Republicans lost 101 seats.*

ARTICLE [XXI.]

SECTION 1. The eighteenth article of amendment to the Constitution of the United States is hereby repealed.

SECTION 2. The transportation or importation into any State, Territory, or possession of the United States for delivery or use therein of intoxicating liquors, in violation of the laws thereof, is hereby prohibited.

SECTION 3. This article shall be inoperative unless it shall have been ratified as an amendment to the Constitution by conventions in the several States, as provided in the Constitution, within seven years from the date of the submission hereof to the States by the Congress.

The Constitution of the United States of America as Amended, House Doc. 102–188, 102d Congress, 2d session (Washington: Government Printing Office, 1992), 22.

124   Senator Huey Long's "Every Man a King" Speech

February 23, 1934

This speech by the flamboyant and controversial Senator Huey Long (D-La.) was not delivered on the floor of the Senate. It was a radio speech, later reprinted in the pages of the Congressional Record. *Huey Long and President Franklin D. Roosevelt were among the first national politicians to effectively utilize radio broadcasts for political purposes. Roosevelt conducted a series of radio addresses popularly called "fireside chats" to assure the country that the Great Depression could be beaten. Long stirred the passions of millions with his "Share Our Wealth" program, which urged a massive redistribution of the wealth of the nation, which he saw as being concentrated in the hands of a few millionaires. Long, a former governor of Louisiana, rose to national prominence as a champion of the poor and the dispossessed of a nation deep in the throes of the Depression. He offered a blend of biblical salvation and economic theory that he pitched in emotion-laded appeals to ordinary Americans who could not share in the American dream or in biblical prophesy because the super-rich hoarded the nation's money.*

During the Great Depression a number of bills to limit the income of individuals came before the House and Senate. All were defeated on various grounds, including arguments that they undermined the capitalist system and imposed a brand of socialism on America. Most Americans rejected such notions even during the hard times of the Depression. In this speech Long called for limitations on individual income, but he was unsure of exactly what amount constituted too much wealth. Long's national popularity led him in August 1935 to announce his candidacy for the Democratic nomination for president. On September 8, 1935, while at the state capitol in Baton Rouge, he was gunned down by a lone gunman and died of his wounds two days later.

Is that a right of life, when the young children of this country are being reared into a sphere which is more owned by 12 men than it is by 120 million people?

Ladies and gentlemen, I have only thirty minutes in which to speak to you this evening, and I, therefore, will not be able to discuss in detail so much as I can write when I have all of the time and space that is allowed me for the subjects, but I will undertake to sketch them very briefly without manuscript or preparation, so that you can understand them so well as I can tell them to you tonight.

I contend, my friends, that we have no difficult problem to solve in America, and that is the view of nearly everyone with whom I have discussed the matter here in Washington and elsewhere throughout the United States—that we have no very difficult problem to solve.

It is not the difficulty of the problem which we have; it is the fact that the rich people of this country—and by rich people I mean the super-rich—will not allow us to solve the problems, or rather the one little problem that is afflicting this country, because in order to cure all of our woes it is necessary to scale down the big fortunes, that we may scatter the wealth to be shared by all of the people.

We have a marvelous love for this government of ours; in fact, it is almost a religion, and it is well that it should be, because we have a splendid form of government and we have a splendid set of laws. We have everything here that we need, except that we have neglected the fundamentals upon which the American government was principally predicated.

How many of you remember the first thing that the Declaration of Independence said? It said, "We hold these truths to be self-evident, that there are certain inalienable rights for the people, and among them are life, liberty, and the pursuit of happiness"; and it said, further, "We hold the view that all men are created equal."

Now, what did they mean by that? Did they mean, my friends, to say that all men were created equal and that that meant that any one man was born to inherit $10 billion and that another child was to be born to inherit nothing?

Did that mean, my friends, that someone would come into this world without having had an opportunity, of course, to have hit one lick of work, should be born with more than it and all of its children and children's children could ever dispose of, but that another one would have to be born into a life of starvation?

That was not the meaning of the Declaration of Independence when it said that all men are created equal or "That we hold that all men are created equal."

Nor was it the meaning of the Declaration of Independence when it said that they held that there were certain rights that were inalienable—the right of life, liberty, and the pursuit of happiness.

Is that right of life, my friends, when the young children of this country are being reared into a sphere which is more owned by 12 men than it is by 120 million people?

Is that, my friends, giving them a fair shake of the dice or anything like the inalienable right of life, liberty, and the pursuit of happiness, or anything resembling the fact that all people are created equal; when we have today in America thousands and hundreds of thousands and millions of children on the verge of starvation in a land that is overflowing with too much to eat and too much to wear?

I do not think you will contend that, and I do not think for a moment that they will contend it.

Now let us see if we cannot return this government to the Declaration of Independence and see if we are going to do anything regarding it. Why should we hesitate or why should we quibble or why should we quarrel with one another to find out what the difficulty is, when we know what the Lord told us what the difficulty is, and Moses wrote it out so a blind man could see it, then Jesus told us all about it, and it was later written in the Book of James, where everyone could read it?

I refer to the Scriptures, now, my friends, and give you what it says not for the purpose of convincing you of the wisdom of myself, not for the purpose, ladies and gentlemen, of convincing you of the fact that I am quoting the Scripture means that I am to be more believed than someone else; but I quote you the Scripture, or rather refer you to the Scripture, because whatever you see there you may rely upon will never be disproved so long as you or your children or anyone may live; and you may further depend upon the fact that not one historical fact that the Bible has ever contained has ever yet been disproved by any scientific discovery or by reason of anything that has been disclosed to man through his own individual mind or through the wisdom of the Lord which the Lord has allowed him to have.

But the Scripture says, ladies and gentlemen, that no country can survive, or for a country to survive it is necessary that we keep the wealth scattered among the people, that nothing should be held permanently by any one person, and that fifty years seems to be the year of jubilee in which all property would be scattered about and returned to the sources from which it originally came, and every seventh year debt should be remitted.

Those two things the Almighty said to be necessary—I should say He knew to be necessary, or else He would not have so prescribed that the property would be kept among the general run of the people, and that everyone would continue to share in it; so that no one man would get half of it and hand it down to a son, who takes half of what was left, and that son hand it down to another one, who would take half of what was left, until, like a snowball going downhill, all of the snow was off of the ground except what the snowball had.

I believe that was the judgment and the view and the law of the Lord, that we would have to distribute wealth ever so often, in order that there could not be people starving to death in a land of plenty, as there is in America today.

We have in America today more wealth, more goods, more food, more clothing, more houses than we have ever had. We have everything in abundance here.

We have the farm problem, my friends, because we have too much cotton, because we have too much wheat, and have too much corn, and too much potatoes.

We have a home-loan problem because we have too many houses, and yet nobody can buy them and live in them.

We have trouble, my friends, in the country, because we have too much money owing, the greatest indebtedness that has ever been given to civilization, where it has been shown that we are incapable of distributing the actual things that are here, because the people have not money enough to supply themselves with them, and because the greed of a few men is such that they think it is necessary that they own everything, and their pleasure consists in the starvation of the masses, and in their possessing things they cannot use, and their children cannot use, but who bask in the splendor of sunlight and wealth, casting darkness and despair and impressing it on everyone else.

. . . .

Now, ladies and gentlemen, if I may proceed to give you some other words that I think you can understand—I am not going to belabor you by quoting tonight—I am going to tell you what the wise men of all ages and all times, down even to the present day, have all said: that you must keep the wealth of the country scattered, and you must limit the amount that any one man can own. You cannot let any man own $300 billion or $400 billion. If you do, one man can own all of the wealth that the United States has in it.

Now, my friends, if you were off on an island where there were one hundred lunches, you could not let one man eat up the hundred lunches, or take the hundred lunches and not let anybody else eat any of them. If you did, there would not be anything else for the balance of the people to consume.

So, we have in America today, my friends, a condition by which about ten men dominate the means of activity in at least 85 percent of the activities that you own. They either own directly everything or they have got some kind of mortgage on it, with a very small percentage to be excepted. They own the banks, they own the steel mills, they own the railroads, they own the bonds, they own the mortgages, they own the stores, and they have chained the country from one end to the other until there is not any kind of business that a small, independent man could go into today and make a living, and there is not any kind of business that an independent man can go into and make any money to buy an automobile with; and they have finally and gradually and steadily eliminated everybody from the fields in which there is a living to be made, and still they have got little enough sense to think they ought to be able to get more business out of it anyway.

If you reduce a man to the point where he is starving to death and bleeding and dying, how do you expect that man to get hold of any money to spend with you? It is not possible.

Then, ladies and gentlemen, how do you expect people to live, when the wherewith cannot be had by the people?

. . . .

Both of these men, Mr. Hoover and Mr. Roosevelt, came out and said there had to be a decentralization of wealth, but neither one of them did anything about it. But, nevertheless, they recognized the principle. The fact that neither one of them ever did anything about it is their own problem that I am not undertaking to criticize; but had Mr. Hoover carried out what he says ought to be done, he would be retiring from the president's office, very probably three years from now, instead of one year ago; and had Mr. Roosevelt proceeded along the lines that he stated were necessary for the decentralization of wealth, he would have gone, my friends, a long way already, and within a few months he would have probably reached a solution of all of the problems that afflict this country today.

But I wish to warn you now that nothing that has been done up to this date has taken one dime away from these big-fortune holders; they own just as much as they did, and probably a little bit more; they hold just as many of the debts of the common people as they ever held, and probably a little bit more; and unless we, my friends, are going to give the people of this country a fair shake of the dice, by which they will all get something out of the funds of this land, there is not a chance on the topside of this God's eternal earth by which we can rescue this country and rescue the people of this country.

It is necessary to save the government of the country, but is much more necessary to save the people of America. We love this country. We love this government. It is a religion, I say. It is a kind of religion people have read of when women, in the name of religion, would take their infant babes and throw them into the burning flame, where they would be instantly devoured by the all-consuming fire, in days gone by; and there probably are some people of the world even today, who, in the name of religion, throw their own babes to destruction; but in the name of our good government people today are seeing their own children hungry, tired, half-naked, lifting their tear-dimmed eyes into the sad faces of their fathers and mothers, who cannot give them food and clothing they both needed, and which is necessary to sustain them, and that goes on day after day, and night after night, when day gets into darkness and blackness, knowing those children would arise in the morning without being fed, and probably go to bed at night without being fed.

Yet in the name of our government, and all alone, those people undertake and strive as hard as they can to keep a good government alive, and how long they can stand that no one knows. If I were in their place tonight, the place where millions are, I hope that I would have what I might say—I cannot give you the word to express the kind of fortitude they have; that is the word—I hope that I might have the fortitude to praise and honor my government that had allowed me here in this land, where there is too much to eat and too much to wear, to starve in order that a handful of men can have so much more than they can ever eat or they can ever wear.

Now, we have organized a society, and we call it "Share Our Wealth Society," a society with the motto "every man a king."

Every man a king, so there would be no such thing as a man or woman who did not have the necessities of life, who would not be dependent upon the whims and caprices and *ipse dixit* of the financial martyrs for a living. What do we propose by this society? We propose to limit the wealth of big men in the country. There is an average of $15,000 in wealth to every family in America. That is right here today.

We do not propose to divide it up equally. We do not propose a division of wealth, but we propose to limit poverty that we will allow to be inflicted upon any man's family. We will not say we are going to try to guarantee any equality, or $15,000 to families. No; but we do say that one third of the average is low enough for any one family to hold, that there should be a guaranty of a family wealth of around $5,000; enough for a home, an automobile, a radio, and the ordinary conveniences, and the opportunity to educate their children; a fair share of the income of this land thereafter to that family so there will be no such thing as merely the select to have those things, and so there will be no such thing as a family living in poverty and distress.

We have to limit fortunes. Our present plan is that we will allow no one man to own more than $50 million. We think that with that limit we will be able to carry out the balance of the program. It may be necessary that we limit it to less than $50 million. It may be necessary, in working out of the plans, that no man's fortune would be more than $10 million or $15 million. But be that as it may, it will still be more than any one man, or any one man and his children and their children, will be able to spend in their lifetimes; and it is not necessary or reasonable to have wealth piled up beyond that point where we cannot prevent poverty among the masses.

Another thing we propose is old-age pension of $30 a month for everyone that is sixty years old. Now, we do not give this pension to a man making $1,000 a year, and we do not give it to him if he has $10,000 in property, but outside of that we do.

We will limit hours of work. There is not any necessity of having overproduction. I think all you have got to do, ladies and gentlemen, is just limit the hours of work to such an extent as people will work only so long as is necessary to produce enough for all of the people to have what they need. Why, ladies and gentlemen, let us say that all of these labor-saving devices reduce hours down to where you do not have to work but four hours a day; that is enough for these people, and then praise be the name of the Lord, if it gets that good. Let it be good and not a curse, and then we will have five hours a day and five days a week, or even less than that, and we might give a man a whole month off during a year, or give him two months; and we might do what other countries have seen fit to do, and what I did in Louisiana, by having schools by which adults could go back and learn the things that have been discovered since they went to school.

We will not have any trouble taking care of the agricultural situation. All you have to do is balance your production with your consumption. You simply have to abandon a particular crop that you have too much of, and all you have to do is store the surplus for the next year, and the government will take it over. When you have good crops in the area in which the crops that have been planted are sufficient for another year, put in your public works in the particular year when you do not need to raise any more, and by that means you get everybody employed. When the government has enough of any particular crop to take care of all the people, that will be all that is necessary; and in order to do all of this, our taxation is going to be to take the billion-dollar fortunes and strip them down to frying size, not to exceed $50 million, and if it is necessary to come to $10 million, we will come to $10 million. We have worked the proposition out to guarantee a limit upon property (and no man will own less than one third the average), and guarantee a reduction of fortunes and a reduction of hours to spread wealth throughout this country. We would care for the old people above sixty and take them away from this thriving industry and give them a chance to enjoy the necessities and live in ease, and thereby lift from the market the labor which would probably create a surplus of commodities.

Those are the things we propose to do. "Every man a king." Every man to eat when there is something to eat; all to wear something when there is something to wear. That makes us all a sovereign.

. . . .

Now, my friends, we have got to hit the root with the ax. Centralized power in the hands of a few, with centralized credit in the hands of a few, is the trouble.

Get together in your community tonight or tomorrow and organize one of our Share Our Wealth societies. If you do not understand it, write me and let me send you the platform; let me give you the proof of it.

This is Huey P. Long talking, United States Senator, Washington, D.C. Write me and let me send you the data on this proposition. Enroll with us. Let us make known to the people what we are going to do. I will send you a button, if I have got enough of them left. We have got a little button that some of our friends designed, with our message around the rim of the button, and in the center "Every man a king." Many thousands of them are meeting through the United States, and every day we are getting hundreds of hundreds of letters. Share Our Wealth societies are now being organized, and people have it within their power to relieve themselves from this terrible situation.

Look at what the Mayo brothers announced this week, these greatest scientists of all the world today, who are entitled to have more money than all the Morgans and the Rockefellers, or anyone else, and yet the Mayos turn back their big fortunes to be used for treating the sick, and said they did not want to lay up fortunes in this earth, but wanted to turn them back where they would do some good; but the other big capitalists are not

willing to do that, are not willing to do what these men, ten times more worthy, have already done, and it is going to take a law to require them to do it.

Organize your Share Our Wealth Society and get your people to meet with you, and make known your wishes to your senators and representatives in Congress.

Now, my friends, I am going to stop. I thank you for this opportunity to talk to you. I am having to talk under the auspices and by the grace and permission of the National Broadcasting System tonight, and they are letting me talk free. If I had the money, and I wish I had the money, I would like to talk to you more often on this line, but I have not got it, and I cannot expect these people to give it to me free except on some rare instance. But, my friends, I hope to have the opportunity to talk with you, and I am writing to you, and I hope that you will get up and help in the work, because the resolution and bills are before Congress, and we hope to have your help in getting together and organizing your Share Our Wealth Society.

Now, that I have but a minute left, I want to say that I suppose my family is listening in on the radio in New Orleans, and I will say to my wife and three children that I am entirely well and hope to be home before many more days, and I hope they have listened to my speech tonight, and I wish them and all of their neighbors and friends everything good that may be had.

I thank you, my friends, for your kind attention, and I hope you will enroll with us, take care of your own work in the work of this government, and share or help in our Share Our Wealth Society.

Robert C. Byrd, *The Senate, 1789–1989*, 4 vols. (Washington, D.C.: Government Printing Office), vol. 3: 587–593. Also printed in the *Congressional Record*, Senate, 73d Congress, 2d session, 3450–3453.

125   Will Rogers on Congress

May 12, 1935

Humor about Congress abounds. It is as American as apple pie to poke fun or lampoon Congress. This has been true from the first Congress more than two hundred years ago and it is true today. Writer Mark Twain said this country had no native criminal class, except Congress.

Few humorists have been as successful at poking fun at Congress as Will Rogers (1879–1935), the cowboy humorist, actor, and homespun philosopher from Oklahoma, who was beloved by millions. Rogers found humor all around him. He said, "All I know is what I read in the papers." His syndicated newspaper columns in the 1920s and 1930s and radio broadcasts made him one of the most widely followed comedians in the country. Among the "papers" he read was the Congressional Record, *the official record of House and Senate debates, which Rogers found to contain many*

hilarious items. As Rogers put it "You see, in Washington they have two of these bodies, Senate and the House of Representatives. That is for the convenience of visitors. If there is nothing funny happening in one, there is sure to be in the other, and in case one body passes a good bill, why, the other can see it in time and kill it."

Rogers died in a airplane crash in Alaska in 1935, along with veteran aviator Wiley Post. Three years later the state of Oklahoma sent a seven-foot six-inch, larger-than-life bronze statue of Will Rogers to the Capitol, where it stands in a corridor outside the House chamber. There, the story goes, he can still keep an eye on Congress.

The document that follows describes Rogers's pride in finding some of his own material in the Congressional Record.

You see, ordinarily you got to work your way up as a humorist and first get into Congress. Then you work your way up into the Senate, and then, if your stuff is funny enough it goes into the *Congressional Record*. But for an outsider to get in there as a humorist without having served his apprenticeship in either the House or the Senate, why, mind you, I'm not bragging, but by golly I feel pretty big about it.

Did I ever tell you about the first time I ever had any stuff in that daily? Well, I'd written some fool thing, and it pertained to the bill that they were arguing—or that they were kidding about, rather—at the time in the Senate. So some Senator read my little article, and as it was during his speech, it naturally went into the *Congressional Record*. So another Senator rose and said, you know how they always do, if you ever see 'em. "Does the gentleman yield?" They always say "gentleman" in there. But the tone—the tone that they put on the word, it would be more appropriate—you know the way they can say "gentleman"—it would sound right if they come right out and said "Does the coyote from Maine yield?" You know what I mean; that's about the way it sounds. So the coyote from Maine says,

"I yield to the polecat from Oregon," for if he don't, the other guy will keep on talking anyhow. You know he don't say "polecat," but he says "gentleman" in such a way that it's almost like polecat. They are very polite in there.

Well, I must get back to my story. When this Senator read my offering, the other Senator said, after all the yielding was over: I object! I object to the remarks of a professional joke maker being put into the *Congressional Record!* You know, meaning me. See? Taking a dig at me. They didn't want any outside fellow contributing. Well, he had me all wrong. Compared to them I'm an amateur, and the thing about my jokes is they don't hurt anybody. You can take 'em or leave 'em. You know what I mean? You know, you can say, well, they're funny, or they're terrible, or they're good, or whatever, but they don't do any harm. You can just pass them by. But with Congress, every time they make a joke it's a law! And every time they make a law, it's a joke.

Bryan B. Sterling and Frances N. Sterling, *Will Rogers' World: Americans Foremost Political Humorist Comments on the Twenties and Thirties—and the Eighties and the Nineties* (New York: M. Evans, 1989), 49–50.

126 *National Labor Relations Board v. Jones and Laughlin Steel Corporation*

April 12, 1937

The National Labor Relations Act, passed by Congress in 1935, gave employees the right to bargain collectively with their employers regarding wages or other conditions of employment. This was a major victory for the labor union movement in the United States. From the standpoint of the Roosevelt administration and the bill's major sponsor, Senator Robert F. Wagner (D-N.Y.), the act was an essential component of national recovery from the Depression. The act established a National Labor Relations Board (NLRB) to mediate labor disputes. The operation of the NLRB was extremely controversial, as employers resented federal regulation and some established unions feared competition from rival unions that had been given new power under the law.

The activities of the NLRB resulted in several important Supreme Court decisions affecting labor relations and U.S. commerce, five of which were decided on the same day. From the standpoint of Congress, the most important of these cases was Na-tional Labor Relations Board v. Jones and Laughlin Steel Cor-poration, which established the right of Congress to regulate labor relations in manufacturing industries to avoid interference with interstate commerce.

In the decision rendered by Chief Justice Charles Evans Hughes, the Court asserted that it was vital to make a distinction between local commercial activities and national commerce and that Con-gress had the authority to step in with laws and regulations to pre-vent obstruction of interstate or foreign commerce. The NLRB had charged the Jones and Laughlin Steel Corporation with discrimina-

tion against union employees and unfairly interfering with at-tempts of company employees to form a union when it fired ten em-ployees from one plant in Pennsylvania who were engaged in union activities. The Court determined this was not merely a local matter but that the practice impeded the "free flow of commerce" and that it was within the authority of the NLRB to deal with the matter.

MR. CHIEF JUSTICE HUGHES delivered the opinion of the Court.

In a proceeding under the National Labor Relations Act of 1935, the National Labor Relations Board found that the re-spondent, Jones & Laughlin Steel Corporation, had violated the Act by engaging in unfair labor practices affecting commerce. The proceeding was instituted by the Beaver Valley Lodge No. 200, affiliated with the Amalgamated Association of Iron, Steel and Tin Workers of America, a labor organization. The unfair labor practices charged were that the corporation was discrimi-nating against members of the union with regard to hire and tenure of employment, and was coercing and intimidating its employees in order to interfere with their self-organization. The discriminatory and coercive action alleged was the discharge of certain employees.

The National Labor Relations Board, sustaining the charge, ordered the corporation to cease and desist from such discrimi-nation and coercion, to offer reinstatement to ten of the employ-ees named, to make good their losses in pay, and to post for thirty days notices that the corporation would not discharge or discriminate against members, or those desiring to become members, of the labor union. As the corporation failed to comply, the Board petitioned the Circuit Court of Appeals to enforce the order. The court denied the petition, holding that the order lay beyond the range of federal power. We granted certiorari.

The scheme of the National Labor Relations Act—which is too long to be quoted in full—may be briefly stated. The first section sets forth findings with respect to the injury to commerce resulting from the denial by employers of the right of employees to organize and from the refusal of employers to accept the procedure of collective bargaining. There follows a declaration that it is the policy of the United States to eliminate these causes of obstruction to the free flow of commerce. The Act then defines the terms it uses, including the terms "commerce" and "affecting commerce." § 2. It creates the National Labor Relations Board, and prescribes its organization. §§ 3–6. It sets forth the right of employees to self-organization and to bargain collectively through representatives of their own choosing. § 7. It defines "unfair labor practices." § 8. It lays down rules as to the representation of employees for the purpose of collective bargaining. § 9. The Board is empowered to prevent the described unfair labor practices affecting commerce and the Act prescribes the procedure to that end. The Board is authorized to petition designated courts to secure the enforcement of its orders. The findings of the Board as to the facts, if supported by evidence, are to be conclusive. If either party, on application to the court, shows that additional evidence is material and that there were reasonable grounds for the failure to adduce such evidence in the hearings before the Board, the court may order the additional evidence to be taken. Any person aggrieved by a final order of the Board may obtain a review in the designated courts with the same procedure as in the case of an application by the Board for the enforcement of its order. § 10. The Board has broad powers of investigation. § 11. Interference with members of the Board or its agents in the performance of their duties is punishable by fine and imprisonment. § 12. Nothing in the Act is to be construed, to interfere with the right to strike. § 13. There is a separability clause to the effect that, if any provision of the Act or its application to any person or circumstances shall be held invalid, the remainder of the Act or its application to other persons or circumstances shall not be affected. § 15. The particular provisions which are involved in the instant case will be considered more in detail in the course of the discussion.

The procedure in the instant case followed the statute. The labor union filed with the Board its verified charge. The Board thereupon issued its complaint against the respondent alleging that its action in discharging the employees in question constituted unfair labor practices affecting commerce within the meaning of § 8, subdivisions (1) and (3), and § 2, subdivisions (6) and (7) of the Act. Respondent, appearing specially for the purpose of objecting to the jurisdiction of the Board, filed its answer. Respondent admitted the discharges, but alleged that

they were made because of inefficiency or violation of rule or for other good reasons, and were not ascribable to union membership or activities. As an affirmative defense, respondent challenged the constitutional validity of the statute and its applicability in the instant case. Notice of hearing was given, and respondent appeared by counsel. The Board first took up the issue of jurisdiction, and evidence was presented by both the Board and the respondent. Respondent then moved to dismiss the complaint for lack of jurisdiction, and, on denial of that motion, respondent, in accordance with its special appearance, withdrew from further participation in the hearing. The Board received evidence upon the merits, and, at its close, made its findings and order.

Contesting the ruling of the Board, the respondent argues (1) that the Act is in reality a regulation of labor relations, and not of interstate commerce; (2) that the Act can have no application to the respondent's relations with its production employees, because they are not subject to regulation by the federal government, and (3) that the provisions of the Act violate § 2 of Article III and the Fifth and Seventh Amendments of the Constitution of the United States.

The facts as to the nature and scope of the business of the Jones & Laughlin Steel Corporation have been found by the Labor Board, and, so far as they are essential to the determination of this controversy, they are not in dispute. The Labor Board has found: the corporation is organized under the laws of Pennsylvania and has its principal office at Pittsburgh. It is engaged in the business of manufacturing iron and steel in plants situated in Pittsburgh and nearby Aliquippa, Pennsylvania. It manufactures and distributes a widely diversified line of steel and pig iron, being the fourth largest producer of steel in the United States. With its subsidiaries—nineteen in number—it is a completely integrated enterprise, owning and operating ore, coal and limestone properties, lake and river transportation facilities, and terminal railroads located at its manufacturing plants. It owns or controls mines in Michigan and Minnesota. It operates four ore steamships on the Great Lakes, used in the transportation of ore to its factories. It owns coal mines in Pennsylvania. It operates towboats and steam barges used in carrying coal to its factories. It owns limestone properties in various places in Pennsylvania and West Virginia. It owns the Monongahela connecting railroad which connects the plants of the Pittsburgh works and forms an interconnection with the Pennsylvania, New York Central, and Baltimore and Ohio Railroad systems. It owns the Aliquippa and Southern Railroad Company, which connects the Aliquippa works with the Pittsburgh and Lake Erie, part of the New York Central system. Much of its product is shipped to its warehouses in Chicago, Detroit, Cincinnati and Memphis—to the last two places by means of its own barges and transportation equipment. In Long Island City, New York, and in New Orleans, it operates structural steel fabricating shops in connection with the warehousing of semi-finished materials sent from its works. Through one of its wholly owned subsidiaries, it owns, leases and operates stores, warehouses and yards for the distribution of equipment and supplies for drilling and operating oil and gas wells and for pipelines, refineries, and pumping stations. It has sales offices in twenty cities in the United States and a wholly owned subsidiary which is devoted exclusively to distributing its product in Canada. Approximately 75 percent of its product is shipped out of Pennsylvania.

Summarizing these operations, the Labor Board concluded that the works in Pittsburgh and Aliquippa "might be likened to the heart of a self-contained, highly integrated body. They draw in the raw materials from Michigan, Minnesota, West Virginia, Pennsylvania, in part through arteries and by means controlled by the respondent; they transform the materials and then pump them out to all parts of the nation through the vast mechanism which the respondent has elaborated."

To carry on the activities of the entire steel industry, 33,000 men mine ore, 44,000 men mine coal, 4,000 men quarry limestone, 16,000 men manufacture coke, 343,000 men manufacture steel, and 83,000 men transport its product. Respondent has about 10,000 employees in its Aliquippa plant, which is located in a community of about 30,000 persons.

. . . .

Practically all the factual evidence in the case, except that which dealt with the nature of respondent's business, concerned its relations with the employees in the Aliquippa plant whose discharge was the subject of the complaint. These employees were active leaders in the labor union. Several were officers, and others were leaders of particular groups. Two of the employees were motor inspectors; one was a tractor driver; three were crane operators; one was a washer in the coke plant, and three were laborers. Three other employees were mentioned in the complaint, but it was withdrawn as to one of them and no evidence was heard on the action taken with respect to the other two.

While respondent criticizes the evidence and the attitude of the Board, which is described as being hostile toward employers and particularly toward those who insisted upon their constitutional rights, respondent did not take advantage of its opportunity to present evidence to refute that which was offered to show discrimination and coercion. In this situation, the record presents no ground for setting aside the order of the Board so far as the facts pertaining to the circumstances and purpose of the discharge of the employees are concerned. Upon that point, it is sufficient to say that the evidence supports the findings of the Board that respondent discharged these men "because of their union activity and for the purpose of discouraging membership in the union." We turn to the questions of law which respondent urges in contesting the validity and application of the Act.

First. The scope of the Act.—The Act is challenged in its entirety as an attempt to regulate all industry, thus invading the reserved powers of the States over their local concerns. It is asserted that the references in the Act to interstate and foreign commerce are colorable, at best; that the Act is not a true regulation of such commerce or of matters which directly affect it, but, on the contrary, has the fundamental object of placing under the compulsory supervision of the federal government all industrial labor relations within the nation. The argument seeks support in the broad words of the preamble (section one) and in the sweep of the provisions of the Act, and it is further insisted that its legislative history shows an essential universal purpose in the light of which its scope cannot be limited by either construction or by the application of the separability clause.

If this conception of terms, intent, and consequent inseparability were sound, the Act would necessarily fall by reason of the limitation upon the federal power which inheres in the constitutional grant, as well as because of the explicit reservation of the Tenth Amendment. *Schechter Corp. v. United States,* 295 U.S. 495, 549, 550, 554. The authority of the federal government may not be pushed to such an extreme as to destroy the distinction, which the commerce clause itself establishes, between commerce "among the several States" and the internal concerns of a State. That distinction between what is national and what is local in the activities of commerce is vital to the maintenance of our federal system.

But we are not at liberty to deny effect to specific provisions, which Congress has constitutional power to enact, by superimposing upon them inferences from general legislative declarations of an ambiguous character, even if found in the same statute. The cardinal principle of statutory construction is to save, and not to destroy. We have repeatedly held that, as between two possible interpretations of a statute, by one of which it would be unconstitutional and by the other valid, our plain duty is to adopt that which will save the act. Even to avoid a serious doubt, the rule is the same. . . .

We think it clear that the National Labor Relations Act may be construed so as to operate within the sphere of constitutional authority. . . .

Thus, in its present application, the statute goes no further than to safeguard the right of employees to self-organization and to select representatives of their own choosing for collective bargaining or other mutual protection without restraint or coercion by their employer.

That is a fundamental right. Employees have as clear a right to organize and select their representatives for lawful purposes as the respondent has to organize its business and select its own officers and agents. Discrimination and coercion to prevent the free exercise of the right of employees to self-organization and representation is a proper subject for condemnation by competent legislative authority. Long ago we stated the reason for labor organizations. We said that they were organized out of the necessities of the situation; that a single employee was helpless in dealing with an employer; that he was dependent ordinarily on his daily wage for the maintenance of himself and family; that, if the employer refused to pay him the wages that he thought fair, he was nevertheless unable to leave the employ and resist arbitrary and unfair treatment; that union was essential to give laborers opportunity to deal on an equality with their employer. *American Steel Foundries v. Tri-City Central Trades Council*, 257 U.S. 184, 209. We reiterated these views when we had under consideration the Railway Labor Act of 1926. Fully recognizing the legality of collective action on the part of employees in order to safeguard their proper interests, we said that Congress was not required to ignore this right, but could safeguard it. Congress could seek to make appropriate collective action of employees an instrument of peace, rather than of strife. We said that such collective action would be a mockery if representation were made futile by interference with freedom of choice. Hence, the prohibition by Congress of interference with the selection of representatives for the purpose of negotiation and conference between employers and employees, "instead of being an invasion of the constitutional right of either, was based on the recognition of the rights of both." . . .

. . . The congressional authority to protect interstate commerce from burdens and obstructions is not limited to transactions which can be deemed to be an essential part of a "flow" of interstate or foreign commerce. Burdens and obstructions may be due to injurious action springing from other sources. The fundamental principle is that the power to regulate commerce is the power to enact "all appropriate legislation" for "its protection and advancement"; to adopt measures "to promote its growth and insure its safety"; "to foster, protect, control and restrain." That power is plenary, and may be exerted to protect interstate commerce "no matter what the source of the dangers which threaten it." Although activities may be intrastate in character when separately considered, if they have such a close and substantial relation to interstate commerce that their control is essential or appropriate to protect that commerce from burdens and obstructions, Congress cannot be denied the power to exercise that control. Undoubtedly the scope of this power must be considered in the light of our dual system of government, and may not be extended so as to embrace effects upon interstate commerce so indirect and remote that to embrace them, in view of our complex society, would effectually obliterate the distinction between what is national and what is local and create a completely centralized government. . . .

That intrastate activities, by reason of close and intimate relation to interstate commerce, may fall within federal control is demonstrated in the case of carriers who are engaged in both interstate and intrastate transportation. There federal control has been found essential to secure the freedom of interstate traffic from interference or unjust discrimination and to promote the efficiency of the interstate service. It is manifest that intrastate rates deal *primarily* with a local activity. But, in rate-making, they bear such a close relation to interstate rates that effective control of the one must embrace some control over the other. Under the Transportation Act, 1920, Congress went so far as to authorize the Interstate Commerce Commission to establish a statewide level of intrastate rates in order to prevent an unjust discrimination against interstate commerce. . . .

. . . When industries organize themselves on a national scale, making their relation to interstate commerce the dominant factor in their activities, how can it be maintained that their industrial labor relations constitute a forbidden field into which Congress may not enter when it is necessary to protect interstate commerce from the paralyzing consequences of industrial war? We have often said that interstate commerce itself is a practical conception. It is equally true that interferences with that commerce must be appraised by a judgment that does not ignore actual experience.

Experience has abundantly demonstrated that the recognition of the right of employees to self-organization and to have representatives of their own choosing for the purpose of collective bargaining is often an essential condition of industrial peace. Refusal to confer and negotiate has been one of the most prolific causes of strife. This is such an outstanding fact in the history of labor disturbances that it is a proper subject of judicial notice, and requires no citation of instances. . . . But with respect to the appropriateness of the recognition of self-organization and representation in the promotion of peace, the question is not essentially different in the case of employees in industries of such a character that interstate commerce is put in jeopardy from the case of employees of transportation companies. And of what avail is it to protect the facility of transportation if interstate commerce is throttled with respect to the commodities to be transported!

These questions have frequently engaged the attention of Congress, and have been the subject of many inquiries. The steel industry is one of the great basic industries of the United States, with ramifying activities affecting interstate commerce at every point. The Government aptly refers to the steel strike of 1919–1920, with its far-reaching consequences. The fact that there appears to have been no major disturbance in that industry in the more recent period did not dispose of the possibilities of future and like dangers to interstate commerce which Congress was entitled to foresee and to exercise its protective power to forestall. It is not necessary again to detail the facts as to respondent's enterprise. Instead of being beyond the pale, we think that it presents in a most striking way the close and intimate relation which a manufacturing industry may have to interstate commerce, and we have no doubt that Congress had constitutional authority to safeguard the right of respondent's employees to self-organization and freedom in the choice of representatives for collective bargaining.

. . . .

The Act has been criticized as one-sided in its application; that it subjects the employer to supervision and restraint and leaves untouched the abuses for which employees may be responsible; that it fails to provide a more comprehensive plan—with better assurances of fairness to both sides and with increased chances of success in bringing about, if not compelling, equitable solutions of industrial disputes affecting interstate commerce. But we are dealing with the power of Congress, not with a particular policy or with the extent to which policy should go. We have frequently said that the legislative authority, exerted within its proper field, need not embrace all the evils within its reach. The Constitution does not forbid "cautious advance, step by step," in dealing with the evils which are exhibited in activities within the range of legislative power. The question in such cases is whether the legislature, in what it does prescribe, has gone beyond constitutional limits.

. . . .

Our conclusion is that the order of the Board was within its competency, and that the Act is valid as here applied. The judgment of the Circuit Court of Appeals is reversed, and the cause is remanded for further proceedings in conformity with this opinion.

Reversed.

301 U.S. 1 (1937).

127 Senator Burton K. Wheeler Opposes President Roosevelt's Court-Packing Scheme

July 9, 1937

When Franklin D. Roosevelt became president in 1933, he launched a series of bold programs designed to speed recovery from the Great Depression. Some of these programs were highly controversial. One, the National Industrial Recovery Act of 1933, was declared unconstitutional by the Supreme Court in 1935. Roosevelt saw the Supreme Court as a major roadblock to implementing the sweeping changes he felt the nation needed to defeat the Depression. With the help of Attorney General Homer S. Cummings, Roosevelt devised a plan to expand the size of the Supreme Court as part of an overall package to reform the judicial branch of government.

Critics of this blatant attempt to fill the Court with justices favorable to Roosevelt's New Deal programs quickly labeled the move a "court-packing scheme." This became the hottest political issue in the nation during the first half of 1937. Members of Congress were disturbed by the plan, not because judicial reform was a bad idea, but because Congress was not consulted in advance. Congressional leaders felt they had been blind-sided by the president, who had not taken them into his confidence on the matter. Senate Majority Leader Joseph T. Robinson (D-Ark.), who was loyal to Roosevelt, pushed the court-packing plan in the Senate and may have succeeded in getting at least part of what Roosevelt wanted when he died suddenly of a heart attack on July 14, 1937, just when debate on the plan was at its peak.

Five days before Robinson's untimely death, Senator Burton K. Wheeler (D-Mont.) delivered a remarkable speech in opposition to the court-packing scheme that placed him at odds with President Roosevelt and his own party. Until that time Wheeler had been a solid supporter of Roosevelt and the New Deal, sponsoring several important pieces of New Deal legislation. His split with the president over court packing played an important role in killing the plan. Just weeks after this speech, and the subsequent death of Majority Leader Robinson, the Senate rejected the court-packing plan.

. . . .

Never before in the history of the Senate of the United States, at least during the 14 or 15 years I have been a Member of it,

have I seen such appeals to the prejudices of the people, to the uninformed, as have been made with reference to this proposed legislation. Never before have I seen on both sides such deep feeling aroused. The reason for it, of course, is that this is a fundamental issue which everyone goes to the very foundation of our Government.

When the bill was first introduced the Attorney General of the United States in a radio speech used this language:

Ladies and gentlemen, only 9 short days have passed since the President sent to the Congress recommendations for the reorganization of the Federal judiciary. Yet in that brief time unfriendly voices have filled the air with lamentations and have vexed our ears with insensate clamor calculated to divert attention from the merits of his proposal.

Why was it that immediately there was aroused such feeling that protests came from the masses of the people of the country against the proposal? It was because they felt that the bill was an attempt on the part of the administration to do by indirection what it did not want to do by direction.

Again, Mr. President, after the appeal was made to the drought-stricken farmers in the Dust Bowl that we must immediately pack the Supreme Court in order to afford relief to those farmers, and after an appeal was made to the flood victims along the Ohio River in order to get them up in favor of the proposal and to cause them to send protests to their Senators who were opposed to it, we found another kind of appeal being made. We found an appeal being made by the Postmaster General of the United States on the ground of party loyalty. He contended that every Democrat ought to support the bill because of party loyalty regardless of its effect upon the Constitution of the United States and regardless of its violation of the spirit of the Constitution.

We heard Mr. Farley saying, "It is in the bag." In another place and at another time he said, "We will let the Senate talk and then we will let the House talk. Then we will call the roll. We have the votes." The press of the country after the last election pronounced Mr. Farley one of the great prognosticators the country had ever seen. Think of it, Mr. President, here in the United States the Postmaster General has said, "We will let the

Senate talk." Certainly our constituents ought to feel very grateful to the Postmaster General for permitting the Members of the Senate of the United States, whom they have elected to office, to speak their minds in the Senate. The constituents of the Members of the House of Representatives ought to feel very grateful to the Postmaster General for condescending to let their Representatives speak with reference to the bill.

Then men were sent into nearly every State in the Union to arouse the labor leaders for the purpose of having them send protests and denunciations of Members of the Senate of the United States who were opposed to the bill. Men were sent into my State. One man was sent there who went to every labor organization in the State. I am told that he was on the Government pay roll. He was seeking to persuade the labor organizations to adopt resolutions not only in favor of the President's bill, but denouncing me. They went even further than that; one of the farm leaders told me that for the first time in his life he was invited to the White House, and it was suggested to him that he should go out and line up the farm organizations in the Northwest against every Member of the House and every Member of the Senate who dared to voice his opposition to the President's bill.

Something has been said about propaganda. We found the Secretary of Agriculture, by the medium of the radio trying to line up the farmers of the country. Why? Not because he knew anything about the Court proposal, not because he was particularly interested in this piece of proposed legislation, but because the Congress of the United States had appropriated money and placed it in his hands to take care of the drought-stricken farmers or those in need of relief; he alone could disburse this money to them, and the implication, of course, was that unless a bill should be passed then the farmers would not be able perhaps to get further appropriations from the Congress.

Then we find the Postmaster General lining up the postmasters throughout the country. We find Mr. Harry Hopkins, of the W.P.A. [Works Progress Administration], on the radio, talking about the Democratic Party and about the Court proposal. Why? Why should the head of Works Progress Administration of the United States be propagandizing and trying to influence the people on relief against Members of the Senate? Hopkins' great influence over relief clients comes from the fact that he disburses money to them. But who appropriated that money? Whose money was it? It was the money of the people of the United States, appropriated by the Congress and turned over to Mr. Hopkins, and yet he is stirring up W. P. A. workers and their dependents against Members of the Senate and Members of the House, and that is the only reason why Hopkins spoke.

That spirit of intolerance with reference to the pending bill has prevailed and pervaded the discussion right down to the present moment. Everyone who does not agree with the administration on this proposal or who disagrees with the Attorney General is denounced as an "economic royalist" and as one who has sold out to Wall Street.

Then we found the same spirit of intolerance prevailing in this chamber yesterday, disclosed by the amazing situation which developed here. When the debate had been proceeding for only a couple of days and the opponents of the bill had not spoken at all, but had merely asked questions of the proponents of the bill who were talking, a practice which has been indulged in by the Senate from time immemorial. when no question of a filibuster was involved at all, but only bona-fide debate on the issues involved in the bill, we were confronted with a sudden appeal for strict application of the rules. Was it because the proponents of the bill are afraid of real debate?

Mr. Farley said, "We have the votes. It is in the bag." If it were "in the bag", why did the proponents desert it? It was deserted and the great prophet of the Democratic party was wrong. They did not have the votes. They do not now have the votes. They do not want the original bill debated because they know that upon legitimate debate they cannot sustain it. They know that while at the outset they undoubtedly had 60 votes in favor of the original bill, which would have added six new Justices to the Supreme Court, after the Members of the Senate heard or read the testimony of those appearing before the Judiciary Committee, and after they had studied the bill, one by one, and then two by two, and then by threes and fours, they deserted that bill, until on the day before yesterday the Democratic leader of the Senate announced that the reason why the proponents of the measure did not try to put forward the other bill was they did not have the votes to pass it. They say they have enough votes at the present time to pass the compromise proposal, and then they appealed to party loyalty. They said to the new Senators who have just been elected, "You ought to vote for this bill because you rode in on the coattails of the President of the United States."

Thank God, I did not ride in on the coattails of the President of the United States! Thank God, I do not have to go to him and ask him whether or not I have to follow the Democratic leader in this new proposal! Those of you who rode in on the coattails of the President of the United States will ride out on the coattails of the President of the United States if that is the only reason you are here.

I did not ride in on the coattails of any President of the United States. I did not come here because I had promised to be 100 percent for the administration and to vote for everything the President wanted.

There are those who were elected to the United States Senate on a platform of "100 percent Roosevelt", but after assuming their seats in this body, when it was politically expedient, they unhesitatingly cast their votes against the administration. Now, however, some such Senators assert that they must vote for this bill because of their campaign promise of supporting the President 100 percent—that pledge is one that they keep or follow, utilize or discard as they deem it politically expedient.

No, Mr. President, I did not come to the Senate on the coattails of anyone; I came to the Senate on my own, and I am responsible for what I do in the Senate. I expect the people of my State to hold me responsible for my actions; and if I go out, I will go out riding on my own coattails and not upon the coattails of anyone else.

Finally, Mr. President, we were told, "If you do not vote for this bill, you will break the President's heart." Oh, dear! What a pity! "You are going to break the President's heart if you do not vote for him on this bill."

If Senators are going to break the President's heart because they do not vote for him on this bill they ought to go back and vote for six new judges instead of voting for the substitute, because we are told that this is not the President's bill. Oh, no; this is not his bill. This is not what the President wanted. He wanted six new judges. And why did he want six new judges? Because some of the proponents of the original bill said, "We cannot trust in less than four judges, and we ought to have six because some of the six might go back on us; but if we cannot get six, the least we will take is four." Finally, however, they have come down and have said, "We do not want six all at one time. That was wrong. That was packing the Court; so now, instead of packing it all at once, we will pack it by slow motion, and we will get the same result."

. . . .

I say now that if a spirit of intolerance is to pervade the Senate, if there is to be an attempt to drive this bill through, if the proponents of the big are going to put pressure on us, if they are going to try to get rough with us, we can get rough as well as they.

The Senator from Kentucky said he had some old dead cats, or something, that he wanted to throw at someone, and intimated that I had said I had some dead cats. Oh, no; he is wrong about that. That is just in line with the intolerance exhibited and the construction other people would put upon my words. But if they have some dead cats they want to throw at me, let them do so. A good many dead cats have been thrown at me; not only dead cats but a lot of other things. Some of which were far worse. [Laughter.]

I do not propose to be intimidated, and the rest of us do not propose to be intimidated, by name callers, or by anyone else, and our opponents might just as well make up their minds to that fact first as last. We are going to have a legitimate debate upon this question before the Senate, regardless of whether Mr. Farley wants us to or whether anybody else wants us to. The country is entitled to it.

. . . .

Mr. HUGHES. Then the objection of the Senator from Montana is not, as I understand, to the purpose of the bill but to the method by which it is sought to effectuate the purpose?

Mr. WHEELER. My contention is that the bill proposes to do something in an unconstitutional way. I want to see the people themselves vote upon the constitutional amendment or upon the proposed; and I say that the people of this country have a right to vote upon such a measure. No President, no Congress, has a right to change the Constitution. When I say that, I say upon the best authority, because I repeat what Presidents of the United States have said, and what the present Attorney General of the United States has said in a speech before

the American Bar Association, to which I shall call the Senate's attention.

Mr. HUGHES. Then, as I understand, the contention of the Senator from Montana is that changing the number of members of the Supreme Court by an act of Congress is changing the Constitution in an unconstitutional way?

Mr. WHEELER. No. Of course, the Congress of the United States has the power to increase the membership of the Supreme Court of the United States.

Mr. HUGHES. Or to decrease it.

Mr. WHEELER. Or to decrease the number of members of the Supreme Court. The Congress of the United States has the power to withhold appropriations for the salaries of the members of the Supreme Court of the United States.

Mr. TYDINGS. Or the salary of the President of the United States.

Mr. WHEELER. Or the salary of the President of the United States; but such would be against the spirit the Constitution. If Senators want to get rid of Mr. Justice Roberts, if Senators want to get rid of Mr. Justice Butler, why do they not do what they can do under the Constitution; that is, refuse to appropriate money to pay the salaries of those Justices? Why do they not do that? Because they know that the people of the United States would not stand for it, and that it would be against the spirit of the Constitution.

Mr. HUGHES. I think I can assure the Senator from Montana that, so far as I am concerned, I would not think of doing any such action with respect to any Justice of the Supreme Court. I would not tear down any Federal institution by denying the necessary support for it. That is as far from my mind as anything possibly can be.

. . . .

Mr. BARKLEY. Mr. President, may I ask the Senator a question in order to clarify the matter?

Mr. WHEELER. Yes.

Mr. BARKLEY. Is it the Senator's contention that under the Constitution the pending bill is unconstitutional?

Mr. WHEELER. Of course, it is constitutional, just as it would be constitutional for the Congress to refuse to appropriate money to pay the salaries of Federal judges. That would be constitutional but it would be against the spirit of the Constitution.

Mr. BARKLEY. Whatever the reasoning and the comparison, the Senator admits that Congress can do this in the way proposed?

Mr. WHEELER. Congress, of course, can refuse to appropriate money for the President of the United States and make it impossible for him to act in the capacity of President. The Congress of the United States can refuse, I repeat, to appropriate the money for Justice Butler, for Justice McReynolds, or for any other Justice of the Supreme Court of the United States by saying that no part of the money appropriated shall be used to pay the salary of a particular Justice.

Mr. BURKE. Mr. President, will the Senator yield there?

Mr. WHEELER. I yield.

Mr. BURKE. On the point raised by the Senator from Kentucky [Mr. Barkley], while it must be admitted that the Constitution leaves it to the Congress entirely to fix the number of the members of the Court, does that necessarily mean that Congress is vested with the authority to turn over to somebody else the right to determine whether the Supreme Court shall consist of 9, 10, 11, or some other number of Justices?

Mr. WHEELER. I wish to consider that point a little later on.

Mr. BURKE. Very well.

Mr. CONNALLY. Mr. President, will the Senator yield for a question?

Mr. BURKE. I yield.

Mr. CONNALLY. In connection with the question of the Senator from Kentucky, let me ask the Senator from Montana a question. The Senator from Kentucky asked if Congress had not the constitutional power to increase the number of judges. Is it not true that Congress has the power to regulate the number of Justices on the Supreme Court for the purpose of making the Court of sufficient size to transact its business and efficiently to dispose of that business, but that Congress has no constitutional power to subtract from or to add to the Court for the purpose of destroying the Court?

Mr. WHEELER. Of course, such an act would be against the spirit of the Constitution. I am sorry the junior Senator from Kentucky [Mr. Logan] is not present, for he said yesterday that the spirit of the Constitution and the letter of the Constitution were the same thing. Let me quote what James Truslow Adams says about that. He says:

To use the letter of the Constitution for a purpose not intended, and subversive to the whole constitutional structure, cannot be considered a constitutional act, although it may be a legal one.

. . . .

Oh, yes, Mr. President, there is a difference between the spirit of the law and the letter of the law. At a hearing a short time ago before the Interstate Commerce Committee when some men came before that committee to testify I said as to certain members of the New York Stock Exchange who were allowing some people to obtain stocks at a price lower than was accorded to the general public that was in the nature of a bribe. They came back saying that it was no violation of the law. I said, "No; it is no violation of the law, but it is morally wrong." So I say it is morally wrong to do by indirection what cannot be done by direction. It is morally wrong to change the Constitution by coercive interpretation. It is morally wrong to put men on the Supreme Court for the express purpose of getting decisions in accordance with the views of Congress or in accordance with the views of the executive department.

I submit that no Senator who really believes in the Constitution of the United States, who believes in a democratic form of government, who believes in and has confidence in the people, can go before his constituents and say, "I did not dare to submit a constitutional amendment to you because I was afraid to trust you. I was afraid you would be corrupted by the 'economic royalists' in Wall Street. I was afraid Mr. Mellon might corrupt the State of Pennsylvania. Therefore I did not care to submit a constitutional amendment to the workers and laborers of Pennsylvania.

. . . .

The minute a Senator is known to be opposed to the President's bill he is denounced as a "defeatist", an "economic royalist", who has sold out to Wall Street. What bigotry! Only those who vote for everything the President wants are liberals. Those whose consciences impel them to disagree even once immediately are "defeatist lawyers" or "economic royalists.". . .

Mr. President, the President did not charge those whose names were mentioned before the Joint Committee on Tax Avoidance with a violation of the letter of the law. He charged them, and the Treasury Department charged them, with having violated the spirit of the law. They were held up and pilloried. I have not any objection to that, but they were pilloried not for breaking the law but for a violation of the spirit of the law doing an illegal act in a legal manner.

We are told that there is great opposition to 5-to-4 decisions. Let us examine that matter for a moment. There is no longer any need for the passage of this bill because of 5-to-4 decisions. There is a vacancy on the Supreme Court. Why has not that vacancy been filled? We all know the reason, and it is not no for me to state it at this time

We do not need to fear 5-to-4 decisions, because we will no longer have them. If the judge to be appointed does not disappoint the proponents of the bill, they can have 6-to-3 decisions, or they can have at least 5-to-4 decisions. The administration can be sure of such decisions on any reasonable proposition. They can be sure of 5-to-4 decisions in their favor. There is no longer any "no man's land." There is no longer any "Mr. Justice Roberts' land." Think what happened when Mr. Justice Van Devanter resigned. Proponents of the bill have been wanting resignations, but when he resigned just think of the statement that was made! "One down and five to go" was the comment made by the Secretary to the President of the United States.

There is a word in use in New England with which many are familiar which describes the sort of discussion that has been taking place on the part of the proponents of the bill, a word that describes it better than any other expression I can think of. That is the word "cheap." It was cheap for the Secretary to the President of the United States to say "One down and five to go", "One down and four to go." It was cheap, Mr. President, for the Postmaster General to say, "We have it in the bag." It was cheap for him to my that he would let the Senate talk; he would let the Congress talk. It was cheap to make the arguments that have been made to intelligent men upon the floor of the Senate. It was cheap, I say, to appeal to Members here and say, "You rode in on the President's coattails, and now you owe it to him to vote as he wants you to vote." It was cheap to say, "You are going to break the President's heart unless you vote for this bill."

What have we come to in this body, when a great issue is before the Senate affecting the Constitution of the United States, affecting the fundamental principles upon which the Government is founded, and Senators are told, "You must vote for the bill because you rode in on the coattails of the President of the United States, and he wants it"? Is that what the people of Mississippi sent the Senator from Mississippi to the Senate for? Were Senators sent here to say "yes", or were they sent here to think?

Mr. President, with reference to 5-to-4 decisions, we are told that we shall have no more of them if this bill is passed. As a matter of fact, under the bill we may not only have 5-to-4 decisions, but we may have 6-to-7 decisions, 7-to-8 decisions, 5-to-5 decisions, or 7-to-7 decisions. What does that mean?

Let me ask my friends who are so bitter against 5-to-4 decisions to consider what may happen under this bill. A district judge out in Podunk declares an act of Congress unconstitutional. The case is appealed directly to the Supreme Court of the United States. The district judge in question, perchance, has been appointed not because of his ability, not because of his legal attainments, but because the Senator wanted him appointed, because he has been the Senator's partner or has been a political friend. He declares the act unconstitutional and the case goes to the Supreme Court. There are 10 members upon the Supreme Court, or 12 members upon the Supreme Court. They divide upon the issue 5 to 5 or 6 to 6. What happens? The decision of the lower court stands. That district judge in Podunk has knocked out the law and held it unconstitutional. There has been no 7-to-5 decision, no 6-to-5 decision; but the single judge out in Podunk, without any legal ability, appointed for purely political reasons, has declared the law unconstitutional and his decision stands. He is the man who ultimately is responsible for its being held unconstitutional—not Roberts, not Hughes, not Brandeis, not Cardozo, not the other Justices, but this judge in Podunk, this judge appointed at the behest of some crooked political boss, perhaps, in one of the great cities of this country that is reeking with political corruption and crookedness.

We are told that that is the constitutional way in which to have the validity of laws of Congress determined; that their constitutionality should be determined not by five men but by one man, and that one man may be a political boss from some corrupt city of the United States.

That is why I have said the substitute bill ought to go back to the committee and be studied. It would not speed up justice, as we were told. It would do nothing of the kind. It would not obviate 5-to-4 decisions. It would result in a condition a thousand times worse than that brought about by 5-to-4 decisions. It would make it possible for cases to be decided by a vote of 7 to 7. It would make it possible for one man, a lower court judge at that, to decide cases; and yet great statesmen want to see that kind of a law placed upon the statute books of the United States. They want to see that kind of a court empowered to pass upon the validity of acts of Congress. That is what they are trying to

force down the throats of the people because they are afraid that if it were not done it might "break the President's heart"!

. . . .

After all, speaking of 5-to-4 decisions, do we want a Supreme Court that simply will agree entirely with our viewpoint? Is that what we want? Let me call attention to the fact that it is out of the clash of opinions that the truth comes. The worse thing that could happen to Congress, the worst thing that could happen to the country, would be to have but one strong political party. We get better legislation in this body because we have a clash of opinions as to proposed legislation. We get better bills out of committees when we have a clash of opinions. The American form of government depends upon the clash of opinions of its people, and not upon a subservient people who are voting as they are told to vote because they are getting hand-outs from the Treasury of the United States.

. . . .

If the contention of those who favor the bill is correct, why have a written Constitution at all? A great many persons in this country think there is not any need for a written Constitution; but why do we have one? We have one, my friends. because my forefathers like the forefathers of most of the Senators, had left foreign shores, where they had seen the tyranny of one-man government in Europe. Some of them had been driven out of England by James I, who said to them, "Unless you conform, I will harass you out of the country"; and he did harass them until they left that country. He drove them to Holland, and then they came to America and settled upon the shores of this great country of ours. They fought the American Revolution; they spilled their blood and many of them died, all up and down the Atlantic seaboard, in order that you and I, their posterity, might have a democratic form of government assured by a written Constitution.

When the framers of the Constitution met in the assembly in Philadelphia, they did not write the Constitution simply to protect themselves, but they remembered some of the things that had occurred before. They remembered the six men of Dorset and the six farm laborers who had assembled for the purpose of petitioning for higher wages, and were banished from England for so doing. So they wrote into the Constitution of the United States a provision that the right of free assemblage should be guaranteed in the United States of America.

They wrote it into the Constitution because those six men were banished from England and sent to Australia. They also wrote into the Constitution that no man should be banished from this country on account of crime. Remembering that Mary, Queen of Scots, before she was beheaded, asked and pleaded that she should be confronted with her accusers, they wrote into the Constitution of the United States that every accused person should be confronted by his accusers, that he should have the right of trial by jury, and that he should have the right to a writ of habeas corpus. They remembered that in European countries the army had been able to enter a man's home and take possession of it; so they wrote into the Constitution of the United States a provision to the effect that no general, no Army officer, no matter whom he might be, in peacetime should be permitted to quarter his troops in the home of a citizen; and if he tried to do so, the citizen could say to him, "Go on down the road."

I might go on and enumerate the other provisions of the Bill of Rights, and say that because of what had been done in Europe the forefathers not only wanted to lay down those principles but they wanted to make those rights inalienable to the people of this country for all time to come.

Oh, but it is said, "What has that to do with the Court-packing bill?" If four men can be put upon the Supreme Bench to override the Constitution of the United States in one particular, they can say as to every other provision of the Constitution of the United States that it shall be inoperative. They can say whatever they choose to say, and make the Bill of Rights become as nothing to the people of this country.

I am told that labor is for the bill and that the farmers are for it. A man was sent out to my State to line up the people. When I went out to Montana, who came out and followed me around to pretty nearly every meeting? The only labor leader who followed me around and made any speeches was the associate editor of the Daily Worker, Mr. Bill Dunn, a man whom I defended some years ago, without charge, when he was indicted for sedition.

He held a meeting and supported the President's proposal in the city of Butte, and in several other places throughout the State. Is he for it because he is for the President of the United States, or is he for it because he believes that it is the first step in tearing down Constitutional government and bringing about a dictatorship?

Mr. President, I say that there is nothing liberal about the proposal before us; there is nothing progressive about it. It has been dressed up in gaudy clothes for the purpose of attracting the fancy of some of the younger generation, who have not given it any serious thought and do not know that the liberties which have become commonplace to us were earned by the lifeblood of our forefathers. Our liberties are so commonplace that few people give any serious consideration to them.

Why should we be zealous about this cause? When we look at world affairs we realize that in Germany in there is a dictator, under whose iron heel are 70,000,000 people. How did be come into power? On what plea did he come into office? He came in under the constitution of Germany. Every step that was taken by him at first was taken in a constitutional way. Mr. Hitler acted "to meet the needs of the times."

Mussolini came into office upon the plea that he would improve economic conditions and he assumed the power of a dictator and abolished the legislative body of Italy and set up his own court, in order that he might "meet the needs of the times" in that country. In every place where a dictatorship has been set up it has been done "in order to meet the needs of the times."

Let me quote Mr. Justice Brandeis. He said:

Experience should teach us to be most on guard to protect our liberty when purposes of government are beneficent. Men born to freedom are naturally alert to repel invasion of their liberty by evil-minded persons. The greatest dangers to liberty lurk in insidious encroachment by men of zeal, well-meaning, but without understanding.

. . . .

I think I stated before upon this floor that the needs of the times are like the shifting sands upon the beach. What may be the needs of the times today may not be the needs of the times tomorrow. If a President comes into office with a great majority behind him, is he going to say, "I have 11,000,000 majority, I have a Congress which is subservient to me, so I am going to increase the members of the Court, because I want men there who are going to decide in accord with the needs of the times"?

There are courts in Germany, there are courts in Italy, there are courts in Russia, and men are placed on them to meet the needs of the times as the dictators see the needs, and those judges do what the dictators want them to do. Can the Democratic Party afford to be placed in the position of saying to the people of this country, "We are going to put men on the Supreme Bench to meet the needs of the times as we see them"?

. . . .

So, my friends, the needs of the times, I repeat, are like shifting sands upon the beach. The needs of the times are one thing today and something else tomorrow. When men are appointed upon the Supreme Court Bench to interpret the Constitution to meet the needs of the times, I say that a step is being taken which is reactionary. A step is being taken which, while it is within the letter of the Constitution, is against the spirit of the Constitution, and I defy anyone who knows the difference between the spirit of the law and the letter of the law to deny that statement.

I think I have once before quoted to this body a statement made by the President of the United States on the question of increasing the Supreme Court of the United States to meet the needs of the times. Why should I be accused of breaking the heart of the President, why should I be accused of being in bad company, when I agree now with the statement which the President of the United States made a few years ago? This is what he said in 1933:

In the face of this congestion the remedy commonly proposed is to add new judges or new courts, but it will readily be seen that, if the problem is what I have stated it to be, such a so-called remedy merely aggravates the complaint. There are, of course, legitimate demands for additional judicial manpower in sections where the population has grown rapidly. But it is easy to see that to apply this remedy in all cases is to add to the ravages of the disease, to contribute to the confusion, and, what is profoundly important at this time, to burden still further an already seriously embarrassed taxpayer.

Senators were told that they rode in on the coattails of the President of the United States and that they ought to support him for that reason; that they ought to support the measure because of party loyalty; that they ought to support the bill be cause some economic royalist disagrees with the President; that they ought to support the measure because some newspaper or some Republican says it is wrong; that they ought to be intimidated and afraid to vote their own convictions. Yes; but who first said that which we who oppose the measure are now saying? The President of the United States, in 1933. When Senators vote against this bill to increase the Supreme Court to "meet the needs of the times", to make it subservient, they are only doing what the President of the United States in 1933 said was the right thing to do. He said it before the Republicans said it. He said it before any of the newspapers he is now criticizing said it. He said it before those now opposed to him in this matter said it. Am I attacking the President of the United States because I am agreeing with what he said in 1933?

Is every Democrat who is opposed to the pending measure trying to break up the Democratic Party because he agrees with what the President said in 1933?

Certainly I want to stand behind the President of the United States. I challenge any Member of the Senate to point to anyone who has stood by the President to a greater degree or tried more earnestly to help secure the enactment of legislation desired by him or supported him in connection with more legislative matters than I have.

It is distressing to have to stand up here and disagree with the President of the United States, with any President of the United States, upon a vital, fundamental issue before the country. Particularly is it distressing for a Senator of the United States to have to stand up and disagree with the President of the United States when he is of his own party. It is even more distressing to me to have to stand up here and disagree with the President of the United States when he has been a personal friend of mine over many years. There is no judgeship dangling before my face, though. [Laughter.] I am not seeking a place upon the circuit court of appeals or upon any other court. The President has been most generous in his treatment of me; he has probably been as friendly to me as he has to any other Member of this body; but there comes a time in the life of every man, whether he was elected on the coattails of the President or not, when his own conscience must tell him whether or not he is going blindly to support the President.

I was the first Member of the Senate to come out openly and espouse Mr. Roosevelt's cause. Where were some of my Democratic colleagues when I was out beating the brush over the country trying to line up delegates in the preconvention campaign? Where were they in Chicago? Where were they after the convention in Chicago? Some of them thought that the lightning was going to strike them in Chicago. [Laughter.]

Not only that, Mr. President, but when some man issues a statement prepared by the Democratic National Committee indicating that I am not a friend of the President of the United States, let me call attention to the fact that I went out to the Chicago convention and spent 10 days there, at my own expense, fighting for Mr. Roosevelt's nomination. I know what went on there; I know what went on on the inside; and I know where every man who is now a Member of the Senate stood in that convention and how he felt with reference to the nomination of Mr. Roosevelt. I know how many of the people who are now on the pay roll of the Government stood at that time, people who now call themselves great liberals. They are liberals only because they think it is popular to be liberal.

Mr. SHIPSTEAD. And it pays.

Mr. WHEELER. And, as the Senator from Minnesota suggests, it pays to be liberal. One can afford to be liberal when he is on the public pay roll.

I know it is being whispered around that Senator Wheeler has changed his economic views; that he has gone back on the President; but I will be fighting the liberal cause when many of the so-called officeholding liberals who are now in Washington will have gone back to the caves of Wall Street to work for the economic royalists.

When does a man become an economic royalist? Does he become one when he fails to support an administration proposal here in Congress? I noticed in this morning's newspapers an item to the effect that the President of the great United States Steel Corporation might be appointed to some diplomatic post. A great liberal; a great progressive! When did he cease to be an economic royalist and become a great progressive liberal? Where were some of these men in 1924? They were supporting the man who they now denounce as the great chief of the Liberty League. Where were they? They were not found espousing the progressive cause at that time, and they will not be found espousing it when it ceases to pay and the patronage stops and the jobs stop and when they cannot get any more projects for their States. Their liberalism continues just as long as they get patronage, pap, and jobs.

Of course, Mr. President, there have been abuses in the Court. I have been one who has disagreed with them, and I expect to disagree with them again, but I am unwilling, on the basis of some specious argument or of some subterfuge that defies the spirit of the Constitution to participate in setting one of the most dangerous precedents that has ever been conceived by this Congress or any other. I am unwilling to go along with a proposal of any kind even if it may be said of me that I am associating with Republicans on the other side.

It is suggested by a Senator near me that half the present Cabinet are Republicans. The Secretary of the Interior went out and made a speech in Chicago in which he referred to "pseudo liberals" and said something about Democrats. I have always had a high regard for the Secretary of the Interior, but it ill behooves him to talk about Democrats and to say anything about somebody trying to break up the Democratic Party or to destroy the Democratic Party. I do not like to become personal in matters of this kind, but when men try to malign others because they disagree with them I say they have no business doing it; they have no business spending the money of the National Democratic Party or the Federal Government to malign Members of the Congress who do not happen to agree upon one issue with the President of the United States.

The bill now pending just does not provide properly for doing what the President wants to do. I give all due credit to the President of the United States for the great things he has accomplished and done since 1933.

. . . .

So, Mr. President, we find George Washington, Andrew Jackson, Abraham Lincoln, Thomas Jefferson, and all the other great leaders denouncing such a proposal and we find George Washington using the word "usurpation." Yet it has been said that this bill proposes simply an "infusion" of new blood. I say it is not merely an infusion of new blood, but it is a transfusion of blood, and that transfusion of blood into the Court will only add confusion to the Nation and to our people. The proponents of the bill want a transfusion of blood, and they want that blood which is to be transfused to match their own blood. . . .

The Senator from Kentucky [Mr. Logan] said the other day that what is wanted is not a Court which believes in the views of Thomas Jefferson, not a Court which believes in the principles of Andrew Jackson, but a Court which believes in the principles of Alexander Hamilton and John Marshall. I have not any objection. I heartily agree that whether we want it or not we are going to have a more centralized government in the city of Washington. We all dislike bureaucracy, and every administration goes out in the campaign and denounces bureaucracy, but each and every one adds to that bureaucracy. Why is that done? It is because of the concentration of wealth that is going on, and because the State legislatures cannot possibly regulate many of the great corporations; so it has to be done by the Federal Government here in Washington. I dislike it, and everybody else dislikes it; but it is not a question of what we like. It is a matter that is going to be forced on the people of the country by the economic conditions which have developed.

But when we want to amend the Constitution, let us not amend it by subterfuge. Let us do it in the way that every great President of the United States including Washington, Jefferson, Jackson, and Wilson has said it should be done. Let us do it under the Constitution. Let us have the amendment submitted to the people of the country. Let us have a vote upon it by the people. Let us not be afraid of it.

It was my recollection that the Attorney General of the United States, somewhere in one of his speeches, stated that the Supreme Court needed an infusion of new blood, or something to that effect, because of the age of the members of the Court, or that the courts of the country in general needed such an infusion. Nobody has stood upon the door of the Senate, however, and said that any man upon the Supreme Bench is incompetent because of his age.

Mr. MCCARRAN. Mr. President, will the Senator yield?

Mr. WHEELER. I yield.

Mr. MCCARRAN. Does the Senator realize the difference between the terms "new blood" and "young blood", as used interchangeably by the President and by the Attorney General and others in discussing this subject? I should like very much to have the Senator express himself on that subject.

Mr. WHEELER. I thank the Senator. I assume that the Senator's interruption is in the nature of a question.

Mr. MCCARRAN. I assumed that it was.

The PRESIDING OFFICER. The Chair understands that the Senator from Nevada asked a question.

Mr. WHEELER. In these technical days I desire to be careful that the interruptions are questions. The question was, as I understood the Senator from Nevada, whether a distinction had been made between "new blood" and "young blood."

First, I wish to continue and say that no one has said that any man upon the Supreme Bench is incompetent by reason of his age; that he is mentally incapacitated. I do not think any man, not even the Senator from Pennsylvania [Mr. Guffey], would charge that Chief Justice Hughes is mentally incompetent by reason of age. I do not think he would charge that Mr. Justice Butler, or Mr. Justice Sutherland, or Mr. Justice Brandeis—who is 80 years old—is mentally incompetent because of his age.

If none of them are mentally incompetent because they have reached a certain age, why say anything about age at the present time? Why try to put them off the Supreme Bench because they are 70 or more years of age, or to put somebody in their place to help them out because they have reached the age of 70 years? And then why change the age limit to 75 years?

Mr. MCCARRAN. Mr. President—

The PRESIDING OFFICER. Does the Senator from Montana yield to the Senator from Nevada?

Mr. WHEELER. I yield.

Mr. MCCARRAN. I rise to a point of order.

The PRESIDING OFFICER. The Senator will state the point of order.

Mr. MCCARRAN. The interpretation of the rules has been invoked in the Senate. May a Senator rise during the course of discussion by another Senator and ask a third Senator a question?

Mr. ROBINSON. Mr. President—

Mr. MCCARRAN. I asked for a ruling by the Chair. I did not ask for a ruling by the leader.

Mr. WHEELER. Under the rule the Senator from Arkansas has invoked, I am afraid I should not be permitted to let him answer the question.

The PRESIDING OFFICER. The Senator from Montana has the floor. Does he yield to the Senator from Arkansas?

Mr. WHEELER. I refuse to yield except for a question. That rule was expressly invoked by the Senator from Arkansas, and I invoke it upon the Senator from Arkansas.

Mr. ROBINSON. That is so. [Laughter.]

The PRESIDING OFFICER (Mr. Duffy in the chair). The Chair thinks the point of order is in the nature of a parliamentary inquiry. In answer to the query of the Senator from Nevada, the present occupant of the Chair will say that a Senator having the floor may not yield for that purpose.

Mr. McCARRAN. In other words, am I to understand the Chair to rule that, though the Senator from Montana has asked the Senator from Pennsylvania a question which the Senator from Pennsylvania has refused to answer, another Senator may not ask the question through the Senator having the floor?

The PRESIDING OFFICER. The present occupant of the Chair believes that the Senator having the floor may not yield for that purpose.

Mr. WHEELER. Mr. President, I was saying that no Member of the Senate of the United States has stood up here in his place and contended for one moment that any member of the present Supreme Court is either unfit or unable to carry on the duties of his office. If it is desired to put men off the Court merely because they are aged, why not point out some man on the Supreme bench who is incapable of performing his duty? If there is no man on the Supreme Bench who is incapable of performing his duty by reason of age, no man there but who can carry on, no man there but who has ability and is able to carry on, why hold them up to scorn before the country? Why humiliate them? Why hold them up before the people of the United States and say, "We want to put another man on the Supreme Bench in Mr. Hughes' place because Mr. Hughes is an aged politician. He ran for President of the United States of America on the Republican ticket"?

What Democrat is there in this body who can go before his people and say, "I wanted to put somebody on the Supreme Bench alongside Mr. Hughes because Mr. Hughes is a politician, because he ran for the Presidency of the United States on the Republican ticket"? Stand up in your place and answer if there is one.

Mr. Justice Brandeis is the oldest man upon the Supreme Bench. He is 80 years of age. For weeks the confirmation of Mr. Justice Brandeis was opposed in this body because he was known as a liberal when he was appointed by President Wilson. A bitter fight was made against him because he was looked upon as a great fighter for the liberal cause, and a determined effort was made to prevent the confirmation of his nomination. He had been fighting for the liberal cause in Massachusetts and throughout the Nation, uncovering the corruption in the old Ballinger case in the Interior Department, fighting the United Shoe Machinery Co. monopoly in the State of Massachusetts, which affected every single little manufacturer in that State and in the other New England States, fighting on the side of the ordinary man, the poor man. He was known as the people's lawyer of the State of Massachusetts. He defended, without pay, men charged with crime. He took up, without compensation or thought of compensation, the defense of the under dog from one end of the country to the other. Since he has been a member of the Supreme Court of the United States he has written more dissenting liberal opinions in favor of the masses of the people than has any other Justice, and now the Democratic Party, because it has the power, wants to humiliate him.

Mr. CONNALLY. Mr. President, will the Senator yield for a question?

The PRESIDING OFFICER. Does the Senator from Montana yield to the Senator from Texas?

Mr. WHEELER. I yield.

Mr. CONNALLY. I desire to ask the Senator a hypothetical question. If the Senator from Montana wanted to remove from the Supreme Court Mr. Justice Butler, Mr. Justice McReynolds, and Mr. Justice Sutherland, but did not care anything about removing Mr. Justice Brandeis, how would he remove those three unless he also removed Mr. Justice Brandeis at the same time?

Mr. WHEELER. I am glad the Senator asked me that question. It is not desired to get Mr. Justice Brandeis off the Bench. The Democratic Party does not want to get him off the Bench. The President does not want to get him off the Bench. Of course, they do not want to humiliate him. The men they want to get off the Bench are Justices Butler, McReynolds, Sutherland, and Hughes. The way the proponents of the bill could do it, if they dared to do it, would be to say, "No part of the appropriation contained in the appropriation bill shall be used to pay the salaries of these men", and just refuse to appropriate money for them, but they do not dare do that. They cannot reduce their salaries, but Congress has the power to refuse to appropriate money for the salary of the President of the United States, for the executive branch, and for the judicial branch. That would be within the Constitution; it would be constitutional, but it would be against the spirit of the Constitution, and it would be immoral to attempt to do it. In trying to get Chief Justice Hughes and other Justices off the Bench, in trying to humiliate them, those behind the pending bill are willing to humiliate a great liberal, and to do it in the name of liberalism in the United States, to do it in the name of progressivism, to do it under the guise of an attempt to do something for the people of the United States.

I am not surprised that someone should say, "A plague on both your houses." Shakespeare used that phrase in Romeo and Juliet. He did not apply it to a labor organization, however, or to a steel trust.

Mr. President, this proposal is not urged on account of the age of the Justices; it is not urged because they are not up with their work. The Solicitor General says they are up with their work, and Chief Justice Hughes in his letter to me pointed out beyond contradiction that the Supreme Court was current with its work, and that the Court never adjourned until every case that was ready for trial had been argued. So that is not the reason. The bill is not urged because the Judges refuse to hear six or seven hundred petitions for writs of certiorari. It is not urged because they denied petitions for certiorari filed by poor people, for, as I pointed out once before, it is not the poor people who apply to the Supreme Court for such writs. It is not the poor man, it is not the farmer whose cattle are killed by the North Western trains, or the Southern trains, or the Seaboard Air Line trains. He goes into the Federal district court and sues the company and obtains a judgment against it for the loss of his stock, or damage to his stock. The railroad employee working upon the road sues for damages in the Federal court, or some man sues because he is run over by a train at a grade crossing. He goes into the Federal court and obtains a judgment in that court.

Who appeals? It is the railroad companies which appeal. They are the ones who want delay; they are the ones who have the long purse. They lose in the district court, and in the circuit court of appeals the judgment is affirmed. When it is affirmed, the railroad company files a petition for a writ of certiorari, and the Supreme Court denies the petition. It says, "You have had your day in court in the district court, and you have had your day in court in the circuit court of appeals." So it is not the poor individual, ninety-nine times out of a hundred, who goes to the Supreme Court with a petition for writ of certiorari. Any trial lawyer who has had any experience knows that what I state is accurate.

Now, let us take the other side. A stockman or a farmer loses his case before a jury. Nine times out of 10 he does not appeal the case to the circuit court of appeals because he has not the money, and his lawyer cannot afford to take the appeal. Assume he does finally raise sufficient money to appeal to the circuit court of appeals, and he loses there. Does he file a petition for a writ of certiorari with the Supreme Court? I challenge anyone to look at the records of the Supreme Court and find where a workingman, or a farmer, or a widow, or an orphan has petitioned the Supreme Court for a writ of certiorari to bring up a case decided against him in the circuit court of appeals. Such cases will not be found, because they are not there.

So when there is an appeal to the prejudices of the American public, when there is an effort to make them think their representatives here are pleading in the interest of the poor and downtrodden widow, when there is talk about delay, it will be found that the denial of such petitions by the Supreme Court has meant speeding up the litigation in this country rather than delaying it. Whoever advised the President on this subject did not know very much about the practice of law in the Federal courts or he never would have written such a letter. I am not condemning the President. I say that he has been misinformed and misadvised with reference to this whole subject. In the very nature of things he has to depend upon advisers, and he has gotten some very poor advice in this matter. Someone lost some cases and was disappointed. Is the Congress of the United States to wreak its vengeance upon individual members of the Supreme Court of the United States because laws have not been construed as we should like to have them construed? Others may take such a course, but I shall not be a party to it.

Mr. President, there is nothing to the argument about the law's delay, so far as the Supreme Court of the United States is concerned; nothing to the charge that the Court is back in its work; nothing to the contentions about age and liberalism, because some of the most liberal men upon the Supreme Court are the oldest, and some of the most liberal men in this body have been the oldest Members of the Senate. I recall that the senior Senator La Follette once said to me that he was more progressive and more liberal in the latter days of his life than he was in the earlier days. Who are looked upon as about the most liberal men in this body? There is the senior Senator from Nebraska [Mr. Norris], one of the oldest men in the body; there is the Senator from California [Mr. Johnson]; there is the Senator from Idaho [Mr. Borah] all looked upon as great liberals and great progressives. The idea of saying that because one is old he shall be proscribed!

Mr. President, in this country no party can survive if it is based upon political bigotry, and no party should survive that bases its existence upon an effort to proscribe men because of their age. No true liberal proscribes a man on account of his race, his color, his creed, or his age; and that is what is being sought by the pending bill.

I have not always agreed with Chief Justice Hughes. I voted against the confirmation of his nomination, as did a great many others. I made a mistake in so voting. I think Mr. Hughes will go down in history as a great Chief Justice. . . .

Mr. President, I saw a Republican landslide in 1920. I saw another Republican landslide in 1924. I saw another Republican landslide in 1928. I saw an overwhelming majority of Republicans in both branches of the Congress of the United States. I saw Mr. Harding come in as President when he thought he had a mandate from the people of the country, and when he had the support of both branches of the Congress. Such a thing may happen again, and it may happen that some of the Members of the Senate who have been appealed to because they came in on the coattails of a Democratic President will go out on the coattails of a Democratic President.

Mr. President, Mr. Harding put Mr. Daugherty in as Attorney General of the United States. Suppose we now set a precedent and say, "Because we have the power, we are going to pack the Supreme Court to get the decisions we want." What would an incoming Republican administration be justified in doing? They would be justified in saying, "You fellows put judges on the bench to make the Court subservient to you, in order to get favorable decisions, and we will do the same thing. We will add to the membership of the Court in order that we may have favorable decisions. Instead of making the membership of the Court 15, we will make it 20. We will reduce the age from 75 to 70 or 65, in order to get rid of the men you have placed on the bench."

What would every progressive, what would every liberal in this body do? They would be standing on their feet denouncing a Harding or a Hoover or anybody else who would propose such a thing. They would say, "You are destroying the Constitution. You are setting up dictatorial powers." They would make the strongest possible arguments against such action, and in what they would say they would be truthful and honest.

. . . .

I could go on, Mr. President, but I do not wish to take up the time of the Senate any longer, except to say that I resent certain statements which have been made, not so far as I am concerned, because whatever is said about me makes little difference. I have had so many things said about me so many times that accusations, whatever they may be, roll off me very easily. But I do resent that some of my colleagues in the Senate of the United States who have supported the President loyally, who have campaigned for him, who have fought for him, should be denounced as desiring to destroy the President of the United States by some paid public officials who never have had to go out and fight a battle before the people of the country themselves, who could not be elected dog catcher in their own community if they had to run for such an office. Yet they set themselves up and denounce Members of the Senate and Members of the other House and break into the public press or go out and make speeches before our constituents against us because we have the temerity to vote our own honest convictions upon public questions confronting the American people.

. . . .

Mr. President, in closing I say that we cannot afford to set such a precedent as the enactment of the pending measure would set. We cannot afford to denounce the members of the Supreme Court and hold them up to ridicule when they are carrying on and voting their honest convictions, whether we agree with them or whether we do not.

The distinguished Senator from Indiana said the members of the Supreme Court are themselves packing the Supreme Court. Well, they were appointed for life. Can the Senator look into their innermost souls and say they are only staying on the Supreme Court in order to pack it? Can the Senator look into the soul and read the mind of Justice Brandeis and say he is staying on the Court because he wants to pack it in favor of the President, and that Justice Hughes wants to stay on the Court in order to pack it in favor of or against the President? I should like to have the Senator tell me how he knows that Justice Sutherland is staying on the Court just to vote against the President. I should like to have him tell me how he knows any one of the present Justices are remaining on the Court in order to pack the Court against the President of the United States. Let the Senator write that down in his notebook and tell me how he knows it when his time comes.

Mr. President, one by one the arguments with reference to the six-man bill were demolished until there was an overwhelming majority in the Senate against that bill, and nobody at heart was for it. Everyone knows that what I am saying is true. So, no one at heart is for the pending bill, because, as everyone knows, it merely provides a slow packing process. As a matter of fact, if I had to choose between packing the Court with six Justices and the method proposed by this bill, I would prefer to pack it with the six at once rather than to pack it in the way which is now proposed. To pack the Court is the reason for the pending bill; and, if we are going to do it, let us put on the six men at once.

We were told there would be no compromise; that we would have to vote it up or vote it down; that no compromise suggestion would be listened to, and that it was "in the bag."

We are now told that the proponents of the measure have got the votes and they are going to try to jam it through. They are going to shut off debate. They have invoked an old rule that I have never before seen invoked in this body during the first 2 or 3 days of debate on a measure, a rule that is violated all the time by every Member of the Senate with impunity. Yet we are told that the proponents of the measure are going to try to force us, pound us, knock the bill down our throat, if you please, in order to put it through. Well, those who are opposed to it will not be the losers if the supporters of the bill should succeed in passing it. The only man who can lose in a fight of that kind is the President of the United States himself.

As I have previously said, I give the President all credit for the great things he has accomplished during the last 4 years for the people of this Nation. We have given him more power than any President of the United States has ever had in peacetime or in war. He has powers that no other President ever had. We delegated to him the power to issue currency and to fix and regulate the value thereof.

He can raise or lower the gold content of the dollar. He can issue $3,000,000,000 of currency. He can remonetize silver up to 16 to 1. He has $2,000,000,000 with which he can buy German marks, British bonds, French francs, or Japanese yen, or take any other course he may desire for the purpose of stabilizing our currency. He can raise or lower the tariff on practically everything that is produced in the United States. He can close the stock markets for a period of 30 days. We have just given him $1,500,000,000 for relief purposes, and he has wide discretionary power in its distribution. We have given him the power to say to the farmers of the country, "We will give you money for not producing crops", and $500,000,000 has been provided for that purpose. He can say to them, "Let this piece of land lie fallow and we will pay you for not planting it." We have given him the power over the economic life and destiny of the American people. He has a substantially subservient Congress. No man in the history of the United States, not even the Father of his Country, ever had reposed in him such vast and extraordinary power. We have given him the power to declare war. We have given him a power over treaties never given to any other President of the United States. He can say to one community, Denver for instance, "I will give you money for a project in your city", or he can say, "I will deny a project to your city." He has the power to say, "I will build a project in Houston, Tex., but I will deny a project to some other place in Texas."

He has a right to say to the people of the State of Illinois or the people of the city of Chicago, "I will build that parkway in your State or that subway in the city of Chicago at the behest of the political bosses of your city, or I will deny it at their behest." He has the right to say the same thing to the city of New York. I am not complaining. Conditions in the country were such that we had to give him that power and I am not complaining about the way he has used it.

But with a subservient Congress, with such tremendous power in the Executive, has not the time come in this Nation when we should say there is a line beyond which no man should pass? Has not the time come when we should say, "No matter how beloved you may be, no matter how profound and wonderful you may be, no matter how much your sympathies are with the masses of the people of the United States, no matter what you want to do, the time has come when we should say there is a line beyond which, under this American

Government of ours and under our Constitution, no man shall pass."

. . . .

Congressional Record, Senate, 75th Congress, 1st session, July 9, 1937, 6966–6981.

128   A Report on Un-American Activities (The Dies Committee)

1939

During the 1920s and 1930s Congress occasionally investigated real or imagined subversive activities of individuals and organizations whose views ran counter to prevailing mainstream political and religious thought in America. In the aftermath of the Russian Revolution of 1917 and the end of World War I, some members of Congress made careers of fighting alien ideologies that they and many of their constituents felt were undermining American values. Chief among these was Bolshevism, or Soviet Communism. The years between the World Wars also saw a great influx of immigrants, who some saw as a threat to America's Anglo-Saxon roots.

Among those in Congress who made a career of fighting unlimited immigration and alien ideologies was Martin Dies Jr. (D-Texas), who entered Congress for the first time in 1931. From his seat on the House Immigration and Naturalization Committee he introduced numerous bills to restrict immigrants or to deport members of the Communist Party who were not citizens. Most of his efforts failed to become law. Some managed to pass the House, only to be defeated in the Senate. A conservative Democrat, Dies opposed organized labor and saw Franklin Roosevelt's New Deal as a program that fostered alien ideas and socialist experiments.

In 1938 Dies became chairman of a special committee to investigate Un-American activities and propaganda. At first it appeared that the investigation would target Nazi propaganda and anti-Semitism from extremist German groups supporting Adolf Hitler. But the committee's real agenda was to investigate the Communist Party in America and its relationship to organized labor and the New Deal.

Opposition to the creation of the Special Committee on Un-American Activities came from New Deal supporters and members who defended civil liberties. Maury Maverick (D-Texas) and John M. Coffee (D-Wash.) argued that deciding what was "Un-American" would be such an arbitrary exercise that it was bound to threaten free speech. But the House voted in favor of the committee and Dies became its chairman. Chairman Dies promised the committee would not smear individuals nor allow its investigations to become a three-ring circus. Events proved him wrong.

The Dies Committee investigations became increasingly sensational and focused on New Deal programs such as the Federal Theater Project, supposedly a hot-bed of Communists and free

thinkers who promoted such radical ideas as interracial dating. Supporters of the New Deal frequently became targets of the committee's investigations. Governor Frank Murphy of Michigan, a New Deal backer, was defeated for reelection after the Dies Committee investigated his role in labor unrest in Michigan, and unfairly portrayed him as a Communist dupe.

The first report of the Dies Committee issued in 1939 is a good indicator of the thinking of the chairman and his committee regarding alien threats to America. More significantly, the public and the press as well as most members of Congress responded favorably to the report. The consensus of public opinion was that subversive activities and alien propaganda were a real challenge that had to be met.

The problem that plagued the Dies Committee was how to investigate serious matters in an objective, bipartisan manner that protected individuals and organizations from unfair smear tactics and protected their constitutional rights under the First Amendment. In this regard the Dies Committee and its permanent successor, the House Un-American Activities Committee (HUAC), failed miserably (see document 134). These two committees represent the darkest chapter in the history of investigations conducted by the House of Representatives. The House has never allowed the full story of the work of these committees to be told. Researchers now have access to the Dies Committee records, but they are still denied access to most of the voluminous records of the HUAC, which remain sealed at the National Archives.

. . . .

II. WHAT ARE UN-AMERICAN ACTIVITIES?

(A) Americanism Defined

In order to determine what activities and propaganda are un-American, we must first define Americanism. No scientific definition will be attempted, but we will undertake to set forth in simple and understandable language what some of the chief principles of Americanism are. In the first place, Americanism is the recognition of the truth that the inherent and fundamental rights of man are derived from God and not from governments, societies, dictators, kings, or majorities. This basic principle of

Americanism is expressed in the Declaration of Independence, where our immortal forefathers said that all men are created equal and that they are endowed by their Creator with certain inalienable rights, chief among which are life, liberty, and the pursuit of happiness. From this declaration and the well-established interpretations that have been put upon it from the beginning of the Republic sown to the present moment, it is clear that Americanism recognizes the existence of a God and the all-important fact that the fundamental rights of man are derived from God and not from any other source. Among these inalienable rights which are the gifts of man from his Creator are: (1) Freedom of worship; (2) freedom of speech, (3) freedom of press; (4) freedom of assemblage; (5) freedom to work in such occupation as the experience, training, and qualifications of a men may enable him to secure and hold; (6) freedom to enjoy the fruits of his work, which means the protection of property rights; (7) the right to pursue happiness with the necessity implication that he dies not harm or injure others in the pursuit of this happiness. Upon this basic principle, the whole structure of the American Government was constructed. The system of checks and balances in the Constitution was wisely conceived and ingeniously constructed to provide every possible guaranty that every citizen of the United States would enjoy and retain his God-given rights. First, the Federal Government was specifically enjoined from exercising any power that was not expressly or by necessity implication granted to it in the Constitution. Second, such powers as the Federal Government was authorized to wield were wisely distributed between the three great departments, the executive the legislative, and the judicial. The essence of Americanism is therefore class, religious, and racial tolerance. It should be emphasized in the strongest language possible that the maintenance of these three forms of tolerance is essential to the preservation of Americanism. They constitute the three great pillars upon which our Constitutional Republic rests, and if any one of these pillars is destroyed, the whole structure of the American system of government will crumble to the earth. Therefore, the man who advocates class hatred is plainly un-American even if he professes racial and religious tolerance. The converse of this proposition is equally true. It is as un-American to hate one's neighbor [if] he has more of this world's material goods as it is to hate him because he was born into another race or worships God according to a different faith.

The American Government was established to guarantee the enjoyment of these fundamental rights. It therefore follows that in America the Government is the servant of the people. The rights of the people are protected through laws and their strict enforcement. For this reason, law and order are essential to the preservation of Americanism while lawlessness and violence are distinctly un-American.

Americanism means the recognition of the God-given rights of man and the protection of those rights under the Constitution through the instrumentality of an independent Congress, an untrammelled judiciary, and a fair and impartial Executive operating under the American system of checks and balances.

Americanism likewise means the protection of an unorganized majority from an organized minority as well as the protection of a helpless minority from an inconsiderate and thoughtless majority.

The characteristic which distinguishes our Republic from the dictatorships of the world is not majority rule but the treatment of minorities. Dictatorships muster huge majorities at the polls, through intimidation and high-powered government propaganda, but these majorities are used for ruthless tyranny over minorities. The majority rule of the American form of government is distinguished by its recognition of certain rights of minorities which majorities cannot alienate.

All of these definitions of Americanism are based upon the Declaration of Independence and the Constitution.

(b) Americanism Contrasted with Communism, Fascism, and Nazi-ism

The simplest and at the same time the most correct definition of communism, fascism, and nazi-ism is that they all represent forms of dictatorship which deny the divine origin of the fundamental rights of man. Since all of these forms of dictatorship deny the divine origin of the rights of man, they assume and exercise the power to abridge or take away any or all of these rights as they see fit. In Germany, Italy, and Russia, the state is everything; the individual nothing. The people are puppets in the hands of the ruling dictators. Rights which we have come to regard as elementary, such as freedom in its sevenfold aspect, either do not exist or if they do exist to any degree are subject to the whims and caprice of the ruling dictators. In all of these countries where these philosophies of government hold sway, the citizen has no rights that the government is required to respect or protect. While the foundation of Americanism is class, racial, and religious tolerance, and the foundation of nazi-ism and fascism is racial and religious hatred, the foundation of communism is class hatred. Americanism is a philosophy of government based upon the belief in God as the Supreme Ruler of the Universe; nazi-ism, fascism, and communism are pagan philosophies of government which either deny, as in the case of the communist, or ignore as in the case of the fascist and nazi, the existence and divine authority of God. Since nazi-ism,. Fascism, and communism are materialistic and pagan, hatred is encouraged. Since Americanism is religious, tolerance is the very essence of its being.

. . . .

VI. SUMMARY OF FINDINGS

While it is true that our committee has only scratched the surface of the un-American and subversive activities of those who are invading America with their alien ideologies, it is also true that we have received abundant evidence to support the following findings with reference to the Communist Party:

It is an integral part of a world revolutionary movement for proletarian internationalism.

It is under direct control of the Third International which has its headquarters in Moscow.

It looks upon Russia as the "fatherland of the revolutionary workers," and cannot claim, therefore, any degree of loyalty to the American form of government.

Whereas it once employed the frank slogan of the "Defense of the Soviet Union," it works today to embroil this country in a foreign war by the propagation of the doctrine of "collective security."

It seeks ultimately the overthrow of the American form of government as established by the Constitution of the United States.

It aims to set up a dictatorship of the proletariat in this country, notwithstanding its present tactical silence on this fundamental tenet of communism.

It rests upon brutal violence despite its present dishonest profession of belief in the processes of democracy.

It is bound by no ordinary ethical limitations in seeking to advance its program.

It aims at the complete confiscation of private property in the means of production, including the socialization of the land.

It hides behind civil liberties in pursuing ends which will destroy civil liberties for all but the ruling few of the proletarian dictatorship.

It works on the principles of leverage in accomplishing its purposes, depending not upon a majority of voters but upon highly disciplined minority.

It is energetically applying the Trojan Horse tactic of penetrating other organizations for the purpose of seeking to control them or, failing that, to destroy them.

It is unusually active in our schools, both openly and subtly insinuating its propaganda into the minds of the students.

It is boring from within the two major political parties.

During the next 2 years, it will concentrate much of its effort in the formation of a national farmer-labor party which will seek to dominate.

It is the enemy of all forms of religion and looks upon faith in God as an out worn superstition.

It is, nevertheless, doing its utmost to make inroads into numerous religious organizations.

In the masquerade of science, it offers the most unscientific approach to human problems which the world has seen since the Dark Ages.

It stifles the creative impulses of the individual by its deadening regimentation.

It is basically a philosophy of hatred which seeks to promote class war.

It is boring from within labor unions on a wide scale, seeking to dominate or wreck the unions for purposes that are alien to the interests of organized wage earners.

It deliberately provokes violence in labor disputes for the purpose of training a revolutionary group in the tactics of civil war.

It seeks to sabotage and cripple our economy on every possible front, with a view to its profiting by the resulting economic crises.

It alines itself with every crack-pot scheme to undermine our system of free enterprise and private initiative.

It has penetrated the Government itself, with the result that some Communists hold key positions in Federal agencies and projects.

It has induced and financed many volunteers to go from this country to fight on the side of the Spanish Loyalist Government.

It aims to incite race war by its special agitation among the Negro population of this country.

It fears to have the spotlight of publicity turned upon its real aims and methods, and will stop at nothing to discredit, if possible, those who fearlessly expose its program and activities.

It seeks to silence all hostile criticism by charging its critics with red-baiting, while, at the same time, it viciously baits those who dare to oppose it.

It resorts to organized campaigns of character assassination wherever the charge of red-baiting dies not suffice to silence its critics.

It tries to exploit any existing discontent for the purpose of building a revolutionary movement which has nothing to do with the solving of the problems from which discontent arises.

It dangles the promise of economic security before the victims of economic distress, offering them a new slavery in the name of emancipation.

It systematically and deliberately deceives many of our people by the use of high-sounding names for organizations which profess laudable objectives, but which, underneath, are designed solely to advance the cause of communism.

It exercises extensive influence among several millions in this country through a device known as the united front.

It persuades thousands of careless or innocent Americans to lend their names for the propaganda purposes of the Communist Party.

It employs numerous "fellow travelers" who outnumber its card-carrying membership, and by the use of these "fellow travelers" extends its influence into organizations and institutions of every description.

Finally, it is diametrically opposed to the principles of Americanism, as set forth in the Constitution and the Declaration of Independence. . . .

VII. RECOMMENDATIONS

Although this committee has worked continuously since the adjournment of Congress and has done everything within its power to get as many facts as possible to the people we have only skimmed the surface. We were able only to hold brief hearings in New York and Detroit. We were urged to conduct hearings in many other cities, such as Chicago, Philadelphia, Pittsburgh, Minneapolis, Milwaukee, Birmingham, Atlanta, New Orleans, San Antonio, Los Angeles, San Francisco, Seattle, and Portland, but due to limited time and funds we were unable to comply with these requests. We had hoped and planned to conduct extensive hearings on the west coast because the evidence before the committee indicates that this area ranks first in the extent of un-American activities and propaganda. We received numerous letters from citizens and public officials in the west coast area urging us to hold hearings there. We have approximately 150 witnesses in the west coast section that should have been heard. However, due to lack of funds we were unable to devote any extensive consideration to west coast activities of Communist, Nazi, and Fascist groups. The situation is so serious on the west coast that it would require 6 months of preparatory investigation before a committee would be ready to conduct hearings, and it is probably that hearing would last 3 or 4 months.

Not only were we unable to investigate un-American activities and propaganda in many important sections of the country, but as a matter of fact, we found it impossible to investigate many of the important phases of un-American activities. Even as to those that we did investigate, we only scratched the surface.

In view of the foregoing, we do not think that the investigation has proceeded far enough to justify us in recommending legislation to Congress. We need and can secure much more information not only from sections of the country that we have investigated but also from the larger areas that we have not even touched before recommending legislation to Congress. Even after we are supplied with full and complete information and facts several months of consideration must be devoted to the question of legislation. This will require expert assistance and thorough research.

It is our recommendation that the House of Representatives adopt a resolution continuing this committee and investigation

for a period of 2 years, and that the House of Representative place at the disposal of the committee not less than $150,000; that the committee continue its investigation along nonpartisan and courageous lines because any investigation conducted along any other line would be more harmful than helpful; that unless the committee is supplied with adequate funds upon the definite understanding that the investigation shall continue along nonpartisan lines, without regard to any other question except the discovery of truth, the investigation should not be continued. No individual or organization engaged in un-American activities should be shielded because of political expediency. The Congress should also require the appropriate departments to cooperate with the committee. The continued success of the committee will depend solely upon the courage, fearlessness, and the thoroughness with which it is conducted, and upon the assumption and maintenance throughout the investigation of a strictly nonpartisan attitude and policy.

Martin Dies, *Chairman,*

Joe Starnes,

John J. Dempsey,

Harold G. Mosier,

Arthur D. Healey,

N. M. Mason,

J. Parnell Thomas,

Special Committee on Un-American Activities.

House Report No. 2, 76th Congress, 1st session, Jan. 3, 1939, 10–11, 118–120, 123–124.

129   Senator Harry S. Truman Calls for Investigation of the National Defense Program

February 10, 1941

In the history of congressional investigations, few can match the success of the Senate Special Committee to Investigate the Defense Program, under the chairmanship of Senator Harry S. Truman (D-Mo.). At the time Truman was a little known senator at the beginning of his second term. As the nation began a massive military buildup in response to the war in Europe, Truman became concerned about the methods used to grant military contracts. He wanted his state of Missouri to receive its fair share of the business. As he studied the issue he discovered a haphazard, wasteful system of expenditures that favored large corporations over small businesses. Truman found gross examples of political favoritism that often included bribery and other payoffs before contracts were awarded. On February 10, 1941, he called for the creation of a committee to investigate the national defense program. On March 1, 1941, the Senate passed a resolution establishing a seven-member Senate committee authorized to investigate the procurement and construction of a full range of military supplies, including

buildings, training camps, munitions, vehicles, aircraft, and warships. Truman became chairman of the committee, which became widely known as the Truman Committee.

The work of the committee was noted for its fairness and efficiency. The committee held hundreds of hearings, conducted many investigations, and issued more than fifty reports to Congress. At the same time it carefully avoided partisanship and did not overly criticize the Roosevelt administration, especially after the United States declared war on Japan and Germany. Truman's work on the committee made him one of the best known senators in the nation and led to his selection as Roosevelt's running mate in the 1944 presidential election. The committee continued in operation until 1948, although it was never quite as effective once Truman left the chairmanship to run for vice president. Estimates vary on how much money the Truman Committee investigations saved the nation by eliminating duplication, making the contracting procedure more efficient, and countering fraudulent practices. Some es-

timates of savings run as high as $30 billion. More importantly, the improved contracting and procurement practices helped to better prepare the nation for the task of providing the war materiel needed to fight World War II.

AWARD OF CONTRACTS UNDER NATION DEFENSE PROGRAM

Mr. TRUMAN. Mr. President, I expect to submit a resolution asking for an investigation of the national-defense program and the handling of contracts.

I feel that it is my duty at this time to place before the Senate certain information which I have, and which I am sure is of vital importance to the success of the national-defense program.

There seems to be a policy in the national-defense set-up to concentrate all contracts and nearly all the manufacturing that has to do with the national defense in a very small area. This area is entirely outside the location which the Army survey, itself, has shown to be safe. The little manufacturer, the little contractor, and the little machine shop have been left entirely out in the cold. The policy seems to be to make the big man bigger and to put the little man completely out of business. There is no reason for this that will stand up, because plans have been presented to the National Defense Committee which would solve the condition of the little manufacturer and the little machine-shop owner.

A perfectly practical and concrete plan was presented by the Mid-Central War Resources Board. A survey of the region within 100 miles of Kansas City was made by this Board, and 160 small machine shops and manufacturing plants were located. It was proposed to combine the facilities of these little machine shops and allow them to take a contract, or contracts, which they could, working as a unit, carry out successfully.

Under this program there would be no housing problem. The shops are in the small towns. The people already have their houses. They are the best workmen and the most loyal citizens in the whole country.

The same sort of a survey was made in St. Louis and the immediate surrounding territory, and the same conditions exist there. I have no doubt that these conditions exist in Iowa, Illinois, and Indiana.

When this matter was put up to the Defense Committee, an effort was made to find out where the machines in these small shops were located so that the big fellows could go and buy them and move them. They are buying these machines wherever they can find them, shipping them to Detroit, Philadelphia, Norfolk, and industrial cities in Massachusetts and Connecticut. They are hiring our young men and moving them to the Atlantic and Pacific seaboards and to Detroit, leaving us denuded of manpower as well as machines. This makes a double housing problem. It leaves our cities with vacant property which is rapidly depreciating in value, and creates a condition at Norfolk, Philadelphia, Detroit, Hartford, Conn., and Los Angeles, Calif., where housing problems have to be met. It just does not make sense. The policy seems to be to make the big men bigger

and let the little men go out of business or starve to death, and they do not seem to care what becomes of the little fellows.

. . . .

Mr. President, under the War Department there are three types of contracts—the lump-sum contract, the purchase-and-hire contract, and the fixed-fee contract. Under the lump-sum contract the contractor is awarded the contract for the work, either on a low-bid basis or on a negotiated lump-sum basis. The purchase-and-hire form of contract was, as it would imply, a straight cost-plus contract. With the cost-plus-a-fixed-fee contract, under which most of the present construction work is being performed, the contractor is selected and a fee for his work fixed. The fixed fee amounts to approximately 3.2 percent. All costs allied with the construction work, including all overhead, blue prints, telephone calls, stenographers, clerks, field inspectors, labor, and material, are paid for by the Government. The fee can be interpreted as a profit to the contractor for the use of his services, and his organization.

I do not pretend to be entirely familiar with the workings of any of these departments. However, the fixed-fee branch is now in the process of being reorganized. General Hartman has been retired, due to overwork. Colonel Somervell, former P. W. A. chieftain of New York City, is now at the head of the fixed-fee branch. Mr. Loving was formerly the construction chief. Colonel Groves is now very important in the construction branch.

Fixed-fee contracts are also being awarded to large industrialists, such as Chrysler, Du Pont, Remington, Atlas, and Hercules. These industrialists are given a fixed fee for the use of their engineering facilities. After the building has been erected and the plant completed by Government money, these industrialists lease the plant and supply the Government with the product of the plant at a fixed cost per unit.

On August 15, the Chrysler Corporation was awarded a contract in the amount of $53,000,000. The fee for construction which is paid by the Government to Chrysler is in the amount of $1. This looks exceedingly patriotic. Nevertheless, during the 1-year period of the Chrysler Corporation's lease of the factory facilities they will produce 1,000 tanks at a cost to the United States Government in the amount of $33,000,000. I doubt if anyone could give the method by which the cost of $33,000 per tank was fixed. Chrysler has full jurisdiction over the spending of all money and the inspection of all work at the job. I am sure the constructing quartermaster at the job is sincere in his effort to guard every penny of the United States Government's money; but with Chrysler having full control, it is almost impossible to do anything else but what Chrysler wants. I do not say that the Chrysler Corporation is performing anything other than its patriotic duty, but I do feel that even the large corporation should be subject to a full accounting for every nickel spent and the profit accrued on every task.

The same procedure followed in the award of the contract to the Chrysler Corporation has been pursued in awarding all contracts to the large corporations. The Remington Co. get $600,000 for acting as advisers to the Government. No one knows what this advice is or what it is worth. In addition to the $600,000, they will receive a profit of no one knows how much for each 30-caliber and 50-caliber shell they produce in a factory which has been financed by the United States Government. After the operating company—the large industrialist—has been selected, an architect, an engineer, and a construction contractor are selected.

Every contractor in the country, with but few exceptions, and every architect and engineer have registered with the Quartermaster General and with the Navy. Each firm presents a portfolio including a statement of the work they have performed. In the past, their present, financial status, and the reasons why they believe they have the ability to perform work under the Government fixed-fee contracts.

The information which the contractor, the architect, and the engineer furnish the Quartermaster General is turned over to the Construction Advisory Board.

The Construction Advisory Board consists of three men, Messrs. P. Blossom, F. Harvey, and F. Dresser. Mr. Blossom is a member of the firm of Sanderson & Porter, engineers and contractors of New York City. Mr. Dresser is a former civil service employee who was employed by the U.S.H.A., has been in business for himself in the Middle West, and has had considerable interest in the Association of General Contractors.

After the information is submitted to the Quartermaster General, it is reviewed by the Board, which interviews the prospective contractor or engineer. The contractor is then given a rating which is filed for future use. The Board could really be considered an indexing committee of contractors and architects throughout the country.

The contractor is supposed to be financially sound. He should have an organization equipped to do the work. He should have done work of a similar character, or at least of similar size. Because he is a local contractor, he is considered conversant with local labor conditions and material markets; and, being in the vicinity of the project, he can serve better than one who is removed from the project because of geographical location. Were these requirements religiously carried out, no one could find fault with them; but the rules do not fit with the facts.

. . . .

In selecting the contractor for the job in question, the Board is supposed to bear in mind the geographical location of the contractor with reference to the job.

The name of the contractor selected by the Board is then submitted to Mr. Loving. Mr. Loving, after perusing the files of the contractor, requests that the contractor come to Washington for negotiations. Contractor No. 1 selected by the Board is then called into conference with Mr. Loving, Mr. O'Brien, and Captain Kirkpatrick and one of the section chiefs. Negotiations then take place, and generally at that meeting the contractor is informed, confidentially, that he has the job.

After negotiations a proceed order, in the form of a letter, is sent to the contractor. Final contracts are drawn up and submitted to the office of the Under Secretary of War for final signature.

One of the first jobs awarded was an $18,115,000 project at Fayetteville, N.C. This contract, strange as it may seem, was awarded to T. A. Loving & Co., at Charlotte, N.C. Mr. Loving, former construction branch chief, bears the same name and is from the same town. It is said that no relationship whatsoever exists between the two Mr. Lovings. Another instance occurred where a contractor and an architect had been because they have special merit for a reasonably small project. The Philadelphia quartermaster depot was awarded to the Ballinger Co. and Wark Co. in the amount of $700,000. Within a month's time this same group received an additional contract in the amount of $9,911,000 as an extra. There were no negotiations. The same thing occurred at Camp Blanding, Fla., Camp Edwards, Mass., and at Camp Meade, Md.

Many of the contracts which have been awarded have been traced to a connection between a member of the contractor's firm and Mr. Dresser, namely, they have been personal friends in the past. This, however, should not effect any criticism. Friends may have been made because of their quality performance. Friendship should not be a handicap to anyone seeking work in the War Department. When a friendship, however, dominates the selection of an inferior contractor, then that selection is wrong. Colonel Wahlbridg of Wahlbridg and Aldinger was a personal friend of Mr. Dresser, so I am told. Wahlbridg & Aldinger of Detroit, and Foley Bros. of St. Paul, Minn., were awarded the $8,000,000 Remington small arms ammunition plant at Lake City, Mo. The two firms were neither geographically located in regard to the Job, nor were they in any way better equipped than local contractors of Kansas and Missouri.

The same policy was followed in letting the contract at Camp Leonard Wood at Rolla, Mo. I am told that the gentlemen who got this contract were dirt movers and had never had a construction job in their lives. They are having much trouble getting organized and are having a great deal of difficulty with local labor conditions.

. . . .

On the Western Cartridge small-arms ammunition plant, to be known as the St. Louis ordnance plant, negotiations were held with two firms who were combined by the Dresser committee. Albert P. Greensfelder, of the Fruco Construction Co., formerly known as the Fruin-Colon Contracting Co., is a personal friend, so I am told, of Mr. Dresser. The Fruco Co. was combined with the Massman Construction Co. Massman is a river contractor. The particular project on which, he was selected to be the contractor is within the city limits of St. Louis, and all the barges which Massman may own would serve no useful purpose for this project. The Fruco Co. had, a month prior to the negotiations, so I am told, a B rating. The second choice for the St. Louis job was Winston, or Winston & Turner, of New York. For some reason Winston has been pushed into practically every job in the Middle West by the Advisory Committee. A short time ago they were awarded, as co-contractors with Sollit Construction Co., the bag-loading plant, at Charlestown, Ind. The operators of this plant were intent on using a contractor close to the job, the H. K. Fergeson Co., of Cleveland. Winston, however, seems to have gotten the job.

At Camp Branding, Fla., Starrett Bros. & Eakin, Inc., general contractors, of New York City, were awarded a $9,000,000 project, and 8 days later, awarded an additional $8,000,000 project—a total of $17,463,777 in construction. This particular job was supposed to be completed January 15, 1941, but as of December 27, 1940, was but 48 percent completed. There has been much discussion on this particular project. Fischbach & Moore, electrical contractors, of New York City, received the contract for the electrical work. So, too, did a New York contracting firm, J. L. Murphy, for all the plumbing work on the project. No one know; why Starrett Bros. & Eakin, of New York City, should have received the contract for this particular project.

One of the first projects that was awarded was the Ellwood ordnance plant at Wilmington, Ill. This project was in the amount of $11,564,000, and was awarded to Mr. Blossom's firm, Sanderson & Porter. Mr. Blossom is on the committee.

I have been informed—and this also needs verification— that John Griffiths & Son Construction Co., of Chicago, were bankrupt 5 years ago, but through a Colonel Paddock, chief Washington representative of the firm, they were awarded a $6,268,669 contract for the construction of Camp Grant in Illinois. At Falmouth, Mass., the Walsh Construction Co., of Boston, a tunnel contractor, received the contract for the construction of Camp Edwards in the amount of $7,000,000 first and $12,000,000 second, a total of $19,697,948 for construction. Fischback-Moore, electrical contractor of New York, is in on this job. The estimated date of completion was February 1 and December 20. To date they are about 70 percent complete. On this particular job, I have been told on good authority that there was a local union consisting of about 100 members who so organized the labor on this job that the 5,000 men employed would have to pay $50 apiece to the local union before they set foot on the job. Labor conditions similar to this have existed on many of the camp jobs, including Fort Dix, Fort Meade, Lake City, St. Louis and Rolla, Mo.

. . . .

I do not believe that any contracts should be let on the basis of friendship or political affiliation. We are facing a national emergency. Patriotism would require that these contracts be let to the man best fitted to carry out the contracts. I believe the Senate ought to go to the bottom of the whole procedure.

It is my opinion, from things I have heard, that the violations of ethics and common-sense procedure are just as flagrant in the letting of contracts for the Navy.

They say the selection of a contractor and architect is based on their financial stability and their past experience. If the contrac-

tor and the architect were selected on the basis of their familiarity with labor and local material markets, and if the contractors were provided with a suitable method of reimbursement, and if the red tape connected with the payments were removed, smaller contracting firms would be judged on the same basis as the larger firms are now judged. Past performance is really no guide for judging a contractor today. In the past 11 years there has been little, if any, industrial expansion. The building industry throughout the United States, as we all know, has suffered for the want of work. The only work that contractors have been performing has been P.W.A. and W.P.A. The firms who were good prior to 1929 not necessarily the firms who are good today.

I am calling the attention of the Senate to these things because I believe most sincerely that they need looking into. I consider public funds to be sacred funds, and I think they ought to have every safeguard possible to prevent their being misused and mishandled.

. . . .

I think the Senate ought to create a special committee with authority to examine every contract that has been let, with authority to find out if the rumors rife in this city have any foundation in fact. This will be a protection to the men who are responsible for letting these contracts, and will also insure a more efficient carrying out of the contract itself.

I have had considerable experience in letting pubic contracts; and I have never yet found a contractor who, if not watched, would not leave the Government holding the bag. We are not doing him a favor if we do not watch him.

When safeguards are removed from a man who is entrusted with funds it does him a disservice, for the simple reason that it is much better to place the necessary guards around public funds and keep men from embezzling them than it is to prosecute men after embezzlement has taken place. When a bank teller is permitted to run loose without bond and without the necessary supervision, in the long run he gets his money mixed up with the money of the bank. The same thing happens in letting Government contracts. I do not like a cost-plus contract. I think it is an abomination; but, under the present conditions, I do not see how else this situation could have been met, although in the time that has been wasted as this matter has been handled, plans and specifications could have been drawn and contracts could have been let to the lowest and best bidder, which is the only proper way to let contracts.

I am particularly alarmed at the concentration of national-defense industrial plants. I am reliably informed that from 70 to 90 percent of the contracts let have been concentrated in an area smaller than England. It undoubtedly is the plan to make the big manufacturers bigger, and let the little men shift for themselves.

I think the "educational order" program ought to be gone into thoroughly. If it is necessary to give Henry Ford and Chrysler and General motors millions of dollars for educational purposes for mass production, then we are certainly out on a limb. I understand that they have been given $11,000,000 apiece for educational purposes. The educational-order program was instituted along in the 1920's and 1930's by the War Department and the Navy Department to educate certain manufacturers in what the Army and the Navy might need in case an emergency should arise. Those educational orders are things of the past, and ought now to be abandoned. They are merely a gift. That phase of our national-defense program should be thoroughly gone into.

I am merely stating what I believe to be conditions that deserve investigation. If nothing is wrong, there will be no harm done. If something is wrong, it ought to be brought to light. The location of these national-defense plants and the profits that are supposed to be made on tanks, planes, and small arms should be a matter of public record, unless we are to have the same old profiteering situation that we had in the last war.

Everyone connected with the national-defense program should have a patriotic interest in seeing that it is properly carried out; and the Senate ought to know whether such persons have this interest, whether they be manufacturers or laboring men.

. . . .

Congressional Record, Senate, 77th Congress, 1st session, Feb. 10, 1941, 830–838.

130   The Lend-Lease Act

March 11, 1941

The Lend-Lease Act gave President Franklin D. Roosevelt broad authority to sell, transfer, exchange, lease, or lend massive amounts of war materiel—ranging from aircraft and ships to food and medical supplies—to any nation when it was deemed to be in the interest of the defense of the United States. Congress passed the program at the request of President Roosevelt, who said the United States should become "the great arsenal of democracy" to aid countries fighting against Nazi Germany, especially Great Britain. It was, in effect, a way of declaring war without going to war. Congress eventually passed the bill by wide margins in both houses, but it generated a heated national debate over the sweeping powers this bill gave the president, concern that passage of lend-lease was really preparation for war, and objections to the high potential cost of the program.

The lend-lease program helped prepare the United States for war by creating a large military buildup almost nine months before the declaration of war on Japan and Germany (see documents 132 and 133). Under this program the United States provided more than $50 billion dollars of aid to its allies by the time the war ended in 1945.

Be it enacted by the Senate and House of Representatives of the United States of America in Congress assembled, That this Act may be cited as "An Act to Promote the Defense of the United States".

SEC. 2. As used in this Act—

(a) The term "defense article" means—

(1) Any weapon, munition, aircraft, vessel, or boat;

(2) Any machinery, facility, tool, material, or supply necessary for the manufacture, production, processing, repair, servicing, or operation of any article described in this subsection;

(3) Any component material or part of or equipment for any article described in this subsection;

(4) Any agricultural, industrial or other commodity or article for defense.

Such term "defense article" includes any article described in this subsection: Manufactured or procured pursuant to section 3, or to which the United States or any foreign government has or hereafter acquires title, possession, or control.

(b) The "defense information" means any plan, specification, design, prototype, or information pertaining to any defense article.

SEC. 3. (a) Notwithstanding the provisions of any other law, the President may, from time to time, when he deems it in the interest of national defense, authorize the Secretary of War, the Secretary of the Navy, or the head of any other department or agency of the Government—

(1) To manufacture in arsenals, factories, and shipyards under their jurisdiction, or otherwise procure, to the extent to which funds are made available therefor, or contracts are authorized from time to time by the Congress, or both, any defense article for the government of any country whose defense the President deems vital to the defense of the United States.

(2) To sell, transfer title to, exchange, lease, lend, or otherwise disposed of, to any such government any defense article, but no defense article not manufactured or procured under paragraph (1) shall in any way be disposed of under this, except after consultation with the Chief of Staff of the Army or the Chief of Naval Operations of the Navy, or both. The value of defense articles disposed of in any way under authority of this paragraph, and procured from funds heretofore appropriated, shall not exceed $1,300,000,000. The value of such shall be determined by the head of the department or agency concerned or such other department, agency or officer as shall be designated in the manner provided in the rules and regulations issued hereunder. Defense articles procured from funds hereafter appropriated to any department or agency of the Government, other than from funds authorized to be appropriated under this Act, shall not be disposed of in any way under authority of this

paragraph except to the extent hereinafter authorized by the Congress in the Acts appropriating such funds or otherwise.

(3) To test, inspect, provide, repair, outfit, recondition, or otherwise to place in good working order, to the extent to which funds are made available therefor, or contracts are authorized from time to time by the Congress, or both, any defense article for any such government, or to procure any or all such services by private contract.

(4) To communicate to any such government any defense information, pertaining to any defense article furnished to such government under paragraph (2) of this subsection.

(5) To release for export any defense article disposed of in any way under this subsection to any such government.

(b) The terms and conditions upon which any such foreign government receives any aid authorized under subsection (a) shall be those which the President deems satisfactory, and the benefit to the United States may be payment or repayment in kind or property, or any other direct or indirect benefit which the President deems satisfactory.

(c) After June 30, 1943, or after the passage of a concurrent resolution by the two Houses before June 30, 1943, which declares that the powers conferred by or pursuant to subsection (a) are no longer necessary to promote the defense of the United States, neither the President nor the head of any department or agency shall exercise any of the powers conferred by or pursuant to subsection (a); except that until July 1, 1946, any of such powers may be exercised to the extent necessary to carry out a contract or agreement with such a foreign government made before July 1, 1943, or before the passage of such concurrent resolution, whichever is the earlier.

(d) Nothing in this Act shall be construed to authorize or to permit the authorization of convoying vessels by naval vessels of the United States.

(e) Nothing in this Act shall be construed to authorize or to permit the authorization of the entry of any American vessel into a combat area in violation of section 8 of the Neutrality Act of 1939.

SEC. 4. All contracts or agreements made for the disposition of any defense article or defense information pursuant to section 3 shall contain a clause by which the foreign government undertakes that it will not, without the consent of the President, transfer title to or possession of such defense article or defense information by gift, sale, or otherwise, or permit its use by anyone not an officer, employee, or agent of such foreign government.

SEC. 5. (a) The Secretary of War, the Secretary of the Navy, or the head of any other department or agency of the Government involved shall, when any such defense article or defense information is exported, immediately inform the department or agency designated by the President to administer section 6 or the Act of July 2, 1940 (54 Stat. 714), of the quantities, character, value, terms of disposition, and destination of the article and information so exported.

(b) The President from time to time, but not less frequently than once every ninety days, shall transmit to the Congress a report of operations under this Act except such information as he deems incompatible with public interest to disclose. Reports provided for under this subsection shall be transmitted to the Secretary of the Senate or the Clerk of the House of Representatives, as the case may be, if the Senate or the House of Representatives, as the case may be, is not in session.

SEC. 6. (a) There is hereby authorized to be appropriated from time to time, out of any money in the Treasury not otherwise appropriated, such amounts as may be necessary to carry out the provisions and accomplish the purposes of this Act.

(b) All money and all property which is converted into money received under section 3 from any government shall, with the approval of the Director of the Budget, revert to the respective appropriation or appropriations out of which funds were expended with respect to the defense article or defense information for which such considerate is received, and shall be available for expenditure for the purpose for which such expended funds were appropriated by law, during the fiscal year in which such funds are received and the ensuing fiscal year; but in no event shall any funds so received be available for expenditure after June 30, 1946.

SEC. 7. The Secretary of War, the Secretary of the Navy, and the head of the department or agency shall in all contracts or agreements for the disposition of any defense article or defense information fully protect the rights of all citizens of the United States who have patent rights in and to any such article or information which is hereby authorized to be disposed of and the payments collected for royalties on such patents shall be paid to the owners and holders of such patents.

SEC. 8. The Secretaries of War and of the Navy are hereby authorized to purchase or otherwise acquire arms, ammunition, and implements of war produced within the jurisdiction of any country to which section 3 is applicable, whenever the President deems such purchase or acquisition to be necessary in the interests of the defense of the United States.

SEC. 9. The President may, from time to time, promulgate such rules and regulations as may be necessary and proper to carry out any of the provisions of this Act; and he may exercise any power or authority conferred on him by this Act through such department, agency, or officer as he shall direct.

SEC. 10. Nothing in this Act shall be construed to change existing law relating to the use of the land and naval forces of the United States, except insofar as such use relates to the manufacture, procurement, and repair of defense articles, the communication of information and other noncombatant purposes enumerated in this Act.

SEC. 11. If any provision of this Act or the application of such provision to any circumstance shall be held invalid, the validity of the remainder of the Act and the applicability of such provision to other circumstances shall not be affected thereby.

Approved, March 11, 1941.

Statutes at Large, 55 (1941–1943), 77th Congress, 1st session, March 11, 1941, 31–33.

131   President Franklin D. Roosevelt Asks Congress to Declare War on Japan

December 8, 1941

In a momentous and dramatic joint session of Congress, President Franklin D. Roosevelt spoke to a packed House chamber on December 8, 1941, to ask Congress to declare war on Japan for its attack on Pearl Harbor the day before. Both the president and Congress were acting out their constitutional roles. Only Congress can declare war. Once war was declared it was up to the president as commander-in-chief of the armed forces to conduct that war.

As the president spoke, he was flanked in the chairs behind the rostrum by Vice President Henry A. Wallace and Speaker of the House Sam Rayburn. The opening sentence of the president's speech electrified the nation, many of whom were just beginning to absorb the news of the tragic loss of life and the devastation that Japan had wreaked on the important naval base in the Hawaiian Islands.

The president kept his message brief. The joint meeting convened in the House chamber at 12:30 P.M. and the president completed his remarks and left the chamber in twelve minutes. The House immediately took up the war resolution, as did the Senate, which arrived back in its chamber just minutes after the conclusion of the president's speech. The Capitol that day appeared as if it was an armed camp. Marine guards with fixed bayonets were stationed on the grounds and steel cables had been strung along the curbs to hold back citizens who had flocked to the Capitol in anticipation of the president's message.

ADDRESS BY THE PRESIDENT

To the Congress of the United States:

Yesterday, December 7, 1941—a date which will live in infamy—the United States of America was suddenly and deliberately attacked by naval and air forces of the Empire of Japan.

The United States was at peace with that nation and, at the solicitation of Japan, was still in conversation with its Government and its Emperor looking toward the maintenance of peace in the Pacific. Indeed, 1 hour after Japanese air squadrons had commenced bombing in Oahu, the Japanese Ambassador to the United States and his colleague delivered to the Secretary of State a formal reply to a recent American message. While this reply stated that it seemed useless to continue the existing diplomatic negotiations, it contained no threat or hint of war or armed attack.

It will be recorded that the distance of Hawaii from Japan makes it obvious that the attack was deliberately planned many days or even weeks ago. During the intervening time the Japanese Government has deliberately sought to deceive the United States by false statements and expressions of hope for continued peace.

The attack yesterday on the Hawaiian Islands has caused severe damage to American naval and military forces. Very many American lives have been lost. In addition American ships have been reported torpedoed on the high seas between San Francisco and Honolulu.

Yesterday the Japanese Government also launched an attack against Malaya.

Last night Japanese forces attacked Hong Kong.

Last night Japanese forces attacked Guam.

Last night Japanese forces attacked the Philippine Islands.

Last night the Japanese attacked Wake Island.

This morning the Japanese attacked Midway Island.

Japan has therefore undertaken a surprise offensive extending throughout the Pacific area. The facts of yesterday speak for themselves. The People of the United States have already formed their opinions and well understand the implications to the very life and safety of our Nation.

As Commander in Chief of the Army and Navy I have directed that all measures be taken for our defense.

Always will we remember the character of the onslaught against us.

No matter how long it may take us to overcome this premeditated invasion, the American people in their righteous might will win through to absolute victory.

I believe I interpret the will of the Congress and of the people when I assert that we will not only defend ourselves to the uttermost but will make very certain that this form of treachery shall never endanger us again.

Hostilities exist. There is no blinking at the fact that our people, our territory, and our interests are in grave danger.

With confidence in our armed forces with the unbounded determination of our people—we will gain the inevitable triumph, so help us God.

I ask that the Congress declare that, since the unprovoked and dastardly attack by Japan on Sunday, December 7, a state of war has existed between the United States and the Japanese Empire.

Franklin D. Roosevelt.

Congressional Record, Senate, 77th Congress, 1st session, Dec. 8, 1941, 9504–9505.

132   Congress Declares War on Japan

December 8, 1941

Within hours of President Franklin D. Roosevelt's speech calling for war with Japan (see document 131), the House and Senate had approved the declaration of war and sent it to the president for his signature. In the House the vote in favor of war was 388–1, with 41 members absent and not voting. Speaker Sam Rayburn expected the vote to be unanimous but one member, Jeannette Rankin (R-Mont.), refused to vote for war. She tried to gain the attention of the Speaker to explain her vote, but Rayburn was in no mood to accommodate her. Rankin had served one term in Congress twenty-four years earlier and had voted against U.S. entry into World War I. This time around she was alone in opposing war. She became the only member of Congress to vote against U.S. entry into both World Wars.

The Senate quickly passed the declaration of war by a vote of 82–0, with 13 members absent and not voting. The absentee rate in both the House and Senate was indicative of the fact that many members were away for the weekend when news arrived of the attack on Pearl Harbor. Many were traveling back to Washington at the time of the president's speech and the House and Senate votes for war.

With the United States already under attack, there was little debate about the war resolution. In the Senate, with Vice President Henry A. Wallace presiding, the declaration of war was introduced by the chairman of the Senate Foreign Relations Committee, Thomas T. Connally (D-Texas), who was quickly interrupted by Senator Arthur H. Vandenberg (R-Mich.). Vandenberg felt compelled to speak since he was one of the most prominent isolationists, who opposed the Lend-Lease Act (see document 130) and was a critic of America's growing entanglement with foreign nations. Vandenberg's isolationism and his stand that America should remain neutral in the growing world conflict had put him at odds with many in his own party and prevented him from being a serious contender for the Republican presidential nomination in 1940. When the Japanese attacked Pearl Harbor, he suddenly and dramatically changed his mind about neutrality and isolationism. In his statement on the floor of the Senate he said, "I have fought every trend that would lead to needless war; but when war comes to us—and particularly when it comes like a thug in the night—I stand with my Commander in Chief for the swiftest and most invincible reply of which our total strength may be capable. It is too late to argue why we face this hazard. The record stands. The historians can settle that conundrum upon another day, when we have finished with this task. For now, it is enough that the attack has come. For now, nothing else will be enough except an answer from 130,000,000 united people that will tell this whole round earth that though America still hates war, America fights when she is violated. And fights until victory is conclusive. God helping her, she can do no other."

Senator Vandenberg's complete change of position regarding the role of the United States in world affairs led him to become one of the major architects of American foreign policy after the war

ended. *As chairman of the Senate Foreign Relations Committee beginning in 1947, he cooperated fully with President Harry Truman and was a major force in securing congressional approval of the United Nations, the North Atlantic Treaty Organization, and other major foreign policy initiatives, such as the Marshall Plan and the Truman Doctrine.*

In the House of Representatives the war resolution was introduced by the Majority Leader John W. McCormack (D-Mass.), who said, "A dastardly attack has been made upon us. This is the time for action." House Minority Leader Joseph Martin (R-Mass.) echoed the sentiment when he said, "We are compelled by this treacherous attack to go to war. From now on there can be no hesitation. We must press the war with unstinted vigor and full efficiency. There can be no peace until the enemy is made to pay in full measure for his dastardly crimes." Only Jeannette Rankin tried to speak out against the war resolution. She was elected in 1940 for her stand as an isolationist opposed to U.S. entry into the war. Her attempt to speak before the war vote was met with booing and jeering from the galleries and from some House members. Speaker Rayburn ignored her and called for the vote on the resolution.

Shortly after it voted for war the House received notice that the Senate had passed its war resolution, S.J. Res. 116, and without objection the House vacated its own resolution and by unanimous consent passed S.J. Res. 116.

[IN THE SENATE]

The Senate having returned to its Chamber (at 12 o'clock and 47 minutes P.M.), it reassembled, and the Vice President resumed the chair.

Mr. BARKLEY. I suggest the absence of a quorum.

The VICE PRESIDENT. The clerk will call the roll. . . .

The VICE PRESIDENT. Eighty-two Senators have answered to their names. A quorum is present.

Mr. CONNALLY. Mr. President, I introduce a joint resolution, and ask for its immediate consideration without reference to a committee.

The VICE PRESIDENT. The joint resolution will be read.

The joint resolution (S.J. Res. 116) declaring that a state of war exists between the Imperial Government of Japan and the Government and the people of the United States and making provision to prosecute the same, was read the first time by its title, and the second time at length, as follows:

Whereas the Imperial Government of Japan has committed unprovoked act of war against the Government and the people of the United States of America: Therefore be it

Resolved, etc., That the state of war between the United States and the Imperial Government of Japan which has thus been thrust the United States is hereby formally declared; and the President is hereby authorized and directed to employ the entire naval and military forces of the

United States and the resources of the Government to carry on war against the Imperial Government of Japan; and, to bring the conflict to a successful termination. all of the resources of the country are hereby pledged by the Congress of the United States.

The VICE PRESIDENT. Is there objection to the present consideration of the Joint resolution?

There being no objection, the Senate Proceeded to consider the Joint resolution.

Mr. CONNALLY. Mr. President, on the passage of the resolution I ask for the yeas and nays.

The yeas and nays were ordered.

Mr. VANDENBERG. Mr. President, I desire to comment briefly on the Joint resolution.

Mr. CONNALLY. Mr. President, those of us on this side of the Chamber are withholding remarks. I was hoping that there would be no comment.

Mr. VANDENBERG. I am sure I shall not interfere with what the Senator has in mind.

Mr. CONNALLY. Of course, the Senator has a right to speak if he insists.

Mr. VANDENBERG. I should not want to proceed further without making the record clear.

Mr. President, out of peaceful Sunday skies, without a word of warning—yes; and even screened by the infamous treachery of pretended amity in pacific negotiations at Washington—like an ambushed murderer, Japan has violated our soil, lulled our citizens, struck at our possessions, assailed our sovereignty, and disclosed to us the pattern of a purpose which reeks with dishonor and with bloody aspiration.

There can be no shadow of a doubt about America's united and indomitable answer to the cruel and ruthless challenge of this tragic hour—the answer not only of the Congress but also of our people at their threatened hearthstones.

To the enemy we answer—you have unsheathed the sword, and by it you shall die.

To the President of the United States we answer—for the defense of all that is America we salute the colors and we forward march.

Mr. President, I am constrained to make this brief statement on my own account, lest there be any lingering apprehension in any furtive mind that previous internal disagreements regarding the wisdom of our policies may encourage the despicable hope that we may weaken from within. I have fought every trend that would lead to needless war; but when war comes to us—and particularly when it comes like a thug in the night—I stand with my Commander in Chief for the swiftest and most invincible reply of which our total strength may be capable. It is too late to argue why we face this hazard. The record stands. The historians can settle that conundrum upon another day, when we have finished with this task. For now, it is enough that the attack has come. For now, nothing else will be enough except an answer from 130,000,000 united people that will tell this whole round earth that though. America still hates war, America fights when she is violated. And fights until victory is conclusive.

God helping her, she can do no other.

Mr. CONNALLY. Mr. President, the issues are so clear and our position was so definitely set forth in the address delivered today by the President of the United States that the Senator from Texas and his associates did not feel that it was necessary to make any address or remarks upon the Joint resolution. We are, of course, glad to have the agreement of the Senator from Michigan.

I therefore ask for the yeas and nays on the passage of the joint resolution.

The VICE PRESIDENT. If there be no amendment proposed. the question is on the engrossment and third reading of the joint resolution.

The joint resolution was ordered to be engrossed for a third reading and was read the third time.

The VICE PRESIDENT. The joint resolution having been read three times, the question is, Shall it pass? On that question the yeas and nays have been demanded and ordered. The clerk will call the roll.

The Chief Clerk proceeded to call the roll.

Mr. WHITE (when Mr. Brewster's name was called). I announce the unavoidable absence of my colleague [Mr. Brewster]. He is flying to Washington at this time. It is a matter of keen regret to him that he was not able to reach here in time to record himself upon this joint resolution. If my colleague were present, he would vote "yea."

Mr. MCNARY (when Mr. Capper's name was called). The senior Senator from Kansas [Mr. Capper] is on his way to Washington. On account of public matters, he has been delayed. If he were present, he would vote "yea."

Mr. MCNARY (when Mr. Holman's name was called). The Junior Senator from Oregon [Mr. Holman] is flying to Washington. He has been absent on account of public matters. If he were present, he would vote "yea."

Mr. BUNKER (when Mr. McCarran's name was called). My colleague [Mr. McCarran] is now on his way to Washington. I am advised that if he were present he would vote "yea."

Mr. O'MAHONEY (when Mr. Schwartz's name was called). My colleague [Mr. Schwartz] left Washington last week by direction of the Senate as a member of the committee to attend the funeral of the late senior Senator from Colorado, Mr. Adams. He has been detained in his return to Washington. If he were present, he would vote "yea."

Mr. MCNARY (when the name of Mr. Thomas of Idaho was called). The junior Senator from Idaho [Mr. Thomas] is absent because of a death in his family. If he were present, he would vote "yea.'"

Mr. LUCAS (when Mr. Walgren's name was called). I desire to state to the Senate that the Junior Senator from Washington [Mr. Walgren] is now on his way to Washington by airplane. If he were present, he would vote "yea" on this joint resolution.

The roll call was concluded.

Mr. HILL. The Senator from Washington [Mr. Bone], who is ill and under the care of a physician, would, if present, vote "yea."

The senior Senator from Arkansas [Mrs. Caraway], the junior Senator Arkansas [Mr. Spencer], from Arizona [Mr. Hayden], and the Senator from Washington [Mr. Wallgren] are absent on official business. They are en route to Washington, but have been unable to reach here in time for this vote. If present, they would vote "yea."

The Senator from Montana [Mr. Wheeler] is necessarily absent but is en route to Washington. If he were present, he would vote "yea."

Mr. DOXEY. I desire to state that my colleague the senior Senator from Mississippi [Mr. Bilbo] is en route to Washington. He has been unavoidably detained. If he were present, he would vote "yea."

Mr. MCFARLAND. I desire to announce that my colleague [Mr. HAYDEN], who is in Arizona on official business, attending a hearing of a subcommittee, is now en route to Washington. If he were present, he would vote "yea."

The result was announced—yeas 82, nays 0. . . .

[IN THE HOUSE OF REPRESENTATIVES]

War Resolution

Mr. MCCORMACK. Mr. Speaker, I move to suspend the rules and pass House Joint Resolution 254, which I send to the desk.

The SPEAKER. The Clerk will read the Joint resolution.

The Clerk read as follows:

Declaring that a state of war exists between the Imperial Government of Japan and the Government and the people of the United States and making provisions to prosecute the same.

Whereas the Imperial Government of Japan has committed repeated acts of war against the Government and the people of the United States of America: Therefore be it

Resolved, etc., That the state of war between the United States and the Imperial Government of Japan which has thus been that upon the United States is hereby formally declared, and that the President be, and he is hereby, authorized and directed to employ the entire naval and military forces of the United States and the resources of the Government to carry on war against the Imperial Government of Japan; and to bring the conflict to a successful termination all of the resources Of the country are hereby pledged by the Congress of the United States.

The SPEAKER. Is a second demanded?

Miss RANKIN of Montana. I object.

The SPEAKER. This is no unanimous-consent request. No objection is in order.

Is a second demanded?

Mr. MARTIN of Massachusetts. Mr. Speaker, I demand a second.

The SPEAKER. Without objection, a second is considered as ordered.

There was no objection.

The SPEAKER. The Chair recognizes the gentleman from Massachusetts [Mr. McCormack].

Mr. MCCORMACK. Mr. Speaker, I yield myself 20 seconds.

Mr. Speaker and my fellow Americans, the President of the United States has just spoken to the Congress and to the American people. A dastardly attack has been made upon us. This is the time for action.

The SPEAKER. The gentleman from Massachusetts [Mr. Martin] is recognized.

Mr. MARTIN of Massachusetts. Mr. Speaker, our Nation is today in the gravest crisis since its establishment as a Republic. All we hold precious and sacred is being challenged by a ruthless, unscrupulous, arrogant foe. We have been the victim of a treacherous attack under cover of darkness. It came at a time when we were trying to establish a basis of peace through mutual understanding. Our ships have been sunk, our planes destroyed, many lives lost, cities and towns under the American flag have been ruthlessly bombed.

No one hates war more than I. Every night I have uttered a silent prayer that America might be spared active involvement in a frightful war. I know the horrors which come with war—the loss of lives, the sacrifices which must be made by all, the sadness and desolation it always brings.

America is challenged. That challenge comes in a ruthless way which leaves but one answer for a liberty-loving, self-respecting people. We are compelled by this treacherous attack to go to war. From now on there can be no hesitation. We must press the war with unstinted vigor and full efficiency. There can be no peace until the enemy is made to pay in full measure for his dastardly crimes.

We in America have wanted peace. We must now fight to uphold our national honor and make secure our freedom.

The attack on our territory will rally every patriotic American to support of the Nation's needs. In shipyards, in factories, in mines, in blast furnaces, on farms, all over this broad land there will be one spontaneous response. The people of America will unanimously meet the attacks of the aggressor and join in an Irresistible effort of increased production. The boys in the training camps and the sailors who maintain the vigils of the sea must have—they will have—the tools and equipment to win this war.

In view of the developments of the past 36 hours, the President's request has my support. When the historic roll is called I hope there will not be a single dissenting vote. Let us show the world we are a united Nation. Let us boldly proclaim we will not permit any force to strike down freedom and progress here in America or replace our way of life with slavery and dictatorship.

God will give us the strength and the courage to drive to victory in a just cause which means all that makes life worth while to the people not only of America but in every country in the world.

[Here the gavel fell.]

Mr. MARTIN of Massachusetts. Mr. Speaker, I yield 3 minutes to the gentleman from New York [Mr. Fish].

Mr. FISH. Mr. Speaker, it is with sorrow and deep resentment against Japan that I rise to support a declaration of war.

I have consistently opposed our entrance into wars in Europe and Asia for the past 3 years, but the vicious, brazen, and dastardly attack by the Japanese Navy and air force while peace negotiations were pending at Washington and in defiance of the President's eleventh-hour personal appeal to the Emperor, makes war inevitable, and necessary.

The time for debate and controversy within America has passed. The time for action has come.

Interventionists and noninterventionists must cease criminations and recriminations, charges and counstercharges against each other, and present a united front behind the President and the Government in the conduct of the war.

There can be only one answer to the treacherous attack of the Japanese and that is war to final victory, cost what it may in blood, treasure, and tears. . . .

Mr. REED of Illinois. Mr. Speaker, our Nation has been struck an insidious, dishonorable, and cowardly blow directed against our fleet, our territory, and our citizens. The perpetrators will find that they have affronted a powerful foe. They will learn that when people accustomed to freedom are assailed they support their Government with every ounce of their strength and endurance. They will find the American people united in a determination to avenge a foul crime and exterminate a foul criminal. There is no disunion in America. The vote on the sanding resolution will demonstrate to the world that our President has behind him a united Congress backed by a united pub-

lic. America aroused will hesitate not an instant and will never rest until the world Is rid of the monsters who planned and executed yesterday's dastardly outrage. Japan will rue the day that the fury of peaceful, liberty loving people was unleashed.

Mr. McCORMACK. Mr. Speaker, I ask for a vote, and on that I demand the yeas and nays.

Miss RANKIN of Montana. Mr. Speaker—

The SPEAKER. The gentleman from Massachusetts demands the yeas and nays. Those who favor taking this vote by the yeas and nays will rise and remain standing until counted.

The yeas and nays were ordered.

Miss RANKIN of Montana. Mr. Speaker, I would like to be heard.

The SPEAKER. The yeas and nays have been ordered. The question is, Will the House suspend the rules and pass the resolution?

Miss RANKIN of Montana. Mr. Speaker, a point of order.

The SPEAKER. A roll call may not be interrupted.

The question was taken; and there were—yeas 388, nays 1, not voting 41. . . .

Congressional Record, Senate, 77th Congress, 1st session, Dec. 8, 1941, 9505–9506; *Congressional Record,* House, 77th Congress, 1st session, Dec. 8, 1941, 9520, 9536.

133   Congress Declares War on Germany and Italy

December 11, 1941

Three days after the declaration of war against Japan, President Franklin D. Roosevelt sent a brief message to Congress. It was read in both chambers by the reading clerks. Earlier that day Germany and its ally, Italy, declared war on the United States in response to the U.S. declaration of war on Japan (see documents 131 and 132). In his message urging Congress to declare war on Germany and Italy, Roosevelt said, "The long known and the long expected has thus taken place. The forces endeavoring to enslave the entire world now are moving toward this hemisphere."

The Senate responded with a 88–0 vote on war with Germany and 90–0 on war with Italy—two more senators having arrived for the vote. In the House the vote was equally lopsided, with 393 members voting in favor of war and 36 not voting. In the case of Italy, the House vote was 399 members for war, with 30 not voting. This time, instead of voting against war as she had in the case of Japan, Jeannette Rankin of Montana voted "present" when the clerk called the role on the votes for war with both Germany and Italy. Shortly after voting, the House received notice that the Senate had passed its war resolution, S.J. Res. 119, and without objection the House vacated its war resolution and by unanimous consent passed the Senate version.

[IN THE SENATE]

The VICE PRESIDENT. The Chair lays before the Senate a message from the President of the United States, which the clerk will read.

The Chief Clerk read as follows:

To the Congress of the United States:

On the morning of December 11 the Government of Germany, pursuing its course of world conquest, declared war against the United States.

The long known and the long expected has thus taken place. The forces endeavoring to enslave the entire world now are moving toward this hemisphere.

Never before has there been a greater challenge to life, liberty, and civilization.

Delay invites greater danger. Rapid and united effort by all the peoples of the world who are determined to remain free will insure a world victory of the forces of justice and of righteousness over the forces of savagery and of barbarism.

Italy also has declared war against the United States.

I therefore request the Congress to recognize a state of war between the United States and Germany and between the United States and Italy.

FRANKLIN D. ROOSEVELT.

The White House, *December 11, 1941.*

The VICE PRESIDENT. The message will be printed and referred to the Committee on Foreign Relations.

Declaration of State of War with Germany

Mr. CONNALLY, from the Committee on Foreign Relations, reported an original joint resolution (S.J. Res. 119) declaring that a state of war exists between the Government of Germany and the Government and the people of the United States, and making provision to prosecute the same, which was read the first time by its title, and the second time at length, as follows:

Whereas the Government of Germany has formally declared war against the Government of the people of the United States of America: Therefore be it

Resolved, etc., That the state of war between the United States and the Government of Germany, which has thus been thrust upon the United States, is hereby formally declared; and the President is hereby authorized and directed to employ the entire naval and military forces of the United States and the resources of the Government to carry on war against the Government of Germany; and, to bring the conflict to a successful termination, all of the resources of the country are hereby pledged by the Congress of the United States.

Mr. CONNALLY. Mr. President, I shall presently ask unanimous consent for the immediate consideration of the joint resolution just read to the Senate. Before the request is submitted, however, I desire to say that, being advised of the declaration of war upon the United States by the Governments of Germany and Italy, and anticipating a message by the President of the United States in relation thereto, and after a conference with the Secretary of State, as chairman of the Committee on Foreign Relations, I called a meeting of the committee this morning and submitted to the committee the course I expected to pursue as chairman and the request which I expected to make.

I am authorized by the Committee on Foreign Relations to say to the Senate that after consideration of the text of the joint resolution which I have reported and after mature consideration of all aspects of this matter, the membership of the Committee on Foreign Relations unanimously approve and agree to the course suggested. One member of the committee was absent, but I have authority to express his views.

Mr. President, I ask unanimous consent for the present consideration of the joint resolution.

The VICE PRESIDENT. Is there objection?

There being no objection, the Senate proceeded to consider the joint resolution (S.J. Res. 119) declaring that a state of war exists between the Government of Germany and the Government and the people of the United States, and making provision to prosecute the same.

The VICE PRESIDENT. The question is on the engrossment and third reading of the joint resolution.

The joint resolution was ordered to be engrossed for a third reading, and was read the third time.

The VICE PRESIDENT. The joint resolution having been read the third time, the question is, shall it pass?

Mr. CONNALLY. On that question I ask for the yeas and nays.

The yeas and nays were ordered, and the Chief Clerk proceeded to call the roll.

Mr. MEAD (when Mr. Wagner's name was called). My colleague the senior Senator from New York [Mr. Wagner] is unavoidably absent today. He has requested me to say that if he were present, he would vote "yea" on the joint resolution.

The roll call was concluded.

Mr. HILL. I announce that the Senator from Washington [Mr. Bone] is absent from the Senate because of illness. I am advised that if present and voting he would vote "yea."

The Senator from Montana [Mr. Wheeler] is absent because of the serious illness of his brother, who is in a hospital in Brookline, Mass., so desperately ill that the Senator from Montana had to leave Washington yesterday for Massachusetts. I am advised that if present the Senator from Montana would vote "yea" on the pending joint resolution.

The Senator from Oklahoma [Mr. Lee], the Senator from Maryland [Mr. Tydings], and the Senator from New Jersey [Mr. Smathers] are unavoidably detained. I am advised that if present and voting these Senators would vote "yea."

Mr. PEPPER. My colleague the senior Senator from Florida [Mr. Andrews] bas been engaged in the conduct of a hearing as chairman of a subcommittee of the Committee on Interstate Commerce, and is striving to reach the Senate Chamber, but has not been able to get here up to this time. He has sent word to me to ask that it be announced that if present and voting he would vote "yea" on the pending joint resolution.

The result was announced—yeas 88, nays 0. . . .

Declaration of State of War with Italy

Mr. CONNALLY, from the Committee on Foreign Relations, reported an original joint resolution (S.J. Res. 120) declaring that a state of war exists between the Government of Italy and the Government and the people of the United States and making provision to prosecute the same, which was read the first time by its title and the second time at length, as follows:

Whereas the Government of Italy has formally declared war against the Government and the people of the United States of America: Therefore be it

Resolved, etc., That the state of war between the United States and the Government of Italy which has thus been thrust upon the United States is hereby formally declared; and the President is hereby authorized and directed to employ the entire naval and military forces of the United States and the resources of the Government to carry on war against the Government of Italy, and, to bring the conflict to a successful termination, all of the resources of the country are hereby pledged by the Congress of the United States.

Mr. CONNALLY. Mr. President, with the same statement which I made earlier with regard to the Senate, Joint Resolution 119 which has just been passed, I ask unanimous consent for the present consideration of Senate Joint Resolution 120.

The VICE PRESIDENT. Is there objection to the present consideration of the joint resolution?

There being no objection, the Senate proceeded to consider the joint resolution (S.J. Res. 120) declaring that a state of war exists between the Government of Italy and the (government and the people of the United States and making provision to prosecute the same.

The VICE PRESIDENT. The question is on the engrossment and third reading of the joint resolution.

The joint resolution was ordered to be engrossed for a third reading, and was read the third time.

The VICE PRESIDENT. The joint resolution having been read the third time, the question is, Shall it pass?

Mr. CONNALLY. Mr. President, on the passage of the joint resolution, I ask for the yeas and nays.

The yeas and nays were ordered, and the legislative clerk proceeded to call the roll.

Mr. MEAD (when Mr. Wagner's name was called). My colleague the senior Senator from New York is unavoidably absent. He requests me to say that if he were present he would vote "yea" on the passage of the joint resolution.

The roll call was concluded.

Mr. HILL. I announce that the Senator from Washington [Mr. Bone] is absent from the Senate because of illness. I am advised that if present and voting he would vote "Yea."

The Senator from Montana [Mr. Wheeler] is absent because of the serious illness of his brother. I am advised that if present and voting he would vote "yea."

The Senator from Oklahoma [Mr. Lee] and the Senator from Maryland [Mr. Tydings] are unavoidably detained. I am advised that if present and voting both Senators would vote "yea."

The result was announced—yeas 90, nays 0. . . .

[IN THE HOUSE OF REPRESENTATIVES]

Declaration of War Against Germany

Mr. McCORMACK. Mr. Speaker, I move to amend the rules and pass House Joint Resolution 256, which I send to the desk and ask to have read.

The Clerk read as follows:

Whereas the Government of Germany has formally declared war against the Government and the people of the United States of America: Therefore be it

Resolved, etc., That the state of war between the United States and the Government of Germany which has thus been thrust upon the United

States to hereby formally declared; and the President is hereby authorized and directed to employ the entire naval and military forces of the United States and the resources of the Government to carry on war against the Government of Germany; and, to bring the conflict to a successful termination, all of the resources of the country as hereby pledged by the Congress of the United States.

The SPEAKER. The question is, will the House suspend the rules and pass the joint resolution?

Mr. McCORMACK. Mr. Speaker, on that I demand the yeas and nays.

The yeas and nays were ordered.

The question was taken; and there were—yeas 393, answered "present" 1, not voting 36. . . .

Declaration of War Against Italy

Mr. McCORMACK. Mr. Speaker, I move to suspend the rule and pass Senate Joint Resolution 120, which I have sent to the Clerk's desk.

The Clerk read as follows:

Whereas the Government of Italy has formally declared war against the Government and the people of the United States of America: Therefore be it

Resolved, etc., That the state of war between the United States and the Government of Italy, which has thus been thrust upon the United States, is hereby formally declared; and the President is hereby authorized and directed to employ the entire naval and military forces of the United States and the resources of the Government to carry on war against the Government of Italy; and, to bring the convict to a successful termination, all of the resources of the country are hereby pledged by the Congress of the United States.

The SPEAKER. The question is, Will the House suspend the rules and pass the resolution?

Mr. McCORMACK. Mr. Speaker, on this vote I ask for the yeas and nays.

The yeas and nays were ordered.

The question was taken; and there were—yeas 399, answered "present" 1, not voting 30. . . .

Congressional Record, Senate, 77th Congress, 1st session, Dec. 11, 1941, 9652–9653; *Congressional Record,* House, 77th Congress, 1st session, Dec. 11, 1941, 9665–9666.

134   Debate Regarding the Establishment of the House Un-American Activities Committee

January 3, 1945

The House Un-American Activities Committee (HUAC), established in 1945, was the most controversial committee ever established by Congress. It grew directly out of its predecessor, the Select Committee on Un-American Activities (the Dies Committee), which was formed in 1938 (see document 128).

The House had conducted two earlier investigations into subversive and un-American activities in relatively minor committees that held hearings in 1930 under the chairmanship of Hamilton Fish (R-N.Y.) and in 1934 under the chairmanship of John McCormack (D-Mass.). With the creation of the Dies Commit-

tee, the controversy surrounding such investigations increased dramatically.

When Martin Dies announced his retirement from Congress at the end of his term in January 1945, many in Congress and in the nation thought the committee he had chaired would cease to exist. But when the 79th Congress convened in January 1945, Representative John D. Rankin (D-Miss.) offered an amendment to the rules of the House that proposed the establishment of a House Un-American Activities Committee to be a permanent standing committee. Even though a substantial number of House members had serious reservations about the establishment of the HUAC, many found themselves unable to vote against an anti-Communist measure during the final roll call vote because of potential repercussions in their districts. The amendment passed 208–186, with 40 not voting.

For a short time HUAC confined itself to noncontroversial investigations that avoided the sensational headlines and charges the Dies Committee had generated. During the 80th Congress, which began in 1947, Representative J. Parnell Thomas (D-N.J.), a former member of the Dies Committee, became chairman of HUAC. Under his leadership the committee set out to expose Communists in all aspects of American life, paying little regard to the consequences to the innocent lives and careers that would be destroyed in the process.

The House Un-American Activities Committee created a climate of fear in America that was successfully exploited by numerous politicians whose careers were launched by anti-Communist crusades. The committee's investigations of Hollywood writers led to the creation of blacklists that kept suspected Communists or Communist sympathizers from working in the movie industry and in radio and television. In 1948 HUAC made headlines when Whittaker Chambers, a senior Time *magazine editor, testified that former State Department official Alger Hiss had been a Communist and Soviet agent. Hiss denied the charges but was later convicted of perjury. In the 1950s HUAC investigations, which often amounted to little more than witch hunts designed to smear political or ideological opponents, led to a climate of fear and conformism that stifled political discourse in schools and public places.*

No committee in the history of Congress has done more to undermine the rights of American citizens as guaranteed by the Constitution. The affects of HUAC investigations of the 1940s and 1950s left an enduring legacy of intolerance and bigotry. Many Americans became disillusioned with excessive government interference in private lives because of the ramifications of HUAC and turned away from civic participation.

By the 1960s the political pendulum began to swing against the extreme measures of HUAC. In some instances violent confrontations took place at anti-HUAC demonstrations. By the mid-1960s HUAC sought unsuccessfully to appease its critics by investigating the Ku Klux Klan. After a number of years of declining influence and controversy, the House finally voted to abolish the committee on January 14, 1975.

RULES OF THE HOUSE

Mr. SABATH. Mr. Speaker, I offer a resolution and ask for its immediate consideration.

The Clerk read the resolution (H. Res. 5), as follows:

Resolved, That the rules of the Seventy-eighth Congress be, and they are hereby, adopted as the rules of the Seventy-ninth Congress.

Mr. RANKIN. Mr. Speaker, I offer an amendment.

The Clerk read as follows:

Amendment offered by Mr. RANKIN: After the word "Congress", at the end of the resolution, strike out the period, insert a comma, and insert the following:

"That rule X of the Rules of the House of Representatives is amended by adding after clause 40a of the first paragraph a new clause to read as follows:

" '40b. On un-American Activities, to consist of 9 members.'

"Rule XI of the Rules of the House of Representatives is amended by adding after clause 40a two new clauses to read as follows:

" '40b. To un-American Activities—to the Committee on un-American Activities.

" '40c. The Committee on Un-American Activities, as a whole or by subcommittee, is authorized to make from time to time investigations of (1) the extent, character, and objects of un-American propaganda activities in the United States, (2) the diffusion within the United States of subversive and un-American propaganda that is instigated from foreign countries or of a domestic origin and attacks the principle of the form of government as guaranteed by our Constitution, and (3) all other questions in relation thereto that would aid Congress in any necessary remedial legislation.

" 'The Committee on Un-American Activities shall report to the House (or to the Clerk of the House if the House is not in session) the results of any such investigation, together with such recommendations as it deems advisable.

" 'For the purpose of any such investigation, the Committee on Un-American Activities, or any subcommittee thereof, is authorized to sit and act at such times and places within the United States, whether or not the House is sitting, has recessed, or has adjourned, to hold such hearings, to require the attendance of such witnesses and the production of such books, papers, and documents, and to take such testimony, as it deems necessary. Subpoenas may be issued under the signature of the chairman of the committee or by any member designated by any such chairman, and may be served by any person designated by any such chairman or member.' "

Mr. RANKIN. Mr. Speaker, the object of this amendment is to extend the life of the Committee on Un-American Activities, usually referred to as the Dies committee, and to make it one of the standing committees of the House.

It also provides for giving that committee the right to report legislation in order that its recommendations may be brought to the floor of the House for consideration in the regular way.

The Dies committee, or the Committee on Un-American Activities, was created in 1938. It has done a marvelous work in the face of all the criticism that has been hurled at its chairman and at its members. I submit that during these trying times the Committee on Un-American Activities has performed a duty second to none ever performed by any committee of this House.

Today, when our boys are fighting to preserve American institutions, I submit it is no time to destroy the records of that committee, it is no time to relax our vigilance. We should carry on in the regular way and keep this committee intact, and above all things, save those records.

There have been more than 5,000 different occasions in which various agencies of this Government have come to this committee for information on un-American activities. That means the Department of State, the Department of War, the Navy Department, the Army Intelligence, the Navy Intelligence, the Department of Justice, and the F.B.I. They have all come to search those records, and have found in them a wealth of information that has gone far toward protecting this Nation from saboteurs of all kinds.

Mr. MUNDT. Mr. Speaker, will the gentleman yield?

Mr. RANKIN. I yield.

Mr. MUNDT. Mr. Speaker, I want to congratulate the gentleman for introducing his amendment. I shall vote for it. As a member of the Dies committee, myself, I know that under the proper chairman such a permanent committee as the gentleman from Mississippi proposes can render a great public services.

Now I would like to ask a question. If the resolution is adopted, as I hope it will be, is it provided that the extensive and highly important records now held by the Dies committee will be turned over to the new committee?

Mr. RANKIN. It is understood that those records will be turned over to this committee. Of course, they are now in the possession of the House. I want to say to you that our policemen in the House Office Building deserve a vote of thanks from this House for protecting those records in the last few days.

The passage of this amendment will not interfere with any orderly procedure, and I do not see how any man in this House can vote against this amendment. I hope it passes unanimously.

. . . .

The SPEAKER. The Chair recognizes the gentleman from Illinois [Mr. Sabath].

Mr. SABATH. Mr. Speaker, in view of the fact that the House a few weeks ago appointed a special committee for the purpose of studying the rules of the House governing its procedure, I move that this resolution be referred to the Committee on Rules.

Mr. RANKIN. Mr. Speaker, I rise in opposition to the motion.

The SPEAKER. That is not a proper motion, the Chair will say, at this time, because there is an amendment to the resolution offered by the gentleman from Illinois which is pending and which must be disposed of.

Mr. SABATH. Mr. Speaker. I move that the amendment be referred to the Committee on Rules.

Mr. RANKIN. Mr. Speaker, I make a point of order. An amendment cannot be referred to a committee. That is out of order. An amendment to a pending motion cannot be referred to a committee.

The SPEAKER. The Chair holds that the amendment must be disposed of.

Mr. RANKIN. That is right.

Mr. COCHRAN. Mr. Speaker, I arise in opposition to the amendment.

Mr. Speaker, there is no doubt but that the amendment is in order, but under the ordinary procedure of the House resolutions creating committees are introduced and referred to the Committee on Rules. This applies to standing committees as well as select committees. There an opportunity is given for a hearing to determine the advisability of bringing the resolution before the House.

What does this resolution to the rules do? In creating the standing committee it likewise provides for the type of legislation that the committee will consider. At the present time legislation of that character is considered by one of the most outstanding committee of this House, the Judiciary Committee.

Much has been said about the preservation of the records of the Dies committee. That is not an issue here in this amendment because there is absolutely nothing in the amendment that provides for placing the record of the Dies committee under the control of the standing committee which the amendment seeks to create.

To place the records of the Dies committee in the hands of a standing committee of the House it would be necessary for the House to pass a resolution authorizing the Clerk of the House to turn the records over to that committee.

I agree with the gentleman from Mississippi that the Dies committee to a certain extend did perform a real public service. That was at a time when all the members of the committee were participating in its deliberations and agreeing upon the procedure that the committee should follow. Later on the committee ceased to function in this way, or at least that charge was made by members of the committee who maintained that the chairman seemed to assume entire responsibility and that statements credited to the committee were issued that members of the committee had never seen or approved. It is no secret that some members of this committee resigned because of their displeasure at the manner in which the committee was being operated.

Every Member of this House is aware that there was an outstanding disagreement between the Department of Justice and the chairman of the committee. Efforts were made to settle this disagreement without success. After the war started the committee was not in full cooperation with the intelligence branches of the Army, Navy, and State Departments, but as time went on this was ironed out. The committee had a tremendous number of names in its files and almost daily the Federal Bureau of Investigation and the Intelligence Division of the Army, Navy, and State Departments would check the files in search of information relative to individuals they were investigating.

The last time the gentleman from Texas, Mr. Dies, appeared before the Committee on Accounts, asking for an additional appropriation, he advised that committee that there was complete harmony between his committee and the Department of Justice and the State, War, and Navy Departments. Today these four agencies of or Government are investigating subversive activities. Millions of dollars have been appropriated for that purpose, for the Federal Bureau of Investigation, and the Intelligence Branches of the State, Army, and the Navy. The Representatives of those agencies can continue checking the records of the Dies committee, with the approval of the Clerk of the House.

In all about $675,000 of the taxpayers' money has been spent by the Dies committee. Officer were opened in New York, Chicago, Philadelphia, Detroit, Los Angeles, and also in Texas.

In recent years the Dies committee has been a one-man committee. Outside of one investigation, meetings were seldom held during the past 2 years. One member of the committee came to me an said he had asked for the names of the employees of the committee of which he was a member, the salaries they were receiving, and the duties that they were performing. He, a member of that committee, said he was denied that information. I told him he could get part of the information if he asked for it. He said that he did ask for it. I said to him then that he should ask again. Then he asked me for it, and I gave the names of the employees and their salaries, but I had no knowledge of what their duties were. I consider the expenditure of public funds a public record, and so long as I am chairman of the Committee on Accounts, unless this House passes a resolution to the contrary, Members of this House can always learn how the money they appropriated is being expended.

Mr. THOMAS of New Jersey. Mr. Speaker, will the gentleman yield?

Mr. COCHRAN. Yes.

Mr. THOMAS of New Jersey. To say, in defense of the chairman of that committee, right along the lines about which the gentleman has spoken, that I know of no time when I served on that committee, and that was some 6 ½ or 7 years, when a member of the committee could not find out at all times just who was employed, and how much that employee was being paid, and I just cannot understand how any member of that committee, even though he might be a new dealer, could ask such a question and not get the answer.

Mr. COCHRAN. And I say to the gentle that I have the utmost confidence in the Member I refer to and that he came to me and told me that he could not get the information.

Mr. RANKIN. Mr. Speaker, will the gentleman yield?

Mr. COCHRAN. I yield.

Mr. RANKIN. I have inquired many times, and I never asked the Dies committee for information in its possession that I did not get it. The War Department never asked the Dies committee for information in its possession that it did not get it; the F.B.I. never asked the Dies committee for information, the Department of Justice and the Department of State never asked the Dies committee for information within its possession that they did not get it right then and there; and at this moment representatives of the State Department and other departments of the Government, are over there getting information from those files to protect us and to protect this Government for which our boys are fighting.

Mr. COCHRAN. Mr. Speaker, let me say to the gentleman from Mississippi that what he enumerates at the moment is correct; but I know that year after year the gentleman from Texas refused the departments the gentleman from Mississippi has named, information they requested.

Mr. THOMAS of New Jersey. I have to deny that statement. That statement, I am sorry, is not true; it is a misstatement.

Mr. COCHRAN. Mr. Speaker, I do not yield to the gentleman from New Jersey. I will let his denial stand but again say there was a time when the chairman of the committee refused to cooperate with the executive branch of the Government.

Mr. THOMAS of New Jersey. There never was a time when we did not give to the departments everything they wanted.

Mr. COCHRAN. Mr. Speaker, we have a rule that provides—and the Speaker has so held—that 3 days after the beginning of a new Congress, and that is today, the records of the Dies committee and every other committee of the House, standing and select, shall be turned over to the Clerk of the House. Further than that, we have a law which provides how the Clerk of the House of Representatives shall handle those records. He has the power to place those records in the Library of Congress. They are valuable records because they contain a tremendous number of names. And how did they get those names? They confiscated mailing lists of so-called subversive organizations they suspected of violating the laws of this country. I have been receiving, from organizations literature of every type. I would not have received that literature had my name not been on such a mailing list. So, if they confiscated the mailing lists of some of these organizations that have been sending out literature over this long period of years, undoubtedly my name is on the list; and so is yours. But that does not mean I was a member of the organization or organizations. I say this matter should be properly handled by the Committee on Rules of this House. If a proper showing can be made to that committee that the rules of the House should be amended and that they should create a standing committee or that a select committee should be provided, the Committee on Rules have the power to report a resolution. Let us proceed in an orderly way as we have done in the past. I hope this amendment will be voted down and then if the gentleman from Mississippi so desires he can offer a resolution that will be referred to the Committee on Rules.

Mr. CASE of South Dakota. Mr. Speaker, will the gentleman yield?

Mr. COCHRAN. I yield.

Mr. CASE of South Dakota. What would be the effect of the adoption of this amendment so far as the finances of the committee are concerned?

Mr. COCHRAN. The committee would have no right to financial assistance other than for a clerk or two because the amendment contains no provision for any special expenses. Certainly if the House creates a standing committee it will give that committee a clerk or two as it does all standing committees.

Mr. CASE of South Dakota. If the gentleman will yield further on that point.

Mr. COCHRAN. I yield.

Mr. CASE of South Dakota. In the past the special resolution creating the Dies committee or the Committee on Un-American Activities, has itself carried an authorization for certain appropriations; is not that correct?

Mr. COCHRAN. No; but the Accounts Committee also feels if the House creates a select committee it is a mandate to allow expenses. It has always carried out the mandate but this is not providing for a select committee.

Mr. CASE of South Dakota. It was done by an accompanying resolution.

Mr. COCHRAN. Yes; the Accounts Committee would bring in a resolution. The Dies committee ends today; there will be no Dies committee after today unless the House creates such a committee. The gentleman from Mississippi desires not to extend the life of the Dies committee but to create a new standing committee of the House. That is what he seeks to do. This new standing committee of the House will have no assistance whatsoever until the Appropriations Committee provides the assistance.

Mr. CASE of South Dakota. If the committee were created as a standing committee of the House by the adoption of the amendment proposed, would it not be true that then its funds would have to come through the Appropriations Committee rather than the Committee on Accounts?

Mr. COCHRAN. Yes; it would go to the Committee on Appropriations. The gentleman said "standing committee"?

Mr. CASE of South Dakota. Yes.

Mr. COCHRAN. It would go to the Appropriations Committee. The Accounts Committee does not handle that appropriation.

Mr. RANKIN. Will the gentleman yield?

Mr. COCHRAN. I yield to the gentle from Mississippi.

Mr. RANKIN. If this amendment is adopted, which I am sure it will be, then this committee will be provided with funds just as any other committee of the House is provided with funds.

Mr. CASE of South Dakota. Coming from the Legislative Appropriations Committee?

Mr. COCHRAN. But not with any money for expenses such as was allowed the Dies committee.

Mr. RANKIN. It would come to the House for funds to carry on its activities.

Mr. CASE of South Dakota. In that case, then, it would be up to the Appropriations Committee to recommend whatever amount it wanted to give them?

Mr. COCHRAN. I say that under the rules of the House the Legislative Subcommittee of the Appropriations Committee would recommend a clerk or two clerks or whatever it desired and it would be carried in a deficiency bill; but there would be no money in a lump sum voted for the standing committee of the House under the amendment that the gentleman has offered.

Mr. MARCANTONIO. Will the gentleman yield?

Mr. COCHRAN. I yield to the gentlemen from New York.

Mr. MARCANTONIO. If this amendment is adopted we will be establishing a standing committee which heretofore has been a select committee, am I correct?

Mr. COCHRAN. That is true to the extent it would have the jurisdiction provided in the amendment.

Mr. EBERHARTER. Will the gentleman yield?

Mr. COCHRAN. I yield to the gentleman from Pennsylvania.

Mr. EBERHARTER. Mr. Speaker, as most Members of the House know, I have for a little over a year been a member of the Special Committee to Investigate Un-American Activities. In my opinion, this is certainly the wrong time to bring up the question as to renewal of the same type of committee.

This is a most controversial question. It is a question that every Member wants to consider at length. It is a question which should take perhaps 2 or 3 days of debate. It is a question involving very, very many important problems and many important decisions.

I call the attention of the Members to the fact that up until the date of the expiration of this committee it required a personnel of 13 employees, which cost thousands of dollars a month. If you are now going to establish a committee to carry on the same kind of activities, you are practically authorizing the expenditure of anywhere from $75,000 to $200,000 a year, and I say this is no time to do anything of that sort.

I may say also that up to the present time I have not seen a piece of paper in the form of any tentative report that is supposed to be presented to the House of Representatives, and I am a member of that committee. If your action today prolongs the committee and it continues to proceed in that manner, I think it is the commencement on the first day this House is in session of a procedure that will lead to disunity. We want to start out in harmony and follow the advice of the Speaker in an endeavor to work in unity and cohesion and to use important reasons for any action we take—not go ahead on passion, prejudice, and on unreliable matter.

Mr. Speaker, this amendment should be defeated if for no other reason than to give us time to think over the question and let us all decide for ourselves. I was under the impression that the minority leader and the minority party had agreed that the further activities of committees of this sort would not be sanctioned in the new Congress.

I hope that the Republican Members as well as the Democratic Members of the House will vote against this amendment.

Mr. MARTIN of Massachusetts. The gentleman has quoted me as being in some agreement about some of these committees being continued. May I inform the gentleman that I have not made any agreement with anyone on any committee.

Mr. EBERHARTER. I beg the gentleman's pardon. I did not say that the gentleman from Massachusetts, the minority leader, had entered into any agreement, but I said it was my understanding, and I will say this, that I have seen published reports in the newspapers to the effect that he would have no objection to the discontinuance of the activities of the Dies committee.

Mr. COCHRAN. Mr. Speaker, I yield to the gentleman from Georgia [Mr. Cox] for an observation.

Mr. COX. Mr. Speaker, I dislike to participate in this discussion, but I would feel ashamed of myself if I did not take the opportunity to publicly express a very deep appreciation of the work done by the so-called Dies committee. Much has been said with reference to the large expenditures made by the committee. As for this, may I say that, in my judgment, the House never made a wiser or a better investment that it made in the setting up of that committee and providing it with funds to carry on its activities.

I feel very deeply about this thing. Frankly, I am not enthusiastic about the setting up of special investigating committees during the new Congress. With respect to what has been said about agreements, let me say that there have been no agreements, but a tacit understanding in certain circles that as few of these committees would be set up as might be possible. The argument that this is a matter for consideration of the Committee on Rules is, in my judgment, not quite—

Mr. MARTIN of Massachusetts. Mr. Speaker, will the gentleman yield for a correction?

Mr. COX. I did not mean to include anybody on this side as being a party to any kind of understanding.

Mr. MARTIN of Massachusetts. That is all right, then.

Mr. COX. As to the argument that this is a matter that should first go to the Committee on Rules, may I say that maybe that would be the wiser course to take, but still to me the argument does not seem entirely valid. The Committee on Rules is the creature of this House, and any recommendation or proposal that that committee might see fit to offer would have to come back to the House. The question raised in the pending amendment is an all-important question, and it is one upon which this House must make a decision sooner or later. Make no mistake about that. The people of this country are very much aroused on this whole question, and they are deeply concerned. They are not willing that the work started by the Dies committee come to an end. In some of the press there has been much shouting over the demise of the Dies committee, but let me say that in the hearts of the people there is a desire that the Congress, at least, meet its responsibility by the setting up of some kind of an agency to stand guard for America.

This decision has to be made. This House may accept this resolution, or it may be rejected. If you turn it down, you may expect a resolution back here to set up another investigating committee, and such a resolution will carry by an overwhelming majority in this body.

If it should be pleasing to the gentleman from Mississippi to withdraw his amendment and let the matter come first to the Committee on Rules, and let a new record be developed, I would make no objection, but as for hearings, hearings have been held and the record is now in the keeping of this House.

Mr. RANKIN. Mr. Speaker, will the gentleman yield?

Mr. COX. I yield to the gentleman from Mississippi.

Mr. RANKIN. If I were to take that course these valuable records that probably involve the fate of this Nation, the safety of the American people, would be dissipated.

Mr. COX. You know the source from which comes this denunciation of the Dies committee. Let me make this observa-

tion. There is a world-wide conspiracy—there is a campaign against constitutional government going on all over the world. The people who are engineering and participating in the furtherance of this campaign are the people who are most often denouncing the work of the Dies committee.

Mr. RANKIN. One of the greatest of American institutions is the American Legion. I hold in my hand the memorial of the American Legion, adopted in Chicago, Ill., on September 18, 1944, memorializing the Congress of the United States to "continue and make permanent the congressional Committee on Un-American Activities."

Mr. COX. May I say to the gentleman that the gentleman from Missouri very kindly yielded to me, and I must not further transgress upon his courtesy.

I do not know what the House may do, but sooner or later decision on this question must be made. and made by this House.

Mr. COCHRAN. Mr. Speaker, I yield such time as he may desire to the gentleman from Massachusetts [Mr. McCormack].

Mr. McCORMACK. Mr. Speaker, this is the opening day of the Seventy-ninth Congress. I hope that on this day we will view this amendment from the angle of reason and from the angle of the legislative history of the very body of which we are Members. I do not know when in the history of our country the National House of Representatives has ever provided by rule for a permanent investigating committee. Mark what we are doing. This is not a question of establishing an investigating committee to investigate conditions that arise from time to time; it is a question of amending the rules of the House to provide for a permanent standing committee that does not consider legislation, but has one subject, one field, the field of investigating and making a report.

The amendment provides:

The Committee on Un-American Activities shall report to the House the results of any such investigation, together with such recommendations as it deems advisable.

You will note, not legislation, recommendations.

Then, further:

The Committee on Un-American Activities as a whole or by subcommittee is authorized to make from time to time investigations.

We are not considering a resolution out of the Committee on Rules for the appointment of a special committee to investigate for the continuance of this session.

We are considering by this amendment the establishment of a permanent committee, a standing committee of the House. I agree with the gentleman from Georgia [Mr. COX]. I hope that the House will not accept this amendment. The merits of it cannot be discussed today. It is a question of whether or not the House shall provide for a standing committee or shall refer this to the Committee on Rules for consideration. I am confident the Committee on Rules will forthwith report a resolution continuing for this Congress the Committee to Investigate Un-American Activities. If that is done, I can assure the gentleman from Mississippi that immediately upon that resolution being reported out, if the House takes such action today, I shall put it on the program for immediate consideration. There is a big difference between establishing a standing committee to investigate and establishing a special investigating committee for a particular Congress. If this amendment is adopted, as far as I know, it will be the first time in the history of this body that a committee of this kind was ever established as a permanent or standing committee.

Mr. RANKIN. Mr. Speaker, will the gentleman yield?

Mr. MCCORMACK. I yield.

Mr. RANKIN. I call the attention of the gentleman from Massachusetts to the fact that this is to be a standing committee. It is to be a legislative committee with powers to make these investigations. This would amend rule 11 of the Rules of the House by adding after clause 40 (a) two new clauses. Section 11 is the one which says to what committees legislation shall be referred, and getting down to this amendment it says:

To the Committee on Un-American Activities—

That is, the legislation which refers to un-American activities to be referred to the Committee on Un-American Activities. Of course, it is a legislative committee.

Mr. MCCORMACK. What type of legislation, that is the question. There is a question of jurisdiction of committees, of other permanent and standing committees. Certainly the existing rules provide the type of bills or resolutions that are referred to a standing committee. This resolution establishing a standing committee, assuming it can recommend legislation, does not set forth the type of legislation.

Mr. ENGEL of Michigan. Mr. Speaker, will the gentleman yield?

Mr. COCHRAN. I yield.

Mr. ENGEL of Michigan. What assurance can the majority leader give the House that the records of the Dies committee will not be destroyed, as charged by the gentleman from Mississippi, if the resolution is defeated?

Mr. MCCORMACK. Mr. Speaker, I think the gentleman's question is a very proper one.

The SPEAKER. If the gentleman from Massachusetts will yield, the Clerk of the House is a sworn officer of the House, and not only the Rules of the House, but the law of the land, provide that they shall be put into his hands and what shall be the disposition of such records. The Chair thinks that answers the question of whether or not these papers are going to be destroyed.

Mr. CITRON. Mr. Speaker, I will say to the gentleman from Massachusetts that we have a penal statute which provides that if the Clerk of the House or any other individual destroys those files, or even takes the files away, he can be sent to the penitentiary.

Mr. MCCORMACK. Mr. Speaker, I am not discussing the merits of this because I voted for the Dies resolution every time it came up. I hope my friend, the gentleman from Mississippi, will withdraw it. I am urging the House to realize that a vote against this is not a vote against a special investigating committee. It is a vote against the procedure that in one-hundred-and-fifty-odd

years of constitutional history, no Congress, no membership of this body, has ever followed to establish a permanent committee of this kind. I hope the amendment will be defeated.

Mr. CITRON. Mr. Speaker, I move the previous question on the amendment and the resolution to final passage.

The previous question was ordered.

Mr. CASE of South Dakota. Mr. Speaker, a parliamentary inquiry.

The SPEAKER. The gentleman will state it.

Mr. CASE of South Dakota. My inquiry has been partly answered by the statement of the Chair, but I now ask, What is the status of the records of the Dies committee at the present time and what will be their status if this amendment should be adopted?

The SPEAKER. This amendment does not change the status of the papers of the Dies committee at all, unless further action of the House is taken. For the information of the House the Chair will read two rules.

First:

RULE XXXVII
PAPERS

The clerks of the several committees of the House shall, within 3 days after the final adjournment of a Congress, deliver to the Clerk of the House all bills, joint resolutions, petitions, and other papers referred to the committee, together with all evidence taken by such committee under the order of the House during the said Congress and not reported to the House; and in the event of the failure or neglect of any clerk of a committee to comply with this rule the Clerk of the House shall, within 3 days thereafter, take into his keeping all such papers and testimony.

Also:

RULE XXXVIII
WITHDRAWAL OF PAPERS

No memorial or other paper presented to the House shall be withdrawn from its files without its leave, and if withdrawn there from certified copies thereof shall be left in the office of the Clerk, but when an act may pass for the settlement of the Claim, the Clerk is authorized to transmit to the officer in charge with the settlement thereof the papers on file in his office relating to such claim, or may loan temporarily to an officer or bureau of the executive departments any papers on file in his office relating to any mutter pending before such officer, or bureau, taking proper receipt therefor.

Those are the rules of the House. The law provides in title II, United States Code, section 147, as follows:

The Clerk of the House of Representatives is authorized and directed to deliver to the Librarian of Congress all bound volumes of original papers, general petitions, printed matter, books, and manuscripts on June 6, 1900, in, or that may thereafter have come Into or may come into, the files of the House, which in his judgment are not required to be retained in the immediate custody of the file clerk; and it shall be the duty of the Librarian of Congress to cause all such matter so delivered to him to be properly classified by Congress and arranged for preservation and ready reference. All of such matter to be held as a part of the files of the House of Representatives, subject to its orders and rules.

The majority leader of the House, with the minority leader and myself, held a conference about these papers and it was decided that they would remain in the committee until today, and be transferred as the rules and law provide unless the House should take further action. So far as the preservation of the papers is concerned, they are in the custody of the Clerk of the House. The Clerk of the House is a sworn officer and he knows his duty.

Mr. RANKIN. Mr. Speaker, a point of order.

The SPEAKER. Just a moment. Does the gentleman want to state a point of order?

Mr. RANKIN. Yes.

Mr. COX. Not against, though.

Mr. RANKIN. Not against.

The SPEAKER. The Chair would like very much to complete the statement the chair started to make.

The House will remember that the McCormack committee, the Committee on Un-American Activities, wound up its work and recommended legislation. Its papers were taken possession of by the Clerk and filed in the Library of Congress. They were looked into by resolution of the Congress. That is the usual method, and it can be done at any time.

Mr. CASE of South Dakota. Mr. Speaker, a further parliamentary inquiry.

The SPEAKER. The gentleman will state it.

Mr. CASE of South Dakota. In the pending amendment, was any order given to the Librarian of Congress with respect to the disposition of these papers?

The SPEAKER. The gentleman heard the amendment read.

Mr. CASE of South Dakota. It was rather Involved in references and at the time it was impossible to tell. The citation the Chair last read from the law stated that the papers would be subject to the order of the House; and I was wondering if the House was proposing to give an order.

The SPEAKER. That is a statutory law, not a rule of the House.

The Chair does not see anything in the pending amendment that makes any disposition whatever of the papers of the so-called Dies committee.

Mr. RANKIN. Mr. Speaker, let me say in that connection in reply to the gentleman from South Dakota [Mr. Case], that some of the men who went over there to look over those papers were prepared to remove them and said they would like to throw them into the Potomac River. I want to see that these records are kept; that is one thing I am striving for.

The SPEAKER. The previous question has been ordered; and, further than that, as far as the occupant of this chair is concerned these papers have been kept intact.

Mr. RANKIN. I am speaking of the ones who went there to look them over.

The SPEAKER. The question is on the amendment.

The question was taken; and on a division (demanded by Mr. Marcantonio) there were—yeas 134, noes 146.

Mr. RANKIN. Mr. Speaker, I ask for the yeas and nays.

The yeas and nays were ordered.

[Editor's Note: The debate and the pending vote on the establishment of the HUAC were temporarily suspended at this point so that several members could be sworn in.]

Mr. RANKIN. Mr. Speaker, I ask that a statement be made as to what we are voting on.

The SPEAKER. The Chair is endeavoring to put the question and will state it if he is allowed to.

The question is on agreeing to the amendment offered by the gentleman from Mississippi [Mr. Rankin]. A roll call has been ordered. Those in favor of the amendment will, when their names are called, answer "yea" and those opposed "nay." The Clerk will call the roll.

The Clerk called the roll; and there were—yeas 208, nays 186, not voting 40. . . .

Congressional Record, House, 79th Congress, 1st session, Jan. 3, 1945, 10–15.

135 Senator Arthur Vandenberg on United States Foreign Policy

January 10, 1945

World War II had a profound impact on the thinking and actions of many members of Congress. Few changed as dramatically as Arthur H. Vandenberg (R-Mich.), who began his conversion from isolationism to internationalism in remarks he made on the floor of the Senate as the Senate was about to declare war on Japan (see document 132). During the war he remained critical of President Franklin D. Roosevelt's conduct of the war and Roosevelt, in turn, kept his distance from Vandenberg's pronouncements on foreign policy.

In this speech before the Senate just months before the end of World War II, Vandenberg shocked many of his Senate colleagues, especially members of his own Republican Party, who had often deferred to Vandenberg on foreign policy issues, by embracing the

goals of President Roosevelt to form a international body dedicated to the maintenance of world peace. Roosevelt met with world leaders at the Yalta Conference to discuss this concept less than a month after Vandenberg's speech. The references in Vandenberg's speech to Dumbarton Oaks referred to a conference held on an estate in Washington, D.C., in 1944, where leaders from Russia, China, the United States, and Great Britain met to shape a new international organization: the United Nations. The Dumbarton Oaks conference paved the way for other meetings in 1945 at Yalta and San Francisco that led to the formation of the United Nations.

Vandenberg's surprise endorsement of Roosevelt's efforts, and the goals of the Dumbarton Oaks conference, had a major impact in removing opposition to the creation of the United Nations. Van-

denberg's position also inspired bipartisan support for the North Atlantic Treaty Organization and the Marshal Plan for the reconstruction of Europe. President Roosevelt had a newfound friend in foreign policy. After Roosevelt's death, President Harry S. Truman and his administration continued to work with Vandenberg to forge a bipartisan foreign policy that would dramatically shape the second half of the twentieth century.

Vandenberg's compelling argument was based on what he saw during World War II. He had been jolted from complacency and isolationism by world events. As he said in this speech: "Since Pearl Harbor, World War II has put the gory science of mass murder into new and sinister perspective. Our oceans have ceased to be moats which automatically protect our ramparts. Flesh and blood now compete unequally with winged steel. War has become an all-consuming juggernaut. If World War III ever unhappily arrives, it will open new laboratories of death too horrible to contemplate. I propose to do everything within my power to keep those laboratories closed for keeps."

Mr. President, I shall detain the Senate less than thirty minutes. I desire to speak about some phases of foreign policy. Because of the solemnity of the subject itself I ask the indulgence of my colleagues that I be permitted at least to make my preliminary statement without interruption.

Mr. President, there are critical moments in the life of every nation which call for the straightest, the plainest, and the most courageous thinking of which we are capable. We confront such a moment now. It is not only desperately important to America, it is important to the world. It is important not only to this generation which lives in blood. It is important to future generations if they shall live in peace.

No man in his right senses will be dogmatic in his viewpoint at such an hour. A global conflict which uproots the earth is not calculated to submit itself to the dominion of any finite mind. The clashes of rival foreign interests, which have motivated wars for countless centuries, are not likely suddenly to surrender to some simple man-made formula, no matter how nobly meditated. Each of us can only speak according to his little lights—and pray for a composite wisdom that shall lead us to high, safe ground. It is only in this spirit of anxious humility that I speak today. Politics, in any such connection, would be as obnoxious at home as they are in manipulations abroad.

Mr. President, we still have two major wars to win. I said "We." That does not mean America alone. It means the continued and total battle fraternity of the United Nations. It must mean one for all and all for one; and it will mean this, unless somewhere in this grand alliance the stupid and sinister folly of ulterior ambitions shall invite the enemy to postpone our victory through our own rivalries and our own confusion. The United Nations, in even greater unity of military action than heretofore, must never, for any cause, permit this military unity to fall apart. If it does, we shall count the cost in mortal anguish, even though we stumble on to a belated, though inevitable victory. And, getting down to what Mr. Churchill would call the

bare bones of the matter, this is an obligation which rests no less upon our allies than. upon us, and no less upon us than upon our allies. First things must come first. History will not deal lightly with any who undermine this aim ere it is achieved. Destiny will one day balance any such ghastly accounts.

We not only have two wars to win, we also have yet to achieve such a peace as will justify this appalling cost. Here again an even more difficult unity is indispensable. Otherwise we shall look back upon a futile, sanguinary shambles and—God save the mark—we shall be able to look forward only to the curse of World War III.

Unfortunately, Mr. President, the morale of unity in war is often threatened by sharply dashing and often disillusioning disclosures which threaten this unity in peace. The two considerations cannot be dissociated. President Roosevelt correctly said in his annual message that "the nearer we come to vanquishing our enemies the more we become inevitably conscious of differences among the victors." He also correctly said that "nations like individuals do not always see alike or think alike, and international cooperation and progress are not helped by any nation assuming that it has a monopoly of wisdom or of virtue." That applies to us. It applies to each of our allies. But when "differences among the victors"—to use the White House phrase—when "differences among the victors," before they have clinched their victory, threaten both the victory and the peace, the hour cannot much longer be postponed when any such trends shall be reversed. We shall not reverse them by our silence upon the issues that are clearly involved; nor, and I say it with great respect, shall we reverse them merely by a generalized restatement of the high aspirations revoked in the recent presidential message. Certainly we shall not reverse them by a snarling process of international recrimination in which every United Nations capital tries to outdo the other in bitter backtalk about the infirmities of each. Such bickering is dangerous—over there or over here. It is water on the Axis wheel. Again I agree wholeheartedly with President Roosevelt when he says:

We must not let such differences divide us and blind us to our more important common and continuing interests in winning the war and building the peace.

On the other hand, I hold the deep belief that honest candor, devoid of prejudice or ire, is our greatest hope and our greatest necessity; and that the government of the United States, above all others, is called at long last to exercise this honest candor not only with its allies but also with its own faithful people.

I hesitate, even now, to say these things, Mr. President, because a great American illusion seems to have been built up—wittingly or otherwise—that we, in the United States, dare not publicly discuss these subjects lest we contribute to international dissension and thus encourage the very thing we all need to cure. But I frankly confess that I do not know why we must be the only silent partner in this grand alliance. There seems to be no fear of disunity, no hesitation in Moscow, when Moscow wants to assert unilateral war and peace aims which collide with ours. There seems to be no fear of disunity, no hesitation in London, when Mr. Churchill proceeds upon his unilateral way to make decisions often repugnant to our ideas and our ideals. Perhaps our allies will plead that their actions are not unilateral; that our president, as Bevin said, has initialed this or that at one of the famous Big Three conferences; that our president, as Churchill said, has been kept constantly "aware of everything that has happened"; in other words, that by our silence we have acquiesced. But that hypothesis would only make a bad matter worse. It would be the final indictment of our silence—the final obituary for open covenants. We, of course, accept no conception that our contribution to unity must be silence, while others say and do what they please, and that our only role in this global tragedy is to fight and die and pay, and that unity for us shall only be the unity which Jonah enjoyed when he was swallowed by the whale.

I hasten to say that any such intolerable conception would be angrily repudiated by every American—from the president down to the last citizen among us. It has not been and is not true. Yet it cannot be denied that our government has not spoken out—to our own people or to our allies—in any such specific fashion as have the others. It cannot be denied, as a result, that too often a grave melancholy settles upon some sectors of our people. It cannot be denied that citizens, in increasing numbers, are crying: "What are we fighting for?" It cannot be denied that our silence—at least our public and official silence—has multiplied confusion at home and abroad. It cannot be denied that this confusion threatens our unity—yes, Mr. President, and already hangs like a cloud over Dumbarton Oaks. So I venture to repeat, with all the earnestness at my command, that a new rule of honest candor in Washington—as a substitute for mystifying silence or for classical generalities—honest candor on the high plane of great ideals—is the greatest contribution we can make to the realities of unity at this moment when enlightened civilization is our common stake.

Let us not mistake the meaning of unity. Unity does not require universal and peremptory agreement about everything. It does not demand a meeting of all minds now in respect to all the minutiae of a postwar world which will take years to stabilize. The president is wholly right in pleading for tolerance upon this score and in warning that we must not expect what he calls perfectionism overnight. Here in the Senate we do not have perpetual agreement between the two sides of the aisle, but we have never failed to have basic unity when crisis calls. The unity I discuss is the overall tie which must continue to bind the United Nations together in respect to paramount fundamentals. We had it once in the original spirit of the Atlantic Charter, and we must get it back again before it is too late.

When Mr. Churchill spoke in the British Parliament last December 15, defending his own current course in Greece and Mr. Stalin's proposed partition of Poland, he said:

There is no doubt that when the time comes the United States will make its own pronouncement upon these matters, bearing in mind, as it will, the practical aspects which these matters assume and also how

much failure on the part of the three greatest powers to work together would damage all our hopes for the future structure of a world government which, whatever else it might fail to do, will at any rate be equipped with all powers necessary to prevent outbreak of future war.

I do not like one of the implications in this quotation. It seems to say that unless we acquiesce in these self-serving unilateral arrangements now being made by great European powers, we shall be the scapegoats to be made responsible for the next war. I would respond categorically to any such abortive thesis by saying that, regardless of the future structure of a world government, an unjust peace, built upon the age-old frictions of international power politics, is the most fatal of all threats which our hopes for the future can possibly confront. But that is not the reason I use the quotation at this point. Of even greater importance is the other implication—namely, that the United States has not spoken; that her official attitude is not dependably recorded; and that, until she does speak, the world cannot find its bearings.

There is no doubt, says Mr. Churchill, that when the time comes the United States will make its own pronouncement.

When the time comes. Mr. President, is the time not here right now?

If it is, Mr. President, what shall we say that we have not already said in the Connally resolution in the Senate and the Fulbright resolution in the House and in the presidential utterances?

It seems to me, Mr. President, that the first thing we must say, beyond misunderstanding, is that we have not altered our original commitments; that we have not lowered our sights; that we have not diluted our dedications; that we are not fighting to pull ancient chestnuts out of alien fires; that the smell of victory is not an anaesthetic which puts our earlier zeals to sleep. We still propose to win this war, come what may. We are fighting to defend America. We still propose to help create the postwar world on a basis which shall stop aggressors for keeps and, so far as humanly possible, substitute justice for force among freemen. We propose to do it primarily for our own sake. We still propose also, to substitute justice for force—if we can—in writing the peace which terminates this war when we deal with the victims of Axis tyranny. That is the road to permanent peace. We still propose that none of the United Nations shall seek aggrandizement, territorial, or otherwise—though conceding that all change is not necessarily aggrandizement. We still propose, outside the Axis, that there shall be no territorial changes which do not accord with the freely expressed wishes of the people concerned. Similarly we still propose to respect the right of all peoples to choose the form of government under which they will five. We still propose to see sovereign rights and self-government restored to those who have been forcibly deprived of them, if it lies within our power.

In a word, Mr. President, it seems to me that the first thing we must do is to reassert, in high places, our American faith in these particular elemental objectives of the so-called Atlantic Charter, which was officially issued as a signed document by the State Department on August 14, 1941; which was officially communicated to the Congress as a signed document by the president of the United States in his message of August 21, 1941; which was embodied in a joint resolution of all the United Nations on January 1, 1942; which was commemorated by the president on August 14, 1943 in a proclamation on the second anniversary of its "signing"—his word—which had a tragic sinking spell when its formal authenticity was amazingly depreciated in a White House press conference fortnight ago, but which the president reembraced in his message of January 6, 1945.

I am sure the president did not anticipate the shocking results of his recent almost jocular, and even cynical, dismissal of the Atlantic Charter as a mere collection of fragmentary notes. It jarred America to its very hearthstones. It seemed to make a mere pretense out of what has been an inspiringly accepted fact. It seemed almost to sanction alien contempts. It seemed to suggest that we have put too much emphasis upon a fighting creed which did not deserve the solemnity which we have been taught to ascribe to it. Coming at a particularly critical moment when these pledges seemed to be at least partially paralyzed in Moscow—and when even Mr. Churchill's memory about the charter was proving to be admittedly fickle—the president's statement was utterly devastating in its impact. He has since sought to repair this damage. I hope he has succeeded. With justification he reminds us in his annual message that there are no rules of easy application—of the charter—to each and every one of this war-torn world's tangled situations. He now says correctly and bravely, "We shall not hesitate to use our influence—and use it now—to secure so far as is humanly possible the fulfillment of these principles." That is the indispensable point. These basic pledges cannot now be dismissed as a mere nautical nimbus. They march with our armies. They sail with our fleets. They fly with our eagles. They sleep with our martyred dead. The first requisite of honest candor, Mr. President, I respectfully suggest, is to relight this torch.

The next thing we need to do, Mr. President, if I may be so bold, in this spirit of honest candor, is to appeal to our allies, in the name of reason, to frankly face the postwar alternatives which are available to them and to us as a means to preserve tomorrow's peace for them and for us. There are two ways to do it. One way is by exclusive individual action in which each of us tries to look out for himself. The other way is by joint action in which we undertake to look out for each other. The first way is the old way which has twice taken us to Europe's interminable battlefields within a quarter century. The second way is the new way in which our present fraternity of war becomes a new fraternity of peace. I do not believe that either we or our allies can have it both ways. They serve to cancel out each other. We cannot tolerate unilateral privilege in a multilateral peace. Yet, that seems to be the fatalistic trend today. I think we must make our choice. I think we must make it wholly plain to our major allies that they, too, must make their choice.

I hasten to make my own personal viewpoint clear. I have always been frankly one of those who has believed in our own self-reliance. I still believe that we can never again—regardless

of collaborations—allow our national defense to deteriorate to anything like a point of impotence. But I do not believe that any nation hereafter can immunize itself by its own exclusive action. Since Pearl Harbor, World War II has put the gory science of mass murder into new and sinister perspective. Our oceans have ceased to be moats which automatically protect our ramparts. Flesh and blood now compete unequally with winged steel. War has become an all-consuming juggernaut. If World War III ever unhappily arrives, it will open new laboratories of death too horrible to contemplate. I propose to do everything within my power to keep those laboratories closed for keeps. I want maximum American cooperation, consistent with legitimate American self-interest, with constitutional process and with collateral events which warrant it, to make the basic idea of Dumbarton Oaks succeed. I want a new dignity and a new authority for international law. I think American self-interest requires it. But, Mr. President, this also requires wholehearted reciprocity. In honest candor I think we should tell other nations that this glorious thing we contemplate is not and cannot be one-sided. I think we must say again that unshared idealism is a menace which we could not undertake to underwrite in the postwar world.

Now, I am not so impractical as to expect any country to act on any final motive other than self-interest. I know of no reason why it should. That is what nations are for. I certainly intend that intelligent and loyal American self-interest shall be just as vigilantly and vigorously guarded as is amply obvious, from time to time, in their own behalf by the actions of our allies. The real question always becomes just this: Where does real self-interest lie?

Here, Mr. President, we reach the core of the immediate problem. Without remotely wanting to be invidious, I use one of many available examples, I would not presume, even under these circumstances, to use it except that it ultimately involves us. Russia's unilateral plan appears to contemplate the engulfment, directly or indirectly, of a surrounding circle of buffer states, contrary to our conception of what we thought we were fighting for in respect to the rights of small nations and a just peace. Russia's announced reason is her insistent purpose never again to be at the mercy of another German tyranny. That is a perfectly understandable reason. The alternative is collective security. Now, which is better, in the long view? That is the question I pose. Which is better, in the long view, from a purely selfish Russian standpoint: To forcefully surround herself with a cordon of unwillingly controlled or partitioned states, thus affronting the opinions of mankind as a means of postwar protection against a renaissance of German aggression, or to win the priceless asset of world confidence in her by embracing the alternative, namely, full and wholehearted cooperation with and reliance on a vital international organization in which all of us shall honorably participate to guarantee that Axis aggression shall never rise again? Well—at that point, Russia, or others like her, in equally honest candor, has a perfect right to reply, "Where is there any such alternative reliance until we know what the

United States will do? How can you expect us to rely on an enigma?"

Now we are getting somewhere. Fear of reborn German aggression in years to come is at the base of most of our contemporary frictions. It is a perfectly human and understandable fear on the part of all neighboring nations which German militarism has twice driven to the valley of the shadow within one generation. Fear of reborn German aggression in years to come is the cause assigned to unilateral plans for Russian postwar expansion. Fear of reborn German aggression is the reason assigned to the proposed partition of Poland. Fear of reborn German aggression gave birth to the Anglo-Soviet agreement of 1942, the Soviet-Czechoslovak agreement of 1943, the Franco-Soviet Treaty of 1944, and to similar unilateral and bilateral actions inevitably yet to come. Fear of reborn German aggression is our apple of discord. This Second World War plagues the earth chiefly because France and Britain did not keep Germany disarmed, according to contract, after World War I. In other words, when we deal with Europe's fear—her justified fear—of another rebirth of German military tyranny in some future postwar era, we are at the heart of the immediate problem which bedevils our Allied relationships.

I propose that we meet this problem conclusively and at once. There is no reason to wait. America has this same self-interest in permanently, conclusively, and effectively disarming Germany and Japan. It is simply unthinkable that America, or any other member of the United Nations, would allow this Axis calamity to reproduce itself again. Whether we Americans do or do not agree upon all the powers that shall reside in an ultimate international council to call upon us for joint military action in behalf of collective security, surely we can agree that we do not ever want an instant's hesitation or doubt about our military cooperation in the peremptory use of force, if needed, to keep Germany and Japan demilitarized. Such a crisis would be the lengthened shadow of the present war. It would be a direct epilogue to the present war. It should be handled as this present war is handled. There should be no more need to refer any such action back to Congress than that Congress should expect to pass upon battle plans today. The commander in chief should have instant power to act, and he should act. I know of no reason why a hard-and-fast treaty between the major allies should not be signed today to achieve this dependable end. We need not await the determination of our other postwar relationships. This problem—this menace—stands apart by itself. Regardless of what our later decision may be in respect to the power that shall be delegated to the president to join our military force with others in a new peace league—no matter what limitations may commend themselves to our ultimate judgments in this regard, I am sure we can agree that there should be no limitations when it comes to keeping the Axis out of piracy for keeps. I respectfully urge that we meet this problem now. From it stem many of today's confusions, doubts and frustrations. I think we should immediately put it behind us by conclusive action. Having done so, most of the reasons given for controversial unilateral and bilat-

eral actions by our allies will have disappeared; and then we shall be able, at least, to judge accurately whether we have found and cured the real hazard to our relationships. We shall have closed ranks. We shall have returned infinitely closer to basic unity.

Then, in honest candor, Mr. President, I think we have the duty and the right to demand that whatever immediate unilateral decisions have to be made in consequence of military need—and there will be such even in civil affairs—they shall all be temporary and subject to final revision in the objective light of the postwar world and the postwar peace league as they shall ultimately develop. As President Roosevelt put it in his annual message:

During the interim period, until conditions permit a genuine expression of the peoples' win, we and our allies have a duty, which we cannot ignore, to use our influence to the end that no temporary or provisional authorities in the liberated countries block the eventual exercise of the peoples' right freely to choose the government and institutions under which, as free men, they are to live.

I agree to that. Indeed, I would go further. I would write it in the bond. If Dumbarton Oaks should specifically authorize the ultimate international organization to review protested injustices in the peace itself, it would at least partially nullify the argument that we are to be asked to put a blank-check warrant behind a future status quo which is unknown to us and which we might be unwilling to defend.

We are standing by our guns with epic heroism. I know of no reason why we should not stand by our ideals. If they vanish under ultimate pressures, we shall at least have kept the record straight; we shall have kept faith with our soldier sons; and we then shall clearly be free agents, unhampered by tragic misunderstandings, in determining our own course when Berlin and Tokyo are in Allied hands. Let me put it this way for myself: I am prepared, by effective international cooperation, to do our full part in charting happier and safer tomorrows. But I am not prepared to guarantee permanently the spoils of an unjust peace. It will not work.

Mr. President, we need honest candor even with our foes. Without any remote suggestion of appeasement—indeed, it seems to me that it is exactly the contrary—I wish we might give these Axis peoples some incentive to desert their own tottering tyrannies by at least indicating to them that the quicker they unconditionally surrender the cheaper will be unconditional surrender's price. Here again we need plain speaking which has been too conspicuous by its absence, and, upon at least one calamitous occasion, by its error.

Mr. President, I conclude as I began. We must win these wars with maximum speed and minimum loss. Therefore we must have maximum Allied cooperation and minimum Allied frictions. We have fabulously earned the right to be heard in respect to the basis of this unity. We need the earliest possible clarification of our relations with our brave allies. We need this clarification not only for the sake of total Allied cooperation in the winning of the war but also in behalf of a truly compensatory peace. We cannot drift to victory. We must have maximum united effort on all fronts. We must have maximum united effort in our councils. And we must deserve the continued united effort of our own people.

I realize, Mr. President, in such momentous problems how much easier it is to be critical than to be correct. I do not wish to meddle. I want only to help. I want to do my duty. It is in this spirit that I ask for honest candor in respect to our ideals, our dedications, and our commitments, as the greatest contribution which government can now make to the only kind of realistic unity which will most swiftly bring our victorious sons back home, and which will best validate our aspirations, our sacrifices, and our dreams.

Congressional Record, Senate, 79th Congress, 1st session, Jan. 10, 1945, 164–167.

136 The Atomic Energy Act

August 1, 1946

The Atomic Energy Act of 1946 marked the beginning of Congress's deep involvement with a vast new scientific and technological age filled with great potential for both good and evil. Congress suddenly found itself with oversight of the powerful new forces unleashed by the atomic age. It would need, as never before, to find ways to upgrade its own ability to understand the social, political, scientific, and technological issues involved.

The atomic age dawned in spectacular and horrifying fashion in August 1945, when the United States dropped two atomic bombs on Japanese cities, the first on Hiroshima on August 6 and the second on Nagasaki on August 9. These powerful new weapons dramatically and quickly contributed to the end of World War II. Congress had funded the secret Manhattan Project that developed this new super weapon, but few members of Congress and few outside the Manhattan Project itself were aware of the consequences of such weapons. With the explosions at Hiroshima and Nagasaki obliterating the cities and killing more than 200,000 persons, the whole world was thrust—without warning and completely unprepared—into the atomic age.

Less than two months after the Japanese bombings President Harry S. Truman sent a message to Congress urging the creation of an atomic energy commission to control research and development of atomic energy. The opening declaration of policy in the Atomic Energy Act succinctly and, with great understatement, described the situation as it existed in 1946: "The significance of the atomic bomb for military purposes is evident. The effect of the use of atomic energy for civilian purposes upon the social, economic, and political structure of today cannot now be determined. It is a field in which unknown factors are involved."

The heated debate in Congress that followed raised complex issues about civilian control, the public's right to know information concerning atomic energy, and issues regarding the government's need for complete secrecy to keep atomic weapons from falling into enemy hands. Some leading scientists argued that atomic energy issues were too complex for one country to control and that atomic energy should be regulated internationally, with all scientists able to share information.

The Atomic Energy Act of 1946 created a five-member civilian commission, appointed by the president with the advice and consent of the Senate, which was to be called the Atomic Energy Commission. Control of the Manhattan Project, which had been under the military, was transferred to the civil commission. The commission would also regulate fissionable material and the dissemination of scientific information. The act also established in Congress a new Joint Committee on Atomic Energy, composed of eighteen members, nine from the Senate and nine from the House. This committee would have oversight of the Atomic Energy Commission. The Joint Committee on Atomic Energy had the power, unusual for a joint committee, to report legislation to Congress on atomic energy issues. Over the next thirty years the Joint Committee on Atomic Energy and the Atomic Energy Commission engaged in a colossal tug of war over the direction of nuclear regulation and the development of weapons and peaceful uses of nuclear energy.

The Atomic Energy Commission lasted until January 1975, when Congress established two new entities in the Energy Reorganization Act of 1974. Replacing the Atomic Energy Commission were the Nuclear Regulatory Commission and the Energy Resource and Development Administration. The Joint Committee on Atomic Energy ceased to exist in 1977 when congressional reorganization transferred oversight of atomic energy issues to other committees in the House and Senate.

DECLARATION OF POLICY

SECTION 1. (a) FINDINGS AND DECLARATION.—Research and experimentation in the field of nuclear chain reaction have attained the stage at which the release of atomic energy on a large scale is practical. The significance of the atomic bomb for military purposes is evident. The effect of the use of atomic energy for civilian purposes upon the social, economic, and political structure of today cannot now be determined. It is a field in which unknown factors are involved. Therefore, any legislation will necessarily be subject to revision from time to time. It is reasonable to anticipate, however, that tapping this new source of energy will cause profound changes in our present life. Accordingly, it is hereby declared to be the policy of the people of the United States that, subject at a times to the paramount objective of assuring the common defense and security, the development and utilization of atomic energy shall, so far as practicable, be directed toward improving the public welfare, increasingly the standard of living, strengthening free competition in private enterprise, and promoting world peace.

(b) PURPOSE OF ACT.—It is the purpose of this Act to effectuate the policies set out in section 1 (a) by providing, among others, for the following major programs relating to atomic energy:

(1) A program of assisting and fostering private research and development to encourage maximum scientific progress;

(2) A program for the control of scientific and technical information which will permit the dissemination of such information to encourage scientific progress, and for the sharing on a reciprocal basis of information concerning the practical industrial application of atomic energy as soon as effective and enforceable safeguards against its use for destructive purposes can be devised;

(3) A program of federally conducted research and development to assure the Government of adequate scientific and technical accomplishment;

(4) A program for Government control of the production, ownership, and use of fissionable material to assure the common defense and security and to insure the broadest possible exploitation of the fields; and

(5) A program of administration which will be consistent with the international arrangements made by the will enable the Congress to be currently informed so as to take further legislative action as may hereafter be appropriate.

ORGANIZATION

SEC. 2. (a) ATOMIC ENERGY COMMISSION.—

(1) There is hereby established an Atomic Energy Commission (herein called the Commission), which shall be composed of five members. Three members shall constitute a quorum of the Commission. The President shall designate one member as Chairman of the Commission.

(2) Members of the Commission shall be appointed by the President, by and with the advice and consent of the Senate. In submitting any nomination to the Senate, the President shall set forth e experience and the qualification's of the nominee. The term of office of each member of the Commission taking office prior to the expiration of two years after the date of enactment of this Act shall expire upon the expiration of such two years. The term of office of each member of the Commission taking office after the expiration of two years from the date of enactment of this Act shall be five years, except that (A) the terms of office of the members first taking office after the expiration of two years from the date of enactment of this Act shall expire, as designated by the President at the time of appointment, one at the end of three years, one at the end of four years, one at the end of five years, one at the end of six years, and one at the end of seven years, after the date of enactment of this Act; and (B) any member appointed to fill a vacancy occurring prior to the expiration of the term for which his predecessor was appointed, shall be appointed for the remainder of such term. Any member of the Commission may be removed by the President for inefficiency, neglect of duty, or malfeasance in office. . . .

RESEARCH

SEC. 3. (a) RESEARCH ASSISTANCE.—The Commission is directed to exercise its powers in such manner as to insure the continued conduct of research and development activities in the fields specified below by private or public institutions or persons and to assist in the acquisition of an ever-expanding fund of theoretical and practical knowledge in such fields. To this end the Commission is authorized and directed to make arrangements (including contracts, agreements, and loans) for the conduct of research and development activities relating to—

(1) nuclear processes;

(2) the theory and production of atomic energy, including processes, materials, and devices related to such production;

(3) utilization of fissionable and radioactive materials, biological, health, or military purposes;

(4) utilization of fissionable and radioactive materials and processes entailed in the production of such materials for all other purposes including industrial uses; and

(5) the protection of health during research and production activities.

. . . .

PRODUCTION OF FISSIONABLE MATERIAL

SEC. 4. (a) DEFINITION.—As used in this Act the term "Produce" when used in relation to fissionable material, means to manufacture; produce, or refine fissionable material, as distinguished from source materials as defined in section 5 (b) (1), or to separate fissionable material from other substances in which such material may be contained or to produce new fissionable material.

(b) PROHIBITION.—It shall be unlawful for any person to own any facilities for the production of fissionable material or for any person to produce fissionable material, except to the extent authorized by subsection (c).

(c) OWNERSHIP AND OPERATION OF PRODUCTION FACILITIES.—

(1) OWNERSHIP OF PRODUCTION FACILITIES.—The Commission, as agent of and on behalf of the United States, shall be the exclusive owner of all facilities for the production of fissionable material other than facilities which (A) are useful in the conduct of research and development activities in the fields specified in section 8, and (B) do not, in the opinion of the Commission, have a potential production rate adequate to enable the operator of such facilities to produce within a reasonable period of time a sufficient quantity of fissionable material to produce an atomic bomb or any other atomic weapon.

(2) OPERATION OF THE COMMISSION'S PRODUCTION FACILITIES.—The Commission is authorized and directed to produce or to provide for the production of fissionable material in its own facilities. To the extent deemed necessary, the Commission is authorized to make, or to continue in effect, contracts with persons obligating them to produce fissionable material in facilities owned by the Commission. The Commission is also authorized to enter into research and development contracts autho-

rizing the contractor to produce fissionable; material in facilities owned by the Commission to the extent that the production of such fissionable material may be incident to the conduct of research and development activities under such contracts. Any contract entered into under this section shall contain provisions (A) prohibiting the contractor with the Commission from subcontracting any part of the work he is obligated to perform under the contract, except as authorized by the Commission, and (B) obligating the contractor to make such reports to the Commission as it may deem appropriate with respect to his activities under the contract, to submit to frequent inspection by employees of the Commission of all such activities, and to comply with safety and security regulations which may be prescribed by the Commission. Any paragraph may be made without regard to the provisions of section 3709 of the Revised Statutes (U.S.C., title 41, sec. 5) upon certification by the Commission that such action is necessary in the interest of the common defense and security, or upon a showing that advertising is not reasonably practicable, and partial and advance payments may be made under such contracts. The President shall determine at least once each year the quantities of fissionable material to be produced under this paragraph.

(3) OPERATION OF OTHER PRODUCTION FACILITIES.—Fissionable material may be produced in the conduct of research and development activities in facilities which, under paragraph (1) above, are not required to be owned by the Commission.

(d) IRRADIATION OF MATERIALS.—For the purpose of increasing the supply of radioactive materials, the Commission and persons lawfully producing or utilizing fissionable material are authorized to expose materials of any kind to the radiation incident to the processes of utilizing fissionable material.

(e) MANUFACTURE OF PRODUCTION FACILITIES.—Unless authorized by the Commission, no person may manufacture, or acquire any facilities for the production of fissionable material. Licenses shall be issued in accordance with such procedures as the Commission may by regulation establish and shall be issued in accordance with such standards and upon such conditions as will restrict the production and distribution of such facilities to effectuate the policies and purposes of this Act. Nothing in this section shall be deemed to require a license for such manufacture, production, transfer, or acquisition incident to or for the conduct of research or development activities in the United States of the types specified in section 8, or to prohibit the Commission from manufacturing or producing such facilities for its own use.

CONTROL OF MATERIALS

SEC. 5. (a) FISSIONABLE MATERIALS.—

(1) DEFINITION.—As used in this Act, the term "fissionable material" means plutonium, uranium enriched in the isotope 235, any other material which the Commission determines to be capable of releasing substantial quantities of energy through nuclear chain reaction of the material, or any material artificially enriched by any of the foregoing; but does not include source materials, as defined in section 5 (b) (1).

(2) GOVERNMENT OWNERSHIP OF ALL FISSIONABLE MATERIAL.—All right, title, and interest within or under the jurisdiction of the United States, in or to any fissionable material, now or hereafter produced, shall be the property of the Commission, and shall be deemed to be vested in the Commission by virtue of this Act. Any person owning any interest in any fissionable material at the time of the enactment of this Act, or owning any interest in any material at the time when such material is hereafter determined to be a fissionable material, or who lawfully produces any fissionable material incident to privately financed research or development activities, shall be paid just compensation therefor. The Commission may, by action consistent with the provisions of paragraph (4) below, authorize any such person to retain possession of such fissionable material, but no person shall have any title in or to any fissionable material.

(3) PROHIBITION.—It shall be unlawful for any person, after sixty days from the effective date of this Act to (A) possess or transfer any fissionable material, except as authorized by the Commission, or (B) export from or import into the United States any fissionable material, or (C) directly or indirectly or indirectly engage in the production of any fissionable material outside of the United States.

(4) DISTRIBUTION OF FISSIONABLE MATERIAL.—Without prejudice thereof, the Commission is authorized to distribute fissionable material owned by it, with or without charge, to applicants requesting such material (A) for the conduct of research or development activities either independently or under contract or other arrangement with the Commission, (B) for use in medical therapy, or (C) for use pursuant to a license issued under the authority of section 7. Such material shall be distributed in such quantities and on such terms that no applicant will be enabled to obtain an amount sufficient to construct a bomb or other military weapon. The Commission is directed to distribute sufficient fissionable material to permit the conduct of widespread independent research and development activity, to the maximum extent practicable. In determining the quantities of fissionable material to be distributed, the Commission shall make such provisions for its own needs and for the conservation of fissionable material as it may determine to be necessary in the national interest for the future development of atomic energy. The Commission shall not distribute any material to any applicant, and shall recall any distributed material from any applicant, who is not equipped to observe or who fails to observe such safety standards to protect health and to minimize danger from explosion or other hazard to life or property as may be established by the Commission, or who uses such material in violation of law or regulation of the Commission or in a manner other than as disclosed in the application therefor.

(5) The Commission is authorized to purchase or otherwise acquire any fissionable material or any interest therein outside the United States, or any interest in facilities for the production of fissionable material, or in real property on which such facilities are located, without regard to the provisions of section 3709 of the Revised Statutes (U.S.C., title 41, sec. 5) upon certification

by the Commission that such action is necessary in the interest of the common defense and security, or upon a showing that advertising is not reasonably practicable, and partial and advance payments may be made under contracts for such purposes. The Commission is further authorized to take, requisition, or condemn, or otherwise acquire any interest in such facilities or real property, and just compensation shall be made therefor.

. . . .

MILITARY APPLICATIONS OF ATOMIC ENERGY

SEC. 6 (a) AUTHORITY.—The Commission is authorized to—

(1) conduct experiments and do research and development work in the military application of atomic energy; and

(2) engage in the production of atomic bombs, atomic, bomb parts, or other military weapons utilizing fissionable materials; except that such activities shall be carried on only to the extent that the express consent and direction of the President of the United States has been obtained, which consent and direction shall be obtained at least once each year.

The President from time to time may direct the Commission (1) to deliver such quantities of fissionable materials or weapons to the armed forces for such use as he deems necessary in the interest of national defense or (2) to authorize the armed forces to manufacture, produce, or acquire any equipment or device utilizing fissionable material or atomic energy as a military weapon.

(b) It shall be unlawful for any person to manufacture, produce, transfer, or acquire any equipment or device utilizing fissionable material or atomic energy as a military weapon except as be authorized by the Commission. Nothing in this subsection shall be deemed to modify the provisions of section 4 of this Act, or to prohibit research activities in respect of military weapons, or to permit the export of any such equipment or device.

UTILIZATION OF ATOMIC ENERGY

SEC. 7. (a) LICENSE REQUIRED.—It shall be unlawful, except as provided in sections 5 (a) (4) (A) or (B) of 6 (a), for any person to manufacture, produce, or export fissionable material or atomic energy or atomic energy with or without such equipment or device, except under and in accordance with a license issued by the Commission authorizing such manufacture, production, export, or utilization. No license may permit any such activity if fissionable material is produced incident to such activity, except as provided in sections 3 and 4. Nothing in this section hall deemed to require a license for the conduct of research or development activities relating to the manufacture of such equipment or devices or the utilization of fissionable the manufacture or use of equipment or devices for medical therapy.

(b) REPORT TO CONGRESS.—Whenever in its opinion any industrial, commercial, or other nonmilitary use of fissionable material or atomic energy has been sufficiently developed to be of practical value, the Commission shall prepare a report to the President stating all the facts with respect to such use, the Commission's estimate of the social, political, economic, and international effects of such use and the Commission's recommendations for necessary or desirable supplemental legislation. The President shall then transmit this report to the Congress together with his commendations. No license for manufacture, production, export, or use shall be issued by the Commission under this section until after (1) a report with respect to such manufacture, production, export, or use has been filed with the Congress; and (2) a period of ninety days in which the Congress was in session has elapsed after the report has been so filed. In computing such period of ninety days, there shall be excluded the days on which of an adjournment of more than three days.

(c) ISSUANCE OF LICENSES.—After such ninety-day period, unless hereafter prohibited by law, the Commission may license such manufacture, production, export, or use in accordance with such procedures and subject to such conditions as it may by regulation establish to effectuate the provisions of this Act. The Commission is authorized and directed to issue licenses on a nonexclusive basis and to supply to the extent available appropriate quantities of fissionable material to licensees (1) whose proposed activities will serve some useful purpose proportionate to the quantities of fissionable material to be consumed; (2) who are equipped to observe such safety standards to protect health and to minimize danger from explosion or other hazard to life or property as the Commission may establish; and (3) who agree to make available to the Commission such technical information and data concerning their activities pursuant to such licenses as the Commission may determine necessary to encourage similar activities by as many licensees as possible. Each such license shall be issued for a specified period, shall be revocable at any time by the Commission in accordance with such procedures as the Commission may establish, and may be renewed upon the expiration of such period. Where activities under any license might serve to maintain or to foster the growth of monopoly, restraint of trade, unlawful competition, or other trade position inimical to the entry of new, freely competitive enterprises in the field, the Commission is authorized and directed to refuse to issue such license or to establish such conditions to prevent these results as the Commission, in consultation with the Attorney General, may determine. The Commission shall report promptly to the Attorney General any information it may have with respect to any utilization of fissionable material or atomic energy which appears to have these results. No license may be given to any person for activities which are not under or within the jurisdiction of the United States, to any foreign government, or to any person within the United States if, in the opinion of the Commission, the issuance of a license to such person would be inimical to the common defense and security.

(d) BYPRODUCT POWER.—If energy which may be utilized is produced in the production of fissionable material, such energy may be used by the Commission, transferred to other Government agencies, or sold to public or private utilities under contracts providing for reasonable resale prices.

CONTROL OF INFORMATION

SEC. 10. (a) POLICY.—It shall be the policy of the Commission to control the dissemination of restricted data in such a manner as to assure the common defense and security. Consistent with such policy, the Commission shall be guided by the following principles:

(1) That until Congress declares by joint resolution that effective and enforceable international safeguards against the use of atomic energy for destructive purposes have been established, there shall be no exchange of information with other nations with respect to the use of atomic energy for industrial purposes; and

(2) That the dissemination of scientific and technical information relating to atomic energy should be permitted and encouraged as to provide that free interchange of ideas and criticisms which is essential to scientific progress.

(b) RESTRICTIONS.—

(1) The term "restricted data" as used in this section means all data concerning the manufacture or utilization of atomic weapons, the production of fissionable material, or the use of fissionable material in the production of power, but shall not include any data which the Commission from time to time determines may be published without adversely affecting the common defense and security.

(2) Whoever, lawfully or unlawfully, having possession of, access to, control over, or being entrusted with, any document, writing, sketch, photograph, plan, model, instrument, appliance, not or information involving or incorporating restricted data—

(A) communicates, transmits, or discloses the same to any individual or person, or attempts or conspires to do any of the foregoing, with intent to injure the United States or with intent to secure an advantage to any foreign nation, upon conviction thereof, shall be punished by death or imprisonment for life (but the penalty of death or imprisonment for life may be imposed only upon recommendation of the jury and only in cases where the offense was committed with intent to injure the United States); or by a fine of not more than $20,000 or imprisonment for not more than twenty years, or both;

(B) communicates, transmits, or discloses the same to an individual or person, or attempts or conspires to do any of the foregoing, with reason to believe such data will be utilized to injure the United States or to secure an advantage to any foreign nation, shall, upon conviction, be punished by a fine of not more than $10,000 or imprisonment for not more than ten years, or both.

(3) Whoever, with intent to injure the United States or with intent to secure an advantage to any foreign nation, acquires or attempts or conspires to acquire any document, writing, sketch, photograph, plan, model, instrument, appliance, note or information involving or incorporating restricted data shall, upon conviction thereof, be punished by death or imprisonment for life (but the penalty of death or imprisonment for life may be imposed only upon recommendation of the jury and only in cases where the offense was committed with intent to injure the United States); or by a fine of not more than $20,000 or imprisonment for not more than twenty years, or both.

(4) Whoever, with intent to injure the United States or with intent to secure an advantage to any foreign nation, removes, conceals, tampers with, alters, mutilates, or destroys any document, writing, sketch, photograph, plan, model, instrument, appliance, or note involving or incorporating restricted data and used by any individual or person in connection with the production of fissionable material, or research or development relating to atomic energy, conducted by the United States, or financed in whole or in part by Federal funds, or conducted with the aid of fissionable material, shall be punished by death or imprisonment for life (but the penalty of death or imprisonment for life may be imposed only upon recommendation of the jury and only in cases where the offense was committed with intent to injure the United States); or by a fine of not more than $20,000 or for not more than twenty years or both.

(5) (A) No person shall be prosecuted for any violation under this section unless and until the Attorney General of the United States has advised the Commission with respect to such prosecution and no such prosecution shall be commenced except upon the express direction of the Attorney General of the United States.

(B) (i) No arrangement shall be made under section 3, no contract shall be made or continued in effect under section 4, and no license shall be issued under section 4 (e) or 7, unless the person with whom such arrangement is made, the contractor or prospective contractor, or the prospective licensee agrees in writing not to permit any individual to have access to restricted data until the Federal Bureau of Investigation shall have made an investigation and report to the Commission on the character, associations, and loyalty of such individual and the Commission shall have determined that permitting such person to have access to restricted data will not endanger the common defense or security.

(ii) Except as authorized by the Commission in case of emergency no individual shall be employed by the Commission until the Federal Bureau of Investigation shall have made an investigation and report to the Commission on the character, association, and loyalty of such individual.

(iii) Notwithstanding the provisions of subparagraphs (i) and (ii), during such period of time after the enactment of this Act as may be necessary to make the investigation, report, and determination required by such paragraphs, (a) any individual who was permitted access to restricted data by the Manhattan Engineer District may be permitted access to restricted data and (b) the Commission may employ any individual who was employed by the Manhattan Engineer District.

(iv) To protect against the unlawful dissemination of restricted data and to safeguard facilities, equipment, materials, and other property of the Commission, the President shall have authority to utilize the services of any Government agency to the extent he may deem necessary or desirable.

(C) All violations of this Act shall be investigated by the Federal Bureau of Investigation of the Department of Justice.

. . . .

JOINT COMMITTEE ON ATOMIC ENERGY

SEC. 15. (a) There is hereby established a Joint Committee on Atomic Energy to be composed of nine Members of the Senate to be appointed by the President of the Senate, and nine Members of the House of Representatives to be appointed by the Speaker of the House of Representatives. In each instance not more than five members shall be members of the same political party.

(b) The joint committee shall make continuing studies of the activities of the Atomic Energy Commission and of problems relating to the development, use, and control of atomic energy. The Commission shall keep the joint committee fully and currently informed with respect to the Commission's activities. All bills, resolutions, and other matters in the Senate or the House of Representatives relating, primarily to the Commission or to the development, use, or control of atomic energy shall be referred to the joint committee. The members of the joint committee who are Members of the Senate shall from time to time report to the Senate, and the members of the joint Committee who are Members of the House of Representatives shall from time to time report to the House, by bill or otherwise their recommendations with respect to matters within the jurisdiction of their respective Houses which are (1) referred to the joint committee or (2) otherwise within the jurisdiction of the joint committee.

(c) Vacancies in the membership of the joint committee shall not affect the power of the remaining members to execute the actions of the joint committee and should be filled in the same manner as in the case of the original selection. The joint committee shall select a chairman and a vice chairman from among its members.

(d) The joint committee, or any duly authorized subcommittee thereof, is authorized to hold such hearings, to sit and act at such places and times, to require, by subpoena or otherwise, the attendance of such witnesses and the production of such books, papers, and documents, to administer such oaths, to take such testimony, to procure such printing and binding, and to make such expenditures as it deems advisable. The cost of stenographic services to report such hearings shall not be in excess of 25 cents per hundred words. The provisions of sections 102 to 104, inclusive, of the Revised Statutes shall apply in case of any failure of any witness to comply with a subpoena or to testify when summoned under authority of this section.

(e) The joint committee is empowered to appoint and fix the compensation of such experts, consultants, technicians, and clerical and assistants as it deems necessary and advisable, but the so fixed shall not exceed the compensation prescribed Act of 1923, as amended, for comparable duties. The committee is authorized to utilize the services, information, facilities, and personnel of the departments and establishments of the Government.

Statutes at Large, 60 (1945–1947), 79th Congress, 2d session, Aug. 1, 1946, 755–775.

137   The Legislative Reorganization Act of 1946

August 2, 1946

The Legislative Reorganization Act of 1946 initiated some of the most important and sweeping changes in the history of Congress. Congress has often reorganized itself through rules changes and other reform efforts. But the major reform of 1946, done by law, was rare for its comprehensiveness and for the long-range affects of the changes.

Following World War II, Congress felt a compelling need to reestablish its ability to match the power of the executive branch in shaping the national agenda. Beginning with the Great Depression but accelerating during World War II, governmental power had shifted dramatically from Congress to the White House. The cumbersome committee structure of the House and Senate often proved inefficient, overlapping, and wasteful while the nation was trying to fight a war. Furthermore, while Congress had the constitutional power of the purse, the executive branch often had the upper hand in the creation and mastery of the details of the budget.

This act cut the number of House standing committees from forty-eight to nineteen. Senate standing committees were reduced from thirty-three to fifteen. The act also strengthened the ability of Congress to create budgets through its own appropriations committees. The bill addressed lobbying issues, congressional pay for members and staff, the education of House and Senate pages, and even remodeling of restaurants in the Capitol. The extended excerpts included here can be read with profit as a fairly detailed outline of the many duties and responsibilities Congress carries out through its committee system.

A significant part of this act was the expansion of a Legislative Reference Service to provide Congress and its committees with well-researched information necessary in the legislative process. This enlarged service helped make it possible for members of Congress to be better informed on a wide variety of topics before them. While the Legislative Reference Service reported to Congress, many of its publications, reports, and bulletins reached the public and helped increase the flow of information about Congress and its functions. The Legislative Reference Service was the forerunner of the Congressional Research Service.

The Legislative Reorganization Act resulted from the work of the Joint Committee on the Organization of Congress, which was established in 1945 under the leadership of Representative Mike Monroney (D-Okla.) and Senator Robert La Follette Jr. (Progressive-Wis.). This reform effort marked the first time that professional political scientists and other congressional experts made a substantial impact on the actual structure of Congress. Congressional analyst George B. Galloway, then at the Brookings Institution in Washington, D.C., became staff director of the committee and played a major role in drafting the bill. Galloway subsequently had a long and distinguished career as a senior specialist for the Legislative Reference Service.

Among its reforms, the Reorganization Act rapidly and substantially increased the size of congressional staff. Staff size doubled in the ten years following the act's passage, and then doubled again by 1966. In recent years critics have cited the size of congressional staff as a symbol of the rapid growth of the size of government since World War II. Supporters of increased staffing point to the increasingly heavy workload of Congress; the complexity of issues, both technical and social in the post-World War world; and the need for Congress to maintain some balance of power in the budget battle that it fights annually with the much larger and more complex executive branch of government.

As important as this act was to the organization of Congress, it was not a cure-all for the modernization of Congress, nor was it a formula that would last indefinitely. One of the major consequences of this act was to concentrate power in the hands of fewer committee chairmen, who held their posts through a seniority system. These powerful chairmen could, and often did, thwart the will of Congress. This became especially obvious during the civil rights movement of the late 1950s and early 1960s, when conservative southerners dominated committees and blocked civil rights legislation. By the 1960s many members of Congress were agitating again for another reorganization of Congress. That movement culminated in the Legislative Reform Act of 1970 (see document 158).

TITLE I—CHANGES IN RULES OF SENATE AND HOUSE

Rule-Making Power of the Senate and House

SEC. 101. The following sections of this title are enacted by the Congress:

(a) As an exercise of the rule-making power of the Senate and the House of Representatives, respective they shall be considered as part of the rules of each House, respectively, or of that House to which they specifically apply; and such rules shall supersede other rules only to the extent that they are inconsistent therewith; and

(b) With full recognition of the constitutional right of either House to change such rules (so far as relating to the procedure in such House) at any time, in the same manner and to the same extent as in the case of any other rule of such House.

Part 1—Standing Rules of the Senate

Standing Committees of the Senate

SEC. 102. Rule XXV of the Standing Rules of the Senate is amended to read as follows:

RULE XXV
"STANDING COMMITTEES

"(1) The following standing committees shall be appointed at the commencement of each Congress, with leave to report by bill or otherwise:

"(a) Committee on Agriculture and Forestry, to consist of thirteen Senators, to which committee shall be referred all proposed legislation, messages, petitions, memorials, and other matters relating to the following subjects.

"1. Agriculture generally.

"2. Inspection of livestock and meat products.

"3. Animal industry and diseases of animals.

"4. Adulteration of seeds, insect pests, and protection of birds and animals in forest reserves.

"5. Agricultural colleges and experiment stations.

"6. Forestry in general, and forest reserves other than those created from the public domain.

"7. Agricultural economics and research.

"8. Agricultural and industrial chemistry.

"9. Dairy industry.

"10. Entomology and plant quarantine.

"11. Human nutrition and home economics.

"12. Plant industry, soils, and agricultural engineering.

"13. Agricultural educational extension services.

"14. Extension of farm credit and farm security.

"15. Rural electrification.

"16. Agricultural production and marketing and stabilization of prices of agricultural products.

"17. Crop insurance and soil conservation.

"(b) Committee on Appropriations, to consist of twenty-one Senators, to which committee shall be referred all proposed legislation, messages, petitions, memorials, and other matters relating to the following subjects:

"1. Appropriation of the revenue for the support of the Government.

"(c) Committee on Armed Services, to consist of thirteen Senators, which committee shall be referred all proposed legislation, messages, petitions, memorials, and other matters relating to the following subjects:

"1. Common defense generally.

"2. The War Department and the Military Establishment generally.

"3. The Navy Department and the Naval Establishment generally.

"4. Soldiers' and sailors' homes.

"5. Pay, promotion, retirement, and other benefits and privileges of members of the armed forces.

"6. Selective service.

"7. Size and composition of the Army and Navy

"8. Forts, arsenals, military reservations, an navy yards.

"9. Ammunition depots.

"10. Maintenance and operation of the Panama Canal, including the administration, sanitation, and government of the Canal Zone.

"11. Conservation, development, and use of naval petroleum and oil shale reserves.

"12. Strategic and critical, materials necessary for the common defense.

"(d) Committee on Banking and Currency, to consist of thirteen Senators, to which committee shall be referred all proposed legislation, messages, petitions, memorials, and other matters relating to the following subjects:

"1. Banking and currency generally.

"2. Financial aid to commerce and industry, other than matters relating to such aid which are specifically assigned to other committees under this rule.

"3. Deposit insurance.

"4. Public and private housing.

"5. Federal Reserve System.

"6. Gold and silver, including the coinage thereof.

"7. Issuance of notes and redemption thereof.

"8. Valuation and revaluation 6f the dollar.

"9. Control of prices of commodities, rents, or services.

"(e) Committee on Civil Service, to consist of thirteen Senators, to which committee shall be referred all proposed legislation, messages, petitions, memorials, and other matters relating to the following subjects:

"1. The Federal civil service generally.

"2. The status of officers and employees of the United States, including classification, and retirement.

"3. The postal service generally, including the railway mail service, mail and pneumatic-tube service; but excluding post roads.

"4. Postal-savings banks.

"5. Census and the collection of statistics generally.

"6. The National Archives.

"(f) Committee on the District of Columbia, to consist of thirteen Senators, to which committee shall be referred all proposed legislation, messages, petitions, memorials, and other matters relating to the following subjects:

"1. All measures relating to the municipal affairs of the District of Columbia in general, other than appropriations therefor, including—

"2. Public health and safety, sanitation, and quarantine regulations.

"3. Regulation of sale of intoxicating liquors.

"4. Adulteration of food and drugs.

"5. Taxes and tax sales.

"6. Insurance, executors, administrators, wills, and divorce.

"7. Municipal and juvenile courts.

"8. Incorporation and organization of societies.

"9. Municipal code and amendments to the criminal and corporation laws.

"(g) (1) Committee on Expenditures in the Executive Department, to consist of thirteen Senators, to which committee shall be referred all proposed legislation, messages, petitions, memorials, and other matters relating to the following subjects:

"(A) Budget and accounting measures, other than appropriations.

"(B) Reorganizations in the executive branch of the Government.

"(2) Such committee shall have the duty of—

"(A) receiving and examining reports of the Comptroller General of the United States and of submitting such recommendations to the Senate as it deems necessary or desirable in connection with the subject matter of such reports;

"(B) studying the operation of Government activities at all levels with a view to determining its economy and efficiency;

"(C) evaluating the effects of laws enacted to reorganize the legislative and executive branches of the Government.

"(D) studying intergovernmental relationships between the United States and the cities and municipalities, and between the United States and international organizations of which the United States is a member.

"(h) Committee on Finance, to consist of thirteen Senators, to which committee shall be referred all proposed legislation, messages, petitions, memorials, and other matters relating to the following subjects:

"1. Revenue measures generally.

"2. The bonded debt of the United States

"3. The deposit of public moneys.

"4. Customs, collection districts, and ports of entry and delivery.

"5. Reciprocal trade agreements

"6. Transportation of dutiable goods.

"7. Revenue measures relating to the insular possessions.

"8. Tariffs and import quotas and matters related thereto.

"9. National social security.

"10. Veterans' measures generally.

"11. Pensions of all the wars of the United States, general and special.

"12. Life insurance issued by the Government on account of service in the armed forces.

"13. Compensation of veterans.

"(i) Committee on Foreign Relations to consist of thirteen Senators, to which committee shall be referred all proposed legislation, messages, petitions, memorials, and other matters relating to the following subjects:

"1. Relations of the United States with foreign nations generally.

"2. Treaties.

"3. Establishment of boundary lines between the United States and foreign nations.

"4. Protection of American citizens abroad and expatriation.

"5. Neutrality.

"6. International conferences and congresses.

"7. The American National Red Cross.

"8. Intervention abroad and declarations of war.

"9. Measures relating to the diplomatic service.

"10. Acquisition of land and buildings for embassies and legations in foreign countries.

"11. Measures to foster commercial intercourse with foreign nations and to safeguard American business in abroad.

"12. United Nations Organization and international financial and monetary organizations.

"13. Foreign loans.

"(j) Committee on Interstate and Foreign Commerce, to consist of thirteen Senators, to which committee shall be referred all proposed legislation, messages, petitions, memorials, and other matters relating to the following subjects:

"1. Interstate and foreign commerce generally.

"2. Regulation of interstate railroads, busses, trucks, and pipe lines.

"3. Communication by telephone, telegraph, radio, and television.

"4. Civil aeronautics.

"5. Merchant marine generally.

"6. Registering and licensing of vessels and small boats.

"7. Navigation and the laws relating thereto, including pilotage.

"8. Rules and international arrangements to prevent collisions at sea.

"9. Merchant marine officers and seamen.

"10. Measures relating to the regulation of common carriers by water and to the on merchant marine vessels, lights and signals, life-saving equipment, and fire protection on such vessels.

"11. Coast and Geodetic Survey.

"12. The Coast Guard, including life-saving service, lighthouses, lightships and ocean derelicts.

"13. United States Coast Guard and Merchant Marine Academies.

"14. Weather Bureau.

"15. Except as provided in paragraph (c), the Panama Canal and interoceanic canals generally.

"16. Inland waterways.

"17. Fisheries and wildlife, including research, restoration, refuges, and conservation.

"18. Bureau of Standards including standardization of weights and measures and the metric system.

"(k) Committee on the Judiciary, to consist of thirteen Senators, to which committee shall be referred all proposed legislation, messages, petitions, memorials, and other matters relating to the following subjects:

"1. Judicial proceedings, civil and criminal, generally.

"2. Constitutional amendments.

"3. Federal courts and judges.

"4. Local courts in the Territories and possessions.

"5. Revision and codification of the statutes of the United States.

"6. National penitentiaries.

"7. Protection of trade and commerce against unlawful restraints and monopolies.

"8. Holidays and celebrations.

"9. Bankruptcy, mutiny, espionage, and counterfeiting.

"10. State and Territorial boundary lines.

"11. Meetings of Congress, attendance of Members, and their acceptance of incompatible offices.

"12. Civil liberties.

"13. Patents, copyrights, and trade-marks.

"14. Patent Office.

"15. Immigration and naturalization.

"16. Apportionment of Representatives.

"17. Measures relating to claims against the United States.

"18. Interstate compacts generally.

"(l) Committee on Labor and Public Welfare, to consist of thirteen Senators, to which committee shall be referred all proposed legislation, messages, petitions, memorials, and other matters relating to the following subjects:

"1. Measures relating to education, labor, or public welfare generally.

"2. Mediation and arbitration of labor disputes.

"3. Wages and hours of labor.

"4. Convict labor and the entry of goods made by convicts into interstate commerce.

"5. Regulation or prevention of importation of foreign laborers under contract.

"6. Child labor.

"7. Labor statistics.

"8. Labor standards.

"9. School-lunch program.

"10. Vocational rehabilitation.

"11. Railroad labor and railroad retirement and unemployment, except revenue measures relating, thereto.

"12. United States Employees' Compensation Commission.

"13. Columbia Institution for the Deaf, Dumb, and Blind; Howard University; Freedmen's Hospital; and Saint Elizabeth's Hospital.

"14. Public health and quarantine.

"15. Welfare of miners.

"16. Vocational rehabilitation and education of veterans.

"17. Veterans' hospitals, medical care and treatment of veterans.

"18. Soldiers' and sailors' civil relief.

"19. Readjustment of servicemen to civil life.

"(m) Committee on Public Lands, to consist of thirteen Senators, to which committee shall be referred all proposed legislation, messages, petitions, memorials, and other matters relating to the following subjects:

"1. Pubic lands generally, including entry, easements, and grazing thereon.

"2. Mineral resources of the public lands.

"3. Forfeiture of land grants and alien ownership, including alien ownership of mineral lands.

"4. Forest reserves and national parks created from the public domain.

"5. Military parks and battlefields. and national cemeteries.

"6. Preservation of prehistoric ruins and objects of interest on the public domain.

"7. Measures relating generally to Hawaii, Alaska, and the insular possessions of the United States, except those affecting their revenue and appropriations.

"8. Irrigation and reclamation, including water supply for reclamation projects, and easements of public lands for irrigation projects.

"9. Interstate compacts relating to apportionment of waters for irrigation purposes.

"10. Mining interests generally.

"11. Mineral land laws and claims and entries thereunder.

"12. Geological survey.

"13. Mining schools and experimental stations.

"14. Petroleum conservation and conservation of the radium supply in the United States.

"15. Relations of the United States with the Indians and the Indian tribes.

"16. Measures relating to the care, education, and management of Indians, including the care and allotment of Indian lands and general and special measures relating to claims which are paid out of Indian funds.

"(n) The Committee on Public Works, to consist of thirteen Senators, to which committee shall be referred all proposed legislation, messages, petitions, memorials, and other matters relating to the following subjects:

"1. Flood control and improvement of rivers and harbors.

"2. Public works for the benefit of navigation, and bridges and dams (other than international bridges and clams).

"3. Water power.

"4. Oil and other pollution of navigable waters.

"5. Public buildings and occupied or improved grounds of the United States generally.

"6. Measures relating to the purchase of sites and construction of post offices, customhouses, Federal courthouses, and Government buildings within the District of Columbia.

"7. Measures relating to the Capitol building and the Senate and House Office Buildings.

"8. Measures relating to the construction or reconstruction, maintenance, and care of the buildings and grounds of the Botanic Gardens, the Library of Congress, and the Smithsonian Institution.

"9. Public reservations and parks within the District of Columbia including Rock Creek Park and the Zoological Park.

"10. Measures relating to the construction or maintenance of roads and post roads.

"(o) (1) Committee on Rules and Administration, to consist of thirteen Senators, to which committee shall be referred all proposed legislation, messages, petitions, memorials, and other matters relating to the following subjects:

"(A) Matters relenting to the payment of money out of the contingent fund of the Senate or creating a charge upon the same; except that any resolution relating to substantive matter within the jurisdiction of any other standing committee of the Senate shall be first referred to such committee.

"(B) Except as provided in paragraph (n) 8, matters relating to the Library of Congress and the Senate Library; statuary and pictures; acceptance or purchase of works of art for the Capitol; the Botanic Gardens; management of the Library of Congress; purchase of books and manuscripts; erection of monuments to the memory of individuals.

"(C) Except as provided in paragraph (n) 8, matters relating to the Smithsonian Institution and the incorporation of similar institutions.

"(D) Matters relating to the election of the President, Vice President, or Members of Congress; corrupt radices; contested elections; credentials and qualifications; Federal elections generally; Presidential succession.

"(E) Matters relating to parliamentary, rules; floor and gallery rules; Senate Restaurant; administration the Senate Office Building of the Capitol; assignment of office space; and services to the Senate.

"(F) Matters relating to printing and correction of the Congressional Record.

"(2) Such committee shall also have the duty of examining all bills, amendments, and joint resolutions after passage by the Senate; and, in cooperation with the Committee on House Administration of the

House of Representatives, of examining all bills and joint resolutions which shall have passed both Houses, to see that the same are correctly enrolled; and when signed by the Speaker of the House and the President of the Senate, shall forthwith present the same, when they shall have originated in the Senate, to the President of the United States in person, and report the fact and date of such presentation to the Senate. Such committee shall also have the duty of assigning office space in the Senate Wing of the Capitol and in the Senate Office Building.

"(3) Each standing committee shall continue and have the power to act until their successors are appointed.

"(3) Each standing committee is authorized to fix the number of its members (but not less than one-third of its entire membership) who for the transaction of such business committee, subject to the provisions of section 133 (d) of the Legislative Reorganization Act of 1946.

"(4) Each Senator shall serve on two standing committees and no more except that Senators of the minority party who are members of Committee on the District of Columbia or on the Committee on Expenditures in the Executive Departments may serve on three standing committees and no more."

Appropriations

SEC. 103. Rule XVI of the Standing Rules of the Senate is amended to read as follows:

"RULE XVI
"AMENDMENTS TO APPROPRIATION BILLS

"1. All general appropriation bills shall be referred to the Committee on Appropriations, and no amendments shall be received to any general bill the effect of which will be to increase an appropriation already contained in the bill, or to add a new item of appropriation, unless it be made to carry out the provisions of some existing law, or treaty stipulation, or Act, or resolution previously passed by the Senate during that session; or unless the same be moved by direction of a standing or select committee of the Senate, or proposed in pursuance of an estimate submitted in accordance with law.

"2. The Committee on Appropriations shall not report an appropriation bill containing amendments proposing new or general legislation or any restriction on the expenditure of the funds appropriated which proposes a limitation not authorized by law if such restriction is to take effect or cease to be effective upon the happening of a contingency, and if an appropriation bill is reported to the Senate or general legislation or any be made against the bill, and if the point is sustained, the bill shall be recommitted to the Committee on Appropriations.

"3. All amendments to general appropriation bills moved by direction of a standing or select committee of the Senate, proposing to increase an appropriation already contained in the bill, or to add new items of appropriation, shall, at least one day before they are considered, be referred to the Committee on Appropriations, and when actually proposed to the bill no amendment proposing to increase the amount stated in such amendment shall be received; in like manner, amendments proposing new items of appropriation to river and harbor bills, establishing post roads, or proposing new post roads, shall, before being considered, be referred to the Committee on Public Works.

"4. No amendment which proposes general legislation shall be received to any general appropriation bill, nor shall any amendment not germane or relevant to the subject matter contained in the bill be received; nor shall any amendment to any item or clause of such bill be received which does not directly relate thereto; nor shall any restriction on the expenditure of the funds appropriated which proposes a limitation not authorized by law be received if such restriction is to take effect or cease to be effective upon the happening of a contingency; and all questions of relevance of amendments under this submitted to the Senate and be decided amendment or restriction to a general appropriation bill may be laid on the table without prejudice to the bill.

"5. No amendment, the object of which is to provide for a private claim, shall be received to any general appropriation bill, unless it be to carry out the provisions- of an existing law or a treaty stipulation, which shall be cited on the face of the amendment.

"6. (a) Three members of the following-named committees, to be selected by their respective committees, shall all be ex officio members of the Committee on Appropriations, to serve on said committee when the annual appropriation bill making appropriations for the purposes specified in the following table opposite the name of the committee is being considered by the Committee on Appropriations:

Name of Committee	Purpose of Appropriation
Committee on Agriculture and Forestry	For the Department of Agriculture.
Committee on Civil Service	For the Post Office Department.
Committee on Armed Services	For the Department of War; for the Department of the Navy.
Committee on the District of Columbia	For the District of Columbia.
Committee Public Works	For Rivers and Harbors.
Committee on Foreign Relations	For the Diplomatic and Consular Service.

"(b) At least one member of each committee enumerated in subparagraph (a), to be selected by his or their respective committees, shall be a member of any conference committee appointed to confer with the House upon the annual appropriation bill making appropriations for the foregoing table opposite the name of his or their respective committee.

"7. When a point of order is made against any restriction on the expenditure of funds appropriated in a general appropriation bill on the ground that the restriction violates this rule, the rule shall be construed strictly and, in case of doubt, in favor of the point of order."

Part 2—Rules of the House of Representatives

Standing Committees of the House of Representatives

SEC. 121. (a) Rule X of the Rules of the House of Representatives is amended to read as follows:

"RULE X
"STANDING COMMITTEES

"(a) There shall be elected by the House, at the commencement of each Congress, the following standing committees:

"1. Committee on Agriculture, to consist of twenty-seven Members.

"2. Committee on Appropriations, to consist of forty-three Members.

"3. Committee on Armed Services, to consist of thirty-three Members.

"4. Committee on Banking and Currency, to consist of twenty-seven Members.

"5. Committee on Post Office and Civil Service, to consist of twenty-five Members.

"6. The Committee on the District of Columbia, to consist of twenty-five Members.

"7. Committee on Education and Labor, to consist of twenty-five Members.

"8. Committee on Expenditures in the Executive Departments, to consist of twenty-five Members.

"9. Committee on Foreign Affairs, to consist of twenty-five Members.

"10. Committee on House Administration, to consist of twenty-five Members.

"11. Committee on Interstate and Foreign Commerce, to consist of twenty-seven Members.

"12. Committee on the Judiciary, to consist of twenty-seven Members.

"13. Committee on Merchant Marine and Fisheries, to consist of twenty-five Members.

"14. Committee on Public Lands, to consist of twenty-five Members.

"15. Committee on Public Works, to consist of twenty-seven Members.

"16. Committee on Rules, to consist of twelve Members.

"17. Committee on Un-American Activities, to consist of nine Members.

"18. Committee on Veterans' Affairs, to consist of twenty-seven Members.

"19. Committee on Ways and Means, to consist of twenty-five Members.

"(b) (1) The Speaker shall appoint all select and conference committees which shall be ordered by the House from time to time.

"(2) At the commencement of each Congress, the House shall elect as chairman of each standing committee one of the Members thereof; in the temporary absence of the chairman, the Member next in rank in the order named in the election of the committee, and so on, as of ten as the case shall happen, shall act as chairman; and in case of a permanent vacancy in the chairmanship of any such committee the house shall elect another chairman.

"(3) All vacancies in standing committees in the House shall be filled by election by the House. Each Member shall be elected to serve on one standing committee and no more; except that Members who are elected to serve on the Committee on the District of Columbia or on the Committee on Un-American Activities may be elected to serve on two standing committees and no more, and Members of the majority party who are elected to serve on the Committee on Expenditures in the Executive Departments or on the Committee on House Administration may be elected to serve on two standing committees and no more."

(b) Rule XI of the Rules of the House of Representatives is amended to read as follows:

"RULE XI
"POWERS AND DUTIES OF COMMITTEES

"(1) All proposed legislation, messages, petitions, memorials, and matters relating to the subjects listed under the standing committees named below shall be referred to such committees, respectively: *Provided,* That unless otherwise provided herein, an matter within the jurisdiction of a standing committee prior to January 2, 1947, of that committee or of the consolidated committee succeeding generally to the jurisdiction of that committee.

"(a) **Committee on Agriculture.**

"1. Agriculture generally.

"2. Inspection of livestock and meat products.

"3. Animal industry and diseases of animals.

"4. Adulteration of seeds, insect pests, and protection of birds and animals in forest reserves.

"5. Agricultural colleges and experiment stations.

"6. Forestry in general, and forest reserves other than those created from the public domain.

"7. Agricultural economics and research.

"8. Agricultural and industrial chemistry.

"9. Dairy industry.

"10. Entomology and plant quarantine.

"11. Human nutrition and home economics.

"12. Plant industry, soils, and agricultural engineering.

"13. Agricultural educational extension services.

"14. Extension of farm credit and farm security.

"15. Rural electrification.

"16. Agricultural production and marketing and stabilization of process of agricultural products.

"17. Crop insurance and soil conservation.

"(b) **Committee on Appropriations.**

"1. Appropriation of the revenue for the support of the Government.

"(c) **Committee on Armed Services.**

"1. Common defense generally.

"2. The War Department and the Military Establishment generally.

"3. The Navy Department and the Naval Establishment generally.

"4. Soldiers' and sailors' homes.

"5. Pay, promotion, retirement, and other benefits and privileges of members of the armed forces.

"6. Selective service.

"7. size and composition of the Army and Navy.

"8. forts, arsenals, military reservations, and navy years.

"9. Ammunition depots.

"10. Conservation, development, and use of naval petroleum and oil shall reserves.

"11. Strategic and critical materials necessary for the common defense.

"12. Scientific research and development in support of the armed services.

"(d) **Committee on Banking and Currency.**

"1. Banking and currency generally.

"2. Financial aid to commerce and industry, other than matters relating to such aid which are specifically assigned to other committees under this rule.

"3. Deposit insurance.

"4. Public and private housing.

"5. Federal Reserve System.

"6. gold and silver, including the coinage thereof.

"7. Issuance of notes and redemption thereof.

"8. Valuation and revaluation of the dollar.

"9. Control of prices of commodities, rents, or services.

"(e) **Committee on Post Office and Civil Service.**

"1. The Federal civil service generally.

"2. The status of officers and employees of the United States, including their compensation, classification, and retirement.

"3. The postal service generally, including the railway mail service, and measures relating to ocean mail and pneumatic-tube service; but excluding post roads.

"4. Postal-savings banks.

"5. Census and the collection of statistics generally.

"6. The National archives.

"(f) **Committee on the District of Columbia.**

"1. All measures relating to the municipal affairs of the District of Columbia in general, other than appropriations therefor, including—

"2. Public health and safety, sanitation, and quarantine regulations.

"3. Regulation of sale of intoxicating liquors.

"4. Adulteration of food and drugs.

"5. Taxes and tax sales.

"6. Insurance, executors, administrators, wills, and divorce.

"7. Municipal and juvenile courts.

"8. Incorporation and organization of societies.

"9. Municipal code and amendments to the criminal and corporation laws.

"(g) **Committee on Education and Labor.**

"1. Measures relating to education or labor generally.

"2. Mediation and arbitration of labor disputes.

"3. Wages and hours of labor.

"4. Convict labor and the entry of goods made by convicts into interstate commerce.

"5. Regulation or prevention of importation of foreign laborers under contract.

"6. child labor.

"7. Labor statistics.

"8. Labor standards.

"9. School-lunch program.

"10. Vocational rehabilitation.

"11. United States Employees' Compensation Commission.

"12. Columbia Institution for the Deaf, Dumb, and Blind; Howard University; Freedmen's Hospital; and Saint Elizabeths Hospital.

"13. Welfare of miners.

"(h) (1) **Committee on Expenditures in the Executive Department.**

"(A) Budget and accounting measures, other than appropriations.

"(B) Reorganizations in the executive branch of the Government.

"(2) Such committee shall have the duty of—

"(A) receiving and examining reports of the Comptroller General of the United States and of submitting such recommendations to the House as it deems necessary or desirable in connection with the subject matter of such reports;

"(B) studying the operation of Government activities at all levels with a view to determining its economy and efficiency;

"(C) evaluating the effects of laws enacted to reorganize the legislative and executive branches of the Government;

"(D) studying intergovernmental relationships between the United States and the States and municipalities, and between the United States and international organizations of which the United States is a member.

"(i) **Committee on Foreign Affairs.**

"1. Relations of the United States with foreign nations generally.

"2. Establishment of boundary lines between the United States and foreign nations.

"3. Protection of American citizens abroad and expatriation.

"4. Neutrality.

"5. International conferences and congresses.

"6. The American National Red Cross.

"7. Intervention abroad and declarations of war.

"8. Measures relating to the diplomatic service.

"9. Acquisition of land and buildings for embassies and legations in foreign countries.

"10. Measures to foster commercial intercourse with foreign nations and to safeguard American business interests abroad.

"11. United National Organizations and international financial and monetary organizations.

"12. Foreign loans.

"(j) (1) **Committee on House Administration.**

"(A) Employment of persons by the House, including clerks for Members and committees, and reporters of debates.

"(B) Expenditure of the contingent fund of the House.

"(C) The auditing and settling of all accounts which may be charged to the contingent fund.

"(D) Measures relating to account of the House generally.

"(E) Appropriations from the contingent fund.

"(F) Measures relating to services to the House, including the House Restaurant and administration of the House Office Buildings and of the House wing of the Capitol.

"(G) Measures relating to the travel of members of the House.

"(H) Measures relating to the assignment of office space for Members and committees.

"(I) Measures relating to the disposition of useless executive papers.

"(J) Except as provided in paragraph (o) 8, matters relating to the Library of Congress and the House Library; statuary and pictures; acceptance or purchase of works of art for the Capitol; the Botanic Gardens; management of the Library of Congress; purchase of books and manuscripts to the memory of individuals.

"(K) Except as provided in paragraph (o) 8, matters relating to the Smithsonian Institution and the incorporation of similar institutions.

"(L) Matters relating to printing and correction of the Congressional Record.

"(M) Measures relating to the election of the President, Vice President, or Members of Congress; corrupt practices; contested elections; credentials and qualifications; and Federal elections generally.

"(2) Such committee shall also have the duty of—

"(A) examining all bills, amendments, and joint resolution after passage by the House; and in cooperation with the Senate Committee on Rules and Administration, of examining all bills and joint resolutions which shall have passed both Houses, to see that they are correctly enrolled; and when signed by the Speaker of the House and the President of the Senate, shall forthwith present the same, when they shall have originated in the House, to the President of the United States in person, and report the fact and date of such presentation to the House;

"(B) reporting to the Sergeant at Arms of the House the travel of Members of the House the travel of Members of the House;

"(C) arranging a suitable program for each day observed by the House of Representatives as a memorial day memory of Members of the Senate and House of Representatives who have died during the preceding period, and to arrange for the publication of the proceedings thereof.

"(k) **Committee on Interstate and Foreign Commerce.**

"1. Interstate and foreign commerce generally.

"2. Regulation of interstate and foreign transportation, except transportation by water not subject to the jurisdiction of the Interstate Commerce Commission.

"3. Regulation of interstate and foreign communications.

"4. Civil aeronautics.

"5. Weather bureau.

"6. Interstate oil compacts; and petroleum and natural gas, except on the public lands.

"7. Securities and exchanges.

"8. Regulation of interstate transmission of power, except the installation of connections between Government water power projects.

"9. Railroad labor and railroad retirement and unemployment, except revenue measures relating thereto.

"10. Public health and quarantine.

"11. Inland waterways.

"12. Bureau of Standards, standardization of weights and measures, and the metric system.

"(l) **Committee on the Judiciary.**

"1. Judicial proceedings, civil and criminal, generally.

"2. Constitutional amendments.

"3. Federal courts and judges.

"4. Local courts in the Territories and possessions.

"5. Revision and codification of the statues of the United States.

"6. National penitentiaries.

"7. Protection of trade and commerce against unlawful restraints and monopolies.

"8. Holidays and celebrations.

"9. Bankruptcy, mutiny, espionage, and counterfeiting.

"10. State and Territorial boundary lines.

"11. Meetings of Congress, attendance of Members, and their acceptance of incompatible offices.

"12. Civil liberties.

"13. Patents, copyrights, and trade-marks.

"14. Patent Office.

"15. Immigration and naturalization.

"16. Apportionment of Representatives.

"17. Measures relating to claims against the United States.

"18. Interstate compacts generally.

"19. Presidential succession.

"(m) **Committee on Merchant Marine and Fisheries.**

"1. Merchant marine generally.

"2. Registering and licensing of vessels and small boats.

"3. Navigation and the laws relating thereto, including pilotage.

"4. Rules and international arrangements to prevent collisions at sea.

"5. Merchant marine officers and seamen.

"6. Measures relating to the regulation of common carriers by water (except matters subject to the jurisdiction of the Interstate Commerce

Commission) and to the inspection of merchant vessels, lights and signals, lifesaving equipment, and fire protection on such vessels.

"7. The Coast Guard, including lifesaving service, lighthouses, lightships, and ocean derelicts.

"8. United States Coast Guard and Merchant Marine Academies.

"9. Coast and Geodetic Survey.

"10. The Panama Canal and the maintenance and operation of the Panama Canal, including the administration, sanitation, and government of the Canal Zone; and interoceanic canals generally.

"11. Fisheries and wildlife, including research, restoration, refuges, and conservation.

"(n) **Committee on Public Lands.**

"1. Public lands generally, including entry, easements, and grazing thereon.

"2. Mineral resources of the public lands.

"3. Forfeiture of land grants and alien ownership, including alien ownership of mineral lands.

"4. Forest reserves and national parks created from the public domain.

"5. Military parks and battlefields, and national cemeteries.

"6. Preservation of prehistoric ruins and objects of interest on the public domain.

"7. Measures relating generally to Hawaii, Alaska, and the insular possessions of the United States, except those affecting the revenue and appropriations.

"8. Irrigation and reclamation, including water supply for reclamation projects, and easements of public lands for irrigation projects, and acquisition of private lands when necessary to complete irrigation projects.

"9. Interstate compacts relating to apportionment of waters for irrigation purposes.

"10. Mining interests generally.

"11. Mineral land laws and claims and entries thereunder.

"12. Geological survey.

"13. Mining schools and experimental stations.

"14. Petroleum conservation on the public lands and conservation of the radium supply in the United States.

"15. Relations of the United States with the Indians and the Indian tribes.

"16. Measures relating to the care, education, and management of Indians, including the care and allotment of Indian lands and general and special measures relating to claims which are paid out of Indian funds.

"(o) **Committee on Public Works.**

"1. Flood control and improvement of rivers and harbors.

"2. Public works for the benefit of navigation, including bridges and dams (other than international bridges and dams).

"3. Water power.

"4. Oil and other pollution of navigable waters.

"5. Public buildings and occupied or improved grounds of the United States generally.

"6. Measures relating to the purchase of sites and construction of post offices, customhouses, Federal courthouses, and Government buildings within the District of Columbia.

"7. Measures relating to the Capitol Building and the Senate and House Office Buildings.

"8. Measures relating to the construction or reconstruction, maintenance, and care of the buildings and grounds of the Botanic Gardens, the Library of Congress, and the Smithsonian Institution.

"9. Public reservations and parks within the District of Columbia, including Rock Creek Park and the Zoological Park.

"10. Measures relating to the construction or maintenance of roads and post roads, other than appropriations therefor; but it shall not be in order for any bill providing general legislation in relation to roads to contain any provision for any specific road, nor for any bill in relation to a specific road to embrace a provision in relation to any other specific road.

"(p) **Committee on Rules.**

"1. The rules, joint rules, and order of business of the House.

"2. Recesses and final adjournments of Congress.

"(q) (1) **Committee on Un-American Activities.**

"(A) Un-American activities.

"(2) The committee on Un-American Activities, as a whole or by subcommittee, is authorized to make from time to time investigations of (i) the extent, character, and objects of un-American propaganda activities in the United States, (ii) the diffusion within the United States of subversive and un-American propaganda that is instigated from foreign countries or of a domestic origin and attacks the principle of the form of government as guaranteed by our Constitution, and (iii) all other questions in relation thereto that would aid Congress in any necessary remedial legislation.

"The Committee on Un-American Activities shall report to the House (or to the Clerk of the House if the House is not in session) the results of any such investigation, together with such recommendations as it deems advisable.

"For the purpose of any such investigation, the Committee on Un-American Activities, or any subcommittee thereof, is authorized to sit and act at such times and places within the United States, whether or not the House is sitting, has recessed, or has adjourned, to hold such hearings, to require the attendance of such books, papers, and documents, and to take such testimony, as it deems necessary. Subpoenas may be issued under the signature of the chairman of the committee or any subcommittee, or by any member designated by any such chairman, and may be served by any person designated by any such chairman or member.

"(r) **Committee on Veterans' Affairs.**

"1. Veterans' measures generally.

"2. Pensions of all the wars of the United States, general and special.

"3. Life insurance issued by the Government on account of service in the armed forces.

"4. Compensation, vocational rehabilitation, and education of veterans.

"5. Veterans' measures generally.

"6. Soldiers' and sailors' civil relief.

"7. Readjustment of servicemen to civil life.

"(s) **Committee on Ways and Means.**

"1. Revenue measures generally

"2. The bonded debt of the United States.

"3. The deposit of public moneys.

"4. Customs, collection districts, and ports of entry and delivery.

"5. Reciprocal trade agreements.

"6. Transportation of dutiable goods.

"7. Revenue measures relating to the insular possessions.

"8. National social security.

"(2) (a) The following-named committees shall have leave to report at any time on the matters herein stated, namely: The Committee on Rules—on rules, joint rules, and order of business; the Committee on House Administration—on the right of a member to his seat, enrolled bills, on all matters referred to it of printing for the use of the House or the two Houses, and on all matters of expenditure of the contingent fund of the House; the Committee on Ways and Means—on bills raising revenue; the Committee on Appropriations—on the general appropriation bills; the Committee on Public Works—on bills authorizing the improvement of rivers and harbors; the Committee on the Public Lands—on bills for the forfeiture of land grants to railroad and other corporations, bills preventing speculation in the public lands, bills for the reservation of the public lands for the benefit of actual and bona fide settlers, and bills for the admission of new States; the Committee on Veterans Affairs—on general pension bills.

"(b) It shall always be in order to call up for consideration a report from the Committee on Rules (except it shall not be called up for consideration on the same day it is presented to the House, unless so determined by a vote of not less than two-thirds of the Members voting, but this provision shall not apply during the last three days of the session), and, pending the consideration thereof, the Speaker may entertain one motion that the House adjourn; but after the result is announced he shall not entertain any other dilatory motion until the said report shall have been fully disposed of. The Committee on Rules shall not report any rule or order which shall provide that business under paragraph 7 of rule XXIV shall be set aside by a vote of less than two-thirds of the Members present; nor shall it report any rule or order which shall operate to prevent the motion to recommit being made as provided in paragraph 4 of rule XVI.

"(c) The Committee on Rules shall present to the House reports concerning rules, joint rules, and order of business, within three legislative days of the time when ordered reported by the committee. If such rule or order is not considered immediately, it shall be referred to the calendar and, if not called up by the Member making the report within seven legislative days thereafter, any member of the Rules Committee may call it up as a question of privilege and the Speaker shall recognize any member of the Rules Committee seeking recognition for that purpose. If the Committee on Rules shall make an adverse report on any resolution pending before the committee, providing for any public bill or joint resolution, on days when it shall be in order to call up motions to discharge committees it shall be in order for any Member of the House to call up for consideration by the House any such adverse report, and it shall be in order to move the adoption by the House of said resolution adversely reported not withstanding the adverse report of the Committee on Rules, and the Speaker shall recognize the Member seeking recognition for that purpose as a question of the highest privilege.

"(d) The Committee on House Administration shall make final report to the House in all contested-election cases not later than six months from the first day of the first regular session of the Congress to which the contestee is elected except in a contest from the Territory of Alaska, in which case the time shall not exceed nine months.

"(e) A standing committee of the House (other than the Committee on Appropriations) shall meet to consider any bill or resolution pending before it (A) on all regular meeting days selected by the committee; (B) upon the call of the chairman of the committee; (C) if the chairman of the committee, after three days' consideration, refuses or fails, upon the request of at least three members of the committee, to call a special meeting of the committee within seven calendar days from the date of said request, then, upon the filing with the clerk of the committee of the written and signed request of a majority of the committee for a called special meeting of the committee, the committee shall meet on the day and hour specified in said written request. It shall be the duty of the clerk of the committee to notify all members of the committee in a usual way of such called special meeting.

"(f) The rules of the House are here by made the rules of it standing committees so far as applicable, except that a motion to recess from day to day is here by made a motion of high privilege in said committee."

Delegates and Resident Commissioner

SEC. 122. Rule XII of the Standing Rules of the House of Representatives is amended to read as follows:

"RULE XII
"DELEGATES AND RESIDENTS COMMISSIONER

"1. The Delegates from Hawaii and Alaska, and the Resident Commissioner to the United Sates from Puerto Rico, shall be elected to serve as additional members on the Committees on Agriculture, Armed Services, and Public Lands; and they shall possess and such committees the same powers and privileges as in the House, and may make any motion except to reconsider."

Reference of Private Claims Bills

SEC. 123. Paragraph 3 of Rule XXI of the Standing Rules of the House of Representatives is amended to read as follows:

"3. No bill for the payment or adjudication of any private claim against the Government shall be referred, except by unanimous consent, to any other than the following committees, namely: To the Committee on Foreign Affairs and to the Committee on the Judiciary."

Part 3 — Provisions Applicable to Both Houses
Private Bills Banned

SEC. 131. No private bill or resolution (including so-called omnibus claims or pension bills), and no amendment to any bill or resolution, authorizing or directing (1) the payment of money for property damages, for the personal injuries or death for which suit maybe instituted under the Federal Tort Claims Act, or for a pension (other than to carry out a provision of law or treaty stipulation); (2) the construction of a bridge across a navigable stream; or (3) the correction of a military or naval record, shall be received or considered in either the Senate or the House of Representatives.

Congressional Adjournment

SEC. 132. Except in time of war or during a national emergency proclaimed by the President, the two Houses shall adjourn sine die not later than the last day (Sundays excepted) in the month of July in each year unless otherwise provided by the Congress.

Committee Procedure

SEC. 133. (a) Each standing committee of the Senate and the House of Representatives (except the Committees on Appropriations) shall fix regular weekly, biweekly, or monthly meetings days for the transaction of business before the committee, and additional meetings maybe called by the chairman as he may deem necessary.

(b) Each such committee shall keep a complete record of all committee action. Such record shall include a record of the votes on any questions on which a record vote is demanded.

(c) It shall be the duty of the chairman of each such a committee to report or cause to be reported promptly to the Senate or House of Representatives, as the case maybe, any measure approved by his committee and to take or cause to be taken necessary steps to bring the matter to a vote.

(d) No measure or recommendation shall be reported from any such committee unless a majority of the committee unless a majority of the committee were actually present.

(e) Each such standing committee shall, so far as practicable, require all witness appearing before it to file in advance written statements of their proposed testimony, and to limit their oral presentations to brief summaries of their argument. The staff of each committee shall prepare digests of such statements for the use of committee members.

(f) All hearing conducted by standing committees or their subcommittees shall be open to the public, except executive session for marking up bills or for voting or where the committee by a majority vote orders an executive session.

Committee Powers

SEC. 134. (a) Each standing committee of the Senate, including any subcommittee of any such committee, is authorized to hold such hearings, to sit and act at such times and places during the sessions, recess, and adjourned periods of the Senate, to require by subpena or otherwise the attendance of such witnesses and the production of such correspondence, books, papers, and documents, to take such testimony and to make such expenditures (not in excess $10,000 for each committee during any Congress) as it deems advisable. Each such committee may make investigations into any matter within its jurisdiction, may report such hearings as may be had by it, and may employ stenographic assistance at a cost not exceeding 25 cents per hundred words. The expenses of the committee shall be paid from the contingent fund of the Senate upon vouchers approved by the chairman.

(b) Every committee and subcommittee serving the Senate and House of Representatives shall report the name, profession and total salary of each staff member employed by it, and shall make an accounting of funds appropriated to it and expended by it to the Secretary of Senate and Clerk of the House of Representatives, as the case may be, at least once every six months, and such information shall be published periodically in the Congressional Directory when and as the same is issued and as Senate and House documents, respectively, every three months.

(c) No standing committee of the Senate or the House, except the Committee on Rules of the House, shall sit, without special leave, while the Senate or the House, as the case may be, is in session.

Conference Rules on Amendments in Nature of Substitute

SEC. 135. (a) In any case in which a disagreement to an amendment in the nature of a substitute has been referred to conferees, it shall be in order for the conferees to report a substitute on the same subject matter; but they may not include in the report matter not committed to them by either House. They may, however, include in their report in any such case matter which is a germane modification of subjects in disagreement.

(b) In any case in which the conferees violate subsection (a), the conference report shall be subject to a point of order.

Legislative Oversight by Standing Committees

SEC. 136. To assist the Congress in appraising the administration of the laws and in developing such amendments or related legislation as it may deem necessary, each standing committee of the Senate and the House of Representatives shall exercise continuous watchfulness of the execution by the administrative agencies concerned of any laws, the subject matter of which is within the jurisdiction of such committee; and, for that purpose, shall study all pertinent reports and data submitted to the Congress by the agencies in the executive branch of the Government.

Decisions on Questions of Committee Jurisdiction

SEC. 137. In any case which a controversy arises as to the jurisdiction of any standing committee of the Senate with respect to any proposed legislation, the question of jurisdiction shall be decided by the presiding officer of the Senate, without debate, in favor of that committee which has jurisdiction over the subject matter which predominates in such proposed legislation; but such decision shall be subject to an appeal.

Legislative Budget

SEC. 138. (a) The Committee on Ways and Means and the Committee on Appropriations of the House of Representatives, and the Committee on Finance and the Committee on Appropriations of the Senate, or duly authorized subcommittees thereof, are authorized and directed to meet jointly at the beginning of each regular session of Congress and after study and consultation, giving due consideration to the budget recommendations of the President, report to their respective Houses a legislative budget for the ensuing fiscal year, including the estimated over-all Federal receipts and expenditures for such year. Such report shall contain a recommendation for the maximum amount to be appropriated for expenditure in such year which shall include such an amount to be reserved for deficiencies as may be deemed necessary by such committees. If the estimated receipts exceed the estimated expenditures, such report shall contain a recommendation for a reduction in public debt. Such report shall be made by February 15.

(b) The report shall be accompanied by a concurrent resolution adopting such budget, and fixing the maximum amount to be appropriated for expenditure in such year. If the estimated expenditures exceed the estimated receipts, the concurrent resolution shall include a section substantially as follows: "That it is the sense of the Congress that the public debt shall be increased in an amount equal to the amount by which the estimated expenditures for the ensuing fiscal year exceed the estimated receipts, such amount being $."

Hearings and Reports by Appropriations Committees

SEC. 139. (a) No general appropriation bill shall be considered in either House unless, prior to the consideration of such bill, printed committee hearings and reports on such bill have been available for at least three calendar days for the Members of the House in which such bill is to be considered.

(b) The committees on Appropriations of the two Houses are authorized and directed, acting jointly, to develop a standard appropriation classification schedule which will clearly define in concise and uniform accounts the subtotals of appropriations asked for by agencies in the executive branch of the Government. That part of the printed hearings containing each such agency's request for appropriations shall be preceded by such a schedule.

(c) No general appropriation bill or amendment thereto shall be received or considered in either House if it contains a provision reappropriating unexpended balances of appropriations; except that this provision shall not apply to appropriations in continuation of appropriations for public works on which work has been commenced.

(d) The Appropriations Committees of both Houses are authorized and directed to make a study of (1) existing permanent appropriations with a view to limiting the number of permanent appropriations and to recommend to their respective Houses what permanent appropriations, if any, should be discontinued; and (2) the disposition of funds resulting from the sale of Government property or services by all departments and agencies in the executive branch of the Government with a view to recommending to their respective Houses a uniform system of control with respect to such funds.

Records of Congress

SEC. 140. (a) The Secretary of the Senate and the Clerk of the House of Representatives are authorized and directed, acting jointly, to obtain at the close of each Congress all of the noncurrent records of the Congress and of each committee thereof and transfer them to the National Archives for preservation, subject to the orders of the Senate or the House, respectively.

(b) The Clerk of the House of Representatives is authorized and directed to collect all of the noncurrent records of the House of Representatives from the First to the Seventy-sixth Congress, inclusive, and transfer such records to the National Archives for preservation, subject to the orders of the Senate or the House, respectively.

Preservation Of Committee Hearings

SEC. 141. The Librarian of the Library of Congress is authorized and directed to have bound at the end of each session of Congress the printed hearings of testimony taken by each committee of the Congress at the preceding session.

Effective Date

SEC. 142. This title shall take effect on January 2, 1947; except that this section and sections 140 and 141 shall take effect on the date of enactment of this Act.

TITLE II—MISCELLANEOUS
Part 1—Statutory Provisions Relating to Congressional Personnel
Increase in Compensation for Certain Congressional Officers

SEC. 201. (a) Effective January 1,1947, the annual basic compensation of the elected officers of the Senate and the House of Representatives (not including the Presiding Officers of the two Houses) shall be increased by 50 per centum; and the provisions of section 501 of the Federal Employees Pay Act of 1945, as amended by section 5 of the Federal Employees Pay Act of 1946, shall not be applicable to the compensation of said elected officers.

(b) There is hereby authorized to be appropriated annually for the "Office of the Vice President" the sum of $23,130; and there is hereby authorized to be appropriated annually for the "Office of the Speaker" the sum of $20,025.

(c) The Speaker, the majority leader and the minority leader of the House of Representatives are each authorized to employ an administrative assistant, who shall receive basic compensation at a rate not to exceed $8,000 a year. There is hereby authorized to be appropriated such sums as may be necessary for the payment of such compensation.

Committee Staffs

SEC. 202. (a) Each standing committee of the Senate and the House of Representatives (other than the Appropriations Committees) is authorized to appoint by a majority vote of the committee not more than four professional staff members in addition to the clerical staffs on a permanent basis without regard to political affiliations and solely on the basis of fitness to perform the duties of the office; and said staff members shall be assigned to the chairman and ranking minority member of such committee as the committee may deem advisable. Each such committee is further authorized to terminate the services by a majority vote of any such professional staff member as it may see fit. Professional staff members shall not engage in any work other than committee business and no other duties may be assigned to them.

(b) Subject to appropriations which it shall be in order to include in appropriation bills, the Committee on Appropriations of each House is authorized to appoint such staff, in addition to the clerk thereof and assistants for the minority, as each such committee, by a majority vote, shall determine to be necessary, such personnel, other than the minority assistants, to possess such qualifications as the committees respectively may prescribe, and the Committee on Appropriations of the House also is authorized to conduct studies and examinations of the organization and operation of any executive agency (including any agency the majority of the stock of which is owned by the Government of the United States) as it may deem necessary to assist it in connection with the determination of matters within its jurisdiction and in accordance with procedures authorized by the committee by a majority vote, including the rights and powers conferred by House Resolution Numbered 50, adopted January 9, 1945.

(c) The clerical staff of each standing committee, which shall be appointed by a majority vote of the committee, shall consist of not more than six clerks, to be attached to the office of the chairman, to the ranking minority member, and to the professional staff, as the committee may deem advisable; and the position of committee janitor is hereby abolished. The clerical staff shall handle committee correspondence and stenographic work, both for the committee staff and for the chairman and ranking minority member on matters related to committee work.

(d) All committee hearings, records, data, charts, and files shall be kept separate and distinct from the congressional office records of the Member serving as chairman of the committee; and such records shall be the property of the Congress and all members of the committee and the respective Houses shall have access to such records. Each committee is authorized to have printed and bound such testimony and other data presented at hearings held by the committee.

(e) The professional staff members of the standing committees shall receive annual compensation, to be fixed by the chairman, ranging from $5,000 to $8,000 and the clerical staff shall receive annual compensation ranging from $2,00 to $8,000.

(f) No committee shall appoint to its staff any experts or other personnel detailed or assigned from any department or agency of the Government, except with the written permission of the Committee on Rules and Administration of the House of Representatives, as the case may be.

(g) No individual who is employed as a professional staff member of any committee as provided in this section shall be eligible for appointment to any office or position in the executive branch of the Government for a period of one year after he shall have ceased to be such a member.

(h) Notwithstanding the foregoing provisions—

(1) the committee employees of the existing Committee on Appropriations of the Senate and of the existing Committee on Appropriations of the Senate and of the existing Committee on Appropriations of the House of Representatives shall be continued on the rolls of the respective appropriations committees established under title I of this Act during the fiscal year 1947, unless sooner removed for cause.

(2) Committee employees of all other existing standing committees of each House shall be continued on the pay rolls of the Senate and House of Representatives, respectively, through January 31, 1947, unless sooner removed for cause by the Secretary of the Senate or the Clerk of the House, as the case may be.

(3) The appropriations for the compensation of committee employees of standing committees of the Senate and of the House of Representatives contained in the Legislative Branch Appropriation Act, 1947, shall be available for the compensation of employees specified in paragraph (2) of this subsection and of employees of the standing committees of the Senate and House of Representatives succeeding to the jurisdiction of the standing committees specified in such Appropriation Act; and in any case in which the legislative jurisdiction of any existing standing committee is transferred to two or more standing committees under title I of this Act, the Committee on Rules and Administration of the Senate with respect to standing committees of the Senate, and the Committee on House Administration, with respect to standing committees of the House, shall allocate such appropriations in an equitable manner.

Legislative Reference Service

SEC. 203. (a) The Librarian of Congress is authorized and directed to establish in the Library of Congress a separate department to be known as the Legislative Reference Service. It shall be the duty of the Legislative Reference Service,

(1) upon request, to advise and assist any committee of either House or any joint committee in the analysis, appraisal, and evaluation of legislative proposals pending before it, or of recommendations submitted to Congress, by the President or any executive agency, and otherwise to assist in furnishing a basis for the proper determination of measures before the committee;

(2) upon request, or upon its own initiative in anticipation of requests, to gather, classify, analyze, and make available, in translations, indexes, digests, compilations and bulletins, and otherwise, data for a bearing upon legislation, and to render such data serviceable to Congress, and committees and Members thereof, without partisan bias in selection or presentation;

(3) to prepare summaries and digest of public hearings before committees of the Congress, and of bills and resolutions of a public general nature introduced in either House.

(b) (1) A director and assistant director of the Legislative Reference Service and all other necessary personnel, shall be appointed by the Librarian of Congress without regard to the civil-service laws and without reference to political affiliations, solely on the ground of fitness to perform the duties of their office. The compensation of all employees shall be fixed in accordance with the provisions of the Classification Act of 1923, as amended: *Provided,* That the grade of senior specialists in each field enumerated in paragraph (2) of this subsection shall not be less than the highest grade in the executive branch of the Government to which research analysts and consultants without supervisory responsibility are currently assigned. All employees of the Legislative Reference Service shall be subject to the provisions of the civil-service retirement laws.

(2) The Librarian of Congress is further authorized to appoint in the Legislative Reference Service senior specialists in the following government and public administration; education; engineering and public works; full employment; housing; industrial organization and corporation finance; international trade, and economic geography; labor; mineral economics; money and banking; price economics; social welfare; taxation and fiscal policy; transportation and communications; and veterans' affairs. Such specialists, together with such other members of the staff as may be necessary, shall be available for special work with the appropriate committees of congress for any of the purposes set out in section 203 (a) (1).

(c) There is hereby authorized to be appropriated for the work of the Legislative Reference Service the following sums: (1) For the fiscal year ending June 30, 1947, $550,000; (2) for the fiscal year ending June 30, 1948, $650,000; (3) for the year ending June 30, 1949, $750,000; and (4) for each fiscal year thereafter such sums as may be necessary to carry on the work of the Service.

SEC. 204. There is hereby authorized to be appropriated for the work of the Office of the Legislative Counsel the following, sums:

(1) For the fiscal year ending June 30, 1947, $150,000;

(2) For the fiscal year ending June 30, 1948, $200,000;

(3) For the fiscal year ending June 30, 1949, $250,000;

(4) For the fiscal year ending June 30, 1950, $250,000; and

(5) For each fiscal year thereafter such sums as may be necessary to carry on the work of the Office.

Studies by Comptroller General

SEC. 205. The Comptroller General is authorized and directed to make a full and complete study of restrictions placed in general appropriation Acts limiting the expenditure of specified appropriations therein, with a view to determining the cost to the Government incident to complying with such restrictions, and to report to the Congress his estimate of the cost of complying with such restrictions and such other recommendations with respect thereto as he deems necessary or desirable.

Expenditure Analysis by Comptroller General

SEC. 206. The Comptroller General is authorized and directed to make an expenditure analysis of each agency in the executive branch of the Government (including Government corporations), which, in the opinion of the Comptroller General, will enable Congress to determine whether public fund have been economically and efficiently administered and expended. Reports on such analyses shall be submitted by the Comptroller General, from time to time, to the Committees on Expenditures in the Executive Departments, to the Appropriations Committees, and to the legislative committees having jurisdiction over legislation relating to the operations of the respective agencies, of the two Houses.

Correction of Military and Naval Records

SEC. 207. The Secretary of War, the Secretary of the Navy, and the Secretary of the Treasury with respect to the Coast Guard, respectively, under procedures set up by them, and acting through boards of civilian officers or employees of their respective departments are authorized to correct any military or naval record where in their judgment such action is necessary to correct an error or to remove an injustice.

Part 2—Statutory Provisions Relating to Committees of Congress

Improvement of Congressional Record

SEC. 221. The Joint Committee on Printing is authorized and directed to provide for printing in the Daily Record the legislative program for the day, together with a list of congressional committee meetings and hearings, and the place of meeting and subject matter; and to cause a brief resume of congressional activities for the previous day to be incorporated in the Record, together with an index of its contents. Such data shall be prepared under the supervision of the Secretary of the Senate and the Clerk of the House of Representatives, respectively.

Joint Committee on Printing

SEC. 222. Section 1 of the Act entitled "An Act Providing for the public printing and binding and the distribution of public documents" approved January 12, 1895 (28 Stat. 601), is amended to read as follows: "That there shall be a Joint Committee on Printing, consisting of the chairman and two members of the Committee on Rules and Administration of the Senate and the chairman and two members of the Committee on House Administration of the House of Representatives, who shall have the powers hereinafter stated."

Joint Committee on the Library

SEC. 223. The Joint Committee of Congress on the Library shall hereafter consist of the chairman and four members of the Committee on Rules and Administration of the Senate and the chairman and four members of the Committee on House Administration of the House of Representatives.

Transfer of Functions

SEC. 224. The functions, powers, and duties imposed by statute, resolution, or rule of either House of Congress on the ef-

fective date of this section on a standing committee of the Senate or the House of Representatives (or the chairman thereof) are, insofar as they are consistent with this Act, hereby transferred to that standing committee created by this Act (or the chairman thereof) to which is transferred the legislative jurisdiction over the subject matter to which such functions, powers, and duties relate; except that the chairman of the Committee on Civil Service of the Senate and the chairman of the Committee on Post Office and Civil Service of the House created by this Act shall be members of the National Archives Council.

Joint Committee on the Economic Report

SEC. 225. Section 5 (b) (3) (relating to the time for filing the report of the Joint Committee on the Economic Report) of the Employment Act of 1946 is amended by striking out "May 1" and inserting in lieu thereof "February 1".

Economic Report of the President

SEC. 226. Section 3 (a) (relating to the time for filing the economic report of the president) of the Employment Act of 1946 is amended by striking out "within 60 days after the beginning of each regular session" and inserting in lieu thereof "at the beginning of each regular session".

Part 3—Provisions Relating to Capitol and Pages

Remodeling of Caucus Rooms and Restaurants

SEC. 241. The Architect of the Capitol is authorized and directed to prepare plans and submit them to Congress at the earliest practicable date for the remodeling (a) of the caucus rooms in the Senate and House Office Buildings to provide improved acoustics and seating facilities and for the presentation of motion picture or other visual displays on matters of national interest; and (b) of the Senate and House Restaurants to provide for more convenient dining facilities.

Assignment of Capitol Space

SEC. 242. The President pro tempore of the Senate and the Speaker of the House of Representatives shall cause a survey to be made of available space within the Capitol which could be utilized for joint committee meetings, meetings of conference committees, and other meeting, requiring, the attendance of both Senators and members of the House of Representatives; and shall recommend the reassignment of such space to accommodate such meetings.

Senate and House Pages

SEC. 243. (a) The Secretary of the Senate and the Clerk of the House of Representatives, acting jointly, are authorized and directed to enter into an arrangement with the Board of Education of the District of Columbia for the education of Congressional pages and pages of the Supreme Court in the public school system of the District. Such arrangement shall include provision for reimbursement to the District of Columbia for any additional expenses incurred by the public school system of the District in carrying out such arrangement.

(b) There are hereby authorized to be appropriated such sums as may be necessary to reimburse the District of Columbia in accordance with the arrangement referred to in subsection (a).

(c) Notwithstanding the provisions of subsections (a) and (b) of this section, said page or pages may elect to attend a private or parochial school of their own choice: *Provided, however,* That such private or parochial school shall be reimbursed by the Senate and House of Representatives only in the same amount as would be paid if the page or pages were attending a public school under the provisions of paragraphs (a) and (b) of this section.

Authorization of Appropriations and Personnel

SEC. 244. All necessary funds required to carry out the provisions of this Act, by the Secretary of the Senate and the Clerk of the House, are hereby authorized to be appropriated, and the Secretary of the Senate and the Clerk of the House are hereby further authorized to employ such administrative assistants as may be necessary in order to carry out the provisions of this Act under their respective jurisdictions.

Effective Date

SEC. 245. This title shall take effect on the date of its enactment; except that sections 202 (a), (b), (c), (e), (f), and (h), 222, 223, 224, and 243 shall take effect on the day on which the Eightieth Congress convenes.

TITLE III—REGULATION OF LOBBYING ACT
Short Title

SEC. 301. This title may be cited as the "Federal Regulation of Lobbying Act".

Definitions

SEC. 302. When used in this title—

(a) The term "contribution" includes a gift, subscription, loan, advance, or deposit of money or anything of value and includes a contract, promise, or agreement, whether or not legally enforceable, to make a contribution.

(b) The term "expenditure" includes a payment, distribution, loan, advance, deposit, or gift of money or anything of value, and includes a contract, promise, or agreement, whether or not legally enforceable, to make an expenditure.

(c) The term "person" includes an individual, partnership, committee, association, corporation, and any other organization or group of persons.

(d) The term "Clerk" means the Clerk of the House of Representatives of the United States.

(e) The term "legislation" means bills, resolutions, amendments, nominations, and other matters pending or proposed in either House of Congress, and includes any other matter, which may be the subject of action by either House.

Detailed Accounts of Contributions

SEC. 303. (a) It shall be the duty of every person who shall in any manner solicit or receive a contribution to any organization or fund for the purposes hereinafter designated to keep a detailed and exact account of,

(1) all contributions of any amount or of any value whatsoever;

(2) the name and address of every person making any such contribution of $500 or more and the date thereof;

(3) all expenditures made by or on behalf of such organization or fund; and

(4) the name and address of every person to whom any such expenditure is made and the date thereof.

(b) It shall be the duty of such person to obtain and keep the receipted bill, stating the particulars, for every expenditure of such funds exceeding $10 in amount, and to preserve all receipted bills and accounts required to be kept by this section for a period of at least two years from the date of the filing of the statement containing such items.

Receipts for Contributions

SEC. 304. Every individual who receives a contribution of $500 or more for any of the purposes hereinafter designated shall within five days after receipt thereof rendered to the person or organization for which such contribution was received a detailed account thereof, including the name and address of the person making such contribution and the date on which received.

Statements to Be Filed with Clerk of House

SEC. 305. (a) Every person receiving any contributions or expending any money for the purposes designated in subparagraph (a) or (b) of section 307 shall file with the Clerk between the first a tenth day of the calendar quarter, a statement containing complete as of the day next preceding the date of filing—

(1) the name and address of each person who has made a contribution of $500 or more not mentioned in the preceding report; except that the first report filed pursuant to this title shall contain the name and address of each person who has made any contribution of $500 or more to such person since the effective date of this title;

(2) the total sum of the contributions made to or for such person during the calendar year and not stated under paragraph (1);

(3) the total sum of all contributions made to or for such person during the calendar year;

(4) the name and address of each person to whom an expenditure in one or more items of the aggregate amount or value, within the calendar year, of $10 or more his been made by or on behalf of such person, and the amount, date, and purpose of such expenditure;

(5) the total sum of all expenditures made by or on behalf of such person during the calendar year and not stated under paragraph (4);

(6) the total sum of expenditures made by or on behalf of such person during the calendar year.

(b) The statements required to be filed by subsection (a) shall be cumulative during the calendar year to which they relate, but where there has been no change in an item reported in a previous statement only the amount need be carried forward.

Statement Preserved for Two Years

SEC. 306. A statement required by this title to be filed with the Clerk—

(a) shall be deemed properly filed when deposited in an established post office within the prescribed time, duly stamped, registered and directed to the Clerk of the House of Representatives of the United States, Washington, District of Columbia, but in the event it is not received, duplicate of such statement shall be promptly filed by the Clerk of its nonreceipt;

(b) shall be preserved by the Clerk for a period of two years constitute part of the public records of his office, shall be open to public inspection.

Persons to Whom Applicable

SEC. 307. The provisions of this title shall apply to any person (except a political committee as defined in the Federal Corrupt Practices Act, and duly organized State or local committees of a political party), who by himself, or through any agent or employee or other persons in any manner whatsoever, directly or indirectly, solicits, collects, or receives money or any other thing of value to be used principally to aid, or the principal purpose of which person is to aid, in the accomplishment of any of the following purposes:

(a) The passage or defeat of the Congress of the United States.

(b) To influence, directly or indirectly, the passage or defeat of any legislation by the Congress of the United States.

Registration with Secretary of the Senate and Clerk of the House

SEC. 308. (a) Any person who shall engage himself for pay or for any consideration for the purpose of attempting to influence the passage or defeat of any legislation by the Congress of the United States shall, before doing anything in furtherance of such object, register with the Clerk of the House of Representatives and the Secretary of the Senate and shall give to those officers in writing and under oath, his name and business address, the name and address of the person by whom he is employed, and in whose interest he appears or works, the duration of such employment, how much he is paid and is to receive, by whom he is paid or is to be paid, how much he is to be paid for expenses, and what expenses are to be included. Each such person so registering, shall, between the first and tenth day of each calendar quarter, so long as his activity continues, file with the Clerk and Secretary a detailed report under oath of all money received and expended by him during the preceding calendar quarter in carrying on his work; to whom paid; for what purposes; and the names of any papers, periodicals, magazines, or other publications in which he has caused to be published any articles or editorials; and the proposed legislation he is employed to support or oppose. The provisions of this section shall not apply to any person who merely appears before a committee of the Congress of the United States in support of or opposition to legislation; nor to any public official acting in his official capacity; nor in the case of any newspaper or

other regularly published periodical (including any individual who owns, publishes, or is employed by any such newspaper or periodical) which in the ordinary course of business publishes news items, editorials, or other comments, or paid advertisements, which directly or defeat of legislation, if such newspaper, periodical, or individual, engages in no further or other activities in connection with the passage or defeat of such legislation, other than to appear before a committee of the Congress of United States in support of or in opposition to such legislation.

(b) All information required to be filed under the provisions of this section with the Clerk of the House of Representatives and the Secretary of the Senate shall be compiled by said Clerk and Secretary, acting jointly, as soon as practicable after the close of the calendar quarter with respect to which such information is filed and shall be printed in the Congressional Record.

Reports and Statements to Be Made Under Oath

SEC. 309. All reports and statements required under this title shall be made under oath, before an officer authorized by law to administer oaths.

Penalties

SEC. 310. (a) Any person who violates any of the provisions of this title, shall, upon conviction, be guilty of a misdemeanor, and shall be punished by a fine of not more than $5,000 or imprisonment for not more than twelve months, or by both such fine and imprisonment.

(b) In addition to the penalties provided for in subsection (a), any person convicted of the misdemeanor specified therein is for a period of three years from the date of such conviction, from attempting to influence, directly or indirectly, the passage of any proposed legislation or from appearing before a committee of the Congress in support of or opposition to proposed legislation; and any person who violates any provision of this subsection shall, upon conviction thereof, be guilty of a felony, and shall be punished by a fine of not more than $10,000, or imprisonment for not more than five years, or by both such fine and imprisonment.

Exemption

SEC. 311. The provisions of this title shall not apply to practices or activities regulated by the Federal Corrupt Practices Act nor be construed as repealing any portion of said Federal Corrupt Practices Act.

. . . .

TITLE VI—COMPENSATION AND RETIREMENT PAY OF MEMBERS OF CONGRESS

Compensation of Members of Congress

SEC. 601. (a) Effective on the day on which the Eightieth Congress convenes, the compensation of Senators, Representatives in Congress, Delegates from the Territories, and the Resident Commissioner from Puerto Rico shall be at the rate of $12,500 per annum each; and the compensation of the Speaker of the House of Representatives and the Vice President of the United States shall be at the rate of $20,000 per annum each.

(b) Effective on the day on which the Eightieth Congress convenes there shall be paid to each Senator, Representative in Congress, Delegate from the Territories, Resident Commissioner from Puerto Rico, an expense allowance of $2,500 per annum to assist in defraying expenses relating to, or resulting from the discharge of his official duties, for which no tax liability shall incur, or accounting be made; such sum to be paid in equal monthly installments.

(c) The sentence contained in the Legislative Branch Appropriation Act, 1946, which reads as follows: "There shall be paid to each Representative and Delegate, and to the Resident Commissioner from Puerto Rico, after January 2, 1945, an expense allowance of $2,500 per annum to assist in defraying expenses related to or resulting from the discharge of his official duties, to be paid in equal monthly installments.", is hereby repealed, effective on the day on which the Eightieth Congress convenes.

(d) The sentence contained in the Legislative Branch Appropriation Act, 1947, which reads as follows: "There shall be paid to each Senator after January 1, 1946, an expense allowance of $2,500 per annum to assist in defraying of expenses related to or resulting from the discharge of his duties, to be paid in equal monthly installments.", is hereby repealed, effective on the day on which the Eightieth Congress convenes.

Retirement Pay of Members of Congress

SEC. 602. (a) Section 3 (a) of the Civil Service Retirement Act of May 29, 1930, is amended by inserting after the words "elective officers" the words "in the executive branch of the Government".

(b) Such Act, as amended, is further amended by adding after section 3 the following new section:

"SEC. 3A. Notwithstanding any other provision of this Act—

"(1) This Act shall not apply to any Member of Congress until he gives notice in writing, while serving as a Member of Congress, to the disbursing officer by whom is salary is paid of his desire to come within the purview of this Act. Such notice may be given by a Member of Congress within six months after the date of enactment of the Legislative Reorganization Act of 1946 or within six months after any date on which he takes an oath of office as a Member of Congress.

"(2) In the case of any Member of Congress who gives notice of his desire to come within the purview of this Act, the amount required to be deposited for the purposes of section 9 with respect to services rendered after the date of enactment of the Legislative Reorganization Act of 1946, shall be a sum equal to 6 per centum of his basic salary, pay, or compensation for such services, together with interest computed at the rate of 4 per centum per annum compounded on December 31 of each year; and the amount to be deducted and withheld from the basic salary, pay, or compensation of each such Member of Congress for the purposes of section 10 shall be a sum equal to 6 per centum of such basic salary, pay, or compensation.

"(3) No Person shall be entitled to receive an annuity as provided d in this section until he shall have become separated from the service af-

ter having had at least six years of service as a Member of Congress and have attained the age of sixty-two years, except that. any such Member who shall have had at least five years of service as a Member of Congress, may, subject to the provisions of section 6 and of paragraph (4) of this section, be retired for disability, irrespective of age, and be paid an annuity computed in accordance with paragraph (5) of this section.

"(4) No Members of Congress shall be entitled to receive an annuity under this Act unless there shall have been deducted and withheld from his basic salary, pay, or compensation for the last five ears of his service as a Member of Congress, or there shall have been deposited under section 9 with respect to such last five years of service, the amounts specified in paragraph (2) of this section with respect to so much of such five years of service as was performed after the date of enactment of the Legislative Reorganization Act of 1946 and the amounts specified in section 9 with respect to so much of such five years of service as was performed prior to such date.

"(5) Subject to the provisions of section 9 and of subsections (c) and (d) of section 4, the annuity of a Member of Congress shall be an amount equal to 2 ½ per centum of his average annual basic salary, pay, or compensation as a Member of Congress multiplied by his years of service as a Member of Congress, but no such annuity shall exceed an amount equal to three-fourths of the salary, pay, or compensation that he is receiving at the time he becomes separated from the service.

"(6) In the case of a Member of Congress who becomes separated from the service before he completes an aggregate of six years of service as a Member of Congress, and who is not retired for disability, the total amount deducted from his basic salary, pay, or compensation as a Member of Congress, together with interest at 4 per centum compounded as of December 31 of each year shall be returned to such Member of Congress. No such Member of Congress shall thereafter this section unless at 4 per centum compounded on December 31 of each year, but interest shall not be required covering any period of separation from the service.

"(7) If any person takes office as a Member of Congress while receiving an annuity as provided in this section, the payment of such annuity shall be suspended during the period for which he holds such office; but, if he gives notice as provided in paragraph (2) of this section, his service as a Member of Congress during such period shall be credited in determining the amount of his subsequent annuity.

"(8) Nothing contained in this Act shall be construed to prevent any person eligible therefor from simultaneously receiving an annuity computed in accordance with this section and an annuity computed in accordance with section 4, but in computing the annuity under section 4 in the case of any person who (A) has had at least six years' service as a Member of Congress, and (B) has served as a Member of Congress at any time after the date of enactment of the Legislative Reorganization Act of 1946, service as a Member of Congress shall not be credited.

"(9) No provision of this or any other Act relating to automatic separation from the service shall be applicable to any Member of Congress.

"(10) As used in this section, the term 'Member of Congress' means a Senator, Representative in Congress, Delegate from a Territory, or the Resident Commissioner from Puerto Rico; and the term 'service as a Member of Congress' shall include the period from the date of the beginning of the term for which a Member of Congress is elected or appointed to the date on which he takes office as such a Member."

Approved August 2, 1946.

Statutes at Large, 57 (1945–1947), 79th Congress, 2d session, Aug. 2, 1946, 812–852.

138   The Presidential Succession Act

July 18, 1947

Congress passed the Presidential Succession Act in 1947 at the request of President Harry S. Truman, who sought to place high-ranking elected officials rather than appointed cabinet members in line to succeed the presidency. Truman had become president when Franklin D. Roosevelt died on April 12, 1945. Under the prevailing order of succession, which had been established in the Presidential Succession Act of 1886, the secretary of state stood next in line for the presidency.

On June 19, 1945, Truman asked Congress to put the Speaker of the House next in line to become president after the vice president. Congress concurred and for the first time in American history, the two highest ranking officials of Congress—the Speaker of the House and the president pro tempore of the Senate—were added to the line of presidential succession. If the line should have to go farther, the act provides for a succession of cabinet officers, beginning with the secretary of state, as was the case with the 1886 act. The Presidential Succession Act of 1947 recognized the importance of the Speaker of the House and the president pro tempore of the Senate as the highest ranking elected officials and the two key officers of Congress mentioned in the Constitution.

AN ACT

To provide for the performance of the duties of the office of President in case of the removal, resignation, death, or inability both of the President and Vice President.

Be it enacted by the Senate and House of Representatives of the United States of America assembled, That (a) (1) if, by reason of death, resignation, removal of office, inability, or failure to qualify, there is neither a President or Vice President to discharge the powers and duties of the office of President, then the Speaker of the House of Representatives shall, upon his resignation as Speaker and as Representative in Congress, act as President.

(2) The same rule shall apply in the case of the death, resignation, removal from office, or inability of an individual acting as President under this subsection.

(b) If, at the time when under subsection (a) a Speaker is to begin the discharge of the powers and duties of the office of President, there is no Speaker, or the Speaker fails to qualify as Acting President, then the President pro tempore of the Senate shall, upon his resignation as President pro tempore and a Senator, act as President.

(c) An individual acting as President under subsection (a) or subsection (b) shall continue to act until the expiration of the then current Presidential term, except that—

(1) if his discharge of the powers and duties of the office is founded in whole or in part on the failure of both the President-

elect and the Vice-President-elect to qualify, then he shall act only until a President or Vice President qualifies; and

(2) if his discharge of the powers and duties of the office is founded in whole or in part on the inability of the President or Vice President, then he shall act only until the removal of the disability of one of such individuals.

(d) (1) If, by reason of death, resignation, removal from office, inability, or failure to qualify, there is no President pro tempore to act as President under subsection (b), then the officer of the United States who is highest on the following list, and who is not under disability to discharge the powers and duties of the office of President shall act as President: Secretary of State, Secretary of the Treasury, Secretary of War, Attorney General, Postmaster General, Secretary of the Navy, Secretary of the Interior, Secretary of Agriculture, Secretary of Commerce, Secretary of Labor.

(2) An individual acting as President under this subsection shall continue to do so until the expiration of the then current Presidential term, but not after a qualified and prior-entitled individual is able to act, except that the removal of the disability of an individual higher on the list contained in paragraph (1) or the ability to qualify on the part of an individual higher on such list shall not terminate his service.

(3) The taking of the oath of office by an individual specified in the list in paragraph (1) shall be held to constitute his resignation from the office by virtue of the holding of which he qualifies to act as President.

(e) Subsections (a), (b), and (d) shall apply only to such officers as are eligible to the office of President under the Constitution. Subsection (d) shall apply only to officers appointed, by and with the advice and consent of the Senate, prior to the time of the death, resignation, removal from office, inability, or failure to qualify, of the President pro tempore, and only to officers not under impeachment by the House of Representatives at the time the powers and duties of the office of the President devolve upon them.

(f) During the period that any individual acts as President under this Act, his compensation shall be at the rate then provided by law in the case of the President.

(g) Sections 1 and 2 of the Act entitled "An Act to provide for the performance of the duties of the office of President in case of the removal, death, resignation, or inability both of the President and Vice President", approved January 19, 1886 (24 Stat. 1; U.S.C., 1940 edition, title 3, secs. 21 and 22), are repealed.

Approved July 18, 1947.

Statutes at Large, 61 (1947–1949), 80th Congress, 1st session, July 18, 1947, 380–381.

139   Senator Joseph R. McCarthy on Communists in Government Service

February 9, 1950

Senator Joseph R. McCarthy (R-Wis.) epitomized the extremes of America's Cold War hysteria. The anti-Communist crusade in the United States began in earnest in the late 1930s with the formation of the Dies Committee in the House of Representatives (see document 128) and grew to agonizing witch-hunt proportions in the conduct of the House Un-American Activities Committee in the 1940s and 1950s. This was one of the darkest and most frightening periods in U.S. history from the standpoint of government intrusion into the lives of ordinary law-abiding citizens (see document 134).

From his position as chairman of the Senate Permanent Subcommittee on Investigations, Joseph McCarthy launched investigations into alleged Communist infiltration and subversion of the federal government. He took the anti-Communist crusade to new levels of intensity in his zeal to rid the nation of real and imagined Communist sympathizers in government and in other places in American society. The nation termed his no-holds-barred tactics, where the ends justified the means, McCarthyism. The rights, liberties, and reputations of citizens were often trampled in the name of "national security." So intense was the frenzy to free the government of subversive elements that entire careers and reputations were ruined by allegations that in most cases contained no proof of wrongdoing.

McCarthy's extreme views and his growing difficulties with alcoholism led to his downfall. Within months of this speech a few brave souls in the Senate, such as Margaret Chase Smith (R-Maine), began denouncing McCarthy's tactics (see document 140). But it took four more years, until December 2, 1954, for the Senate to vote to censure McCarthy for behavior that was "contemptuous, contumacious, and denunciatory." Just months before his censure, during the Army-McCarthy hearings, the entire nation had the chance to see his denunciatory style on television (see document 144). This turned many Americans against him, as they saw firsthand his callous disregard for common decency.

In this speech McCarthy's first made his accusation that there were known Communists in the U.S. State Department. McCarthy spoke before the Ohio County Women's Republican Club, in Wheeling, West Virginia, at an event commemorating Lincoln's birthday. He spoke from notes, but a version of the speech was later reconstructed and read into the Congressional Record. *This speech lifted McCarthy from obscurity to national and international attention and launched his career as an anti-Communist crusader.*

Ladies and gentlemen, tonight as we celebrate the one hundred and forty-first birthday of one of the greatest men in American history, I would like to be able to talk about what a glorious day today is in the history of the world. As we celebrate the birth of this man who with his whole heart and soul hated war, I would like to be able to speak of peace in our time, of war being outlawed, and of worldwide disarmament. These would be truly appropriate things to be able to mention as we celebrate the birthday of Abraham Lincoln.

Five years after a world war has been won, men's hearts should anticipate a long peace, and men's minds should be free from the heavy weight that comes with war. But this is not such a period—for this is not a period of peace. This is a time of the "cold war." This is a time when all the world is split into two vast, increasingly hostile armed camps—a time of a great armaments race.

Today we can almost physically hear the mutterings and rumblings of an invigorated god of war. You can see it, feel it, and hear it all the way from the hills of Indochina, from the shores of Formosa, right over into the very heart of Europe itself.

The one encouraging thing is that the "mad moment" has not yet arrived for the firing of the gun or the exploding of the bomb which will set civilization about the final task of destroying itself. There is still a hope for peace if we finally decide that no longer can we safely blind our eyes and close our ears to those facts which are shaping up more and more clearly. And that is that we are now engaged in a show-down fight—not the usual war between nations for land areas or other material gains, but a war between two diametrically opposed ideologies.

The great difference between our western Christian world and the atheistic Communist world is not political, ladies and gentlemen, it is moral. There are other differences, of course, but those could be reconciled. For instance, the Marxian idea of confiscating the land and factories and running the entire economy as a single enterprise is momentous. Likewise, Lenin's invention of the one-party police state as a way to make Marx's idea work is hardly less momentous.

Stalin's resolute putting across of these two ideas, of course, did much to divide the world. With only those differences, however, the East and the West could most certainly still live in peace.

The real, basic difference, however, lies in the religion of immoralism—invented by Marx, preached feverishly by Lenin, and carried to unimaginable extremes by Stalin. This religion of immoralism, if the Red half of the world wins—and well it may—this religion of immoralism will more deeply wound and damage mankind than any conceivable economic or political system.

Karl Marx dismissed God as a hoax, and Lenin and Stalin have added in clear-cut unmistakable language their resolve that no nation, no people who believe in a God, can exist side by side with their communistic state.

Karl Marx, for example, expelled people from his Communist party for mentioning such things as justice, humanity, or morality. He called this soulful ravings and sloppy sentimentality.

While Lincoln was a relatively young man in his late thirties, Karl Marx boasted that the Communist specter was haunting Europe. Since that time, hundreds of millions of people and vast areas of the world have fallen under Communist domination. Today, less than one hundred years after Lincoln's death, Stalin brags that this Communist specter is not only haunting the world, but is about to completely subjugate it.

Today we are engaged in a final, all-out battle between communistic atheism and Christianity. The modern champions of communism have selected this as the time. And, ladies and gentlemen, the chips are down—they are truly down.

Lest there be any doubt that the time has been chosen, let us go directly to the leader of communism today—Joseph Stalin. Here is what he said—not back in 1928, not before the war, not during the war—but two years after the last war was ended: "To think that the Communist revolution can be carried out peacefully, within the framework of a Christian democracy, means one has either gone out of one's mind and lost all normal understanding, or has grossly and openly repudiated the Communist revolution."

And this is what was said by Lenin in 1919, which was also quoted with approval by Stalin in 1947: "We are living," said Lenin, "not merely in a state, but in a system of states, and the existence of the Soviet Republic side by side with Christian states for a long time is unthinkable. One or the other must triumph in the end. And before that end supervenes, a series of frightful collisions between the Soviet Republic and the Bourgeois states will be inevitable."

Ladies and gentlemen, can there be anyone here tonight who is so blind as to say that the war is not on? Can there be anyone who fails to realize that the Communist world has said, "The time is now"—that this is the time for the showdown between the democratic Christian world and the Communist atheistic world?

Unless we face this fact, we shall pay the price that must be paid by those who wait too long.

Six years ago, at the time of the first conference to map out the peace—Dumbarton Oaks—there was within the Soviet orbit 180 million people. Lined up on the antitotalitarian side there were in the world at that time roughly 1.625 billion people. Today, only six years later, there are 800 million people under the absolute domination of Soviet Russia—an increase of over 400 percent. On our side, the figure has shrunk to around 500 million. In other words, in less than six years the odds have changed from 9 to 1 in our favor to 8 to 5 against us. This indicates the swiftness of the tempo of Communist victories and American defeats in the cold war. As one of our outstanding historical figures once said, "When a great democracy is destroyed, it will not be because of enemies from without, but rather because of enemies from within."

The truth of this statement is becoming terrifyingly clear as we see this country each day losing on every front.

At war's end we were physically the strongest nation on earth and, at least potentially, the most powerful intellectually and morally. Ours could have been the honor of being a beacon in the desert of destruction, a shining living proof that civilization was not yet ready to destroy itself. Unfortunately, we have failed miserably and tragically to arise to the opportunity.

The reason why we find ourselves in a position of impotency is not because our only powerful potential enemy has sent men to invade our shores, but rather because of the traitorous actions of those who have been treated so well by this nation. It has not been the less fortunate or members of minority groups who have been selling this nation out, but rather those who have had all the benefits that the wealthiest nation on earth has had to offer—the finest homes, the finest college education, and the finest jobs in government we can give.

This is glaringly true in the State Department. There the bright young men who are born with silver spoons in their mouths are the ones who have been worst.

Now I know it is very easy for anyone to condemn a particular bureau or department in general terms. Therefore, I would like to cite one rather unusual case—the case of a man who has done much to shape our foreign policy.

When Chiang Kai-shek was fighting our war, the State Department had in China a young man named John S. Service. His task, obviously, was not to work for the communization of China. Strangely, however, he sent official reports back to the State Department urging that we torpedo our ally Chiang Kai-shek and stating, in effect, that communism was the best hope of China.

Later, this man—John Service—was picked up by the Federal Bureau of Investigation for turning over to the Communists secret State Department information. Strangely, however, he was never prosecuted. However, Joseph Grew, the under secretary of state, who insisted on his prosecution, was forced to resign. Two days after Grew's successor, Dean Acheson, took over as under secretary of state, this man—John Service—who had been picked up by the FBI and who had previously urged that communism was the best hope of China, was not only reinstated in the State Department but promoted. And finally, under Acheson, placed in charge of all placements and promotions.

Today, ladies and gentlemen, this man Service is on his way to represent the State Department and Acheson in Calcutta—by far and away the most important listening post in the Far East.

Now, let's see what happens when individuals with Communist connections are forced out of the State Department. Gustave Duran, who was labeled as (I quote) "a notorious international Communist," was made assistant to the assistant secretary of state in charge of Latin American affairs. He was taken into the State Department from his job as a lieutenant colonel in the Communist International Brigade. Finally, after intense congressional pressure and criticism, he resigned in 1946 from the State Department—and, ladies and gentlemen, where do you think he is now? He took over a high-salaried job as chief of Cultural Activities Section in the office of the assistant secretary general of the United Nations.

Then there was a Mrs. Mary Jane Kenny, from the Board of Economic Warfare in the State Department, who was named in an FBI report and in a House committee report as a courier for the Communist party while working for the government. And where do you think Mrs. Kenny is—she is now an editor in the United Nations Document Bureau.

Another interesting case was that of Julian H. Wadleigh, economist in the Trade Agreements Section of the State Department for eleven years and was sent to Turkey and Italy and other countries as United States representative. After the statute of limitations had run so he could not be prosecuted for treason, he openly and brazenly not only admitted but proclaimed that he had been a member of the Communist party ... that while working for the State Department he stole a vast number of secret documents ... and furnished these documents to the Russian spy ring of which he was a part.

You will recall last spring there was held in New York what was known as the World Peace Conference—a conference which was labeled by the State Department and Mr. Truman as the sounding board for Communist propaganda and a front for Russia. Dr. Harlow Shapley was the chairman of that conference. Interestingly enough, according to the news release put out by the department in July, the secretary of state appointed Shapley on a commission which acts as liaison between UNESCO and the State Department.

This, ladies and gentlemen, gives you somewhat of a picture of the type of individuals who have been helping to shape our foreign policy. In my opinion the State Department, which is one of the most important government departments, is thoroughly infested with Communists.

I have in my hand fifty-seven cases of individuals who would appear to be either card carrying members or certainly loyal to the Communist party, but who nevertheless are still helping to shape our foreign policy.

One thing to remember in discussing the Communists in our government is that we are not dealing with spies who get thirty pieces of silver to steal the blueprints of a new weapon. We are dealing with a far more sinister type of activity because it permits the enemy to guide and shape our policy.

In that connection, I would like to read to you very briefly from the testimony of Larry E. Kerley, a man who was with the counter espionage section of the FBI for eight years. And keep in mind as I read this to you that at the time he is speaking, there was in the State Department Alger Hiss, the convicted Alger Hiss; John Service, the man whom the FBI picked up for espionage—Julian Wadleigh, who brazenly admitted he was a spy and wrote newspaper articles in regard thereto, plus hundreds of other bad security risks.

The FBI, I may add, has done an outstanding job, as all persons in Washington, Democrats and Republicans alike, agree. If J. Edgar Hoover had a free hand, we would not be plagued by Hisses and Wadleighs in high positions of power in the State Department. The FBI has only power to investigate.

Here is what the FBI man said.

In accordance with instructions of the State Department to the FBI, the FBI was not even permitted to open an espionage case against any Russia suspect without State Department approval.

Mr. ARENS. Did the State Department ever withhold from the Justice Department the right to intern suspects?

Mr. KERLEY. They withheld the right to get out process for them which, in effect, kept them from being arrested, as in the case of Schevchenko and others.

Mr. ARENS. In how many instances did the State Department decline to permit process to be served on Soviet agents?

Mr. KERLEY. Do you mean how many Soviet agents were affected?

Mr. ARENS. Yes.

Mr. KERLEY. That would be difficult to say because there were so many people connected in one espionage ring, whether or not they were directly conspiring with the ring.

Mr. ARENS. Was that order applicable to all persons?

Mr. KERLEY. Yes; all persons in the Soviet-espionage organization.

Mr. ARENS. What did you say the order was as you understood it or as it came to you?

Mr. KERLEY. That no arrests of any suspects in the Russian-espionage activities in the United States were to be made without the prior approval of the State Department.

Now the reason for the State Department's opposition to arresting any of this spy ring is made rather clear in the next question and answer.

"Senator O'CONOR. Did you understand that that was to include also American participants?

"Mr. KERLEY. Yes; because if they were arrested that would disclose the whole apparatus, you see.

In other words they could not afford to let the whole ring which extended into the State Department be exposed.

This brings us down to the case of one Alger Hiss who is important not as an individual any more, but rather because he is so representative of a group in the State Department. It is unnecessary to go over the sordid events showing how he sold out the nation which had given him so much. Those are rather fresh in all of our minds.

However, it should be remembered that the facts in regard to his connection with this international Communist spy ring were made known to the then Under Secretary of State Berle three days after Hitler and Stalin signed the Russo-German alliance pact. At that time one Whittaker Chambers—who was also part of the spy ring—apparently decided that with Russia on Hitler's side, he could no longer betray our nation to Russia. He gave Under Secretary of State Berle—and this is all a matter of record—practically all, if not more, of the facts upon which Hiss' conviction was based.

Under Secretary Berle promptly contacted Dean Acheson and received word in return that Acheson (and I quote) "could vouch for Hiss absolutely"—at which time the matter was dropped. And this, you understand, was at a time when Russia was an ally of Germany. This condition existed while Russia and Germany were invading and dismembering Poland, and while the Communist groups here were screaming "warmonger" at the United States for their support of the allied nations.

Again in 1943, the FBI had occasion to investigate the facts surrounding Hiss' contacts with the Russian spy ring. But even after that FBI report was submitted, nothing was done.

Then late in 1948—on August 5—when the Un-American Activities Committee called Alger Hiss to give an accounting, President Truman at once issued a presidential directive ordering all government agencies to refuse to turn over any information whatsoever in regard to the Communist activities of any government employee to a congressional committee.

Incidentally, even after Hiss was indicted—it is interesting to note that the president still labeled the exposé of Hiss as a "red herring."

If time permitted, it might be well to go into detail about the fact that Hiss was Roosevelt's chief adviser at Yalta when Roosevelt was admittedly in ill health and tired physically and mentally . . . and when, according to the secretary of state, Hiss and Gromyko drafted the report on the conference.

According to the then Secretary of State Stettinius, here are some of the things that Hiss helped to decide at Yalta. (1) The establishment of a European High Commission; (2) the treatment of Germany—this you will recall was the conference at which it was decided that we would occupy Berlin with Russia occupying an area completely circling the city, which, as you know, resulted in the Berlin airlift which cost thirty-one American lives; (3) the Polish question; (4) the relationship between UNRRA and the Soviet; (5) the rights of Americans on control commissions of Rumania, Bulgaria, and Hungary; (6) Iran; (7) China—here's where we gave away Manchuria; (8) Turkish Straits question; (9) international trusteeships; (10) Korea.

Of the results of this conference, Arthur Bliss Lane of the State Department had this to say: "As I glanced over the document, I could not believe my eyes. To me, almost every line spoke of a surrender to Stalin."

As you hear this story of high treason, I know that you are saying to yourself, "Well, why doesn't the Congress do something about it?" Actually, ladies and gentlemen, one of the important reasons for the graft, the corruption, the dishonesty, the disloyalty, the treason in high government positions—one of the most important reasons why this continues is a lack of moral uprising on the part of the 140 million American people. In the light of history, however, this is not hard to explain.

It is the result of an emotional hangover and a temporary moral lapse which follows every war. It is the apathy to evil which people who have been subjected to the tremendous evils of war feel. As the people of the world see mass murder, the destruction of defenseless and innocent people, and all of the crime and lack of morals which go with war, they become numb and apathetic. It has always been thus after war.

However, the morals of our people have not been destroyed. They still exist. This cloak of numbness and apathy has only needed a spark to rekindle them. Happily, this spark has finally been supplied.

As you know, very recently the secretary of state proclaimed his loyalty to a man guilty of what has always been considered as the most abominable of all crimes—of being a traitor to the people who gave him a position of great trust. The secretary of state in attempting to justify his continued devotion to the man who sold out the Christian world to the atheistic world, referred to Christ's Sermon on the Mount as a justification and reason therefor, and the reaction of the American people to this would have made the heart of Abraham Lincoln happy.

When this pompous diplomat in striped pants, with a phony British accent, proclaimed to the American people that Christ on the Mount endorsed communism, high treason, and betrayal of a sacred trust, the blasphemy was so great that it awakened the dormant indignation of the American people.

He has lighted the spark which is resulting in a moral uprising and will end only when the whole sorry mess of twisted, warped thinkers are swept from the national scene so that we may have a new birth of national honesty and decency in government.

Congressional Record, Senate, 81st Congress, 2d session, Feb. 20, 1950, 1954–1957. McCarthy read a transcribed copy of this address in the Senate on Feb. 20, 1950, as part of a longer speech. The ellipses in this text appear in the version printed in the *Congressional Record.* The whereabouts of the original recording of the speech made on Feb. 9, 1950, in Wheeling, West Virginia, is unknown.

140 Senator Margaret Chase Smith's Declaration of Conscience

June 1, 1950

Senator Margaret Chase Smith (R-Maine) was willing to give her Senate colleague and fellow Republican Joseph McCarthy the benefit of the doubt when others attacked him for his Wheeling, West Virginia, speech accusing the State Department of harboring Communists (see document 139). But her attitude changed quickly as McCarthy continued to make unsubstantiated charges of Communists in government service. When she delivered this speech on the floor of the Senate, McCarthy was in the chamber, sitting nearby. Scrupulously following Senate rules that prohibit personal attacks on fellow senators, Smith, a freshman senator and the only woman in the Senate at the time, never once mentioned McCarthy's name. But it was clear to all that he was the subject of
her remarks. Six other Republican senators endorsed her statement. When she finished, McCarthy left the chamber without attempting to rebut this speech. Later he referred to Smith and her fellow cosigners as "Snow White and the Seven Dwarfs."

Other senators failed to pay much attention to Smith's remarks. Most were still too wary or frightened of McCarthy's growing political power. But many newspaper editorials and civic organizations praised her for her courage, as did President Harry S. Truman who told her during a Capitol Hill luncheon that "your Declaration of Conscience was one of the finest things that has happened here in Washington in all my years in the Senate and the White House." Truman said this even though the speech con-

tained many partisan jabs at the Democratic administration. Overall the tone of the speech was one of reason, fairness, and decency that stood as a beacon of courage, eloquence, and sanity even as McCarthyism continued to grow in the nation.

Mr. President, I would like to speak briefly and simply about a serious national condition. It is a national feeling of fear and frustration that could result in national suicide and the end of everything that we Americans hold dear. It is a condition that comes from the lack of effective leadership either in the legislative branch or the executive branch of our government.

That leadership is so lacking that serious and responsible proposals are being made that national advisory commissions be appointed to provide such critically needed leadership.

I speak as briefly as possible because too much harm has already been done with irresponsible words of bitterness and selfish political opportunism. I speak as simply as possible because the issue is too great to be obscured by eloquence. I speak simply and briefly in the hope that my words will be taken to heart.

Mr. President, I speak as a Republican. I speak as a woman. I speak as a United States senator. I speak as an American.

The United States Senate has long enjoyed worldwide respect as the greatest deliberative body in the world. But recently that deliberative character has too often been debased to the level of a forum of hate and character assassination sheltered by the shield of congressional immunity.

It is ironical that we senators can in debate in the Senate, directly or indirectly, by any form of words, impute to any American who is not a senator any conduct or motive unworthy or unbecoming an American—and without that non-senator American having any legal redress against us—yet if we say the same thing in the Senate about our colleagues we can be stopped on the grounds of being out of order.

It is strange that we can verbally attack anyone else without restraint and with full protection, and yet we hold ourselves above the same type of criticism here on the Senate floor. Surely the United States Senate is big enough to take self-criticism and self-appraisal. Surely we should be able to take the same kind of character attacks that we "dish out" to outsiders.

I think that it is high time for the United States Senate and its members to do some real soul searching and to weigh our consciences as to the manner in which we are performing our duty to the people of America and the manner in which we are using or abusing our individual powers and privileges.

I think that it is high time that we remembered that we have sworn to uphold and defend the Constitution. I think that it is high time that we remembered that the Constitution, as amended, speaks not only of the freedom of speech but also of trial by jury instead of trial by accusation.

Whether it be a criminal prosecution in court or a character prosecution in the Senate, there is little practical distinction when the life of a person has been ruined.

Those of us who shout the loudest about Americanism in making character assassinations are all too frequently those who, by our own words and acts, ignore some of the basic principles of Americanism—

The right to criticize.

The right to hold unpopular beliefs.

The right to protest.

The right of independent thought.

The exercise of these rights should not cost one single American citizen his reputation or his right to a livelihood nor should he be in danger of losing his reputation or livelihood merely because he happens to know someone who holds unpopular beliefs. Who of us does not? Otherwise none of us could call our souls our own. Otherwise thought control would have set in.

The American people are sick and tired of being afraid to speak their minds lest they be politically smeared as "Communists" or "Fascists" by their opponents. Freedom of speech is not what it used to be in America. It has been so abused by some that it is not exercised by others.

The American people are sick and tired of seeing innocent people smeared and guilty people whitewashed. But there have been enough proved cases, such as the Amerasia case, the Hiss case, the Coplon case, the Gold case, to cause nationwide distrust and strong suspicion that there may be something to the unproved, sensational accusations.

As a Republican, I say to my colleagues on this side of the aisle that the Republican party faces a challenge today that is not unlike the challenge which it faced back in Lincoln's day. The Republican party so successfully met that challenge that it emerged from the Civil War as the champion of a united nation—in addition to being a party which unrelentingly fought loose spending and loose programs.

Today our country is being psychologically divided by the confusion and the suspicions that are bred in the United States Senate to spread like cancerous tentacles of "know nothing, suspect everything" attitudes. Today we have a Democratic administration which has developed a mania for loose spending and loose programs. History is repeating itself—and the Republican party again has the opportunity to emerge as the champion of unity and prudence. The record of the present Democratic administration has provided us with sufficient campaign issues without the necessity of resorting to political smears. America is rapidly losing its position as leader of the world simply because the Democratic administration has pitifully failed to provide effective leadership.

The Democratic administration has completely confused the American people by its daily contradictory grave warnings and optimistic assurances, which show the people that our Democratic administration has no idea of where it is going.

The Democratic administration has greatly lost the confidence of the American people by its complacency to the threat of communism here at home and the leak of vital secrets to Russia through key officials of the Democratic administration. There are enough proved cases to make this point without diluting our criticism with unproved charges.

Surely these are sufficient reasons to make it clear to the American people that it is time for a change and that a Republican victory is necessary to the security of the country. Surely it is clear that this nation will continue to suffer so long as it is governed by the present ineffective Democratic administration.

Yet to displace it with a Republican regime embracing a philosophy that lacks political integrity or intellectual honesty would prove equally disastrous to the nation. The nation sorely needs a Republican victory. But I do not want to see the Republican party ride to political victory on the Four Horsemen of Calumny—fear, ignorance, bigotry, and smear.

I doubt if the Republican party could do so, simply because I do not believe the American people will uphold any political party that puts political exploitation above national interest. Surely we Republicans are not that desperate for victory.

I do not want to see the Republican party win that way. While it might be a fleeting victory for the Republican party, it would be a more lasting defeat for the American people. Surely it would ultimately be suicide for the Republican party and the two-party system that has protected our American liberties from the dictatorship of a one-party system.

As members of the minority party, we do not have the primary authority to formulate the policy of our government. But we do have the responsibility of rendering constructive criticism, of clarifying issues, of allaying fears by acting as responsible citizens.

As a woman, I wonder how the mothers, wives, sisters, and daughters feel about the way in which members of their families have been politically mangled in Senate debate—and I use the word "debate" advisedly.

As a United States senator, I am not proud of the way in which the Senate has been made a publicity platform for irresponsible sensationalism. I am not proud of the reckless abandon in which unproved charges have been hurled from this side of the aisle. I am not proud of the obviously staged, undignified countercharges which have been attempted in retaliation from the other side of the aisle.

I do not like the way the Senate has been made a rendezvous for vilification, for selfish political gain at the sacrifice of individual reputations and national unity. I am not proud of the way we smear outsiders from the floor of the Senate and hide behind the cloak of congressional immunity and still place ourselves beyond criticism on the floor of the Senate.

As an American, I am shocked at the way Republicans and Democrats alike are playing directly into the Communist design of "confuse, divide, and conquer." As an American, I do not want a Democratic administration "whitewash" or "coverup" any more than I want a Republican smear or witch hunt.

As an American, I condemn a Republican Fascist just as much as I condemn a Democrat Communist. I condemn a Democrat Fascist just as much as I condemn a Republican Communist. They are equally dangerous to you and me and to our country. As an American, I want to see our nation recapture the strength and unity it once had when we fought the enemy instead of ourselves.

It is with these thoughts that I have drafted what I call a Declaration of Conscience. I am gratified that the senator from New Hampshire [Mr. Tobey], the senator from Vermont [Mr. Aiken], the senator from Oregon [Mr. Morse], the senator from New York [Mr. Ives], the senator from Minnesota [Mr. Thye], and the senator from New Jersey [Mr. Hendrickson] have concurred in that declaration and have authorized me to announce their concurrence.

The declaration reads as follows:

STATEMENT OF SEVEN REPUBLICAN SENATORS

1. We are Republicans. But we are Americans first. It is as Americans that we express our concern with the growing confusion that threatens the security and stability of our country. Democrats and Republicans alike have contributed to that confusion.

2. The Democratic administration has initially created the confusion by its lack of effective leadership, by its contradictory grave warnings and optimistic assurances, by its complacency to the threat of communism here at home, by its oversensitiveness to rightful criticism, by its petty bitterness against its critics.

3. Certain elements of the Republican party have materially added to this confusion in the hopes of riding the Republican party to victory through the selfish political exploitation of fear, bigotry, ignorance, and intolerance. There are enough mistakes of the Democrats for Republicans to criticize constructively without resorting to political smears.

4. To this extent, Democrats and Republicans alike have unwittingly, but undeniably, played directly into the Communist design of "confuse, divide, and conquer."

5. It is high time that we stopped thinking politically as Republicans and Democrats about elections and started thinking patriotically as Americans about national security based on individual freedom. It is high time that we all stopped being tools and victims of totalitarian techniques—techniques that, if continued here unchecked, will surely end what we have come to cherish as the American way of life.

Margaret Chase Smith, *Maine*
Charles W. Tobey, *New Hampshire*
George D. Aiken, *Vermont*
Wayne L. Morse, *Oregon*
Irving M. Ives, *New York*
Edward J. Thye, *Minnesota*
Robert C. Hendrickson, *New Jersey*

Congressional Record, Senate, 81st Congress, 2d session, June 1, 1950, 7894–7895.

141   General Douglas MacArthur Speaks Before a Joint Meeting of Congress

April 19, 1951

"Old soldiers never die; they just fade away" became a world-famous phrase after General Douglas MacArthur used it in his address before a packed joint meeting of Congress on April 19, 1951. But the significance of his speech did not reside in this poignant phrase alone. Just eight days before MacArthur delivered this speech, President Harry S. Truman had charged the general with insubordination and relieved him of command of the United Nations armed forces in the Korean conflict. At the time MacArthur was the highest ranking general and one of the most distinguished military men of his generation. MacArthur and Truman disagreed over the conduct of the war. MacArthur wanted an all-out war against Communism in Asia. This included the pursuit of Communist troops in North Korea across the Chinese border into China and the bombing of supply lines inside China. Truman, fearing a much wider war, possibly World War III, refused to authorize the incursion into Chinese territory.

MacArthur decided to appeal for support in the Congress, where he had many friends, especially among members of the Republican Party. On March 20, 1951, he had written a letter to House Minority Leader Joseph Martin (R-Mass.) in which he said that the way to fight a war was "meeting force with maximum counterforce," adding that "if we lose the war to Communism in Asia the fall of Europe is inevitable. . . ." MacArthur did not mention President Truman directly or their ongoing feud over taking the war in Korea across the border into China. In Martin's memoir, My First Fifty Years in Politics, *he recounted how disturbed he was by this letter, realizing its publication would cause trouble with President Truman and his administration. At the same time, Martin agreed with MacArthur's assessment of the situation in Korea and the need to aggressively assault Communism with a maximum military effort. As debate continued to rage in Congress over the conduct of the Korean conflict, Martin decided that MacArthur's letter should be made public to clear the air. He read it aloud from the floor of the House, entering it into the public debate. "I anticipated that it would cause a jolt, and it did, here and abroad," Martin wrote in his memoir. What Martin did not anticipate was that this would be the last straw for President Truman. Less than a week after MacArthur's letter became public, Truman fired MacArthur, causing a national storm of criticism against Truman for his actions.*

The congressional reaction to the firing, especially among Republicans, was one of shock and dismay. Some talked of impeaching Truman, but cooler heads prevailed, citing Truman's constitutional authority as commander-in-chief. Martin asked House Speaker Sam Rayburn (D-Texas) to permit a joint meeting of Congress to allow MacArthur to speak. Many Republicans thought MacArthur would be a likely contender for the Republican presidential nomination in 1952, and that his speech before Congress could help that cause. Rayburn did not agree with MacArthur's position on the war in Korea, but he agreed to allow MacArthur to speak, following precedent established earlier, where returning generals had been invited before Congress in honor of their service to the nation.

When MacArthur addressed Congress it was a moment of great emotion and high political theater in the nation's capital and around the world. As Martin recalled, "It was a drama that forced gasps from men and women who were long hardened to the excitements of public life." MacArthur's address was covered live on national television, with an estimated audience of 30 million viewers and countless others listening in on radio. MacArthur delivered his address with a deliberate, polished, oratorical style that added to the drama of the occasion. By the time MacArthur came to the conclusion of his remarks, emotions on both sides of the aisle were primed for his final sentimental lines. When he said "Good-by" there was hardly a dry eye in the chamber. Many said it was MacArthur's finest hour.

The next day a crowd estimated at 7.5 million people came out to cheer this national hero at a ticker tape parade in New York City. Others were quietly glad that MacArthur had been fired. His conduct of the Korean conflict may have led to a much larger and deadlier conflict in Asia. Truman, according to biographer David McCullough, did not watch MacArthur's performance before Congress but he did read the speech later and declared it to be "a bunch of damn bullshit."

. . . .

The Doorkeeper announced General of the Army Douglas MacArthur.

General of the Army Douglas MacArthur, escorted by the committee of Senators and Representatives, entered the Hall of the House of Representatives and stood at the Clerk's desk. [Applause, the Members rising.]

The SPEAKER. Members of the Congress, it is my great pleasure and a distinct privilege to present to you General of the Army Douglas MacArthur. [Applause, the Members rising.]

ADDRESS OF GENERAL OF THE ARMY DOUGLAS MACARTHUR

General MACARTHUR. Mr. President, Mr. Speaker, and distinguished Members of the Congress, I stand on this rostrum with a sense of deep humility and great pride—humility in the wake of those great American architects of our history who have stood here before me, pride in the reflection that this forum of legislative debate represents human liberty in the purest form yet devised. [Applause.] Here are centered the hopes, and aspirations, and faith of the entire human race.

I do not stand here as advocate for any partisan cause, for the issues are fundamental and reach quite beyond the realm of partisan consideration. They must be resolved on the highest plane of national interest if our course is to prove sound and our future protected. I trust, therefore, that you will do me the justice of receiving that which I have to say as solely expressing the considered viewpoint of a fellow American. I address you with neither rancor nor bitterness in the fading twilight of life with but one purpose in mind—to serve my country. [Applause.]

The issues are global and so interlocked that to consider the problems of one sector, oblivious to those of another, is but to court disaster for the whole.

While Asia is commonly referred to as the gateway to Europe, it is no less true that Europe is the gateway to Asia, and the broad influence of the one cannot fail to have its impact upon the other.

There are those who claim our strength is inadequate to protect on both fronts—that we cannot divide our effort. I can think of no greater expression of defeatism. [Applause]. If a potential enemy can divide his strength on two fronts, it is for us to counter his effort.

The Communist threat is a global one. Its successful advance in one section threatens the destruction of every other sector. You cannot appease or otherwise surrender to communism in Asia, without simultaneously undermining our efforts to halt its advance in Europe. [Applause.]

Beyond pointing out these general truisms, I shall confine my discussion to the general areas of Asia. Before one may objectively assess the situation now existing there, he must comprehend something of Asia's past and the revolutionary changes which have marked her course up to the present. Long exploited by the so-called colonial powers, with little opportunity to achieve any degree of social justice, individual dignity, or a higher standard of life such as guided our own noble administration of the Philippines, the peoples of Asia found their opportunity in the war just past to throw off the shackles of colonialism, and now see the dawn of new opportunity, a heretofore unfelt dignity and the self-respect of political freedom.

Mustering half of the earth's population and 60 percent of its natural resources, there peoples are rapidly consolidating a new force, both moral and material, with which to raise the living standard and erect adaptations of the design of modern progress to their own distinct cultural environments. Whether one adheres to the concept of colonization or not, this is the direction of Asian progress and it may not be stopped. It is a corollary to the shift of the world economic frontiers, as the whole epicenter of world affairs rotates back toward the area whence it started. In this situation it becomes vital that our own country orient its policies in consonance with this basic evolutionary condition rather than pursue a course blind to the reality that the colonial era is now past and the Asian peoples covet the right to shape their own free destiny. What they seek now is friendly guidance, understanding, and support, not imperious direction [applause]; the dignity of equality, not the shame of subjugation. Their prewar standards of life, pitifully low, is infinitely lower now in the devastation left in war's wake. World ideologies play little part in Asian thinking and are little understood. What the peoples strive for is the opportunity for a little more food in their stomachs, a little better clothing on their backs, a little firmer roof over their heads, and the realization of the normal nationalist urge for political freedom. These political-social condition have but an indirect bearing upon our own national security, but do form a backdrop to contemporary planning which must be thoughtfully considered if we are to avoid the pitfalls of unrealism.

Of more direct and immediate bearing upon our national security are the changes wrought in the strategic potential of the Pacific Ocean in the course of the past war. Prior thereto, the western strategic frontier of the United States lay on the littoral line of the Americas with an exposed island salient extending out through Hawaii, Midway, and Guam to the Philippines. That salient proved not an outpost of strength but an avenue of weakness along which the enemy could and did attack. The Pacific was a potential area of advance for any predatory force intent upon striking at the bordering land areas.

All this was changed by our Pacific victory. Our strategic frontier then shifted to embrace the entire Pacific Ocean which became a vast moat to protect us as long as we hold it. Indeed, it acts as a protective shield for all of the Americas and all free lands of the Pacific Ocean area. We control it to the shores of Asia by a chain of islands extending in an arc from the Aleutians to the Mariannas held by us and our free allies.

From this island chain we can dominate with sea and air power every Asiatic port from Vladivostok to Singapore and prevent any hostile movement into the Pacific. Any predatory attack from Asia must be a amphibious effort. No amphibious force can be successful without control of the sea lands and the air power those lanes in its avenue of advance. With naval and air supremacy and modest ground elements to defend bases, any major attack from continental Asia toward us or our friends of the Pacific would be doomed to failure. Under such conditions the Pacific no longer represents menacing avenues of approach for a prospective invader—it assumes instead the friendly aspect of a peaceful lake. Our line of defense is a natural one and can be maintained with a minimum of military effort and expense. It envisions not attack against anyone nor does it provide the bastions essential for offensive operations, but properly maintained would be an invincible defense against aggression.

The holding of this littoral defense line in the western Pacific is entirely dependent upon holding all segments thereof, for any major breach of that line by an unfriendly power would render vulnerable to determined attack every other major segment. This is a military estimate as to which I have yet to find a military leader who will take exception. [Applause.]

For that reason, I have strongly recommended in the past as a matter of military urgency that under no circumstances must Formosa fall under Communist control. [Applause.] Such an eventuality would at once threaten the freedom of the Philippines and the lost of Japan, and might well force our western frontier back to the coasts of California, Oregon, and Washington.

. . . .

While I was not consulted prior to the President's decision to intervene in support of the Republic of Korea, that decision, from a military standpoint, proved a sound one [applause] as we hurled back the invaders and decimated his forces. Our victory was complete and our objectives within reach when Red China intervened with numerically superior ground forces. This created a new war and an entirely new situation—a situation not contemplated when our forces were committed against the North Korean invaders—a situation which called for new decisions in the diplomatic sphere to permit the realistic adjustment of military strategy. Such decisions have not been forthcoming. [Applause.]

While no man in his right mind would advocate sending our ground forces into continental China and such was never given a thought, the new situation did urgently demand a drastic revision of strategic planning if our political aim was to defeat this new enemy as we had defeated the old. [Applause.]

While no man in his right mind would advocate sending our ground forces into continental China and such was never given a thought, the new situation did urgently demand a drastic revision of strategic planning if our political aim was to defeat this new enemy as we had defeated the old. [Applause.]

Apart from the military need as I saw it to neutralize the sanctuary protection given the enemy north of the Yalu, I felt that military necessity in the conduct of the war made mandatory:

1. The intensification of our economic blockade against China;

2. The imposition of a naval blockade against the China coast;

3. Removal of restrictions on air reconnaissance of China's coast areas and of Manchuria [applause];

4. Removal of restrictions on the forces of the Republic of China on Formosa with logistical support to contribute to their effective operations against the common enemy. [Applause.]

For entertaining these views, all professionally designed to support to our forces committed to Korea and bring hostilities to an end with the lease possible delay and at a saving of countless American and Allied lives, I have been severely criticized in lay circles, principally abroad, despite my understanding that from a military standpoint the above views have been fully shared in the past by practically every military leader concerned with the Korean campaign, including our own Joint Chiefs of Staff. [Applause, the Members rising.]

I called for reinforcements, but was informed that reinforcements were not available. I made clear that if not permitted to destroy the build-up bases north of the Yalu; if not permitted to utilize the friendly Chinese force of some 600,000 men on Formosa; if not permitted to blockade the China coast to prevent the Chinese Reds from getting succor from without; and if there were to be no hope of major reinforcements, the position of the command from the military standpoint forbade victory. We could hold in Korea by constant maneuver and at an approximate area where our supply line advantages were in balance with the supply line disadvantages of the enemy, but we could hope at best for only an indecisive campaign, with its terrible and constant attrition upon our forces if the enemy

utilized his full military potential. I have constantly called for the new political decisions essential to a solution. Efforts have been made to distort my position. It has been said, in effect, that I am a warmonger. Nothing could be further from the truth. I know war as few other men now living know it, and nothing to me is more revolting. I have long advocated its complete abolition as its very destructiveness on both friend and foe has rendered it useless as a means of settling international disputes.

. . . .

But once war is forced upon us, there is no other alternative than to apply every available means to bring it to a swift end. War's very object is victory—not prolonged indecision. [Applause.] In war, indeed, there can be no substitute for victory. [Applause.]

There are some who for varying reasons would appease Red China. They are blind to history's clear lesson. For history teaches with unmistakable emphasis that appeasement but begets new and bloodier war. It points to no single instance where appeasement has led to more than a sham peace. Like blackmail, it lays the basis for new and successively greater demands, until, as in blackmail, violence becomes the only other alternative. Why, my soldiers asked of me, surrender military advantages to an enemy in the field? I could not answer. [Applause.] Some may say to avoid spread of the conflict into an all-out war with China; others, to avoid Soviet intervention. Neither explanation seems valid. For China is already engaging with the maximum power it can commit and the Soviet will not necessarily mesh its actions with our moves. Like a cobra, any new enemy will more likely strike whenever it feels that the relativity in military or other potential is in its favor on a world-wide basis.

The tragedy of Korea is further heightened by the fact that as military action is confined to its territorial limits, it condemns that nation, which it is our purpose to save, to suffer the devastating impact of full naval and air bombardment, while the enemy's sanctuaries are fully protected from such attack and devastation. Of the nations of the world, Korea alone, up to now, is the sole one which has risked its all against communism. The magnificence of the courage and fortitude of the Korean people defies description. [Applause.] They have chosen to risk death rather than slavery. Their last words to me were "Don't scuttle the Pacific." [Applause.]

I have just left your fighting sons in Korea. They have met all tests there and I can report to you without reservation they are splendid in every way. [Applause.] It was my constant effort to preserve them and end this savage conflict honorably and with the least loss of time and a minimum sacrifice of life. Its growing bloodshed has caused me the deepest anguish and anxiety. Those gallant men will remain often in my thoughts and in my prayers always. [Applause.]

I am closing my 52 years of military service. [Applause.] When I joined the Army even before the turn of the century, it was the fulfillment of all my boyish hopes and dreams. The world has turned over many times since I took the oath on the plain at West Point, and the hopes and dreams have long since vanished. But I still remember the refrain of one of the most popular barrack ballads of that day which proclaimed most proudly that—

"Old soldiers never die; they just fade away."

And like the old soldier of that ballad, I now close my military career and just fade away—an old soldier who tried to do his duty as God gave him the light to see that duty.

Good-by.

Congressional Record, House, 82d Congress, 1st session, April 19, 1951, 4123–4125. Bracketed comments in the text regarding applause are as they appeared in the *Congressional Record*.

142   Conclusions of the Kefauver Committee on Organized Crime

May 1, 1951

In 1950 and 1951 the Senate began investigations, under the chairmanship of Estes Kefauver (D-Tenn.), into organized crime. Hearings by the Kefauver Committee were the first of many congressional attempts to define the nature of organized crime in the United States and address concern about the operations of major crime families, known collectively as the Mafia. While earlier investigations at the state and local levels, including crime commissions in Illinois and California, had addressed the issue, the Kefauver Committee dramatically thrust the subject onto the national scene through the use of televised hearings, which were a novelty in the 1950s when television was still in its infancy. For millions of Americans, these televised hearings were their first exposure to the workings of a congressional investigation.

On January 5, 1950, Kefauver introduced a resolution in the Senate calling for the creation of a committee to investigate organized crime. Kefauver responded to numerous press stories that described an American crime wave. In his statement in support of his resolution, he said: "Responsible and nationally known reporters and magazine writers have for the past several years been writing of a national crime syndicate which they allege is slowly but surely through corruption gaining control of, or improper influence in, many cities throughout the United States." Noting the lack of federal legislation to attack organized crime, Kefauver called for a full investigation of what could be done at the federal level. The Senate did not adopt his resolution immediately due to arguments over which committee should conduct the investigation. Eventually the Senate approved a five-member special committee composed of members of the Senate Judiciary and Commerce committees, under Kefauver's chairmanship.

The significance of the work of the Kefauver Committee was its ability to focus public attention on the issue of organized crime rather than any specific legislation that resulted from the work of the committee. Among the major recommendations of the committee were the establishment of a "racket squad" in the Justice Department and a "special fraud squad" in the Federal Bureau of Investigation, the creation of an independent Federal Crime Commission, the regulation of gambling casinos so the Internal Revenue Service could monitor the daily records of gambling operations, and the regulation of interstate gambling.

Kefauver became one of the best known and most respected members of Congress, due largely to his work on this committee and the television exposure that came with it. He was a Democratic candidate for the presidential nomination in 1952 and 1956 and was nominated for vice president as Adlai Stevenson's running mate in 1956.

GENERAL CONCLUSIONS

1. Organized criminal gangs operating in interstate commerce are firmly entrenched in our large cities in the operation of many different gambling enterprises such as bookmaking, policy, slot machines, as well as other rackets such as the sale and distribution of narcotics and commercialized prostitution. They are the survivors of the murderous underworld wars of the prohibition era. After the repeal of the prohibition laws, these groups and syndicates shifted their major criminal activities to gambling. However many of the crime syndicates continued to take an interest in other rackets such as narcotics, prostitution, labor and business racketeering, black marketing, etc.

2. Criminal syndicates in this country make tremendous profits and are due primarily to the ability of such gangs and syndicates to secure monopolies in the illegal operations in which they are engaged. These monopolies are secured by persuasion, intimidation, violence, and murder. The committee found in some cities that law-enforcement officials aided and protected gangsters and racketeers to maintain their monopolistic position in particular rackets. Mobsters who attempted to compete with these entrenched criminal groups found that they and their followers were being subjected to arrest and prosecution while protected gang operations were left untouched.

3. Crime is on a syndicated basis to a substantial extent in many cities. The two major crime syndicates in this country are the Accardo-Guzik-Fischette syndicate, whose headquarters are Chicago; and the Costello-Adonis-Lansky syndicate based on New York. Evidence of the operations of the Accardo-Guzik-Fischette syndicate was found by the committee in such places as Chicago, Kansas City, Dallas, Miami, Las Vegas, Nev., and the west coast. Evidence of the Costello-Adonis-Lansky operations was found in New York City, Saratoga, Bergen County,

N.J., New Orleans, Miami, Las Vegas, the west coast, and Havana, Cuba. These syndicates, as well as other criminal gangs throughout the country, enter profitable relationships with each other. There is also a close personal, financial, and social relationship between top-level mobsters in different areas of the country.

4. There is a sinister criminal organization known as the Mafia operating throughout the country with ties in other nations, in the opinion of committee. The Mafia is the direct descendant of a criminal organization of the same name originating in the island of Sicily. In this country, the Mafia has also been known as the Black Hand and the Unione Siciliano. The membership of the Mafia today is not confined to persons of Sicilian origin. The Mafia is a loose-knit organization specializing in the sale and distribution of narcotics, the conduct of various gambling enterprises, prostitution, and other rackets based on extortion and violence. The Mafia is the binder which ties together the two major criminal syndicates as well as numerous other criminal groups throughout the country. The power of the Mafia is based on a ruthless enforcement of its edicts and its own law of vengeance, to which have been creditably attributed throughout the country.

5. Despite known arrest records and well-documented criminal reputations, the leading hoodlums in the country remain, for the most part, immune from prosecution and punishment, although underlings of their gangs may, on occasion, be prosecuted and punished. This quasi-immunity of top-level mobsters can be ascribed to what is popularly known as the "fix." The fix is not always the direct payment of money to law-enforcement officials, although the committee has run across considerable evidence of such bribery. The fix may also come about through the acquisition of political power by contributions to political organizations or otherwise, by creating economic ties with apparently respectable and reputable businessmen and lawyers, and by buying public good will through charitable contributions and press relations.

Gambling Supports Big-Time Rackets

6. Gambling profits are the principal support of big-time racketeering and gangsterism. These profits provide the financial resources and are converted into big-time racketeers, businessmen, and alleged philanthropists. Thus, the $2 horse bettor and the 5-cent numbers player are not only suckers because they are gambling against hopeless odds, but they also provide the moneys which enable underworld characters to undermine our institutions.

The legalization of gambling would not terminate the widespread predatory activities of criminal gangs and syndicates. The history of legalized gambling in Nevada and in other parts of the country gives no assurance that mobsters and racketeers can be converted into responsible businessmen through the simple process of obtaining State and local licenses for their gambling enterprises. Gambling, moreover, historically has been associated with cheating and corruption.

The committee has not seen any workable proposal for controlled gambling which would eliminate the gangsters or the corruption.

7. Rapid transmission of racing information and gambling information about other sporting events is indispensable to big-time bookmaking operations. This information is presently being provided by a monopoly operated by the Continental Press Service. The Continental Press Service, at critical times and in crucial places where monopoly of bookmaking is at stake, yields to the domination and control of the Accardo-Guzik-Fischetti crime syndicate, to which it is beholden for its own monopoly in the wire-service field. The wire service is so vital to large bookmakers that they are compelled to pay what the traffic will bear to the Continental Press Service. This mikes it possible for the Accardo-Guzik-Fischetti crime syndicate to participate in the profits of bookmaking operations throughout the country.

8. The backbone of the wire service which provides gambling information to bookmakers is the leased wires of the Western-Union Telegraph Co. This company, in many parts of the country has not been fully cooperative with law-enforcement officials who have been trying to suppress organize criminal rackets which make use of its facilities to be used by bookmakers, Western Union has given aid and comfort to those engaged in violation of gambling laws. In some cases, Western Union officials and employees actually participated in bookmaking conspiracies by accepting bets and transmitting them to bookmakers. It should be noted that during the latter months of the committee's investigation, Western Union has taken steps to prevent this practice and has been more cooperative with the committee.

In many areas, of which New York is a notable example, the telephone companies have cooperated fully with law-enforcement officials. However, in still other areas, telephone companies have been much less cooperative. Local legislation is apparently necessary in many states to require telephone company officials to refuse facilities and remove existing facilities of suspected bookmakers and to call to the attention of local law-enforcement officials the use of telephone facilities by bookmakers.

9. Crime is largely a local problem. It must be attacked primarily at the local level, with supplementary aid, where appropriate, from State and Federal authorities. The conduct of various forms of gambling enterprises, houses of prostitution, the distribution of narcotics, the use of intimidation, violence, and murder to achieve gang objectives are all violations of State laws. The public must insist upon local and State law-enforcement agencies meeting this challenge, and must not be deceived by the aura of romanticism and respectability, deliberately cultivated by the communities' top mobsters.

10. The Federal Government has the basic responsibility of helping the States and local governments in eliminating the interstate activities and interstate aspects of organized crime, and in facilitating exchange of information with appropriate safeguards between the Federal Government and local and State law-enforcement agencies as well as between law-enforcement agencies in the various States.

The task of dealing with organized crime is so great that the public must insist upon the fullest measure of cooperation between law-enforcement agencies at all levels of Government without buck-passing. The committee feels that it has fully demonstrated the need for such cooperation. The time for action has arrived.

11. Wide-open gambling operations and racketeering conditions are supported by out-and-out corruption in many places. The wide-open conditions which were found in these localities can easily be cleaned up by vigorous law enforcement. This has been demonstrated in the past in different communities and has received added life of our committee. The outstanding example which ran wide-open through the racing season of 1949 but was closed down tight in 1950.

12. Venal public officials have had the effrontery to testify before the committee that they were elected on "liberal" platforms calling for wide-open towns. The committee believes that these officials were put in office by gamblers and with gamblers' money, and that in the few cases where the public was convinced that gambling is good for business, this myth was deliberately propagated by the paid publicists of the gambling interests. In many wide-open communities, so-called political leaders and law-enforcement officials have sabotaged efforts of civic-minded citizens to combat such wide-open conditions and the crime and corruption that they entailed.

13. The Treasury of the United States has been defrauded of huge sums of money in tax revenues by racketeers and gangsters engaged in organized criminal activities. Huge sums in cash handled by racketeers and gangsters are not reflected in their income tax returns. Income tax records filed with the Federal Government have been inadequate since, as a rule, it contained no listing of the sources of income nor any itemization of the expenses. Gangsters and racketeers, moreover, do not keep books and records from which it might be possible to check tax returns.

14. Mobsters and racketeers have been assisted by some tax accountants and tax lawyers in defrauding the Government. These accountants and lawyers have prepared and defended income tax returns which they knew to be inadequate. At the very least, those who are guilty of -such practices could be convicted of a misdemeanor and sent to jail for a year for every year in which they have failed to comply with the law.

The Bureau of Internal Revenue states that it has, to the best of its ability, considering its limited manpower, been investigating these returns. It states further that when it pursues the case of one of these individuals, it prefers to set up against him a case of criminal tax evasion which is a felony, rather than the lesser offense of failing to keep proper books and records, which is a misdemeanor.

Despite this, the committee believes that the Bureau of Internal Revenue could, and should, make more frequent use of the sanctions provided for failure to keep proper books and records than it has heretofore. In any event, the Bureau of Internal Revenue should insist on adequate returns and proper books.

While the great majority of agents of the Bureau of Internal Revenue are honest and efficient, there have been relatively few instances in different parts of the country of lack of vigorous and effective action to collect income taxes from gangsters and racketeers.

15. A major question of legal ethics has arisen in that there are a number of lawyers in different parts of the country whose relations to organized criminal gangs and individual mobsters pass the line of reasonable representation. Such lawyers become true "mouthpieces" for the mob. In individual cases, they have become integral parts of the criminal conspiracy of their clients.

16. Evidence of this infiltration by organized crime into legitimate business has been found, particularly in connection with the sale and distribution of liquor, real-estate operations, night clubs, hotels, automobile agencies, restaurants, taverns, cigarette-vending companies, jukebox concerns, laundries, the manufacture of clothing, and the transmission of racing and sport news. In some areas of legitimate activity, the committee has found evidence of the use by gangsters of the same methods of intimidation and violence as are used to secure monopolies in criminal enterprise. Gangster infiltration into business also aggravates the possibility of black markets during a period of national emergency such as we are now experiencing. Racketeers also have used labor unions as fronts to enable them to exploit legitimate businessmen.

17. In some instances legitimate businessmen have aided the interests of the underworld by awarding lucrative contracts to gangsters and mobsters in return for help in handling employees, defeating attempts at organization, and in breaking strikes. And the committee has had testimony showing that unions are used in the aid of racketeers and gangsters, particularly on the New York water front.

RECOMMENDATIONS
Introduction

The committee has received many recommendations for controlling organized crime and improving the enforcement of the criminal law and the administration of criminal justice. Those recommendations have been received from a variety of sources: from public officials, experts on law enforcement, lawyers, accountants, and interested laymen. They all have been given careful attention.

The committee is convinced that there is no single panacea for the widespread social, economic, and political evils that have been uncovered in the many cities in which it has made investigations and held hearings. The committee feels, nevertheless, that while organized crime cannot be completely eliminated from our society, this is no reason for defeatism for vigorous law enforcement can control organized crime to the point there it is no longer a menace to our institutions.

Any program for controlling organized crime must take into account the fundamental nature of our governmental system. The enforcement of the criminal law is primarily a State and local responsibility. While channels of interstate communication and interstate commerce may be used by organized criminal gangs and syndicates, their activities are in large measure violations of local criminal statutes. When criminal gangs and syndicates engage in bookmaking operations, operate gambling casinos or slot machines, engage in policy operations, peddle narcotics, operate houses of prostitution, use intimidation or violence to secure monopoly in any area of commercial activity, commit assaults and murder to eliminate competition, they are guilty of violating State laws and it is upon State and local prosecuting agencies, police and courts, that the major responsibility for the detection, apprehension, prosecution, and punishment of offenders rests.

The crisis of law enforcement which has been uncovered by the committee is basically a State and a local crisis. The Federal Government does not have responsibility for the widespread gambling and vice conditions it has found in such places as the Miami area; the parishes outside of New Orleans; the Covington-Newport areas of Kentucky; Bergen County, N.J.; several counties in California, Illinois, and Saratoga, N.Y. The responsibility is basically one that must be shared by local and State agencies of law enforcement as well as by the citizens of the various communities who tolerated such conditions. Nor can a remedy for these conditions be found merely by shrugging off local and State responsibility and declaring that only the Federal Government can do the job of cleaning up wide open conditions. As J. Edgar Hoover pointed out in his statement to this committee, to this committee, "The Federal Government can never be a satisfactory substitute for local self-government in the enforcement field."

The Federal Government, moreover, can do relatively little to assist local citizens and officials in the removal of local law-enforcement officials who have accepted money from gangsters and racketeers or who have actually participated in criminal operations. The Federal Government can do little about the influence which gangsters and racketeering elements exert upon local political The Federal Government can do even less about the inefficiency and ineffectiveness of local law-enforcement agencies. Nor can the Federal Government correct the diffusion of responsibility and the "buck passing" which take place between independent law-enforcement agencies operating in the same county or in the same metropolitan area. Finally the Federal Government can do nothing to correct the misguided leniency of State and local judges who impose small fines or short jail sentences in racketeering situations.

While the Federal police and prosecuting agencies cannot be substituted for State and local law enforcement in dealing with organized crime, the Federal Government still has a major and vital responsibility in this field. The Federal Government must provide leadership and guidance in the struggle against organized crime, for the criminal gangs and syndicates have Nation-wide ramifications. It should establish additional techniques to provide maximum coordination in law-enforcement agencies to insure complete efficiency. It must help work out techniques for securing better interstate cooperation for dealing with crime. In addition, the Federal Government is under certain positive obligations to use powers presently available to it against organized criminal gangs. It is the responsibility of the Federal Government to see that the channels of interstate commerce, transportation, communication, and the United States mails are not used to facilitate the operations of organized criminal gangs and syndicates. It is up to the Federal Government to see that gangsters and racketeers are stripped of as much of their ill-gotten gains as possible through vigorous enforcement of the income-tax laws. Only the Federal Government can take affirmative action to rid our shores of alien criminals who have become members of predatory criminal groups. Finally, the Federal Government has the responsibility for revision of existing statutes where legal technicalities are permitting the guilty to escape just punishment.

. . . .

Senate Report No. 307, 82d Congress, 1st session, "Third Interim Report of the Special Committee to Investigate Organized Crime in Interstate Commerce," pursuant to S. Res. 202, 81st Congress, 1–7.

143   Speaker Joseph Martin's Account of a Shooting on the Floor of the House

March 1, 1954

Speaker Joseph Martin (R-Mass.) thought someone had set off some firecrackers in the House gallery until he looked into the visitor's gallery and saw several pistols pointed in his direction. This account from Martin's memoir, My First Fifty Years in Politics, describes one of the most violent days in the history of the Capitol from the perspective of an eyewitness. On March 1, 1954, three persons, two men and a woman, members of an extremist group supporting independence for Puerto Rico, began firing on members of the House of Representatives assembled on the floor of the *House chamber. Although no one was killed, five House members—Benton Jensen (R-Iowa), Alvin Bentley (R-Mich.), Clifford Davis (D-Tenn.), George Fallon (D-Md.), and Kenneth Roberts (D-Ala.)—were wounded in the gunfire; Bentley was seriously injured. Fortunately, among the members on the floor that day were two physicians, Walter Judd (R-Minn.) and Arthur Miller (R-Neb.), who administered first aid until medical teams arrived. At the time of the shooting, more than two hundred members were on the floor.*

The first to open fire was Lolita Lebrón, who shouted "Puerto Rico is not free!" The three terrorists sprayed thirty rounds of bullets down on the chamber, pausing only to reload their automatic pistols, as members sought cover under their seats. They had come prepared to die for their acts, according to a note found in their possession afterwards. As they ran out of the House gallery, the would-be assassins were captured and thrown to the floor by a House page, a staff member of the Foreign Affairs Committee, several members of Congress, and some visitors who had witnessed the shooting. A fourth accomplice was arrested afterwards at a bus terminal. All were identified as belonging to the same extremist group that had made an assassination attempt on President Harry S. Truman four years earlier at Blair House, across the street from the White House. All received long prison sentences for their deeds.

In the aftermath of this shooting the House debated the question of tighter security for the chamber, including a proposal to wall off the visitor's gallery with bulletproof glass. This notion was rejected on the grounds that the elected representatives of the people should not be walled off from the public. The Capitol would remain open to visitors and citizens would be welcomed to the galleries to watch the deliberations. (For a general discussion of other incidents of violence in the Capitol, see the headnote to document 102.)

In this account, Speaker Martin refers to several members of Congress seeking shelter from the gunfire under their desks. The House chamber had bench seating, not individual desks. He may have been referring to the two large desks in the chamber often used by committee chairmen and House leaders during the introduction and discussion of legislation. One of these desks, on the Republican side of the chamber, still has a bullet hole in one of its drawers.

On March 1, 1954, when I was again Speaker in the Eighty-third Congress, I was presiding over what was, until a few seconds after 2:30 P.M., an uneventful session of the House. The measure we were about to consider was the "wetback" bill to permit federal supervision of migrant Mexican farm workers. At about two-thirty I called for a standing vote on a rule to bring it up. Two hundred forty-three members were present.

As I was counting the vote, starting with the Republicans on the left-hand side of the aisle as I faced them, a firecracker— or so I thought—was set off up in Gallery 11 at the extreme end of the chamber to my left. Too busy to take note of the disturbance at the moment, the thought flashed through my mind that I would order the sergeant-at-arms up to deal with the pranksters as soon as I had completed the count. When a second and third report followed in rapid succession, I swung around in exasperation.

Instead of seeing firecrackers, as I had expected, I found myself looking, at a distance, at the muzzle of a pistol. As I gaped, I saw three assailants—a woman and two men (I later learned that there was a third man whom I could not see)—and they all seemed to be aiming German pistols at me.

Bullets whistled through the chamber in the wildest scene in the entire history of Congress. Pandemonium spread so fast that control of the House was wrenched from my hands.

White plaster came sifting down from two bullet holes in the ceiling. Two more bullets struck the wall of Gallery 4, and one ripped into the door of that gallery. The walnut paneling behind the Democratic seats was pierced. A chair on the Democratic side and another on the Republican side were struck. Two bullets hit the majority table with such impact that a splinter flew into the face of Leo Allen, who was standing beside it.

Seconds before, the young woman, who was dressed in gray and whose name I later learned was Mrs. Lolita Lebrón, had been waving a flag and screaming. Now she was holding a Luger in both hands, firing indiscriminately into the panic-stricken House. One of the men was shooting from a crouch; another was standing and aiming over his head.

The three looked to me like Mexicans, and I had a fleeting thought that they must have been driven to this madness by some grotesque misconception of the wetback bill. It was not until later that I learned that they were Puerto Rican nationalists conducting a fanatical demonstration on behalf of Puerto Rican independence, very much as Oscar Collazo and Griselio Torresola had done at Blair House when they tried to assassinate President Truman on November 1, 1950.

In the Press Gallery above me C. P. Trussell, of *The New York Times*, was struck on the cheek by plaster from the ceiling. William Belcher, a sixty-year-old doorkeeper, collapsed in the excitement. As on the earlier occasion of Mr. Kemmerer's visit, some members simply stood or sat at their desks, frozen in surprise and horror, while others dived to the floor and scrambled under desks and chairs.

"The House stands recessed," I declared, unhindered by any parliamentarian.

"That was the greatest understatement of all time," one of my colleagues told me later. Understatement or not, I darted clear of my chair and ducked behind a marble pillar behind the Speaker's desk. From there, protected against the firing, I could command a clear view of what was happening on the floor.

On the Democratic side, Representative Kenneth Roberts of Alabama had just resumed his seat after I had counted his vote. He crossed his left leg over his right knee, and suddenly gasped, "I'm hit!" Blood was seeping from his left leg. On hands and knees he crawled to the end of his row of seats where Representative Percy Priest of Tennessee removed his own necktie and applied it above the wound as a tourniquet.

Representative George H. Fallon of Maryland was shot in the hip. He tried to stand, but his leg gave way, toppling him to the floor behind some seats where he lay helpless until the shooting ended.

At the sound of shots, Representative Clifford Davis of Tennessee began sliding off his chair to take cover under his desk. He was too late. A bullet passed through the calf of his leg.

On the Republican side, Representative Alvin M. Bentley of Michigan was walking down the aisle when the firing started. Dropping to his knees, he crawled between the first and second rows of desks in a desperate search for protection, which he never found. A bullet struck him underneath the right armpit and tore clear through his body, penetrating two lobes of his right lung, opening a hole in his diaphragm, shattering his liver and traversing his stomach.

Representative Ben F. Jensen of Iowa, still waiting to be counted by me, was standing at his seat in the fifth row. He had just turned to speak to his Iowa colleague, Representative Thomas E. Martin, when a bullet hit him between his neck and right shoulder and ripped through the back muscles to lodge near his left shoulder blade.

"He got me!" Jensen cried, believing that he had been the victim of someone bearing a personal grudge. Jensen steadied himself against a chair and then staggered for an exit. Just as he reached a door, his strength gave out, and he collapsed across the threshold to the floor of the Speaker's Lobby.

Another member, rushing for the same door, saw Jensen fall and supposed that he had been shot from the lobby.

"My God, they're in here too!" he yelled. "They're in the corridor!"

At another exit two large men, Representatives Martin Dies of Texas and Frank W. Boykin of Alabama, arrived together at the same moment on their flight from the floor. Unheeding one another, they became wedged together in the doorway as they tried to scramble through simultaneously. Later, after they had frantically struggled free, Boykin said to Dies, "Say who was that guy who got caught between us in the doorway?"

While some were struck and others felled, Representative James E. Van Zandt of Pennsylvania, a decorated Navy veteran of both world wars, managed to break from the chamber, as La Guardia had done twenty-two years earlier, and race up to Gal-

lery 11. He pinned one of the assailants to the floor, while the others were seized by attendants or fled, soon to be captured.

In the bedlam on the floor two members of the House who were physicians, Representatives Walter H. Judd of Minnesota and A. L. Miller of Nebraska, had rushed to the aid of Bentley, who lay moaning, the most seriously wounded of the five who had been struck. Happily, he and the others recovered from their wounds in the hospital.

There had never been such a scene since Sergeant Boston Corbett, the religious crank who claimed to be the slayer of John Wilkes Booth, shot up the Kansas House of Representatives in 1887. One of our members who was wounded had, as chance would have it, taken the pledge the day before. As he was being carried out to an ambulance, an old colleague of his looked at him sadly.

"I told you something would happen if you did that," he said.

After this episode all sorts of schemes were brought to me for increasing the protection of members of the House against similar attacks. We did indeed tighten up the security arrangements a good deal. Nevertheless I rejected the most ambitious proposal, one that called for installation of bullet-proof glass around the front of the galleries. For one thing, I was advised that the weight of this glass would be too great for the galleries to support. For another, I felt that, danger or not, Americans do not want their Congress walled off from the people by glass.

Joe Martin, *My First Fifty Years in Politics* (New York: McGraw-Hill, 1960), 216–220.

144   An Excerpt from the Army-McCarthy Hearings

June 9, 1954

Television played an important role in the downfall of Senator Joseph McCarthy, whose crusade to expose Communists in office in the United States had taken him to such extremes that he was willing to attack high-ranking government officials, including the president of the United States, and smear innocent persons to make his point. For more than four years McCarthy relentlessly made charges about the number of Communist subversives in government, first in the State Department and later in other offices, such as the Government Printing Office and the Foreign Service (see documents 139 and 140), McCarthy played on the public fear and uncertainty generated by the Cold War, the Korean conflict, and growing tensions between Russia and the United States to increase his personal power. He claimed that Communist influence inside the government was undermining the ability of the United States to win the Cold War.

In 1953 McCarthy, then chairman of the Senate Government Operations Committee, began an investigation of the U.S.

Army, claiming that Communist spies were operating from a highly secret Army Signal Corps facility at Fort Monmouth, New Jersey. McCarthy hired a team of like-minded prosecutors and former FBI agents to carry out his investigations. Chief among McCarthy's investigators was Roy M. Cohn, a former prosecutor from New York, who, like his boss, was willing to see Communists behind every bush.

When McCarthy began his investigation of the army, he ran afoul of President Dwight D. Eisenhower. At first Eisenhower kept his distance from fellow Republican McCarthy, but McCarthy's investigation of the army incurred his wrath. Eisenhower was one of the nation's most distinguished military men and formerly the supreme commander of allied forces in World War II. The Senate, with Eisenhower's encouragement, began its own investigation of McCarthy and his investigations. A special subcommittee of McCarthy's own Government Operations Committee, under the chairmanship of Karl E. Mundt (R-S.D.), conducted the investi-

gation. *Eisenhower urged that the hearings be televised so the American people could see McCarthy's crude and insensitive tactics firsthand.*

The turning point in the Army-McCarthy hearings, and the beginning of the rapid downfall of McCarthy as a political force in the United States, occurred on June 9, 1954, when army counsel Joseph Welch was questioning McCarthy's chief investigator, Roy Cohn. McCarthy took offense at Welch's questioning and decided to indirectly attack Welch's integrity by exposing one of Welch's own staff—a young attorney named Fred Fisher—as a Communist sympathizer. McCarthy's use of the personal smear backfired in dramatic fashion before a nationally televised audience when Welch explained Fisher's circumstances and said to McCarthy: "Let us not assassinate this lad further, Senator. You have done enough. Have you no sense of decency, sir, at long last? Have you left no sense of decency?"

The Senate held hearings beginning August 31, 1954, to decide if it would censure McCarthy for his inflammatory charges and his contemptuous behavior. Anticipating the vote on his censure, McCarthy lashed out at the Senate in November, saying his censure would be a victory for Communists and that the Senate was playing into the hands of the Communist Party. On December 2, 1954, the Senate censured him. With Democrats gaining the control of the Senate in 1955, McCarthy lost his chairmanship and his ability to conduct further investigations. He remained in the Senate—isolated, bitter, and stripped of power—until his death at the age of forty-eight, caused by alcoholism, in 1957.

. . . .

Mr. WELCH. I want to come back, Mr. Cohn, to the item that we were talking about this morning. I gathered, to sum it up a little, that as early as the spring, which must mean March or April, you knew about this situation of possible subversives and security risks, and even spies at Fort Monmouth, is that right?

Mr. COHN. Yes, sir.

Mr. WELCH. And I think you have used the word "disturbing," that you found it a disturbing situation?

Mr. COHN. Yes, sir.

Mr. WELCH. And you had, so to speak, only a sort of glimpse in it. you couldn't tell how big it was or how little it was, could you?

Mr. COHN. Not at the beginning, sir.

Mr. WELCH. And you probably knew enough about Fort Monmouth or found out quickly enough about Fort Monmouth, to know it was a sensitive place, didn't you?

Mr. COHN. Yes, sir.

Mr. WELCH. And I am sure the knowledge that you had was a source, Mr. Cohn, to one in your position, of some anxiety for the Nation's safety, wasn't it?

Mr. COHN. It was one situation among a number of serious situations; yes, sir.

Mr. WELCH. Well, I don't know how many worries you have, but I am sure that was, to you, a disturbing and alarming situation.

Mr. COHN. Well, sir, it was certainly serious enough for me to want to check into it and see how many facts we could check out and—

Mr. WELCH. And stop it as soon as possible?

Mr. COHN. Well, it was a question of developing the—

Mr. WELCH. But the thing that we have to do is stop it, isn't it?

Mr. COHN. Stop what, sir?

Mr. WELCH. Stop the risk.

Mr. COHN. Stop the risk, sir?

Mr. WELCH. Yes.

Mr. COHN. Yes, what we had to do was stop the risk and—

Mr. WELCH. That is right, get the people suspended or get them on trial or fire them or do something, that is right, isn't it?

Mr. COHN. Partly, sir.

Mr. WELCH. Sir?

Mr. COHN. Partly, sir.

Mr. WELCH. But it is primarily the thing, isn't it?

Mr. COHN. Well, the thing came up—

Mr. WELCH. Mr. Cohn, if I told you now that we had a bad situation at Monmouth, you would want to cure it by sundown, if you could, wouldn't you?

Mr. COHN. I am sure I couldn't, sir.

Mr. WELCH. But you would like to, if you could?

Mr. COHN. Sir—

Mr. WELCH. Isn't that right?

Mr. COHN. No, what I want—

Mr. WELCH. Answer me. That must be right. It has to be right.

Mr. COHN. What I would like to do and what can be done are two different things.

Mr. WELCH. Well, if you could be God and do anything you wished, you would cure it by sundown, wouldn't you?

Mr. COHN. Yes, sir.

Mr. WELCH. And you were that alarmed about Monmouth?

Mr. COHN. It doesn't go that way.

Mr. WELCH. I am just asking how it does go. When you find there are Communists and possible spies in a place like Monmouth, you must be alarmed, aren't you?

Mr. COHN. Now you have asked me how it goes, and I am going to tell you.

Mr. WELCH. No; I didn't ask you how it goes. I said aren't you alarmed when you find it is there?

Mr. COHN. Whenever I hear that people have been failing to act on FBI information about Communists, I do think it is alarming, I would like the Communists out, and I would like to be able to advise this committee of why people who have the responsibility for getting them out haven't carried out their responsibility.

Mr. WELCH. Yes, but what you want first of all, Mr. Colin, and let's be fair with each other, what you want first of all, if it is within your power, is to get them out, isn't it?

Mr. COHN. I don't know if I draw a distinction as to what ought to come first, Mr. Welch.

Mr. WELCH. It certainly ranks terrifically high, doesn't it?

Mr. COHN. It was a situation that I thought should be developed, and we did develop it.

Mr. WELCH. When did you first meet Secretary [of the Army Robert T.] Stevens?

Mr. COHN. I first met Secretary Stevens September 7 I believe it was.

Mr. WELCH. September 7? Where were you, sir?

Mr. COHN. Washington.

Mr. WELCH. Where in Washington?

Mr. COHN. I don't remember where I was when I met him. It was in this building, either at lunch or in a hearing room, something like that.

Mr. WELCH. And you knew that he was the new Secretary of the Army?

Mr. COHN. Yes; I did know he was the Secretary of the Army.

Mr. WELCH. And you must have had high hopes about him, didn't you?

Mr. COHN. I don't think I gave it too much thought, sir.

Mr. WELCH. Anybody wants the Secretary of the Army to do well, no matter what party he is from, do we not?

Mr. COHN. Surely, sir.

Mr. WELCH. And on September 7, when you met him, you had in your bosom this alarming situation about Monmouth, is that right?

Mr. COHN. Yes; I knew about Monmouth, then. Yes, sir.

Mr. WELCH. And you didn't tug at his lapel and say, "Mr. Secretary, I know something about Monmouth that won't let me, sleep nights"? You didn't do it, did you?

Mr. COHN. I don't—as I testified, Mr. Welch, I don't know whether I talked to Mr. Stevens about it then or not. I know that on the 16th I did. Whether I talked to him on the 7th or not, is something I don't know.

Mr. WELCH. Don't you know that if you had really told him what your fears were, and substantiated them to any extent, lie could have jumped in the next day with suspensions?

Mr. COHN. No, sir.

Mr. WELCH. Did you then have any reason to doubt his fidelity?

Mr. COHN. No, sir.

Mr. WELCH. Or his honor?

Mr. COHN. No.

Mr. WELCH. Or his patriotism?

Mr. COHN. No.

Mr. WELCH. And yet, Mr. Cohn, you didn't tell him what you knew?

Mr. COHN. I don't know whether I did or not. I told him some of the things I knew, sir. I don't think I told him everything I knew on the first occasion. After the first 2 or 3 occasions, I think he had a pretty good idea of what we were working on.

Mr. WELCH. Mr. Cohn, tell me once more: Every time you learn of a Communist or a spy anywhere, is it your policy to get them out as fast as possible?

Mr. COHN. Surely, we want them out as fast as possible, sir.

Mr. WELCH. And whenever you learn of one from now on, Mr. Cohn, I beg of you, will you tell somebody about them quick?

Mr. COHN. Mr. Welch, with great respect, I work for the committee here. They know how we go about handling situations of Communist infiltration and failure to act on FBI information about Communist infiltration. If they are displeased with the speed with which I and the group of men who work with me proceed, if they are displeased with the order in which we move, I am sure they will give me appropriate instructions along those lines, and I will follow any which they give me.

Mr. WELCH. May I add my small voice, sir, and say whenever you know about a subversive or a Communist or a spy, please hurry. Will you remember those words?

Senator MCCARTHY. Mr. Chairman.

Mr. COHN. Mr. Welch, I can assure you, sir, as far as I am concerned, and certainly as far as the chairman of this committee and the members, and the members of the staff, are concerned, we are a small group, but we proceed as expeditiously as is humanly possible to get out Communists and traitors and to bring to light the mechanism by which they have been permitted to remain where they were for so long a period of time.

Senator MCCARTHY. Mr. Chairman, in view of that question—

Senator MUNDT. Have you a point of order?

Senator MCCARTHY. Not exactly, Mr. Chairman, but in view of Mr. Welch's request that the information be given once we know of anyone who might be performing any work for the Communist Party, I think we should tell him that he has in his law firm a young man named Fisher whom he recommended, incidentally, to do work on this committee, who has been for a number of years a member of an organization which was named, oh, years and years ago, as the legal bulwark of the Communist Party, an organization which always swings to the defense of anyone who dares to expose Communists. I certainly assume that Mr. Welch did not know of this young man at the time he recommended him as the assistant counsel for this committee, but he has such terror and such a great desire to know where anyone is located who may be serving the Communist cause, Mr. Welch, that I thought we should just call to your attention the fact that your Mr. Fisher, who is still in your law firm today, whom you asked to have down here looking over the secret and classified material, is a member of an organization, not named by me but named by various committees, named by the Attorney General, as I recall, and I think I quote this verbatim, as "the legal bulwark of the Communist Party." He belonged to that for a sizable number of years, according to his own admission, and he belonged to it long after it had been exposed as the legal arm of the Communist Party.

Knowing that, Mr. Welch, I just felt that I had a duty to respond to your urgent request that before sundown, when we know of anyone serving the Communist cause, we let the agency know. We are now letting you know that your man did belong to this organization for either 3 or 4 years, belonged to it long after he was out of law school.

I don't think you can find anyplace, anywhere, an organization which has done more to defend Communists—I am again quoting the report—to defend Communist, to defend espionage agents, and to aid the Communist cause, than the man whom you originally wanted down here at your right hand instead of Mr. St. Clair.

I have hesitated bringing that up, but I have been rather bored with your phony requests to Mr. Cohn here that he personally get every Communist out of government before sundown. Therefore, we will give you information about the young man in your own organization.

I am not asking you at this time to explain why you tried to foist him on this committee. Whether you knew he was a member of that Communist organization or not, I don't know. I assume you did not, Mr. Welch, because I get the impression that, while you are quite an actor, you play for a laugh, I don't think you have any conception of the danger of the Communist Party. I don't think you yourself would ever knowingly aid the Communist cause. I think you are unknowingly aiding it when you try to burlesque this hearing in which we are attempting to bring out the facts, however.

Mr. WELCH. Mr. Chairman.

Senator MUNDT. Mr. Welch, the Chair should say he has no recognition or no memory of Mr. Welch's recommending either Mr. Fisher or anybody else as counsel for this committee.

I will recognize Mr. Welch.

Senator MCCARTHY. Mr. Chairman, I will give you the news story on that.

Mr. WELCH. Mr. Chairman, under these circumstances I must have something approaching a personal privilege.

Senator MUNDT. You may have it, sir. It will not be taken out of your time.

Mr. WELCH. Senator McCarthy, I did not know—Senator, sometimes you say "May I have your attention?"

Senator MCCARTHY. I am listening to you. I can listen with one ear.

Mr. WELCH. This time I want you to listen with both.

Senator MCCARTHY. Yes.

Mr. WELCH. Senator McCarthy, I think until this moment—

Senator MCCARTHY. Jim, will you get the news story to the effect that this man belonged to this Communist-front organization? Will you get the citations showing that this was the legal arm of the Communist Party, and the length of time that he belonged, and the fact that he was recommended by Mr. Welch? I think that should be in the record.

Mr. WELCH. You won't need anything in the record when I have finished telling you this.

Until this moment, Senator, I think I never really gaged your cruelty or your recklessness. Fred Fisher is a young man who went to the Harvard Law School and came into my firm and is starting what looks to be a brilliant career with us.

When I decided to work for this committee I asked Jim St. Clair, who sits on my right, to be my first assistant. I said to Jim, "Pick somebody in the firm who works under you that you would like." He chose Fred Fisher and they came down on an afternoon plane. That night, when he had taken a little stab at trying to see what the case was about, Fred Fisher and Jim St. Clair and I went to dinner together. I then said to these two young men, "Boys, I don't know anything about you except I have always liked you, but if there is anything funny in the life of either one of you that would hurt anybody in this case you speak up quick."

Fred Fisher said, "Mr. Welch, when I was in law school and for a period of months after, I belonged to the Lawyers Guild," as you have suggested, Senator. He went on to say, "I am secretary of the Young Republicans League in Newton with the son of Massachusetts' Governor, and I have the respect and admiration of my community and I am sure I have the respect and admiration of the 25 lawyers or so in Hale & Dorr."

I said, "Fred, I just don't think I am going to ask you to work on the case. If I do, one of these days that will come out and go over national television and it will just hurt like the dickens."

So, Senator, I asked him to go back to Boston.

Little did I dream you could be so reckless and so cruel as to do an injury to that lad. It is true he is still with Hale & Dorr. It is true that he will continue to be with Hale & Dorr. It is, I regret to say, equally true that I fear he shall always bear a scar needlessly inflicted by you. If it were in my power to forgive you for your reckless cruelty, I will do so. I like to think I am a gentleman, but your forgiveness will have to come from someone other than me.

Senator MCCARTHY. Mr. Chairman.

Senator MUNDT. Senator McCarthy?

Senator MCCARTHY. May I say that Mr. Welch talks about this being cruel and reckless. He was just baiting; he has been baiting Mr. Cohn here for hours, requesting that Mr. Cohn, before sundown, get out of any department of Government anyone who is serving the Communist cause.

I just give this man's record, and I want to say, Mr. Welch, that it has been labeled long before he became a member, as early as 1944—

Mr. WELCH. Senator, may we not drop this? We know he belonged to the Lawyers Guild, and Mr. Cohn nods his head at me. I did you, I think, no personal injury, Mr. Cohn.

Mr. COHN. No, sir.

Mr. WELCH. I meant to do you no personal injury, and if I did, I beg your pardon.

Let us not assassinate this lad further, Senator. You have done enough. Have you no sense of decency, sir, at long last? Have you left no sense of decency?

Senator MCCARTHY. I know this hurts you, Mr. Welch. But I may say, Mr. Chairman, on a point of personal privilege, and I would like to finish it—

Mr. WELCH. Senator, I think it hurts you, too, sir.

Senator MCCARTHY. I would like to finish this.

Mr. Welch has been filibustering this hearing, he has been talking day after day about how he wants to get anyone tainted with communism out before sundown. I know Mr. Cohn would rather not have me go into this. I intend to, however, Mr. Welch talks about any sense of decency. If I say anything which is not the truth, then I would like to know about it.

The foremost legal bulwark of the Communist Party, its front organizations, and controlled unions, and which, since its inception, has never failed to rally to the legal defense of the Communist Party, and individual members thereof, including known espionage agents.

Now, that is not the language of Senator McCarthy. That is the language of the Un-American Activities Committee. And I can go on with many more citations. It seems that Mr. Welch is pained so deeply he thinks it is improper for me to give the record, the Communist-front record, of the man whom he wanted to foist upon this committee. But it doesn't pain him at all— there is no pain in his chest about the unfounded charges against Mr. Frank Carr; there is no pain there about the attempt to destroy the reputation and take the jobs away from the young men who were working in my committee.

And, Mr. Welch, if I have said anything here which is untrue, then tell me. I have heard you and every one else talk so much about laying the truth upon the table that when I hear—and it's completely phony, Mr. Welch. I have listened to you for a long time—when you say "Now, before sundown, you must get these people out of Government," I want to have it very clear, very clear that you were not so serious about that when you tried to recommend this man for this committee.

And may I say, Mr. Welch, in fairness to you, I have reason to believe that you did not know about his Communist-front record at the time you recommended him. I don't think you would have recommended him to the committee if you knew that.

I think it is entirely possible you learned that after you recommended him.

Senator MUNDT. The Chair would like to say again that he does not believe that Mr. Welch recommended Mr. Fisher as counsel for this committee, because he has through his office all the recommendations that were made. He does not recall any that came from Mr. Welch, and that would include Mr. Fisher.

Senator MCCARTHY. Let me ask Mr. Welch. You brought him down, did you not, to act as your assistant?

Mr. WELCH. Mr. McCarthy, I will not discuss this with you further. You have sat within 6 feet of me, and could have asked me about Fred Fisher. You have brought it out. If there is a God in heaven, it will do neither you nor your cause any good. I will not discuss it further. I will not ask Mr. Cohn any more questions. You, Mr. Chairman, may, if you will, call the next witness.

. . . .

Hearing Before the Special Subcommittee on Investigations of the Committee on Government Operations, United States Senate, 83d Congress, 2d session, Pursuant to S. Res. 189, Part 59, June 9, 1954, 2424–2430. Special Senate Investigation on Charges and Countercharges Involving Secretary of the Army Robert T. Stevens, John G. Adams, H. Struve Hensel and Senator Joe McCarthy, Roy M. Cohn, and Francis P. Carr (Washington: Government Printing Office, 1954).

145   The Creation of the Interstate Highway System (The Federal-Aid Highway Act of 1956)

June 29, 1956

On June 26, 1956, as the Senate considered a highway funding bill that contained provisions for the creation of an interstate highway system, Senator Thomas E. Martin (R-Iowa) summed up the magnitude of the bill before them. "I should like to say," said Senator Martin, "that the road bill is the biggest undertaking the United States has ever attempted, outside of war." The passage of the Federal-Aid Highway Act of 1956—which contained, in Section 108, a description of the planned system—was a landmark piece of congressional legislation because it was a law that profoundly changed the United States, in some instances in ways not anticipated by Congress. This bill is an excellent example of a law that affects the lives of all citizens, directly or indirectly, on an daily basis, whether they are traveling the interstate system or not.

The 1950s was a time of great economic expansion and development within the United States. It was also a time of great concern over national security. These two forces met in the creation of *the interstate highway system. The proposed system would link the nation for defense purposes as well as provide for the demands of an ever-increasing motoring public. Automobiles were relatively scarce in the 1930s, and limited in production during World War II, as automobile plants turned out the machinery of war instead of cars. The age of the automobile began in earnest in the 1950s, as ownership of a private passenger automobile came within reach of millions of Americans. This, combined with the rise of shipping of goods by truck, led to a thirteen-year plan to develop an interconnecting national highway system. It was, as Senator Martin said during consideration of the bill in the Senate, the largest single appropriation outside of wartime expenditures in the history of the nation up to that time.*

This massive system of highways changed the face of American cities, often dividing neighborhoods along racial or ethnic lines, contributing to the rise of the shopping mall and the decline of tra-

ditional main streets in small- and medium-sized towns across the nation. The decision to spend billions on highway transportation also contributed to the decline of mass urban transit systems and passenger travel by train. It was a bill that contributed to considerable change in American culture and the American economy. Scholars are still studying both the positive and negative affects of this massive system of transportation, the last components of which were completed in the early 1990s, encompassing more than 45,000 miles of highways, bridges, and tunnels.

TITLE I—FEDERAL-AID HIGHWAY ACT OF 1956

. . . .

SEC. 108. National System of Interstate and Defense Highways.

(a) INTERSTATE SYSTEM.—It is hereby declared to be essential to the national interest to provide for the early completion of the "National System of Interstate Highways", as authorized and designated in accordance with section 7 of the Federal-Aid Highway Act of 1944 (58 Stat. 838). It is the intent of the Congress that the Interstate System be completed as nearly as practicable over a thirteen-year period and that the entire System in all the States be brought to simultaneous completion. Because of its primary importance to the national defense, the name of such system is hereby changed to the "National System of Interstate and Defense Highways". Such National System of Interstate and Defense Highways is hereinafter in this Act referred to as the "Interstate System".

(b) AUTHORIZATION OF APPROPRIATIONS.—For the purpose of expediting the construction, reconstruction, or improvement, inclusive of necessary bridges and tunnels, of the Interstate System, including extensions thereof through urban areas, designated in accordance with the provisions of section 7 of the Federal-Aid Highway Act of 1944 (58 Stat. 838), there is hereby authorized to be appropriated the additional sum of $1,000,000,000 for the fiscal year ending June 30, 1957, which sum shall be in addition to the authorization heretofore made for that year, the additional sum of $1,700,000,000 for the fiscal year ending June 30, 1958, the additional sum of $2,000,000,000 for the fiscal year ending June 30, 1959, the additional sum of $2,200,000,000 for the fiscal year ending June 30, 1960, the additional sum of $2,200,000,000 for the fiscal year ending June 30, 1961, the additional sum of $2,200,000,000 for the fiscal year ending June 30, 1962, the additional sum of $2,200,000,000 for the fiscal year ending June 30, 1963, the additional sum of $2,200,000,000 for the fiscal year ending June 30, 1964, the additional sum of $2,200,000,000 for the fiscal year ending June 30, 1965, the additional sum of $2,200,000,000 for the fiscal year ending June 30, 1966, the additional sum of $2,200,000,000 for the fiscal year ending June 30, 1967, the additional sum of $1,500,000,000 for the fiscal year ending June 30, 1968, and the additional sum of $1,025,000,000 for the fiscal year ending June 30, 1969.

(C) APPORTIONMENTS FOR 1957, 1958, AND 1959.—The additional sums herein authorized for the fiscal years ending June 30, 1957, June 30, 1958, and June 30, 1959, shall be apportioned among the several States in the following manner: one-half in the ratio which the population of each State bears to the total population of all the States, as shown by the latest available Federal census: *Provided,* That no State shall receive less than three-fourths of 1 per centum of the money so apportioned; and one-half in the manner now provided by law for the apportionment of funds for the Federal-aid primary system. The additional sum herein authorized for the fiscal year ending June 30, 1957, shall be apportioned immediately upon enactment of this Act. The additional sums herein authorized for the fiscal years ending June 30, 1958, and June 30, 1959, shall be apportioned on a date not less than six months and not more than twelve months in advance of the beginning of the fiscal year for which authorized.

(d) APPORTIONMENTS FOR SUBSEQUENT YEARS BASED UPON REVISED ESTIMATES OF COST.—All sums authorized by this section to be appropriated for the fiscal years 1960 through 1969, inclusive, shall be apportioned among the several States in the ratio which the estimated cost of completing, the Interstate System in each State, as determined and approved in the manner provided in this subsection, bears to the sum of the estimated cost of completing the Interstate System in all of the States. Each apportionment herein authorized for the fiscal years 1960 through 1969, inclusive, shall be made on a date as far in advance of the beginning of the fiscal year for which authorized as practicable but in no case more than eighteen months prior to the beginning of the fiscal year for which authorized. As soon as the standards provided for in subsection (i) have been adopted, the Secretary of Commerce, in cooperation with the State highway departments, shall make a detailed estimate of the cost of completing the Interstate System as then designated, after taking into account all previous apportionments made under this section based upon such standards and in accordance with rules and regulations adopted by him and applied uniformly to all of the States. The Secretary of Commerce shall transmit such estimate to the Senate and the House of Representatives within ten days subsequent to January 2, 1958. Upon approval of such estimate by the Congress by concurrent resolution, the Secretary of Commerce shall use such approved estimate in making apportionments for the fiscal years ending June 30, 1960, June 30, 1961, and June 30, 1962. The Secretary of Commerce shall make a revised estimate of the cost of completing the then designated Interstate System, after taking into account all previous apportionments made under this section, in the same manner as stated above, and transmit the same to the Senate and the House of Representatives within ten days subsequent to January 2, 1962. Upon approval of such estimate by the Congress by concurrent resolution, the Secretary of Commerce shall use such approved estimate in making apportionments for the fiscal years ending June 30, 1963, June 30, 1964, June 30, 1965, and June 30, 1966. The Secretary of Commerce shall make a revised estimate of the cost of completing the then designated Interstate System, after taking into account all previous apportionments made under this section, in the same manner as stated above, and transmit the same to the Senate and the House of Representatives within ten days subsequent to January 2, 1966, and annually thereafter through and including January 2, 1968. Upon approval of any such estimate by the Congress by concurrent resolution, the Secretary of Commerce shall use such approved estimate in making apportionments for the fiscal year which begins next following the fiscal year in which such report is transmitted to the Senate and the House of Representatives. Whenever the Secretary of Commerce, pursuant to this subsection, requests and receives estimates of cost from the State highway departments, he shall furnish copies of such estimates at the same time to the Senate and the House of Representatives.

(e) FEDERAL SHARE.—The Federal share payable on account of any project on the Interstate System provided for by funds made available under the provisions of this section shall be increased to 90 per centum of the total cost thereof, plus a percentage of the remaining 10 per centum of such cost in any State containing unappropriated and unreserved public lands and nontaxable Indian lands, individual and tribal, exceeding 5 per centum of the total area of all lands therein equal to the percentage that the area of such lands in such State is of its total area: *Provided,* That such Federal share payable on any project in any State shall not exceed 95 per centum of the total cost of such project.

. . . .

Statutes at Large, 70 (1956), 84th Congress, 2d session, June 29, 1956, 374–402.

146   *Watkins v. United States*

June 17, 1957

In the Watkins v. United States *decision, delivered by Chief Justice Earl Warren, the Supreme Court recognized and affirmed the broad powers of Congress to conduct investigations, but at the same time it offered a stinging criticism of the abuse of that power by the House Un-American Activities Committee (HUAC, see document 134). This case and one from 1959,* Barenblatt v. United States, *which also involved a witness before the HUAC, would define how the Supreme Court addressed difficult questions regarding balancing the constitutional rights of witnesses before congressional committees with the congressional power to compel them to testify.*

In this case John T. Watkins, an official of the Farm Equipment Workers International Union, was subpoenaed to testify before the HUAC about union activities and his relation to the Communist Party in the 1940s. He had been implicated by two earlier witnesses before the committee. In his testimony of April 19, 1954, Watkins readily and freely admitted to his association with members of the Communist Party, his occasional contributions to the party, and his attendance at party meetings. He also made it clear that he was not a "card-carrying" member of the Communist Party and never had been. When he was asked to testify about other individuals and their relationship with the Communist Party, he refused. He told the committee he was perfectly willing to answer questions about himself or others he knew for a fact to have been party members. He told the committee he did not believe it had the right to "undertake the public exposure of persons because of their past activities." The House of Representatives, at the request of the HUAC, directed the U.S. attorney general to bring a criminal indictment against Watkins. He waived his right to a jury trial and was found guilty. Watkins was fined $100 and sentenced to one year in jail, with the sentence suspended. He was placed on probation. The Court of Appeals in the District of Columbia upheld the conviction, and the case went to the Supreme Court.

The decision in this case was ultimately settled on some narrow questions. But the language of the decision is sweeping in its criticism of the House Un-American Activities Committee and reflected the growing national sentiment that the committee had often abused its powers to investigate. Even though this particular congressional investigation was looking into Communist activity in labor unions, many of the witnesses had nothing to do with unions. The Court declared that a congressional inquiry was not an end in itself but had to be related to a "legitimate task of Congress," and that Congress did not have the "general authority to expose the private affairs of individuals without justification in terms of the functions of Congress."

The Court's decision said the resolution authorizing the HUAC was vague and did not sufficiently define the scope of the committee's jurisdiction. "It would be difficult," Chief Justice Warren wrote, "to imagine a less explicit authorizing resolution. Who can define the meaning of 'unAmerican'?" Watkins's conviction was overturned, the House Un-American Activities Committee was soundly rebuked, but the power of Congress to conduct investigations and compel witnesses to testify was left in tact.

In Barenblatt v. United States, *a witness before the HUAC refused to testify about whether he had ever been a member of the Communist Party. In this decision the Court reversed much of its opinion in the* Watkins *case. This time around Chief Justice Warren found himself in the minority. Much of the sharp criticism of the HUAC that appeared in his* Watkins *decision, as well as the grounds on which the* Watkins *decision rested (that the inquiry was too vague to compel Watkins's testimony), was set aside in an opinion written by Justice John Marshall Harlan.*

In the Barenblatt *case, the witness based his refusal to testify primarily on the First Amendment's protection of free speech and the right to privately held beliefs, a reference to the religious clause of the First Amendment. He was convicted for his failure to testify and sentenced to six months in jail. The Court affirmed the HUAC's authority to compel testimony and said the vagueness of the investigation was insufficient constitutional grounds to deny a duly authorized committee of Congress its power to compel a witness to testify. In the majority opinion the Court held that the long history of House approval of the HUAC demonstrated that the House had "clothed the Committee with pervasive authority to investigate Communist activities in this country." The Court declared "that the balance between the individual and the governmental interests here at stake must be struck in favor of the latter, and that therefore the provisions of the First Amendment have not been offended."*

. . . .

MR. CHIEF JUSTICE WARREN delivered the opinion of the Court.

. . . .

We start with several basic premises on which there is general agreement. The power of the Congress to conduct investigations is inherent in the legislative process. That power is broad. It encompasses inquiries concerning the administration of existing laws as well as proposed or possibly needed statutes. It includes surveys of defects in our social, economic or political system for the purpose of enabling the Congress to remedy them. It comprehends probes into departments of the Federal Government to expose corruption, inefficiency or waste. But, broad as is this power of inquiry, it is not unlimited. There is no general authority to expose the private affairs of individuals without justification in terms of the functions of the Congress. This was freely conceded by the Solicitor General in his argument of this case. Nor is the Congress a law enforcement or trial agency. These are functions of the executive and judicial departments of government. No inquiry is an end in itself; it must be related to, and in furtherance of, a legitimate task of the Congress. Investigations conducted solely for the personal aggrandizement of the investigators or to "punish" those investigated are indefensible.

It is unquestionably the duty of all citizens to cooperate with the Congress in its efforts to obtain the facts needed for intelligent legislative action. It is their unremitting obligation to respond to subpoenas, to respect the dignity of the Congress and its committees and to testify fully with respect to matters within the province of proper investigation. This, of course, assumes that the constitutional rights of witnesses will be respected by the Congress as they are in a court of justice. The Bill of Rights is applicable to investigations as to all forms of governmental action. Witnesses cannot be compelled to give evidence against themselves. They cannot be subjected to unreasonable search and seizure. Nor can the First Amendment freedoms of speech, press, religion, or political belief and association be abridged.

The rudiments of the power to punish for "contempt of Congress" come to us from the pages of English history. The origin of privileges and contempts extends back into the period of the emergence of Parliament. The establishment of a legislative body which could challenge the absolute power of the monarch is a long and bitter story. In that struggle, Parliament made broad and varied use of the contempt power. Almost from the beginning, both the House of Commons and the House of Lords claimed absolute and plenary authority over their privileges. This was an independent body of law, described by Coke as *lex parliamenti.* Only Parliament could declare what those privileges were or what new privileges were occasioned, and only Parliament could judge what conduct constituted a breach of privilege.

. . . .

The history of contempt of the legislature in this country is notably different from that of England. In the early days of the United States, there lingered the direct knowledge of the evil effects of absolute power. Most of the instances of use of compulsory process by the first Congresses concerned matters affecting the qualification or integrity of their members or came about in inquiries dealing with suspected corruption or mismanagement of government officials. Unlike the English practice, from the very outset the use of contempt power by the legislature was deemed subject to judicial review.

There was very little use of the power of compulsory process in early years to enable the Congress to obtain facts pertinent to the enactment of new statutes or the administration of existing laws. The first occasion for such an investigation arose in 1827 when the House of Representatives was considering a revision of the tariff laws. In the Senate, there was no use of a fact-finding investigation in aid of legislation until 1859. In the Legislative Reorganization Act, the Committee on Un-American Activities was the only standing committee of the House of Representatives that was given the power to compel disclosures.

It is not surprising, from the fact that the Houses of Congress so sparingly employed the power to conduct investigations, that there have been few cases requiring judicial review of the power. The Nation was almost one hundred years old before the first case reached this Court to challenge the use of compulsory process as a legislative device, rather than in inquiries concerning the elections or privileges of Congressmen. In *Kilbourn v. Thompson,* 103 U.S. 168, decided in 1881, an investigation had been authorized by the House of Representatives to learn the circumstances surrounding the bankruptcy of Jay Cooke & Company, in which the United States had deposited funds. The committee became particularly interested in a private real estate pool that was a part of the financial structure. The Court found that the subject matter of the inquiry was "in its nature clearly judicial and therefore one in respect to which no valid legislation could be enacted." The House had thereby exceeded the limits of its own authority.

Subsequent to the decision in *Kilbourn,* until recent times, there were very few cases dealing with the investigative power.

The matter came to the fore again when the Senate undertook to study the corruption in the handling of oil leases in the 1920's. In *McGrain v. Daugherty,* 273 U.S. 135, and *Sinclair v. United States,* 279 U.S. 263, the Court applied the precepts of Kilbourn to uphold the authority of the Congress to conduct the challenged investigations. The Court recognized the danger to effective and honest conduct of the Government if the legislature's power to probe corruption in the executive branch were unduly hampered.

. . . .

In the decade following World War II, there appeared a new kind of congressional inquiry unknown in prior periods of American history. Principally this was the result of the various investigations into the threat of subversion of the United States Government, but other subjects of congressional interest also contributed to the changed scene. This new phase of legislative inquiry involved a broad-scale intrusion into the lives and affairs of private citizens. It brought before the courts novel questions of the appropriate limits of congressional inquiry. Prior cases, like *Kilbourn, McGrain* and *Sinclair,* had defined the scope of investigative power in terms of the inherent limitations of the sources of that power. In the more recent cases, the emphasis shifted to problems of accommodating the interest of the Government with the rights and privileges of individuals. The central theme was the application of the Bill of Rights as a restraint upon the assertion of governmental power in this form.

It was during this period that the Fifth Amendment privilege against self-incrimination was frequently invoked and recognized as a legal limit upon the authority of a committee to require that a witness answer its questions. Some early doubts as to the applicability of that privilege before a legislative committee never matured. When the matter reached this Court, the Government did not challenge in any way that the Fifth Amendment protection was available to the witness, and such a challenge could not have prevailed. It confined its argument to the character of the answers sought and to the adequacy of the claim of privilege. *Quinn v. United States,* 349 U.S. 155; *Emspak v. United States,* 349 U.S. 190; *Bart v. United States,* 349 U.S. 219.

A far more difficult task evolved from the claim by witnesses that the committees' interrogations were infringements upon the freedoms of the First Amendment. Clearly, an investigation is subject to the command that the Congress shall make no law abridging freedom of speech or press or assembly. While it is true that there is no statute to be reviewed, and that an investigation is not a law, nevertheless an investigation is part of lawmaking. It is justified solely as an adjunct to the legislative process. The First Amendment may be invoked against infringement of the protected freedoms by law or by lawmaking.

Abuses of the investigative process may imperceptibly lead to abridgment of protected freedoms. The mere summoning of a witness and compelling him to testify, against his will, about his beliefs, expressions or associations is a measure of governmental interference. And when those forced revelations concern matters that are unorthodox, unpopular, or even hateful to the general public, the reaction in the life of the witness may be disastrous. This effect is even more harsh when it is past beliefs, expressions or associations that are disclosed and judged by current standards rather than those contemporary with the matters exposed. Nor does the witness alone suffer the consequences. Those who are identified by witnesses and thereby placed in the same glare of publicity are equally subject to public stigma, scorn and obloquy. Beyond that, there is the more subtle and immeasurable effect upon those who tend to adhere to the most orthodox and uncontroversial views and associations in order to avoid a similar fate at some future time. That this impact is partly the result of non-governmental activity by private persons cannot relieve the investigators of their responsibility for initiating the reaction.

. . . .

Accommodation of the congressional need for particular information with the individual and personal interest in privacy is an arduous and delicate task for any court. We do not underestimate the difficulties that would attend such an undertaking. It is manifest that despite the adverse effects which follow upon compelled disclosure of private matters, not all such inquiries are barred. *Kilbourn v. Thompson* teaches that such an investigation into individual affairs is invalid if unrelated to any legislative purpose. That is beyond the powers conferred upon the Congress in the Constitution. *United States v. Rumely* makes it plain that the mere semblance of legislative purpose would not justify an inquiry in the face of the Bill of Rights. The critical element is the existence of, and the weight to be ascribed to, the interest of the Congress in demanding disclosures from an unwilling witness. We cannot simply assume, however, that every congressional investigation is justified by a public need that overbalances any private rights affected. To do so would be to abdicate the responsibility placed by the Constitution upon the judiciary to insure that the Congress does not unjustifiably encroach upon an individual's right to privacy nor abridge his liberty of speech, press, religion or assembly.

Petitioner has earnestly suggested that the difficult questions of protecting these rights from infringement by legislative inquiries can be surmounted in this case because there was no public purpose served in his interrogation. His conclusion is based upon the thesis that the Subcommittee was engaged in a program of exposure for the sake of exposure. The sole purpose of the inquiry, he contends, was to bring down upon himself and others the violence of public reaction because of their past beliefs, expressions and associations. In support of this argument, petitioner has marshalled an impressive array of evidence that some Congressmen have believed that such was their duty, or part of it.

We have no doubt that there is no congressional power to expose for the sake of exposure. The public is, of course, entitled to be informed concerning the workings of its government. That cannot be inflated into a general power to expose where the predominant result can only be an invasion of the private rights of individuals. But a solution to our problem is not to be found in testing the motives of committee members for this purpose. Such is not our function. Their motives alone would not vitiate an investigation which had been instituted by a House of Congress if that assembly's legislative purpose is being served.

Petitioner's contentions do point to a situation of particular significance from the standpoint of the constitutional limitations upon congressional investigations. The theory of a committee inquiry is that the committee members are serving as the representatives of the parent assembly in collecting information for a legislative purpose. Their function is to act as the eyes and ears of the Congress in obtaining facts upon which the full legislature can act. To carry out this mission, committees and subcommittees, sometimes one Congressman, are endowed with the full power of the Congress to compel testimony. In this case, only two men exercised that authority in demanding information over petitioner's protest.

An essential premise in this situation is that the House or Senate shall have instructed the committee members on what they are to do with the power delegated to them. It is the responsibility of the Congress, in the first instance, to insure that compulsory process is used only in furtherance of a legislative purpose. That requires that the instructions to an investigating committee spell out that group's jurisdiction and purpose with sufficient particularity. Those instructions are embodied in the authorizing resolution. That document is the committee's charter. Broadly drafted and loosely worded, however, such resolutions can leave tremendous latitude to the discretion of the investigators. The more vague the committee's charter is, the greater becomes the possibility that the committee's specific actions are not in conformity with the will of the parent House of Congress.

The authorizing resolution of the Un-American Activities Committee was adopted in 1938 when a select committee, under the chairmanship of Representative Dies, was created." Several years later, the Committee was made a standing organ of the House with the same mandate. It defines the Committee's authority as follows:

"The Committee on Un-American Activities, as a whole or by subcommittee, is authorized to make from time to time investigations of (1) the extent, character, and objects of un-American propaganda activities in the United States, (2) the diffusion within the United States of subversive and un-American propaganda that is instigated from foreign countries or of a domestic origin and attacks the principle of the form of government as guaranteed by our Constitution, and (3) all other questions in relation thereto that would aid Congress in any necessary remedial legislation."

It would be difficult to imagine a less explicit authorizing resolution. Who can define the meaning of "un-American"? What is that single, solitary "principle of the form of government as guaranteed by our Constitution"? There is no need to dwell upon the language, however. At one time, perhaps, the resolution might have been read narrowly to confine the Committee to the subject of propaganda. The events that have transpired in the fifteen years before the interrogation of petitioner make such a construction impossible at this date.

The members of the Committee have clearly demonstrated that they did not feel themselves restricted in any way to propaganda in the narrow sense of the word. Unquestionably the Committee conceived of its task in the grand view of its name. Un-American activities were its target, no matter how or where manifested. Notwithstanding the broad purview of the Committee's experience, the House of Representatives repeatedly approved its continuation. . . .

. . . There is a wide gulf between the responsibility for the use of investigative power and the actual exercise of that power. This is an especially vital consideration in assuring respect for constitutional liberties. Protected freedoms should not be placed in danger in the absence of a clear determination by the House or the Senate that a particular inquiry is justified by a specific legislative need.

It is, of course, not the function of this Court to prescribe rigid rules for the Congress to follow in drafting resolutions establishing investigating committees. That is a matter peculiarly within the realm of the legislature, and its decisions will be accepted by the courts up to the point where their own duty to enforce the constitutionally protected rights of individuals is affected. An excessively broad charter, like that of the House Un-American Activities Committee, places the courts in an untenable position if they are to strike a balance between the public need for a particular interrogation and the right of citizens to carry on their affairs free from unnecessary governmental interference. It is impossible in such a situation to ascertain whether any legislative purpose justifies the disclosures sought and, if so, the importance of that information to the Congress in furtherance of its legislative function. The reason no court can make this critical judgment is that the House of Representatives itself has never made it. Only the legislative assembly initiating an investigation can assay the relative necessity of specific disclosures.

. . . .

Since World War II, the Congress has practically abandoned its original practice of utilizing the coercive sanction of contempt proceedings at the bar of the House. The sanction there imposed is imprisonment by the House until the recalcitrant witness agrees to testify or disclose the matters sought, provided that the incarceration does not extend beyond adjournment. The Congress has instead invoked the aid of the federal judicial system in protecting itself against contumacious conduct. It has become customary to refer these matters to the United States Attorneys for prosecution under criminal law.

The appropriate statute is found in 2 U.S.C. § 192. It provides:

"Every person who having been summoned as a witness by the authority of either House of Congress to give testimony or to produce papers upon any matter under inquiry before either House, or any joint committee established by a joint or concurrent resolution of the two Houses of Congress, or any committee of either House of Congress, willfully makes default, or who, having appeared, refuses to answer any question pertinent to the question under inquiry, shall be deemed guilty of a misdemeanor, punishable by a fine of not more than $1,000 nor less than $100 and imprisonment in a common jail for not less than one month nor more than twelve months."

In fulfillment of their obligation under this statute, the courts must accord to the defendants every right which is guaranteed to defendants in all other criminal cases. Among these is the right to have available, through a sufficiently precise statute, information revealing the standard of criminality before the commission of the alleged offense. Applied to persons prosecuted under § 192, this raises a special problem in that the statute defines the crime as refusal to answer "any question pertinent to the question under inquiry." Part of the standard of criminality, therefore, is the pertinency of the questions propounded to the witness.

. . . .

The Government believes that the topic of inquiry before the Subcommittee concerned Communist infiltration in labor. In his introductory remarks, the Chairman made reference to a bill, then pending before the Committee, which would have penalized labor unions controlled or dominated by persons who were, or had been, members of a "Communist-action" organization, as defined in the Internal Security Act of 1950. The Subcommittee, it is contended, might have been endeavoring to determine the extent of such a problem.

This view is corroborated somewhat by the witnesses who preceded and followed petitioner before the Subcommittee. Looking at the entire hearings, however, there is strong reason to doubt that the subject revolved about labor matters. The published transcript is entitled: Investigation of Communist Activities in the Chicago Area, and six of the nine witnesses had no connection with labor at all.

The most serious doubts as to the Subcommittee's "question under inquiry," however, stem from the precise questions that petitioner has been charged with refusing to answer. Under the terms of the statute, after all, it is these which must be proved pertinent. Petitioner is charged with refusing to tell the Subcommittee whether or not he knew that certain named persons had been members of the Communist Party in the past. The Subcommittee's counsel read the list from the testimony of a previous witness who had identified them as Communists. Although this former witness was identified with labor, he had not stated that the persons he named were involved in union affairs. Of the thirty names propounded to petitioner, seven were completely unconnected with organized labor. One operated a beauty parlor. Another was a watchmaker. Several were identified as "just citizens" or "only Communists." When almost a quarter of the persons on the list are not labor people, the inference becomes strong that the subject before the Subcommittee was not defined in terms of Communism in labor.

The final source of evidence as to the "question under inquiry" is the Chairman's response when petitioner objected to the questions on the grounds of lack of pertinency. The Chairman then announced that the Subcommittee was investigating "subversion and subversive propaganda." This is a subject at least as broad and indefinite as the authorizing resolution of the Committee, if not more so.

Having exhausted the several possible indicia of the "question under inquiry," we remain unenlightened as to the subject to which the questions asked petitioner were pertinent. Certainly, if the point is that obscure after trial and appeal, it was not adequately revealed to petitioner when he had to decide at his peril whether or not to answer. Fundamental fairness demands that no witness be compelled to make such a determination with so little guidance. Unless the subject matter has been made to appear with undisputable clarity, it is the duty of the investigative body, upon objection of the witness on grounds of pertinency, to state for the record the subject under inquiry at that time and the manner in which the propounded questions are pertinent thereto. To be meaningful, the explanation must describe what the topic under inquiry is and the connective reasoning whereby the precise questions asked relate to it.

The statement of the Committee Chairman in this case, in response to petitioner's protest, was woefully inadequate to convey sufficient information as to the pertinency of the questions to the subject under inquiry. Petitioner was thus not accorded a fair opportunity to determine whether he was within his rights in refusing to answer, and his conviction is necessarily invalid under the Due Process Clause of the Fifth Amendment.

We are mindful of the complexities of modern government and the ample scope that must be left to the Congress as the sole constitutional depository of legislative power. Equally mindful are we of the indispensable function, in the exercise of that power, of congressional investigations. The conclusions we have reached in this case will not prevent the Congress, through its committees, from obtaining any information it needs for the proper fulfillment of its role in our scheme of government. The legislature is free to determine the kinds of data that should be collected. It is only those investigations that are conducted by use of compulsory process that give rise to a need to protect the rights of individuals against illegal encroachment. That protection can be readily achieved through procedures which prevent the separation of power from responsibility and which provide the constitutional requisites of fairness for witnesses. A measure of added care on the part of the House and the Senate in authorizing the use of compulsory process and by their committees in exercising that power would suffice. That is a small price to pay if it serves to uphold the principles of limited, constitutional government without constricting the power of the Congress to inform itself.

The judgment of the Court of Appeals is reversed, and the case is remanded to the District Court with instructions to dismiss the indictment.

It is so ordered.

354 U.S. 178 (1957).

147 Senator Strom Thurmond's Record-Setting Filibuster

August 28–29, 1957

Senator Strom Thurmond (R-S.C.) has been in the Senate so long that he has become an institution unto himself. At the age of ninety-five (as this book goes to press), he holds and continues to add to his record as the oldest person to serve in the Senate. He broke the record at the age of ninety-three years and ninety-four days on March 8, 1996. He is also the longest serving member in the history of the Senate, a record he broke on May 25, 1997, with forty-one years and ten months of service. He was a high school teacher in South Carolina in the 1920s, a lawyer and state senator in the 1930s, and a circuit court judge in the late 1930s and early 1940s. He served in the U.S. Army during World War II as a paratrooper, rising to the rank of major general in the U.S. Army Reserve. He was governor of South Carolina from 1947 to 1951. He ran for president of the United States in 1948 as the candidate of the segregationist States Rights Party (known as Dixiecrats). First appointed to the Senate as a Democrat in 1954, Thurmond was elected to the Senate as a write-in candidate in 1954, resigned in 1955, was reappointed to fill his own seat, and has served in the Senate since that time. He switched from the Democratic to the Republican Party in 1964.

Senator Thurmond holds the record for the longest Senate filibuster in history. A filibuster is a parliamentary tactic to delay the proceedings of the Senate. Over a two-day period beginning 8:45 P.M. on August 28 and continuing until 9:12 A.M. the next morning, he held the floor of the Senate for twenty-four hours and eighteen minutes in his attempt to block passage of the Civil Rights Act of 1957 (see document 148). He hoped that his filibuster would cause an outpouring of opposition from southern states that would help defeat the bill. But this did not happen. Nor did any other southern senator, even those who would vote against the bill, join Thurmond in this one-man effort. Although his views on civil rights would change over the next several decades, at the time of this filibuster Thurmond was a leading segregationist and opponent of federal civil rights legislation.

Some filibuster's occurred in the early history of the House, but there are different rules in the House and Senate regarding debate. House members are strictly limited in the time they have for debate, while Senate rules provide for unlimited debate. Although the Senate may, under certain circumstances, and with the consent of all members, limit the time it allows for debate, in most cases once senators gain recognition to speak they may hold the floor until they yield, or until the Senate can invoke cloture—a process to end debate that required a two-thirds vote of the senators present at the time of the filibuster. During the time they hold the floor senators may speak about any subject they wish. Thurmond, in order to kill time, read at length from state laws, constitutional histories, Supreme Court decisions, and newspaper clippings, all of which amounted to a long-winded, disjointed, civics lesson attempting to prove the folly of federal civil rights legislation.

Under Senate rules, a senator may yield for the purpose of a question, or for other business to proceed, as long as it is stipulated that the senator speaking does not yield the floor or leave the chamber. In this filibuster, Senator Thurmond was interrupted numerous times as other senators tried to end his filibuster or make a few points of their own. The filibuster was suspended briefly so a new member of the Senate, William Proxmire (D-Wis.), could be sworn in as a senator. Thurmond sustained himself with throat lozenges and a pocket full of malted milk tablets. He managed to sneak in a sandwich from the cloak room during the time Senator Proxmire was being sworn in. Through all these interruptions Thurmond continued to hold the floor.

Thurmond's delaying tactics were more symbolic than effective. Less that two weeks after this filibuster, the Senate passed the Civil Rights Act of 1957. This filibuster stands as a symbol of southern opposition to the Civil Rights movement of the 1950s and 1960s. Other filibusters on civil rights would follow this one, including a prolonged struggle to delay passage of the 1964 Civil Rights act.

Mr. THURMOND. Mr. President, I rise to speak against the so-called voting-right bill H.R. 6127, which bill was passed by the House of Representatives. It came to the Senate without being referred to a committee and was placed on the Senate Calendar, which is something unusual and out of ordinary procedure. The bill was then amended by the Senate and returned to the House, after which time the House amended it again by adopting what was called a compromise. The compromise as well as the bill is entirely unreasonable, and I hope that the Senate will not pass the bill.

There are mainly three reasons why I feel the bill should not be passed. The first is that it is unnecessary.

STATE LEGISLATION PROTECTING THE VOTING RIGHTS OF CITIZENS

Every State has enacted some legislation making it unlawful to intimidate a voter or to hinder him in the exercising of his voting rights. Penalties have been provided for such violations.

I now expect to take up the voting laws in each of the 48 States and show that each of the States affords adequate protection to the voting right. The first is Alabama.

. . . .

Mr. THURMOND. I have read the election laws of every State in the Union, from Alabama to Wyoming, showing that the States now have, on their statute books and in their constitutions, provisions to protect the right to vote. The accuracy of the statutes which I have just recited is confirmed by the Legislative Reference Service of the Library of Congress.

No one can say that any State, from Alabama through Wyoming, does not have statutes to protect the right to vote.

The bill before the Senate is called a right-to-vote bill. Why is it called that? Every State has statutes to protect the right to vote. The sovereign States are protecting their citizens in the right to vote. Yet there is a big cry and a big hue about the voting law. As a matter of fact, the only thing that instigated this bill was the desire of both parties, the Democratic and the Republican, to play to minority votes. That is the purpose of the bill. It is purely political. Why do we need a Federal law when every State has a statute to protect the right to vote? And who is in a better position to protect the right to vote than the officials of the States.

Suppose the voting laws of all the States were abrogated and violated. Does the Federal Government have a policy system which would enable it to send officials into every State to police the election laws of every State? If so, it would change our entire concept of the Government of this Nation.

The Constitution of the United States was written in 1789, in Philadelphia. It was ratified by nine Colonies which made them States and created the union; 2 years later the Bill of Rights was adopted; and in the 10th amendment, which is a part of the Bill of Rights, it is provided that all powers not specifically delegated to the Federal Government are reserved to the States. There is nothing in the Constitution that delegates those powers to the Federal Government. Therefore, those rights are reserved to the States, and it is unlawful and unconstitutional for Congress to attempt to pass a law that will set up an administration which will attempt to bring about a policing of all the elections in all the 48 States of this Nation.

Some persons say, "Well, the States won't enforce the voting laws. We have got to have a Federal law. Some States deny the vote to citizens." I question that. Has there been a single instance brought before the Judiciary Committee of the Senate of the United States and proof presented that anyone has been denied the vote? From my understanding, and from the minority report which was submitted by some members of the Judiciary Committee, that has not been the case. So why does the Federal Government want to enter a field into which it has no constitutional authority to enter? As a matter of fact, the Federal Government already has a statute, I say to those who say the States are not protecting the right to vote. I am wondering if the Members of the Senate and of the House of Representatives have overlooked the Federal statute. I shall read that statute, so that Senators can know that we now have a Federal statute to protect the right to vote.

I shall read several provisions. The last one is the most applicable, and one on which I shall comment a little more, but I want to start with chapter 29 of title 18 of the Criminal Code and Criminal Procedure.

. . . .

During the delivery of Mr. Thurmond's remarks,

Mr. JOHNSON of Texas. Mr. President, will the distinguished Senator from South Carolina yield to me, with the understanding—

Mr. THURMOND. I will yield for a question.

Mr. JOHNSON of Texas. Mr. President, I should like to ask the Senator if he would be agreeable to yielding to me for the purpose of making a brief announcement, with the understanding that the announcement appear at the conclusion of his remarks, with the further understanding that when he resumes after the interruption it will no be counted as a second speech, and with the further understanding that the Senator retain the floor.

Mr. THURMOND. If unanimous consent is obtained, and there is no objection on the part of the majority leader or minority leader, I will do so.

The PRESIDING OFFICER (Mr. Johnston of South Carolina in the chair). Is there objection to the request of the Senator from Texas? The Chair hears none, and it is so ordered.

Mr. JOHNSON of Texas. Mr. President, I am pleased to announce that the Senator-elect, Mr. William Proxmire, from the State of Wisconsin, who was on yesterday chosen by the citizens of Wisconsin in a landslide vote, is present, ready, and prepared to take the oath of office.

. . . .

Thursday, August 29, 1957

[Continuation of Senate proceedings of Wednesday, August 28, 1957, from 2 A.M. Thursday, August 29]

Mr. THURMOND. Mr. President, I now wish to take up Chief Justice Taft's opinion on jury trials in contempt cases. Considerable has been said about what Chief Justice Taft said concerning contempt and jury trials. Chief Justice Taft was at one time President of the United States. He was a great man and a great American. His opinions are highly revered, but some of his opinions have been quoted out of context or when not applicable. I wish to take up at this time his opinions on jury trials in contempt cases.

. . . .

Mr. President, here is another article from the Charleston (S.C.) News and Courier. It is entitled "Trial by Jury Right of All Americans" and it appears in the June 5, 1957, issue of the News and Courier, and has this to say:

. . . .

Mr. President, I have an article from the May 10, 1957, issue of the Charleston (S.C.) News and Courier. It is entitled "The Civil-Rights Fight and Trial-by-Jury Issue" and was written by the distinguished southern newspaperman, Dr. John Temple Graves. Here is what it has to say on the jury-trial issue:

. . . .

As I have said before, Mr. President—to digress there—the only purpose of this so-called right-to-vote bill is to advance the cause of the national political parties with the minorities and to advance the cause of certain politicians. If it were not for the purpose of both parties playing to the minorities and advancing the cause of certain politicians to high offices, I do not believe this bill would ever have been introduced. It is a disgrace to the United States even to have the Congress consider such an abominable and obnoxious bill.

. . . .

Mr. KNOWLAND. Mr. President, will the Senator from South Carolina yield for a question, with the understanding that he will not lose his right to the floor, and the understanding that that it will not be considered a second speech or jeopardize the Senator's right to the floor?

Mr. THURMOND. If unanimous consent is granted, under the conditions which the distinguished Senator has outlined, I will be please to yield.

The PRESIDING OFFICER. Is there objection to the request of the Senator from California? The Chair hears none, and it is so ordered.

Mr. KNOWLAND. Mr. President, I shall preface my question by this brief statement of fact, namely, since the House has adopted a sine die adjournment resolution, and there is no fixed period for adjournment, and the Senate can, and in my judgment will, continue in session as long as it is necessary to complete its business, I put these questions in all seriousness to the distinguished Senator from South Carolina:

First. What is the Senator's purpose by his interesting but prolonged remarks? Is it a matter of education of the Senate or of the country?

Second. Is it to establish a record of discussion on the floor of the Senate?

Third. Is it merely to delay a vote on the civil rights bill, which is the pending business?

Fourth. Is it to prevent a final vote on H.R. 6127, the so-called civil rights bill?

Fifth. Is it to make friends and to influence other Senators in the southern position?

Sixth. Is it to emphasize to the Senator the need for a change, beginning in January, of rule XXII?

There may be other reasons, but I should be very much interested—and I believe the Senate would be interested also—if the Senator from South Carolina would agree to indicate the purpose of his prolonged address.

Mr. THURMOND. I would merely say that my purpose in making the extended address if for educational purposes—to educate the Senate and the people of the country. There is no question in my mind that the so-called civil-rights bill violates the Constitution of the United States. I do not believe the Senator was in the Chamber when I spoke earlier and cited a decision pointing out that criminal contempt has been held to be a crime and that under the Constitution of the United States it is provided that a man charged with crime shall get a jury trial.

The so-called compromise bill provides that if a person is sentenced by a judge by being fined more than $300 or imprisoned for more than 45 days, he will get a jury trial. The Constitution does not say that. The Constitution provides that if he is charged with a crime, he shall get a jury trial.

I believe in the Constitution. I believe that the Constitution is clear. I hope the Senator will take the time one of these days—probably he will not have an opportunity soon—to read the address I have made in which I have gone into these matters and have tried to delineate them and point them out for the benefit of the American people, as well as for the benefit of the Senate.

Mr. KNOWLAND. Mr. President, will the Senator yield?

Mr. THURMOND. I am confident that the pending bill is a dangerous bill in a number of ways. I have pointed out that it is necessary that every State in the Nation have laws to protect the right to vote. The Senator's own State of California has such laws. I started with the State of Alabama and read the laws for every State. Those laws were confirmed to be accurate by the Library of Congress. I read the State laws beginning with Alabama and ending with Wyoming. Every State in the Nation has laws to protect the right to vote.

I say there is no need for the pending bill. This is a matter that comes under the Constitution, and it should be left to the States. It is a State matter. It is not a Federal matter.

Furthermore, the Federal Government has invaded the field. It has already invaded the field. I believe it made a mistake when it did so.

. . . .

Mr. KNOWLAND. Mr. President, will the Senator yield under the same conditions as heretofore stated?

Mr. THURMOND. I yield under the same conditions.

Mr. KNOWLAND. I can assure the Senator, whether we make that proviso in our remarks back and for the, the Senator will be fully protected in his right to the floor.

Mr. THURMOND. I shall be pleased to yield to the Senator from California under those conditions.

Mr. KNOWLAND. I did listen to the earlier part of the Senator's address. I was in the Chamber at the time. I must confess that for several hours I did get some sleep and was able to freshen up and to change my clothes, and I am now back in the Chamber.

Mr. THURMOND. I notice that the Senator looks very fresh at about 6:45 in the morning.

Mr. KNOWLAND. Yes. I am glad to be here with the Senator. Of course, the question which obviously disturbed a majority of the two Houses of Congress was that the statutes which are now on the statute books were not effective in protecting those constitutional rights. The Senators who felt that way are just as sincere as the Senator from South Carolina. I know the senator from South Carolina has a deep conviction and is one of the ablest Members of the Senate. However, I refer to the provisions of section 1 of the 15th amendment of the Constitution, which provides:

The right of citizens of the United States to vote shall not be denied or abridged by the United States or by any State on account of race, color, or previous condition of servitude.

Section 2 of the 15th amendment reads:

The Congress shall have power to enforce this article by appropriate legislation.

Both sections point up the fundamental constitutional right of American citizens and clearly underscore the fact that Congress not only has the right, but the responsibility in this field.

. . . .

Mr. JOHNSON of Texas. Mr. President, will the Senator from South Carolina yield?

Mr. THURMOND. I yield for a question.

Mr. JOHNSON of Texas. Mr. President, would the Senator from South Carolina be willing to yield to me for the purpose of submitting a unanimous-consent request to the Senate to the effect that when the Senator-elect from Wisconsin appears the telegram of the Governor of the Sate of Wisconsin may be read and the oath be administered by unanimous consent of the Senate, without my field from South Carolina losing the floor thereby, and that his remarks thereafter shall not count as a second speech against, and that this interruption be placed in another portion of the *Record*?

Mr. THURMOND. Mr. President, I yield under those conditions.

Mr. JOHNSON of Texas. Mr. President, I ask unanimous consent that when the Senator-elect from Wisconsin appears in the Chamber the clerk may read the telegram from the Governor of Wisconsin and that the Senate give its consent to the oath being administered to the Senator-elect.

The PRESIDING OFFICER. Is there objection to the unanimous-consent request of the Senator from Texas? The Chair thinks it also includes the provision that the Senator from South Carolina [Mr. Thurmond] shall not lose the floor.

Mr. JOHNSON of Texas. All the conditions enumerated, Mr. President.

Mr. KNOWLAND. Mr. President, reserving the right to object—and, of course, I shall not object—I should like to be associated with the unanimous-consent request made by the distinguished majority leader.

Mr. JOHNSON of Texas. Mr. President, I make the request on behalf of the minority leader and myself. I wish to make it abundantly clear that when the Senator-elect from Wisconsin appears consent will have already been given to his being sworn in after the telegrams have been read; and that the Senator from South Carolina will still retain the floor and will be protected in his right to the floor and in the fact that he has made only one speech on this subject. Also, Mr. President, I request that the interruption be placed in the *Record* at the conclusion of the remarks of the Senator from South Carolina.

The PRESIDING OFFICER. Is there objection? The Chair hears none, and the request is agreed to.

Mr. JOHNSON of Texas. I thank the Senator from South Carolina for yielding.

. . . .

[Mr. THURMOND.] Mr. President, there are many things in this bill. I am not against civil rights, and I am not against civil rights, and I am not against civil rights, and I am not against voting. As I have said, the finest civil rights are those in the Bill of Rights. I am for genuine civil rights, not this so-called political civil rights.

Both national parties that are pushing civil rights bills, this right to vote and other bills, are not doing it because they love the Negro. The southern white man does more for the Negro than any other man in any part of the country. This bill is motivated purely by politics. It is a political bill.

We might as well face the facts as they are. Both parties are trying to play to get the Negro vote, and, in some States, if the Negroes vote as a bloc, which they should not do, they are herded to the polls like sheep and voted. If they vote as individual citizens, which they should, this would not occur. But for some reason, both parties think that they are going to vote as a bloc. I do not know how a few leaders do it, or just how it is done. But it is unfortunate, and it is unfair to the Negro, because it takes him out of the category of an individual. It takes away his dignity. It takes away his sanctity as an individual, in which he can take pride in himself, his accomplishments and his race and not be led around like a bull with a ring in his nose. But that is the feeling of both parties in this country. They think they can vote the Negroes in a bloc, and they are making this play on these civil rights bills, so-called. They are not civil rights bills. They are so-called civil rights bills. The politicians are pushing these so-called civil rights bills to make a play and try to get the vote of the Negroes in certain doubtful States.

I have some good friends who are Negroes. I have helped many of them. I have represented them in lawsuits. I have loaned them money. I value the friendship of many Negroes, and I hate to see them treated like they are being treated. I hope that their real leaders, there genuine leaders, who are sincerely interested in them, will wake up some day and inform the members of their race just what is going on.

. . . .

Mr. President, if I have helped to bring home to the American people, the citizens of this Nation, the heartfelt conviction which I hold, namely, that this bill is unwise, unnecessary, and unconstitutional, then I shall have done what I believe to be my duty.

I should like to believe that some have been convinced by my arguments, and that my arguments have been accepted on the basis on which I intended them to be accepted—as arguments against what I am convinced is bad proposed legislation, proposed legislation which never should have been introduced, and which never should be approved by the Senate.

Mr. President, I urge every Member of this body to consider this bill most carefully. I hope the Senate will see fit to kill it.

I expect to vote against the bill. [Laughter.]

Mr. President, I wish to extend my sincerest gratitude to the officials of the Senate, to those who have come in to listen to this debate, to the various Senators who have listened to this debate from time to time; to the clerks and the attaches, and to all who did everything they could to make me as comfortable as possible during the 24 hours and 22 minutes I have spoken.

Mr. President, I am deeply grateful for these courtesies, and again I want to thank the President Officer and the others for their courtesies extended to me, and with this I now give up the floor, and suggest the absence of a quorum.

. . . .

Congressional Record, Senate, 85th Congress, 1st session, Aug. 28–29, 1957, 16263–16456.

148   The Civil Rights Act of 1957

September 9, 1957

The Civil Rights Act of 1957, introduced at the request of the Eisenhower administration, is not as sweeping in scope as the Civil Rights Act of 1964, but it was the important first step toward creating meaningful and much needed civil rights legislation in the United States. This act was the first civil rights legislation passed in eighty years. Earlier efforts in the 1950s to pass civil rights legislation were defeated due to the opposition of southern segregationists in Congress. Once the bill became law it opened the door for further debate and additional legislation on the subject of civil rights.

The most significant part of this bill was the creation of a Civil Rights Commission and a separate division devoted to civil rights within the U.S. Department of Justice. The law was supposed to protect voting rights, but did little to help in this area. The law put the burden of complaints regarding voting problems squarely on the shoulders of individuals, who were required to file formal complaints when they had been discriminated against at the polls.

The difficulty Congress had in passing this legislation highlighted the fact that many key House and Senate committees were in the hands of southern segregationists, who were opposed to the passage of the bill and delayed its consideration (see document 147). Chief among the opponents of civil rights legislation in the House was the Rules Committee chairman, Howard W. Smith (D-Va.), who had a powerful grip on how legislation was handled once it got to the floor of the House. Judge Smith, as he was known, was notorious for delaying legislation. He had his own brand of absentee filibustering—disappearing to his farm in Virginia to delay action on bills. In the Senate, Richard Russell (D-Ga.) and James O. Eastland (D-Miss.) were leaders in opposing civil rights legislation. The key supporter of the legislation in the Senate was Lyndon B. Johnson (D-Texas), to whom the lion's share of credit goes for passage of the bill.

The Civil Rights Act of 1957 passed during mounting national pressure to pass such a law. The 1954 Supreme Court decision in Brown v. Board of Education, *which declared segregation in schools to be unconstitutional, and the boycotts in 1955 of segregated buses in Montgomery, Alabama, helped create a climate of urgency for the passage of this legislation.*

AN ACT

To provide means of further securing and protecting the civil rights of persons within the jurisdiction of the United States.

Be it enacted by the Senate and House of Representatives of the United States of America in Congress assembled,

Part I—Establishment of the Commission on Civil Rights

SEC. 101. (a) There is created in the executive branch of the Government a Commission on Civil Rights (hereinafter called the "Commission").

(b) The Commission shall be composed of six members who shall be appointed by the President by and with the advice and consent of the Senate. Not more than three of the members shall at any one time be of the same political party.

(c) The President shall designate one of the members of the Commission as Chairman and one as Vice Chairman. The Vice Chairman shall at as Chairman in the absence or disability of the Chairman, or in the event of a vacancy in that office.

(d) Any vacancy in the Commission shall not affect its powers and shall be filled in the same manner, and subject to the same limitation with respect to party affiliations as the original appointment was made.

(e) Four members of the Commission shall constitute a quorum.

Duties of the Commission

SEC. 104. (a) The Commission shall—

(1) investigate allegations in writing under oath or affirmation that certain citizens of the United States are being deprived of their right to vote and have that vote counted by reason of their color, race, religion, or national origin; which writing, under oath or affirmation, shall set forth the facts upon which such beliefs are based;

(2) study and collect information concerning legal developments constituting a denial of equal protection of the laws under the Constitution; and

(3) appraise the laws and policies of the Federal Government with respect to equal protection of the laws under the Constitution.

(b) The Commission shall submit interim reports to the President and to the Congress at such times as either the Commission or the President shall deem desirable, and shall submit to the President and to the Congress a final comprehensive report of its activities, findings, and recommendations not later than two years from the date of the enactment of this Act.

(c) Sixty days after the submission of its final report and recommendations the Commission shall cease to exist.

SEC. 105. (a) There shall be a full-time staff director for the Commission who shall be appointed by the President by and with the advice and consent of the Senate and who shall receive compensation at a rate, to be fixed by the President, not in excess of $22,500 a year. The President shall consult with the Commission before submitting the nomination of any person for appointment to the position of staff director. Within the limitations of its appropriations, the Commission may appoint such other personnel as it deems advisable, in accordance with the civil service and classification laws, and my procure services as authorized by section 15 of the Act of August 2, 1946 (60 Stat. 810; 5 U.S.C. 55a), but at rates for individuals not in excess of $50 per diem.

(b) The Commission shall not accept or utilize services of voluntary or uncompensated personnel, and the term "whoever" as used in paragraph (g) of section 102 hereof shall be construed to mean a person whose services are compensated by the United States.

(c) The Commission may constitute such advisory committees within States composed of citizens of that State and may consult with governors, attorneys general, and other representatives of State and local governments, and private organizations, as it deems advisable.

(d) Members of the Commission, and members of advisory committees constituted pursuant to subsection (c) of this section, shall be exempt from the operation of sections 281, 283, 284, 434, and 1914 of title 18 of the United States Code, and section 190 of the Revised Statutes (5 U.S.C. 99).

(e) All Federal agencies shall cooperate fully with the Commission to the end that it may effectively carry out its functions and duties.

(f) The Commission, or on the authorization of the Commission any subcommittee of two or more members, at least one of whom shall be of each major political party, may, for the purpose of carrying out the provisions of this Act, hold such hearings and act at such times and places as the Commission or such authorized subcommittee may deem advisable. Subpenas for the attendance and testimony of witnesses or the production of written or other matter may be issued in accordance with the rules of the Commission as contained in section 102 (j) and (k) of this Act, over the signature of the Chairman of the Commission or of such subcommittee, and may be served by any person designated by such Chairman.

(g) In case of contumacy or refusal to obey a subpena, any district court of the United States or the United States court of any Territory or possession, or the District Court of the United States for the District of Columbia, within the jurisdiction of which said person guilty of contumacy or refusal to obey is found or resides or transacts business, upon application by the Attorney General of the United States shall have jurisdiction to issue to such person an order requiring such person to appear before the Commission or a subcommittee thereof, there to produce evidence if so ordered, or there to give testimony touching the matter under investigation; and any failure to obey such order of the court may be punished by said court as a contempt thereof.

Appropriations

SEC. 106. There is hereby authorized to be appropriated, out of any money in the Treasury not otherwise appropriated, so much as may be necessary to carry out the provisions of this Act.

Part IV—To Provide Means of Further Securing and Protecting the Right to Vote

SEC. 131. Section 2004 of the Revised Statutes (42 U.S.C. 1971), is amended as follows:

(a) Amend the catch line of said section to read, "Voting rights".

(b) Designate its present text with the subsection symbol "(a)".

(c) Add, immediately following the present text, four new subsections to read as follows:

"(b) No person, whether acting under color of law or otherwise, shall intimidate, threaten, coerce, or attempt to intimidate, threaten or coerce any other person for the purpose of interfering with the right of such other person to vote or to vote as he may choose, or of causing such other person to vote for, or not to vote for, any candidate for the office of President, Vice President, presidential elector, Member of the Senate, or Member of the House of Representatives, Delegates or Commissioners from the Territories or possessions, at any general, special, or primary election held solely or in part for the purpose of selecting any such candidate.

"(c) Whenever any person has engaged or there are reasonable grounds to believe that any person is about to engage in any act or practice which would deprive any other person of any right or privilege secured by subsection (a) or (b), the Attorney General may institute for the United States, or in the name of the United States, a civil action or other proper proceeding for preventive relief, including an application for a permanent or temporary injunction, restraining order, or other order. In any proceeding hereunder the United States shall be liable for costs the same as a private person.

"(d) The district courts of the United States shall have jurisdiction of proceedings instituted pursuant to this section and shall exercise the same without regard to whether the party aggrieved shall have exhausted any administrative or other remedies that may be provided by law.

"(e) Any person cited for an alleged contempt under this Act shall be allowed to make his full defense by counsel learned in the law; and the court before which he is cited or tried, or some judge thereof, shall immediately, upon his request, assign to him such counsel, not exceeding two, as he may desire, who shall have free access to him at all reasonable hours. He shall be allowed, in his defense to make any proof that he can produce by lawful witnesses, and shall have the like process of the court to compel his witnesses to appear at his trial or hearing, as is usually granted to compel witnesses to appear on behalf of the

prosecution. If such person shall be found by the court to be financially unable to provide for such counsel, it shall be the duty of the court to provide such counsel."

. . . .

Statutes at Large, 71 (1957), 85th Congress, 1st session, Sept. 9, 1957, 634–638.

149   Creation of the House Committee on Science and Astronautics and the Senate Committee on Aeronautical and Space Sciences

July 21 and 24, 1958

The Constitution of the United States only uses the word science *on one occasion, in Article I, Section 8, Clause 8, where it states Congress has the power to* "promote the Progress of Science and useful Arts, by securing for limited Times to Authors and Inventors the exclusive Right to heir respective Writings and Discoveries. . . ." *But it was clearly understood that it was within the power of Congress to address the issues of technology and science. Congress regularly dealt with scientific matters in the nineteenth century, often through military activities and research. In the post-World War II era, science and technology have become major concerns of Congress, as exemplified by the Atomic Energy Act of 1946 (see document 136) and the creation of the National Science Foundation in 1950.*

The creation of standing House and Senate committees to address the technical and scientific issues related to the exploration of outer space was dramatically spurred by the Soviet Union's launching of a small satellite know as Sputnik I *on October 4, 1957. The fact that the Soviet Union beat the United States into space with the first artificial satellite galvanized the United States into action like few single events in American history. Members of Congress and their military advisers feared that the United States could be attacked with powerful rockets capable of launching satellites into space. Congress passed the National Defense Education Act in 1958 to encourage scientific research and training in colleges. It created the National Aeronautic and Space Administration (NASA) in 1958, and three years later President John F. Kennedy challenged the nation to put a man on the moon before the end of the 1960s.*

Within days of one another in July 1958 the House and Senate each created new standing committees to deal with the challenges of space sciences and technology. These committees would play important roles in overseeing the work of NASA and building a space program that would put men on the moon and engage in the ongoing exploration of the universe.

The following excerpts from the Congressional Record *document the efforts in the House and Senate to amend the rules and create new committees to handle space issues. Richard Bolling (D-Mo.) introduced the rules change in the House, stating:* "To pre-

vent duplication of effort it is important that scientific research and development in the field of outer space, and the problems pertaining to the same, be closely coordinated. This can best be done through the establishment of a standing committee having across-the-board jurisdiction in this area which has, in the last few years, assumed great significance." In the Senate the rules change was introduced by Lyndon B. Johnson (D-Texas), who said: "Exploration of space will require a cooperative undertaking unmatched in all previous history. It calls for the mobilizing of tremendous resources—materials, manpower, and brain power."*

[IN THE HOUSE, JULY 21, 1958]

. . . .

Mr. BOLLING. Mr. Speaker, by direction of the Committee on Rules, I call up House Resolution 580 and ask for its immediate consideration.

The Clerk read as follows:

Resolved, That the Rules of the House of Representatives are hereby amended as follows:

Rule X, clause 1, is hereby amended by inserting after (p) the following:

"(q) committee on Science and Astronautics to consist of 25 members."

. . . .

[Mr. BOLLING.] Mr. Speaker, House Resolution 580, reported from the Committee on Rules, amends the rules of the House to provide for the establishment of a new standing legislative committee to be known as the Committee on Science and Astronautics. The committee will consist of 25 members and will have jurisdiction over the exploration and control of outer space and astronautic research and development, including resources, personnel, equipment, and facilities.

The standing committee will take over, and continue, the work started by the House Select Committee on Astronautics and Space Exploration. Certain functions of the Committee on

Interstate and Foreign Commerce and the Armed Services Committee will be transferred to this committee, namely legislation relating to the scientific agencies—the Bureau of Standards, the National Advisory Committee for Aeronautics and the National Science Foundation. The chairman of the Interstate and Foreign Commerce Committee and the Armed Services Committee agree with there proposed transfers. The committee will also cooperate with the Executive in the operation of the Space Agency.

To prevent duplication of effort it is important that scientific research and development in the field of outer space, and the problems pertaining to the same, be closely coordinated. This can best be done through the establishment of a standing committee having across-the-board jurisdiction in this area which has, in the last few years, assumed great significance. I urge the adoption of House Resolution 580.

Mr. Speaker, to the best of my knowledge, there is no opposition to this resolution.

. . . .

[IN THE SENATE, JULY 24, 1958]

. . . .

Mr. JOHNSON of Texas. Mr. President, the resolution creates a Standing Committee on Aeronautical and Space Sciences, similar to the House committee. The resolution was unanimously approved yesterday by the Committee on Rules and Regulations.

The resolution now before the Senate for consideration represents a needed form of legislative organization to meet the challenge of a new universe which is opening before us with startling rapidity.

In the short space of a year, our whole concept of our position in the universe has changed completely. We have discovered that we are no longer bound irrevocably to the earth.

The magnitude of the changes that are before us is evident from the mere fact that it is possible for us to set up this new committee without any significant reduction in the jurisdiction of existing committees of the Congress. We are dealing with a new dimension which brings new and previously unknown responsibilities.

The new committee would have jurisdiction over the newly created National Aeronautics and Space Administration. Its responsibilities would cover aeronautic and space sciences.

It will not, however, have legislative jurisdiction over defense aeronautical and space activities, nor will it have jurisdiction over civil aviation matters except those included in the research aeronautical and space activity which is the responsibility of the new Aeronautics and Space Administration.

The committee would be composed of 15 members. Membership on it would be regarded as a third committee assignment.

Exploration of space will require a cooperative undertaking unmatched in all previous history. It calls for the mobilizing of tremendous resources—materials, manpower, and brain power.

Congress has done many things to launch this venture. We have appropriated money for research. We have appropriated money for development. We have created a new agency to direct and guide the effort.

One more step remains to be taken in this session. It is to provide the mechanism through which Congress itself can play a role.

It is urgent that Congress place itself in such a position, We are dealing with a dimension which will occupy the minds and dominate the lives of men for centuries to come I hope that this resolution will be approved speedily by the Senate.

Congressional Record, House, 85th Congress, 2d session, July 21, 1958, 14513; July 24, 1958, 14857–14858.

150   The Twenty-Third Amendment to the Constitution

Submitted to the States, June 17, 1960; Ratified, April 3, 1961

Congress has the constitutional authority to "exercise exclusive Legislation" regarding the District of Columbia (Article I, Section 8, Clause 17). Since the federal government moved to the District of Columbia in 1800, Congress has yet to give the citizens of the District the same level of voting rights enjoyed by those in the fifty states (see documents 35 and 42 for additional background on the District of Columbia). The Twenty-Third Amendment to the Constitution gave District of Columbia residents the right to vote in presidential elections and provided for electors in the electoral college. The political struggle to get this minimum amount of participation took decades to achieve. In 1960, when Congress finally approved the measure and sent it to the states for ratification, there was considerable opposition from Republicans, who saw the dis-

trict as a solid bastion of the Democratic Party, and from southern Democrats, who were leery of fully enfranchising a large African American population. As measured in the 1960 census, African Americans comprised 54 percent of the total district population. Partisan politics and racism have played major roles in any attempt to expand voting rights and the right to representation for district residents.

Although this amendment was not ratified in time for district citizens to vote in the 1960 elections, it became an issue in the presidential campaign that year. Fortunately, both the Democratic candidate, John F. Kennedy, and the Republican candidate, Richard Nixon, endorsed the amendment. It was ratified quickly by the necessary thirty-eight states, but indicative of the racial un-

dertones in the ratification process, none of the former Confederate states ever ratified this amendment.

The voters of the District of Columbia have consistently and overwhelmingly voted for the Democratic candidate in every presidential election since 1964.

ARTICLE [XXIII.]

SECTION 1. The District constituting the seat of Government of the United States shall appoint in such manner as the Congress may direct:

A number of electors of President and Vice President equal to the whole number of Senators and Representatives in Congress to which the District would be entitled if it were a State, but in no event more than the least populous State; they shall be in addition to those appointed by the States, but they shall be considered, for the purposes of the election of President and Vice President, to be electors appointed by a State; and they shall meet in the District and perform such duties as provided by the twelfth article of amendment.

SEC. 2. The Congress shall have power to enforce this article by appropriate legislation.

The Constitution of the United States of America as Amended, House Doc. 102–188, 102d Congress, 2d session (Washington: Government Printing Office, 1992), 23.

151 A Joint Meeting of Congress to Honor Astronaut John H. Glenn Jr.

February 26, 1962

Following the Soviet Union's successful launch of the first artificial satellite in 1957, the United States moved quickly to address the issues of technology and science (see document 149). During the 1960s the world would witness one of the most remarkable scientific and technical feats ever undertaken—a massive program to send human beings to the moon and return them safely. Congress played a key role in creating the National Aeronautic and Space Administration (NASA), which conducted the space program, and Congress also created its own committees to oversee and fund the space program.

The "space race" with the Soviet Union became intense following the launch of Sputnik I. It became apparent that this tiny satellite was not all the Soviets were capable of launching. On November 3, 1958, the Soviets placed a dog into earth orbit. It was the first living creature to venture into space. On April 12, 1961, the Soviet Union beat the United States in the race to place a human being in orbit, when Major Yuri A. Gagarin orbited the earth for two hours in a five-ton capsule and returned safely.

The first U.S. manned spaceflight occurred on May 5, 1961, when Project Mercury astronaut Alan B. Shepard Jr. flew a suborbital flight that lasted about fifteen minutes. While this closed the gap in the space race, the United States was still behind Soviet accomplishments in space. Later that same month President John F. Kennedy challenged Congress and the nation to send a man to the moon and return him safely before the end of the decade. On February 20, 1962, John Glenn Jr. became the first American to complete an orbital flight in his Project Mercury capsule named Friendship 7. He circled the earth three times in a flight that lasted about five hours. While still behind in the space race, the United States celebrated John Glenn's flight as a great triumph and embraced him as a national hero for his exploits. He was honored with an appearance before a joint meeting of Congress and appeared in a number of ticker tape parades. The other Mercury astronauts were also present at the joint meeting of Congress, except for one, Gordon Cooper, who was returning from a NASA tracking station in Australia at the time of the joint meeting.

John Glenn, a Marine Corps fighter pilot in World War II and the Korean conflict, was one of the original group of astronauts, joining in 1959. He retired as an astronaut in 1964. In 1974 he was elected to the U.S. Senate as a Democrat from the state of Ohio and was reelected three times. In 1997 he announced his intentions to retire from the Senate at the end of his term in 1998 and to return to space. At the age of seventy-seven he became the oldest man in space when he served as a payload specialist on the space shuttle Discovery, launched October 29, 1998.

At 12 o'clock and 53 minutes P.M., the Doorkeeper announced the President pro tempore and Members of the U.S. Senate who entered the Hall of the House of Representatives, the President pro tempore taking the chair at the right of the Speaker, and the Members of the Senate the seats reserved for them.

The SPEAKER. On the part of the House the Chair appoints as members of the committee to escort Lieutenant Colonel Glenn into the Chamber, the gentleman from Oklahoma [Mr. Albert], the gentleman from Louisiana [Mr. Boggs], the gentleman from Georgia [Mr. Vinson], the gentleman from California [Mr. George P. Miller], the gentleman from Indiana [Mr. Halleck], the gentleman from Illinois [Mr. Arends], and the gentleman from Massachusetts [Mr. Martin].

The PRESIDENT PRO TEMPORE. On the part of the Senate the Chair appoints as members of the committee of escort the Senator from Montana [Mr. Mansfield], the Senator from Georgia [Mr. Russell], the Senator from Oklahoma [Mr. Kerr], the Senator from Arkansas [Mr. Fulbright], the Senator from Illinois [Mr. Dirksen], the Senator from Massachusetts [Mr. Saltonstall], the Senator from Wisconsin [Mr. Wiley], and the Senator from California [Mr. Kuchel].

The Doorkeepers announced the ambassadors, ministers, and charges d'affaires of foreign governments.

The ambassadors, ministers, and charges d'affaires of foreign governments entered the Hall of the House of Representatives and took the seats reserved for them.

The Doorkeeper announced the Chief Justice of the United States and the Associate Justices of the Supreme Court.

The Chief Justice of the United States and the Associate Justices of the Supreme Court entered the Hall of the House of Representatives and took the seats reserved for them in front of the Speaker's rostrum.

At 1 o'clock and 6 minutes P.M., Lieutenant Colonel Glenn's fellow astronauts, Virgil I. Grissom, Alan B. Shepard, Jr., Donald K. Slayton, Malcom S. Carpenter, and Walter M. Schirra entered the Chamber. [Applause, the Members rising.]

The Doorkeeper announced the Cabinet of the President of the United States.

The members of the Cabinet of the President of the United States entered the Hall of the House of Representatives and took the seats reserved for them in front of the Speaker's rostrum.

At 1 o'clock and 8 minutes P.M., the Vice President entered the Chamber and assumed the chair vacated by the President pro tempore at the right of the Speaker.

At 1 o'clock and 13 minutes P.M., the Doorkeeper announced Lieutenant Colonel Glenn.

Lieutenant Colonel Glenn, accompanied by the committee of escort, entered the Chamber and stood at the Clerk's desk. [Applause, the Members rising.]

The SPEAKER. Members of the Congress, it is a privilege, and I deem it a high honor to present to you a brave, a courageous American, a hero in World War II and in the Korean conflict, who recently in a most notable manner added glory and prestige to our country, the first U.S. astronaut to have achieved orbital flight, Lt. Col. John H. Glenn, Jr., U.S. Marine Corps. [Applause, the Members rising.]

Lieutenant Colonel GLENN. Mr. Speaker, Mr. President, Members of the Congress, I am only too aware of the tremendous honor that is being shown us at this joint meeting of the Congress today. When I think of past meetings that involved heads of state and equally notable persons, I can only say I am most humble to know that you consider our efforts to be in the same class.

This has been a great experience for all of us present and for all Americans, of course, and I am certainly glad to see that pride in our country and its accomplishments is not a thing of the past. [Applause.]

I still get a hard-to-define feeling inside when the flag goes by—and I know that all of you do, too. Today as we rode up Pennsylvania Avenue from the White House and saw the tremendous outpouring of feeling on the part of so many thousands of our people I got this same feeling all over again. Let us hope that none of us ever loses it. [Applause.]

The flight of *Friendship 7* on February 20 involved much more than one man in the spacecraft in orbit. [Applause.] I

would like to have my parents stand up, please. [Mr. and Mrs. John Glenn, Sr., stood and received the rising applause of the Members.]

My wife's mother and Dr. Castor. [Dr. and Mrs. H. W. Castor stood and received the rising applause of the Members.]

My son and daughter, David and Carolyn. [David and Carolyn Glenn rose and received the rising applause of the Members.]

And the real rock in my family, my wife, Annie. [Mrs. John H. Glenn, Jr., rose and received the applause of the Members.]

There are many more people, of course, involved in our flight in *Friendship 7;* many more things involved, as well as people. There was the vision of Congress that established this national program of space exploration. Beyond that, many thousands of people were involved, civilian contractors and many subcontractors in many different fields; many elements— civilian, civil service, and military, all blending their efforts toward a common goal.

To even attempt to give proper credit to all the individuals on this team effort would be impossible. But let me say that I have never seen a more sincere, dedicated, and hard-working group of people in my life. [Applause.]

From the original vision of the Congress to consummation of this orbital flight has been just over 3 years. This, in itself, states eloquently the case for the hard word and devotion of the entire Mercury team. This has not been just another job. It has been a dedicated labor such as I have not seen before. It has involved a cross cut of American endeavor with many different disciplines cooperating toward a common objective.

Friendship 7 is just another beginning, a successful experiment. It is another plateau in our step-by-step program of increasingly ambitious flights. The earlier flights of Alan Shepard and Gus Grissom were steppingstones toward *Friendship 7.* My flight in the *Friendship 7* spacecraft will, in turn, provide additional information for use in striving toward future flights that some of the other gentlemen you see here will take part in. [Applause.]

Scott Carpenter here, who was my backup on this flight; Walt Schirra, Deek Slayton, and one missing member, who is still on his way back from Australia, where he was on the tracking station, Gordon Cooper. A lot of direction is necessary for a project such as this, and the Director of Project Mercury since its inception has been Dr. Robert Gilruth, who certainly deserves a hand here. [Applause.]

I have been trying to introduce Walt Williams. I do not see him here. There he is up in the corner. [Applause.]

He was the Associate Director of Mercury, and was in the unenviable position of being Operational Director. He is a character, no matter how you look at him. He says hold the countdown, and one thing and another.

With all the experience we have had so far, where does this leave us?

There are the building blocks upon which we shall build much more ambitious and more productive portions of the program.

As was to be expected, not everything worked perfectly on my flight. We may well need to make changes—and these will be tried out on subsequent 3-orbit flights, later this year, to be followed by 18-orbit, 24-hour missions.

Beyond that, we look forward to Project Gemini—a two-man orbital vehicle with greatly increased capability for advanced experiments. There will be additional rendezvous in space, technical and scientific observations—then, Apollo orbital, circumlunar and finally, lunar landing flights.

What did we learn from the *Friendship 7* flight that will help us attain these objectives?

Some specific items have already been covered briefly in the news reports. And I think it is of more than passing interest to all of us that information attained from these flights is readily available to all nations of the world. [Applause.]

The launch itself was conducted openly and with the news media representatives from around the world in attendance. [Applause.] Complete information is released as it is evaluated and validated. This is certainly in sharp contrast with similar programs conducted elsewhere in the world and elevates the peaceful intent of our program. [Applause.]

Data from the *Friendship 7* flight is still being analyzed. Certainly, much more information will be added to our storehouse of knowledge.

But these things we do know. The Mercury spacecraft and systems design concepts are sound and have now been verified during manned flight. We also proved that man can operate intelligently in space and can adapt rapidly to this new environment.

Zero g., or weightlessness—at least for this period of time—appears to be no problem. As a matter of fact, lack of gravity is a rather fascinating thing.

Objects within the cockpit can be parked in midair. For example, at one time during the flight, I was using a hand held camera. Another system needed attention; so it seemed quite natural to let go of the camera, take care of the other chore in the spacecraft, then reach out, grasp the camera and go back about my business.

It is a real fascinating feeling, needless to say.

There seemed to be little sensation of speed although the craft was traveling at about 5 miles per second—a speed that I too find difficult to comprehend.

In addition to closely monitoring onboard systems, we were able to make numerous outside observations.

The view from that altitude defies description.

The horizon colors are brilliant and sunsets are spectacular. It is hard to beat a day in which you are permitted the luxury of seeing four sunsets.

I think after all of our talk of space, this morning coming up from Florida on the plane with President Kennedy, we had the opportunity to meet Mrs. Kennedy and Caroline before we took off. I think Caroline really cut us down to size and put us back in the proper position. She looked up, upon being introduced, and said, "Where's the monkey?" [Laughter.]

And I did not get a banana pellet on the whole ride.

Our efforts today and what we have done so far are but small building blocks in a huge pyramid to come.

But questions are sometimes raised regarding the immediate payoffs from our efforts. What benefits are we gaining from the money spent? The real benefits we probably cannot even detail. They are probably not even known to man today. But exploration and the pursuit of knowledge have always paid dividends in the long run—usually far greater than anything expected at the outset. [Applause.]

The story has been told of Disraeli, Prime Minister of England at the time, visiting the laboratory of Faraday, one of the early experimenters with basic electrical principles. After viewing various demonstrations of electrical phenomena, Disraeli asked, "But of what possible use is it?" Faraday replied, "Mister Prime Minister, what good is a baby?"

That is the stage of development in our program today—in its infancy. And it indicates a much broader potential impact, of course, than even the discovery of electricity did. We are just probing the surface of the greatest advancements in man's knowledge of his surroundings that has ever been made, I feel. There are benefits to science across the board. Any major effort such as this results in research by so many different specialties that it is hard to even envision the benefits that will accrue in many fields.

Knowledge begets knowledge. The more I see, the more impressed I am—not with how much we know—but with how tremendous the areas are that are as yet unexplored.

Exploration, knowledge, and achievement are good only insofar as we apply them to our future actions. Progress never stops. We are now on the verge of a new era, I feel.

Today, I know that I seem to be standing alone on this great platform—just as I seemed to be alone in the cockpit of the *Friendship 7* spacecraft. But I am not. There were with me then—and with me now—thousands of Americans and many hundreds of citizens of many countries around the world who contributed to this truly international undertaking voluntarily and in a spirit of cooperation and understanding.

On behalf of all of those people, I would like to express my and their heartfelt thanks for the honors you have bestowed upon us here today.

We are all proud to have been privileged to be part of this effort, to represent our country as we have. As our knowledge of the universe in which we live increases, may God grant us the wisdom and guidance to use it wisely.

Thank you, gentlemen. [Applause, the Members rising.]

At 1 o'clock and 32 minutes P.M., Lieutenant Colonel Glenn, accompanied by the committee of escort, retired from the Hall of the House of Representatives.

. . . .

Congressional Record, House, 87th Congress, 2d session, Feb. 26, 1962, 2901–2903.

152   Senator Everett Dirksen on the Civil Rights Act of 1964

June 10, 1964

Senator Everett McKinley Dirksen (R-Ill.) played a key role in passage of the Civil Rights Act of 1964, both behind the scenes in negotiations and on the floor of the Senate. Using the words of the French writer Victor Hugo, Dirksen told his senate colleagues that "stronger than all the armies is an idea whose time has come." His address in the Senate on June 10, 1964, was the finest of his career and a landmark in terms of its eloquence and effectiveness in helping to break the Senate filibuster that was blocking passage of this major civil rights bill.

Passage of the Civil Rights Act of 1964, the most comprehensive and sweeping civil rights legislation in almost a hundred years, was not an easy matter. Proposed by President John F. Kennedy in early 1963, the bill suffered delays in both the House and Senate. In addition to opposition from southern Democrats, many of whom opposed integration, some Republicans in the Senate opposed the bill because of its provisions regarding federal enforcement of the law.

The bill's passage came in the midst of many public demonstrations in favor of a civil rights bill. The most notable of these occurred on August 28, 1963, when Dr. Martin Luther King Jr. lead a massive March on Washington, backed by major civil rights organizations, religious groups, and labor organizations. When President Kennedy was assassinated on November 22, 1963, the new president, Lyndon B. Johnson, urged passage of the bill to help complete President Kennedy's legacy. The House finally passed it in February 1964, shifting the fight to the Senate.

Everett Dirksen, the Senate minority leader and a longtime supporter of civil rights, was key to getting Republican votes in favor of the bill. He negotiated behind the scenes with Senate Majority Leader Mike Mansfield (D-Mont.) and Senator Hubert Humphrey (D-Minn.) as well as with Justice Department officials and the White House to come up with a bill that Republicans could support in the Senate. He managed to amend the House version of the bill by shifting the burden of enforcement of the bill from federal to state and local authorities in most instances. While this change won over some Republicans, especially in the Midwest, southern Democrats remained opposed to the bill and continued to filibuster against its passage.

In order to break the logjam of opposition in the Senate and end the filibuster, supporters of the bill had to garner enough votes to invoke cloture, the Senate parliamentary process that requires a vote of two-thirds of the senators present to end debate and allow the bill to be voted on. On June 10, 1964, Dirksen took the floor to call for an end to the filibuster. Dirksen appealed to his fellow Republicans by reminding them of their party heritage, which began with support of civil rights, but he also appealed to all senators that this was a moral issue whose time had come. He said at the conclusion of his remarks: "Today let us not be found wanting in whatever it takes by way of moral and spiritual substance to face up to the issue and to vote cloture." The speech was timely and moving, delivered in Dirksen's finest oratorical style. The Senate voted to

end the filibuster later the same day as Dirksen's speech. It was the first time cloture had been used successfully on a civil rights bill. After the Civil Rights Act of 1964 passed the Senate, it went back to the House, where the Senate amendments were agreed to. The bill was signed into law by President Johnson on July 2, 1964.

Mr. President, it is a year ago this month that the late President Kennedy sent his civil rights bill and message to the Congress. For two years, we had been chiding him about failure to act in this field. At long last, and after many conferences, it became a reality.

After nine days of hearings before the Senate Judiciary Committee, it was referred to a subcommittee. There it languished and the administration leadership finally decided to await the House bill.

In the House it traveled an equally tortuous road. But at long last, it reached the House floor for action. It was debated for 64 hours; 155 amendments were offered; 34 were approved. On February 10, 1964, it passed the House by a vote of 290 to 130. That was a 65-percent vote.

It was messaged to the Senate on February 17 and reached the Senate calendar on February 26. The motion to take up and consider was made on March 9. That motion was debated for sixteen days and on March 26 by a vote of 67 to 17 it was adopted.

It is now 4 months since it passed the House. It is 3½ months since it came to the Senate calendar. Three months have gone by since the motion to consider was made. We have acted on one intervening motion to send the bill back to the Judiciary Committee and a vote on the jury trial amendment. That has been the extent of our action.

Sharp opinions have developed. Incredible allegations have been made. Extreme views have been asserted. The mail volume has been heavy. The bill has provoked many long-distance telephone calls, many of them late at night or in the small hours of the morning. There has been unrestrained criticism about motives. Thousands of people have come to the Capitol to urge immediate action on an unchanged House bill.

For myself, I have had but one purpose and that was the enactment of a good, workable, equitable, practical bill having due regard for the progress made in the civil rights field at the state and local level.

I am no Johnnie-come-lately in this field. Thirty years ago, in the House of Representatives, I voted on antipoll tax and antilynching measures. Since then, I have sponsored or cosponsored scores of bills dealing with civil rights.

At the outset, I contended that the House bill was imperfect and deficient. That fact is now quite generally conceded. But the debate continued. The number of amendments submitted increased. They now number nearly four hundred. The stalemate continued. A backlog of work piled up. Committees could not function normally. It was an unhappy situation and it was becoming a bit intolerable.

It became increasingly evident that to secure passage of a bill in the Senate would require cloture and a limitation on debate. Senate aversion to cloture is traditional. Only once in thirty-five years has cloture been voted. But the procedure for cloture is a standing rule of the Senate. It grew out of a filibuster against the Armed Ship bill in 1917 and has been part of the standing rules of the Senate for forty-seven years. To argue that cloture is unwarranted or unjustified is to assert that in 1917, the Senate adopted a rule which it did not intend to use when circumstances required or that it was placed in the rulebook only as to be repudiated. It was adopted as an instrument for action when all other efforts failed.

Today the Senate is stalemated in its efforts to enact a civil rights bill, one version of which has already been approved by the House by a vote of more than 2 to 1. That the Senate wishes to act on a civil rights bill can be divined from the fact that the motion to take up was adopted by a vote of 67 to 17.

There are many reasons why cloture should be invoked and a good civil rights measure enacted.

First. It is said that on the night he died, Victor Hugo wrote in his diary, substantially this sentiment:

Stronger than all the armies is an idea whose time has come.

The time has come for equality of opportunity in sharing in government, in education, and in employment. It will not be stayed or denied. It is here.

The problem began when the Constitution makers permitted the importation of persons to continue for another twenty years. That problem was to generate the fury of civil strife seventy-five years later. Out of it was to come the Thirteenth Amendment ending servitude, the Fourteenth Amendment to provide equal protection of the laws and dual citizenship, the Fifteenth Amendment to prohibit government from abridging the right to vote.

Other factors had an impact. Two and three-quarter million young Negroes served in World Wars I, II, and Korea. Some won the Congressional Medal of Honor and the Distinguished Service Cross. Today they are fathers and grandfathers. They brought back impressions from countries where no discrimination existed. These impressions have been transmitted to children and grandchildren. Meanwhile, hundreds of thousands of colored have become teachers and professors, doctors and dentists, engineers and architects, artists and actors, musicians and technicians. They have become status minded. They have sensed inequality. They are prepared to make the issue. They feel that the time has come for the idea of equal opportunity. To enact the pending measure by invoking cloture is imperative.

Second. Years ago, a professor who thought he had developed an uncontrovertible scientific premise submitted it to his faculty associates. Quickly they picked it apart. In agony he cried out, "Is nothing eternal?" To this one of his associates replied, "Nothing is eternal except change."

Since the act of 1875 on public accommodations and the Supreme Court decision of 1883 which struck it down, America has changed. The population then was 45 million. Today it is 190 million. In the Pledge of Allegiance to the Flag we intone, "One nation, under God." And so it is. It is an integrated nation. Air, rail, and highway transportation make it so. A common language makes it so. A tax pattern which applies equally to white and nonwhite makes it so. Literacy makes it so. The mobility provided by eighty million autos makes it so. The accommodations laws in thirty-four states and the District of Columbia makes it so. The fair employment practice laws in thirty states make it so. Yes, our land has changed since the Supreme Court decision of 1883.

As Lincoln once observed:

The occasion is piled high with difficulty and we must rise with the occasion. As our case is new, so we must think anew and act anew. We must first disenthrall ourselves and then we shall save the Union.

To my friends from the South, I would refresh you on the words of a great Georgian named Henry W. Grady. On December 22, 1886, he was asked to respond to a toast to the new South at the New England society dinner. His words were dramatic and explosive. He began his toast by saying:

There was a South of slavery and secession—that South is dead. There is a South of union and freedom—that South thank God is living, breathing, growing every hour.

America grows. America changes. And on the civil rights issue we must rise with the occasion. That calls for cloture and for the enactment of a civil rights bill.

Third. There is another reason—our covenant with the people. For many years, each political party has given major consideration to a civil rights plank in its platform. Go back and reexamine our pledges to the country as we sought the suffrage of the people and for a grant of authority to manage and direct their affairs. Were these pledges so much campaign stuff or did we mean it? Were these promises on civil rights but idle words for vote-getting purposes or were they a covenant meant to be kept? If all this was mere pretense, let us confess the sin of hypocrisy now and vow not to delude the people again.

To you, my Republican colleagues, let me refresh you on the words of a great American. His name is Herbert Hoover. In his day he was reviled and maligned. He was castigated and calumniated. But today his views and his judgment stand vindicated at the bar of history. In 1952 he received a volcanic welcome as he appeared before our national convention in Chicago. On that occasion he commented on the Whig party, predecessor of the Republican party, and said:

The Whig party temporized, compromised upon the issue of freedom for the Negro. That party disappeared. It deserved to disappear. Shall the Republican party receive or deserve any better fate if it compromises upon the issue of freedom for all men?

To those who have charged me with doing a disservice to my party because of my interest in the enactment of a good civil rights bill—and there have been a good many who have made that charge—I can only say that our party found its faith in the Declaration of Independence in which a great Democrat, Jefferson by name, wrote the flaming words:

We hold these truths to be self-evident that all men are created equal.

That has been the living faith of our party. Do we forsake this article of faith, now that equality's time has come or do we stand up for it and insure the survival of our party and its ultimate victory. There is no substitute for a basic and righteous idea. We have a duty—a firm duty—to use the instruments at hand—namely, the cloture rule—to bring about the enactment of a good civil rights bill.

Fourth. There is another reason why we dare not temporize with the issue which is before us. It is essentially moral in character. It must be resolved. It will not go away. Its time has come. Nor is it the first time in our history that an issue with moral connotations and implications has swept away the resistance, the fulminations, the legalistic speeches, the ardent but dubious arguments, the lamentations and the thought patterns of an earlier generation and pushed forward to fruition.

More than sixty years ago came the first efforts to secure federal pure food and drug legislation. The speeches made on this floor against this intrusion of federal power sound fantastically incredible today. But it would not be stayed. Its time had come and since its enactment, it has been expanded and strengthened in nearly every Congress.

When the first efforts were made to ban the shipment of goods in interstate commerce made with child labor, it was regarded as quite absurd. But all the trenchant editorials, the bitter speeches, the noisy onslaughts were swept aside as this limitation on the shipment of goods made with sweated child labor moved on to fulfillment. Its time had come.

More than eighty years ago came the first efforts to establish a civil service and merit system to cover federal employees. The proposal was ridiculed and drenched with sarcasm. Some of the sharpest attacks on the proposal were made on this very Senate floor. But the bullet fired by a disappointed office seeker in 1880 which took President Garfield's life was the instrument of destiny which placed the Pendleton Act on the federal statute books in 1883. It was an idea whose time had come.

When the New York legislature placed a limit of ten hours per day and six days per week upon the bakery workers in that State, this act was struck down by the U.S. Supreme Court. But in due time came the eight-hour day and the forty-hour week and how broadly accepted this concept is today. Its time had come.

More than sixty years ago, the elder La Follette thundered against the election of U.S. senators by the state legislatures. The cry was to get back to the people and to first principles. On this Senate floor, senators sneered at his efforts and even left the chamber to show their contempt. But fifty years ago, the Constitution was amended to provide for the direct election of senators. Its time had come.

Ninety-five years ago came the first endeavor to remove the limitation on sex in the exercise of the franchise. The comments made in those early days sound unbelievably ludicrous. But on and on went the effort and became the Nineteenth Amendment to the Constitution. Its time had come.

When the eminent Joseph Choate appeared before the Supreme Court to assert that a federal income tax statute was unconstitutional and communistic, the Court struck down the work of Congress. Just twenty years later in 1913 the power of Congress to lay and collect taxes on incomes became the Sixteenth Amendment to the Constitution itself.

These are but some of the things touching closely the affairs of the people which were met with stout resistance, with shrill and strident cries of radicalism, with strained legalisms, with anguished entreaties that the foundations of the Republic were being rocked. But an inexorable moral force which operates in the domain of human affairs swept these efforts aside and today they are accepted as parts of the social, economic and political fabric of America.

Pending before us is another moral issue. Basically it deals with equality of opportunity in exercising the franchise, in securing an education, in making a livelihood, in enjoying the mantle of protection of the law. It has been a long, hard furrow and each generation must plow its share. Progress was made in 1957 and 1960. But the furrow does not end there. It requires the implementation provided by the substitute measure which is before us. And to secure that implementation requires cloture.

Let me add one thought to these observations. Today is an anniversary. It is in fact the one hundredth anniversary of the nomination of Abraham Lincoln for a second term for the presidency on the Republican ticket. Two documents became the blueprints for his life and his conduct. The first was the Declaration of Independence which proclaimed the doctrine that all men are created equal. The second was the Constitution, the preamble to which began with the words:

We, the people ... do ordain and establish this Constitution for the United States of America.

These were the articles of his superb and unquenchable faith. Nowhere and at no time did he more nobly reaffirm that faith than at Gettysburg 101 years ago when he spoke of "a new nation, conceived in liberty and dedicated to the proposition that all men are created equal."

It is to take us further down that road that a bill is pending before us. We have a duty to get that job done. To do it will require cloture and a limitation on debate as provided by a standing rule of the Senate which has been in being for nearly fifty years. I trust we shall not fail in that duty.

That, from a great Republican, thinking in the frame of equality of opportunity—and that is all that is involved in this bill.

To those who have charged me with doing a disservice to my party—and there have been many—I can only say that our party found its faith in the Declaration of Independence, which was penned by a great Democrat, Thomas Jefferson by name. There he wrote the great words:

We hold these truths to be self-evident, that all men are created equal.

That has been the living faith of our party. Do we forsake this article of faith, now that the time for our decision has come?

There is no substitute for a basic ideal. We have a firm duty to use the instrument at hand; namely, the cloture rule, to bring about the enactment of a good civil rights bill.

I appeal to all senators. We are confronted with a moral issue. Today let us not be found wanting in whatever it takes by way of moral and spiritual substance to face up to the issue and to vote cloture.

Congressional Record, Senate, 88th Congress, 2d session, June 10, 1964, 13319–13320.

153 Senator Wayne Morse Opposes the Tonkin Gulf Resolution

August 5, 1964

The United States' long war against North Vietnam was conducted without the benefit of a formal declaration of war. But when Congress passed the Southeast Asia Resolution, better known as the Tonkin Gulf Resolution, on August 7, 1964, it gave President Lyndon Johnson broad powers to conduct war even with the absence of a formal declaration. This resolution was extremely popular at the time of its passage. Two identical versions of the resolution—S.J. Res. 189 and H.J. Res. 1145—circulated before both bodies passed H.J. Res. 1145 and sent it to President Johnson, who signed it into law on August 10. The House passed it by a vote of 416–0. It had overwhelming support in the Senate, where it passed 88–2. The only two senators who voted against the resolution were Wayne Morse (D-Ore.) and Ernest Gruening (D-Alaska).

Morse, an often cantankerous and fiercely independent senator, was a stickler for constitutional authority. He had spoken out often against the rise of presidential power in relation to the powers of Congress. He was against the United States unilaterally engaging in war in Southeast Asia, preferring to see the conflict settled through negotiations and the involvement of the United Nations. Morse was a staunch defender of the constitutional principle that only Congress could declare war. On August 5, 1964, one day after the United States launched a series of major air strikes against North Vietnam, Morse found himself in a tiny minority when he opposed giving the president authority to fight a wider war in Southeast Asia. His speech in opposition to the Tonkin Gulf Resolution is a landmark of Congress, not because his argument convinced his colleagues to change their votes. Quite the contrary. It is a landmark because it spoke to important issues of presidential and congressional power. At the time it was one lone speech of opposition to a war what would eventually unfold as a great tragedy in American foreign policy, a war that seriously divided the people of the United States and eventually tarnished the reputation of President Johnson.

President Johnson was looking for a way to win reelection to the presidency in 1964. Part of his strategy, and that of his top aides, was to find a way to take decisive action in the war in Vietnam and undermine Republican criticism that the Democratic Party was soft on Communism and indecisive in handling the situation in Southeast Asia. His aides suggested as early as February 1964 that he needed a resolution from Congress to make it possible for

him to conduct a more aggressive war against North Vietnam. By May 1964 the resolution calling for congressional support to commit U.S. troops in any Southeast Asian nation that was threatened by Communist aggression had been drafted and was awaiting the go-ahead from the president before it was submitted to Congress.

The event that precipitated the introduction of the resolution occurred in the Tonkin Gulf, the open waters bordering Vietnam. A U.S. destroyer, the Maddox, was ordered into the gulf to conduct electronic surveillance of North Vietnamese military activities. The North Vietnamese formally protested the activities of the Maddox, but the Maddox stayed in the gulf, supposedly in international waters, continuing to gather intelligence. On August 2, 1964, North Vietnamese gun boats attacked the Maddox in a brief skirmish that did no harm to the destroyer and resulted in the sinking or damaging of three of the gun boats. The commander of the Maddox claimed he was always in international waters, while the North Vietnamese claimed they were acting in self-defense and that the Maddox was in their territorial water. While the circumstances and details of this encounter remained murky, subsequent events in the Tonkin Gulf on August 4, when it appeared the Maddox may have been attacked a second time, prompted Secretary of War Robert McNamara to recommend retaliation. President Johnson concurred and the United States launched air raids into North Vietnam. This incident, despite the lack of confirmation of what actually happened in the Tonkin Gulf, was enough to set in motion Johnson's plans to expand the war and take tough action against Communist forces before the fall presidential election. On the evening of August 4, the president spoke to the nation in a televised broadcast announcing the action he had taken. The next day in a message to Congress he explained the situation and said: "As President of the United States, I have concluded that I should now ask the Congress, on its part, to join in affirming the national determination that all such attacks will be met, and that the United States will continue in its basic policy of assisting the free nations of the area to defend their freedom."

The president's message to Congress, reprinted below, was read on the floor of the Senate just before Senator Morse rose to voice his objections. But it was too late. The newspaper reports and public reaction to a U.S. destroyer being attacked by a Communist nation, and the swift and decisive response to launch air strikes, met with public approval. Johnson had found the incident and the right timing to ensure that Congress would support him. Following his remarks on August 5, Morse continued to object privately in a meeting with Secretary McNamara that whatever happened in the Tonkin Gulf, the United States was implicated—we were not just innocent bystanders attacked without provocation. In Michael Beschloss's edited book, Taking Charge: The Johnson White House Tapes, 1963–64 *(Simon and Schuster, 1997), there is a taped conversation between McNamara and President Johnson on August 6, 1964, when McNamara told the President: "I had a hell of a time with Morse. . . . I think I finally shut him up." Three decades later, in* In Retrospect: The Tragedy and Lessons of Vietnam *(Time Books, 1995), his own book about the Vietnam War and his role in it, McNamara admitted that the incidents in the Tonkin Gulf in August 1964, which he did not fully understand at the time, were used as an excuse and an opportunity to escalate the war—something he had in mind all along. In his address to the Senate, Morse said, "I stand on this issue as I have stood before in the Senate, perfectly willing to take the judgment of history as to the merits of my cause."*

TO PROMOTE THE MAINTENANCE OF INTERNATIONAL PEACE AND SECURITY IN SOUTHEAST ASIA—MESSAGE FROM THE PRESIDENT. . . .

Mr. HUMPHREY. Mr. President, did I correctly understand there is a message from the President of the United States at the desk?

The PRESIDING OFFICER. The Senator is correct.

Mr. HUMPHREY. I believe it is of sufficient importance, since it relates to a grave international situation, that it be read.

Mr. MORSE. I agree with the Senator.

The PRESIDING OFFICER. The message from the President of the United States will be read.

The Legislative clerk read the message, as follows:

To the Congress of the United States:

Last night I announced to the American people that the North Vietnamese regime had conducted further deliberate attacks against U.S. naval vessels operating in international waters, and that I had therefore directed air action against gunboats and supporting facilities used in these hostile operations. This air action has now been carried out with substantial damage to the boats and facilities. Two U.S. aircraft were lost in the action.

After consultation with the leaders of both parties in the Congress, I further announced a decision to ask Congress for a resolution expressing the unity and determination of the United States in supporting freedom and in protecting peace in southeast Asia.

These latest actions of the North Vietnamese regime have given a new and grave turn to the already serious situation in southeast Asia. Our commitments in that area are well known to the Congress. They were first made in 1954 by President Eisenhower. They were further defined in the Southeast Asia Collective Defense Treaty approved by the Senate in February 1955.

This treaty with its accompanying protocol obligates the United States and other members to act in accordance with their constitutional processes to meet Communist aggression against any of the parties or protocol states.

Our policy is southeast Asia has been consistent and unchanged since 1954. I summarized it on June 2 in four simple propositions:

1. America keeps her word. Here as elsewhere, we must and shall honor our commitments.

2. The issue is the future of southeast Asia as a whole. A threat to any nation in that region is a threat to all, and a threat to us.

3. Our purpose is peace. We have no military, political, or territorial ambitions in the area.

4. This is not just a jungle war, but a struggle for freedom on every front of human activity. Our military and economic assistance to South Vietnam and Laos in particular has the purpose of helping these countries to repel aggression and strengthen their independence.

The threat to the free nations of southeast Asia has been long clear. The North Vietnamese regime has constantly sought to take over South Vietnam and Laos. This Communist regime has violated the Geneva accords for Vietnam. It has systematically conducted a campaign of subversion, which includes the direction, training, and supply of personnel and arms for the conduct of guerrilla warfare in South Vietnamese territory. In Laos, the North Vietnamese regime has maintained military forces, used Laotian territory for infiltration into South Vietnam, and most recently carried out combat operations—all in direct violation of the Geneva agreements of 1962.

In recent months, the actions of the North Vietnamese regime have become steadily more threatening. In May, following new acts of Communist aggression in Laos, the United States undertook reconnaissance flights over Laotian territory, at the request of the Government of Laos. These flights had the essential mission of determining the situation in territory where Communist forces were preventing inspection by the International Control Commission. When the Communists attacked these aircraft, I responded by furnishing escort fighters with instructions to fire when fired upon. Thus, these latest North Vietnamese attacks on our naval vessels are not the first direct attack on Armed Forces of the United States.

As President of the United States, I have concluded that I should now ask the Congress, on its part, to join in affirming the national determination that all such attacks will be met, and that the United States will continue in its basic policy of assisting the free nations of the area to defend their freedom.

As I have repeatedly made clear, the United States intends no rashness, and seeks no wider war. We must make it clear to all that the United States is united in its determination to bring about the end of Communist subversion and aggression in the area. We seek the full and effective restoration of the international agreements signed in Geneva in 1954, with respect to South Vietnam, and again at Geneva in 1962, with respect to Laos.

I recommend a resolution expressing the support of the Congress for all necessary action to protect our Armed Forces and to assist nations covered by the SEATO Treaty. At the same time, I assure the Congress that we shall continue readily to explore any avenues of political solution that will effectively guarantee the removal of Communist subversion and the preservation of the independence of the nations of the area.

The resolution could well be based upon similar resolutions enacted by the Congress in the past—to meet the threat to Formosa in 1955, to meet the threat to the Middle East in 1957, and to meet the threat to Cuba in 1962. It could state in the simplest terms the resolve and support of the Congress for action to deal appropriately with attacks against our Armed Forces and to defend freedom and preserve peace in southeast Asia in accordance with the obligations of the United States under the Southeast Asia Treaty. I urge the Congress to enact such a resolution promptly and thus to give convincing evidence to the aggressive Communist nations, and to the world as a whole, that our policy in southeast Asia will be carried forward—and that the peace and security of the area will be preserved.

The events of this week would in any event have made the passage of a congressional resolution essential. But there is an additional reason for doing so at a time when we are entering on 3 months of political campaigning. Hostile nations must understand that in such a period the United States will continue to protect its national interests, and that in these matters there is no division among us.

LYNDON B. JOHNSON

The White House, *August 5, 1964.*

Mr. FULBRIGHT. Mr. President, I send to the desk a joint resolution on behalf of myself, the Senator from Iowa [Mr. Hickenlooper], the Senator from Georgia [Mr. Russell], and the Senator from Massachusetts [Mr. Saltonstall], and ask unanimous consent that it be referred to the Committee on Foreign Relations and the Committee on Armed Services, sitting jointly.

The PRESIDING OFFICER. Without objection, the joint resolution will be received, and referred, as requested.

The joint resolution (S.J. Res. 189) to promote the maintenance of international peace and security in southeast Asia, was received, read twice by its title, and ordered to be referred to the Committees on Foreign Relations and Armed Services, jointly.

Mr. MORSE. Mr. President, I rise to speak in opposition to the joint resolution which has been introduced.

Mr. STENNIS. Mr. President, will the Senator yield to me so that I may request that the joint resolution be read?

Mr. MORSE. I shall be glad to have the joint resolution read.

Mr. STENNIS. Mr. President, may we have order? Will the Chair request the staff, and Senators also, to cease speaking so that we may hear what is going on?

The PRESIDING OFFICER. The Senate will be in order. The resolution will be read.

The joint resolution (S.J. Res. 189) was read, as follows:

Whereas naval units of the Communist regime in Vietnam, in violation of the principles of the Charter of the United Nations and of international law, have deliberately and repeatedly attacked United States naval vessels lawfully present in international waters, and have thereby created a serious threat to international peace;

Whereas these attacks are part of a deliberate and systematic campaign of aggression that the Communist regime in North Vietnam has been waging against its neighbors and the nations joined with them in the collective defense of their freedom;

Whereas the United States is assisting the peoples of southeast Asia to protect their freedom and has no territorial, military or political ambitions in that area, but desires only that these peoples should be left in peace to work out their own destinies in their own way: Now, therefore, be it

Resolved by the Senate and House of Representatives of the United States of America in Congress assembled, That the Congress approves and supports the determination of the President, as Commander in Chief, to take all necessary measures to repel any armed attack against the forces of the United States and to prevent further aggression.

SEC. 2. The United States regards as vital to its national interest and to world peace the maintenance of international peace and security in southeast Asia. Consonant with the Constitution and the Charter of the United Nations and in accordance with its obligations under the Southeast Asia Collective Defense Treaty, the United States is, therefore, prepared, as the President determines, to take all necessary steps, including the use of armed force, to assist any member of protocol state of the Southeast Asia Collective Defense Treaty requesting assistance in defense of its freedom.

SEC. 3. This resolution shall expire when the President shall determine that the peace and security of the area is reasonably assured by international conditions created by action of the United Nations or otherwise, except that it may be terminated earlier by concurrent resolution of the Congress.

Mr. MORSE. Mr. President, I rise to speak in opposition to the joint resolution. I do so with a very sad heart. But I consider the resolution, as I considered the resolution of 1955, known as the Formosa resolution, and the subsequent resolution, known as the Middle East resolution, to be naught but a resolution which embodies a predated declaration of War.

Article I, section 8 of our Constitution does not permit the President to make war at his discretion. Therefore I stand on this issue as I have stood before in the Senate, perfectly willing to take the judgment of history as to the merits of my cause. I note in passing that the warnings which the Senator from New York, Mr. Lehman, and the senior Senator from Oregon uttered in 1955 in opposition to the Formosa Resolution have been proved to be correct by history. I am satisfied that history will render a final verdict in opposition to the joint resolution introduced today.

Mr. President, I shall not yield during the course of my speech, although I shall be very glad to yield to respond to questions afterward.

The senior Senator from Oregon has no illusions as to the reactions which will be aroused in some quarters in this Republic. However, I make the speech because it represents the convictions of my conscience and because I consider it essential to make in keeping the sworn trust that I undertook when I came into this body on four different occasions and was sworn in as a senator from the State of Oregon, pledging myself to uphold the Constitution.

I have one other remark by way of preface, not contained in the manuscript. I yield to no other Senator, or to anyone else in this country in my opposition to communism and all that communism stands for.

In our time a great struggle, which may very well be a deathlock struggle, is going on in the world between freedom on the one hand and the totalitarianism of communism on the other.

However, I am satisfied that that struggle can never be settled by war. I am satisfied that if the hope of anyone is that the struggle between freedom and communism can be settled by war, and that course is followed, both freedom and communism will lose, for there will be no victory in that war.

Because of our own deep interest in the struggle against communism, we in the United States are inclined to overlook some of the other struggles which are occupying others. We try to force every issue into the context of freedom every issue into the context of freedom versus communism. That is one of our great mistakes in Asia. There is much communism there, and much totalitarianism in other forms. We say we are opposing communism there, but that does not mean we are advancing freedom, because we are not.

Senators will note as I proceed in the presentation of my case in opposition to the resolution that I believe the only hope for the establishment of a permanent peace in the world is to practice our oft-repeated American professing that we believe in the substitution of the rule of law for the jungle law of military force as a means of settling disputes which threaten the peace of the world.

The difficulty with that professing or preaching by the United States is that the United States, like some Communist nations, does not practice it.

I wish to make one last introductory remark in the hope that more will understand the message of this speech, although we sometimes deplore the possibility of understanding on a subject matter that stirs so much emotion, so much feeling, and so much passion in the minds of so-called superpatriots, who seem to feel that if one raises any question or expresses any criticism of the policies of our country in the field of foreign policy, one's very patriotism is subject to question.

In the hope that there may be those who may wish to understand the basic tenet of the foreign policy philosophy of the senior Senator from Oregon, I wish to repeat what some of my colleagues have heard me say before.

My foreign policy philosophy is based on a great teaching of a great teacher in this body, one who undoubtedly exercised more influence on me in the field of foreign policy than any other person; a great Republican, who became chairman of the Committee on Foreign Relations; who was one of the architects of the San Francisco Charter; who joined with Franklin Delano Roosevelt in the announcement of that great statement in the field of foreign policy, that politics should stop at water's edge. I refer, of course, to the incomparable Arthur Vandenberg, of Michigan.

Senators within my hearing have heard me say before that I was deeply moved by that dramatic account of Arthur Vandenberg, in which he told, so many times, how he ceased being the leading isolationist in the Senate and became the leading internationalist. It was before the atomic bomb was finally perfected, but after it was known that the atomic bomb would be successful in its perfection.

Franklin Roosevelt called to the White House late one night the leaders of Congress, the leading scientists of the country, who were working on the bomb at that time, and the military leaders of our Defense Establishment who were still stationed in Washington. As Arthur Vandenberg used to say, "We were briefed, and the conference continued until the wee hours of the morning. The scientists convinced all that there was no question that the bomb would work. Then the discussion turned to the implications of this great discovery of science."

Senator Vandenberg used to say to us, "When I came out of the White House in the wee hours of that morning, I knew that while I had been in there that night, the world had so shrunken that there no longer was any place in American politics for an isolationist."

It was then that the great record of internationalism was begun to be made by the incomparable Vandenberg. I paraphrase him, but accurately, for my speech today rests upon this tenet, this unanswerable teaching of Vandenberg. This speech is my challenge today to the members of our Government and the people of my country to follow that teaching, for I do not believe that there is an implementation of any other teaching that can offer mankind any hope for peace. Unless mankind proceeds to adopt the procedures that will make possible permanent peace, both Western civilization and Communist civilization are headed for annihilation. In my judgment, we cannot find reputable scientists who will testify that either civilization could survive a nuclear war.

That tenet of Vandenberg's is as follows: There is no hope for permanent peace in the world until all the nations—not merely those we think are friendly—but until all the nations are willing to establish a system of international justice through law, to the procedures of which will be submitted each and every international dispute that threatens the peace of the world, anywhere in the world, for final and binding determination, to be enforced by an international organization, such as the United Nations.

I am aware of all the criticisms of that tenet. But I have yet to hear a criticism that either destroys or weakens the tenet. One of the almost pro forma criticisms is that it is idealistic, it is impractical, unrealistic. The fact is that only ideals are practical. The only practicality we shall experience in the field of foreign policy or any other field of human behavior is an ideal put to work.

Vandenberg left us this great ideal. It will take years to implement it. But we must always move forward, not backward. We are moving in Asia today, but the movement of the United States in Asia is not in the direction of Vandenberg's principle.

It makes no difference who says that our objective is peace, even if he be the President of the United States. Our actions speak louder than words; and our actions in Asia today are the actions of warmaking.

As I speak on the floor of the Senate at this moment, the United States is making war in Asia.

I shall never give up, short of the actual passage of a declaration of war, my prayerful hope for peace and my prayerful hope that we will substitute the ideal of the rule of law through the only international organization that exists and that has any hope, in my judgment, of applying the rule—the United Nations.

Asia Policy Is Catching Up with Us

Thus I say that the incident that has inspired the joint resolution we have just heard read is as much the doing of the United States as it is the doing of North Vietnam. For 10 years, the role of the United States in South Vietnam has been that of a provocateur, every bit as much as North Vietnam has been a provocateur. For 10 years, the United States, in South Vietnam, has violated the Geneva agreement of 1954. For 10 years, our military policies in South Vietnam have sought to impose a military solution upon a political and economic problem. For 10 years the Communist nations of that part of the world have also violated the Geneva accord of 1954. Not only do two wrongs not make one right, but also I care not how many wrongs we add together, we still do not come out with a summation except a summation of wrong—never a right.

The American effort to impose by force of arms a government of our own choosing upon a segment of the old colony of Indochina has caught up with us.

Our violations of the Geneva accord have caught up with us. Our violations of the United Nations Charter have caught up with us.

Our failure to apply the provisions of the Southeast Asia Treaty have caught up with us. We have been making covert war in southeast Asia for some time, instead of seeking to keep the peace. It was inevitable and inexorable that sooner or later we would have to engage in overt acts of war in pursuance of that policy, and we are now doing so.

There never was a time when it was possible for us to impose a government upon the people of South Vietnam without constant fighting to keep it in power. There never was a time when it would be possible to "bring the boys home by 1965,"—as was once promised—or on any other date. There never was a time when the war could be fought and won in South Vietnam alone, because the Khanh junta—and any of its successors and predecessors—could not survive without massive and direct American military backing that was possible only if the war were expanded.

So the war has at last been expanded—as the Senator from Alaska and I for the last 5 months, in speech after speech on the floor of the Senate, have forewarned was inevitable if we continued our course of action. That course of action, of unilateral military action on the part of the United States, is irreconcilable with our professings as to the application of the rule of law for the settlement of disputes which threaten the peace of the world or any region thereof.

Whether the choice of expanding it was that of North Vietnam or South Vietnam is still in doubt. But I am satisfied that the present rulers of South Vietnam could not long continue their civil war unless the war were expanded.

The United States is, of course, a full partner in the Government of South Vietnam. I am satisfied that ever since 1954, when the United States did not sign the Geneva accords but instead started down the road of unilateral military action in South Vietnam, we have become a provocateur of military conflict in southeast Asia and marched in the opposite direction from fulfilling our obligations under the United Nations Charter. I am satisfied, further, that officials of both the Pentagon and the State Department during those years have ill advised the White House in respect to what our course of action should be in southeast Asia from the standpoint of a sound foreign policy.

In recent months, evidence has been mounting that both the Pentagon and the State Department were preparing to escalate the war into North Vietnam. Many of the policies they have initiated and the statements they have made in public have been highly provocative of military conflict beyond the borders of South Vietnam.

When the high emotionalism of the present crisis has passed, and historians of the future will disclose the some of the provocative things that have occurred, I have no doubt that they will disclose that for quite some time past, there have been violations of the North Vietnamese border and the Cambodian border by South Vietnam, as well as vice versa.

I am also satisfied that they will disclose that the United States was not an innocent bystander. We will not receive a verdict of innocence form the jury box of history on several counts.

Our extensive military aid to South Vietnam was a violation of the Geneva accords in the first instance. Our sending troops into South Vietnam, even under the semantic camouflage of designation as military advisers, was a violation of the Geneva accords. In fact, both of those two counts were also a clear violation of the spirit and intent of the peaceful purposes of the United Nations Charter itself.

Any violation of the borders of Cambodia and North Vietnam by the South Vietnamese were not conducted in a vacuum so far as U.S. assistance was concerned.

We assisted not only with material, but we advised on war plans, and our military presence in South Vietnam served as an ever-present strong back-stop to the South Vietnamese. I doubt if their military leaders acted at any time without the tacit approval of their American advisers.

Tonkin Bay Incident Provoked by South Vietnam

In a very recent incident which was the forerunner to the attacks on American destroyers in the Tonkin Bay, it is known that South Vietnamese naval vessels bombarded two North Vietnamese islands within 3 to 5 or six miles of the main coast of North Vietnam. Of course, the national waters of North Vietnam extend, according to our international claims, 3 miles seaward from the eastern extremity of those islands and 12 miles seaward under national water boundary claims of North Vietnam. While the South Vietnamese vessels were attacking the North Vietnamese islands, the newspapers tell us that U.S. vessels of war were patrolling Tonkin Bay, presumably some 6 to 11 miles off the shore of North Vietnam.

Was the U.S. Navy standing guard while vessels of South Vietnam shelled North Vietnam? That is the clear implication of the incident.

In regard to the international waters, a subject which is one of the highly disputed and still unsettled questions of international law, I believe that the position of the United States is the sounder position. I believe that the 3-mile limit has the better support of under international law principles. But we have neighbors to the south of us in Latin America who do not accept that principle and insist on a 12-mile limit—in one instance, as I recall, a longer limit. Time and time again international incidents arise between the United States and Latin American countries, when American fishing boats get within the limits of the claimed national waters of our South American neighbors and are towed into port. Then begins the exchange of notes and conferences in an effort to have those men released.

The U.S. Government knew that the matter of national and international waters was a controversial issue in Tonkin Bay. The United States also knew that the South Vietnamese vessels planned to bomb, and did bomb, two North Vietnamese islands within 3 to 6 miles of the coast of North Vietnam. Yet, these war vessels of the United States were in the vicinity of that bombing, some miles removed.

Can anyone question that even their presence was a matter of great moral value to South Vietnam? Or the propaganda value to the military totalitarian tyrant and despot who rules South Vietnam as an American puppet—General Khanh, who is really, when all is said and done, the leader whom we have put in charge of an American protectorate called South Vietnam?

It should be unnecessary to point out either to the Senate or to the American people that the position of the United States and its people would be if the tables were reversed and Soviet warships or submarines were to patrol 5 to 11 miles at sea while Cuban naval vessels bombarded Key West....

These facts are as well known to the world as they are to officials of the U.S. Government. They mean that our charges of aggression against North Vietnam will be greeted by considerable snickering abroad.

So, too, will the pious phrases of the resolution about defending freedom in South Vietnam. There is no freedom in South Vietnam. I think even the American people know that to say we are defending freedom in South Vietnam is a travesty upon the word. We are defending General Khanh from being overthrown; that is all. We are defending a clique of military generals and their merchant friends who live well in Saigon, and who need a constantly increasing American military force to protect their privileged position.

Repetitious as these remarks may seem to those who have heard me speaking on Asian policy over the last 5 months, nevertheless, the facts of our obligations under international law, and the stupidity of our policy in southeast Asia remain the same. I am aware that my words will not be popular with many, and will unacceptable to some. But the times demand wisdom more than they demand popularity.

If war is really to important to be left to the generals, then the American people are going to have to make themselves heard soon on U.S. policy in Asia. The only hope that remains for diplomatic action in our activities in the former Indochinese peninsula is the vague hope that a large enough military buildup and a forceful enough threat to expand the war will cause Red China and North Vietnam to retreat from Laos and to cease their support of the rebels in South Vietnam.

When this retreat and this cessation of support to the Vietcong has occurred, then and only then, say our diplomatic spokesmen, might the United States consider a United Nations action in the area, or a new 14-power conference.

Such an American foreign policy is in direct violation of our international legal obligations, including our obligations under the United Nations Charter. What is worse, we have threatened war where no direct threat to American security is at stake. Many journalists who reflect this Government policy in their writings have resorted to fear arguments, seeking to create the impression that unless the United States uses its military might

in South Vietnam and other parts of Asia, the security of the United States will be threatened and communism will run rampant over all of Asia. They are men of little faith in the strength of joint efforts of peaceful nations, who by solemn treaty have bound themselves together to enforce the peace through the application of the procedures of international law. They would take the United States outside the framework of where we are today, along with North Vietnam, Red China, South Vietnam, the Pathet Lao in Laos, and possibly others.

Likewise, there are many congressional politicians who would evade their responsibilities as to American foreign policy in Asia by use of the specious argument that "foreign policy is a matter for the executive branch of the Government. That branch has information no Congressman has access to." Of course, such an alibi for evading congressional responsibility in the field of foreign policy may be based on lack of understanding, or a convenient forgetting of our system of checks and balances that exists and should be exercised in the relationships between and among our three coordinate and coequal branches of government.

Granted that there are many in Congress who would prefer to pass the buck to the White House, the State Department, and the Pentagon Building in respect to our unilateral American military action in Asia. And this resolution gives them the vehicle. Nevertheless, I am satisfied that once the American people come to understand the facts involved in the ill-fated military operations in Asia, they will hold to an accounting those Members of Congress who abdicate their responsibilities in the field of foreign policy.

It is an elementary principle of constitutional law that the executive branch of government cannot spend taxpayers' money in the field of foreign policy, or for any other purpose except when the appropriations are passed by law.

Article I, section 9, of the Constitution reads:

No money shall be drawn from the Treasury but in consequence of appropriations made by law.

It is also elementary that before an appropriation law can be passed, an authorization bill approving of the policy requested by the President must be passed.

These legal requirements under our constitutional system give the Congress a check and voice in determining American foreign policy. Likewise, the Constitution in several other respects places checks upon the executive branch of Government in the field of foreign policy.

Under article I, section 8 of the Constitution, the power to declare war is vested in the Congress. No president has the legal authority under the Constitution to send American boys to their death on a battlefield in the absence of a declaration of war, and in the absence of a prior treaty commitment calling for that action in prescribed circumstances.

There has been a tendency in the historic debate that is taking place on United States-Asian policy for those who favor American unilateral military action in Asia to substitute the waving of the flag into tatters for a reasoned discussion of our international law obligations. Of course, that is no way to pay respect the flag. If we are to go to war in Asia we should at least stay within the provisions of the Constitution. But a war in Asia should be recognized as being unthinkable, and every effort within reason and honor should be made to avoid it. That is why I have urged that as a substitute for American unilateral military action in South Vietnam we should appeal to the SEATO organization, and to the United Nations, for joint action on the part of the members thereof, in accordance with the provisions of those two charters, in an endeavor to substitute a keeping of the peace, for the making of the war in Asia. . . .

Congressional Record, Senate, 88th Congress, 2d session, Aug. 5, 1964, 18132–18136.

154　*Powell v. McCormack*

June 16, 1969

The case of Powell v. McCormack *was fraught with emotion and public controversy. The Supreme Court's decision in this case confirmed the strict nature of the constitutionally defined qualifications for office in the House of Representatives. The Court ruled that the House had unconstitutionally kept Adam Clayton Powell Jr. (D-N.Y.) from taking his seat in the House in 1967.*

Powell was one of the most powerful, charismatic, and controversial members of the House of Representatives during his tenure from 1945 to 1971. A Baptist minister, he was a pioneer civil rights leader in Harlem beginning in the 1930s and one of the first African American members of the House to challenge the segregated facilities of nation's capital, including the all-white House restaurant. He championed legislation to outlaw the poll tax, which kept black voters from voting in many southern states, and led in the cause to desegregate the U.S. armed forces. His efforts to eliminate racial discrimination from all aspects of American life became known as the "Powell Amendment," which he sought to add to many bills before Congress. He assumed the chairmanship of the House Committee on Education and Labor in 1961 and played an important role in the passage of major social legislation to promote education, help the needy and the handicapped, and provide for a minimum wage for all working Americans. These programs became hallmarks of the Kennedy and Johnson administrations.

In the mid-1960s, while at the height of his power, Powell came under attack from his long-time political enemies and from some members of his own committee for his slipshod and fraudulent management of the committee's budget, including payments to his wife for work she did not do; his frequent absence from Congress on extended vacations in the Bahamas; and his inability to appear in his own district in Harlem, where he was subject to arrest for failure to pay a slander judgment against him. The House stripped Powell of his committee chairmanship on January 9, 1967, and refused to allow him to take his seat in the House (even though he had been properly elected) until the completion of a Judiciary Committee investigation of his use of committee funds. The important distinction in this case was that Powell was excluded from taking his seat in the 90th Congress. Article I, Section 5 of the Constitution provides for expulsion of a member by a two-thirds vote, but it does not provide for being excluded from taking a seat after being elected to that seat. Instead of accepting the Judiciary Committee's resolution that Powell be censured, fined, and stripped of seniority, the House amended the resolution to call for excluding Powell from the House. The Speaker ruled that a majority vote, not a two-thirds vote, would be sufficient to amend the Judiciary Committee's resolution. The House then overwhelmingly voted to exclude Powell from taking his seat. Three months after he was excluded he was reelected to fill his own seat on April 11, 1967. Powell chose not to appear to be sworn in.

In the meantime, Powell and some of his constituents in his Harlem district sued the House. Their suit named Speaker John W. McCormack (D-Mass.) and the officers of the House, including the clerk, the House sergeant-at-arms, and the House doorkeeper, plus members of the House who had investigated him, and charged them with denying him his seat in the 90th Congress, denying him his salary, and keeping him from appearing on the floor of the House.

The Supreme Court ruled that Powell was entitled to be seated in the 90th Congress because the Constitution provides only three qualifications for office: age, citizenship, and residency—all of which he met (see Article I, Section 2, Clause 2). The Court said Congress could not add qualifications for office. Congress did not have the constitutional authority to exclude a duly elected member of Congress. They did have the right to expel a sitting member after a two-thirds vote of the House. By the time the Court rendered its decision, the 90th Congress had ended and Powell had already been reseated in the 91st Congress.

Although Powell won his case regarding his seating in the 90th Congress, he was stripped of his seniority in the 91st Congress. He did not appear in the House after his election to the 91st Congress in 1968 until the Supreme Court case was settled in June 1969. He narrowly lost the nomination for reelection in 1970, returned to the ministry of the Abyssinian Baptist Church in Harlem, and died in 1972.

Powell v. McCormack *stands as a strong reminder that the Constitution provides specific qualification for office and that these qualifications cannot be added to or subtracted from without a constitutional amendment. In recent years a number of states have launched a movement to limit the number of terms a member of*

Congress can serve. Those who advocate term limits for members of Congress are proposing a qualification for office based on the length of service. The *Powell* case suggests that in order for such a qualification to be constitutional, it will require an amendment to the Constitution.

. . . .

MR. CHIEF JUSTICE WARREN delivered the opinion of the Court.

. . . .

I V.

Exclusion or Expulsion.

The resolution excluding petitioner Powell was adopted by a vote in excess of two-thirds of the 434 Members of Congress—307 to 116. 113 Cong. Rec. 5037-5038. Article I, § 5, grants the House authority to expel a member "with the Concurrence of two thirds." Respondents assert that the House may expel a member for any reason whatsoever and that, since a two-thirds vote was obtained, the procedure by which Powell was denied his seat in the 90th Congress should be regarded as an expulsion, not an exclusion. Cautioning us not to exalt form over substance, respondents quote from the concurring opinion of Judge McGowan in the court below:

"Appellant Powell's cause of action for a judicially compelled seating thus boils down, in my view, to the narrow issue of whether a member found by his colleagues ... to have engaged in official misconduct must, because of the accidents of timing, be formally admitted before he can be either investigated or expelled. The sponsor of the motion to exclude stated on the floor that he was proceeding on the theory that the power to expel included the power to exclude, provided a ⅔ vote was forthcoming. It was. Therefore, success for Mr. Powell on the merits would mean that the District Court must admonish the House that it is form, not substance, that should govern in great affairs, and accordingly command the House members to act out a charade." 129 U.S. App. D.C., at 383–384, 395 F. 2d, at 606–607.

Although respondents repeatedly urge this Court not to speculate as to the reasons for Powell's exclusion, their attempt to equate exclusion with expulsion would require a similar speculation that the House would have voted to expel Powell had it been faced with that question. Powell had not been seated at the time House Resolution No. 278 was debated and passed. After a motion to bring the Select Committee's proposed resolution to an immediate vote had been defeated, an amendment was offered which mandated Powell's exclusion. Mr. Celler, chairman of the Select Committee, then posed a parliamentary inquiry to determine whether a two-thirds vote was necessary to pass the resolution if so amended "in the sense that it might amount to an expulsion." 113 Cong. Rec. 5020. The Speaker replied that "action by a majority vote would be in accordance with the rules." *Ibid.* Had the amendment been regarded as an attempt to expel Powell, a two-thirds vote would have been constitutionally required. The Speaker ruled that the House was voting to exclude Powell, and we will not speculate what the re-

sult might have been if Powell had been seated and expulsion proceedings subsequently instituted.

Nor is the distinction between exclusion and expulsion merely one of form. The misconduct for which Powell was charged occurred prior to the convening of the 90th Congress. On several occasions the House has debated whether a member can be expelled for actions taken during a prior Congress and the House's own manual of procedure applicable in the 90th Congress states that "both Houses have distrusted their power to punish in such cases." Rules of the House of Representatives, H.R. Doc. No. 529, 89th Cong., 2d Sess., 25 (1967); see G. Galloway, History of the House of Representatives 32 (1961). The House rules manual reflects positions taken by prior Congresses. For example, the report of the Select Committee appointed to consider the expulsion of John W. Langley states unequivocally that the House will not expel a member for misconduct committed during an earlier Congress:

"[I]t must be said that with practical uniformity the precedents in such cases are to the effect that the House will not expel a Member for reprehensible action prior to his election as a Member, not even for conviction for an offense. On May 23, 1884, Speaker Carlisle decided that the House had no right to punish a Member for any offense alleged to have been committed previous to the time when he was elected a Member, and added, 'That has been so frequently decided in the House that it is no longer a matter of dispute.'" H.R. Rep. No. 30, 69th Cong., 1st Sess., 1–2 (1925).

Members of the House having expressed a belief that such strictures apply to its own power to expel, we will not assume that two-thirds of its members would have expelled Powell for his prior conduct had the Speaker announced that House Resolution No. 278 was for expulsion rather than exclusion.

Finally, the proceedings which culminated in Powell's exclusion cast considerable doubt upon respondents' assumption that the two-thirds vote necessary to expel would have been mustered. These proceedings have been succinctly described by Congressman Eckhardt:

"The House voted 202 votes for the previous question leading toward the adoption of the [Select] Committee report. It voted 222 votes against the previous question, opening the floor for the Curtis Amendment which ultimately excluded Powell.

"Upon adoption of the Curtis Amendment, the vote again fell short of two-thirds, being 248 yeas to 176 nays. Only on the final vote, adopting the Resolution as amended, was more than a two-thirds vote obtained, the vote being 307 yeas to 116 nays. On this last vote, as a practical matter, members who would not have denied Powell a seat if they were given the choice to punish him had to cast an aye vote or else record themselves as opposed to the only punishment that was likely to come before the House. Had the matter come up through the processes of expulsion, it appears that the two-thirds vote would have failed, and then members would have been able to apply a lesser penalty."

We need express no opinion as to the accuracy of Congressman Eckhardt's prediction that expulsion proceedings would have produced a different result. However the House's own views of the extent of its power to expel combined with the Congressman's analysis counsel that exclusion and expulsion are not fungible proceedings. The Speaker ruled that House

Resolution No. 278 contemplated an exclusion proceeding. We must reject respondents' suggestion that we overrule the Speaker and hold that, although the House manifested an intent to exclude Powell, its action should be tested by whatever standards may govern an expulsion. . . .

VII.

Conclusion.

To summarize, we have determined the following:

(1) This case has not been mooted by Powell's seating in the 91st Congress. (2) Although this action should be dismissed against respondent Congressmen, it may be sustained against their agents. (3) The 90th Congress' denial of membership to Powell cannot be treated as an expulsion. (4) We have jurisdiction over the subject matter of this controversy. (5) The case is justiciable.

Further, analysis of the "textual commitment" under Art. 1, § 5 (see Part VI, B (1)), has demonstrated that in judging the qualifications of its members Congress is limited to the standing qualifications prescribed in the Constitution. Respondents concede that Powell met these. Thus, there is no need to remand this case to determine whether he was entitled to be seated in the 90th Congress. Therefore, we hold that, since Adam Clayton Powell, Jr., was duly elected by the voters of the 18th Congressional District of New York and was not ineligible to serve under any provision of the Constitution, the House was without power to exclude him from its membership.

Petitioners seek additional forms of equitable relief, including mandamus for the release of petitioner Powell's back pay. The propriety of such remedies, however, is more appropriately considered in the first instance by the courts below. Therefore, as to respondents McCormack, Albert, Ford, Celler, and Moore, the judgment of the Court of Appeals for the District of Columbia Circuit is affirmed. As to respondents Jennings, Johnson, and Miller, the judgment of the Court of Appeals for the District of Columbia Circuit is reversed and the case is remanded to the United States District Court for the District of Columbia with instructions to enter a declaratory judgment and for further proceedings consistent with this opinion.

It is so ordered.

395 U.S. 486 (1969).

155   A Joint Meeting of Congress to Honor the Apollo 11 Astronauts

September 16, 1969

In one of the greatest scientific and technical feats and one of the greatest acts of exploration in world history, the National Aeronautic and Space Administration (NASA) successfully sent men to the moon and returned them safely to earth. On July 20, 1969, astronaut Neil A. Armstrong descended the ladder of his lunar module, named Eagle, and became the first human to set foot on the moon. The two other astronauts on the Apollo 11 flight were Edwin "Buzz" Aldrin and Michael Collins. It was the eleventh launch of the Apollo program, designed to fulfill President John F. Kennedy's 1961 challenge to place a man on the moon before the end of the decade. Millions of persons worldwide watched on television as Armstrong set foot on the moon. He became an instant national hero, as did the other astronauts. All three Apollo 11 astronauts spoke briefly before a joint meeting of Congress on September 16, 1969. Armstrong acknowledged the role of Congress in the space program when he said, "It was here in these Halls that our venture really began. Here the Space Act of 1958 was framed, the chartering document of the National Aeronautics and Space Administration. And here in the years that followed the key decisions that permitted the successive steps of Mercury and Gemini and Apollo were permitted."

While there was general adulation of the astronauts and pride in the tremendous feat they had accomplished, the space program had its critics from the beginning. Most critics focused on the billions of dollars expended on the space program at a time when the United States was engaged in a war in Vietnam and struggling at home to end poverty in America. Michael Collins addressed this criticism in his remarks before Congress when he said, "We cannot launch our planetary probes from a springboard of poverty, discrimination, or unrest. But neither can we wait until each and every terrestrial problem has been solved."

Presiding over this joint meeting was Speaker of the House John W. McCormack (D-Mass.) and Vice President Spiro T. Agnew.

The SPEAKER of the House presided.

At 12 o'clock and 19 minutes P.M, the Doorkeeper (William M. Miller) announced the Vice President and Members of the U.S. Senate who entered the Hall of the House of Representatives, the Vice President taking the chair at the right of the Speaker, and the Members of the Senate the seats reserved for them.

The SPEAKER. The Chair appoints as members of the committee on the part of the House to escort our distinguished visitors into the Chamber the gentleman from Oklahoma, Mr. Albert; the gentleman from Louisiana, Mr. Boggs; the gentleman from Louisiana, Mr. Hebert; the gentleman from California, Mr. Miller; the gentleman from New Jersey, Mr. Rodino; the gentleman from Michigan, Mr. Gerald R. Ford; the gentleman from Illinois, Mr. Arends; the gentleman from Pennsylvania, Mr. Fulton; and the gentleman from Ohio, Mr. McCulloch.

The VICE PRESIDENT. On behalf of the Senate the Vice President appoints the following Senators to escort our distinguished astronauts into the Chamber: Senator Richard Russell, of Georgia; Senator Mike Mansfield, of Montana; Senator Clinton Anderson, of New Mexico; Senator Edward M. Kennedy, of Massachusetts; Senator Robert C. Byrd, of West Virginia; Senator Hugh Scott, of Pennsylvania; Senator Margaret Chase Smith, of Maine; Senator Milton R. Young, of North Dakota; and Senator Gordon Allott, of Colorado.

The Doorkeeper announced the ambassadors, ministers, and charges d'affaires of foreign governments.

The ambassadors, ministers, and charges d'affaires of foreign governments entered the Hall of the House of Representatives and took the seats reserved for them.

The Doorkeeper announced the Cabinet of the President of the United States.

The members of the Cabinet of the President of the United States entered the Hall of the House of Representatives and took the seats reserved for them in front of the Speaker's rostrum.

At 12 o'clock and 34 minutes P.M, the Doorkeeper announced the Apollo 11 astronauts.

Mr. Neil A. Armstrong; Lt. Col. Michael Collins, U.S. Air Force; and Col. Edwin E. Aldrin, Jr., U.S. Air Force, accompanied by the committee of the escort, entered the Chamber and stood at the Clerk's desk.

[Applause, the Members rising.]

The SPEAKER. My distinguished colleagues of the Congress, we are honoring today three men who represent the best in America and whose coordinated skill, fantastic daring, and visionary drive have made history that constitutes a turning point of paramount importance in the journey of mankind. I have the high honor and official and personal pleasure of presenting to you the crew of Apollo 11, who successfully made the historic journey to the moon, Neil A. Armstrong, Col. Edwin E. Aldrin, Jr., and Lt. Col. Michael Collins.

The Chair recognizes Mr. Armstrong.

Mr. ARMSTRONG. Mr. Speaker, Mr. President, Members of Congress, distinguished guests, we are greatly honored that you have invited us here today. Only now have we completed our journey to land on and explore the moon, and return. It was here in these Halls that our venture really began. Here the Space Act of 1958 was framed, the chartering document of the National Aeronautics and Space Administration. And here in the years that followed the key decisions that permitted the successive steps of Mercury and Gemini and Apollo were permitted.

Your policies and the marvels of modern communication have permitted people around the world to share the excitement of our exploration. And, although you have been informed of the results of the Apollo 11, we are particularly pleased to have this opportunity to complete our work by reporting to you and through you to the American people. My colleagues share the honor of presenting this report. First, it is my pleasure to present Col. Edwin Aldrin.

Colonel ALDRIN. Distinguished ladies and gentlemen, it is with a great sense of pride as an American and with humility as a human being that I say to you today what no men have been privileged to say before: "We walked on the moon." But the footprints at Tranquillity Base belong to more than the crew of Apollo 11. They were put there by hundreds of thousands of people across this country, people in Government, industry, and universities, the teams and crews that preceded us, all who strived throughout the years with Mercury, Gemini, and Apollo. Those footprints belong to the American people and you, their representatives, who accepted and supported the inevitable challenge of the moon. And, since we came in peace for all mankind those footprints belong also to all people of the world. As the moon shines impartially on all those looking up from our spinning earth so do we hope the benefits of space exploration will be spread equally with a harmonizing influence to all mankind.

Scientific exploration implies investigating the unknown. The result can never be wholly anticipated. Charles Lindbergh said, "Scientific accomplishment is a path, not an end; a path leading to and disappearing in mystery.

Our steps in space have been a symbol of this country's way of life as we open our doors and windows to the world to view our successes and failures and as we share with all nations our discovery. The Saturn, Columbia, and Eagle, and the extravehicular mobility unit have proved to Neil, Mike, and me that this Nation can produce equipment of the highest quality and dependability. This should give all of us hope and inspiration to overcome some of the more difficult problems here on earth. The Apollo lesson is that national goals can be met where there is a strong enough will to do so.

The first step on the moon was a step toward our sister planets and ultimately toward the stars. "A small step for a man," was a statement of fact, "a giant leap for mankind," is a hope for the future.

What this country does with the lessons of Apollo apply to domestic problems, and what we do in further space exploration programs will determine just how giant a leap we have taken.

Thank you.

Mr. ARMSTRONG. Now I should like to present Col. Michael Collins.

Colonel COLLINS. Mr. President, Members of Congress, and distinguished guests: One of the many things I have very much enjoyed about working for the Space Agency, and for the Air Force, is that they have always given me free rein, even to the extent of addressing this most august assemblage without coaching, without putting any words in my mouth. Therefore, my brief remarks are simply those of a free citizen living in a free country and expressing free thoughts that are purely my own.

Many years before there was a space program my father had a favorite quotation: "He who would bring back the wealth of the Indies must take the wealth of the Indies with him." This we have done. We have taken to the moon the wealth of this Nation, the vision of its political leaders, the intelligence of its scientists, the dedication of its engineers, the careful craftsmanship of its workers, and the enthusiastic support of its people. We have brought back rocks. And I think it is a fair trade. For just as the Rosetta stone revealed the language of ancient Egypt, so may these rocks unlock the mystery of the origin of the moon, of our earth, and even of our solar system.

During the flight of Apollo 11, in the constant sunlight between the earth and the moon, it was necessary for us to control the temperature of our spacecraft by a slow rotation not unlike that of a chicken on a barbecue spit. As we turned, the earth and the moon alternately appeared in our windows. We had our choice. We could look toward the Moon, toward Mars, toward our future in space—toward the new Indies—or we could look back toward the Earth, our home, with its problems spawned over more than a millennium of human occupancy.

We looked both ways. We saw both, and I think that Is what our Nation must do.

We can ignore neither the wealth of the Indies nor the realities of the immediate needs of our cities, our citizens, or our civics. We cannot launch our planetary probes from a springboard of poverty, discrimination, or unrest. But neither can we wait until each and every terrestrial problem has been solved. Such logic 200 years ago would have prevented expansion westward past the Appalachian Mountains, for assuredly the eastern seaboard was beset by problems of great urgency then, as it is today.

Man has always gone where he has been able to go. It is that simple. He win continue pushing back his frontier, no matter how far it may carry him from his homeland.

Someday in the not-too-distant future, when I listen to an earthling step out onto the surface of Mars or some other planet, just as I listened to Neil step out onto the surface of the Moon, I hope I hear him say: "I come from the United States of America."

Mr. ARMSTRONG. We landed on the Sea of Tranquillity, in the cool of the early lunar morning, when the long shadows would aid our perception.

The sun was only 10%, above the horizon. While the earth turned through nearly a full day during our stay, the sun at Tranquillity Base rose barely 11%—a small fraction of the month-long lunar day. There was a peculiar sensation of the duality of time—the swift rush of events that characterizes all our lives—and the ponderous parade which marks the aging of the universe.

Both kinds of time were evident—the first by the routine events of the flight, whose planning and execution were detailed to fractions of a second—the latter by rocks around us, unchanged throughout the history of man—whose 3-billion-year-old secrets made them the treasure we sought.

The plaque on the Eagle which summarized our hopes bears this message:

Here men from the planet earth first set foot upon the moon July 1969 A.D.

We came in peace for all mankind. Those nineteen hundred and sixty-nine years had constituted the majority of the age of Pisces, a 12th of the great year. That is measured by the thousand generations the precession of the earth's axis requires to scribe a giant circle in the heavens.

In the next 20 centuries, the age of Aquarius of the great year, the age for which our young people have such high hopes, humanity may begin to understand its most baffling mystery—where are we going?

The earth is, in fact, traveling many thousands of miles per hour in the direction of the constellation Hercules—to some unknown destination in the cosmos. Man must understand his universe in order to understand his destiny.

Mystery however is a very necessary ingredient in our lives. Mystery creates wonder and wonder is the basis for man's desire to understand. Who knows what mysteries will be solved in our lifetime, and what new riddles will become the challenge of the new generations?

Science has not mastered prophesy. We predict too much for next year yet far too little for the next 10. Responding to challenge is one of democracy's great strengths. Our successes in space lead us to hope that this strength can be used in the next decade in the solution of many of our planet's problems. Several weeks ago I enjoyed the warmth of reflection on the true meanings of the spirit of Apollo.

I stood in the highlands of this Nation, near the Continental Divide, introducing to my sons the wonders of nature, and pleasures of looking for deer and for elk.

In their enthusiasm for the view they frequently stumbled on the rocky trails, but when they looked only to their footing, they did not see the elk. To those of you who have advocated looking high we owe our sincere gratitude, for you have granted us the opportunity to see some of the grandest views of the Creator.

To those of you who have been our honest critics, we also thank, for you have reminded us that we dare not forget to watch the trail. We carried on Apollo 11 two flags of this Union that had flown over the Capitol, one over the House of Representatives, one over the Senate. It is our privilege to return them now in these Halls which exemplify man's highest purpose—to serve one's fellow man.

We thank you, on behalf of all the men of Apollo, for giving us the privilege of joining you in serving—for all mankind.

[Applause, the Members rising.]

(Thereupon, the flags were presented to the Speaker and to the Vice President.)

The SPEAKER. I think we would be remiss on this occasion if we did not, in paying the highest honor that the Congress can pay to any person—to invite them and receive them in joint meeting—also honor what might be termed the unseen astronauts, the wives of our distinguished friends. I am going to ask the wives of the astronauts to rise: Mrs. Armstrong, Mrs. Collins, Mrs. Aldrin.

[Applause, the Members rising.]

The VICE PRESIDENT. On behalf of the Members of the Senate, we are very grateful for the presentation of this flag. We watched with great interest the Apollo program proceed and are conscious of the thrust of the need, in the words of the gentleman who spoke here this morning, the need being balance and the need to meet the problems of our society wherever they arise.

I can assure you that this memento will not fall into that category but will be kept and appreciated with the dignity that it deserves.

Thank you very much.

The SPEAKER. On behalf of the House of Representatives I want to express our sincere thanks to the members of the Apollo 11 for the thought and for the action in carrying this flag, presented to the House, to the moon and flying it on the moon. These two flags are probably two of the most precious flags, not only of our own country, but of any other country. We extend to you the deep thanks of the Members of the House of Representatives and assure you that every care and caution will be taken, because this will be forever one of the most treasured possessions of this great Chamber.

[Applause, the Members rising.]

At 12 o'clock and 59 minutes P.M, Mr. Neil A. Armstrong, Lt. Col. Michael Collins, U.S. Air Force, Col. Edwin E. Aldrin, Jr., U.S. Air Force, accompanied by the committee of escort, retired from the Hall of the House of Representatives.

· · · ·

Congressional Record, House, 91st Congress, 1st session, Sept. 16, 1969, 25609–25611.

156   Senator Frank Church on the War in Vietnam and Cambodia

May 1, 1970

Senator Frank Church (D-Idaho) was at the center of a small group of senators from both parties, including Senator John Sherman Cooper (R-Ky.), who were opposed to the war in Vietnam and sought a negotiated settlement or a unilateral withdrawal of U.S. troops to end the fighting. Church was constantly on guard to oppose further escalations of the war into neighboring countries such as Cambodia and Laos and urged Congress to take a more aggressive role in bringing the war to an end. On April 30, 1970, President Richard Nixon told the nation in a televised address that he had ordered U.S. troops into Cambodia. This set in motion a series of extraordinary events in the Senate, led by Church and Cooper, to convince Congress to cut off funds to support the expansion of the war into Cambodia. Church stepped up his criticism of the Nixon administration's conduct of the war, arguing that the war continued primarily because the United States could not admit it was a mistake in the first place. Nixon's announcement also revitalized the antiwar movement at home, leading to thousands of protests on college campuses nationwide.

As the Vietnam War continued with no apparent end in sight, it began to take a serious toll on American politics in addition to the frightful increase in battle casualties. President Lyndon Johnson's earlier decisions to escalate the war (see document 153) helped him win the presidency in 1964, but four years later he refused to run again. His inability to find a way to end the war had ruined his chances for reelection. Hubert Humphrey became the Democratic candidate but was unable to distance himself from the policies of Lyndon Johnson, who continued to bomb North Vietnam even as the presidential campaign got underway. The Republican candidate, Richard M. Nixon, won the election by a narrow margin and entered the White House in 1969, suggesting during the campaign that he had a plan to end the war. He was elected with a golden opportunity to break with past conduct of the war and negotiate a settlement to the conflict.

The Nixon administration engaged in negotiations with the North Vietnamese in a series of failed efforts in Paris and in secret negotiations conducted by Henry Kissinger, the president's chief adviser on Vietnam, first as head of the National Security Council and later as secretary of state. At the same time, within months of assuming the presidency, President Nixon had ordered highly secret bombings inside Cambodia.

In response to Nixon's address to the nation on the invasion of Cambodia, Frank Church took to the floor of the Senate the next day in opposition not only to the invasion of Cambodia, but also to the other strategy of the Nixon administration, called "Vietnamization"—the idea that the U.S. goal in Vietnam was to get the South Vietnamese to the point where they could successfully fight their own war and then U.S. troops could be withdrawn. In the meantime national criticism of Nixon's invasion of Cambodia led to massive student protests that forced hundreds of campuses to suspend classes. Five days after President Nixon's address, Ohio National Guard troops that had been called to Kent State University to control student demonstrations shot and killed four students and wounded nine others.

The war continued for another three years, even though there were other attempts to end it emanating from Congress, such as the McGovern-Hatfield Amendment (see document 157). Unfortunately, Congress was unable to find a successful constitutional formula for limiting the president in his role as commander-in-chief, especially once the United States was in the middle of a war. Congress addressed the issue of presidential power in a substantial manner in the War Powers Act of 1973 (see document 163).

WAR WITHOUT END
Congress Must Draw the Line

Mr. CHURCH. Mr. President, when President Nixon took office 15 months ago, he had two good choices and one bad one for dealing with the war in Vietnam. The promising choices were a negotiated peace based on a compromise coalition government in Saigon, coupled with the swift withdrawal of American forces; or, failing an agreement, a unilateral disengagement by the United States based on a phased but steady and complete withdrawal of American forces. In order to pursue either of these courses in those early days of his administration when all options were open to him, the President would have had to acknowledge the futility of our continued military intervention in Vietnam. He would have had to admit—at least to himself—the impossibility of sustaining at any acceptable cost an anti-Communist regime in Saigon, allied with, dependent on, and supported by the United States.

This, of course, had long been the coveted objective of American policy in Indochina. Mr. Nixon was unprepared to abandon it. The result was the rejection of the two possible means of bring the war to an early end and the adoption instead of the policy known as "Vietnamization." The tactics of the new course of action soon became clear: instead of escalating, we were going to de-escalate, albeit by very gradual stages and over an indefinite period of time; instead of pouring in ever larger numbers of American troops, we were going to gradually substitute South Vietnamese forces in their place and thus keep the war going until the insurgents finally gave up their effort to displace the Saigon regime. Lost to view throughout the year 1969 was the fact that the new policy was only new in the means it employed; the objective remained unchanged.

We are still trying to maintain an anti-Communist regime, resistant to the North, in the southern half of a divided Vietnam. We are still determined to pursue an objective that makes necessary a permanent American military presence in Indochina. We are still bent upon preserving an American bridgehead on the mainland of Asia, next door to China. That is the meaning of Vietnamization.

In January 1969 Mr. Nixon inherited the leadership of an angry, divided, and demoralized country. He had at that time a better opportunity than he will ever have again to diagnose and treat the cause of the country's agony. In keeping with his own record and outlook, however, the new President did not perceive anything fundamentally wrong with the old policy. Instead, he saw only the symptoms: The high casualties, the inflated rhetoric, the student unrest, the Johnson style, and the so-called credibility gap.

It did not occur to Mr. Nixon that the policy itself was deeply unsound, extraneous to American interests, and offensive to American values. The result was a change in tactics but not in goals. The policy has been repackaged; new improved methods of salesmanship have been adopted; an optimistic new vocabulary has been introduced, full of bright promises of "peace with honor." Hopes of our troops, people everywhere are saying that

Vietnam is no longer an issue. Or at least they were saying that until yesterday.

But the war goes on. American combat strength in South Vietnam has been reduced, but the war itself is spreading beyond the borders of Vietnam and has become an Indochina war. Nor is there any end in sight. The administration has consistently refused to say—and perhaps does not even know—when if ever the American involvement will be brought to an end. Our withdrawal is said to be "irreversible," but the President continues to warn of "strong and effective measures" if the enemy takes military advantage of it. Such as a measure, as the Senate well knows, was dramatically announced to the American people last night. How can a process of irreversible withdrawal can be reconciled with these "strong and effective measures" is not explained; nor is it explained what possible reason we might have for supposing that the enemy will not "take advantage" of our withdrawals.

The Nixon administration has led us into a fundamental contradiction through its temporizing policy of scaled-down but indefinite warfare. The Johnson policy at least moved in one direction: an extravagant objective was matched by extravagant means but retained the objective. The result is a masterpiece of incongruity, a design well conceived for futility and failure.

Sooner or later we are going to have to make a choice, matching our methods to our goals. If we continue to pursue the same extravagant objective in South Vietnam, the American military occupation of that country will have to be extended indefinitely. The alternative is to change the objective, to alter the policy. The latter, as I shall try once again to show, is the course of realism. Once we have chosen that course, once we have bitten the bullet of acknowledging past error, the means of extricating ourselves will pose no insuperable problems. Once we admit that this war is not now and never has been essential to American security, there should be no great difficulty about ending it. Until we do admit it, the war will go on.

I. A War Not in Our Interest

It is no easy thing to admit an error but, as events have shown the scale and consequences of our mistaken venture in Vietnam, more and more Americans have been coming of the opinion that it is better to acknowledge a mistake than to perpetuate it. Even for those not directly involved, a good deal of maturity is required for facing up to a mistaken course of action. For statesmen and soldiers who have had personal involvement with the war in Vietnam, a high degree of fortitude and integrity is required. Nonetheless, an increasing number of men who have found it necessary to express their doubts about its justification. Late last year, for example, a former Air Cavalry captain who lost his right arm and both legs when he picked up a live grenade at Khe Sanh, summed up his own personal distress in these words:

To the devastating psychological effect of getting maimed, paralyzed, or in some way unable to reenter American life as you left it, is the added psychological weight that it may not have been worth it: that the war may have been a cruel hoax, an American tragedy that left a small minority of young American males holding the bag.

Distasteful though it is, we must review the reasons for our initial involvement in Vietnam. This is not just a case of confession being good for the soul. We need to understand the past so that we can act more wisely in the future. A clear comprehension of past mistakes is the only reliable insurance against repeating them. I do not agree, therefore, with President Nixon's assertion in his speech of May 14, 1969, that the "urgent question" is "not whether we should have entered on this course, but what is required of us today." The two, I believe, are connected: In order to determine "what is required of us today," it is indispensable that we understand why we did what we did in the past, and whether we should have done it.

If indeed the decision to intervene with an American Army in 1965 was wise and sound, that would suggest that we now should continue the fight, with whatever force may be necessary, and for whatever time may be required. If, on the other hand, the intervention of 1965 was the result of faulty judgment, then it makes no sense to continue the war for a single day longer than is required to liquidate it in a decent and orderly way. There can be no cure without honest diagnosis. Yet, the administration refuses even to think about past decisions in a critical or analytical way. Instead, it clings tenaciously and defensively to the discredited old arguments. The result is indecision and incongruity. As best as I can make it out—and I do not think I can make it out with any real clarity—the administration's position seems to be that the war is and always has been necessary and justified, but that political considerations rule out a greater military effort to win it, while they cannot bring themselves to end it either by a negotiated compromise or a phased-out, complete withdrawal.

The single most important source of this paralyzing ambiguity is the continuing prevalence of the myth so implicit in the President's remarks last evening—a myth of which Mr. Nixon himself was one of the principal perpetrators: the notion that communism is a single, unified, centrally directed, conspiratorial force unalterably committed to conquest of the world. Though often denied, the notion keeps turning up. Mr. Rusk used to warn of the danger of a "world cut in two by Asian communism." Mr. Nixon referred last November 3 to "those great powers who have not yet abandoned their goals of world conquest," and he predicted that American withdrawal from Vietnam would "spark violence wherever our commitments help maintain the peace—in the Middle East, in Berlin, eventually even in the Western Hemisphere." The President did not say how the spark would spread, but the explanation of why he thinks it would is implicit in his words: It is the old notion of the world Communist conspiracy, nurtured and sustained against all the compelling evidence which shows that, except in those areas such as Western Europe where the Russians bring direct physical power to bear, world communism has broken down into its national components, to such a degree that today communism is scarcely more united a force in the world that anticommunism.

Mr. President (Mr. Spong), in the case of Vietnam, it belabors the obvious—at least it would if the obvious were not under such steady challenge—to assert once again that the real force behind the long internal struggle is not ideology but Vietnamese nationalism. In his recent book on President Johnson's decision to end the escalation and initiate peace negotiations, Mr. Townsend Hoopes, the former Under Secretary of the Air Force, analyzed the war as follows:

North Vietnam was fighting *primarily* to achieve an unfulfilled national purpose. While it was, to be sure, fully aware of the implications for the wider application of the Mao-Ho-Giap insurgency doctrine, it was fighting not an abstractly ideological war, but a very particular war—in a particular place, characterized by a particular kind of terrain and weather, peopled by a particular breed of men, and above all, conditioned by a particular history. What really drove Ho's sacrificial legions was not the dream of world conquest, nor even the notion of generating a new momentum for Communist advance and triumph throughout Asia. What motivated Hanoi and enabled its leadership to hold 19 million primitive people to endless struggle and sacrifice against odds that were statistically ludicrous was the goal of national independence.

If our hands were cleared of the burden and our minds cleared of the Communist monolith obsession, we would perceive readily that the small country of North Vietnam, with which we have been at war for the last 5 years, is an authentically independent country, pursuing its own national objectives. These are the expulsion of foreign influence, the reunification of Vietnam and, quite probably, the establishment of their own dominant influence in all of former French Indochina. Though disagreeable to the United States and hardly benevolent, these designs are by no means to be confused with a conspiracy for the conquest of Asia. North Vietnamese ambitions are far less ideological, and much too restricted by the power limitations of a small, undeveloped country to possibly be a serious threat to the United States, or even to those Southeast Asian countries which have any real measure of political coherence and support from their own populations.

Some Americans argue that we must stay in South Vietnam in order to prevent the population from falling under the yoke of a Communist dictatorship. Whatever altruism that idea may have in the abstract, it has little merit in actuality. For most of the people of Southeast Asia—certainly for the Vietnamese—there is no available democratic alternative. The choice lies between the harsh but relatively efficient and purposeful Communist dictatorship of the North and the equally harsh but corrupt and incompetent non-Communist dictatorship of the South.

Ideology in any case is of little consequence to poor and underdeveloped societies. Their requirements are more basic: they need governments which will refrain from robbing and plundering them, which will permit them the use and benefit of the land on which they live, and perhaps give them some assistance in cultivating it; which will provide basic medical services to protect them from common diseases; and which will provide at least elementary education for their children. Perhaps the time will come when political philosophy will acquire some importance for the villagers of Vietnam, Laos, and Cambodia. In the meantime, nothing could be further from their needs than those warring political ideologies which agitate the minds of statesmen in Washington, Moscow, and Peking.

To suppose in any case that the regime we are defending in South Vietnam has any knowledge of, interest in, or commitment to, democratic freedoms requires a greater capacity for self-delusion than is to be found among any but that dwindling band of old-school cold warriors whose demeaning definition of a democratic government is any regime, however decadent, which preaches undying hostility to communism.

Another superficially compelling rationalization for our continued participation in this war, in which we have no vital interest of our own, is the threat of a massacre in South Vietnam if we should leave. Raising this specter in his speech of November 3, Mr. Nixon warned that our "precipitate withdrawal would inevitably allow the Communists to repeat the massacres which followed their takeover in the North 15 years before."

Last evening, I must add, the President, once again, raised the same outmoded specter in his address. Even if it were as certain as the President takes it to be that a victorious Vietcong would murder large numbers of South Vietnamese civilians, it is not a rational policy to hold off this calamity by perpetuating the killing of both Vietnamese and Americans in this endless war. Even if the Communists were to do everything that Mr. Nixon fears, it is doubtful that they could match the daily, continuing bloodbath of the war itself.

For this has become a war of indiscriminate killing on both sides. Unable to distinguish between soldiers and civilians, as likely to have a grenade thrown at him by a woman or child as by an identifiable soldier, the American GI has learned to shoot first and ask questions later. He is doing no more than any of us would do under the circumstances—but he is doing it.

This war in which the enemy is indistinguishable from the people is the real bloodbath in Vietnam. To continue it so as to prevent possible Communist reprisals after the war is to rely on the same perverse logic as that contained in the now famous words of the American major who said after the Tet offensive in 1968: "We had to destroy Ben Tre in order to save it."

If once we made the decision that we were going to withdraw from Vietnam—finally and completely—it should be possible to have guarantees for the lives of South Vietnamese civilians included among the provisions of a negotiated settlement. The North Vietnamese—for what it is worth—insist that they have no intention of perpetuating a peacetime massacre. They say that they are prepared to live and even cooperate with anyone who favors the "independence, peace and neutrality" of South Vietnam.

If in the end we should withdraw without a formal peace settlement, it would be a matter of honor to provide asylum for those South Vietnamese who might be unwilling to trust their fate to Communist promises. If it came to that, it would be far better to open our own gates to those who felt themselves endangered than to keep on sending Americans to die for them in their own land. As for the Saigon generals, there should be ample facilities for them on the French Riviera.

On all counts, the evidence is overwhelming that this war is not necessary, that, indeed, its continuation is immensely detrimental both to our own interests and to those of the peoples involved. We keep fighting in Vietnam because we are not yet willing to acknowledge that we should never have gone there in the first place. The result is a policy of pure contradiction: torn between its stubborn adherence to the war and its political need to get out of it, the Nixon administration has devised a policy with no chance of ending it, and every chance of perpetuating it into the indefinite future—the policy called Vietnamization.

II. Vietnamization

The official logic of Vietnamization is that, by some miraculous means, we are going to strengthen our bargaining hand by weakening our military effort. It is indeed a unique strategy, quite probably unprecedented in the history of warfare: bringing pressure to bear on the enemy by withdrawing from the battlefield. As the President explained it in his press conference of December 8, 1969, gradual American withdrawal is supposed to induce Hanoi to negotiate on our terms and because, as he put it, "Once we are out and the South Vietnamese are there, they will have a much harder individual to negotiate with * * *"

If the President was speaking of Mr. [Nguyen Van] Thieu's attitude toward negotiations, there can be no argument: He is much harder. But the President neglected to mention that it is not the political toughness of the South Vietnamese that is going to count if American forces are withdrawn but their military toughness, and in that department—despite the optimism expressed by the President in his speech of April 20—they are hardly a match for their Communist adversaries. That, let it never be forgotten, is why we went there with half a million American troops in the first place.

Novel as it may be, Vietnamization is a dangerous and unsound policy, more likely to lead to that "defeat and humiliation" which President Nixon so rightly deplores that to anything resembling an "honorable" peace. What it comes down to in plain commonsense terms is that, when you reduce your strength, you reduce your bargaining power. Thus far, our withdrawals have not been sufficient to make a major difference in the military balance. But, by the spring of 1971, when American forces are scheduled to be reduced to around 250,000 men, the military balance will be significantly altered—unless the ARVN [Army of the Republic of Vietnam] shows a far greater capacity of improving its effectiveness than we have any reason now to expect. What, then, if the Communists undertake a massive offensive aimed at winning the war outright? Would we reescalate the war, taking those "strong and effective measures" of which President Nixon has repeatedly warned, or would we accept the defeat?

Neither American military personnel in Vietnam nor the South Vietnamese themselves are sanguine about the prospects of Vietnamization. According to staff members of the Senate Foreign Relations Committee who went on a study trip to Vietnam in December 1969, American military officers have very little to say about the prospect for South Vietnamese military self-sufficiency, and when they do talk about it, it is in the time span of 2 to 4 years. President Thieu said recently that the withdrawal of American ground combat forces by the end of 1970 was an "impossible goal" and that, instead, "it will take many years" to remove these forces. President Nixon said nothing in his speech of April 20 to indicate a different assessment on his part.

Congress is as much in the dark as everybody else about the timetable for Vietnamization. Even in closed session of the Senate Foreign Relations Committee, the Secretaries of States and Defense have consistently declined to indicate how long the process is expected to take and how many Americans might remain in South Vietnam for the indefinite future. It is well to remember that there are still 50,000 American soldiers in Korea, 17 years after the end of the Korean war, despite the fact that the Republic of Korea has a large and effective army of its own, a defensible frontier, and freedom from internal subversion. How many Americans may be required to sustain the Saigon regime, which has none of the assets of South Korea? The administration steadfastly refuses to divulge the answer. That, I think, is because it has no answer.

III. An Indochina War

Even if it worked, Vietnamization would be a futile policy, because it no longer covers the situation in Southeast Asia. "I feel," the late Vietnam expert Bernard Fall once remarked, "like it is 1913, and I am an expert on Serbia who is about to be outstripped by events." The import of Fall's apprehension was that Vietnam might one day be consumed in a far wider conflict just as the Serbian controversy was consumed and then forgotten in the flames of World War I. One hopes it will never comes to that, but the spread of hostilities to Laos and Cambodia has already made it obsolete to speak of a Vietnamese war. In fact, with or without official recognition, we are now quite busily engaged in what Fall had the prescience several years ago to perceive as a "second Indochina war," a sequel to the struggle between the Vietminh and the French for domination of the entire Indochinese peninsula.

Increasingly the North Vietnamese and even the Chinese are referring to the conflicts in Vietnam, Laos, and Cambodia as a single "struggle for Indochina." As Mr. Stanley Karnow, one of the most perceptive journalists reporting from Indochina, commented recently:

The Communists are making it clear that they are prepared to expand the war over the artificial boundaries that separate the Indochinese states, and there is no reason to doubt their intentions.

There is hope as well as menace in this new situation, depending upon how the Nixon administration responds to it. If it follows the counsel of some of its military and civilian advisers in Vietnam and expands American military activities in Laos and Cambodia, then a predictable spiral of challenge and response will soon put an end both to Vietnamization and deescalation of the war. If, on the other hand, Mr. Nixon and his advisers see what Bernard Fall perceived long ago, that there can

be no solution to Vietnam except in the context of a general solution to Indochina, they might then revise their entire strategy and put us for the first time on a sensible course toward peace.

Stalemated by superior American firepower in Vietnam, the Communists appear to have embarked upon a general Indochinese strategy aimed at surrounding and isolating the American position in South Vietnam.

In Laos, despite a momentary abatement of hostilities, the military strength of the American-supported army of Meo tribesmen appears to be slowly deteriorating. Although the Communists have made no thrust toward the administrative capital of Vientiane, their dominance over northeastern Laos is virtually unchallenged except by continuing American air attacks. these air strikes, according to reports, are being conducted round the clock, amounting to an estimated 18,000 sorties a month. Meanwhile, despite fearful harassment from the air, the North Vietnamese continue to move supplies across the Plain of Jars toward the few remaining anti-Communist strongholds in northeastern Laos.

As an American diplomat recently explained to a diligent reporter:

The important thing is that the clandestine army is being destroyed and the U.S. bombing cannot stop it. This happens every day, in little skirmishes you never hear about. When Long Tieng finally crumbles, the Communists will have consolidated their own on northeast Laos. American bombing can make life hell for them, but it cannot stop them. Laos, in its typically leisurely way, is going down the drain.

In truth, our position in Laos borders on helplessness. Secretary of State Rogers all but confessed as much in a television statement on March 17. "We hope," he said, "that what they are up to is to make their negotiating position a little stronger. We hope that they do not intend to overrun Laos."

Whatever the precise Communist objective in Laos, it is already having the effect of undermining the foundations of the Nixon Vietnamization policy. In a military sense, it raises the long-term prospect of locking American forces into a beleaguered South Vietnamese enclave, while North Vietnam establishes its hegemony over the rest of Indochina.

Aside from continuing our indecisive bombing campaign in Laos and hoping for the best, the administration has two equally distasteful alternatives. It can simply give up any further hope for salvaging Laos and thereby see its Vietnamization strategy undermined by indirection; or it can send American ground forces, or a greatly increased number of Thais, into the Laotian war thereby abandoning the Vietnamization strategy and reverting to escalation. In the latter event, there is no telling where the escalation would stop. In a phrase reminiscent of the days before their "volunteers" swarmed into Korea in 1950, the Chinese have already responded to the entry of Thai forces into Laos with the warning that they "will not sit idly by."

The situation is hardly more promising in Cambodia; it may indeed be worse. With more bravado than wisdom, the new regime of General Lon Nol has undertaken to drive the North Vietnamese and Vietcong forces out of the borderlands of Cambodia. The trouble is that the weak Cambodian Army is in no position to do it unless it receives a massive injection of American arms, and that, in fact, is exactly what appears to be in the offing.

With indeterminate but unmistakable American support—support, incidentally, that was revealed more fully to the American people last evening—South Vietnamese troops have been striking at North Vietnamese and Vietcong units inside Cambodia. The Communists in turn have called on the Cambodian people to overthrow their new government and are using their forces within Cambodia to weaken the new regime. The Phnom Penh regime, for its part, is showing itself impotent against the Vietcong, while its troops, with or without official approval, have committed atrocious mass murders of Vietnamese civilians living in Cambodia.

It has long been the desire of American and South Vietnamese military officials to attack the Communist sanctuaries in Cambodia. From a purely military standpoint this is understandable, but the political implications are ominous. They raise the possibility of escalation in still another direction, under circumstances the Thieu government must surely welcome as a golden opportunity to put an end to American troop withdrawals by plunging the United States into a wider, Indochinese war.

Mr. Nixon and his advisers may feel tempted to come to the support of the anti-Communist but relatively powerless new regime in Phnom Penh. On the other hand, the administration must surely recognize the risks involved in an expansion of the war into Cambodia. The Vietcong and North Vietnamese have already turned that formerly neutral country into a battleground, and done so with the blessing of the ousted Prince Sihanouk, who has cloaked the Communists with legitimacy by creating a government in exile and by calling for a national liberation army to fight "with other anti-imperialist peoples forces of fraternal countries."

It escapes my understanding how, under these altered circumstances, the administration still fails to recognize that it is involving itself in an Indochina war which can only be resolved by an Indochina strategy. To continue relying on Vietnamization under these circumstances is comparable, in Bernard Fall's World War I analogy, to throwing resources into Serbia long after the Western Front had exploded. The Communists have made it abundantly clear that they are not going to allow us to press our military advantage in Vietnam without circumventing it by exploiting the power vacuums in Laos and Cambodia. Even more to the point, they have made it abundantly clear that, although they cannot expel us from Indochina, they are able and determined to thwart the policy of Vietnamization. The premise of that policy is that American intervention can be reduced to a level at which it may be sustained indefinitely without undue political disruption at home. That premise has been discredited by events in Laos and Cambodia, if not indeed by conditions in Vietnam as well. We are going to have to plunge into Indochina all the way and face the enormous consequences at home and abroad, or we are going to have to get out.

IV. The Way Out

The obvious and desirable way out is through a negotiated political settlement. President Nixon, however, appears to have given up on the Paris negotiations, insisting that the only alternative to Vietnamization is "immediate precipitate withdrawal." The North Vietnamese Government, he told Congress in his report of February 18, "has adamantly refused even to discuss our proposals" and, further, "has insisted that we must unconditionally and totally accept its demands for unilateral U.S. withdrawal and for the removal of the leaders of the Government of South Vietnam." He repeated this in scarcely altered words on April 20.

Reports by numerous unofficial and foreign observers suggest that the President's reading of the North Vietnamese position is inaccurate. Reputable individuals who have met with North Vietnamese officials both in Hanoi and in Paris assert that they do not insist on a complete American withdrawal prior to the conclusion of a settlement, nor do they demand a Vietcong takeover of South Vietnam. What they do insist upon, according to these observers, is an American commitment to a definite schedule for complete withdrawal of American forces and a traditional coalition regime to rule in Saigon until such time as a permanent government can be constituted. What the North Vietnamese and Vietcong are not able to accept are the following: an indefinite American presence; the continuation of the present South Vietnamese constitution—known to them as the "Johnson constitution"—which prohibits Communists from any participation in the government; and control of the election procedure for a permanent government by the present Saigon regime.

Aside from the continued presence of American forces in Indochina, the crucial question is quite simple: Who is going to rule South Vietnam? That is what the war is all about.

. . . .

Congressional Record, Senate, 91st Congress, 2d session, May 1, 1970, 13829–13832.

157   Senate Debate on the McGovern-Hatfield Amendment

September 1, 1970

The Senate debate over the McGovern-Hatfield amendment, which proposed a withdrawal of U.S. troops from Vietnam by the end of 1971, is an important reflection of the sharp divisions the war caused in the nation and in the halls of Congress. The escalation of the antiwar protests that spread across the United States in the spring and summer of 1970 in the wake of President Richard Nixon's order to send U.S. troops into Cambodia (see document 156) prompted the Nixon administration to investigate the seriousness of domestic unrest over the Vietnam War. The president appointed former governor of Pennsylvania William Scranton to conduct the investigation and issue a report. The Scranton commission said the war in Vietnam had seriously divided the nation, like no other time since the Civil War. The people of the United States, the report concluded, wanted U.S. troops withdrawn. Most Americans wanted an end to the war, although many were divided as to the best means of ending it. Congress was similarly divided on the issue. The Scranton commission warned of continuing unrest and serious damage to the stability of the nation unless the war was concluded.

Senators George McGovern (D-S.D.) and Mark Hatfield (R-Ore.) drafted an amendment to the military procurement bill for fiscal year 1971 that called for the withdrawal of U.S. troops by December 31, 1971. The Senate debated the proposal and rejected it by a vote of 55–39. The debate revealed growing opposition to the war within the Senate. It also revealed that there was serious opposition to ending U.S. involvement suddenly, as would be the case if the McGovern-Hatfield amendment was adopted. According to Stanley Karnow, in his Vietnam: A History *(Viking Press, 1983), President Nixon dismissed the amendment as the work of "radical liberals" in the Senate and said he would only start to worry "when the Right starts wanting to get out, for whatever reason. . . ." Nixon referred to the McGovern-Hatfield amendment as a "bug-out" proposal.*

In his remarks in support of his own amendment George McGovern indirectly answered the president's flip characterization of the McGovern-Hatfield amendment when he said:

Every Senator here is partly responsible for that human wreckage at Walter Reed and Bethesda Naval and all across our land—young men without legs, or arms, or genitals, or faces, or hopes.

There are not many of these blasted and broken boys who think this war is a glorious venture.

Do not talk to them about bugging out, or national honor, or courage.

The excerpts from the lengthy debate on September 1, 1970, included here contain remarks from only a few of those who spoke for or against the amendment. In addition to the remarks of McGovern and Hatfield, excerpts from the following senators are presented: Stephen Young (D-Ohio); Charles Percy (R-Ill.); Stuart Symington (D-Mo.); John Stennis (D-Miss.); Ralph Yarborough (D-Texas); Mike Mansfield (D-Mont.); Barry Goldwater (R-Ariz.); Bob Dole (R-Kan.); and Henry "Scoop" Jackson (D-Wash.).

SUPPORT FOR THE McGOVERN-HATFIELD AMENDMENT

Mr. YOUNG of Ohio. I wish to speak briefly and to the point on an important matter before the Senate today. I shall take great pride today in voting in favor of ending our war in Vietnam just as soon as we can. Of course, I shall record my vote in favor of the amendment pending before us.

It was the most horrendous mistake ever made by any President of the United States to involve us in a war in Vietnam—a little country of no importance whatsoever to the defense of the United States.

I feel that I am able to speak with some authority on this matter for the reason that in 1965 I spent nearly a month in Southeast Asia. I was in every area of South Vietnam. Also, I was in Korea and Thailand as well. At that time, despite the fact that we had guaranteed the neutrality of Laos, our war planes, disguised, were bombing areas of Laos.

As a member of the Armed Services Committee, my vote, on most occasions, has been a minority vote. I am happy to report, however, that the distinguished senior Senator from Missouri (Mr. Symington), and the distinguished Senator form Hawaii (Mr. Inouye) and I filed the first majority report ever filed with respect to authorizations for military appropriations.

In the Committee on Armed Services, time after time I have heard Senators, considered the greatest war hawks in this body, say that we should never have been involved in the war in Vietnam, but since we are in there we should see it through. Confucius, the great Chinese philosopher, centuries before the birth of our Saviour, said:

A man who makes a mistake and does not correct it makes another mistake.

That is also true of a nation, If a nation like ours makes a serious mistake and then does not correct it, it makes another mistake.

. . . .

But what happened soon after President Johnson became President? We have witnessed this in the Senate in recent years. It is evident that President Johnson was given poor advice by generals of the Joint Chief of Staff and Secretary of State Rusk.

He yielded deference and devotion to the military. This has also been demonstrated under President Nixon. He was elected largely because he promised the people of this country that he had a secret plan to end the war in Vietnam, That is still his secret. Instead of the war nearing its end, it had been expanded and extended and our combat planes and our B-52's are dumping napalm bombs and explosive bombs throughout Southeast Asia.

The war is no longer called our intervention in Vietnam, or the Vietnam war, it is the Indochina war. We are carrying on where the French left off.

We have an opportunity today in the Senate of the United States to give voice to the fact that 35 or 40 Senators—or more, I hope—are giving notice that we intend to refuse to vote for any appropriations unless this war or involvement over there is ended by the end of next year.

. . . .

Mr. PERCY. Mr. President, I do not intend to vote for the McGovern-Hatfield amendment. I have had grave reservations about it from its inception as an effective means of ending the war. Although its authors have made commendable and frequent efforts to modify its most controversial features, I still feel it would detract from our efforts to negotiate a settlement of the war which would end the war, not just American participation in the war.

I take second place to no Senator in my deep desire and commitment to end the war in Vietnam. I have believed for many years that the war has not been in our national interest, does not effect our own vital national security, and should be ended.

I continue to believe that the way to end the war is to promote meaningful negotiations, and I am not dissuaded by the failure so far of the Paris talks, because recent appointment of Ambassador Bruce and the return to Paris of Xuan Thuy have set the stage for a new era of negotiations. I have been doing everything I can to urge the President, Secretary Rogers, and Dr. Kissinger to give Ambassador Bruce a green light for peace.

. . . .

Mr. SYMINGTON. Mr. President, last May the original text of this McGovern-Hatfield amendment was presented to Congress and the American people.

At that time, many voiced their approval of this amendment. Others, however, although they favored the idea of setting some sort of timetable for the withdrawal of troops from Vietnam, had objections to some of the provisions contained in the original amendment.

During the intervening 3 months, supporters of the amendment have worked earnestly to develop language which would meet most of these objections, without sacrificing the original intent.

I believe the time devoted to this end has proven to be well worth the effort and commend the final product the Senate has before it today.

This amendment, as now drafted, should go a long way in answering any questions which some had about the earlier version; and all Senators who are interested in preserving the role of the Senate in matters of foreign policy should support it.

Some criticized the withdrawal date of June 30, 1971, in the original amendment as a "cut-and-run" policy; but the December 31, 1971, date for "orderly termination of military operations" and "the safe and systematic withdrawal of remaining Armed Forces" can hardly be characterized in any such manner.

Surely, 16 more months for the orderly termination of this costly war, one that has now dragged in for more than 5 years, is a reasonable timetable.

In addition, of particular concern to many with respect to the original version was that it would "tie the hands" of the President, militarily as well as diplomatically.

That concern has been laid to rest.

The amendment now provides that if the President finds in meeting the termination date of December 31, 1971, the Armed Forces of the United States are exposed to "unanticipated clear and present danger," he may suspend the withdrawal for 60 days; and so report these findings to Congress within 10 days in order that Congress can authorize a further extension.

Diplomatically, I believe the setting of a withdrawal date, combined with this provision of flexibility, could well provide a long overdue stimulus to the progress of the peace talks in Paris.

. . . .

Mr. MCGOVERN. Mr. President, I yield myself 2 minutes to reply to the excellent statement of the Senator from Missouri, who is a senior member of the Committee on Foreign Relations and the Committee on Armed Services. I commend him for the support that he brings to this amendment.

As the Senator knows, during most of the discussion and debate, the amendment has had a number of critics but very few positive defenders of our present course in Vietnam. Very few people understand why we have become so heavily involved in Indochina.

Most of the opponents of the amendment have contented themselves largely with criticism of the amendment, without making very mush of a defense of the alternative, which is what is taking place in Vietnam now.

Does not the Senator think that the burden of proof really ought not to be on those who call for underinvolvement, who call simply for flexibility for the President, who are opposed to the surrender of the constitutional responsibilities that are placed on Congress? It seems to me that the burden of proof ought to be on those who, according to a recent projection by two defense experts, recommend a situation in which we would keep a residual force in Vietnam over a period running, perhaps, to 1975, which could lead to the death of another 15,000 Americans and the expenditure of another $50 billion.

The PRESIDING OFFICER. The time of the Senator from South Dakota has expired.

Mr. MCGOVERN. I yield myself an additional minute.

Does not the Senator think that the burden of proof ought to be on those who defend that kind of course rather than the termination of the war?

Mr. SYMINGTON. If I may answer somewhat indirectly, under the Constitution Congress should have some say as to where, when, and how the youth of America are to be sent to fight and die for this country. We have had more than half a million

Americans in Germany for over a quarter of a century, We have had some 60,000 military in Korea for over 20 years. We have hundreds of thousands in Southeast Asia. This policy will break the back of the economy of the United States if we are not more careful.

It is such world "baby-sitting" policies which make it impossible in my State of Missouri to have adequate schools, adequate hospitals, adequate control of pollution, adequate care for our aged and ill. Too many people in my State live in a manner in which they should not live as citizens of the most prosperous Nation in the world.

As has been well said, all this is now getting tot he point where we are taking money from the poor people in a rich country so as to give it to the rich people in poor countries.

. . . .

Mr. HATFIELD. Mr. President, I, too, wish to express my appreciation for the eloquent statement by the distinguished Senator from Missouri (Mr. Symington) because it contributes greatly to the debate that has been taking place on the floor of the Senate.

Let us put aside all the rhetoric about whether or not we are supporting the President and whether or not we are undermining the negotiations in Paris or whether or not we are retreating into a new isolationism. These are not the real issues; they are not what are at stake here today. Rather, let us simply examine what the amendment prescribes. It says that the Congress supports the President in his currently announced withdrawal plan, that the Congress believes that the withdrawal should be completed by the end of 1971—an opinion shared by the majority of Americans—and that if the President finds it necessary or advisable to maintain troops beyond that time, then he should simply obtain the authorization of Congress.

To be opposed to that proposition is to believe that the executive branch should be able to chart any course of policy in Indochina and maintain any level of troops there into 1972 and beyond without the Congress saying a single word.

It is the difference between those who would yield to the idolatry of the Presidency, those who would grant what amounts to one-man rule, and those who believe in the wisdom of the constitutional process which is designed to guide this country.

We who support the amendment believe that we have been granted, by the people and by our Constitution, an obligation and a duty to exercise a role in the determination of the policies guiding our Nation. We have constructed the amendment not to be in opposition and confrontation to the Executive, but simply as a means to share in the responsibility which is ours.

Today, we shall choose to assume that responsibility, or to continue to abdicate it.

The future of our institutions is at stake this morning. We have a chance to begin the renewal of our constitutional system. We have the chance to demonstrate that Government is truly by the people and for the people.

. . . .

Mr. STENNIS. Mr. President, I plead with the Senate that as of now we should not stampede. Let us go right on down the road we are going, retaining whatever power the Chief Executive has as a negotiator and as a peacemaker. He is a man of discernment.

We should let him use whatever discretion he can exercise. We should not only let him do that, but we should also keep the responsibility on him.

I fell that the President is trying to do everything he can. If I did not feel that way, I would not say what I am saying.

I think that sometimes we need someone to rock the boat, but not now in this matter.

I hope that by a clearcut, clean, and large majority the Senate rejects the amendment.

. . . .

Mr. YARBOROUGH. Mr. President, Yesterday I placed before the Senate petitions bearing the names of more than 10,000 persons from my home city of Austin, Tex., requesting that all American troops be withdrawn from Southeast Asia by June 30, 1971. We are now about to vote on a request to the President to withdraw such troops by December 31, 1971. In so doing, we are asking the President to carry out his pledge to the American people in 1968 to settle the war in Southeast Asia. All the Hatfield-McGovern amendment does is to request the President to settle the war more than 2 years after he promised to settle it.

The President won the 1968 election by 0.43 percent—less than one-half of 1 percent—by promising to settle the war. What is wrong with voting, nearly 2 years after the promise was made, to ask the President to settle it? It should help him; he can point to congressional action as demanding and requesting it. We take the responsibility off his back and place it on our own. This I am willing to do.

The war is not and Indochina war; it is an American war, fought in every instance by Americans and their hired mercenaries, South Vietnamese, Korean, Philippine, Thai—save only a token force of Australian and New Zealanders. We have poured over $110 billion into Indochina, have lost over 338,000 of our men dead and wounded, more that twice our losses in the Korean conflict and more than our total losses in World War I.

We have killed hundreds of thousands of South Vietnamese civilians and wounded over a million more. We have burned their villages, poisoned their fields and forests, virtually destroyed their civilization. The civilized world stands shocked at our ruling that is proper and legal for an American military man to kill women and children if he suspects that they sympathize with the Vietcong.

Who wants us in South Vietnam? Not the South Vietnamese people, not the North Vietnamese people, not the Vietnamese people. Our own polls show that they want us out. Then what validity is there in our continuing to stay, to send back a long list each week of American boys dead and wounded because we hire people to kill their own people, and some of our own are lost in the process.

It takes courage to vote for this measure—far more than to vote against it. Wayne Morse, Joe Clark, Ernest Gruening, and I are examples of the price one risks in voting against those who make billions off this unwise, stupid war. A director of Lockheed Aircraft ran against me and spent $6.5 million to gain my seat. That is a small price to pay if it gains one vote in the Senate for those who want this war to continue. But I have faith that right makes might, and that right and wisdom will prevail here in the Halls of Congress, as I believe it now does in the hearts and minds of the American people.

We have a chance today to vote for our little, timid request to the President to do by 1972 what should have been done 10 years earlier. The measure is years late, but it is never too late to start on a course of wisdom and justice.

Neither side here has a patent on patriotism. It is just as patriotic to oppose the senseless killings and monstrous concentration jails, as it is to support them. A percentage of Americans taught the pleasure of killing in Vietnam will be unable to reorient themselves on their return to America, and murder in the street will continue here. . . .

The terrible truth which we in this country must face is that the Indochina war is a mistake. It is not a Democratic mistake or a Republican mistake, but rather an American mistake. It resulted from and has been prolonged by our blind obedience to a foreign policy that simply cannot work in the nuclear age. Instead of recognizing our blunder, both the Democratic and Republican administrations have continued to follow these outmoded theories with the result being a wider and more costly war.

During this tragic period in our history, attempts are constantly being made to justify our continued involvement in this military misadventure. The American people have been subjected to a continuing flow of speeches, programs, conferences, and promises regarding the war. Out of this war has come a series of words and slogans such as "pacification" and lately "Vietnamization" which are ushered in with great pomp and ceremony, only to evaporate in the hard light of reality. The American people have had their patience and trust strained to the breaking point They are no longer willing to accept without question such shallow and fruitless plans for ending the war as Vietnamization or put their trust in so-called secret plans such as the one to which President Nixon continually refers. What they want is positive proof that Congress will put a stop to the killing of Americans in Indochina.

The amendment we have offered gives our people the action they have called for. Since it is obvious that the administration does not know how to end this war or lacks the will to do so, it is Congress' responsibility to end it and end it now.

Our country cannot continue to bear the cost of this immoral and fruitless conflict. As of August 22, 1970, the Department of Defense reports that 43,418 of America's finest young people have died in battle in Southeast Asia. Another 8, 425 persons have perished as a result of disease and injuries sustained in these foreign lands. This means that over 51,000 young lives have been abruptly ended before they reach their most productive years. In addition to the tragic loss of life, over 287,000 of our servicemen have been wounded, some crippled for life. Another 1,556 of our troops are either missing or prisoners of war. This is twice as many dead and wounded as we suffered in the Korean conflict, and more than our total casualties in World War II.

We can only wonder what the world has lost by the death of these young people. The man who could have cured cancer might have been among them. We will never know how many potential teachers, lawyers, doctors, engineers, scientists, and artists we have lost. Nothing we can say will bring the dead back to life or restore the wounded and crippled to health. We can, however, insure that no more of their generation will be sacrificed in this purposeless struggle.

In addition to the terrible loss of life, this war has played havoc with the economy of the Nation and halted progress in many vital domestic areas. Never in the history of our Nation have we been subjected to runaway inflation and rising unemployment at the same time. The cost of war is being felt on every domestic front. There is not enough money to build and expand medical schools, so that doctors can be trained to treat our sick. Students cannot obtain loans to continue their education. Colleges and universities are turning away students because they cannot build facilities to accommodate them. The average American cannot purchase a suitable home or borrow money from a bank without paying interest at the rate of 9 to 10 percent a year.

In 1969, the Government admitted spending $29 billion on the Indochina war. This year it plans to commit another $20 to 25 billion on this struggle. Let us stop and think what this money could be used for in this country. As one author has suggested, the cost of 1 month of the war by itself could provide enough food to end hunger among 10 million Americans, finance the annual cost of State and local police forces, and train 100,000 scientists. The cost of 1 year of this war would be more than sufficient to double the social security benefits of 20 million Americans.

Instead of spending America's tax dollars where they would benefit the majority of our people. The administration continues to throe billions on the blood-soaked battlefields of Vietnam, Cambodia, and Laos, while attacking funds for education and health as inflationary. War is inflationary, the most inflationary of all physical governmental actions. Education is not inflationary.

. . . .

[Mr. MANSFIELD] The Senate cannot evade its share of responsibility for the answer to such questions. The dead and wounded are not the President's responsibility alone. The burden falls on all of us. What we do or do not in conjunction with the President, in the end, will determine the end of the road.

We cannot say, "Leave it to the President," and then wash our hands of the matter. The Senate so said at the beginning of this ill-fated military involvement, a half decade ago. We left it to a President. We raised no caveat. All in the name of leaving to the President, we endorsed a war which we did not expect to begin. In the same name, by rejecting Hatfield-McGovern, will we now hail an American military withdrawal which has yet to take place?

. . . .

Mr. GOLDWATER. Mr. President, I do not think there is any question in any Senator's mind that this has been a wrong war. I do not think the idea of our getting into it was particularly wrong, but we never meant to win this war, and when you do not mean to win a war, for God's sake, so not get into a war. This is the first war in the history of our country which history will say we lost because we did not go into it with the will on the part of any President who participated in getting us into the war to win it. We could have won it. We could have won it 6 years ago, and in my opinion, had we used our power correctly, the war might never have started. But we allowed it to start.

It has been an expensive war, one of the most expensive in our history, not just in money, but that becomes inconsequential when we compare money against men. It has divided our country as probably no war in the history of this country except the War Between the States has divided us. And it need not have divided our country had we gone into this war and had we made a decision to go into the war and at the same time made up our minds to win the war.

I hope that never in the history of this country will anything like this ever again be perpetrated against the American people. I think it has been a shame and a crime. I think history is going to blacken the names of those Presidents who got us into this position and refused to do anything about it.

It has weakened us in the eyes of the world. As I talk to friends around the world, it shocks me to hear what people are saying about the United States and the United States inability to make up its mind, inability to separate national politics from international policy, international policy on which depends the whole peace and freedom of the world. And yet we do not seem to have the courage—if I may say, the guts—to stand up and face it.

It rather sickens me to hear amendments coming up like this. I know it is perfectly within our constitutional rights to offer amendments like this, to control the spending by the President so that we might end the war, but I have to remind us that our President inherited these wrongs. He did not create them. He is the first President we have had to do anything about changing those wrongs. He is the man charged with the responsibility of going to war and emerging with peace.

We have some constitutional rights in this general area but, Mr. President, they are very, very fuzzy, and I would suggest to those who are constantly bringing up this type of amendment that they do as I have so often suggested—that if they are not happy with the warmaking powers of the Congress, if they are not happy with the strategic, tactical, and force level decision-making powers of the Executive, let us offer constitutional amendments to the people to correct that. If we are not happy with the powers given to the President as Commander in Chief under the Constitution, then let us change it by constitutional amendment. Let us not try to get it changed by congressional edict.

I hope the amendment is soundly defeated. Even though I recognize the right of the Senators to offer it, I think it comes at a poor time in our history, when we are trying to engage an enemy in meaningful talks. I so not think we are giving our negotiators any kind of handle at all. I hate to say this, but we are helping Hanoi every time we seek to hamper the President in ending a war that need never have started, I said that 6 long years ago, but, unfortunately, people would not listen.

. . . .

Mr. DOLE. Mr. President, we have about concluded the Madison Avenue effort costing hundreds of thousands of dollars to sell the so-called "end the war" amendment which I have designated the "lose the peace" amendment—to the U.S. Senate. For the first time in history, U.S. Senators have raised funds directly to be used to lobby their fellow Senators. It is fair to say, excluding those who have Presidential ambitions, the vote today will for all practical purposes be a vote of confidence in the Vietnamization policy of President Nixon.

The various versions of the so-called "end the war amendment" should prove to everyone the impossibility and impracticability of attempting to fix a date. While the sponsors would impose a fixed date on the President, it is interesting to note that they have had difficulty arriving at a date themselves.

First the war was to end on December 1, 1970; then December 31, 1970; then April 30, 1971; then December 31, 1971; and now March 1, 1972.

It seems strange, indeed, that the sponsors, having used five different, arbitrary dates in an effort to attract votes, would now seek to hamstring the President who has been extracting us from South Vietnam.

I can imagine what the critics would be saying if President Nixon had changed his mind five different times on troop withdrawals or on South Vietnamese policy.

The hard facts are that the President and only the President is the Commander in Chief—that the President and only the President can negotiate peace, and that despite the appeal of the so-called "end the war" amendment—which I designate the "end the peace" amendment—it can best be characterized as a shallow appeal to the emotions and anxieties of good Americans who are weary of 7 years of war.

Politics might dictate supporting the amendment, but I believe the great majority of Senators have confidence in President Nixon's policies because he is demonstrating that we may achieve peace with honor—rather than retreat and defeat.

To those who say that 40 votes would be a moral victory, I say 40 votes for the amendment would be a moral defeat for this country.

. . . .

[Mr. JACKSON.] I believe, Mr. President, that the "amendment-to-end-the-war" will not achieve the objective. The supporters of the amendment have failed completely to convince me that the total number of lives lost in this tragic conflict will be fewer if the amendment is passed than if we carry out an orderly withdrawal in the absence of statutory compulsion. It is entirely possible, for example, that passage of the amendment will serve, not to shorten the war, but to deepen the intransigence of the North Vietnamese at Paris and further liberate their armed forces to concentrate on the destruction of innocent civilians in Cambodia and Laos.

As our withdrawal proceeds, the only leverage we have with which to promote the chance of a negotiated settlement lies in the uncertainty that surrounds the President's timetable. This leverage applies not only to Hanoi—which must view with displeasure our efforts to strengthen the South Vietnamese—but also to Saigon whose cooperation will be essential to any negotiated settlement. If we establish a date certain for the withdrawal of the last American soldier, our capacity to influence the South Vietnamese will vanish. And what is worse, the spirit of cooperation essential to the collaborative training mission of the Vietnamization program may be turned, to enmity and bitterness.

For this reason, I believe it is mistaken to assume that if the McGovern-Hatfield amendment were adopted Vietnamization could go forward successfully in the months before December 31, 1971. It might well collapse entirely under the burden of a seriously demoralized South Vietnam and an invigorated North Vietnamese military force.

Moreover, Mr. President, I am opposed to the rigid inflexibility that would result from the legal requirements that all armed forces be withdrawn by December 31, 1971. . . .

Mr. DOLE. Mr. President, I received a very forcefully worded and concise statement of opposition to the McGovern-Hatfield amendment. It is remarkable in that its brevity adds to the impact of its message by saying in a few words all that is really necessary to know about the amendment.

The statement was in the form of a telegram from J. Milton Patrick, national commander of the American Legion. It was sent from Portland, Oreg., where the Legion is holding its national convention.

I believe that Mr. Patrick's statement expresses the feelings of millions of Americans, both members of the Legion and other citizens.

I ask unanimous consent that the text of the telegram be inserted in the *Record* at this point.

There being no objection, the telegram was ordered to be printed in the *Record*, as follows:

August 27, 1970.

HON. ROBERT DOLE,
U.S. Senate,
Washington, D.C.:

The American Legion strongly opposes the Hatfield-McGovern amendment to FY-71 military procurement authorization act, This amendment would compel the United States to withdraw forces from Viet Nam and ham-string the President's efforts to achieve a just and honorable peace in that war torn country. The action called for by this amendment would in effect hand over all Indochina to Communism and make a terrible mockery of the sacrifices we have made to insure the right of South Vietnam to self determination. We urge you to oppose the passage of the Hatfield-McGovern amendment and to encourage your colleagues to do likewise.

J. Milton Patrick,
National Commander of the American Legion.

Mr. MCGOVERN. Mr. President, the vote we are about to cast could be one of the most significant votes Senators will ever cast.

I have lived with this vote night and day since last April 30—the day before the Cambodian invasion—the day this amendment was first submitted.

I thank God this amendment was submitted when it was, because, as every Senator knows, in the turbulent days following the invasion of Cambodia and the tragedy at Kent State University, this amendment gave a constructive rallying point to millions of anguished citizens across this war-weary land.

I believe that, along with the Cooper-Church amendment the pending amendment helped to keep the Nation from exploding this summer. It was the lodestar that inspired more mail, more telegrams, more eager young visitors to our offices, more political action, and more contributions from doctors, lawyers, workers, and housewives than any other initiative of Congress in this summer of our discontent.

Now this question is about to be resolved. What is the choice it presents us? It presents us with an opportunity to end a war we never should have entered. It presents us with an opportunity to revitalize constitutional government in America by restoring the war powers the Founding Fathers obliged the Congress to carry.

It gives us an opportunity to correct the drift toward one-man rule in the crucial areas of war and peace.

All my life, I have heard Republicans and conservative Democrats complaining about the growth of centralized power in the Federal executive.

Vietnam and Cambodia have convinced me that the conservatives were right. Do they really believe their own rhetoric? We have permitted the war power which the authors of the Constitution wisely gave to us as the people's representatives to slip out of our hands until it now resides behind closed doors at the State Department, the CIA, the Pentagon, and the basement of the White House. We have foolishly assumed that war was too complicated to be trusted to the people's forum—the Congress of the United States. The result has been the cruelest, the most barbaric, and the most stupid war in our national history.

Every Senator here is partly responsible for sending 50,000 young Americans to an early grave. This Chamber reeks of blood.

Every Senator here is partly responsible for that human wreckage at Walter Reed and Bethesda Naval and all across our land—young men without legs, or arms, or genitals, or faces, or hopes.

There are not many of these blasted and broken boys who think this war is a glorious venture.

Do not talk to them about bugging out, or national honor, or courage.

It does not take any courage at all for a Congressman, or a Senator, or a President to wrap himself in the flag and say we are staying in Vietnam, because it is not our blood that is being shed.

But we are responsible for those young men and their lives and their hopes.

And if we do not end this damnable war, those young men will some day curse us for our pitiful willingness to let the Executive carry the burden that the Constitution places on us.

So before we vote, let us ponder the admonition of Edmund Burke, the great parliamentarian of an earlier day:

A conscientious man would be cautious how he dealt in blood.

Mr. MANSFIELD. Mr. President, I ask for the yeas and nays.

The yeas and nays were ordered.

. . . .

The result was announced—yeas 39, nays 55. . . .

So the McGovern-Hatfield amendment (No. 862) was rejected.

. . . .

Congressional Record, Senate, 91st Congress, 2d session, Sept. 1, 1970, 30566–30683.

---

158   The Legislative Reorganization Act of 1970

October 26, 1970

The Legislative Reorganization Act of 1970 proposed the first major reorganization of Congress since 1946 (see document 137). Congress sought to open more of its activities, especially committee hearings, to public scrutiny. This included making provisions for televising more congressional hearings. It also increased the professionalism of the standing committee staff of the House and Senate and expanded the Legislative Reference Service, renaming it the Congressional Research Service. This legislation clearly reflected Congress's growing need for highly qualified staff to assist with the complexities of a technical society and provide expertise in dozens of specialized areas of knowledge. This far-ranging reform bill also introduced the use of electronic equipment for conducting roll call votes in the House of Representatives. It called for the creation of "a standardized information and data processing system for budgetary and fiscal data." The concern of Congress for opening more of its operations to public scrutiny even extended to the creation of a Capitol Guide Service, with uniformed guides to provide visitors with tours of the Capitol.

This reform grew out of the work of the Joint Committee on the Organization of Congress, created in 1965 under the leadership of Senator Mike Monroney (D-Okla.) and Representative Ray Madden (D-Ind.). Other members of Congress wanted even more sweeping changes, especially in the area of the seniority system by which members moved up in the ranks to important chairmanships. Richard Bolling (D-Mo.), an aggressive reformer in the House, had called for limitations on the powers of committee chairman in two influential books on reforming Congress, House Out of Order *(1965) and* Power in the House *(1968). In 1974 Bolling chaired the influential Select Committee on Committees, which examined in considerable detail the entire committee structure of the House and addressed many of the issues that were not incorporated in the Legislative Reorganization Act of 1970 (see document 159).*

TITLE I—THE COMMITTEE SYSTEM
Rulemaking Power of Senate and House

SEC. 101. The following sections of this title are enacted by the Congress—

(1) insofar as applicable to the Senate, as an exercise of the rulemaking power of the Senate and, to the extent so applicable, those sections are deemed a part of the Standing Rules of the Senate, superseding other individual rules of the Senate only to the extent that those sections are inconsistent with those other individual Senate rules, subject to and with full recognition of the power of the Senate to enact or change any rule of the Senate at any time in its exercise of its constitutional right to determine the rules of its proceedings; and

(2) insofar as applicable to the House of Representatives, as an exercise of the rulemaking power of the House of Representatives, subject to and with full recognition of the power of the House, of Representatives to enact or change any rule of the House at any time in its exercise of its constitutional right to determine the rules of its proceedings.

Calling of Committee Meetings

. . . .

Each standing committee of the Senate shall fix regular biweekly, or monthly meetings days for the transaction of business before the committee and additional meetings may be called by the chairman as he may deem necessary. If at least three members of any such committee desire that a special meeting of the committee be called by the chairman, those members may file in the offices of the committee their written request to the chairman for that special meeting. Immediately upon the filing of the request, the clerk of the committee shall notify the chairman of the filing of the request. If, within three calendar days after the filing of the request, the chairman does not call the requested special meeting, to be held within seven calendar days after the filing of the request, a majority of the members of the committee may file in the offices of the committee their written notice that a special meeting of the committee will be held, specifying the date and hour of that special meeting. The committee shall meet on that date and hour. Immediately upon the filing of the notice, the clerk of the committee shall notify all members of the committee that such special meeting will be held and inform them of its date and hour. If the chairman of any such committee is not present it any regular, additional, or special meeting of the committee, the ranking member of the majority party on the committee who is present shall prescribe at meeting.

. . . .

. . . Meetings for the transaction of business of each standing committee of the Senate, other than for the conduct of hearings, shall be open to the public except during executive sessions for marking up bills or for voting or when the committee by majority vote orders an executive session.

. . . .

The vote of the committee to report a measure or matter shall require the concurrence of a majority of the members of the committee who are present. No vote of any member of any such committee to report a measure or matter may be cast by proxy if rules adopted by such committee forbid the casting of votes for that purpose by proxy, however, proxies shall not be voted for such purpose except when the absent committee member has been informed of the, matter on which he is being recorded and has affirmatively requested that he be so recorded. Action by any such committee in reporting any measure or matter in accordance with the requirements of this subsection shall constitute the ratification by the committee of all action theretofore taken by the committee with respect to that measure or matter, including votes taken upon the measure. or matter or any amendment thereto, and no point of order shall lie with respect to that measure or matter on the ground that such previous action with respect thereto by such committee was not taken in compliance with such requirements. Whenever any such committee by roll call vote reports any measure or matter, the report of the committee upon such measure or matter shall include a tabulation of the votes cast in favor of and the votes cast in opposition to such measure or matter by each member of the committee. Nothing contained in this subsection shall abrogate the power of any committee of the Senate to adopt rules—

(1) providing for proxy voting on all matters other than the reporting of a measure or matter, or

(2) providing in accordance, with the rules of the Senate for a lesser number as a quorum for any action other than the reporting of a measure or matter.

. . . No vote by any member of any committee with respect to any measure or matter may be cast by proxy unless such committee, by written rule adopted by the committee, permits voting by proxy and requires that the proxy authorization shall be in writing, shall designate the person who is to execute the proxy authorization, and shall be limited to a specific measure or matter and any amendments or motions pertaining thereto.

. . . .

. . . Each committee of the House (except the Committee or Rules) shall make public announcement of the date, place, and subject matter of any hearing to be conducted by the committee on any measure or matter at least one week before the commencement of that hearing, unless the committee determines that there is good cause to begin such hearing at an earlier date. If the committee makes that determination, the committee shall make such public announcement a the earliest possible date. Such public announcement also shall be published in the Daily Digest portion of the Congressional Record as soon as possible after such public announcement is made by the committee.

Open Committee Hearings

. . . Each hearing conducted by each standing, select, or special committee of the Senate (except the Committee on Appropriations) shall be open to the public except when the committee determines that the testimony to be taken at that hearing may relate to a matter of national security, may tend to reflect adversely on the character or reputation of the witness or any other individual, or may divulge matters deemed confidential under other provisions of law or Government regulation.

. . . .

(2) Each hearing conducted by each committee shall be open to the public except when the committee, by majority vote, determines otherwise.

. . . .

Broadcasting of Committee Hearings

SEC. 116. . . . Whenever any such hearing is open to the public, that hearing may be broadcast by radio or television, or both, under such rules as the committee may adopt.

(b) Rule XI of the Rules of the House of Representatives is amended by adding at the end thereof the following new clause:

33. (a) It is the purpose of this clause to provide a means, In conformity with acceptable standards of dignity, propriety, and decorum, by which committee hearings which are open to the public may be covered, by television broadcast, radio broadcast, and still photography, or by any of such methods of coverage—

(1) for the education, enlightenment, and information of the general public, on the basis of accurate and impartial news coverage, regarding the operations, procedures, and practices of the House as a legislative and representative body and regarding the measures, public issues, and other matters before the House and its committees, the consideration thereof, and the action taken thereon; and

(2) for the development of the perspective and understanding of the general public with respect to the role and function of the House under the Constitution of the United States as an organ of the Federal Government.

(b) In addition, it is the intent of this clause that radio and television tapes and television film of any coverage under this clause shall not be used, or made available for use, as partisan political campaign material to promote or oppose the candidacy of any person for elective public office.

(c) It is, further, the intent of this clause that the general conduct each meeting of any hearing or hearings covered, under authority of this clause, by television broadcast, radio broadcast, and still photography, or by any of such methods of coverage, and the personal behavior of the committee members and staff, other Government officials and personnel, witnesses, television, radio, and press media personnel, and the general public at the hearing shall be, in strict conformity with and observance of the acceptable standards of dignity, propriety, courtesy, and decorum traditionally observed by the House in its operations and shall not be such as to—

(A) distort the objects and purposes of the hearing or the activities of committee members in connection with that hearing or in connection with the general work of the committee or of the House; or

(B) cast discredit or dishonor oil the House, the committee, or any Member or bring the House, the committee, or any Member into disrepute.

(d) The coverage of committee hearings by television broadcast, radio broadcast, or still photography is a privilege made available House and shall be permitted and conducted only in strict conformity with the purposes, provisions, and requirements of this clause.

. . . .

(1) If the television or radio coverage of the hearing is to be presented to the, public as live coverage, that coverage shall be conducted and presented without commercial sponsorship.

(2) No witness served with a subpena by the committee shall be required against his will to be, photographed at any hearing or to give evidence or testimony while the broadcasting of that hearing, by radio or television, is being conducted. At the request of any such witness who does not wish to be subjected to radio, television, or still photography coverage, all lenses shall be covered and all microphones used or coverage turned off. . . .

Recording of Roll Calls and Quorum Calls Through Electronic Equipment in the House

SEC. 121 . . .

5. In lieu of the calling of the names of Members in the manner provided for under the preceding provisions of this Rule, upon any roll call or quorum, call, the names of such Members voting or present may be recorded through the use of appropriate electronic equipment. In any such case, the Clerk shall enter

in the Journal and publish in the Congressional Record, in alphabetical order in each category, a list of the names of those Members recorded as voting in the affirmative, of those Members recorded as voting in the negative, and of those members voting present, as the case may be, as if their names had been called in the manner provided for under such preceding provisions.

. . . .

TITLE II—FISCAL CONTROLS
Part I—Budgetary and Fiscal Information and Data
Budgetary and Fiscal Data Processing System

SEC. 201. The Secretary of the Treasury and the Director of the Office of Management and Budget, in cooperation with the Comptroller General of the United States, shall develop, establish, and maintain, insofar as practicable, for use by all Federal agencies, a standardized information and data processing system for budgetary and fiscal data.

Budget Standard Classifications

SEC. 202. (a) The Secretary of the Treasury and the Director of the Office of Management and Budget, in cooperation with the Comptroller General, shall develop, establish, and maintain standard classifications of programs, activities, receipts, and expenditures of Federal agencies in order—

(1) to meet the needs of the various branches of the Government; and

(2) to facilitate the development, establishment, and maintenance of the data processing system under section 201 through the utilization of modern automatic data processing techniques.

. . . .

Availability to Congress of Budgetary, Fiscal, and Related Data

SEC. 203. Upon request of any committee of either House, or of any Joint committee of the two Houses, the Secretary of the Treasury and the Director of the Office of Management and Budget shall

(1) furnish to such committee or joint committee information as to the location and nature of data available in the various Federal agencies with respect to programs, activities, receipts, and expenditures of such agencies; and

(2) to the extent feasible, prepare for such committee, or joint committee summary tables of such data.

Assistance to Congress by General Accounting Office

SEC. 204. (a) The Comptroller General shall review and analyze the results of Government programs and activities carried on under existing law, including the making of cost benefit studies, when ordered by either House of Congress, or upon his own initiative, or when requested by any committee of the House of Representatives or the Senate, or any joint committee of the two Houses, having jurisdiction over such programs and activities.

(b) The Comptroller General shall have available in the General Accounting Office employees who are expert in analyzing and conducting cost benefit studies of Government programs. Upon request of any committee of either House or any joint committee of the two Houses, the Comptroller General shall assist such committee or joint committee, or the staff of such committee or joint committee—

(1) in analyzing cost benefit studies furnished by any Federal agency to such committee or joint committee; or

(2) in conducting cost benefit studies of programs under the jurisdiction of such committee or joint committee.

. . . .

TITLE III—SOURCES OF INFORMATION

Part 1—Staffs of Senate and House Standing Committees

Increase in Professional Staffs of Senate Standing Committees; Senate Minority Professional and Clerical Staffs; Fair Treatment for Senate Minority Staffs

SEC. 301. . . . (a) Each standing committee of the Senate (other that the Committee on Appropriations) is authorized to appoint, by majority vote of the committee, not more than six professional staff members in addition to the clerical staffs. Such professional staff members shall be assigned to the chairman and the ranking minority member of such committee as the committee may deem advisable, except that whenever a majority of the minority members of such committee so request, two of such professional staff members may be selected for appointment by majority vote of the minority members and the committee shall appoint any staff members so selected. A staff member or members appointed pursuant to a request by the minority members of the committee shall be assigned to such committee business as such minority members deem advisable. Services of professional staff members appointed by majority vote of the committee may be terminated by a majority vote of the committee and services of professional staff members appointed pursuant to a request by the minority members of the committee shall be terminated by the committee when a majority of such minority members so request. Professional staff members authorized by this subsection shall be appointed on a permanent basis, without regard to political affiliation, and solely on the basis of fitness to perform the duties of their respective positions. Such professional staff members shall not engage in any work other than committee business and no other duties may be assigned to them.

. . . .

Part 2—Congressional Research Service

Improvement of Research Facilities of Congress

SEC. 321. (a) Section 203 of the Legislative Reorganization Act of 1946, as amended (2 U.S.C. 166) is amended to read as follows:

CONGRESSIONAL RESEARCH SERVICE

SEC. 203. (a) The Legislative Reference Service in the Library of Congress is hereby continued as a separate department in the Library of Congress and is redesignated the "Congressional Research Service".

(b) It is the policy of Congress that—

(1) the Librarian of Congress shall, in every possible way, encourage, assist, and promote the Congressional Research Service in—

(A) rendering to Congress the most effective and efficient service,

(B) responding most expeditiously, effectively, and efficiently to the special needs of Congress, and

(C) discharging its responsibilities to Congress; and

(2) the Librarian of Congress shall grant and accord to the Congressional Research Service complete research independence and the maximum practicable administrative independence consistent with these objectives.

. . . .

(e) The Librarian of Congress is authorized to appoint in the Congressional Research Service, upon the recommendation of the Director, Specialists and Senior Specialists in the, following broad fields:

(1) agriculture;

(2) American government and public administration;

(3) American public law;

(4) conservation;

(5) education;

(6) engineering and public works;

(7) housing;

(8) industrial organization and corporation finance;

(9) international affairs;

(10) international trade and economic geography;

(11) labor and employment;

(12) mineral economics;

(13) money and banking;

(14) national defense;

(15) price economics;

(16) science;

(17) social welfare;

(18) taxation and fiscal policy;

(19) technology;

(20) transportation and communications;

(21) urban affairs;

(22) veterans affairs; and

(23) such other broad fields as the Director may consider appropriate.

Such Specialists and Senior Specialists, together with such other employees of the Congressional Research Service as may be necessary, shall be available for special work with the committees and Members of the Senate and House of Representatives and the joint committee of Congress for any of the purposes of subsection (d) of this section.

. . . .

Part 3—Parliamentary Precedents of the House of Representatives
Periodic Compilation of Parliamentary Precedents of the House of Representatives

SEC. 331. (a) The Parliamentarian of the House of Representatives, at the beginning of the fifth fiscal year following the completion and publication of the parliamentary precedents of the House authorized by the Legislative Branch Appropriation Act, 1966 (79 Stat. 270; Public Law 89-90), and at the beginning of each fifth fiscal year thereafter, shall commence the compilation and preparation for printing of the parliamentary precedents of the House of Representatives, together with such other materials as may be useful in connection therewith, and an index digest of such precedents and other materials. Each such compilation and preparation for printing of the parliamentary precedents of the House shall be, completed by the close of the fiscal year immediately following the fiscal year in which such work is commenced.

(b) As so compiled and prepared, such precedents and other materials and index digest shall be printed on pages of such size, and in such type and format, as the parliamentarian may determine and shall be printed in such numbers and for such distribution as may be provided by low enacted prior to printing.

(c) For the purpose of carrying out each such compilation and preparation, the Parliamentarian may

(1) subject to the approval of the Speaker, appoint (as employees of the House of Representatives) clerical and other personnel and fix their respective rates of pay; and

(2) utilize the services of personnel of the Library of Congress and the Government Printing Office.

. . . .

TITLE IV—CONGRESS AS AN INSTITUTION
Part 1—Joint Committee on Congressional Operations
Establishment of Joint Committee on Congressional Operations

SEC. 401. (a) There is hereby created a Joint Committee on Congressional Operations (hereafter in this Part referred to as the "Joint Committee").

(b) The Joint Committee shall be composed of ten members as follows:

(1) five Members of the Senate, appointed by the President pro tempore of the Senate, three from the majority party and two from the minority party; and

(2) five Members of the House of Representatives appointed by the Speaker of the House of Representatives, three from the majority party and two from the minority party.

(c) Vacancies in the membership of the Joint Committee shall not affect the power of the remaining members to execute the functions of the joint Committee and shall be filled in the same manner as in the case of the original appointment.

(d) The Joint Committee shall select a chairman and a vice chairman from among its members at the beginning of each Congress. The vice chairman shall act in the place and stead of the chairman in the, absence of the chairman. The chairmanship and the vice chairmanship shall alternate between the, Senate and the House of Representatives with each Congress. The chairman during each even numbered Congress shall be selected by the Members of the House of Representatives on the Joint Committee from among their number and the chairman during each odd-numbered Congress shall be selected by the Members of the Senate on the Joint Committee from among their number. The vice chairman during each Congress shall be chosen in the same manner from that House of Congress other than the House of Congress of which the chairman is a Member.

Duties of the Joint Committee

SEC. 402. (a) The Joint Committee shall—

(1) make a continuing study of the organization and operation of the Congress of the United States and shall recommend improvements in such organization and operation with a view toward strengthening Congress, simplifying its operations, improving its relationships with other branches of the United States government, and enabling it better to meet its responsibilities under the Constitution of the United States; and

(2) identify any court proceeding or action which, in the opinion of the Joint Committee, is of vital interest to the Congress, or to either House of the Congress, as a constitutionally established institution of the Federal Government and call such proceeding or action to the attention of that House of the Congress which is specifically concerned or to both Houses of the Congress if both Houses are concerned.

. . . .

Part 4—The Capitol Guide Service
Establishment and Operation of the Capitol Guide Service

SEC. 441. (a) There is hereby established an organization under the Congress of the United States, to be designated the "Capitol Guide Service," which shall be subject to the direction, supervision, and control of a Capitol Guide Board consisting of the Architect of the Capitol, the Sergeant at Arms of the Senate, and the Sergeant at Arms of the House of Representatives.

(b) The Capitol Guide Service is authorized and directed to provide guided tours of the interior of the United States Capitol Building for the education and enlightenment of the general public, without charge for such tours. All such tours shall be conducted in compliance with regulations prescribed by the Capitol Guide Board.

. . . .

TITLE V—OFFICE OF THE LEGISLATIVE
COUNSEL
Subtitle A—House of Representatives
Part 1—Purpose, Policy, and Function
Establishment

SEC. 501. There is established in the House of Representatives an Office to be known as the Office of the Legislative Counsel, referred to hereinafter in this subtitle as the "Office".

Purpose and Policy

SEC. 502. The purpose of the Office shall be to advise and assist the House of Representatives, and its committees and Members, in the achievement, of a clear, faithful, and coherent expression of legislative policies. The Office shall maintain impartiality as to issues of legislative policy to be determined by the House of Representatives, and shall not, advocate the adoption or rejection of any legislation except when duly requested by the Speaker or a committee to comment on a proposal directly affecting the functions of the Office. The Office shall maintain the attorney-client relationship with respect to all communications between it and any Member or committee of the House.

Functions

SEC. 503. The functions of the Office shall be as follows:

(1) Upon request of the managers on the part, of the House at any conference oil the disagreeing votes of the two Houses, to advise and assist the managers on the part of the House in the course of the conference, and to assist the committee of confer-ence in the preparation of the conference report and any accompanying explanatory statement.

(2) Upon request of any committee of the House, or any joint committee having authority to report legislation to the House, to advise and assist the committee in the consideration of any legislation before it, and to assist the committee, in the preparation of drafts of any such legislation, amendments thereto, and reports thereon.

(3) Upon request of any Member having control of time during the consideration of any legislation by the House, to have in attendance on the floor of the House not more than two members of the staff of the Office (and, in his discretion, the Legislative Counsel) to advise and assist such Member and, to the extent feasible, any other Member, in the course of such consideration.

(4) Upon request of any Member, subject to such reasonable restrictions as the Legislative Counsel may impose with the approval of the Speaker on the proportion of the resources of the Office which may be devoted to the requests of any one Member, to prepare drafts of legislation and to furnish drafting advice with respect to drafts of legislation prepared by others.

(5) At the direction of the Speaker, to perform on behalf of the House of Representatives any legal services which are within the capabilities of the Office and the performance of which would not be inconsistent with the provisions of section 502 or the preceding provisions of this section.

. . . .

Statutes at Large, 84 (1970), 91st Congress, 2d session, Oct. 26, 1970, 1140–1204.

159   The Twenty-Sixth Amendment to the Constitution

Submitted to the States, March 23, 1971; Ratified, July 5, 1971

Until the Twenty-Sixth Amendment, the Constitution had left determination of the minimum voting age to the discretion of the states. Most states set that minimum at age twenty-one. During World War II, with eighteen-year-old soldiers fighting around the world, the House of Representatives held hearings on the question of lowering the voting age to eighteen, but no legislation resulted and the discretion to change the voting age remained where it always had been, in the state legislatures. In 1943 Georgia lowered its voting age to eighteen. Sixteen years later Kentucky also lowered its voting age to eighteen. In the late 1960s, as the war in Vietnam expanded, public and congressional support for a constitutional amendment that would provide eighteen-year-olds the right to vote gained momentum. It finally passed Congress in 1971 and was quickly ratified.

This amendment significantly expanded the franchise in the United States, but it did not cause any major changes in American politics, as some observers had predicted it would. Voters between the ages of eighteen and twenty-one did not register and vote in sufficient numbers to have much impact on the nature of political parties or the national issues before the electorate. Neither congressional elections nor presidential elections saw much impact from the newly enfranchised young voters. It remains to be seen in future elections if this amendment is a landmark only because it expanded the electorate, or if young voters increase their participation in national politics and play a more direct role in determining the kind of country they want to live in and helping to chart the political course of the nation in the new century.

ARTICLE [XXVI.]

SECTION 1. The right of citizens of the United States, who are eighteen years of age or older, to vote shall not be denied or abridged by the United States or by any State on account of age.

SEC. 2. The Congress shall have power to enforce this article by appropriate legislation.

The Constitution of the United States of America as Amended, House Doc. 102–188, 102d Congress, 2d session (Washington: Government Printing Office, 1992), 26.

160 *Gravel v. United States*

June 29, 1972

The Constitution provides in Article I, Section 6, Clause 1 that members of the House or Senate are protected from arrest in all cases "except Treason, Felony, and Breach of the Peace" when they are attending sessions of Congress or going to and from their official business in Congress. The same clause also states that "for any Speech or Debate in either House, they shall not be questioned in any other Place." In the case of Gravel v. United States, *the Supreme Court extended the "speech or debate" protection to include congressional aides working on behalf of a member of Congress. At the same time, the Court ruled that congressional aides were not exempt from being called in a grand jury investigation regarding matters that were not directly related to the legislative process.*

This case grew out of one of the most intriguing chapters in the debate over U.S. involvement in the Vietnam War. In 1971 a top-secret Defense Department report, entitled "History of the United States Decision-Making Process on Viet Nam Policy," was leaked to the press and to members of Congress by Daniel Ellsberg, one of the authors of the report. The public release of the so-called Pentagon Papers stirred a major controversy that placed official statements regarding the conduct of the war at odds with information held in secret. The New York Times *began publishing excerpts of the report on June 13, 1971, and was joined shortly thereafter by the* Washington Post.

The Nixon administration attempted to stop the dissemination of the Pentagon Papers. Two days after the first installment appeared in the New York Times, *the Department of Justice obtained a court order temporarily halting the publication of further installments. Despite the court order, the* Washington Post *began publishing its series of excerpts on June 18. Both newspapers were named in a suit brought by the Justice Department to cease publication of the Pentagon Papers. On June 30, 1971, the Supreme Court ruled that the newspapers had the right to publish the Pentagon Papers and that the government had not made a sufficient case to restrain them from doing so.*

In the meantime, Senator Mike Gravel (D-Alaska), the chairman of the Subcommittee on Buildings and Grounds of the Senate Public Works Committee, had obtained a copy of the entire forty-seven volume report. He read parts of it to a meeting of his subcommittee on June 29, 1971, the night before the Supreme Court ruled to allow newspaper publication to continue. Gravel then proceeded to place all forty-seven volumes into the public record. The

senator was assisted in this endeavor by a newly hired aide, Leonard S. Rodberg, who made arrangements with two publishers, Beacon Press and the Massachusetts Institute of Technology Press, to print the report.

When the grand jury investigating the release of the Pentagon Papers issued subpoenas to the publishers of the Pentagon Papers and to members of the senator's staff, including Rodberg, Senator Gravel moved in federal court to quash the subpoenas. The Justice Department cross-appealed and the case went to the Supreme Court, which rendered its decision on June 29, 1972, a year after Gravel's first release of the documents. By this time the contents of the Pentagon Papers had been widely disseminated and contributed in a major way to the debate over U.S. involvement in Southeast Asia.

. . . .

Opinion of the Court by Mr. JUSTICE WHITE, announced by Mr. JUSTICE BLACKMUN.

. . . .

I

Because the claim is that a Member's aide shares the Member's constitutional privilege, we consider first whether and to what extent Senator Gravel himself is exempt from process or inquiry by a grand jury investigating the commission of a crime. Our frame of reference is Art. I, § 6, cl. 1, of the Constitution:

"The Senators and Representatives shall receive a Compensation for their Services, to be ascertained by Law, and paid out of the Treasury of the United States. They shall in all Cases, except Treason, Felony and Breach of the Peace, be privileged from Arrest during their Attendance at the Session of their respective Houses, and in going to and returning from the same; and for any Speech or Debate in either House, they shall not be questioned in any other Place."

The last sentence of the Clause provides Members of Congress with two distinct privileges. Except in cases of "Treason, Felony and Breach of the Peace," the Clause shields Members from arrest while attending or traveling to and from a session of their House. History reveals, and prior cases so hold, that this part of the Clause exempts Members from arrest in civil cases only. . . .

... It is, therefore, sufficiently plain that the constitutional freedom from arrest does not exempt Members of Congress from the operation of the ordinary criminal laws, even though imprisonment may prevent or interfere with the performance of their duties as Members. *Williamson* v. *United States, supra;* cf. *Burton* v. *United States* (1906). Indeed, implicit in the narrow scope of the privilege of freedom from arrest is, as Jefferson noted, the judgment that legislators ought not to stand above the law they create but ought generally to be bound by it as are ordinary persons. T. Jefferson, Manual of Parliamentary Practice, S. Doc. No. 92–1, p. 437 (1971).

In recognition, no doubt, of the force of this part of § 6, Senator Gravel disavows any assertion of general immunity from the criminal law. But he points out that the last portion of § 6 affords Members of Congress another vital privilege—they may not be questioned in any other place for any speech or debate in either House. The claim is not that while one part of § 6 generally permits prosecutions for treason, felony, and breach of the peace, another part nevertheless broadly forbids them. Rather, his insistence is that the Speech or Debate Clause at the very least protects him from criminal or civil liability and from questioning elsewhere than in the Senate, with respect to the events occurring at the subcommittee hearing at which the Pentagon Papers were introduced into the public record. To us this claim is incontrovertible. The Speech or Debate Clause was designed to assure a co-equal branch of the government wide freedom of speech, debate, and deliberation without intimidation or threats from the Executive Branch. It thus protects Members against prosecutions that directly impinge upon or threaten the legislative process. We have no doubt that Senator Gravel may not be made to answer—either in terms of questions or in terms of defending himself from prosecution—for the events that occurred at the subcommittee meeting. Our decision is made easier by the fact that the United States appears to have abandoned whatever position it took to the contrary in the lower courts.

Even so, the United States strongly urges that because the Speech or Debate Clause confers a privilege only upon "Senators and Representatives," Rodberg himself has no valid claim to constitutional immunity from grand jury inquiry. In our view, both courts below correctly rejected this position. We agree with the Court of Appeals that for the purpose of construing the privilege a Member and his aide are to be "treated as one," *United States* v. *Doe,* 455 F. 2d, at 761; or, as the District Court put it: the "Speech or Debate Clause prohibits inquiry into things done by Dr. Rodberg as the Senator's agent or assistant which would have been legislative acts, and therefore privileged, if performed by the Senator personally." *United States* v. *Doe,* 332 F. Supp., at 937–938. Both courts recognized what the Senate of the United States urgently presses here: that it is literally impossible, in view of the complexities of the modern legislative process, with Congress almost constantly in session and matters of legislative concern constantly proliferating, for Members of Congress to perform their legislative tasks without the help of aides and assistants; that the day-to-day work of such aides is so critical to the Members' performance that they must be treated as the latter's alter egos; and that if they are not so recognized, the central role of the Speech or Debate Clause—to prevent intimidation of legislators by the Executive and accountability before a possibly hostile judiciary, *United States* v. *Johnson* (1966)—will inevitably be diminished and frustrated.

. . . .

It is true that the Clause itself mentions only "Senators and Representatives," but prior cases have plainly not taken a literalistic approach in applying the privilege. The Clause also speaks only of "Speech or Debate," but the Court's consistent approach has been that to confine the protection of the Speech or Debate Clause to words spoken in debate would be an unacceptably narrow view. Committee reports, resolutions, and the act of voting are equally covered; "[i]n short, . . . things generally done in a session of the House by one of its members in relation to the business before it." *Kilbourn* v. *Thompson* 204 (1881), quoted with approval in *United States* v. *Johnson.* Rather than giving the Clause a cramped construction, the Court has sought to implement its fundamental purpose of freeing the legislator from executive and judicial oversight that realistically threatens to control his conduct as a legislator. We have little doubt that we are neither exceeding our judicial powers nor mistakenly construing the Constitution by holding that the Speech or Debate Clause applies not only to a Member but also to his aides insofar as the conduct of the latter would be a protected legislative act if performed by the Member himself.

. . . .

The United States fears the abuses that history reveals have occurred when legislators are invested with the power to relieve others from the operation of otherwise valid civil and criminal laws. But these abuses, it seems to us are for the most part obviated if the privilege applicable to the aide is viewed, as it must be, as the privilege of the Senator, and invocable only by the Senator or by the aide on the Senator's behalf, and if in all events the privilege available to the aide is confined to those services that would be immune legislative conduct if performed by the Senator himself. This view places beyond the Speech or Debate Clause a variety of services characteristically performed by aides for Members of Congress, even though within the scope of their employment. It likewise provides no protection for criminal conduct threatening the security of the person or property of others, whether performed at the direction of the Senator in preparation for or in execution of a legislative act or done without his knowledge or direction. Neither does it immunize Senator or aide from testifying at trials or grand jury proceedings involving third-party crimes where the questions do not require testimony about or impugn a legislative act. Thus our refusal to distinguish between Senator and aide in applying the Speech or Debate Clause does not mean that Rodberg is for all purposes exempt from grand jury questioning.

II

We are convinced also that the Court of Appeals correctly determined that Senator Gravel's alleged arrangement with Beacon Press to publish the Pentagon Papers was not protected speech or debate within the meaning of Art. 1, § 6, cl. 1, of the Constitution.

. . . .

Prior cases have read the Speech or Debate Clause "broadly to effectuate its purposes," *United States* v. *Johnson,* and have included within its reach anything "generally done in a session of the House by one of its members in relation to the business before it." *Kilbourn* v. *Thompson,* 103 U. S., at 204; *United States* v. *Johnson.* Thus, voting by Members and committee reports are protected; and we recognize today—as the Court has recognized before, *Kilbourn* v. *Thompson*; *Tenney* v. *Brandhove* (1951)—that a Member's conduct at legislative committee hearings, although subject to judicial review in various circumstances, as is legislation itself, may not be made the basis for a civil or criminal judgment against a Member because that conduct is within the "sphere of legitimate legislative activity.". . .

But the Clause has not been extended beyond the legislative sphere. That Senators generally perform certain acts in their official capacity as Senators does not necessarily make all such acts legislative in nature. Members of Congress are constantly in touch with the Executive Branch of the Government and with administrative agencies—they may cajole, and exhort with respect to the administration of a federal statute—but such conduct, though generally done, is not protected legislative activity. *United States* v. *Johnson* decided at least this much. "No argument is made, nor do we think that it could be successfully contended, that the Speech or Debate Clause reaches conduct, such as was involved in the attempt to influence the Department of Justice, that is in no wise related to the due functioning of the legislative process."

Legislative acts are not all-encompassing. The heart of the Clause is speech or debate in either House. Insofar as the Clause is construed to reach other matters, they must be an integral part of the deliberative and communicative processes by which Members participate in committee and House proceedings with respect to the consideration and passage or rejection of proposed legislation or with respect to other matters which the Constitution places within the jurisdiction of either House. As the Court of Appeals put it, the courts have extended the privilege to matters beyond pure speech or debate in either House, but "only when necessary to prevent indirect impairment of such deliberations." *United States* v. *Doe.*

Here, private publication by Senator Gravel through the cooperation of Beacon Press was in no way essential to the deliberations of the Senate; nor does questioning as to private publication threaten the integrity or independence of the Senate by impermissibly exposing its deliberations to executive influence. The Senator had conducted his hearings; the record and any report that was forthcoming were available both to his committee and the Senate. Insofar as we are advised, neither Congress nor the full committee ordered or authorized the publication." We cannot but conclude that the Senator's arrangements with Beacon Press were not part and parcel of the legislative process.

There are additional considerations. Article I, § 6, cl. 1, as we have emphasized, does not purport to confer a general exemption upon Members of Congress from liability or process in criminal cases. Quite the contrary is true. While the Speech or Debate Clause recognizes speech, voting, and other legislative acts as exempt from liability that might otherwise attach, it does not privilege either Senator or aide to violate an otherwise valid criminal law in preparing for or implementing legislative acts. If republication of these classified papers would be a crime under an Act of Congress, it would not be entitled to immunity under the Speech or Debate Clause. It also appears that the grand jury was pursuing this very subject in the normal course of a valid investigation. The Speech or Debate Clause does not in our view extend immunity to Rodberg, as a Senator's aide, from testifying before the grand jury about the arrangement between Senator Gravel and Beacon Press or about his own participation, if any, in the alleged transaction, so long as legislative acts of the Senator are not impugned.

III

Similar considerations lead us to disagree with the Court of Appeals insofar as it fashioned, tentatively at least, a nonconstitutional testimonial privilege protecting Rodberg from any questioning by the grand jury concerning the matter of republication of the Pentagon Papers. This privilege, thought to be similar to that protecting executive officials from liability for libel, see *Barr* v. *Matteo* (1959), was considered advisable "[t]o the extent that a congressman has responsibility to inform his constituents. . . ." But we cannot carry a judicially fashioned privilege so far as to immunize criminal conduct proscribed by an Act of Congress or to frustrate the grand jury's inquiry into whether publication of these classified documents violated a federal criminal statute. The so-called executive privilege has never been applied to shield executive officers from prosecution for crime, the Court of Appeals was quite sure that third parties were neither immune from liability nor from testifying about the republication matter, and we perceive no basis for conferring a testimonial privilege on Rodberg as the Court of Appeals seemed to do.

IV

We must finally consider, in the light of the foregoing, whether the protective order entered by the Court of Appeals is an appropriate regulation of the pending grand jury proceedings.

Focusing first on paragraph two of the order, we think the injunction against interrogating Rodberg with respect to any act, "in the broadest sense," performed by him within the scope of his employment, overly restricts the scope of grand jury inquiry. Rodberg's immunity, testimonial or otherwise, extends only to legislative acts as to which the Senator himself would be immune. The grand jury, therefore, if relevant to its investigation into the possible violations of the criminal law, and absent Fifth Amendment objections, may require from Rodberg answers to questions relating to his or the Senator's arrangements, if any, with respect to republication or with respect to third-party conduct under valid investigation by the grand jury, as long as the questions do not implicate legislative action of the Senator. Neither do we perceive any constitutional or other privilege that shields Rodberg, any more than any other witness, from grand jury questions relevant to tracing the source of obviously highly classified documents that came into the Senator's possession and are the basic subject matter of inquiry in this case, as long as no legislative act is implicated by the questions.

Because the Speech or Debate Clause privilege applies both to Senator and aide, it appears to us that paragraph one of the order, alone, would afford ample protection for the privilege if it forbade questioning any witness, including Rodberg: (1) concerning the Senator's conduct, or the conduct of his aides, at the June 29, 1971, meeting of the subcommittee; (2) concerning the motives and purposes behind the Senator's conduct, or that of his aides, at that meeting; (3) concerning communications between the Senator and his aides during the term of their employment and related to said meeting or any other legislative act of the Senator; (4) except as it proves relevant to investigating possible third-party crime, concerning any act, in itself not criminal, performed by the Senator, or by his aides in the course of their employment, in preparation for the subcommittee hearing. We leave the final form of such an order to the Court of Appeals in the first instance, or, if that court prefers, to the District Court.

The judgment of the Court of Appeals is vacated and the cases are remanded to that court for further proceedings consistent with this opinion.

So ordered.

408 U.S. 606 (1972).

161 A Resolution to Establish the Senate Watergate Committee

February 7, 1973

The word Watergate *has entered the English language as the name for one of the most serious and prolonged congressional investigations in U.S. history. While most Americans know the general outcome of these investigations, which resulted in the resignation of President Richard M. Nixon on August 9, 1974, few can recall the congressional process, or the exact charges, that led to the resignation of a president. This volume contains three pivotal documents that illuminate key aspects of the investigation. In addition to the resolution establishing the Senate investigation of presidential campaign activities in the election of 1972, the debate over impeachment by the House Judiciary Committee (document 165) and the articles of impeachment of Richard M. Nixon (document 166) are also presented.*

The Watergate scandal began with a seemingly minor matter, when five men were arrested for breaking into the headquarters of the Democratic National Committee offices on June 17, 1972. The offices were located in the posh office and apartment complex along the Potomac River in Washington, D.C., known as the Watergate. This burglary soon implicated high-ranking officials in the Nixon administration and, after a lengthy investigation, the president of the United States himself, who learned of the break-in three days after the event and participated in the complex cover-up of the crime. The president initially tried to keep the Federal Bureau of Investigation from investigating the incident by urging the Central Intelligence Agency to declare the matter a case of national security. Later, President Nixon agreed to find hush money to keep the burglars quiet. The story unfolded in a slow and often agonizing manner through the pages of the Washington Post, *where two reporters, Bob Woodward and Carl Bernstein, doggedly pursued the facts. Even though the scandal broke before the 1972 presidential elections, nothing at first linked it to Nixon. He was reelected in a landslide that November.*

The Senate Select Committee on Presidential Campaign Activities began its hearings in May 1973, under the chairmanship of Senator Sam Ervin (D-N.C.). During the first three months of hearings, sixty-three witnesses testified about the attempted burglary at the Watergate complex and the subsequent cover-up. The key witness was John Dean, the former counsel to the president, who admitted his involvement in the cover-up and implicated other officials, including Attorney General John Mitchell, top White House aides John Erhlichman and H. R. Haldeman, and President Nixon himself. The Senate investigation also uncovered an elaborate system for taping conversations in the White House that eventually led to the discovery of the hard evidence needed to implicate the president in the cover-up of the Watergate break-in. Subsequent investigation by the Senate Select Committee focused on broader issues of campaign finance irregularities and the use of political "dirty tricks" and sabotage of Democratic candidates. The committee issued a report of more than 2,000 pages in July 1974, revealing a corrupt pattern of practices carried on at the highest levels of the Nixon administration, often involving the president of the United States.

S. RES. 60

Resolved,

SECTION 1. (a) That there is hereby established a select committee of the Senate, which may be called, for convenience of expression, the Select Committee on Presidential Campaign Activities, to conduct an investigation and study of the extent, if any, to which illegal, improper, or unethical activities were engaged in by any persons, acting either individually or in combination with others, in the presidential election of 1972, or in any related campaign or canvass conducted by or in behalf of any person seeking nomination or election as the candidate of any political party for the office of President of the United States in such election, and to determine whether in its judgment any occurrences which may be revealed by the investigation and study indicate the necessity or desirability of the enactment of new congressional legislation to safeguard the electoral process by which the President of the United States is chosen.

(b) The select committee created by this resolution shall consist of seven Members of the Senate, four of whom shall be appointed by the President of the Senate from the majority Members of the Senate upon the recommendation of the majority leader of the Senate, and three of whom shall be appointed by the President of the Senate from the minority Members of the Senate upon the recommendation of the minority leader of the Senate. For the purposes of paragraph 6 of rule XXV of the Standing Rules of the Senate, service of a Senator as a member, chairman, or vice chairman of the select committee shall not be taken into account.

(c) The select committee shall select a chairman and vice chairman from among its members, and adopt rules of procedure to govern its proceedings. The vice chairman shall preside over meetings of the select committee during the absence of the chairman, and discharge such other responsibilities as may be assigned to him by the select committee or the chairman. Vacancies in the membership of the select committee shall not affect the authority of the remaining members to execute the functions of the select committee and shall be filled in the same manner as original appoints to it are made.

(d) A majority of the members of the select committee shall constitute a quorum for the transaction of business, but the select committee may fix a lesser number as a quorum for the purpose of taking testimony or depositions.

SEC. 2. That the select committee is authorized and directed to do everything necessary or appropriate to make the investigation and study specified in section 1(a). Without abridging or limiting in any way the authority conferred upon the select committee by the preceding sentence, the Senate further expressly authorizes and directs the select committee to make a complete investigation and study of the activities of any and all persons or groups of persons or organizations of any kind which have any tendency to reveal the full facts in respect to the following matters or questions:

(1) The breaking, entering, and bugging of the headquarters or offices of the Democratic National Committee in the Watergate Building in Washington, District of Columbia;

(2) The monitoring by bugging, eavesdropping, wiretapping, or other surreptitious means of conversations or communications occurring in whole or in part in the headquarters or offices of the Democratic National Committee in the Watergate Building in Washington, District of Columbia;

(3) Whether or not any printed or typed or written document or paper of other material was surreptitiously removed from the headquarters or offices of the Democratic National Committee in the Watergate Building in Washington, District of Columbia, and thereafter copied or reproduced by photography or any other means for the information of any person or political committee or organization;

(4) The preparing, transmitting or any political committee or any organization of any report or information concerning the activities mentioned in subdivision (1), (2), or (3) of this section, and the information contained in any such report;

(5) Whether any persons, acting individually or in combination with others, planned the activities mentioned in subdivision (1), (2), (3), or (4) of this of this section, or employed any of the participants in such activities to participate in them, or made any payments or promises of payments of money or other things of value to the participants in such activities or their families for their activities, or for concealing the truth in respect to them or any of the persons having any connection with them or their activities, and, if so, the source of the moneys used in such payments, and the identities and motives of the persons planning such activities or employing the participants in them;

(6) Whether any persons participating in any of the activities mentioned in subdivision (1), (2), (3), (4), or (5) of this section have been induced by bribery, coercion, threats, or any other means whatsoever to plead guilty to the charges preferred against them in the District Court of Columbia or to conceal or fail to reveal any knowledge of any of the activities mentioned in subdivision (1), (2), (3), (4), or (5) of this section, and if so, the identities of the persons inducing them to do such things, and the identities of any other persons or any committees or organizations for whom they acted;

(7) Any effort to disrupt, hinder, impede, or sabotage in any way any campaign, canvass or activity conducted by or in behalf of any person seeking nomination or elections as the candidate of any political party for the office of President of the United 1972 by infiltrating any political committee or organization or headquarters of offices or home or whereabouts of the person seeking such nomination or election or of any person aiding him in so doing, or by bugging or eavesdropping or wiretapping the conversations, communications, plans, headquarters, offices, home, or whereabouts of the person seeking such nomination or election or of any other persons assisting him in so doing, or by exercising surveillance over the person seeking such nomination or election or of any person assisting him in so doing, or by reporting to any other person or to any political committee or organization any information obtained by such infiltration, eavesdropping, bugging, wiretapping, or surveillance;

(8) Whether any person, acting individually or in combination with others, or political committee or organization induced any of the activities mentioned in subdivision (7) of this section or paid any of the participants in any such activities for

their services, and, if so, the identities of such persons, or committee, or organization, and the source of the funds used by them to procure or finance such activities;

(9) Any fabrication, dissemination, or publication of any false charges or other false information having the purpose of discrediting any person seeking nomination or election as the candidate of any political party to the office of President of the United States in 1972;

(10) The planning of any of the activities mentioned in subdivision (7), (8), or (9) of this section, the employing of the participants in such activities, and the source of any moneys or things of value which may have been given or promised o the participants in such activities for their services, and the identities of any persons or committees or organizations which may have been involved in any way in the planning procuring, and financing of such activities;

(11) Any transactions or circumstances relating to the source, the control, the transmission, the transfer, the deposit, the storage, the concealment, the expenditure, or use in the United States or in any other country, or any moneys or other things of value collected or received for actual or pretended use in the presidential election of 1972 or in any related campaign or canvass or activities preceding or accompanying such election by any person, group of persons, committee, or organization of any kind acting or professing to act in behalf of any national political party or in support of or in opposition to any person seeking nomination or election to the office of President of the United States in 1972;

(12) Compliance or noncompliance with any Act of Congress requiring the reporting of the receipt or disbursement or use of any moneys or other things of value mentioned in subdivision (11) of this section;

(13) Whether any of the moneys or things of value mentioned in subdivision (11) of this section were placed in any secret fund or place of storage for use in financing any activity which was sought to be concealed from the public, and, if so, what disbursement or expenditure was made of such secret fund, and the identities of any person or group of persons or committee or organization having any control over such secret fund or the disbursement or expenditure of the same;

(14) Whether any books, checks, canceled checks, communication, correspondence, documents, papers, physical evidence, records, recordings, tapes, or materials relating to any of the matters or questions the select committee is authorized and directed to investigate and study have been concealed, suppressed, or destroyed by any persons acting individually or in combination with other, and, if so, the identities and motives of any such persons or groups of persons;

(15) Any other activities, circumstances, materials, or transactions having a tendency to prove or disprove that persons acting either individually or in combination with others, engaged in any illegal, improper, or unethical activities in connection with the presidential election of 1972 or any campaign, canvass, or activity related to such election;

(16) Whether any of the existing laws of the United States are inadequate, either in their provision or manner of enforcement to safeguard the integrity or parity of the process by which Presidents are chosen.

SEC. 3. (1) To enable the select committee to make the investigation and study authorized and directed by this resolution, the Senate hereby empowers the select committee as an agency of the Senate (1) to employ and fix the compensation of such clerical, investigatory, legal, technical, and other assistants as it deems necessary or appropriate; (2) to sit and act at any time or place during sessions, recesses, and adjournment periods of the Senate; (3) to hold hearings for taking testimony on oath or to receive documentary or physical evidence relating to the matters and questions it is authorized to investigate or study; (4) to require by subpoena or otherwise the attendance as witnesses of any persons who the select committee believes have knowledge or information concerning any of the matters or questions it is authorized to investigate and study; (5) to require by subpoena or order any department, agency, officer, or employee of the executive branch of the United States Government, or any private person, firm, or corporation, or any officer or former officer of employee of any political committee or organization to produce for its consideration or for use as evidence in its investigation and study any books, checks, canceled checks, correspondence, communications, document, papers, physical evidence, records, recording, tapes, or materials relating to any of the matters or questions it is authorize to investigate and study which they or any of them may have in their custody or under their control; (6) to make to the Senate any recommendations it deems appropriate in respect to the willful failure or refusal of any person to appear before it in obedience to a subpoena or order, or in respect to the willful failure or refusal of any person to answer questions or give testimony in his character as a witness during his appearance before it, or in respect to the willful failure or refusal of any officer or employee of the executive branch of the United States Government or any person, firm, or corporation, or any officer or former officer or employee of any political committee or organization, to produce before the committee any books, checks, canceled checks, correspondence, communications, documents, financial records, papers, physical evidence, records, recordings, tapes, or materials in obedience to any subpoena or order; (7) to take depositions any other testimony on oath anywhere within the United States or in any other country; (8) to procure the temporary or intermittent services of individual consultants, or organizations thereof, in the same manner and under the same conditions as a standing committee of the Senate may procure such services under section 202(i) of the Legislative Reorganization Act of 1946; (9) to use on a reimbursable basis, with the prior consent of the Government department or agency concerned and the Committee on Rules and Administration, the services of personnel of any such department or agency; (10) to use on a reimbursable basis or otherwise with the prior consent of the chairman of any other of the senate committees or the chairman of any subcommittee of any committee of the Senate the facilities or services of any members of the staffs of such other Senate committees or any subcommittees of such other Senate committees whenever the select committee or its chairman deems that such action is necessary or appropriate to enable the select committee to make the investigation and study authorized and directed by this resolution; (11) to have access through the agency of any members of the select committee, chief majority counsel, minority counsel, or any of its investigatory assistants jointly designated by the chairman and the ranking minority members to any data, evidence, information, report, analysis, or document or paper relating to any of the matters or questions which it is authorized and directed to investigate and study in the custody or under the control of any department, agency, officer, or employee of the executive branch of the United States Government having the power under the laws of the United States to investigate any alleged criminal activities or to prosecute persons charged with crimes against the United States which will aid the select committee to prepare for or conduct the investigation and study authorized and directed by this resolution; and (12) to expend to the extent it determines necessary or appropriate any moneys made available to it by the Senate to perform the duties and exercises the powers conferred upon it by this resolution and to make the investigation and study it is authorized by this resolution to make.

(b) Subpoenas may be issued by the select committee acting through the chairman or any other member designated by him, and may be served by any person designated by such chairman or other member anywhere within the borders of the United States. The chairman of the select committee, or any other member thereof, is hereby authorized to administer oaths to any witnesses appearing before the committee.

(c) In preparing for or conducting the investigation and study authorized and directed by this resolution, the select committee shall be empowered to exercise the powers conferred upon committees of the Senate by section 6002 of title 18 of the United States code or any other Act of Congress regulating the granting of immunity to witnesses.

SEC. 4. The select committee shall have authority to recommend the enactment of any new congressional legislation which its investigation considers it is necessary of desirable to safeguard the electoral process by which the President of the United States is chosen.

SEC. 5. The select committee shall make a final report of the results of the investigation and study conducted by it pursuant to this resolution, together with its findings and its recommendations as to new congressional legislation it deems necessary or desirable, to the Senate at the earliest practicable date, but no later then February 28, 1974. The select committee may also submit to the Senate such interim reports as it considers appropriate. After submission of its final report, the select committee shall have three calendar months to close its affairs, and on the expiration of such three calendar months shall cease to exist.

SEC. 6. The expenses of the select committee through February 28, 1974, under this resolution shall not exceed $500,000, of which amount not to exceed $25,000 shall be available for the procurement of the services of individual consultants or organization thereof. Such expenses shall be paid from the contingent fund of the Senate upon vouchers approved by the chairman of the select committee. The minority members of the select committee shall have one-third of the professional staff of the select committee (including a minority counsel) and such part of the clerical staff as may be adequate.

. . . .

Congressional Record, Senate, 93d Congress, 1st session, Feb. 7, 1973, 3849–3851.

162   The War Powers Resolution

November 7, 1973

The Constitution gives Congress the power to declare war and to raise and support an army and a navy (Article I, Section 8, Clauses 11–16). It also gives the role of commander-in-chief of the armed forces to the president of the United States (Article II, Section 2). Throughout American history tension and often conflict have occurred between the executive and legislative branches over this war-making authority. Before World War II, and especially through most of the nineteenth century, Congress was the dominant branch of government in terms of setting the national agenda and deciding matters of war and peace. Since World War II the power has shifted to the White House, not only because of the unprecedented growth of the government during the 1940s but also because of the nature of warfare itself. With the advent of atomic weapons, super-sonic aircraft, and intercontinental ballistic missiles, the potential for devastating wars to be launched and fought in hours or days meant that the president had to be ready to act quickly to a crisis without waiting for Congress to debate the matter first.

In 1951 President Harry S. Truman sent U.S. ground troops to Europe without seeking advance congressional approval. This action sparked a lengthy debate in the Senate regarding the powers of the president to move on his own in such matters, but Congress left Truman's decision standing and approved it after the fact. During the Cuban missile crisis in October 1962 the United States came to the brink of war with the Soviet Union during a tense thirteen-day standoff. President John F. Kennedy was ready to use his powers as commander-in-chief, without the advance approval of Congress, which was in adjournment at the time. In 1964 Congress, acting on murky information, passed the Gulf of Tonkin Resolution, which gave President Johnson broad powers to engage in warfare in Vietnam without an actual declaration of war (see document 153). When President Richard Nixon ordered the bombing of Cambodia in 1970 (see document 156), many members of Congress became concerned that they had lost far too much war-making authority to the executive branch. Congress, like the nation itself, became torn on the entire policy of the conduct of the war in Southeast Asia.

The War Powers Resolution of 1973 represented the culmination of years of debate on the subject. It was the best effort of Congress to reestablish its constitutional authority to declare war and limit the unilateral actions of presidents. President Nixon vetoed the resolution, saying it would interfere with the president's ability to defend the United States. Congress passed it over his veto. The resolution did not strip the president of any authority. Rather, it reestablished a partnership in the decision-making process with Congress, which remains to this day.

The statement of purpose and policy in the resolution read like a basic lesson in the Constitution, reminding everyone of what the Constitution states on the subject. The resolution called for a timetable during which Congress must be notified of any hostile action, preferably in advance; if not, notification must be within forty-eight hours of the action. It also required that the president withdraw troops from action within sixty days unless Congress extended the time period by resolution.

The War Powers Resolution remains a point of friction between presidents and Congress in their ongoing constitutional struggle over the power to make war. Since its passage, not all of its provisions have been fully met. Presidents Gerald Ford, Jimmy Carter, and Ronald Reagan all initiated military action on foreign soil without the prior approval of Congress, although in most instances they complied with the provision of notification within forty-eight hours. President Reagan ignored the War Powers Resolution by failing to notify Congress on several occasions, including sending military advisers to El Salvador in 1981 and troops to Lebanon and the Sinai in 1982, Grenada and Chad in 1983, and to the Persian Gulf in 1987. As the United States prepares for new kinds of warfare, including undeclared wars against international terrorism, the likelihood of continued conflict over the War Powers Resolution remains and is not easily resolved.

JOINT RESOLUTION CONCERNING THE WAR POWERS OF CONGRESS AND THE PRESIDENT

Resolved by the Senate and House of Representatives of the United States of America in Congress assembled,

Short Title

SECTION 1. This joint resolution may be cited as the "War Powers Resolution".

Purpose and Policy

SEC. 2. (a) It is the purpose of this joint resolution to fulfill the intent of the framers of the Constitution of the United States and insure that the collective judgment of both the Congress and the President will apply to the introduction of the United States Armed Forces into hostilities, or into situations where imminent involvement in hostilities is clearly indicated by the circumstances, and to the continued use of such forces in hostilities or in such situations.

(b) Under article I, section 8, of the Constitution, it is specifically provided that the Congress shall have the power to make all laws necessary and proper for carrying into execution, not only its own powers but also all other powers vested by the Constitution in the Government of the United States, or in any department or officer thereof.

(c) The constitutional powers of the President as Commander-in-Chief to introduce United States Armed Forces into hostilities, or into situations where imminent involvement in hostilities is clearly indicated by the circumstances, are exercised only pursuant to (1) a declaration of war, (2) specific statutory authorization, or (3) a national emergency created by attack upon the United States, its territories or possessions, or its armed forces.

Consultation

SEC. 3. The President in every possible instance shall consult with Congress before introducing United States Armed Forces into hostilities or into situations where imminent involvement in hostilities is clearly indicated by the circumstances, and after every such introduction shall consult regularly with the Congress until United States Armed Forces are no longer engaged in hostilities or have been removed from such situations.

Reporting

SEC. 4. (a) In the absence of a declaration of war, in any case in which United States Armed Forces are introduced—

(1) into hostilities or into situations where imminent involvement in hostilities is clearly indicated by circumstances;

(2) into the territory, airspace or waters of a foreign nation, while equipped for combat, except for deployment which relate solely to supply, replacement, repair, or training of such forces; or

(3) in numbers which substantially enlarge United States Armed Forces equipped for combat already located in a foreign nation;

the President shall submit within 48 hours to the Speaker of the House of Representatives and to the President pro tempore of the Senate a report, in writing, setting forth—

(A) the circumstances necessitating the introduction of United States Armed Forces;

(B) the constitutional and legislative authority under which such introduction took place; and

(C) the estimated scope and duration of the hostilities or involvement.

(b) The President shall provide such other information as the Congress may request in the fulfillment of its constitutional responsibilities with respect to committing the Nation to war and to the use of United States Armed Forces abroad.

(c) Whenever United States Armed Forces are introduced into hostilities or into any situation described in subsection (a) of this section, the President shall, so long as such armed forces continue to be engaged in such hostilities or situation, report to the Congress periodically on the status of such hostilities or situation as well as on the scope and duration of such hostilities or situation, but in no event shall he report to the Congress less often than once every six months.

Congressional Action

SEC. 5. (a) Each report submitted pursuant to section 4 (a) (1) shall be transmitted to the Speaker of the House of Representatives and to the President pro tempore of the Senate on the same calendar day. Each report so transmitted shall be referred to the Committee on Foreign Affairs of the House of Representatives and to the Committee on Foreign Relations of the Senate for appropriate action. If, when the report is transmitted, the Congress has adjourned sine die or has adjourned for any period in excess of three calendar days, the Speaker of the House of Representatives and the President pro tempore of the Senate, if they deem it advisable (or if petitioned by at least 30 percent of the membership of their respective Houses) shall jointly request the President to convene Congress in order that it may consider the report and take appropriate action pursuant to this section.

(b) Within sixty calendar days after a report is submitted or is required to be submitted pursuant to section 4 (a) (1), whichever is earlier, the President shall terminate any use of United States Armed Forces with respect to which such report was submitted (or required to be submitted), unless the Congress (1) has declared war or has enacted a specific authorization for such use of United States Armed Forces, (2) has extended by law such sixty-day period, or (3) is physically unable to meet as a result of an armed attack upon the United States. Such sixty-day period shall be extended for not more than an additional thirty days if the President determines and certifies to the Congress in writing that unavoidable military necessity respecting the safety of United States Armed Forces requires the continued use of such armed forces in the course of bringing about a prompt removal of such forces.

(c) Notwithstanding subsection (b), at any time that United States Armed Forces are engaged in hostilities outside the territory of the United States, its possessions and territories without a declaration of war or specific statutory authorization, such forces shall be removed by the president if the Congress so directs by concurrent resolution.

Congressional Priority Procedures for Joint Resolution or Bill

SEC. 6. (a) Any joint resolution or bill introduced pursuant to section 5(b) at least thirty calendar days before the expiration of the sixty-day period specified in such section shall be referred to the Committee on Foreign Affairs of the House of Representatives or the Committee on Foreign Relations of the Senate, as the case may be, and such committee shall report one such joint resolution or bill, together with its recommendations, not later than twenty-four calendar days before the expiration of the sixty-day period specified in such section, unless such House shall otherwise determine by the yeas and nays.

(b) Any joint resolution or bill so reported shall become the pending business of the House in question (in the case of the Senate the time for debate shall be equally divided between the proponents and the opponents), and shall be voted on within three calendar days thereafter, unless such House shall otherwise determine by yeas and nays.

(c) Such a joint resolution or bill passed by one House shall be referred to the committee of the other House named in subsection (a) and shall be reported out not later than fourteen calendar days before the expiration of the sixty-day period specified in section 5 (b). The joint resolution or bill so reported shall become the pending business of the House in question and shall be voted on within three calendar days after it has been reported, unless such House shall otherwise determine by yeas and nays.

(d) In the case of any disagreement between the two Houses of Congress with respect to a joint resolution or bill passed by both Houses, conferees shall be promptly appointed and the committee of conference shall make and file a report with respect to such resolution or bill not later than four calendar days before the expiration of the sixty-day period specified in section 5 (b). In the event the conferees are unable to agree within 48 hours, they shall report back to their respective Houses in disagreement. Notwithstanding any rule in either House concerning the printing of conference reports in the Record or concerning the printing of conference reports in the Record or concerning any delay in the consideration of such reports, such reports shall be acted on by both Houses not later than the expiration of such sixty-day period.

Congressional Priority Procedures for Concurrent Resolution

SEC. 7 (a) Any concurrent resolution introduced pursuant to section 5 (c) shall be referred to the Committee on Foreign Affairs of the House of Representatives or the Committee on Foreign Relations of the Senate, as the case may be, and one such concurrent resolution shall be reported out by such committee together with its recommendations within fifteen calendar days, unless such House shall otherwise determine by the yeas and nays.

(b) Any concurrent resolution so reported shall become the pending business of the House in question (in the case of the Senate the time for debate shall be equally divided between the proponents and the opponents) and shall be voted on within three calendar days thereafter, unless such House shall otherwise determine by yeas and nays.

(c) Such a concurrent resolution passed by one House shall be referred to the committee of the other House named in subsection (a) and shall be reported out by such committee together with its recommendations within fifteen calendar days and shall thereupon become the pending business of such

House and shall be voted upon within three calendar days, unless such House shall otherwise determine by yeas and nays.

(d) In the case of any disagreement between the two Houses of Congress with respect to a concurrent resolution passed by both Houses, conferees shall be promptly appointed and the committee of conference shall make and file a report with respect to such concurrent resolution within six calendar days after the legislation is referred to the committee of conference. Notwithstanding any rule in either House concerning the printing of conference reports in the Record or concerning any delay in the consideration of such reports, such report shall be acted on by both Houses not later than six calendar days after the conference report is filed. In the event the conferees are unable to agree within 48 hours, they shall report back to their respective Houses in disagreement.

Interpretation of Joint Resolution

SEC. 8. (a) Authority to introduce United States Armed Forces into hostilities or into situations of wherein involvement in hostilities is clearly indicated by the circumstances shall not be inferred—

(1) from any provision of law (whether or not in effect before the date of the enactment of this joint resolution), including any provision contained in any appropriation Act, unless such provision specifically authorizes the introduction of United States Armed Forces into hostilities or into such situations and states that it is intended to constitute specific statutory authorization within the meaning of this joint resolution; or

(2) from any treaty heretofore or hereafter ratified unless such treaty is implemented by legislation specifically authorizing the introduction of United States Armed Forces into hostilities or into such situations and stating that it is intended to constitute specific statutory authorization within the meaning of this joint resolution.

(b) Nothing in this joint resolution shall be construed to require any further specific statutory authorization to permit members of United States Armed Forces to participate jointly with members of the armed forces of one or more foreign countries in the headquarters operations of high-level military commands which were established prior to the date of enactment of this joint resolution and pursuant to the United Nations Charter or any treaty ratified by the United States prior to such date.

(c) For purposes of this joint resolution, the term "introduction of United States Armed Forces" includes the assignment of members of such armed forces to command, coordinate, participate in the movement of, or accompany the regular or irregular military forces in of any foreign country or government when such military forces are engaged, or there exists an imminent threat that such forces will become engaged, in hostilities.

(d) Nothing in this joint resolution—

(1) is intended to alter the constitutional authority of the Congress or the President, or the provisions of existing treaties; or

(2) shall be construed as granting any authority to the President with respect to the introduction of United States Armed Forces into hostilities or into situations wherein involvement in hostilities is clearly indicated by the circumstances which authority he would not have had in the absence of this joint resolution.

Separability Clause

SEC. 9. If any provision of this joint resolution or the application thereof to any person or circumstance is held invalid, the remainder of the joint resolution and the application of such provision to any other person or circumstance shall not be affected thereby.

Effective Date

SEC. 10. This joint resolution shall take effect on the date of its enactment.

. . . .

Statutes at Large, 93d Congress, 1st session, Nov. 7, 1973, 555–560 .

163   The Reorganization of the District of Columbia Government

December 24, 1973

The right of citizens of the District of Columbia to fully participate in governing themselves, to the extent afforded citizens of the fifty states, has never been fully realized. The Constitution gives Congress the power to rule in the District of Columbia (see documents 35, 42, and 88). In 1973, for the first time in a century, the government of the District of Columbia was completely reorganized to provide for an increased level of self-government, commonly referred to as "home rule."

The District of Columbia Self-Government and Governmental Reorganization Act of 1973 allowed Washington residents to elect a mayor and city council and gave them broad powers to administer the city. This legislation replaced the commissioner form of government that had been in force since 1874. At the same time, Congress did not relinquish any of its constitutional authority to ultimately control the district government. Title VI of this legislation clearly states that "notwithstanding any other provision of this

Act, the Congress of the United States reserves the right, at any time, to exercise its constitutional authority as legislature for the District, by enacting legislation for the District on any subject, whether within or without the scope of legislative power granted to the Council by this Act. . . ."

TITLE I

. . . .

SEC. 101. This Act may be cited as the "District of Columbia Self-Government and Governmental Reorganization Act."

Statement of Purposes

SEC. 102. (a) Subject to the retention by Congress of the ultimate legislative authority over the Nation's Capital granted by article 1, section 8, of the Constitution, the intent of Congress is to delegate certain legislative powers to the government of the District of Columbia: authorize the election of certain local officials by the registered qualified electors in the District of Columbia; grant to the inhabitants of the District of Columbia powers of local self-government; to modernize, reorganize, and otherwise improve the governmental structure of the District of Columbia; and, to the greatest extent possible, consistent with the constitutional mandate, relieve Congress of the burden of legislating upon essentially local District matters.

(b) Congress further intends to implement certain recommendations of the Commission on the Organization of the Government of the District of Columbia and take certain other actions irrespective of whether the charter for greater self-government provided for in title IV of this Act is accepted or rejected by the registered qualified electors of the District of Columbia.

. . . .

TITLE IV—THE DISTRICT CHARTER
Part A—The Council

. . . .

Creation and Membership

SEC. 401. (a) There is established a Council of the District of Columbia; and the members of the Council shall be elected by the registered qualified electors of the District.

(b) (1) The Council established under subsection (a) shall consist of thirteen members elected on a partisan basis. The Chairman and four members shall be elected at large in the District, and eight members shall be elected one each from the eight election wards established, from time to time, under the District of Columbia Election Act. The term of office of the members of the Council shall be four years, except as provided in paragraph (3), and shall begin at noon on January 2 of the year following their election.

(2) In the case of the first election held for the office of member of the Council after the effective date of this title, not more, than two of the at-large members (excluding the Chairman) shall be nominated by the same political party. Thereafter, a political party may nominate a number of candidates for the office of at-large member of the Council equal to one less than the total number of at-large members (excluding the Chairman) to be elected in such election.

(3) Of the members first elected after the effective date of this title, the Chairman and two members elected at-large and four of the members elected from election wards shall serve for four-year terms; and two of the at-large members and four of the members elected from election wards shall serve for two-year terms. The members to serve the four-year terms and the members to serve the two-year terms shall be determined by the Board of Elections by lot, except that not more than one of the at-large members nominated by any political party shall serve for any such four-year term.

(c) The Council may establish and select such Other officers and employees as it deems necessary and appropriate to carry out the functions of the Council.

(d) (1) In the event of a vacancy in the Council of a member elected from a ward, the Board of Elections shall hold a special election in such ward to fill such vacancy on the first Tuesday Occurring more than one hundred and fourteen days after the date on which such vacancy occurs, unless the Board of Elections determines that such vacancy could be more practicably filled in a special election held on the same day as the next general election to be held in the District occurring within sixty days of the date on which a special election would otherwise have been held under the provisions of this subsection. The person elected as a member to fill a vacancy on the Council shall take office on the day on which the Board of Elections certifies his election, and shall serve as a member of the Council only for the remainder of the term during which such vacancy occurred.

(2) In the event of a vacancy in the office of Mayor, and if the Chairman becomes a candidate for the office of Mayor to fill such vacancy, the office of Chairman shall be deemed vacant as of the date of the filing of his candidacy. In the event of a vacancy in the Council of a member elected at large, other than a vacancy in the office of Chairman, who is affiliated with a political party, the central committee of such political party shall a point a person to fill such vacancy, until the Board of Elections can hold a special election to fill such vacancy, and such special election shall be held on the first Tuesday occurring more than one hundred and fourteen days after the date on which such vacancy occurs unless the Board of Elections determines that such vacancy could be more practicably filled in a special election held on the same day as the next general election to be held in the District occurring within sixty days of the date on which a special election would otherwise be held under the provision of this subsection. The person appointed to fill such vacancy shall take office on the date of his appointment and shall serve as a

member of the Council until the day on which the Board certifies the election of the member elected to fill such vacancy in either a special election or a general election. The person elected as a member to fill such a vacancy on the Council shall take office on the day on which the Board of Elections certifies his election, and shall serve as a member of the Council only for the remainder of the term during which such vacancy occurred. With respect to a vacancy on the Council of a member elected at large who is not affiliated with any political party, the Council shall appoint a similarly nonaffiliated person to fill such vacancy until such vacancy can be filled in a special election in the manner prescribed in this paragraph. Such person appointed by the Council shall take office and serve as a member at the same time and for the same term as a member appointed by a central committee of a political party.

(3) Notwithstanding any other provision of this section, at no time shall there be more than three members (including the Chairman) serving at large on the Council who are affiliated with the same political party.

. . . .

Powers of the Council

SEC. 404. (a) Subject to the limitations specified in title VI of this Act, the legislative power granted to the District by this Act is vested in and shall be exercised by the Council in accordance with this Act. In addition, except as otherwise provided in this Act, all functions granted to or imposed upon, or vested in or transferred to the District of Columbia Council, as established by Reorganization Plan Numbered 3 of 1967, shall be carried out by the Council in accordance with the, provisions of this Act.

(b) The Council shall have authority to create, abolish, or organize any office, agency, department, or instrumentality of the government of the District and to define the powers, duties, and responsibilities of any such office, agency, department, or instrumentality.

(c) The Council shall adopt and publish rules of procedures which shall include provisions for adequate public notification of intended actions of the Council.

(d) Every act shall be published and codified upon becoming law as the Council may direct.

(e) An act passed by the Council shall be presented by the Chairman of the Council to the Mayor, who shall, within ten calendar days (excluding Saturdays, Sundays, and holidays) after the act is presented to him, either approve or disapprove such act. If the Mayor shall approve such act, he shall indicate the same by affixing his signature thereto, and such act shall become law subject to the provisions of section 602(c). If the Mayor shall disapprove such act, he shall, within ten calendar days (excluding Saturdays, Sundays, and holidays) after it is presented to him, return such act to the Council setting forth in writing his reasons for such disapproval. If any act so passed shall not be returned to the Council by the Mayor within ten calendar days after it shall have been presented to him, the

Mayor shall be deemed to have approved it, and such act shall become law subject to the provisions of section 602(c). If, within thirty calendar days after an act has been timely returned by the Mayor to the Council with his disapproval, two-thirds of the members of the Council present and voting vote to reenact such act, the act so reenacted shall be transmitted by the Chairman to the President of the United States. Subject to the provisions of section 602(c), such act, except any act of the Council submitted to the President in accordance with the Budget and Accounting Act, 1921, shall become law at the, end of the thirty day period beginning on the, date of such transmission, unless during such period the President disapproves such act.

(f) In the case of any budget act adopted by the Council pursuant to section 446 of this Act and submitted to the Mayor in accordance with subsection (e) of this section, the Mayor shall have power to disapprove any items or provisions, or both, of such act and approve the remainder. In any case in which the Mayor so disapproves of any item or provision, he shall append to the act when he signs it a statement of the item or provision which he disapproves, and shall, within such ten-day period, return a copy of the act and statement with his objections to the Council. If, within thirty calendar days after any such item or provision so disapproved has been timely returned by the Mayor to the Council, two-thirds of the members of the Council present and voting vote, to reenact any such item or provision, such item or Provision so reenacted shall be transmitted by the Chairman to the President of the United States. In any case in which the Mayor fails to timely return any such item or provision so disapproved to the Council, the Mayor shall be deemed to have approved such item or provision not returned, and such item or provision not, returned shall be transmitted by the Chairman to the President of the United States.

. . . .

Part B—The Mayor

. . . .

SEC. 421. (a) There is established the Office of the Mayor of the District of Columbia; and the Mayor shall be elected by the registered qualified electors of the District.

(b) The Mayor established by subsection (a) shall be elected, on a partisan basis, for a term of four years beginning at noon on January 2 of the year following his election.

(c) (1) No person shall hold the Office of Mayor unless he (A) is a qualified elector, (B) has resided and been domiciled in the District for one year immediately preceding the day on which the general or special election for Mayor is to be held, and (C) is not engaged in any employment (whether as an employee or as a self-employed individual) and holds no public office or position (other than his employment in and position as Mayor), for which he is compensated in an amount in excess of his actual expenses in connection therewith, expect that nothing in this clause shall be construed as prohibiting such person, while holding the Office of Mayor, from serving as a delegate or alternate delegate to a convention of a political party nominating candidates for President and Vice President of the United States, or from holding an appointment in the reserve component of an armed force of the United States other than a member serving on active duty under a call for more than thirty days. The Mayor shall forfeit his office upon failure to maintain the qualifications required by this paragraph.

(2) To fill a vacancy in the Office of Mayor, the Board of Elections shall hold a special election in the District on the first Tuesday occurring more than one hundred and fourteen days after the date on which such vacancy occurs, unless the Board of Elections determines that such vacancy could be more practicably filled in a special election held on the same day as the next general election to be held in the District occurring within sixty days of the date on which a special election would otherwise have been held under the provisions of this paragraph. The person elected Mayor to fill a vacancy in the Office of Mayor shall take office on the day on which the Board of Elections certifies his election, and shall serve as Mayor only or the remainder of the term during which such vacancy occurred. When the Office of Mayor becomes vacant the Chairman shall become Acting Mayor and shall serve from the date such vacancy occurs until the date on which the Board of Elections certifies the election of the new Mayor at which time he shall again become Chairman.

. . . .

Powers and Duties

SEC. 422. The executive power of the District shall be vested in the Mayor who shall be the chief executive officer of the District government. In addition, except as otherwise provided in this Act, all functions granted to or vested in the Commissioner of the District of Columbia, as established under Reorganization plan Numbered 3 of 1967, shall be carried out by the Mayor in accordance with this Act. The Mayor shall be responsible for the proper execution of all laws relating to the District, and for the proper administration of the affairs of the District coming under his jurisdiction or control, including but not limited to the following powers, duties, functions:

(1) The Mayor shall administer all laws relating to the appointment, promotion, discipline, separation, and other conditions of employment of personnel in the office of the Mayor, personnel in executive departments of the District, and members of boards, commissions, and other agencies. . . .

Municipal Planning

SEC. 423. (a) The Mayor shall be the central planning agency for the District. He shall be responsible for the coordination of planning activities of the municipal government and the preparation and implementation of the District's elements of the comprehensive plan for the National Capital which may include land use elements, urban renewal and redevelopment elements, a multi-year program of municipal public works for the District, and physical, social, economic, transportation, and population elements. The Mayor's planning responsibility shall not extend to Federal and international projects and developments in the District, as determined by the National Capital Planning Commission, or to the United States Capitol buildings and grounds . . . or to any extension thereof or addition thereto, or to buildings and grounds under the care of the Architect of the Capitol.

. . . .

Part C—The Judiciary
Judicial Powers

SEC. 431. (a) The judicial powers of the District is vested in the District of Columbia Court of Appeals and the Superior Court of the District of Columbia. The Superior Court has jurisdiction of any civil action or other matter (at law or equity) brought to the District and of any criminal case under any law applicable exclusively to the District. The Superior Court has no jurisdiction over any civil or criminal matter over which the United States court has exclusive jurisdiction pursuant to an Act of Congress. The Court of Appeals has jurisdiction of appeals from the Superior Court and, to the extent provided by law, to review orders and decisions of the Mayor, the Council, or any agency of the District. The District of Columbia courts shall also have jurisdiction over any other matters granted to the District of Columbia courts or other provisions of law.

. . . .

Enactment of Appropriations by Congress

SEC. 446. The Council, within fifty calendar days after the receipt of the budget proposal from the Mayor, and after public hearing, shall by act adopt an annual budget for the District of Columbia government. Any supplements thereto shall also be adopted by act by the Council after public hearing. Such budget so adopted shall be submitted by the Mayor to the President for transmission by him to the Congress. No amount may be obligated or expended by any officer or employee of the District of Columbia government unless such amount has been approved by Act of Congress, and then only according to such Act. Notwithstanding any other provision of this Act, the Mayor shall not transmit any annual budget or amendments or supplements thereto, to the President of the United States until the completion of the budget procedures contained in this Act.

. . . .

TITLE IV—FEDERAL PAYMENT
Duties of the Mayor, Council, and Federal Office of Management and Budget

SEC. 501 (a) It shall be the duty of the Mayor in preparing an annual budget for the government of the District to develop meaningful intercity expenditure and revenue comparisons based on data supplied by the Bureau of the Census, and to identify elements of cost and benefits to the District which result from the unusual role of the District as the Nation's Capital. The results of the studies conducted by the Mayor under this subsection shall be made available to the Council and to the Federal Office of Management and Budget for their use in reviewing and revising the Mayor's request with respect to the level of the appropriation for the annual Federal payment to the District. Such Federal payment should operate to encourage efforts on the part of the government of the District to maintain and increase its level of revenues and to seek such efficiencies and economies in the management of its programs as are possible.

. . . .

TITLE VI—RESERVATION OF CONGRESSIONAL AUTHORITY

Retention of Congressional Authority

SEC. 601. Notwithstanding any other provision of this Act, the Congress of the United States reserves the right, at any time, to exercise its constitutional authority as legislature for the District, by enacting legislation for the District on any subject, whether within or without the scope of legislative power granted to the Council by this Act, including legislation to amend or repeal any law in force in the District prior to

or after the enactment of this Act and any act passed by the Council.

Limitations on the Council

SEC. 602. (a) The Council shall have no authority to pass any act contrary to the provisions of this Act except as specifically provided in this Act, or to—

(1) impose any tax on property of the United States or any of the several States;

(2) lend the public credit for support of any private undertaking;

(3) enact any act , or enact any act to amend or repeal any Act of Congress, which concerns the functions or property of the United States or which is not restricted in its application exclusively in or to the District;

(4) enact any act, resolution, or rule with respect to any provision of title 11 of the District of Columbia Code (relating to organization and jurisdiction of the District of Columbia courts);

(5) impose any tax on the whole or any portion of the personal income, either directly or at the source thereof, of any individual not a resident of the District (the terms "individual" and "resident" to be understood for the purposes of this paragraph as they are defined in section 4 of title I of the District of Columbia Income and Franchise Tax Act of 1947)....

Statutes at Large 87 (1973), 93d Congress, 1st session, Dec. 24, 1973, 774–836.

---

164   The Congressional Budget and Impoundment Control Act of 1974

July 12, 1974

When Congress passed the Budget and Accounting Act of 1921 (see document 117), it helped bring order to the chaotic and decentralized manner in which the annual budget had been prepared. The 1921 act made the president and the executive branch the central organizing mechanism for budget preparation and set up a Bureau of the Budget (later renamed the Office of Management and Budget). This gave the executive branch considerable control over the details of the budget. Congress continued to consider the budget in pieces. Numerous committees and subcommittees, especially the House and Senate Appropriations Committees, the House Ways and Means Committee, and the Senate Finance Committee, each dealt with parts of the overall budget, but there was no overall coordination of spending targets and revenue projections. In the years following passage of the 1921 act, Congress saw a slow but steady loss of its constitutional power of the purse to the executive branch. By the late 1960s the matter had festered into a major crisis.

During the administration of President Richard Nixon from 1969 to 1973, pressure grew in Congress to change the budget

process. Nixon, in an effort to control inflation and limit federal spending, frequently fought with Congress over reducing expenditures, often resorting to vetoes of spending bills. Nixon also sought to control spending with which his administration disagreed by impounding funds that Congress had appropriated. In other words, he refused to spend the money that Congress had allotted for specific programs. During these same years inflation continued to rise and the federal budget continued to grow, with increased deficits.

The Congressional Budget and Impoundment Control Act of 1974 established House and Senate Budget Committees, which were composed, in part, of members of the House and Senate Appropriations Committees, the House Ways and Means Committee, and the Senate Finance Committee. Staffed by experts in budgetary matters, these committees gave Congress important new tools to analyze the president's budget and decide on an overall spending strategy that set limits on what individual committees could spend. Title X of the bill, known as the Impoundment Control Act of 1974, placed limits on the president's ability to arbitrarily impound funds that Congress had appropriated by requiring him to report to Congress on all funds that might be rescinded or deferred. The act also created an important new agency, the Congressional Budget Office, to provide expertise to the House and Senate Budget Committees and provide Congress with the kind of specialists found in the president's Office of Management and Budget.

The 1974 act shifted the beginning of the federal government's fiscal year from July 1 to October 1. While giving Congress more time, the act also established budget deadlines, a strictly controlled timeframe for the congressional response to the president's budget. As a result of the passage of this act Congress was able to reassert itself in determining annual spending priorities, recapturing a good portion of its power of the purse that had been eroded since the passage of the Budget and Accounting Act of 1921.

TITLE I—ESTABLISHMENT OF HOUSE AND SENATE BUDGET COMMITTEES

Budget Committee of the House Representatives

SEC. 101. (a) Clause 1 of Rule X of the Rules of the House of Representatives is amended by redesignating paragraphs (e) through (u) as paragraphs (f) through (v), respectively, and by inserting after paragraph (d) the following new paragraph:

"(e) Committee on the Budget, to consist of twenty-three Members as follows:

"(1) five members who are members of the Committee on Appropriations;

"(2) five Members who are members of the Committee on Ways and Means;

"(3) eleven Members who are members of other standing committees;

"(4) one Member from the leadership of the majority party; and

"(5) one Member from the leadership of the minority party. No Member shall serve as a member of the Committee on the Budget during more than two Congresses in any period of five successive Congresses beginning after 1974 (disregarding for this purpose any service performed as a member of such committee for less than a full session in any Congress). All selections of Members to serve on the committee shall be made without regard to seniority."

(b) Rule X of the Rules of the House of Representatives is amended by adding at the end thereof the following new clause:

"6. For carrying out the purposes set forth in clause 5 of Rule XI, the Committee on the Budget or any subcommittee thereof is authorized to sit and act at such times and places within the United States, whether the House is in session, has recessed, or has adjourned, to hold such hearings, to require the attendance of such witnesses and the production of such books or papers or documents or vouchers by subpoena or otherwise, and to take such testimony and records, as it deems necessary. Subpoenas may be issued over the signature of the chairman or member. The chairman of the committee, or any member thereof, may administer oaths to witnesses."

. . . .

Budget Committee of the Senate

SEC. 102. (a) Paragraph 1 of rule XXV of the Standing Rules of the Senate is amended by adding at the end thereof the following new subparagraph:

"(r)(1) Committee on the Budget, to which committee shall be referred all concurrent resolutions on the budget (as defined in section 3(a)(4) of the Congressional Budget Act of 1974) and all other matters required to be referred to that committee under titles III and IV of that Act, and messages, petitions, memorials, and other matters relating thereto.

"(2) Such committee shall have the duty—

"(A) to report the matters required to be reported by it under titles III and IV of the Congressional Budget Act of 1974;

"(B) to make continuing studies of the effect on budget outlays of relevant existing and proposed legislation and to report the results of such studies to the Senate on a recurring basis;

"(C) to request and evaluate continuing studies of tax expenditures, to devise methods of coordinating tax expenditures, policies, and programs with direct budget outlays, and to report the results of such studies to the Senate on a recurring basis; and

"(D) to review, on a continuing basis, the conduct by the Congressional Budget Office of its functions and duties."

. . . .

TITLE II—CONGRESSIONAL BUDGET OFFICE

Establishment of Office

SEC. 201. (a) IN GENERAL.—

(1) There is established an office of the Congress to be known as the Congressional Budget Office (hereinafter in this title referred to as the "Office"). The Office shall be headed by a Director; and there shall be a Deputy Director who shall perform such duties as may be assigned to him by the Director and, during the absence or incapacity of the Director or during a vacancy in that office, shall act as Director.

(2) The Director shall be appointed by the Speaker of the House of Representatives and the President pro tempore of the Senate after considering recommendations received from the Committees on the Budget of the House and the Senate, without regard to political affiliation and solely on the basis of his fitness to perform his duties. The Deputy Director shall be appointed by the Director.

. . . .

(d) RELATIONSHIP TO EXECUTIVE BRANCH.—The Director is authorized to secure information, data, estimates, and statistics directly from the various departments, agencies, and establishments of the executive branch of Government and the regulatory agencies and commissions of the Government. All such departments, agencies, establishments, and regulatory agencies and commissions shall furnish the director any available material which he determines to be necessary in the performance of his duties and functions (other than material the disclosure of which would be a violation of law). The Director is also authorized, upon agreement with the head of any such department, agency, establishment, or regulatory agency or commission, to utilize its services, facilities, and personnel with or without reimbursement; and the head of each such department, agency, establishment, or regulatory agency or commission is authorized to provide the Office such services, facilities, and personnel.

(e) RELATIONSHIP TO OTHER AGENCIES OF CONGRESS.—In carrying out the duties and functions of the Office, and for the purpose of coordinating the operations of the Office with those of other congressional agencies with a view to utilizing most effectively the information, services, and capabilities of all such agencies in carrying out the various responsibilities assigned to each, the Director if authorized to obtain information, data, estimates, and statistics developed by the General Accounting Office, the Library of Congress, and the Office of Technology Assessment, and (upon agreement with them) to utilize their services, facilities, and personnel with or without reimbursement. The Comptroller General, the Librarian of Congress, and the Technology Assessment Board are authorized to provide the Office with the information, data, estimates, and statistics, and the services, facilities, and personnel, referred to in the preceding sentence.

. . . .

(f) REPORTS TO BUDGET COMMITTEES.—

(1) One or before April 1 of each year, the Director shall submit to the Committees on the Budget of the House of Representatives and the Senate a report, for the fiscal year commencing on October 1 of that year, with respect to fiscal policy, including (A) alternative levels of total revenues, total new budget authority, and total outlays (including related surpluses and deficits), and (B) the levels of tax expenditures under existing law, taking into account projected economic factors and any changes in such levels based on proposals in the budget submitted by the President for such fiscal year. Such report shall also include a discussion of national budget priorities, including alternative ways of allocating budget authority and budget outlays for such fiscal year among major programs or functional categories, taking into account how such alternative allocations will meet major national needs and affect balance growth and development of the United States.

(2) The Director shall from time to time submit to the Committees on the Budget of the House of Representatives and the Senate such further reports (including reports revising the report required by paragraph (1)) as may be necessary or appropriate to provide such Committees with information, data, and analyses for the performance of their duties and functions.

(g) USE OF COMPUTERS AND OTHER TECHNIQUES.—The Director may equip the Office with up-to-date computer capability (upon approval of the Committee on House Administration of the House of Representatives and the Committee on Rules and Administration of the Senate), obtain the services of experts and consultants in computer technology, and develop techniques for the evaluation of budgetary requirements.

Public Access to Budget Data

SEC. 203. (a) RIGHT TO COPY.—Except as provided in subsections (c) and (d), the Director shall make all information, data, estimates, and statistics obtained under sections 201(d) and 201(e) available for public copying during normal business hours, subject to reasonable rules and regulations, and shall to the extent practicable, at the request of any person, furnish a copy of any such information, data, estimates, or statistics upon payment by such person of the cost of making and furnishing such copy.

. . . .

TITLE III—CONGRESSIONAL BUDGET PROCESS
Timetable

SEC. 300. The timetable with respect to the congressional budget process for any fiscal year is as follows:

On or before:	Action to be completed:
November 10	President submits current services budget.
15th day after Congress meets	President submits his budget.
March 15	Committees and joint committees submit reports to Budget Committees.
April 1	Congressional Budget Office submits report to Budget Committees.
April 15	Budget Committees report first concurrent resolution on the budget to their Houses.
May 15	Committees report bills and resolutions authorizing new budget authority.
May 15	Congress completes action on the first concurrent resolution on the budget.
7th day after Labor Day	Congress completes action on bills and resolutions providing new budget authority and new spending authority.
September 15	Congress completes action on second required concurrent resolution on the budget.
September 25	Congress completes action on reconciliation bill or resolution, or both, implementing second required concurrent resolution.
October 1	Fiscal year begins.

. . . .

TITLE VI—AMENDMENTS TO BUDGET AND ACCOUNTING ACT, 1921

Matters to Be Included in President's Budget

SEC. 601. Section 201 of the Budget and Accounting Act, 1921 (31 U.S.C. 11), is amended by adding at the end thereof the following new subsections:

"(d) The Budget transmitted pursuant to subsection (a) for each fiscal year shall set for the separately the items enumerated in section 301(a)(1)–(5) of the Congressional Budget Act of 1974.

"(e) The Budget transmitted pursuant to subsection (a) for each fiscal year shall set forth the levels of tax expenditures under existing law for such fiscal year (the tax expenditure budget), taking into account projected economic factors, and any changes in such existing levels based on proposals contained in such Budget. For purposes of this subsection, the terms 'tax expenditures' and 'tax expenditures budget' have the means given to them by section 3(a)(3) of the Congressional Budget Act of 1974.

"(f) The Budget transmitted pursuant to subsection (a) for each fiscal year shall contain—

"(1) a comparison, for the last completed fiscal year, of the total amount of outlays estimated in the Budget transmitted pursuant to subsection (a) for each major program involving uncontrollable or relatively uncontrollable outlays and the total amount of outlays made under each such major program during such fiscal year;

"(2) a comparison, for the last completed fiscal year, of the total amount of revenues estimated in the Budget transmitted pursuant to subsection (a) and the total amount of revenues received during such year, and, with respect to each major revenue source, the amount of revenues estimated in the Budget transmitted pursuant to subsection (a) and the amount of revenues received during such year; and

"(3) an analysis and explanation of the difference between each amount set forth pursuant to paragraphs (1) and (2) as the amount of outlays or revenues estimated in the Budget submitted under subsection (a) for such fiscal year and the corresponding amount set forth as the amount of outlays made or revenues received during such fiscal year.

"(g) The President shall transmit to the Congress, on or before April 10 and July 15 of each year, a statement of all amendments to or revisions in the budget authority requested, the estimated outlays, and the estimated receipts for the ensuing fiscal year set forth in the Budget transmitted pursuant to subsection (a) (including any previous amendments or revisions proposed on behalf of the executive branch) that he deems necessary and appropriate based on the most current information available. Such statement shall contain the effect of such amendments and revisions on the summary data submitted under subsection (a) and shall include such supporting detail as is practicable. The statement transmitted on or before July 15 of any year may be included in the supplemental summary required to be transmitted under subsection (b) during such year. The Budget transmitted under subsection (b) during such year. The Budget transmitted to the Congress pursuant to subsection (a) for any fiscal year, or the supporting detail transmitted in connection therewith, shall include a statement of all such amendments and revisions with respect to the fiscal year in progress made before the date of transmission of such Budget.

. . . .

TITLE X—IMPOUNDMENT CONTROL

Disclaimer

SEC. 1001. Nothing contained in this Act, or in any amendments made by this Act, shall be construed as—

(1) asserting or conceding the constitutional powers or limitations of either the Congress or the President;

(2) ratifying or approving any impoundment heretofore or hereafter executed or approved by the President or any other Federal officer or employee, except insofar as pursuant to statutory authorization then in effect;

(3) affecting in any way the claims or defenses of any party to litigation concerning any impoundment; or

(4) superseding any provision of law which requires the obligation of budget authority or the making of outlays thereunder.

. . . .

Rescission of Budget Authority

SEC. 1012. (a) TRANSMITTAL OF SPECIAL MESSAGE.—Whenever the President determines that all or part of any budget authority will not be required to carry out the full objectives or scope of programs for which it is provided or that such budget authority should be rescinded for fiscal policy or other reasons (including the termination of authorized projects or activities for which budget authority has been provided), or whenever all or part of budget authority provided for only one fiscal year is to be reserved from obligation for such fiscal year, the President shall transmit to both Houses of Congress a special message specifying—

(1) the amount of budget authority which he proposes to be rescinded or which is to be so reserved;

(2) any account, department, or establishment of the Government to which such budget authority is available for obligation, and the specific project or governmental functions involved;

(3) the reasons why the budget authority should be rescinded or is to be so reserved;

(4) to the maximum extent practicable, the estimated fiscal, economic, and budgetary effect of the proposed rescission or of the reservation; and

(5) all facts, circumstances, and considerations relating to or bearing upon the proposed rescission or the reservation

and the decision to effect the proposed rescission or the reservation, and to the maximum extent practicable, the estimated effect of the proposed rescission or the reservation upon the objects, purposes, and programs for which the budget authority is provided.

(b) REQUIREMENT TO MAKE AVAILABLE FOR OBLIGATION.—Any amount of budget authority proposed to be rescinded or that is to be reserved as set forth in such special message shall be made available for obligation unless, within the prescribed 45-day period, the Congress has completed action on a rescission bill rescinding all or part of the amount proposed to be rescinded or that is to be reserved.

Disapproval of Proposed Deferrals of Budget Authority

SEC. 1013. (a) TRANSMITTAL OF SPECIAL MESSAGE.—Whenever the President, the Director of the Office of Management and Budget, the head of any department or agency of the United States, or any officer or employee of the United States proposes to defer any budget authority provided for a specific purpose or project, the President shall transmit to the House of Representatives and the Senate a special message specifying—

(1) the amount of the budget authority proposed to be deferred;

(2) any account, department, or establishment of the Government to which such budget authority is available for obligation, and the specific projects or governmental functions involved;

(3) the period of time during which the budget authority is proposed to be deferred;

(4) the reasons for the proposed deferral, including any legal authority invoked by him to justify the proposed deferral;

(5) to the maximum extent practicable, the estimated fiscal, economic, and budgetary effect of the proposed deferral; and

(6) all facts, circumstances, and considerations relating to or bearing upon the proposed deferral and the decision to effect the proposed deferral, including an analysis of such facts, circumstances, and considerations in terms of their application to any legal authority and specific elements of legal authority invoked by him to justify such proposed deferral, and to the maximum extent practicable, the estimated effect of the proposed deferral upon the objects, purposes, and programs for which the budget authority is provided.

A special message may include one or more proposed deferrals of budget authority. A deferral may not be proposed for any period of time extending beyond the end of the fiscal year in which the special message proposing the deferral is transmitted to the House and the Senate.

(b) REQUIREMENT TO MAKE AVAILABLE FOR OBLIGATION.—Any amount of budget authority proposed to be deferred, as set forth in a special message transmitted under subsection (a), shall be made available for obligation if either House of Congress passes an impoundment resolution disapproving such proposed deferral.

(c) EXCEPTION.—The provisions of this section do not apply to any budget authority proposed to be rescinded or that is to be reserved as set forth in a special message required to be transmitted under section 1012.

. . . .

Procedure in House and Senate

SEC. 1017. (a) REFERRAL.—Any rescission bill introduced with respect to a special message or impoundment resolution introduced with respect to a proposed deferral of budget authority shall be referred to the appropriate committee of the House of Representatives or the Senate, as the case may be.

(b) DISCHARGE OF COMMITTEE.—

(1) If the committee to which a rescission bill or impoundment resolution has been referred has not reported it at the end of 25 calendar days of continuous session of the congress after its introduction, it is in order to move either to discharge the committee from further consideration of the bill or resolution or to discharge the committee from further consideration of any other rescission bill with respect to the same special message or impoundment resolution with respect to the same proposed deferral, as the case may be, which has been referred to the committee.

(2) A motion to discharge may be made only by an individual favoring the bill or resolution, may be made only if supported by one-fifth of the members of the House involved (a quorum being present), and is highly privileged in the House and privileged in the Senate (except that it may not be made after the committee has reported a bill or resolution with respect to the same special message or the same proposed deferral, as the case may be); and debate thereon shall be limited to not more than 1 hour, the time to be divided in the House equally between those favoring and those opposing the bill or resolution, and to be divided in the Senate equally between, and controlled by, the majority leader and the minority leader or their designees. An amendment to the motion is not in order, and it is not in order to move to reconsider the vote by which the motion is agreed to or disagreed to.

(c) FLOOR CONSIDERATION IN THE HOUSE.—

(1) When the committee of the House of Representatives has reported, or has been discharged from further consideration of, a rescission bill or impoundment resolution, it shall at any time thereafter be in order (even though a previous motion to the same effect has been disagreed to) to move to proceed to the consideration of the bill or resolution. The motion shall be highly privileged and not debatable. An amendment to the motion shall not be in order, nor shall it be in order to move to reconsider the vote by which the motion is agreed to or disagreed to.

. . . .

(d) FLOOR CONSIDERATION IN THE SENATE.—

(1) Debate in the Senate on any rescission bill or impoundment resolution, and all amendments thereto (in the

case of a rescission bill) and debatable motions and appeals in connection therewith, shall be limited to not more than 10 hours. The time shall be equally divided between, and controlled by, the majority leader and the minority leader or their designees.

(2) Debate in the Senate on any amendment to a rescission bill shall be limited to 2 hours, to be equally divided between, and controlled by, the mover and the manager of the bill. Debate on any amendment to an amendment, to such a bill, and debate on any debatable motion or appeal in connection with such a bill or an impoundment resolution shall be limited to 1 hour, to be equally divided between, and controlled by, the mover and the manager of the bill or resolution, except that in the event the manager of the bill or resolution is in favor of any such amendment, motion, or appeal, the time in opposition thereto, shall be controlled by the minority leader or his designee. No amendment that is not germane to the provisions of rescission bill shall be received. Such leaders, or either of them,

may, from the time under their control on the passage of a rescission bill or impoundment resolution, allot additional time to any Senator during the consideration of any amendment, debatable motion, or appeal.

(3) A motion to further limit debate is not debatable. In the case of a rescission bill, a motion to recommit (except a motion to recommit with instructions to report back within a specified number of days, not to exceed 3, not counting any day on which the Senate is not in session) is not in order. Debate on any such motion to recommit shall be limited to one hour, to be equally divided between, and controlled by, the mover and the manager of the concurrent resolution. In the case of an impoundment resolution, no amendment or motion to recommit is in order.

. . . .

Statutes at Large, 88 (1974), 93d Congress, 2d session, July 12, 1974, 297–339.

165   The House Judiciary Committee Debates the Impeachment of President Richard M. Nixon

July 24, 1974

One of the most awesome powers of Congress is the ability to impeach and remove a president from office. Such a procedure, constitutional scholars agree, should not be entered into lightly or for frivolous or partisan reasons. The first president ever impeached was Andrew Johnson in 1868 (see documents 81 and 82). While some members of Congress occasionally threatened to impeach other presidents, it was not until 1974, more than a hundred years after Andrew Johnson's impeachment, that the House of Representatives began the formal process of impeaching another president, Richard M. Nixon (R-Calif.) on charges stemming from the investigation of the Watergate scandal (see document 161). The House of Representatives began another impeachment process on October 9, 1998, when it passed a resolution to begin a formal inquiry into the impeachment of President William Jefferson Clinton (see document 189).

The fact that impeachment proceedings are rare also signifies that they are difficult and complex processes. There are many unanswered questions about what constitutes an impeachable offense. The Constitution gives the power to impeach to the House of Representatives (Article I, Section 2, Clause 5) and the power to try impeached officials to the Senate (Article I, Section 3, Clause 6). The constitutional reasons for impeaching a president or other high-ranking government officials are contained in Article II, Section 4, which states: "The President, Vice President and all civil Officers of the United States, shall be removed from Office on Impeachment for, and Conviction of, Treason, Bribery, or other high Crimes and Misdemeanors."

When the House Judiciary Committee was charged by a vote of the full House with the task of beginning impeachment hearings, it took up its task with great seriousness, as can be seen in the debate that follows. The members of the House Judiciary Committee, under the chairmanship of Peter Rodino (D-N.J.), represented a cross-section of Democrats and Republicans, liberals and conservatives. It was hardly a nonpartisan, objective group, however. Many were political defenders of President Nixon and others were strong political opponents. Nonetheless, Democrats and Republicans on the committee comported themselves in a manner that exhibited fairness, seriousness of purpose, and the avoidance of overt partisan bickering. Their deliberations can serve as a model of conduct in such matters. Compared to the wildly partisan debacle of Andrew Johnson's impeachment process, the House Judiciary Committee in 1974 truly distinguished itself. The committee's solemn vote on the articles of impeachment led to President Nixon's resignation on August 9, 1974, before the full House could take up the matter.

As this debate reveals, the members of the committee looked to history, past precedent, the Framers of the Constitution, and the authors of the Federalist (see document 3) for guidance on what constituted an impeachable offense. They made a determination in the case of Richard Nixon, but they did not solve the problem of defining "high Crimes and Misdemeanors." When Gerald R. Ford assumed the presidency following Nixon's resignation, he pardoned Nixon. President Ford also offered his opinion on what was an impeachable offense: "The only honest answer is that an impeachable offense is whatever a majority of the House of Represen-

tatives considers it to be at a given moment in history; conviction results from whatever offense or offenses two-thirds of the other body [Senate] considers to be sufficiently serious to require removal from office."

STATEMENT OF HON. PETER W. RODINO, JR., A REPRESENTATIVE IN CONGRESS FROM THE 10TH CONGRESSIONAL DISTRICT OF THE STATE OF NEW JERSEY

The CHAIRMAN. Before I begin, I hope you will allow me a personal reference. Throughout all of the painstaking proceedings of this committee, I as the chairman have been guided by a simple principle, the principle that the law must deal fairly with every man. For me, this is the oldest principle of democracy. It is this simple, but great principle which enables man to live justly and in decency in a free society.

It is now almost 15 centuries since the Emperor Justinian from whose name the word "justice" is derived, established this principle for the free citizens of Rome. Seven centuries have now passed since the English barons proclaimed the same principle by compelling King John, at the point of the sword, to accept a great doctrine of Magna Carta, the doctrine that the king, like each of his subjects, was under God and the law.

Almost two centuries ago the Founding Fathers of the United States reaffirmed and refined this principle so that here all men are under the law, and it is only the people who are sovereign. So speaks our Constitution, and it is under our Constitution, the supreme law of our land, that we proceed through the sole power of impeachment.

We have reached the moment when we are ready to debate resolutions whether or not the Committee on the Judiciary should recommend that the House of Representatives adopt articles calling for the impeachment of Richard M. Nixon.

Make no mistake about it. This is a turning point, whatever we decide. Our judgment is not concerned with an individual but with a system of constitutional government.

It has been the history and the good fortune of the United States, ever since the Founding Fathers, that each generation of citizens, and their officials have been, within tolerable limits, faithful custodians of the Constitution and of the rule of law.

For almost 200 years every generation of Americans has taken care to preserve our system, and the integrity of our institutions, against the particular pressures and emergencies to which every time is subject.

This committee must now decide a question of the highest constitutional importance. For more than 2 years, there have been serious allegations by people of good faith and sound intelligence, that the President, Richard M. Nixon, has committed grave and systematic violations of the Constitution.

Last October, in the belief that such violations had in fact occurred, a number of impeachment resolutions were introduced by Members of the House and referred to our committee by the Speaker. On February 6, the House of Representatives, by a vote of 410 to 4, authorized and directed the committee on the Judiciary to investigate whether sufficient grounds exist to impeach Richard M. Nixon, President of the United States.

The Constitution specifies that the grounds for impeachment shall be, not partisan consideration, but evidence of "treason, bribery, or other high crimes and misdemeanors."

Since the Constitution vests the sole power of impeachment in the House of Representatives, it falls to the Judiciary Committee to understand even more precisely what "high crimes and misdemeanors" might mean in the terms of the Constitution and the facts before us in our time.

The Founding Fathers clearly did not mean that a President might be impeached for mistakes, even serious mistakes, which he might commit in the faithful execution of his office. By "high crimes and misdemeanors" they meant offenses more definitely incompatible with our Constitution.

The Founding Fathers, with their recent experience of monarchy and their determination that government be accountable and lawful, wrote into the Constitution a special oath that the President, and only the President, must take at his inauguration. In that oath, the President swears that he will take care that the laws be faithfully executed. The Judiciary Committee has for 7 months investigated whether or not the President has seriously abused his power, in violation of that oath and the public trust embodied in it.

We have investigated fully and completely what within our constitution and traditions would be grounds for impeachment. For the past 10 weeks, we have listened to the presentation of evidence in documentary form, to tape recordings of 19 Presidential conversations, and to the testimony of nine witnesses called before the entire committee.

We have provided a fair opportunity for the President's counsel to present the President's views to the committee. We have taken care to preserve the integrity of the process in which we are engaged.

We have deliberated. We have been patient. We have been fair. Now, the American people, the House of Representatives, the Constitution, and the whole history of our Republic demand that we make up our minds.

As the English statesman, Edmund Burke said during an impeachment trial in 1788; "It is by this tribunal that statesmen who abuse their power are accused by statesmen and tried by statesmen, not upon the niceties of a narrow jurisprudence, but upon the enlarged and solid principles of state morality."

Under the Constitution and under our authorization from the House, this inquiry is neither a court of law nor a partisan proceeding. It is an inquiry which must result in a decision—a judgment based on the facts.

In his statement of April 30, 1973, President Nixon told the American people that he had been deceived by subordinates into believing that none of the members of his administration or his personal campaign committee were implicated in the

Watergate break-in, and that none had participated in efforts to cover up that illegal activity.

A critical question this committee must decide is whether the President was deceived by his closest political associates or whether they were in fact carrying out his policies and decisions. This question must be decided one way or the other.

It must be decided whether the President was deceived by his subordinates into believing that his personal agents and key political associates had not been engaged in a systematic coverup of the illegal political intelligence operation, of the identities of those responsible, and of the existence and scope of other related activities; or whether, in fact, Richard M. Nixon, in violation of the sacred obligation of his constitutional oath, has used the power of his high office for over 2 years to cover up and conceal responsibility for the Watergate burglary and other activities of a similar nature.

In short, the committee has to decide whether in his statement of April 30 and other public statements the President was telling the truth to the American people, or whether that statement and other statements were part of a pattern of conduct designed not to take care that the laws were faithfully executed, but to impede their faithful execution for his political interest and on his behalf.

There are other critical questions that must be decided. We must decide whether the President abused his power in the execution of his office.

The great wisdom of our founders entrusted this process to the collective wisdom of many men. Each of those chosen to toil for the people at the great forge of democracy—the House of Representatives—has a responsibility to exercise independent judgment. I pray that we will each act with the wisdom that compels us in the end to be but decent men who seek only the truth.

Let us be clear about this. No official, no concerned citizen, no Representative, no member of this committee, welcomes an impeachment proceeding. No one welcomes the day when there has been such a crisis of concern that he must decide whether "high crimes and misdemeanors," serious abuses of official power or violations of public trust, have in fact occurred.

Let us also be clear. Our own public trust, our own commitment to the Constitution, is being put to the test. Such tests, historically, have come to the awareness of most peoples too late—when their rights and freedoms under the law were already so far in jeopardy and eroded that it was no longer in the people's power to restore constitutional government by democratic means.

Let us go forward. Let us go forward into debate in good will, with honor and decency, and with respect for the views of one another. Whatever we now decide, we must have the integrity and the decency, the will, and the courage to decide rightly.

Let us leave the Constitution as unimpaired for our children as our predecessors left it to us.

I now recognize the gentleman from Michigan.

Mr. HUTCHINSON. Thank you, Mr. Chairman.

I certainly agree with the opening paragraphs of your statement and I want to compliment you upon a statement in which you have strong and firm belief, although I would disagree with parts of it. I certainly wanted to say that I certainly compliment you upon its opening several paragraphs.

We now proceed to consider the large mass of evidential material which was assembled during many months and presented to us by committee staff, and by the testimony of witnesses who appeared before us.

During the next few days, we will be weighing the evidence and acting upon it. After a period of general debate, we will be discussing amendments and voting upon them. And finally, the end product of our deliberations will be manifest. Either we shall by majority vote have recommended on or more grounds for impeachment against the President, or all of those proposed for adoption will have been defeated in our deliberations.

The people will have an unusual glimpse into the discussions of those charged with the decision making in a unique judicial process. But perhaps ours is more of a political that a judicial function after all. The fact is that, of course, judges and juries deliberate behind closed doors, but by the committee's action in opening these discussions it has, in effect, determined that our function is more political than judicial. I think the public should know that until now the only decisions made by this committee have been procedural ones. No substantive matter has yet been resolved.

Early in the inquiry the staff submitted a memorandum on what constitutes an impeachable offense within the meaning of the Constitution, but the committee took no action upon it, it being recognized that no definition could be drawn which would be agreed to probably by most members. Thus, as of this minute, the committee has not resolved just what an impeachable offense is.

As the staff assembled evidence, many of us felt that the committee should decide and give some direction to the staff as to the scope of the inquiry. We thought the committee should direct to the staff to those areas of inquiry in which the committee itself determined that there might be merit so that time and effort would not be consumed in frivolous or otherwise nonmeritorious allegations. But such a course of action would have required the committee to make decisions of substance, and no decisions were made.

The articles of impeachment which are to be exhibited tonight are, like any legislative bill, merely a vehicle upon which the committee may work its will. They will be open to additions, deletions, amendments, and substitutions. Each member of this committee individually weighing the evidence against his own concept of what warrants impeachment will come to his own conclusion on how he votes on the articles in their final form. Each of us is struck by the enormity of the decisions that we are called upon to make.

As I see it, and I state only my personal views, a vote for an article of impeachment means that a member is convinced that the article states an offense for which the President should be removed from office, and that there is evidence which supports the charge beyond a reasonable doubt.

Unlike criminal jurisprudence, there is discretion in the court to make the sentence fit the crime. The Constitution mandates that conviction on impeachment shall carry with it the removal from office, nothing less.

It seems to me that, then, that in determining in my own mind whether a specific charge states an impeachable offense, I would have to decide whether I thought the offense charged is of sufficient gravity to warrant removal of the President from office because of it. In other words, some offenses may be charged for which there is convincing evidence, and still such offenses may not, in the judgment of a member, be so serious as to justify impeachment and removal of a President of the United States from office.

Earlier today, the Supreme Court announced that the President of the United States is required by law to comply with a certain subpena duces tecum served upon him in the case of the *United States* v. *Mitchell and others,* by submission of the subpenaed material to the trial judge for his private examination, and that the judge shall deliver to the Prosecutor only those portions which are relevant to the case, returning the balance of the documentation to the President without disclosing its contents.

Since this committee has requested the tapes of the same conversations from the President, and then subpenaed them, the question arises whether our committee should proceed further until the availability of the additional evidence to the committee is determined. Many members on this side, Mr. Chairman, feel strongly that we should not, we believe the American people will expect us to examine and weigh all available evidence before we decide the momentous and most difficult issue before us.

Even now, Mr. Chairman, we hope that the Chair will consider whether, in view of the events of today, the committee ought not first to determine to postpone consideration of articles of impeachment until the evidence now that has become available through the Court can be made available to this committee.

The CHAIRMAN. I recognize the gentleman from Massachusetts, Mr. Donohue.

Mr. DONOHUE. Thank you, Mr. Chairman.

Pursuant to the procedural resolution which this committee adopted yesterday, I move that the committee report to the House a resolution together with articles of impeachment, impeaching Richard M. Nixon, President of the United States.

Now, a copy of this resolution is at the clerk's desk and I understand a copy is also before each member.

The CHAIRMAN. I recognize the gentleman from Massachusetts for purpose of general debate on his resolution for not to exceed 15 minutes and every other member of the committee will be recognized for purposes of debate not to exceed 15 minutes following Mr. Donohue's presentation.

Mr. Donohue.

STATEMENT OF HON. HAROLD D. DONOHUE, A REPRESENTATIVE IN CONGRESS FROM THE THIRD CONGRESSIONAL DISTRICT OF THE STATE OF MASSACHUSETTS

Mr. DONOHUE. Thank you again, Mr. Chairman.

This is a historic debate and the motions I have just offered to this committee have their roots in the most fundamental precept of free men, that no individual is above the law.

On July 20, 1787, the Constitutional Convention had before it the great question, "Shall the Executive be removable on impeachment?"

Mr. Gouverneur Morris, a delegate to that Convention, spoke forcibly in opposition. He wanted no impeachment clause in the draft of our Constitution. But he listened intently as first Benjamin Franklin and then James Madison argued on behalf of such a clause and finally just before the question was voted, Mr. Gouverneur Morris announced that his opinion had been changed by the arguments presented in debate.

The impeachment clause was adopted by the Convention and became section 4 of article II of the Constitution of the United States and the sole power of impeachment was vested in the House of Representatives under article I, section 2 of the Constitution.

Now, pursuant to that constitutional power, House Resolution 803 as stated by our distinguished chairman was adopted by the House of Representatives on February 6 by a vote of 410 to 4. That resolution directed this committee to investigate fully and completely whether sufficient grounds exist for the House of Representatives to exercise its constitutional authority to impeach the President of the United States.

For the past several months, as also has been stated, this committee has been continuously engaged in the careful conduct of this Presidential impeachment inquiry. . . .

Now, Mr. Chairman, those conversations to which I have just referred took place in the White House, in the President's own office, the Oval Office, the absolute center of executive power of the United States. That was Richard Nixon, our President, your President and mine, conferring with his Chief of Staff and his Counsel. There they were in the Oval Office, plotting, planning and conspiring together to cover up and contain evidence of violations of our law, to obstruct our system of justice, and to impede a congressional committee in the discharge of its lawful duties, and their planning was followed up by a lot of overt acts. Their efforts were successful. The Patman committee was prevented from conducting its investigation and that, Mr. Chairman, was on September 15, 1972, more than 6 months before March 21, 1973, the date on which the President states he learned for the first time about the coverup operation.

I submit, Mr. Chairman, that this is enough direct and undisputed evidence to support a conviction of conspiracy in a criminal court.

And that connects President Richard Nixon directly to conduct which is a clear breach of his oath of office, and his duty to take care that the laws are faithfully executed.

I have another instance, Mr. Chairman, of direct proof that the President was personally involved in this coverup operation, in this obstruction of justice. You will recall, Mr. Chairman, before Haldeman met with the President on June 23, Haldeman had received a report from Dean that he had had a meeting with Acting FBI Director Gray. Gray had told Dean that the FBI's theories of Watergate included both the theory that it was a political CRP operation, and the theory that it was a CIA operation.

Gray also told Dean of the 32, $100 bills. Now, this was relayed directly by Haldeman to the President. But the President, nevertheless, passed on the instructions that the FBI should not investigate in Mexico because it might interfere with the activities of the CIA.

Mr. Chairman, my time has expired. But, I respectfully submit that rather than relying entirely upon circumstantial evidence we have direct evidence coming out of the mouth of the President of the United States that he not only condoned but he directed these coverup operations.

The CHAIRMAN. I recognize the gentleman from Mississippi, Mr. Lott, for general debate.

STATEMENT OF HON. TRENT LOTT, A REPRESENTATIVE IN CONGRESS FROM THE FIFTH CONGRESSIONAL DISTRICT OF THE STATE OF MISSISSIPPI

Mr. LOTT. Thank you, Mr. Chairman.

The CHAIRMAN. For a period not to exceed 15 minutes.

Mr. LOTT. Thank you.

This has truly been an awesome, time-consuming and exhausting task, and I really wonder if any of us here really can appreciate what this moment in history could mean to the future of our country. And while at various points along the way I have really been somewhat disgusted with this committee's proceedings, such as when we spent an hour earlier this week trying to decide not whether or not to have television cameras, but whether or not to have lights for the television cameras. I must admit in all candidness that it has been very fair and I must take this opportunity to thank the chairman for his consideration of this particular member.

And also, Mr. Chairman, I was particularly impressed with several of the comments that you made in your opening statement last night. And I would like to refer to those.

"Make no mistake about it, this is a turning point whatever we decide. Our judgment is not concerned with an individual, but with a system of constitutional government."

I believe that.

Further quoting: "For almost 200 years, every generation of Americans has taken care to preserve our system and the integrity of our institutions against the particular pressures and emergencies to which every time is subject." And I subscribe to that.

Quoting further:

"The Founding Fathers clearly did not mean that a President might be impeached for mistakes, even serious mistakes."

These quotes I would like to direct some of my attention to. But first, let me go back and put our present situation into the proper perspective. We are now in the final stages of review of some 15 months of the most intensive investigation of any President of the United States, perhaps any man. The Senate select committee or the Watergate Committee spent some months and over $2 million in its investigation. The grand jury in Washington, D.C., has spent over $225, 000 in their proceedings since June 1972. The Special Prosecutors have been at their task since May 1973 and at a cost of over $2.8 million. And the House Judiciary Committee staff of some 100 have been working since January at a cost of over $1.17 million.

There are reams of paper, thousands of pages, volumes of material, grand jury evidence, other congressional committee investigation papers and transcripts, tapes, logs, handwritten memos, and on, and on and on. The sheer weight in pounds is overwhelming.

Could any man withstand such scrutiny, could any man go through all of this without some evidence of a questionable statement under pressure, or while frustrated, or even without revealing some mistakes? I submit no. And where was the similar counterbalancing presentation of the other side of the story? Was the whole picture revealed properly? Was it in the Senate Watergate Committee? No.

Was it in the grand jury or even in this committee? In this committee the staff was nonpartisan, and I must give credit where credit is due, for a fair presentation, until, of course, very recently and that is understandable. But, except for a last-minute shift in the minority counsel, the arguments against impeachment, the cons, the other side of the story, would not have been presented.

Yes, the President's counsel, James St. Clair, was properly allowed to sit in this presentation of evidence and eventually to participate on a limited basis. His was the only argument on behalf of the President until the last presentation by Mr. Garrison. However, he was the President's counsel, not the committee counsel, not my counsel.

There was not a staff structure for a balanced presentation, in my opinion, and perhaps I share the blame for that.

An interesting aside is the fact that, as I get into procedure, is that last night at 7:30 we received the proposed articles of impeachment, the night the debate began. Quite often we have been faced with being hit at the last minute with what we are fixing to vote on, but regardless of that, we are now preparing to vote on articles of impeachment.

I have tried to maintain a restrained position because I think it has been incumbent upon every member to listen and keep his mouth shut until he had enough to make his decision. But; I must also be frank in saying that I have approached this task from the standpoint that point that the President was innocent, like any man, under such proceedings, and should be presumed innocent until there was clear and convincing evidence to, the contrary. You cannot impeach a President because you don't like his philosophy, or on the basis of innuendo or contradicted evidence.

In my opinion, you cannot impeach a President for a half a case or on the basis of parts of several cases put together.

And we are not faced with impeaching John Dean or John Mitchell, or Magruder or any of these others. We are faced with impeaching the President. The line must be drawn directly to the President, clearly to the President.

This has not been done.

The President had several aides that served him and this country poorly. The legal processes are now dealing with them. But, for every bit of evidence implicating the President, there is evidence to the contrary. What is at stake here is the Presidency, and this is what has worried me all along.

In my part of the country we do worry about these institutions, we do still hold institutions that made this grand country great, dear, and important. We have to consider the best interests of this country now and in the long run. We cannot allow political considerations or circumstantial evidence to be the basis for impeaching the first President of the United States in over 100 years. And I might add, in so many ways, the best President in that period of time.

I think this is a classic example here of how perhaps all of us in this committee have gotten so deep in the forest that we have lost sight of the forest. We are now analyzing every diseased tree and I think we have got to look beyond that.

Let us take a look at a couple of specifics. There is not one iota of evidence that the President had any prior knowledge whatsoever of the Watergate break-in. And I don't want to get into quoting half a passage. But I guess we could do that on each one, one would be quoting something and the other to the contrary and the that's my point. So much contradicting evidence.

The President himself, in the transcript of March 13, referred to the Watergate break-in like this. "What a stupid thing, pointless. That was the stupid thing."

The President did not participate in the Watergate coverup. True, he did not immediately throw all possibly involved immediately to the wolves. Would you, without knowing all of the facts dismissed, your principle aide?

But, upon learning from Dean on March 21 the real seriousness of what was happening, he started taking a series of actions to find really what the truth, the whole story, was. The President on March 22 said that Hunt could not demand blackmail money, they just wouldn't go along with that, and he instructed Dean to prepare a report for him of what had really gone on. He never got that report.

The Attorney General was advised to report directly to the President. Members of the White House were instructed to go to the grand jury and to tell the truth. I think it is important that you have got to look at what eventually happened. I think that you must consider the fact that the President waived executive privilege for his closest aides, including his counsel.

That is what really happened.

And we could go on, and on and on.

With regard to Ellsberg's psychiatrist break-in, Charles Colson testified before this committee that he was convinced that the President did not know in advance of the break-in.

I will make no comment on the part of the article that deals with the contempt of Congress charge because I think it is so ludicrous that it deserves no comment.

No, what is really the genesis of all of this? What was the beginning of the whole thing? Now, I am not saying that or other things weren't important and I had my difficult moments, particularly with the conversation of March 21, which I have satisfied myself that the President did not order that payment.

But, the beginning really was with the bombing of Cambodia and the impoundment of funds. And look at that. The bombing of Cambodia led to the eventual end of the longest war in this country's history. It was one of the important ingredients.

And then impoundment. Presidents have been impounding funds since Thomas Jefferson, and Kennedy and Johnson both percentage-wise impounded more than President Nixon. I think it is interesting in a recent article in the Washington Post of August 2, 1971, where it came out that under the Kennedy administration, through Assistant Attorney General Burke Marshall there was a plan called Stick it to Mississippi, my home State.

"Stick it to Mississippi." Remember that. And what was involved was the impoundment of funds on some three dozen projects to force Mississippi to comply with certain Justice Department decrees and court decrees. It is impoundment. It is impoundment any way you look at it. But, when it is impoundment of some other area, then it is a different horse.

Now, many of those here have talked about the youth of America, and although I have grown older in the last few months, I guess I am still the youngest member of this committee. And I have been concerned at what impact Watergate would have on the young people of America. But, I think maybe in the final analysis they see all of this more clearly than we do. And I really think the young people that I have talked to, and I have talked to a lot of them, have dedicated themselves to making this system better by working within the system. And no matter what we finally do in Congress, the Presidency will be treated more carefully by future Presidents. So I think we must take care to see that we don't do irreparable damage to the longest single existing form of government in the history of man.

My question, in the final analysis, will be this: As strongly as I, as I disapproved of the policies of President Kennedy and Johnson, would I have voted to impeach them based on the evidence before this committee.

Thank you, Mr. Chairman.

The CHAIRMAN. I recognize the gentleman from Ohio, Mr. Seiberling, for purposes of general debate only for a period of not to exceed 15 minutes.

Mr. Seiberling.

STATEMENT OF HON. JOHN F. SEIBERLING, A REPRESENTATIVE IN CONGRESS FROM THE 14TH CONGRESSIONAL DISTRICT OF THE STATE OF OHIO

Mr. SEIBERLING. Thank you, Mr. Chairman.

I appreciate you traditional fairness in permitting me to speak out of order. I had to be on the floor of the House in connection with action on a very important strip mining control bill which I have worked on for many months.

Mr. Chairman, I am also at the age where I have to admit that I've got to put on my glasses. I am not the youngest member on this committee by any means.

As we approach a decision, it is well to remind ourselves that those who founded our country 200 years ago foresaw the possibility of the very situation that confronts us today and made provision for it. The power to impeach the President is expressly granted by the Constitution of the United States. The power was given to the Congress by the Founding Fathers for one purpose, to protect the Republic against the possible abuse of powers of the Presidency by a person who had been elected to serve in that office for a fixed term of 4 years.

Other countries, including Great Britain, our parent country, have a different system. There the chief executive can be turned out of office at the will of the Legislature.

Having rejected that system in favor of a powerful chief executive elected for a fixed term, the authors of our Constitution adopted the impeachment process as the necessary and only constitutional procedure for removal of a President prior to the end of his term.

If the Founding Fathers were concerned with the abuse of power by a chief executive in a small fledgling country, how much more would they be concerned today, when the President presides over an executive branch with employees numbering in the millions, is responsible for annually collecting and spending hundreds of billions of dollars and holds the power of life and death over the people of this country and indeed the entire world.

The authors of the Constitution wisely refrained from specifying the precise actions which would justify impeachment except to indicate that they were " high" crimes and "high" misdemeanors, such as treason and bribery. Clearly, the Founding Fathers were saying that impeachable conduct is conduct that strikes at the very existence of the constitutional system or the integrity of the Government itself.

The nature of their concern becomes even more apparent when we consider the oath which the Constitution requires the President to take before entering on the execution of his of lice—an oath to "preserve, protect, and defend the Constitution of the United States."

Mr. Petersen, Assistant Attorney General, and head of the Criminal Justice Division of the Department of Justice, in answer to a number of questions and in answer again specifically to a question asked by Mr. Sandman, stated that there is no evidence, there is no evidence to implicate the President of the United States in any criminal action. Now, this comes from the head of the Criminal Justice Division, from the man who has made the investigation, from a career man, from a man whose reputation and integrity are beyond reproach.

And yet, Mr. Dean says otherwise. I can only say that I do not believe Mr. Dean, and I don't believe the American people will believe Mr. Dean.

If I have to choose between Mr. Dean and the President as to who is telling the truth, I have no difficulty in that regard.

Now, let us turn to the tape of the morning of April 16, 1973, and what does the President say to Mr. Dean, in regard to his testimony before the Grand Jury? The President says: "Don't lie. Don't do it, John. Tell the truth. That is the thing I have told everyone here. Tell the truth. Don't lie. Understand what I say. Don't lie about me either." In effect he says later on go to the Grand Jury. Go down and testify. Go down and tell the truth. Do not claim executive privilege. Do not claim attorney-client privilege. I waive that.

Mr. Chairman, and members of this committee, does this sound like a man who wants to cover up? What more can a President do but to tell his staff, as he did, to tell the truth and not to claim executive privilege on the Watergate break-in.

Mr. Chairman, let me say that I listened with interest to your opening statement and I concur with that portion of your statement in which you say that we must deal fairly with every man. It is my hope that we adopt that principle expounded by you in our final and most crucial deliberations.

I look forward with interest to the discussion of the particular articles of impeachment that may be set forth and I invite those who propose impeachment to martial the hard facts in support of their position.

They have a duty and a responsibility to do so and I, Mr. Chairman, will exercise my duty and responsibility to consider the hard facts if they can be shown.

Thank you, Mr. Chairman, and I wish to yield the balance of my time to Mr. Latta.

The CHAIRMAN. The gentleman from New Jersey has 1 minute and 5 seconds remaining which will be yielded to Mr. Latta at the appropriate time.

I recognize the gentlelady from Texas, Ms. Jordan, for the purpose of general debate, not to exceed a period of 15 minutes.

STATEMENT OF HON. BARBARA JORDAN, A REPRESENTATIVE IN CONGRESS FROM THE 18TH CONGRESSIONAL DISTRICT OF THE STATE OF TEXAS

Ms. JORDAN. Thank you, Mr. Chairman.

Mr. Chairman, I join my colleague, Mr. Rangel, in thanking you for giving the junior members of this committee the glorious opportunity of sharing the pain of this inquiry. Mr. Chairman, you are a strong man and it has not been easy but we have tried as best we can to give you as much assistance as possible.

Earlier today we heard the beginning of the Preamble to the Constitution of the United States, We, the people. It is a very eloquent beginning. But when that document was completed on the 17th of September in 1787 I was not included in that "We, the people." I felt somehow for many years that George Washington and Alexander Hamilton just left me out by mistake. But through the process of amendment, interpretation and court decision I have finally been included in "We, the people."

Today, I am an inquisitor, I believe hyperbole would not be fictional and would not overstate the solemness that I feel right now. My faith in the Constitution is whole, it is complete, it is total. I am not going to sit here and be an idle spectator to the diminution, the subversion, the destruction of the Constitution.

"Who can so properly be the inquisitors for the nation as the representatives of the nation themselves?" (Federalist No. 65) The subject of its jurisdiction are those offenses which proceed from the misconduct of public men. That is what we are talking about. In other words, the jurisdiction comes from the abuse of violation of some public trust. It is wrong, I suggest, it is a misreading of the Constitution for any member here to assert that for a member to vote for an Article of Impeachment means that that member must be convinced that the President should be removed from office. The Constitution doesn't say that. The powers relating to impeachment are an essential check in the hands of this body, the legislature, against and upon the encroachment of the Executive. In establishing the division between the two branches of the legislature, the House and the Senate, assigning to the one the right to accuse and to the other the right to judge, the Framers of this Constitution were very astute. They did not make the accusers and the judges the same person.

We know the nature of impeachment. We have been talking about it awhile now. "It is chiefly designed for the President and his high ministers" to somehow be called into account. It is designed to "bridle" the Executive if he engages in excesses. "It is designed as a method of national inquest into the conduct of public men." (Hamilton, Federalist No. 65) The Framers confined in the Congress the power if need be, to remove the President in order to strike a delicate balance between a President swollen with power and grown tyrannical; and preservation of the independence of the Executive. The nature of impeachment is a narrowly channeled exception to the separation of powers maxim, the Federal Convention of 1787 said that. It limited impeachment to high crimes and misdemeanors and discounted and opposed the term, "maladministration." "It is to be used only for great misdemeanors," so it was said in the North Carolina ratification convention. And in the Virginia ratification convention: "We do not trust our liberty to a particular branch. We need one branch to check the others."

The North Carolina Ratification Convention: "No one need be afraid that officers who commit oppression will pass with immunity."

"Prosecutions of impeachments will seldom fail to agitate the passions of the whole community," said Hamilton in the Federalist Papers No. 65. "And to divide it into parties more or less friendly or inimical to the accused." I do not mean political parties in that sense.

The drawing of political lines goes to the motivation behind impeachment; but impeachment must proceed within the confines of the constitutional term, "high crime and misdemeanors."

Of the impeachment process, it was Woodrow Wilson who said that "nothing short of the grossest offenses against the plain law of the land will suffice to give them speed and effectiveness. Indignation so great as to overgrow party interest may secure a conviction; but nothing else can."

Commonsense would be revolted if we engaged upon this process for petty reasons. Congress has a lot to do. Appropriations, tax reform, health insurance, campaign finance reform, housing, environmental protection, energy sufficiency, mass transportation. Pettiness cannot be allowed to stand in the face of such overwhelming problems. So today we are not being petty. We are trying to be big because the task we have before us is a big one.

This morning in a discussion of the evidence we were told that the evidence which purports to support the allegations of misuse of the CIA by the President is thin. We are told that that evidence is insufficient. What that recital of the evidence this morning did not include is what the President did know on June 23, 1972. The President did know that it was Republican money, that it was money from the Committee for the Re-Election of the President, which was found in the possession of one of the burglars arrested on June 17.

What the President did know on June 23 was the prior activities of E. Howard Hunt, which included his participation in the break-in of Daniel Ellsberg's psychiatrist, which included Howard Hunt's participation in the Dita Beard ITT affair, which included Howard Hunt's fabrication of cables designed to discredit the Kennedy administration.

We were further cautioned today that perhaps these proceedings ought to be delayed because certainly there would be new evidence forthcoming from the President of the United States. There has not even been an obfuscated indication that this committee would receive any additional materials from the President. The committee subpena is outstanding and if the President wants to supply that material, the committee sits here.

That fact is that on yesterday, the American people waited with great anxiety for 8 hours, not knowing whether their President would obey an order of the Supreme Court of the United States.

At this point I would like to juxtapose a few of the impeachment criteria with some of the President's actions.

Impeachment criteria: James Madison, from the Virginia Ratification Convention. "If the President be connected in any suspicious manner with any person and there be grounds to believe that he will shelter him, he may be impeached."

We have heard time and time again that the evidence reflects payment to the defendants of money. The President had knowledge that these funds were being paid and that these were funds collected for the 1972 Presidential campaign.

We know that the President met with Mr. Henry Petersen 27 times to discuss matters related to Watergate and immediately thereafter met with the very persons who were implicated in the information Mr. Petersen was receiving and transmitting to the President. The words are, "if the President be connected in any suspicious manner with any person and there be grounds to believe that he will shelter that person, he may be impeached."

Justice Story: "Impeachment is intended for occasional and extraordinary cases where a superior power acting for the whole people is put into operation to protect their rights and rescue their liberties from violations."

We know about the Huston plan. We know about the break-in of the psychiatrist's office. We know that there was absolute complete direction in August 1971 when the President instructed Ehrlichman to "do whatever is necessary." This instruction led to a surreptitious entry into Dr. Fielding's office.

"Protect their rights." "Rescue their liberties from violation."

The South Carolina Ratification Convention impeachment criteria: Those are impeachable "who behave amiss or betray their public trust."

Beginning shortly after the Watergate break-in and continuing to the present time the President has engaged in a series of public statements and actions designed to thwart the lawful investigation by Government prosecutors. Moreover, the President has made public announcements and assertions bearing on the Watergate case which the evidence will show he knew to be false.

These assertions, false assertions, impeachable, those who misbehave. Those who "behave amiss or betray their public trust."

James Madison again at the Constitutional Convention: "President is impeachable if he attempts to subvert the Constitution."

The Constitution charges the President with the task of taking care that the laws be faithfully executed, and yet the President has counseled his aides to commit perjury, willfully disregarded the secrecy of grand jury proceedings, concealed surreptitious entry, attempted to compromise a Federal judge while publicly displaying his cooperation with the processes of criminal justice.

"A President is impeachable if he attempts to subvert the Constitution."

If the impeachment provision in the Constitution of the United States will not reach the offenses charged here, then perhaps that 18th century Constitution should be abandoned to a 20th century paper shredder. Has the President committed offenses and planned and directed and acquiesced in a course of conduct which the Constitution will not tolerate? That is the question. We know that. We know the question. We should now forthwith proceed to answer the question. It is reason, and not passion, which must guide our deliberations, guide our debate, and guide our decision.

. . . .

U.S. House of Representatives, Committee on the Judiciary, Hearings, *Debate on Articles of Impeachment*, July 24, 25, 26, 27, 29, and 30, 1974, 93d Congress, 2d session, July 24, 1974 (Washington, D.C.: U.S. Government Printing Office, 1974), 1–6, 86–90, 110–113.

166   The Articles of Impeachment Against President Richard M. Nixon

August 4, 1974

"Watergate," the long ordeal that tested the strength of constitutional government in the United States, reached its culmination when the House Committee on the Judiciary voted three articles of impeachment against President Richard M. Nixon. President Nixon resigned from office five days later, thus preventing further action on the impeachment process. Only one previous president of the United States, Andrew Johnson, had ever been impeached (see document 82), although an impeachment inquiry against President William J. Clinton is underway as this volume goes to press (see document 189). Nixon certainly would have been impeached by the full House and tried in the Senate had he not resigned. On September 8, 1974, the new president, Gerald R. Ford, pardoned Richard Nixon, declaring "our long national nightmare is over." Ford said he wanted to spare the country an extended, bitter trial that would only further divide the nation.

Many observers of American politics consider this action by the House Judiciary Committee to be one of the finest moments in the history of the House of Representatives. The proceedings followed a two-year long politically charged and highly dramatic investigation that revealed large-scale corruption in the Nixon White House, which eventually led to prison sentences for twenty men, including several top White House officials. The House Judiciary Committee, chaired by Peter Rodino (D-N.J.), conducted its grim but necessary constitutional duty with dignity and determination that upheld the principles and the letter of the U.S. Constitution. There were thirty-eight members on the House Judiciary Committee—twenty-one Democrats and seventeen Republicans—all of whom were lawyers.

The vote on the articles was not unanimous, but it was decisive. On Article I the vote was 27–11; Article II was 28–10; and Article III was 21–17.

RESOLUTION

Impeaching Richard M. Nixon, President of the United States, of high crimes and misdemeanors.

Resolved, That Richard M. Nixon, President of the United States, is impeached for high crimes and misdemeanors, and that the following articles of impeachment be exhibited to the Senate:

Articles of impeachment exhibited by the House of Representatives of the United States of America in the name of itself and of all of the people of the United States of America, against Richard M. Nixon, President of the United States of America, in maintenance and support of its impeachment against him for high crimes and misdemeanors.

Article I

In his conduct of the office of President of the United States, Richard M. Nixon, in violation of his constitutional oath faithfully to execute the office of President of the United States and, to the best of his ability, preserve, protect and defend the Constitution of the United States, and in violation of his constitutional duty to take care that the laws be faithfully executed, has prevented, obstructed, and impeded the administration of justice, in that:

On June 17, 1972, and prior thereto, agents of the Committee for the Re-election of the President committed unlawful entry of the headquarters of the Democratic National Committee in Washington, District of Columbia, for the purpose of securing political intelligence. Subsequent thereto, Richard M. Nixon, using the powers of his high office, engaged personally and through his subordinates and agents in a course of conduct or plan designed to delay, impede, and obstruct the investigation of such unlawful entry; to cover up, conceal and protect those responsible; and to conceal the existence and scope of other unlawful covert activities.

The means used to implement this course of conduct or plan have included one or more of the following:

(1) making or causing to be made false or misleading statements to lawfully authorized investigative officers and employee of the United States;

(2) withholding relevant and material evidence or information from lawfully authorized investigative officers and employees of the United States;

(3) approving, condoning, acquiescing in, and counseling witnesses with respect to the giving of false or misleading statements to lawfully authorized investigative officers and employee of the United States and false or misleading testimony in duly instituted judicial and Congressional proceedings;

(4) interfering or endeavoring to interfere with the conduct of investigations by the Department of Justice of the United States, the Federal Bureau of Investigation, the office of Watergate Special Prosecution Force, and Congressional Committees;

(5) approving, condoning, and acquiescing in, the surreptitious payment of substantial sums of money for the purpose of obtaining the silence or influencing the testimony of witnesses, potential witnesses or individuals who participated in such illegal entry and other illegal activities;

(6) endeavoring to misuse the Central Intelligence Agency, an agency of the United States;

(7) disseminating information received from officers of the Department of Justice of the United States to subjects of investigations conducted by lawfully authorized investigative officers and employee of the United States, for the purpose of aiding and assisting such subjects in their attempts to avoid criminal liability;

(8) making false or misleading public statements for the purpose of deceiving the people of the United States into believing that a thorough and complete investigation had been conducted with respect to allegations of misconduct on the part of personnel of the executive branch of the United States and personnel of the Committee for the Reelection of the President, and that there was no involvement of such personnel in such misconduct; or

(9) endeavoring to cause prospective defendants, and individuals duly tried and convicted, to expect favored treatment and consideration in return for their silence or false testimony, or rewarding individuals for their silence or false testimony.

In all of this, Richard M. Nixon has acted in a manner contrary to his trust as President and subversive of constitutional government, to the great prejudice of the cause of law and justice and to the manifest injury of the people of the United States.

Wherefore Richard M. Nixon, by such conduct, warrants impeachment and trial, and removal from office.

Article II

Using the powers of the office of President of the United States, Richard M. Nixon, in violation of his constitutional oath faithfully to execute the office of President of the United States, and to the best of his ability preserve, protect and defend the Constitution of the United States, and in disregard of his constitutional duty to take care that the laws be faithfully executed, has repeatedly engaged in conduct violating the constitutional right of citizens, impairing the due and proper administration of justice in the conduct of lawful inquiries, of contravening the law of governing agencies of the executive branch and the purposes of these agencies.

This conduct has included one or more of the following:

(1) He has, acting personally and through his subordinates and agents, endeavored to obtain from the Internal Revenue Service in violation of the constitutional rights of citizens, confidential information contained in income tax returns for purposes not authorized by law; and to cause, in violation of the constitutional rights of citizens, income tax audits or other income tax investigations to be initiated or conducted in a discriminatory manner.

(2) He misused the Federal Bureau of Investigation, the Secret Service and other executive personnel in violation or disregard of the constitutional rights of citizens by directing or authorizing such agencies or personnel to conduct or continue electronic surveillance or other investigations for purposes unrelated to national security, the enforcement of laws or any other lawful function of his office.

He did direct, authorize or permit the use of information obtained thereby for purposes unrelated to national security, the enforcement of laws or any other lawful function of his office. And he did direct the concealment of certain records made by the Federal Bureau of Investigation of electronic surveillance.

(3) He has, acting personally and through his subordinates and agents, in violation or disregard of the constitutional rights of citizens, authorized and permitted to be maintained a secret investigative unit within the office of the President, financed in part with money derived from campaign contributions, which unlawfully utilized the resources of the Central Intelligence Agency, engaged in covert and unlawful activities, and attempted to prejudice the constitutional right of an accused to a fair trial.

(4) He has failed to take care that the laws were faithfully executed by failing to act when he knew or had reason to know that his close subordinates endeavored to impede and frustrate lawful inquiries by duly constituted executive, judicial and legislative entities concerning the unlawful entry into the headquarters of the Democratic National Committee and the cover-up thereof and concerning other unlawful activities including those relating to the confirmation of Richard Kleindienst as Attorney General of the United States, the electronic surveillance of private citizens, the break-in into the offices of Dr. Lewis Fielding and the campaign financing practices of the Committee to Re-elect the President.

(5) In disregard of the rule of law he knowingly misused the executive power by interfering with agencies of the executive branch including the Federal Bureau of Investigation, the Criminal Division and the office of Watergate special prosecution force of the Department of Justice, and the Central Intelligence Agency, in violation of his duty to take care that the laws be faithfully executed.

In all of this Richard M. Nixon has acted in a manner contrary to his trust as President and subversive of constitutional government to the great prejudice of the cause of law and justice and to the manifest injury of the people of the United States.

Wherefore, Richard M. Nixon, by such conduct warrants impeachment and trial and removal from office.

Article III

In his conduct of the office of President of the United States, Richard M. Nixon, contrary to his oath faithfully to execute the office of President of the United States and to the best of his ability to preserve, protect and defend the Constitution of the United States, and in violation of his constitutional duty to take care that the laws be faithfully executed, has failed without lawful cause or excuse to produce papers and things, as directed by duly authorized subpoenas issued by the Committee on the Judiciary of the House of Representatives on April 11, 1974, May 15, 1974, May 30, 1974, and June 24, 1974, and willfully disobeyed such subpoenas.

The subpoenaed papers and things were deemed necessary by the committee in order to resolve by direct evidence fundamental factual questions relating to Presidential direction, knowledge or approval of actions demonstrated by other evidence to be substantial grounds for impeachment of the President.

In refusing to produce these papers and things Richard M. Nixon, substituting his judgment as to what materials were necessary for the inquiry, interposed the powers of the Presidency against the lawful subpoenas of the House of Representatives, thereby assuming for himself functions and judgments necessary to the exercise of the sole power of impeachment vested by the Constitution in the House of Representatives.

In all this, Richard M. Nixon has acted in a manner contrary to his trust as President and subversive of constitutional government, to the great prejudice of the cause of law and justice, and to the manifest injury of the people of the United States.

Wherefore, Richard M. Nixon, by such conduct warrants impeachment and trial and removal from office.

House of Representatives, *House Report* 93–1305, House Committee on the Judiciary, 93d Congress, 2d session, "Impeachment of Richard M. Nixon, President of the United States," August 20, 1974, 1–4.

167   The Bolling-Martin Report on Reform of House Committees

October 8, 1974

This influential report is little known except by experts on the committee system of Congress and committee members and staff who function within the committee system of the House. The report represented an ambitious attempt at reform of the House committee system, but its recommendations were never completely adopted. In the next Congress in 1975, with its influx of a large class of freshman Democrats called "Watergate Babies," the House

finally adopted some of the recommendations in this report. Nevertheless, this report offered a clear statement about the importance of committees to the functioning of Congress. It is also gave a ringing endorsement to the importance of professional staff to the functioning of the committee system.

The report took as its operating premise that "committees are the nerve ends of Congress—the gatherers of information, the sifters of alternatives, the refiners of legislation. Few organizations are so critical to the continued effectiveness of Congress as a policy-making body."

The Legislative Reorganization Act of 1946 (see document 137) led to a concentration of power in the hands of a few senior committee chairman. It also led to a substantial increase in the size of congressional staff. In the next major reorganization of the legislative branch in 1970 (see document 158), Congress continued toward openness of committee meetings, upgraded the professional staff, and instituted other important reforms, but the committee system itself still suffered from inequities of workload and jurisdictional problems.

Spurred by the aggressive reform efforts of Richard Bolling (D-Mo.), the House Select Committee on Committees sought major reform of the House committee system by attempting to clear up overlapping jurisdictional disputes between committees, establish a more equitable workload between the committees, and limit members from serving on more than one of the key legislative committees. The Select Committee on Committees provided a ranking of the committees in order of their importance, into category A and category B status.

The cochairman of the House Select Committee on Committees was Dave Martin (R-Neb.), who managed to convince most Republicans to favor the proposed reforms. But it was Bolling's own Democratic Party, and its powerful committee chairmen, who rejected these reforms because they did not want their own power and prestige weakened.

I. Summary

On January 31, 1973 the House of Representative passed House Resolution 132, which established a ten-member bipartisan Select Committee on Committees charged with conducting a "thorough and complete" study of the House Rules X and XI. These two rules establish the standing committees of the House, define their jurisdictions, and regulate their procedures. After much deliberation and with the benefit of testimony from Members of the House, the academic community, and public witnesses as well as from informal conversations with both House members and committee staff, the House and its committees more deliberative, responsive, and efficient. The select committee members unanimously agree that these comprehensive proposals will improve significantly the operations of the House of Representatives. This action comes at a time when the public's faith in the institutions of government is low.

What follows in this summary are highlights of the select committee's proposals.

Jurisdiction

In consolidating and updating committee jurisdictions, the Select Committee on Committees proposes a committee structure consisting of fifteen ("A") committees of equal stature on which membership would be limited to one per Members, and seven in addition to their assignment on one of the fifteen. The present jurisdiction of each of the fifteen committees has been modified to a greater or lesser extent in order more appropri-

ately to meet the needs of the House. The fifteen major committees are as follows: Agriculture and Forestry, Appropriations, Armed Services, Banking, Currency and Housing, Commerce and Health, Education, Energy and Environment, Foreign Affairs, Government Operations, Judiciary, Labor, Public Works and Transportation, Rules, Science and Technology, and Ways and Means.

Of the seven additional ("B") committees proposed by the select committee all but one presently exist and that one, the Committee on the Budget, awaits legislative action. The other six committees, which all have revised jurisdiction except for the last one listed, are the Committees on House administration, Standards of Official Conduct, Merchant Marine and Fisheries, Small Business, the District of Columbia, and Veterans' Affairs. Small Business no longer would be a select committee and now would have legislative authority over the Small Business Administration, in addition to the oversight authority it already has.

In the proposals of the select committee the same number of standing committees now in the House is retained, 22 (if one includes the Permanent Select Committee on Small Business). The present Committees on Post Office and Civil Service (primarily absorbed into Labor) and Internal Security (absorbed into Government Operations) would be abolished.

Referral of Legislation

Because overlap in jurisdiction is likely to continue regardless of committee realignments, the select committee believes that a procedure to accommodate the inevitable conflict between committees is imperative. Indeed, a major defect of present House procedure is the prohibition against the referral of legislation to several committees. This prohibition results in legitimate interests not being heard and reflects an undesirable rigidity in the procedures of the House. The select committee therefore strongly endorses a procedure permitting the Speaker to refer bills and resolutions to more than one committee, to split legislation for purposes of referral, and to refer legislation sequentially to committees. In addition, the Speaker, subject to the approval of the House, would be able to constitute special *ad hoc* committees from the membership of committees having legislative jurisdiction, to consider matters that, on those rare occasions, would best be handled by such a special unit.

Inevitably, the actual referral of legislation will at times cause controversy. Present practice in the House provides no workable, effective means of appeal. At times, a committee may try to block the granting of a rule to achieve an accommodation but this procedure is both awkward and inappropriate. The select committee therefore proposes a simple appeals procedure, which need not be used often, that utilizes the Rules Committee but is subject to review on the floor.

Oversight

The Select Committee on Committees firmly believes that the oversight responsibilities of the House committees are important and too often shunted aside by the press of other business. Oversight, which is not just an additional activity to do when time permits but a function mandated by law, is an integral part of a committee's job. After all, committees ought to review the administrative, fiscal, futures, and program consequences of their legislation.

The select committee proposes to strengthen committee oversight in the House by: (1) Requiring each standing committee other than Appropriations to establish a separate subcommittee on oversight; (2) Enhancing the role of the Committee on Government Operations by: (a) requiring the committee to assemble an oversight agenda for the House at the beginning of each year, (b) permitting the committee to conduct investigations in areas where other committees are studying similar subjects, a practice not now permitted, (c) granting privileged status on the floor to those amendments offered by Government Operations that are based upon their oversight findings, and (d) requiring other committees to include in their reports pertinent oversight findings of the Government Operations Committee; (3) Authorizing the standing committee of the House to review and study the impact of tax policy affecting subjects within their jurisdiction; and (4) Permitting a few committees to conduct non-legislative special oversight, that is, oversight of policy areas for which they have a logical responsibility but which in part and by necessity are found within the legislative jurisdiction of other committees. For example, the Committee on Education is authorized to examine but not legislate upon educational programs placed for special reasons in other committees so that the Educational Committee can carry on comprehensive consideration of educational policies and programs.

The oversight activity envisioned by the select committee should not be confused with the committee's recommendations on "legislative review." The latter denotes a legislative responsibility and authority. The former, "oversight," does not. It is limited to study, review, and investigations. In only two instances, however, does the select committee propose such legislative review.

Transitional Devices

In order to facilitate the reforms proposed, the select committee believes that it should be the sense of the House that the Members who by these reforms may be required to leave one of two committees should be allowed to select the committee on which they wish to remain. It is also recommended that a Member who presently serves on a committee which has significant jurisdiction transferred may be permitted to join that committee to which the jurisdiction is assigned, with his or her service on the former committee appropriately recognized.

Committee Staffs

The professional and clerical staffs of the standing committees are a necessary component of the committee system in the House. No longer simply an asset, committee staffs have become essential. The select committee therefore reviewed the subject of staffing carefully and has agreed: (1) To increase the number of standing professional and clerical staff members al-lowed a committee from six to 18 and four to 12, respectively. This will make the staff provisions of Rule XI more realistic and encouraging less reliance upon committee expense (investigative) resolutions as a source of committee staffing. (2) to allow the minority members of a committee the opportunity to select one-third of the 30 staff so provided and one-third of the funds for staff under expense resolutions. However, the select committee realizes that some committees employ non-partisan staff and may wish to continue this practice. The select committee does not want to foreclose such an option, so its proposals specifically permit the use of non-partisan or partly non-partisan committee staff.

Voting by Proxy

The Select Committee on Committees proposes to ban voting by proxy in committees and subcommittees. The select committee believe that such a prohibition will improve attendance at committee meetings and thus enhance participation of and deliberation by committee members. Furthermore, it will ensure actual Member involvement in the deliberations and decisions of the committees and subcommittees.

Subpoena Power

The select committee certain standardized procedures and safeguards covering subpoenas that would apply uniformly to all committees. The Committees on Appropriations, Government Operations, and Standards of Official Conduct would continue to have standing subpoena authority, while others would be required to receive House authorization for each activity or series of activities. However, in the case of all committees a majority of the membership of each committee would be necessary to authorize the issuance of a subpoena or group of subpoenas. Compliance could be enforced only as authorized or directed by the House.

Appointment of Conferees

Conference committee are a critical step in the legislative process. More often than not what is reported form conference is accepted by the House and likely to become law. Thus, the appointment of conferees is itself important. By rule conferees are appointed by the Speaker. In practice they are selected by the chairman of the committee going to conference. On occasion these conferees have on the floor or in committee voted against positions they are expected to uphold in conference. Both they and the House are then placed in a difficult—and unnecessary—position. The select committee thus recommends that clause 2 of Rule X be revised so that at least a majority of the conferees have supported the position of the House as determined by the Speaker, who will continue to appoint conferees.

Updating of Committee Jurisdictions

Twenty-eight years have passed since the House last revised its committee jurisdictions. Given the speed with which new problems emerge and the certainty that the jurisdictional realignments proposed will require updating, the select committee believes that the House cannot afford to wait another 28 years before revising committee jurisdictions. Hence the select committee proposes that the House members of the Joint Committee on Congressional Operations conduct a continuing study of committee jurisdictions and periodically prepare a report of its findings for submission to the Committee on Rules. The Rules Committee, which retains jurisdiction over the Rules of the House, may submit the matter to the full House.

Support Commissions

The management of information, the utilization of available space, and the further development of administrative services are all critical to the operations of the House of Representatives. In the future, as demands increase, the House will become even more dependent upon these support services. Information, space, and administrative services raise complex problems, but not to simple solutions. The select committee believes that these problems require careful and expert analysis and that the time available do not permit such an analysis to be done by the committee. Thus it recommends a House Commission on Information and a House Commission on Administrative Services and Facilities, to undertake thorough and complete examinations of these areas, reporting back to the House by the end of the term of the next Congress.

Legislative Classification Office

To be most useful, program and budget information available to House committees should like authorizations, appropriations, committee jurisdictions, and agency program to the basic statutes. At present such a linkage does not exist so that the committees' legislative and oversight responsibilities, which require precise, timely, and unable information, suffer. The Select Committee on Committees, after an extensive study conducted on its behalf by the General Accounting Office, proposes to remedy the situation by the establishment in the House of Legislative Classification Office to develop the necessary cross-reference system.

Law Revision Counsel

The select committee is concerned about the large body of Federal laws in need of revision and codification. It therefore proposes an Office of Law Revision Counsel, to codify the laws of the United States and to submit each title as it is prepared to the Judiciary Committee for enactment into positive law. The office shall be supervised by a Law Revision Counsel appointed by the Speaker.

Early Organization

Too often the House of Representatives at the beginning of a Congress does not organize committees until late February or early March. The time lost is considerable, especially as viewed late in the session when a crowded calendar occasionally forces the House to act hastily. The time should be spent discharging legislative and oversight responsibilities, not in organizing the committees, a task which could well be done prior to the time Congress convenes. The select committee proposes that the House better utilize its limited time by organizing committee in the period after the November elections but before Christmas. The majority and minority leaders, after consultation with the Speaker, would call their colleagues together and complete their organization task so that the business of the House could start when the new year begins.

II. General Statement

A. The Importance of Committees

Committees are the nerve ends of Congress—the gatherers of information, the sifters of alternatives, the refiners of legislation. Few organizations are so critical to the continued effectiveness of Congress as a policy-making body. "It is not far from the truth to say," wrote Woodrow Wilson in 1885, "that congress in session is Congress on public exhibition, whilst Congress in its committee-rooms is congress at work." This observation is, if anything, even more accurate today.

If they perform their tasks successfully, the committees sustain the vitality of congress as an equal partner in national policy making. Public policy is, of course, the outgrowth of many individuals, opinions, and influences. Often, individuals are given credit for policy innovations that are in fact the product of many people working over a period of months or even years. A common question is, "Where do policies originate?" To a greater extent that most observers realize, the answer lies in the committee and subcommittee rooms of the House.

Committees serve legislative policy-making in a variety of ways. Most obviously, they enable a large number of measures, many of them extraordinarily complex and technical, to be developed through expert study. By dividing its membership into a number of work groups the House is able to consider simultaneously dozens of proposed laws. Through the committee device, the House is able to winnow out the important from the unimportant, the workable from the unworkable. The committee system is, therefore, a technique for effectively utilizing time and energy in the development of quality legislation.

Especially through the hearing process, the committees serve also as arenas for the expression of the multitude of viewpoints which are found in our society. By serving as channels for national concerns, committees help to resolve tensions as well as to solve problem. By maintaining themselves as listening-posts for citizens' concerns, the committees form a vital link in the representative process.

Finally, committees perform an oversight function. They help to insure that legislative programs are properly administered by executive officials. In doing so, committees develop refinements and alternatives to existing public policies.

B. Historical Background

The committee system is as old as the House of Representatives itself, having been established out of precedents drawn from the English House of Commons, the colonial assemblies, and the Continental Congress. Although during its first quarter century the House relied primarily upon select committees and the Committee of the Whole, the first standing committee dates from 1789. As the 19th century advanced, select committees were converted into standing committees, which grew in number until by 1905 there were no less than 61 of them. Various consolidations, culminating with the Legislative Reorganization Act of 1946 (which combined 48 committees into 19), brought the number to approximately its present level.

No less than 77 different committees have existed in the House at one time or another. The names of these committees, their year of establishment and other pertinent information, are listed in Appendix A, found at the end of this report. The list of the names of these committees reflects the growing diversity of public business and, consequently, the rising workload of the House. Such a committee list may be viewed, moreover, as a reflection of American history, for the creation (and, in some instances, the abolition) of each major committee corresponded with important historical events or shifting public problems.

The legislative duties of the House of Representatives—once relatively limited in scope, small in volume, and simple in content—have grown to staggering proportions. When the first House convened (1789–90), only 142 bills were introduced and 85 reports filed from committees (mainly select committees). In the 92nd Congress (1971–72) no less then 17,230 bills were introduced and 1,637 committee reports prepared. A few indicators of the contemporary workload of the House serve eloquently to convey the picture:

The average House workload, 80th through 92nd Congresses (1946–72)

Category	Average per Congress
Bills introduced	13,711
Committee reports	2,456
Public laws passed	790
Private laws passed	618
Total laws and resolutions	1,408
Presidential messages	185
Presidential messages referred to committees	167
Executive communications	2,372

Source: Final House calendars

In recent decades, legislative business has kept the House and its committees in virtually continuous session.

Legislative business has mounted in scope and complexity as well as in sheer volume. Legislators in the early years of the Republic, meeting in Washington a few months at a time, enjoyed the opportunity of digesting at leisure the handful of major questions placed before Congress. Today's House of Representatives, responding to increased demands generated for a larger population, more complex technology, and broader governmental involvement, must cope with a variety of issues that in the past was left to State and local governments, or deemed entirely outside the scope of governmental activity. Even a cursory glance at the activity of House committees (on topics ranging alphabetically from "abandoned automobiles" to "zoos") indicates the pressures toward division of labor, specialization, and technical expertise—all characteristics manifested today in the House committee system.

Virtually all contemporary legislation originates from, or is at least refined by, committee deliberations. Division of labor in the House has reached a very advanced stage. Despite the consolidations of the 1946 Reorganization Act, subcommittee proliferation since then has brought the number of separate working groups in the House to an all-time high. No less then 184 separate committees and subcommittees competed for the time and attention of Members during the 93d Congress (1973–74):

Committees and subcommittees, 93d Congress

Standing and select committees	27
Joint committees	9
Standing and select subcommittees	132
Joint subcommittees	16
Total	184

By any set of standards, then, the House of Representatives is a complicated organization.

The rise of the committee system, so crucial to the processing of a burgeoning workload, has changed the House of Representatives as a deliberative and a representative body. In its early days, for example, the House maintained close control and supervision over the activities of its committees. Legislative subjects were generally referred to a committee of the Whole in order to develop the outlines of legislation, after which they were committed to select committees for specific drafting of bills. These *ad hoc* bodies were required to report back to the House, whether favorably or unfavorably, and were dissolved when they completed their assignment. Moreover, bill introduction and referral were strictly controlled by the House. When standing committees were created, assuming something of their modern form, they received their rights and powers from the parent body. Committees were regarded as creatures of the House and were subject to its direction.

As the standing committees proliferated, their influence and prestige grew. Increasingly they became autonomous in their operations. By 1885 Woodrow Wilson, then a graduate student of Johns Hopkins University, characterized congressional government as government by the standing committees of Congress. At the turn of the century Mary Follett, an incisive student of the House, observed that "Congress no longer exercises its lawful function of lawmaking; that has gone to the committees as completely as in England it has passed to the Cabinet."

In spite of periodic attempts at consolidation and reorganization, committee and even subcommittee autonomy has become even more pronounced in recent decades. "The role of the House is now largely limited to ratifying decisions made by its committees," one long-time observer of the House wrote in 1959.

Committees nowadays have developed an independent sovereignty of their own, subject only to very infrequent reversals and modifications of their powers by House party leaders backed by large and insistent majorities.

Committee autonomy has been encouraged by two 20th-century trends which have had a considerable impact on the life of the House of Representatives. First, the retrenchment of partisan leadership which followed in the wake of the 1910 "revolt" against Speaker Joseph G. Cannon served to disperse power and enhance the independence of the committees. Moreover, as Members have come to make careers out of their service in the House (the average Members of the 93rd Congress has served in the House more than 11 years), tenure developed traditions and habits that are often independent of the House as a whole.

Aside from sporadic attempts to consolidate the jurisdictions of the proliferating committees, the first broad-scale effort to bring order to the committees of the House was the Legislative Reorganization Act of 1946. "Modernization of the standing committee system," writes the historian George B. Galloway, staff director for the Joint committee on the Organization of Congress (79th Congress), the LaFollette-Monroney Committee, "was the first objective of the Act and the keystone in the arch of congressional reform." Among the goals of the 1946 Act were the following: streamlining and simplifying the committee structure; elimination of the use of special or select committees; clarification of committee jurisdictions; regularization and publication of committee procedures; improvement of committee staff aids; reduction of the over-all workload of Congress; strengthening legislative oversight of administration; and reorganization of the budgetary process.

The 1946 Act was a broad set of proposals that has influenced the operations of the House ever since. For the first time a large body of the precedents which had accumulated concerning committee jurisdictions was codified and embodied in the House rules. The entire legislative domain, as it was then understood, was thus set forth and divided into categories, each assigned to a separate standing committee. In the process obsolete committees were eliminated or consolidated, responsibility for programs was focused, and many potential jurisdictional conflicts were avoided. The Act also laid the groundwork for a modern staff system to support committee operations.

Not all of the objects of the 1946 Act were achieved. Perhaps the most conspicuous failure was the inability to coordinate the congressional budgetary process—a defect which is only now receiving the attention it deserves. Of equal importance, by reducing the number of standing committees and hardening their jurisdictional lines, the Act tended to strengthen the seniority system, reinforce committee autonomy, and inhibit the ability of the House to adapt to new configurations of public programs.

Twenty years later (in the 89th Congress) a second Joint Committee on the Organization of the Congress reexamined the state of Congress and its committees. A number of its recommendations eventually found their way into the Legislative Reorganization Act of 1970 (P.L. 91–510). Although it covered many of the same topics as the earlier measure, the 1970 Act was more modest in scope. A definitive assessment is as yet impossible, but the Act's major impact upon the committees is probably its regularization of committee procedures and its provision underscoring the committees' responsibility to the parent houses. In the House of representatives, these provisions are closely tied to changes initiated by the House Democratic Caucus and House Republican Conference (1970–1973).

In the important area of committee jurisdictions, the Joint Committee proposed a limited number of refinements rather than wholesale changes. Of the proposals that were made, few were adopted. The Senate accepted only two jurisdictional alterations, the House none at all.

Inevitably, time has outrun the committee system created by the 1946 Act. The legislators who labored on the LaFollette-Monroney Committee could not possibly have predicted the changes in congressional responsibilities which have occurred in the last three decades. Legislative topics which preoccupy us today—environmental protection, energy conservation, and medical insurance, to name a few—were only dimly perceived in the post-World War II years. As a result even the most careful reading of Rules X and XI, which govern committee structure and jurisdiction, yields but a fragmentary view of the tasks performed by House committees.

Other considerations argue for a thoroughgoing review of House organization. In the years since 1946, the prerogatives of the legislative branch have been under constant pressure from activism in the executive and judicial branches. Many serious breaches have been allowed to occur in the system of checks and balances embodied in the Constitution. The Founding Fathers; wisdom—in distrusting any single branch of government and in devising mechanisms for blending and checking powers—has been vindicated repeatedly throughout our history. Moreover, the Congress—and especially the House of Representatives—is uniquely a representative institution. The type of citizen access provided by this body must not be allowed to lose its power to influence public policy.

Congress must put its house in order if the imbalance of powers is to be combated. Imbalances frequently occur not because one branch usurps another's powers, but because one branch moves into a vacuum caused by another's ineffectiveness. To the extent that congressional powers have ebbed as a result of failure to develop timely and coherent responses to public problems, Congress has itself to blame for the predicament. And to the extent that better organization will strengthen the ability of Congress to fulfill its constitutional duties, periodic changes are justified to help preserve congressional powers from further decline.

Citizen confidence in the Federal Government is at a low ebb. A public opinion survey conducted late in 1973 by the Louis Harris organization found that only 29 percent of the American people expressed "a great deal of confidence" in the U.S. House of Representatives. This figure has dropped 10 percentage points since 1965, and ranks below the confidence citizens express in the medical profession, higher education, local police forces, and even local trash collection. While it is our view that this represents an unfair appraisal of the performance of this body, the mere existence of such a widespread feeling among the public is cause for sober reflection.

The public is asking searching questions about our institutions of government. They will insist upon institutional arrangements that are efficient, economical, and designed to give timely and responsive consideration to the business before us. And they will continue to expect that we will structure our work with the public welfare paramount in our minds.

It is therefore appropriate that the House undertake periodic inquiry into the health of its standing committee system. As the LaFollette-Monroney Committee concluded in presenting its proposals for committee reorganization,

We feel that there is nothing sacrosanct in the present arrangement of our committees. A study of the committee system of both Houses reveals that since the first Congress the committees have undergone many realignments and changes as conditions demanded. As the "workshop of Congress" the committee structure, more than any other arm of the legislative branch, needs frequent modernization to bring its efficiency up to the requirements of the day.

Since the work of that committee, there has been no comprehensive examination of the operation and effectiveness of the House committee system. Yet many piecemeal changes have occurred in the last 28 years, and the need for systematic review is as acute as it was in 1946.

The committees of the House have undergone continuous change and evolution in the past and must continue to adapt to meet future needs. As Speaker Carl Albert has noted, "the committee system is a pragmatic instrument." As public problems have shifted, new committees have been created and old ones consolidated or phased out. Diverse practices have been employed to select personnel for committees and even to select committee leaders. Staff resources have grown in the post-World War II era, as have innovative techniques for hearings and supporting research. Committee rules have been modified to meet new demand. In short, there is nothing fixed or immutable about the current committee structure.

Change is a new law of life, for institutions as well as individuals. Thomas Jefferson, who drafted the original set of rules by which the House conducts its business, fervently believed that periodic institutional renewal was a necessity. Those who have shaped the House's institutional growth over the years, leaders and reformers alike, have realized the need for modification in the face of changing tasks. In this spirit the Select Committee undertook its review of the committee system of the House of Representatives.

. . . .

D. Basic Objectives of the Select Committee's Recommendations

As the select committee studied the problems of House committee organization, certain basic themes emerged. In the process of receiving testimony, examining documents prepared by experts, and refining ideas through thoughtful and spirited discussion, members of the committee reached general consensus on the fundamental problems to be dealt with in this report. While individual members had differing views over the priority to be assigned to various problems, they are unanimous in concluding that the following goals should be achieved if the House is to deal realistically with its organizational shortcomings.

1. The jurisdictional responsibilities of House committees should be thoroughly modernized.

In the 28 years since the House was last reorganized, the shape of national problems has changed so dramatically that jurisdictional lines are tangled, workloads unbalanced, and overlap and confusion all too frequent. Some committees are severely overburdened; others could be more effectively utilized. Overlaps, which are tolerable and even desirable if kept at moderate levels, have in certain fields reached the point where coherent policy formation is hampered. The proposals . . . are designed to balance and realign workloads in accord with contemporary national concerns.

2. The House should be organized to give coherent consideration to broad, pressing national problems.

The select committee proposes that the House consolidate the legislative and review responsibilities of its committees in such fields as: energy and environment, research and development, manpower, health, transportation and foreign affairs. . . . For example, today, no less than 12 House committees have significant responsibilities for energy legislation; 5 committees have major environmental legislation. Where the breadth of a problem demands examination from different viewpoints, cooperative arrangements among committees should be instituted. . . .

3. The House of Representatives should take steps to limit committee assignments.

In particular, the select committee recommends that all committees which deal with broad segments of public policy be considered exclusive—that is, single assignments for their members among those committees. . . . Such a policy will concentrate Members' energies, encourage deliberation within committees, and facilitate scheduling. It hopes to eliminate the problems Members frequently face when they are scheduled to be in several different meetings at the same time. The select committee believes that citizens have a right to expect the House to schedule its business so that each Member can devote concerted attention to his or her committee responsibilities, while discharging constituency responsibilities at the same time.

4. Committee jurisdictions should be equalized to afford each Member of the House an opportunity to participate meaningfully in decisions affecting the lives of their constituents.

Thus the select committee has tried to balance workloads of the House's major committees . . .—an innovation which will promote not only equity but also efficiency in House deliberations.

5. As creatures of the House, committees should be able to attract a broadly representative membership and embrace a variety of viewpoints on the question within their jurisdiction.

Committee assignments are sought for a variety of reasons, most notably the needs of the Members' constituents and the Members' background and training. It is inevitable, therefore, that not all committees will be equally attractive to all Members. However, the select committee recommends . . . combining jurisdictions which in addition to being logically related, will compel the interest of a wide variety of Members. The objective is to foster representative viewpoints within those committees.

6. Concrete incentives for legislative oversight should be provided, along with workable mechanisms for building upon those incentives.

Members and public witnesses alike agree that Congress badly needs to intensify its review of Government programs once they have been enacted—to assure that objectives are being met and that Federal dollars are wisely spent. Therefore, the select committee is advancing a series of recommendations aimed at multiplying both incentives and opportunities for conducting oversight. . . . Subject matter committees and the Government Operations Committee must range widely and examine carefully the implementation and cost-effectiveness of Federal programs.

7. The House should take immediate steps to develop greater coordination and more professional management for its information resources, supporting services, and physical planning.

In the past, the House has neglected to plan and coordinate its supporting activities in these areas. This committee has explored these problems and has reviewed many possible solutions. It proposes the creation of a Legislative Classification Office, which will develop and disseminate information concerning the linkages between appropriations for programs and subsequent executive outlays to carry out those programs. Because in many of these matters the House cannot act alone, but rather must rely upon cooperation for other institutions, the select committee is also recommending the creating of temporary bodies with the power to review and analyze proposed solutions to these problems. . . .

8. The House should implement a procedure to assure continuous review of jurisdictional assignments and encourage cooperation among committees dealing with related matters.

Ultimate authority for delegating work to its committees rests with the House as a whole. The House has not exercised this authority actively or on a continuing basis, and has sponsored no comprehensive inquiry during the past 28 years. However meritorious this committee's jurisdictional recommendations may be, the House will still need to adjust its organization in future years as situations and issues change. It is therefore recommending . . . a process for continuous review of House organization, to give maximum flexibility in adjusting to new and unforeseen problems.

The select committee has concluded that rigid adherence to any sort of "ideal model" for organizing the House would be not only unfeasible but unwise as well. It examined various models, so that it could gain whatever insights it could from them. However, it has resisted suggesting that the House adopt preconceived or inflexible modes of operation. Rather, the report assumes that compromises must necessarily be reached among organizing principles and competing goals. Where choice had to be made, the committee tended to opt for more detailed scheduling and more rational assignment of workloads, while retaining enough "slack in the system" to permit flexibility and competition among diverse viewpoints.

Legislative institutions, especially large and complex ones like the House of Representatives, must strive to retain as much organizational flexibility as possible. While the select committee suggests modernization of procedures and jurisdictions, we are under no illusions that this will resolve tomorrow's challenges. Its recommendations for continuing review—a kind of institutional "preventive maintenance"—reflect this conviction. Although periodic housecleanings are useful, change is better seen as the creation of mechanisms which themselves will permit the institution to adapt to changing circumstances when the arise.

It goes without saying that the select committee tried to avoid making its decisions on the basis of whether specific governmental policies would thereby be advanced or retarded. Not infrequently the committee was urged to take certain courses of action for such reason. In every case this approach was rejected. Its paramount concern is that every measure be the outgrowth of a vigorous exchange of viewpoints. The effectiveness of the House of Representatives in policy making was the object which members of this committee placed above all other considerations, both personal and philosophical; and it is this objective that the select committee asks its colleagues to keep foremost as they ponder the recommendations.

PRINCIPAL RECOMMENDATIONS ON COMMITTEE STRUCTURE, JURISDICTION, AND OPERATION

I. Jurisdictional Realinements

A. The Select Committee's Proposal for Committee Structure

The House places primary reliance upon the work of its committees. A legislative body of 439 Members, Delegates and Commissioners does not usually lend itself to extended floor debate and full Member participation in the details of drafting legislation; instead, the floor is the place for weighing broad policy alternatives and settling particular points at issue. The House thus works its will on the detailed work which flows from its committees. But for this process to work well, it is essential that the committee system itself avoid defects which would jeopardize seriously the legislative product.

The committee system is used to provide division of labor and specialization to bring added competence to the Members. It inevitably carries with it problems of policy coordination and also scheduling problems for the participants.

There are many conceivable methods of organizing the work of the House. Many comprehensive plans for a committee system, as well as specific recommendations, were made during the select committee's hearings, and in written and oral communications. Some plans called for less than a dozen committees, and others had about three times that number. Some proposals followed the pattern of departments in the executive branch, and some stressed parallelism with the Senate. A few recommendations represented a complete overhaul of jurisdictions; others made only minor adjustments in the present system. There were proposals for strengthening party leadership, and proposals which would lessen the role of the party; for increasing the influence of seniority, and for decreasing such influence; for promoting the role of subcommittees, and for promoting the full committees.

The diversity of opinions was impressive; one concludes that there is no perfect committee system, no ideal solution which would satisfy all interested parties. In the words of its chairman, the select committee faced an "impossible task."

As a result of its extensive deliberations, the select committee has concluded that rigid adherence to any sort of ideal model for organizing the House would be not only unfeasible but unwise as well. Compromises must necessarily be reached among competing goals. Moreover, a high degree of flexibility is desirable in a legislative institution, and mechanisms are needed which will permit the institution to adapt to changing circumstances. Committee reorganization, therefore, is more than an attempt to establish a certain number of committees with names and jurisdictions; it is a total package of proposals, each affecting the others, and all contributing to the legislative process.

A thorough comprehension of the select committee's recommendations require study of the entire resolution and its accompanying explanatory report. Virtually all parts of the proposal are interrelated and interact to achieve a balanced whole.

The select committee recommendation is built around the concept of one committee assignment per Member. However, several practical considerations require the retention of some second assignments for Members. But the primary objective is to provide exclusive assignments for each Member to minimize scheduling conflicts, and with each committee sufficiently comprehensive in its responsibilities to represent a full and responsible assignment of roughly equal importance and equal workload for every Member. As much as possible, important jurisdictions are grouped to provide one-stop, coherent policy consideration, and additional mechanisms are provided to bring coordination among the separate committees when necessary. Historically, as new subjects or problems develop, more committee have been created, and/or existing committees have captured new areas of jurisdiction. The select committee plan provides for procedures to meet future changes.

Committee jurisdictions cannot be considered in the abstract, however; such factors as committee number and size, scheduling of meetings, coordination and integrating of committees, the total responsibilities of a Member, and the characteristics of the House are as important in the organization of a committee system as is the identification of substantive areas of legislation. For example, the number of committees, and their overlapping membership, causes many Members to have meeting conflicts and militates against specialization. The present scheduling diffi-

culties, a major source of discontent and inefficiency, are illuminated with factual analysis . . . and they are alarming.

Unduly heavy committee schedules can influence the role of the Congressman and the House in the legislative process. The House can be justly proud of the competence its Members have developed in the subject matter of their assigned committees, in the personal participation of Members rather than delegation to committee and personal staff, and in the responsiveness of the institution to the larger needs of society. As the Members' committee responsibilities increase, however, other important functions and services must suffer.

A major goal of the select committee was to recommend a committee structure which would decrease schedule conflicts and improve the Members' ability properly to focus their energies and talents.

The select committee also recommends that the committee jurisdictions be such that the consideration of comprehensive public policies is enhanced. Too often policy consideration is fragmented and split; a comprehensive view of issues is needed, a rational system for determining what is going on. House committees should be organized to give coherent consideration to a number of pressing policy problems whose handling has been fragmented, e.g. energy resource utilization, research and development, health care, transportation, environmental protection, and foreign affairs.

As in society itself, legislative issues today are not isolated issues but are interrelated in a very complex way to each other. The structure and operation of the House committee system must reflect this "act of life" of modern policy making. The need is to develop mechanisms and procedures which encourage cooperation among committees dealing with related matters. Furthermore, because of the continuously "shifting sands of policy issue," procedures must exist which assure a continuous review of jurisdictional assignments.

In summary, the select committee believes that the committee system of the House should concentrate Members' energies, encourage deliberation within committees, facilitate scheduling, and provide each Member with an opportunity for meaningful participation in making decisions within a significant public policy field. These guidelines lead the committee to recommend major committees nearly equal in size (not over 35 members, except the Appropriations Committee). The essential characteristic of this system is that each Member has *one* major committee assignment, rather than two or more. In addition to the major policy committees, certain other committees exist to perform specific functions, or for a jurisdiction with special characteristics. Membership on these committees would be second committee assignments for their members. Based upon the constraints of a desirable committee size and scheduling problems, and upon a rational grouping of major public policy areas, plus the requirements for "B" committees, the select committee recommends that there be 15 major committees and 7 other committees. The resolution provides for changes in committee structure which could be utilized if this number need be changed as problems of transition to the new system are resolved, or jurisdictional needs come and go.

The system recommended by the select committee is as follows:

"A"

1. Agriculture
2. Appropriations
3. Services
4. Banking, Currency, and Housing
5. Commerce and Health
6. Education
7. Energy and Environment
8. Foreign Affairs
9. Government Operations
10. Judiciary
11. Labor
12. Public Works and Transportation
13. Rules
14. Science and Technology
15. Ways and Means

"B"

1. Budget
2. District of Columbia
3. House Administration
4. Merchant Marine and Fisheries
5. Small Business
6. Standards of Official Conduct
7. Veterans' Affairs

House of Representatives [Committee Print], *Staff Report of the Select Committee on Committees,* "Committee Reform Amendments of 1974: Explanation of H. Res. 988 as Adopted by the House of Representatives, October 8, 1974," 93d Congress, 2d session, October 1974, 3–26.

168 *Buckley v. Valeo*

January 30, 1976

The 1976 Supreme Court decision in Buckley v. Valeo *struck down important provisions of the Federal Election Campaign Act of 1971, which had been significantly amended in 1974. The election law revisions came in the wake of campaign abuses that surfaced during the Watergate investigations. The high court's decision in this case has profoundly influenced the conduct and financing of political campaigns for seats in congressional and presidential elections. The affects of this monumental case continue to weigh heavily on subsequent efforts on the part of Congress to reform campaign financing.*

The 1974 amendments to the Federal Election Campaign Act of 1971 were so sweeping that they amounted to a complete overhaul of existing campaign laws. The main provisions of the act, as amended, were designed to restrict spending by candidates running for office, place limits on the amount that individuals and political committees could contribute, and require disclosure of campaign contributors. The law also provided for some public financing of presidential campaigns through voluntary check-offs on federal income tax returns. The law established the Federal Elections Commission, with four members appointed by House and Senate leaders and two appointed by the president. The clerk of the House and the secretary of the Senate were also named to the commission, whose purpose was to ensure compliance with the election laws.

The law was quickly challenged on January 2, 1975, by several plaintiffs representing a cross-section of the political spectrum, including Senator James L. Buckley (C-N.Y.); former senator Eugene McCarthy (D-Minn.); Human Events, Inc., publishers of a conservative political magazine; the New York Civil Liberties Union, Inc.; and the Libertarian Party. They charged that the limits on campaign expenditures and contributions limited freedom of speech and that public financing as provided for in the law discriminated against minority party candidates who would have a harder time qualifying for the funds.

The Supreme Court upheld parts of the law and struck down other parts. The lengthy decision was rendered "per curiam," by all members of the Court, except Justice John Paul Stevens, who did not participate in the case. Several of the justices separately dissented on parts of the decision. The major parts of the election law that the ruling upheld included setting limits on how much individuals and political committees could give to a candidate and provisions relating to public financing of presidential primary and general elections. The Court also upheld provisions of the law that called for disclosure of campaign contributions and campaign expenditures of more than a $100. The Court declared that the method of appointing members to the Federal Election Commission was unconstitutional because legislative appointees were performing executive functions, violating the doctrine of separation of powers.

The most controversial aspect of the decision was the Court's determination that setting limits on campaign spending was unconstitutional. The decision stated:

A restriction on the amount of money a person or group can spend on political communication during a campaign necessarily reduces the quantity of expression by restricting the number of issues discussed, the depth of their exploration, and the size of the audience reached. This is because virtually every means of communicating ideas in today's mass society requires the expenditure of money. The distribution of the humblest handbill or leaflet entails printing, paper, and circulation costs. Speeches and rallies generally necessitate hiring a hall and publicizing the event. The electorate's increasing dependence on television, radio, and other mass media for news and information has made these expensive modes of communication indispensable instruments of effective political speech.

The Court, in linking the issue of money with the First Amendment issue of freedom of speech, presented a monumental challenge to reformers seeking to limit the ever increasing costs of political campaigns. One of the defendants in Buckley v. Valeo, *Francis R. Valeo, the secretary of the Senate, was named in his capacity as a member of the Federal Elections Commission (as was the clerk of the House). Valeo said, in an interview conducted by the Senate Historical Office in 1986, "I knew the minute that they took off the limitations on personal expenditures that you were setting up a Senate of millionaires, or people who could rely on other people's money for their support. . . . The Senate has become too much a money place."*

Because of the importance of this case to the issue of campaign finance reform, the excerpts of the decision of the Court are presented here at some length, although appendices, footnotes, separate dissenting opinions, and some citations have been omitted.

Per Curiam. [Mr. Justice STEVENS took no part in the consideration of decision of these cases.]

These appeals present constitutional challenges to the key provisions of the Federal Election Campaign Act of 1971 (Act), and related provisions of the Internal Revenue Code of 1954, all as amended in 1974.

The Court of Appeals, in sustaining the legislation in large part against various constitutional challenges, viewed it as "by far the most comprehensive reform legislation [ever] passed by Congress concerning the election of the President, Vice-President, and members of Congress" (1975). The statutes at issue, summarized in broad terms, contain the following provisions: (a) individual political contributions are limited to $1,000 to any single candidate per election, with an over-all annual limitation of $25,000 by any contributor; independent expenditures by individuals and groups "relative to a clearly identified candidate" are limited to $1,000 a year; campaign spending by candidates for various federal offices and spending for national conventions by political parties are subject to prescribed limits; (b) contributions and expenditures above certain threshold levels must be reported and publicly disclosed; (c) a system for public funding of Presidential campaign activities is established by Subtitle H of the Internal Revenue Code; and (d) a Federal Election Commission is established to administer and enforce the legislation.

This suit was originally filed by appellants in the United States District Court for the District of Columbia. Plaintiffs included a candidate for the Presidency of the United States, a United States Senator who is a candidate for reelection, a potential contributor, the Committee for a Constitutional Presidency—McCarthy '76, the Conservative Party of the State of New York, the Mississippi Republican Party, the Libertarian Party, the New York Civil Liberties Union, Inc., the American Conservative Union, the Conservative Victory Fund, and Human Events, Inc. The defendants included the Secretary of the United States Senate and the Clerk of the United States House of Representatives, both in their official capacities and as ex officio members of the Federal Election Commission. The Commission itself was named as a defendant. Also named were the Attorney General of the United States and the Comptroller General of the United States.

Jurisdiction was asserted under 28 U.S.C. §§ 1331, 2201, and 2202, and § 315(a) of the Act, 2 U.S.C. § 437h(a) (1970 ed.,

Supp. IV). The complaint sought both a declaratory judgment that the major provisions of the Act were unconstitutional and an injunction against enforcement of those provisions. Appellants requested the convocation of a three-judge District Court as to all matters and also requested certification of constitutional questions to the Court of Appeals, pursuant to the terms of § 315(a). The District Judge denied the application for a three-judge court and directed that the case be transmitted to the Court of Appeals. That court entered an order stating that the case was "preliminarily deemed" to be properly certified under § 315(a). Leave to intervene was granted to various groups and individuals. After considering matters regarding factfinding procedures, the Court of Appeals entered an order en banc remanding the case to the District Court to (1) identify the constitutional issues in the complaint; (2) take whatever evidence was found necessary in addition to the submissions suitably dealt with by way of judicial notice; (3) make findings of fact with reference to those issues; and (4) certify the constitutional questions arising from the foregoing steps to the Court of Appeals. On remand, the District Judge entered a memorandum order adopting extensive findings of fact and transmitting the augmented record back to the Court of Appeals.

On plenary review, a majority of the Court of Appeals rejected, for the most part, appellants' constitutional attacks. The court found "a clear and compelling interest" in preserving the integrity of the electoral process. On that basis, the court upheld, with one exception, the substantive provisions of the Act with respect to contributions, expenditures, and disclosure. It also sustained the constitutionality of the newly established Federal Election Commission. The court concluded that, notwithstanding the manner of selection of its members and the breadth of its powers, which included nonlegislative functions, the Commission is a constitutionally authorized agency created to perform primarily legislative functions. The provisions for public funding of the three stages of the Presidential selection process were upheld as a valid exercise of congressional power under the General Welfare Clause of the Constitution, Art. I, § 8.

In this Court, appellants argue that the Court of Appeals failed to give this legislation the critical scrutiny demanded under accepted First Amendment and equal protection principles. In appellants' view, limiting the use of money for political purposes constitutes a restriction on communication violative of the First Amendment, since virtually all meaningful political communications in the modern setting involve the expenditure of money. Further, they argue that the reporting and disclosure provisions of the Act unconstitutionally impinge on their right to freedom of association. Appellants also view the federal subsidy provisions of Subtitle H as violative of the General Welfare Clause, and as inconsistent with the First and Fifth Amendments. Finally, appellants renew their attack on the Commission's composition and powers.

At the outset, we must determine whether the case before us presents a "case or controversy" within the meaning of Art. III of the Constitution. Congress may not, of course, require this

Court to render opinions in matters which are not "cases or controversies." *Aetna Life Ins. Co. v. Haworth* (1937). We must therefore decide whether appellants have the "personal stake in the outcome of the controversy" necessary to meet the requirements of Art. III. *Baker* v. *Carr* (1962). It is clear that Congress, in enacting 2 U.S.C. § 437h (1970 ed., Supp. IV), intended to provide judicial review to the extent permitted by Art. III. In our view, the complaint in this case demonstrates that at least some of the appellants have a sufficient "personal stake" in a determination of the constitutional validity of each of the challenged provisions to present a real and substantial controversy admitting of specific relief through a decree of a conclusive character, as distinguished from an opinion advising what the law would be upon a hypothetical state of facts. *Aetna Life Ins. Co. v. Haworth,* supra at 241.

I. CONTRIBUTION AND EXPENDITURE LIMITATIONS

The intricate statutory scheme adopted by Congress to regulate federal election campaigns includes restrictions on political contributions and expenditures that apply broadly to all phases of and all participants in the election process. The major contribution and expenditure limitations in the Act prohibit individuals from contributing more than $25,000 in a single year or more than $1,000 to any single candidate for an election campaign and from spending more than $1,000 a year "relative to a clearly identified candidate." Other provisions restrict a candidate's use of personal and family resources in his campaign and limit the over-all amount that can be spent by a candidate in campaigning for federal office.

The constitutional power of Congress to regulate federal elections is well established and is not questioned by any of the parties in this case. Thus, the critical constitutional questions presented here go not to the basic power of Congress to legislate in this area, but to whether the specific legislation that Congress has enacted interferes with First Amendment freedoms or invidiously discriminates against nonincumbent candidates and minor parties in contravention of the Fifth Amendment.

A. General Principles

The Act's contribution and expenditure limitations operate in an area of the most fundamental First Amendment activities. Discussion of public issues and debate on the qualifications of candidates are integral to the operation of the system of government established by our Constitution. The First Amendment affords the broadest protection to such political expression in order "to assure [the] unfettered interchange of ideas for the bringing about of political and social changes desired by the people." *Roth* v. *United States* (1957). Although First Amendment protections are not confined to "the exposition of ideas," *Winters* v. *New York* (1948), there is practically universal agreement that a major purpose of that Amendment was to protect the free discussion of governmental affairs, . . . of course in-

clud[ing] discussions of candidates. . . . *Mills* v. *Alabama* (1966). This no more than reflects our "profound national commitment to the principle that debate on public issues should be uninhibited, robust, and wide-open," *New York Times Co.* v. *Sullivan* (1964). In a republic where the people are sovereign, the ability of the citizenry to make informed choices among candidates for office is essential, for the identities of those who are elected will inevitably shape the course that we follow as a nation. As the Court observed in *Monitor Patriot Co.* v. *Roy* (1971), it can hardly be doubted that the constitutional guarantee has its fullest and most urgent application precisely to the conduct of campaigns for political office.

The First Amendment protects political association as well as political expression. The constitutional right of association explicated in *NAACP* v. *Alabama* (1958), stemmed from the Court's recognition that [e]ffective advocacy of both public and private points of view, particularly controversial ones, is undeniably enhanced by group association.

Subsequent decisions have made clear that the First and Fourteenth Amendments guarantee " 'freedom to associate with others for the common advancement of political beliefs and ideas,' " a freedom that encompasses " '[t]he right to associate with the political party of one's choice.' " *Kusper* v. *Pontikes* (1973), quoted in *Cousins* v. *Wigoda* (1975).

It is with these principles in mind that we consider the primary contentions of the parties with respect to the Act's limitations upon the giving and spending of money in political campaigns. Those conflicting contentions could not more sharply define the basic issues before us. Appellees contend that what the Act regulates is conduct, and that its effect on speech and association is incidental, at most. Appellants respond that contributions and expenditures are at the very core of political speech, and that the Act's limitations thus constitute restraints on First Amendment liberty that are both gross and direct.

In upholding the constitutional validity of the Act's contribution and expenditure provisions on the ground that those provisions should be viewed as regulating conduct, not speech, the Court of Appeals relied upon *United States* v. *O'Brien* (1968). The O'Brien case involved a defendant's claim that the First Amendment prohibited his prosecution for burning his draft card because his act was " 'symbolic speech' " engaged in as a " 'demonstration against the war and against the draft.' " On the assumption that "the alleged communicative element in O'Brien's conduct [was] sufficient to bring into play the First Amendment," the Court sustained the conviction because it found "a sufficiently important governmental interest in regulating the nonspeech element" that was "unrelated to the suppression of free expression" and that had an "incidental restriction on alleged First Amendment freedoms . . . no greater than [was] essential to the furtherance of that interest." . . . The Court expressly emphasized that O'Brien was not a case where the alleged governmental interest in regulating conduct arises in some measure because the communication allegedly integral to the conduct is itself thought to be harmful. . . .

We cannot share the view that the present Act's contribution and expenditure limitations are comparable to the restrictions on conduct upheld in O'Brien. The expenditure of money simply cannot be equated with such conduct as destruction of a draft card. Some forms of communication made possible by the giving and spending of money involve speech alone, some involve conduct primarily, and some involve a combination of the two. Yet this Court has never suggested that the dependence of a communication on the expenditure of money operates itself to introduce a nonspeech element or to reduce the exacting scrutiny required by the First Amendment. For example, in *Cox* v. *Louisiana* (1965), the Court contrasted picketing and parading with a newspaper comment and a telegram by a citizen to a public official. The parading and picketing activities were said to constitute conduct "intertwined with expression and association," whereas the newspaper comment and the telegram were described as a "pure form of expression" involving "free speech alone," rather than "expression mixed with particular conduct." . . .

Even if the categorization of the expenditure of money as conduct were accepted, the limitations challenged here would not meet the O'Brien test because the governmental interests advanced in support of the Act involve "suppressing communication." The interests served by the Act include restricting the voices of people and interest groups who have money to spend and reducing the over-all scope of federal election campaigns. Although the Act does not focus on the ideas expressed by persons or groups subject to its regulations, it is aimed in part at equalizing the relative ability of all voters to affect electoral outcomes by placing a ceiling on expenditures for political expression by citizens and groups. Unlike O'Brien, where the Selective Service System's administrative interest in the preservation of draft cards was wholly unrelated to their use as a means of communication, it is beyond dispute that the interest in regulating the alleged "conduct" of giving or spending money "arises in some measure because the communication allegedly integral to the conduct is itself thought to be harmful." . . .

Nor can the Act's contribution and expenditure limitations be sustained, as some of the parties suggest, by reference to the constitutional principles reflected in such decisions as *Cox* v. *Louisiana,* supra; *Adderley* v. *Florida* (1966); and *Kovacs* v. *Cooper* (1949). Those cases stand for the proposition that the government may adopt reasonable time, place, and manner regulations, which do not discriminate among speakers or ideas, in order to further an important governmental interest unrelated to the restriction of communication. In contrast to O'Brien, where the method of expression was held to be subject to prohibition, *Cox, Adderley,* and *Kovacs* involved place or manner restrictions on legitimate modes of expression—picketing, parading, demonstrating, and using a sound truck. The critical difference between this case and those time, place, and manner cases is that the present Act's contribution and expenditure limitations impose direct quantity restrictions on political communication and association by persons, groups, candidates, and

political parties in addition to any reasonable time, place, and manner regulations otherwise imposed.

A restriction on the amount of money a person or group can spend on political communication during a campaign necessarily reduces the quantity of expression by restricting the number of issues discussed, the depth of their exploration, and the size of the audience reached. This is because virtually every means of communicating ideas in today's mass society requires the expenditure of money. The distribution of the humblest handbill or leaflet entails printing, paper, and circulation costs. Speeches and rallies generally necessitate hiring a hall and publicizing the event. The electorate's increasing dependence on television, radio, and other mass media for news and information has made these expensive modes of communication indispensable instruments of effective political speech.

The expenditure limitations contained in the Act represent substantial, rather than merely theoretical, restraints on the quantity and diversity of political speech. The $1,000 ceiling on spending "relative to a clearly identified candidate," 18 U.S.C. § 608(e)(1) (1970 ed., Supp. IV), would appear to exclude all citizens and groups except candidates, political parties, and the institutional press from any significant use of the most effective modes of communication. Although the Act's limitations on expenditures by campaign organizations and political parties provide substantially greater room for discussion and debate, they would have required restrictions in the scope of a number of past congressional and Presidential campaigns and would operate to constrain campaigning by candidates who raise sums in excess of the spending ceiling.

By contrast with a limitation upon expenditures for political expression, a limitation upon the amount that any one person or group may contribute to a candidate or political committee entails only a marginal restriction upon the contributor's ability to engage in free communication. A contribution serves as a general expression of support for the candidate and his views, but does not communicate the underlying basis for the support. The quantity of communication by the contributor does not increase perceptibly with the size of his contribution, since the expression rests solely on the undifferentiated, symbolic act of contributing. At most, the size of the contribution provides a very rough index of the intensity of the contributor's support for the candidate. A limitation on the amount of money a person may give to a candidate or campaign organization thus involves little direct restraint on his political communication, for it permits the symbolic expression of support evidenced by a contribution but does not in any way infringe the contributor's freedom to discuss candidates and issues. While contributions may result in political expression if spent by a candidate or an association to present views to the voters, the transformation of contributions into political debate involves speech by someone other than the contributor.

Given the important role of contributions in financing political campaigns, contribution restrictions could have a severe impact on political dialogue if the limitations prevented candidates and political committees from amassing the resources necessary for effective advocacy. There is no indication, however, that the contribution limitations imposed by the Act would have any dramatic adverse effect on the funding of campaigns and political associations. The over-all effect of the Act's contribution ceilings is merely to require candidates and political committees to raise funds from a greater number of persons and to compel people who would otherwise contribute amounts greater than the statutory limits to expend such funds on direct political expression, rather than to reduce the total amount of money potentially available to promote political expression.

The Act's contribution and expenditure limitations also impinge on protected associational freedoms. Making a contribution, like joining a political party, serves to affiliate a person with a candidate. In addition, it enables like-minded persons to pool their resources in furtherance of common political goals. The Act's contribution ceilings thus limit one important means of associating with a candidate or committee, but leave the contributor free to become a member of any political association and to assist personally in the association's efforts on behalf of candidates. And the Act's contribution limitations permit associations and candidates to aggregate large sums of money to promote effective advocacy. By contrast, the Act's $1,000 limitation on independent expenditures "relative to a clearly identified candidate" precludes most associations from effectively amplifying the voice of their adherents, the original basis for the recognition of First Amendment protection of the freedom of association. See *NAACP* v. *Alabama.* The Act's constraints on the ability of independent associations and candidate campaign organizations to expend resources on political expression "is simultaneously an interference with the freedom of [their] adherents," *Sweezy* v. *New Hampshire* (1957) (plurality opinion). . . .

In sum, although the Act's contribution and expenditure limitations both implicate fundamental First Amendment interests, its expenditure ceilings impose significantly more severe restrictions on protected freedoms of political expression and association than do its limitations on financial contributions.

B. Contribution Limitations
1. The $1,000 Limitation on Contributions by Individuals and Groups to Candidates and Authorized Campaign Committees

Section 608(b) provides, with certain limited exceptions, that no person shall make contributions to any candidate with respect to any election for Federal office which, in the aggregate, exceed $1,000.

The statute defines "person" broadly to include "an individual, partnership, committee, association, corporation or any other organization or group of persons." . . . The limitation reaches a gift, subscription, loan, advance, deposit of anything of value, or promise to give a contribution, made for the purpose of influencing a primary election, a Presidential preference primary, or a general election for any federal office. . . . The $1,000 ceiling applies regardless of whether the contribution is given to the candidate, to a committee authorized in writing by

the candidate to accept contributions on his behalf, or indirectly via earmarked gifts passed through an intermediary to the candidate. . . . The restriction applies to aggregate amounts contributed to the candidate for each election—with primaries, runoff elections, and general elections counted separately, and all Presidential primaries held in any calendar year treated together as a single election campaign. . . .

Appellants contend that the $1,000 contribution ceiling unjustifiably burdens First Amendment freedoms, employs overbroad dollar limits, and discriminates against candidates opposing incumbent officeholders and against minor party candidates in violation of the Fifth Amendment. We address each of these claims of invalidity in turn.

(a) As the general discussion in Part I-A, supra, indicated, the primary First Amendment problem raised by the Act's contribution limitations is their restriction of one aspect of the contributor's freedom of political association. The Court's decisions involving associational freedoms establish that the right of association is a "basic constitutional freedom," *Kusper* v. *Pontikes,* that is "closely allied to freedom of speech and a right which, like free speech, lies at the foundation of a free society." *Shelton* v. *Tucker* (1960). See, e.g., *Bates* v. *Little Rock* (1960); *NAACP* v. *Alabama,* supra at 460–461; *NAACP* v. *Button,* supra at 452 (Harlan, J., dissenting). In view of the fundamental nature of the right to associate, governmental "action which may have the effect of curtailing the freedom to associate is subject to the closest scrutiny." *NAACP* v. *Alabama,* supra at 460–461. Yet, it is clear that "[n]either the right to associate nor the right to participate in political activities is absolute." *CSC* v. *Letter Carriers* (1973). Even a "'significant interference' with protected rights of political association" may be sustained if the State demonstrates a sufficiently important interest and employs means closely drawn to avoid unnecessary abridgment of associational freedoms. *Cousins* v. *Wigoda,* supra at 488; *NAACP* v. *Button,* supra at 438; *Shelton* v. *Tucker,* supra at 488.

Appellees argue that the Act's restrictions on large campaign contributions are justified by three governmental interests. According to the parties and *amici,* the primary interest served by the limitations and, indeed, by the Act as a whole, is the prevention of corruption and the appearance of corruption spawned by the real or imagined coercive influence of large financial contributions on candidates' positions and on their actions if elected to office. Two "ancillary" interests underlying the Act are also allegedly furthered by the $1,000 limits on contributions. First, the limits serve to mute the voices of affluent persons and groups in the election process and thereby to equalize the relative ability of all citizens to affect the outcome of elections. Second, it is argued, the ceilings may to some extent act as a brake on the skyrocketing cost of political campaigns and thereby serve to open the political system more widely to candidates without access to sources of large amounts of money.

It is unnecessary to look beyond the Act's primary purpose—to limit the actuality and appearance of corruption resulting from large individual financial contributions—in order to find a constitutionally sufficient justification for the $1,000 contribution limitation. Under a system of private financing of elections, a candidate lacking immense personal or family wealth must depend on financial contributions from others to provide the resources necessary to conduct a successful campaign. The increasing importance of the communications media and sophisticated mass-mailing and polling operations to effective campaigning make the raising of large sums of money an ever more essential ingredient of an effective candidacy. To the extent that large contributions are given to secure a political quid pro quo from current and potential office holders, the integrity of our system of representative democracy is undermined. Although the scope of such pernicious practices can never be reliably ascertained, the deeply disturbing examples surfacing after the 1972 election demonstrate that the problem is not an illusory one.

Of almost equal concern as the danger of actual quid pro quo arrangements is the impact of the appearance of corruption stemming from public awareness of the opportunities for abuse inherent in a regime of large individual financial contributions. In *CSC* v. *Letter Carriers,* supra, the Court found that the danger to "fair and effective government" posed by partisan political conduct on the part of federal employees charged with administering the law was a sufficiently important concern to justify broad restrictions on the employees' right of partisan political association. Here, as there, Congress could legitimately conclude that the avoidance of the appearance of improper influence "is also critical . . . if confidence in the system of representative Government is not to be eroded to a disastrous extent." . . .

Appellants contend that the contribution limitations must be invalidated because bribery laws and narrowly drawn disclosure requirements constitute a less restrictive means of dealing with "proven and suspected quid pro quo arrangements." But laws making criminal the giving and taking of bribes deal with only the most blatant and specific attempts of those with money to influence governmental action. And while disclosure requirements serve the many salutary purposes discussed elsewhere in this opinion, Congress was surely entitled to conclude that disclosure was only a partial measure, and that contribution ceilings were a necessary legislative concomitant to deal with the reality or appearance of corruption inherent in a system permitting unlimited financial contributions, even when the identities of the contributors and the amounts of their contributions are fully disclosed.

The Act's $1,000 contribution limitation focuses precisely on the problem of large campaign contributions—the narrow aspect of political association where the actuality and potential for corruption have been identified—while leaving persons free to engage in independent political expression, to associate actively through volunteering their services, and to assist to a limited but nonetheless substantial extent in supporting candidates and committees with financial resources. Significantly, the Act's contribution limitations in themselves do not undermine to any material degree the potential for robust and effective discussion of candidates and campaign issues by individual citizens, associations, the institutional press, candidates, and political parties.

We find that, under the rigorous standard of review established by our prior decisions, the weighty interests served by restricting the size of financial contributions to political candidates are sufficient to justify the limited effect upon First Amendment freedoms caused by the $1,000 contribution ceiling.

(b) Appellants' first overbreadth challenge to the contribution ceilings rests on the proposition that most large contributors do not seek improper influence over a candidate's position or an officeholder's action. Although the truth of that proposition may be assumed, it does not undercut the validity of the $1,000 contribution limitation. Not only is it difficult to isolate suspect contributions but, more importantly, Congress was justified in concluding that the interest in safeguarding against the appearance of impropriety requires that the opportunity for abuse inherent in the process of raising large monetary contributions be eliminated.

A second, related overbreadth claim is that the $1,000 restriction is unrealistically low because much more than that amount would still not be enough to enable an unscrupulous contributor to exercise improper influence over a candidate or officeholder, especially in campaigns for state-wide or national office. While the contribution limitation provisions might well have been structured to take account of the graduated expenditure limitations for congressional and Presidential campaigns, Congress' failure to engage in such fine tuning does not invalidate the legislation. As the Court of Appeals observed, [i]f it is satisfied that some limit on contributions is necessary, a court has no scalpel to probe, whether, say, a $2,000 ceiling might not serve as well as $1,000. . . . Such distinctions in degree become significant only when they can be said to amount to differences in kind. Compare *Kusper* v. *Pontikes* (1973), with *Rosario* v. *Rockefeller* (1973).

(c) Apart from these First Amendment concerns, appellants argue that the contribution limitations work such an invidious discrimination between incumbents and challengers that the statutory provisions must be declared unconstitutional on their face. In considering this contention, it is important at the outset to note that the Act applies the same limitations on contributions to all candidates regardless of their present occupations, ideological views, or party affiliations. Absent record evidence of invidious discrimination against challengers as a class, a court should generally be hesitant to invalidate legislation which on its face imposes evenhanded restrictions. Cf. *James* v. *Valtierra* (1971).

There is no such evidence to support the claim that the contribution limitations in themselves discriminate against major party challengers to incumbents. Challengers can and often do defeat incumbents in federal elections. Major party challengers in federal elections are usually men and women who are well known and influential in their community or State. Often such challengers are themselves incumbents in important local, state, or federal offices. Statistics in the record indicate that major party challengers as well as incumbents are capable of raising large sums for campaigning. Indeed, a small but nonetheless significant number of challengers have in recent elections outspent their incumbent rivals. And, to the extent that incumbents generally are more likely than challengers to attract very large contributions, the Act's $1,000 ceiling has the practical effect of benefiting challengers as a class. Contrary to the broad generalization drawn by the appellants, the practical impact of the contribution ceilings in any given election will clearly depend upon the amounts in excess of the ceilings that, for various reasons, the candidates in that election would otherwise have received and the utility of these additional amounts to the candidates. To be sure, the limitations may have a significant effect on particular challengers or incumbents, but the record provides no basis for predicting that such adventitious factors will invariably and invidiously benefit incumbents as a class. Since the danger of corruption and the appearance of corruption apply with equal force to challengers and to incumbents, Congress had ample justification for imposing the same fundraising constraints upon both.

The charge of discrimination against minor party and independent candidates is more troubling, but the record provides no basis for concluding that the Act invidiously disadvantages such candidates. As noted above, the Act, on its face treats, all candidates equally with regard to contribution limitations. And the restriction would appear to benefit minor party and independent candidates relative to their major party opponents, because major party candidates receive far more money in large contributions. Although there is some force tax appellants' response that minor party candidates are primarily concerned with their ability to amass the resources necessary to reach the electorate, rather than with their funding position relative to their major party opponents, the record is virtually devoid of support for the claim that the $1,000 contribution limitation will have a serious effect on the initiation and scope of minor party and independent candidacies. Moreover, any attempt to exclude minor parties and independents en masse from the Act's contribution limitations overlooks the fact that minor party candidates may win elective office or have a substantial impact on the outcome of an election.

In view of these considerations, we conclude that the impact of the Act's $1,000 contribution limitation on major party challengers and on minor party candidates does not render the provision unconstitutional on its face.

2. The $5,000 Limitation on Contributions by Political Committees

Section 608(b)(2) permits certain committees, designated as "political committees," to contribute up to $5,000 to any candidate with respect to any election for federal office. In order to qualify for the higher contribution ceiling, a group must have been registered with the Commission as a political committee under 2 U.S.C. § 433 (1970 ed., Supp. IV) for not less than six months, have received contributions from more than 50 persons, and, except for state political party organizations, have

contributed to five or more candidates for federal office. Appellants argue that these qualifications unconstitutionally discriminate against ad hoc organizations in favor of established interest groups and impermissibly burden free association. The argument is without merit. Rather than undermining freedom of association, the basic provision enhances the opportunity of bona fide groups to participate in the election process, and the registration, contribution, and candidate conditions serve the permissible purpose of preventing individuals from evading the applicable contribution limitations by labeling themselves committees.

3. Limitations on Volunteers' Incidental Expenses

The Act excludes from the definition of contribution the value of services provided without compensation by individuals who volunteer a portion or all of their time on behalf of a candidate or political committee.... Certain expenses incurred by persons in providing volunteer services to a candidate are exempt from the $1,000 ceiling only to the extent that they do not exceed $500. These expenses are expressly limited to (1) "the use of real or personal property and the cost of invitations, food, and beverages, voluntarily provided by an individual to a candidate in rendering voluntary personal services on the individual's residential premises for candidate-related activities," ... (2) "the sale of any food or beverage by a vendor for use in a candidate's campaign at a charge [at least equal to cost but] less than the normal comparable charge," (3) "any unreimbursed payment for travel expenses made by an individual who on his own behalf volunteers his personal services to a candidate," ...

If, as we have held, the basic contribution limitations are constitutionally valid, then surely these provisions are a constitutionally acceptable accommodation of Congress' valid interest in encouraging citizen participation in political campaigns while continuing to guard against the corrupting potential of large financial contributions to candidates. The expenditure of resources at the candidate's direction for a fundraising event at a volunteer's residence or the provision of in-kind assistance in the form of food or beverages to be resold to raise funds or consumed by the participants in such an event provides material financial assistance to a candidate. The ultimate effect is the same as if the person had contributed the dollar amount to the candidate and the candidate had then used the contribution to pay for the fundraising event or the food. Similarly, travel undertaken as a volunteer at the direction of the candidate or his staff is an expense of the campaign and may properly be viewed as a contribution if the volunteer absorbs the fare. Treating these expenses as contributions when made to the candidate's campaign or at the direction of the candidate or his staff forecloses an avenue of abuse without limiting actions voluntarily undertaken by citizens independently of a candidate's campaign.

4. The 25,000 Limitation on Total Contributions During any Calendar Year

In addition to the $1,000 limitation on the nonexempt contributions that an individual may make to a particular candidate for any single election, the Act contains an over-all $25,000 limitation on total contributions by an individual during any calendar year.... A contribution made in connection with an election is considered, for purposes of this subsection, to be made in the year the election is held. Although the constitutionality of this provision was drawn into question by appellants, it has not been separately addressed at length by the parties. The over-all $25,000 ceiling does impose an ultimate restriction upon the number of candidates and committees with which an individual may associate himself by means of financial support. But this quite modest restraint upon protected political activity serves to prevent evasion of the $1,000 contribution limitation by a person who might otherwise contribute massive amounts of money to a particular candidate through the use of unearmarked contributions to political committees likely to contribute to that candidate, or huge contributions to the candidate's political party. The limited, additional restriction on associational freedom imposed by the over-all ceiling is thus no more than a corollary of the basic individual contribution limitation that we have found to be constitutionally valid.

C. Expenditure Limitations

The Act's expenditure ceilings impose direct and substantial restraints on the quantity of political speech. The most drastic of the limitations restricts individuals and groups, including political parties that fail to place a candidate on the ballot, to an expenditure of $1,000 "relative to a clearly identified candidate during a calendar year."... Other expenditure ceilings limit spending by candidates, their campaigns, and political parties in connection with election campaigns. . . . It is clear that a primary effect of these expenditure limitations is to restrict the quantity of campaign speech by individuals, groups, and candidates. The restrictions, while neutral as to the ideas expressed, limit political expression "at the core of our electoral process and of the First Amendment freedoms." *Williams* v. *Rhodes* (1968).

1. The $1,000 Limitation on Expenditures "Relative to a Clearly Identified Candidate"

Section 608(e)(1) provides that [n]o person may make any expenditure . . . relative to a clearly identified candidate during a calendar year which, when added to all other expenditures made by such person during the year advocating the election or defeat of such candidate, exceeds $1,000.

The plain effect of § 608(e)(1) is to prohibit all individuals, who are neither candidates nor owners of institutional press facilities, and all groups, except political parties and campaign organizations, from voicing their views "relative to a clearly identified candidate" through means that entail aggregate expenditures of more than $1,000 during a calendar year. The provision, for example, would make it a federal criminal offense for a person or association to place a single one-quarter page advertisement "relative to a clearly identified candidate" in a major metropolitan newspaper.

Before examining the interests advanced in support of § 608(e)(1)'s expenditure ceiling, consideration must be given

to appellants' contention that the provision is unconstitutionally vague. Close examination of the specificity of the statutory limitation is required where, as here, the legislation imposes criminal penalties in an area permeated by First Amendment interests. . . . The test is whether the language of § 608(e)(1) affords the "[p]recision of regulation [that] must be the touchstone in an area so closely touching our most precious freedoms." *NAACP* v. *Button.*

The key operative language of the provision limits "any expenditure . . . relative to a clearly identified candidate." Although "expenditure," "clearly identified," and "candidate" are defined in the Act, there is no definition clarifying what expenditures are "relative to" a candidate. The use of so indefinite a phrase as "relative to" a candidate fails to clearly mark the boundary between permissible and impermissible speech, unless other portions of § 608(e)(1) make sufficiently explicit the range of expenditures covered by the limitation. The section prohibits "any expenditure . . . relative to a clearly identified candidate during a calendar year which, when added to all other expenditures . . . advocation the election or defeat of such candidate, exceeds $1,000." (Emphasis added.) This context clearly permits, if indeed it does not require, the phrase "relative to" a candidate to be read to mean "advocating the election or defeat of" a candidate.

But while such a construction of § 608(e)(1) refocuses the vagueness question, the Court of Appeals was mistaken in thinking that this construction eliminates the problem of unconstitutional vagueness altogether. . . . For the distinction between discussion of issues and candidates and advocacy of election or defeat of candidates may often dissolve in practical application. Candidates, especially incumbents, are intimately tied to public issues involving legislative proposals and governmental actions. Not only do candidates campaign on the basis of their positions on various public issues, but campaigns themselves generate issues of public interest. In an analogous context, this Court in *Thomas* v. *Collins* (1945), observed:

[W]hether words intended and designed to fall short of invitation would miss that mark is a question both of intent and of effect. No speaker, in such circumstances, safely could assume that anything he might say upon the general subject would not be understood by some as an invitation. In short, the supposedly clear-cut distinction between discussion, laudation, general advocacy, and solicitation puts the speaker in these circumstances wholly at the mercy of the varied understanding of his hearers and consequently of whatever inference may be drawn as to his intent and meaning.

Such a distinction offers no security for free discussion. In these conditions it blankets with uncertainty whatever may be said. It compels the speaker to hedge and trim. . . .

The constitutional deficiencies described in *Thomas* v. *Collins* can be avoided only by reading § 608(e)(1) as limited to communications that include explicit words of advocacy of election or defeat of a candidate, much as the definition of "clearly identified" in § 608(e)(2) requires that an explicit and unambiguous reference to the candidate appear as part of the communication. This is the reading of the provision suggested by the nongovernmental appellees in arguing that "[f]unds spent to propagate one's views on issues without expressly calling for a candidate's election or defeat are thus not covered." We agree that, in order to preserve the provision against invalidation on vagueness grounds, § 608(e)(1) must be construed to apply only to expenditures for communications that, in express terms advocate the election or defeat of a clearly identified candidate for federal office.

We turn then to the basic First Amendment question—whether § 608(e)(1), even as thus narrowly and explicitly construed, impermissibly burdens the constitutional right of free expression. The Court of Appeals summarily held the provision constitutionally valid on the ground that "section 608(e) is a loophole-closing provision only" that is necessary to prevent circumvention of the contribution limitations. . . . We cannot agree.

The discussion in Part I-A, supra, explains why the Act's expenditure limitations impose far greater restraints on the freedom of speech and association than do its contribution limitations. The markedly greater burden on basic freedoms caused by § 608(e)(1) thus cannot be sustained simply by invoking the interest in maximizing the effectiveness of the less intrusive contribution limitations. Rather, the constitutionality of § 608(e)(1) turns on whether the governmental interests advanced in its support satisfy the exacting scrutiny applicable to limitations on core First Amendment rights of political expression.

We find that the governmental interest in preventing corruption and the appearance of corruption is inadequate to justify § 608(e)(1)'s ceiling on independent expenditures. First, assuming, arguendo, that large independent expenditures pose the same dangers of actual or apparent quid pro quo arrangements as do large contributions, § 608(e)(1) does not provide an answer that sufficiently relates to the elimination of those dangers. Unlike the contribution limitations' total ban on the giving of large amounts of money to candidates, § 608(e)(1) prevents only some large expenditures. So long as persons and groups eschew expenditures that, in express terms advocate the election or defeat of a clearly identified candidate, they are free to spend as much as they want to promote the candidate and his views. The exacting interpretation of the statutory language necessary to avoid unconstitutional vagueness thus undermines the limitation's effectiveness as a loophole-closing provision by facilitating circumvention by those seeking to exert improper influence upon a candidate or officeholder. It would naively underestimate the ingenuity and resourcefulness of persons and groups desiring to buy influence to believe that they would have much difficulty devising expenditures that skirted the restriction on express advocacy of election or defeat, but nevertheless benefited the candidate's campaign. Yet no substantial societal interest would be served by a loophole-closing provision designed to check corruption that permitted unscrupulous persons and organizations to expend unlimited sums of money in order to obtain improper influence over candidates for elective office. Cf. *Mills* v. *Alabama*.

Second, quite apart from the shortcomings of § 608(e)(1) in preventing any abuses generated by large independent expenditures, the independent advocacy restricted by the provision does not presently appear to pose dangers of real or apparent corruption comparable to those identified with large campaign contributions. The parties defending § 608(e)(1) contend that it is necessary to prevent would-be contributors from avoiding the contribution limitations by the simple expedient of paying directly for media advertisements or for other portions of the candidate's campaign activities. They argue that expenditures controlled by or coordinated with the candidate and his campaign might well have virtually the same value to the candidate as a contribution and would pose similar dangers of abuse. Yet such controlled or coordinated expenditures are treated as contributions, rather than expenditures under the Act. Section 608(b)'s contribution ceilings, rather than § 608(e)(1)'s independent expenditure limitation, prevent attempts to circumvent the Act through prearranged or coordinated expenditures amounting to disguised contributions. By contrast, 608(e)(1) limits expenditures for express advocacy of candidates made totally independently of the candidate and his campaign. Unlike contributions, such independent expenditures may well provide little assistance to the candidate's campaign, and indeed may prove counterproductive. The absence of prearrangement and coordination of an expenditure with the candidate or his agent not only undermines the value of the expenditure to the candidate, but also alleviates the danger that expenditures will be given as a quid pro quo for improper commitments from the candidate. Rather than preventing circumvention of the contribution limitations, § 608(e)(1) severely restricts all independent advocacy despite its substantially diminished potential for abuse.

While the independent expenditure ceiling thus fails to serve any substantial governmental interest in stemming the reality or appearance of corruption in the electoral process, it heavily burdens core First Amendment expression. For the First Amendment right to "'speak one's mind . . . on all public institutions'" includes the right to engage in "'vigorous advocacy' no less than 'abstract discussion.'" *New York Times Co.* v. *Sullivan*, quoting *Bridges* v. *California* (1941), and *NAACP* v. *Button*. Advocacy of the election or defeat of candidates for federal office is no less entitled to protection under the First Amendment than the discussion of political policy generally or advocacy of the passage or defeat of legislation. It is argued, however, that the ancillary governmental interest in equalizing the relative ability of individuals and groups to influence the outcome of elections serves to justify the limitation on express advocacy of the election or defeat of candidates imposed by § 608(e)(1)'s expenditure ceiling. But the concept that government may restrict the speech of some elements of our society in order to enhance the relative voice of others is wholly foreign to the First Amendment, which was designed "to secure 'the widest possible dissemination of information from diverse and antagonistic sources,'" and "'to assure unfettered interchange of ideas for the bringing about of political and social changes desired by the people.'" *New York*

Times Co. v. *Sullivan,* supra at 266, 269, quoting *Associated Press* v. *United States* (1945), and *Roth* v. *United States.* The First Amendment's protection against governmental abridgment of free expression cannot properly be made to depend on a person's financial ability to engage in public discussion. Cf. *Eastern R. Conf.* v. *Noerr Motors* (1961). The Court's decisions in *Mills* v. *Alabama* (1966), and *Miami Herald Publishing Co.* v. *Tornillo* (1974), held that legislative restrictions on advocacy of the election or defeat of political candidates are wholly at odds with the guarantees of the First Amendment. In Mills, the Court addressed the question whether a State, consistently with the United States Constitution, can make it a crime for the editor of a daily newspaper to write and publish an editorial on election day urging people to vote a certain way on issues submitted to them. . . .

We held that "no test of reasonableness can save [such] a state law from invalidation as a violation of the First Amendment." . . . Yet the prohibition of election day editorials invalidated in Mills is clearly a lesser intrusion on constitutional freedom than a $1,000 limitation on the amount of money any person or association can spend during an entire election year in advocating the election or defeat of a candidate for public office. More recently, in Tornillo, the Court held that Florida could not constitutionally require a newspaper to make space available for a political candidate to reply to its criticism. Yet, under the Florida statute, every newspaper was free to criticize any candidate as much as it pleased so long as it undertook the modest burden of printing his reply. . . . The legislative restraint involved in Tornillo thus also pales in comparison to the limitations imposed by § 608(e)(1).

For the reasons stated, we conclude that § 608(e)(1)'s independent expenditure limitation is unconstitutional under the First Amendment.

2. Limitation on Expenditures by Candidates from Personal or Family Resources

The Act also sets limits on expenditures by a candidate "from his personal funds, or the personal funds of his immediate family, in connection with his campaigns during any calendar year." § 608(a)(1). These ceilings vary from $50,000 for Presidential or Vice Presidential candidates to $35,000 for senatorial candidates, and $25,000 for most candidates for the House of Representatives.

The ceiling on personal expenditures by candidates on their own behalf, like the limitations on independent expenditures contained in § 608(e)(1), imposes a substantial restraint on the ability of persons to engage in protected First Amendment expression. The candidate, no less than any other person, has a First Amendment right to engage in the discussion of public issues and vigorously and tirelessly to advocate his own election and the election of other candidates. Indeed, it is of particular importance that candidates have the unfettered opportunity to make their views known so that the electorate may intelligently evaluate the candidates' personal qualities and their positions on vital public issues before choosing among them on election day. Mr. Justice Brandeis' observation that, in our country "public discussion is a political duty," *Whitney* v. *California* (1927) (concurring opinion), applies with special force to candidates for public office. Section 608(a)'s ceiling on personal expenditures by a candidate in furtherance of his own candidacy thus clearly and directly interferes with constitutionally protected freedoms.

The primary governmental interest served by the Act—the prevention of actual and apparent corruption of the political process—does not support the limitation on the candidate's expenditure of his own personal funds. As the Court of Appeals concluded:

Manifestly, the core problem of avoiding undisclosed and undue influence on candidates from outside interests has lesser application when the monies involved come from the candidate himself or from his immediate family. . . .

Indeed, the use of personal funds reduces the candidate's dependence on outside contributions, and thereby counteracts the coercive pressures and attendant risks of abuse to which the Act's contribution limitations are directed.

The ancillary interest in equalizing the relative financial resources of candidates competing for elective office, therefore, provides the sole relevant rationale for § 608(a)'s expenditure ceiling. That interest is clearly not sufficient to justify the provision's infringement of fundamental First Amendment rights. First, the limitation may fail to promote financial equality among candidates. A candidate who spends less of his personal resources on his campaign may nonetheless outspend his rival as a result of more successful fundraising efforts. Indeed, a candidate's personal wealth may impede his efforts to persuade others that he needs their financial contributions or volunteer efforts to conduct an effective campaign. Second, and more fundamentally, the First Amendment simply cannot tolerate § 608(a)'s restriction upon the freedom of a candidate to speak without legislative limit on behalf of his own candidacy. We therefore hold that § 608(a)'s restriction on a candidate's personal expenditures is unconstitutional.

3. Limitations on Campaign Expenditures

Section 608(c) places limitations on over-all campaign expenditures by candidates seeking nomination for election and election to federal office. Presidential candidates may spend $10,000,000 in seeking nomination for office, and an additional $20,000,000 in the general election campaign. §§ 608(c)(1)(A), (B). The ceiling on senatorial campaigns is pegged to the size of the voting-age population of the State, with minimum dollar amounts applicable to campaigns in States with small populations. In senatorial primary elections, the limit is the greater of eight cents multiplied by the voting-age population or $100,000, and, in the general election, the limit is increased to 12 cents multiplied by the voting-age population, or $150,000. §§ 608(c)(1)(C), (D). The Act imposes blanket $70,000 limitations on both primary campaigns and general election campaigns for the House of Representatives, with the exception that the senatorial ceiling applies to campaigns in States entitled to only one Representative. §§ 608(c)(1)(C)(E). These ceilings are to be adjusted upwards at the beginning of each calendar year by the average percentage rise in the consumer price index for the 12 preceding months. § 608(d).

No governmental interest that has been suggested is sufficient to justify the restriction on the quantity of political expression imposed by § 608(c)'s campaign expenditure limitations. The major evil associated with rapidly increasing campaign expenditures is the danger of candidate dependence on large contributions. The interest in alleviating the corrupting influence of large contributions is served by the Act's contribution limitations and disclosure provisions, rather than by § 608(c)'s campaign expenditure ceilings. The Court of Appeals' assertion that the expenditure restrictions are necessary to reduce the incentive to circumvent direct contribution limits is not persuasive. . . . There is no indication that the substantial criminal penalties for violating the contribution ceilings, combined with the political repercussion of such violations, will be insufficient to police the contribution provisions. Extensive reporting, auditing, and disclosure requirements applicable to both contributions and expenditures by political campaigns are designed to facilitate the detection of illegal contributions. Moreover, as the Court of Appeals noted, the Act permits an officeholder or successful candidate to retain contributions in excess of the expenditure ceiling, and to use these funds for "any other lawful purpose." . . . This provision undercuts whatever marginal role the expenditure limitations might otherwise play in enforcing the contribution ceilings.

The interest in equalizing the financial resources of candidates competing for federal office is no more convincing a justification for restricting the scope of federal election campaigns. Given the limitation on the size of outside contributions, the financial resources available to a candidate's campaign, like the number of volunteers recruited, will normally vary with the size and intensity of the candidate's support. There is nothing invidious, improper, or unhealthy in permitting such funds to be spent to carry the candidate's message to the electorate. Moreover, the equalization of permissible campaign expenditures might serve not to equalize the opportunities of all candidates, but to handicap a candidate who lacked substantial name recognition or exposure of his views before the start of the campaign.

The campaign expenditure ceilings appear to be designed primarily to serve the governmental interests in reducing the allegedly skyrocketing costs of political campaigns. Appellees and the Court of Appeals stressed statistics indicating that spending for federal election campaigns increased almost 300% between 1952 and 1972 in comparison with a 57.6% rise in the consumer price index during the same period. Appellants respond that, during these years, the rise in campaign spending lagged behind the percentage increase in total expenditures for commercial advertising and the size of the gross national product. In any event, the mere growth in the cost of federal election cam-

paigns, in and of itself, provides no basis for governmental restrictions on the quantity of campaign spending and the resulting limitation on the scope of federal campaigns. The First Amendment denies government the power to determine that spending to promote one's political views is wasteful, excessive, or unwise. In the free society ordained by our Constitution, it is not the government, but the people—individually, as citizens and candidates, and collectively, as associations and political committees—who must retain control over the quantity and range of debate on public issues in a political campaign.

For these reasons, we hold that § 608(c) is constitutionally invalid.

In sum, the provisions of the Act that impose a $1,000 limitation on contributions to a single candidate, § 608(b)(1), a $5,000 limitation on contributions by a political committee to a single candidate, § 608(b)(2), and a $25,000 limitation on total contributions by an individual during any calendar year, § 608(b)(3), are constitutionally valid. These limitations, along with the disclosure provisions, constitute the Act's primary weapons against the reality or appearance of improper influence stemming from the dependence of candidates on large campaign contributions. The contribution ceilings thus serve the basic governmental interest in safeguarding the integrity of the electoral process without directly impinging upon the rights of individual citizens and candidates to engage in political debate and discussion. By contrast, the First Amendment requires the invalidation of the Act's independent expenditure ceiling, § 608(e)(1), its limitation on a candidate's expenditures from his own personal funds, § 608(a), and its ceilings on over-all campaign expenditures, § 608(e). These provisions place substantial and direct restrictions on the ability of candidates, citizens, and associations to engage in protected political expression, restrictions that the First Amendment cannot tolerate.

II. REPORTING AND DISCLOSURE REQUIREMENTS

Unlike the limitations on contributions and expenditures imposed by 18 U.S.C. § 608 (1970 ed., Supp. IV), the disclosure requirements of the Act, 2 U.S.C. § 431 et seq. (1970 ed., Supp. IV), are not challenged by appellants as per se unconstitutional restrictions on the exercise of First Amendment freedoms of speech and association. Indeed, appellants argue that "narrowly drawn disclosure requirements are the proper solution to virtually all of the evils Congress sought to remedy." . . . The particular requirements embodied in the Act are attacked as overbroad—both in their application to minor party and independent candidates and in their extension to contributions as small as $11 or $101. Appellants also challenge the provision for disclosure by those who make independent contributions and expenditures, § 434(e). The Court of Appeals found no constitutional infirmities in the provisions challenged here. We affirm the determination on overbreadth and hold that § 434(e), if narrowly construed, also is within constitutional bounds.

The first federal disclosure law was enacted in 1910. Act of June 25, 1910, c. 392, 36 Stat. 822. It required political committees, defined as national committees and national congressional campaign committees of parties, and organizations operating to influence congressional elections in two or more States, to disclose names of all contributors of $100 or more; identification of recipients of expenditures of $10 or more was also required. . . . Annual expenditures of $50 or more "for the purpose of influencing or controlling, in two or more States, the result of" a congressional election had to be reported independently if they were not made through a political committee. . . . In 1911, the Act was revised to include pre-nomination transactions such as those involved in conventions and primary campaigns. . . .

Disclosure requirements were broadened in the Federal Corrupt Practices Act of 1925 (Title III of the Act of Feb. 28, 1925), 43 Stat. 1070. That Act required political committees, defined as organizations that accept contributions or make expenditures "for the purpose of influencing or attempting to influence" the Presidential or Vice Presidential elections (a) in two or more States or (b) as a subsidiary of a national committee, § 302(c), 43 Stat. 1070, to report total contributions and expenditures, including the names and addresses of contributors of $100 or more and recipients of $10 or more in a calendar year. . . . The Act was upheld against a challenge that it infringed upon the prerogatives of the States in *Burroughs* v. *United States* (1934). The Court held that it was within the power of Congress "to pass appropriate legislation to safeguard [a Presidential] election from the improper use of money to influence the result." . . . Although the disclosure requirements were widely circumvented, no further attempts were made to tighten them until 1960, when the Senate passed a bill that would have closed some existing loopholes. . . . The attempt aborted because no similar effort was made in the House.

The Act presently under review replaced all prior disclosure laws. Its primary disclosure provisions impose reporting obligations on "political committees" and candidates. "Political committee" is defined in § 431(d) as a group of persons that receives "contributions" or makes "expenditures" of over $1,000 in a calendar year. "Contributions" and "expenditures" are defined in lengthy parallel provisions similar to those in Title 18, discussed above. Both definitions focus on the use of money or other objects of value "for the purpose of . . . influencing" the nomination or election of any person to federal office.

Each political committee is required to register with the Commission, § 433, and to keep detailed records of both contributions and expenditures, §§ 432(c), (d). These records must include the name and address of everyone making a contribution in excess of $10, along with the date and amount of the contribution. If a person's contributions aggregate more than $100, his occupation and principal place of business are also to be included. . . . These files are subject to periodic audits and field investigations by the Commission. . . .

Each committee and each candidate also is required to file quarterly reports. . . . The reports are to contain detailed finan-

cial information, including the full name, mailing address, occupation, and principal place of business of each person who has contributed over $100 in a calendar year, as well as the amount and date of the contributions. . . . They are to be made available by the Commission "for public inspection and copying." . . . Every candidate for federal office is required to designate a "principal campaign committee," which is to receive reports of contributions and expenditures made on the candidate's behalf from other political committees and to compile and file these reports, together with its own statements, with the Commission. . . .

Every individual or group, other than a political committee or candidate, who makes "contributions" or "expenditures" of over $100 in a calendar year "other than by contribution to a political committee or candidate" is required to file a statement with the Commission. . . . Any violation of these recordkeeping and reporting provisions is punishable by a fine of not more than $1,000 or a prison term of not more than a year, or both. . . .

A. *General Principles*

Unlike the over-all limitations on contributions and expenditures, the disclosure requirements impose no ceiling on campaign-related activities. But we have repeatedly found that compelled disclosure, in itself, can seriously infringe on privacy of association and belief guaranteed by the First Amendment. . . .

We long have recognized that significant encroachments on First Amendment rights of the sort that compelled disclosure imposes cannot be justified by a mere showing of some legitimate governmental interest. Since *NAACP* v. *Alabama,* we have required that the subordinating interests of the State must survive exacting scrutiny. We also have insisted that there be a "relevant correlation" or "substantial relation" between the governmental interest and the information required to be disclosed. . . . This type of scrutiny is necessary even if any deterrent effect on the exercise of First Amendment rights arises not through direct government action, but indirectly, as an unintended but inevitable result of the government's conduct in requiring disclosure. *NAACP* v. *Alabama,* supra at 461. Cf. *Kusper* v. *Pontikes.*

Appellees argue that the disclosure requirements of the Act differ significantly from those at issue in *NAACP* v. *Alabama and its progeny,* because the Act only requires disclosure of the names of contributors, and does not compel political organizations to submit the names of their members.

As we have seen, group association is protected because it enhances "[e]ffective advocacy." *NAACP* v. *Alabama,* supra at 460. The right to join together "for the advancement of beliefs and ideas," ibid., is diluted if it does not include the right to pool money through contributions, for funds are often essential if "advocacy" is to be truly or optimally "effective." Moreover, the invasion of privacy of belief may be as great when the information sought concerns the giving and spending of money as when it concerns the joining of organizations, for "[f]inancial transactions can reveal much about a person's activities, associations, and beliefs." *California Bankers Assn.* v. *Shultz* (1974) (POWELL, J., concurring). Our past decisions have not drawn fine lines between contributors and members, but have treated them interchangeably. In Bates, for example, we applied the principles of *NAACP* v. *Alabama* and reversed convictions for failure to comply with a city ordinance that required the disclosure of "dues, assessments, and contributions paid, by whom and when paid." See also *United States* v. *Rumely* (1953) (setting aside a contempt conviction of an organization official who refused to disclose names of those who made bulk purchases of books sold by the organization).

The strict test established by *NAACP* v. *Alabama* is necessary because compelled disclosure has the potential for substantially infringing the exercise of First Amendment rights. But we have acknowledged that there are governmental interests sufficiently important to outweigh the possibility of infringement, particularly when the "free functioning of our national institutions" is involved. *Communist Party* v. *Subversive Activities Control Bd.*

The governmental interests sought to be vindicated by the disclosure requirements are of this magnitude. They fall into three categories. First, disclosure provides the electorate with information "as to where political campaign money comes from and how it is spent by the candidate" in order to aid the voters in evaluating those who seek federal office. It allows voters to place each candidate in the political spectrum more precisely than is often possible solely on the basis of party labels and campaign speeches. The sources of a candidate's financial support also alert the voter to the interests to which a candidate is most likely to be responsive, and thus facilitate predictions of future performance in office.

Second, disclosure requirements deter actual corruption and avoid the appearance of corruption by exposing large contributions and expenditures to the light of publicity. This exposure may discourage those who would use money for improper purposes either before or after the election. A public armed with information about a candidate's most generous supporters is better able to detect any post-election special favors that may be given in return. And, as we recognized in *Burroughs* v. *United States,* Congress could reasonably conclude that full disclosure during an election campaign tends "to prevent the corrupt use of money to affect elections." In enacting these requirements, it may have been mindful of Mr. Justice Brandeis' advice:

Publicity is justly commended as a remedy for social and industrial diseases. Sunlight is said to be the best of disinfectants; electric light the most efficient policeman.

Third, and not least significant, recordkeeping, reporting, and disclosure requirements are an essential means of gathering the data necessary to detect violations of the contribution limitations described above.

The disclosure requirements, as a general matter, directly serve substantial governmental interests. In determining whether these interests are sufficient to justify the requirements, we must look to the extent of the burden that they place on individual rights.

It is undoubtedly true that public disclosure of contributions to candidates and political parties will deter some individuals who otherwise might contribute. In some instances, disclosure may even expose contributors to harassment or retaliation. These are not insignificant burdens on individual rights, and they must be weighed carefully against the interests which Congress has sought to promote by this legislation. In this process, we note and agree with appellants' concession that disclosure requirements—certainly in most applications—appear to be the least restrictive means of curbing the evils of campaign ignorance and corruption that Congress found to exist. Appellants argue, however, that the balance tips against disclosure when it is required of contributors to certain parties and candidates. We turn now to this contention.

B. Application to Minor Parties and Independents

Appellants contend that the Act's requirements are overbroad insofar as they apply to contributions to minor parties and independent candidates because the governmental interest in this information is minimal, and the danger of significant infringement on First Amendment rights is greatly increased.

1. Requisite Factual Showing

In *NAACP* v. *Alabama,* the organization had made an uncontroverted showing that, on past occasions, revelation of the identity of its rank-and-file members [had] exposed these members to economic reprisal, loss of employment, threat of physical coercion, and other manifestations of public hostility, and the State was unable to show that the disclosure it sought had a "substantial bearing" on the issues it sought to clarify. . . . Under those circumstances, the Court held that "whatever interest the State may have in [disclosure] has not been shown to be sufficient to overcome petitioner's constitutional objections." . . .

The Court of Appeals rejected appellants' suggestion that this case fits into the *NAACP* v. *Alabama* mold. It concluded that substantial governmental interests in "informing the electorate and preventing the corruption of the political process" were furthered by requiring disclosure of minor parties and independent candidates, . . . and therefore found no tenable rationale for assuming that the public interest in minority party disclosure of contributions above a reasonable cutoff point is uniformly outweighed by potential contributors' associational rights. . . .

The court left open the question of the application of the disclosure requirements to candidates (and parties) who could demonstrate injury of the sort at stake in *NAACP* v. *Alabama.* No record of harassment on a similar scale was found in this case. [n83] We agree with the Court of Appeals' conclusion that *NAACP* v. *Alabama* is inapposite where, as here, any serious infringement on First Amendment rights brought about by the compelled disclosure of contributors is highly speculative.

It is true that the governmental interest in disclosure is diminished when the contribution in question is made to a minor party with little chance of winning an election. As minor parties usually represent definite and publicized viewpoints, there may be less need to inform the voters of the interests that specific candidates represent. Major parties encompass candidates of greater diversity. In many situations, the label "Republican" or "Democrat" tells a voter little. The candidate who bears it may be supported by funds from the far right, the far left, or any place in between on the political spectrum. It is less likely that a candidate of, say, the Socialist Labor Party will represent interests that cannot be discerned from the party's ideological position.

The Government's interest in deterring the "buying" of elections and the undue influence of large contributors on officeholders also may be reduced where contributions to a minor party or an independent candidate are concerned, for it is less likely that the candidate will be victorious. But a minor party sometimes can play a significant role in an election. Even when a minor party candidate has little or no chance of winning, he may be encouraged by major party interests in order to divert votes from other major party contenders.

We are not unmindful that the damage done by disclosure to the associational interests of the minor parties and their members and to supporters of independents could be significant. These movements are less likely to have a sound financial base, and thus are more vulnerable to fall-offs in contributions. In some instances, fears of reprisal may deter contributions to the point where the movement cannot survive. The public interest also suffers if that result comes to pass, for there is a consequent reduction in the free circulation of ideas both within and without the political arena.

There could well be a case, similar to those before the Court in *NAACP* v. *Alabama* and *Bates,* where the threat to the exercise of First Amendment rights is so serious, and the state interest furthered by disclosure so insubstantial, that the Act's requirements cannot be constitutionally applied. But no appellant in this case has tendered record evidence of the sort proffered in *NAACP* v. *Alabama.* Instead, appellants primarily rely on "the clearly articulated fears of individuals, well experienced in the political process." . . . At best they offer the testimony of several minor party officials that one or two persons refused to make contributions because of the possibility of disclosure. On this record, the substantial public interest in disclosure identified by the legislative history of this Act outweighs the harm generally alleged.

2. Blanket Exemption

Appellants agree that "the record here does not reflect the kind of focused and insistent harassment of contributors and members that existed in the *NAACP* cases." They argue, however, that a blanket exemption for minor parties is necessary lest irreparable injury be done before the required evidence can be gathered.

Those parties that would be sufficiently "minor" to be exempted from the requirements of § 434 could be defined, appellants suggest, along the lines used for public financing purposes, . . as those who received less than 25% of the vote in past elections. Appellants do not argue that this line is constitution-

ally required. They suggest as an alternative defining "minor parties" as those that do not qualify for automatic ballot access under state law. Presumably, other criteria, such as current political strength (measured by polls or petition), age, or degree of organization, could also be used.

The difficulty with these suggestions is that they reflect only a party's past or present political strength, and that is only one of the factors that must be considered. Some of the criteria are not precisely indicative of even that factor. Age, or past political success, for instance, may typically be associated with parties that have a high probability of success. But not all long-established parties are winners—some are consistent losers—and a new party may garner a great deal of support if it can associate itself with an issue that has captured the public's imagination. None of the criteria suggested is precisely related to the other critical factor that must be considered, the possibility that disclosure will impinge upon protected associational activity.

An opinion dissenting in part from the Court of Appeals' decision concedes that no one line is "constitutionally required." It argues, however, that a flat exemption for minor parties must be carved out, even along arbitrary lines, if groups that would suffer impermissibly from disclosure are to be given any real protection. An approach that requires minor parties to submit evidence that the disclosure requirements cannot constitutionally be applied to them offers only an illusory safeguard, the argument goes, because the "evils" of "chill and harassment . . . are largely incapable of formal proof." This dissent expressed its concern that a minor party, particularly a new party, may never be able to prove a substantial threat of harassment, however real that threat may be, because it would be required to come forward with witnesses who are too fearful to contribute but not too fearful to testify about their fear. A strict requirement that chill and harassment be directly attributable to the specific disclosure from which the exemption is sought would make the task even more difficult.

We recognize that unduly strict requirements of proof could impose a heavy burden, but it does not follow that a blanket exemption for minor parties is necessary. Minor parties must be allowed sufficient flexibility in the proof of injury to assure a fair consideration of their claim. The evidence offered need show only a reasonable probability that the compelled disclosure of a party's contributors' names will subject them to threats, harassment, or reprisals from either Government officials or private parties. The proof may include, for example, specific evidence of past or present harassment of members due to their associational ties, or of harassment directed against the organization itself. A pattern of threats or specific manifestations of public hostility may be sufficient. New parties that have no history upon which to draw may be able to offer evidence of reprisals and threats directed against individuals or organizations holding similar views.

Where it exists, the type of chill and harassment identified in *NAACP* v. *Alabama* can be shown. We cannot assume that courts will be insensitive to similar showings when made in future cases. We therefore conclude that a blanket exemption is not required.

C. Section 434(e)

Section 434(e) requires "[e]very person (other than a political committee or candidate) who makes contributions or expenditures" aggregating over $100 in a calendar year "other than by contribution to a political committee or candidate" to file a statement with the Commission. Unlike the other disclosure provisions, this section does not seek the contribution list of any association. Instead, it requires direct disclosure of what an individual or group contributes or spends.

In considering this provision, we must apply the same strict standard of scrutiny, for the right of associational privacy developed in *NAACP* v. *Alabama* derives from the rights of the organization's members to advocate their personal points of view in the most effective way. . . .

Appellants attack § 434(e) as a direct intrusion on privacy of belief, in violation of *Talley* v. *California* (1960), and as imposing "very real, practical burdens . . . certain to deter individuals from making expenditures for their independent political speech" analogous to those held to be impermissible in *Thomas* v. *Collins* (1945).

1. The Role of § 434(e)

The Court of Appeals upheld § 434(e) as necessary to enforce the independent expenditure ceiling imposed by 18 U.S.C. § 608(e)(1) (1970 ed., Supp. IV). . . .

If . . . Congress has both the authority and a compelling interest to regulate independent expenditures under section 608(e), surely it can require that there be disclosure to prevent misuse of the spending channel. . . .

We have found that § 608(e)(1) unconstitutionally in fringes upon First Amendment rights. If the sole function of § 434(e) were to aid in the enforcement of that provision, it would no longer serve any governmental purpose.

But the two provisions are not so intimately tied. The legislative history on the function of § 434(e) is bare, but it was clearly intended to stand independently of § 608(e)(1). It was enacted with the general disclosure provisions in 1971 as part of the original Act, while § 608(e)(1) was part of the 1974 amendments. Like the other disclosure provisions, § 434(e) could play a role in the enforcement of the expanded contribution and expenditure limitations included in the 1974 amendments, but it also has independent functions. Section 434(e) is part of Congress' effort to achieve "total disclosure" by reaching "every kind of political activity" in order to insure that the voters are fully informed and to achieve through publicity the maximum deterrence to corruption and undue influence possible. The provision is responsive to the legitimate fear that efforts would be made, as they had been in the past, to avoid the disclosure requirements by routing financial support of candidates through avenues not explicitly covered by the general provisions of the Act.

2. Vagueness Problems

In its effort to be all-inclusive, however, the provision raises serious problems of vagueness, particularly treacherous where, as here, the violation of its terms carries criminal penalties and fear of incurring these sanctions may deter those who seek to exercise protected First Amendment rights.

Section 434(e) applies to "[e]very person . . . who makes contributions or expenditures." "Contributions" and "expenditures" are defined in parallel provisions in terms of the use of money or other valuable assets "for the purpose of . . . influencing" the nomination or election of candidates for federal office. It is the ambiguity of this phrase that poses constitutional problems.

Due process requires that a criminal statute provide adequate notice to a person of ordinary intelligence that his contemplated conduct is illegal, for "no man shall be held criminally responsible for conduct which he could not reasonably understand to be proscribed." . . .

There is no legislative history to guide us in determining the scope of the critical phrase "for the purpose of . . . influencing." It appears to have been adopted without comment from earlier disclosure Acts. Congress "has voiced its wishes in [most] muted strains," leaving us to draw upon "those common sense assumptions that must be made in determining direction without a compass." *Rosado* v. *Wyman* (1970). Where the constitutional requirement of definiteness is at stake, we have the further obligation to construe the statute, if that can be done consistent with the legislature's purpose, to avoid the shoals of vagueness. . . .

In enacting the legislation under review, Congress addressed broadly the problem of political campaign financing. It wished to promote full disclosure of campaign-oriented spending to insure both the reality and the appearance of the purity and openness of the federal election process. Our task is to construe "for the purpose of . . . influencing," incorporated in § 434(e) through the definitions of "contributions" and "expenditures," in a manner that precisely furthers this goal.

In Part I, we discussed what constituted a "contribution" for purposes of the contribution limitations set forth in 18 U.S.C. § 608(b) (1970 ed., Supp. IV). We construed that term to include not only contributions made directly or indirectly to a candidate, political party, or campaign committee, and contributions made to other organizations or individuals but earmarked for political purposes, but also all expenditures placed in cooperation with or with the consent of a candidate, his agents, or an authorized committee of the candidate. The definition of "contribution" in § 431(e), for disclosure purposes, parallels the definition in Title 18 almost word for word, and we construe the former provision as we have the latter. So defined, "contributions" have a sufficiently close relationship to the goals of the Act, for they are connected with a candidate or his campaign.

When we attempt to define "expenditure" in a similarly narrow way, we encounter line-drawing problems of the sort we faced in 18 U.S.C. § 608(e)(1) (1970 ed., Supp. IV). Although the phrase, "for the purpose of . . . influencing" an election or nomination, differs from the language used in § 608(e)(1), it shares the same potential for encompassing both issue discussion and advocacy of a political result. The general requirement that "political committees" and candidates disclose their expenditures could raise similar vagueness problems, for "political committee" is defined only in terms of amount of annual "contributions" and "expenditures," and could be interpreted to reach groups engaged purely in issue discussion. The lower courts have construed the words "political committee" more narrowly. To fulfill the purposes of the Act, they need only encompass organizations that are under the control of a candidate or the major purpose of which is the nomination or election of a candidate. Expenditures of candidates and of "political committees," so construed, can be assumed to fall within the core area sought to be addressed by Congress. They are, by definition, campaign-related.

But when the maker of the expenditure is not within these categories—when it is an individual other than a candidate or a group other than a "political committee"—the relation of the information sought to the purposes of the Act may be too remote. To insure that the reach of § 434(e) is not impermissibly broad, we construe "expenditure" for purposes of that section in the same way we construed the terms of § 608(e)—to reach only funds used for communications that expressly advocate the election or defeat of a clearly identified candidate. This reading is directed precisely to that spending that is unambiguously related to the campaign of a particular federal candidate.

In summary, § 434(e), as construed, imposes independent reporting requirements on individuals and groups that are not candidates or political committees only in the following circumstances: (1) when they make contributions earmarked for political purposes or authorized or requested by a candidate or his agent, to some person other than a candidate or political committee, and (2) when they make expenditures for communications that expressly advocate the election or defeat of a clearly identified candidate.

Unlike 18 U.S.C. § 608(e)(1) (1970 ed., Supp. IV), § 434(e), as construed, bears a sufficient relationship to a substantial governmental interest. As narrowed, § 434(e), like § 608(e)(1), does not reach all partisan discussion, for it only requires disclosure of those expenditures that expressly advocate a particular election result. This might have been fatal if the only purpose of § 434(e) were to stem corruption or its appearance by closing a loophole in the general disclosure requirements. But the disclosure provisions, including § 434(e), serve another, informational interest, and, even as construed, § 434(e) increases the fund of information concerning those who support the candidates. It goes beyond the general disclosure requirements to shed the light of publicity on spending that is unambiguously campaign-related, but would not otherwise be reported because it takes the form of independent expenditures or of contributions to an individual or group not itself required to report the names of its contributors. By the same token, it is not fatal that § 434(e) encompasses purely independent expenditures uncoordinated with a particular candidate or his agent. The corruption potential of these expenditures may be significantly different, but the informational interest can be as strong as it is in coordinated spending, for disclosure helps voters to define more of the candidates' constituencies.

Section 434(e), as we have construed it, does not contain the infirmities of the provisions before the Court in *Talley* v. *California* (1960), and *Thomas* v. *Collins* (1945). The ordinance found wanting in *Talley* forbade all distribution of handbills that did not contain the name of the printer, author, or manufacturer, and the name of the distributor. The city urged that the ordinance was aimed at identifying those responsible for fraud, false advertising, and libel, but the Court found that it was "in no manner so limited." . . . Here, as we have seen, the disclosure requirement is narrowly limited to those situations where the information sought has a substantial connection with the governmental interests sought to be advanced. Thomas held unconstitutional a prior restraint in the form of a registration requirement for labor organizers. The Court found the State's interest insufficient to justify the restrictive effect of the statute. The burden imposed by § 434(e) is no prior restraint, but a reasonable and minimally restrictive method of furthering First Amendment values by opening the basic processes of our federal election system to public view.

D. Thresholds

Appellants' third contention, based on alleged overbreadth, is that the monetary thresholds in the recordkeeping and reporting provisions lack a substantial nexus with the claimed governmental interests, for the amounts involved are too low even to attract the attention of the candidate, much less have a corrupting influence.

The provisions contain two thresholds. Records are to be kept by political committees of the names and addresses of those who make contributions in excess of $10, § 432(c)(2), and these records are subject to Commission audit, § 438(a)(8). If a person's contributions to a committee or candidate aggregate more than $100, his name and address, as well as his occupation and principal place of business, are to be included in reports filed by committees and candidates with the Commission, § 434(b)(2), and made available for public inspection, § 438(a)(4).

The Court of Appeals rejected appellants' contention that these thresholds are unconstitutional. It found the challenge on First Amendment grounds to the $10 threshold to be premature, for it could "discern no basis in the statute for authorizing disclosure outside the Commission. . . ; and hence no substantial 'inhibitory effect' operating upon" appellants. The $100 threshold was found to be within the "reasonable latitude" given the legislature "as to where to draw the line." We agree.

The $10 and $100 thresholds are indeed low. Contributors of relatively small amounts are likely to be especially sensitive to recording or disclosure of their political preferences. These strict requirements may well discourage participation by some citizens in the political process, a result that Congress hardly could have intended. Indeed, there is little in the legislative history to indicate that Congress focused carefully on the appropriate level at which to require recording and disclosure. Rather, it seems merely to have adopted the thresholds existing in similar disclosure laws since 1910. But we cannot require Congress to establish that it has chosen the highest reasonable threshold. The line is necessarily a judgmental decision, best left in the context of this complex legislation to congressional discretion. We cannot say, on this bare record, that the limits designated are wholly without rationality.

We are mindful that disclosure serves informational functions, as well as the prevention of corruption and the enforcement of the contribution limitations. Congress is not required to set a threshold that is tailored only to the latter goals. In addition, the enforcement goal can never be well served if the threshold is so high that disclosure becomes equivalent to admitting violation of the contribution limitations.

The $10 recordkeeping threshold, in a somewhat similar fashion, facilitates the enforcement of the disclosure provisions by making it relatively difficult to aggregate secret contributions in amounts that surpass the $100 limit. We agree with the Court of Appeals that there is no warrant for assuming that public disclosure of contributions between $10 and $100 is authorized by the Act. Accordingly, we do not reach the question whether information concerning gifts of this size can be made available to the public without trespassing impermissibly on First Amendment rights. . . .

In summary, we find no constitutional infirmities in the recordkeeping, reporting, and disclosure provisions of the Act.

III. PUBLIC FINANCING OF PRESIDENTIAL ELECTION CAMPAIGNS

A series of statutes for the public financing of Presidential election campaigns produced the scheme now found in § 6096 and Subtitle H of the Internal Revenue Code of 1954, 26 U.S.C. §§ 6096, 9001–9012, 9031–9042 (1970 ed., Supp. IV). [n115] Both the District Court, 401 F. Supp. 1235, and the Court of Appeals sustained Subtitle H against a constitutional attack. Appellants renew their challenge here, contending that the legislation violates the First and Fifth Amendments. We find no merit in their claims and affirm.

A. Summary of Subtitle H

Section 9006 establishes a Presidential Election Campaign Fund (Fund), financed from general revenues in the aggregate amount designated by individual taxpayers, under § 6096, who on their income tax returns may authorize payment to the Fund of one dollar of their tax liability in the case of an individual return or two dollars in the case of a joint return. The Fund consists of three separate accounts to finance (1) party nominating conventions, § 9008(a), (2) general election campaigns, § 9006(a), and (3) primary campaigns, § 9037(a).

Chapter 95 of Title 26 which concerns financing of party nominating conventions and general election campaigns, distinguishes among "major," "minor," and "new" parties. A major party is defined as a party whose candidate for President in the most recent election received 25% or more of the popular vote. § 9002(6). A minor party is defined as a party whose candidate received at least 5% but less than 25% of the vote at the most recent election. § 9002(7). All other parties are new parties, § 9002(8), including both newly created parties and those receiving less than 5% of the vote in the last election.

Major parties are entitled to $2,000,000 to defray their national committee Presidential nominating convention expenses, must limit total expenditures to that amount, § 9008(d), and may not use any of this money to benefit a particular candidate or delegate, § 9008(c). A minor party receives a portion of the major party entitlement determined by the ratio of the votes received by the party's candidate in the last election to the average of the votes received by the major parties' candidates. § 9008(b)(2). The amounts given to the parties and the expenditure limit are adjusted for inflation, using 1974 as the base year. § 9008(b)(5). No financing is provided for new parties, nor is there any express provision for financing independent candidates or parties not holding a convention.

For expenses in the general election campaign, § 9004(a)(1) entitles each major party candidate to $20,000,000. This amount is also adjusted for inflation. . . . To be eligible for funds the candidate must pledge not to incur expenses in excess of the entitlement under § 9004(a)(1) and not to accept private contributions except to the extent that the fund is insufficient to provide the full entitlement. . . . Minor party candidates are also entitled to funding, again based on the ratio of the vote received by the party's candidate in the preceding election to the average of the major party candidates. . . . Minor party candidates must certify that they will not incur campaign expenses in excess of the major party entitlement and that they will accept private contributions only to the extent needed to make up the difference between that amount and the public funding grant. . . . New party candidates receive no money prior to the general election, but any candidate receiving 5% or more of the popular vote in the election is entitled to post-election payments according to the formula applicable to minor party candidates. . . . Similarly, minor party candidates are entitled to post-election funds if they receive a greater percentage of the average major party vote than their party's candidate did in the preceding election; the amount of such payments is the difference between the entitlement based on the preceding election and that based on the actual vote in the current election. . . . A further eligibility requirement for minor and new party candidates is that the candidate's name must appear on the ballot, or electors pledged to the candidate must be on the ballot, in at least 10 States. . . .

Chapter 96 establishes a third account in the Fund, the Presidential Primary Matching Payment Account. . . . This funding is intended to aid campaigns by candidates seeking Presidential nomination "by a political party," . . . in "primary elections," . . .

The threshold eligibility requirement is that the candidate raise at least $5,000 in each of 20 States, counting only the first $250 from each person contributing to the candidate.... In addition, the candidate must agree to abide by the spending limits in § 9035.... Funding is provided according to a matching formula: each qualified candidate is entitled to a sum equal to the total private contributions received, disregarding contributions from any person to the extent that total contributions to the candidate by that person exceed $250.... Payments to any candidate under Chapter 96 may not exceed 50% of the over-all expenditure ceiling accepted by the candidate....

B. Constitutionality of Subtitle H

Appellants argue that Subtitle H is invalid (1) as "contrary to the 'general welfare,'" Art. I, § 8, (2) because any scheme of public financing of election campaigns is inconsistent with the First Amendment, and (3) because Subtitle H invidiously discriminates against certain interests in violation of the Due Process Clause of the Fifth Amendment. We find no merit in these contentions.

Appellants' "general welfare" contention erroneously treats the General Welfare Clause as a limitation upon congressional power. It is rather a grant of power, the scope of which is quite expansive, particularly in view of the enlargement of power by the Necessary and Proper Clause. *M'Culloch* v. *Maryland,* 4 Wheat. 316, 420 (1819). Congress has power to regulate Presidential elections and primaries, *United States* v. *Classic* (1941); *Burroughs* v. *United States* (1934); and public financing of Presidential elections as a means to reform the electoral process was clearly a choice within the granted power. It is for Congress to decide which expenditures will promote the general welfare:

[T]he power of Congress to authorize expenditure of public moneys for public purposes is not limited by the direct grants of legislative power found in the Constitution.

United States v. *Butler* (1936). See *Helvering* v. *Davis* (1937). Any limitations upon the exercise of that granted power must be found elsewhere in the Constitution. In this case, Congress was legislating for the "general welfare"—to reduce the deleterious influence of large contributions on our political process, to facilitate communication by candidates with the electorate, and to free candidates from the rigors of fundraising.... Whether the chosen means appear "bad," "unwise," or "unworkable" to us is irrelevant; Congress has concluded that the means are "necessary and proper" to promote the general welfare, and we thus decline to find this legislation without the grant of power in Art. I, § 8.

Appellants' challenge to the dollar check-off provision (§ 6096) fails for the same reason. They maintain that Congress is required to permit taxpayers to designate particular candidates or parties as recipients of their money. But the appropriation to the Fund in § 9006 is like any other appropriation from the general revenue except that its amount is determined by reference to the aggregate of the one- and two-dollar authorization on taxpayers' income tax returns. This detail does not constitute the appropriation any less an appropriation by Congress. The fallacy of appellants' argument is therefore apparent; every appropriation made by Congress uses public money in a manner to which some taxpayers object. Appellants next argue that, "by analogy" to the Religion Clauses of the First Amendment, public financing of election campaigns, however meritorious, violates the First Amendment. We have, of course, held that the Religion Clauses—"Congress shall make no law respecting an establishment of religion, or prohibiting the free exercise thereof"—require Congress, and the States through the Fourteenth Amendment, to remain neutral in matters of religion. E.g., *Abington School Dist.* v. *Schempp* (1963). The government may not aid one religion to the detriment of others or impose a burden on one religion that is not imposed on others, and may not even aid all religions. E.g., *Everson* v. *Board of Education* (1947). See Kurland, Of Church and State and the Supreme Court, 29 *U.Chi.L.Rev.* 1, 96 (1961). But the analogy is patently inapplicable to our issue here. Although "Congress shall make no law ... abridging the freedom of speech, or of the press," Subtitle H is a congressional effort not to abridge, restrict, or censor speech, but rather to use public money to facilitate and enlarge public discussion and participation in the electoral process, goals vital to a self-governing people. Thus, Subtitle H furthers, not abridges, pertinent First Amendment values. Appellants argue, however, that as constructed public financing invidiously discriminates in violation of the Fifth Amendment. We turn therefore to that argument.

Equal protection analysis in the Fifth Amendment area is the same as that under the Fourteenth Amendment. *Weinberger* v. *Wiesenfeld* (1975), and cases cited. In several situations concerning the electoral process, the principle has been developed that restrictions on access to the electoral process must survive exacting scrutiny. The restriction can be sustained only if it furthers a "vial" governmental interest, *American Party of Texas* v. *White* (1974), that is achieved by a means that does not unfairly or unnecessarily burden either a minority party's or an individual candidate's equally important interest in the continued availability of political opportunity.

Lubin v. *Panish* (1974). See *American Party of Texas* v. *White*, supra, at 780; *Storer* v. *Brown* (1974). These cases, however, dealt primarily with state laws requiring a candidate to satisfy certain requirements in order to have his name appear on the ballot. These were, of course, direct burdens not only on the candidate's ability to run for office, but also on the voter's ability to voice preferences regarding representative government and contemporary issues. In contrast, the denial of public financing to some Presidential candidates is not restrictive of voters' rights and less restrictive of candidates'. Subtitle H does not prevent any candidate from getting on the ballot or any voter from casting a vote for the candidate of his choice; the inability, if any, of minor party candidates to wage effective campaigns will derive not from lack of public funding but from their inability to raise private contributions. Any disadvantage suffered by operation of the eligibility formulae under Subtitle

H is thus limited to the claimed denial of the enhancement of opportunity to communicate with the electorate that the formulae afford eligible candidates. But eligible candidates suffer a countervailing denial. As we more fully develop later, acceptance of public financing entails voluntary acceptance of an expenditure ceiling. Noneligible candidates are not subject to that limitation. Accordingly, we conclude that public financing is generally less restrictive of access to the electoral process than the ballot-access regulations dealt with in prior cases. In any event, Congress enacted Subtitle H in furtherance of sufficiently important governmental interests and has not unfairly or unnecessarily burdened the political opportunity of any party or candidate.

It cannot be gainsaid that public financing as a means of eliminating the improper influence of large private contributions furthers a significant governmental interest.... In addition, the limits on contributions necessarily increase the burden of fundraising, and Congress properly regarded public financing as an appropriate means of relieving major party Presidential candidates from the rigors of soliciting private contributions.... The States have also been held to have important interests in limiting places on the ballot to those candidates who demonstrate substantial popular support. E.g., *Storer* v. *Brown,* supra at 736; *Lubin* v. *Panish,* supra at 718-719; *Jenness* v. *Fortson* (1971); *Williams* v. *Rhodes.* Congress' interest in not funding hopeless candidacies with large sums of public money, S. Rep. No. 93–689, supra at 7, necessarily justifies the withholding of public assistance from candidates without significant public support. Thus, Congress may legitimately require "some preliminary showing of a significant modicum of support," *Jenness* v. *Fortson,* supra at 442, as an eligibility requirement for public funds. This requirement also serves the important public interest against providing artificial incentives to "splintered parties and unrestrained factionalism." *Storer* v. *Brown,* supra at 736; S. Rep. No. 93–689, supra at 8; H.R. Rep. No. 93–1239, p. 13 (1974). Cf. *Bullock* v. *Carter* (1972).

At the same time Congress recognized the constitutional restraints against inhibition of the present opportunity of minor parties to become major political entities if they obtain widespread support. S. Rep. No. 93–689, supra at 8–10; H.R. Rep. No. 93–1239, supra, at 13. As the Court of Appeals said, provisions for public funding of Presidential campaigns . . . could operate to give an unfair advantage to established parties, thus reducing, to the nation's detriment . . . the "potential fluidity of American political life." . . .

1. General Election Campaign Financing

Appellants insist that Chapter 95 falls short of the constitutional requirement in that its provisions supply larger, and equal, sums to candidates of major parties, use prior vote levels as the sole criterion for pre-election funding, limit new party candidates to post-election funds, and deny any funds to candidates of parties receiving less than 5% of the vote. These provisions, it is argued, are fatal to the validity of the scheme, because they work invidious discrimination against minor and new parties in violation of the Fifth Amendment. We disagree.

As conceded by appellants, the Constitution does not require Congress to treat all declared candidates the same for public financing purposes. As we said in *Jenness* v. *Fortson,* there are obvious differences in kind between the needs and potentials of a political party with historically established broad support, on the one hand, and a new or small political organization on the other.... Sometimes the grossest discrimination can lie in treating things that are different as though they were exactly alike, a truism well illustrated in *Williams* v. *Rhodes.* Since the Presidential elections of 1856 and 1860, when the Whigs were replaced as a major party by the Republicans, no third party has posed a credible threat to the two major parties in Presidential elections. Third parties have been completely incapable of matching the major parties' ability to raise money and win elections. Congress was, of course, aware of this fact of American life, and thus was justified in providing both major parties full funding and all other parties only a percentage of the major party entitlement. Identical treatment of all parties, on the other hand, "would not only make it easy to raid the United States Treasury, it would also artificially foster the proliferation of splinter parties."... The Constitution does not require the Government to "finance the efforts of every nascent political group," *American Party of Texas* v. *White,* merely because Congress chose to finance the efforts of the major parties.

Furthermore, appellants have made no showing that the election funding plan disadvantages nonmajor parties by operating to reduce their strength below that attained without any public financing. First, such parties are free to raise money from private sources, and, by our holding today, new parties are freed from any expenditure limits, although admittedly those limits may be a largely academic matter to them. But since any major party candidate accepting public financing of a campaign voluntarily assents to a spending ceiling, other candidates will be able to spend more in relation to the major party candidates. The relative position of minor parties that do qualify to receive some public funds because they received 5% of the vote in the previous Presidential election is also enhanced. Public funding for candidates of major parties is intended as a substitute for private contributions; but for minor party candidates such assistance may be viewed as a supplement to private contributions since these candidates may continue to solicit private funds up to the applicable spending limit. Thus, we conclude that the general election funding system does not work an invidious discrimination against candidates of nonmajor parties.

Appellants challenge reliance on the vote in past elections as the basis for determining eligibility. That challenge is foreclosed, however, by our holding in *Jenness* v. *Fortson,* that popular vote totals in the last election are a proper measure of public support. And Congress was not obliged to select instead from among appellants' suggested alternatives. Congress could properly regard the means chosen as preferable, since the alternative of petition drives presents cost and administrative problems in validating signatures, and the alternative of opinion polls might be thought inappropriate, since it would involve a Government agency in the business of certifying polls or conducting its own investigation of support for various candidates, in addition to serious problems with reliability.

Appellants next argue, relying on the ballot access decisions of this Court, that the absence of any alternative means of obtaining pre-election funding renders the scheme unjustifiably restrictive of minority political interests. Appellants' reliance on the ballot access decisions is misplaced. To be sure, the regulation sustained in *Jenness* v. *Fortson,* for example, incorporated alternative means of qualifying for the ballot, and the lack of an alternative was a defect in the scheme struck down in *Lubin* v. *Panish.* To suggest, however, that the constitutionality of Subtitle H therefore hinges solely on whether some alternative is afforded overlooks the rationale of the operative constitutional principles. Our decisions finding a need for an alternative means turn on the nature and extent of the burden imposed in the absence of available alternatives. We have earlier stated our view that Chapter 95 is far less burdensome upon and restrictive of constitutional rights than the regulations involved in the ballot access cases. . . . Moreover, expenditure limits for major parties and candidates may well improve the chances of nonmajor parties and their candidates to receive funds and increase their spending. Any risk of harm to minority interests is speculative due to our present lack of knowledge of the practical effects of public financing and cannot overcome the force of the governmental interests against use of public money to foster frivolous candidacies, create a system of splintered parties, and encourage unrestrained factionalism.

Appellants' reliance on the alternative means analyses of the ballot access cases generally fails to recognize a significant distinction from the instant case. The primary goal of all candidates is to carry on a successful campaign by communicating to the voters persuasive reasons for electing them. In some of the ballot access cases, the States afforded candidates alternative means for qualifying for the ballot, a step in any campaign that, with rare exceptions, is essential to successful effort. Chapter 95 concededly provides only one method of obtaining pre-election financing; such funding is, however, not as necessary as being on the ballot. . . . Plainly, campaigns can be successfully carried out by means other than public financing; they have been up to this date, and this avenue is still open to all candidates. And, after all, the important achievements of minority political groups in furthering the development of American democracy were accomplished without the help of public funds. Thus, the limited participation or nonparticipation of nonmajor parties or candidates in public funding does not unconstitutionally disadvantage them.

Of course, nonmajor parties and their candidates may qualify for post-election participation in public funding and in that sense the claimed discrimination is not total. Appellants contend, however that the benefit of any such participation is illusory due to § 9004(c), which bars the use of the money for any purpose other than paying campaign expenses or repaying loans that had been used to defray such expenses. The only meaningful use for post-election funds is thus to repay loans; but loans, except from national banks, are "contributions" subject to the general limitations on contributions, 18 U.S.C. § 591(e) (1970 ed., Supp. IV). Further, they argue, loans are not readily available to nonmajor parties or candidates before elections to finance their campaigns. Availability of post-election funds therefore assertedly gives them nothing. But, in the nature of things, the willingness of lenders to make loans will depend upon the pre-election probability that the candidate and his party will attract 5% or more of the voters. When a reasonable prospect of such support appears, the party and candidate may be an acceptable loan risk, since the prospect of post-election participation in public funding will be good.

Finally, appellants challenge the validity of the 5% threshold requirement for general election funding. They argue that, since most state regulations governing ballot access have threshold requirements well below 5%, and because, in their view, the 5% requirement here is actually stricter than that upheld in *Jenness* v. *Fortson* (1971), the requirement is unreasonable. We have already concluded that the restriction under Chapter 95 is generally less burdensome than ballot access regulations. Further, the Georgia provision sustained in *Jenness* required the candidate to obtain the signatures of 70% of all eligible voters, without regard to party. To be sure, the public funding formula does not permit anyone who voted for another party in the last election to be part of a candidate's 5%. But, under Chapter 95, a Presidential candidate needs only 5% or more of the actual vote, not the larger universe of eligible voters. As a result, we cannot say that Chapter 95 is numerically more, or less, restrictive than the regulation in *Jenness.* In any event, the choice of the percentage requirement that best accommodates the competing interests involved was for Congress to make. . . . Without any doubt, a range of formulations would sufficiently protect the public fisc and not foster factionalism, and would also recognize the public interest in the fluidity of our political affairs. We cannot say that Congress' choice falls without the permissible range.

2. Nominating Convention Financing

The foregoing analysis and reasoning sustaining general election funding apply in large part to convention funding under Chapter 95 and suffice to support our rejection of appellants' challenge to these provisions. Funding of party conventions has increasingly been derived from large private contributions, see H.R. Rep. No. 93–1239, p. 14 (1974), and the governmental interest in eliminating this reliance is as vital as in the case of private contributions to individual candidates. The expenditure limitations on major parties participating in public financing enhance the ability of nonmajor parties to increase their spending relative to the major parties; further, in soliciting private contributions to finance conventions, parties are not subject to the $1,000 contribution limit pertaining to candidates. We therefore conclude that appellants' constitutional challenge to the provisions for funding nominating conventions must also be rejected.

3. Primary Election Campaign Financing

Appellants' final challenge is to the constitutionality of Chapter 96, which provides funding of primary campaigns. They contend that these provisions are constitutionally invalid (1) because they do not provide funds for candidates not running in party primaries and (2) because the eligibility formula actually increases the influence of money on the electoral process. In not providing assistance to candidates who do not enter party primaries, Congress has merely chosen to limit at this time the reach of the reforms encompassed in Chapter 96. This Congress could do without constituting the reforms a constitutionally invidious discrimination. . . .

We also reject as without merit appellants' argument that the matching formula favors wealthy voters and candidates. The thrust of the legislation is to reduce financial barriers and to enhance the importance of smaller contributions. Some candidates undoubtedly could raise large sums of money, and thus have little need for public funds, but candidates with lesser fundraising capabilities will gain substantial benefits from matching funds. In addition, one eligibility requirement for matching funds is acceptance of an expenditure ceiling, and candidates with little fundraising ability will be able to increase their spending relative to candidates capable of raising large amounts in private funds.

For the reasons stated, we reject appellants' claims that Subtitle H is facially unconstitutional.

C. Severability

The only remaining issue is whether our holdings invalidating 18 U.S.C. §§ 608(a), 608(c), and 608(e)(1) require the conclusion that Subtitle H is unconstitutional. There is, of course, a relationship between the spending limits in § 608(c) and the public financing provisions; the expenditure limits accepted by a candidate to be eligible for public funding are identical to the limits in § 608(c). But we have no difficulty in concluding that Subtitle H is severable.

Unless it is evident that the Legislature would not have enacted those provisions which are within its power, independently of that which is not, the invalid part may be dropped if what is left is fully operative as a law.

Champlin Refining Co. v. *Corporation Commission* (1932). Our discussion of "what is left" leaves no doubt that the value of public financing is not dependent on the existence of a generally applicable expenditure limit. We therefore hold Subtitle H severable from those portions of the legislation today held constitutionally infirm.

IV. THE FEDERAL ELECTION COMMISSION

The 1974 amendments to the Act create an eight-member Federal Election Commission (Commission) and vest in it primary and substantial responsibility for administering and enforcing the Act. The question that we address in this portion of the opinion is whether, in view of the manner in which a majority of its members are appointed, the Commission may, under the Constitution, exercise the powers conferred upon it. We find it unnecessary to parse the complex statutory provisions in order to sketch the full sweep of the Commission's authority. It will suffice for present purposes to describe what appear to be representative examples of its various powers.

Chapter 14 of Title 2 makes the Commission the principal repository of the numerous reports and statements which are required by that chapter to be filed by those engaging in the regulated political activities. Its duties under § 438(a) with respect to these reports and statements include filing and indexing, making them available for public inspection, preservation, and auditing and field investigations. It is directed to "serve as a national clearinghouse for information in respect to the administration of elections." . . .

Beyond these recordkeeping, disclosure, and investigative functions, however, the Commission is given extensive rule-making and adjudicative powers. . . .

The Commission's enforcement power is both direct and wide-ranging. It may institute a civil action for (i) injunctive or other relief against "any acts or practices which constitute or will constitute a violation of this Act," . . . (ii) declaratory or injunctive relief "as may be appropriate to implement or con[s]true any provisions" of Chapter 95 of Title 26, governing administration of funds for Presidential election campaigns and national party conventions . . . and (iii) "such injunctive relief as is appropriate to implement any provision" of Chapter 96 of Title 26, governing the payment of matching funds for Presidential primary campaigns. . . . If, after the Commission's post-disbursement audit of candidates receiving payments under Chapter 95 or 96, it finds an overpayment, it is empowered to seek repayment of all funds due the Secretary of the Treasury. . . . In no respect do the foregoing civil actions require the concurrence of or participation by the Attorney General; conversely, the decision not to seek judicial relief in the above respects would appear to rest solely with the Commission. With respect to the referenced Title 18 sections, provides that, if, after notice and opportunity for a hearing before it, the Commission finds an actual or threatened criminal violation, the Attorney General, "upon request by the Commission . . , shall institute a civil action for relief." Finally, as "[a]dditional enforcement authority," § 456(a) authorizes the Commission, after notice and opportunity for hearing, to make "a finding that a person . . . while a candidate for Federal office, failed to file" a required report of contributions or expenditures. If that finding is made within the applicable limitations period for prosecutions, the candidate is thereby disqualified from becoming a candidate in any future election for Federal office for a period of time beginning on the date of such finding and ending one year after the expiration of the term of the Federal office for which such person was a candidate.

The body in which this authority is reposed consists of eight members. The Secretary of the Senate and the Clerk of the

House of Representatives are ex officio members of the Commission without the right to vote. Two members are appointed by the President pro tempore of the Senate "upon the recommendations of the majority leader of the Senate and the minority leader of the Senate." Two more are to be appointed by the Speaker of the House of Representatives, likewise upon the recommendations of its respective majority and minority leaders. The remaining two members are appointed by the President. Each of the six voting members of the Commission must be confirmed by the majority of both Houses of Congress, and each of the three appointing authorities is forbidden to choose both of their appointees from the same political party.

A. Ripeness

Appellants argue that given the Commission's extensive powers the method of choosing its members under § 437c(a)(1) runs afoul of the separation of powers embedded in the Constitution, and urge that, as presently constituted, the Commission's "existence be held unconstitutional by this Court." Before embarking on this or any related inquiry, however, we must decide whether these issues are properly before us. Because of the Court of Appeals' emphasis on lack of "ripeness" of the issue relating to the method of appointment of the members of the Commission, we find it necessary to focus particularly on that consideration in this section of our opinion.

We have recently recognized the distinction between jurisdictional limitations imposed by Art. III and "[p]roblems of prematurity and abstractness" that may prevent adjudication in all but the exceptional case. *Socialist Labor Party* v. *Gilligan* (1972). In *Regional Rail Reorganization Act Cases* (1974), we stated that "ripeness is peculiarly a question of timing," and therefore the passage of months between the time of the decision of the Court of Appeals and our present ruling is, of itself, significant. We likewise observed in the *Reorganization Act Cases*:

Thus, occurrence of the conveyance allegedly violative of Fifth Amendment rights is in no way hypothetical or speculative. Where the inevitability of the operation of a statute against certain individuals is patent, it is irrelevant to the existence of a justiciable controversy that there will be a time delay before the disputed provisions will come into effect.

The Court of Appeals held that of the five specific certified questions directed at the Commission's authority, only its powers to render advisory opinions and to authorize excessive convention expenditures were ripe for adjudication. The court held that the remaining aspects of the Commission's authority could not be adjudicated, because, "[in] its present stance, this litigation does not present the court with the concrete facts that are necessary to an informed decision." . . .

Since the entry of judgment by the Court of Appeals, the Commission has undertaken to issue rules and regulations under the authority of § 438(a)(10). While many of its other functions remain as yet unexercised, the date of their all but certain exercise is now closer by several months than it was at the time the Court of Appeals ruled. Congress was understandably most concerned with obtaining a final adjudication of as many issues as possible litigated pursuant to the provisions of § 437h. Thus, in order to decide the basic question whether the Act's provision for appointment of the members of the Commission violates the Constitution, we believe we are warranted in considering all of those aspects of the Commission's authority which have been presented by the certified questions.

Party litigants with sufficient concrete interests at stake may have standing to raise constitutional questions of separation of powers with respect to an agency designated to adjudicate their rights. *Palmore* v. *United States* (1973); *Glidden Co.* v. *Zdanok* (1962); *Coleman* v. *Miller*. In *Glidden*, of course, the challenged adjudication had already taken place, whereas in this case appellants' claim is of impending future rulings and determinations by the Commission. But this is a question of ripeness, rather than lack of case or controversy under Art. III, and, for the reasons to which we have previously adverted we hold that appellants' claims as they bear upon the method of appointment of the Commission's members may be presently adjudicated.

B. The Merits

Appellants urge that, since Congress has given the Commission wide-ranging rulemaking and enforcement powers with respect to the substantive provisions of the Act, Congress is precluded under the principle of separation of powers from vesting in itself the authority to appoint those who will exercise such authority. Their argument is based on the language of Art. II, § 2, cl. 2, of the Constitution, which provides in pertinent part as follows:

[The President] shall nominate, and by and with the Advice and Consent of the Senate, shall appoint . . . all other Officers of the United States, whose Appointments are not herein otherwise provided for, and which shall be established by Law: but the Congress may by Law vest the Appointment of such inferior Officers, as they think proper, in the President alone, in the Courts of Law, or in the Heads of Departments.

Appellants' argument is that this provision is the exclusive method by which those charged with executing the laws of the United States may be chosen. Congress, they assert, cannot have it both ways. If the Legislature wishes the Commission to exercise all of the conferred powers, then its members are, in fact, "Officers of the United States," and must be appointed under the Appointments Clause. But if Congress insists upon retaining the power to appoint, then the members of the Commission may not discharge those many functions of the Commission which can be performed only by "Officers of the United States," as that term must be construed within the doctrine of separation of powers.

Appellee Commission and *amici* in support of the Commission urge that the Framers of the Constitution, while mindful of the need for checks and balances among the three branches of the National Government, had no intention of denying to the Legislative Branch authority to appoint its own officers. Congress, either under the Appointments Clause or under its grants of substantive legislative authority and the Necessary and

Proper Clause in Art. I, is, in their view, empowered to provide for the appointment to the Commission in the manner which it did because the Commission is performing "appropriate legislative functions.". . .

1. Separation of Powers

. . . Our inquiry, of necessity, touches upon the fundamental principles of the Government established by the Framers of the Constitution, and all litigants and all of the courts which have addressed themselves to the matter start on common ground in the recognition of the intent of the Framers that the powers of the three great branches of the National Government be largely separate from one another.

James Madison, writing in the Federalist No. 47, defended the work of the Framers against the charge that these three governmental powers were not *entirely* separate from one another in the proposed Constitution. He asserted that, while there was some admixture, the Constitution was nonetheless true to Montesquieu's well known maxim that the legislative, executive, and judicial departments ought to be separate and distinct.

The reasons on which Montesquieu grounds his maxim are a further demonstration of his meaning. "When the legislative and executive powers are united in the same person or body," says he, there can be no liberty, because apprehensions may arise lest the same monarch or senate should enact tyrannical laws to execute them in a tyrannical manner. . . .

Yet it is also clear from the provisions of the Constitution itself, and from the Federalist Papers, that the Constitution by no means contemplates total separation of each of these three essential branches of Government. The President is a participant in the lawmaking process by virtue of his authority to veto bills enacted by Congress. The Senate is a participant in the appointive process by virtue of its authority to refuse to confirm persons nominated to office by the President. The men who met in Philadelphia in the summer of 1787 were practical statesmen, experienced in politics, who viewed the principle of separation of powers as a vital check against tyranny. But they likewise saw that a hermetic sealing off of the three branches of Government from one another would preclude the establishment of a Nation capable of governing itself effectively.

Mr. Chief Justice Taft, writing for the Court in *Hampton & Co.* v. *United States* (1928), after stating the general principle of separation of powers found in the United States Constitution, went on to observe:

[T]he rule is that, in the actual administration of the government, Congress or the Legislature should exercise the legislative power, the President or the State executive, the Governor, the executive power, and the Courts or the judiciary the judicial power, and in carrying out that constitutional division into three branches, it is a breach of the National fundamental law if Congress gives up its legislative power and transfers it to the President, or to the Judicial branch, or if, by law, it attempts to invest itself or its members with either executive power or judicial power. This is not to say that the three branches are not coordinate parts of one government, and that each, in the field of its duties, may not invoke the action of the two other branches insofar as the action in-

voked shall not be an assumption of the constitutional field of action of another branch. In determining what it may do in seeking assistance from another branch, the extent and character of that assistance must be fixed according to common sense and the inherent necessities of the governmental coordination.

More recently, Mr. Justice Jackson, concurring in the opinion and the judgment of the Court in *Youngstown Sheet & Tube Co.* v. *Sawyer* (1952), succinctly characterized this understanding:

While the Constitution diffuses power the better to secure liberty, it also contemplates that practice will integrate the dispersed powers into a workable government. It enjoins upon its branches separateness but interdependence, autonomy but reciprocity.

The Framers regarded the checks and balances that they had built into the tripartite Federal Government as a self-executing safeguard against the encroachment or aggrandizement of one branch at the expense of the other. . . .

2. The Appointments Clause

The principle of separation of powers was not simply an abstract generalization in the minds of the Framers: it was woven into the document that they drafted in Philadelphia in the summer of 1787. Article I, § 1, declares: "All legislative Powers herein granted shall be vested in a Congress of the United States." Article II, § 1, vests the executive power "in a President of the United States of America," and Art. III, § 1, declares that "the judicial Power of the United States, shall be vested in one supreme Court, and in such inferior Courts as the Congress may from time to time ordain and establish."

The further concern of the Framers of the Constitution with maintenance of the separation of powers is found in the so-called "Ineligibility" and "Incompatibility" Clauses contained in Art. I, § 6:

No Senator or Representative shall, during the Time for which he was elected, be appointed to any civil Office under the Authority of the United States, which shall have been created, or the Emoluments whereof shall have been increased during such time; and no Person holding any Office under the United States, shall be a Member of either House during his Continuance in Office.

It is in the context of these cognate provisions of the document that we must examine the language of Art. II. § 2, cl. 2, which appellants contend provides the only authorization for appointment of those to whom substantial executive or administrative authority is given by statute. Because of the importance of its language, we again set out the provision:

[The President] shall nominate, and by and with the Advice and Consent of the Senate, shall appoint Ambassadors, other public Ministers and Consuls, Judges of the supreme Court, and all other Officers of the United States whose Appointments are not herein otherwise provided for, and which shall be established by Law: but the Congress may by Law vest the Appointment of such inferior Officers as they think proper in the President alone, in the Courts of Law, or in the Heads of Departments.

. . . We think that the term "Officers of the United States," as used in Art. II, defined to include "all persons who can be said to hold an office under the government" in *United States* v. *Ger-*

maine, supra, is a term intended to have substantive meaning. We think its fair import is that any appointee exercising significant authority pursuant to the laws of the United States is an "Officer of the United States," and must, therefore, be appointed in the manner prescribed by § 2, cl. 2, of that Article.

If "all persons who can be said to hold an office under the government about to be established under the Constitution were intended to be included within one or the other of these modes of appointment," *United States* v. *Germaine,* supra, it is difficult to see how the members of the Commission may escape inclusion. If a postmaster first class, *Myers* v. *United States* (1926), and the clerk of a district court, *Ex parte Hennen,* 13 Pet. 230 (1839), are inferior officers of the United States within the meaning of the Appointments Clause, as they are, surely the Commissioners before us are, at the very least, such "inferior Officers" within the meaning of that Clause.

Although two members of the Commission are initially selected by the President, his nominations are subject to confirmation not merely by the Senate, but by the House of Representatives as well. The remaining four voting members of the Commission are appointed by the President pro tempore of the Senate and by the Speaker of the House. While the second part of the Clause authorizes Congress to vest the appointment of the officers described in that part in "the Courts of Law, or in the Heads of Departments," neither the Speaker of the House nor the President pro tempore of the Senate comes within this language.

The phrase "Heads of Departments," used as it is in conjunction with the phrase "Courts of Law," suggests that the Departments referred to are themselves in the Executive Branch or at least have some connection with that branch. While the Clause expressly authorizes Congress to vest the appointment of certain officers in the "Courts of Law," the absence of similar language to include Congress must mean that neither Congress nor its officers were included within the language "Heads of Departments" in this part of cl. 2.

Thus, with respect to four of the six voting members of the Commission, neither the President, the head of any department, nor the Judiciary has any voice in their selection.

The Appointments Clause specifies the method of appointment only for "Officers of the United States" whose appointment is not "otherwise provided for" in the Constitution. But there is no provision of the Constitution remotely providing any alternative means for the selection of the members of the Commission or for anybody like them. Appellee Commission has argued, and the Court of Appeals agreed, that the Appointments Clause of Art. II should not be read to exclude the "inherent power of Congress" to appoint its own officers to perform functions necessary to that body as an institution. But there is no need to read the Appointments Clause contrary to its plain language in order to reach the result sought by the Court of Appeals. Article I, § 3, cl. 5, expressly authorizes the selection of the President pro tempore of the Senate, and § 2, cl. 5, of that Article provides for the selection of the Speaker of the House.

Ranking nonmembers, such as the Clerk of the House of Representatives, are elected under the internal rules of each House, and are designated by statute as "officers of the Congress." There is no occasion for us to decide whether any of these member officers are "Officers of the United States" whose "appointment" is otherwise provided for within the meaning of the Appointments Clause, since, even if they were such officers, their appointees would not be. Contrary to the fears expressed by the majority of the Court of Appeals, nothing in our holding with respect to Art. II, § 2, cl. 2, will deny to Congress "all power to appoint its own inferior officers to carry out appropriate legislative functions."

Appellee Commission and *amici* contend somewhat obliquely that, because the Framers had no intention of relegating Congress to a position below that of the coequal Judicial and Executive Branches of the National Government, the Appointments Clause must somehow be read to include Congress or its officers as among those in whom the appointment power may be vested. But the debates of the Constitutional Convention, and the Federalist Papers, are replete with expressions of fear that the Legislative Branch of the National Government will aggrandize itself at the expense of the other two branches. The debates during the Convention, and the evolution of the draft version of the Constitution, seem to us to lend considerable support to our reading of the language of the Appointments Clause itself.

An interim version of the draft Constitution had vested in the Senate the authority to appoint Ambassadors, public Ministers, and Judges of the Supreme Court, and the language of Art. II as finally adopted is a distinct change in this regard. We believe that it was a deliberate change made by the Framers with the intent to deny Congress any authority itself to appoint those who were "Officers of the United States." The debates on the floor of the Convention reflect at least in part the way the change came about.

On Monday, August 6, 1787, the Committee on Detail to which had been referred the entire draft of the Constitution reported its draft to the Convention, including the following two articles that bear on the question before us:

Article IX, § 1: "The Senate of the United States shall have power . . . to appoint Ambassadors, and Judges of the Supreme Court."

Article X, § 2: "[The President] shall commission all the officers of the United States, and shall appoint officers in all cases not otherwise provided for by this Constitution."

It will be seen from a comparison of these two articles that the appointment of Ambassadors and Judges of the Supreme Court was confided to the Senate, and that the authority to appoint—not merely nominate, but to actually appoint—all other officers was reposed in the President.

During a discussion of a provision in the same draft from the Committee on Detail which provided that the "Treasurer" of the United States should be chosen by both Houses of Congress, Mr. Read moved to strike out that clause, "leaving the appointment of the Treasurer as of other officers to the Executive." Opposition to Read's motion was based not on objection to the principle of executive appointment, but on the particular nature of the office of the "Treasurer."

On Thursday, August 23, the Convention voted to insert after the word "Ambassadors" in the text of draft Art. IX the words "and other public Ministers." Immediately afterwards, the section as amended was referred to the "Committee of Five." The following day, the Convention took up Art. X. Roger Sherman objected to the draft language of § 2 because it conferred too much power on the President, and proposed to insert after the words "not otherwise provided for by this Constitution" the words "or by law." This motion was defeated by a vote of nine States to one. On September 3, the Convention debated the Ineligibility and Incompatibility Clauses which now appear in Art. I, and made the Ineligibility Clause somewhat less stringent.

Meanwhile, on Friday, August 31, a motion had been carried without opposition to refer such parts of the Constitution as had been postponed or not acted upon to a Committee of Eleven. Such reference carried with it both Arts. IX and X. The following week, the Committee of Eleven made its report to the Convention, in which the present language of Art. II, § 2, cl. 2, dealing with the authority of the President to nominate is found, virtually word for word, as § 4 of Art. X. The same Committee also reported a revised article concerning the Legislative Branch to the Convention. The changes are obvious. In the final version, the Senate is shorn of its power to appoint Ambassadors and Judges of the Supreme Court. The President is given not the power to appoint public officers of the United States, but only the right to nominate them, and a provision is inserted by virtue of which Congress may require Senate confirmation of his nominees.

It would seem a fair surmise that a compromise had been made. But no change was made in the concept of the term "Officers of the United States," which, since it had first appeared in Art. X, had been taken by all concerned to embrace all appointed officials exercising responsibility under the public laws of the Nation.

Appellee Commission and *amici* urge that, because of what they conceive to be the extraordinary authority reposed in Congress to regulate elections, this case stands on a different footing than if Congress had exercised its legislative authority in another field. There is, of course, no doubt that Congress has express authority to regulate congressional elections, by virtue of the power conferred in Art. I, § 4. This Court has also held that it has very broad authority to prevent corruption in national Presidential elections. *Burroughs* v. *United States* (1934). But Congress has plenary authority in all areas in which it has substantive legislative jurisdiction, *M'Culloch* v. *Maryland*, 4 Wheat. 316 (1819), so long as the exercise of that authority does not offend some other constitutional restriction. We see no reason to believe that the authority of Congress over federal election practices is of such a wholly different nature from the other grants of authority to Congress that it may be employed in such a manner as to offend well established constitutional restrictions stemming from the separation of powers.

The position that, because Congress has been given explicit and plenary authority to regulate a field of activity, it must therefore have the power to appoint those who are to administer the regulatory statute is both novel and contrary to the language of the Appointments Clause. Unless their selection is elsewhere provided for, all officers of the United States are to be appointed in accordance with the Clause. Principal officers are selected by the President with the advice and consent of the Senate. Inferior officers Congress may allow to be appointed by the President alone, by the heads of departments, or by the Judiciary. No class or type of officer is excluded because of its special functions. The President appoints judicial, as well as executive, officers. Neither has it been disputed—and apparently it is not now disputed—that the Clause controls the appointment of the members of a typical administrative agency even though its functions, as this Court recognized in *Humphrey's Executor* v. *United States* (1935), may be "predominantly quasi-judicial and quasi-legislative," rather than executive. The Court in that case carefully emphasized that, although the members of such agencies were to be independent of the Executive in their day-to-day operations, the Executive was not excluded from selecting them. Appellees argue that the legislative authority conferred upon the Congress in Art. I, § 4, to regulate "the Times, Places and Manner of holding Elections for Senators and Representatives" is augmented by the provision in § 5 that "Each House shall be the Judge of the Elections, Returns and Qualifications of its own Members." Section 5 confers, however, not a general legislative power upon the Congress, but rather a power "judicial in character" upon each House of the Congress. *Barry* v. *United States ex rel. Cunningham* (1929). The power of each House to judge whether one claiming election as Senator or Representative has met the requisite qualifications, *Powell* v. *McCormack* (1969), cannot reasonably be translated into a power granted to the Congress itself to impose substantive qualifications on the right to so hold such office. Whatever power Congress may have to legislate, such qualifications must derive from § 4, rather than § 5, of Art. I.

Appellees also rely on the Twelfth Amendment to the Constitution insofar as the authority of the Commission to regulate practices in connection with the Presidential election is concerned. This Amendment provides that certificates of the votes of the electors be "sealed [and] directed to the President of the Senate," and that the "President of the Senate shall, in the presence of the Senate and House of Representatives, open all the certificates, and the votes shall then be counted." The method by which Congress resolved the celebrated disputed Hayes-Tilden election of 1876, reflected in 19 Stat. 227, supports the conclusion that Congress viewed this Amendment as conferring upon its two Houses the same sort of power "judicial in character," *Barr* v. *United States ex rel. Cunningham*, supra at 613, as was conferred upon each House by Art. I, § 5, with respect to elections of its own members.

We are also told by appellees and *amici* that Congress had good reason for not vesting in a Commission composed wholly of Presidential appointees the authority to administer the Act, since the administration of the Act would undoubtedly have a bearing on any incumbent President's campaign for reelection. While one cannot dispute the basis for this sentiment as a practical matter, it would seem that those who sought to challenge incumbent Congressmen might have equally good reason to fear a Commission which was unduly responsive to members of Congress whom they were seeking to unseat. But such fears, however rational, do not, by themselves, warrant a distortion of the Framers' work.

Appellee Commission and *amici* finally contend, and the majority of the Court of Appeals agreed with them, that, whatever shortcomings the provisions for the appointment of members of the Commission might have under Art. II, Congress had ample authority under the Necessary and Proper Clause of Art. I to effectuate this result. We do not agree. The proper inquiry when considering the Necessary and Proper Clause is not the authority of Congress to create an office or a commission, which is broad indeed, but rather its authority to provide that its own officers may make appointments to such office or commission.

So framed, the claim that Congress may provide for this manner of appointment under the Necessary and Proper Clause of Art. I stands on no better footing than the claim that it may provide for such manner of appointment because of its substantive authority to regulate federal elections. Congress could not, merely because it concluded that such a measure was "necessary and proper" to the discharge of its substantive legislative authority, pass a bill of attainder or ex post facto law contrary to the prohibitions contained in § 9 of Art. I. No more may it vest in itself, or in its officers, the authority to appoint officers of the United States when the Appointments Clause, by clear implication, prohibits it from doing so. . . .

3. The Commission's Powers

Thus, on the assumption that all of the powers granted in the statute may be exercised by an agency whose members have been appointed in accordance with the Appointments Clause, the ultimate question is which, if any, of those powers may be exercised by the present voting Commissioners, none of whom was appointed as provided by that Clause. Our previous description of the statutory provisions . . . disclosed that the Commission's powers fall generally into three categories: functions relating to the flow of necessary information—receipt, dissemination, and investigation; functions with respect to the Commission's task of fleshing out the statute—rulemaking and advisory opinions; and functions necessary to ensure compliance with the statute and rules—informal procedures, administrative determinations and hearings, and civil suits.

Insofar as the powers confided in the Commission are essentially of an investigative and informative nature, falling in the same general category as those powers which Congress might delegate to one of its own committees, there can be no question that the Commission as presently constituted may exercise them. . . .

But when we go beyond this type of authority to the more substantial powers exercised by the Commission, we reach a different result. The Commission's enforcement power, exemplified by its discretionary power to seek judicial relief, is authority that cannot possibly be regarded as merely in aid of the legislative function of Congress. A lawsuit is the ultimate remedy for a breach of the law, and it is to the President, and not to the Congress, that the Constitution entrusts the responsibility to "take Care that the Laws be faithfully executed." Art. II, § 3.

Congress may undoubtedly under the Necessary and Proper Clause create "offices" in the generic sense and provide such method of appointment to those "offices" as it chooses. But Congress' power under that Clause is inevitably bounded by the express language of Art. II, § 2, cl. 2, and, unless the method it provides comports with the latter, the holders of those offices will not be "Officers of the United States." They may, therefore, properly perform duties only in aid of those functions that Congress may carry out by itself, or in an area sufficiently removed from the administration and enforcement of the public law as to permit their being performed by persons not "Officers of the United States."

This Court observed more than a century ago with respect to litigation conducted in the courts of the United States:

Whether tested, therefore, by the requirements of the Judiciary Act, or by the usage of the government, or by the decisions of this court, it is clear that all such suits, so far as the interests of the United States are concerned, are subject to the direction, and within the control of, the Attorney General. . . .

The Court echoed similar sentiments 59 years later in *Springer* v. *Philippine Islands*. . . .

Not having the power of appointment unless expressly granted or incidental to its powers, the legislature cannot engraft executive duties upon a legislative office, since that would be to usurp the power of appointment by indirection, though the case might be different if the additional duties were devolved upon an appointee of the executive.

We hold that these provisions of the Act, vesting in the Commission primary responsibility for conducting civil litigation in the courts of the United States for vindicating public rights, violate Art. II, § 2, cl. 2, of the Constitution. Such functions may be discharged only by persons who are "Officers of the United States" within the language of that section.

All aspects of the Act are brought within the Commission's broad administrative powers: rulemaking, advisory opinions, and determinations of eligibility for funds and even for federal elective office itself. These functions, exercised free from day-to-day supervision of either Congress or the Executive Branch, are more legislative and judicial in nature than are the Commission's enforcement powers, and are of kinds usually performed by independent regulatory agencies or by some department in the Executive Branch under the direction of an Act of Congress. Congress viewed these broad powers as essential to effective and impartial administration of the entire substantive framework of the Act. Yet each of these functions also represents the performance of a significant governmental duty exercised pursuant to a public law. While the President may not insist that such functions be delegated to an appointee of his removable at will, *Humphrey's Executor* v. *United States* (1935), none of them operates merely in aid of congressional authority to legislate or is sufficiently removed from the administration and enforcement of public law to allow it to be performed by the present Commission. These administrative functions may therefore be exercised only by persons who are "Officers of the United States."

It is also our view that the Commission's inability to exercise certain powers because of the method by which its members have been selected should not affect the validity of the Commission's administrative actions and determinations to this date, including its administration of those provisions, upheld today, authorizing the public financing of federal elections. The past acts of the Commission are therefore accorded de facto validity, just as we have recognized should be the case with respect to legislative acts performed by legislators held to have been elected in accordance with an unconstitutional apportionment plan. . . . We also draw on the Court's practice in the apportionment and voting rights cases and stay, for a period not to exceed 30 days, the Court's judgment insofar as it affects the authority of the Commission to exercise the duties and powers granted it under the Act. This limited stay will afford Congress an opportunity to reconstitute the Commission by law or to adopt other

valid enforcement mechanisms without interrupting enforcement of the provisions the Court sustains, allowing the present Commission in the interim to function de facto in accordance with the substantive provisions of the Act. . . .

CONCLUSION

In summary, we sustain the individual contribution limits, the disclosure and reporting provisions, and the public financing scheme. We conclude, however, that the limitations on campaign expenditures, on independent expenditures by individuals and groups, and on expenditures by a candidate from his personal funds are constitutionally infirm. Finally, we hold that most of the powers conferred by the Act upon the Federal Election Commission can be exercised only by "Officers of the United States," appointed in conformity with Art. II, § 2, cl. 2, of the Constitution, and therefore cannot be exercised by the Commission as presently constituted.

In No. 75–436, the judgment of the Court of Appeals is affirmed in part and reversed in part. The judgment of the District Court in No. 75–437 is affirmed. The mandate shall issue forthwith, except that our judgment is stayed, for a period not to exceed 30 days, insofar as it affects the authority of the Commission to exercise the duties and powers granted it under the Act.

So ordered.

424 U.S. 1 (1976).

---

169   The House Investigation of Korean-American Relations (Koreagate)

October 31, 1978

Beginning in the late 1960s as a result of the Adam Clayton Powell case (see document 154) and accelerated by the "long national nightmare" of Watergate (see documents 161 and 165), numerous changes were made in government ethics laws affecting both the legislative and executive branches of government. These changes were designed to foster improved ethical standards in government. Both the House and Senate upgraded the status of their respective ethics committees to the rank of permanent committees.

In 1976 the Washington Post *first reported on an ongoing Justice Department investigation that was billed as "the most sweeping allegations of congressional corruption ever investigated by the federal government." It became known as "Koreagate," a variation of the word* Watergate. *According to the investigation, at least 115 members of the House and Senate supposedly took illegal gifts from agents of the South Korean government, which operated an aggressive influence peddling scheme that spent upwards of a million dollars a year to bribe government officials and journalists. Testimony revealed it to be fairly common practice for South Korean officials to hand members of Congress, or sometimes their spouses, envelopes containing large amounts of money. The blame for this*

illegal activity was placed on Park Chung Hee, president of the Republic of Korea, and several of his key operatives in the United States, most notably Tongsun Park, who fled the country when the scandal broke. He later returned in 1978 to testify.

Both the House and Senate held investigations. Beginning in early 1977, the hearings focused on the activities of South Korean agents in the United States. The House Committee on Standards of Official Conduct (often called the Ethics Committee) laid down ground rules that prohibited the mention of the names of any House members who were implicated in the scandal. Later, as the investigation progressed, the testimony got specific about individual members caught up in the influence-peddling scheme. In his testimony, Tongsun Park implicated three former House members as being the largest recipients of his money, even though his evasive and incomplete answers left most of the investigators wondering about the credibility of his remarks. These three individuals—Otto E. Passman (D-La.), Richard Hanna (D-Calif.), and Cornelius Gallagher (D-N.J.)—each supposedly received hundreds of thousands of dollars in payments, although the charges against these men were eventually dropped. Another group of beneficiaries named in Tong-

sun Park's federal indictment included twenty-five incumbent and former members of Congress, most of whom received cash amounting from a few hundred to a few thousand dollars.

This excerpt from the House investigation reveals a complex pattern of corruption that grew out of South Korean fears that U.S. interest in the Republic of Korea was waning and that something had to be done to bolster U.S. support of South Korean interests. While the investigation pointed to a pattern of corruption and bribery in South Korea involving some officials of the U.S. government, journalists, professors, and executives of U.S. corporations, the House and Senate cleared the vast majority of incumbent members implicated in one way or another in the scandal. Several House members received reprimands, a mild form of official rebuke.

The Senate Select Committee on Ethics concluded their investigation with no recommendation for disciplinary action against any incumbent or former member of the Senate.

. . . .

THE SCANDAL BREAKS

Beginning in the Spring of 1975, there was a series of revelations of questionable activities by the Korean Government which were to have a serious impact on Korean-American relations.

At a May 16 hearing of the Subcommittee on Multinational Corporations of the Senate Foreign Relations Committee, the chairman of Gulf Oil Co. revealed that under Korean Government pressure Gulf had paid the DRP $1 million in 1967 and $3 million in 1971. The Gulf revelations have never been published in Korea, and foreign publications carrying the story were censored.

In early 1975, certain intelligence information which the State Department characterized as implying extralegal attempts by the Korean Government to influence members of Congress and their staff was brought to the attention of Philip Habib, then Assistant Secretary of State for East Asian and Pacific Affairs. Habib immediately showed the information to Secretary of State Kissinger and more detailed information was sought, at the request of the President.

On June 10, at hearings of this subcommittee regarding human rights in South Korea, former Korean diplomat Lee Jai Hyon outlined a plan for ROK influence activities in the United States as it had been explained to him and other embassy staff by the KCIA prior to Lee's defection in 1973. One aspect of the plan outlined by Lee was to "buy off American leaders—particularly in Congress." Lee testified that he personally had seen Ambassador Kim Dong Jo stuffing $100 bills into envelopes prior to visiting Capitol Hill. There was little public reaction to Lee's revelations at that time, but his testimony led the subcommittee to begin an examination of KCIA activities in the United States which in turn culminated in this Investigation of Korean-American Relations.

In late 1975 Assistant Secretary of State Habib received additional intelligence information. Secretary of State Kissinger obtained President Ford's authorization to transmit the informa-

tion received from Habib to the Justice Department. The ensuing investigation had a major impact on Korean-American relations in the succeeding years.

During the fall of 1976, American newspapers printed a number of articles on South Korean influence activities in the United States, specifically investigating Tongsun Park and the Justice Department's investigation. In the midst of this publicity, Tongsun Park left the United States in mid-October. A few days later, on October 26, a front-page article with a banner headline appeared in the Washington Post about the extent of Korean influence-buying in Congress and the central role played by Tongsun Park.

The Park Chung Hee Government, shaken by the publicity, took a series of steps to curtail the influence operations and to limit the inquiries into its activities. On November 9, Yang Doo Won, who, as noted above, had been in charge of many influence operations, was dismissed by President Park. In November 23, the New York Times reported that KCIA officer Kim Sang Keun was being recalled to Seoul. However, Kim requested political asylum in the United States, fearing that he would be held responsible for the publicity over the scandal.

Following the defection of Kim Sang Keun, the ROK Government became concerned that other KCIA officials might defect. In early December, Seoul sent a high-ranking KCIA official to Washington to persuade station chief Kim Yung Hwan to return to Korea; Kim did return. Other persons intimately involved in Korean influence activities also left the United States during this time. For example, in November and December Hahn Kwang Neun of the Hankooli Shinmoon and General Kang Young Research Institute on Korean Affairs both left the United States.

On December 4, President Park ousted the director of the KCIA, Shin Jik Soo, and replaced him with Construction Minister Kim Jae Kyu. Seoul drastically reduced the number of KCIA personnel in the United States. They were ordered to assume a low profile by confining their activities to collection of intelligence from overt sources, or through liaison and to refrain from anything that might be considered coercion, manipulation, or attempts to influence.

The unfolding scandal became a factor complicating the Carter administration's conduct of relations with South Korea. During his campaign for the presidency, Carter made a statement condemning political repression in South Korea and calling for a phased withdrawal of all U.S. ground troops. The scandal in Washington intensified the controversy over Korea in Congress and among the public. By the beginning of 1977, when this Investigation of Korean-American Relations was initiated, all three issues—troop withdrawal, human rights, and the scandal—had become entangled and seemed certain to complicate Korean-American relations for some time to come.

. . . .

Documents Relating to Tongsun Park's Activities

When Federal agents searched Tongsun Park's residence in Washington, they found a number of documents, written in Korean, which appeared to be carefully drawn plans for intelligence and influence operations in the United States. All but one appeared to have been written in 1970. The remaining one, entitled "The U.S. Congressional Delegation's Visit to Korea," was apparently written in 1974. An additional document dated September 30, 1972, was found in Park's house by one of his employees.

Tongsun Park denied having had any part in composing the documents, but one contained notations in what appeared to be his handwriting, and there were many accurate descriptions of his activities. Park suggested that Steve Kim had composed the documents. (Kim was a frequent visitor to Park's house while serving as an aide to KCIA Director Lee Hu Rak and later as KCIA station chief in Mexico City.) Kim Sang Keun, after inspecting the documents in the original Korean, concluded that the author had used the terms, format and writing style of the KCIA.

The document entitled "Plans for Korea's Foreign Policy Toward the United States" contained a detailed section on "Invitation Diplomacy": Inviting Senators, Congressmen, media figures, and other prominent Americans to Korea where they could be persuaded to support Korea's position on foreign aid bills and other issues. The plan recounted in detail the results of past invitations to certain Congressmen and concluded that these efforts had been "almost 100 percent successful." In selecting targets for "Invitation Diplomacy," the plan said:

The main targets are U.S. senators and congressmen who are in the position to help Korea. The invitees shall include members of the academia, financial, and media circles on the basis of their involvement in the issues that may arise between Korea and the U.S.

The plan named individual Congressmen, Senators, journalists, and businessmen who were to receive special attention, including invitations to visit Korea. However, the invitations were not to be made directly by KCIA personnel:

It is recommended that invitations be sent out by the speaker of the Assembly or by the Prime Minister, and by a cabinet minister if otherwise inappropriate.

Under a section entitled "Conduct of Diplomacy through Advancing Interests of Senators and Congressmen," the plan advocated harnessing ROK economic policies to the goal of influencing U.S. foreign policy. Business firms within the district of a particular Congressman or Senator were to receive assistance in investing in Korea. Examples of how a Congressman or Senator had been won over by ROK economic assistance to his district were cited. At one point the plan stated:

We give continuous support to the larger firms which have invested in Korea already (Gulf, Caltex, American Airlines, Fairchild) so that we can win over the members of Congress in whose districts the headquarters of such firms are located.

In one revealing passage the plan noted an additional advantage to encouraging economic relationships in congressional districts:

The commissions derived from buying their products and other business transactions can be used to fund our activities. We will have the cake and eat it too.

The subcommittee found numerous ways in which the Korean Government was able to "have the cake and eat it too." Programs and activities designed to advance ROK interests were funded through outside sources, and various means, thereby saving money for the Korean Government and obscuring the relationship between the activity and the government. Rice commissions, for example, helped finance the George Town Club and other Tongsun Park projects. Through the Korean Cultural and Freedom Foundation and its project Radio of Free Asia, the Korean Government was also able to guide and control pro-Government activities which were being financed, wholly or partly, from U.S. sources.

In the same 1970 plan, $380,000 was requested immediately for contributions to the fall 1970 congressional election campaigns. Future budgetary needs were to be met as follows:

2. How To Raise the Funds:
    (a) The first year (1970): As proposed in the attached paper, $380,000 should be raised in Korea.
    (b) The second year (1971) budget:
        (1) Rice imports (Office of Supply and Ministry of Agriculture and Forestry): $100,000–$130,000.
        (2) Farming equipment imports such as bulldozers (Office of Supply and the Agricultural Promotion Corporation): $200,000–$300,000.
        (3) M-16 weapons (Ministry of Defense): $100,000–$150,000.
        (4) Others: $100,000–$200,000.
            Total: $500,000–$780,000.
    (c) Future budget:
It is recommended that the 70 percent of the net income—gross income minus expenses—generated by the Agency-assisted future business activities be allocated to support activities for diplomacy toward the Untied [sic] States.

The subcommittee was particularly interested in the reference to the need to raise $100,000 to $150,000 through M-16 weapons, since the coproduction agreement between Colt Industries and the Korean Government did not call for any commissions from which such an amount could be siphoned. However, the subcommittee teamed that in March 1971, Mickey Kim, acting for Park Chong Kyu, requested a contribution from Colt, ostensibly for the 1971 election campaign of Park Chung Hee. Colt officials initially agreed and drew a check for $100,000 payable to Mickey Kim, but on the advice of counsel decided against the contribution.

The 1970 plan also contained a section entitled "Diplomacy Through Offered Intelligence." It defined "offered intelligence" as "* * * intelligence obtained from the other side in return for providing accurate intelligence of ours to them in order to achieve specific objectives." The stated objective was to provide the United States with intelligence favorable to Korea, and:

    (a) In our diplomacy toward the United States, the most effective approach is to utilize this type of intelligence, that is, offered intelligence.
    (b) By providing the United States with appropriate intelligence advantageous to Korea, we may effect [sic] them to make judgments favorable to Korea.

In addition to influencing U.S. judgments, the plan envisioned acquiring the capacity to anticipate future U.S. policy:

2. Sensing the United States policymakers' view before policy is formulated.

(a) As explained above, we will be able to approach high officials of the Central Intelligence Agency and Mr. Kissinger by giving our favorable information about Korea in such a way that we will be able to assume a role of a bridge between the two governments.

(b) Through this, the United States side would naturally approach us to sound out feasibility of their policies toward Korea before the policies are firmly formulated.

(c) When this happens, we will be able to obtain United States plans in advance and have a chance to evaluate such plans and take appropriate measures.

In the 1974 document entitled "The United States Congressional Delegation's Visit to Korea," there was extensive analysis of the benefits reaped from past cultivation of Congressmen. The document also reported on a meeting between Tongsun Park and former Vice President Agnew and included the comment:

While vice president, Mr. Agnew personally participated in the U.S. policy formulation toward Korea and attended the National Security Council meetings for four to five years, and, thus, he is knowledgeable of the Korean policy of the U.S. government, in particular of the State Department and the Central Intelligence Agency. He also knows other secret diplomatic issues.

The suggestion was that Tongsun Park would be able to obtain classified information on diplomatic and national security issues by cultivating Mr. Agnew.

Tongsun Park did make business offers to Agnew and other former officials in the Nixon and Ford administrations. Park and Agnew entered into a business relationship in 1974; in 1975 Park hired former White House aide William Timmons as a public relations consultant; and in 1976 Park hired former Attorney General Richard Kleindienst as counsel for his company, Pacific Development, Inc. Park explained his friendships with Congressmen and his overtures to former high-ranking U.S. officials such as Agnew by messing his personal business ambitions, which might be furthered by having influential friends and associates.

There were numerous indications that personal ambition rather than patriotic desire lay behind many of Tongsun Park's plans and activities. It led him to distort and exaggerate the extent of his influence and ability to carry out missions for the ROK Government. Nevertheless, a comparison of the activities and plans described in the documents found in Park's home with another KCIA document and with actual events showed repeated attempts by the KCIA—some successful—to carry out the stated objectives.

Annual KCIA plans

The subcommittee's investigation revealed that by at least the mid-1970's the KCIA had annual written plans for operations in the United States. A copy of one such plan, that for 1976, was obtained by the subcommittee. Also examined was another plan for an earlier year. Both plans envisaged the recruitment of Americans—including Government officials, Members of Congress, journalists, scholars, religious leaders, businessmen, and leaders of citizens' organizations—for the purpose of swaying American public opinion and official policy in favor of the Park Government. Both plans also called for operations to counteract American and Korean critics of the ROK Government.

. . . .

THE JUSTICE DEPARTMENTS BRIBERY INVESTIGATION

In the fall of 1974, Philip Habib became Assistant Secretary of State for East Asian and Pacific Affairs, after having served as Ambassador to the Republic of Korea since 1971. At the time of his return to the State Department, the ROK Government had been expressing deep concern to executive branch officials and Members of Congress and their aides over hearings on human rights in South Korea being held by the Subcommittee on International Organizations and the Subcommittee on Asian and Pacific Affairs. Shortly thereafter, in December, Congress reduced military assistance to South Korea by $90 million because of the ROK Government's human rights record.

In early February 1975, intelligence information came to the Assistant Secretary's attention concerning KCIA attempts to influence the opinions of key Americans. He showed it to Secretary of State Kissinger, who in 1978 told the subcommittee that the information—

* * * indicated that there might be some attempt not to lobby but to bribe Congressmen. * * * I took it to the President. The President asked me whether the information was conclusive, and I told him it did not seem to be. He asked me to watch it, and when we had further information, to come back to him.

In late October 1975, Habib obtained intelligence information of a more precise nature, which Kissinger then discussed with the President. Although the intelligence community was reluctant to have the information turned over to investigative agencies, the President ordered that it be made available to them. Pursuant to his orders, Assistant Secretary Habib, accompanied by State Department Legal Adviser Monroe Leigh, delivered the information to Acting Attorney General Robert Bork in mid-November.

At the Department of Justice, the Foreign Agents Registration Section was continuing its efforts to determine whether Tongsun Park should be required to register as an agent of the Korean Government. Justice's investigation of Korean bribery and payoffs became full-scale in mid-1976 when the newly created Public Integrity Section took over the investigative files developed by the Registration Section and the intelligence information transmitted by the State Department. As of October 1978, the investigation had resulted in five indictments and two convictions. Tongsun Park was indicted on September 6, 1977, and later was granted immunity from prosecution in return for cooperation with the investigation. Another Korean agent of influence, Hancho Kim, was indicted on September 27, 1977, and convicted on April 8, 1978. Former Congressman Richard

Hanna was indicted on September 6, 1977. After entering a partial plea of guilty, he was sentenced to 6-30 months in prison on April 25, 1978. Former Congressman Otto Passman was indicted on February 6, 1978, and Grover Connell, a rice dealer, was indicted on May 25, 1978. Passman and Connell were still awaiting trial in October 1978.

CONCLUSION

By the end of 1971, agencies of the executive branch had sufficient information to warrant taking steps to alter certain questionable conduct by Korean Government officials and agents. The State Department and the U.S. Embassy in Seoul regarded Tongsun Park as an unregistered Government agent, a nuisance counterproductive to normal government-to-government relations who was offering gifts of cash to Congressmen. Both the Department and the Embassy presumed he was connected with the KCIA. State believed that Radio of Free Asia was controlled by the KCIA and that it was using financial contributions from Americans for unknown purposes, since broadcast facilities apparently were provided free of charge by the Korean Government. Because Radio of Free Asia's sponsors included prominent Americans, the Department was worried about the possibility of a scandal. State had some indication that Kim Kwang, an aide to Congressman Neil Gallagher, was a KCIA agent reporting on the activities of Gallagher's subcommittee. Officials at State also suspected that Suzi Park Thomson, an aide to Speaker Carl Albert, was working for the KCIA.

The FBI had information that convinced its own officials that "criminal activities are strongly indicated," that a KCIA agent working as a Congressman's aide had made a "payoff" to the Congressman; that Tongsun Park had made payments to a Congressman from money received in rice deals; that a Congressman had sought campaign contributions from President Park and had recommended that Tongsun Park not only be put in charge of all lobbying and influence efforts in the United States, but also should be named chief ROK agent for rice purchases from the United States.

No effective action was taken to deal with any of these reported activities. When the State Department asked the Department of Justice to investigate Radio of Free Asia, Tongsun Park, and other Korean matters, Justice and the FBI did no more than interview the head of Radio of Free Asia and run a file check before closing the case. According to Ambassador Porter, the problems caused by Tongsun Park Hai reached "serious dimensions," and he complained to ROK Government leader. However, as Tongsun Park's activities continued undeterred, the problem was not given attention at the top level of the State Department. Officials at State were under the impression that the FBI was investigating Kim Kwang in 1971 when in fact the FBI was not.

With respect to the FBI's information indicating criminal activity, Director J. Edgar Hoover favored instituting a national security intercept in the matter of the alleged bribery of a Congressman by a KCIA agent. The subcommittee found no evidence of the idea being pursued further. Hoover sent the information indicating criminal activity to Attorney General Mitchell and National Security Adviser Kissinger, but with a statement that the "information is extremely sensitive and such as to preclude any investigation whatsoever." Accordingly, neither Mitchell nor Kissinger took action, other than Mitchell's informing Speaker Albert about the report on Albert's aide. According to Albert, the Attorney General and he said that there was no cause to dismiss the aide, Suzi Park Thomson, because she did not have access to classified material.

The failure to share information among executive branch agencies accounts partly for the failure to take effective action regard questionable Korean activities. When the Department of Agriculture queried the appropriate agencies to determine if Tongsun Park was connected with the ROK Government at a time when he was to become a selling agent for rice deals under the Food for Peace program, the reply was in the negative. This was despite the fact that the agencies had information strongly indicating that Tongsun Park was working with the KCIA. When the State Department asked Justice to investigate Radio of Free Asia, Tongsun Park, and other matters in 1971, Justice applied the "third agency" rule and failed to provide the FBI with State's information that Tongsun Park had offered money to Congressmen. Justice, for its own part, did nothing with that information. Donald Ranard, the State Department's Director of Korean Affairs, was cut off from information about KCIA operative Kim Kwang, whose work with Congressman Gallagher's subcommittee could have had a direct bearing on matters of concern to Ranard's office.

Priorities established at the highest level of the U.S. Government resulted in insufficient attention to lower-priority matters by senior officials. Subordinates, responding to the priority concerns of attention to periodic intelligence plans and activities. Since officials at all levels were busy with other matters, a cumulative record was not maintained. A record would have shown a pattern of growing and interrelated activities. Donald Ranard did compile a list of some of the suspicious activities in connection with State's request for an investigation in 1971, but Justice failed to take advantage of the information.

Forceful measures against ROK influence activities would have run counter to the primary concern of U.S. policy toward South Korea in the early 1970's: Participation by Korean forces in the Vietnam war. In addition, there were related Priority concerns: to accomplish the reduction of U.S. troops in Korea with minimum adverse consequences to Korean-American relations; and to maintain credibility for the U.S. position in Korea as a firm commitment to resist the threat of Communist aggression. Preoccupation with these concerns led to a permissive attitude toward questionable Korean activities in the United States.

Ambassador Porter recalled how the situation appeared to him from Seoul:

I sensed a good deal of permissiveness * * * I think there was at least one case referred to Justice * * * and never aimed to happen. The Congress * * * was certainly aware of its contacts, or a lot of contacts with people like Tungston Park * * * I assumed * * * the lack of reaction from Washington where it was all happening right here in our front yard * * * was due to a lack of desire to make things difficult for an ally who was contributing so much to the Vietnam effort.

The State Department, a policy agency with the least amount of information indicating criminal activity, consistently took the most initiative for action against Korean influence activities. The Justice Department, a law enforcement agency with the most information indicating criminal activity, took the least initiative. Prior to 1975, the only decisive action taken was that of the State Department when it requested the recall of KCIA station chief Yang Doo Won in 1973 for harassment of Koreans in the United States. A request by State to Justice for an investigation brought only perfunctory action. After Yang departed the United States, harassment as well as other improper KCIA activities continued. In 1975, the chairman of the Subcommitttee on International Organizations asked Justice to investigate a former Korean diplomat's allegation of a nine-point KCIA plan to buy support in the United States. The Justice Department took no active interest in the matter, so the subcommittee began an inquiry which led to the Investigation of Korean-American Relations.

It was only when concern was elevated to the level of the President and the Secretary of State that Justice undertook a full investigation. Again, the initiative came from the State Department, specifically from Philip Habib, Assistant Secretary for East Asian and Pacific Affairs. As Ambassador to Korea from 1971 to 1974, Habib had become increasingly suspicious about the way Korean officials were attempting to influence Americans. His annoyance over Tongsun Park's activities led to an order that Embassy personnel have nothing to do with Park. Park Chong Kyu's gift of $10,000 to a White House aide was returned and followed with a strong remonstrance from Habib. After he returned to the United States amid heightened Korean influence activities in Congress over a reduction in military assistance and criticism of human rights violation, Habib requested intelligence information. What he received in February 1915 was of a more specific nature than anything he had seen previously, strongly implying attempts to bribe Congressmen. He immediately took the information to Secretary of State Kissinger. In 1971, Kissinger had known of an alleged bribery of a Congressman by the KCIA, but this was the first intelligence he had seen alleging briber of more than one. Kissinger brought the matter to President Ford's attention. Since the information was not conclusive, the President asked for further information. In October, when Habib received intelligence which was much more definite, the President ordered that it be turned over to the Attorney General.

Even after the Korean bribery investigation was well underway, there was continuing reluctance by the Department of Justice to look into questions of improper activities involving the Korean Government. In 1976, Under Secretary of State Habib requested an investigation by Justice to determine whether Rev. Sun Myung Moon, Pak Bo Hi, and several of the organizations associated with Moon, should be required to register under the Foreign Agents Registration Act. Justice refused to investigate, citing the absence of prima facie evidence that the Unification Church is not a bona fide religious organization. The refusal noted also that the 1971 investigation of Radio of Free Asia, requested by State, had concluded with insufficient evidence to establish that Radio of Free Asia was an agent of a foreign principal.

The decision of Justice not to investigate Moon's activities in 1976 was based partly on the results of a pro forma investigation in 1971 when decisions were made not to investigate strong indications of criminal activity by persons involved in the Korean Government's influence campaign. A serious pursuit of those indications could have forestalled the scandal 5 years later. It is significant that in 1975 Assistant Secretary Habib—unaware of the earlier information—acted on information alleging criminal activity which was not more serious than that which was known by the Justice Department in 1971.

RECOMMENDATIONS

In addition to monitoring the activities in the United States of the intelligence services of unfriendly countries, appropriate agencies should monitor more closely the activities of other intelligence services which may present special problems for the United States. Current lists of all foreign intelligence officials assigned to the United States should be maintained. The Justice Department should take steps necessary for the effective enforcement of the Foreign Agents Registration Act, as well as other related statutes such as 50 U.S.C. 851–857. The State Department should be prepared to act firmly whenever activities by foreign intelligence services appear to violate U.S. laws.

To assist the Director of Central Intelligence in transmitting classified information to the Justice Department, there should be created within the Justice Department a mechanism for the routine receipt and appropriate handling of such information.

The Department of Justice and the Federal Bureau of Investigation should be treated as one agency for purposes of the "third agency rule," which prevents a third agency from receiving from a second agency classified information originally obtained from another agency.

If during the normal course of operations the Director of Central Intelligence becomes aware that Members of Congress or members been contacted or designated for contact by persons known to be or suspected of being foreign intelligence agents, such information to the leadership and the Select Committee on Intelligence of the appropriate House of Congress.

Written statements or articles provided to Members of Congress by foreign governments, agents of foreign governments or by Americans acting on their behalf, should be identified as such when placed in the Congressional Record or in the records of congressional hearings.

The State Department should enter into negotiations with the Republic of Korea for a formal extradition treaty with this country.

ADDITIONAL VIEWS BY HON. EDWARD J. DERWINSKI AND HON. WILLIAM F. GOODLING

The Minority had serious doubts about this investigation when it was first proposed in 1977. The questionable activities carried out by South Korea in the United States—which were the inspiration for the investigation—had for the most part ceased, as this report documents, by the time the inquiry got underway in April 1977 believed in the beginning that there were several other serious problems to which the Subcommittee could have turned its energies rather than to add to its burdens an investigation already being carried out, or contemplated, by the House and Senate ethics committees, as well as by the several agencies of the Executive Branch.

Nevertheless, once the investigation started, the Minority Members gave it full cooperation. It was our aim, among other things, to help provide objectivity and perspective to the investigation itself and to the final report. We believe we have made a positive contribution in this regard.

This report describes in detail the nature and extent of South Korea's actions. It provides valuable insights into questions often treated superficially by the media and sheds light on some heretofore unexamined areas. The report thereby contributes to a clearer understanding of a complex Korean-American relationship—a comprehension of which has often been absent or simply obscured by rhetoric.

All this notwithstanding, the Members of the Minority have believed that, from the start, the scope of the investigation was far too broad; indeed, the Subcommittee's mandate itself encompassed too much. Thus, a highly diligent staff attempted to accomplish more than the time and resources could allow. Qualified and dedicated, the staff members labored extremely hard throughout the investigative stage, and their efforts to produce a detailed and comprehensive final report were exceptional.

By the same token, the volume of information acquired in the course of the inquiry was so great that the members of the Subcommittee obviously could not familiarize themselves with it all. Having worked long and diligently with the Chairman of this of the Majority have signed this report in the same spirit of cooperation which him characterized our collaboration throughout the investigation. Our signatures, however, are not an imprimatur for all the complex details uncovered, or all the conclusions and recommendations arrived at, by the large and industrious staff.

There were, moreover, some differences of perception, interpretation and emphasis between the Majority and Minority Members. These differences, though not many, mitigate against a blanket endorsement of the report.

This investigation found its origins, of course, in South Korean wrongdoing . With respect to these misdeeds, the Minority endorses the view of Harold Brown, Secretary of Defense, when he spoke of allegations of South Korean bribery and improper influence:

We condemn such actions as a serious misinterpretation of our governmental process and of the mores of the American people. At the same time, we must not let the Tongsun Park affair obscure our basic national interest in Korea.

To look at Korea solely in terms of this scandal without regard to our security interests and responsibilities would endanger not only South Korea and its but the stability of northeast Asia and the security of this country as well. (As quoted in the New York Times, Feb. 23, 1978.)

This statement offers a perspective which the Minority believes should be emphasized. Another is one arrived at by The Washington Post in a perceptive editorial on June 14, 1978. The editorial said in part:

Whatever South Korean officials did on the Hill back in the early 1970's, they were surely motivated only by a desire to serve their country. It is not hard to imagine that the Koreans, apprehensive about what American policy might be after Vietnam, thought it might be prudent to take out a little insurance on Capitol Hill. They could well have thought that they would not be the first to act in this way.

The misdeeds detailed by this report can in no way be condoned, but the basic interests of the United States must nevertheless remain paramount in any assessment of these activities. Moreover, the enormous apprehension of the Koreans about their national survival must be understood completely before one can judge the "Korean scandal" properly.

The point made at the end of The Washington Post editorial is also particularly relevant in viewing the Korean problem. There are, and have been for decades, other operations of influence in this country—some conducted by allies, as in the case of the Republic of Korea, some by more-or-less neutrals or occasional friends, and some by those who have acted consistently as virtual enemies. During hearings conducted by the subcommittee the word "subversion" was used more than once to characterize South Korea's attempts to better her position vis-à-vis the U.S. Congress and other agencies of power in America. The media, of course, seized upon that dramatic word for its headlines. There has been no evidence, however, to determine that the ROK ever attempted "to overthrow or destroy" or "to overturn from beneath," which are normal definitions of the word "subversion."

Indeed, the whole point of the Korean excesses would be missed if they are not viewed in that light. The Koreans have done some bad things; of that there is no doubt. They have misunderstood our mores, as Secretary Brown has observed, and they have misused our institutions. Nevertheless, as this report clearly documents, they were keying, however misdirected their operations, to restore and strengthen long-established ties with the U.S. They were not even remotely trying to overturn or destroy our system of government on which they depend so much. In comparison, the Soviet Union, for example, has been sponsoring agents of influence in this country since before the Republic of Korea exited. That is the kind of influence and the kind of activity which can correctly be called "subversive."

The Minority also believes that the course of the investigation was sometimes shaped by preconceptions. The goals were optimistic but evidence did not always materialize in the precise form to support the objectives.

The Minority also notes the obvious—that the matter of questionable corporate payments to officials abroad is not limited to South Korea. It is a way of life in a number of areas of the world.

There were also mechanical problems which precluded an unqualified acceptance of the report by the Minority. With the adjournment of Congress on October 15, 1978, most of the Members of the Subcommittee left Washington before a completed draft of the report could be reviewed. We, therefore, were unable to read the report in its entirety.

Despite these real reservations and concerns over various aspects of this report, the Minority wishes to assert its particular support of the finding of the section on the Moon organization. We believe that no member of the Subcommittee was in any way interested in interfering with the religious rights of Sun Myung Moon or his followers. There was complete agreement, nonetheless, that the political and commercial activities of the Moon organizational complex may have violated U.S. laws and deserve to be investigated thoroughly. For several years a few states in the U.S. have attempted to cope with the Moon organization despite inadequate coordination that only the Federal Government can provide. As this report shows, the Moon operation is national—indeed international—in scope.

It has long deserved the close scrutiny of the Federal Government, and it is difficult to understand why the appropriate agencies of the Executive Branch have not long since taken action against those activities of the Moon Organization which are illegal.

That South Korea was particularly bold and active in its operations contributed to the shock when its activities were eventually publicized. Whatever caused the South Koreans to act as they did and what American officials contributed to that process are well set forth in this document. One may differ in the interpretation of the events as spelled out in this report, but it is obvious there is much to be learned from this investigation.

Finally, the Minority believes that most of the problems discussed in this final document have already been solved. Those that remain can now be approached with the valuable perspective gained from this inquiry. The Minority Members trust that the Korean-American interrelationships will now have reached a point of mutual understanding and that henceforth relations will only continue to improve.

EDWARD J. DERWINSKI.
WILLIAM F. GOODLING.

House of Representatives [Committee Print], Subcommittee on International Organizations of the Committee on International Relations, "Investigation of Korean-American Relations," 95th Congress, 2d session, Oct. 31, 1978, 46–439.

170   Immigration and Naturalization Service v. Chadha

June 23, 1983

This seemingly simple case about an immigrant who came to the United States as a student and sought to stay in this country when his visa expired had a profound effect on congressional power and Congress's longtime use of a controversial devise known as the legislative veto.

The Constitution (Article I, Section 7, Clause 2) provides the process for a bill to become a law. A bill must pass both houses of Congress and then be signed by the president before it becomes law. If the president vetoes the bill, Congress can, with a two-thirds vote in each house, override that veto. Once a bill becomes law, the law remains until it is amended or abolished by another act of Congress or until it is declared unconstitutional by the Supreme Court.

Congress introduced an additional wrinkle to this process, the legislative veto, in 1932 as part of an appropriations bill for fiscal year 1933. The legislative veto was designed to allow either House of Congress the opportunity to veto plans of President Herbert Hoover to reorganize parts of the executive branch. Congress wanted to make sure it approved of the plan and, if not, wanted the power to reject what it disliked.

For the next half century, until the legislative veto was struck down in the Chadha decision, language providing for a legislative

veto found its way into more than two hundred laws. In all cases the purpose was to give Congress some control over blocking executive branch action short of passing a law. The legislative veto came in various forms. It could require action by both the House and Senate (a two-house veto) or by the House or Senate acting alone (a one-house veto). In a few instances a single committee of the House or Senate could launch the legislative veto. While presidents complained that the legislative veto encroached on the powers of the executive branch, Congress became more and more fond of this device as a check on executive power.

The case that eventually unraveled the legislative veto began in 1974 when a Kenya-born East Indian named Jagdish Rai Chadha, who had entered the United States legally on a student visa, sought an extension of his stay in the United States after his visa had expired. The Immigration and Naturalization Service (INS) suspended his deportation pending further review of the case. Congress, during the height of the anti-Communist crusade in 1952, had amended the Immigration and Nationality Act to give itself the authority to override individual cases before the INS. In late 1975 the House voted to override the INS suspension of Chadha's deportation and ordered him to be deported. Chadha filed suit, ar-

guing that it was unconstitutional for Congress to overrule an executive branch decision. The Justice Department saw this case as an opportunity to strike down the legislative veto. The House and Senate joined the suit to protect the line-item veto.

Chief Justice Warren Burger rendered the majority decision of the Supreme Court, which voted 7–2 to declare the legislative veto unconstitutional. For Mr. Chadha, it meant that he could stay in the United States. Long before the decision was reached, however, he had married an American citizen and started a family. For Congress, it meant the loss of a power never explicitly granted in the Constitution. The legislative veto had made it possible for legislators to engage in the micro-management of executive branch responsibilities without going through the regular constitutional process of how a bill becomes a law.

The references in this excerpt from the Chadha *decision to "Section 244(c)(2)" refer to a section of the Immigration and Nationality Act. Under this act the attorney general has the power to make decisions regarding deportations. Section 244(c)(2) of the act, which was the legislative veto component of the bill, reads as follows:*

(2) In the case of an alien specified in paragraph (1) of subsection (a) of this subsection—

if during the session of the Congress at which a case is reported, or prior to the lose of the session of the Congress next following the session at which a case is reported, either the Senate or the House of Representatives passes a resolution stating in substance that it does not favor the suspension of a deportation, the Attorney General shall thereupon deport such alien or authorize the alien's voluntary departure at his own expense under the order of deportation in the manner provided by law. If, within the time above specified, neither the Senate nor the House of Representatives shall pass such a resolution, the Attorney General shall cancel deportation proceedings.

. . . .

IV

The Constitution sought to divide the delegated powers of the new Federal Government into three defined categories, Legislative, Executive, and Judicial, to assure, as nearly as possible, that each branch of government would confine itself to its assigned responsibility. The hydraulic pressure inherent within each of the separate Branches to exceed the outer limits of its power, even to accomplish desirable objectives, must be resisted.

Although not "hermetically" sealed from one another, *Buckley v. Valeo* [1976], the powers delegated to the three Branches are functionally identifiable. When any Branch acts, it is presumptively exercising the power the Constitution has delegated to it. See *J. W. Hampton & Co. v. United States* (1928). When the Executive acts, he presumptively acts in an executive or administrative capacity as defined in Art. II. And when, as here, one House of Congress purports to act, it is presumptively acting within its assigned sphere.

Beginning with this presumption, we must nevertheless establish that the challenged action under § 244(c)(2) is of the kind to which the procedural requirements of Art. 1, § 7, apply. Not every action taken by either House is subject to the bicameralism and presentment requirements of Art. I. See *infra,* at 955, and nn. 20, 21. Whether actions taken by either House are, in law and fact, an exercise of legislative power depends not on their form but upon "whether they contain matter which is properly to be regarded as legislative in its character and effect." S. Rep. No. 1335, 54th Cong., 2d Sess., 8 (1897).

Examination of the action taken here by one House pursuant to § 244(c)(2) reveals that it was essentially legislative in purpose and effect. In purporting to exercise power defined in Art. I, § 8, cl. 4, to "establish an uniform Rule of Naturalization," the House took action that had the purpose and effect of altering the legal rights, duties, and relations of persons, including the Attorney General, Executive Branch officials and Chadha, all outside the Legislative Branch. Section 244(c)(2) purports to authorize one House of Congress to require the Attorney General to deport an individual alien whose deportation otherwise would be canceled under §244. The one-House veto operated in these cases to overrule the Attorney General and mandate Chadha's deportation; absent the House action, Chadha would remain in the United States. Congress has acted and its action has altered Chadha's status.

The legislative character of the one-House veto in these cases is confirmed by the character of the congressional action it supplants. Neither the House of Representatives nor the Senate contends that, absent the veto provision in §244(c)(2), either of them, or both of them acting together, could effectively require the Attorney General to deport an alien once the Attorney General, in the exercise of legislatively delegated authority, had determined the alien should remain in the United States. Without the challenged provision in § 244(c)(2), this could have been achieved, if at all, only by legislation requiring deportation. Similarly, a veto by one House of Congress under § 244(c)(2) cannot be justified as an attempt at amending the standards set out in § 244(a)(1), or as a repeal of § 244 as applied to Chadha. Amendment and repeal of statutes, no less than enactment, must conform with Art. I.

The nature of the decision implemented by the one-House veto in these cases further manifests its legislative character. After long experience with the clumsy, time-consuming private bill procedure, Congress made a deliberate choice to delegate to the Executive Branch, and specifically to the Attorney General, the authority to allow deportable aliens to remain in this country in certain specified circumstances. It is not disputed that this choice to delegate authority is precisely the kind of decision that can be implemented only in accordance with the procedures set out in Art. I. Disagreement with the Attorney General's decision on Chadha's deportation—that is, Congress' decision to deport Chadha—no less than Congress' original choice to delegate to the Attorney General the authority to make that decision, involves determinations of policy that Congress can implement in only one way; bicameral passage followed by presentment to the

President. Congress must abide by its delegation of authority until that delegation is legislatively altered or revoked.

Finally, we see that when the Framers intended to authorize either House of Congress to act alone and outside of its prescribed bicameral legislative role, they narrowly and precisely defined the procedure for such action. There are four provisions in the Constitution, explicit and unambiguous, by which one House may act alone with the unreviewable force of law, not subject to the President's veto:

(a) The House of Representatives alone was given the power to initiate impeachments. Art. I, § 2, cl. 5;

(b) The Senate alone was given the power to conduct trials following impeachment on charges initiated by the House and to convict following trial. Art. I, § 3, cl. 6;

(c) The Senate alone was given final unreviewable power to approve or to disapprove Presidential appointments. Art. II, § 2, cl. 2;

(d) The Senate alone was given unreviewable power to ratify treaties negotiated by the President. Art. II, § 2, cl. 2.

Clearly, when the Draftsmen sought to confer special powers on one House, independent of the other House, or of the President, they did so in explicit, unambiguous terms. These carefully defined exceptions from presentment and bicameralism underscore the difference between the legislative functions of Congress and other unilateral but important and binding one-House acts provided for in the Constitution. These exceptions are narrow, explicit, and separately justified; none of them authorize the action challenged here. On the contrary, they provide further support for the conclusion that congressional authority is not to be implied and for the conclusion that the veto provided for in § 244(c)(2) is not authorized by the constitutional design of the powers of the Legislative Branch.

Since it is clear that the action by the House under §244(c)(2) was not within any of the express constitutional exceptions authorizing one House to act alone, and equally clear that it was an exercise of legislative power, that action was subject to the standards prescribed in Art. I. The bicameral requirement, the Presentment Clauses, the President's veto, and Congress' power to override a veto were intended to erect enduring checks on each Branch and to protect the people from the improvident exercise of power by mandating certain prescribed steps. To preserve those checks, and maintain the separation of powers, the carefully defined limits on the power of each Branch must not be eroded. To accomplish what has been attempted by one House of Congress in this case requires action in conformity with the express procedures of the Constitution's prescription for legislative action: passage by a majority of both Houses and presentment to the President.

The veto authorized by § 244(c)(2) doubtless has been in many respects a convenient shortcut; the "sharing" with the Executive by Congress of its authority over aliens in this manner is, on its face, an appealing compromise. In purely practical terms, it is obviously easier for action to be taken by one House without submission to the President; but it is crystal clear from the records of the Convention, contemporaneous writings and debates, that the Framers ranked other values higher than efficiency. The records of the Convention and debates in the states preceding ratification underscore the common desire to define and limit the exercise of the newly created federal powers affecting the states and the people. There is unmistakable expression of a determination that legislation by the national Congress be a step-by-step, deliberate and deliberative process.

The choices we discern as having been made in the Constitutional Convention impose burdens on governmental processes that often seem clumsy, inefficient, even unworkable, but those hard choices were consciously made by men who had lived under a form of government that permitted arbitrary governmental acts to go unchecked. There is no support in the Constitution or decisions of this Court for the proposition that the cumbersomeness and delays often encountered in complying with explicit constitutional standards may be avoided, either by the Congress or by the President. See *Youngstown Sheet & Tube Co. v. Sawyer* (1952). With all the obvious flaws of delay, untidiness, and potential for abuse, we have not yet found a better way to preserve freedom than by making the exercise of power subject to the carefully crafted restraints spelled out in the Constitution.

v

We hold that the congressional veto provision in § 244(c)(2) is severable from the Act and that it is unconstitutional. Accordingly, the judgment of the Court of Appeals is

Affirmed.

462 U.S. 919 (1983).

171 Speaker Tip O'Neill's Words Are Taken Down During Debate with Representative Newt Gingrich

May 15, 1984

It is rare for a Speaker of the House to be declared out of order during a debate on the floor of the House. When this happened in 1984, it was a symbolic event that focused attention on a new confrontational style being used by some members of the Republican Party, especially Newt Gingrich (D-Ga.), who rose to prominence by aggressively and often rudely challenging his political opponents. The debate that occurred on May 15, 1984, pitted Thomas P. "Tip" O'Neill (D-Mass.), the seventy-one-year-old Speaker, who had served in the House for thirty-two years at the time of this incident, against Gingrich, a brash forty-one-year-old former history professor who had served five years in the House at the time of the incident. O'Neill was near the end of his long career in the House. Gingrich was a rising star of the Republican Party. Eleven years after this debate, Gingrich became Speaker himself.

In 1979, when the House began regular televised proceedings of House debates, nobody took to the new procedure quicker and more effectively that Gingrich and several of his Republican colleagues. They used time known as "Special Orders" at the end of the regular legislative day to speak for up to an hour on any topic of their choosing. Under the House rules and practice at the time, the television camera was fixed on the member who held the floor. Often during Special Orders, the chamber would be empty of other members, with only a few clerks, the presiding officer, the parliamentarian, and the person speaking. Often the member speaking, even though the chamber was empty, would gesture and make references to his colleagues in the House as if they were actually in the room. This looked effective on television, since the camera never left the person speaking.

Under House rules and practice going back to 1808, when any member, during the course of debate, utters disorderly or objectionable language, his words may be "taken down"—a parliamentary procedure that requires the clerk to literally write down the offensive language so the presiding officer (the Speaker, chairman of the Committee of the Whole, or other person presiding), can rule on the matter and determine if the words are inappropriate. If they are considered disorderly or inappropriate, the member uttering the offensive language is admonished by the chair. The incident could lead to censure of the member, although in most instances it is usually enough to suffer the embarrassment of being called out of order. If the offending member apologizes for the offensive language, the incident is usually quickly dropped.

The immediate backdrop of the debate that led to the rising tensions between the Speaker and some of the Republican members of the House was debate over controversial legislation to fund the war against the leftist governments in El Salvador and Nicaragua. During the months of April and May 1984, the debate was intense in the House and Senate, with the Reagan administration and House Republicans getting their way against a divided Democratic Party.

The struggle over aid to the contra rebels in Central America generated some of the most bitter debates in Congress during the first term of the Reagan administration. Just five days before the confrontation between Speaker O'Neill and Gingrich, the House voted to grant aid to the contra rebels. Gingrich, in early debate, had also made unfavorable references to Edward Boland (D-Mass.), one of Speaker O'Neill's dearest friends with whom he shared a Washington apartment. It was Boland who had championed several amendments, the first in 1983, that prohibited U.S. aid for the purpose of overthrowing the Nicaraguan government. Also taking part in this debate was Jim Wright (D-Texas), then majority leader of the House and an outspoken foe of aid to the contra rebels; he would later succeed O'Neill as Speaker. Wright and Gingrich would clash many times in the years ahead, and Gingrich would eventually level ethics charges against Wright that would lead to his resignation as Speaker in 1989 (see document 174).

Three years after this incident of May 15, 1984, after he had retired from Congress, Tip O'Neill wrote about this debate in his autobiography, Man of the House *(1987). He described Gingrich as someone who did his "best to undermine the dignity of the House." He said of the aggressive right wing Republicans: "What really infuriated me about these guys is that they had no real interest in legislation. As far as they were concerned, the House was no more than a pulpit, a sound stage from which to reach the people at home. If the TV cameras were facing the city dump, that's where they'd be speaking."*

Just days before this debate, after listening to one of Gingrich's allies, Robert Walker (R-Pa.), speak against Boland, as if he was still in the chamber, O'Neill, in an uncharacteristic rash act, ordered the television cameras that were supposed to remain fixed on the speaker to scan the chamber, revealing it to be empty and making Walker look like a fool. Speaker O'Neill later admitted that he should have warned his colleagues that he was going to do this. His temper got the best of him. He was still angry when he came to the floor of the House, not as the presiding officer but as another member in the well of the House to chastise Gingrich. But the Speaker's temper did not serve him well. The Speaker lost this round to Gingrich, Walker, and Trent Lott (R-Miss.). Lott called for the Speaker's words to be taken down when the Speaker, literally shaking with anger, said to Gingrich, "My personal opinion is this: you deliberately stood in that well before an empty House and challenged these people, and you challenged their Americanism, and it is the lowest thing that I have ever seen in my thirty-two years in Congress."

Mr. GINGRICH. If I might continue for just a moment and then I will be glad to yield, let me just say, because I think there is a more serious issue here I want to get to, that in any event we were in fact attempting to inform the Members, and if the Members would look, for example, at the CONGRESSIONAL RECORD on May 4 on a colloquy which involved the gentleman from Oregon (Mr. Weaver) and the gentleman from Pennsylvania (Mr. Walker) and myself, on that particular day we had been informed by staff that there was a document in the Speaker's lobby which could I think legitimately be characterized as propaganda for the Nicaraguan Government. And I consciously, and if you read the text of this colloquy, I consciously avoided naming any Member, although we had every reason to believe we knew who put it there, until finally forced by Mr. Weaver, at which point the gentleman from Pennsylvania checked with the staff and reported what the staff told him. But in fact precisely the opposite of what the Speaker said yesterday, we have not attempted to embarrass or engage Members except in a context where we are inviting them to come to the floor and defend their position.

Now let me continue if I might to one other point and then I will be glad, I believe we will have the time, and I am certain if we were to run out of the time the distinguished—

Mr. WRIGHT. I want the gentleman to yield, if he will, at that point.

Mr. GINGRICH. I will.

Mr. WRIGHT. Did I understand the gentleman to characterize a letter that was signed by some of the Members of the U.S. House of Representatives as a propaganda document?

Mr. GINGRICH. No.

Mr. WRIGHT. For the Communist government, is that what the gentleman said?

Mr. GINGRICH. No.

Mr. WRIGHT. It sounded as though that was what he was saying.

Mr. GINGRICH. I am not quite certain I understand the gentleman from Texas.

Mr. WRIGHT. I am not certain I understand the gentleman from Georgia. But I want to make it abundantly clear that we do understand what we are talking about. When we begin impugning one another's patriotism, then we cross a bar which should not be crossed.

The gentleman has written letters and made speeches, written letters to newspapers throughout the country impugning the acts of Members of this Congress which should not have been undertaken in a civil procedure. This House has always assumed the sincerity of one another whether we agree or not.

One of the great things about democracy is that it assumes our ability to disagree without being disagreeable.

But you know, we have gone through periods in our history—

Mr. GINGRICH. If I may reclaim my time—

Mr. WRIGHT. The gentleman surely may reclaim his time but I would like to have an answer.

Mr. GINGRICH. I want to give you an answer.

Mr. WRIGHT. The gentleman has written some speeches for newspapers.

I thought the gentleman said that he was willing to engage in debate. Now he is willing to engage in debate when the Members are not here whose patriotism he impugns, but he is not willing to engage in debate when we are here. Now that is the question, and the gentleman has raised a question of patriotism.

The SPEAKER pro tempore (Mr. Moakley). The gentleman declines to yield any further.

Mr. GINGRICH. Reclaiming my time for a moment, I win tender to the very distinguished majority leader the simple proposition that I will yield you as much time as you desire if in return you will insure me that this dialog will continue until I am finished. But if your side is determined to yield me only 1 hour, which is the correct rule of the House, for you to turn around and control the calendar as you do, and impugn my willingness to debate has certainly not been our past relationship.

Mr. WRIGHT. If the gentleman would yield on that point?

Mr. GINGRICH. I will yield.

Mr. WRIGHT. I should like to make note of the fact that in the past 30 days the gentleman from Georgia has asked for 27 hours. Now if that is not enough time, I do not know how much time the gentleman needs.

I have asked him to yield for a colloquy so that I might understand exactly what it is that he was accusing Members of this House of having done.

Mr. GINGRICH. I will now answer you. I will now answer you.

Mr. WRIGHT. Very good. That was what I was hopeful of.

Mr. GINGRICH. I am frankly surprised that the very distinguished gentleman from Texas should raise the letter as a possible example of Communist propaganda.

I was referring, and if you will check the CONGRESSIONAL RECORD of May 3, to a very specific document which is referred to I believe by the bishops in their Easter statement as a deliberate effort by the Nicaraguan Government to propagandize using the women of Nicaragua. I was referring to a very specific Nicaraguan document which is covered on pages, I believe it is 10989 through 10998. And I am frankly—I was stunned. I listened carefully to the gentleman from Texas because I was stunned that he would consider anyone who imagined his very legitimate letter, which I disagree with and question the wisdom of, as though it were Communist propaganda.

Mr. WRIGHT. If the gentleman would yield further, I appreciate that elucidation, and I think perhaps the gentleman might understand my misunderstanding his intent, given the fact that he has repeatedly cast aspersions upon the good faith of Members of this House in his repeated 1-hour speeches.

Now, we have not interrupted the gentleman, we have not bothered him, we have allowed him to say whatever he wanted to say. None of us have engaged him in dialog.

But the gentleman just seems intent on repetitiously questioning the good will, and the good faith, and the patriotism of his colleagues.

Mr. GINGRICH. Let me reclaim.

You just made a very serious assertion, which is paralleled by what the Speaker said yesterday, and frankly very helpful, because you lead me precisely into the assertion that I think is the most devastating and which compelled me to rise.

The Speaker said, and I quote: "Giving the thought and the idea that Members of Congress were un-American." The Speaker, I think, raises a question which goes to the very heart of this system and a system which the gentleman from Texas very eloquently described.

Let me make my position very, very clear to the distinguished gentleman from Texas. Whether—we are talking about two different issues here for those Members who have not been engaged. One issue is the letter to Commandante Ortega which I have raised very serious questions about, which appeared as late as yesterday's Washington Post, which I addressed an American Bar Association standing committee on last week and which I think legitimately, as a matter of constitutional law and process deserves to be debated in its own right.

The second is a document written by Frank Gregorsky, which is a Republican study committee study that looks back at the record of 14 years of some Members of this body, projecting what would happen in foreign policy and then what happened in reality.

Now let me be just as blunt and straightforward as I can, because I think this is where the Speaker was totally unfair yesterday and what we are seeing comes all too close to resembling a McCarthyism of the left. We believe it is legitimate in the system of this House to raise two sets of questions; first about the "Dear Commandante" letter.

Is it truly appropriate for Members of this body to write a foreign dictator in a period when the United States is in conflict with the Government and to send that letter saying what that letter said? I happen to think if you read the Logan Act and I would suggest to you there are not many Members who went back and read the debate in 1799. I have.

There is no question but that the Founding Fathers felt strongly that members of the legislative branch should not be involved. That is a structural question; it is not—

Mr. WRIGHT. Would the gentleman yield for a question?

Mr. GINGRICH. Let me finish, and I will yield in just a second.

Mr. WRIGHT. Is the gentleman implying that Members of the Congress—is the gentleman implying that—

Mr. GINGRICH. I do not yield yet.

Mr. WRIGHT. That they have broken the law? Is that what the gentleman is saying?

Mr. GINGRICH. I reclaim my time. Let me continue for a second and then I will yield, but let me focus first on the "Dear Comandante" letter.

There are legitimate structural questions which if you read, for example, the American Law Division's two passages studying the Logan Act, if you go back and read the original debate in 1799, those are legitimate questions; whether or not in fact, not because they are bad people, not because they do not mean well, but in the effect of their action, the gentleman who signed that letter made a serious mistake and a mistake of long-term consequence.

I think that is a legitimate question to raise, it is a question worth debating in its own right.

The second point I raised, which is largely contained in the Gregorsky paper, is the issue when you look at statements of gentlemen in this body, statements about South Vietnam, about Laos, about Cambodia, about Angola, about Afghanistan, about Ethiopia, about Grenada, about Nicaragua, and now about El Salvador, and you see a consistent, what some of us would regard as inaccurate, judgment; not I say to you, and I say this as strongly as I can, not a question of their patriotism, not a question of their good intentions, not a question of their decency.

Mr. WRIGHT. If the gentleman would yield.

Mr. GINGRICH. I will not yield yet.

It is a question of their judgment, a question of the historical record, a question of what they said and what happened in reality.

Now I think those are very serious charges, not as the Speaker would characterize them of charging anyone as being un-American. It is perfectly American to be wrong, it is to have bad judgment; it is perfectly legitimate for people to believe in a philosophy which does not work, I am not in any sense and I resent bitterly the idea that, starting with the gentleman from Wisconsin the night I put this in the RECORD who got up promptly and used the terms, referring to the Senator from Wisconsin, is it wrong for those of us who were 9 or 10 at that time, to ask the question what has happened in the intervening 30 years?

Is it wrong for those of us who have grown up as historians who believe in looking at history to raise questions of history?

Is it wrong for us to go back and do the research and lay it out?

Mr. O'NEILL. Will the gentleman yield.

Mr. GINGRICH. I am always delighted to yield to our distinguished Speaker.

Mr. O'NEILL. Very interesting the way the gentleman talks, as an apologist for the remarks that he made the other day. Let us look at the truth of the thing. Let us look at the truth.

Mr. GINGRICH. I reclaim my time for 1 minute.

Mr. O'NEILL. I want to know why you went back to 1970 and 1971.

Mr. GINGRICH. I reclaim my time, Mr. Speaker, just to make the point.

Mr. O'NEILL. I thought you said you would give to the Speaker the courtesy.

Mr. GINGRICH. I reclaim my time to simply make the point that I am not in any sense apologizing. Had the Speaker been here for this whole dialog, you would understand; I am explaining, I am putting in context. I am not apologizing. He used the term—

Mr. O'NEILL. Would the gentleman yield for just a question?

Mr. GINGRICH. I now yield.

Mr. O'NEILL. The gentleman yields.

As Speaker of the House, I was notified personally, every Member of this House was notified on May 8 by the Postmaster that they were delaying 4 and 5 days, that is No. 1. Were you not informed at that particular time that you were delayed 4 or 5 days that the mail was not coming through because of the tremendous amount of mail?

Mr. GINGRICH. The Speaker was apparently not on the floor a few moments ago when I explained specifically that my staff had asked the Postmaster if a Member-to-Member letter could be delivered internally that day, or if it were better to deliver it by page? And we were assured it was appropriate to deliver it by mail. It would be appropriate.

Mr. O'NEILL. Is not it amazing to you that a staff member would receive one answer and the Members of Congress received another? Particularly a Member?

Mr. GINGRICH. Let me make a point, and then I will yield to my friend from California.

My point to the Speaker is, as you pointed out again to us yesterday, you are in charge of this House If you are saying to me that your postmaster is incapable of delivering from one Member to another the mail in the system you run, then I think you may want to appoint a commission to look into the Post Office; that is not my job as a single Member.

Mr. THOMAS of California. Will the gentleman yield?

Mr. GINGRICH. I yield to the gentleman from California.

Mr. THOMAS of California. I thank the gentleman from Georgia for yielding.

Surely the Speaker is not unaware of what goes on in the committees of this House. And that the chairman of the House Administration or the subcommittee chairman have not informed the Speaker that we have already in the Committee on House Administration voted to have additional staff to deal with the backlog—

Mr. O'NEILL. Now, listen; we are just getting away from the issue.

Mr. THOMAS of California. May I reclaim my time.

Mr. O'NEILL. We are getting away from the issue. The issue comes down to one thing.

Mr. THOMAS of California. Regular order.

The SPEAKER pro tempore. The gentleman from Georgia controls the time.

Mr. O'NEILL. I would like to have a dialog on what happened. You are making accusations—

Mr. THOMAS of California. Regular order, Mr. Speaker.

The SPEAKER pro tempore. The gentleman from Georgia is recognized.

Mr. O'NEILL. You are making accusations that I—

Mr. THOMAS of California. Regular order, Mr. Speaker.

Mr. O'NEILL. Will the gentleman yield?

Mr. GINGRICH. In just one moment, Mr. Speaker.

I yield to the gentleman from California, and then I yield to the distinguished Speaker.

Mr. THOMAS of California. I thank the gentleman from Georgia for yielding. And we have already in committee begun to make amends for the backlog which involves outside mail coming into Members and Members mail going to the outside.

I think there can be no question, if the Speaker would inform himself in terms of decisions that have already been made in committees chaired by his party, that the internal mail question was not at issue. It was the external, coming from Members and to Members, that was at issue. And therefore any discussion about the Postmaster's position on internal mail is simply an informed one.

I thank the gentleman for yielding.

Mr. GINGRICH. OK. I would be delighted to yield to our distinguished Speaker, if he wishes to continue this, Mr. Speaker.

Mr. O'NEILL. You yield to me. I just want to say this.

Mr. GINGRICH. Please use the mike.

Mr. O'NEILL. There is no question in my mind that the arguments and statements that I said on this floor came to me by complaint of the Members.

First, that they had not been notified. I do not believe that they were notified. I believe that truly, that they did not get the mail in their office, No. 1.

No. 2, the sense of your letter here: "I am inviting you to hear a dialog on my perception of what American policy and foreign affairs should be. I am going to go back," you did not tell them you were going to go back to 1970 to get clips, 1972 in the instance of Mr. Edward Boland, the gentleman whom I have the greatest respect for; chairman of our Intelligence Committee. And you were going to ask him a question as to their policy and how they felt about the Vietnam war and the question of "Did you beat your wife lately?" "I want you to come in and answer the questions of the philosophy that you had then."

You talk about Angola, you did not—you do not talk about Angola, how during the Eisenhower administration we were for the very, very people that later on the Nixon people were opposed to. Change in strategy. You do not say anything about things of that nature. Very interesting.

My personal opinion is this: You deliberately stood in that well before an empty House and challenged these people, and you challenged their Americanism, and it is the lowest thing that I have ever seen in my 32 years in Congress.

Mr. GINGRICH. Mr. Speaker, if I may reclaim my time, let me say first of all that—

Mr. LOTT. Mr. Speaker, I demand that the Speaker's words be taken down.

The SPEAKER pro tempore. Words will be taken down.

The Clerk will report the words.

The Clerk read as follows:

My personal opinion is this: you deliberately stood in that well before an empty House and challenged these people and you challenged their Americanism and it is the lowest thing that I have ever seen in my 32 years in Congress.

Mr. LOTT. Mr. Speaker, has the Chair ruled?

The SPEAKER pro tempore. The Chair has not ruled.

Mr. LOTT. If the Chair would rule, I have a request that I would like to make.

The SPEAKER pro tempore. The Chair feels that that type of characterization should not be used in debate.

Mr. LOTT. Mr. Speaker, I ask unanimous consent at this point that the Speaker be allowed to continue in order.

The SPEAKER pro tempore. Is there objection to the request of the gentleman from Mississippi?

Mr. THOMAS of California. Mr. Speaker, reserving the right to object will the gentleman from Mississippi indicate to me the intent and purpose of that unanimous-consent request.

Mr. LOTT. Mr. Speaker, will the gentleman yield?

Mr. THOMAS of California. I yield to the gentleman from Mississippi.

Mr. LOTT. Mr. Speaker's words have been taken down. The Chair has ruled that they were not in proper order or conduct on this floor.

And based on that I now ask that the Speaker be allowed to continue in order so that we can continue this debate and so that the Speaker can more properly state his position.

Mr. THOMAS of California. And that requires unanimous consent?

Mr. LOTT. I am asking for that unanimous consent. Our point has been made. I think that we want to change the tenor of this debate and we should now proceed on a higher plane with this debate.

Mr. THOMAS of California. Mr. Speaker, I shall not object.

The SPEAKER pro tempore. Is there objection to the request of the gentleman from Mississippi?

There was no objection.

Mr. GINGRICH. If I may reclaim my time for a moment, Mr. Speaker, let me read to this body part of what was put in that night so that you can understand why I am so sensitive and why I am so upset by some of the allegations our friends on the left have made.

And I quote, and this is in the RECORD. This is on page 11426 on May 8:

The necessary question still gets lost in the rhetorical mud. It's a question national Democrats could answer convincingly in 1955 or 1965, but can't now. That question has nothing to do with motivation or patriotism, and everything to do with results and reality. Conservatives, Republicans and traditional Democrats ought to ask it the right way:

Can the Democrats manage U.S. foreign affairs based on their view of the world? Based on the record of the recent past, will their policies work?

Effectiveness and competence is the standard for judging, not motivation. Any fair-minded (or merely cautious) critic should take as a given the patriotism of any Democrat. Republicans eager to save Central America from Radical blunders must make it a point to endorse the patriotism and sincerity of every Democrat they take to task for being, objectively speaking, blind to reality.

Radicalized Democrats would prefer Joe McCarthy launch every debate. Their opponents must instead make Al Smith the keynote: "Let's look at the record, my friend."

Conservatives, Republicans and traditional Democrats must be instructors in reality not evaluators of motivation.

Let me just say before I yield, if you think for just a moment of what in a moment of passion our very distinguished Speaker said a few moments ago, you think of what in a moment of passion the other night our distinguished colleague from Wisconsin said.

In many ways it is my patriotism being impugned. I am as sincerely committed to the survival of this country, Mr. Speaker, as you are. I am as sincerely committed as Mr. Wright.

Mr. O'NEILL. I am not questioning the gentleman's patriotism, I am questioning his judgment. I also question the judgment of the Chair.

I was expressing my opinion. As a matter of fact, I was expressing my opinion very mildly, because I think much worse than what I said.

Mr. WEBER. I thank my colleague for yielding.

And as long as the Speaker is on the floor, I would like to ask the Speaker to respond to a question. We are spending a lot of time here discussing very emotionally charged words. I have a strong bias in favor of the position of the gentleman from Georgia, but I would ask the Speaker a question—

Mr. O'NEILL. Will the gentleman yield?

Mr. WEBER. If I can conclude my question. The point is, the Speaker has accused—

Mr. O'NEILL. I do not mind anybody expressing their opinion if there are Members on the floor.

Mr. THOMAS of California. Mr. Speaker, regular order.

Mr. O'NEILL. The gentleman, Mr. Weaver, could identify him, and the gentleman, Mr. Walker, if they would express their opinion to the Members on the floor, we would be fine.

PARLIAMENTARY INQUIRY

Mr. WEBER. A point of parliamentary inquiry.

Do the rules of this body apply to the Speaker of the House? That is a serious parliamentary inquiry, Mr. Speaker.

The SPEAKER pro tempore. Does the gentleman from Georgia yield for a parliamentary inquiry?

Mr. GINGRICH. I yield for a parliamentary inquiry.

Mr. WEBER. My parliamentary inquiry, Mr. Speaker, is: Do the rules of the House apply to the Speaker of the House?

The SPEAKER pro tempore. The rules of the House apply to all Members of the House.

Mr. WEBER. Including the Speaker of the House?

The SPEAKER pro tempore. All Members of the House.

Mr. WEBER. I thank the gentleman for answering my parliamentary inquiry.

Will the gentleman yield?

Mr. GINGRICH. I yield to the gentleman from Minnesota.

Mr. WEBER. I thank the gentleman for yielding.

My question of the Speaker is, since the Speaker has on several occasions accused the gentleman from Georgia, as well as others of us implicit[l]y of impugning the patriotism of Members on this side of the aisle, and accusing them of un-American activity, I think we minimally have a right to know the specific statements to which the Speaker is referring.

Mr. OBEY. Would the gentleman yield on that point for an answer?

Mr. WEBER. Would the Speaker be willing to tell us specifically which statements he was referring to when he accused the gentleman from Georgia of calling Members on his side of the aisle un-American?

Mr. OBEY. Will the gentleman yield on that point for an answer?

Mr. GINGRICH. I have the time.

Mr. O'NEILL. Will the gentleman yield?

Mr. GINGRICH. I yield to the gentleman from Massachusetts.

Mr. O'NEILL. I would yield to Mr. Obey.

Mr. GINGRICH. You do not have the right to yield, Mr. Speaker. I yielded to you.

Mr. OBEY. Will the gentleman yield to me to answer that question?

The SPEAKER pro tempore. The gentleman from Georgia has yielded to the gentleman from Massachusetts.

Mr. GINGRICH. I would be glad to hear from the gentleman from Massachusetts. It is his statement in the RECORD yesterday, his statement on the floor, which led me to rise to a point of personal privilege.

Mr. WRIGHT. I wonder if the gentleman would yield to me so that I might respond to that question.

Mr. WEBER. Will the gentleman yield?

Mr. GINGRICH. I yield to the gentleman from Minnesota.

Mr. WEBER. The point is, the special orders taken out on this subject, although they were involving primarily the gentleman from Georgia, also included my name, the name of the gentleman from Pennsylvania. I consider it a very high form of criticism when I am accused of impugning the patriotism of another Member. That criticism did not come from the gentleman from Wisconsin or the gentleman from Texas. It came from the Speaker of the House. And I would like the Speaker, not the gentleman from Texas, not the gentleman from Wisconsin, but the Speaker to tell us exactly what he was referring to.

I thank the gentleman for yielding.

Mr. DELLUMS. Will the gentleman from Georgia yield to me?

Mr. GINGRICH. Not for the moment.

Let me say again, just two points, as colleagues—and I will yield to you just a moment, Mr. Wright.

Let me say two things, because we get rather excited here, and this is an exciting topic.

First of all, the Speaker made the allegation earlier that I read my paper into the RECORD when the House was empty and implied that it is because I was afraid to be criticized.

Now, I think we are proving today that we are willing to rise in the House when there are a number of Members in the House, and we are willing to talk with some of the most eloquent and intelligent Members of the Democratic Party and that we are not trying to hide anything. I just wanted to make that point.

Second, we had said in our letter, and I think we are all on our side still committed, to the gentleman from Wisconsin, the gentleman from New York, the gentleman from California, if they wish to arrange a special order, that is fine. We would be delighted, at their convenience, to stand here and to debate in a way which is appropriate. But—

Mr. WRIGHT. I wonder if the gentleman would yield—

Mr. GINGRICH. In 1 second.

Mr. WRIGHT. In order that I might provide a reply to the question—

Mr. GINGRICH. In 1 second I will be glad to yield.

Mr. WRIGHT. Offered to the Speaker by the gentleman.

Mr. GINGRICH. I just want to say that the reason we are trying to focus on the Speaker is because it is the Speaker, with the full majesty and weight of his position, who yesterday made certain allegations, which at this point, at least, he has not yet answered to.

Mr. O'NEILL. Would the gentleman yield?

Mr. GINGRICH. Would you prefer I—I was going to yield to Mr. Wright, but I will yield to you, Mr. Speaker.

Mr. O'NEILL. You have an audience. You do not normally have that in the 26 hours you presented this case to the public. But the interesting fact is, the whole tenor of your remarks, going back to 1970, and Dave Obey, and going back to 1972, taking out of context on Mr. Boland, you were there for one purpose and one purpose alone, in my opinion, and that was to imply that Members on this side were un-American in their activities. You stopped. You waited. Your motions.

Would you respond? You knew that there was nobody here. You knew that there was nobody here. I have asked you a question about a policy that happened 12 years ago. Do you still feel the same way? It may be wrong today. Governments change; Members of the Congress change their minds. Have you beaten your wife lately? I want you to come to the floor of the House and answer the question that I think

Mr. GINGRICH. Mr. Speaker—

Mr. O'NEILL. No. Just a moment. That, I think is going to put you in a bad light.

You know, the interesting thing is, we are prepared, I believe, tonight during special orders—you sent the letter out. Tonight during special orders we are going to ask this—signed by three. The majority of the people did not even get it or they got it about 3 days later.

Mr. GINGRICH. Mr. Speaker—

Mr. O'NEILL. Did you do that deliberately?

Mr. GINGRICH. I reclaim my time.

Mr. O'NEILL. I do not know.

Mr. GINGRICH. I reclaim my time.

Mr. O'NEILL. I would just hate to think that a man would deliberately do what I feel that you did.

The SPEAKER pro tempore. The gentleman from Georgia reclaims his time.

Mr. GINGRICH. I reclaim my time, Mr. Speaker, because you just once again made the same points. First, your post office may or may not have delivered the mail we were assured your post office would deliver; second, I have to confess to you, Mr. Speaker, I have a bias in favor of history. I have a graduate degree in history. I think history matters. And since the gentlemen who made the history are still in this body, still voting, still speaking, I think the weight of their record matters.

Mr. LOTT. Will the gentleman yield for a question?

Mr. GINGRICH. I will be glad to yield to the distinguished gentleman from Mississippi.

Mr. LOTT. Since the whole thrust of the questioning on the other side has had to do with notice and whether Members were informed that they would be referred to, I just wonder if the gentleman on yesterday or at any point received notice that he would be referred to on the subject matter which prompted him to ask for this point of personal privilege? Did you receive any notice before or during that your name would be referred to?

Mr. GINGRICH. As the distinguished gentleman from Mississippi knows, the first indication I have that the Speaker would refer to me on the floor of the House—and I must say, Mr. Speaker, that I read with considerable interest the quote of you in this morning's paper, which said: "I have never seen anything so low to attack a man when he is not in the Hall."

Since I was not in the Hall yesterday when you talked, but—

Mr. WRIGHT. Will the gentleman yield for a somewhat serious distinction to be made?

Mr. GINGRICH. I yield to the gentleman from Texas.

Mr. WRIGHT. I do not think anybody in this House would deny to the gentleman from Georgia or any of his colleagues the right to question the wisdom or the judgment of any of us. Sometimes we disagree on the Democratic side and sometimes you disagree on the Republican side on questions of judgment.

Basically, however, whether you write a letter to someone or not, if you rise late at night, after the House's business has been concluded and everybody has gone home and nobody is here and question that Member's patriotism or his good faith, then I think that—

Mr. GINGRICH. When has that been done, Mr. Wright?

Mr. WRIGHT. That is the point that I wanted to raise. I know the gentleman does not consider the things he has written and said so harshly critical of certain Members of our Congress as questioning their patriotism and good faith, but let me just read to the gentleman, since he read something from the morning paper attributed to the Speaker, let me read from yesterday morning's newspaper, the Washington Post, an article written by Mr. Gingrich, in which he attempts to characterize a communication signed by 10 Members of the Congress, including the chairman of the Intelligence Committee of the House, and others of us, in the following words. This is from the article written by the gentleman from Georgia, referring to a document written by Members of the Congress:

Their letter goes on in two places to invite the Nicaraguan Communists to establish their policy with an eye to weakening conservative forces in America. In an election year this letter is a virtual teaching document to bring Third World Soviet colonies into the process of manipulating American politics and politicians.

Now, it seems to me that that is a harsh statement and one which borders upon, if it does not invade, the well placed injunction against questioning one another's patriotism or one another's loyalty.

Mr. GINGRICH. If I may reclaim my time for a second, Mr. Wright.

Mr. WRIGHT. The letter—

Mr. GINGRICH. Let me reclaim my time. I will yield again but let me reclaim my time for a second so I can answer your specific allegation.

Mr. WRIGHT. I want to make plain that what the gentleman said was not true.

Mr. GINGRICH. Let me simply say to the very distinguished gentleman from Texas that, having read the Logan Act debates, having read all the legal documents produced by the Library of Congress on this topic, having talked with two of the leading experts in this country, having addressed the American Bar Association's standing committees on national security law and on executive-legislative branch relations on this very topic, I think that the gentleman from Texas, rather than attacking me for having raised this issue, should be suggesting that the House form a special task force to look at this very serious question not in any sense—and let me make this very clear: I am fairly certain I know I how that letter came to be signed. I am fairly certain the 10 gentlemen who signed it signed it with the best of intentions.

If you will read the January 1799 debate, you will discover that the Founding Fathers talk about precisely that kind of case and they say even if your intentions are of the best, you should not do it because it violates the Constitution. I would simply suggest if the gentleman from Texas would look at the context, as a historian, of what I am trying to say, he will probably join me in being very concerned and hoping those letters are not signed.

. . . .

Congressional Record, House, 98th Congress, 2d session, May 15, 1984, 12199–12204.

172   Senate Hearings on the Supreme Court Nomination of Robert H. Bork

September 15 and 18, 1987

The Senate's rejection of President Ronald Reagan's nomination of Robert H. Bork, a judge on the Court of Appeals in the District of Columbia, to a seat on the Supreme Court in 1987 was a bitter battle filled with political charges and countercharges. Bork's supporters felt the Senate had unfairly treated a distinguished, *highly qualified, scholarly judge by attacking his conservative views and engaging in character assassination. Critics of the Bork rejection claimed that this partisan action by the Senate Judiciary Committee, then in the hands of Democrats under the chairmanship of Senator Joseph R. Biden Jr. (D-Del.), was an unusual use of its authority to reject the president's nominee. But a look into the history of the Senate's nomination process reveals that it has not been uncommon for the Senate to reject a high court nominee.*

The Constitution gives the Senate the power to confirm the president's nominees as ambassadors, consuls, public ministers, members of the Supreme Court, and other officers, including military officers (Article II, Section 2, Clause 2). The vast majority of presidential nominations and confirmations by the Senate are handled in a routine manner, with a minimum of political controversy. During the 97th Congress (1981–1983), for example, a much higher than average number of confirmations occurred. During that Congress President Reagan made 184,973 nominations, of which 184,844 were confirmed.

As the political or public profile of the nomination increases, there is often a corresponding increase in political maneuvering. Nominees to the president's cabinet sometimes generate controversy, but the Senate usually bows to the right of a president to name his own team. Less than 5 percent of cabinet nominations have been rejected by the Senate since 1789.

In the case of nominations to the Supreme Court, the Senate has exercised its power more strenuously because of the high profile nature of this appointment and the fact that the appointment is for life to an independent branch of government. The nomination process for high court nominees has often involved political maneuvering and a great deal of controversy. Only 108 individuals have served on the Supreme Court in its entire history. Since 1793 twenty-seven nominees have been rejected by the Senate or withdrew their names before final action in the Senate. The unsuccessful nominees represent about 25 percent of the total who have served on the high court. This rate runs even higher if the names are included of those who withdrew from the process before their nomination reached the Senate. Following Judge Bork's failed nomination, for example, President Reagan's next nominee for the high court, Douglas H. Ginsberg, withdrew from consideration just days after his nomination because of a political firestorm regarding the fact that he admitted he had smoked marijuana.

Sometimes, even when a nominee was eventually confirmed, the political fight for the nomination captured and held the public's attention. This was the case in 1991 during the highly charged confirmation hearings of Clarence Thomas. Thomas labeled the process a "high-tech lynching" because of the charges of alleged sexual impropriety brought against him during the hearings.

Senator Edward M. Kennedy (D-Mass.) led the opposition to Bork's nomination, casting Bork in public statements as no friend of women and minorities and as a judge who would not uphold the rights of individual privacy. Supporters of Judge Bork, including Senator Alan Simpson (R-Wyo.), portrayed Bork as the victim of a massive, expensive, smear campaign orchestrated in the media that totally distorted Bork's record. The hearings, while tense with undertones, represented an interesting philosophical debate about the nature of the American legal system.

In the end, one Republican on the Senate Judiciary Committee sided with all of the Democrats in rejecting Bork's nomination by a vote of 5–9. The committee then voted to send the nomination to the floor of the Senate with an unfavorable recommendation. This led to a highly partisan and acrimonious debate in the Senate, which only added to the polarized feelings over Bork's nomination. When the full Senate voted, it rejected Bork by a vote of 42–58.

OPENING STATEMENT OF SENATOR EDWARD M. KENNEDY

Senator KENNEDY. Good morning, Judge Bork.

From the beginning, America has set the highest standards for our highest Court. We insist that a nominee should have outstanding ability and integrity. But we also insist on even more than those who sit on the Supreme Court must deserve the special title we reserve for only nine federal judges in the entire country, the title that sums up in one word the awesome responsibility on their shoulders—the title of "Justice."

Historically, America has set this high standard because the Justices of the Supreme Court have a unique obligation: to serve as the ultimate guardians of the Constitution, the rule of law, and the liberty and the quality of every citizen. To fulfill these responsibilities, to earn the title of "Justice," a person must have special qualities:

A commitment to individual liberty as the cornerstone of American democracy.

A dedication to equality for all Americans, especially those who have been denied their full measure of freedom, such as women and minorities.

A respect for justice for all whose rights are too readily abused by powerful institutions, whether by the power of government or by giant concentrations of power in the private sector.

A Supreme Court Justice must also have respect for the Supreme Court itself, for our constitutional system of government, and for the relationship between Congress and the President.

Indeed, it has been said that the Supreme Court is the umpire of the federal system because it has the last word about justice in America. Above all, therefore, a Supreme Court nominee must posses the special quality that enables a justice to render justice. This is the attribute whose presence we describe by the words such as fairness, impartiality, open-mindedness, and judicial temperament, and whose absence we call prejudice or bias.

These are the standards by which the Senate must evaluate any judicial nominee. And by these standards, Robert Bork falls short of what Americans demand of a man or woman as a Justice on the Supreme Court. Time and again, in his public record over more than a quarter of a century, Robert Bork has shown that he is hostile to the rule of law and the role of the courts in protecting individual liberty.

He has harshly opposed—and is publicly itching to overrule—many of the great decisions of the Supreme Court that seek to fulfill the promise of justice for all Americans.

He is instinctively biased against the claims of the average citizen and in favor of concentrations of power, whether that is governmental or private.

And in conflicts between the legislative and executive branches of government, he has repeatedly expressed a clear contempt for Congress and an unbridled trust in the power of the President.

Mr. Bork has said many extreme things in his comments of a lifetime in the law. We already have a more extensive record of his work and writings than perhaps we have had for any other Supreme Court nominee in history.

It is easy to conclude from the public record of Mr. Bork's published views that he believes women and blacks are second-class citizens under the Constitution. He even believes that, in the relation to the executive, Members of Congress are second-class citizens, yet he is asking the Senate to confirm him.

The strongest case against this nomination is made by the word of Mr. Bork himself. In an article he wrote in 1963, during the battle to desegregate lunch counters, motels, hotels, and other public accommodations in America, he referred to the civil rights principle underlying that historic struggle as a principle of unsurpassed ugliness.

Ten years later, he recanted his opposition, but in the time since then he has consistently demonstrated his hostility towards equal justice for all.

As recently as June of this year, he ridiculed a Supreme Court decision prohibiting sex discrimination and suggested that the extension of the equal protection clause to women trivializes the Constitution.

In Robert Bork's America, there is no room at the inn for blacks and no place in the Constitution for women, and in our America there should be no seat on the Supreme Court for Robert Bork.

Mr. Bork has been equally extreme in his opposition to the right to privacy. In an article in 1971, he said, in effect, that a husband and wife have no greater right to privacy under the Constitution than a smokestack has to pollute the air.

President Reagan has said that this controversy is pure politics, but that is not the case. I and others who oppose Mr. Bork have often supported nominees to the Supreme Court by Republican Presidents, including many with whose philosophy we disagree. I voted for the confirmation of Chief Justice Burger and also Justices Blackmun, Powell, Stevens, O'Connor and Scalia. But Mr. Bork is a nominee of a different stripe. President Reagan has every right to take Mr. Bork's reactionary ideology into account in making the nomination, and the Senate has every right to take that ideology into account in acting on the nomination.

Now, Mr. Bork's supporters are understandably seeking to change his spots and deflect attention from the public record of his controversial career. He will have ample opportunity in these hearings to explain, or explain away, the extraordinarily extreme and biased positions he has taken. But a switch at a convenient time should not be sufficient to make Mr. Bork one of the nine.

Some observers are predicting a bitter battle over this nomination and have suggested that the struggle is reminiscent of the great confrontations over civil rights and equal justice in the past. But those confrontations were inevitable and irrepressible. All Americans should realize that the confrontation over this nomination is the result of a deliberate decision by the Reagan administration. Rather than selecting a real judicial conservative to fill Justice Powell's vacancy, the President has sought to appoint an activist of the right whose agenda would turn us back to the battles of a bitterly divided America, reopening issues long thought to be settled and wounds long thought to be healed.

I for one am proud of the accomplishments of America in moving towards the constitutional ideas of liberty and equality and justice under law. I am also proud of the role of the Senate in ensuring that Supreme Court nominees adhere to the tradition of fairness, impartiality, and freedom from bias.

I believe the American people strongly reject the administration's invitation to roll back the clock and relive the more troubled times of the past. I urge the committee and the Senate to reject the nomination of Mr. Bork.

. . . .

OPENING STATEMENT OF SENATOR ORRIN G. HATCH

Senator HATCH. Thank you. I want to welcome you to the committee, Judge Bork, and I would just state that I think it is important that potential Justices be treated with fairness too; not with inflammatory mischaracterizations; not with distorted statistics; not with misleading methodology leading up to these type of statements and statistics, and certainly not with the selective use of evidence, a lot of which I have seen by your critics in this particular matter.

Mr. Chairman, I feel honored to welcome to the committee one of the most qualified individuals ever nominated to serve on the United States Supreme Court. His resume—outstanding law student, successful trial practitioner, leading law professor, esteemed author and lecturer, excellent Solicitor General, and respected judge on the District of Columbia Circuit—speaks for itself.

Nonetheless a few details might demonstrate the quality of his life's work. He was not merely one of the top law students at the University of Chicago, but he was the managing editor of the Law Review, as has been stated. He was not merely one of the top law professors for 15 years, but the holder of two endowed chairs. He was not merely an excellent Solicitor General, but successfully represented the United States before the Supreme Court in hundreds of cases during his 4-year tenure. He was not merely another appellate judge, but a judge who in at least 416 total cases was never once reversed on appeal. Moreover, the Supreme Court six times adopted his dissenting opinion when he had the courage to dissent from the majority of his judicial colleagues.

Now, this is a jurist who, in the words of President Carter's legal counsel, Lloyd Cutler, will be counted by history as belonging alongside a few select justices, like Oliver Wendell Holmes, Louis Brandeis, Felix Frankfurter, Potter Stewart—whose wife is here with you today and whom I have a great deal of admiration and respect for, of course, her husband—and Lewis Powell, as well.

You have been paid an even higher tribute than even that endorsement, however, Judge Bork. That tribute is found in the witness list of those who have volunteered to testify in you behalf, and I will just mention a few. That list includes, as we have seen, a former President, a former Chief Justice, six former Attorney Generals of both parties, twelve top leaders of law enforcement officers, seven law school deans, twelve leading law professors in this country, four top anti-trust lawyers, three bar leaders, several of your former colleagues at the Department of Justice, and other influential lawyers and organizational heads. If an individual can be judged by the company he keeps, then you are unrivaled.

In light of these remarkable credentials, it is hard to understand why your nomination would generate controversy. The answer is found in one word, which is tragic in this judicial context, and that word is "politics." Judge Bork is experiencing the kind of innuendo and intrigue that usually accompanies a campaign for the U.S. Senate. Many Senators are experienced at running that kind of campaign but it has no place in a judicial nominating proceeding. Federal judges are not politicians and ought not to be judged like politicians.

The great danger I see in the impending ideological inquisition is injury to the independence and integrity of the Supreme Court and the whole federal judiciary. When we undertake to judge a judge according to political rather than legal criteria, we have stripped the judicial office of all that makes it a distinct separated power. If the general public begins to measure judges by a political yardstick and if the judges themselves begin to base their decisions on political criteria, we will have lost the reasoning processes of the law which have served us so well to check political excesses and fervor over the past 200 years. I would ask any American if they would wish to have their life, liberty and property resting on the decision of judges who are more worried about what the newspaper might say about the case than they are about life, liberty or property.

Recognizing precisely this danger, the Senate has refused to employ political litmus tests while confirming 53 justices over this past century. Senate precedent does not support subjecting judicial nominees to ideological inquisitions.

Moreover, the Constitution itself does not support that practice. Based on the common sense observation that a diverse congressional body would have difficulty overcoming jealousies and politics to select the best candidate, the framers in 1878—200 years ago, just 2 days from now—unanimously voted to vest the nomination power in the President. The Senate, however, was given a checking function. In the words of Alexander Hamilton, the advice and consent function was to prevent "nepotism" and "unfit characters." The advice and consent function is a checking function, not a license to expert political influence on another branch, not a license to control the outcome of future cases by overriding the President's prerogatives.

Despite the lessons of Senate precedent and the Constitution and despite the political damage to the independence and integrity of the judiciary, we are likely to witness a bruising political campaign before your nomination comes to a final vote in the Senate. It is not difficult to outline in advance the type of campaign it will be.

In the first place, you will be labeled. Even though political litmus tests do not work well with judges, you will be branded an extreme conservative. Of course, this will require some explanation as to why you voted with your Carter-appointed colleague, Judge Ruth Ginsburg—who is a great judge, by the way—in 90 percent of the cases in which you both sat, or with your Carter-appointed colleague, Judge Abner Mikva, in 83 percent of the cases in which you both sat.

The next tactic will be to extract a few quotes from 15-year-old articles while you were a law professor and ignore your judicial actions. For example, we have already heard allegations that you might allow censorship of free speech. In fact, anyone who wants to know your views on censorship would merely need to read your Lebron decision where you held that the D.C. Metro authorities violated Mr. Lebron's free speech rights by refusing to let him hang a poster that was extremely critical of President Reagan. In fact, those posters are going up today. You were even willing to allow the embarrassment of the President who appointed you to uphold his rights. In my mind, actions speak louder than words.

Another tactic will be to selectively use evidence. For evidence. For instance, we have already seen criticism that your *Dronenburg* decision denied homosexuals a special constitutional protection. The evidence that these critics consistently ignore is that the Supreme Court reached precisely the same decision and the same result in the *Bowers* v. *Hardwick* case.

Still another tactic, familiar to political campaigns is to accuse you of ethical violations. In that vein, we have heard too much recently about the so-called Saturday Night Massacre. In fact, this was one of your finest hours. You were not the cause of Watergate but you were part of the solution. As a precondition of carrying out the President's order, you gained a commitment that the investigation would go forth without further interference. You had to make a difficult decision on the spur of the moment. Even then you had to be convinced by Attorney General Richardson not to resign, but the evidence that your decision was correct is history. Because you preserved the investigation, the President was later forced to resign and several others were prosecuted. The performance that you gave, it seems to me, deserves commendation, not criticism.

It will not end there. Inconsistent charges will be hurled at you. For example, you will be called both an "extremist" and "the one vote likely to tip the balance." You cannot be both, unless those making the charge are the extremists themselves because the four other justices, includes one—Justice White—appointed by President John Kennedy, and two—Scalia and O'Connor—who were unanimously approved by the Senate. Unless they are also extremists, I do not see how you can change anything there. Consistency, I think you can conclude, will not be a hallmark of this debate.

We could discuss likely political tactics for a long time. The important thing to remember is that these political charges betray themselves. As Hodding Carter, an official from the previous Democratic administration, candidly observed, quote "The nomination of Judge Bork forces liberals like me to confront a reality we don't want to confront, which is that we are depending in large part on the least democratic institution, with a small "d", in government to defend what it is we no longer are able to win out there in the electorate," unquote.

That is really what is involved here, and I think he was candid and honest enough to state it in those succinct, candid terms.

This is the reason that politics are injected into this proceeding, because many politicians are hoping to win from unelected judges what they cannot win in the Congress or with the people of this United States of America. My fear, however, is that the price of a politicized judiciary is too high to pay in exchange for a short-term policy set of gains. If judges fear to uphold the Constitution due to political pressures or sense that their judicial careers might be advanced by reading that document in the smokey back rooms of political intrigue, then the Constitution will no longer be the solid anchor holding our nation in place during the times of storm and crisis. Instead, the Constitution will just become part of that political storm, blowing hot and cold whenever the wind changes. That is a price that we in this country cannot afford to pay, and I think it is important that the American people understand that here.

I commend you for subjecting yourself to this situation and I commend you for the work that you have done and for the respect that you have from people who are truly learned in the law all over this country and who set aside political gain.

Thank you for being here and thanks for accepting this nomination.

The CHAIRMAN. Thank you, Senator.

[Prepared statement follows:]

STATEMENT OF ROBERT H. BORK

I want to begin by thanking the President for placing my name in nomination for this extremely important position. I am both flattered and humbled to have been selected. If confirmed, I assure the Senate that I will approach the enormous task ahead energetically and enthusiastically and will endeavor to the best of my ability to live up to the confidence placed in me.

I also want to thank President Ford and Senators Dole and Danforth and Congressman Fish for their warm remarks in itroducing me to the Senate and this Committee.

I would like to add a few remarks at the outset on a subject of central interest in this hearing: my understanding of how a judge should go about his or her work. That may also be described as my philosophy of the role of the judge in a constitutional democracy.

The judge's authority derives entirely from the fact that he is applying the law and not his own personal values. That is way the American public accepts the decisions of its courts, accepts even decisions that nullify laws a majority of the electorate or of their representatives voted for. The judge, to deserve that trust and authority, must be every bit as governed by law as is Congress, the President, the state governors and legislatures, and the American people. No one, including the judge, can be above the law. Only in that way will justice be done and the freedoms of Americans assured.

How should a judge go about finding the law? The only legitimate way is by attempting to discern what those who made the law intended. The intentions of the lawmakers govern, whether the lawmakers are the Congress of the United States enacting a statute or those who ratified our Constitution and its various amendments. Where the words are precise and the facts simple that is a relatively easy task. Where the words are general, as is the case with some of the most profound protections of our liberties in the Bill of Rights and the Civil War amendments, the task is far more complex—it is to find the principle or value that was intended to be protected and see that it is protected. As I wrote in an opinion, the judge's responsibility "is to discern how the framers' values, defined in the context of the world they knew, apply in the world we know."

If a judge abandons intention as his guide, there is no law available to him and he begins to legislate a social agenda for the American people. That goes well beyond his legitimate authority. He or she diminishes liberty instead of enhancing it.

That is why I agree with Judge Learned Hand, one of the great jurists in our history. He wrote that the judge's "authority and his immunity depend upon the assumption that he speaks with the mouth of others: the momentum of his utterances must be greater than any which his personal reputation and character can command, if it is to do the work assigned to it—if it is to stand against the passionate resentments arising out of the interests he must frustrate." To state that another way, the judge must speak with the authority of the past and yet accommodate that past to the present.

The past, however, includes not only the intentions of those who first made the law, it also includes those past judges who interpreted and applied it in prior cases. That is why a judge must give great respect to precedent. It is one thing as a legal theorist to criticize the reasoning of a prior decision, even to criticize it severely, as I have done. It is another and more serious thing altogether for a judge to ignore or overturn a prior decision. That requires much careful thought.

Times come, of course, when even a venerable precedent can and should be overruled. The primary example of a proper overruling is *Brown* v. *Board of Education*, the case which outlawed racial segregation accomplished by government action. Brown overturned the rule of separate but equal laid down 58 years before in *Plessy* v. *Ferguson*. Yet Brown, delivered with the authority of a unanimous court, was clearly correct and represents perhaps the greatest moral achievement of our constitutional law.

Nevertheless, overruling should be done sparingly and cautiously. Respect for precedent is part of the great tradition of our law, just as is fidelity to the intent of those who ratified the Constitution and enacted our statutes.

That does not mean that constitutional law is static. It will evolve as judges modify doctrine to meet new circumstances and new technologies. Thus, today we apply the first amendment's guarantee of the freedom of the press to radio and television and we apply to electronic surveillance the fourth amendment's guarantee of privacy for the individual against unreasonable searches of his or her home.

I can put the matter no better than I did in an opinion on my present court. Speaking of the judge's duty, I said:

The important thing, the ultimate consideration, is the constitutional freedom that is given into our keeping. A judge who refuses to see new threats to an established constitutional value, and hence provides a crabbed interpretation that robs a provision of its full, fair and reasonable meaning, fails in his judicial duty. That duty, I repeat, is to ensure that the powers and freedoms the framers specified are made effective in today's circumstances.

But I must add that when a judge goes beyond this and reads entirely new values into the Constitution, values the framers and ratifiers did not put there, he deprives the people of their liberty. That liberty, which the Constitution clearly envisions, is the liberty of the people to set their own social agenda through the processes of democracy. Conservative judges frustrated that process in the mid-1930's, by using the fourteenth amendment's supposed guarantee of a liberty of contract to strike down laws designed to protect workers and labor unions. That was wrong then and it would be wrong now.

My philosophy of judging is neither liberal nor conservative. It is simply a philosophy of judging which gives the Constitution a full and fair interpretation but, where the Constitution is silent, leaves the policy struggles to Congress, the President, the legislatures and executives of the fifty states, and to the American people.

I welcome this opportunity to come before the Committee and answer whatever questions the members may have. I am quite willing to discuss with you my judicial philosophy and the approach I take to deciding cases with this Committee. I cannot, of course, commit myself as to how I might vote on any particular case and I know you would not wish me to do that.

Let me note in closing that I sit here today as one who has been fortunate to have enjoyed in my professional career a rich experience in four major areas of the law: private practice; the academic world; government experience; and the judiciary. I have been an associate, junior partner, and senior partner in one of the nation's major law firms. I have been a professor of law at Yale University, holding two named chairs, as Chancellor Kent Professor, once held by William Howard Taft, and as the first Alexander M. Bickel Professor of Public Law. For almost four years I served as Solicitor General of the United States, in which capacity I argued about 35 cases before the Supreme Court of the United States. Finally, for the past five and one-half years I have been a judge on the United States Court of Appeals for the District of Columbia Circuit, where I have written over 150 opinions and participated in over 400 decisions. I have a

record in each of these areas of the law and it is for this Committee and the Senate to judge that record.

I will be happy to answer the Committee's questions.

. . . .

The CHAIRMAN. Let me begin. I want to begin to try to understand better and lay out your record in this round of questioning that I have. I want to talk a little bit about what you have said and what you believe about the role of the courts and what that role is in society, and as you said, your judicial philosophy.

Judge Bork, I am sure you know the one question to be raised in these hearings is whether or not you are going to vote to overturn Supreme Court decisions, which is obviously your right as a Supreme Court Justice, if you are confirmed.

In 1981 in testimony before the Congress, you said "there are dozens of cases" in which Supreme Court made a wrong decision. This January, in remarks before the Federalist Society, you implied that you would have no problem in overruling decisions based on a philosophy or a rationale that you rejected.

In an interview with the District Lawyer magazine in 1985, you were asked if you could identify cases that you think should be reconsidered. You said, I again quote, "Yes, I can but I won't."

Would you be willing for this committee to identify the "dozens of cases" that you think should be reconsidered?

Judge BORK. Mr. Chairman, to do that I am afraid I would have to go out and start back through the casebooks again to pick out the ones.

I do not know how many should be reconsidered. I can discuss with you the grounds upon, the way in which I would reconsider them.

Let me mention that Federalist Society talk which was given from scribbled notes. I had some notes, but I scribbled something in the margin which I got up and said in response to another speaker. It was that a non-originalist decision—by which I mean a decision which does not relate to a principle or value the ratifiers enacted in the Constitution—could be overruled.

If you look at the next paragraph of that talk, which was a written out part and not the extemporized part, it contradicts that statement. The very next paragraph states that the enormous expansion of the commerce power, Congress' power under the commerce clause of the Constitution, is settled, and it is simply too late to go back and reconsider that, even though it appears to be much broader than anything the framers or the ratifiers intended.

So there is, in fact, a recognition on my part that stare decisis or the theory of precedent is important. In fact, I would say to you that anybody who believes in original intention as the means of interpreting the Constitution has to have a theory of precedent, because this Nation has grown in ways that do not comport with the intentions of the people who wrote the Constitution—the commerce clause is one example—and it is simply too late to go back and tear that up.

I cite you the *Legal Tender* cases. These are extreme examples admittedly. Scholarship suggests that the framers intended to prohibit paper money. Any judge who today thought he would go back to the original intent really ought to be accompanied by a guardian rather than be sitting on a bench.

The CHAIRMAN. I could not agree with you more, Judge, but when you and I had our brief discussion a month or so ago, a similar question was raised by me or by you—I cannot recall who—and you pointed out that you cite the commerce clause and the legal tender decisions as examples.

Can you give us any other examples of the numerous decisions you have criticized that might fall in that category of being settled doctrine now and would cause such upheaval to change? Because you know there have been many decisions you have criticized that have been decided from 1942 on after the commerce clause.

Judge BORK. All right. I criticized these cases on the basis of the reasoning or lack of reasoning that the courts offered. For example, the case has come up and was mentioned, I think, in your opening statement, *Shelley* v. *Kraemer*. *Shelley* v. *Kraemer* was a case decided under the 14th amendment. The 14th amendment, as we all know, applies only when government acts, when government coerces and denies equal protection of the laws or due process.

That was a racial covenant, restrictive covenant case, and the Court held that when a State court enforced that contract, that was action by the government; and, hence, the 14th amendment applied to private action.

I have never been for racially restrictive covenants. I argued in the Supreme Court that racially discriminatory private contracts were covered by Section 1981, a famous post-Civil War enactment, and outlawed as such by that statute. That was *Runyon* v. *McCrary*.

The CHAIRMAN. What year was the statute, Judge? Do you know?

Judge BORK. No, I do not offhand.

The CHAIRMAN. Did it ante-date the *Shelley* case?

Judge BORK. Oh, yes. But it just had not been applied. It was a post-Civil War statute.

The difficulty with *Shelley* was not that it struck down a racial covenant, which I would be delighted to see happen, but that it adopted a principle which, if generally adopted, would turn almost all private action into action to be judged by the Constitution.

Let me give you an example. If people at a dinner party get into a political argument, and the guest refuses to leave when asked to do so by the host, and finally the host calls the police to have the unwanted guest ejected, under *Shelley* v. *Kraemer* that would become State action, and the guest could raise the first amendment. His first amendment rights would have been violated because a private person got sick of his political diatribe and asked him to leave and the police assisted him.

In that way, any contract action, any tort action, any kind of action can be turned into a constitutional case. Now, I am not alone in criticizing *Shelley* v. *Kraemer*. I think I have here Professor Herbert Wechsler who has criticized it. Professor Tribe

has said that, "[t]o contemporary commentators . . . *Shelley* and [another case] appear as highly controversial decisions. In neither case, the critical consensus has it, is the Court's finding of State action [Government coercion] supported by any reasoning which would suggest that the 'State action' [doctrine] is a meaningful requirement rather than an empty formality."

There have been some suggestions that my constitutional philosophy or my reasoning about these cases is in some sense eccentric. It is not in the least bit. All of these cases have been criticized. In fact, *Shelley* v. *Kraemer* has never been applied again. It has had no generative force. It has not proved to be a precedent. As such, it is not a case to be reconsidered. It did what it did; it adopted a principle which the Court has never adopted again. And while I criticized the case at the time, it is not a case worth reconsidering.

The CHAIRMAN. Well, let's talk about another case. Let's talk about the *Griswold* case. Now, while you were living in Connecticut, that State had a law—I know you know this, but for the record—that made it a crime for anyone, even a married couple, to use birth control. You indicated that you thought the law was "nutty," to use your words and I quite agree. Nevertheless, Connecticut, under that "nutty" law, prosecuted and convicted a doctor and the case finally reached the Supreme Court.

The Court said that the law violated a married couple's constitutional right to privacy. You criticized this opinion in numerous articles and speeches, beginning in 1971 and as recently as July 26th of this year. In your 1971 article, "Neutral Principles and Some First Amendment Problems," you said that the right of married couples to have sexual relations without fear of unwanted children is no more worthy of constitutional protection by the courts than the right of public utilities to be free of pollution control laws.

You argued that the utility company's right or gratification, think you referred to it, to make money and the married couple's right or gratification to have sexual relations without fear of unwanted children, as "the cases are identical." Now, I am trying to understand this. It appears to me that you are saying that the government has as much right to control a married couple's decision about choosing to have a child or not, as that government has a right to control the public utility's right to pollute the air. Am I misstating your rationale here?

Judge BORK. With due respect, Mr. Chairman, I think you are. I was making the point that where the Constitution does not speak—there is no provision in the Constitution that applies to the case—then a judge may not say, I place a higher value upon a marital relationship than I do upon an economic freedom. Only of the Constitution gives him some reasoning. Once the judge begins to say economic rights are more important than marital rights or vice versa, and if there is nothing in the Constitution, the judge is enforcing his own moral values, which I have objected to. Now, on the *Griswold* case itself—

The CHAIRMAN. Can we stick with that point a minute to make sure I understand it?

Judge BORK. Sure.

The CHAIRMAN. So that you suggest that unless the Constitution, I believe in the past you used the phrase, textually identifies, a value that is worthy of being protected, then competing values in society, the competing value of a public utility, in the example you used, go out and make money—that economic right has no more or less constitutional protection than the right of a married couple to use or not use birth control in their bedroom. Is that what you are saying?

Judge BORK. No, I am not entirely, but I will straighten it out. I was objecting to the way Justice Douglas, in that opinion, *Griswold* v. *Connecticut,* derived this right. It may be possible to derive an objection to an anti-contraceptive statute in some other way. I do not know.

But starting from the assumption, which is an assumption for purposes of my argument, not a proven fact, starting from the assumption that there is nothing in the Constitution, in any legitimate method of constitutional reasoning about either subject, all I am saying is that the judge has now way to prefer one to the other and the matter should be left to the legislatures who will then decide which competing gratification, or freedom, should be placed higher.

The CHAIRMAN. Then I think I do understand it, that is, that the economic gratification of a utility company is as worthy of as much protection as the sexual gratification of a married couple, because neither is mentioned in the Constitution.

Judge BORK. All that means is that the judge may not choose.

The CHAIRMAN. Who does?

Judge BORK. The legislature.

The CHAIRMAN. Well, that is my point, so it is not a constitutional right. I am not trying to be picky here. Clearly, I do not want to get into a debate with a professor, but it seems to me that what you are saying is what I said and that is, that the Constitution—if it were a constitutional right, if the Constitution said anywhere in it, in your view, that a married couple's right to engage in the decision of having a child or not having a child was a constitutionally-protected right of privacy, then you would rule that right exists. You would not leave it to a legislative body no matter what they did.

Judge BORK. That is right.

The CHAIRMAN. But you argue, as I understand it, that no such right exists.

Judge BORK. No, Senator, that is what I tried to clarify. I argued that the way this unstructured, undefined right of privacy that Justice Douglas elaborated, that the way he did it did not prove its existence.

The CHAIRMAN. You have been a professor now for years and years, everybody has pointed out and I have observed, you are one of the most well-read and scholarly people to come before this committee. In all your short life, have you come up with any other way to protect a married couple, under the Constitution, against an action by a government telling what they can or cannot do about birth control in their bedroom? Is there any constitutional right, anywhere in the Constitution?

Judge BORK. I have never engaged in that exercise. What I was doing was criticizing a doctrine the Supreme Court was creating which was capable of being applied in unknown ways in the future, in unprincipled ways. Let me say something about *Griswold* v. *Connecticut.* Connecticut never tried to prosecute any married couple for the use of contraceptives. That statute was used entirely through an aiding and abetting clause in the general criminal code to prosecute birth control clinics that advertised. This is what it was about.

The CHAIRMAN. But, in fact, they did prosecute a doctor, didn't they, for giving advice?

Judge BORK. Well, I was at Yale when that case was framed by Yale professors. That was not a case of Connecticut going out and doing anything. What happened was some Yale professors sued to have that—because they like this kind of litigation—to have that statute declared unconstitutional. It got up to the Supreme Court under the name of *Poe* v. *Ullman.* The Supreme Court refused to take the case because there was no showing that anybody ever got prosecuted.

They went back down and engaged in enormous efforts to get somebody, have a right to pass a law telling a married couple, or anyone else, that behind—let's stick with the married couple for a minute—behind their bedroom door, telling them they can or cannot use birth control? Does the majority have the right to tell a couple that they cannot use birth control?

Judge BORK. There is always a rationality standard in the law, Senator. I do not know what rationale the State would offer or what challenge the married couple would make. I have never decided that case. If it ever comes before me, I will have to decide it. All I have done was point out that the right of privacy, as defined or undefined by Justice Douglas, was a free-floating right that was not derived in a principled fashion from constitutional materials. That is all I have done.

The CHAIRMAN. Judge, I agree with the rationale offered in the case. Let me just read it to you and it went like this. I happen to agree with it. It said, in part, "would we allow the police to search the sacred precincts of marital bedrooms for telltale signs of contraceptives? The very idea is repulsive to the notions of privacy surrounding the marriage relationship. We deal with the right of privacy older than the Bill of Rights. Marriage is a coming together for better or worse, hopefully enduring, and intimate to the degree of being sacred. The association promotes a way of life, not causes. A harmony of living, not political face. A bilateral loyalty, not a commercial or social projects."

Obviously, that Justice believes that the Constitution protects married couples, anyone.

Judge BORK. I could agree with almost every—I think I could agree with every word you read but that is not, with respect, Mr. Chairman, the rationale of the case. That is the rhetoric at the end of the case. What I objected to was the way in which this right of privacy was created and that was simply this. Justice Douglas observed, quite correctly, that a number of provisions of the Bill of Rights protect aspects of privacy and indeed they do and indeed they should.

But he went on from there to say that since a number of the provisions did that and since they had emanations, by which I think he meant buffer zones to protect the basic right, he would find a penumbra which created a new right of privacy that existed where no provision of the Constitution applied, so that he—

The CHAIRMAN. What about the ninth amendment?

Judge BORK. Wait, let me finish with Justice Douglas.

The CHAIRMAN. All right.

Judge BORK. He did not rest on the ninth amendment. That was Justice Goldberg.

The CHAIRMAN. Right. That is what I was talking about.

Judge BORK. Yes. And I want to discuss first Judge Douglas and then I would be glad to discuss Justice Goldberg.

The CHAIRMAN. Okay.

Judge BORK. Now you see, in that way, he could have observed, equally well, the various provisions of the Constitution protect individual freedom and therefore, generalized a general right of freedom that would apply where no provision of the Constitution did. That is exactly what Justice Hugo Black criticized in dissent in that case, in some heated terms—and Justice Potter Stewart also dissented in that case.

So, in observing that *Griswold* v. *Connecticut* does not sustain its burden, the judge's burden of showing that the right comes from constitutional materials, I am by no means alone. A lot of people, including Justices, have criticized that decision.

The CHAIRMAN. I am not suggesting whether you are alone or in the majority. I am just trying to find out where you are. As I here you, you do not believe that there is a general right of privacy that is in the Constitution.

Judge BORK. Not one derived in that fashion. There may be other arguments and I do not want to pass upon those.

The CHAIRMAN. Have you ever thought of any? Have you ever written about any?

Judge BORK. Yes, as a matter of fact, Senator, I taught a seminar with Professor Bickel starting in about 1963 or 1964. We taught a seminar called Constitutional Theory. I was then all in favor of *Griswold* v. *Connecticut.* I thought that was a great way to reason. I tried to build a course around that, only I said: we can call it a general right of freedom, and let's then take the various provisions of the Constitution, treat them the way a lawyer treats common law cases, extract a more general principle and apply that.

I did that for about 6 or 7 years, and Bickel fought me every step of the way; said it was not possible. At the end of 6 or 7 years, I decided he was right.

The CHAIRMAN. Judge, let's go on. There have been a number of cases that flow from the progeny of the *Griswold* case, all relying on *Griswold,* the majority view, with different rationales offered, that there is a right of privacy in the Constitution, a general right of privacy, a right of privacy derived from the due process, from the 14th amendment, a right of privacy, to use the Douglas word—the penumbra, which you criticize, and a right Goldberg suggested in the *Griswold* case, from the ninth

amendment. It seems to me, if you cannot find a rationale for the decision of the *Griswold* case, then all the succeeding cases are up for grabs.

Judge BORK. I have never tried to find a rationale and I have not been offered one. Maybe somebody would offer me one. I do not know if the other cases are up for grabs or not.

The CHAIRMAN. Wouldn't they have to be if they are based on the same rationale?

Judge BORK. Well, it may be that—I have written that some of these cases were wrongly decided, in my opinion. For some of them I can think of rationales that would make them correctly decided but wrongly reasoned. There may be other ways, that a generalized and undefined right of privacy—one of the problems with the right of privacy, as Justice Douglas defined it, or did not define it, is not simply that it comes out of nowhere, that it does not have any rooting in the Constitution, it is also that he does not give it any contours, so you do not know what it is going to mean from case to case.

The CHAIRMAN. Let's talk about another basic right, at least I think a basic right, the right not to be sterilized by the government. The Supreme Court addressed that right in the famous case, *Skinner* v. *Oklahoma.* Under Oklahoma law, someone convicted of certain crimes faced mandatory sterilization. In 1942, Mr. Skinner had been convicted of his third offense and therefore, faced sterilization, brought his case to the Supreme Court. The Court said that the State of Oklahoma could not sterilize him. Let me read something from the Court's opinion.

"We are dealing with legislation which involves one of the basic civil rights of man. Marriage and procreation are fundamental in the very existence and survival of a race. There is no redemption for the individual whom the law touches. Any experiment which the State conducts is to his irreparable injury. He is forever deprived of a basic liberty."

Judge, you said that Supreme Court decision is improper and intellectually empty. I would like to ask you, do you think that there is a basic right, under the Constitution, not to forcibly sterilized by the State?

Judge BORK. There may well be, but not on the grounds stated there. I hate to keep saying this, Mr. Chairman, much of my objection is to the way some members of the Court, not always the whole Court, has gone about deriving these things. In *Skinner* v. *Oklahoma,* I think it might have been better to say that the statute does not have a reasonable basis because there is no scientific evidence upon which to rest the thought that criminality—that was, not then, I do not know anything about the state of scientific evidence now—that criminality is really genetically carried.

The CHAIRMAN. But if there was, they would be able to sterilize?

Judge BORK. Well, I do not know. The second thing about that statute, in this case, is that Justice Douglas did say something which is quite correct and he did not need to talk about procreation and fundamental rights to do it. That is, he noted that the statute made distinctions, for example, between a robber and an embezzler. The embezzler was not subject to this kind of thing.

He had gone on and pointed out that those distinctions really sterilized, in effect, blue collar criminals and exempted white collar criminals, and indeed, appeared to have some taint of a racial basis to it, he could have arrived at the same decision in what I would take to be a more legitimate fashion.

The CHAIRMAN. I thought that under the equal protection clause, that was the essence of it and you have written—I may be mistaken—I thought you had written that there is no basis under the equal protection clause for having arrived at that conclusion.

Judge BORK. Not the way he did it. What the Court was doing with the equal protection clause for many years, and to which I objected more generally in this article, is that they would decide whether a whole group was in or out and then they would decide what level of scrutiny they would give to the statute to see whether it was constitutional or not.

I think that derives—and I hate to get into a technical question—but I think it derives from a footnote in the *Carolene Products* case, in which they were supposed to look at groups, as such. It would be much better if instead of taking groups as such and saying this group is in, that group is out, if they merely used a reasonable basis test and asked whether the law had a reasonable basis. I think the statute, in *Skinner* v. *Oklahoma,* the sterilization statute, would have failed under a reasonable basis test.

The CHAIRMAN. So you have to find a reasonable basis. If there is one, you could sterilize. If there is not one, you cannot. It seems to me that it comes down to a basic difference. You do not believe the Constitution recognizes what I consider to be a basic liberty, a basic liberty not to be sterilized.

Judge BORK. I agree that this is a basic liberty, and I agree that family life is a basic liberty and so forth. But the fact is we know that legislatures can, constitution, regulate some aspects of sexuality.

The CHAIRMAN. True.

Judge BORK. We know that legislatures do and can constitutionally regulate some aspects of family life. There is no question, I think, that these things are subject to some regulation. We have divorce laws, custody laws, child beating laws and so forth. The question always becomes, under the equal protection clause, has the legislature a reasonable basis for the kind of thing it does here.

The sterilization law would probably require an enormous or perhaps impossible degree of justification.

The CHAIRMAN. I hope so.

Judge, my time is about up, but with regard to the *Griswold* case, you are quoted in 1985—you were a judge at this time, although this statement was not made in your judicial capacity— as saying, "I don't think there is a supportable method of constitutional reasoning underlying the *Griswold* decision."

So obviously, you thought about it, and you at least at that point concluded you could not find one.

It seems to me, Judge—and as I said, there are many more cases I would like to talk to you about, and I appreciate you engaging in this dialogue—that you say that a State can impact upon marital relations and can impact upon certain other relations, and it seems to me that there are certain basic rights that they cannot touch. And what you seem to be saying to me is that a State legislature can theoretically, at least, pass a law sterilizing, and we will see what the courts say. It is not an automatic, it is not basic. Right now, if any State legislature in the country asked counsel for the legislature, "Could we pass a law, sterilizing?" I suspect the immediate response from counsel would be, "No, you cannot do that"—not only politically, but constitutionally.

Have any State legislative bodies said, "Can we decide on whether or not someone can or cannot use contraceptives," not any reasonable basis, I imagine all counsel would say "No" flatly; cannot even get into that area.

And it seems to me you are not saying that. You are saying that it is possible that can happen, and in *Griswold* you are saying that there is no principle upon which they could reach the result—not the rationale, you say; you say the result.

Judge BORK. Well, I think I was talking about the principle underlying that one. But I should say—

The CHAIRMAN. Well, wait, let me stop you there, Judge, because I want to make sure I understand. The principle underlying that one is the basic right to privacy, right, and from that flows all these other cases, all the way down to Franz, which you spoke to all the way down to *Roe* v. *Wade.* They all are premised upon that basic principle that you cannot find.

I am not saying you are wrong. I just want to make sure I understand what you are saying.

Judge BORK. Well, I do not think all those cases necessarily follow. They used the right of privacy in some of those cases, and it was not clear why it was a right of privacy.

I should say that I think not only Justices Black and Stewart could not find it—and Gerald Gunther, who is a professor at Stanford and an authority in these matters, has criticized the case; and Professor Philip Kurland has referred to *Griswold* v. *Connecticut* as a "blatant usurpation."

The CHAIRMAN. But most did find it; the majority did find it though, didn't they?

Judge BORK. Yes. But I am just telling you, Senator, that a lot of people have thought the reasoning of that case was just not reasoning.

The CHAIRMAN. My time is up. Judge, I want to make it clear, I am not suggesting there is anything extreme about your reasoning. I am not suggesting it is conservative or liberal. I just want to make sure I understand it. And as I understand what you have said in the last 30 minutes, a State legislative body, a government, can, if it so chose, pass a law saying married couples cannot use birth control devices.

Judge BORK. Senator, Mr. Chairman, I have not said that; I do not want to say that. What I am saying to you is that if that law is to be struck down, it will have to be done under better constitutional argumentation than was present in the *Griswold* opinion.

The CHAIRMAN. Again, I will end, to quote you, sir, you said, "The truth is that the Court could not reach the result in *Griswold* through principle." I assume you are talking about constitutional principle.

Judge BORK. I do not know—what is that from?

The CHAIRMAN. I am referring to your 1971 article. That is the quote in the 1971 article. And then you said—

Judge BORK. Do you have a page number for that, Senator?

The CHAIRMAN. I will get the page. Sorry—a 1982 speech while you were Judge, speaking at Catholic University. You said, "The result in *Griswold* could not have been reached by proper interpretation of the Constitution." End of quote. We will dig it out for you here to show you—I believe you all sent it to us, so that is how we got it.

Judge BORK. Okay. Yes.

The CHAIRMAN. Well, my time is up. I appreciate it. We will do more of this.

. . . .

[SEPTEMBER 18]

. . . .

Senator KENNEDY. Well, I think the record will speak for itself. I have no further questions of the nominee. I would like to just use the remaining 2 or 3 minutes for a comment. I think Mr. Bork has claimed that he is only applying neutral principles, but there is something wrong with neutral principles if the result is that Congress and the courts must be neutral in the face of discrimination because of race, they must be neutral in the face of discrimination against women and in the face of gross invasions by the Government of individual citizen's rights to privacy.

Above all, a Supreme Court Justice may be fair, but in lifetime of writings on the public record, Mr. Bork has shown his bias against women and minorities and in favor of big business and Presidential power. It is small comfort to minorities to know that some years after the Civil Rights Act was passed over his opposition, Mr. Bork changed his mind and said that it had worked all right. But if you had your way, Mr. Bork, no one would ever have known how the Civil Rights Act would work.

Mr. Bork is against the one man, one vote decision of the Supreme Court, which says that everyone's vote should count equally and the same. He would allow majorities to write laws that give greater weight to some people's vote than others and that is the very opposite of democracy. Mr. Bork asks us to judge him on his record, as a judge, but in his own speeches, as a judge, he has shown little respect for past decisions of the Supreme Court.

Again and again on the public record, he has suggested that he is prepared to roll back the clock, return to more troubled times, uproot decades of settled law in order to write his own ideology into law. And in these hearings this week , he has asked us to believe that he can make a U-turn in these areas of fundamental importance. The question all of us are asking is who is the real Robert Bork and what risks are we taking for the future if he becomes a Justice of the Supreme Court with the last word about justice in America.

The White House strategy, in these proceedings, has been clear. Mr. Bork's balloon was losing altitude in the Senate, and he has been rapidly jettisoning the baggage of a lifetime in opposition to individual liberty and equal justice. President Reagan has failed to achieve his ideological agenda in Congress and is not entitled to achieve it by an ideological nomination to the Supreme Court that could reverse the progress of the past and tilt the country far beyond the end of his term.

America is ready to move forward with the Supreme Court, not backward. But Mr. Bork is out of step with the Congress, out of step with the country, out of step with the Constitution and many of the most fundamental issues facing America. Mr. Bork is a walking constitutional amendment and he should not be confirmed by the Senate.

Judge BORK. Senator, if those charges were not so serious, the discrepancy between the evidence and what you say would be highly amusing. I have not asked that either the Congress nor the courts be neutral in the face of racial discrimination. I have upheld the laws that outlaw racial discrimination. I have consistently supported *Brown* v. *Board of Education* in my writings long ago. I have never written a word hostile to women.

I have never written a word hostile to privacy. I have complained about the reasoning of one Supreme Court case. I have never written a word or made a decision from which you can infer that I am pro-big business at the expense of other people. And as far as Presidential power is concerned, I have rarely dealt with that, but when I have, it is on constitutional principles and upon occasion, as in the pocket veto matter, you will find me squarely opposing Presidential power.

I have no ideological agenda and if I did, it would not do me any good because nobody else on the Court has an ideological agenda and I do not intend, if confirmed, to be the only person up there, running around with a political agenda. In fact, nothing in my record suggests I have a political or ideological agenda.

Senator KENNEDY. Well, Mr. Chairman, I think my time is expired and I think the record speaks for itself. We have had an opportunity to review those items in previous questioning and the members will have to make their own judgment.

Judge BORK. I agree with that, Senator Kennedy.

The CHAIRMAN. The Senator from Wyoming.

Senator SIMPSON. Thank you, Mr. Chairman. Mr. Chairman, I have shared with you and I practiced law for 18 years and have legislated for 24 and I have enjoyed that thoroughly. In these last for days, I have become totally convinced of what I thought was inadequacy, but has actually proven to be a great, remarkable asset. I never wrote any books. I wrote a lot of briefs. There are no written speeches of Al Simpson. I knew I was on the right track years ago.

The CHAIRMAN. I think you will find a bunch of them are taped, Al. I am finding that out right now. [Laughter.]

And not all of them turn out to be mine either. [Laughter and applause.]

Senator SIMPSON. Well, next question please. That is typical of your grace in this situation and like you and I like that. You need that. Keep your humor, it sure throws the rest of them off. They do not know what the hell to do with it. But, I never wrote any stuff. I worked hard and I worked hard to be a great lawyer and I work hard to be a great legislator or statesman. I work hard because I do not like to make an ass out of myself. There really is nothing else in it for me.

And when you said this morning—it was very moving—when you said something to the effect—and it was just two or three words, so I must be pretty close to it—that you did not want to go down in history or to be disgraced in history, that you have said and stated your position absolutely clearly and if anyone could believe that you are going to go on the Supreme Court and not do it all differently, you would be disgraced in history. Isn't that what you said?

Judge BORK. I did indeed. I should make an additional point. I also took an oath, when I came in here before this committee, to tell the truth and I take an oath very seriously and that is what I have done is told the truth.

Senator SIMPSON. Well, I think that is something for people to hear very clearly. Indeed, you did take an oath and you take that oath very seriously and you have a belief in a higher being and that is what makes the oath worth taking. That is how that works. That ain't corny. That is the way it is.

But again, back to writings. It was curious to me and it has been like a law school seminar in some situations to hear you and my fine friend from Pennsylvania discussing certain areas of the law in a highly honed way. For me to listen to this is educational and very fascinating how you get into it and both can bat it around—and others. And Senator Metzenbaum with his antitrust. Having never written a book—this fellow said he had written in the area of probate—he wrote a very provocative book called "The Role of the Decedent in Estate Planning." I could have written a book like that and I thought that is the only title I could have probably gotten away with.

But, I had an awful lot of fun practicing law in a profession that I dearly loved and I wrote some awfully stupid letters. People still bring them to my attention. I tried some really goofy cases, losers, total losers. In pro bono—we really did not get going on pro bono until I was about 3 or 4 years into the practice, about 1963. Somebody said, you know, we ought to do some pro bono. We said, well we will so the Park County Bar Association said we will do, you know, blank hours a month, each of us and check the book.

I do not know how many lawyers did it that way. We did. We thought we were pro bono automatically. We were charging 10 bucks an hour for our work. So, pro bono was not what it is now.

That again is kind of what this whole thing is about. We are judging you on the basis of September 18th, 1987, when they forgot everything that was swirling around in 1964 and 1971 and 1980, whenever. That's, I think, total distortion.

Back to that extraordinary case, the "illegal" case, that you did something illegal. Well, I tell you, I used to use Black's law dictionary only when I was in extremity. The word "vacate" in Black's law dictionary says "To amend, to set aside, to cancel, or rescind; to render an act void; to vacate an entry of record or judgment." It is not synonymous with "suspend," which means to stay enforcement of judgment or decree—to put an end to.

I hope we can put an end to what must be another goofy case where the party that won didn't want to go any further with it.

Now, you don't have to be a real wizard to know that must be a real turkey. And it was vacated. And that ought to be the end of that, surely.

So I guess that we, who support your nomination—I guess we kind of come out and say, ah, that's crazy, how can that be? But obviously, that isn't enough, because those on the other side say highly dramatic things: you have shocked my senses, you have left me limp, I cannot believe that I have read, you have stunned me.

Well, I tell you, why wouldn't someone in America be alarmed to see the distortion of your record. How would anyone not, any sensible American not be disturbed if they read your record? The word "poll tax" is immediately equated with racism. I think we all ought to get awfully tired of that; that case had nothing to do with racism, nothing. The words "poll tax" have a marvelous connotation—no, a hideous connotation of racism. And you would have trashed it in a minute, would you not, if it had anything to do with racism?

Judge BORK. Of course, the basis of my discussion of that case was that it had nothing to do with racism and therefore it was a little hard to follow some of the reasoning. I should say—I've just been handed the opinion in that case, Senator, and Justice Hugo Black dissented from that ruling that the poll tax was automatically unconstitutional, even when there was no racism. And in his dissent, he said:

"It should be pointed out at once that the Court's decision is to no extent based on a finding that the Virginia law, as written or as applied, is being used as a device or a mechanism to deny Negro citizens of Virginia the right to vote on account of their color. Apparently the Court agrees with the district court below, and with my brothers Harlan and Stewart, that this record would not support any finding that the Virginia poll tax law the Court invalidates has any such effect."

That is, any such discriminatory effect. Hugo Black said that very plainly, and indeed, the Court did not claim that there was any racial animus in that poll tax.

Senator SIMPSON. Yet that has been presented day after day, hour after hour, on the hour—in fact, they all are presented on the hour, or on the half hour—the same ones; and they always have the charged word "anti-black," "racist," "sterilization of your fellow human beings," "contraceptives," "homosexuality," "sexual preference," "women's rights." You know, really, what a bizarre exercise. It must be something for you to observe—and you are observing it, you are living it.

How do you feel about it all?

Judge BORK. Senator, I have not yet had time to gather my thoughts on the entire matter. Let me say it is not terribly enjoyable.

Senator SIMPSON. No, I think not, but I think it will be concluded shortly. And it's been a very fair hearing—and a good one, and you like it somewhere down in there.

Judge BORK. Oh, Senator, I love it. [Laughter.]

Senator SIMPSON. All right, now, several Senators have gone through the list of your actions and views and cases and amicus briefs, and the full-page newspaper ads have continued in harsh and hysterical tones, and repeated and supplemented your "record", which is really so grossly distorted, from prior writings and speeches. And, you know, when I ask who these groups are, I never really can find out; it's really getting to be a phantom kind of a networking operation now—they are running out of gas, or money, and nobody really takes any responsibility. I wasn't going to used the word "credit"—that would be a disservice.

But other items in these listings and in these advertisings are not only unfair, in my mind—and in some cases outrageous; they are dishonest—I will use that term—and they are lies—I will even use that term, because that's more perfunctory and more real, and one that I'd love to stick with: lies. And those words that people know, words like "lie."

Going over this list that we have heard this morning—and I've had my list over the last 3 days—on what you have done on the court, which are not anything more than things of the record, which are precise and irrefutable; they are in the statutes, in the law books. So when we get to what is the point, what kind of a Justice will this man be as a Supreme Court judge, it is quite helpful to see what he was as an appellate judge. And I am not going to go through the cases that have already been reported about female Foreign Service officers entitled to the same pay as similarly employed male officers—you did that; holding that intentional sex discrimination can be inferred solely on statistical evidence—a marvelous pro-civil rights decision; female stewardesses may not be paid less than male pursers with similar jobs; two cases on title 7, which were liberally construed, which in effect kept the courthouse door open for aggrieved people who claimed employment discrimination—that hasn't been quoted before, and that's *Nordell* v. *Heckler* and *Tyrell* v. *U.S. Postal Service*—you kept the door open, other people were trying to shut it on blacks and others; the senior military officers case and the promotion decision on the black officer—you did that, you opened that door for him; the South Carolina vote where there was an at-large election without first proving that the changes would have no discriminatory effect against blacks—you did that, you opened that door, that isn't something you talk about on a podium or sing about—you did it. That's not the view of a judge who is hostile to women and minorities; it sounds to me like a very compassionate man.

I hope the people of America are seeing that in you, a judge who has expanded civil rights during every bit of his writings and decisions instead of pinching it down and shutting it off. The earlier Robert Bork, you know, who wrote all those provocative law review articles—well, that's you, too. Theory, I read that yesterday what you said about as you opened and prefaced those remarks in that law review article, and how you ended it.

What was interesting to me was that when you were Solicitor General you filed several briefs supporting the rights of minorities and rights of women when you didn't even have to, didn't you?

Judge BORK. True.

Senator SIMPSON. That's pretty clear. You get a lot of flak on that, but that's what the system is supposed to be all about.

So then you filed an amicus brief urging and arguing that single-sex schools are unconstitutional and illegal—that was a Philadelphia case. You filed these because you felt it was the right thing to do under the law. We've all heard several times— and yet it keeps coming back up when they talk about you as being a racist, that you alone took a pretty firm stand in your original law firm and stopped the prejudice against another Jewish lawyer in the firm.

Then you filed another brief—and you mentioned on your first day, Section 1981, which is an old statute—I don't remember the date of it, but I know if we had ever put the right English on the cue ball on that one years ago we could have saved a lot of time in the civil rights laws, wouldn't you agree?

Judge BORK. That's entirely true.

Senator SIMPSON. You bet. So 1981, Section 1981, is a most important civil rights statute. And you filed a brief which said it was the most important one prior to the Civil Rights Act of 1964.

Judge BORK. I didn't say it prior to 1964, that's right; I said the statute was the most important one before the 1964 one.

Senator SIMPSON. When applied to racially discriminatory private contracts.

Well, Gordon Humphrey has reviewed some of those, Orrin Hatch has reviewed some of those.

You filed another amicus brief, successfully arguing the 14th amendment gave the Congress the complete power to remedy State or local violations of the amendment. Now, that one decision right there is probably the most critical one of getting things done under the civil rights law, is that not correct?

Judge BORK. I think so.

Senator SIMPSON. That one has escaped people, apparently— *Fitzpatrick* v. *Bitzer*. That was absolutely essential to the federal elimination of racial discrimination, is that not true?

Judge BORK. I guess so. Senator, I don't have that—I'm afraid I filed so many briefs in my time—

Senator SIMPSON. I'm sure that's true. But, in any event, it was essential—and you did that. Then you represented the position of unions—you went through those other cases. And no one has really presented any honest evidence of you doing these heinous things in this country, and that really—well, that galls me—I'm not going to ask you what it does with you. Because I believe in fairness. You know, you can play this game of politics—and I love it, I can bat around it, chew up in it, snarl, and then go off and have a light glass of ale with some guys who I vote with 5 percent of the time—but that's fun for me, because that's the way I practiced law.

So to hear these things said about you—the best and most attractive phrase, it just seems weird, absolutely weird, to hear that when the cases are there. I think it shows how much we are talking past each other with regard to you. I hope we are somewhere listening in this process and that our colleagues on the floor will be listening, because it would be a great disservice to talk past each other as regards to you. And if it's not being heard, that would be indeed too bad. And if that happens and goes on, they will not know about you.

I was interested again in that issue of precedent and overruling and so on. I don't know how you can get any more clear than that—I really don't—because in the same article that is being used to drum you about the head and shoulders, this "District Lawyer" article—you said it all in there, that, you know, if things had been built up, regulations and governmental institutions and private expectations had built up around that, it's too late, even if a justice or judge became certain that broad interpretation is wrong in the matter of original intent, to tear it up and overturn it. That's what you said. And then at the end of that article you said "If the Justices have become convinced that a decision cannot be squared with the Constitution, they ought to consider overruling it. But the Court should be careful"—these are your words—"If a particular decision has become the basis for a large array of social and economic institutions, overruling it could be disastrous." You said that, didn't you?

Judge BORK. Yes, I certainly did.

Senator SIMPSON. In the same article that was referred to moments ago—I believe; maybe it was a different one, but it was certainly from the "District lawyer."

Judge BORK. That's the same article—same interview.

Senator SIMPSON. Here's a statement, call it "Guess Who" time.

He is a dangerous radical. The general opinion is that he is a very able lawyer, a man of keen intellect, but that, as a matter of intellectual honesty, he is not entirely trustworthy. He will distort the Court's decisions for generations; he will take his seat equipped with a variety of preconceived notions and firmly held opinions relating only remotely, if at all, to the questions of law, but rather to the questions of a purely political nature concerning social issues.

Now, that was a comment about Justice Louis Brandeis. The year was 1916.

Did you think he panned out all right?

Judge BORK. I certainly did.

Senator SIMPSON. In the end?

Judge BORK. I certainly did. He's become one of the giants of the Court.

Senator SIMPSON. He made the grade.

Judge BORK. That's right.

Senator SIMPSON. He is not disgraced in history, is he?

Judge BORK. Certainly not, certainly not. The names of Holmes and Brandeis, I suppose, will live as long as our jurisprudence does.

Senator SIMPSON. Well, they will be to all of us who love the law and practiced it and to the people who it affects—and that's everybody else. That was a comment about Justice Brandeis.

How about this one? "He has a record of continued hostility to the law, of continual war on the Constitution. He has already taken sides with the executive branch. He would be but their echo." The National Organization for Women warned that if he were confirmed, "justice for women would be ignored or further delayed, which means justice denied."

That is a comment about Lewis Powell. What do you think of that one?

Judge BORK. They appear to have missed the mark rather substantially.

Senator SIMPSON. I think so. One more—and a final one.

We opposed his confirmation not solely because of his consistent opposition to women's rights, but, more importantly, because he has demonstrated that his legal opinions on women's issues are based on an apparent personal philosophy and not on the facts and laws and cases before him. Thus he lacks the fairness and the impartiality requisite for appointment to the Supreme Court of the United States.

That's about Justice John Paul Stevens. What do you think about that comment?

Judge BORK. Just as the comment about Justice Powell, when I said they missed the mark very substantially, was being a bit wry; they missed the missed the mark by 180 degrees.

Senator SIMPSON. Well, indeed they have, and they have fired all the grapeshot in their cannon at you, and they missed it just as badly. And I think history will bear that out.

I'm interested in another thing—oh, I know one I wanted to cover. Back to the issue of equal protection. How much time to I have, please? Forget it, they are not going to keep track.

The CHAIRMAN. Just keep going.

Senator SIMPSON. The issue of equal protection—

The CHAIRMAN. About 6 or 7 minutes, Senator, but, if you need more time, take it.

Senator SIMPSON. You noted that the military draft—I think this is important, I want you to hear this little scheme here.

Judge BORK. All Right.

Senator SIMPSON. Heh, heh, heh. [Laughter.]

That the draft was a good example of a case where distinctions based on race were improper, but distinctions bases on gender were not improper. Now, I should point out to you—I know this is hideous—that a majority of the Senators agreed with the finding of the Supreme Court on that, and your example, that gender-based distinctions are acceptable in certain rare circumstances. On June 10, 1980, the U.S. Senate itself voted to exclude women from President Carter's draft plan by a vote of 51 to 40. A number of people on this panel participated in that vote, six of us sitting right here, three Republicans, three Democrats, to exclude women from the draft.

Now, I just want to make a point that Congress was quite willing to make a gender-based distinction in this case, present criticisms and dire comments notwithstanding. I think that's kind of important to kind of touch on occasionally. That's real life.

The first amendment, that is a troubling thing. I cannot believe that anyone is going to try to blast you away on the first amendment. I do not know of anybody that has done more.

There should not be a person in this country to believe that you would not broaden it. You have said you would, and, as I say, your favorite guy that was doing posters over there, that you allowed him to do that, has done some ever-new ones now. I want to get over and see them, and they are on the wall.

And you gave him all the ability to do that, to raise hell about this President, your President, his President, and he is doing it again. It is opinion, it is his expression, and, that is real life.

You did that, didn't you, in that case?

Judge Bork. Right.

Senator Simpson. I have read that case, and it is fascinating, and of course several have read about the fact that you must be willing to bear criticism, disparagement, and even wounding assessments. We all have been through that one. We have been there.

But I loved what you went on to say. You said:

> Perhaps it would be better if disputation were conducted in measured phrases, and calibrated assessments, and with strict avoidance of the ad hominem, better, that is, if the opinion and editorial pages of the public press were modeled on The Federalist Papers.
>
> But that is not the world in which we live, ever have lived, or ever likely to know, and the law of the first amendment must not try to make public disputes safe and comfortable for all the participants. That would only stifle the debate.
>
> In our world, the kind of commentary that the columnists have engaged in here is the coin in which the controversialists are commonly paid.

I like that. That is pretty gutsy, strong, fair, firm, protective of the first amendment, and people.

Well, I am going to conclude here, but I hope everyone sees the essence of what is happening here, the essence of this cause against Judge Bork. I do not want anybody to miss this.

The opponents of Robert Bork are the opponents of any kind of change in the Supreme Court in my view. They really wanted to halt Sandra Day O'Connor. They really did. But they could not really challenge that remarkable, steady, personable lady. They just could not do anything with her.

And she is a tremendous lady, and jurist. They really wanted to toss Rehnquist off the side of the ship. But as they frothed at the mouth there, they finally sobered up and realized he was already on the Court. That was a dazzling thing for them to decide, that finally, they thought, well, we will kick him off as Chief Justice but he is still going to be there, and then they are going to bring in somebody else.

That brought a note of sobriety to their cause. He was already on the Court. And with Scalia, they saw another bright, dedicated, articulate spirited man, and they had already spurted all the venom out their glands with Rehnquist when he came along, and they were exhausted from the attempt to land the fatal strike on Rehnquist and they slipped back to their lair, or den, whichever you wish—

Senator DeConcini. Will the Senator yield just for a clarification.

Senator Simpson. Yes.

Senator DeConcini. My recollection on the Sandra Day O'Connor, that it was the National Right to Life that testified in opposition to her. The president of that group is a friend of mine, and from Arizona. I had big arguments with her, and she came and testified here in opposition to Sandra O'Connor.

I just thought the record ought to show that. I know the Senator wants to know that all of those so-called radical groups are properly identified, and I do not consider that a radical group.

Senator Simpson. I will finish and then you can go on with your explanations. You know, you name them. I am just talking about the fact that there were groups. I do not consider that group a radical group.

What had they learned in the fray after they went through that exercise? They learned really only one thing as I see it.

They learned that you were next. They knew the minute—I think their worst fears were realized—that you are the "live" round that was coming at them the next time, and they went to work.

And when Scalia raised his right hand on his oath, they raised the stakes, and they said "Get Bork. He's next. Can't possibly miss him on the next selection. That's him."

And they put their researchers and minions to work, and they readied their fund-raising apparatus, and they cranked up the networking, and hours and days of work in a non-unanimous decision venture. Every utterance. I mean, you know, when you are dragging stuff out of a question and answer session at a school in 1985, and then hearing in—you know—that took a lot of work. A lot of people have done a lot of work.

The Chairman. Senator, if I can interrupt you just hold on that point because I think it is very important.

I want the record to show that I went to Judge Bork yesterday, and gave him a full transcript, told him that that tape had been sent, unsolicited, to several people, apparently. I know I was sent a tape. And I did not want him to be caught unaware by anything. I had the tape transcribed, I gave it to him, told him I would not ask him any questions about that tape, and for a full day, to give him a full opportunity to look at it, and I am sure the tape was sent to other people by a student up there, as I recall.

I may be mistaken. So I just do not want you to think that all of a sudden, out of the heavens, came this—

Senator Simpson. No, no.

The Chairman. And then I was asked by a colleague whether or not it could be played. So I just did not want anyone to think that Judge Bork was not fully aware that (a) there was a tape and (b) he had a written transcript, and even outlined—I believe my staff even circled or pointed out for you where that point was.

Judge Bork. No, I was not caught by surprise, Mr. Chairman.

The Chairman. I am not suggesting you think you were.

Judge Bork. And I was not disturbed by it because it is an unexceptional remark, and it is the only time I did not add a qualification which I have added on every other occasion. So that does not bother me at all.

Senator SIMPSON. Mr. Chairman, I have before me, right here, the excerpt from the question and answer question. It was handed to me this morning.

The CHAIRMAN. I am not suggesting, Alan, in any way, that you should have known that. I just wanted everyone to know, though that Judge Bork knew of that, and possibly, if I had thought about it, I should have handed the transcript to everyone.

But obviously, the most important person to be aware of it was Judge Bork, and that is all I meant to state. I am not trying to make any more of it than it is.

Senator SIMPSON. Mr. Chairman, I will conclude in 2 minutes, and I promise that, from these notes that were thoughtfully prepared by me, because I am trying to figure where it all started.

And as I say it, it started when Scalia was approved in the most remarkable fashion. That was a remarkable confirmation hearing.

So then they set up their early-warning system: if Robert Bork is nominated it will be destructive, it will be contentious. And then they said this to the American people, after Judge Lewis Powell announced his retirement.

They said if Robert Bork is nominated it will be destructive, contentious, quote, "time-consuming"—whatever that connotation—we know what that means in the Senate. It will be a struggle. It will be a watershed, shifting the balance, and, there was a kind of a warning to our President that he should not do this.

When the President nominated you they detonated the package, they were ready to do that, and they did it in a way I think where the shards and the chunks from the explosion, you know, were destined to be a little hurtful and painful, and injure.

Because they really do not care about that. The personal anguish of that to you is not important to those kind, and yet they will tell you they represent the oppressed and the disenfranchised, and the powerless, and those who need care. But give them another human being to gnaw on and they will do it in a rather extraordinarily tough, mean, nasty fashion.

So what that they maligned your character, which is all we have in life. Your life style. Why wouldn't any thoughtful American be stunned, and deeply concerned in the full burst of all that, as they fired that around the United States? They were saying you were a racist, a sexist, one who would deny women their rights. A segregationist. A peeper at the keyhole. An invader of privacy Insensitive to homosexuals, and in favor of mandatory sterilization of your fellow man and woman.

Who wouldn't be frightened by that, or deeply appalled and concerned?

Well, I think the American people are terribly fair. They hear, and they know, and you have been right there for four days, and the interested ones have been observing the process, and they have to see you and know your persona is a most extraordinary man, with a dazzling record. A creative, thoughtful man with an agile, adroit and facile mind.

And the American people, and our colleagues would, in my mind, Mr. Chairman, be ill-served, and very certainly cruelly short-changed if you are to be rejected in these proceedings. Thank you.

. . . .

U.S. Senate, Senate Hearing 100–1011, Part 1, Hearings Before the Committee on the Judiciary, 100th Congress, 1st session, September 15–19, 21–23, 25, 28, and 30, 1987.

173   A Poem to the Congress of the United States

March 2, 1989

It is a rare and special event when a poet speaks to Congress. On March 2, 1989, as part of a joint meeting of Congress to commemorate its 200th anniversary, Howard Nemerov (1920–1991), the poet laureate of the United States, delivered a short poem on the role of the legislative branch in the life of the nation. No poet had addressed Congress since 1959, when Carl Sandburg delivered an address about Abraham Lincoln on the 150th anniversary of Lincoln's birth.

The bicentennial commemoration of Congress in 1989 came at a time when Congress was racked with scandal and, according to opinion polls, was generally mistrusted by the public. The Speaker of the House, Jim Wright (D-Texas), who presided at the joint meeting celebrating Congress's two-hundredth birthday, was himself under the cloud of a House investigation that would lead him, less than three months later, to become the first Speaker in history to be forced to resign from office (see document 174).

Nemerov faced a difficult challenge. What does a poet say before a two-hundred-year-old institution that is celebrating its long,

rich, diverse history, while at the same time facing a serious internal crisis and high levels of public mistrust? The fair balance Nemerov struck that day, the masterful way in which he cut to the essence of the importance of Congress to the people of the United States, and the humor with which he concluded the poem sounded just the right note for the occasion. Those assembled in the House chamber responded with enthusiastic applause, appreciation, and laughter. As he left the podium and sat down next to the historian David McCullough, who was also on the program that day, Nemerov said to McCullough, "It worked."

The poet recognized the central importance of Congress to our system of representative democracy with his stunning opening line: "Here at the fulcrum of us all." He spoke of the importance of compromise and balance to the conflicts before Congress "Lest our enterprise collapse in silence." The poem concluded with a whimsical but insightful analysis of the zeal of the reformer tempered with the need to be cautious. Sometimes the role of Congress is to innovate and sometimes its role is to apply the brakes. Knowing when to forge ahead with innovation and when to apply the brakes to change can determine the success or failure of a Congress, and perhaps of the nation itself.

TO THE CONGRESS OF THE UNITED STATES
ENTERING ITS THIRD CENTURY, WITH PREFACE

Because reverence has never been America's thing, this verse in your honor will not begin "O thou." But the great respect our country has to give may you all continue to deserve, and have.

Here at the fulcrum of us all,
The feather of truth against the soul
Is weighed, and had better be found to balance
Lest our enterprise collapse in silence.

For here the million varying wills
Get melted down, get hammered out
Until the movie's reduced to stills
That tell us what the law's about.

Conflict's endemic in the mind:
Your job's to hear it in the wind

And compass it in opposites,
And bring the antagonists by your wits

To being one, and that the law
Thenceforth, until you change your minds
Against and with the shifting winds
That this and that way blow the straw.

So it's a republic, as Franklin said,
If you can keep it; and we did
Thus far, and hope to keep our quarrel
Funny and just, and though with this moral:—

Praise without end for the go-ahead zeal
Of whoever it was invented the wheel;
But never a word for the poor soul's sake
That thought ahead, and invented the brake.

Congressional Record, House, 101st Congress, 1st session, March 2, 1989, H501. The poem was later published in Howard Nemerov, *Trying Conclusions: New and Selected Poems, 1961–1991* (Chicago: University of Chicago Press, 1991), 142. In the *Congressional Record* version, all first lines of the poem were capitalized. In the version published in *Trying Conclusions,* all lines begin with lower case letters. Reprinted courtesy of Mrs. Howard Nemerov.

174   The Resignation Speech of Speaker Jim Wright

May 31, 1989

Never before in the history of the House of Representatives had a Speaker of the House been forced to resign from office. But after a year of investigation by an outside attorney hired by the House Committee on Standards of Official Conduct, Speaker Jim Wright (D-Texas) decided to give up his office. Charges had been filed against him by Newt Gingrich (R-Ga.) and Common Cause, a citizen's advocacy group. Wright was charged with numerous violations of House ethics rules regarding the sale of his book, Reflections of a Public Man, *and other violations related to the limits on outside income. According to the committee's report, Wright had used bulk book sales in place of speaking fees to skirt the income provisions, since book royalties were exempted from the rules and income from speeches was not. The lengthy ethics report contained a statement of alleged violations, with sixty-nine counts in five categories. It was alleged that Wright had received the equivalent of free housing from George Mallick, a Fort Worth developer, and that the Speaker's wife Betty had received a salary from an investment company the Wrights had formed with Mallick, even though there was no evidence that work was done for this salary.*

In his speech, Wright argued in his own defense about the various charges against him before saying, near the end of the speech:

Well, I tell you what, I am going to make you a proposition: Let me give you back this job you gave to me as a propitiation for all of this season of bad will that has grown up among us. Let me give it back to you. I will re-

sign as Speaker of the House effective upon the election of my successor, and I will ask that we call a caucus on the Democratic side for next Tuesday to choose a successor.

I do not want to be a party to tearing up this institution. I love it.

To tell you the truth, this year it has been very difficult for me to offer the kind of moral leadership that our institution needs. Because every time I try to talk about the needs of the country, about the needs for affordable homes—both Jack Kemp's idea and the ideas we are developing here—every time I try to talk about the need for a minimum wage, about the need for day dare centers, embracing ideas on both sides of the aisle, the media have not been interested in that. They wanted to ask me about petty personal finances.

Jim Wright served thirty-four years in the House of Representatives and rose in the leadership ranks, serving for ten years as the House majority leader while Thomas P. "Tip" O'Neill's was Speaker (1977–1987). Wright was elected Speaker at the opening of the 100th Congress in January 1987 and was reelected Speaker in the 101st Congress in 1989, serving in that capacity until his resignation on June 6, 1989.

The climate of scandal that swirled in the House of Representatives in the 1980s and 1990s had many complex roots, some of which could be traced to new and stricter ethics rules in the House and Senate, the establishment of standing committees dealing with ethics issues in both houses of Congress, and the willingness of both parties to use violations of ethics rules to attack and in some cases destroy their political opponents. John M. Barry's account of the fall of Speaker Wright, The Ambition and the Power *(1989), suggests that the real driving force behind the case against Wright was the fear on the part of Gingrich and other Republicans that Wright was a serious threat to Republican Party interests, especially in the area of foreign policy, where Wright showed a strong willingness to challenge President Ronald Reagan's policy in Central America. Wright sought to place his stamp on Latin American policy, a subject long of great interest to him. Not since Henry Clay had a Speaker sought such a direct involvement in foreign policy decision-making.*

In his memoir, Worth It All *(1993), Wright showed no bitterness toward his political enemies in Congress or in the executive branch. "If I have a major regret," he wrote, "it is that my talents for leadership were inadequate to the task of united and conciliating the harshly divergent factions within our Congress into a reasonably harmonious consensus toward the problems besetting our nation. I resigned as Speaker because it was apparent to me that such leadership was needed and that it had eluded my capacities. Striving for conciliation, I had reaped polarization. It was time for someone else."*

On the day Speaker Wright delivered his resignation speech, the House chamber was packed with members and staff and the galleries were filled to capacity. There were only a few empty seats, on the Republican side of the aisle. All who were assembled felt the gravity of the situation. The chamber, and the packed galleries, had a solemn cast. News of the Speaker's impending resignation had swept Capitol Hill, although he did not officially announce it until near the end of his remarks. Several of his staff members wept openly, but quietly, along the rails in the back of the chamber.

. . . .

Mr. WRIGHT. Mr. Speaker, for 34 years I have had the great privilege to be a Member of this institution, the people's House, and, I shall forever be grateful for that wondrous privilege. I never cease to be thankful to the people of the 12th District of Texas for their friendship and their understanding and their partiality, toward me.

Eighteen times they have voted to permit me the grand privilege of representing them here in this repository of the democratic principles.

Only a few days ago, even in the face of the news accounts and bitter criticisms, they indicated in a poll taken by the leading newspaper in the district that 78 percent of them approved of my services, and that includes 73 percent of the Republicans in my district. I am very proud of that.

And you, my colleagues—Democrats and Republicans—I owe a great deal to you. You have given me the greatest gift within your power to give. To be the Speaker of the U.S. House of Representatives is the grandest opportunity that can come to any lawmaker anywhere in the Western World, so I would be deeply remiss if I did not express my sincere appreciation to you for that opportunity.

I would hope that I have reflected credit upon the people of my district who know me best, perhaps, and upon the people of this House who, next to them, know me best.

I am proud of a number of things that we have done together while you have let me be your Speaker. I am proud of the record of the 100th Congress.

Many people feel that it was the most responsive and productive Congress in perhaps 25 years, and all of you who were here in that Congress had a part in that.

Many of the things we did were truly bipartisan in character. Together we made it possible for great leaps forward be made in such things as U.S. competitiveness in the world. Together we fashioned the beginnings of a truly effective war on drugs—to stamp out that menace to the streets and schools and homes of our Nation.

We began the effort to help the homeless, and we still have work to do to make housing affordable to low-income Americans so that there will not be any homeless in this country.

We did things to help abate the financial disaster of catastrophic illness, to provide for welfare reform, clean water, and a great many other things that I shall not detail.

For your help, your great work, and for permitting me to be a part of this institution while that was happening, I thank you and I shall forever be grateful for your cooperation.

I love this institution. I want to assure each of you that under no circumstances, having spent more than half my life here, this House being my home, would I ever knowingly or intentionally do or say anything to violate its rules or detract from its standards. All of us are prone to human error.

The Speaker of the House is, in fact, the chief enforcer of the rules of the House. It is really a wonderful thing that any Member of the House may, at his or her will, bring questions against any other Member and under our rules the case must be investigated. I have no quarrel with that, nor do I have any criticism of the people who serve on the Committee on Standards of Official Conduct. That is a thankless job, and we have to have such a committee.

For nearly a year I have ached to tell my side of the story. True, the questions which I have to respond to keep changing. But today silence is no longer tolerable, nor, for the good of the House, is it even desirable.

So without any rancor and without any bitterness, without any hard feelings toward anybody, I thank you for indulging me as I answer to you, and to the American people, for my honor, my reputation, and all the things I have tried to stand for all these years.

For the past year, while the Committee on Standards of Official Conduct has had these matters under advisement, I have ached for the opportunity to speak. Almost daily I besought the committee to let me come and answer whatever questions the Members had on their minds.

Finally, on the 14th of September, 1988, they gave me 1 day in which to respond. I gratefully went and spent the whole morning and the whole afternoon, answering as candidly and as freely as I possibly could, any question that anyone asked. I believe when I left everyone was reasonably well satisfied.

Suffice it to say that the five original charges were dropped, dismissed. In their place, however, came three additional charges. Well, some said 69. But the 69 are actually just a matter of multiple counting of the 3.

In April the committee said, well, the members thought there was some reason to believe that rules may have been violated in these three basic areas.

I owe it to you, and to the American people, to give a straightforward answer on those three areas.

While I am convinced that I am right, maybe I am wrong. I know that each of us, as Benjamin Franklin suggested, should be careful to doubt a little his own infallibility.

Before those charges were issued, press leaks filtered out almost daily, tarnishing my reputation and, by inference, spilling over to the reputation of this institution.

I pleaded for the privilege to come and answer those questions. Under the rules, that was not permitted to me. And the charges were formally made.

So let us look at them—one by one—dispassionately.

The committee has raised three basic questions. It does not say there is clear and convincing proof that I violated the rules; it does not say that the committee knows I violated the rules. The committee said it had some reason to believe I may have violated the rules. For these last few weeks I have been trying to understand that and get an opportunity to address it.

Now is the day; I am going to do it now.

The three questions are these: One relates to my wife Betty's employment at $18,000 a year for some 4 years by a small investment corporation which she and I formed with friends of ours, George and Marlene Mallick. Did the salary and the attendant benefits of that employment—the use of an apartment when she was in Fort Worth on company business and the use of a company-owned car—constitute merely a sham and subterfuge and a gift from our friend Mr. Mallick? Betty's employment and those things related to it—were they gifts?

Members have read in the papers the suggestion made by committee counsel that I may have received up to $145,000 in gifts from my friend, Mr. Mallick. Half of it, $72,000, was Betty's income, Betty's salary. The other half involved the use of a car and use of an apartment. The question is whether this is right or wrong. Let us look at it.

Betty's employment—was this a gift? The first question, I suppose Members might be asking, is why was Betty working for the corporation. Why did we put her to work at $18,000 a year? The answer is very simple. She was the only one of the four of us who had the time and the inclination to handle the job—to look into the investment opportunities that our investment corporation was created to explore. George Mallick was too busy looking after his own interests. He has business interests of his own. Marlene Mallick was raising a family. I was busy being a Member of Congress and majority leader. I did not have any time to spend on it. Betty alone, among all of us, had the time, the opportunity, the experience, and the desire to give effort and energy to exploring and promoting investment opportunities.

She did, indeed, perform work. It paid off for the little corporation. She did it well. She studied and followed the stock market on regional stocks. I had brought into the corporation some that I had owned personally, in my personal estate. Betty advised us as to the best time to sell, the best time to buy, and the corporation made some money on those regional stocks. Not a lot of money by some people's standards, but we made some money. Betty's work paid for her salary, several times over.

She made very frequent contacts with a drilling company that was working on a series of exploratory west Texas gas wells, in which each of the partners had an interest, having all borrowed money from the corporation in order to invest. She visited the site of drilling and maintained contact with the company for us.

She went to New York and studied the gemstone business and the corporation made an investment in gemstones. We made some money on that. Betty also looked Into the possibility of the corporation, Mallightco, building an apartment complex for young people but she concluded that the interest rates were unfavorable. Betty also spent a considerable amount of time studying the wine culture industry which was then just getting started in Texas. She made an economic study that concluded it was too speculative for a little corporation of our type.

She looked into other prospective investments such as a small and limited partnership in the movie, "Annie," and a prospective venture in sulfur extraction, but advised against both of those investments. It was lucky for us that she did because people investing in them lost money.

Now I want to include for printing in the RECORD affidavits from several business people who know from their personal experience and attest to the work that Betty did in this regard. There will appear in the RECORD, at this point, an affidavit by Pamela L. Smith, one by Kay P. Snyder, one by John Freeman, one by Louis A. Parris, Jr., and one by J. B. Williams, all attesting to their personal knowledge of the things Betty did in working for the corporation at $18,000 a year.

. . . .

The outside counsel employed by the committee has suggested that Mrs. Wright's employment somehow amounted to as gift. I do not know why, but he assumed that the services she rendered could not have been worth $18,000 a year. How he concludes that she did not perform duties is to me a mystery.

On page 20 of the statement of alleged violation, there is a very strange suggestion that, "there was no evidence either supporting or establishing that the money paid to Mrs. Wright was in return for identifiable services or work products." Frankly, I do not know exactly what Mr. Phelan means by "work products."

Does he want so many pages of old shorthand notes? So many pages of typed manuscript? Betty was not a carpenter.

Is a woman's mental study, her time and her advice. not to be counted as a work product? How the committee could conclude that there was "no evidence" that Betty performed duties is very puzzling to me. There certainly is no evidence that she did not.

When I was before the committee, that was not one of the things that was being considered. The committee did not ask me to go into any elaborate details as I have just done—to tell them the things that she did.

The committee assumed—assumed—there was no evidence. Oh, but there was evidence. Both the people of whom questions were asked, aside from myself, Mr. Mallick and Pamela Smith, testified that she did indeed work.

Mr. Phelan's report says that Pamela Smith could not identify any more than maybe 12 days in the whole 4-year period in which Betty worked. That is an inaccurate representation of what Mrs. Smith said. Pamela Smith, both in this affidavit and in her testimony before the committee, clearly said she saw Betty there from 5 to 7 days every month including weekends. Mrs. Smith spoke of her knowledge of Betty doing work in Washington and New York and elsewhere. So there was surely evidence.

Well, is one to conclude that my wife's services to a little corporation were worth less than $18,000? For most of her adult life Mrs. Wright has been a business person. She has been an officer in a large hotel, an officer in a successful real estate and construction firm, and a professional staff person on a congressional committee.

She was making more than $18,000 when she worked for the congressional committee.

And here is the irony, the supreme irony: In 1976, when I was elected majority leader, Betty voluntarily left her job as a professional staff person on the committee so as to avoid any criticism of this institution or of her husband on the grounds that we both were on the public payroll. How many colleagues in the House and the Senate do Members know whose wives are on the public payroll, doing good work? Yet Betty did not want to be the cause for even unfounded criticism. She was legally entitled to continue. She had occupied that job before our marriage. But she chose to leave, to save the institution and her husband from unwanted criticism. That is the kind of person she is.

Now it just seems to me that there is not any justification at all for any person even raising a question about whether she earned her $18,000 a year. Should a Member of Congress have to prove that his wife earned that much money? Bear in mind, this money was not paid by Mr. Mallick. The money was paid by the corporation of which Betty and I were half owners.

In addition to charging that Betty's salary was a gift, the outside counsel contends, in summing up $145,000 in gifts, that Betty had the use of the company car. That is true, she did. For the first 3 years it was used largely by Mr. and Mrs. Mallick. The next 4 years, Betty had most use of it.

It was not Mr. Mallick's car, it was the company car. The company bought and paid for it. We owned half of it. The next 4 years Betty had most of the use of it.

I have done what I can to resolve any doubt. I wanted to do the right thing—the honorable thing. I bought and paid for that car out of my personal funds.

The trustee of my blind trust, at my instruction, paid the corporation full book value for the car on the day Betty first started driving it on company business, plus interest. The interest amounted to about $3,000.

What more can I do? Does that make it right? That has already been done.

Concerning the apartment, Betty and I have been more than anxious to do what is right and honorable about that. We did not think there was anything wrong with paying a per diem rate. The apartment was not held out for rent to anybody else. It was not owned for rental purposes. The Mallick family did not want anybody also in the apartment. The family owned about six apartments in this unit or complex. They held those apartments out for their employees and their families. There would not have been anybody in the apartment paying any amount of money at all if they had not permitted us, when we were in town, to occupy the apartment. We paid on a daily basis for our use of that apartment.

But in an effort to resolve any doubt, last year I told Mr. Mallick that I did not like the situation being criticized. He said "Ralph Lotkin, the counsel for the Committee on Standards, said it was all right." Mr. Mallick pointed out that 4 years ago, there was in the Fort Worth Star-Telegram newspaper a statement quoting the chief counsel of the Committee on Standards. Mr. Lotkin, as saying that he did not see anything improper with the per diem arrangement on the apartment. I relied on that.

Nevertheless, last year I said to George Mallick, "I want to buy the apartment, George. I want to pay you for it." I did. I paid the amount suggested as appraised by two real estate persons in Fort Worth, $58,000. Now, if anybody thinks that is too low a price, I will sell it to you today for $58,000.

Well, I just wanted to clear the air and remove doubts and say that if we made a mistake, we have done what we can to set things right. I do not think we violated any rules. I think you are entitled to know that, and my respect for you leads me to want to tell you that.

The second alleged violation is based on the assumption that Betty's employment and the job benefits that she had were gifts, and the further assumption that George Mallick, our friend and business partner, had a direct interest in influencing legislation, which would make it a violation of the rules for us to accept gifts from him.

Now how does the committee arrive at that suggestion? I have known Mr. Mallick for more than 25 years. He has been my friend. He has been a good, decent, hard-working man, a man of Lebanese extraction. His father had a wholesale grocery store in Fort Worth. His grandfather came there with a wagon, a cart. George has been a moderately successful businessman.

Never once in all the years I have known this man has he ever asked me to vote for or against any piece of legislation—not once. That is not the basis of our friendship. That is not the way our relationship goes. You have friends like that; they do not ask you for anything. All they want is to be a friend. Not one time has he asked me to intercede with any administrative agency of government in his behalf or in behalf of any institution in which he has an interest—not once.

How do they say that he had a direct interest in influencing legislation? Well, on page 58 of the committee report, it is suggested that simply because he was in the real estate business and because he had some oil and gas investments, the committee might "infer"—that is the word—the committee might infer that he could be deemed a person with an interest of a direct nature in legislation.

The committee suggested he might have an interest in the Tax Code. Well, who does not? Every taxpayer has an interest in the Tax Code. Anybody who ever expects to receive Social Security has an interest in the Security laws. All people have an interest of some kind in the results of legislation; do they not?

That is not what we are talking about. We are talking about whether or not they have an interest in trying to influence the course of legislation.

Now where would you go to find out what that means? If somebody wants to association with you in some way and be in business with you back home in a perfectly legal way, where would you go to find out whether they have an interest in legislation or not? Whom would you consult if you were in doubt about it? I was not in doubt, but suppose you were. Would you think you could consult the publications of the committee or consult the people who wrote the rules?

Well, the people who wrote the rules do not thing George Mallick had an interest in legislation. David Obey was the chairman of the committee that drafted those rules. He asserts clearly, emphatically, and unambiguously, both in an affidavit and an op ed he wrote for the Washington Post, the definition that does not fit George Mallick's case. Mr. Mallick does not have an interest in legislation, as defined under the rules, the rules that David and his committee wrote.

Harold Sawyer, a former Republican Member from Michigan who served on that committee along with David Obey, says the same thing. I have an affidavit from Mr. Sawyer in which he states exactly that same conclusion.

And there is an affidavit of Donald F. Terry, who is currently employed by the Committee on Small Business, but who was a staff member of the Commission on Administrative Review, which was charged in 1976 with responsibility for drafting new rules of official conduct for the House. Most of what he refers to has to do with the question of book royalties, and I shall come to that next.

But in these matters, these three people who had a great deal to do with writing the rule say that is not what they intended when they wrote the rule. I offer these for printing in the RECORD. . . .

Where else might you turn if you were in doubt? Might you not possibly go to the committee itself and see advisory opinions it has given? Here is the publication the committee sends to all of us to tell us what is and what is not legal. Each year we receive this as instructions for filling out our financial disclosure, statements. Appendix E is an advisory opinion No. 10

which defines who has a direct interest in legislation under the rules. It says:

If the Member does not believe that the donor of the gift has a distinct or special interest in the congressional legislative process which set him clearly apart from the general public, then the Member should feel free to accept such gifts.

That is the official advice from the committee given to every Member. Then it defines, in summary, who has an interest in legislation as prohibited under the rule. It's given four classes. That is all.

Listed first are registered lobbyist. George Mallick is not a registered lobbyist.

Next comes any person who employs a registered lobbyist. George Mallick never did that.

Third, it refers to somebody who directs or operates a political action committee. George Mallick has never done that.

And finally, any other individual which the Member "knows"—not "should know" or "ought to suspect or ought to infer," but which the Member knows has distinct or special interest in influencing or affecting the legislative process. The definition is not just somebody who has got an interest financially in the outcome of legislation. Not at all. It is rather somebody you know who has a direct or special interest in influencing the outcome of the legislative process which sets that individual apart from the general public.

My colleagues, that was just simply not the case with George Mallick. He had no direct interest in legislation of any type.

Now we have motions before the committee to set aside that presumption of Mr. Mallick's having a interest in legislation. Personally, I do not have reason to believe he has.

The only thing the committee has suggested is that in 1986 his son borrowed money from a savings and loan to build it shopping center, wholly apart and separate from any investments Betty and I had. Then in 1987, the lending institution had to foreclose on the son's loans.

But note the years involved here. Betty was employed, purportedly as a gift, from 1981 to 1984. Mr. Mallick could not have known in 1981 and 1984 that his son was going to borrow money in 1986, and that the thing would go bad in 1987, and that an economic decline would make it possible for him to pay off his note on time. He could not have known that in any way.

I ask my colleagues: "Would you stretch this rule to the point of saying it covers that just anybody who has a member of his family who owes money to a bank or a savings and loan?"

Of course my colleagues would not. That would cover more than half the citizens of the country.

The people who wrote the rules do not believe that Mr. Mallick is covered. So I think under all reasonable circumstances that our dismissal motion ought to be agreed to. Our motion ought to be agreed to, if rules mean anything—if we are not just going to turn the whole thing on its head and change the rules by whim every time we turn around.

Now the third count that remains in the statement of alleged violations which concerns the sales of a book called "Reflections of a Public Man," which I wrote and which was sold sometimes in bulk quantities to people who took it and gave it away to other people—students, newspapers, public officials, and members of their organizations. Did I want these books circulated widely? Of course I did. My colleagues know that I wanted to get the widest possible distribution of the book. A book that you write, you know, is a part of you. You think of it as a child almost.

Now this book probably is not great literature, but I like it. Marty Tolchin of the New York Times; John Bilber, president of Boston University; Jim Lehrer of the MacNeil/Lehrer Report; and Dr. Bill Tucker, chancellor of TCU, all said nice things about it. And I appreciate that.

Now, the contention of the committee, as I understand it, is that the publication of this book, from which I got $3.25 for every one that sold, was a kind of a sham and a subterfuge in itself and an overall scheme for me to exceed and violate the outside earnings limitation on a Member of Congress. Do my colleagues think that I would so something like that?

The purpose of the book was to publish something that could be sold at a small price and get wide distribution. If monetary gain had been my primary interest, do my colleagues not think I would have gone to one of the big Madison Avenue publishers—the houses that give writers big advances?

I know people who have received advances before a single book sells from those big companies—advances twice or three times as much as I got in the total sale of all those books. If it had been a scheme to get around outside earning limits, that is what I might have done.

I hear that a woman author of a book called "Mayflower Madam," got $750,000 in advance royalties. Our former Speaker, Mr. O'Neill, is said to have received $1 million for his excellent and readable book in advance before any of them were sold. I have read that a woman named Kitty Kelly received as much as $2 million in advance royalties for a book she has written on Nancy Reagan and which, as I understand it, is not even an authorized biography. Well, so much for that.

It is true, I think, that people on my staff were eager to sell these books. They knew I wanted them sold. I have got to accept full responsibility for that if it was wrong. But the rule does not say it was wrong.

It could not have been an overall scheme to avoid outside earning limits because the rules are clear. They are not equivocal. The rules expressly exempt royalty income, and that, too, is attested to by the gentleman from Wisconsin (Mr. Obey), and it is attested to by Donald Terry who gives the rationale. There were not any exceptions; book royalties were exempted.

Now maybe book royalties should not have been exempt. But the rules clearly say that they are.

Maybe somebody got the impression that buying a book was a price of getting me to make a speech. I never intended that impression. I never suggested that. I hope that friends of mine did not.

Of all the books that were sold, the committee suggests that seven cases involved instances where individuals associated with organizations to which I made speeches bought multiple copies of the book and distributed them among members of the organization or others.

Now I have not been permitted to see a copy of their testimony, so I do not know exactly what the witness said. I have asked people on my staff, "Did you tell these folks that they had to buy these books or I wouldn't make a speech?" and they said, "no, they did not."

The total amount, as I figure, from all of those sales involved only about $7,700. That is what I received.

My colleagues know I would do whatever was necessary, whatever was right. If any of those people were under the impression that I was not going to make a speech to them unless they bought a bunch of books, and if they wanted their money back, I would give them that money. I do not want the money. That is not important. What is important is a person's honor and his integrity.

During that 3-year period, the committee says there were seven instances where I made speeches to groups that bought copies of these books. In that period, I made at least 700 speeches for which I did not get any honorarium at all, and no one offered to sell anybody a book. Do my colleagues suppose that, if this had been an overall scheme, that there would not have been a wider kind of an experience than that? I do not know. I am Just saying to my colleagues that I did not intend to violate the outside earning limitation, and I do not believe legally that I did.

Some of the rest of my colleagues make a lot of speeches. I ask, "How many speeches do you suppose you make that you don't get anything for?" Most of us make many.

One other thing about the book that I suppose needs elaboration involves the allegation in the statement of alleged violations that a man named S. Gene Payte, a reputable businessman in Fort Worth, paid for more books than he got from the publisher. That is what was said in the report of the outside counsel.

S. Gene Payte, upon reading report, issued an affidavit that is no ambiguous at all. Here is what Mr. Payte says. I will read in part this affidavit and put the whole thing in the RECORD.

He says:

I have read the Report of Special Outside Counsel Richard J. Phelan on the Preliminary Inquiry conducted pursuant to the Committee's June 9, 1988 resolution, as it relates to my testimony. I also have reviewed the transcript of my deposition testimony. The Report, and also the conclusions reached by the Special Counsel, ignores much of the most pertinent testimony in the transcript, takes certain statements out of context, distorts clear statements of fact and in general, fails fairly and accurately to summarize the matters as to which I testified.

And the conclusion reached by the Special Counsel that Wright violated the rule was, quoting the, affidavit "based on his [Mr. Phelan's] categorical assertion that, 'Gene Payte did not receive the books?' "

The Special Counsel asserts,

Payte

And I am quoting—

Testified that he only received between 300 and 500 copies of the old book for his $6,000 and makes the flat statement, "Gene Payte did not receive the books." Citing as authority Payte's transcript, on page 77.

Now here is what Payte says:

On, the contrary. I did not so testify. I stated not once, but three times, that I believed 1,000 books were delivered to me.

And he cites the transcript of this testimony, pages 27, 40. and 41.

Mr. Payte goes on:

The Special Counsel ignores this testimony. Instead, he cites Transcript 77. That citation does not support the Special Counsel's assertion. Transcript 77 shows that Congressman Myers—not I—made the comment, "I believe you said you received 300 to 500 books."

I did not confirm his recollection, my reply being, "I would like to have the new books." . . . In fact, I never so testified.

So this is a copy of that affidavit which I should like to submit for the RECORD, together with a copy of a letter that was sent by the committee to Mr. Payte after he issued this affidavit telling him he ought not to comment.

. . . .

What do you think of that? A private citizen, a reputable citizen of my community, is misquoted in a document published at public expense, and sent widely to newspapers throughout the country. It is widely cited as authority, uncritically, and assumed to be accurate. The citizen being misquoted issues in affidavit to straighten it out so that he is not misquoted in the public record, and then he is warned by the committee that he might be held in violation and in contempt of Congress if he does not shut up.

First amendment rights supersede any rules of any committee, and any citizen of the United States ought to have the right to have his own testimony correctly characterized and not be threatened, or silenced by a House committee. Any House committee owes to a citizen of the United States that right and that privilege.

Well, those are basically the matters pending before the committee in our motion to dismiss. Those motions could clear the air.

Rules are important, just as the constancy of what a law means is important. The committee can resolve these particular legal issues as to what constitutes direct interest in legislation and whether or not book royalties are exempt, as the rules say they are.

I think it is important for the motions to be ruled upon, and I earnestly hope the committee will look at it from that standpoint and grant our motions.

Members are entitled to know what the rules mean and if they still mean what they meant when they were written and promulgated.

Now, maybe the rules need to be changed. If so, let us change them in a legal, orderly way. Let us vote on them. Let us vote to change them. Maybe the whole process needs some change and clarification.

You know, the House may want to consider establishing a House to whom Members can look for official advice and then rely on that advice.

The rules of the committee itself might need some reconsideration.

I have gone through this agonizing experience for about a year now. Almost every day there is a new story and a newspaper leak without any chance for me to know what is coming next, no chance for me to go to the committee and answer it and say, "Hey, wait a minute. That is not correct. That is not right."

Maybe the committee which is currently required to sit both as a kind of grand jury and a petit jury ought to have a different composition, rather than having those who issue the statement of alleged violations being the same people who have to judge them. I think it clearly is difficult to expect Members who publicly announce reason to believe there is a violation to reverse their position at the hearing stage and dismiss charges against a Member. And maybe once a report of alleged violations is issued, the committee rules ought to allow the Member to respond expeditiously.

To deny a Member the opportunity to reply quickly can cause serious political injury. It is unfair. Once alleged violations are announced, the committee ought to release immediately to the Member all the evidence that it has to backup what it has alleged.

In my case, for example, the committee has yet to release any witness testimony or documents that it obtained during the investigation.

Why hide the evidence? What is there to hide? This ought not to be the kind of proceeding in which strategic maneuvering is allowed to override fundamental principles of fair play.

I urge the abolition of the gag order, too, which the committee says forbids any witness who comes and makes a deposition from discussing publicly or telling his side of the thing.

In addition charges which the committee concludes are unfounded should not be published and widely disseminated as though they were true and bear the imprimatur of the committee's approval.

Now, there are other things you ought to consider. I am not trying to give you an exhaustive list of what might happen. I know there are others who have views that am equally relevant.

Perhaps we want to consider an outright abolition of all honoraria and speaking fees. Maybe we want to do that in exchange for a straightforward honest increase in the salary for members of all three branches of Government. I do not know. It is up to the House.

It is intolerably hurtful to our Government that qualified members of the executive and legislative branches are resigning because of ambiguities and confusion surrounding the ethics laws and because of their own consequent vulnerability to personal attack. That is a shame, but it is happening and it is grievously hurtful to our society.

When vilification becomes an accepted form of political debate, when negative camp becomes a full-time occupation, when members of each may become self-appointed vigilantes carrying out personal vendettas against members of the other party. In God's name that is not what this institution is supposed to be all about. When vengeance becomes more desirable than vindication and harsh personal attacks upon one another's motives and one another's character drown out the quiet logic of serious debate on important issues—things that we ought to be involving ourselves in—surely that is unworthy of our institution, unworthy of our American political process.

All of us in both political parties must resolve to bring this period of mindless cannibalism to an end. There has been enough of it.

I pray to God that we will do that and restore the spirit that always existed in this House. When I first came here, all those years ago in 1955, this was a place where a man's word was his bond, and his honor and the truth of what he said to you were assumed. He did not have to prove it.

I remember one time Cleve Bailey of West Virginia in a moment of impassioned concern over a tariff bill jumped up and made an objection to the fact that Chet Holifield had voted. In those days we shouted our answers to the votes, and Mr. Holifield was there in the back, and Bailey said, "I object to the vote of the gentleman from California being counted." He said, "He was not in the Chamber when his name was called and, therefore, he is not entitled to vote."

It was a close vote. Speaker Rayburn grew as red as a tomato, and I thought he was going to break the gavel when he hammered and said, "The Chair always takes the word of a Member," and then because I was sitting over here behind Cleve Bailey, I heard other Members come and say, "Cleve, you are wrong. Chet was back there behind the rail. I was standing there by him when he answered. His answer just was not heard." Others said he should not have said that. Cleve Bailey, the crusty old West Virginian, came down and abjectly, literally with tears in his eyes, apologized for having questioned the word of a fellow Member. We need that.

Have I made mistakes? Oh, boy, how many? I have made a lot of mistakes—mistakes in judgment. Oh yes, a lot of them. I will make some more.

Let me just comment on this briefly, because it is such a sensational thing, and injury has been done to me in this particular moment because of it. John Mack—and many of you remember him, know him, and I think a lot of you like him and respect him. I helped John one time in his life when he was about 20 years old. I did not know him and had never met him. I did not know the nature of the crime of which he had been convicted. I knew only that John Mack was a young man whom my daughter had known in high school. My daughter was married to his brother, incidentally, and that is how she knew about John. She mentioned it to me. All I knew was that he had been convicted of assault and that he had served 27 months in the Fairfax County jail.

Contrary to what has been published, I did not intervene with the court. I did not suggest anything to the court. I did not have anything to do with his sentencing. I really did not know and did not inquire, and maybe that is bad judgment. I did not inquire as to the exact nature of the crime.

The sheriff's office in Fairfax County called me and asked me if I would know of any job that I could help this young man get. They wanted to parole him. They said he had been a model rehabilitative prisoner. I gave him a job as a file clerk at $9,000 a year, and he really blossomed and grew and developed.

Those of the Members who know him found the story hard to conceive, as I did, when finally just 2 years ago I read in the newspaper the precise nature of that crime. It just did not fit his character. John was married and had two beautiful children. He was wonderfully responsible. I think he had become a very fine person.

Was that bad judgment to hire John? Maybe so. It does not have any thing to do with the rules, but it got all mixed up with it, I do not think though that it is bad judgment to try to give a young man a second chance. Maybe I should have known more about him. But in this case I think he has turned out well.

I do not believe that America really stands for the idea that a person once convicted should forever be condemned, but I think maybe he ought to have a second chance, and that is what I thought in the case of John Mack. Good judgment or bad, I believe in giving somebody a second chance.

Have I contributed unwittingly to this manic idea of a frenzy of feeding on other people's reputations? Have I caused a lot of this? Maybe I have. God, I hope I have not, but maybe I have. Have I been too partisan? Too insistent? Too abrasive? Too determined to have my way? Perhaps. Maybe so.

If I have offended anybody in the other party, I am sorry. I never meant to. I would not have done so intentionally. I have always tried to treat all of our colleagues, Democrats and Republicans with respect.

Are there things I would do differently if I had them to do over again? Oh, boy, how many may I name for you?

Well, I tell you what, I am going to make you a proposition: Let me give you back this job you gave to me as a propitiation for all of this season of bad will that has grown up among us. Let me give it back to you. I will resign as Speaker of the House effective upon the election of my successor, and I will ask that we call a caucus on the Democratic side for next Tuesday to choose a successor.

I do not want to be a party to tearing up this institution. I love it.

To tell you the truth, this year it has been very difficult for me to offer the kind of moral leadership that our institution needs. Because every time I try to talk about the needs of the country, about the needs for affordable homes—both Jack Kemp's idea and the ideas we are developing here—every time I try to talk about the need for a minimum wage, about the need for day dare centers, embracing ideas on both sides of the aisle, the media have not been interested in that. They wanted to ask me about petty personal finances.

You do not need that for a Speaker. You need somebody else, so I want to give you that back, and will have a caucus on Tuesday.

Then I will offer to resign from the House sometime before the end of June. Let that be a total payment for the anger and hostility we feel toward each other.

Let us not try to get even with each other. Republicans, please, do not get it in your heads you need to get somebody else because of John Tower. Democrats, please, do not feel that you need to get somebody on the other side because of me. We ought to be more mature than that.

Let us restore to this institution the rightful priorities of what is good for this country. Let us all work together to try to achieve them.

The Nation has important business, and it cannot afford these distractions, and that is why I offer to resign.

I have enjoyed these years in Congress. I am grateful, for all of you have taught me things and been patient with me.

Horace Greeley had a quote that Harry Truman used to like:

Fame is a vapor, popularity an accident. Riches take wings. Those who cheer today may curse tomorrow. Only one thing endures: character.

I am not a bitter man. I am not going to be. I am a lucky man. God has given me the privilege of serving in this, the greatest law making institution on Earth, for a great many years, and I am grateful to the people of my district in Texas and grateful to you, my colleagues, all of you.

God bless this institution. God bless the United States. [Applause.]

. . . .

Congressional Record, House, 101st Congress, 1st session, May 31, 1989, 10431–10441. Affidavits mentioned in the text have been omitted.

175   Senator Robert Byrd on the War in the Persian Gulf

January 12, 1991

Senator Robert C. Byrd (D-W.Va.) is one of the rare members of the modern Senate who has devotedly studied the great orators of the Senate's history. He is a dedicated student of the Senate's rich two-century history and is the author of a four-volume history of the Senate as well as The Senate of the Roman Republic *(1995). Many of his speeches have defended the U.S. Constitution and the prerogatives of the Senate. He often speaks as the conscience of the Senate, sprinkling his remarks with references to American history and the history of ancient Rome (see document 182). Such was the case with his speech on U.S. entry into war with Iraq. It stands as a landmark in the great tradition of Senate oratory, something that, in the age of television and sound bites, is rapidly becoming a lost art in American politics.*

The sudden Iraqi invasion of Kuwait on August 2, 1990, quickly plunged the House and Senate into debate over the proper response to such blatant aggression. A United Nations resolution condemned the invasion and demanded withdrawal of Iraqi troops. President George Bush harshly condemned the invasion, froze Iraqi assets in the United States, and imposed economic sanctions on Iraq. After these actions failed to get Iraqi troops out of Kuwait, and as Iraq's dictator Saddam Hussein refused to pay attention to the many nations of the world who protested his actions, President Bush asked Congress for the authority to use power to eject Iraq from Kuwait.

U.S. forces and troops from other nations were already in the Persian Gulf when the House and Senate took up the debate. While presidents of the United States have broad powers to deploy troops in an emergency under the War Powers Resolution (see document 162), Congress—and only Congress—has the power to declare

war. The debate in both chambers of Congress was spirited and thoughtful. Many observers rank the debate on the Gulf War among the more substantial congressional debates in recent history.

Senator Byrd urged caution and patience before rushing into war. He did not think war would solve the problems of the region. Despite his warnings, the Senate voted 52–47 in favor of granting the president the authority he sought to use force to liberate Kuwait. U.S. and allied forces waged a brief but extremely intense war that devastated the army of Saddam Hussein and liberated Kuwait. As Senator Byrd predicted, the war did not solve the problems related to the dictatorship of Saddam Hussein. In the aftermath of the war, despite the euphoria of a highly successful military engagement, the nagging question remained about the proper role of the United States. Should the United States, because of its unsurpassed military power, be the policeman of the entire world?

Mr. President, this is my thirty-ninth year in Congress. This is my thirty-third year in the U.S. Senate. I have cast a total of 12,822 votes during these thirty-nine years in Congress.

This vote today troubles me. I have cast difficult votes before: For example, in the case of the Panama Canal treaties and the Civil Rights Act of 1964. There are three or four votes that I regret having cast, one of them being my vote in opposition to the 1964 Civil Rights Act. But this vote today I think, Mr. President, may be the most important vote that I shall have cast in my career, certainly up to this point.

I represent a state that is a patriotic state. My state is second to none in the number of men who died in the Korean War and in the Vietnam War—the percentage of deaths in proportion to the eligible male population at that time.

Stonewall Jackson, one of the greatest of all generals, was born in Clarksburg, what is now West Virginia. I was born during the administration of Woodrow Wilson in 1917 during the First World War. My mother died when I was a little less than one year old on Armistice Day of 1918.

So, Mr. President, coming from a state which broke away from the Old Dominion during the Civil War to become the thirty-fifth star in the galaxy of stars; coming from a state, the motto of which is "Mountaineers are always free"; coming from this background, my natural instincts are to support the president today.

The spirit of patriotism has a natural force which urges me in that direction, not just because it is President Bush or not just because the president seeks a vote in support of the second resolution which will be voted on today, but because there is that spirit of patriotism that runs in the veins of the Anglo-Saxon and Germanic peoples and those from southern and eastern Europe who hewed the forests and fought the savages and plowed the fields of West Virginia.

That would be my first instinct, my "gut" reaction, my "gut" feeling, to use a somewhat familiar idiom.

But the question before the Senate today is too grave a question to be decided by the neigh of a horse or by a gut feeling. It is one which engages the heart and the mind as well as the visceral impulse, and so I have sought to bring my mind and heart and all that is within me to bear on this grave issue.

Mr. President, what is the question? The question, as I see it, is whether the Senate will stamp its imprimatur on the second resolution which authorizes the president to go to war at any time after midnight on Tuesday next, January 15, unless provoked by Iraq before that time, or whether to support and vote for the first resolution, of which I am a cosponsor, and which would say to the president, "Stay the course yet a little while; let sanctions have more time."

It is not an easy decision for me. Socrates, when asked whether it was better to marry or not, replied, "Whichever you do, you will repent it."

Mr. President, I will not repent the vote that I am about to cast, and that is that we stay the course for now, give peace a further chance to work. Its pulse beat is not dead. It is still alive. Let us not cut off the life support mechanism just yet.

There are those who say that it is up to Hussein as to whether or not we go over the brink next Tuesday after midnight. Mr. President, that is our decision and not Hussein's.

Fabius Buteo was the head of the Roman delegation that called on the council of Carthage in the year 218 B.C. The Romans delivered an ultimatum to the Carthaginian council. The question was whether or not the Carthaginian council chose war or peace. Fabius Buteo said that within the fold of his toga he held both war and peace and asked the Carthaginian council, "Which do you choose?" The council answered, "It is your choice." Fabius then, with a symbolic gesture, said, "Then I will

let fall war." And the Carthaginian council shouted, "We accept it." And so it was in this very casual way that these two great Mediterranean powers in that day chose to go to war, a war which Livy, the Roman historian, who lived between the years 59 B.C. and 17 A.D., characterized as "the most memorable of all wars" ever waged—the Second Punic War.

Mr. President, I think that we stand at a moment so grave and that the responsibility is so great upon us that we should not cavalierly be hurried into an action that may cost this country its treasure and its blood beyond what the cost may be otherwise if we stay the course for yet a little time.

Decisions of war and peace are the gravest choices that political leaders of our country are ever called on to make. In these decisions, our duty as leaders of a free society is to act judiciously above all else, keeping in mind our national interests as we discern those interests from the coldest facts.

Right now, the gravity of the choices facing the president and the Congress requires us to assess our national interests by a totally calm and rational standard. We ought not personalize or politicize the looming conflict. To do so would cloud our judgment at a time in our lives and in our careers that demands from us absolute lucidity.

We would make a mistake in going to war to kick someone's rear. I will not use the word that has been heard around here. We all know what is meant. We should not go to war in vengeance and indignation, or through any emotional distraction that might shorten our ability rationally to judge the outcome of our actions or the ways in which that outcome might affect our long-term national interests.

Mr. President, those who will oppose the first resolution and support the second resolution say that we are at our peak now, our legions are brimful, our cause is ripe; that "we must take the current when it serves or lose our ventures."

Mr. President, delay does not help Saddam. Delay will help the United States. We can use that time. Delay will cause Saddam to need additional spare parts. It will cost him in new equipment. It will cost him in treasure. He has no additional reservoir from which to get his manpower, nothing like that which the United States has. The United States can restore spare parts. It can restore equipment that has been cannibalized for spare parts. Saddam cannot.

We are told that the coalition may fall apart if we delay. Mr. President, I do not believe that. If a coalition will fall apart staying the course with sanctions, and the embargo, which has been overwhelmingly supported by the United Nations, then what might we expect the coalition to do if there is a war?

They say that American support may dwindle; the support of the American people may lessen. I do not believe that. I think that the support of the American people will grow if we measure our actions, let the embargo have more time, and let diplomacy work.

Mr. President, this is one senator who, while he will not vote today to authorize war as of one minute past midnight next Tuesday, January 15, this senator will vote for a declaration of war a few months down the road. I have said this to the president of the United States at the White House.

I believe the support here in the Senate would be stronger for such an authorization six months from today. Why not six months? It was earlier envisaged that it might take a year or longer for the sanctions to work. Another six months would not total a year.

I think the consensus would be stronger here in the Senate if we measure our actions, and be patient. There are those who say, well, there is a religious holiday coming, and we should act before the religious holiday. The Ramadan will begin, as I understand it, on March 17 and end on April 16. And then there are the intensely warm months of June, July, and August.

There are those who say let us hurry, let us get our bid in, let us act now before the religious holiday, and before the hot months arrive.

Mr. President, Machiavelli advised the prince to study history; to study those who made war and to study the reasons for their victories or their defeats, so that one would emulate the former and avoid the latter; and he advised the prince to choose someone whom the Prince should emulate, as Alexander the Great did Achilles, as Caesar did Alexander the Great, and as Scipio Africanus did Cyrus.

Byron said "History with all her volumes vast, hath but one page." Mr. President, let us consult history.

In 218, Hannibal had just crossed the Alps and lost 20,000 of his men out of the 46,000 who left the Rhone River just sixteen or eighteen days before. At the battle of the Trebbia, he was confronted with two Roman consular armies. The Roman military system consisted of two or more consular armies. There were two consuls, each elected for one year. Each consul had command of two legions. So, there were at least four legions facing Hannibal at the battle of the Trebbia.

The two Roman consuls were Publius Cornelius Scipio and Tiberius Sempronius Longus. Longus wanted to rush into battle with Hannibal. Scipio advised waiting through the winter, biding their time.

Longus was impetuous and eager to fight immediately. A battle was fought. Longus lost the battle, and, with it, fifteen thousand men.

Mr. President, here, too, we are confronted with a weather problem. There is no doubt about it. But that will pass in time. We can utilize that time to good advantage.

Some say the United States will suffer if we do not support the president. I took an oath, Mr. President, to support and defend, not the president of the United States, whether he be a Democrat, such as Jimmy Carter, or a Republican like Ronald Reagan or George Bush, but to defend the Constitution of the United States. That is where my responsibility lies, and I intend to do that.

I think it is better to be wise than simply tough. Patience does not damage prestige. Our prestige will not suffer if President Bush does not win this vote.

What about the future prestige of our country in the Middle East if we go to war now? As Admiral Crowe summed it up in recent hearings:

Even in winning, we could lose. Dealing effectively in the Arab world will take all our resources of creativity and patience. And, thus, even a quick "knockout" of Iraqi forces may well unleash a cascade of outcomes and reactions that reduce our long-term ability to influence events in that region.

We are tied to the complexities of the Middle East in part because of oil dependency and energy reality, which might not be so severe if the Reagan administration had not dismantled the national energy policy that I put into place with Scoop Jackson and others in this Senate when I was majority leader during the presidency of President Carter. But that is behind us. That national energy policy was dismantled. We have done little since to solve the energy dependency situation.

Meanwhile, we have been able to accomplish next to nothing to solve the Palestinian crisis. These and the continued stark discrepancy between the haves and the have-nots in the Middle East, fueling a growing anti-Western Arab nationalism, are in the deep contours of the Middle East landscape. Unless we roll up our sleeves on these fundamental questions in the region and work with a true international coalition to solve them, we will have no end to the series of sorry episodes that have weighted us down for more than a decade now.

War will not solve the root problems of the Middle East; we have said that, and we have known it. Only with a long-term commitment with resolve, patience, dedication, and the will to succeed, will we be able to address the complexities of the region.

It is said that sanctions are not working. Mr. President, sanctions are working. Saddam's spare parts cannot be replenished. His equipment that is cannibalized for the purpose of securing spare parts cannot be made whole again. With us, it is different.

I have been a strong supporter of the president's decisive action to respond to the defensive needs of Saudi Arabia and to punish Iraq for its invasion of Kuwait through an economic embargo. These twin goals have been largely successful up to now.

Who expected them to work completely by now? Even the president did not expect them to work so quickly. Meantime, Saudi Arabia has been safeguarded from Iraqi invasion. And the economic stranglehold being tightened around Iraq's economy has not only denied Hussein any economic benefit from the aggression, but has also begun to cripple the Iraqi economy. These actions have enjoyed substantial and continued support from the American people and from the Congress, as well as from the international community.

Mr. President, I say to those who say sanctions are not working: have we forgotten so soon the celebrations of last year when we so correctly congratulated ourselves on the crumbling of the Soviet Empire in Eastern Europe, after more than forty years? Forty years of patience, willpower, strength, and resolve. We were patient for forty years. What has happened to that patience?

Let us remember the lessons of history. Edward Gibbon wrote of the Battle of Hadrianople. The Roman Empire was divided into the western empire and the eastern empire. Valens was the emperor of the east. He was the brother of Valentinian, and the uncle of Gratian, who was the emperor of the west. The Goths had gathered just a dozen miles from Hadrianople. Gratian, emperor of the west, was on his way to assist his uncle, the emperor of the east, but Valens was impetuous. He did not want to wait and share the glory of a victory over the Goths with Gratian, his nephew. So Valens rushed on to the field, and in one afternoon, two-thirds of the Roman army was destroyed. Almost as many Romans were killed and captured as died at the Battle of Cannae in 216 B.C. Had Valens exercised patience until Gratian could arrive with his legions, the Romans might have won, and the Goths might have been defeated. Valens lost his life in the battle.

Mr. President, a superpower does not have to be impatient. Aristotle told the story that had been related to him by Antisthenes, a sardonic fable about the hares and the lions. The hares addressed the assembly and demanded that all should have equality. But the lions said, "Where are your claws and your teeth?"

Mr. President, a superpower has claws and has teeth. A superpower, as against this Third World power, does not have to be impatient or impetuous. A superpower does not have to feel rushed. We can afford to be patient and let sanctions work.

They say the morale of our soldiers will suffer if we give the embargo more time to work. Mr. President, we should have thought about this before we proceeded to double our forces in Saudi Arabia and terminate the rotation policy in the Middle East. Nothing damages morale more than early, large losses of life.

Mr. President, the nation is fixated on the so-called countdown or the deadline established by the United Nations resolution demanding that Iraq evacuate its forces from Kuwait by January 15.

Such self-imposed pressures need not dominate our provisions about what actions to take in the Persian Gulf. The UN resolution only asks member governments to decide for themselves how best to implement the demand that Iraq evacuate Kuwait. Why are we in such a rush to go to war when many avenues of diplomacy are apparently still being explored by the United Nations, by the French, by the Soviet Union and others?

Mr. President, how much time do I have remaining?

The ACTING PRESIDENT pro tempore. The senator from West Virginia, the president pro tempore, has 13½ minutes remaining of this time.

Mr. BYRD. I thank the Chair.

Mr. President, the sanctions are working. Nobody disputes that. Granted, they have not yet accomplished the goal of driving Saddam out of Kuwait. But who would expect them to have done that in these few short months. I heard the distinguished senator from Georgia [Mr. Nunn] say yesterday, I believe, that Saddam Hussein had not been able to sell one drop of oil. Oil is the backbone of the Iraqi economy, and without the sale of oil, Hussein's currency is going to dry up. He will not be able to buy anything after yet a little while. So the pressure on Saddam increases.

Mr. President, we ourselves could use that time; we could use the time for another six months. Let Ramadan pass. Let the hot months of June and July and August pass. We could make good use of that time.

I recently read that an American general said that our forces are not ready yet to go on the offensive. A little more time would enable our forces to get ready. I cannot believe that our forces would not benefit from additional training in the desert, that they might become better acclimated to that harsh climate. A little more time, and all the buildup that we have read about can then be in place.

Mr. President, I have been disconcerted by reading that there is still a divided command in the desert; that we have not yet unified all of the allied forces under one command. Mr. President, I think it would be a mistake to go on the offensive until there is a unified command. I am not a military man. I never served in any war. I built ships in World War II. I was a welder in shipyards in Baltimore, Maryland, and Tampa, Florida. But common sense would tell me, there should be only one commander at the top.

Again, let us resort to history. Hannibal, who has been proclaimed by some as "the greatest soldier that the world has ever seen," knew that under the Roman military system there was a divided command. There were two consuls. Each had two legions. And there was jealousy between the two consuls. Hannibal knew this. He did not have this problem. Hannibal exercised a single command; there was one brain and one will behind his planning, his designs, and his actions.

At the battle of Cannae, which took place on August 2, 216 B.C., Paulus and Varro, the two Roman consuls, were at variance. Varro wanted to meet Hannibal on the plain. Paulus wanted to meet Hannibal in a hillier region. They daily rotated their commands and on August 2, it was Varro's day to command all of the Roman legions. Both Livy and Polybius, the Roman historian and the Greek historian, respectively, agree that there were eight Roman legions, 5,000 men in a legion, 40,000 Romans with an equal number of allies, totaling 80,000 foot soldiers and horsemen, but the wind, the sun, and the dust were in the faces of the Romans that afternoon. The Roman armies were devastated. It was Hannibal's greatest victory in his fifteen years in Italy. That was the lesson of Cannae. That was the lesson of a divided command.

Fabius Maximus initiated a policy of *cunctatio,* "putting off" or avoiding battle with Hannibal's forces, knowing that Hannibal, like Saddam Hussein, could not replenish his resources. He could win battles, but he could not take walls and earthened works around cities.

Knowing that Hannibal would run out of "spare parts"—he had lost his elephants, and, in time, he lost his Nubian horsemen, his excellent cavalry—Fabius Maximus implemented his policy of *cunctatio,* patience, avoid a battle just now, let Hannibal's forces decline by attrition. In the long run, the policy of avoiding battle with Hannibal proved to be effective.

Mr. President, a majority of the American people do not believe that we should rush into war immediately. I now read from the *Washington Post* of January 11, this paragraph:

While most Americans appear willing to go to war at some point after Tuesday if Iraq continues to occupy Kuwait, the latest Post-ABC poll continues to show that only a minority of Americans want that war to begin when the deadline expires.

Mr. President, something should be said about the cost of a war in treasure. We are going to end up paying for most of Operation Desert Shield ourselves, as we will discover when the supplemental appropriations measures are submitted. We will end up fueling our deficit with a war and borrowing from the Germans and Japanese at Treasury bill auctions to fund our budget deficit because they would not provide the money up front to help us.

Our projected deficit, as of now, for fiscal year 1991 is $320 billion. This is an American operation with a superficial covering of internationalism. It is a bitter pill for the American people to swallow, coated with the noble embroidery of international collective burden sharing, and they will be swallowing the economic consequences of such a war for years to come.

According to the Veterans' Administration, 72,000 World War I veterans are alive today, after seventy-three years; 8.6 million World War II veterans are living; 3.9 million veterans of the Korean war are living; 7.7 million Vietnam veterans are alive. Society will be paying for health care and pensions for these veterans for many years to come, as we should.

For fiscal year 1991, the Veterans' Administration will provide in pension payments, readjustment benefits, and support for the Home Loan Guarantee Program in the amounts broken out by specific war service: World War I, $737 million; World War II, $11.3 billion; Korean war, $3.3 billion; Vietnam, $8.3 billion; total $23.637 billion. So, if war comes, the U.S. government will be paying the costs for decades to come.

Mr. President, there is a serious question of burden sharing here. I was provoked and insulted and embittered when I read in the *Washington Post* of Saturday, January 5, an Associated Press story headlined "Japanese Application to Gulf Ended."

And I now read therefrom:

Japan's lone aid team in Saudi Arabia has returned home, and officials were unsure today whether the government would send more.

The seven doctors and nurses who made up Japan's second medical team all had left by Dec. 28, the Foreign Ministry said today, ending a mission plagued by too few volunteers and what critics say is the Japanese people's unwillingness to consider Iraq's occupation of Kuwait their problem.

Both missions drew only a total of two dozen volunteers. Two ministry officials who accompanied the second team are the only Japanese personnel still among the more than half-million U.S.-led troops massed in the Persian Gulf region.

Critics say Japan's inability to put together a 100-member medical team as promised in September reflects an insular mentality that has undercut government efforts to do more than send $4 billion to help pay for the troop deployment and aid poor states in the area that have suffered from boycotting Iraq.

"We are still not sure whether we really can . . . make a meaningful contribution," said a Foreign Ministry official, speaking on condition of anonymity. He said another medical mission was possible but "has not been worked out yet."

In a poll last month, 62 percent of Japanese questioned opposed sending anything more than financial aid to the gulf.

So, Mr. President, while the American people will send their doctors to the Persian Gulf, while the American people will do without adequate medical care, will do without their medical personnel to a high degree, the Japanese will not even send a volunteer team—a volunteer medical mission to the Persian Gulf.

Mr. President, the United States is working nearly alone in this effort. It is clear that many, if not most, of our major allies in Europe do not share our enthusiasm for this adventure. Money is not pouring into our treasury in a genuine burden-sharing act by our allies. The administration is about to embark on the second phase of "Operation Tin Cup." We have to go around begging for contributions for this effort.

I salute and congratulate the president of the United States and Secretary Baker for the leadership that they have demonstrated, for their dedication, for their skill, and for their success to a point, in marshaling the strength of the United Nations behind this effort.

But the total amount of cash and in-kind contributions provided by our allies as of the last report from DOD is less than $5 billion, an embarrassingly small sum. According to that report, the Germans have provided some $272 million and the Japanese some $426 million. Together, the two economic giants of Germany and Japan have hardly spoken eloquently with their pocketbooks. They have only opted to hold our coats, while we take on Hussein.

Mr. President, I think this is a shame and a disgrace, that Germany and Japan, two countries which will benefit far more than will the United States, two countries whose dependence on the oil from the Middle East far exceeds our own need, will stand by and cynically watch American men and women shed their blood in the sands of the Arabian desert and refuse to help to finance, from their treasuries, the cost of this effort.

Mr. President, I have difficulty finding the words adequately to express my feeling that such nations would stand by. It is a monstrous disgrace and the American people will remember it.

Mr. President, Herodotus wrote of the words that Croesus spoke to Cyrus the Great, that "peace was better than war because in peace the sons did bury their fathers, while in war the fathers did bury their sons." How appropriate at this moment.

Mr. President, let Hussein get no comfort from the vote today. I anticipate that the resolution offered by Senator Nunn and others will not carry. But, as the chairman of the Appropriations Committee, I can assure Mr. Hussein that there will be no division here if war comes.

I pray that the president will exercise patience and take time. He has it within his hands. But Saddam must know that we will all stand together and that, whatever the cost, the Senate will do its duty. We will not let down our men and our women in the Middle East.

Mr. President, I know what it is to lose a grandson, and I know that there are many fathers and mothers and grandparents and wives and brothers and sisters who pray each night that their sons and daughters, their relatives, will come back home safely. I know what it is to lose a grandson. The greatest sorrow of my life was the loss of Michael. Let us hope for the best.

So, Mr. President, in the words of the Epistle to the Hebrews, "Let us run with patience the race that is set before us."

U.S. Congress, Senate, *Congressional Record*, 102d Congress, 1st session, Jan. 12, 1991, S537–560.

176   Congress Authorizes Use of Military Force Against Iraq

January 14, 1991

The Constitution provides that only Congress can declare war. The Constitution also provides that the president is commander-in-chief of the armed forces. The conflict over the exercise of this important power has provided some of the most significant clashes between the executive and legislative branches. In recent times the Gulf of Tonkin Resolution of 1964 gave President Lyndon Johnson broad discretion to commit troops to Vietnam (see document 153). In 1973 Congress sought to gain firmer control over the power to declare war with the War Powers Resolution (see document 162). The 1991 resolution authorizing military use against Iraq shows how tightly drawn the struggle between Congress and the executive can become over the constitutional power of declaring war.

When Iraq invaded its tiny neighbor of Kuwait on August 2, 1990, Congress began a serious and intense debate over the nature and extent of U.S. military involvement in the Gulf region (see document 175). This debate lead to a joint resolution authorizing the use of U.S. armed forces. Nowhere did the resolution state explicitly that the United States declared war on Iraq. In this case the resolution was proceeded by a series of "whereas" clauses that state the reasons for authorizing military intervention. The authorization was cloaked in references to various United Nations resolutions and to references to the War Powers Resolution. Many members of Congress were fearful that a broad authorization of war powers in this instance could lead to a repeat what happened following the Gulf of Tonkin Resolution, when the Vietnam War escalated dramatically and went on for years. Congress finally agreed to allow military use against Iraq, but this resolution makes clear that Congress did not want the president or the Pentagon to think that it had in any way abdicated its authority under the War Powers Resolution. The fact that Iraqi troops were quickly expelled from Kuwait and the Iraqi army was defeated in a matter of days meant the legal requirements placed on President George Bush and his military commanders did not come directly into contention.

H.J. RES. 77

To authorize the use of United States Armed Forces pursuant to United Nations Security Council Resolution 678.

Whereas the Government of Iraq without provocation invaded and occupied the territory of Kuwait on August 2, 1990;

Whereas both the House of Representatives (in H. J. Res. 658 of the 101st Congress) and the Senate (in S. Con. Res. 147 of the 101st Congress) have condemned Iraq's invasion of Kuwait and declared their support for international action to reverse Iraq's aggression;

Whereas, Iraq's conventional, chemical, biological, and nuclear weapons and ballistic missile programs and its demonstrated willingness to use weapons of mass destruction pose a grave threat to world peace;

Whereas the international community has demanded that Iraq withdraw unconditionally and immediately from Kuwait and that Kuwait's independence and legitimate government be restored;

Whereas the United Nations Security Council repeatedly affirmed the inherent right of individual or collective self-defense in response to the armed attack by Iraq against Kuwait in accordance with Article 51 of the United Nations Charter;

Whereas, in the absence of full compliance by Iraq with its resolutions, the United Nations Security Council in Resolution 678 has authorized member states of the United Nations to use all necessary means, after January 15, 1991, to uphold and implement all relevant Security Council resolutions and to restore international peace and security in the area; and

Whereas Iraq has persisted in its illegal occupation of, and brutal aggression against Kuwait: Now, therefore, be it

Resolved by the Senate and House of Representatives of the United States of America in Congress assembled,

Section 1. Short Title.

This joint resolution may be cited as the "Authorization for Use of Military Force Against Iraq Resolution".

Sec. 2. Authorization for Use of United States Armed Forces.

(a) AUTHORIZATION.—The President is authorized, subject to subsection (b), to use United States Armed Forces pursuant to United Nations Security Council Resolution 678 (1990) in order to achieve implementation of Security Council Resolutions 660, 661, 662, 664, 665, 666, 667, 669, 670, 674, and 677.

(b) Requirement for Determination That Use of Military Force Is Necessary.—Before exercising the authority granted in subsection (a), the President shall make available to the Speaker of the House of Representatives and the President pro tempore of the Senate his determination that—

(1) the United States has used all appropriate diplomatic and other peaceful means to obtain compliance by Iraq with the United Nations Security Council resolutions cited in subsection (a), and

(2) that those efforts have not been and would not be successful in obtaining such compliance.

(c) War Powers Resolution Requirements.—

(1) Specific Statutory Authorization.—Consistent with section 8(a)(1) of the War Powers Resolution, the Congress declares that this section is intended to constitute specific statutory authorization within the meaning of section 5(b) of the War Powers Resolution.

(2) Applicability of Other Requirements.—Nothing in this resolution supersedes any requirement of the War Powers Resolution.

Sec. 3. Reports to Congress.

At least once every 60 days, the President shall submit to the Congress a summary on the status of efforts to obtain compliance by Iraq with the resolutions adopted by the United Nations Security Council in response to Iraq's aggression.

Approved January 14, 1991.

Congressional Record, House, 102d Congress, 1st session, January 12, 1991, H443. The resolution passed Congress and was signed into law by the president on January 14, 1991.

177   The Senate Select Committee on Ethics Reports on the Investigation of the Keating 5

November 20, 1991

In late 1990 and early 1991 the Senate investigated five senators who had been accused of improperly interceding on behalf of the California-based Lincoln Savings and Loan Association, which was headed by Charles H. Keating Jr., a wealthy and prominent thrift industry figure. The five senators—Alan Cranston (D-Calif.), Dennis DeConcini (D-Ariz.), John Glenn (D-Ohio), John McCain (R-Ariz.), and Donald W. Riegle (D-Mich.)—became known as the "Keating 5." This major investigation explored the complex and often murky dealings between those who make large donations to Senate campaigns and the favors such donors expected for their money. The inquiry highlighted the need for campaign finance reform, one of the most important but largely unresolved issues before Congress in the 1990s.

The senators under investigation denied any wrongdoing, arguing that they had done no more for Keating than they would for any constituent who came to them for assistance. Keating had given $1.5 million to the campaign chests or to the political causes supported by the five senators. In 1987 the senators met on two occasions with federal regulators looking into the operations of Lincoln Savings and Loan, which had come under scrutiny for its high-risk investments. The investigation hinged on a determination of the dividing line between the normal and legal conduct of a senator in aiding constituents and illegal conduct, where money bought the direct influence of a senator.

In April 1989 Lincoln Savings and Loan filed for bankruptcy and was seized by the federal government. Keating was jailed briefly in 1990 on charges of securities fraud. The failure of Lincoln Savings and Loan sent shock waves through the savings and loan industry. It came to symbolize the massive failure of this industry to police itself and avoid highly speculative practices that put at risk the savings of millions of depositors. Many people lost their life savings or were otherwise seriously financially crippled by the failure of Lincoln Savings and Loan and other similar associations across the country. The financial mess created by Keating cost the American taxpayers $2 billion, as part of one of the worst financial crises ever to hit the United States.

The document provided here is an appendix to the report of the Senate Select Committee on Ethics investigating the matter. This appendix provided the best summary of the findings against the five senators. Two of the senators, Glenn and McCain, were found to have exercised bad judgment but were not punished in any manner, other than the bad publicity generated by the investigation. Senators Riegle and DeConcini received stronger rebukes for their aggressive intercession on behalf of Keating with federal regulators. In the case of Riegle, the ethics committee said: "The Committee finds that Senator Riegle took steps to assist Lincoln Savings & Loan Association with its regulatory problems at a time that Charles Keating was raising substantial campaign funds for Senator Riegle." While the Senate ethics committee did not condone Riegle's behavior, it concluded that he had broken no laws and had not violated Senate ethics rules as they stood at the time. Only Senator Cranston was found to have violated Senate ethics rules. The ethics committee reported: "From April 1987 through April 1989, Senator Cranston personally, or through Senate staff, contacted the Federal Home Loan Bank Board on behalf of Lincoln, during a period when Senator Cranston was soliciting and accepting substantial contributions from Mr. Keating. On at least four occasions, these contacts were made in close connection with the solicitation or receipt of contributions." Cranston was reprimanded by the ethics committee and the full Senate did not take further ac-

tion. Earlier, Cranston announced that he would not seek reelection when his term was up in January 1993. He also stepped down in 1991 as the majority whip of the Senate.

APPENDIX E.—STATEMENT OF THE SELECT COMMITTEE ON ETHICS FOLLOWING HEARINGS INVOLVING SENATORS CRANSTON, DECONCINI, GLENN, MCCAIN, AND RIEGLE

Introduction

The United States Senate Select Committee on Ethics initiated Preliminary Inquiries into allegations of misconduct by Senator Alan Cranston, Senator Dennis DeConcini, Senator John Glenn, Senator John McCain, and Senator Donald Riegle, in connection with their actions on behalf of Charles H. Keating, Jr. and Lincoln Savings and Loan Association. In the course of its Preliminary Inquiries, the Committee held hearings over a two-month period which began November 15, 1990. These hearings were conducted for the purpose of determining whether there is sufficient credible evidence of possible violations by any of the five Senators involved in the Preliminary Inquiries. Because this process was investigatory in nature, a wide net was cast and evidence was admitted with few limitations.

The Committee has met on more than a dozen occasions to consider the evidence produced at the hearings and the written arguments of Special Counsel and counsel for each of the Respondent Senators. The task of the Committee has been to sort through this exhaustive record to ascertain the relevant facts, and to identify any evidence of wrongdoing and any exculpatory evidence.

Findings and Recommendations

Having deliberated at length upon the issues presented, the Committee has weighed the relevant evidence and makes the following findings and recommendations:

Intervention in the Administrative Process

It is a necessary function of a Senator's office to intervene with officials of the executive branch and independent regulatory agencies on behalf of individuals when the facts warrant, and it is a Senator's duty to make decisions on whether to intervene without regard to whether they have contributed to the Senator's campaigns or causes. Ample evidence was received during the hearings showing that Senators should and do provide essential constituent services. In this case, each of the Senators under inquiry had information that reasonably caused concern about the fairness of the Federal Home Loan Bank's examination of Lincoln Savings and Loan Association (Lincoln), and which was sufficient to justify the Senator's contacting Bank Board personnel.

The degree of intervention with the regulators varied as to each Senator. The evidence clearly shows that their contacts with federal regulators regarding Lincoln did not cause the eventual failure of Lincoln or the thrift industry in general.

Prior to April 1987, four of the Senators (Cranston, DeConcini, Glenn, and McCain) had officially expressed opposition to or raised questions about the adoption of a "Direct Investment Rule," promulgated by the Federal Home Loan Bank Board (FHLBB). This Rule was opposed by many Members of Congress and a large number of thrift organizations. The Committee has concluded that, when considered without regard to any contribution or other benefit, the opposition expressed or the questions raised about the Direct Investment Rule did not violate any law or Senate rule.

There were two meetings between Federal Home Loan Bank personnel and groups of Senators. The first, on April 2, 1987 between Federal Home Loan Bank Board Chairman Edwin Gray and four Senators (Cranston, DeConcini, Glenn, and McCain), ended when Chairman Gray advised the Senators that he had no knowledge about the Lincoln examination being conducted by the San Francisco Federal Home Loan Bank (FHLB), and indicated that he would arrange a meeting with, and suggested that they could obtain the information they sought from, the San Francisco FHLB personnel. When considered without regard to any contribution or other benefit, no Senator violated any law or Senate rule by merely attending the meeting.

One week later, on April 9, 1987, there was a second meeting in Washington between four representatives of the San Francisco Federal Home Loan Bank and five Senators (DeConcini, Glenn, McCain, Riegle; and Cranston making a one-minute appearance). One of the FHLB personnel wrote an account of the meeting in reasonable detail, which was amplified by testimony. The Committee finds that, when considered without regard to any contributions or other benefit, no Senator, merely by virtue of his attendance at this meeting, violated any law or Senate rule. At this second meeting, the FHLB representatives advised the Senators that a "criminal referral" was going to be filed relative to the conduct of certain unnamed officials of Lincoln.

Following the two meetings, neither Senator McCain nor Senator Riegle took any action on behalf of Lincoln.

Ten months after the April meetings, Senator Glenn was host at a luncheon meeting he arranged for Mr. Charles Keating to meet House Speaker Jim Wright. There is disputed evidence as to whether Lincoln's problems with the FHLBB were discussed at this meeting. The weight of the evidence indicates that Senator Glenn's participation did not go beyond serving as host and there is no evidence that Senator Glenn was asked to or did take any action on behalf of Lincoln.

Between February and mid-April 1989, Senator DeConcini made several telephone calls to FBB members and other regulatory officials urging prompt consideration of applications for the sale of Lincoln.

In 1987 following the April meetings, and in 1988, Senator Cranston set up a meeting between FHLBB Chairman M. Danny Wall and Mr. Keating, and made several telephone inquiries to Chairman Wall on behalf of Lincoln. Additionally, in 1989, Senator Cranston made calls to FHLB Board members and other regulatory officials urging consideration of applications for the sale of Lincoln.

The Committee finds that, when considered without regard to any contribution or other benefit, none of the activities of Senator Cranston, Senator DeConcini, or Senator Glenn concerning Mr. Keating or Lincoln, following the April 1987 meetings, violated any law or Senate rule.

Official Actions and Campaign Contributions

While the Committee has concluded that none of the Senators' actions described above, when considered without regard to any contribution or other benefit, violated any law or Senate rule, each act must also be examined against more general ethical standards to determine if there was any impropriety because of any relation between those actions and campaign contributions or other benefits provided by Mr. Keating and his associates.

It is a fact of life that candidates for the Senate must solicit and receive assistance in their campaigns, including the raising of campaign funds. Such fund-raising is authorized and regulated by law, and contributions and expenditures under the Federal Election Campaign Act are required to be publicly disclosed. Additionally, contributions under the Federal Election Campaign Act are not personal gifts to candidates.

Mr. Keating, his associates, and his friends contributed $49,000 for Senator Cranston's 1984 presidential Campaign and his 1986 Senatorial Campaign. Mr. Keating also gave corporate funds at the behest of Senator Cranston: $85,000 to the California Democratic Party 1986 get-out-the-vote campaign; $850,000 in 1987 and 1988 to several voter registration organizations with which Senator Cranston was affiliated; and $10,000 to PAC affiliated with Senator Cranston in January 1989. Mr. Keating's Lincoln Savings and Loan also made a $300,000 line of credit available to Senator Cranston's campaign in the fall of 1986 on an expedited basis, although the loan was not used.

Mr. Keating, his associates, and his friends contributed $31,000 to Senator DeConcini's 1982 Senatorial Campaign and $54,000 to his 1988 Senatorial Campaign.

Mr. Keating contributed a total of $200,000 in corporate funds to the non-federal account of Senator Glenn's multi-candidate PAC in 1985 and 1986. Mr. Keating, his associates, and his friends contributed $24,000 for Senator Glenn's Senatorial Campaign, and $18,200 for his Presidential Campaign. Senator Glenn received no contribution from or through Mr. Keating after February 1986.

Mr. Keating, his associates, and his friends contributed $56,000 for Senator McCain's two House races in 1982 and 1984, and $54,000 for his 1986 Senate race. Mr. Keating also provided his corporate plane and/or arranged for payment for the use of commercial or private aircraft on several occasions for travel by Senator McCain and his family, for which Senator McCain ultimately provided reimbursement when called upon to do so. Mr. Keating also extended personal hospitality to Senator McCain for vacations at a location in the Bahamas in each of the calendar years 1983 through 1986.

Mr. Keating organized and hosted a Riegle re-election campaign fund-raising event in March 1987 in Detroit at his company's Pontchartrain Hotel. As a result of Mr. Keating's efforts, approximately $78,250 was raised from Keating associates and friends for Senator Riegle's 1988 campaign.

Based on all the available evidence, the Committee has concluded that in the case of each of the five Senators, all campaign contributions from Mr. Keating and his associates under the Federal Election Campaign Act were within the established legal limits, and were properly reported. Similarly, from the available evidence, the Committee concludes that the Senators' solicitation or acceptance of all contributions made in these cases to state party organizations, political action committees, and voter registration organizations were, standing alone, not illegal or improper; nor did any such contribution constitute a personal gift to any Senator.

With respect to each Senator, there remains the question of whether any actions taken by the Senator, standing alone or in combination with contributions or other benefits, constitutes improper conduct or an appearance of impropriety. The Committee has examined the specific conduct of each Senator and has determined that under the totality of the circumstances: the conduct of each of the five Senators reflected poor judgment; the conduct of some of the Senators constituted at least an appearance of improper conduct; and the conduct of one Senator may have been improper.

The Committee believes that every Senator must always endeavor to avoid the appearance that he, the Senate, or the governmental process may be influenced by campaign contributions or other benefits provided by those with significant legislative or governmental interests. Nonetheless, if an individual or organization which contributed to a Senator's campaigns or causes has a case which the Senator reasonably believes he is obliged to press because it is in the public interest or the cause of justice or equity to do so, then the Senator's obligation is to pursue that case. In such instances, the Senator must be mindful of the appearance that may be created and take special care to try to prevent harm to the public's trust in him and the Senate.

The Committee believes that appearances of impropriety are particularly likely to arise where a Senator takes action on behalf of a contributor. Such appearances are even more difficult to avoid when large sums are being raised from individuals or corporations for unregulated "soft money" accounts and for independent expenditures by third parties. Over 80 percent of the funds raised by Mr. Keating for or on behalf of the five Senators was "soft money."

A full report respecting the Committee's decisions will be issued at the earliest possible date. . . .

Specific Findings

The Committee finds that there is substantial credible evidence that provides substantial cause for the Committee to conclude that Senator Cranston may have engaged in improper conduct reflecting upon the Senate and, therefore, has voted to proceed to an Investigation (see attached). The Investigation will proceed as expeditiously as possible.

The Committee's conclusions in the cases concerning the other four Senators are also set forth in attachments.

Recommendations to the Senate

Section 2(a)(3) of Senate Resolution 338 (88th Congress) places a duty upon the Committee to recommend additional rules or regulations to the Senate, where the Committee has determined that such rules or regulations are necessary or desirable to insure proper standards of conduct by Members, officers, and employees in the performance of their official duties.

In fulfilling its duty under this section, the Committee will make the following recommendations to the Senate in its Final Report on the Preliminary Inquiries.

Recommendation for a Bi-Partisan Task Force on Constituent Service

As noted in the course of the Committee's hearings, the Senate has no specific written standards embodied in the Senate rules respecting contact or intervention with federal executive or independent regulatory agency officials. While unknown to many Senators, there are general guidelines. These are best expressed in House Advisory Opinion No. 1 and the writings of Senator Paul Douglas.

The Committee believes that the Senate should adopt written standards in this area. A specific proposal should be developed either by the Senate Rules Committee or by a bipartisan Senate Task Force created for this purpose. The Rules Committee or Task Force will, of course, need to address the special ethical problems which may arise when such contact or intervention is sought by individuals who have contributed to the Senator's campaigns or causes.

Such standards could be similar to House Advisory Opinion No. 1 or could be more specific. Until such time as such Committee or Task Force has finished its work and the Senate has adopted specific standards respecting contact or intervention with executive or independent regulatory agencies, all Senators are encouraged to use House Advisory Opinion No. 1 as a source of guidance for their actions.

The Committee hopes that the adoption of specific standards governing contact or intervention by Senators with executive or independent regulatory agencies will minimize the potential for appearances of impropriety. Members of the Committee are especially mindful that the success of any democratic government, designed to execute the will of a free people, is ultimately dependent on the public's confidence in the integrity of the governmental process and those who govern.

Recommendation for Bi-Partisan Campaign Reform

The inquiries in these five cases have shown the obvious ethical dilemmas inherent in the current system by which political activities are financed. The Committee notes that over 80 percent of the funds at issue were not disclosed funds raised by candidates for Senate or House campaigns under the Federal Election Campaign Act. Rather, such funds were undisclosed, unregulated funds raised for independent expenditures, political party "soft money," and a non-federal political action committee. Any campaign finance reform measure will have to address these mechanisms for political activities, as well as campaign fundraising and expenditures directly by candidates, in order to deal meaningfully and effectively with the issues presented in these cases.

The Committee urges the leadership and Members of both the Senate and the House to work together in a bipartisan manner to address the urgent need for comprehensive campaign finance reform. The reputation and honor of our institutions demand it.

Resolution for Investigation

Whereas, the Select Committee on Ethics on December 21 1989 initiated a Preliminary Inquiry into allegations of misconduct by Senator Alan Cranston, and notified Senator Cranston of such action; and

Whereas, the Committee retained Special Counsel Robert S. Bennett to assist the Committee in conducting the Preliminary Inquiry into the allegations, and received and considered a report related thereto; and

Whereas, in the course of its Preliminary Inquiry the Committee held hearings from November 15, 1990 through January 16, 1991 and heard evidence relating to the allegations; and

Whereas, the Committee received and considered post-hearing memoranda from Special Counsel and counsel for Respondent Senators;

It is therefore Resolved:

(a) That the Committee finds that there is substantial credible evidence that provides substantial cause for the Committee to conclude that, in connection with his conduct relating to Charles H. Keating, Jr., and Lincoln Savings and Loan Association, Senator Cranston may have engaged in improper conduct that may reflect upon the Senate, as contemplated in Section 2(a)(1) of S. Res. 338, 88th Congress, as amended. To wit, there is substantial credible evidence that provides substantial cause for the Committee to conclude, based upon the totality of the circumstances, including but not limited to the following conduct or activities, that Senator Cranston engaged in an impermissible pattern of conduct in which fund raising and official activities were substantially linked:

(1) From April 1987 through April 1989, Senator Cranston personally, or through Senate staff, contacted the Federal Home Loan Bank Board on behalf of Lincoln, during a period when Senator Cranston was soliciting and accepting substantial contributions from Mr. Keating. On at least four occasions, these contacts were made in close connection with the solicitation or receipt of contributions. These four occasions are as follows:

(i) As a result of a solicitation from Senator Cranston in early 1987, Mr. Keating, on March 3, 1987, contributed $100,000 to America Votes, a voter registration organization.

This contribution was made during the period leading to Senator Cranston's participation in the April 2 and April 9 meetings with Federal Home Loan Bank Board Chairman Edwin J. Gray and the San Francisco regulators.

(ii) In the fall of 1987, Senator Cranston solicited from Mr. Keating a $250,000 contribution, which was delivered to the Senator personally by Mr. Keating's employee James Grogan on November 6, 1987. When the contribution was delivered, Mr. Grogan and Senator Cranston called Mr. Keating, who asked if the Senator would contact new Federal Home Loan Bank Board Chairman M. Danny Wall about Lincoln. Senator Cranston agreed to do so, and made the call six days later.

(iii) In January 1988, Mr. Keating offered to make an additional contribution and also asked Senator Cranston to set up a meeting for him with Chairman Wall. Senator Cranston did so on January 20, 1988 and Chairman Wall and Mr. Keating met eight days later. On February 10, 1988 Senator Cranston personally collected checks totaling $500,000 for voter registration groups.

(iv) In early 1989, at the time that Senator Cranston was contacting, Bank Board officials about the sale of Lincoln, he personally or through Joy Jacobson, his chief fund raiser, solicited another contribution. (This contribution was never made. American Continental Corporation declared bankruptcy on April 13, 1989.)

(2) Senator Cranston's Senate office practices further evidenced an impermissible pattern of conduct in which fund raising and other official activities were substantially linked. For example Joy Jacobson (who was not a member of his Senate staff and who had no official Senate duties or substantive expertise), engaged in the following activities with Senator Cranston's knowledge, permission, at his direction, or under his supervision:

(i) Senator Cranston's fund raiser repeatedly scheduled and attended meetings between Senator Cranston and contributors in which legislative or regulatory issues were discussed.

(ii) Senator Cranston's fund raiser often served as the intermediary for Mr. Keating or Mr. Grogan when they could not reach the Senator or Carolyn Jordan, the Senator's banking aide.

(iii) Senator Cranston received several memoranda from Ms. Jacobson which evidenced her understanding that contributors were entitled to special attention and special access to official services. Senator Cranston never told her that her understanding was incorrect, nor did he inform her that such a connection between contributions and official actions was improper.

(b) That the Committee, pursuant to Committee Supplementary Procedural Rules 3(d)(5) and 4(f)(4), shall proceed to an Investigation under Committee Supplementary Procedural Rule 5; and

(c) That Senator Cranston shall be given timely written notice of this resolution and the evidence supporting it, and informed of a respondent's rights pursuant to the Rules of the Committee.

Decision of the Committee Concerning Senator McCain

Based on the evidence available to it, the Committee has given consideration to Senator McCain's actions on behalf of Lincoln Savings & Loan Association. The Committee concludes that Senator McCain exercised poor judgment in intervening with the regulators. The Committee concludes that Senator McCain's actions were not improper nor attended with gross negligence and did not reach the level of requiring institutional action against him. The Committee finds that Senator McCain took no further action after the April 9, 1987, meeting when he learned of the criminal referral.

The Committee reaffirms its prior decision that it does not have jurisdiction to determine the issues of disclosure or reimbursement pertaining to flights provided by American Continental Corporation while Senator McCain was a Member of the House of Representatives. The Committee did consider the effect of such on his state of mind and judgment in taking steps to assist Lincoln Savings & Loan Association.

Senator McCain has violated no law of the United States or specific Rule of the United States Senate; therefore, the Committee concludes that no further action is warranted with respect to Senator McCain on the matters investigated during the preliminary inquiry.

Decision of the Committee Concerning Senator Glenn

Based on the evidence available to it, the Committee has given consideration to Senator Glenn's actions on behalf of Lincoln Savings & Loan Association. The Committee concludes that Senator Glenn, although believing that the Lincoln matter was in the process of resolution, exercised poor judgment in arranging a luncheon meeting between Mr. Keating and Speaker Wright in January, 1988, some eight months after Senator Glenn learned of the criminal referral. There is disputed evidence as to whether Lincoln's problems with the Federal Home Loan Bank Board (FHLBB) were discussed at that meeting. The evidence indicates that Senator Glenn's participation did not go beyond serving as host. The Committee further concludes that Senator Glenn's actions were not improper or attended with gross negligence and did not reach the level requiring institutional action against him.

Senator Glenn has violated no law of the United States or specific Rule of the United States Senate; therefore, the Committee concludes that no further action is warranted with respect to Senator Glenn on the matters investigated during the preliminary inquiry.

Decision of the Committee Concerning Senator Riegle

Based on the evidence available to it, the Committee has given consideration to Senator Riegle's actions on behalf of Lincoln Savings & Loan Association. The Committee finds that Senator Riegle took steps to assist Lincoln Savings & Loan Association with its regulatory problems at a time that Charles Keating was raising substantial campaign funds for Senator Riegle. During the course of the hearings, possible conflicts arose concerning actions on the part of Senator Riegle that caused the Committee concern, but the Committee finds that the evidence indicates no deliberate intent to deceive. The evidence shows that Senator Riegle took no further action after the April 9, 1987, meeting where he learned of the criminal referral.

While the Committee concludes that Senator Riegle has violated no law of the United States or specific Rule of the United States Senate, it emphasizes that it does not condone his conduct. The Committee has concluded that the totality of the evidence shows that Senator Riegle's conduct gave the appearance of being improper and was certainly attended with insensitivity and poor judgment. However, the Committee finds that his conduct did not reach a level requiring institutional action.

The Committee concludes that no further action is warranted with respect to Senator Riegle on the matters investigated during the preliminary inquiry.

Decision of the Committee Concerning Senator DeConcini

Based on the evidence available to it, the Committee has given consideration to Senator DeConcini's actions on behalf of Lincoln Savings & Loan Association. While aggressive conduct by Senators in dealing with regulatory agencies is sometimes appropriate and necessary, the Committee concludes that Senator DeConcini's aggressive conduct with the regulators was inappro-

priate. The Committee further concludes that the actions of Senator DeConcini after the April 9, 1987, meeting where he learned of the criminal referral, were not improper in and of themselves.

While the Committee concludes that Senator DeConcini has violated no law of the United States or specific Rule of the United States Senate, it emphasizes that it does not condone his conduct. The Committee has concluded that the totality of the evidence shows that Senator DeConcini's conduct gave the appearance of being improper and was certainly attended with insensitivity and poor judgment. However, the Committee finds that his conduct did not reach a level requiring institutional action.

The Committee therefore concludes that no further action is warranted with respect to Senator DeConcini on the matters investigated during the preliminary inquiry.

U.S. Senate, Select Committee on Ethics, *Report 102–223* (Vol. 1), "Investigation of Senator Alan Cranston," Appendix E., 102d Congress, 1st session, November 20, 1991, 46–56.

178   The Twenty-Seventh Amendment to the Constitution

Submitted to the States, September 25, 1789; Ratified, May 18, 1992

It took the states 203 years to ratify the Twenty-Seventh Amendment, which decrees that no salary increase can take place until an election cycle for the House of Representatives intervenes. James Madison proposed the amendment in 1789 as one of twelve amendments to the Constitution (see document 15). By 1791 the states had ratified ten of the twelve, which collectively constitute the Bill of Rights. The two other amendments failed to be ratified by the required number of states when first proposed. But Congress had not included a time limit regarding the expiration of the amendment if it failed ratification. Time limits became common practice in the twentieth century. Technically, this 1789 proposal remained on the books. Only six states ratified the amendment from 1789 to 1791. Ohio later ratified the amendment in 1873. After more than a century of inactivity, Wyoming ratified it 1978, followed by a slow but increasing trickle of state ratifications in the 1980s. With New Jersey's ratification of the amendment on May 7, 1992, the necessary three-quarters of the states had ratified the amendment. The archivist of the United States, Don Wilson, announced on May 18, 1992, that the amendment had become a valid part of the Constitution. In the meantime, Illinois had also ratified the amendment on May 12, 1992.

Credit for reviving this amendment and urging states to pass it goes largely to Gregory Watson, a staff member of the Texas state legislature, who made the issue a personal cause and was instrumental in convincing a sufficient number of state legislatures to take up the matter. Fueled partly by the public reaction to rapidly increasing congressional salaries in the 1970s and 1980s and the age-old debate over what is proper pay for a member of Congress (see documents 18, 49, 86, and 94), the movement succeeded. The

annual salary of a member of Congress, both House and Senate, stood at $57,500 in 1978. By 1992, the year the Twenty-Seventh Amendment was ratified, annual pay had more than doubled to $129,500. Some opponents of the amendment argued that the ratification process should have been nullified long ago because the amendment did not express a contemporary opinion on the subject and did not reflect the true will of the people. Congress addressed this issue in 1983 when, bowing to public pressure, it passed a resolution agreeing to accept ratification of this amendment if the requisite number of states eventually approved it. Nine years later that eventuality became a reality.

The purpose of the amendment was to make Congress accountable, although indirectly, to the voters regarding any raise in salary. Supposedly, if a sufficient number of voters are opposed to the raise, they will express their views at the ballot box, since such a raise can only take effect following an election cycle for the House. Since ratification of the amendment in 1992, Congress has not proposed a salary increase, although a cost of living adjustment increased the annual salary to $133,600 in 1993. Since that time Congress has rejected several proposed cost of living increases and the salary has remained at 1993 levels.

(ARTICLE XXVII.)

No law, varying the compensation for the services of the Senators and Representatives, shall take effect, until an election of Representatives shall have intervened.

The Constitution of the United States of America as Amended, House Doc. 102–188, 102d Congress, 2d session (Washington: Government Printing Office, 1992), 27.

179   *Nixon v. United States*

January 13, 1993

In Nixon v. United States *the Supreme Court made an important ruling regarding the Senate's power of impeachment. It upheld the Senate's right to determine its own rules with respect to the impeachment power without interference from the courts.*

Walter L. Nixon Jr., the chief judge of the U.S. District Court for the Southern District of Mississippi, was convicted of perjury before a grand jury investigating bribery charges against him. Nixon was sentenced to jail, but he refused to resign his seat on the federal bench and continued to draw his salary as a federal judge while in prison. On May 10, 1989, the House of Representatives impeached Judge Nixon for high crimes and misdemeanors for his false testimony before the grand jury and for bringing disrepute on the federal judiciary.

When the impeachment reached the Senate it fell under Rule XI of the Senate rules, which provides for the creation of a "committee of Senators to receive evidence and take testimony at such times and places as the committee may determine, and for such purpose the committee so appointed and the chairman thereof, to be elected by the committee, shall (unless otherwise ordered by the Senate) exercise all the powers and functions conferred upon the Senate and the Presiding Officer of the Senate, respectively, under the rules of procedure and practice of the Senate when sitting on impeachment trials." Rule XI also required the impeachment committee to report to the full Senate in writing, including the transcript of the hearings, so that it could vote on the impeachment. Rule XI provides further that the full Senate may decide to call witnesses to appear before it.

Judge Nixon challenged Rule XI, saying that it infringed upon the rights of the full Senate to hear the evidence in an impeachment trial. The Supreme Court ruled that the Senate had the right to determine its procedures for trying an impeachment. As Chief Justice William H. Rehnquist said in the decision of the court: "In the case before us, there is no separate provision of the Constitution that could be defeated by allowing the Senate final authority to determine the meaning of the word 'try' in the Impeachment Trial Clause." The Senate used the same procedure in trying the Nixon case that it used in the impeachments of two other federal judges, Harry T. Claiborne in 1986 and Alcee Hastings in 1989.

CHIEF JUSTICE REHNQUIST delivered the opinion of the Court.

Petitioner Walter L. Nixon, Jr., asks this Court to decide whether Senate Rule XI, which allows a committee of Senators to hear evidence against an individual who has been impeached and to report that evidence to the full Senate, violates the Impeachment Trial Clause, Art. 1, §3 cl. 6. That Clause provides that the "Senate shall have the sole Power to try all Impeachments." But before we reach the merits of such a claim we must decide whether it is "justiciable," that is, whether it is a claim that may be resolved by the courts. We conclude that it is not.

Nixon, a former Chief Judge of the United States District Court for the Southern District of Mississippi, was convicted by a jury of two counts of making false statements before a federal grand jury and sentenced to prison. See *United States v. Nixon* (CA5 1987). The grand jury investigation stemmed from reports that Nixon had accepted a gratuity from a Mississippi businessman in exchange for asking a local district attorney to halt the prosecution of the businessman's son. Because Nixon refused to resign from his office as a United States District Judge, he continued to collect his judicial salary while serving out his prison sentence. See H. R. Rep. No. 101–36, p. 13 (1989).

On May 10, 1989, the House of Representatives adopted three articles of impeachment for high crimes and misdemeanors. The first two articles charged Nixon with giving false testimony before the grand jury and the third article charged him with bringing disrepute on the Federal Judiciary. . . .

After the House presented the articles to the Senate, the Senate voted to invoke its own Impeachment Rule XI, under which the presiding officer appoints a committee of Senators to "receive evidence and take testimony." Senate Impeachment Rule XI, reprinted in Senate Manual, S. Doc. No. 101–1, p.186 (1989). The Senate committee held four days of hearings, during which 10 witnesses, including Nixon, testified. . . . Pursuant to Rule XI, the committee presented the full Senate with a complete transcript of the proceeding and a Report stating the uncontested facts and summarizing the evidence on the contested facts. . . . Nixon and the House impeachment managers submitted extensive final briefs to the full Senate and delivered arguments from the Senate floor during the three hours set aside for oral argument in front of that body. Nixon himself gave a personal appeal, and several Senators posed questions directly to both parties. . . . The Senate voted by more than the constitutionally required two-thirds majority to convict Nixon on the first two articles. . . . The presiding officer then entered judgment removing Nixon from his office as United States District Judge.

Nixon thereafter commenced the present suit, arguing that Senate Rule XI violates the constitutional grant of authority to the Senate to "try" all impeachments because it prohibits the whole Senate from taking part in the evidentiary hearings. See Art. 1, § 3, cl. 6. Nixon sought a declaratory judgment that his impeachment conviction was void and that his judicial salary and privileges should be reinstated. The District Court held that his claim was nonjusticiable, and the Court of Appeals for the District of Columbia Circuit agreed. . . . We granted certiorari. . . .

A controversy is nonjusticiable—i.e., involves a political question—where there is "a textually demonstrable constitutional commitment of the issue to a coordinate political department; or a lack of judicially discoverable and manageable standards for resolving it. . . ." But the courts must, in the first instance, interpret the text in question and determine whether and to what extent the issue is textually committed. . . . As the discussion that follows makes clear, the concept of a textual commitment to a coordinate political department is not completely separate from the concept of a lack of judicially discoverable and manageable standards for resolving it; the lack of judicially manageable standards may strengthen the conclusion that there is a textually demonstrable commitment to a coordinate branch.

In this case, we must examine Art. 1, § 3, cl. 6, to determine the scope of authority conferred upon the Senate by the Framers regarding impeachment. It provides:

"The Senate shall have the sole Power to try all Impeachments. When sitting for that Purpose, they shall be on Oath or Affirmation. When the President of the United States is tried, the Chief Justice shall preside: And no Person shall be convicted without the Concurrence of two thirds of the Members present."

The language and structure of this Clause are revealing. The first sentence is a grant of authority to the Senate, and the word "sole" indicates that this authority is reposed in the Senate and nowhere else. The next two sentences specify requirements to which the Senate proceedings shall conform: The Senate shall be on oath or affirmation, a two-thirds vote is required to convict, and when the President is tried the Chief Justice shall preside.

Petitioner argues that the word "try" in the first sentence imposes by implication an additional requirement on the Senate in that the proceedings must be in the nature of a judicial trial. From there petitioner goes on to argue that this limitation precludes the Senate from delegating to a select committee the task of hearing the testimony of witnesses, as was done pursuant to Senate Rule XI. " '[T]ry' means more than simply 'vote on' or 'review' or 'judge.' In 1787 and today, trying a case means hearing the evidence, not scanning a cold record.". . . Petitioner concludes from this that courts may review whether or not the Senate "tried" him before convicting him.

There are several difficulties with this position which lead us ultimately to reject it. The word "try," both in 1787 and later, has considerably broader meanings than those to which petitioner would limit it. Older dictionaries define try as "[t]o examine" or "[t]o examine as a judge." See 2 S. Johnson, A Dictionary of the English Language (1785). In more modern usage the term has various meanings. For example, try can mean "to examine or investigate judicially," "to conduct the trial of," or "to put to the test by experiment, investigation, or trial." Webster's Third New International Dictionary 2457 (1971). Petitioner submits that "try," as contained in T. Sheridan, Dictionary of the English Language (1796), means "to examine as a judge; to bring before a judicial tribunal." Based on the variety of definitions, however, we cannot say that the Framers used the word "try" as an implied limitation on the method by which the Senate might proceed in trying impeachments. "As a rule the Constitution speaks in general terms, leaving Congress to deal with subsidiary matters of detail as the public interests and changing conditions may require. . . ." *Dillon* v. *Gloss* (1921).

The conclusion that the use of the word "try" in the first sentence of the Impeachment Trial Clause lacks sufficient precision to afford any judicially manageable standard of review of the Senate's actions is fortified by the existence of the three very specific requirements that the Constitution does impose on the Senate when trying impeachments: The Members must be under oath, a two-thirds vote is required to convict, and the Chief Justice presides when the President is tried. These limitations are quite precise, and their nature suggests that the Framers did not intend to impose additional limitations on the form of the Senate proceedings by the use of the word "try" in the first sentence.

Petitioner devotes only two pages in his brief to negating the significance of the word "sole" in the first sentence of Clause 6. As noted above, that sentence provides that "[t]he Senate shall have the sole Power to try all Impeachments." We think that the word "sole" is of considerable significance. Indeed, the word "sole" appears only one other time in the Constitution—with respect to the House of Representatives' "*sole* Power of Impeachment." Art. 1, § 2, cl. 5 (emphasis added). The commonsense meaning of the word "sole" is that the Senate alone shall have authority to determine whether an individual should be acquitted or convicted. The dictionary definition bears this out. "Sole" is defined as "having no companion," "solitary," "being the only one," and "functioning . . . independently and without assistance or interference." Webster's Third New International Dictionary 2168 (1971). If the courts may review the actions of the Senate in order to determine whether that body "tried" an impeached official, it is difficult to see how the Senate would be "functioning . . . independently and without assistance or interference."

Nixon asserts that the word "sole" has no substantive meaning. To support this contention, he argues that the word is nothing more than a mere "cosmetic edit" added by the Committee of Style after the delegates had approved the substance of the Impeachment Trial Clause. There are two difficulties with this argument. First, accepting as we must the proposition that the Committee of Style had no authority from the Convention to alter the meaning of the Clause, see 2 Records of the Federal Convention of 1787, p. 553 (M. Farrand ed. 1966) (hereinafter Farrand), we must presume that the Committee's reorganization or rephrasing accurately captured what the Framers meant in their unadorned language. See *Powell* v. *McCormack*. That is, we must presume that the Committee did its job. This presumption is buttressed by the fact that the Constitutional Convention voted on, and accepted, the Committee of Style's linguistic version. . . . We agree with the Government that "the word 'sole' is entitled to no less weight than any other word of the text, because the Committee revision perfected what 'had been agreed to' ." . . . Second, carrying Nixon's argument to its logical conclusion would constrain us to say that the *second to last draft* would govern in every instance where the Committee of Style added an arguably substantive word. Such a result is at odds with the fact that the Convention passed the Committee's version, and with the well-established rule that the plain language of the enacted text is the best indicator of intent.

Petitioner also contends that the word "sole" should not bear on the question of justiciability because Art. II, § 2, cl. 1, of the Constitution grants the President pardon authority "except in Cases of Impeachment." He argues that such a limitation on the President's pardon power would not have been necessary if the Framers thought that the Senate alone had authority to deal with such questions. But the granting of a pardon is in no sense an overturning of a judgment of conviction by some other tribunal; it is "[a]n executive action that mitigates or sets aside *punishment* for a crime." Black's Law Dictionary 1113 (6th ed. 1990) (emphasis added). Authority in the Senate to determine procedures for trying an impeached official, unreviewable by the courts, is therefore not at all inconsistent with authority in the President to grant a pardon to the convicted official. The exception from the President's pardon authority of cases of impeachment was a separate determination by the Framers that executive clemency should not be available in such cases.

Petitioner finally argues that even if significance be attributed to the word "sole" in the first sentence of the Clause, the authority granted is to the Senate, and this means that "the Senate—not the courts, not a lay jury, not a Senate Committee—shall try impeachments.". . . It would be possible to read the first sentence of the Clause this way, but it is not a natural reading. Petitioner's interpretation would bring into judicial purview not merely the sort of claim made by petitioner, but other similar claims based on the conclusion that the word "Senate" has imposed by implication limitations on procedures which the Senate might adopt. Such limitations would be inconsistent with the construction of the Clause as a whole, which, as we have noted, sets out three express limitations in separate sentences.

The history and contemporary understanding of the impeachment provisions support our reading of the constitutional language. The parties do not offer evidence of a single word in the history of the Constitutional Convention or in contemporary commentary that even alludes to the possibility of judicial review in the context of the impeachment powers. . . . This silence is quite meaningful in light of the several explicit references to the availability of judicial review as a check on the Legislature's power with respect to bills of attainder, *ex post facto* laws, and statutes. See The Federalist No. 78, p. 524 (J. Cooke ed. 1961) ("Limitations . . . can be preserved in practice no other way than through the medium of the courts of justice").

The Framers labored over the question of where the impeachment power should lie. Significantly, in at least two considered scenarios the power was placed with the Federal Judiciary. . . . Indeed, James Madison and the Committee of Detail proposed that the Supreme Court should have the power to determine impeachments. . . . Despite these proposals, the Convention ultimately decided that the Senate would have "the sole Power to try all Impeachments." Art. I, §3, cl. 6. According to Alexander Hamilton, the Senate was the "most fit depositary of this important trust" because its Members are representatives of the people. The Supreme Court was not the proper body because the Framers "doubted whether the members of that tribunal would, at all times, be endowed with so eminent a por-

tion of fortitude as would be called for in the execution of so difficult a task" or whether the Court "would possess the degree of credit and authority" to carry out its judgment if it conflicted with the accusation brought by the Legislature—the people's representative. . . . In addition, the Framers believed the Court was too small in number: "The awful discretion, which a court of impeachments must necessarily have, to doom to honor or to infamy the most confidential and the most distinguished characters of the community, forbids the commitment of the trust to a small number of persons.". . .

There are two additional reasons why the Judiciary, and the Supreme Court in particular, were not chosen to have any role in impeachments. First, the Framers recognized that most likely there would be two sets of proceedings for individuals who commit impeachable offenses—the impeachment trial and a separate criminal trial. In fact, the Constitution explicitly provides for two separate proceedings. See Art. I, §3, cl. 7. The Framers deliberately separated the two forums to avoid raising the specter of bias and to ensure independent judgments:

"Would it be proper that the persons, who had disposed of his fame and his most valuable rights as a citizen in one trial, should in another trial, for the same offence, be also the disposers of his life and his fortune? Would there not be the greatest reason to apprehend, that error in the first sentence would be the parent of error in the second sentence? That the strong bias of one decision would be apt to overrule the influence of any new lights, which might be brought to vary the complexion of another decision?" The Federalist No. 65, p. 442 (J. Cooke ed. 1961)

Certainly judicial review of the Senate's "trial" would introduce the same risk of bias as would participation in the trial itself.

Second, judicial review would be inconsistent with the Framers' insistence that our system be one of checks and balances. In our constitutional system, impeachment was designed to be the *only* check on the Judicial Branch by the Legislature. On the topic of judicial accountability, Hamilton wrote:

"The precautions for their responsibility are comprised in the article respecting impeachments. They are liable to be impeached for malconduct by the house of representatives, and tried by the senate, and if convicted, may be dismissed from office and disqualified for holding any other. *This is the only provision on the point, which is consistent with the necessary independence of the judicial character, and is the only one which we find in our own constitution in respect to our own judges.*". . . (emphasis added).

Judicial involvement in impeachment proceedings, even if only for purposes of judicial review, is counterintuitive because it would eviscerate the "important constitutional check" placed on the Judiciary by the Framers. . . . Nixon's argument would place final reviewing authority with respect to impeachments in the hands of the same body that the impeachment process is meant to regulate.

Nevertheless, Nixon argues that judicial review is necessary in order to place a check on the Legislature. Nixon fears that if the Senate is given unreviewable authority to interpret the Impeachment Trial Clause, there is a grave risk that the Senate will usurp judicial power. The Framers anticipated this objection and created two constitutional safeguards to keep the Senate in check. The first safeguard is that the whole of the impeachment power is divided between the two legislative bodies, with the House given the right to accuse and the Senate given the right to judge.... This split of authority "avoids the inconvenience of making the same persons both accusers and judges; and guards against the danger of persecution from the prevalency of a factious spirit in either of those branches." The second safeguard is the two-thirds supermajority vote requirement. Hamilton explained that "[a]s the concurrence of two-thirds of the senate will be requisite to a condemnation, the security to innocence, from this additional circumstance, will be as complete as itself can desire.". . .

In addition to the textual commitment argument, we are persuaded that the lack of finality and the difficulty of fashioning relief counsel against justiciability. See *Baker* v. *Carr*. We agree with the Court of Appeals that opening the door of judicial review to the procedures used by the Senate in trying impeachments would "expose the political life of the country to months, or perhaps years, of chaos." This lack of finality would manifest itself most dramatically if the President were impeached. The legitimacy of any successor, and hence his effectiveness, would be impaired severely, not merely while the judicial process was running its course, but during any retrial that a differently constituted Senate might conduct if its first judgment of conviction were invalidated. Equally uncertain is the question of what relief a court may give other than simply setting aside the judgment of conviction. Could it order the reinstatement of a convicted federal judge, or order Congress to create an additional judgeship if the seat had been filled in the interim?

Petitioner finally contends that a holding of nonjusticiability cannot be reconciled with our opinion in *Powell* v. *McCormack* (1969). The relevant issue in *Powell* was whether courts could review the House of Representatives' conclusion that Powell was "unqualified" to sit as a Member because he had been accused of misappropriating public funds and abusing the process of the New York courts. We stated that the question of justiciability turned on whether the Constitution committed authority to the House to judge its Members' qualifications, and if so, the extent of that commitment.... Article I, § 5, provides that "Each House shall be the Judge of the Elections, Returns and Qualifications of its own Members." In turn, Art. I, §2, specifies three requirements for membership in the House: The candidate must be at least 25 years of age, a citizen of the United States for no less than seven years, and an inhabitant of the State he is chosen to represent. We held that, in light of the three requirements specified in the Constitution, the word "qualifications"—of which the House was to be the Judge—was of a precise, limited nature....

Our conclusion in *Powell* was based on the fixed meaning of "[q]ualifications" set forth in Art. I, § 2. The claim by the House that its power to "be the Judge of the Elections, Returns and Qualifications of its own Members" was a textual commitment of unreviewable authority was defeated by the existence of this separate provision specifying the only qualifications which might be imposed for House membership. The decision as to whether a Member satisfied these qualifications was placed with the House, but the decision as to what these qualifications consisted of was not.

In the case before us, there is no separate provision of the Constitution that could be defeated by allowing the Senate final authority to determine the meaning of the word "try" in the Impeachment Trial Clause. We agree with Nixon that courts possess power to review either legislative or executive action that transgresses identifiable textual limits. As we have made clear, "whether the action of [either the Legislative or Executive Branch] exceeds whatever authority has been committed, is itself a delicate exercise in constitutional interpretation, and is a responsibility of this Court as ultimate interpreter of the Constitution.". . . But we conclude, after exercising that delicate responsibility, that the word "try" in the Impeachment Trial Clause does not provide an identifiable textual limit on the authority which is committed to the Senate.

For the foregoing reasons, the judgment of the Court of Appeals is

Affirmed.

506 U.S. 224 (1993).

180 Conclusions of the Special Prosecutor Regarding the Iran-Contra Investigation

August 4, 1993

Events that became known as the Iran-contra affair led to the most serious constitutional crisis during the presidency of Ronald Reagan. This conflict pitted the will of Congress against the powers of the executive branch. Congressional investigations in the House and Senate were launched over secret arms sales to Iran in order to finance war efforts in Nicaragua, where the Reagan administra-tion supported contra rebels fighting to overthrow the leftist Sandinista government. At issue was the president's behavior in the matter and how much he knew about the arms sales. Neither President Reagan nor Vice President George Bush were held accountable for any wrongdoing in the matter, although fourteen others, including several top White House aids, were charged with crimes.

In 1984 Congress passed the second of three "Boland Amendments," named for Edward Boland (D-Mass.), chairman of the House Intelligence Committee. This amendment specifically banned aid to the contra rebels from the funds of the Central Intelligence Agency, the Pentagon, or any other part of the U.S. government. To skirt the will of Congress, and the law in the matter, Marine Lieutenant Colonel Oliver North began a clandestine operation from the White House to secretly sell arms to Iran and divert the money to the contra rebels. North also raised funds from wealthy conservatives in the United States who were willing to help underwrite the war against the Sandinistas, whom many conservatives saw as a puppet regime of the Soviet Union. Other members of the Reagan administration secretly sought help from leaders in foreign governments, including King Fahd of Saudi Arabia, who funneled upwards of $2 million per month to the contra rebels.

In December 1986 the U.S. Court of Appeals for the District of Columbia appointed an independent counsel, Lawrence E. Walsh, to investigate the sale and shipment of arms to Iran and the diversion of funds from such sales to Nicaragua. The independent counsel's investigation led to charges against fourteen individuals. All were convicted of various crimes mentioned in the document that follows. Two prominent figures in the case—Oliver North and John Poindexter—had their convictions overturned on appeal and President Bush pardoned two others in 1992.

In 1993, five years after President Reagan left office and a year after President Bush was defeated for reelection, the independent counsel submitted a three-volume Final Report of the Independent Counsel for Iran/Contra Matters *to the U.S. Court of Appeals for the District of Columbia. The court ordered the* Final Report *to be released to the public. Although much of the evidence contained in the report was revealed in one form or another earlier in the investigation, this* Final Report *presented a clear statement of the issues involved in the complex web of deception, law breaking, and lies known as Iran-contra. The* Final Report *documented examples of the abuse of executive power and the inability and unwillingness of Congress to take firm action to correct the situation, despite House and Senate investigations into the matter. In the statements of former presidents Reagan and Bush included in volume III of the* Final Report *(see document 181) the Iran-contra matter was portrayed not as a major constitutional crisis, but as a disagreement over foreign policy between Congress and the White House.*

EXECUTIVE SUMMARY

In October and November 1986, two secret U.S. Government operations were publicly exposed, potentially implicating Reagan Administration officials in illegal activities. These operations were the prevision of assistance to the military activities of the Nicaraguan contra rebels during an October 1984 to October 1986 prohibition on such aid, and the sale of U.S. arms to Iran in contravention of stated U.S. policy and in possible violation of arms-export controls. In late November 1986, Reagan Administration officials announced that some of the proceeds from the sale of U.S. arms to Iran had been diverted to the contras.

As a result of the exposure of those operations, Attorney General Edwin Meese III sought the appointment of an independent counsel to investigate and, if necessary, prosecute possible crimes arising from them.

The Special Division of the United States Court of Appeals for the District of Columbia Circuit appointed Lawrence E. Walsh as Independent Counsel on December 19, 1986, and charged him with investigating:

(1) the direct or indirect sale, shipment, or transfer since in or about 1984 down to the present, of military arms, materiel, or funds to the government of Iran, officials of that government, persons, organizations or entities connected with or purporting to represent that government, or persons located in Iran;
(2) the direct or indirect sale, shipment, or transfer of military arms, materiel or funds to any government, entity, or person acting, or purporting to act as an intermediary in any transaction referred to above;
(3) the financing or funding of any direct or indirect sale, shipment or transfer referred to above;
(4) the diversion of proceeds from any transaction described above to or for any person, organization, foreign government, or any faction or body of insurgents in any foreign country, including, but not limited to Nicaragua;
(5) the provision or coordination of support for persons or entities engaged as military insurgents in armed conflict with the government of Nicaragua since 1984.

This is the final report of that investigation.

Overall Conclusions

The investigations and prosecutions have shown the high-ranking Administration officials violated laws and executive orders in Iran/contra matter.

Independent Counsel concluded that:

—sales of arms to Iran contravened United States Government policy and may have violated the Arms Export Control Act;
—the provision and coordination of support to the contras violated the Boland Amendment ban on aid to military activities in Nicaragua;
—the policies behind both the Iran and contra operations were fully reviewed and developed at the highest levels of the Reagan Administration;
—although there was little evidence of National Security Council level knowledge of most of the actual contra-support operations, there was no evidence that any NSC [National Security Council] member dissented from the underlying policy—keeping the contras alive despite congressional limitations on contra support;
—Iran operations were carried out with the knowledge of, among others, President Ronald Reagan, Vice President George Bush, Secretary of State George P. Shultz, Secretary of Defense Caspar W. Weinberger, Director of Central Intelligence William J. Casey, and national security advisers Robert C. McFarlane and John M. Poindexter; of these officials, only Weinberger and Shultz dissented from the policy decision, and Weinberger eventually acquiesced by ordering the Department of Defense to provide the necessary arms; and
—large volumes of highly relevant, contemporaneously created documents were systematically and willfully withheld from investigators by several Reagan Administration officials.
—following the revelation of these operations in October and November 1986, Reagan Administration officials deliberately deceived the Congress and the public about the level and extent of official knowledge of and support for these operations.

In addition, Independent Counsel concluded that the off-the-books nature of the Iran and contra operations gave line-level personnel the opportunity to commit money crimes.

Prosecutions

In the course of Independent Counsel's investigation, 14 persons were charged with criminal violations. There were two broad classes of crimes charged: Operational crimes, which largely concerned the illegal use of funds generated in the course of the operations, and "cover-up" crimes, which largely concerned false statements and obstructions after the revelation of the operations. Independent Counsel did not charge violations of the Arms Export Control Act or Boland Amendment. Although apparent violations of these statutes provided the impetus for the cover-up, they are not criminal statutes and do not contain any enforcement provisions.

All of the individuals charged were convicted, except for one CIA official whose case was dismissed on national security grounds and two officials who received unprecedented pre-trial pardons by President Bush following his electoral defeat in 1992. Two of the convictions were reversed on appeal on constitutional grounds that in no way cast doubt on the factual guilt of the men convicted. The individuals charged and the disposition of their cases are:

(1) Robert C. McFarlane: pleaded guilty to four counts of withholding information from Congress;

(2) Oliver L. North: convicted of altering and destroying documents, accepting an illegal gratuity, and aiding and abetting in the obstruction of Congress; conviction reversed on appeal;

(3) John M. Poindexter: convicted of conspiracy, false statements, destruction and removal of records, and obstruction of Congress; conviction reversed on appeal;

(4) Richard V. Secord: pleaded guilty to making false statements to Congress;

(5) Albert Hakim: pleaded guilty to supplementing the salary of North;

(6) Thomas G. Clines: convicted of four counts of tax-related offenses for failing to report income from the operations;

(7) Carl R. Channell: pleaded guilty to conspiracy to defraud the United States;

(8) Richard R. Miller: pleaded guilty to conspiracy to defraud the United States;

(9) Clair E. George: convicted of false statements and perjury before Congress;

(10) Duane R. Clarridge: indicted on seven counts of perjury and false statements; pardoned before trial by President Bush;

(11) Alan D. Fiers, Jr.: pleaded guilty to withholding information from Congress;

(12) Joseph F. Fernandez: indicted on four counts of obstruction and false statements; case dismissed when Attorney General Richard L. Thornburgh refused to declassify information needed for his defense;

(13) Elliott Abrams: pleaded guilty to withholding information from Congress;

(14) Caspar W. Weinberger: charged with four counts of false statements and perjury; pardoned before trial by President Bush.

At the time President Bush pardoned Weinberger and Clarridge, he also pardoned George, Fiers, Abrams, and McFarlane.

The Basic Facts of Iran/contra

The Iran/contra affair concerned two secret Reagan Administration policies whose operations were coordinated by National Security Council staff. The Iran operation involved efforts in 1985 and 1986 to obtain the release of Americans held hostage in the Middle East through the sale of U.S. weapons to Iran, despite an embargo on such sales. The contra operations from 1984 through most of 1986 involved the secret governmental support of contra military and paramilitary activities in Nicaragua, despite congressional prohibition of this support.

The Iran and contra operations were merged when funds generated from the sale of weapons to Iran were diverted to support the Contra effort in Nicaragua. Although this "diversion" may be the most dramatic aspect of Iran/contra, it is important to emphasize that both the Iran and contra operations, separately, violated United States policy and law. The ignorance the "diversion" asserted by President Reagan and his Cabinet officers on the National Security Council in no way absolves them of responsibility for the underlying Iran and contra operations.

The secrecy concerning the Iran and contra activities was finally pierced by events that place thousands of miles apart in the fall of 1986. The first occurred on October 5, 1986, when Nicaraguan government soldiers downed an American cargo plane that was carrying military supplies to contra forces; the one surviving crew member, American Eugene Hasenfus, was taken into captivity and stated that he was employed by the CIA. A month after the Hasenfus shootdown, President Reagan's secret sale of U.S. arms to Iran was reported by a Lebanese publication on November 3. The joining of these two operations was made public on November 25, 1986, when Attorney General Meese announced that Justice Department officials had discovered that some of the proceeds from the Iran arms sales been diverted to the contras.

When these operations ended, the exposure of the Iran/contra affair generated a new round of illegality. Beginning with the testimony of Elliott Abrams and others in October 1986 and continuing through the public testimony of Caspar W. Weinberger on the last day of congressional hearings in the summer of 1987, senior Reagan Administration officials engaged in a concerted effort to deceive Congress and the public about their knowledge of and support for the operations.

Independent Counsel has concluded that the President's most senior advisers and the members on the National Security Council participated in the strategy to make National Security staff members McFarland, Poindexter and North the scapegoats whose sacrifice would protect the Reagan Administration in its final years. In an important sense, this strategy succeeded. Independent Counsel discovered much of the best evidence of the cover-up in final year of active investigation, too late for most prosecutions.

Scope of Report

This report provides an account of the Independent Counsel's investigation, the prosecutions, the basis for decisions not to prosecute, and overall observations and conclusions on the Iran/contra matters.

Part I of the report sets out the underlying facts of the Iran and contra operations. Part II describes the criminal investigation of those underlying facts. Part M provides an analysis of the central operational conspiracy. Parts IV through IX are agency-level reports of Independent Counsel's investigations and cases: the National Security staff, the private operatives who assisted the NSC staff, Central Intelligence Agency officials, Department of State officials, and White House officials and Attorney General Edwin Meese III.

Volume I of this report concludes with a chapter concerning political oversight and the rule of law, and a final chapter containing independent Counsel's observations. Volume II of the report contains supporting documentation. Volume III is a classified appendix.

Because many will read only sections of the report, each has been written with completeness, even though this has resulted in repetition of factual statements about central activities.

The Operational Conspiracy

The operational conspiracy was the basis for Count One of the 23-count indictment returned by the Grand Jury March 16, 1988, against Poindexter, North, Secord, and Hakim. It charged the four with conspiracy to defraud the United States by deceitfully:

(1) supporting military operations in Nicaragua in defiance of congressional controls;

(2) using the Iran arms sales to raise funds to be spent at the direction of North, rather than the U.S. Government; and

(3) endangering the Administration's hostage-release effort by overcharging Iran for the arms to generate unauthorized profits to fund the contras and for other purposes.

The charge was upheld as a matter of law by U.S. District Judge Gerhard A. Gesell even though the Justice Department, in a move that Judge Gesell called "unprecedented," filed an amicus brief supporting North's contention that the charge should be dismissed. Although Count One was ultimately dismissed because the Reagan Administration refused to declassify information necessary to North's defense, Judge Gesell's decision established that high government officials who engage in conspiracy to subvert civil laws and the Constitution have engaged in criminal acts. Trial on Count One would have disclosed the Government-wide activities that supported North's Iran and contra operations.

Within the NSC, McFarlane pleaded guilty in March 1988 to four counts of withholding information from Congress in connection with his denials that North was providing the contras with military advice and assistance. McFarlane, in his plea agreement, promised to cooperate with Independent Counsel by providing truthful testimony in subsequent trials.

Judge Gesell ordered severance of the trials of the four charged in the conspiracy indictment because of the immunized testimony given by Poindexter, North and Hakim to Congress.

North was tried and convicted by a jury in May 1989 of altering and destroying documents, accepting an illegal gratuity and aiding and abetting in the obstruction of Congress. His conviction was reversed on appeal in July 1990 and charges against North were subsequently dismissed in September 1991 on the ground that trial witnesses were tainted by North's nationally televised, immunized testimony before Congress. Poindexter in April 1990 was convicted by a jury on five felony counts of conspiracy, false statements, destruction and removal of records and obstruction of Congress. The Court of Appeals reversed his conviction in November 1991 on the immunized testimony issue.

The Flow of Funds

The illegal activities of the private citizens involved with the North and Secord operations are discussed in detail in Part V. The off-the-books conduct of the two highly secret operations circumvented normal Administration accountability and congressional oversight associated with covert ventures and presented fertile ground for financial wrongdoing. There were several funding sources for the contras' weapons purchases from the covert-action Enterprise formed by North, Secord and Hakim:

(1) donations from foreign countries;

(2) contributions from wealthy Americans sympathetic to President Reagan's contra support policies; and

(3) the diversion of proceeds from the sale of arms to Iran.

Ultimately, all of these funds fell under the control of North, and through him, Secord and Hakim.

North used political fundraisers Carl R. Channell and Richard R. Miller to raise millions of dollars from wealthy Americans, illegally using a tax-exempt organization to do so. These funds, along with the private contributions, were run through a network of corporations and Swiss bank accounts put at North's disposal by Secord and Hakim, through which transactions were concealed and laundered. In late 1985 through 1986 the Enterprise became centrally involved in the arms sales to Iran. As a result of both the Iran and contra operations, more than $47 million flowed through Enterprise accounts.

Professional fundraisers Channell and Miller pleaded guilty in the spring of 1987 to conspiracy to defraud the Government by illegal use of a tax-exempt foundation to raise contributions for the purchase of lethal supplies for the contras. They named North as an unindicted co-conspirator.

Secord pleaded guilty in November 1989 to a felony, admitting that he falsely denied to Congress that North had personally benefited from the Enterprise. Hakim pleaded guilty to the misdemeanor count of supplementing the salary of North. Lake Resources Inc., the company controlled by Hakim to launder the Enterprise's money flow, pleaded guilty to the corporate felony of theft of Government property in diverting the proceeds from the arms sales to the contras and for other unauthorized purposes. Thomas G. Clines was convicted in September 1990 of four tax-related felonies for failing to report all of his income from the Enterprise.

Agency Support of the Operations

Following the convictions of those who were most central to the Iran/contra operations, Independent Counsel's investigation focused on the supporting roles played by Government officials in other agencies and the supervisory roles of the NSC principals. The investigation showed that Administration officials who claimed initially that they had little knowledge about the Iran arms sales or the illegal contra-resupply operation North directed were much better informed than they professed to be. The Office of Independent Counsel [OIC] obtained evidence that Secretaries Weinberger and Shultz and White House Chief of Staff Donald T. Regan, among others, held back information that would have helped Congress obtain a much clearer view of the scope of the Iran/contra matter. Contemporaneous notes of Regan and Weinberger, and those dictated by Shultz, were withheld until they were obtained by Independent Counsel in 1991 and 1992.

The White House and Office of the Vice President

As the White House section of this report describes in detail, the investigation found no credible evidence that President Reagan violated any criminal statute. The OIC could not prove that Reagan authorized or was aware of the diversion or that he had knowledge of the extent of North's control of the contra-resupply network. Nevertheless, he set the stage for the illegal activities of others by encouraging and, in general terms, ordering support of the contras during the October 1984 to October 1986 period when funds for the contras were cut off by the Boland Amendment, and in authorizing the sale of arms to Iran, in contravention of the U.S. embargo on such sales. The President's disregard for civil laws enacted to limit presidential actions abroad—specifically the Boland Amendment, the Arms Export Control Act and congressional-notification requirements in covert-action laws—created a climate in which some of the Government officers assigned to implement his policies felt emboldened to circumvent such laws.

President Reagan's directive to McFarlane to keep the contras alive "body and soul" during the Boland cut-off period was viewed by North, who was charged by McFarlane to carry out the directive, as an invitation to break the law. Similarly, President Reagan's decision in 1985 to authorize the sale of arms to Iran from Israeli stocks, despite warnings by Weinberger and Shultz that such transfers might violate the law, opened the way for Poindexter's subsequent decision to authorize the diversion. Poindexter told Congress that while he made the decision on his own and did not tell the President, he believed the President would have approved. North testified that he believed the President authorized it.

Independent Counsel's investigation did not develop evidence that proved that Vice President Bush violated any criminal statute. Contrary to his public pronouncements, however, he was fully aware of the Iran arms sales. Bush was regularly briefed, along with the President, on the Iran arms sales, and he participated in discussions to obtain third-country support for the contras. The OIC obtained no evidence that Bush was aware of the diversion. The OIC teamed in December 1992 that Bush had failed to produce a diary containing contemporaneous notes relevant to Iran/contra despite requests made in 1987 and again in early 1992 for the production of such material. Bush refused to be interviewed for a final time in light of evidence developed in the latter stages of OIC's investigation, leaving unresolved a clear picture of his Iran/contra involvement. Bush's pardon of Weinberger on December 24, 1992 preempted a trial in which defense counsel indicated that they intended to call Bush as a witness.

The chapters on White House Chief of Staff Regan and Attorney General Edwin Meese III focus on their actions during the November 1986 period, as the President and his advisers sought to control the damage caused by the disclosure of the Iran arms sales. Regan in 1992 provided Independent Counsel with copies of notes showing that Poindexter and Meese attempted to create a false account of the 1985 arms sales from Israeli stocks, which they believed were illegal, in order to protect the President. Regan and the other senior advisers did not speak up to correct the false version of events. No final legal determination on the matter had been made. Regan said he did not want to be the one who broke the silence among the President's senior advisers, virtually all of whom knew the account was false.

The evidence indicates that Meese's November 1986 inquiry was more of a damage-control exercise than an effort to find the facts. He had private conversations with the President, the Vice President, Poindexter, Weinberger, Casey and Regan without taking notes. Even after teaming of the diversion, Meese failed to secure records in NSC staff offices or take other prudent steps to protect potential evidence. And finally, in reporting to the President and his senior advisers, Meese gave a false account of what he had been told by stating that the President did not know about the 1985 HAWK shipments, which Meese said might have been illegal. The statute of limitations had run on November 1986 activities before OIC obtained its evidence. In 1992, Meese denied recollection of the statements attributed to him by the notes of Weinberger and Regan. He was unconvincing, but the passage of time would have been expected to raise a reasonable doubt of the intentional falsity of his denials if he had been prosecuted for his 1992 false statements.

The Role of CIA Officials

Director Casey's unswerving support of President Reagan's contra policies and of the Iran arms sales encouraged some CIA officials to go beyond legal restrictions in both operations. Casey was instrumental in pairing North with Secord as a contra-support team when the Boland Amendment in October 1994 forced the CIA to refrain from direct or indirect aid. He also supported the North-Secord combination in the Iran arms sales, despite deep reservations about Secord within the CIA hierarchy.

Casey's position on the contras prompted the chief of the CIA's Central American Task Force, Alan D. Fiers, Jr., to "dovetail" CIA activities with those of North's contra-resupply network, in violation of Boland restrictions. Casey's support for the NSC to direct the Iran arms sales and to use arms dealer Manucher Ghorbanifar and Secord in the operation, forced the CIA's Directorate of Operations to work with people it distrusted.

Following the Hasenfus shootdown in early October 1986, George and Fiers lied to Congress about U.S. Government involvement in contra resupply, to, as Fiers put it, "keep the spotlight off the White House." When the Iran arms sales became public in November 1986, three of Casey's key office officers—George, Clarridge and Fiers—followed Casey's lead in misleading Congress.

Four CIA officials were charged with criminal offense—George the deputy director for operations and the third highest-ranking CIA official; Clarridge, chief of the European Division; Fiers; and Fernandez. George was convicted of two felony counts of false statements and perjury before Congress. Fiers pleaded guilty to two misdemeanor counts of withholding information from Congress. The four counts of obstruction and false statements against Fernandez were dismissed when the Bush Administration refused to declassify information needed for his defense. Clarridge was awaiting trial on seven counts of perjury and false statements when he, George and Piers were pardoned by President Bush.

State Department Officials

In 1990 and 1991, Independent Counsel received new documentary evidence in the form of handwritten notes suggesting that Secretary Shultz's congressional testimony painted a misleading and incorrect picture of his knowledge of the Iran arms sales. The subsequent investigation focused on whether Shultz or other Department officials deliberately misled or withheld information from congressional or OIC investigators.

The key notes, taken by M. Charles Hill, Shultz's executive assistant, were nearly verbatim, contemporaneous accounts of Shultz's meetings within the department and Shultz's reports to Hill on meetings the secretary attended elsewhere. The Hill notes and similarly detailed notes by Nicholas Platt, the State Department's executive secretary, provided the OIC with a detailed account of Shultz's knowledge of the Iran arms sale. The most revealing of these notes were not provided to any Iran/contra investigation until 1990 and 1991. The notes show that—contrary to his early testimony that he was not aware of details of the 1985 arms transfers—Shultz knew that the shipments were planned and that they were delivered. Also in conflict with his congressional testimony was evidence that Shultz was aware of the 1986 shipments.

Independent Counsel concluded that Shultz's early testimony was incorrect, if not false, in significant respects, and misleading, if literally true, in others. When questioned about the discrepancies in 1992, Shultz did not dispute the accuracy of the Hill notes. He told OIC that he believed his testimony was accurate at the time and he insisted that if he had been provided with the notes earlier, he would have testified differently. Independent Counsel declined to prosecute because there was a reasonable doubt that Shultz's testimony was willfully false at the time it was delivered.

Independent Counsel concluded that Hill had willfully withheld relevant notes and prepared false testimony for Shultz in 1987. He declined to prosecute because Hill's claim of authorization to limit the production of his notes and the joint responsibility of Shultz for the resulting misleading testimony, would at trial have raised a reasonable doubt, after Independent Counsel had declined to prosecute Shultz.

Independent Counsel's initial focus on the State Department had centered on Assistant Secretary Elliott Abrams' insistence to Congress and to the OIC that he was not aware of North's direction of the extensive contra-resupply network in 1985 and 1986. As assistant secretary of state for inter-American affairs, Abrams chaired the Restricted Inter-Agency Group, or RIG, which coordinated U.S. policy in Central America. Although the OIC was skeptical about Abrams' testimony, there was insufficient evidence to proceed against him until additional documentary evidence inculpating him was discovered in 1990 and 1991, and until Fiers, who represented the CIA on the RIG, pleaded guilty in July 1991 to withholding information from Congress. Fiers provided evidence to support North's earlier testimony that Abrams was knowledgeable about North's contra-supply network. Abrams pleaded guilty in October 1991 to two counts of withholding information from Congress about secret Government efforts to support the contras, and about his solicitation of $10 million to aid the contras from the Sultan of Brunei.

Secretary Weinberger and Defense Department Officials

Contrary to their testimony to the presidentially appointed Tower Commission and the Select Iran/contra Committees of Congress, Independent Counsel determined that Secretary Weinberger and his closest aides were consistently informed of proposed and actual arms shipments to Iran during 1985 and 1986. The key evidence was handwritten notes of Weinberger, which he deliberately withheld from Congress and the OIC until they were discovered by independent counsel in late 1991. The Weinberger daily diary notes and notes of significant White House and other meetings contained highly relevant, contemporaneous information that resolved many questions left unanswered in early investigations.

The notes demonstrated that Weinberger's early testimony—that he had only vague and general information about Iran arms sales in 1985—was false, and that he in fact had detailed information on the proposed arms sales and the actual deliveries. The notes also revealed that Gen. Colin Powell, Weinberger's senior military aide, and Richard L. Armitage, assistant secretary of defense for international security affairs, also had detailed knowledge of the 1985 shipments from Israeli stocks. Armitage and Powell had testified that they did not learn of the November 1985 HAWK missile shipment until 1986.

Weinberger's notes provided detailed accounts of high-level Administration meetings in November 1986 in which the President's senior advisers were provided with false accounts of the Iran arms sales to protect the President and themselves from the consequences of the possibly illegal 1995 shipments from Israeli stocks.

Weinberger's notes provided key evidence supporting the charges against him, including perjury and false statements in connection with his testimony regarding the arms sales, his denial of the existence of notes and his denial of knowledge of Saudi Arabia's multi-million dollar contribution to the contras. He was pardoned less than two weeks before trial by President Bush on December 24, 1992.

There was little evidence that Powell's early testimony regarding the 1985 shipments and Weinberger's notes was willfully false. Powell cooperated with the various Iran/contra investigations and, when his recollection was refreshed by Weinberger's notes, he readily conceded their accuracy. Independent Counsel declined to prosecute Armitage because the OIC's limited resources were focused on the case against Weinberger and because the evidence against Armitage, while substantial, did not reach the threshold of proof beyond a reasonable doubt.

The Reagan, Bush and Casey Segments

The Independent Counsel Act requires a report as to persons not indicted as well as those indicted. Because of the large number of persons investigated, those discussed in individual sections of this report are limited to those as to whom there was a possibility of indictment. In addition there are separate sections on President Reagan and President Bush because, although criminal proceedings against them were always unlikely, they were important subjects of the investigation, and their activities were important action taken with respect to others.

CIA Director Casey is a special case. Because Casey was hospitalized with a fatal illness before Independent Counsel was appointed, no formal investigation of Casey was ever undertaken by the OIC. Casey was never able to give his account, and he was unable to respond to allegations of wrongdoing made about him by others, most prominently North, whose veracity is subject to serious question. Equally important, fundamental questions could not be answered regarding Casey's state of mind, the impact, if any, of his fatal illness on his conduct and his intent.

Under normal circumstances, a prosecutor would hesitate to comment on the conduct of an individual whose activities and actions were not subjected to rigorous investigation, which might exculpate that individual. Nevertheless, after serious deliberation, Independent Counsel concluded that it was in the public interest that this report expose as full and complete an account of the Iran/contra matter as possible. This simply could not be done without an account of the, role of Director Casey.

Observations and Conclusions

This report concludes with Independent Counsel's observations and conclusions. He observes that the governmental problems presented by Iran/contra are not those of rogue opera-

tions, but rather those of Executive Branch efforts to evade congressional oversight. As this report documents, the competing roles of the attorney general—adviser to the President and top law enforcement officer—come into irreconcilable conflict in the case of high-level Executive Branch wrongdoing. Independent Counsel concludes that congressional oversight alone cannot correct the deficiencies that result when an attorney abandons the law-enforcement responsibilities of that office and undertakes, instead, to protect the President.

Independent Counsel asks the Congress to review the difficult and delicate problem posed to the investigations and prosecutions by congressional grants of immunity to principals. While recognizing the important responsibility of Congress for investigating such matters thoroughly, Congress must realize that grants of use immunity to principals in such highly exposed as the Iran/contra affair will virtually rule out successful prosecution.

Independent Counsel also addresses the problem of the Classified Information Procedures Act (CEPA) in cases steeped in highly classified information, such as many of the Iran/contra prosecutions. Under the Act, the attorney general has unrestricted discretion to decide whether to declassify information necessary for trial, even in cases in which Independent Counsel has been appointed because of the attorney general's conflict of interest. This discretion is inconsistent with the perceived need for independent counsel, particularly in cases in which officers of the intelligence agencies that classify information are under investigation. This discretion gives the attorney general the power to block almost any potentially embarrassing prosecution that requires the declassification of information. Independent Counsel suggests that the attorney general implement standards that would permit independent review of a decision to block a prosecution of an officer within the Executive Branch and legitimate congressional oversight.

Classified Information

In addition to the unclassified Volumes I and II of this report, a brief classified report, Volume M, has been filed with the Special Division. The classified report contains references to material gathered in the investigation of Iran/contra that could not be declassified and could not be concealed by some substitute form of discussion.

. . . .

PART XI: CONCLUDING OBSERVATIONS

The underlying facts of Iran/contra are that, regardless of criminality, President Reagan, the secretary of state, the secretary of defense, and the director of central intelligence and their necessary assistants committed themselves, however reluctantly, to two programs contrary to congressional policy and contrary to national policy. They skirted the law, some of them broke the law, and almost all of them tried to cover up the President's willful activities.

What protection do the people of the United States have against such a concerted action by such powerful officers? The Constitution provides for congressional oversight and congressional control of appropriations, but if false information is given to Congress, these checks and balances are of lessened value. Further, in the give and take of the political community, congressional oversight is often overtaken and subordinated by the need to keep Government functioning, by the need to anticipate the future, and by the ever-present requirement of maintaining consensus among the elected officials who are the Government.

The disrespect for Congress by a popular and powerful President and his appointees was obscured when Congress accepted the tendered concept of a runaway conspiracy of subordinate officers and avoided the unpleasant confrontation with a powerful President and his Cabinet. In haste to display and conclude its investigation of this unwelcome issue, Congress destroyed the most effective lines of inquiry by giving immunity to Oliver L. North and John M. Poindexter so that they could exculpate and eliminate the need for the testimony of President Reagan and Vice President Bush.

Immunity is ordinarily given by a prosecutor to a witness who will incriminate someone more important than himself Congress gave immunity to North and Poindexter, who incriminated only themselves and who largely exculpated those responsible for the initiation, supervision and support of their activities. This delayed and infinitely complicated the effort to prosecute North and Poindexter, and it largely destroyed the likelihood that their prompt conviction and appropriate sentence would induce meaningful cooperation.

These important political decisions were properly the responsibility of Congress. It was for the Committees to decide whether the welfare of the nation was served or endangered by a continuation of its investigation, a more deliberate effort to test the self-serving denials presented by Cabinet officers and to search for the full ramifications of the activities in question. Having made this decision, however, no one could gainsay the added difficulties thrust upon Independent Counsel. These difficulties could be dealt with only by the investment of large amounts of additional time and large amounts of expense.

The role of Independent Counsel is not well understood. Comparisons to United States attorneys, county district attorneys, or private law offices do not conceive the nature of Independent Counsel. Independent Counsel is not an individual put in charge of an ongoing agency as an acting U.S. attorney might be; he is a person taken from private practice and told to create a new agency, to carry out the mission assigned by the court. It is not as though he were told to step in and try a case on the calendar of an ongoing office with full support of the Government behind him, as it would be behind the United States attorney. He is told to create an office and to confront the Government without any expectation of real cooperation, and, indeed, with the expectation of hostility, however veiled. That hostility will manifest itself in the failure to declassify information, in the suppression of documents, and in all of the evasive techniques of highly skilled and large, complex organizations.

The investigation into Iran/contra nevertheless demonstrates that the rule of law upon which our democratic system of government depends can be applied to the highest officials even when they are operating in the secret areas or diplomacy and national security.

Despite extraordinary difficulties imposed by the destruction and withholding of records, the need to protect classified information, and the congressional grants of immunity to some of the principals involved, Independent Counsel was able to bring criminal charges against nine government officers and five private citizens involved in illegal activities growing out of the Iran/contra affair.

More importantly, the investigation and the prosecutions arising out of it have provided a much more accurate picture of how two secret Administration policies keeping the contras alive "body and soul" during the Boland cutoff period and seeking the release of Americans held hostage by selling arms to Iran veered off into criminality.

Evidence obtained by Independent Counsel establishes that the Iran/contra affair was not an aberrational scheme carried out by a "cabal of zealots" on the National Security Council staff, as the congressional Select Committees concluded in their majority report. Instead, it was the product of two foreign policy directives by President Reagan which skirted the law and which were executed by the NSC staff with the knowledge and support of high officials in the CIA, State and, Defense departments, and to a lesser extent, officials in other agencies.

Independent Counsel found no evidence of dissent among his Cabinet officers from the President's determination to support the contras after federal law banned the use of appropriated funds for that purpose in the Boland Amendment in October 1984. Even the two Cabinet officers who opposed the sale of arms to Iran on the grounds that it was illegal and bad policy—Defense Secretary Caspar W. Weinberger and Secretary of State George P. Shultz—either cooperated with the decision once made, as in the case of Weinberger, or stood aloof from it while being kept informed of its progress, as was the case of Shultz.

In its report section titled "Who Was Responsible," the Select Committees named CIA Director William Casey, National Security Advisers Robert C. McFarlane and John M. Poindexter, along with NSC staff member Oliver L. North, and private sector operatives Richard V. Secord and Albert Hakim. With the exception of Casey who died before he could questioned by the OIC, Independent Counsel and obtained criminal convictions of charges of each of the men named by Congress. There is little doubt that, operationally, these men were central players.

But the investigation and prosecutions have shown that these six were not out-of-control mavericks who acted alone without the knowledge or assistance of others. The evidence establishes that the central NSC operatives kept their superiors—including Reagan, Bush, Shultz, Weinberger and other high officials—informed of their efforts generally, if not in detail, and their superiors either condoned or turned a blind eye to them. When it was required, the NSC principals and their private sector operatives received the assistance of high-ranking officers in the CIA, the Defense Department, and the Department of State.

Of the 14 persons charged criminally during the investigation, four were convicted of felony charges after trial by jury, seven pleaded guilty either to felonies or misdemeanors, and one had his case dismissed because the Administration refused to declassify information deemed necessary to the defendant by the trial judge. Two cases that were awaiting trial were aborted by pardons granted by President Bush. As this report explained earlier, many persons who committed crimes were not charged. Some minor crimes were never investigated and some that were investigated were not solved. But Independent Counsel believes that to the extent possible, the central Iran/contra crimes were vigorously prosecuted and the significant acts of obstruction were fully charged.

Fundamentally, the Iran/contra affair was the first known criminal assault on the post-Watergate rules governing the activities of national security officials. Reagan Administration officials rendered these rules ineffective by creating private operations, supported with privately generated funds that successfully evaded executive and legislative oversight and control. Congress was defrauded. Its appropriations restrictions having been circumvented, Congress was led to believe that the Administration was following the law. Numerous congressional inquiries were thwarted through false testimony and the destruction and concealment of government records.

The destruction and concealment of records and information, beginning at the twilight of Iran/contra and continuing throughout subsequent investigations, should be of particular concern. Oliver North's destruction of records in October and November 1986 caused an irretrievable loss of information to the executive agencies responsible for regulating clandestine activities, to Congress, and to Independent Counsel. John Poindexter's efforts to destroy NSC electronic mail nearly resulted in comparable damage. CIA Costa Rican Station Chief Joseph F. Fernandez attempted to hide phone records that would have revealed his contacts with Enterprise activities.

This sort of obstruction continued even after Independent Counsel's appointment. In the course of his work, Independent Counsel located large caches of handwritten notes and other documents maintained by high officials that were never relinquished to investigators. Major aspects of Iran/contra would never have been uncovered had all of the officials who attempted to destroy or withhold their records of the affair succeeded. Had these contemporaneous records been produced to investigators when they were initially requested, many of the troublesome conflicts between key witnesses would have been resolved, and timely legal steps taken toward those who feigned memory lapses or lied outright.

All of this conduct—the evasions of the Executive branch and the Congress, the lies, the conspiracies, the acts of obstruction—had to be addressed by the criminal justice system.

The path Independent Counsel embarked upon in late 1986 had been a long and arduous one. When he hired 10 attorneys in early 1987, Independent Counsel's conception of the operational conspiracy—with its array of Government officials and private contractors, its web of secret foreign accounts, and its world-wide breadth—was extremely hazy. Outlining an investigation of a runaway conspiracy disavowed by the President was quite different from the ultimate investigation of the President and three major agencies, each with the power to frustrate an investigation by persisting in the classification of non-secret but embarrassing information. Completing the factual mosaic required examining pieces spread worldwide in activities that occurred over a three-year period by officials from the largest agencies of government and a host of private operatives who, by necessity, design and training, worked secretly and deceptively.

The Role of Independent Counsel

Given the enormous autonomous power of both the Legislative and Executive branches in the modern state, the rightly celebrated constitutional checks and balances are inadequate, alone, to preserve the rule of law upon which our democracy depends.

As Watergate demonstrated, the checks and balances reach their limits in the case of criminal wrongdoing by Executive branch officials. The combination of an aggressive press, simple crimes, the White House tapes, and principled defiance by Department of Justice-appointed counsel all combined to bring Watergate to its conclusion without an independent counsel statute. It was apparent then, however, as it should be now in light of Iran/contra, that the competing roles of the attorney general, as a member of the Cabinet and presidential adviser on the one hand and chief law enforcement officer on the other, create an irreconcilable conflict of interest.

As Iran/contra demonstrated, congressional oversight alone cannot make up for deficiencies that result when an attorney general abandons that law-enforcement role in cases of Executive branch wrongdoing. Well before Attorney General Meese sought an independent counsel in December 1986, he had become, in effect, the President's defense lawyer, to the exclusion of his responsibilities as the nation's top law enforcement officer. By that time, crucial documents had already been destroyed and false testimony given.

Congress, with all the investigatory powers it wields in the oversight process, was not able to uncover many of these documents or disprove much of that false testimony. That inability is structural, and does not result from ill will, impatience, or character flaw on the part of any legislator. With good reason, Congress's interest in investigating Executive branch wrongdoing extends no farther than remedying perceived imbalances in its relations with the Executive branch. Except in the case of impeachment, Congress's interest does not, and should not, extend to the law-enforcement goals of deterrence, retribution and punishment.

In normal circumstances, these law-enforcement goals are the province of the Justice Department, under the direction of the attorney general. As the chief law enforcement officer of the United States, the attorney general represents the people of the United States—not the President, the Cabinet or any political party. When the attorney general cannot so represent the people, the rule of law requires that another, independent institution assume that responsibility. That is the historic role of the independent counsel.

Problems Posed by Congressional Immunity Grants

The magnitude of Iran/contra does not by itself explain why Independent Counsel took so long to complete the task assigned by the Special Division which appointed him. The word "independent" in Independent Counsel is not quite accurate as a description of his work. Time and again this Independent Counsel found himself at the mercy of political decisions of the Congress and the Executive branch. From the date of his appointment on December 19, 1986, Independent Counsel had to race to protect his investigations and prosecutions from the congressional grants of immunity to central Enterprise conspirators. At the same time, he had to wait almost one year for records from Swiss banks and financial organizations vital to his work. Once Congress granted immunity, Independent Counsel had to insulate himself and his staff from immunized disclosures, postponing the time he could get a wider view of the activities he was investigating.

Despite extraordinary efforts to shield the OIC from exposure to immunized testimony, the North and Poindexter convictions were overturned on appeal on the immunity issue. While the appellate panels did not find the prosecution was "tainted" by improper exposure to the immunized testimony of North or Poindexter, they ruled that the safeguards utilized by the trial courts did not ensure that witnesses' testimony was not affected by the immunized testimony.

Although Independent Counsel warned the Select Committees of the possibility that granting use immunity to principals in the Iran/contra matter might make it impossible to prosecute them successfully, he has never contended that Congress should refrain from granting use immunity to compel testimony in such important matters as Iran/contra. In matters of great national concern, Independent Counsel recognizes that intense public interest and the need for prompt and effective congressional oversight of intelligence activities may well force the Congress to act swiftly and grant immunity to principals.

But, in light of the experience of Independent Counsel in the Iran/contra cases, Congress should be aware of the fact that future immunity grants, at least in such highly publicized cases, will likely rule out criminal prosecution.

Congressional action that precludes, or makes it impossible to sustain, a prosecution has more serious consequences than simply one less conviction. There is a significant inequity when more peripheral players are convicted while central figures in a criminal enterprise escape punishment. And perhaps more fundamentally, the failure to punish governmental lawbreakers feeds the perception that public officials are not wholly accountable for their actions. In Iran/contra, it was President Reagan who first asked that North and Poindexter be given immunity so that they could exculpate him from responsibility for the diversion. A few months later, the Select Committees did that—granting immunity without any proffer to ensure honest testimony.

The Classified Information Procedures Act

After Independent Counsel brought the principal operational conspiracy cases, he was forced to dismiss the central conspiracy charges against North, Poindexter, Hakim and Secord because the Administration, which had opposed the charge in the first instance, refused to declassify the information needed to proceed in the North case. Later, the entire case against Joseph F. Fernandez, the CIA's station chief in Costa Rica, was dismissed when the Administration declined to declassify information necessary for the trial. In both instances, Independent Counsel concluded that the classified information in question was already publicly known, but the Administration declined to engage in meaningful consultation with Independent Counsel before making its decision.

In any prosecution of a national security official, a tension inevitably arises between the Executive branch's duty to enforce the criminal law and its obligation to safeguard the national security through protecting classified information. The Classified Information Procedures Act (CIPA) was enacted in 1980 to assist the Department of Justice and other Executive branch agencies in resolving this tension in a manner consistent with our nation's commitment to the rule of law. Under CIPA, only the attorney general has the authority to make the decision between the Government's need to enforce the law and the Government's need to withhold information for national security masons. If the intelligence agencies decline to declassify information deemed necessary by the trial court for the fair trial of a case, only the attorney general can overrule them. Likewise, if the attorney general decides that the information should not be disclosed, he is empowered to file a CIPA § 6(e) affidavit to prohibit the disclosure. Current law does not require that the attorney general's decision to withhold classified material from disclosure at trial meet any objective or articulated standard. No court can challenge the substance of a § 6(e) affidavit; no litigant has standing to contest the attorney general's decision to file one.

The Administration the power to make the CIPA process work when it wants to, as in the case of alleged spies or in the trial of former Panamanian dictator Manuel Noriega. Since CEPA became law in 1980, no attorney general killed a prosecution by filing a § 6(e) affidavit until Attorney General Richard Thornburgh forced the dismissal of the Fernandez case in November 1989. As the Fernandez and North cases show, the Administration also has the power to derail the CIPA process when, for reasons of its own, it chooses not to make it work.

The attorney general's unrestricted CIPA § 6(e) authority becomes questionable when an independent counsel, rather than the Justice Department, has jurisdiction over the prosecution. An independent counsel is appointed only when the attorney general determines, after a preliminary investigation, that high-level officials within the Executive branch may have been involved in criminal activity or that the Department of Justice may be perceived to have a conflict of interest. The problems of conflict are compounded in CIPA because the issue involves classified information controlled by an intelligence agency in a case charging one or more of the officials of that agency in criminal activity. Congress could not have intended that CEPA—a statute designed to facilitate trials involving classified information used by the attorney general to control prosecutions of independent counsel.

Final Thoughts

The Iran/contra investigation will not end the kind of abuse of power that it addressed any more than the Watergate investigation did. The criminality in both affairs did not arise primarily out of ordinary venality or greed, although some of those charged were driven by both. Instead, the crimes committed in Iran/contra were motivated by the desire of persons in high office to pursue controversial policies and goals even when the pursuit of those policies and goals was inhibited or restricted by executive orders, statutes or the constitutional system of checks and balances.

The tone in Iran/contra was set by President Reagan. He directed that the contras be supported, despite a ban on contra aid imposed on him by Congress. And he was willing to trade arms to Iran for the release of Americans held hostage in the Middle East, even if doing so was contrary to the nation's stated policy and possibly in violation of the law.

The lesson of Iran/contra is that if our system of government is to function properly, the branches of government must deal with one another honestly and cooperatively. When disputes arise between the Executive and Legislative branches, as they surely will, the laws that emerge from such disputes must be obeyed.

When a President, even with good motive and intent, chooses to skirt the laws or to circumvent them, it is incumbent upon his subordinates to resist, not join in. Their oath and fealty are to the Constitution and the rule of law, not to the man temporarily occupying the Oval Office. Congress has the duty and the power under our system of checks and balances to ensure that the President and his Cabinet officers are faithful to their oaths.

Final Report of the Independent Counsel for Iran/Contra Matters, Vol. 1: Investigations and Prosecutions, August 4, 1993 (Washington, D.C.: U.S. Government Printing Office, 1993), xiii–xxi, 561–566.

181   Statements of Presidents Bush and Reagan Regarding Their Role in Iran-Contra

December 3, 1993

The Iran-contra affair was the most significant constitutional crisis between the executive branch and Congress during the presidency of Ronald Reagan (see document 180 for background). The Iran-contra investigation by independent counsel Lawrence E. Walsh took almost seven years to complete. As part of the Final Report of the Independent Counsel for Iran/Contra Matters, published for the first time in 1993, former presidents Ronald Reagan and George Bush submitted statements for the record, through their attorneys, that gave their views on the Iran-contra affair. The independent counsel's investigation concluded that both President Reagan and then Vice President Bush, as well as other top administration officials, had knowledge of the Iran operations.

In Bush's statement, he concluded that the investigation had "largely been an inquiry into a political dispute between a Republican Administration and a Democratic Congress over foreign policy." While recognizing the affair as a serious constitutional struggle between Congress and the White House over the conduct of foreign policy, Bush objected to the independent counsel's attempt to turn this partisan political struggle into criminal behavior. In his statement Bush also explained why, on Christmas eve 1992— just weeks before his term of office was up—he pardoned former

secretary of defense Caspar Weinberger and others convicted in the Iran-contra affair.

In the statement prepared by President Reagan's attorneys, Reagan concluded that "the Iran-Contra Independent Counsel has misused and abused the reporting process that is mandated by the independent counsel statute. The Final Report *unfairly and unnecessarily injures the rights and reputations of individuals, relies on innuendo, speculation, and conjecture instead of proof, violates established standards governing the conduct of prosecutors, and improperly relies on secret grand jury materials to support the Independent Counsel's many accusations."*

[STATEMENT OF FORMER PRESIDENT GEORGE H. W. BUSH]
Introduction

The investigation conducted by the Office of Independent Counsel ("OIC") under Judge Lawrence Walsh has largely been an inquiry into a political dispute between a Republican administration and a Democratic Congress over foreign policy. OIC has spent over six years and $40 million trying to give a criminal hue to the serious constitutional struggle over separation of powers between the Congress and the Executive in the foreign policy area. While the Report speculates that laws were broken by certain Administration officials other than President Bush, the real thrust of its conclusions relate to purported contravention of government *policy*. The Independent Counsel's authorizing legislation did not contemplate the investigation of such policy differences.

Congress has used the Independent Counsel statute as a tool for inserting itself into foreign policy, which is reserved under the Constitution to the Executive. An attempt to criminalize public policy differences jeopardizes any President's ability to govern. By seeking to craft criminal violations from a political foreign policy dispute, OIC was cast in a biased Position from the beginning. Notwithstanding this inherent bias, however, the Report does not and cannot dispute that:

(1) President Bush was unaware of the contra diversion as he has always maintained;

(2) President Bush told the truth in both his 1988 deposition to the OIC, which subsequently he released to the public, and in his 1987 FBI interview; and

(3) President Bush never violated any criminal statute.

Furthermore, despite statements or inferences in the Report to the contrary:

(1) President Bush issued the pardons of Caspar Weinberger and others because he believed it was the right and courageous thing to do. He was not concerned about the upcoming trials nor that he might be called as a witness by the defense.

(2) President Bush completely cooperated with OIC's investigation. As the Report even states, he told his staff to "give them [OIC] everything."

(3) President Bush had no idea that his personal, political thoughts, dictated well after the events of Iran-contra, were responsive to any OIC document requests until a member of his staff discovered them in a safe and reviewed them in late September 1992. President Bush immediately directed that the diary be turned over to White House Counsel Boyden Gray for his review, which was done. Mr. Gray subsequently produced the diary to OIC in December.

(4) President Bush's diary was exculpatory and would have had no material effect on the investigation had it been produced sooner. The Report acknowledges that the contents of the diary did not justify a reopening of the investigation.

(5) President Bush, through King & Spalding, provided OIC with thousands of additional documents in 1993 that related, generally to Iran-contra, even though OIC had declared months earlier that the investigation was finished.

(6) President Bush would have a to a final interview/deposition under reasonable conditions. OIC refused to negotiate and decided to simply declare in its Report that the President was uncooperative.

I. Iran Arms Sale

• President Bush has always acknowledged that he was aware that arms were sold to Iran. The Report offers nothing new on this issue.

• On December 3, 1986, then Vice-President Bush told the American public about his knowledge of the Iran arms initiative immediately after the story broke:

I was aware of our Iran initiative and I support the President's decision. I was not aware of and I oppose any diversion of funds, any ransom payments, or any circumvention of the will of the Congress, the law or the United States of America.

Speech to American Enterprise Institute ("AEI")....

This statement was accurate, and the Report offers no evidence to the contrary. Inexplicably, however the Report contends that President Bush's public statements conflicted with his deposition testimony and FBI interview, all of which reflected his knowledge of the Iran arms sales. The Report is simply wrong.

• Most importantly President Bush did not believe there was anything illegal about the arms sale to Iran. In fact, after six years of investigation and expenditures of $40 million, OIC *remains* unsure whether any laws were violated by the arms sale. As the Report acknowledges, the Reagan Administration Justice Department issued an opinion that the shipments of U.S. weapons to Iran *did not violate the law*. President Bush was never advised by anyone that the Iran arms shipments were illegal.

II. Contra diversion

• President Bush was unaware of the contra diversion until the news of the diversion broke publicly in November 1986. The Report confirms this fact.

• Moreover, the Report found that there was an effort to keep then Vice-President Bush and his staff in the dark about the entire resupply effort:

There was no credible evidence obtained that the Vice-President or any member of his staff directly or actively participated in the contra resupply effort that existed during the Boland Amendment prohibition on military aid to the contras. To the contrary, the OVP's [Office of the Vice President] staff was largely excluded from RIG meetings when contra matters were discussed and during which North openly discussed operational details of his contra efforts.

The Pardons

• OIC contends that defense counsel for Caspar Weinberger indicated their intent to call President Bush as a witness. In fact, President Bush was never subpoenaed or included on any witness list.

• The sole allusion to the possibility that Secretary Weinberger's counsel might attempt to call President Bush occurred two weeks before the Weinberger trial was to commence in a pre-trial conference during which numerous matters were discussed. The possibility that President Bush would actually be called to testify was always remote. Furthermore, there was little chance that President Bush would actually be required to testify even if called. Secretary Weinberger's counsel did not give any notice to the White House of an intent to call President Bush nor was it likely that counsel could have made the required showing that President Bush would provide any testimony that Could not have been obtained through other means. The slim possibility that he could be called as a witness was not a factor in issuing the pardons.

IV. President Bush's Diary

- President Bush issued the pardons of Caspar Weinberger and others on December 24, 1992.
- That evening, Judge Walsh publicly proclaimed President Bush to be a "subject" of his investigation on ABC's *Nightline* for allegedly failing to produce earlier a personal diary of primarily political thoughts. The public pronouncement constituted a remarkable departure from prevailing prosecutorial standards of conduct. Judge Walsh then began a new investigation into the timing of the production of the Bush diary, *a diary that was exculpatory* and contained information that would have helped, not hurt, President Bush's reelection chances.
- At the time of Judge Walsh's proclamation, OIC had already reviewed the diary and was aware of its personal, political nature. As OIC later stated in its Report, the Bush diary did not warrant a reopening of the investigation.
- As the Report also acknowledges, "Bush's notes themselves proved not as significant" as others. In fact, the diary was made *after* the events of Iran-contra and corroborated his lack of knowledge as events were uncovered.
- The Report implies that President Bush was aware that his diary dictation was responsive to OIC's document requests and purposefully did not produce the material. In support, the Report cites a 1987 Bush diary entry that indicates surprise at Secretary Shultz' production of his personal, contemporaneous notes dictated immediately following meetings with President Reagan. Contrary to the Report's implication, President Bush never believed that his random, personal dictation on a variety of issues, contemporaneous only with the aftermath and not the events of Iran-contra, was responsive to any OIC document request until September 1992 when his staff reviewed the diary. President Bush *was* concerned, however, that by keeping their own, sometimes unreliable notes of confidential communications with the President, cabinet members could have a chilling effect upon the ability of the Executive to benefit from frank and candid discussions. Hence, the passage in his diary relating to Secretary Shultz notes.

- The bottom line is that President Bush turned over all of his responsive documents on Iran-contra.

V. President Bush's Cooperation

- Completely at odds with the Report's implication of willful withholding of documents is the following passage in the Report:

Related to the issue of the diary was the production of the chron files. When the Iran/contra document request was circulated, *Bush instructed [Suzie] Peake to "just give them everything."* (Emphasis added.)

- The Report fails to acknowledge that Peake was one of the people who typed the dictated diary. If President Bush was trying to withhold the diary, he never would have given Peake such an instruction. Furthermore, none of the other staff members who had knowledge of President Bush's diary dictation, Don Rhodes, Jack Steel, and Betty Green, believed that the diary was responsive to OIC's document requests.
- The Report does acknowledge that when the diary was discovered in a personal safe by Patty Presock in late September 1992, President Bush, who was in the middle of the campaign, immediately stated "let's call Boyden and he can sort it out." Mr. Gray subsequently reviewed and turned over the diary to OIC. President Bush's policy was always to provide OIC whatever material it requested.

A. 1993 Document Production

- The Report contends that in 1993 King & Spalding adopted a "very narrow approach to the OIC document request, allowing production of only those materials that related to the production of the diary." The report asserts that King & Spalding claimed that all other documents requested wore protected by the attorney-client privilege. Again, OIC's position is contrary to the facts.
- By letter dated January 27, 1993 . . . King & Spalding informed OIC as follows:

Although it is our understanding that the [OIC is] investigating the delay in the production of President Bush's November/December 1986 dictation transcripts, consistent with your request *we will nevertheless provide you non-privileged documents which related generally to Iran-contra* (emphasis added).

- In accordance with our representation, King & Spalding reviewed 111 boxes of files stored at the National Archives and produced approximately 6,500 pages of non-privileged documents related to Iran-contra and unrelated to the diary production issue. King & Spalding also produced all documents, regardless of privilege, related to the diary production.
- OIC lawyers originally directed King & Spalding to review 400 boxes of documents stored at the Bush Presidential Materials Project in College Station, Texas but later backed off once they realized the breadth of their request. (*See* letter dated February 22, 1993, Attachment 3). King & Spald-

ing subsequently produced 326 pages of documents from College Station relating to the diary production issue.

- Finally, King & Spalding also produced President Bush's "chron" files to OIC in their entirety, constituting in excess of 29,000 pages of documents. (The chron files had been made available to OIC prior to then Vice-President Bush's deposition in 1988.) Only a total of 14 documents were withheld because of attorney-client privilege. President Bush never asserted, as would be his right, executive privilege over any documents.

B. Interview of George Bush

- President Bush fully cooperated with the OIC investigation. He voluntarily gave a 5 hour videotaped deposition to OIC lawyers in 1988 covering the entire subject of Iran-contra. In addition, he was interviewed at length by the FBI. In all respects, he was truthful and candid—the Report never contends otherwise.

- The Report, however, contends that the investigation of President Bush was somehow incomplete, citing OIC's inability to question President Bush further in 1993. As is evident by the following chronology, OIC had effectively finished its investigation in September 1992 and absent the issuance of the pardons would never have sought another deposition of President Bush.

- In the summer of 1992, OIC indicated to the White House that it might seek additional information from President Bush in the form of interrogatories. Later in the summer, OIC postponed until after the election any request for additional information.

- In September 1992, OIC reported to the special D.C. Court of Appeals panel (the "Special Panel") that the investigation was complete, barring unforeseen developments at the upcoming Weinberger and Claridge trials. The Report's admission that OIC had concluded its investigation is inconsistent with any need or even desire on the part of OIC to interview President Bush again on the substance of Iran-contra.

- After the election, OIC remained silent regarding the notion of obtaining additional information from President Bush through interrogatories.

- OIC did not renew its request for responses to interrogatories even after the White House informed OIC on December 11, 1992 about the discovery of President Bush's personal dictation.

- It was the issuance of the pardons on December 24, 1992 that triggered OIC's deposition request to President Bush and the general reopening of the investigation.

- In its Report, OIC misstated the negotiations, or lack thereof, surrounding a possible second Bush deposition in 1993. The following are the facts.

- First, *Judge Walsh turned down Griffin Bell's offer to have Judge Walsh conduct President Bush's deposition.* Judge Walsh stated that he was too busy preparing the Report

and that it would be necessary for his deputy, Craig Gillen, to conduct the deposition.

- In addition to Judge Walsh's refusal to conduct the deposition, OIC refused to consider any reasonable limitations on the deposition, including the following specific proposals:

  (1) That the deposition be conducted in Houston or any location other than OIC's office in D.C.

  (2) That there be some general understanding of the time to be devoted to the deposition. OIC would not even commit to finishing in one day.

  (3) That there be an agreement as to the scope of the questioning. We would have considered favorably a request to explore new Iran/contra material or issues, in addition to the questions surrounding production of the diary. OIC made no counterproposal.

  (4) That the inquiry be conducted, as originally contemplated, through interrogatories.

  (5) That there be some assurances concerning the purpose of the inquiry and OIC's intent.

. . . .

- OIC never discussed with King & Spalding lawyers any one of these proposals, as King & Spalding fully expected OIC would. Mr. Gillen's response in his February 26, 1993 letter . . . was that "further negotiation was pointless." In fact, OIC refused to negotiate on any points.

- If OIC believed that President Bush had important additional information as the Report suggests, OIC would have negotiated over the terms of a voluntary deposition. If President Bush remained an "important witness," despite having already submitted to a lengthy deposition and FBI interview OIC would have issued a grand jury subpoena. OIC's excuse for not doing so, the absence of an "appropriate likelihood of a criminal prosecution," misstates the standard for issuance of a grand jury subpoena to a witness.

VI. Remaining Questions for President Bush

- The Report lists seven areas of inquiry that OIC would have covered with President Bush had another deposition occurred in 1993. Any deposition would have been cumulative of the previous wide-ranging deposition and FBI interview conducted of President Bush.

- Three months before the pardons issued, OIC represented to the Special Panel that the investigation was finished. Thereafter, no circumstances changed that warranted another deposition of President Bush. Certainly, the diary produced in December 1992 did not warrant an additional deposition on the substance of Iran-contra. OIC's own Report stated "They [the diaries] did not justify re-opening the investigation."

- President Bush's knowledge of Iran-contra has been explored to exhaustion, beginning with his December 3, 1986 speech to AEI, continuing with his 5 hour deposition by OIC, his FBI interview and countless press conferences and inquiries. OIC's suggestion that the investigation of President Bush was "regrettably incomplete" is nonsense.

[STATEMENT OF FORMER PRESIDENT RONALD W. REAGAN]

Preliminary Statement

President Reagan first learned in November of 1986 that proceeds from United States Government arms sales to Iran may have been diverted to assist the Nicaraguan resistance movement. He responded immediately by opening the records of his Administration to congressional investigators and to an independent investigating commission headed by former Senator John Tower. He waived of executive privilege and instructed his subordinates to cooperate fully with all investigations. He asked his Attorney General to seek the appointment of an independent counsel to investigate and, where appropriate, to prosecute any violations of criminal law arising from the events that became known as Iran-Contra.

Lawrence E. Walsh was appointed on December 19, 1986, to serve as Iran-Contra Independent Counsel. President Reagan cooperated fully with that investigation from its inception. He provided the Independent Counsel with unlimited access to the records of his Administration. He answered the Independent Counsel's questions under oath in writing and in person. He allowed the Independent Counsel access to all relevant portions of his diaries. He denied no information to the Independent Counsel. His cooperation has been both unlimited and unlimited and unstinting.

President Reagan has never publicly criticized any aspect of the investigation or conduct of Independent Counsel Walsh. He has refrained from any statement or conduct that might in any way be perceived as an impediment to the investigation. He declined requests to pardon individuals being investigated by the Independent Counsel. He did everything within his power to ensure that the Independent Counsel had the fullest authority and unfettered discretion to conduct his investigation.

The Independent Counsel has now completed his almost seven-year investigation, and it is now both appropriate and necessary for former President Reagan to respond. As many others have commented, and as his Final Report reveals, the Independent Counsel has permitted his investigation to become both excessive and vindictive. He has abused his authority. He has used his office to intimidate and harass individuals and otherwise to damage the lives of the persons he was given license to investigate. He and his Final Report have violated the policies of the Department of Justice that he was required by law to uphold, and he has disregarded the standards and ethics imposed uniformly on public prosecutors. His Final Report exceeds the authority given to him by law. He has used it to disseminate false and unfounded speculation, opinion and innuendo. His Final Report is not a chronicle of facts, but a prolonged justification of his own excessive investigation and a defamation of the individuals he was empowered to investigate.

Independent Counsel Walsh found no credible evidence of personal wrongdoing by President Reagan or violation by the former President of any criminal laws. *See, e.g., Final Report of the Independent Counsel for Iran/Contra Matters*, Vol. 1, at xiii (Aug. 4, 1993) ("[T]he investigation found *no* credible evidence that President Reagan violated any criminal statute.") (emphasis added) [hereinafter *Final Report*] ... (the former President's conduct *fell well short of criminality*") (emphasis added). Yet in his Final Report the Independent Counsel attempts to indict President Reagan for alleged misconduct by others and to hint, without the benefit of any evidence, at wrongdoing by the former President himself.

The Independent Counsel's Final Report is the product of almost seven-year's work involving sixty-eight lawyers and hundreds of investigators. It is several hundred pages and several hundred-thousand words long. It is based upon years of secret grand jury interrogations to which only the Independent Counsel has had access. It is therefore impossible for anyone injured by the Report adequately to respond to it without comparable resources and access to the same materials. However, the following pages respond to the principal assertions and conclusions of the Independent Counsel. They demonstrate that, except for matters already considered by Congress and the courts, the Independent Counsel's speculation and conclusions regarding alleged misconduct by many individuals, including former President Reagan, are without foundation, and reflect, at best, a misunderstanding of the events he has investigated and a slanted and completely misleading rendition of them.

Executive Summary
The Facts of Iran-Contra

The essential facts of Iran-Contra are as follows:

1. In the summer of 1985, the Reagan Administration, at the urging and with the assistance of the Israeli government, determined to explore forming a relationship with moderates in the government of Iran who were preparing to seek power upon the death of Ayatollah Khomeini. The Iranians offered to demonstrate their "bona fides" by attempting to assist the United States in achieving the release of American hostages being held in Lebanon. To demonstrate the good faith of the United States in engaging in these discussions, the United States agreed to sell a limited amount of arms to these moderate an government officials. President Reagan was informed of and approved the initiative, which at first involved Israel's shipment of U.S.-made TOW and HAWK missiles to Iran, and, subsequently involved direct shipments of a limited amount of arms to Iran by the United States. Three hostages were released during the eighteen-month Iran initiative, which was first publicly reported on November 3, 1986, and terminated shortly thereafter.

2. Beginning in 1983, Congress sought to impose a series of legal restrictions on the use of certain appropriated funds by the Reagan Administration to support the Nicaraguan Democratic Resistance, or "Contras," in their efforts to resist the excesses and expansionism of the communist "Sandinistas," who had seized

control of the Nicaraguan government in 1979. Congress enacted and subsequently repeatedly amended appropriations riders, the so-called Boland Amendments, to restrict certain Executive Branch agencies from providing certain types of aid to the Contras. President Reagan acted in compliance with the Boland Amendments and directed his subordinates to do so as well.

3. In connection with a preliminary investigation of the Iranian arms sales directed by Attorney General Edwin Meese III over the weekend of November 21–23, 1986, the Attorney General's staff discovered a memorandum in the files of Lt. Col. Oliver L. North indicating that funds from the Iranian arms transactions may have been diverted to support the Contras. President Reagan was first informed on November 24, 1986, that a diversion may have occurred, and on November 25, 1986, the President and the Attorney General held a press conference to disclose the discovery of the possible diversion of funds. President Reagan moved immediately thereafter to assist congressional investigations of these events, authorized the creation of an independent Executive Branch investigation and urged the appointment of an independent counsel by the Judiciary to conduct a third investigation. He opened the records of his Administration to these three separate independent investigations.

Response of Former President Reagan to the Independent Counsel's Final Report

The Response of former President Reagan to the Final Report demonstrates the following:

1. The Iran-Contra Independent Counsel has misused and abused the reporting process that is mandated by the independent counsel statute. The Final Report unfairly and unnecessarily injures the rights and reputations of individuals, relies on innuendo, speculation and conjecture instead of proof, violates established standards governing the conduct of prosecutors, and improperly relies on secret grand jury materials to support the Independent Counsel's many accusations.

2. The Independent Counsel's principal accusation in his Final Report is that officials at the highest levels of the Reagan Administration engaged in a "cover-up" designed to conceal the fact that President Reagan had contemporaneous knowledge of the 1985 arms shipments. There was, however, no "cover-up." To the contrary, President Reagan repeatedly insisted, both publicly and privately, that the complete facts of Iran-Contra be publicly aired and that his Administration cooperate fully with investigators. Moreover, the evidence is overwhelming that the essential facts of the an initiative were readily and repeatedly disclosed by President Reagan and his top advisers. The contemporaneous notes of participants in the meetings referred to by the Independent Counsel independently refute the notion of a cover-up and demonstrate that the Independent Counsel has falsely depicted the events that he purports to describe. In fact, President Reagan's knowledge of the 1985 arms transactions supports, not undermines, the legality of those transactions.

3. The Independent Counsel's contention that President Reagan and his senior advisers and Cabinet officials partici-

pated in a strategy to make National Security Council ("NSC") staff member Lt. Col. North, and National Security Advisers Robert C. McFarlane and John M. Poindexter "scapegoats" with respect to Iran-Contra is demonstrably false. President Reagan took full responsibility for the an initiative from the outset. He also accepted responsibility for all actions within the *scope* of his instructions taken by his subordinates in support of the Contras. But he was not aware of and could not responsibly be blamed for the diversion of funds to the Contras, the destruction of records by individuals acting contrary to his instructions or other conduct that was not authorized or sanctioned. The "scapegoat" theory of the Independent Counsel has been advanced and repeatedly rejected since the first public revelation of Iran-contra, and was rejected by the Independent Counsel himself in the cases that he prosecuted. His Final Report adds nothing to the record except his own, internally inconsistent, personal theory.

4. The Independent Counsel repeatedly seeks to convey the impression that high-ranking Reagan Administration officials, including the President, violated civil laws and Executive Orders in carrying out the Iranian initiative, particularly with regard to the 1985 arms shipments. But there is, in fact, strong authority supporting the legality of the Iranian arms shipments. The President had the power and responsibility to take certain measures to advance U.S. policies and interests and the constitutional discretion to protect the lives and liberty of Americans in foreign countries. The President properly relied on legal experts to ensure that his actions were lawful, as the Independent Counsel grudgingly acknowledges. The Iranian initiative was consistent with other applicable laws, and the Independent Counsel has provided no reasoned legal analysis to the contrary.

5. Although the Independent Counsel concedes that there is "*no* credible evidence that the President authorized or was aware of the diversion of profits from the Iran arms sales to assist the contras," *Final Report*, Vol. 1, at 443 (emphasis added), his Final Report indulges in the irresponsible speculation that the President must have known about the diversion. However, that speculation has no evidentiary support whatsoever, and is directly contradicted by the findings of the Tower Commission and the Congressional Committees that investigated Iran-Contra. President Reagan has consistently, unequivocally and categorically stated that he had no knowledge of the diversion, and every bit of credible evidence in the record—including the voluminous record compiled by Independent Counsel Walsh—is consistent with the President's clear and unwavering position on this point. The Independent Counsel's Report adds nothing new beyond his capricious speculation.

6. The Independent Counsel asserts that President Reagan is responsible for "set[ting] the stage" for alleged violations of the law by his subordinates by expressing his continuing Public support for the Contras. . . . However, President Reagan gave repeated instructions to members of his Administration to follow the law and abide by the Boland restrictions. The activities

authorized by President Reagan complied with the Boland Amendments and all other laws of the United States. The Independent Counsel has been unable to establish that any conduct by the President the various vague appropriations riders referred to as the Boland Amendments.

Final Report of the Independent Counsel for Iran/Contra Matters, Vol. III: Comments and Materials Submitted by Individuals and Their Attorneys Responding to Volume I of the Final Report, December 3, 1993 (Washington, D.C.: U.S. Government Printing Office, 1993), 21–35, 639–646. References to attachments in George Bush's statement have been omitted.

182   Senator Robert C. Byrd Opposes the Line-Item Veto

October 18, 1993

The line-item veto became a hotly debated political issue in the 1980s and 1990s as a device to control federal spending. "Line item" refers to a specific line and a specific amount in any of the appropriations bills that comprise the federal budget. Under the proposed line-item veto method, after Congress had passed an appropriations bill, the president could strike out—or veto—specific items without vetoing the entire bill. Those who supported this device claimed it would make it possible for the president to eliminate waste in the federal budget, especially "pork-barrel" legislation that members of Congress inserted in the bill to benefit their own districts. Critics of the line-item veto claimed that it undermined one of the most important powers of the legislative branch, the power of the purse, and it gave the president the authority to make law—a power not granted to that office in the Constitution.

This speech, the fourteenth and last in a series that Senator Robert C. Byrd (D-W.Va.) delivered on the subject of the line-item veto, is a landmark example of Senate oratory at its finest (see also document 175). Byrd was a staunch opponent of the line-item veto because of its infringement on the powers of Congress. In this speech, the line-item veto itself is hardly mentioned, except near the end of the senator's remarks when he makes reference to "quack remedies such as line-item vetoes." Instead, this speech is a history lesson, based on the experience of the ancient Roman Senate, on the perils to our Republic if Congress willingly weakens its own legislative authority. In preparation for this series of speeches Senator Byrd read extensively about the Roman Senate, eventually publishing a book on that subject. He made a strong comparison between the problems that led to the eventual decline of the power of the Roman Senate with current trends in the U.S. Senate, including the line-item veto, which, he argued, seriously undermined the constitutional authority and power of the legislative branch of government.

Despite Byrd's arguments, Congress approved the line-item veto, which was signed into law April 9, 1996 (Public Law 104–130). President William J. Clinton became the first president to veto specific spending items from appropriations bills approved by Congress. Although the line-item veto idea has been around since Civil War times and has, in various forms, been adopted by many state legislatures, this represented the first time in U.S. history that the concept had been applied to the federal budget.

On June 25, 1998, the Supreme Court struck down the line-item veto as unconstitutional in its decision in Clinton v. City of New York *(see document 188).*

Mr. President, this is the fourteenth in my series of speeches on the line-item veto, with particular reference to the Roman Republic and the Roman Senate. When I began this series of one-hour speeches on May 5, I spoke of Montesquieu, the eminent French philosopher and author who had greatly influenced the Founding Fathers with his political theory of checks and balances and separation of powers.

What influenced Montesquieu in his espousal of this political system? Montesquieu was greatly influenced by the history of the development of the English constitution and by the history of the people of Rome. So impressed was Montesquieu with the Romans that he, in fact, developed and published a work of his own on the subject. Almost midway between the *Persian Letters* in 1721 and the *Spirit of the Laws* in 1748, Montesquieu published, in 1734, his *Considerations on the Causes of the Greatness of the Romans and their Decline*, which is the least well-known of the three.

I have also stated a number of times that if we are to have a better appreciation and understanding of the Constitution—its separation of powers, and checks and balances, and the power over the purse—then we should follow in Montesquieu's tracks and study Roman history as he did, and that is what we have been doing together during these past several months.

What have we acquired to pay us for our pains? What have we learned that can be applicable to our own time, our own country, and to the political questions of today concerning checks and balances and the control over the purse? Let us see.

Mr. President, I hold that human nature is like a molecule of water. It has never changed. That which was H_2O at the beginning of creation, when "the spirit of God moved upon the face of the waters" is still H_2O today, two atoms of hydrogen and one atom of oxygen. And that which was human nature when Adam and Eve fell from grace, is still human nature today. It has never changed. And as human nature has not changed from the beginning, but is still motivated by the same emotions and instincts and needs and drives—love and hate and fear and greed and hunger, and so on, the history of man's actions will always have a way of repeating itself.

So, as we who live today contribute to the flow of history's unceasing stream, we will find it worth our while to examine the events of past ages, their causes and their consequences, in order that we might better understand the causes and possible consequences of the phenomena, the happenings, the events, and the actions of our own life and times.

Napoleon said, "Let my son often read and reflect on history. This is the only true philosophy." So, we have elected, as did Montesquieu, to look to Roman history for guidance.

Roman power derived from Roman virtue, basically; in other words, from great moral qualities. The average Roman, as we have noted, was simple, steadfast, honest, courageous, law-abiding, patriotic, and reverent, and his leaders were men of uncommon dedication and acumen.

From the earliest times, the Romans possessed a profound reverence for national tradition, a firm conviction of being the special object and instrument of destiny, and a strong sense of individual responsibility and obligation to that tradition and to the fulfillment of that destiny.

There spring to mind several parallels between the history of the Romans and the history of our own Republic, one such parallel being that the same old virtues which lent sturdiness and integrity to the early Romans, also gave stability and substance and strength and character to our own national life in the early years of its formation and development.

The Roman family was the cornerstone of the Roman social structure, and the family setting instilled in its members the self-discipline, the respect for authority, the veneration of ancestors, and the reverence for the gods that lent stability to Roman society and iron discipline to the Roman legions.

The Roman family unit was, indeed, a religious organization, a community of worship centered around the cult of the hearth and the cult of the dead. Each morning and evening, the entire family, including the slaves, offered prayers and sacrifices to the departed ancestors at the family hearth, the ever-burning flame of which symbolized both the unity and the continuity of the Roman family.

Because of their pastoral tradition, the Romans, like the Jews of the Old Testament, sacrificed animals to their gods. Reverence and the idea of obligation—inherent in the Roman conception of the relation between gods and men—inevitably developed among the Romans a strong sense of duty, a moral factor of inestimable worth.

Mr. President, we have seen that same strong tradition of family and religious values prevalent in the formation and development of our own country, from colonial times down to the mid-twentieth century. The erosion of these values in America over the last fifty to sixty years has signified a decline in the moral and spiritual strength of this nation, as it did in the Roman state.

We have seen in both the Roman and American psyches a sense of Manifest Destiny, and the same urge to extend territorial frontiers. We saw in the territorial expansion of the Roman city state what amounted to an overexpansion. We saw the drain that was placed upon Roman manpower, and the burden that was imposed upon the administration of the far-flung provinces. While, in our own case, territorial expansion has long since ceased, in recent years we have spent billions of dollars in space exploration, and we stand in danger of overextending our international commitments and our financial capability to sustain and underwrite them.

We have been talking about that a good bit lately.

We have also drawn Roman and American parallels in the vanishing peasantry from the land and the decline in small family farms, the consequences of which have been increasing unemployment and crime and poverty in the cities, and a growing welfare dependence upon the state.

During the centuries of the early and middle Republic, public office in Rome could be obtained only through virtue, and brought with it no pay, no salary, no benefit other than honor, and the opportunity to prove one's self worthy of being preferred for further toils on behalf of the state.

In the last century of the Republic, the old citizen soldiery and the old moral structure of integrity and dedication to the cause of country gave way to greed, graft, corruption, venality, and political demagoguery, much of which we see in our own time and in our own country. The self-serving ambitions of Roman generals and politicians led to violence, civil wars, and military domination by standing armies made up of professional soldiers. In our own Republic today, the military-industrial complex, against which President Eisenhower warned, can pose a threat to the system.

So, Mr. President, there are sundry similarities between our own history and the history of the Romans.

Now, let us turn to the consideration of the Roman political system. In the Roman Republic, the political organization was complex, and it was also experimental, unlike that of Lycurgus, the Spartan lawgiver of the ninth century B.C.

Lycurgus united in his constitution all of the good and distinctive features of the best governments, so that none of the principal parts should unduly grow and predominate. But inasmuch as the force of each part would be neutralized by that of the others, neither of them should prevail and outbalance another. Therefore, the constitution should remain in a state of equilibrium.

Lycurgus then, foreseeing by a process of reasoning whence and how events would naturally happen, constructed his constitution untaught by adversity. But, while the Romans would achieve the same final result, according to Polybius, they did not reach it by any process of reasoning but by the discipline of many trials and struggles. And, by always choosing the best, in the light of the experience gained, they reached the same result as Lycurgus.

Let us consider the Roman system as it was seen by Polybius, the Greek historian, who lived in Rome from 168 B.C. after the Battle of Pydna, until after 150 B.C., at a time when the Roman

Republic was at a pinnacle of majesty that excited his admiration and comment.

Polybius viewed the Roman constitution as having three elements: the executive, the Senate, and the people, with their respective share of power in the state regulated by a scrupulous regard to equality and equilibrium.

Let us examine the separation of powers in the Roman Republic as explained by Polybius. The consuls—representing the executive—were the supreme masters of the administration of the government when remaining in Rome. All of the other magistrates, except the tribunes, were under the consuls and took their orders from the consuls. The consuls brought matters before the Senate that required its deliberation and they saw to the execution of the Senate's decrees. In matters requiring the authorization of the people, the consuls summoned the popular meetings, presented the proposals for their decision, and carried out the decrees of the majority.

In matters of war, the consuls imposed such levies upon the allies as the consuls deemed appropriate, and made up the roll for soldiers and selected those who were suitable. Consuls had absolute power to inflict punishment upon all who were under their command, and had all but absolute power in the conduct of military campaigns.

As to the Senate—we are talking about the separation of powers—as to the Senate, it had complete control over the treasury and regulated receipts and disbursements alike. The quaestors could not issue any public money to the various departments of the state without a decree of the Senate. The Senate controlled the money for the repair and construction of public works and public buildings throughout Italy, but this money could not be obtained by the censors, who oversaw the contracts for public works and public buildings, except by the grant of the Senate.

The Senate also had jurisdiction over all crimes in Italy requiring a public investigation, such as treason, conspiracy, poisoning, or willful murder, as well as controversies between and among allied states. Receptions for ambassadors and matters affecting foreign states were the business of the Senate.

What part of the constitution was left to the people? The people participated in the ratification of treaties and alliances, and decided questions of war and peace. The people passed and repealed laws, and bestowed public offices on the deserving, which, according to Polybius, "are the most honorable rewards for virtue."

Polybius, having described the separation of powers under the Roman constitution, how did the three parts of state check and balance each other?

Mr. President, during the past several months, I have often referred to the various checks that the consuls, the tribunes, the Senate and the assemblies exercised against each other. And I have paid particular attention to the veto power of the Roman Senate and the tribunes.

Incidentally, Henry Clay, who believed that the veto power of American presidents was "despotic" and ought to be circum-

scribed, stated in a Senate floor speech that the veto "originated in the institution of the tribunician power in ancient Rome," and had "been introduced from the practice under the empire into the monarchies of Europe."

Polybius explains the checks and balances of the Roman constitution, as he had observed them firsthand. Remember, he was living in Rome at the time.

What were the checks upon the consuls, the executive? The consul—whose power over the administration of the government when in the city, and over the military when in the field, appeared absolute—still had need of the support of the Senate and the people. The consul needed supplies for his legions, but without a decree of the Senate, his soldiers could be supplied with neither corn nor clothes nor pay. Moreover, all of his plans would be futile if the Senate shrank from danger, or if the Senate opposed his plans or sought to hamper them. Therefore, whether the consul could bring any undertaking to a successful conclusion depended upon the Senate, which had the absolute power, at the end of his one-year term, to replace him with another consul or to extend his command.

Even to the successes of the consuls on the field of battle, the Senate had the power to add distinction and glory, or to obscure their merits, for unless the Senate concurred in recognizing the achievements of the consuls and in voting the money, there could be no celebration or public triumph.

The consuls were also obliged to court the favor of the people, so here is the check of the people against the consul, for it was the people who would ratify, or refuse to ratify, the terms of peace. But most of all, the consuls, when laying down their office at the conclusion of their one-year term, would have to give an accounting of their administration, both to the Senate and to the people. So, it was necessary that the consuls maintain the good will of both the Senate and the people.

What were the checks against the Senate? The Senate was obliged to take the multitude into account and respect the wishes of the people, for in matters directly affecting the senators—for instance, in the case of a law diminishing the Senate's traditional authority, or depriving senators of certain dignities, or even actually reducing the property of senators—in such cases, the people had the power to pass or reject the law in their assembly.

In addition, according to Polybius, if the tribunes imposed their veto, the Senate would not only be unable to pass a decree, but could not even hold a meeting. And because the tribunes must always have a regard for the people's wishes, the Senate stood in awe of the multitude and could not neglect the feelings of the people.

But as a counterbalance, what check was there against the people? We have seen the checks against the consuls; we have described the checks against the Senate. What about the people? According to Polybius, the people were far from being independent of the Senate, and were bound to take its wishes into account, both collectively and individually.

For example, contracts were given out in all parts of Italy by the censors for the repair and construction of public works and public buildings. Then there was the matter of the collection of revenues from rivers and harbors and mines and lands—everything, in a word, that came under the control of the Roman government. In all of these things, the people were engaged, either as contractors or as pledging their property as security for the contractors, or in selling supplies, or making loans to the contractors, or as engaging in the work and in the employ of the contractors.

"Over all these transactions," says Polybius, "the Senate has complete control." For example, it could extend the time on a contract and thus assist the contractors; or in the case of unforeseen accident, it could relieve the contractors of a portion of their obligation; or it could even release them altogether if they were absolutely unable to fulfill the contract.

So, there were many ways in which the Senate could inflict great hardships upon the contractors; or, on the other hand, grant great indulgences to the contractors. But in every case, the appeal was to the Senate.

The Senate's ace card lay in its control over the purse strings. Also, the judges were selected from the Senate, at the time of Polybius, for the majority of trials in which the charges were heavy. Consequently, the people were cautious about resisting or actively opposing the will of the Senate, because they were uncertain as to when they might need the Senate's aid. For a similar reason, the people did not rashly resist the will of the consuls, because one and all might, in one way or another, become subject to the absolute power of the consuls at some point in time.

Polybius sums it up in this way: "When any one of the three classes becomes puffed up, and manifests an inclination to be contentious and unduly encroaching, the mutual interdependency of all the three, and the possibility of the pretensions of any one being checked and thwarted by the others, must plainly check this tendency. And so the proper equilibrium is maintained by the impulsiveness of the one part being checked by its fear of the other."

Polybius' account may not have been an exact representation of the true state of the Roman system, but he was on the scene, and he was writing to tell us what he saw with his own eyes—not through the eyes of someone else. What better witness could we have?

The theory of a mixed constitution—that is what ours is, a mixed constitution, checks and balances, and separation of powers—the theory of a mixed constitution had had its great measure of success in the Roman Republic. It is not surprising, therefore, that the Founding Fathers of the United States should have been familiar with the works of Polybius, or that Montesquieu should have been influenced by the checks and balances and separation of powers in the Roman constitutional system, a clear element of which was the control over the purse, vested solely in the Senate in the heyday of the Republic.

Mr. President, in my presentations today and heretofore on this subject, I have drawn many parallels between our own Republic and the historical meanderings of that ancient Republic that rose and declined along the banks of the Tiber River, a parallel which induced someone in an earlier American generation to name the tiny stream that once flowed across the present-day Mall, "Tiber Creek." It is my own sincere prayer, however, that the United States will not follow a course parallel to the Roman Republic into an inexorable decline and decadence.

Mr. President, worthy scholars and thoughtful authors have exhausted rivers of ink in attempting to analyze the decline and fall of the Roman Republic and the subsequent empire. Among the foremost of these author-historians is Edward Gibbon. Gibbon's *Decline and Fall of the Roman Empire* is an incontestable historical classic, and no competent grasp of Roman historiography can be achieved without taking Gibbon into consideration. If senators have not read his volumes, they should read them.

Whereas Polybius wrote about the rise of the Roman Republic and its greatness, Gibbon wrote about the decline and fall of the Roman Empire, which followed on after the Republic collapsed.

However, Gibbon outlines a case for Rome's decline and fall with which few, if any, subsequent historians will agree. Gibbon asserts that Christianity was the cause of Rome's decline and ultimate fall.

Gibbon's assertion is not an atheist's diatribe against Christianity, as some people might assume. Gibbon's position is that Christianity's "other-worldly" orientation, its exclusivistic monotheism, its withdrawal from the larger society, its condemnation of Mediterranean culture, its fostering of monasticism, and its contemplative emphasis, when taken together, refocused the people's attention on spiritual values to the detriment of the practicality, the civic activism, and the aggressiveness that characterized and gave rise to the Roman attitude toward life.

Conversely, while Gibbon is acquainted with and recounts most of the evidences of Rome's decline that have nothing to do with Christianity—moral decadence, tyrannical emperors, barbarian incursions, the decline of the small family farms, the vanishing peasantry, the depletion of soils and accessible mineral resources, and the collapse of faith in the old gods—Gibbon treats these as being merely coincidental to Rome's decline—minor distractions and sideshows around the center ring's main event, namely, Christianity's gnawing away at the empire's superstructure.

Certainly, no informed student of Roman history can ignore Gibbon's achievement, both as a historian and as an interpreter of ancient Roman civilization. But though the *Decline and Fall of the Roman Empire* is an undeniable classic, Gibbon has not written the last word on ancient Rome. Indeed, during the roughly two centuries since Gibbon wrote his masterpiece, we have witnessed a revolution in historical methodology and a reformation in our comprehension of the causes of Rome's failure. For example, Will Durant, who made his political and cultural influence felt earlier in this century, broadly represents a twentieth-century perspective on the causes of Rome's decline and decay. In *The Story of Civilization*, Will Durant asserts that

Rome was already in decline before Christianity emerged on the scene.

An eroding faith in the old Greco-Roman pantheon of deities, a decline in family life, rotting public and individual morality; the corrosion of discipline, patriotism, and the military esprit; abandonment of the land by the peasant classes, agricultural decline, deforestation; civil wars, class struggle, international warfare, praetorian intrigues and conspiracies, assassinations, violence, and civil disorders; bureaucratic despotism, economic depression, stifling taxes, and corruption in government; mad emperors, pestilences, and plague; games and circuses, free bread, and the welfare mob—all of these wore away the moral and spiritual and social underpinnings of the Roman state, and accelerated its plunge into hopeless impotence and eventual obscurity as a military power and territorial empire.

Against such a backdrop of crises, fecklessness, and drift, Christianity served, not as a cause of decay and collapse, but as a lifeboat for a despairing populace. Rome was already a cracked shell when Christianity ascended the stage.

But, perhaps most tellingly, Durant declares:

The political causes of decay were rooted in one fact—increasing despotism destroyed the citizens' civic sense and dried up statesmanship at its source. . . . The Senate, losing ever more of its power and prestige, . . . relapsed into indolence, subservience, or venality; and the last barrier fell that might have saved the state from militarism and anarchy.

In short, Rome's fate was sealed by the one-by-one donations of power and prerogative that the Roman Senate plucked from its own quiver and voluntarily delivered into the hands, first, of Julius Caesar and Octavian, and then into the trust of the succession of Caligulas, Neros, Commoduses, and Elagabaluses who followed, until at last, the ancient and noble ideals of the Roman Republic had been dissolved into the stinking brew of imperial debauchery, tyranny, megalomania, and rubble into which the Roman Empire eventually sank.

At the height of the Republic, the Roman Senate had been the one agency with the authority, the perspective, and the popular aura to debate, investigate, commission, and correct the problems that confronted the Roman state and its citizens. But the Senate's loss of will and its eagerness to hand its responsibilities over to a one-man government—a man on a "white horse"—a dictator, and later an emperor, doomed Rome and predestined Rome's decline and ultimate fall.

Mr. President, those "political midwives" attendant on the birth of our own Republic—George Washington, Alexander Hamilton, Benjamin Franklin, James Madison, James Wilson, Elbridge Gerry, Oliver Ellsworth, and others—were some of the wisest men alive at that time, in this or any other country. Many had served in the Continental and Confederation congresses and in state legislatures. All of them were experienced and reflective men.

Many of those constitutional framers were well acquainted with Cicero, Polybius, Livius, Tacitus, and Plutarch, and the glories of the classical Roman Republic. Those brilliant men borrowed freely from the best of ancient Rome, and purposefully and deliberately christened the upper chamber of the Congress "the Senate."

Just as carefully, they set in place a system of checks and balances and separation of powers, and lodged the control of the purse in the "people's branch" to prevent the rise of a new coinage of imperial executives in the federation that they created.

Mr. President, in our own times we see the same problems, the same kinds of dilemmas that the hand of history wrote large upon Rome's slate, being written upon America's slate. In difficult times or in crises, many people grow impatient, as they grew impatient during the French Revolution and elevated Napoleon to the emperorship; as they grew impatient during the Russian Revolution and elevated Lenin to head of state; as they grew impatient in depression-era Germany and elevated Adolf Hitler to the presidency and the chancellorship; as they grew impatient in Cuba and elevated Fidel Castro to the dictatorship.

We, too, have reached a stage where we seem to remain in a state of crisis, semicrisis, or pseudocrisis. The American people have grown impatient and are demanding solutions to serious problems—problems that do not lend themselves to easy and quick solutions. The solutions to these problems will be painful and will take time, perhaps years, to succeed.

This is not a truth that some people want to hear. Many would rather believe that quack remedies such as line-item vetoes and enhanced rescissions powers in the hands of presidents will somehow miraculously solve our current fiscal situation and eliminate our monstrous budget deficits.

Of course, some people would, perhaps, prefer to abolish the Congress altogether and institute one-man government from now on. Some people have no patience with constitutions, for that matter.

Mr. President, let us study Rome. The basic lesson that we should remember for our purposes here is, that when the Roman Senate gave away its control of the purse strings, it gave away its power to check the executive. From that point on, the Senate declined and, as we have seen, it was only a matter of time. Once the mainstay was weakened, the structure collapsed and the Roman Republic fell.

This lesson is as true today as it was two thousand years ago. Does anyone really imagine that the splendors of this capital city stand or fall with mansions, monuments, buildings, and piles of masonry? These are but bricks and mortar, lifeless things, and their collapse or restoration means little or nothing when measured on the great clock-tower of time. But the survival of the American constitutional system, the foundation upon which the superstructure of the Republic rests, finds its firmest support in the continued preservation of the delicate mechanism of checks and balances, separation of powers, and the control of the purse, solemnly instituted by the Founding Fathers. For over two hundred years, from the beginning of the Republic to this very hour, it has survived in unbroken continuity. We received it from our fathers. Let us as surely hand it on to our sons and daughters.

Mr. President, I close my series of reflections on the ancient Roman Republic with the words of Daniel Webster from his speech in 1832 on the centennial anniversary of George Washington's birthday:

Other misfortunes may be borne or their effects overcome. If disastrous war should sweep our commerce from the ocean, another generation may renew it. If it exhaust our Treasury, future industry may replenish it. If it desolate and lay waste our fields, still, under a new cultivation, they will grow green again and ripen to future harvests. It were but a trifle even if the walls of yonder Capitol were to crumble, if its lofty pillars should fall, and its gorgeous decorations be all covered by the dust of the valley. All these might be rebuilt. But who shall re-construct the fabric of demolished government? Who shall rear again the well-proportioned columns of constitutional liberty? Who shall frame together the skillful architecture which unites national sovereignty with state rights, individual security, and public prosperity? No. If these columns fall, they will be raised not again. Like the Colosseum and the Parthenon, they will be destined to a mournful, a melancholy immortality. Bitterer tears, however, will flow over them than were ever shed over the monuments of Roman or Grecian art. For they will be the remnants of a more glorious edifice than Greece or Rome ever saw: the edifice of constitutional American liberty.

Congressional Record, Senate, 103d Congress, 1st session, October 18, 1993, S13561–65 (daily edition).

183   The House Republicans' Contract with America

September 27, 1994

This document, the brain-child of House Republican whip Newt Gingrich (R-Ga.) and Dick Armey (R-Texas), is a landmark of political rhetoric and political aspirations that helped the Republican Party gain control of the House of Representatives for the first time in forty years. The contract was designed to appeal to voters who were concerned about the growth of big government, who believed that most members of Congress were "career" politicians who had been in office too long, and who were fed up with the scandals that had racked the House in the late 1980s and early 1990s, including the resignation of Speaker Jim Wright and scandals involving the House post office and House bank.

The Contract with America was soundly criticized and even ridiculed by Democrats as a cheap political ploy. Nonetheless it served several important functions for House Republicans running for office in 1994. Most incumbent House Republicans, and those Republicans running for office for the first time, signed the contract in a public ceremony on the steps of the Capitol on September 27, 1994. Altogether 367 Republican candidates signed the document. The goals of the contract gave the candidates an appearance of solidarity of purpose. The contract was a rallying point for action to clean up the perceived mess in Washington. While some Republicans made the contract the centerpiece of their campaigns, others ignored it or played down its significance.

Once the Republicans won a majority of seats in the House for the first time since the congressional elections of 1952, the contract played a different role. With Newt Gingrich elected Speaker, and with Dick Armey the new House majority leader, the Contract with America became a blueprint for an aggressive legislative agenda, modeled in part on the historic first "100 Days" of the Franklin Roosevelt administration during the Great Depression, when dramatic action helped restore public confidence in government. The new Speaker wanted to quickly stamp his new leadership on the House and he used the Contract with America as his agenda. The House worked at a blistering pace during the first 100 days of the 104th Congress in the opening months of 1995. The

House worked late into the night on many occasions to push through the provisions of the contract. In his first speech as Speaker, Gingrich spoke of the need to quickly pass the ten items of the Contract with America (see document 184).

Speaker Gingrich managed to push most of the provisions of the Contract with America through the House in the early months of 1995. The term limits provision of the contract failed to pass the House, as some Republicans lost interest in that measure once they were in the majority. The failure of the Contract with America in practical congressional terms was that the agenda it proclaimed to be the most pressing for the nation was not shared with the same degree of enthusiasm or the same level of priority in the Senate, even though the Senate had a Republican majority. The new Republican House majority eventually had to realize that passing bills in one house of Congress does not mean those same bills will succeed in the other body or eventually be signed into law by the president. Most of the contract's provisions failed to pass the Senate and at the end of the first session of the 104th Congress only two of the ten proposals in the contract had been enacted into law: internal reforms in the House of Representatives and the elimination of unfunded mandates—laws that required state spending without providing for the necessary funds. Subsequently Congress passed the line-item veto, one of the goals of the Contract with America, only to have the Supreme Court declare it unconstitutional in 1998 (see document 188).

As Republican Members of the House of Representatives and as citizens seeking to join that body we propose not just to change its policies, but even more important, to restore the bonds of trust between the people and their elected representatives. That is why, in this era of official evasion and posturing, we offer instead a detailed agenda for national renewal, a written commitment with no fine print.

This year's election offers the chance, after four decades of one-party control, to bring to the House a new majority that will transform the way Congress works. That historic change would be the end of government that is too big, too intrusive, and too easy with the public's money. It can be the beginning of a Congress that respects the values and shares the faith of the American family.

Like Lincoln, our first Republican president, we intend to act "with firmness in the right, as God gives us to see the right." To restore accountability to Congress. To end its cycle of scandal and disgrace. To make us all proud again of the way free people govern themselves.

On the first day of the 104th Congress, the new Republican majority will immediately pass the following major reforms, aimed at restoring the faith and trust of the American people in their government:

First, require all laws that apply to the rest of the country also apply equally to the Congress;

Second, select a major independent auditing firm to conduct a comprehensive audit of Congress for waste, fraud, or abuse;

Third, cut the number of House committees, and cut committee staff by one-third;

Fourth, limit the terms of all committee chairs;

Fifth, ban the casting of proxy votes in committee;

Sixth, require committee meetings to be open to the public;

Seventh, require a three-fifths majority vote to pass a tax increase;

Eighth, guarantee an honest accounting of our federal budget by implementing zero baseline budgeting.

Thereafter, within the first hundred days of the 104th Congress, we shall bring to the House Floor the following bills, each to be given full and open debate, each to be given a clear and fair vote, and each to be immediately available this day for public inspection and scrutiny.

The Fiscal Responsibility Act

A balanced budget/tax limitation amendment and a legislative line-item veto to restore fiscal responsibility to an out-of-control Congress, requiring them to live under the same budget constraints as families and businesses.

The Taking Back Our Streets Act

An anti-crime package including stronger truth in sentencing, "good faith" exclusionary rule exemptions, effective death penalty provisions, and cuts in social spending from this summer's crime bill to fund prison construction and additional law enforcement to keep people secure in their neighborhoods and kids safe in their schools.

The Personal Responsibility Act

Discourage illegitimacy and teen pregnancy by prohibiting welfare to minor mothers and denying increased AFDC for additional children while on welfare, cut spending for welfare pro-

grams, and enact a tough two-years-and-out provision with work requirements to promote individual responsibility.

The Family Reinforcement Act

Child support enforcement, tax incentives for adoption, strengthening rights of parents in their children's education, stronger child pornography laws, and an elderly dependent care tax credit to reinforce the central role of families in American society.

The American Dream Restoration Act

A $500-per-child tax credit, begin repeal of the marriage tax penalty, and creation of American Dream Savings Accounts to provide middle-class tax relief.

The National Security Restoration Act

No U.S. troops under UN command and restoration of the essential parts of our national security funding to strengthen our national defense and maintain our credibility around the world.

The Senior Citizens Fairness Act

Raise the Social Security earnings limit, which currently forces seniors out of the workforce, repeal the 1993 tax hikes on Social Security benefits, and provide tax incentives for private long-term care insurance to let older Americans keep more of what they have earned over the years.

The Job Creation and Wage Enhancement Act

Small business incentives, capital gains cut and indexation, neutral cost recovery, risk assessment/cost-benefit analysis, strengthening of the Regulatory Flexibility Act and unfunded mandate reform to create jobs and raise worker wages.

The Common Sense Legal Reforms Act

"Loser pays" laws, reasonable limits on punitive damages, and reform of product liability laws to stem the endless tide of litigation.

The Citizen Legislature Act

A first-ever vote on term limits to replace career politicians with citizen legislators.

Further, we will instruct the House Budget Committee to report to the floor and we will work to enact additional budget savings, beyond the budget cuts specifically included in the legislation described above, to ensure that the federal budget deficit will be less than it would have been without the enactment of these bills.

Respecting the judgment of our fellow citizens as we seek their mandate for reform, we hereby pledge our names to this *Contract with America.*

The document was obtained from the Web site of Speaker Newt Gingrich, *http://speakernews.house.gov/contract.htm.*

184   Newt Gingrich Addresses the House Upon His Election as Speaker

January 4, 1995

Newt Gingrich (R-Ga.) was elected Speaker of the House for the first time on January 4, 1995, at the opening session of the 104th Congress. His election marked a landmark occasion in the history of the House because he was the first Republican Speaker elected in forty years of unbroken control of the House by a succession of Democratic Speakers. The last Republican Speaker was Joseph Martin (R-Mass.), elected Speaker for the last time in the 83d Congress, which met from 1953 to 1955.

As part of the traditional ceremony, the candidate for Speaker from the minority party turns over the Speaker's gavel to the newly elected Speaker. In this instance, Richard Gephardt (D-Mo.) was the Democratic Party candidate who turned the gavel over to Newt Gingrich. The new Speaker began his remarks by thanking a number of individuals, including Robert H. Michel (R-Ill.), the long-time minority leader of the House, and then launched into his ambitious plans to start pushing legislation immediately to fulfill the Contract with America (see document 183).

Newt Gingrich's rise to power in the House corresponded with a growing atmosphere of aggressive partisanship in which Gingrich played a key role. In this speech he attempted to hold out an olive branch to Democrats and pledged cooperation with them. As Gingrich flexed his muscle as the new king of Capitol Hill, the Democrats in the chamber were experiencing a completely different set of emotions. They were in shock. House Democrats were just beginning to realize what it was like to be in the minority, out of power and out of control of the House leadership for the first time in four decades. A process of major adjustments had begun for both parties.

Mr. GINGRICH. Let me say first of all that I am deeply grateful to my good friend, Dick Gephardt. When my side maybe over-reacted to your statement about ending 40 years of Democratic rule, I could not help but look over at Bob Michel, who has often been up here and who knows that everything Dick said was true. This is difficult and painful to lose, and on my side of the aisle, we have for 20 elections been on the losing side. Yet there is something so wonderful about the process by which a free people decides things.

In my own case, I lost two elections, and with the good help of my friend Vic Fazio came close to losing two others. I am sorry, guys, it just did not quite work out. Yet I can tell you that every time when the polls closed and I waited for the votes to come in, I felt good, because win or lose, we have been part of this process.

. . . .

This is a historic moment. I was asked over and over, how did it feel, and the only word that comes close to adequate is overwhelming. I feel overwhelmed in every way, overwhelmed by all the Georgians who came up, overwhelmed by my extended family that is here, overwhelmed by the historic mo-

ment, I walked out and stood on the balcony just outside of the Speaker's office, looking down the Mall this morning, very early. I was just overwhelmed by the view, with two men I will introduce and know very, very well. Just the sense of being part of America, being part of this great tradition is truly overwhelming.

I have two gavels. Actually, Dick happened to use one. Maybe this was appropriate. This was a Georgia gavel I just got this morning, done by Dorsey Newman of Tallapoosa. He decided that the gavels he saw on TV weren't big enough or strong enough, so he cut down a walnut tree in his backyard, make a gavel, put a commemorative item on it, and sent it up here.

So this is a genuine Georgia gavel, and I am the first Georgia Speaker in over 100 years. The last one, by the way, had a weird accent, too. Speaker Crisp was born in Britain. His parents were actors and they came to the United States—a good word, by the way, for the value we get from immigration.

Second, this is the gavel that Speaker Martin used. I am not sure what it says about the inflation of Government, to put them side by side, but this was the gavel used by the last Republican Speaker.

. . . .

I could not help but think as a way I wanted to start the Speakership and to talk to every Member, that in a sense these young people around us are what this institution is really all about. Much more than the negative advertising and the interest groups and all the different things that make politics all too often cynical, nasty, and sometimes frankly just plan miserable, what makes politics worthwhile is the choice, as Dick Gephardt said, between what we see so tragically on the evening news and the way we try to work very hard to make this system of free, representative self-government work. The ultimate reason for doing that is these children, the country they will inherit, and the world they will live in.

We are starting the 104th Congress. I do not know if you have ever thought about this, but for 208 years, we bring together the most diverse country in the history of the world. We send all sorts of people here. Each of us could find at least one Member we thought was weird. I will tell you, if you went around the room the person chosen to be weird would be different for virtually every one of us. Because we do allow and insist upon the right of a free people to send an extraordinary diversity of people here.

Brian Lamb of C-SPAN read to me Friday a phrase from de Tocqueville that was so central to the House. I have been reading Remini's biography of Henry Clay and Clay, as the first strong Speaker, always preferred the House. He preferred the House to the Senate although he served in both. He said the House is more vital, more active, more dynamic, and more common.

This is what de Tocqueville wrote: "Often there is not a distinguished man in the whole number. Its members are almost all obscure individuals whose names bring no associations to mind. They are mostly village lawyers, men in trade, or even persons belonging to the lower classes of society."

If we include women, I do not know that we could change much. But the word "vulgar" in de Tocqueville's time had a very particular meaning. It is a meaning the world would do well to study in this room. You see, de Tocqueville was an aristocrat. He lived in a world of kings and princes. The folks who come here do so by the one single act that their citizens freely chose them. I do not care what your ethnic background is, or your ideology. I do not care if you are younger or older. I do not care if you are born in America or it you are a naturalized citizen. Everyone of the 435 people have equal standing because their citizens freely sent them. Their voice should be heard and they should have a right to participate. It is the most marvelous act of a complex giant country trying to argue and talk. And, as Dick Gephardt said, to have a great debate, to reach great decisions, not through a civil war, not by bombing one of our regional capitals, not by killing a half million people, and not by having snipers. Let me say unequivocally, I condemn all acts of violence against the law by all people for all reasons. This is a society of law and a society of civil behavior.

Here we are as commoners together, to some extent Democrats and Republicans, to some extent liberals and conservatives, but Americans all. Steve Gunderson today gave me a copy of the "Portable Abraham Lincoln." He suggested there is much for me to learn about our party, but I would also say that it does not hurt to have a copy of the portable F.D.R.

This is a great country of great people. If there is any one factor or acts of my life that [strikes] me as I stand up here as the first Republican in 40 years to do so. When I first became whip in 1989, Russia was beginning to change, the Soviet Union as it was then. Into my whip's office one day came eight Russians and a Lithuanian, members of the Communist Party, newspaper editors. They asked me, "What does a whip do?"

They said, "In Russia we have never had a free parliament since 1917 and that was only for a few months, so what do you do?"

I tried to explain, as Dave Bonior or Tom DeLay might now. It is a little strange if you are from a dictatorship to explain you are called the whip but you do not really have a whip, you are elected by the people you are supposed to pressure—other members. If you pressure them too much they will not reelect you. On the other hand [if] you do not pressure them enough they will not reelect you. Democracy is hard. It [is] frustrating.

So our group came into the Chamber. The Lithuanian was a man in his late sixties, and I allowed him to come up here and sit and be Speaker, something many of us have done with constituents. Remember, this is the very beginning of perestroika and glasnost. When he came out of the chair, he was physically trembling. He was almost in tears. He said, "Ever since World War II, I have remembered what the Americans did and I have never believed the propaganda. But I have to tell you, I did not think in my life that I would be able to sit at the center of freedom."

It was one of the most overwhelming, compelling moments of my life. It struck me that something I could not help but think of when we were here with President [Nelson] Mandela. I went over and saw Ron Dellums and thought of the great work Ron had done to extend freedom across the planet. You get that sense of emotion when you see something so totally different that you had expected. Here was a man who reminded me first of all that while presidents are important, they are in effect an elected kingship, that this and the other body across the way are where freedom has to be fought out. This is the tradition I hope that we will take with us as we go to work.

Today we had a bipartisan prayer service. Frank Wolf made some very important points. He said, "We have to recognize that many of our most painful problems as a country are moral problems, problems of dealing with ourselves and with life."

He said character is the key to leadership and we have to deal with that. He preached a little bit. I do not think he thought he was preaching, but he was. It was about a spirit of reconciliations. He talked about caring about our spouses and our children and our families. If we are not prepared to model our own family life beyond just having them here for 1 day, if we are not prepared to care about our children and we are not prepared to care about our families, then by what arrogance do we think we will transcend our behavior to care about others? This is why with Congressman Gephardt's help we have established a bipartisan task force on the family. We have established the principle that we are going to set schedules we stick to so families can count on time to be together, built around school schedules so that families can get to know each other, and not just by seeing us on C-SPAN.

I will also say that means one of the strongest recommendations of the bipartisan committee, is that we have 17 minutes to vote. This is the bipartisan committee's recommendations, not just mine. They pointed out that if we take the time we spent in the last Congress where we waited for one more Member, and one more, and one more, that we literally can shorten the business and get people home if we will be strict and firm. At one point this year we had a 45-minute vote. I hope all of my colleagues are paying attention because we are in fact going to work very hard to have 17 minute votes and it is over. So, leave on the first bell, not the second bell. OK?

This may seem particularly inappropriate to say on the first day because this will be the busiest day on opening day in congressional history.

I want to read just a part of the Contract With America. I don't mean this as a partisan act, but rather to remind all of us what we are about to go through and why. Those of us who ended up in the majority stood on these steps and signed a contract and here is part of what it says:

On the first day of the 104th Congress the new Republican majority will immediately pass the following reforms aimed at renewing the faith and trust of the American people in their government: First, require all laws that apply to the rest of the country also to apply equally to the Congress. Second, select a major, independent auditing firm to conduct a comprehensive audit of Congress for waste, fraud or abuse. Third, cut the number of House committees and committee staffs by a third. Fourth, limit the terms of all committee chairs. Fifth, ban the casting of proxy votes in committees. Sixth, require committee meetings to be open to the public. Seven, require a three-fifths majority vote to pass a tax increase. Eight, guarantee an honest accounting of our federal budget by implementing zero baseline budgeting.

Now, I told Dick Gephardt last night that if I had to do it over again I would have pledged within 3 days that we will do these things, but that is what we said. So we have ourselves in a little bit of a box here.

Then we go a step further. I carry a T.V. Guide version of the contract with me at all times.

We then say that within the first 100 days of the 104th Congress we will bring to the House floor the following bills, each to be given full and open debate, each to be given a full and clear vote, and each to be immediately available for inspection. We made it available that day. We listed 10 items. A balanced budget amendment and line item veto, a bill to stop violent criminals, emphasizing among other things an effective and enforceable death penalty. Third was welfare reform. Fourth, legislation protecting our kids. Fifth was to provide tax cuts for families. Sixth was a bill to strengthen our national defense. Seventh was a bill to raise the senior citizens' earning limit. Eighth was legislation rolling back Government regulations. Ninth was a commonsense legal reform bill, and tenth was congressional term limits legislation.

Our commitment on our side, this is an absolute obligation, is first of all to work today until we are done. I know that is going to inconvenience people who have families and supporters. But we were hired to do a job and we have to start today to prove we will do it. Second, I would say to our friends in the Democratic Party that we are going to work with you, and we are really laying out a schedule working with the minority leader to make sure that we can set dates certain to go home. That does mean that if 2 or 3 weeks out we are running short we will, frankly, have longer sessions Tuesday, Wednesday, and Thursday. We will try to work this out on a bipartisan basis to, in a workmanlike way, get it done. It is going to mean the busiest early months since 1933.

Beyond the Contract I think there are two giant challenges. I know I am a partisan figure. But I really hope today that I can speak for a minute to my friends in the Democratic Party as well as my own colleagues, and speak to the country about these two challenges so that I hope we can have a real dialog. One challenge is to achieve a balanced budget by 2002. I think both Democratic and Republican Governors will say we can do that but it is hard. I do not think we can do it in a year or two. I do not think we ought to lie to the American people. This is a huge, complicated job.

The second challenge is to find a way to truly replace the current welfare state with an opportunity society.

Let me talk very briefly about both challenges. First, on the balanced budget I think we can get it done. I think the baby boomers are now old enough, that we can have an honest dialog about priorities, about resources, about what works, and what does not work. Let me say I have already told Vice President Gore that we are going to invite him to address a Republican conference. We would have invited him in December but he had to go to Moscow, I believe there are grounds for us to talk together and to work together, to have hearings together, and to have task forces together. If we set priorities, if we apply the principles of Edwards Deming and of Peter Drucker we can build on the Vice President's reinventing government effort and we can focus on transforming, not just cutting. The choice becomes not just do you want more or do you want less, but are there ways to do it better? Can we learn from the private sector, can we learn from Ford, IBM, from Microsoft, from what General Motors has had to go through? I think on a bipartisan basis we owe it to our children and grandchildren to get this Government in order and to be able to actually pay our way. I think 2002 is a reasonable timeframe. I would hope that together we could open a dialog with the American people.

I have said that I think Social Security ought to be off limits, at least for the first 4 to 6 years of the process, because I think it will just destroy us if we try to bring it into the game. But let me say about everything else, whether it is a Medicare, or it is agricultural subsidies, or it is defense or anything that I think the greatest Democratic President of the 20th century, and in my judgment the greatest President of the 20th century, said it right. On March 4, 1933, he stood in braces as a man who had polio at a time when nobody who had that kind of disability could be anything in public life. He was President of the United States, and he stood in front of this Capitol on a rainy March day and he said, "We have nothing to fear but fear itself." I want every one of us to reach out in that spirit and pledge to live up to that spirit and I think frankly on a bipartisan basis, I would say to Members of the Black and Hispanic Caucuses that I would hope we could arrange by late spring to genuinely share districts. You could have a Republican who frankly may not know a thing about your district agree to come for a long weekend with you, and you will agree to go for a long weekend with them. We begin a dialog and an openness that is totally different than people are used to seeing in politics in America. I believe if we do that we can then create a dialog that can lead to a balanced budget.

But I think we have a greater challenge, I do want to pick up directly on what Dick Gephardt said, because he said it right. No Republican here should kid themselves about it. The greatest leaders in fighting for an integrated America in the 20th century were in the Democratic Party. The fact is, it was the liberal wing of the Democratic Party that ended segregation. The fact is that it was Franklin Delano Roosevelt who gave hope to a Nation that was in distress and could have slide into dictatorship. Every Republican has much to learn from studying what the Democrats did right.

But I would say to my friends in the Democratic Party that there is much to what Ronald Reagan was trying to get done.

There is much to what is being done today by Republicans like Bill Weld, and John Engler, and Tommy Thompson, and George Allen, and Christy Whitman, and Pete Wilson. There is much we can share with each other.

We must replace the welfare state with an opportunity society. The balanced budget is the right thing to do. But it does not in my mind have the moral urgency of coming to grips with what is happening to the poorest Americans.

I commend to all Marvin Olasky's "The Tragedy of American Compassion." Olasky goes back for 300 years and looked at what has worked in America, how we have helped people rise beyond poverty, and how we have reached out to save people. He may not have the answers, but he has the right sense of where we have to go as Americans.

I do not believe that there is a single American who can see a news report of a 4-year-old thrown off of a public housing project in Chicago by other children and killed and not feel that a part of your heart went, too. I think of my nephew in the back, Kevin, and how all of us feel about our children. How can any American read about an 11-year-old buried with his Teddy bear because he killed a 14-year-old, and then another 14-year-old killed him, and not have some sense of "My God, where has this country gone?" How can we not decide that this is a moral crisis equal to segregation, equal to slavery? How can we not insist that every day we take steps to do something?

I have seldom been more shaken than I was after the election when I had breakfast with two members of the Black Caucus. One of them said to me, "Can you imagine what it is like to visit a first-grade class and realize that every fourth or fifth young boy in that class may be dead or in jail within 15 years? And they are your constituents and you are helpless to change it?" For some reason, I do not know what, maybe cause I visit a lot of schools, that got through. I mean, that personalized it. That made it real, not just statistics, but real people.

Then I tried to explain part of my thoughts by talking about the need for alternatives to the bureaucracy, and we got into what I think frankly has been a pretty distorted and cheap debate over orphanages.

Let me say, first of all, my father, who is here today, was a foster child. He was adopted as a teenager. I am adopted. We have relatives who were adopted. We are not talking out of some vague impersonal Dickens "Bleak House" middle-class intellectual model. We have lived the alternatives.

I believe when we are told that children are so lost in the city bureaucracies that there are children who end up in dumpsters, when we are told that there are children doomed to go to schools where 70 or 80 percent of them will not graduate, when we are told of public housing projects that are so dangerous that if any private sector ran them they would be put in jail, and the only solution we are given is, "Well, we will study it, we will get around to it," my only point is that this is unacceptable. We can find ways immediately to do things better, to reach out, break through the bureaucracy and give every young American child a better chance.

Let me suggest to you Morris Schectman's new book. I do not agree with all of it, but it is fascinating. It is entitled "Working Without a Net." It is an effort to argue that in the 21st century we have to create our own safety nets. He draws a distinction between caring and caretaking. It is worth every American reading.

He said caretaking is when you bother me a little bit, and I do enough, I feel better because I think I took care of you. That is not any good to you at all. You may be in fact an alcoholic and I just gave you the money to buy the bottle that kills you, but I feel better and go home. He said caring is actually stopping and dealing with the human being, trying to understand enough about them to genuinely make sure you improve their life, even if you have to start with a conversation like, "If you will quit drinking, I will help you get a job." This is a lot harder conversation than, "I feel better. I gave him a buck or 5 bucks."

I want to commend every Member on both sides to look carefully. I say to those Republicans who believe in total privatization, you cannot believe in the Good Samaritan and explain that as long as business is making money we can walk by a fellow American who is hurt and not do something. I would say to my friends on the left who believe there has never been a government program that was not worth keeping, you cannot look at some of the results we now have and not want to reach out to the humans and forget the bureaucracies.

If we could build that attitude on both sides of this aisle, we could be an amazingly different place, and the country would begin to be a different place.

We have to create a partnership. We have to reach out to the American people. We are going to do a lot of important things. Thanks to the House Information System and Congressman Vern Ehlers, as of today we are going to be on line for the whole country, every amendment, every conference report. We are working with C-SPAN and others, and Congressman Gephardt has agreed to help on a bipartisan basis to make the building more open to television, more accessible to the American people. We have talk radio hosts here today for the first time. I hope to have a bipartisan effort to make the place accessible for all talk radio hosts of all backgrounds, no matter their ideology. The House Historian's office is going to be more aggressively run on a bipartisan basis to reach out to Close Up, and to other groups to teach what the legislative struggle is about. I think over time we can and will this Spring rethink campaign reform and lobbying reform and review all ethics, including the gift rule.

But that isn't enough. Our challenge shouldn't be just to balance the budget or to pass the Contract. Our challenge should not be anything that is just legislative. We are supposed to, each one of us, be leaders. I think our challenge has to be set as our goal, and maybe we are not going to get there in 2 years. This ought to be the goal that we go home and we tell people we believe in: that there will be a Monday morning when for the entire weekend not a single child was killed anywhere in America; that there will be a Monday morning when every child in the country went to a school that they and their parents thought prepared them as citizens and prepared them to compete in the world market; that there will be a Monday morning where it was easy to find a job or create a job, and your own Government did not punish you if you tried.

We should not be happy just with the language of politicians and the language of legislation. We should insist that our success for America is felt in the neighborhoods, in the communities, is felt by real people living real lives who can say, "Yes, we are safer, we are healthier, we are better educated, America succeeds."

This morning's closing hymn at the prayer service was the Battle Hymn of the Republic. It is hard to be in this building, look down past Grant to the Lincoln Memorial and not realize how painful and how difficult that battle hymn is. They key phrase is, "As he died to make men holy, let us live to make men free."

It is not just political freedom, although I agree with everything Congressman Gephardt said earlier. If you cannot afford to leave the public housing project, you are not free. If you do not know how to find a job, you are not free. If you cannot find a place that will educate you, you are not free. If you are afraid to walk to the store because you could get killed, you are not free.

So as all of us over the coming months sing that song, "As he died to make men holy, let us live to make men free," I want us to dedicate ourselves to reach out in a genuinely nonpartisan way to be honest with each other. I promise each of you that without regard to party my door is going to be open. I will listen to each of you. I will try to work with each of you. I will put in long hours, and I will guarantee that I will listen to you first. I will let you get it all out before I give you my version, because you have been patient with me today, and you have given me a chance to set the stage.

But I want to close by reminding all of us how much bigger this is than us. Because beyond talking with the American people, beyond working together, I think we can only be successful if we start with our limits. I was very struck this morning with something Bill Emerson uses, a very famous quote of Benjamin Franklin, at the point where the Constitutional Convention was deadlocked. People were tired, and there was a real possibility that the Convention was going to break up. Franklin, who was quite old and had been relatively quiet for the entire Convention, suddenly stood up and was angry, and he said:

I have lived, sir, a long time, and the longer I live the more convincing proofs I see of this truth, that God governs in the affairs of men, and if a sparrow cannot fall to the ground without His notice, is it possible that an empire can rise without His aid?

At that point the Constitutional Convention stopped. They took a day off for fasting and prayer.

Then, having stopped and come together, they went back, and they solved the great question of large and small States. They wrote the Constitution, and the United States was created. All I can do is pledge to you that, if each of us will reach out prayerfully and try to genuinely understand each other, if we will recognize that in this building we symbolize America, and that we have an obligation to talk with each other, then I think a year from now we can look on the 104th Congress as a truly amazing institution without regard to party, without regard to ideology. We can say, "Here, America comes to work, and here we are preparing for those children a better future."

Thank you. Good luck and God bless you.

Congressional Record, House, 104th Congress, 1st session, January 4, 1995, H4–H8.

185   Final Report of the Senate Whitewater Investigation (Majority Views)

June 17, 1996

"Whitewater" is a shorthand term to describe the many phases of the longest running investigation of a sitting president in American history. Charges first surfaced during the 1992 presidential election that William J. Clinton and his wife Hillary Rodham Clinton were allegedly involved in illegal investments and dealings with the Whitewater Development Corporation and the Madison Guaranty Savings and Loan Association in the Clintons' home state of Arkansas. As the Whitewater investigations unfolded, various charges were made that spread over more than twenty years of the Clintons' public life, both before and after President Clinton's election to office. The Arkansas phase of Whitewater was investigated by Justice Department special counsel Robert B. Fiske Jr. and then by an independent counsel appointed to the case, Kenneth W. Starr (see document 189).

A Washington phase of Whitewater was investigated by the Senate beginning in May 1995. This investigation involved a probe

of White House staff to determine if the Clinton administration had attempted to interfere with an investigation of Madison Guaranty Savings and Loan Association by the Resolution Trust Corporation, a federal agency established to rescue failed savings and loan institutions. The Senate inquiry, conducted by the Special Committee to Investigate Whitewater Development Corporation and Related Matters, was chaired by Senator Alphonse D'Amato (R-N.Y.). The D'Amato investigation could not escape the charges of partisanship leveled against it. The committee faced a constant tug-of-war between Republicans and Democrats over the conduct of the committee's work. In the end Republicans and Democrats issued separate reports that drew completely different conclusions based on the same evidence. The Republicans concluded that the Clinton White House abused its power to thwart investigations into the financial affairs of the president and first lady. The Democratic minority report concluded that neither the president nor the first lady had tried to impede the ongoing investigations and that neither had abused the power of the White House (see document 186).

Various aspects of Starr's Whitewater investigation were still ongoing in late 1998, although the independent counsel's focus changed dramatically when his office undertook yet another investigation of President Clinton—a probe into a sexual affair between the president and a "young subordinate employee" in the White House (see document 189).

FINAL REPORT
Preface

On May 17, 1995, the United States Senate, by a vote of 96–3, adopted Senate Resolution 120, which established the Special Committee to Investigate Whitewater Development Corporation and Related Matters (hereinafter the "Special Committee"), to be administered by the Committee on Banking, Housing, and Urban Affairs (the "Banking Committee"). Resolution 120 charged the Special Committee with the responsibility to conduct an extensive investigation into and to hold public hearings on specified matters relating to the President's and Mrs. Clinton's investment in Whitewater Development Corporation ("Whitewater") along with James and Susan McDougal, Madison Guaranty Savings and Loan Association ("Madison Guaranty"), and related matters.

In discharging its responsibilities under Resolution 120, the Special Committee deposed 274 witnesses and held 60 days of public hearings, during which 136 witnesses testified. The Committee also reviewed approximately 1 million pages of documents produced by the President and Mrs. Clinton, the White House, various federal agencies, and a number of individual witnesses.

Resolution 120 authorized the Committee to investigate and to hold public hearings into three general subject areas. Section 1(b)(1) authorized investigation into whether White House officials engaged in improper conduct in handling papers in Deputy White House Counsel Vincent Foster's office following his death on July 20, 1993—the so-called Foster Phase of the Special Committee's inquiry.

With respect to the Washington Phase of the inquiry, Section 1(b)(2) authorized investigation into whether the White House improperly interfered with any investigations or prosecutions by various federal agencies relating to, among other things, Whitewater, Madison Guaranty related entities, and Capital Management Services, Inc. ("CMS").

Finally, in the Arkansas Phase, 1(b)(3) of Resolution 120 authorized the Special Committee to investigate, among other things, the activities of Whitewater, Madison Guaranty, CMS, Lasater & Co., and the work and billing practices of the Rose Law Firm relating to Madison Guaranty.

1. The Foster Phase

During the 103d Congress, the Banking Committee, pursuant to Senate Resolution 229, conducted an inquiry into the case of Mr. Foster's death and the conduct of the subsequent investigation of his death by the United States Park Police. On

July 15, 1994, Special Counsel Robert B. Fiske, Jr. advised the Banking Committee that "public hearings on the subject of the handling of documents in Mr. Foster's office while this investigation is continuing could prejudice our investigation." Accordingly, the Banking Committee's public hearings on July 29, 1994 into the cause of Mr. Foster's death excluded inquiry into the handling of documents in Mr. Foster's office.

At the conclusion of the Banking Committee's hearings in the summer of 1994, the following matters, among others, were identified for future inquiry relating to Mr. Foster's death:

the White House interference into the Park Police search of Mr. Foster's office;

the presence of White House counsel staff during standard Park Police investigatory interviews;

the White House insistence that the Park Police investigation proceed with Department of Justice [DOJ] involvement to the extent that DOJ was "calling the shots" and "setting up protocol" and the Park Police were "stand[ing] and waiting for permission to do our job"; and

the late delivery of the note in Mr. Foster's office to Park Police, discovered by White House counsel.

On April 22, 1995, Independent Counsel Kenneth W. Starr advised the Chairman and Ranking Member of the Banking Committee that his investigation would not be hindered or impeded by a Senate inquiry into the way in which White House officials handled documents in Mr. Foster's office following his death.

Accordingly, the Special Committee commenced its investigation and public hearings into whether White House officials engaged in improper conduct in handling documents in Mr. Foster's office at the time of his death. The Special Committee recognizes that Mr. Foster's death remains a source of much grief to his family and friends. In conducting its inquiry under section 1(b)(1) of Resolution 120, the Committee sought to balance carefully the need to protect the privacy of the Foster family and its duty to carry out fully the mandate of the Senate.

2. The Washington Phase

Resolution 120 directed the Special Committee to review the handling of several federal investigations relating to the Whitewater real estate venture; Madison Guaranty McDougal's S&L, the failure of which cost American taxpayers more than $60 million; and CMS, a small business investment company owned by David Hale, who made illegal loans to James and Susan McDougal in part to finance the Whitewater investment. Specifically, section 1(b)(2) of the Resolution authorized the Special Committee to conduct an investigation and public hearings into the following matters:

(A) whether any persona has improperly handled confidential Resolution Trust Corporation ("RTC") information relating to Madison Guaranty or Whitewater, including whether any person has improperly communicated such information to individuals referenced therein;

(B) whether the White House has engaged in improper contacts with any other agency or department in the government with regard to confidential RTC information relating to Madison Guaranty or Whitewater;

(C) whether the Department of Justice has improperly handled RTC criminal referrals relating to Madison Guaranty or Whitewater;

(D) whether RTC employees have been improperly importuned, prevented, restrained, or deterred in conducting investigations or making enforcement recommendations relating to Madison Guaranty or Whitewater; and

(E) whether the report issued by the Office of Government Ethics on July 31, 1994, or related transcripts of deposition testimony—

(i) were improperly released to White House officials or others prior to their testimony before the Committee on Banking, Housing, and Urban Affairs pursuant to Senate Resolution 229 (103d Congress); or

(ii) were used to communicate to White House officials or to others confidential RTC information relating to Madison Guaranty or Whitewater.

In conducting the inquiry mandated during this so-called "Washington Phase" of the investigation, the Special Committee examined whether the President and Mrs. Clinton—or their agents—misused the power of the presidency in responding to a series of investigations of the Whitewater matter. As in the past, the Senate sought to serve as the public's watchdog, to expose abuses of the public trust.

Of necessity, the Special Committee inquired into the investigative and prosecutorial process of Executive Branch agencies to determine whether the laws were properly and faithfully executed. Congress has a duty to investigate allegations that the normal investigative and prosecutorial processes of the Executive Branch have been compromised. More important, Congress has the constitutional obligation to ensure that the President's private interests have not been elevated above the public good.

3. The Arkansas Phase

This is the beginning of the Whitewater matter. In this phase of its inquiry, the Senate charged the Special Committee with investigating the complex web of intermingled funds, fraudulent transactions, political favors, and conflicted relationships which comprise the "20 years of public life in Arkansas" that Mrs. Clinton did not want an independent counsel, among others, to look into.

Specifically, Section 1(b)(3) of Resolution 120 authorized an investigation and public hearings into the following matters:

(A) the operations, solvency, and regulation of Madison Guaranty Savings & Loan Association, and any subsidiary, affiliate, or other entity owned or controlled by Madison Guaranty Savings and Loan Association;

(B) the activities, investments, and tax liability of Whitewater Development Corporation and, as related to Whitewater

Development Corporation, of its officers, directors, and shareholders;

(C) the policies and practices of the RTC and the Federal banking agencies (as that term is defined in section 3 of the Federal Deposit Insurance Act) regarding the legal representation of such agencies with respect to Madison Guaranty Savings and Loan Association;

(D) the handling by the RTC, the Office of Thrift Supervision, the Federal Deposit Insurance Corporation, and the Federal Savings and Loan Insurance Corporation of civil or administrative actions against parties regarding Madison Guaranty Savings and Loan Association.

(E) the sources of funding and the lending practices of Capital Management Services, Inc., and its supervision and regulation by the Small Business Administration, including any alleged diversion of funds to Whitewater Development Corporation;

(F) the bond underwriting contracts between Arkansas Development Finance Authority and Lasater & Company; and

(G) the lending activities of Perry County Bank, Perryville, Arkansas, in connection with the 1990 Arkansas gubernatorial election.

These various subjects, seemingly disparate, are nevertheless woven together by common and recurring themes of abuse of power, fraud on federal institutions and theft of public funds, and frequent neglect, if not deliberate disregard, of professional, ethical and, at times, legal standards.

The Special Committee completed its task under Resolution 120 in a bipartisan manner. With few notable exceptions, the Special Committee conducted its investigation and public hearings by mutual consent between the Chairman and Ranking Member, thus obviating the need for votes by the Special Committee.

Because the testimony of witnesses before the Special Committee was often contradictory, incomplete, or inaccurate as to important events and actions, the Committee placed particular emphasis on available documentary evidence. Unfortunately, throughout its inquiry, the Committee was hindered by parties unduly delaying the production of, or withholding outright, documents critical to its investigation. Although the White House was most often and most notably engaged in this course of action, the pattern of noncooperation extended to other parties, as this Report lays out more fully in the Washington Phase of the Special Committee's inquiry.

This Report of the Special Committee is divided into three separate but interrelated parts. Part 1 focuses on the Foster Phase of the inquiry, into whether White House officials engaged in improper conduct in the handling of documents in Mr. Foster's office at the time of his death. Part 2 summarizes the Special Committee's investigation into the Washington Phase and discusses the handling of federal investigations into Whitewater and related matters, the Administration's attempts to interfere with these investigations, and the White House's attempts to interfere with Congressional inquiries into the Administration's alleged improprieties. Part 3 centers on the

Arkansas Phase and details the transactions and activities that comprise Governor Clinton's web of political, personal, and business relationships—a web that includes, among others, Whitewater, Madison, CMS, James McDougal, David Hale, and Danny Ray Lasater. Each Part begins with a separate, detailed outline and concludes with respective endnotes.

These three parts are interrelated because the entire story of Whitewater is not simply the sum of its parts. Rather, seeping through the pages that follow are clearly identifiable patterns of motivation, conduct, and, at times, concealment. Beyond discrete judgments of impropriety in particular instances, therefore, the Special Committee has examined the evidence and reached conclusions that transcend any individual persons, actions, or events but rather illuminate patterns of conduct behind the Whitewater affair.

The Conclusions of the Special Committee are summarized at the beginning of each Part. They do not answer all questions and allegations that have surfaced, but, taken together, they provide a comprehensive survey of the facts uncovered by the Special Committee in its 13 months of investigation. And they offer a full, fair, and often troubling picture of the inner workings of government that the Senate, by an overwhelming mandate, charged the Special Committee to present to the American people.

. . . .

Conclusions of the Special Committee

"Bernie, are you hiding something?"—Philip Heymann, former Deputy Attorney General.

Whitewater is a "can of worms you shouldn't open."—Vincent Foster's handwritten notes.

"HRC 'doesn't want [an independent counsel] poking into 20 years of public life in Arkansas.' "—Diary of Roger Altman, former Deputy Secretary of Treasury, quoting Margaret Wiliams, Chief of Staff to the First Lady.

"Ms. Thomases and the First Lady may have been concerned about anyone having unfettered access to Mr. Foster's office."—Associate White House Counsel Stephen Neuwirth.

The death of White House Deputy Counsel Vincent W. Foster, Jr. on July 20, 1993 marked the first time since the death of Secretary of Defense James Forrestal in 1949 that a high-ranking U.S. official took his own life. Now, almost three years later, the circumstances surrounding Mr. Foster's tragic death remain the subject of much speculation and even suspicion. Against the backdrop of the death of a high-ranking U.S. official, this controversy has been fueled by a series of misguided actions taken by senior White House officials to shield the documents in Mr. Foster's office from independent career law enforcement investigators and to spirit the documents to the White House Residence.

As Deputy Counsel to the President, Mr. Foster was the number two lawyer in the White House. He worked on the most important public issues faced by the new Clinton Admin-

istration. At the time of his death, Mr. Foster also was one of the Clintons' key advisors on Whitewater and Travelgate. These matters are now the subject of criminal investigations by Independent Counsel Kenneth Starr. In fact, by July 20, 1993, federal investigators already were examining Madison Guaranty Savings and Loan Association, the S&L at the center of the Whitewater affair, as well as the controversial firing in May 1993 of seven career White House Travel Office employees. Mr. Foster's office contained important evidence of actions that the Clintons and senior White House officials took with respect to Whitewater and Travelgate.

The Special Committee's investigation into the handling of Mr. Foster's documents was among the most important matters of inquiry under Resolution 120. It raised the question, once again in our nation's history, whether the power of the White House was misused to served the purely private ends of the President and his associates: specifically, whether senior officials took improper steps, in their handling of Mr. Foster's documents, to cover up embarrassing revelations or even crimes relating to Whitewater and Travelgate.

Often, the successful prosecution of financial crimes and public corruption depends on the documentary trail left by the perpetrators of such wrongdoing. For example, Independent Counsel Starr recently obtained the convictions of Arkansas Governor Jim Guy Tucker and James and Susan McDougal, the owners of Madison Guaranty and the Clintons' partners in the Whitewater real estate development, in part on the basis of more than 600 documents introduced into evidence. By the same token, the concealment or removal of documents can seriously delay or derail investigation of financial malfeasance.

The White House undeniably mishandled the review of documents in Mr. Foster's office following his death. Department of Justice and Park Police investigators told the Special Committee that their investigations were hindered and impeded by the refusal of senior White House officials to allow them to review Mr. Foster's documents. The questions before the Committee, then, is whether senior White House officials simply committed an inexplicable series of blunders and misjudgments or whether these officials deliberately interfered with the investigations into Mr. Foster's death and, perhaps, into the Whitewater and Travelgate affairs.

After careful review of all the evidence, the Special Committee concludes that senior White House Counsel, engaged in a pattern of highly improper conduct in their handling of the documents in Mr. Foster's office following his death. These senior White House officials deliberately prevented career law enforcement officers from the Department of Justice and Park Police from fully investigating the circumstances surrounding Mr. Foster's death, including whether he took his own life because of troubling matters involving the President and Mrs. Clinton. At every turn, senior White House officials prevented Justice Department and Park Police investigators from examining the documents in Mr. Foster's office, particularly those relating to the Whitewater and Travelgate affairs then under investigation.

This pattern of concealment and obstruction continues even to the present day. The special Committee concludes that senior White House officials and other close Clinton associates were not candid in their testimony before the Committee. Specifically, the Committee concludes that Margaret Williams, Chief of Staff to the First Lady, Susan Thomases, a New York attorney and close advisor to Mrs. Clinton, Bernard Nussbaum, then-White House Counsel, and Webster Hubbell, former Associate Attorney General and now-convicted felon, all provided inaccurate and incomplete testimony to the Committee in order to conceal Mrs. Clinton's pivotal role in the decisions surrounding the handling of Mr. Foster's documents following his death.

Finally, the Special Committee concludes that the misconduct surrounding the handling of Mr. Foster's documents is a part of a larger and more troubling pattern, that began in Arkansas in the 1980s and has continued in Washington during the Clinton Administration, in which the Clintons and their associates have sought to hinder, impede and control investigations into Madison Guaranty S&L and the Whitewater real estate investment. Parts of this larger pattern include (i) Mrs. Clinton's decision in 1988—when federal investigators were examining possible misconduct leading to Madison Guaranty's failure just two years before—to order the destruction of records relating to her representation of this S&L; (ii) Mr. Foster's and Mr. Hubbell's improper and unauthorized 1992 removal of Rose Law Firm records and files relating to Mrs. Clinton's representation of this corrupt S&L; and (iii) and the improper communication to White House officials during the fall of 1993 of confidential information relating to ongoing criminal investigations of Madison Guaranty and of Capital Management Services, Inc., a small business investment company also central to the Whitewater affair.

. . . .

Our nation rests on the principle that all Americans are equal under the law. No one, including the President, is entitled to special treatment in a civil or criminal investigation of their conduct. The power of the presidency may not be used to obtain a legal defense for the President and his associates unavailable to other citizens.

During the 1992 presidential campaign, questions surfaced about the relationship of then-Governor Clinton and Mrs. Clinton and James McDougal, the owner of Madison Guaranty Savings and Loan Association ("Madison Guaranty") and the Clintons' partner in the Whitewater Development Corporation, Inc. ("Whitewater"). Within the past month, a jury in Little Rock, Arkansas convicted Mr. McDougal, his former wife, Susan, and Arkansas Governor Jim Guy Tucker of numerous federal crimes relating to the activities of Madison Guaranty and, in part, the operation of Whitewater.

The McDougal-Tucker convictions grew out of an investigation begun during the 1992 presidential campaign by investigators of the Resolution Trust Corporation ("RTC"). This RTC investigation culminated in a series of criminal referrals to the United States Attorney's Office in Little Rock naming the Clintons as witnesses to suspected criminal activity. These significant convictions also rested on a parallel inquiry begun in 1992 by the Small Business Administration ("SBA") of Capital Management Services, Inc. ("CMS"), a small business investment company.

Within months of the inauguration of President Clinton, senior Administration officials began to take steps to minimize the legal and political damage to the Clintons arising from these investigations. These officials seriously misused their public offices for the Clintons' private benefit, obtained confidential law enforcement information from the RTC and SBA relating to investigations touching on the Clintons, and they attempted to interfere in ongoing law enforcement investigations.

During hearings in the summer of 1994, the Senate Banking Committee examined—in deference to the investigation of Special Counsel Robert Fiske—only the propriety of certain communications in late 1993 and early 1994 between senior officials of the White House and the Treasury Department concerning confidential RTC criminal referrals involving Madison and Whitewater. The White House then claimed that its receipt of this confidential law enforcement information was appropriate to allow the President to respond to press inquiries and to protect the President from inadvertently engaging in meetings that later could prove embarrassing. No one—and certainly no member of the Banking Committee—asserted that the President was entitled to use such information to further his personal legal interests.

Rather than being limited to the narrow question before the Banking Committee in the 103d Congress, and without objection by Independent Counsel Kenneth Starr, the Special Committee examined all aspects of the Clinton Administration's response to ongoing investigations of Whitewater and related matters. This broader inquiry revealed that in 1993 and 1994, senior Administration officials took steps that went far beyond what was necessary to respond to press inquiries. Indeed, when the full picture is examined, the claim that Administration officials were innocently gathering information so they could respond to press inquiries collapses entirely.

After careful review of all the evidence, including evidence obtained by the Banking Committee during the summer of 1994, the Special Committee concludes that senior Administration officials—in the White House, the Treasury and Justice Departments, the RTC and the SBA—engaged in a pattern of highly improper conduct in responding to investigations of the Clinton's involvement in Whitewater and related matters.

This pattern cannot be explained as the result of a series of lapses in judgment. The Committee concludes that these Administration officials deliberately misused their public offices to advance the purely private interests of the President and Mrs. Clinton. Raising the possibility of obstruction of justice, they repeatedly attempted to hinder, impede and control investigations of Whitewater and related matters by the RTC, the Justice Department, the Inspectors General of the RTC and Treasury Departments, and even the Senate.

Because of misdeeds of the White House, perhaps the American people will never know the full extent to which the highly improper actions of Administration officials prejudiced the outcome of inquires involving Whitewater, Madison Guaranty and related matters. But the available facts clearly demonstrate that Administration officials improperly used the power of their offices in a wrongful attempt to ensure that ongoing federal investigations resulted in the least amount of legal and political damage to the President and Mrs. Clinton.

. . . .

The convictions of three of the President and Mrs. Clinton's close Arkansas business and political associates in the recently concluded Tucker-McDougal trial in Little Rock marked a key turning point in the ongoing Whitewater affair. The jury's guilty findings against Governor Jim Guy Tucker and James and Susan McDougal, the Clinton's Whitewater business partners, demonstrate the seriousness of the matters under investigation in the Committee's Arkansas Phase. Simply put, Whitewater can no longer be responsibly dismissed as "a cover-up without a crime."

The Arkansas jury unanimously concluded that James McDougal operated Madison Guaranty as, in effect, a criminal enterprise. The failure of Madison Guaranty cost American taxpayers more than $60 million. It is now clear that Madison and CMS, a small business investment company run by David Hale, were piggy banks for the Arkansas political elite.

Eight of the 24 counts of conviction relate directly to the Clintons' investment in Whitewater. The jury convicted on all of the counts concerning a loan from CMS to Susan McDougal's firm, Master Marketing. According to the testimony of an FBI agent at the Tucker-McDougal trial, approximately $50,000 of the loan was used to pay the expenses of Whitewater. Moreover, Mr. Hale testified at the trial that he discussed this fraudulent loan with then-Governor Clinton. Unfortunately, the Committee never heard the important testimony of Mr. Hale, who asserted his constitutional right not to testify. The Committee was unable to secure sufficient votes to grant Mr. Hale limited use immunity.

The recently-discovered Rose Law Firm billing records provide important new evidence relating to the Arkansas Phase.

The records reveal Mrs. Clinton's previously undisclosed personal representation of Mr. McDougal's S&L before state regulators, seeking permission to raise additional money through the sale of stock. The records also show that Mrs. Clinton was repeatedly called on to do work related to the Madison land deal, known as Castle Grande, which federal S&L regulators found involved a series of fraudulent transactions. The Special Committee concludes that Mrs. Clinton's work on Castle Grande related to an effort to conceal the true nature of activities at Madison Guaranty.

The Special Committee also uncovered evidence that Mr. Clinton himself took an active role in obtaining one of the original Whitewater loans—one apparently approved as a favor after the bank's political lobbyist intervened. And Mr. Clinton's accountant testified that when he raised objections to early parts of Mr. McDougal's Whitewater proposal, Mr. Clinton pulled him aside and told him to "back off."

During the 1980s, Mr. McDougal and his allies obtained favorable results from their dealings with the Arkansas state government under Governor Clinton. At a time when Mr. McDougal was carrying the Clintons on their Whitewater loans, Mr. McDougal had a say in the making of state appointments, enjoyed personal access to the Governor and won valuable state leases for Madison. The Special Committee concludes that Governor Clinton's official and personal dealings with Mr. McDougal raised an apparent, if not an actual, improper conflict of interest.

Finally, the Clintons were not "passive" investors in the Whitewater real estate venture, as they have claimed. Indeed, the Clintons participated in important meetings concerning the Whitewater investment. The Special Committee concludes that the Clintons took an active role in obtaining and extending Whitewater-related loans.

. . . .

Senate Report 104–280, 104th Congress, 2d session, Investigation of Whitewater Development Corporation and Related Matters, Final Report of the Special Committee to Investigate Whitewater Development Corporation and Related Matters, Together with Additional and Minority Views (Washington: U.S. Government Printing Office, 1996), 1–5, 8–10, 137–139, 288–289.

186   Final Report of the Senate Whitewater Investigation (Minority Views)

June 17, 1996

When the Senate's special committee investigating the Whitewater affair finished its inquiry (see document 185 for background), both a majority report and a minority report were issued. These reports came to opposite conclusions and provided no resolution of the matters under investigation.

Congressional investigations throughout American history have been influenced by partisan considerations, since all such investigations occur in a highly charged political atmosphere. In the most productive congressional investigations partisanship, while present, has been tempered by other factors, not the least of which is the leadership of the investigating committee. The Senate Whitewater investigation was a blatantly partisan investigation in which the public interest seemed secondary to party goals. Part of the partisanship in this investigation was generated by Alphonse D'Amato (R-N.Y.), the acerbic chairman of the Senate Special Committee to Investigate Whitewater Development Corporation and Related Matters. His aggressive and combative style contributed little to an atmosphere of impartiality during the hearings. Democrats on the committee were equally dogged in their defense of President William J. Clinton. A comparison of the conclusions of the Republican majority (see document 185) with those of the Democratic minority presented here reveals how far apart both sides were and how little light was shed on the matters under investigation.

MINORITY VIEWS TO THE FINAL REPORT OF THE SPECIAL COMMITTEE TO INVESTIGATE WHITEWATER DEVELOPMENT CORPORATION AND RELATED MATTERS OF SENATORS SARBANES, DODD, KERRY, BRYAN, BOXER, MOSELEY-BRAUN, MURRAY, AND SIMON

Summary of Conclusions

I. Preface

The central question that faced the Special Committee is: Did Bill Clinton misuse the powers of the Presidency? The answer is a clear and unequivocal "no."

A secondary question is whether, prior to his election as President, Mr. Clinton used his official position in the State of Arkansas improperly to provide favored treatment to business associates or others. In its exhaustive review of various allegations extending back to the 1970s in some instances, the Committee examined in excruciating detail a number of matters in Arkansas ranging from the handling of water and sewer legislation to state regulation of the sale of alcoholic beverages. Again, the clear conclusion is that then-Governor Clinton did not abuse his office.

Having failed to tarnish the President, the Majority turned its attention to Mrs. Clinton's private law practice in Arkansas more than ten years ago. The Majority launched a massive hunt for some way in which to contradict statements made by Mrs. Clinton during the last four years. Again, no credible evidence has been put forward to show that Mrs. Clinton engaged in any improper, much less illegal, conduct.

The public deserves an objective report that separates the facts developed in the Senate Whitewater inquiry from the superheated and untenable conclusions that pervade the Majority's report. Unfortunately, the extension of these hearings directly into the presidential campaign season has provoked a high degree of partisanship, which has undermined the objectivity of this investigation. Partisanship has colored the Majority's decisions in conducting the inquiry and in reaching conclusions that clearly are intended for political impact. It is now evident that this Committee's business easily could have been concluded within the original February 29, 1996 deadline.

When a parallel situation presented itself as the Iran-Contra hearings threatened to spill over into the political season, Democrats concurred in bringing the hearings to a prompt close. That was the right decision and one that future Senate committees should follow as a more worthy precedent than the Whitewater example.

The Majority's pattern throughout these hearings has been to construct conclusions first and then to discard the facts as they become inconvenient. One after another, the partisan conspiracy theories about Whitewater—from the alleged shredding of documents at the Rose Law Firm, to the so-called "mystery phone call," to the "all-important" White House e-mails—have turned into dry holes.

Lacking any credible case against the President, the Majority is now engaging in a blatantly political game of "tag" by tarring several witnesses with unsupportable suggestions of perjury in a bid to grab media attention. The political grandstanding of these "perjury referrals" is a tactic also used after the 1994 hearings. Margaret Williams, for instance—a favorite target of the Majority—has passed two lie detector tests, which corroborate her testimony that she did not remove documents from Foster's office on the night of his death. Yet, the Majority seeks to discount Williams's lie detector tests—performed first by a retired FBI polygraph instructor and confirmed by a present FBI expert under the supervision of the Independent Counsel. In the bargain, the Majority report takes on the reliability of polygraph testing, which the FBI has depended on for decades in investigations involving the highest levels of national security.

Taken as a whole, the Majority's approach to its report has been to hammer evidence—no matter how ill-fitting—into the precast mold of its conclusions. A perfect example of this refusal to modify its preordained conclusion by reference to the facts is revealed by the Majority's treatment of the April 5, 1985 fundraiser hosted by James McDougal for Governor Clinton at Madison Guaranty Savings and Loan. The Majority began the inquiry with the conclusion that there was a quid pro quo involving the fundraiser and the decision of an Arkansas state agency—ADFA—to lease office space from Madison Guaranty. To a fair-minded investigator, two obstacles to reading such a conclusion would be presented: (1) the fact that the lease for office space was entered into more than a full year before the McDougal fundraiser, and (2) the evidence showed that Governor Clinton played no role in selecting the office site or negotiating the terms of the lease. When the evidence at the public hearing demonstrated the circumstances under which the Madison space was chosen, a Member of the Majority registered his consternation at this departure from the Republican game plan:

Mr. Chairman, isn't the point here simply to draw a conclusion that [then-Governor Clinton] played a major role in the selection of this building?

Inconveniently, the evidence once again rebutted the preconceived conclusion, yet that conclusion is the one relied upon by the Majority in its final report.

More than finding no abuse of office by Bill Clinton, the evidence gathered by the Committee shows that then-Governor Clinton demonstrated independence from political supporters doing business with State government. Three examples from the Committee's exhaustive review of Governor Clinton's twelve-year tenure as governor of Arkansas are representative of our findings in this area. In 1983, Marlin Jackson, the Arkansas State Banking Commissioner, informed Governor Clinton of bank regulatory problems at the Bank of Kingston, a small bank in northern Arkansas that James McDougal purchased after leaving a senior post in Governor Clinton's first administration. Jackson testified that he mentioned the Bank of Kingston problem as a "litmus test" to see if the young governor would seek to influence Jackson and obtain favorable treatment for a political supporter. Clinton passed Jackson's test. Jackson testified that Governor Clinton told him:

You do whatever you need to do to be a good, no, to be a great Bank Commissioner and don't worry about the political consequences. It doesn't matter who is involved. I'll take the political heat. You just do whatever you need to do to be a great Bank Commissioner.

Four years later, in another situation involving James McDougal, Governor Clinton showed the same good judgment and respect for the independence of state regulatory officials. McDougal requested a meeting with Governor Clinton and State Health Department officials to present a grievance about unfair treatment by state sanitarians inspecting sewage disposal systems at one of the Madison Guaranty real estate developments. McDougal behaved badly at the meeting, attacking the Health Department officials and accusing them of misconduct. Governor Clinton supported the state officials at the meeting. He reprimanded McDougal for his conduct in front of Health Department officials. Most important, after the meeting, Governor Clinton pulled aside Tom Butler, the Deputy Director of the State Health Department, and told him to "do what you have to do, and you will not hear another word from me." Once again, Governor Clinton made it perfectly clear to a state regulator that James McDougal should not receive any special treatment.

One final example of Governor Clinton's actions in Arkansas is worth noting. About 1984, Dan Lasater, a strong political supporter of Governor Clinton who had helped Clinton regain the Governor's office in 1982 after an upset loss in 1980, requested a meeting to complain to the Governor that his investment firm was not getting its fair share of the state bond business. Governor Clinton met with Lasater, listened to his complaint, then told him that he should make his case to the appropriate State officials. Although it would have been easy for him to do so, Governor Clinton did not tell Lasater that he would intervene in the matter. Lasater left the meeting "disappointed" that he had not obtained the result he had hoped to obtain. Again, Governor Clinton did not intervene on behalf of a political supporter.

These examples lead a fair-minded reader to the same conclusion that will follow from a review of the entire, lengthy report: Governor Clinton did not misuse his office, as Governor of Arkansas, or as President.

These examples also underscore another important point. Governor Clinton, of course, was an elected public official when these events took place. As an elected official he was answerable to his constituents, and it was his responsibility to listen to their complaints. All elected public officials, at the state, local, and even the national level, must do this—it is part of the job. To do this job properly, however, a public official must exercise good judgment, so as to be responsive to constituents without going too far and interfering with the actions of career government officials who also are discharging their responsibilities. Governor Clinton's actions some ten years ago in Arkansas, as illustrated, met the test then of proper conduct by an elected official, and they meet that test now.

The venom with which the Majority focuses its attack on Hillary Rodham Clinton is surprising, even in the context of the investigation. No attempt is made to place into perspective the relative importance to the American people of whether Mrs. Clinton has a special recollection today of every memorandum, phone call, and detail of every case she handled in her private law practice in Little Rock over a decade ago.

Every act is portrayed in its most sinister light, every failure of recollection is treated as though the standard for human experience is total recall and photographic memory.

Perhaps the most sensationalized conclusions of the Majority involved the handling of Vincent Foster's papers. The crux of the disagreement between White House Counsel Bernard Nussbaum and Deputy Attorney General Philip Heymann was whether Nussbaum's insistence on being the one to review Foster's files in the presence of Justice Department lawyers and law enforcement officials would create an unfortunate appearance problem for the White House. Heymann agreed that, legally, the Park Police investigators had no right to enter the office and search the files, nor could Justice Department lawyers obtain a search warrant or subpoena. While Heymann was clearly prescient about the public and political fallout from Nussbaum's decision, who is to say that Nussbaum wasn't right also in believing that even if the Justice Department lawyers had taken part in the search, critics of the Administration would simply charge a broader conspiracy?

Irresponsible claims of possible obstruction of justice simply ignore the testimony of law enforcement officials who came before the Committee: that the investigation into Vincent Foster's death—the only investigation involving the review of the office files—was not obstructed; that the investigators were provided every document or file they requested; that the investigators had absolutely no interest in reviewing financial records or files involving personal investments of the Clintons such as Whitewater; and that the investigator's interest was limited to reviewing a suicide note or other information bearing on the cause for Foster's suicide.

The Majority's pursuit of White House officials involved in searching for a suicide note in the aftermath of Foster's death is equally irresponsible. Senator Dodd captured the spirit of the Majority's onslaught during a hearing in November, 1995:

Senator Dodd. Mr. Chairman, just on this point, and I think it is very important, this gets to the reality. But what I was getting at earlier and what we're doing here in a sense is there are sort of three fact situations. You get a witness that says well, I don't recall. The immediate accusation is your being disingenuous.

If you have witnesses with conflicting testimony, the allegation is someone's lying. And if you have witnesses that have consistent statements, its a conspiracy.

This is getting ridiculous. So you're trapped no matter what you say * * * You're either disingenuous, lying or conspiring, and that's just foolishness.

The game of leaking information has marred the Committee's credibility throughout these proceedings. Often, distorted or even baseless charges have been disseminated through faceless leaks. The recent, well-orchestrated leak of the Majority report is but part of a pattern.

The supposed short-term benefits of leaking will be offset by the longer-term diminution of credibility that the Majority must suffer for these blatantly political and unfair tactics.

The Minority report was not leaked. It was released according to the rules. In it, the subjects set forth in Senate Resolution 120 are analyzed according to the testimony and documents presented. We look forward to the opportunity to present the facts to the American public in contrast to the overheated assertions by the Majority, which have characterized its approach to this investigation.

Not including the Senate Banking Committee's hearings in 1994, the Senate Whitewater Committee in 1995 and 1996 met for more than 300 hours in open sessions, taking 10,729 pages of hearing testimony in 51 hearings and 8 public meetings. The Committee received hearing testimony from 159 witnesses and took more than 35,000 pages of deposition testimony from 245 persons. Hundreds of thousands of pages of documents have been provided to the Committee by various government departments, agencies, and individuals.

The White House has produced more than 15,000 pages of documents, and the Clintons' attorney has produced nearly 30,000 pages more.

Direct costs of the various Whitewater inquiries now exceed $31,849,795 (as of May, 1996), including: $400,000 from the Senate Banking Committee's 1994 hearings (Senate Resolution 229), $950,000 through the initial charter of the D'Amato hearings (Senate Resolution 120, approved May 17, 1995), and another $450,000 for an extension this year approved by the Senate (Senate Resolution 246, approved April 17, 1996); $3,800,000 for the Resolution Trust Corporation's contract with the Pillsbury, Madison & Sutro law firm, for the production of its report; and $26,249,795 by the Office of the Independent Counsel (through May, 1996). Costs of the various Whitewater inquiries in the House of Representatives and agency work to comply with inquiries while not separately accounted for amount to significant additional sums.

This has been the longest-running congressional investigation of any sitting president, far longer than Watergate or Iran-Contra—both of which involved actual abuse of government power. The facts gathered by the Committee are more than enough to close this chapter. The American people deserve to know, and now can take comfort in knowing, that this year-long investigation shows no misconduct or abuse of power by their President or First Lady.

. . . .

Senate Report 104–280, 104th Congress, 2d session, *Investigation of Whitewater Development Corporation and Related Matters, Final Report of the Special Committee to Investigate Whitewater Development Corporation and Related Matters, Together with Additional and Minority Views* (Washington: U.S. Government Printing Office, 1996), 395–399.

187   A Ruling on the Election of Speaker Newt Gingrich

January 7, 1997

The House faced a dramatic and precedent-setting situation at the opening of the 105th Congress on January 7, 1997. The Speaker of the House, Newt Gingrich (R-Ga.), who became the first Republican Speaker to be elected to the House in forty years when he assumed the post in 1995, was under investigation for violations of House ethics rules. Just days before the opening of the 105th Congress Gingrich had publicly admitted that he had brought discredit on the House. In the weeks preceding the January 7 start of the new Congress, Gingrich learned that a subcommittee of the House Committee on Standards of Official Conduct (known as the House ethics committee) had voted 4–0 to bring charges against him that related to his improper use of funds from a political action committee called GOPAC and his attempts to mislead the House ethics committee during the investigation.

Democrats, and even a few Republicans, stated that if the Speaker was guilty of the charges against him, he should not be re-elected Speaker. Under House rules, members found guilty of ethics violations face a series of punishments ranging from the mildest sanction, a reprimand, to a more serious punishment, a censure, and the most serious of all, expulsion from the House of Representatives. If the House recommended censure as the proper punishment, Gingrich would be stripped of the speakership. At the time of the convening of the 105th Congress the final report of the ethics committee had not been completed and no decision regarding the committee's findings of guilt or innocence had been announced. Critics of the Speaker blamed the ethics committee for deliberately delaying the completion of their report until after the election for Speaker took place.

The House of Representatives "reinvents" itself anew on the opening day of each new session of Congress every two years. The House must swear in all 435 members, adopt the rules that will govern its conduct, and elect the Speaker of the House and other officers. In this practice the House is quite different from the Senate, which is known as a "continuous body" because only one-third of its membership is elected every two years and its rules do not have to be readopted in total every two years when a new Congress begins. Senate leaders are not automatically reelected at the beginning of each Congress, unless, of course, there is a change in party control of the chamber.

Until the election of the Speaker is completed at the opening session of each new Congress, the presiding officer is the clerk of the House. In this instance the clerk was Robin H. Carle, selected by Newt Gingrich and elected by the Republican majority in the House. She was the first woman to hold the office of clerk of the House. When the moment came to call for the election of the Speaker, Representative John Boehner (R-Ohio) placed the name of Newt Gingrich in nomination. When the clerk turned to the Democratic side for the customary nomination from that party, Representative Vic Fazio (D-Calif.) took the opportunity to object to the election of the Speaker, arguing that it should be postponed until the ethics committee report on Gingrich was completed.

The clerk ruled that there was ample precedent to support an immediate vote on the election of the Speaker. When Fazio challenged the ruling of the clerk, his motion was defeated on a straight party-line vote. This ruling established the primacy of the election of the Speaker over any attempt to postpone the election. The Speaker had successfully dodged a political bullet. Gingrich was then elected Speaker for his second term.

Two weeks later, on January 21, 1997, with the findings of the ethics committee in the hands of the House of Representatives, the House voted overwhelmingly, 395–28, to reprimand the Speaker for his violations of House rules. In addition, the House vote approved the ethics committee's recommendation that a "penalty" of $300,000 be imposed on the Speaker to reimburse the committee's expenses for the time and effort it took to unravel Gingrich's misleading information—a sanction never imposed before in the history of Congress. The ethics committee's use of the word penalty *was carefully chosen to minimize the appearance that the Speaker had been fined for wrongdoing. The Speaker and his defenders consistently corrected members of the press and Democratic critics who called the $300,000 penalty a* fine.

The CLERK. Pursuant to law and to precedent, the next order of business is the election of the Speaker of the House of Representatives for the 105th Congress.

Nominations are now in order.

The CLERK recognizes the gentleman from Ohio [Mr. Boehner].

Mr. BOEHNER. Madam Clerk, as chairman of the Republican Conference, I am honored and privileged to welcome my colleagues, their families, and the American people to this historic day.

Two years ago we began a new chapter in American history, one of faith in the strength, creativity and goodness of Americans; one where we humbly recognize that although the people sent us here to do their business, we cannot do our job without their consent and their support.

With their support, we began to change America by reforming Washington. And together, we will ensure our reforms improve Americans' quality of life. We will balance the budget, provide permanent tax relief, safer streets, better schools, a cleaner environment, and longer healthier lives with more affordable health care. It is an ambitious agenda, but it is what we were sent here to do. And we owe the American people nothing less.

With pride in what we have accomplished in the past and anticipation of what we can do together in the future, I am directed by a unanimous vote of the Republican Conference to present the name of the Honorable Newt Gingrich, a Representative-elect from the State of Georgia, for election to the office of Speaker of the House of Representatives for the 105th Congress.

QUESTION OF PRIVILEGE OFFERED BY MR. FAZIO OF CALIFORNIA

The CLERK. The Clerk now recognizes the gentleman from California [Mr. Fazio] for a nomination.

Mr. FAZIO of California. Madam Clerk, I rise to a question of the highest constitutional privilege. I offer a resolution which calls for the postponement of the election of the Speaker of the House until the Committee on Standards of Official Conduct completes its work on the matters concerning Representative Newt Gingrich of Georgia. The resolution requires the House to proceed immediately to the election of an interim Speaker who will preside over the House until that time.

I ask for the immediate consideration of the resolution.

The CLERK. Section 30 of the Revised Statutes of the United States, which is codified in section 25 of title 2, United States Code, reads in part as follows:

At the first session of Congress after every general election of Representatives, the oath of office shall be administered by any Member of the House of Representatives to the Speaker; and by the Speaker to all Members and Delegates present, and to the Clerk, previous to entering on any other business.

This has been the law since June 1, 1789.

The precedent recorded in Hinds' Precedents of the House at volume 1, section 212, recites that, "at the organization of the House the motion to proceed to the election of a Speaker is of the highest privilege." On that occasion, the Clerk stated that "the duty of the House to organize itself is a duty devolved upon it by law, and any matter looking to the performance of that duty takes precedence in all parliamentary bodies of all minor questions."

The CLERK cites both the statute and the precedent as controlling her decision, consistent with the modern practice of the House, to recognize nominations for Speaker.

Mr. FAZIO of California. Madam Clerk, given the unprecedented nature of the circumstance, I urge that the Clerk permit the Representatives-elect a vote on the motion that I have submitted.

The CLERK. Is the gentleman from California appealing the ruling of the Clerk?

Mr. FAZIO of California. Madam Clerk, if the gentlewoman does not permit a vote under the extraordinary circumstance we face today, I would appeal the ruling of the Clerk.

The CLERK. The gentleman may appeal from the Clerk's ruling on the question of order as to the priority of business.

The question is, Shall the decision of the Clerk stand as the judgment of the House?

Mr. BOEHNER. Madam Clerk, I move to lay the appeal on the table.

Mr. FAZIO of California. Madam Clerk, on that I demand the yeas and nays on the motion to table made by the majority.

The CLERK. The question is on the motion offered by the gentleman from Ohio [Mr. Boehner] to lay the appeal on the table.

The question was taken; and the Clerk announced that the yeas and nays appeared to have it.

Mr. FAZIO of California. Madam Clerk, on that I demand the yeas and nays.

The yeas and nays were ordered.

The vote was taken by electronic device, and there were— yeas 222, nays 210, not voting 0. . . .

Congressional Record, House, 105th Congress, 1st session, January 7, 1997, H2–H3. Downloaded from the Library of Congress's "Thomas" Web site: http://thomas.loc.gov/home/thomas2.html.

188   Clinton v. City of New York

June 25, 1998

The controversy over the line-item veto, which had occupied considerable time and energy in American politics for almost two decades (see document 182), finally reached partial resolution in April 1996, when Congress passed a bill to give the president the authority to use a version of the line-item veto. President William J. Clinton endorsed this Republican initiative, one of the key provisions of the House Republicans' Contract with America (see document 183), and signed the bill into law.

The law took affect on January 1, 1997, and was immediately challenged in federal court by a group of six senators and representatives, led by Senator Robert C. Byrd (D-W.Va.), who filed suit on grounds that the law gave the president more authority to change law than was granted in the Constitution. On April 10, 1997, Judge Thomas J. Jackson, of the United States District Court for the District of Columbia, in the case of Byrd v. Raines, *struck down the Line Item Veto Act because Congress had delegated to the president powers they could not constitutionally surrender. The act, according to Judge Jackson, violated the law-making procedures described in Article I of the Constitution. The Supreme Court then ruled that the members of Congress who brought the suit did not have the standing to do so because they could not demonstrate that they had in any way been injured or affected by the law. The Supreme Court ordered the district court to dismiss the case for lack of jurisdiction.*

President Clinton, two months after the court challenge had been dismissed, became the first president in history to use the line-item veto on several bills. Once he did so, a new lawsuit was filed by several parties who could demonstrate that they were concretely affected by the president's actions—the City of New York, two hospital associations, and two unions representing health care em-

ployees. A related case was also filed by thirty potato growers in Idaho, the Snake River Potato Growers, Inc., and an individual farmer who claimed financial loss when the president "unilaterally canceled provisions of duly enacted statutes."

On June 25, 1998, the Supreme Court ruled that "our decision rests on the narrow ground that the procedures authorized by the Line Item Veto Act are not authorized by the Constitution." The high court determined that the procedures outlined in the Line Item Veto Act gave the president more authority than he had under the provisions of Article I, regarding what a president could do with legislation coming to him for signature. The Supreme Court did not rule on the various merits of the line-item veto. What the Court did say was that it would require an amendment to the Constitution to allow the president more authority to unilaterally change legislation. "The Line Item Veto Act," Justice John Paul Stevens wrote, "authorizes the President himself to effect the repeal of laws, for his own policy reasons, without observing the procedures set out in Article I, §7. The fact that Congress intended such a result is of no moment. Although Congress presumably anticipated that the President might cancel some of the items in the Balanced Budget Act and in the Taxpayer Relief Act, Congress cannot alter the procedures set out in Article I, §7, without amending the Constitution."

. . . .

IV

The Line Item Veto Act gives the President the power to "cancel in whole" three types of provisions that have been signed into law: "(1) any dollar amount of discretionary budget authority; (2) any item of new direct spending; or (3) any limited tax benefit." (1994 ed., Supp. II). It is undisputed that the New York case involves an "item of new direct spending" and that the Snake River case involves a "limited tax benefit" as those terms are defined in the Act. It is also undisputed that each of those provisions had been signed into law pursuant to Article I, §7, of the Constitution before it was canceled.

The Act requires the President to adhere to precise procedures whenever he exercises his cancellation authority. In identifying items for cancellation he must consider the legislative history, the purposes, and other relevant information about the items. . . . He must determine, with respect to each cancellation, that it will "(i) reduce the Federal budget deficit; (ii) not impair any essential Government functions; and (iii) not harm the national interest." §691(a)(A). Moreover, he must transmit a special message to Congress notifying it of each cancellation within five calendar days (excluding Sundays) after the enactment of the canceled provision. See §691(a)(B). It is undisputed that the President meticulously followed these procedures in these cases.

A cancellation takes effect upon receipt by Congress of the special message from the President. See §691b(a). If, however, a "disapproval bill" pertaining to a special message is enacted into law, the cancellations set forth in that message become "null and void." *Ibid.* The Act sets forth a detailed expedited procedure for the consideration of a "disapproval bill," see §691d, but no such bill was passed for either of the cancellations involved in these cases.

A majority vote of both Houses is sufficient to enact a disapproval bill. The Act does not grant the President the authority to cancel a disapproval bill, see §691(c), but he does, of course, retain his constitutional authority to veto such a bill.

The effect of a cancellation is plainly stated in §691e, which defines the principal terms used in the Act. With respect to both an item of new direct spending and a limited tax benefit, the cancellation prevents the item "from having legal force or effect." (1994 ed., Supp. II).

Thus, under the plain text of the statute, the two actions of the President that are challenged in these cases prevented one section of the Balanced Budget Act of 1997 and one section of the Taxpayer Relief Act of 1997 "from having legal force or effect." The remaining provisions of those statutes, with the exception of the second canceled item in the latter, continue to have the same force and effect as they had when signed into law.

In both legal and practical effect, the President has amended two Acts of Congress by repealing a portion of each. "[R]epeal of statutes, no less than enactment, must conform with Art. I." *INS v. Chadha.* There is no provision in the Constitution that authorizes the President to enact, to amend, or to repeal statutes. Both Article I and Article II assign responsibilities to the President that directly relate to the lawmaking process, but neither addresses the issue presented by these cases. The President "shall from time to time give to the Congress Information on the State of the Union, and recommend to their Consideration such Measures as he shall judge necessary and expedient . . . ." Art. II, §3.

Thus, he may initiate and influence legislative proposals. Moreover, after a bill has passed both Houses of Congress, but "before it become[s] a Law," it must be presented to the President. If he approves it, "he shall sign it, but if not he shall return it, with his Objections to that House in which it shall have originated, who shall enter the Objections at large on their Journal, and proceed to reconsider it." Art. I, §7, cl. 2.

His "return" of a bill, which is usually described as a "veto," is subject to being overridden by a two-thirds vote in each House.

There are important differences between the President's "return" of a bill pursuant to Article I, §7, and the exercise of the President's cancellation authority pursuant to the Line Item Veto Act. The constitutional return takes place *before* the bill becomes law; the statutory cancellation occurs *after* the bill becomes law. The constitutional return is of the entire bill; the statutory cancellation is of only a part. Although the Constitution expressly authorizes the President to play a role in the process of enacting statutes, it is silent on the subject of unilateral Presidential action that either repeals or amends parts of duly enacted statutes.

There are powerful reasons for construing constitutional silence on this profoundly important issue as equivalent to an express prohibition. The procedures governing the enactment of statutes set forth in the text of Article I were the product of the great debates and compromises that produced the Constitution itself. Familiar historical materials provide abundant support for the conclusion that the power to enact statutes may only "be exercised in accord with a single, finely wrought and exhaustively considered, procedure." *Chadha.* Our first President understood the text of the Presentment Clause as requiring that he either "approve all the parts of a Bill, or reject it in toto."

What has emerged in these cases from the President's exercise of his statutory cancellation powers, however, are truncated versions of two bills that passed both Houses of Congress. They are not the product of the "finely wrought" procedure that the Framers designed.

At oral argument, the Government suggested that the cancellations at issue in these cases do not effect a "repeal" of the canceled items because under the special "lockbox" provisions of the Act, a canceled item "retain[s] real, legal budgetary effect" insofar as it prevents Congress and the President from spending the savings that result from the cancellation. . . .

The text of the Act expressly provides, however, that a cancellation prevents a direct spending or tax benefit provision "from having legal force or effect." That a canceled item may have "real, legal budgetary effect" as a result of the lockbox procedure does not change the fact that by canceling the items at issue in these cases, the President made them entirely inoperative as to appellees. Section 968 of the Taxpayer Relief Act no longer provides a tax benefit, and §4722(c) of the Balanced Budget Act of 1997 no longer relieves New York of its contingent liability.

Such significant changes do not lose their character simply because the canceled provisions may have some continuing financial effect on the Government. The cancellation of one section of a statute may be the functional equivalent of a partial repeal even if a portion of the section is not canceled.

V

The Government advances two related arguments to support its position that despite the unambiguous provisions of the Act, cancellations do not amend or repeal properly enacted statutes in violation of the Presentment Clause. First, relying primarily on *Field* v. *Clark* (1892), the Government contends that the cancellations were merely exercises of discretionary authority granted to the President by the Balanced Budget Act and the Taxpayer Relief Act read in light of the previously enacted Line Item Veto Act. Second, the Government submits that the substance of the authority to cancel tax and spending items "is, in practical effect, no more and no less than the power to 'decline to spend' specified sums of money, or to 'decline to implement' specified tax measures."... Neither argument is persuasive.

. . . .

The Line Item Veto Act authorizes the President himself to effect the repeal of laws, for his own policy reasons, without observing the procedures set out in Article 1, §7. The fact that Congress intended such a result is of no moment. Although Congress presumably anticipated that the President might cancel some of the items in the Balanced Budget Act and in the Taxpayer Relief Act, Congress cannot alter the procedures set out in Article 1, §7, without amending the Constitution.

Neither are we persuaded by the Government's contention that the President's authority to cancel new direct spending and tax benefit items is no greater than his traditional authority to decline to spend appropriated funds. The Government has reviewed in some detail the series of statutes in which Congress has given the Executive broad discretion over the expenditure of appropriated funds. For example, the First Congress appropriated "sum[s] not exceeding" specified amounts to be spent on various Government operations.... In those statutes, as in later years, the President was given wide discretion with respect to both the amounts to be spent and how the money would be allocated among different functions. It is argued that the Line Item Veto Act merely confers comparable discretionary authority over the expenditure of appropriated funds. The critical difference between this statute and all of its predecessors, however, is that unlike any of them, this Act gives the President the unilateral power to change the text of duly enacted statutes. None of the Act's predecessors could even arguably have been construed to authorize such a change.

VI

Although they are implicit in what we have already written, th profound importance of these cases makes it appropriate to emphasize three points.

First, we express no opinion about the wisdom of the procedures authorized by the Line Item Veto Act. Many members of both major political parties who have served in the Legislative and the Executive Branches have long advocated the enactment of such procedures for the purpose of Censuring greater fiscal accountability in Washington."... The text of the Act was itself the product of much debate and deliberation in both Houses of Congress and that precise text was signed into law by the President. We do not lightly conclude that their action was unauthorized by the Constitution. We have, however, twice had full argument and briefing on the question and have concluded that our duty is clear.

Second, although appellees challenge the validity of the Act on alternative grounds, the only issue we address concerns the "finely wrought" procedure commanded by the Constitution. *Chadha.* We have been favored with extensive debate about the scope of Congress' power to delegate law-making authority, or its functional equivalent, to the President. The excellent briefs filed by the parties and their *amici curiae* have provided us with valuable historical information that illuminates the delegation issue but does not really bear on the narrow issue that is dispositive of these cases. Thus, because we conclude that the Act's cancellation provisions violate Article 1, §7, of the Constitution, we find it unnecessary to consider the District Court's alternative holding that the Act "impermissibly disrupts the balance of powers among the three branches of government."...

Third, our decision rests on the narrow ground that the procedures authorized by the Line Item Veto Act are not authorized by the Constitution. The Balanced Budget Act of 1997 is a 500-page document that became "Public Law 105–33" after three procedural steps were taken: (1) a bill containing its exact text was approved by a majority of the Members of the House of Representatives; (2) the Senate approved precisely the same text; and (3) that text was signed into law by the President. The Constitution explicitly requires that each of those three steps be taken before a bill may "become a law." Art. 1, §7. If one paragraph of that text had been omitted at any one of those three stages, Public Law 105–33 would not have been validly enacted. If the Line Item Veto Act were valid, it would authorize the President to create a different law one whose text was not voted on by either House of Congress or presented to the President for signature. Something that might be known as "Public Law 105–33 as modified by the President" may or may not be desirable, but it is surely not a document that may "become a law" pursuant to the procedures designed by the Framers of Article I, §7, of the Constitution.

If there is to be a new procedure in which the President will play a different role in determining the final text of what may "become a law," such change must come not by legislation but through the amendment procedures set forth in Article V of the Constitution. Cf. *U.S. Term Limits, Inc.* v. *Thornton* (1995).

The judgment of the District Court is affirmed.

It is so ordered.

189   A Resolution Authorizing an Impeachment Investigation of President William Jefferson Clinton

October 8, 1998

The House of Representatives, upon recommendation of the House Judiciary Committee, voted on October 8, 1998, to authorize an investigation of President William J. Clinton to see if there were grounds for his impeachment. This was only the third time in American history that the House moved this far in the constitutional process of removing a president from office. Only one president—Andrew Johnson in 1868—has been impeached by a vote of the entire House (see documents 81 and 82). Johnson remained in office when the Senate failed by one vote to convict him of the charges brought by the House. President Richard Nixon resigned from office in 1974 following a vote in the House Judiciary Committee on articles of impeachment (see documents 165 and 166).

Although the resolution made no reference to any specific high crimes and misdemeanors, and did not specify particular topics or alleged crimes that should be investigated, it was clear that the impetus for the resolution was the findings of Independent Counsel Kenneth W. Starr regarding the actions of the president concerning a sexual affair with a former White House intern.

The unfolding of this highly charged political and constitutional drama will be a landmark in congressional history regardless of the eventual outcome. There are many unprecedented aspects to this five-year investigation of the president by an independent counsel, who was originally appointed to investigate alleged crimes in the Whitewater matter (see documents 185 and 186).

On January 16, 1998, the independent counsel's investigation of Whitewater-related matters shifted its focus to a sexual affair between the president and a "young subordinate employee" in the White House. Seven months later, on August 17, 1998, President Clinton testified before a grand jury in the matter and also publicly admitted to an improper relationship with Monica Lewinsky.

On September 9, 1998, the independent counsel turned over to the House of Representatives a 435-page report of his findings related to the president and Lewinsky, including thousands of pages of documents and the transcripts and tapes of the president's grand jury testimony. The Starr Report, as the independent counsel's report quickly became known around the world, listed eleven acts by the president that the independent counsel believed to be grounds for impeachment. Most of the eleven items related to lying about the sexual affair and obstructing the investigation of it. The next day the House ordered the Starr Report to be printed as a House document. Complete with graphic details documenting the sexual affair, the Starr Report was instantly and widely disseminated in newspapers, books, and on the Internet.

During House debate on September 10, 1998, to provide for the release of the Starr Report, House Rules Committee Chairman Gerald B. H. Solomon (R-N.Y.) said: "In some senses, we are in uncharted waters. There has never been a report from an independent counsel detailing possible impeachable offenses by a President." He added: "This is a very grave day for the House of Repre-

sentatives, indeed it is a solemn time for our nation. Today we will do what we are compelled to do under the Constitution not because we desire it, but because it is our duty. In order to most judiciously fulfill these constitutional duties, I encourage all of the Members to approach this sensitive matter with the dignity and decorum which befits the most deliberative body in the world."

On October 8, 1998, after nearly a month of public exposure to the details of the Clinton-Lewinsky affair, the House authorized its judiciary committee to investigate the grounds for possible impeachment. The debate was partisan in nature, revealing that the House had not resolved the many issues related to this impeachment inquiry. All Republicans voted for the resolution, while 175 Democrats voted against it. Only 31 Democrats supported the measure. The final tally was 258–176. (The one Independent member, Bernard Sanders of Vermont, voted against the resolution.)

AUTHORIZING THE COMMITTEE ON THE JUDICIARY TO INVESTIGATE WHETHER SUFFICIENT GROUNDS EXIST FOR THE IMPEACHMENT OF WILLIAM JEFFERSON CLINTON, PRESIDENT OF THE UNITED STATES

. . . .

H. Res. 581

Resolved, That the Committee on the Judiciary, acting as a whole or by any subcommittee thereof appointed by the chairman for the purposes hereof and in accordance with the rules of the committee, is authorized and directed to investigate fully and completely whether sufficient grounds exist for the House of Representatives to exercise its constitutional power to impeach William Jefferson Clinton, President of the United States of America. The committee shall report to the House of Representatives such resolutions, articles of impeachment, or other recommendations as it deems proper.

SEC. 2. (a) For the purpose of making such investigation, the committee is authorized to require—

(1) by subpoena or otherwise—

(A) the attendance and testimony of any person (including at a taking of a deposition by counsel for the committee); and

(B) the production of such things; and

(2) by interrogatory, the furnishing of such information as it deems necessary to such investigation.

(b) Such authority of the committee may be exercised—

(1) by the chairman and the ranking minority member acting jointly, or, if either declines to act, by the other acting alone, except that in the event either so declines, either shall have the right to refer to the committee for decision the ques-

tion whether such authority shall be so exercised and the committee shall be convened promptly to render that decision; or

(2) by the committee acting as a whole or by subcommittee.

Subpoenas and interrogatories so authorized may be issued over the signature of the chairman, or ranking minority member, or any member designated by either of them, and may be served by any person designated by the chairman, or ranking minority member, or any member designated by either of them. The chairman, or ranking minority member, or any member designated by either of them (or, with respect to any deposition, answer to interrogatory, or affidavit, any person authorized by law to administer oaths) may administer oaths to any witness. For the purposes of this section, "things" includes, without limitation, books, records, correspondence, logs, journals, memorandums, papers, documents, writings, drawings, graphs, charts, photographs, reproductions, recordings, tapes, transcripts, printouts, data compilations from which information can be obtained (translated if necessary, through detection devices into reasonably usable form), tangible objects, and other things of any kind.

Congressional Record, House, 105th Congress, 2d session, October 8, 1998 (Part 1—daily edition), H10015.

190   The Resignation of Speaker Newt Gingrich

November 6, 1998

Three days after the congressional elections of November 3, 1998, Speaker of the House Newt Gingrich (R-Ga.) surprised his supporters and critics alike by announcing that he would not be a candidate for Speaker in the 106th Congress, which was scheduled to begin in January 1999. Gingrich's statement was issued as a press release and also appeared on the Speaker's Web site. Even though Gingrich had been easily reelected to his seat representing the sixth district of Georgia and his party retained its majority in the House of Representatives, House Republicans expressed dismay and anger with Gingrich that the Democrats picked up five House seats in this off-year election. This moderate gain by the Democrats was a matter of great concern for Republican leaders, as the party not in control of the White House has usually gained an average of twenty-seven seats in off-year elections.

Gingrich, who played a key role in promoting the investigation of President William J. Clinton, may have misjudged the public's obsession with the Clinton-Lewinsky sex scandal (see document 189). Republican strategists evidently alienated voters when they launched in the closing days of the campaign a $10 million advertising blitz that focused on the presidential scandal.

The poor Republican showing in the election was only part of the Speaker's growing problems within his own party. Just weeks before the 1998 elections, with eight of the thirteen annual appropriations bills unfinished, the Republican-controlled House and Senate passed a massive omnibus bill, 4,000 pages in length, containing a total appropriation of approximately $500 billion. Republicans were angry that the Clinton administration and the House and Senate Democrats were able to gain too many concessions in this bill, which undermined the Republican agenda, especially in the area of a proposed tax cut that never materialized. Much of the blame for the budget fiasco focused on Gingrich, just as it had in 1995 when a failed budget showdown with President Clinton led to a temporary shutdown of the federal government.

Only a handful of Speakers in the history of Congress have resigned the office. Henry Clay resigned as Speaker in 1814 to become a treaty negotiator for the United States to end the War of 1812. Clay also resigned the speakership once for personal financial reasons, returning to Kentucky in 1820.

Thomas Brackett Reed (R-Maine) resigned from office on September 4, 1899, three months before the start of the 56th Congress. While he was one of the most powerful Speakers in the history of the House, Reed was philosophically out of step with the majority of the Republican Party over the issue of U.S. acquisition of the Philippines, Hawaii, and other territory as a result of the Spanish-American War. At the time Reed was considered a potential presidential contender. When asked if his party might nominate him for president after he resigned as Speaker, he replied with his characteristic wit: "They could do worse, and probably will." The Republican presidential nomination went to William McKinley, a supporter of U.S. territorial expansion.

While other Speakers have declined to run for reelection or were not reelected as Speaker for various reasons, it was not until 1989 that another Speaker, Jim Wright (D-Texas), resigned while in office, effective June 6, 1989. Wright left in response to ethics charges brought against him by Newt Gingrich and others (see document 174).

While it is too early to fully evaluate the legacy of Gingrich's speakership, it is safe to say that he was the key architect of Republican Party success in 1994, when, for the first time in four decades, Republicans were able to gain control of the House of Representatives. Gingrich sought to stamp his own personality and leadership style on the House as have few Speakers in this century. He reminded the nation that the office of the Speaker can be a bully pulpit for setting the national agenda. But the personal drive and aggressive style that made him successful in his rise from back-bench critic to the office of the Speaker did not serve him well once in the office of Speaker. As his statement of resignation suggested, the Re-

publican Party needed new leaders who could "both reconcile and discipline . . . work together and communicate effectively." At the time this volume went to press, Speaker Gingrich had announced only that he would not be a candidate for Speaker in the 106th Congress. News accounts speculated that he would also announce that he was resigning his seat in the House, sometime before the start of the 106th Congress on January 5, 1999.

A MESSAGE FROM THE SPEAKER

Today I have reached a difficult personal decision. I will not be a candidate for Speaker of the 106th Congress. The Republican conference needs to be unified, and it is time for me to move forward where I believe I still have a significant role to play for our country and our party. My party will have my full support, and I will do all I can to help us win in 2000.

I urge my colleagues to pick leaders who can both reconcile and discipline, who can work together and communicate effectively. They have my prayers and my thoughts as they undertake this task.

I want to thank everyone whose friendship and support has made these years enjoyable. Marianne and I are grateful to the citizens of Georgia who gave us the wonderful opportunity to represent them and to my Republican colleagues who became our extended family. Thank you and God bless you.

Newt Gingrich
Speaker of the House

The statement was obtained from the Web site of Speaker Newt Gingrich, *http://speakernews.house.gov.*

Bibliography

GENERAL REFERENCES

Bacon, Donald C., Roger H. Davidson, and Morton Keller, eds. *The Encyclopedia of the United States Congress,* 4 vols. New York: Simon & Schuster, 1995.

Biographical Directory of the United States Congress, 1774–1989: Bicentennial Edition. Washington, D.C.: U.S. Government Printing Office, 1989.

Christianson, Stephen G. *Facts About the Congress.* New York: H. W. Wilson, 1996.

Congressional Quarterly. *Congress A to Z,* 2d ed. Washington, D.C.: Congressional Quarterly, 1993.

Congressional Quarterly. *Guide to Congress,* 4th ed. Washington, D.C.: Congressional Quarterly, 1991.

Levy, Leonard W., and Louis Fisher, eds. *Encyclopedia of the American Presidency,* 4 vols. New York: Simon & Schuster, 1994.

BOOKS AND ARTICLES

Allen, W. B., ed. *Works of Fisher Ames as Published by Seth Ames,* Vols. I and II. Reprint. Indianapolis: LibertyClassics, 1983.

Ashby, LeRoy, and Rod Gramer. *Fighting the Odds: The Life of Senator Frank Church.* Pullman: Washington State University Press, 1994.

Baker, Richard Allan. *The Senate of the United States: A Bicentennial History.* Malabar, Fla.: Robert E. Krieger Publishing, 1988.

Baker, Richard Allan, and Roger H. Davidson. *First Among Equals: Outstanding Senate Leaders of the Twentieth Century.* Washington, D.C.: Congressional Quarterly, 1991.

Barry, John M. *The Ambition and the Power.* New York: Viking Press, 1989.

Beschloss, Michael R., ed. *Taking Charge: The Johnson White House Tapes, 1963–1964.* New York: Simon & Schuster, 1997.

Bickford, Charlene, Kenneth R. Bowling, Helen E. Veit, William C. DiGiacomantonio, and Linda Grant DePauw, eds. *Documentary History of the First Federal Congress of the United States of America.* 14 vols. to date. Baltimore: Johns Hopkins University Press, 1972—.

Biskupic, Joan, and Elder Witt. *The Supreme Court and the Powers of the American Government.* Washington, D.C.: Congressional Quarterly, 1997.

Blain, James G. *Twenty Years of Congress: From Lincoln to Garfield with a Review of the Events Which Led to the Political Revolution of 1860,* 2 vols. Norwich, Conn.: Henry Bill Publishing, 1884.

Bolling, Richard. *House Out of Order.* New York: E. P. Dutton, 1964.

———. *Power in the House: A History of the Leadership of the House of Representatives.* New York: Capricorn Books, 1968.

Bowling, Kenneth R., and Helen E. Veit, eds. *The Diary of William Maclay and Other Notes on Senate Debates.* Baltimore: Johns Hopkins University Press, 1988.

Bradley, Phillips, ed. *Democracy in America, by Alexis de Tocqueville: The Henry Reeve Text as Revised by Francis Bowen,* 2 vols. New York: Alfred A. Knopf, 1963.

Brown, George Rothwell. *The Leadership of Congress.* Indianapolis: Bobbs-Merrill, 1922.

Bryce, James. *The American Commonwealth,* 2 vols. [originally published in 1893]. New York: Macmillan, 1901.

Byrd, Robert C. *The Senate, 1789–1989,* 4 vols. Washington: U.S. Government Printing Office, 1989–1993.

———. *The Senate of the Roman Republic: Addresses on the History of Roman Constitutionalism.* Washington, D.C.: U.S. Government Printing Office, 1995.

Cannon, Clarence. *Cannon's Precedents of the House of Representatives, Including References to Provisions of the United States Constitution, the Laws, and Decisions of the United States Senate.* Washington: U.S. Government Printing Office, 1935.

Carr, Robert K. *The House Committee on Un-American Activities, 1945–1950.* Ithaca, N.Y.: Cornell University Press, 1952.

Cunningham, Noble E., Jr., ed. *Circular Letters of Congressmen to their Constituents, 1789–1829,* 3 vols. Chapel Hill: University of North Carolina Press, 1978.

Currie, James T. *The United States House of Representatives.* Malabar, Fla.: Robert E. Krieger Publishing, 1988.

Davidson, Roger H., and Walter J. Oleszek. *Congress and Its Members,* 4th ed. Washington, D.C.: CQ Press, 1994.

Davidson, Roger H., Walter J. Oleszek, Susan Webb Hammond, and Raymond W. Smock. *Masters of the House: Congressional Leadership over Two Centuries.* Boulder, Colo.: Westview Press, 1998.

Dickens, Charles. *American Notes* [originally published in 1842], 2 vols. New York: St. Martin's, 1985.

Druckman, Mason. *Wayne Morse: A Political Biography.* Portland: Oregon Historical Society Press, 1997.

Emery, Fred. *Watergate: The Corruption of American Politics and the Fall of Richard Nixon.* New York: Time Books, 1994.

Fenno, Richard F., Jr. *Home Style: House Members in Their Districts.* Boston: Little, Brown, 1978.

Foner, Eric. *Reconstruction: America's Unfinished Revolution, 1863–1877.* New York: Harper & Row, 1988.

Gillespie, Ed, and Bob Schellhas, eds. *Contract with America: The Bold Plan by Rep. Newt Gingrich, Rep. Dick Armey and the House Republicans to Change the Nation.* New York: Time Books, 1994.

Haines, Wilder H. "The Congressional Caucus of Today," in *The American Political Science Review,* Vol. IX. Baltimore, Md.: Waverly Press, 1915.

Hamilton, Charles V. *Adam Clayton Powell, Jr.: The Political Biography of an American Dilemma.* New York: Collier Books, 1991.

Hinsdale, Burke A., ed. *The Works of James Abram Garfield,* 2 vols. Boston: James B. Osgood and Co., 1883.

Jackson, Carlton. *Presidential Vetoes, 1792–1945.* Athens: University of Georgia Press, 1967.

Jefferson, Thomas. *A Manual of Parliamentary Practice for the Use of the Senate of the United States* [reprint of first edition, 1801, Senate Doc. 103–8]. Washington: U.S. Government Printing Office, 1993.

Jensen, Merrill, Robert A. Becker, Gordon DenBoer, et al., eds. *The Documentary History of the First Federal Elections 1788–1790,* 4 vols. Madison: University of Wisconsin Press, 1976–1989.

Johnson, Andrew. *Trial of Andrew Johnson, President of the United States, on Impeachment by the House of Representatives for High Crimes and Misdemeanors,* 3 vols. Washington, D.C.: U.S. Government Printing Office, 1868.

Josephy, Alvin M. *The American Heritage History of the Congress of the United States.* New York: American Heritage, 1975.

Karnow, Stanley. *Vietnam: A History.* New York: Viking Press, 1983.

Kutler, Stanley I. *The Wars of Watergate: The Last Crisis of Richard Nixon.* New York: W. W. Norton, 1990.

Luce, Robert. *Legislative Assemblies: Their Framework, Make-Up, Character, Characteristics, Habits and Manners.* Boston: Houghton Mifflin, 1924.

McNamara, Robert S. *In Retrospect: The Tragedy and Lesson of Vietnam.* New York: Time Books, 1995.

MacNeil, Neil. *Forge of Democracy: The House of Representatives.* New York: David McKay Company, 1963.

Martin, Joe. *My First Fifty Years in Politics, As Told to Robert J. Donovan.* New York: McGraw-Hill, 1960.

Mikva, Abner J., and Patti B. Saris. *The American Congress: The First Branch.* New York: Franklin Watts, 1983.

Nemerov, Howard. *Trying Conclusion: New and Selected Poems, 1961–1991.* Chicago: University of Chicago Press, 1991.

O'Neill, Thomas P., Jr. (with William Novak). *Man of the House: The Life and Political Memoirs of Speaker Tip O'Neill.* New York: Random House, 1987.

Peters, Ronald M., Jr. *The American Speakership: The Office in Historical Perspective,* 2d ed. Baltimore: Johns Hopkins University Press, 1997.

_____. *The Speaker: Leadership in the U.S. House of Representatives.* Washington, D.C.: Congressional Quarterly, 1995.

Peterson, Merrill, D. *The Great Triumvirate: Webster, Clay, and Calhoun.* New York: Oxford University Press, 1987.

Pierson, George Wilson. *Tocqueville in America.* Reprint. Baltimore: Johns Hopkins University Press, 1996.

Remini, Robert V. *Henry Clay: Statesman for the Union.* New York: W. W. Norton, 1991.

_____. *Daniel Webster: The Man and His Time.* New York: W. W. Norton, 1997.

Ritchie, Donald A. *Press Gallery: Congress and the Washington Correspondents.* Cambridge, Mass.: Harvard University Press, 1991.

Sargent, Nathan. *Public Men and Events: From the Commencement of Mr. Monroe's Administration, in 1817, to the Close of Mr. Fillmore's Administration, in 1853,* Vol. II. Philadelphia: J. B. Lippincott, 1875.

Schlesinger, Arthur, Jr., and Roger Bruns, eds. *Congress Investigates: A Documentary History, 1792–1974,* 5 vols. New York: Chelsea House Publishers in association with R. R. Bowker, 1975.

Starr, Kenneth W. *The Starr Report: The Findings of Independent Counsel Kenneth W. Starr on President Clinton and the Lewinksy Affair.* New York: PublicAffairs, 1998.

Sterling, Bryan B., and Frances N. Sterling. *Will Rogers's World: America's Foremost political Humorist Comments on the Twenties and Thirties—and on the Eighties and Nineties.* New York: M. Evans, 1989.

Tocqueville, Alexis de. *Democracy in America* [originally published in 1835], 2 vols. New York: Alfred A. Knopf, 1963.

Wright, Jim. *Worth It All: My War for Peace.* Washington, D.C.: Brassey's (U.S.), 1993.

Wilson, Woodrow. *Congressional Government: A Study in American Politics* [originally published in 1885]. Reprint of 15th ed. Gloucester, Mass.: Peter Smith, 1973.

NEWSPAPER ARTICLES

Boston Gazette, March 26, 1812, "A New Species of Monster which appeared in Essex South District in January last" [cartoon on the gerrymander].

Frank Leslie's Illustrated Newspaper, February 20, 1858, "The Congressional Row."

Washington Post, April 22, 1889 and May 6, 1889, "The House Rules: Majorities, not Minorities Must Govern" [survey].

Washington Post, March 1, 1890, "Nearly a Fatal Shot: Ex-Congressman Taulbee Wounded by Correspondent Kincaid."

Washington Post, July 3, 1915, "Blast Shakes Capitol and Wrecks Reception Room on Senate Side."

GOVERNMENT PUBLICATIONS

American State Papers, various volumes.

Annals of Congress, various volumes.

Committee Reform Amendments of 1974, Explanation of H. Res. 988 as Adopted by the House of Representatives, October 8, 1974. Washington, D.C.: U.S. Government Printing Office, 1974.

Confirmation Hearings on Federal Appointments: Hearings Before the Committee on the Judiciary United States Senate, 100th Congress, 2d session, on Confirmation Hearings on Appointments to the Federal Judiciary. Washington, D.C.: U.S. Government Printing Office, 1989.

Congressional Globe, various issues.

Congressional Record, various issues.

Hearings of the Committee on the Judiciary House of Representatives, Ninety-Third Congress, Second Session, pursuant to H. Res.

803: A Resolution Authorizing and Directing the Committee on the Judiciary to Investigate Whether Sufficient Grounds Exist for the House of Representatives to Exercise its Constitutional Power to Impeach Richard M. Nixon, President of the United States. Washington, D.C.: U.S. Government Printing Office, 1974.

House Report, *Investigation of Un-American Activities and Propaganda: Report of the Special Committee on Un-American Activities pursuant to H. Res. 282 (75th Congress).* Washington, D.C.: U.S. Government Printing Office, 1939.

Investigation of Korean-American Relations: Report of the Subcommittee on International Organizations of the committee on International Relations, United States House of Representatives. Washington, D.C.: U.S. Government Printing Office, 1978.

Investigations of Senators Joseph R. McCarthy and William Benton pursuant to S. Res. 187 and S. Res. 304: Report of the Subcommittee on Privileges and Elections to the Committee on Rules and Administration. Washington, D.C.: U.S. Government Printing Office, 1952.

Register of Debates in Congress, various volumes.

Senate Report, Nos. 205–254, *Investigation of Senator Alan Cranston. United States Congressional Series Set, Serial Number 14051.* Washington: U.S. Government Printing Office, 1993.

Senate Report, *Investigation of Whitewater Development Corporation and Related Matters: Final Report of the Special Committee to Investigate Whitewater Development Corporation and Related Matters together with Additional and Minority Views.* Washington, D.C.: U.S. Government Printing Office, 1996.

Senate Report, *Third Interim Report of the Special Committee to Investigate Organized Crime in Interstate Commerce pursuant to S. Res. 202 (81st Congress): A Resolution to Investigate Gambling and Racketeering Activities.* Washington, D.C.: U.S. Government Printing Office, 1951.

Statutes at Large, various volumes.

Tansill, Charles C., ed. *Documents Illustrative of the Formation of the Union of the American States.* House document no. 398, 69th Congress, 1st session. Washington, D.C.: U.S. Government Printing Office, 1927.

Walsh, Lawrence E. *Final Report of the Independent Counsel for Iran/Contra Matters,* 3 vols. Washington D.C.: U.S. Government Printing Office, 1993.

Index

Abington School District v. Schempp, 523
Abrams, Elliott, 589
Acheson, Dean, 402, 403
Adams, Clarence, 271
Adams, John
  Indian treaties, 70
  as president pro tempore of the Senate, 53,
    54–55, 98
  presidential election (1800), 94–96
  on presidential title, 57
  relationship with Maclay, 55
  as vice president
    address to the Senate, 54–55
    election notification, 47–48
Adams, John Quincy
  gag rule opponent, 158
  de Tocqueville's visit to America, 149
  War of 1812 negotiator, 111–113
Adams, William, War of 1812 negotiator, 113
Adderley v. Florida, 509
Aetna Life Insurance Co. v. Haworth, 508
African Americans. *See also* Slavery; Slaves
  voting rights, 221
Agnew, Spiro T., honoring Apollo 11 astronauts,
  448–451
Aiken, George D., 406
Aldrin, Edwin "Buzz," Jr., 448, 449, 451
Allen, William, war with Mexico, 167
Allen, William C., 84
Alricks, Ann, 102–103
American Commonwealth (Bryce), 257–261,
  261–266
American Notes (Dickens), 160–163
American Party of Texas v. White, 523, 524
American State Papers series, 117
American System, Henry Clay on, 149, 150–158
Americanism, defined, 352–353
Ames, Fisher
  on the first Congress, 49
  and first quorum of the House, 47
  on House Elections Committee, 52
  on Jay Treaty, 49
Ames, Oakes, and Credit Mobilier scandal, 223–224
Annals of Congress, 117
Anthony, Henry Bowen, 201
Anthony, Susan B., 228–230
Anti-Saloon League, 309, 310
Apollo II space program, 448–451
Apportionment
  for first Congress, 19–21
  limiting size of the House, 299–300
  proportion of suffrage, 7–9
Apportionment Act, 83–84
Appropriations, origination of revenue bills,
  18–19, 21–23, 24
Archbold, John D., 301–303
Archer, William Segar
  establishment of Senate Press Gallery, 160
  war with Mexico, 168
Arens, Henry Martin, 403
Armey, Dick, Contract with America, 608–609
Armstrong, James, 48
Armstrong, Neil A., 448–451
Articles of Confederation, 25
Articles of impeachment, 216–221, 495–497. *See
  also* Johnson, Andrew; Nixon, Richard
Ashmore, John Durant, 196
Associated Press v. U.S., 515
Atomic Energy Act of 1946, 379–384

Bacon, Augustus Octavius, 304
Bacon, Donald C., 325
Bailey, Cleve, 571
Bailey, Theodorus, 95
Baker v. Carr, 508
Baldwin, Abraham
  at Federal Convention of 1787, 7
  investigation of General St. Clair, 80
Banks, Nathaniel P., 225
Barbour, James, 113
Barenblatt v. United States, 421–422
Barkley, Alben William, 343, 362
Barksdale, William, 193–194
Barnwell, Robert, 80
Barr v. Mateo, 471
Barry v. United States ex rel. Cunningham, 530
Bart v. United States, 423
Bassett, Richard, 47, 53
Bates v. Little Rock, 510
Bayard, James A.
  presidential election, 95, 96
  press gallery in the Senate, 159
  on seating of senators from West Virginia, 200
  War of 1812 negotiator, 111–113
Bayly, Thomas Henry, war with Mexico, 169
Bayne, Thomas McKee, 267
Beaumont, August de, 149
Beck, James B., 225
Beckley, John, as first clerk of the House, 47
Bedinger, George M., 103, 104
Belcher, William, 414
Benson, Egbert, 52
Bentley, Alvin, 413, 414
Benton, Thomas Hart
  opposes Compromise of 1850, 177–181
  on de Tocqueville's views on Congress, 149
  war with Mexico, 168
  Webster-Hayne debate, 139
  on westward expansion, 132
Bernstein, Carl, 472
Beschloss, Michael, 441
Beveridge, Albert J., Philippines policy, 274–282
Biden, Joseph R., Jr., 548–549
Bill of Rights, Madison resolution on, 59–67
Bingham, John Armor, 196, 197, 224
Blackmun, Harry Andrew, 469–472
Blaine, James G.
  on Congress at the beginning of the Civil War,
    199–202
  and Credit Mobilier scandal, 223–224
  Mulligan Letters corruption controversy,
    232–238
Blair, Francis P., Jr., 201
Bland, Richard P., 267
Bliss, Cornelius N., 301
Blount, James Henderson, 267, 268, 269
Bocok, Thomas Stanley, 197
Boland Amendments, 588
Boland, Edward, 542, 588
Bolling, Richard, 432–433, 463, 497–506
Bombing incidents. *See under* Violence in the
  Capitol
Borah, William E.
  opposes League of Nations, 315–320
  opposes Versailles Treaty, 323–325
Bork, Robert H., Supreme Court nomination,
  546–563
Boudinot, Elias
  first presidential election, 48

House investigation of General St. Clair, 79, 80
  House Rules Committee chairman, 50, 52
Bourn, Sylvanus, 48
Boyer, Benjamin, and Credit Mobilier scandal, 223,
  224
Boykin, Frank W., 415
Bradley, Joseph, 239
Brandeis, Louis Dembitz, 349
Breckinridge, John C., 200
Breckinridge, William C., 267, 268
Brent, Robert, 99
Bricker, John W., 270
Bridges v. California, 514
Bright, Jesse D., 201
Brooks, James, 223, 224
Brooks, Preston, Sumner beating, 183–185
Broome, [Delegate], at Federal Convention of
  1787, 15, 20
Brown v. Board of Education, 430
Browning, W. J., 273
Bryan, William Jennings, income tax proponent,
  284
Bryce, James, on the House of Representatives,
  257–261
Buchanan, James, congressional investigation of,
  195–197
Buckley, James L., 506
Buckley v. Valeo, 506–532
Budget and Accounting Act of 1921, 320–323,
  482
Bullock v. Carter, 524
Bunker, Berkeley Lloyd, 363
Burch, S., 110
Bureau of the Budget, creation of, 320, 321–322
Burke, Aedanus, constitutional amendments, 61
Burke, Edward Raymond, 343, 344
Burke, James Frances, 287
Burleson, Albert Sidney, 296, 297, 298
Burnett, Henry Cornelius, 196
Burr, Aaron, presidential election (1800), 94–96
Burroughs v. United States, 518, 523, 530
Bush, George, and Iran-contra affair, 587, 588,
  597–601
Butler, Andrew, Sumner beating, 183–185
Butler, Benjamin Franklin, 224
Butler, General Benjamin F., 200
Butler, Josiah, 117
Butler, Pierce
  at Federal Convention of 1787, 3, 5, 7, 8, 12, 13,
    15, 18, 20
  Indian treaties, 70
Byrd, Robert C.
  opposes line-item veto, 603–608, 624
  on Persian Gulf War, 572–577
  on Senate rule, 53
  on Webster-Hayne debate, 138

Caldwell, Josiah, 237, 238
Calhoun, John C.
  Clay on death of, 175–176
  debates with Webster, 171
  war with Mexico, 166–167
  and Webster-Hayne debate, 132
California Bankers Assn. v. Shultz, 518
Cambodia, U.S. invasion, 451–456, 476
Cameron, Simon, 201
Campaign finance
  Buckley v. Valeo case, 506–532
  Clapp Committee investigations, 301–304

contributions and expenditure limitations, 506, 508–516
Covode Committee investigations, 195–197
of presidential campaigns, 522–526
reporting and disclosure requirements, 516–522
Campbell, Lewis D., 185
Cannon, Joseph Gurney, 256, 284–298, 325
Capital, location of. *See* Seat of government
Capitol Building. *See also* Violence in Congress
bombing incidents, 304–307
burning of, 109–110, 304
laying of cornerstone, 84–85
Capitol Guide Service, 463, 467
Capitol police
bombing incident investigation, 304–307
salaries, 227
shootings of, 270
The Capitol's Four Cornerstones (Allen), 84
Carlile, John Snyder, 200
Carpenter, Scott, 435
Carrington, Colonel, 46
Carroll, Daniel
appointed to elections committee, 52
at Federal Convention of 1787, 23
at Washington inauguration, 56, 57
Carter, Jimmy, 476
Case, Francis Higbee, 370, 371, 373–374
Casey, Donald, 591–592, 593
Census, accuracy of, 31
Census Act of 1790, 74–76
Chambers, Whittaker, 403
Champlin, Christopher G., 95
Champlin Refining Co. v. Corp. Commission, 526
Channell, Carl R., 589
Chase, Salmon Portland, 201
Cheney, Ward, 235
Chestnut, Jacob J., 272
Church, Frank, on Vietnam conflict, 448–456
Circular letters, 77
Citron, William Michael, 373
Civil Rights Act of 1866, 209–211
Civil Rights Act of 1957, 426, 430–432
Civil Rights Act of 1964, 437–440
Civil Rights Commission, creation of, 430–431
Civil Service reform, 249–251, 251–254
Claiborne, William Charles Cole, 95
Clapp Committee, 301–304
Clapp, Moses E., 301
Clark, Abraham, 80, 81
Clark, Daniel, 201
Clark, Frank, 298
Clark, James Beauchamp "Champ," 285, 286, 289–290
Clarridge, Duane R., 589
Clay, Henry
American System proponent, 149, 150–158
debates with Webster, 171
eulogy for John C. Calhoun, 175–176
and Missouri Compromise, 125–126
press gallery in the Senate, 159–160
resignation from the Senate, 163–166
War of 1812 negotiator, 108, 111–113
Clayton, Henry De Lamar, 291–292
Clayton, John Middleton, war with Mexico, 167–168
Clerk of the House
duties of, 52
first, John Beckley, 47
and loss of records during War of 1812, 109–110
Clines, Thomas G., 589
Clinton, George, 48
Clinton v. City of New York, 622–626
Clinton, William Jefferson "Bill"
impeachment inquiry, 487
impeachment investigation, 627–628
line-item veto, 603, 624
Whitewater investigation, 614–619, 619–622
Clymer, George, 52
Cobb, Williamson Robert Winfield, 197
Cochran, John Joseph, 369–373

Cochrane, John, 197
Coffee, John M., 352
Cohn, Roy M., 415, 416, 417
Coleman v. Miller, 527
Colfax, Schuyler, 213, 223
Collamer, Jacob, 201
Collins, Michael, 448, 449, 451
Committees. *See standing committees under* House of Representatives; Senate
Communist Party investigations. *See* House Special Committee on Un-American Activities; House Un-American Activities Committee
Communist Party v. Subversive Activities Control Bd., 518
Communists
in government service, 401–404
in the U.S. Army, 415–419
Compensation Act, 71–73
Compensation of Members of Congress, 114–116
Compromise of 1850, 171, 176, 177–181
Compton, Barnes, 268
Congress
descriptions of
by Ames (Fisher), of first Congress, 49
by Blaine (James G.), at beginning of the Civil War, 199–202
by Bryce (James), 257–261, 262–266
by Dickens (Charles), 160–163
by Garfield (James), 241–242
by Longworth (Nicholas), 325–327
by de Tocqueville (Alexis), 149–150
by Rogers (Will), 336–337
by Wilson (Woodrow), 254–255
first quorum, 47–48
history of, 116–117
investigative powers, 79–81. *See also* Congressional investigations
legislative reorganization, 384–399
powers and functions, 25–27
staff size, 385
Congress, First Federal. *See* First Federal Congress
Congressional Budget and Impoundment Control of Act of 1974, 320, 482–487
Congressional Budget Office, establishment of, 483–484
Congressional committees. *See standing committees under* House of Representatives; Senate
Congressional elections
first elections, 45–46
representatives elected by the people, 1–2
senators elected by the people, 300
senators elected by state legislatures, 2–10, 14–15
Congressional Government (Wilson), 254, 256
Congressional investigations
of campaign finance, 195–197, 301–304
and contempt of Congress, 244–247
of General St. Clair, 79–81
Iran-contra affair, 587–597
of Keating Five, 578–583
limitations to, 244–247
of national defense program, 355–359
of presidents
Buchanan, James, 195–197
Clinton, William J., 614–619, 627–628
Nixon, Richard, 472–475, 487–496
Teapot Dome scandal, 328–330
Un-American activities, 352–355, 367–374
Watergate affair, 472–475
Whitewater affair, 614–619
Congressional letters, 77
Congressional petitions
of Alricks, Ann, regarding divorce, 102–103
of Anthony, Susan B., for voting rights, 228–230
of Jones, Absalom, regarding fugitive slaves, 92–93
of Sanduskie warriors, 105–106
on slavery, "gag rule" on, 158
Congressional quorums, 47–48

Connally, Thomas Terry "Tom," 344–347, 349, 362–363, 366, 367
Conscience, Declaration of (Smith), 404–406
Constitution (U.S.)
amendments, 25, 59–67
(12th), 94, 100
(13th), 204
(14th), 211–212, 228
(15th), 221–222
(16th), 284
(17th), 300
(18th), 309, 310
(19th), 228, 310
(20th), 331–332
(21st), 310, 332
(23d), 433–434
(27th), 59, 114, 468–469, 583
Article I
commerce clause, 127
District of Columbia government, 230–232
powers of Congress, 25–27
war powers declaration, 108–109
Article II, oath of office, 58–59
Preamble, 25
ratification, 45, 46, 59
Speech or Debate Clause, 469–472
Continental Navy, 86
Contract with America, 608–609
Cooper, George William, 267, 268
Cooper, Gordon, 435
Cooper, John Sherman, 451
Corruption in government, 40
bribery of members accusations, 223–225
campaign finance, 195–197
Credit Mobilier scandal, 223–225
Keating Five investigation, 578–583
and Koreagate, 532–539
Mulligan Letters, 232–238
political patronage reform, 249–254
Court system, federal, 73–74
Cousins v. Wigoda, 510
Covert, James Way, 267
Covode, John, 195–197
Cowles, Charles H., 267, 269
Cox, Edward Eugene, 371–372, 374
Cox v. Louisiana, 509
Craige, Francis Burton, 196
Cranston, Alan, 578–583
Credit Mobilier scandal, 223–225
Crisp, Charles Frederick, 267, 268, 269
CSC v. Letter Carriers, 510, 511
Cuban missile crisis, 475
Cumberland Road Act, 104–105
Cummings, Homer S., 341

Dalton, Tristram
Indian treaties, 71
on presidential title, 57
Dalzell, John, 267, 285, 286, 287, 288, 292
D'Amato, Alphonse, Whitewater investigation, 614, 620
Dane, Nathan, 132, 140
Daniel Webster: The Man and His Time (Remini), 138, 171
Daugherty, Harry M., 328
Davidson, Roger H., 284
Davis, Clifford, 413, 414
Davis, David, 222
Davis, Garrett, war with Mexico, 166, 168–169
Davis, Jefferson
farewell address to the Senate, 197–199
Dawes, Henry Laurens, 223, 224–225
Dayton, [Delegate], at Federal Convention of 1787, 18
Dean, John, 472
Declarations of war
with Germany, 307–309
with Great Britain and Ireland, 108–109
with Spain, 273

DeConcini, Dennis, 578–583
Defense program investigation, 355
Democracy in America (de Tocqueville), 149
Dempsey, John J., 355
Dent, George, 95
Derwinski, Edward J., on Koreagate, 538–539
Dickens, Charles, description of Congress, 160–163, 257
Dickinson, Philemon, at Federal Convention of 1787, 5, 6, 7, 10, 23
Dies Committee. *See* House Special Committee on Un-American Activities
Dies, Martin, Jr., 352, 355, 368, 415
Diggs, Charles, 231
Dirksen, Everett McKinley, and Civil Rights Act of 1964, 437–440
Distilled Spirits Act, 78–79
District of Columbia
    establishment of federal district, 76
    government reorganization, 230–232
    home rule, 99, 231, 478–482
    House Committee on, 106–107
    voting rights for citizens of, 433–434
District of Columbia Self-Government and Governmental Reorganization Act of 1873, 478–482
Divorces, petition for, 102–103
Dixon, James, 201
Documents Illustrative of the Formation of the American States (Tansill, ed.), 1
Dole, Robert "Bob," 457, 461, 462
Domestic Revenue Act, 78–79
Donohue, Harold Daniel, 490–491
Douglas, Albert, 289, 290, 292
Douglas, Stephen, and Kansas-Nebraska Act, 181–183
Doxey, Wall, 364
Dred Scott Decision (*Scott v. Sanford*), 185–192, 211
Dumbarton Oaks conference, 374
Duran, Gustave, 402
Durham, Israel W., 303
Duties. *See also* Taxes
    on distilled spirits, 78–79
    Tariff Bill, 67–69, 78
Dwight, John Wilbur, 297, 298

Eastern R. Conf. v. Noerr Motors, 515
Eastland, James O., 430
Eberharter, Herman Peter, 371
Edmundson, Henry, Sumner beating, 183–185
Eighteenth amendment to the Constitution, 309
Eisenhower, Dwight D., and McCarthy investigations, 415–416
Elections. *See* Congressional elections; Presidential elections; Vice presidential elections
Electoral Commission of 1877, 238–240
Eliot, Thomas Dawes, 224
Ellsberg, Daniel, 469
Ellsworth, Oliver
    at Federal Convention of 1787, 9, 10, 11–12, 14–15, 17
    communications with clerk of the House, 57
    first quorum of the Senate, 47, 48
    Indian treaties, 70, 71
    Senate rules committee, 53
    vice presidential duties, 55
Ellsworth, Roger, federal court system, 73
Elmer, Jonathan, 47
Emory, Major General William H., 214, 219
Emspak v. United States, 423
Engel, Albert Joseph, 373
Enloe, Benjamin A., 267, 268
Erhlichman, John, 472
Ervin, Sam, 472
Etheridge, Emerson, 201
Ethics in government. *See* Corruption in government
Everson v. Bd. of Education, 523

Fallon, George H., 413, 414
Farley, James Aloysius, 341–342
Federal budget process, 320–323, 482–487
Federal Convention of 1787, notes of debate, 1–25
Federal court system, 73–74
Federal district. *See also* District of Columbia
    establishment of, 76
    government of, 99
    House District of Columbia Committee, 106–107
Federal Election Campaign Act of 1971, 506
Federal Election Commission, establishment of, 506, 526–532
Federal government, power over state governments, 118–124, 127–132
Federal-Aid Highway Act of 1956, 419–421
Federalist, 28–45, 487, 528. *See also* Hamilton, Alexander; Jay, John; Madison, James
    47, 528
    52, 28
    53, 28–30
    54, 30–31
    55, 31–33
    56, 33
    57, 33–34
    58, 34–35
    59, 36
    62, 36–38
    63, 38–40
    64, 40–42
    65, 42–43
    66, 43–45
Fernandez, Joseph F., 589
Fessenden, William Pitt, 201
Few, William, 47
Fiers, Alan D., Jr., 589
Fifteenth amendment to the Constitution, 221–222
Filibuster, record-setting, 426–430
Fillmore, Millard, 171
    majority views, 614–619
    minority views, 619–622
Findley, William, 104, 107
First branch. *See* House of Representatives
First Federal Congress, 76
Fish, Hamilton, 364–365, 367
Fisher, Fred, 416, 418
Fisher, Warren, Jr., 235, 237
Fiske, Robert B., Jr., 614
Fitzgerald, John Joseph, 293–294
Fitzsimons, Thomas, House investigation of General St. Clair, 80, 81
Flag (U.S.)
    burning of, 118
    design of, 117–118
    preservation of Fort McHenry flag, 331
Flinn, William, 303
Florence, Thomas Birch, 195–197
Foelker, Otto Godfrey, 286, 290
Foot, Samuel A., 132
Foot, Solomon, 201
Foote, Henry, 177
Ford, Gerald, 476, 487–488, 495
Foreign policy
    Arthur Vandenberg on, 374–379
    Philippines-U.S. policy, 274–282
Foster, Abiel, 95
Foster, Lafayette Sabine, 201, 213
Fourteenth amendment to the Constitution, 211–212
Fowler, John, 95
France, XYZ Affair, 91–92
Franklin, Benjamin
    at Federal Convention of 1787, 8, 17, 19
    on the republic, 25
Frost, J. T., 109–110
Frye, William Pierce, 237
Fugitive Slave Act of 1793, 92–93
Fulbright, James William, 442

Gagarin, Yuri A., 434
Gaines, Joseph Holt, 289
Gales, Joseph, Jr., 116–117
Gallagher, Cornelius, 532
Gallatin, Albert
    presidential election, 95
    War of 1812 negotiator, 111–113
Galloway, George B., 385
Gambier, Lord James, War of 1812 negotiator, 111–113
Garfield, James Abram
    assassination of, 250
    and Credit Mobilier scandal, 223
    describing Congress, 241–242
    on House rules, 286
General Accounting Office (GAO), creation of, 320, 322–323
George, Clair E., 589
Germany
    World War I declaration, 307–309
    World War II declaration, 365–367
Gerry, Elbridge
    at Federal Convention of 1787, 1, 2, 3, 6, 7, 8, 13, 14, 17, 18, 19, 21, 22, 24
    and gerrymandering, 107
Gerrymandering, origins of, 107–108
Ghorum, [Delegate], at Federal Convention of 1787, 11, 12, 14, 15, 20
Gibbons, Thomas, 127, 132
Gibbons v. Ogden, 127–132
Gibson, John M., 270
Giles, William B., House investigation of General St. Clair, 79, 80, 81
Gilman, Nicholas, 52
Gingrich, Newt
    charges against Speaker Wright, 564
    Contract with America, 608–609
    debate with Tip O'Neill, 542–548
    ethics violations, 622–624
    resignation, 628–629
    as Speaker of the House, 610–614
Ginsberg, Douglas H., 549
Glenn, John H., Jr., 434–436, 578–583
Glidden Co. v. Zdanok, 527
Glover, John Montgomery, 238
Goldsborough, Robert, 111
Goldwater, Barry, 457, 461–462
Good, James W., budgetary reform, 320
Goodhue, Benjamin, constitutional amendments, 60
Goodling, William F., on Koreagate, 538–539
Goulburn, Henry, War of 1812 negotiator, 111–113
Government ethics. *See* Corruption in government
Government, seat of. *See* Seat of government
Governments in antiquity, 40
Gravel, Mike, 469
Gravel v. United States, 469–472
Great Britain
    Jay Treaty with, 88–90
    War of 1812, 108–109
"Great Compromise" (Connecticut Compromise), 1
Great Depression, Huey Long's "Every Man a King" speech, 333–336
Great Triumvirate: Webster, Clay, and Calhoun (Peterson), 171
Gregg, Andrew, 104
Grew, Joseph, 402
Griswold, Roger
    dispute with Lyon, 91–92
    presidential election (1800), 95
Gronna, Asle Jorgenson, 295, 307
Grow, Galusha A.
    brawl on House floor, 193–194
    Buchanan investigation, 196–197
    as Speaker of the House, 201
Gunn, James, Indian treaties, 70
Gwin, William M., 201

Habib, Philip, 533, 535
Hakim, Albert, 589
Haldeman, H. R., 472
Hale, John P., 201
Hamilton, Alexander
    and army defeat under General St. Clair, 79–81
    Federalist papers, 28–45
    mint, establishment of, 81
    and presidential veto, 84
    on tariffs, 67, 78
    at Federal Convention of 1787, 9, 10–11, 12, 14,
        16–17, 25
Hamilton, Robert, 235
Hammond, Susan Webb, 284
Hampton & Co. v. United States, 528
Hancock, John, 48
Hanna, Richard, 532, 535–536
Harding, Warren G., 323
Hardwick, Thomas William, 297
Harper, Robert Goodloe, 92
Harris, John Thomas, 197
Harrison, Robert H., 48
Hartley, Thomas, House investigation of General
    St. Clair, 80–81
Hatch, Orrin G., Bork Supreme Court nomination,
    550–552
Hatfield, Mark, opposes Vietnam war, 457–463
Haver v. Yaker, 222
Hayes, Everis Anson, 294
Hayes, Rutherford B., 238–240
Hayes, Walter Ingalls, 268
Hayne, Robert Y., debate with Daniel Webster,
    132–137, 138–148
Healey, Arthur D., 355
Helvering v. Davis, 523
Hendrickson, Robert C., 406
Henry Clay: Statesman for the Union (Remini), 171,
    176
Hickman, John, 193–194
Hill, Joseph Lister, 363–364, 366, 367
Hillhouse, James, 80
Hindman, Thomas Carmichael, 196
Hiss, Alger, 367, 403, 404
Hitchcock, Gilbert Monell, 307–309
Hoar, George Frisbie
    on Philippines self-government, 282–283
    U.S. policy toward Philippines, 274
Holman, William Steele, 225
Hopkins, Harry, 342
Horr, Roswell G., 247
House Out of Order (Bolling), 463
House of Representatives. *See also* Clerk of the
        House; Representatives; Sergeant-at-arms;
        Speaker of the House
    biennial elections, 28–30
    bill procedures, 51
    brawl on the floor of, 193–194
    Bryce's description of, 257–261
    Committee on Elections, 50, 103
    Committee on the Judiciary, 487–495
    Committee on Privileges, 91–92
    Committee on Public Lands, creation of, 103–104
    Committee on Science and Astronautics, 432–433
    committee procedures, 51–52
    committee system reform, 497–506
    creation of, 1
    election of members, 25, 26, 28–30
    eligibility of members, 12–14
    first quorum, 47
    Legislative Counsel Office, 468
    powers and functions, 25–27
    public gallery, 159
    purposes of, 33
    records destroyed during War of 1812, 109–110
    rules of procedure, 49–53, 243–244, 266–270,
        284–298
    salaries for members, 227–228
    Select Committee to Investigate Alleged
        Corruption in Government, 195–197

size of, 299–300
special investigative committee, on army defeat
    under General St. Clair, 79–81
standing committees, 103–104, 384, 388–392,
    464, 466, 497–506
term of office, 10–11
de Tocqueville's description of, 149–150
House Special Committee on Un-American
    Activities (Dies Committee), 352–355, 367,
    401
House Un-American Activities Committee
    (HUAC), 352, 367–374, 401, 421–425
Hughes, Charles Evans, 337–341
Hughes, James Hurd, 343
Humphrey, Hubert, 437, 441
    as presidential candidate, 451
Humphrey's Executor v. United States, 530, 532
Hunt, Ward, 228
Hunter, Robert Mercer Taliaferro, 200
Huntington, Benjamin, 52
Huntington, Samuel, 48
Hunton, Eppa, 234

Immigration and Naturalization Service v. Chadha,
    539–541
Impeachment
    presidential
        of Clinton, William, 627–628
        of Johnson, Andrew, 216–221, 627
        of Nixon, Richard, 495–497
Impeachment powers, 26, 42–43
    of Congress discussed, 24
    impeachable offense, 487
    Senate as court of impeachment, 43–45
    Senate vs. Supreme Court, 42–43
    Senate's power of impeachment, 584–587
Imperialism (U.S.), Philippines policy, 274–283
In Retrospect: The Tragedy and Lessons of Vietnam
    (McNamara), 441
Inaugurations, presidential, of George Washing-
    ton, 56–57
Inaugurations (presidential), and "Lame Duck"
    amendment, 331–332
Income tax, federal, 202–204, 284
Indian treaties, 69–71
Indians, hostilities with, 79–81
Interstate commerce, 127–132
Interstate highway system, 104–105, 419–421
Iran-contra investigations, 587–597, 597–603
Iraq. *See* Persian Gulf War
Ireland, War of 1812, 108–109
Isolationism
    opposition to League of Nations, 315–320
    opposition to Versailles Treaty, 323–325
Italy, World War II declaration, 365–367
Ives, Irving M., 406
Izard, Ralph
    at Washington inauguration, 56, 57
    Indian treaties, 70

Jackson, Andrew
    assassination attempt, 272
    opposes Clay's American System, 149, 150
    veto of Second Bank recharter, 118, 150
Jackson, Henry "Scoop," 457, 462
Jackson, James
    constitutional amendments, 60
    on Louisiana Purchase, 101
Jackson, Thomas J., 624
James, Ollie Murray, 287, 297
James v. Valtierra, 511
Japan, World War II declaration, 361, 362–365
Jay, John
    Federalist 64, 28, 40–42
    presidential election (1789), 48
    presidential election (1800), 94
Jay Treaty, 49, 88–90
Jefferson, Thomas
    House rules of procedure, 50, 98

library purchased for Library of Congress, 96–97,
    110–111
and the Louisiana Purchase Treaty, 100
presidential election (1800), 94–96
and presidential veto, 83
Jenckes, Thomas A., 250
Jenifer, [Delegate], at Federal Convention of 1787,
    14
Jenness v. Fortson, 524, 525
Jensen, Benton, 413, 415
Johnson, Andrew
    impeachment of, 205, 213–216, 216–221, 627
    presidential reconstruction plan, 204, 212
    as senator, 200
Johnson, Lyndon Baines
    Civil Rights Act supporter, 427, 429, 430
    and space exploration, 432, 433
    and Tonkin Gulf Resolution, 440, 441–442, 476
    and Vietnam war, 451
Johnson, Richard M., compensation of members of
    Congress, 114–116
Johnson, William Samuel
    at Federal Convention of 1787, 15, 25
    presidential election, 47, 48
Joint Committee on the Organization of Congress,
    385
Jones, Absalom, 92–93
Jordan, Barbara, 493–495
Journal of proceedings, 26, 116
Judd, Walter H., 413, 415
Judiciary Act of 1789, 73–74

Kansas-Nebraska Act, 181–183, 185
Karnow, Stanley, 457
Kasson, John Adam, 235
Keating, Charles H., Jr., 578–583
Keating Five, 578–583
Kefauver Committee, 410–413
Kefauver, Estes, 410–413
Keifer, Joseph Warren, 288
Keitt, Laurence
    and brawl on the House floor, 193–194
    Sumner beating, 183–185
Kelley, William Darrah, 223–224, 235
Kennedy, Edward M., Bork Supreme Court nomi-
    nation, 549–550, 558
Kennedy, John F.
    assassination, 437
    and Civil Rights Act, 437
    and Cuban missile crisis, 475–476
    and space exploration, 433, 434
Kenny, Mary Jane, 402
Kerley, Larry E., 403
Key, Francis Scott, 330
Key, Philip Barton, 106–107
Kilbourn, Hallet, 244
Kilbourn v. Thompson, 244–247, 422–423, 471
Kincaid, Charles E., shooting of Taulbee, 270–272
King, Rufus, at Federal Convention of 1787, 2, 7–8,
    10, 11, 12, 13, 21, 25
King, Martin Luther, Jr., 437
Kissinger, Henry, 451
Kittera, John Wilkes, 80
Knott, James Proctor, 234, 235, 237, 238
Knowland, William Fife, 428
Knox, General Henry
    and army defeat under General St. Clair, 79–81
    Indian treaties, 70–71
Knox, Philander C., 303
Koreagate, 532–539
Korean conflict, MacArthur relieved of command,
    407
Kovacs v. Cooper, 509
Kusper v. Pontikes, 508, 511

La Follette, Robert, Jr., 385
Labor unions, collective bargaining rights, 337–341
"Lame Duck" amendment, 331–332
Landrum, John Morgan, 196

Lane, James H., 200
Langdon, John, as first president pro-tempore, 47, 48
Latham, Milton S., 201
Latrobe, Benjamin Henry, 109
Laurance, John, 67
League of Nations, opposition to, 315–320
Lee, Richard Henry, 47, 48
  at Washington inauguration, 56, 57
  constitutional amendments, 67
  Indian treaties, 70, 71
  Senate rules committee, 53
Legislative Reorganization Act of 1946, 384–399, 498
Legislative Reorganization Act of 1970, 463–468, 498
Lend-Lease Act, 359–360
Lenroot, Irvine Luther, 291
Lewinsky, Monica, 627, 629
Library of Congress
  Congressional Research Service, 463, 466–467
  establishment of, 96–97
  fire of 1851, 304
  Legislative Reference Service, 395, 463
  purchase of the library of Thomas Jefferson, 110–111
Lincoln, Abraham
  addressing Congress at beginning of the Civil War, 202
  assassination, 204
  call for troops for the Civil War, 200
  Wilmot Proviso supporter, 170
Lincoln, Benjamin, 48
Line-item veto. See Veto
Linn, Lewis Fields, 160
Livermore, Samuel, constitutional amendments, 67
Livingston, Robert, swearing in George Washington, 56
Lobbying, regulation of, 397–398
Lodge, Henry Cabot, 315
Long, Huey, "Every Man a King" speech, 333–336
Longworth, Nicholas, as Speaker of the House, 325–327
Lott, Trent, 491–492, 543
Loudenslager, Henry Clay, 297
Louisiana Purchase, Senate debate on, 100–101
Lubin v. Panish, 523, 524
Lucas, Scott Wike, 363
Luther v. Borden, 207
Lynn, James, 95
Lyon, General Nathaniel, 200
Lyon, Matthew, dispute with Griswold, 91–92

Maas, Melvin, 272
MacArthur, General Douglas, speech before Congress, 407–410
Mace, as symbol for the House, 50
Mack, John, 571
Maclay, William
  at first quorum of the Senate, 47
  diary of, 55–57, 69–71
  on the inauguration of George Washington, 56–57
  as member of first Senate rules committee, 53
  relationship with John Adams, 55
  on vice presidential duties, 55–56
Macon, Nathaniel, 92, 95
Madden, Martin Barnaby, 297
Madden, Ray, 463
Madison, James
  Bill of Rights resolution, 59–67
  constitutional amendments, 60, 61, 62–66, 67
  election campaign, 46–47
  Federal Convention of 1787, notes on, 1–25
  Federalist papers, 28–45
  House investigation of General St. Clair, 81
  letter to Randolph, 46–47
  and War of 1812, 108, 111
Magruder, Colonel George, 109–110

Magruder, Patrick, 109
Man of the House (O'Neill), 542
Mann, James Robert, 287, 288, 289, 293
Mansfield, Mike, 437, 457, 460–461
Manual of Parliamentary Procedure (Jefferson), 50, 98
Marcantonio, Vito Anthony, 371
March on Washington (1963), 437
Marshall, John
  Gibbons v. Ogden decision, 127–132
  McCullough v. Maryland decision, 118–124
Marshall, Thomas Riley, 307–308
Martin, Dave, House committee system reform, 497–506
Martin, Eben Wever, 288, 289, 290–291, 292
Martin, Joseph William, Jr., 362, 364, 371, 372, 407
  on shooting on the House floor, 413–415
Martin, L., at Federal Convention of 1787, 9, 13, 19
Martin, Thomas E., 415
  interstate highway system, 419–421
Mason, Jonathan, at Federal Convention of 1787, 1–2, 4, 7, 9, 10, 12, 13, 18–19, 21, 24
Mason, George, and bill of rights, 59
Mason, James, 171
Mason, N. M., 355
Masters of the House: Congressional Leadership Over the Centuries (Davidson, Hammond, and Smock), 284
Maverick, Maury, 352
McCain, John, 578–583
McCall, Samuel Walker, 292, 294
McCarran, Patrick Anthony, 348, 349
McCarthy, Eugene, 506
McCarthy, Joseph R.
  on Communists in government service, 401–404
  U.S. Army investigations, 415–419
McCarthyism, 401
McComb, Henry S., 223
McCormack, John William
  honoring Apollo 11 astronauts, 448
  and House Un-American Activities Committee, 372–373
  and Powell case, 446–448
  World War II war declarations, 362, 364, 365, 367
McCrary, George W., 225
McCreary, James B., 267, 268, 271
McCullough, David, 407, 563
McCullough, James W., 118
McCullough v. Maryland, 118–124, 523, 530
McDougall, James A., 201
McFarland, Ernest William, 364
McFarlane, Robert C., 589
McGovern, George, opposes Vietnam War, 457–463
McGovern-Hatfield Amendment, 451, 457–463
McGrain, John J., 328
McGrain v. Daugherty, 244, 328–330, 423
McHenry, [Delegate], at Federal Convention of 1787, 23, 24
McKinley, William, and Spanish-American War, 273
McLean, General, 200
McNamara, Robert, 440, 441
McNary, Charles Linza, 363
Mead, James Michael, 366, 367
Members, House of Representatives. See Representatives
Memorial of Sundry Citizens of the City of Washington in the District of Columbia, 99
Mexican war, 166–169
Miami Herald Publishing Co. v. Tornillo, 515
Miler, Richard R., 589
Miles, William Porcher, 197
Miller, Arthur L., 413, 415
Miller, Samuel Freeman, 244–247
Mills, Roger Q., 286
Mills v. Alabama, 508, 514, 515
Milton, John, 48
Minor v. Happersett, 228

Minot, George Richards, 49
Mint, establishment of, 81–83
Missouri Compromise, 125–126, 181, 185–192
Mitchell, John, 472
Money, establishment of the Mint, 81–83
Monitor Patriot Co. v. Roy, 508
Monroe, James, 46, 104
Monroney, Mike, 385, 463
Montgomery, William, 197
Morehead, James Turner, war with Mexico, 167
Morgan, John P., 301
Morgan, John P., Jr., 305
Morrill, Lot M., 201
Morris, Edward, 196
Morris, Gouverneur, at Federal Convention of 1787, 6, 18, 19, 22, 24, 25
Morris, Lewis R., 95
Morris, Robert, 47, 70
Morse, Wayne Lyman
  Declaration of Conscience, 406
  opposes Tonkin Gulf Resolution, 440–446
Moser, Harold D., 138
Mosier, Harold G., 355
Mott, Lucretia, 228
Muenter, Erich, 305
Muhlenberg, Frederick Augustus C.
  on congressional pay, 247
  as first Speaker of the House, 47
Mulligan, James, 232
Mulligan Letters, 232–238
Mundt, Karl Earl, 369, 415, 417, 418, 419
Murdock, Victor, 293
Murphy, Frank, 352
My First Fifty Years in Politics (Martin), 407, 413

NAACP v. Alabama, 508, 510, 517, 518, 519, 520
NAACP v. Button, 510, 513, 514
National Aeronautic and Space Administration (NASA), space program, 434, 448
National anthem, designation of, 330–331
National highway system. See Interstate highway system
National Industrial Recovery Act of 1933, 341
National Intelligencer, 116–117
National Labor Relations Board v. Jones and Laughlin Steel Corporation, 337–341
National Prohibition Act (Volstead Act), 310–314
Native Americans, petition regarding land titles, 105–106
Navy (U.S.), establishment of, 86–87
Negroes. See Slaves
Nemerov, Howard, poem to Congress, 563–564
Nesmith, James W., 201
New Deal programs, 341, 352
New York Times Co. v. Sullivan, 514, 514–515
Niblack, William E., 225
Nicholas, John, 92
Nicholson, Joseph Hopper, 104
Niles, John, 159
Nineteenth amendment to the Constitution, 310
Nixon, Richard
  article of impeachment against, 495–497
  on Cambodian invasion, 451, 476
  impeachment debates, 487–495
  voting rights, 433
  Watergate investigations, 472–475
Nixon v. United States, 584–587
Nixon, Walter L., Jr., 584–587
Noell, John William, 197
Norris, George E.
  revolt against Speaker Cannon, 284–298
  twentieth amendment to the Constitution, 331–332
North Atlantic Treaty Organization (NATO), 375
North, Oliver L., 588, 589
Northwest Ordinance of 1787, 132, 140

Oath of Office Act, 58–59
Obey, David Ross, 546, 547

O'Connor, Herbert Romulus, 403
O'Ferrall, Charles Triplett, 268
Office of Management and Budget (OMB). *See under its earlier name* Bureau of the Budget
Ogden, Aaron, 127, 132
Olmsted, Marlin Edgar, 294
O'Mahoney, Joseph Christopher, 363
O'Neill, Thomas P. "Tip," debate with Newt Gingrich, 542–548
Organized crime, Kefauver Committee report on, 410–413
Orr, James, 193
Otis, Harrison G., 95
Otis, Samuel, as Senate secretary, 55
Outhwaite, Joseph Hodson, 268

Page, John, constitutional amendments, 62, 67
Palmore v. United States, 527
Papers of Daniel Webster: Speeches and Formal Writings (Wiltse and Moser), 138
Park Chung Hee, 532
Passman, Otto E., 532
Paterson, William, 47, 48
    federal court system, 73
Patterson, General Robert, 200
Patterson, James, and Credit Mobilier scandal, 223
Patterson, [Delegate], at Federal Convention of 1787, 20
Patterson, William, at Washington inauguration, 57
Payne, Sereno Elisha, 298
Pendleton, George Hunt, 250, 251
Pennington, A. C. M., 185
Pennypacker, Samuel W., 303
Penrose, Boies, campaign financing investigation, 301–304
Pentagon Papers controversy, 469–472
People of Colour, Freemen within the City of Philadelphia, 92
Percy, Charles, 457, 458
Persian Gulf War, 572–577, 577–578
Peterson, Merrill D., 171
Petitions. *See* Congressional petitions
Peyton, Samuel Oldham, 197
Philadelphia, seat of government, 76–77
Philippines, U.S. policy, 274–282
Pierce, George, at Federal Convention of 1787, 5
Pierpont, Francis H., 200
Pinckney, Charles Coatesworth, 94
Pinckney, Thomas, 95, 96
Pinkney, William, at Federal Convention of 1787, 3, 5, 7, 8, 9, 10, 12, 15, 17, 18, 19, 20, 25
Poindexter, John, 589
Poland, Luke P., 223, 225
Political patronage, 241–254
Polk, James K.
    opposes Wilmot Proviso, 174
    war with Mexico, 166
Pollack v. Farmers' Loan and Trust Co., 284
Pomeroy, Samuel C., 200
Post, Wiley, 336
Potter, John, 193–194
Powell, Adam Clayton, Jr., 446–448, 532
Powell, Elizabeth, 25
Powell v. McCormack, 446–448
Power in the House (Bolling), 463
President
    executive privilege, 88
    oath of office, 58
    presidential succession, 400
    title for, 57–58
    treaty making powers, 40–42
    veto powers, 83–84
President pro tempore of the Senate
    duties, 54–55
    and presidential succession, 400
Presidential elections
    (1789) first election, 47–48
    (1800), 94–96

(1876), 238–240
(1904), 301–304
(1908), 301–304
House role, 94–96
public financing of, 522–526
separate balloting for, 102
Presidential inaugurations. *See* Inaugurations (presidential)
Presidential Succession Act, 400
Press Gallery: Congress and the Washington Correspondents (Ritchie), 159
Priest, Percy, 414
Prince, George Washington, 295
Prohibition (of alcohol), 309, 310–314, 332
Proxmire, William, 426
Public land policy, as issue in Webster-Hayne debates, 132–148
Publius (*pen name*). *See* Hamilton, Alexander; Jay, John; Madison, James

Quinn v. United States, 423
Quitman, John, 193–194

Rager, Scott, 284
Rand, [Delegate], at Federal Convention of 1787, 2
Randall, Samuel Jackson, 224, 286
Randolph, [Delegate], at Federal Convention of 1787, 3, 10, 11, 15, 20, 21, 23
Randolph, Edmund
    establishment of Library of Congress, 96
    letter from Madison, 46–47
Rankin, Jeanette, 310, 362, 364, 365
Rankin, John D., 368–369, 370, 371, 372, 373, 374
Rayburn, Sam, 361, 362, 407, 571
Read, George, 57
    at Federal Convention of 1787, 5, 6, 14, 15, 16
Reagan, Ronald, 476
    and Iran-contra affair, 587, 588, 601–603
Reapportionment. *See* Apportionment
Reconstruction Act of 1867, 211, 212–213
Reconstruction period, 205–209
Reed, Chauncey William, 365
Reed, Thomas Brackett, 266–270, 284
Reflections of a Public Man (Wright), 564
Register of Debates, 117, 132
Rehnquist, William H., 584–587
Reigle, Donald W., 578–583
Remini, Robert V., 138, 171, 176
Representatives
    absence procedures, 52
    apportionment of members, 30–31, 34–35
    biennial elections, 28–30
    characteristics of, 33–34
    elections, regulation of, 36
    elections of, 1–5, 28–30
    knowledge of constituent interests, 33
    number of, 26, 31–33
    qualifications of, 25, 28
    term limits, 28, 34, 35
    vacancies, 26
Revenue bills. *See* Appropriations
Ritchie, Donald A., 159
Rittenhouse, David, 81
Rives, William Cabell, 160
Roberts, Kenneth, 413, 414
Robertson, Thomas Bolling, 117
Robinson, Joseph T., 341, 348
Rodberg, Leonard S., 469
Rodenberg, William August, 287, 288, 297
Rodino, Peter W. , Jr., 487, 488–490, 495
Rogers, John Henry, 267
Rogers, Will, on Congress, 336–337
Roosevelt, Franklin Delano. *See also* New Deal programs
    fireside chats, 333
    Lend-Lease Act, 359–360
    Supreme Court expansion scheme, 341–352
    World War II declarations, 361, 365–367

Roosevelt, Theodore
    assassination attempt, 301
    presidential election (1904), 301–304
Rosado v. Wyman, 520
Rosario v. Rockefeller, 511
Roth v. United States, 508, 515
Russell, Jonathan, War of 1812 negotiator, 111–113
Russell, Richard, 430
Rutledge, John, Jr.
    at Federal Convention of 1787, 3, 7, 8, 9–10, 13, 14, 20, 21, 23
    first presidential eletion, 48

Sabath, Adolph Joachim, 297, 368, 369
St. Clair, General Arthur, 79–81
Salaries
    compensation and retirement pay, 398–399
    for government officials, 225–228
    of members, 11–12, 17–18, 26, 71–73, 225–228, 583
    pay increases, 59, 114–116
    reducing congressional, 247–249
"Salary Grab" Act of 1793, 225–228
Sargent, Aaron, 228
Savings and loan industry, 578–583
Schenck, General Robert C., 200
Schirra, Walt, 435
Schureman, James, 47
Scofield, Glenni William, 224
Scott, Colonel Thomas A., 237
Scott, Thomas, 47
Scott v. Sanford. See Dred Scott decision
Seat of government, establishing, 76–77
Seaton, William W., 116–117
Secession from the Union
    Jefferson Davis's farewell address, 197–199
    Webster opposition to, 171–175
Second Bank of the United States, 118–124
Second branch. *See* Senate
Secord, Richard V., 589
Sedgwick, Theodore, House investigation of General St. Clair, 81
Seiberling, John F., 493
Senate. *See also* Congressional elections; President pro tempore of the Senate
    Adams's vice presidential address, 54–55
    Bryce's description of, 262–266
    Committee on Aeronatutical and Space Sciences, 432–433
    committee assignments during Civil War, 201
    creation of, 1
    election of members, 26, 300
    equality of representation, 36–37
    first quorum, 47–48
    impeachment powers, 26
    powers and functions, 25–27
    press gallery, 159–160
    purposes, 37–40
    rules of procedure, 53–54
    salaries for members, 225–227
    standing committees, 113, 384, 385–388, 463–464, 466
    term of office, 15–17
    de Tocqueville's description of, 149–150
    treaties, power of advise and consent, 69–71
    treaty making powers, 222
The Senate (Byrd), 138
Senate Special Committee to Investigate the Defense Program, 355–359
Senators
    appointment by state legislatures, 37
    elections of, 26
    number of, 26, 37
    qualifications of, 36–37
    term limits, 37–38
Seney, Joshua, House investigation of General St. Clair, 80
Sergeant-at-arms
    duties of, 56

fees for, 53
lifting Mace to restore order, 193–194
symbol of office, 50, 52, 53
Service, John S., 402
Seventeenth amendment to the Constitution, 300
Sevier, John, circular letter of, 77
Seward, William Henry, 201
Shapley, Harlow, 403
Shepard, Alan B., Jr., 434
Sherley, Joseph Swagar, 296, 297
Sherman, Roger
at Federal Convention of 1787, 1, 3, 4, 5, 7, 8, 9, 10, 11, 12, 13, 14, 15, 16, 24
constitutional amendments, 61, 66
Shipstead, Henrik, 347
Shooting incidents at the Capitol. See under Violence in Congress
Shultz, Charles, 592
Simmons, James Fowler, 201
Simpson, Alan, Bork Supreme Court nomination, 549, 559–563
Sinclair, Harry F., 328
Sinclair v. United States, 328, 423
Site of government, 45–46
Sixteenth amendment to the Constitution, 284
Slave trade, abolition of, 113
Slavery. See also Compromise of 1850; Kansas-Nebraska Act; Missouri Compromise; Wilmot Proviso
abolition of, 204
Dred Scott decision, 185–192
House "gag rule" on, 158
as issue in Webster-Hayne debates, 132–148
prohibition of, 125–126
Slaves
fugitive slave rights, 92–93
and representative apportionment, 31, 32
Slayton, Deek, 435
Smilie, John, 104
Smith, Howard W., 430
Smith, Margaret Chase, Declaration of Conscience, 401, 404–406
Smith, Samuel H., 110, 111
Smith, William
constitutional amendments, 60
House investigation of General St. Clair, 80
Smock, Raymond W., 284
Socialist Labor Party v. Gilligan, 527
Solomon, Gerald B. H., 627
Somes, Daniel Eton, 197
Space exploration
congressional committees on, 432–433
honoring Apollo 11 astronauts, 448–451
honoring John Glenn, 434–435
Spaight, Richard Dobbs, at Federal Convention of 1787, 2, 14
Spanish-American War, declared, 108
Speaker of the House
duties of, 50
Gingrich address, 610–614
Gingrich resignation, 628–629
Longworth on the Congress, 325–327
and presidential succession, 400
revolt against Joseph Cannon, 284–298
role of, 254, 256–257
Wright resignation, 564–572
Speight, Jesse, war with Mexico, 167
Spinner, F. E., 185
Springer v. Philippine Islands, 531
Springer, William McKendree, 269
Stanton, Edwin M., 214–215, 216–219
Stanton, Elizabeth Cady, 228, 310
"Star Spangled Banner" (national anthem), 330–331
Starnes, Joe, 355
Starr, Kenneth W., Whitewater investigation, 614, 615, 627
Steele, John, House investigation of General St. Clair, 80, 81

Stennis, John Cornelius, 442, 457, 459
Stevens, John Paul, on line-item veto, 624
Stevens, Thaddeus
on impeachment of Andrew Johnson, 213–216
on Reconstruction, 205–209
as senator during Civil War, 201
Stone, William Joel, 304
Storer v. Brown, 523, 524
Strong, Caleb, 47, 53
at Federal Convention of 1787, 10
federal court system, 73
Suffrage. See Voting rights
Sumner, Charles
beating in Congress, 183–185
committee appointment, 201
Sumter, Thomas, constitutional amendments, 66–67
Supreme Court
Bork nomination, 548–563
establishment of, 73–74
expansion of size of, 341–352
impeachment powers, 42–43
nominations, 549
Supreme Court cases
Abington School District v. Schempp, 523
Adderley v. Florida, 509
Aetna Life Insurance Co. v. Haworth, 508
American Party of Texas v. White, 523, 524
Associated Press v. U.S., 515
Baker v. Carr, 508
Barenblatt v. U.S., 421–422
Barr v. Mateo, 471
Barry v. United States ex rel. Cunningham, 530
Bates v. Little Rock, 510
Bridges v. California, 514
Brown v. Board of Education, 430
Buckley v. Valeo, 506–532
Bullock v. Carter, 524
Burroughs v. United States, 518, 523, 530
California Bankers Assn. v. Shultz, 518
Champlin Refining Co. v. Corp. Commission, 526
Clinton v. City of New York, 622–626
Coleman v. Miller, 527
Communist Party v. Subversive Activities Control Bd., 518
Cousins v. Wigoda, 510
Cox v. Louisiana, 509
CSC v. Letter Carriers, 510, 511
Eastern R. Conf. v. Noerr Motors, 515
Emspak v. U.S., 423
Everson v. Bd. of Education, 523
Gibbons v. Ogden, 127–132
Glidden Co. v. Zdanok, 527
Gravel v. U.S., 469–472
Hampton & Co. v. U.S., 528
Haver v. Yaker, 222
Helvering v. Davis, 523
Humphrey's Executor v. U.S., 530, 532
Immigration and Naturalizaion Service v. Chadha, 539–541
James v. Valtierra, 511
Jenness v. Fortson, 424, 525
Kilbourn v. Thompson, 244–247, 422–423, 471
Kovacs v. Cooper, 509
Kusper v. Pontikes, 508, 511
Lubin v. Panish, 523, 524
Luther v. Borden, 207
McCullough v. Maryland, 118–124, 523, 530
McGrain v. Daugherty, 244, 328–330, 423
Miami Herald Publishing Co. v. Tornillo, 515
Mills v. Alabama, 508, 514, 515
Minor v. Happersett, 228
Monitor Patriot Co. v. Roy, 508
NAACP v. Alabama, 508, 510, 517, 518, 519, 520
NAACP v. Button, 510, 513, 514
National Labor Relations Board v. Jones and Laughlin Steel Corp., 337–341
New York Times Co. v. Sullivan, 514, 514–515
Nixon v. U.S., 584–587
Palmore v. U.S., 527

Pollack v. Farmers' Loan and Trust Co., 284
Powell v. McCormack, 446–448
Quinn v. U.S., 423
Rosado v. Wyman, 520
Roth v. U.S., 508, 515
Scott v. Sanford, 185–192, 211
Sinclair v. U.S., 328, 423
Socialist Labor Party v. Gilligan, 527
Springer v. Philippine Islands, 521
Storer v. Brown, 523, 524
Talley v. California, 520, 521
Tenney v. Brandhove, 471
Texas v. Johnson, 118
Thomas v. Collins, 513, 521
United States v. Butler, 523
United States v. Classic, 523
United States v. Doe, 471
United States v. Germaine, 528–529
United States v. Johnson, 471
United States v. O'Brien, 508–509
United States v. Rumely, 423
Watkins v. U.S., 421–425
Weinberger v. Wiesenfeld, 523
Williams v. Rhodes, 513, 524
Winters v. New York, 508
Youngstown Sheet & Tube Co. v. Sawyer, 528
Swift, Dean, 201
Symington, Stuart, 457, 458–459

Taft Commission, 320
Taft, William Howard
budgetary reform, 320
presidential election (1908), 301
Taking Charge: The Johnson White House Tapes, 1963–64 (Beschloss), 441
Taliaferro, Benjamin, 95
Talley v. California, 520, 521
Tallmadge, James, Jr., prohibition of slavery, 125
Taney, Roger B.
Dred Scott decision, 186–192
relationship with Thaddeus Stevens, 205
Tansill, Charles C., 1
Tariff Bill, 67–69, 78
Taulbee, William Preston, shooting of, 270–272
Taulbee-Kincaid incident, 270–272
Tawney, James Albertus, 287, 288, 294, 295, 296, 298
Taxes. See also Duties; Income tax
on distilled spirits, 78–79
federal government authority, 78
Taylor, Abner, 267
Taylor, General Zachary, war with Mexico, 166
Taylor, Miles, 195
Taylor, William, prohibition of slavery, 125–126
Tazewell, Littleton W., 95, 96
Teapot Dome scandal, 328–330
Telfair, Edward, 48
Teller, Henry M., 273
Tenney v. Brandhove, 471
Term limits
for congressional members, 28, 34, 35, 37–38
constitutionality of, 447
Texas v. Johnson, 118
Thirteenth amendment to the Constitution, 204
Thirty Years View (Benton), 149
Thomas, Clarence, 549
Thomas, J. Parnell, 355, 368
Thomas, Jesse B., prohibition of slavery, 125–126
Thomas, John Parnell, 370
Thomas, Lorenzo P., 214–215, 216, 218
Thomas v. Collins, 513, 521
Thomas, William Marshall
debate with Gingrich, 545, 546
on House mail distribution, 545
Thompson, John G., 244
Thompson, John R., 201
Thomson, Charles, as Senate secretary, 48, 57
Thurmond, Strom, record-setting filibuster, 426–430

Thye, Edward J., 406
Tilden, Samuel J., 238–240
Tobey, Charles W., 406
Tocqueville, Alexis de, 149–150, 257
Tongsun Park, 532, 535
Tonkin Gulf Resolution, 440–446, 476
Treaties
    power of making, 27, 40–42
    Senate advice and consent powers, 69–71
    Senate power of, 222
Treaty of Ghent, 109, 111–113
Truman, Harry S.
    assassination attempt (1950), 414
    on the Declaration of Conscience, 404
    defense program investigation, 355–359
    foreign policy, 375
    and Presidential Succession Act, 400
    relieves General MacArthur of command, 407
    and war powers, 475
Trussell, C. P., 414
Twelfth amendment to the Constitution, 102
Twentieth amendment to the Constitution,
    331–332
Twenty Years of Congress: From Lincoln to Garfield
    (Blaine), 200
Twenty-first amendment to the Constitution, 332
Twenty-seventh amendment to the Constitution,
    583
Twenty-sixth amendment to the Constitution,
    468–469
Twenty-third amendment to the Constitution,
    433–434
Tydings, Millard Evelyn, 343

Un-American activities. See House Special Com-
    mittee on Un-American Activities; House
    Un-American Activities Committee
Underwood, John William Henderson, 196
Underwood, Oscar Wilder, 293, 298
United Nations, creation of, 374
United States v. Butler, 523
United States v. Classic, 523
United States v. Doe, 471
United States v. Germaine, 528–529
United States v. Johnson, 471
United States v. O'Brien, 508–509
United States v. Rumely, 423

Valeo, Francis R., and campaign finance reform,
    506–532
Van Devanter, Willis, 328–330
Van Zandt, James E., 415
Vandenberg, Arthur H.
    U.S. foreign policy, 374–379
    World War II declaration, 362, 363
Varnum, Joseph B., 105
Venable, Abraham B.
    House investigation of General St. Clair, 80
    report on Lyon-Griswold dispute, 91–92
Versailles Treaty, 323–325
Veto
    legislative veto, 539–541
    line-item veto, 603–608, 622–626
    presidential, 83–84
Vice president
    Adams address to the Senate, 54–55
    duties of, 55–56
Vice presidential elections
    first election, 47–48
    separate balloting for, 102

Vietnam: A History (Karnow), 457
Vietnam conflict
    Frank Church opposition to, 451–456
    McGovern-Hatfield amendment for U.S. troop
        withdrawal, 457–463
    Pentagon papers, 469–472
    Tonkin Gulf Resolution, 440–446
Vining, John
    constitutional amendments, 67
    House investigation of General St. Clair, 79, 80, 81
Violence in the Capitol
    Benton-Foote incident, 177
    bombing incidents, 304–307
    House floor brawl, 193–194
    Jackson (Andrew) assassination attempt, 270
    Lyon-Griswold dispute, 91–92
    shootings at the Capitol, 270, 413–415
    Sumner (Charles) beating, 183–185
    Taulbee-Kincaid shooting incident, 270–272
Volstead Act, 309, 310–314, 332
Volstead, Andrew J., 310
Voting rights
    for African Americans, 221–222
    constitutional definition of, 28
    for District of Columbia citizens, 433–434
    minimum age requirements, 468
    for women, 228–230, 310

Wadleigh, Julian H., 402–403
Wagner, Robert F., 337
Walker, Robert, 542
Walker, Robert John, 159
Wallace, Henry A., 361, 362
Walsh, Lawrence E., 588
Walton, Sam, 271
War declarations, 108–109, 166–169
    nondeclared wars, 108
    Persian Gulf War, 577–578
    Spanish-American War, 273
    Tonkin Gulf Resolution, 440–446
    War of 1812, 108–109
    War powers resolution, 475–478
    World War I (with Germany), 307–309
    World War II (with Germany and Italy), 365–367
    World War II (with Japan), 361, 362–365
War of 1812
    declared, 108–109
    peace negotiations, 111–112
War Powers Act of 1973, 451, 475–478
Warren, Earl, 421–425
Washburn, Cadwallader, 193–194
Washington, D.C. See District of Columbia
Washington, George
    at Capitol cornerstone laying ceremony, 84–86
    executive privilege, 88
    oath of office and, 58
    presidential election notification, 47–48
    presidential inauguration of, 56–57
    presidential veto, 83–84
    treaty making power of the president, 69–71
    Whiskey Rebellion commander–in–chief, 78
Watergate affair, 472–475, 487–495, 495–497
Watkins, John T., 421
Watkins v. United States, 421–425
Watson, Gregory, 583
Watterson, George, appointed librarian of
    Congress, 111
Weber, John Vincent, 546
Webster, Daniel
    on Constitution and the Union, 171–175

    debate with Robert Hayne, 132–137, 138–148
    public land policy, 132–137, 138–148
    salary issue, 114
Webster-Hayne debate, 132–148
Weinberger, Caspar W., 589, 592–593
Weinberger v. Wiesenfeld, 523
Welch, Joseph, 416, 417, 418, 419
West Virginia, creation of, 200
Wheeler, Burton K., 341–352
Wheeler, Wayne B., 310
Whiskey Rebellion, 78
White, Alexander, 52
    constitutional amendments, 61–62
    on Louisiana Purchase, 100
White, Byron Raymond, 469–472
White, Wallace Humphrey, Jr., 363
Whitewater investigation
    majority view, 614–619
    minority view, 619–622
Willey, Waitman Thomas, 200
Williams v. Rhodes, 513, 524
Williamson, Hugh
    at Federal Convention of 1787, 5, 11, 15, 17, 18,
        24, 25
    House investigation of General St. Clair, 80
Wilmot, David
    prohibitions on expansion of slavery, 169–170
    war with Mexico, 166
Wilmot Proviso, 169–170, 174, 185
Wilson, Don, 583
Wilson, Henry, 201
Wilson, John, 110
Wilson, John Lockwood, 267
Wilson, William, at Federal Convention of 1787,
    2–4, 5–6, 8, 9, 10, 11, 12, 13, 14, 17, 18, 19, 22,
    24
Wilson, Woodrow
    League of Nations supporter, 315
    on the Senate, 254–255
    on the Speaker of the House's role, 256–257
    and the Versailles Treaty, 323
    veto of Prohibition bill, 310
    World War I war declaration, 307–309
Wiltse, Charles M., 138
Wingate, Paine
    at first quorum of the Senate, 47
    Indian treaties, 71
Winslow, Warren, 196
Winters v. New York, 508
Woodward, Bob, 472
World War I. See also Versailles Treaty
    declaration of, 108, 307–309
    Reparation Commission, 323–325
World War II
    declared, 108
    war with Germany and Italy declared, 365–366
    war with Japan declared, 361, 362–365
Worth It All (Wright), 565
Wright, Jim
    debate with Newt Gingrich, 542–544, 547, 548
    resignation as Speaker of the House, 542, 563,
        564–572

XYZ Affair, 91–92

Yaker, Peter, 222
Yarborough, Ralph, 457, 459–460
Yoder, Samuel, 271
Young, Stephen, 457–458
Youngstown Sheet & Tube Co. v. Sawyer, 528